Street by Street

C000184257

MERSEYSIDE

Enlarged areas BIRKENHEAD, BOOTLE, ELLESMERE PORT, LIVERPOOL, RUNCORN, ST HELENS, SOUTHPORT, WARRINGTON, WIDNES, WIGAN

Plus Ashton-in-Makerfield, Bebington, Chorley, Crosby, Formby, Heswall, Hoylake, Kirkby, Maghull, Neston, Ormskirk, Skelmersdale, Wallasey, West Kirby

2nd edition November 2004
© Automobile Association Developments Limited 2004

Original edition printed May 2001

Ordnance Survey® This product includes map data licensed from Ordnance Survey ® with the permission of the Controller of Her Majesty's Stationery Office. © Crown copyright 2004. All rights reserved. Licence number 399221.

All rights reserved. No part of this publication may be reproduced, stored in a retrieval system, or transmitted in any form or by any means – electronic, mechanical, photocopying, recording or otherwise – unless the permission of the publisher has been given beforehand.

Published by AA Publishing (a trading name of Automobile Association Developments Limited, whose registered office is Southwood East, Apollo Rise, Farnborough, Hampshire, GU14 0JW, UK. Registered number 1878835).

Mapping produced by the Cartography Department of The Automobile Association. (A02238)

A CIP Catalogue record for this book is available from the British Library.

Printed and bound by Leo, China.

The contents of this atlas are believed to be correct at the time of the latest revision. However, the publishers cannot be held responsible for loss occasioned to any person acting or refraining from action as a result of any material in this atlas, nor for any errors, omissions or changes in such material. This does not affect your statutory rights. The publishers would welcome information to correct any errors or omissions and to keep this atlas up to date. Please write to Publishing, The Automobile Association, Fanum House (FH17), Basing View, Basingstoke, Hampshire, RG21 4EA.

Ref: MX048z

Key to map pages	ii–iii
Key to map symbols	iv–1
Enlarged map pages	2-21
Main map pages	22-167
Index – towns & villages	168
Index – streets	169-210
Index – featured places	210-215
Acknowledgements	215

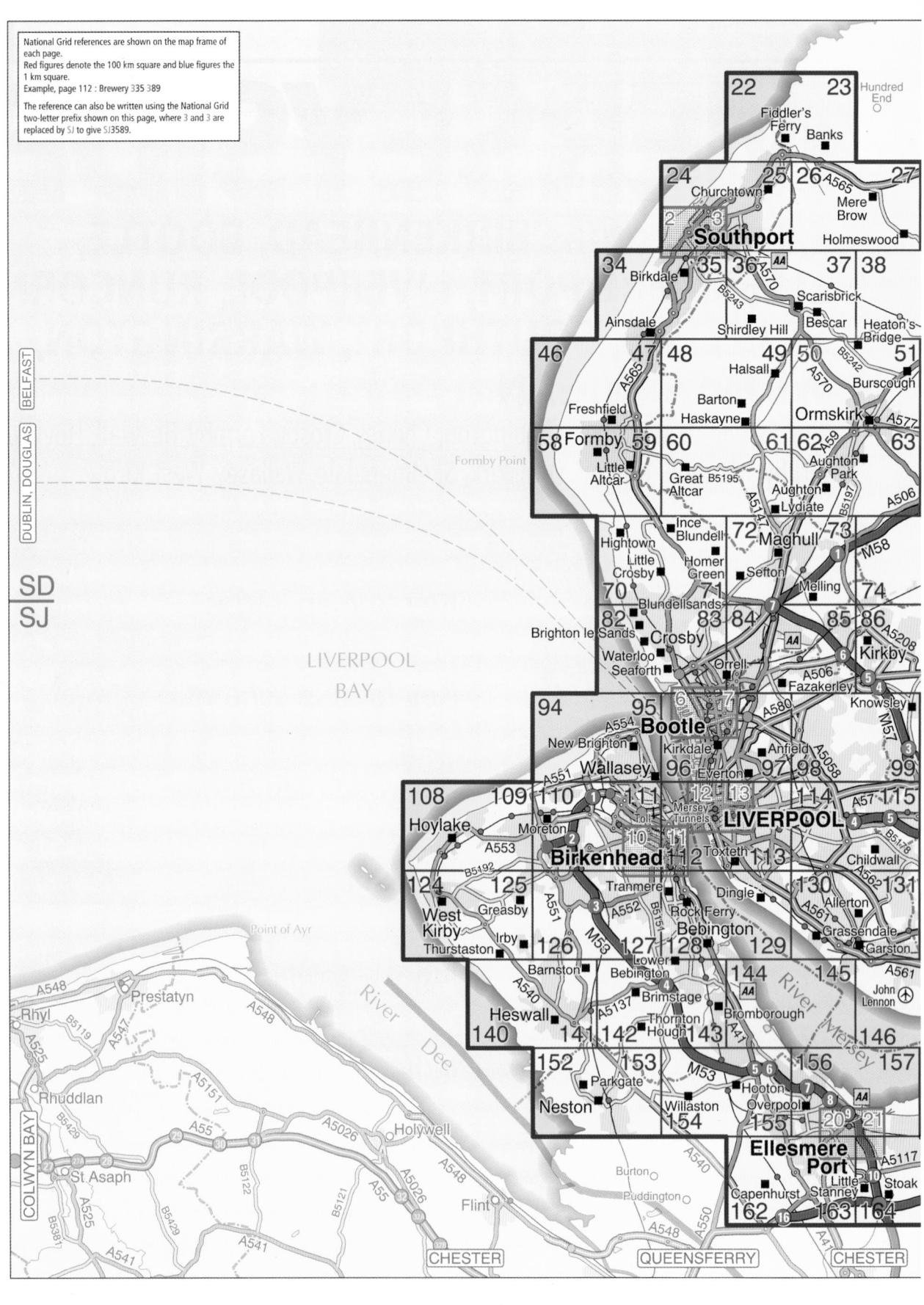

National Grid references are shown on the map frame of each page.
Red figures denote the 100 km square and blue figures the 1 km square.
Example, page 112 : Brewery 335 389

The reference can also be written using the National Grid two-letter prefix shown on this page, where 3 and 3 are replaced by SJ to give SJ3589.

Scale of enlarged map pages   1:10,000   6.3 inches to 1 mile

0   1/4   miles   1/2   3/4

0   1/4   1/2   kilometres   3/4   1   1 1/4

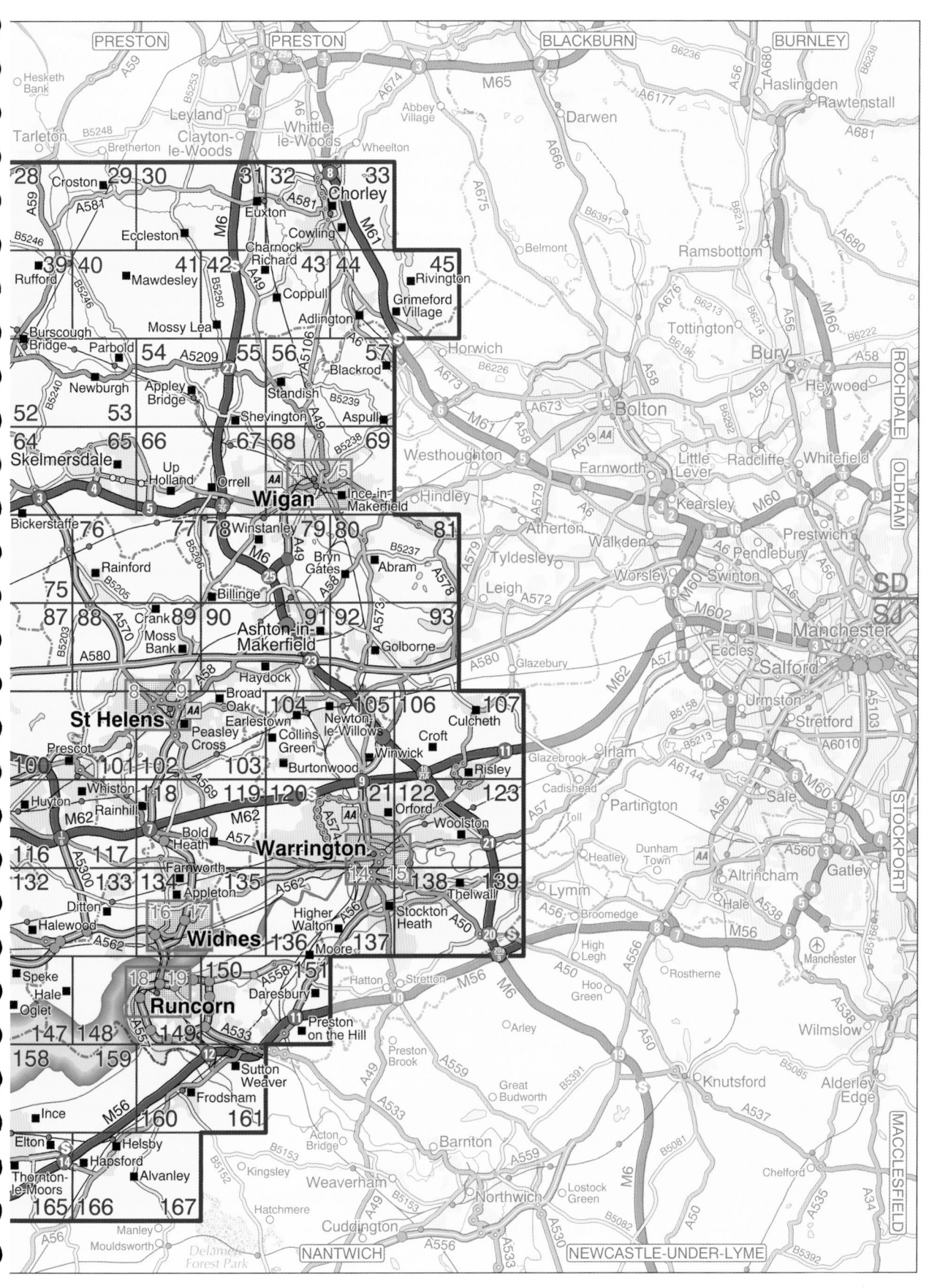

iv

Junction 9	Motorway & junction
Services	Motorway service area
	Primary road single/dual carriageway
Services	Primary road service area
	A road single/dual carriageway
	B road single/dual carriageway
	Other road single/dual carriageway
	Minor/private road, access may be restricted
← ←	One-way street
	Pedestrian area
	Track or footpath
	Road under construction
	Road tunnel
AA	AA Service Centre
P	Parking
P+	Park & Ride
	Bus/coach station
	Railway & main railway station
	Railway & minor railway station
⊖	Underground station

⊖	Light railway & station
	Preserved private railway
LC	Level crossing
	Tramway
	Ferry route
	Airport runway
	County, administrative boundary
	Mounds
93	Page continuation 1:17,500
7	Page continuation to enlarged scale 1:10,000
	River/canal, lake
	Aqueduct, lock, weir
465 Winter Hill	Peak (with height in metres)
	Beach
	Woodland
	Park
	Cemetery
	Built-up area
	Featured building
	City wall

A&E	Hospital with 24-hour A&E department
PO	Post Office
📖	Public library
i	Tourist Information Centre
i	Seasonal Tourist Information Centre
⛽⛽	Petrol station, 24 hour Major suppliers only
†	Church/chapel
🚻	Public toilets
♿	Toilet with disabled facilities
PH	Public house AA recommended
🍴	Restaurant AA inspected
Madeira Hotel ▄	Hotel AA inspected
🎭	Theatre or performing arts centre
🎥	Cinema
⚑	Golf course
▲	Camping AA inspected
🚐	Caravan site AA inspected
▲🚐	Camping & caravan site AA inspected
🎢	Theme park
⛪	Abbey, cathedral or priory

♜	Castle
🏛	Historic house or building
Wakehurst Place NT	National Trust property
Ⓜ	Museum or art gallery
🐎	Roman antiquity
⊥	Ancient site, battlefield or monument
⛭	Industrial interest
❋	Garden
◉	Garden Centre Garden Centre Association Member
💐	Garden Centre Wyevale Garden Centre
🌲	Arboretum
🛒	Farm or animal centre
🦌	Zoological or wildlife collection
🦜	Bird collection
🦆	Nature reserve
🐟	Aquarium
V	Visitor or heritage centre
⛤	Country park
⌒	Cave
🌾	Windmill
🛢	Distillery, brewery or vineyard

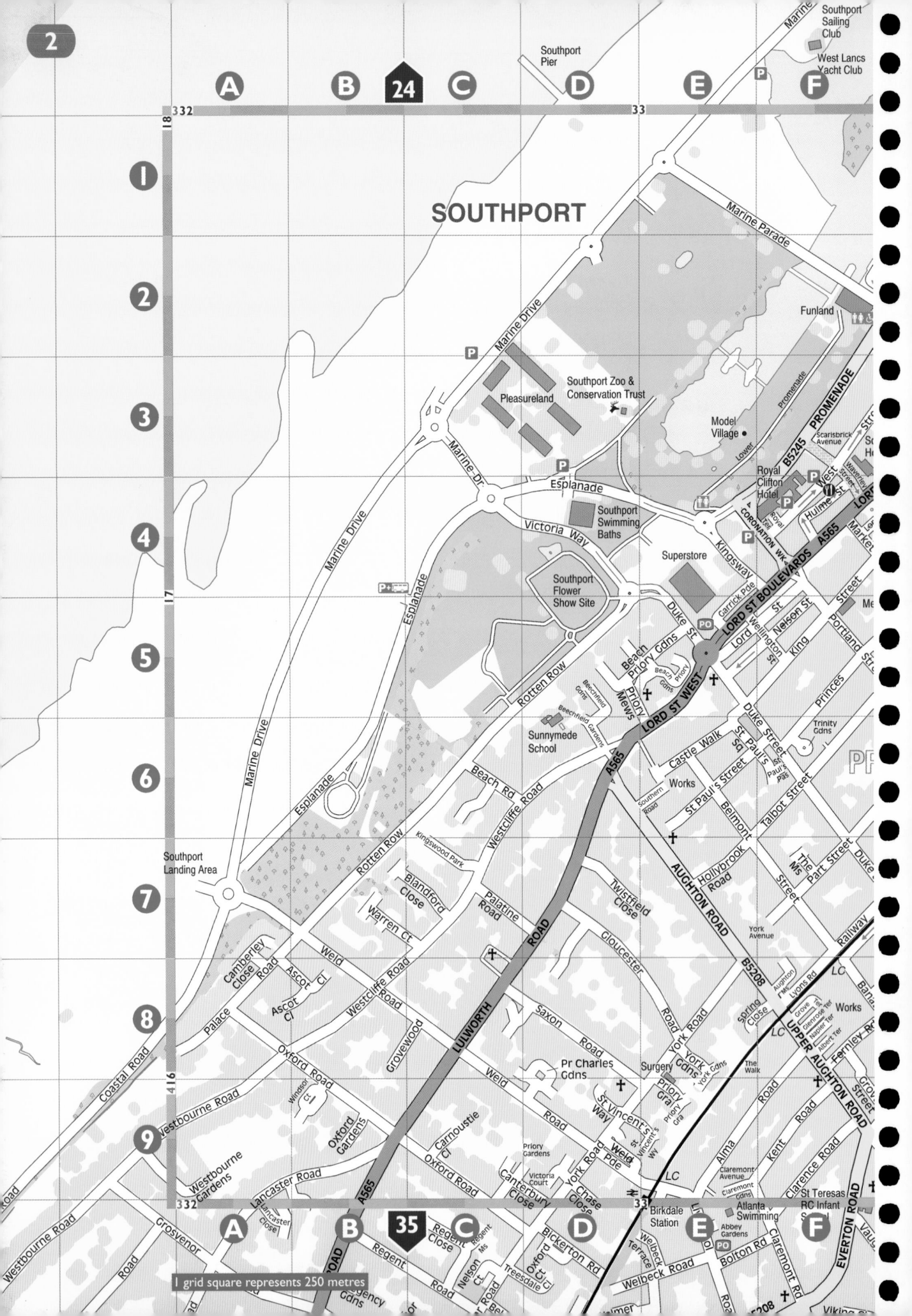

SOUTHPORT

A B 24 C D E F

Southport Pier

Marine Drive

Southport Sailing Club

West Lancs Yacht Club

Marine Parade

Funland

Pleasureland

Southport Zoo & Conservation Trust

Model Village

Lower

PROMENADE

B5245

Scarisbrick Avenue

Marine Dr.

Esplanade

Royal Clifton Hotel

West Street

Marine Drive

Victoria Way

Southport Swimming Baths

Superstore

CORONATION WK

Royal

Kingsway

LORD ST BOULEVARDS

A565

Market Street

LORD

Southport Flower Show Site

Carrick Pde

Lord

Wellington St

Nelson St

King Street

Portland

Esplanade

Beach

Priory Gdns

Beach Gdns

PO

St

Castle Walk

St Paul's Street

Princes

Trinity Gdns

PR

Rotten Row

Priory Mews

LORD ST WEST

Beechfield Gdns

Beechfield Gardens

St Paul's Square

St Paul's Pas

Duke Street

Sunnymede School

Works

St Paul's Street

Belmont

Talbot Street

Beach Rd

Southern Road

The

Westcliffe Road

Hollybrook Road

Part Street

Duke

A565

Kingswood Park

AUGHTON ROAD

York Avenue

Southport Landing Area

Blandford Close

Warren Ct

Palatine Road

Twistfield Close

Gloucester

B5208

Railway

LC

Rotten Row

Camberley Close

Weld Road

Ascot Cl

Westcliffe Road

Grovewood

LULWORTH

Spring Close

Grove

Glenrose Ter

Napier Ter

Albert Ter

UPPER AUGHTON ROAD

Works

Palace

Ascot Ct

ROAD

Saxon Road

York Road

York Gdns

LC

Fernley Rd

Grove Street

Oxford Road

Windsor Ct

Weld Road

Pr Charles Gdns

Surgery

Priory Gra

The Walk

Westbourne Road

Oxford Gardens

Carnoustie

St Vincent's Way

York Gdns

Priory Gra

Alma Road

Kent Road

Claremont Road

Westbourne Gardens

Canterbury Close

Priory Gardens

Weld Pde

York Road

Chase Close

St Vincent's Wy

Claremont Avenue

Claremont Gdns

EVERTON ROAD

St Teresas RC Infant

Coastal Road

Lancaster Close

Oxford Road

Victoria Court

Bickerton Rd

LC

Birkdale Station

Atlanta Swimming

Abbey Gardens

PO

Bolton Rd

Vaux

Lancaster Road

A565

Regent Close

Regent

Nelson Ms

Treesdale

Welbeck Terrace

Welbeck Road

A B 35 C D E F

Grosvenor Road

Regent Road

Regency Gdns

Bickerton

Viking Rd

B5208

Westbourne Road

1 grid square represents 250 metres

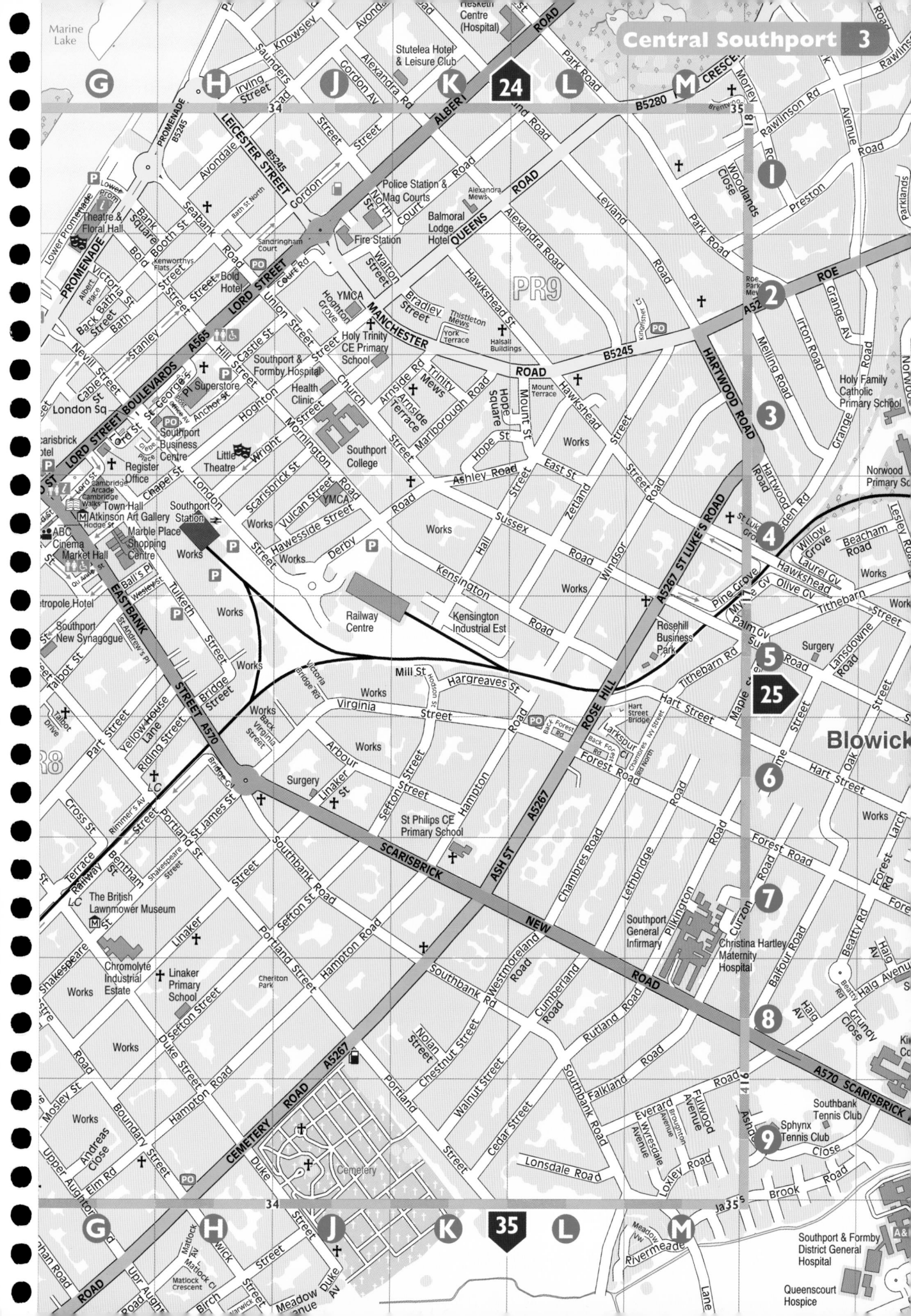

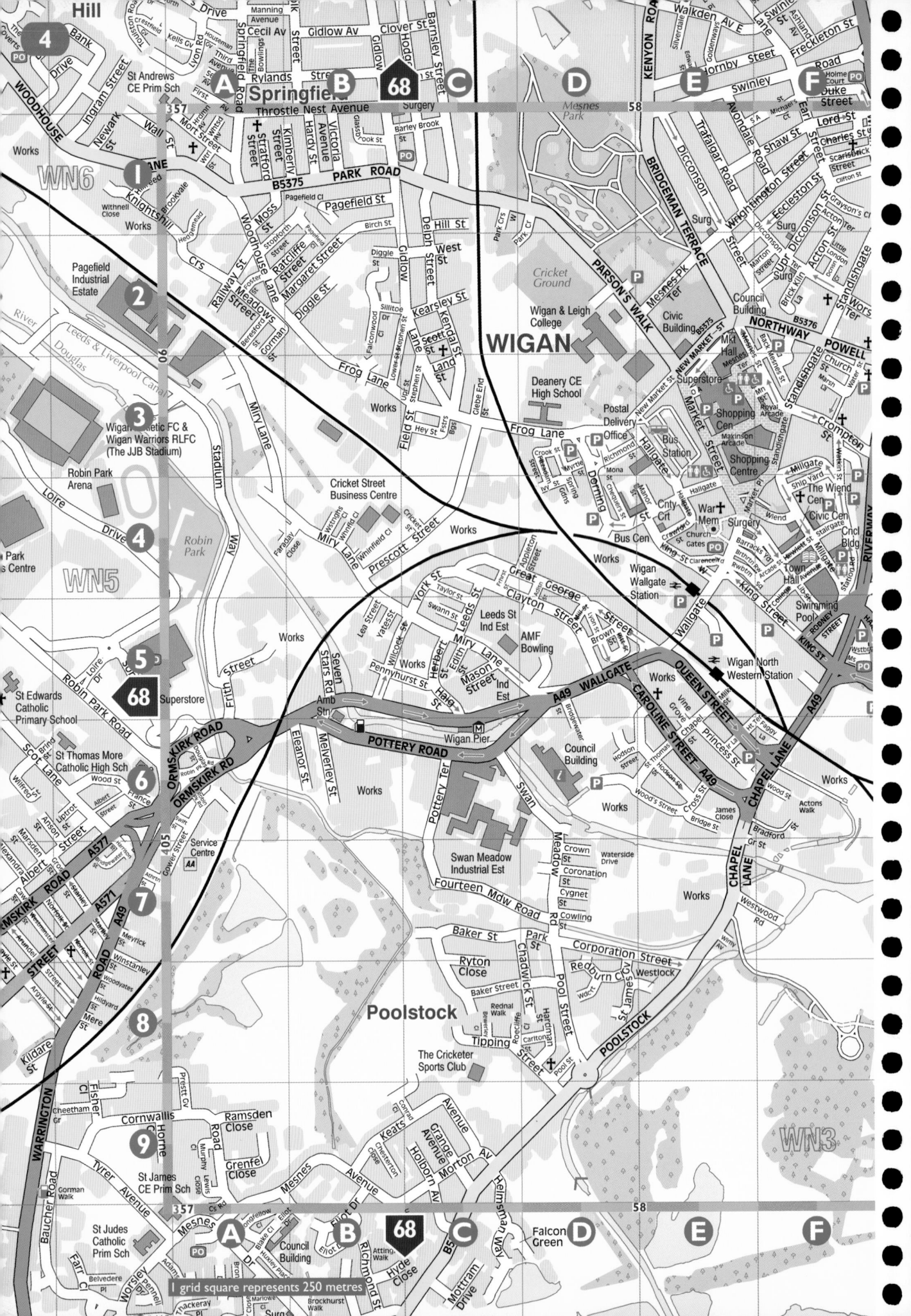

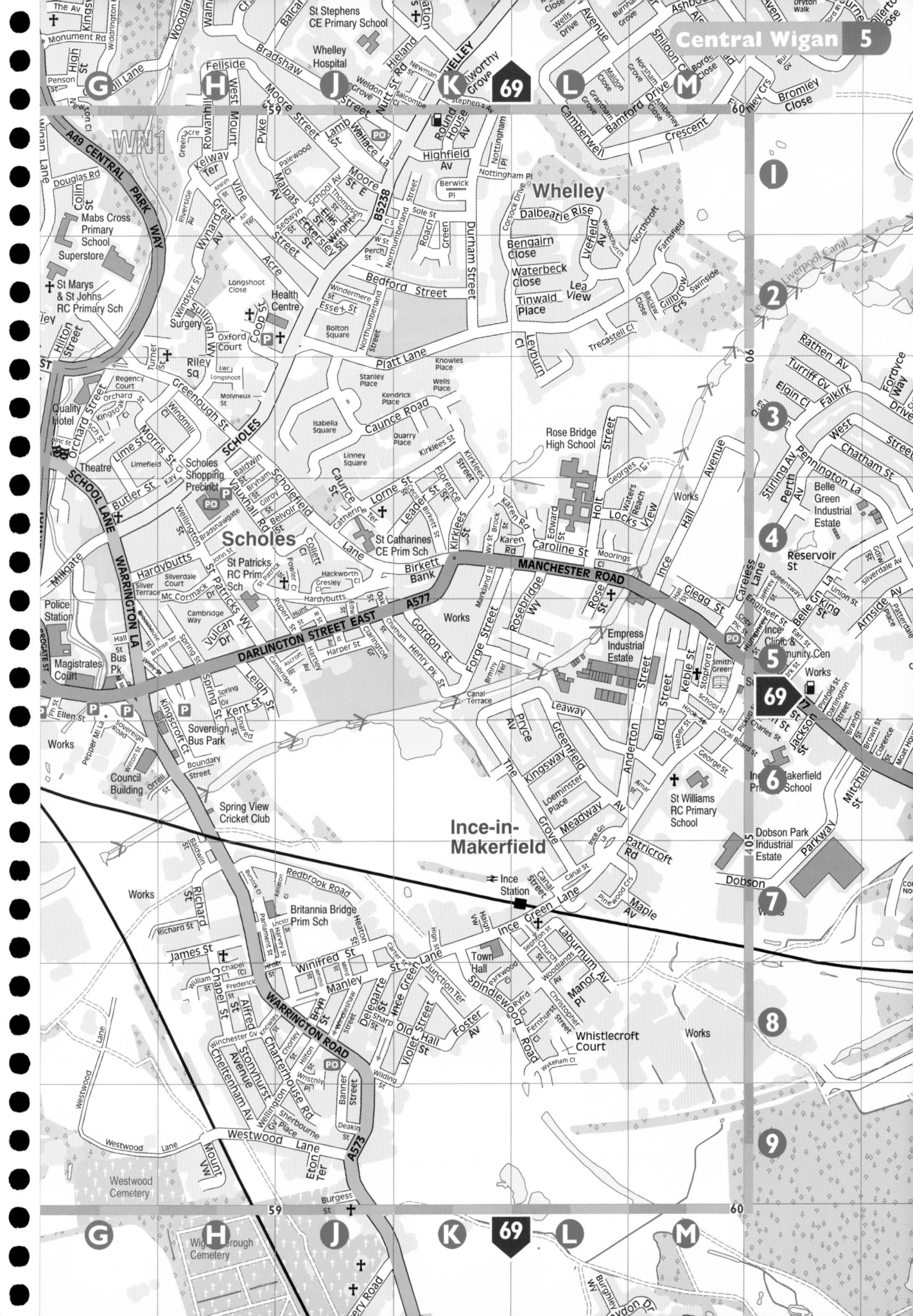

BOOTLE

1 grid square represents 250 metres

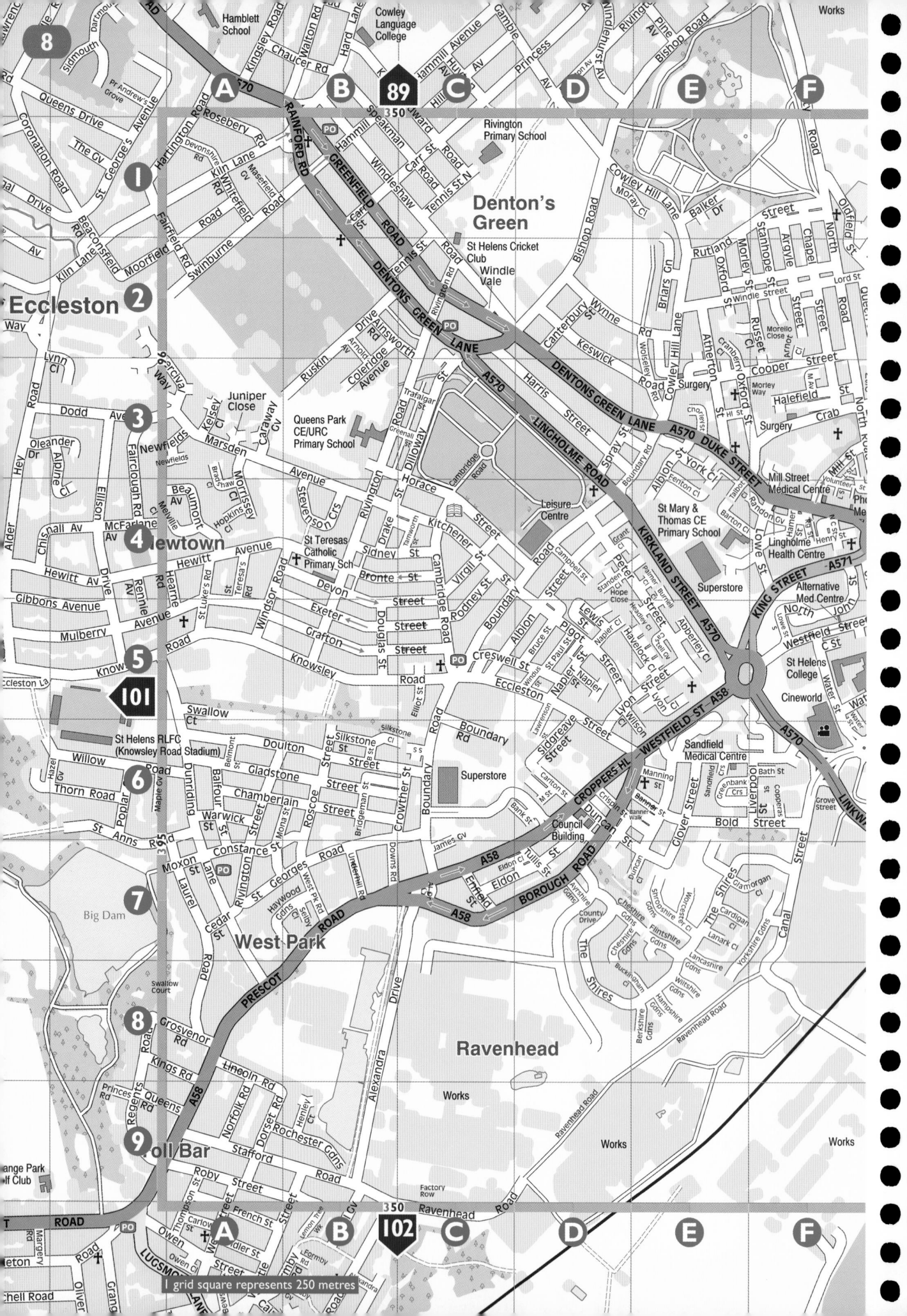

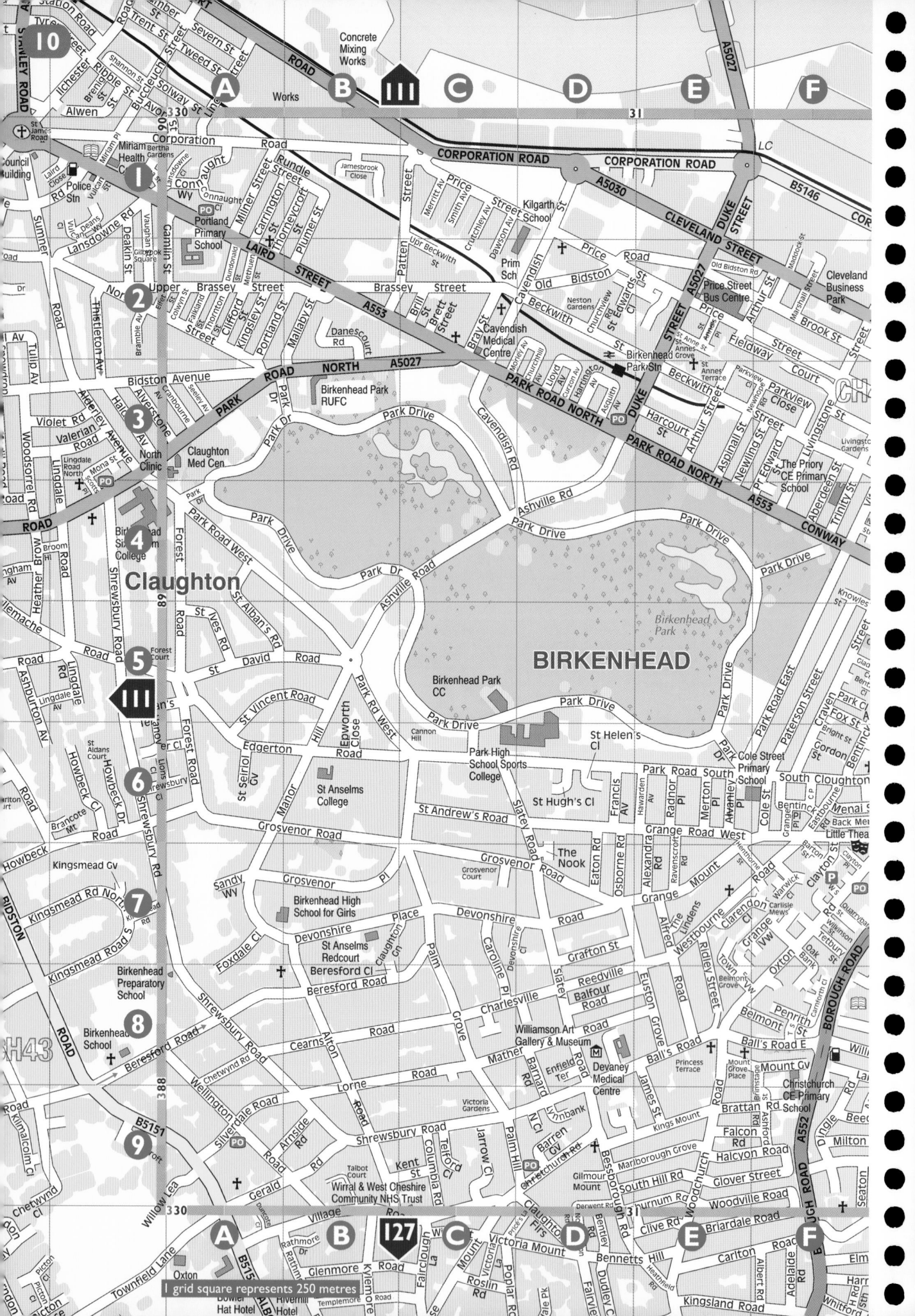

BIRKENHEAD

Claughton

1 grid square represents 250 metres

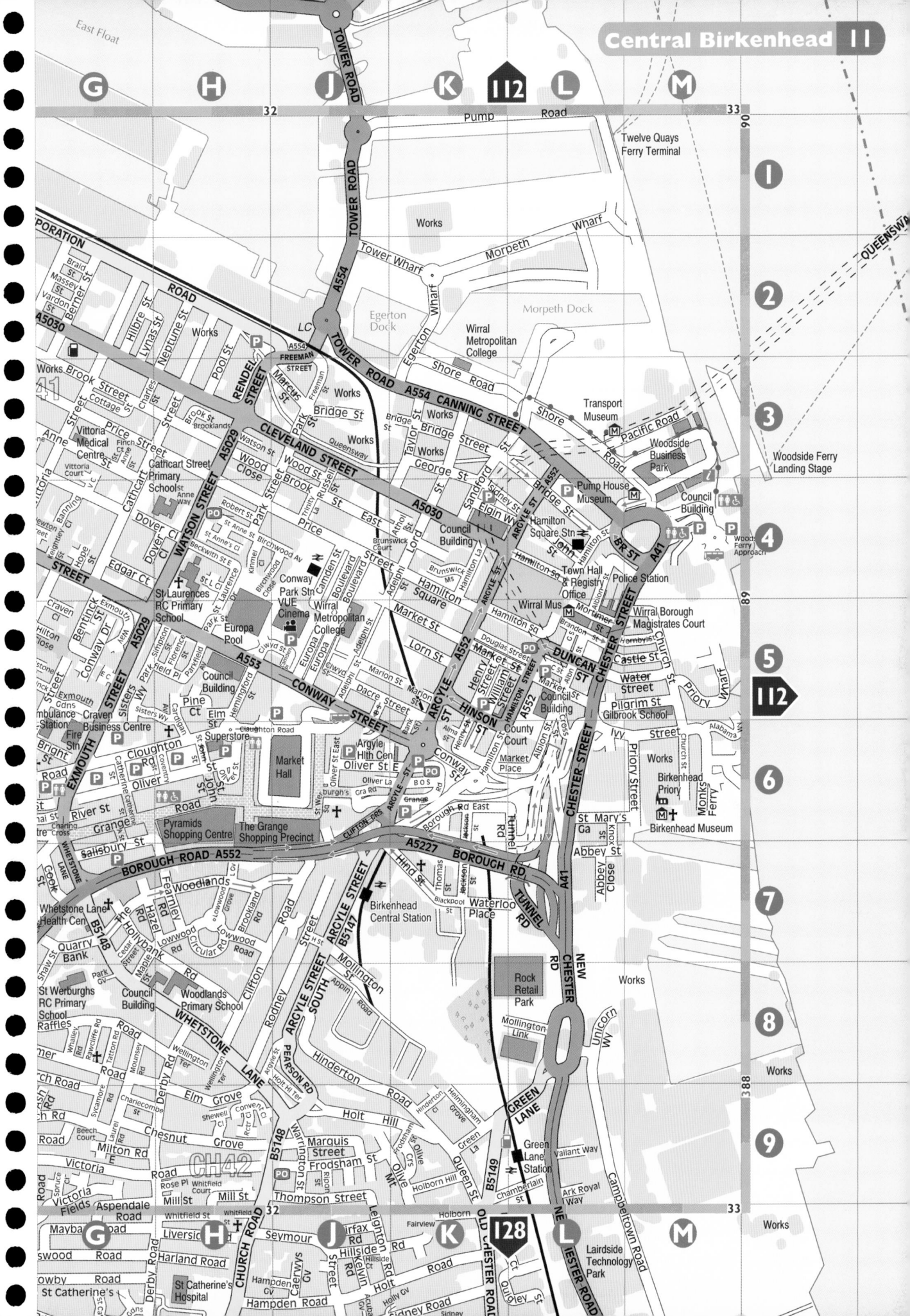

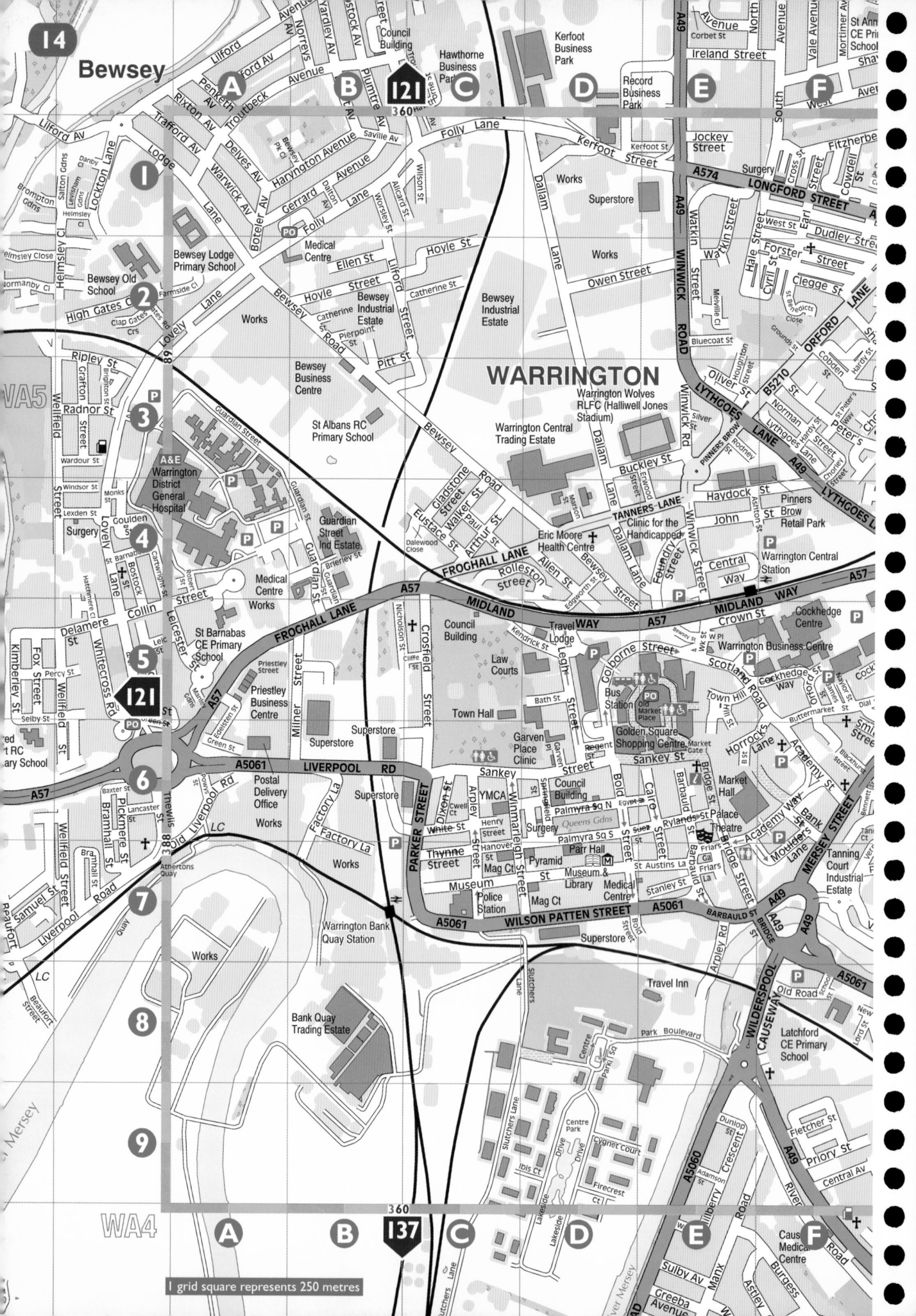

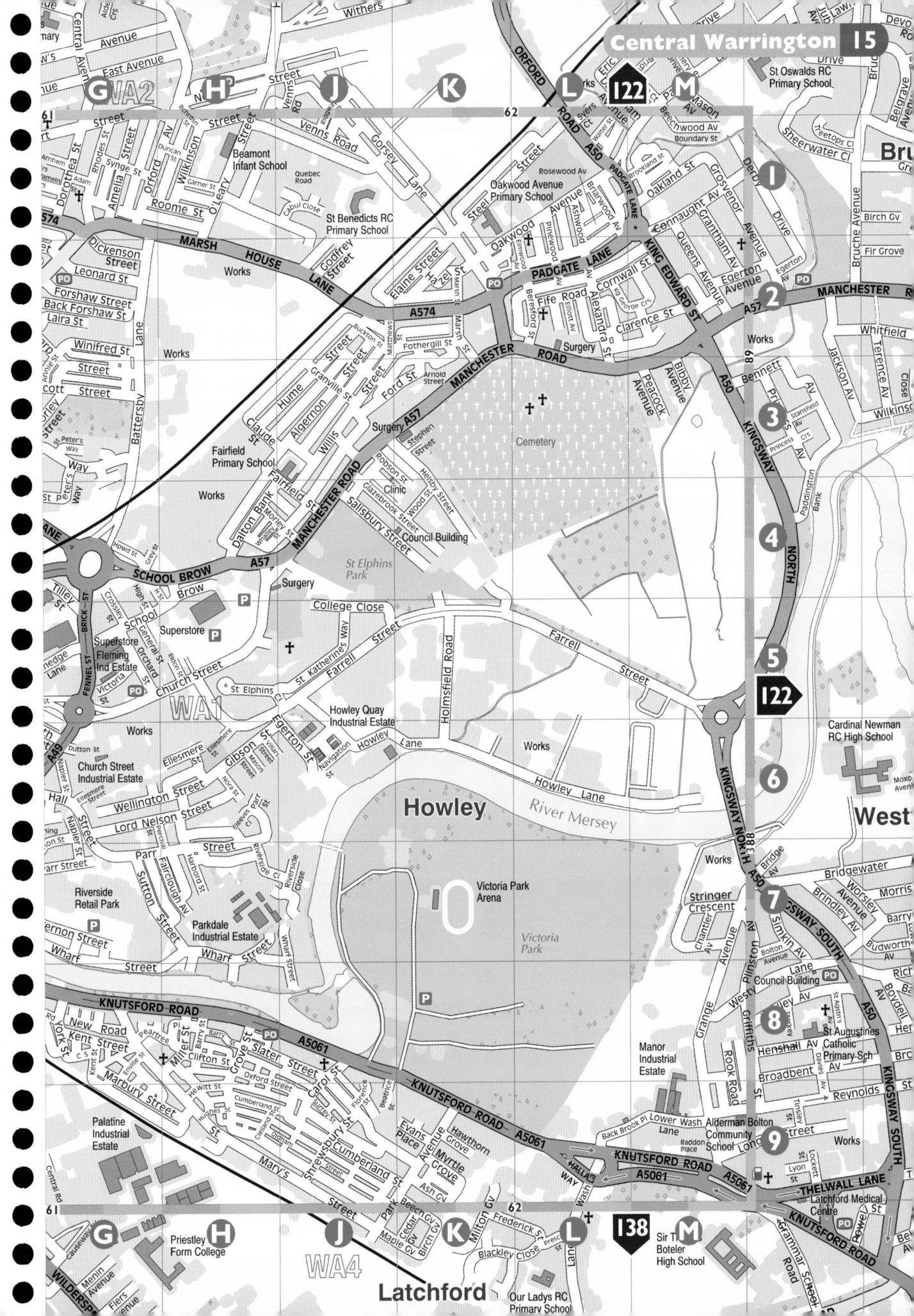

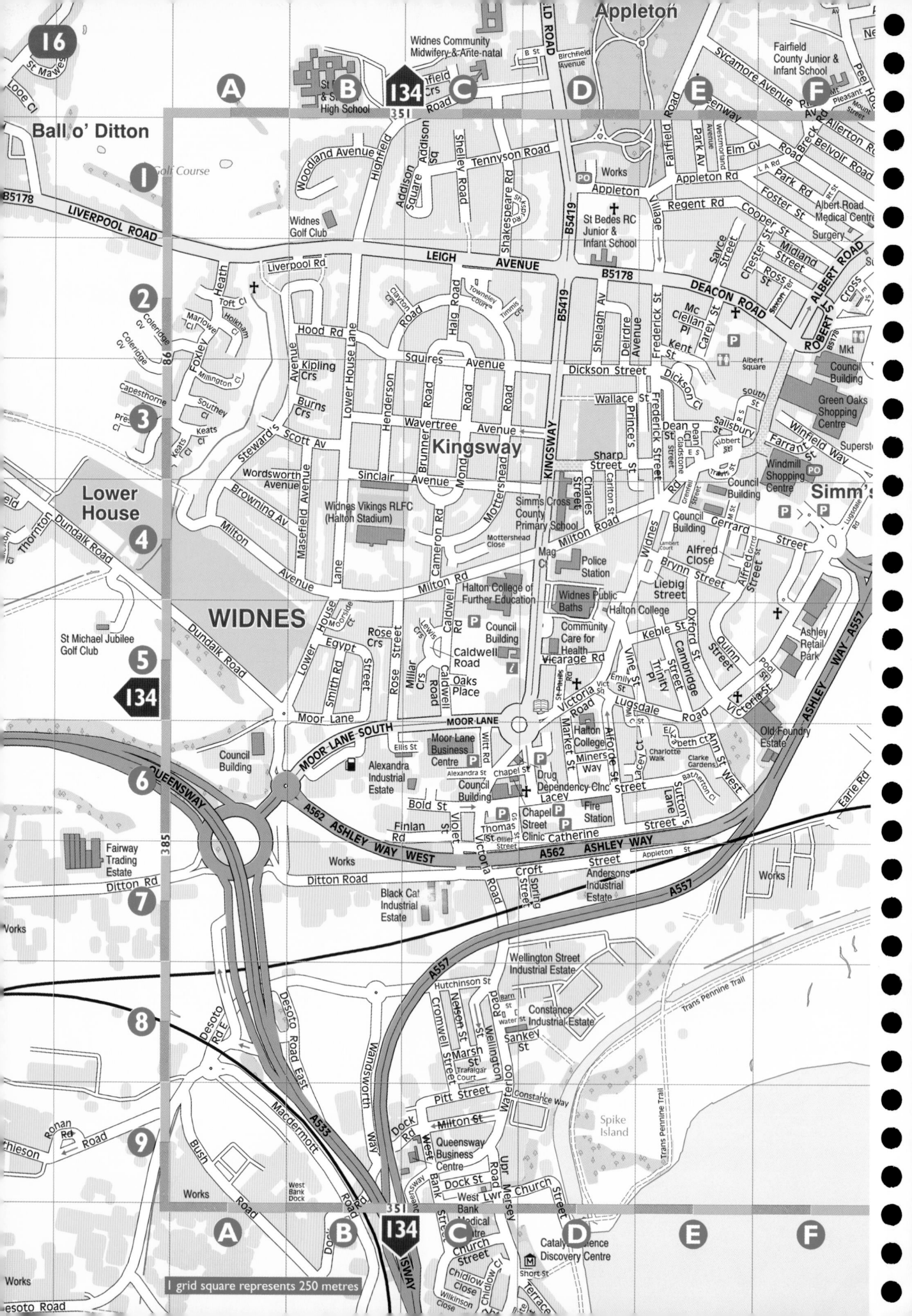

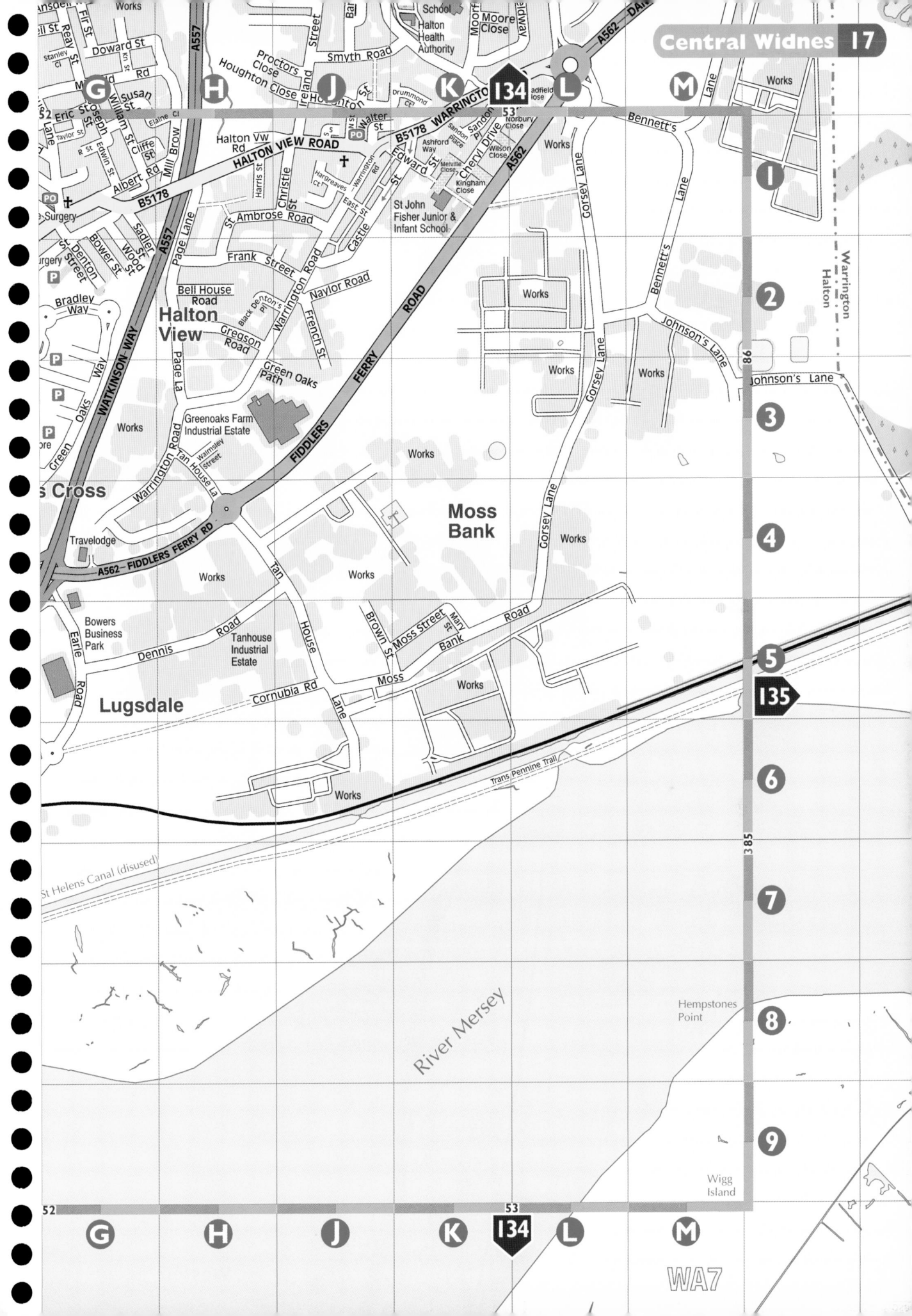

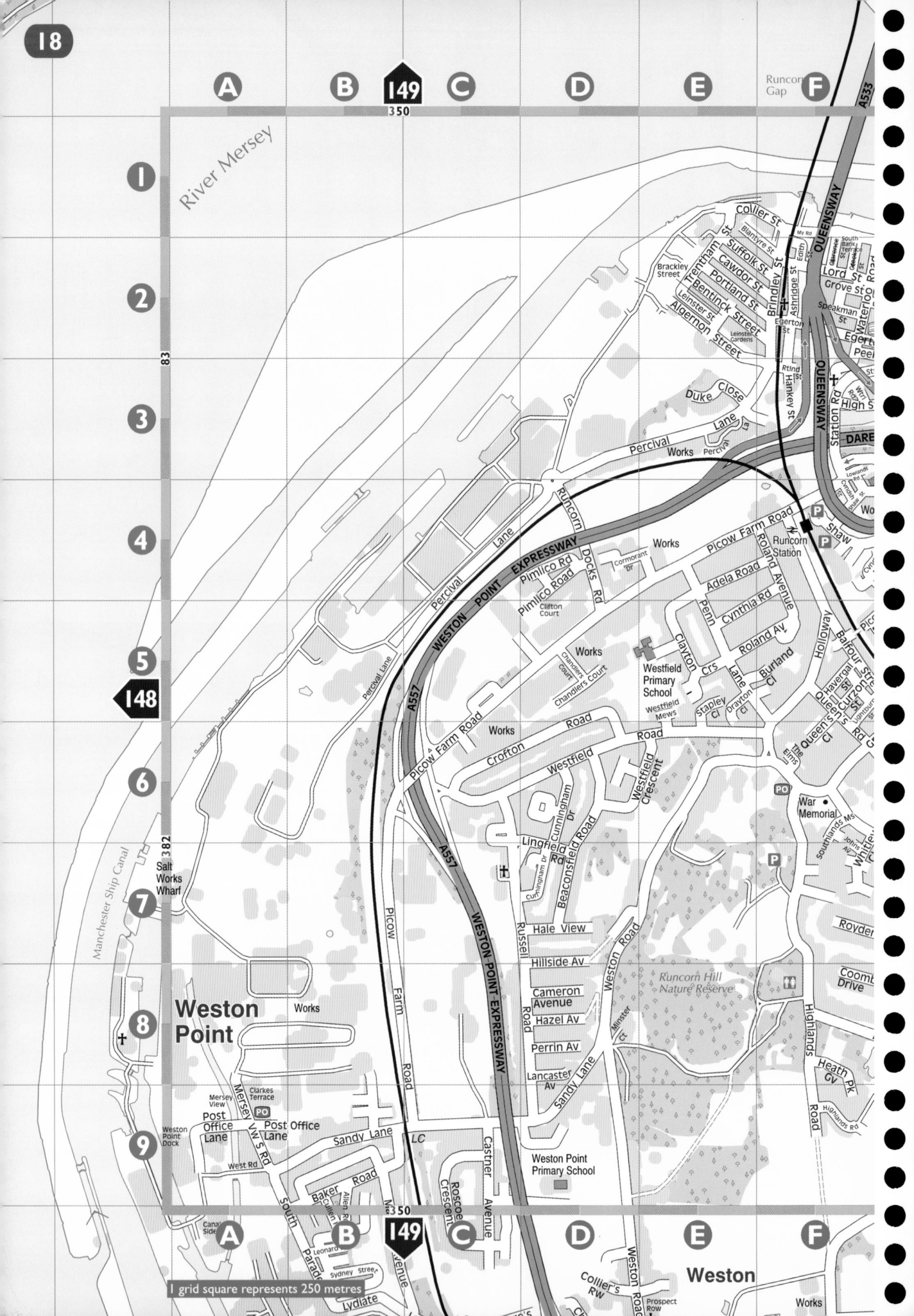

A   B   149   C   D   E   F
        350

Runcorn
Gap

River Mersey

I

2

83

3

4

5

148

6

382

7

Salt
Works
Wharf

Manchester Ship Canal

Weston
Point

8

Works

9

Mersey
View

Clarkes
Terrace

Post
Office
Lane

PO

Post Office
Lane

Weston
Point
Dock

West Rd

Canal
Side

A   B   149   C   D   E   F

Weston

Collier St
St
Biarritz St
My Rd
South
Banks
Terrace
Edith St
Suffolk St
Ashridge St
Brackley
Street
Trentham St
Cawdor St
Brindley St
Lord
Grove st
St
Portland St
Bentinck Street
Leinster st
Speakman
St
Leinster
Gardens
Egerton
St
Algernon
Street
Waterloo
Egerton
St
Peel
Duke
Close
Hankey St
High St
Rtind St
Percival
Percival
Lane
Works
Percival
DARE
Lowlands
Rd

Runcorn
Lane
P
Shaw
Percival
Lane
Works
Picow Farm Road
Runcorn
Station
P
WESTON POINT EXPRESSWAY
Pimlico Rd
Docks Rd
Cormorant
Dr
Roland Avenue
Adela Road
A557
Pimlico Road
Clifton
Court
Penn
Cynthia Rd
Roland Av
Clayton
Burland
Cl
Holloway
Balfour
Str
Works
Chandlers
Court
Westfield
Primary
School
Crs
Lane
Stapley
Cl
Drayton
Queens
Cl
Curzon
Queen's
Rd
Westfield
Mews
Picow Farm Road
Chandlers Court
Westfield
Road
Elms
Crofton
Westfield
Road
Westfield
Crescent
PO
War
Memorial
Works
Cunningham
Dr
Beaconsfield Road
Southlands
Whitlel
A557
Lingfield
Rd
Cunningham Dr
P
Picow
Farm
Road
Hale View
Russell
Hillside Av
Weston Road
Runcorn Hill
Nature Reserve
Royden
Cameron
Avenue
Coomb
Drive
Hazel Av
Minster
Ct
Perrin Av
Sandy Lane
Highlands
Heath
Gv
WESTON POINT EXPRESSWAY
Lancaster
Av
Castner Avenue
Sandy Lane
LC
Highlands Rd
Road
Weston Point
Primary School
Weston
Road
Sandy Lane
South
Parade
Baker
Road
Allen
Cullen
Leonard
Roscoe
Crescent
Collier's
Rw
Sydney Stree
Lydiate
Prospect
Row
A350
Works

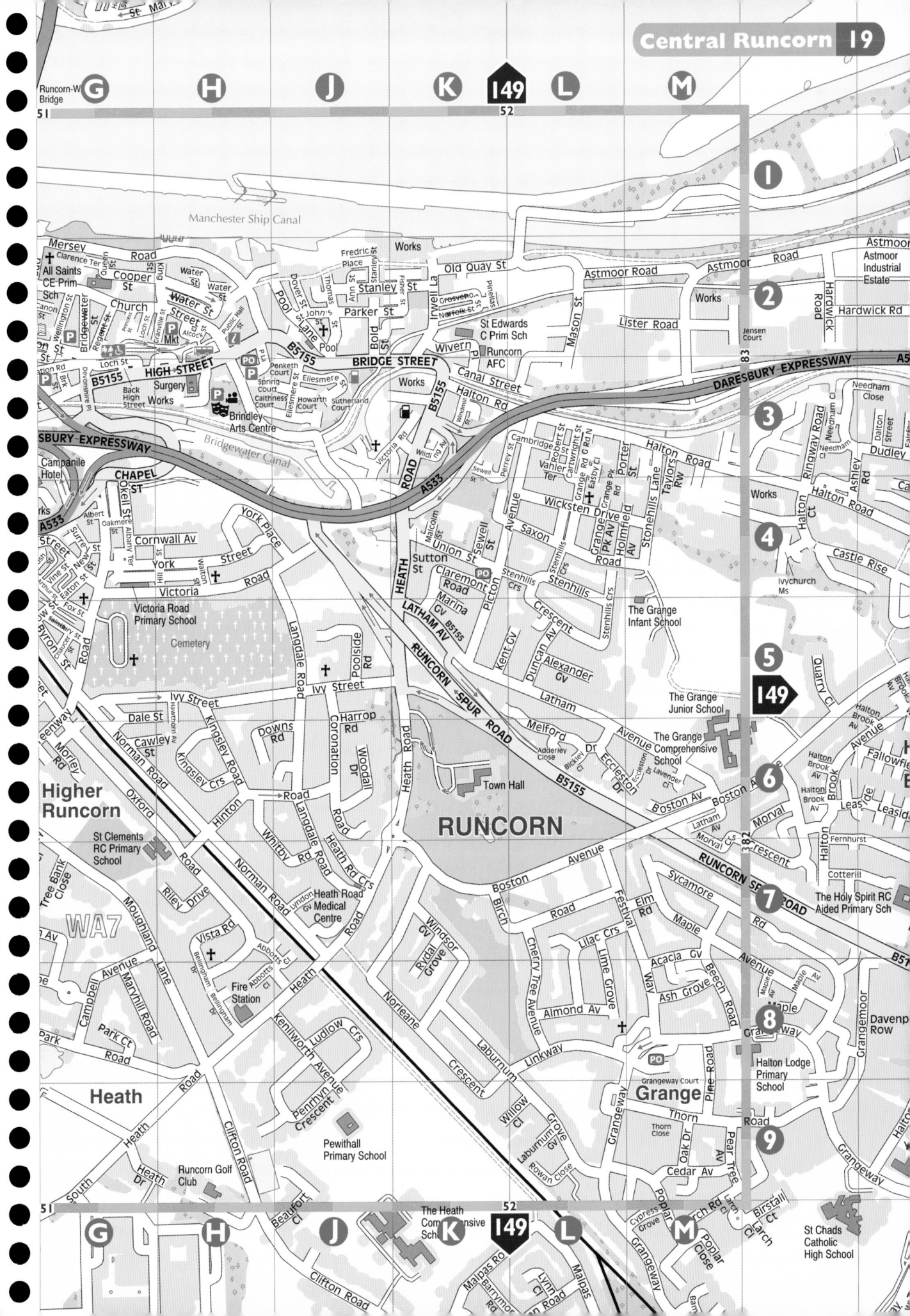

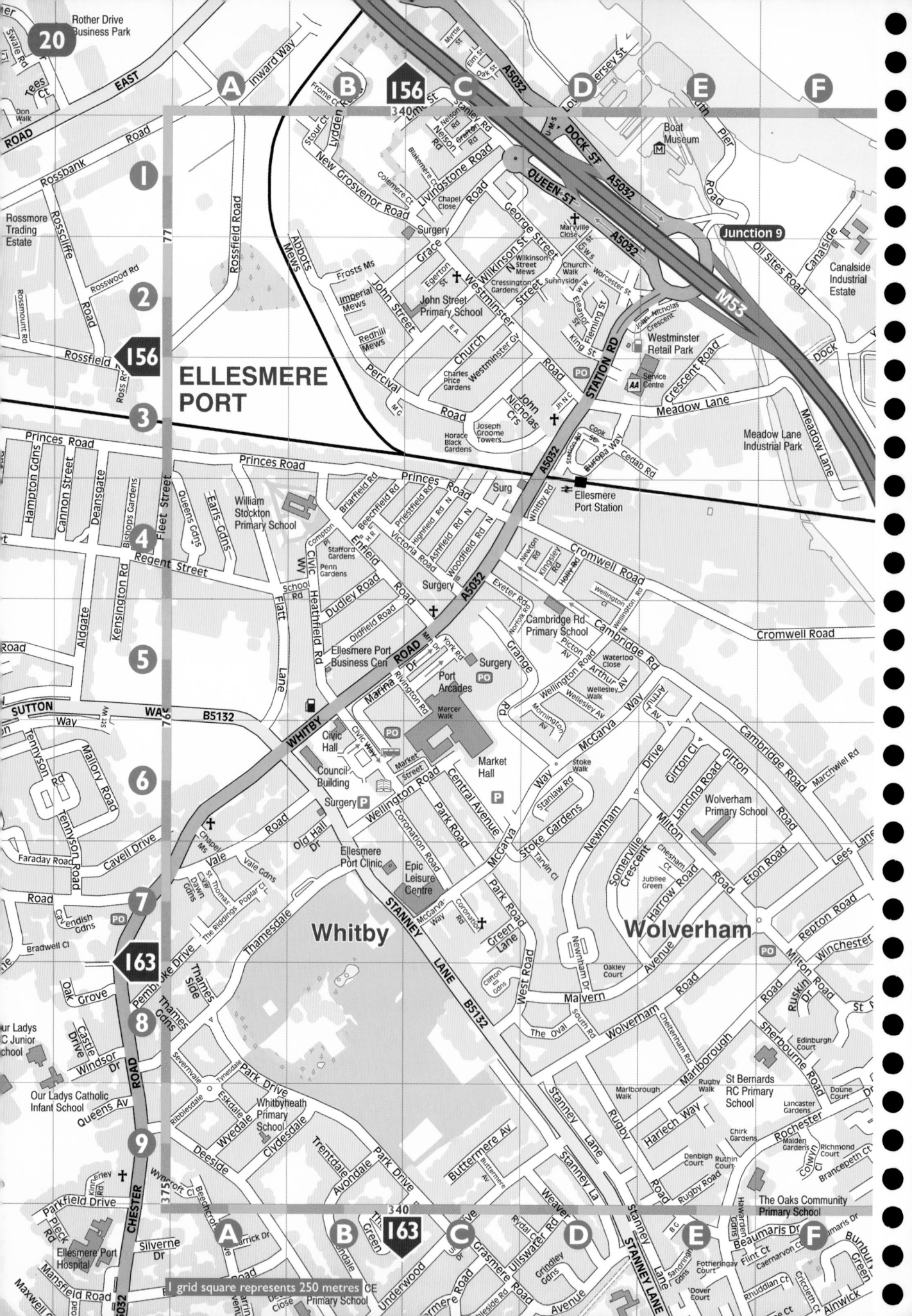

ELLESMERE
PORT

Whitby

Wolverham

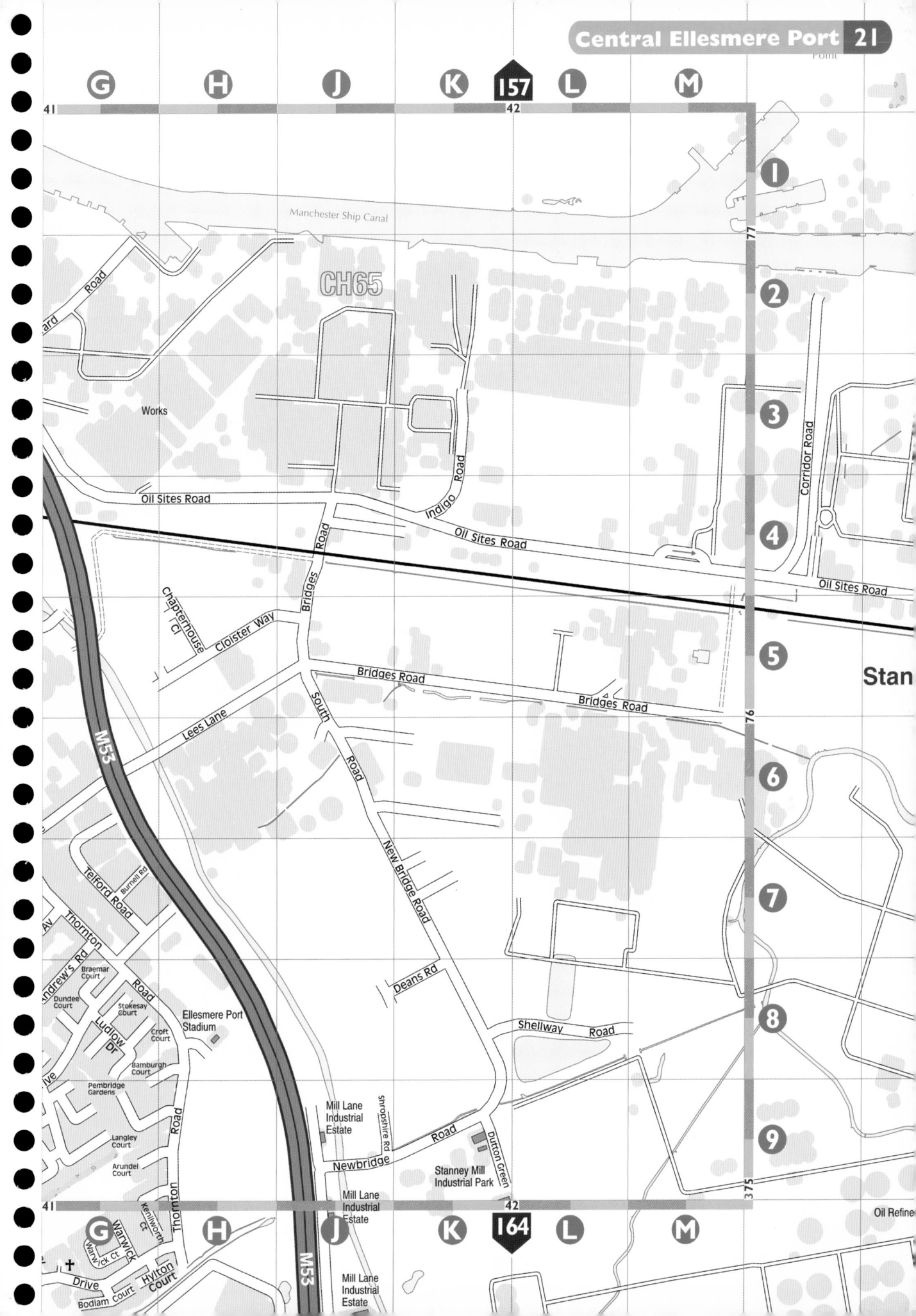

Point

G H J K **157** L M

41 42

Manchester Ship Canal

CH65

Works

Oil Sites Road

Indigo Road

Oil Sites Road

Corridor Road

Oil Sites Road

Bridges Road

Chapterhouse Ct

Cloister Way

Bridges Road

Bridges Road

Lees Lane

South Road

Stan

M53

Telford Road

Burnell Rd

Thornton

New Bridge Road

Andrew's Rd

Braemar Court

Dundee Court

Stokesay Court

Road

Croft Court

Ellesmere Port Stadium

Ludlow Dr

Bamburgh Court

Drive

Pembridge Gardens

Deans Rd

Shellway Road

Langley Court

Road

Mill Lane Industrial Estate

Shropshire Rd

Dutton Green

Arundel Court

Newbridge

Road

Stanney Mill Industrial Park

Thornton

Mill Lane Industrial Estate

1
2
3
4
5
6
7
8
9

77

76

375

41 42

Oil Refine

Warwick Ct

Kenilworth Ct

Warwick

Hylton Court

Drive

Bodlam Court

Mill Lane Industrial Estate

A   B   C   D   E   F

335   36   37

24

I

2

23

3

4

22

5

6

21

7

Works

P

arshside
eserve

8

420

335

Marine Drive

Marshside Road

Stanley

1 grid square represents 500 metres

Lancashire County
Sefton

Crossens
Marsh

Fiddler's
Ferry

Banks Road

Skipton Avenue
Harrogate Way
Crossens Way
Marine Drive
Primrose Cl
Ilkley Av
Whitby
Felview
Meadow
BROW
Bartons Cl
WATER LANE

Menhale Close
Glencoyne Drive
Treen Close
Parkstone Gy
Truro Cl
Dawlish
Millar's Pace
Crediton Av
Melrose Avenue
Eamont Avenue
Ferry Side Lane
Norbury Rd
Kingston Crs
Primrose Cl

Seaton Way
Northam Close
Salcombe Crescent
Seacroft Crescent
Fylde Road
Ferry Side Lane
Works

Salwick Close
Pilling Close
Totnes Drive
Sandburn Crescent
Works
Meadpark Drive

Marine Drive

Works

The Causeway
Tarvin Cl
Woodlea Wy
Turnbury Cl
Primary
School
Byfr Cl

Pool Street

Ridge Cl
Poolside Walk
Holmdale Road
Douglas Brade Road
Ribble Avenue
Asland Gardens
Drewitt Crs

Brook Street
Land
Lane
Works

Elswick Road
Garstang Road
Freckleton Road
Hornby Road
Inskip Road
Catton Close
Seaton Wy
Coyford Dr
burn
Fylde Road

A   B   C   25   D   E   F

Crossens

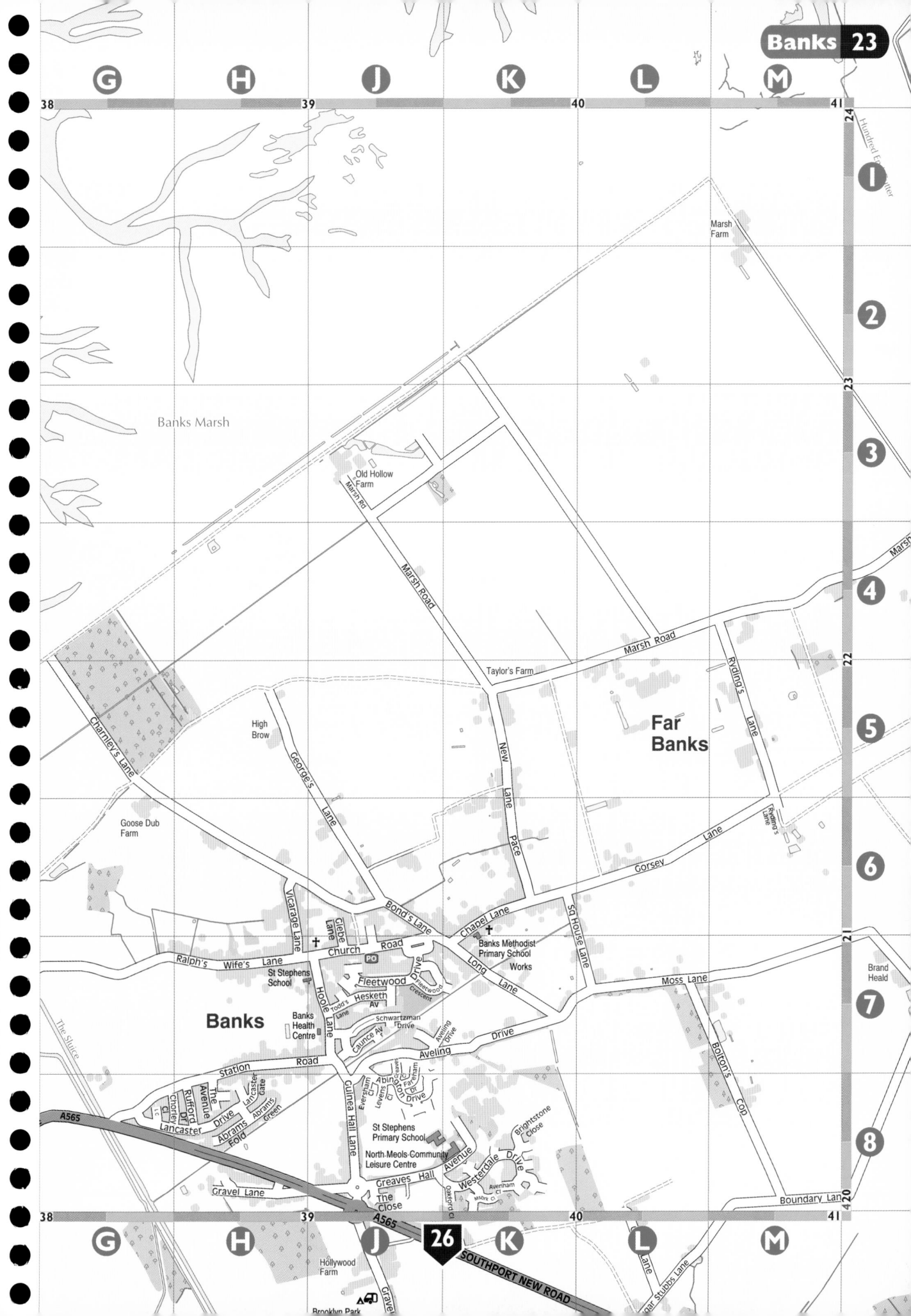

Marshside RSPB
Reserve

Marshside
Sands

Golf

SOUTHPORT

Southport
Pier

Southport
Sailing Club

West Lancs
Yacht Club

Marine Lake

Golf Course

Southport
Municipal
Golf Club

Hesketh
Centre
(Hospital)

Stutelea Hotel
& Leisure Club

PARK CRES

ALBERT ROAD

PARK CRESC

Theatre &
Floral Hall

Police Station &
Mag Courts

Fire Station

Funland

Pleasureland

Southport Zoo &
Conservation Trust

Model
Village

Royal
Clifton
Hotel

Esplanade

Southport
Swimming
Baths

Southport Flower
Show Site

Superstore

Sunnymede
School

Beach
Road

Southport &
Formby Hosp
Health
Clinic

Southport
College

Primary
School

YMCA

MANCHESTER ROAD

Kensington
Industrial
Estate

Kensington
Ind Est

Railway
Centre

Rosehill
Business
Park

Register
Office

Southport
Business
Gen

Art Gal

Marble Place
Shopping Cen

ABC
Cinema

Metropole
Hotel

Southport
New
Synagogue

ST LUKE'S

Works

Works

Mill St

Hargreaves
St

Virginia
St

Works

Surgery

St Philips
CE Primary School

ASH STREET

ROSE HILL

NEW ROAD

SCARISBRICK

Southport
General
Infirmary

Southport
Landing Area

West
School

Castle WK

St Paul's
St

AUGHTON ROAD

LULWORTH ROAD

A565

Gloucester Rd

Saxon Road

Palatine
Road

York Avenue

The British Lawnmower Museum

Chromolyte
Ind Est

Cheriton
Park

Linaker
Prim Sch

CEMETERY ROAD

A5267

Camberley CI
Palace Road

Ascot
Close

Westcliffe

Warren
Cres

Blandford
Close

Birkdale
Station

Swimming

Infant
School

VERTON R

1 grid square represents 500 metres

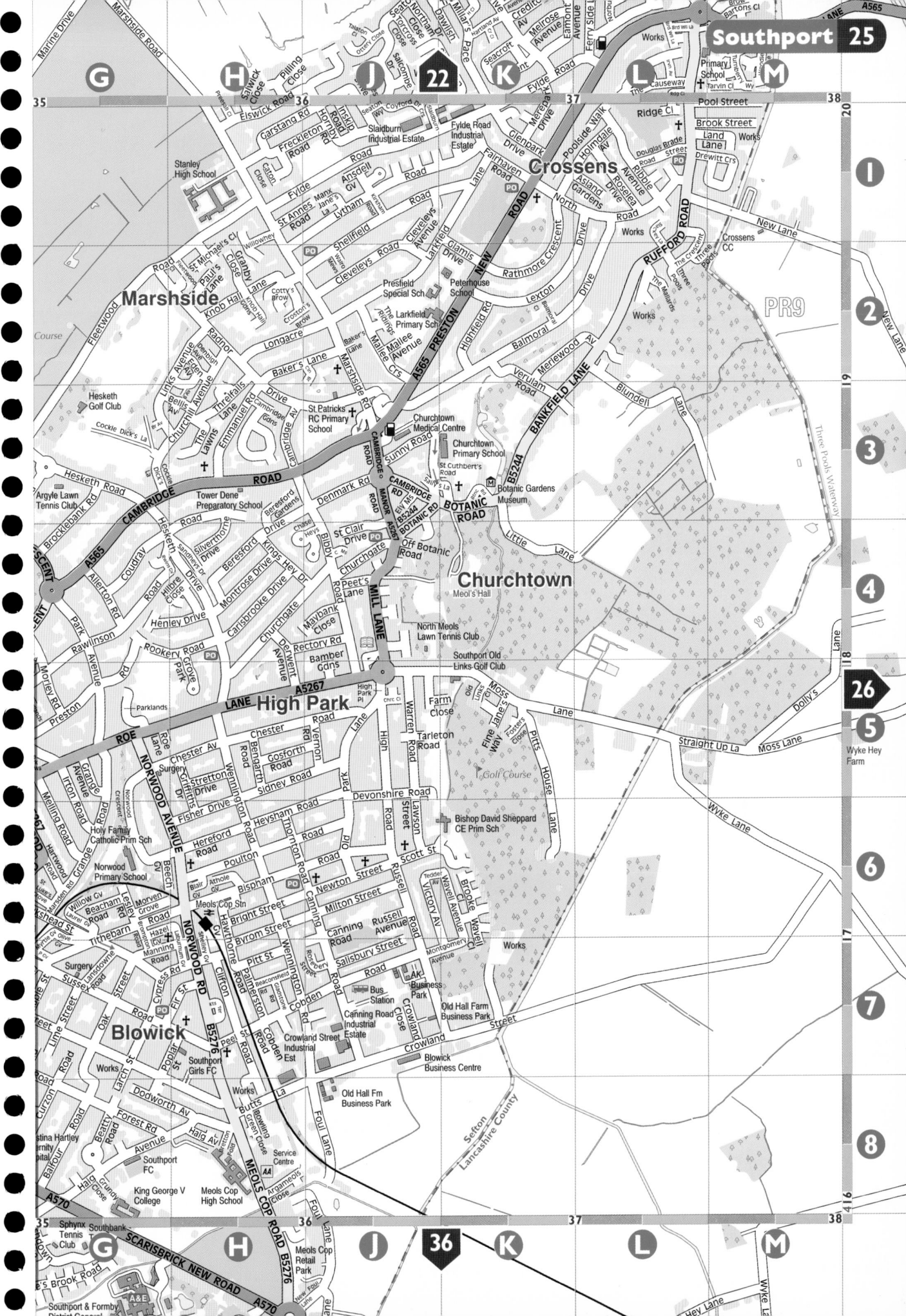

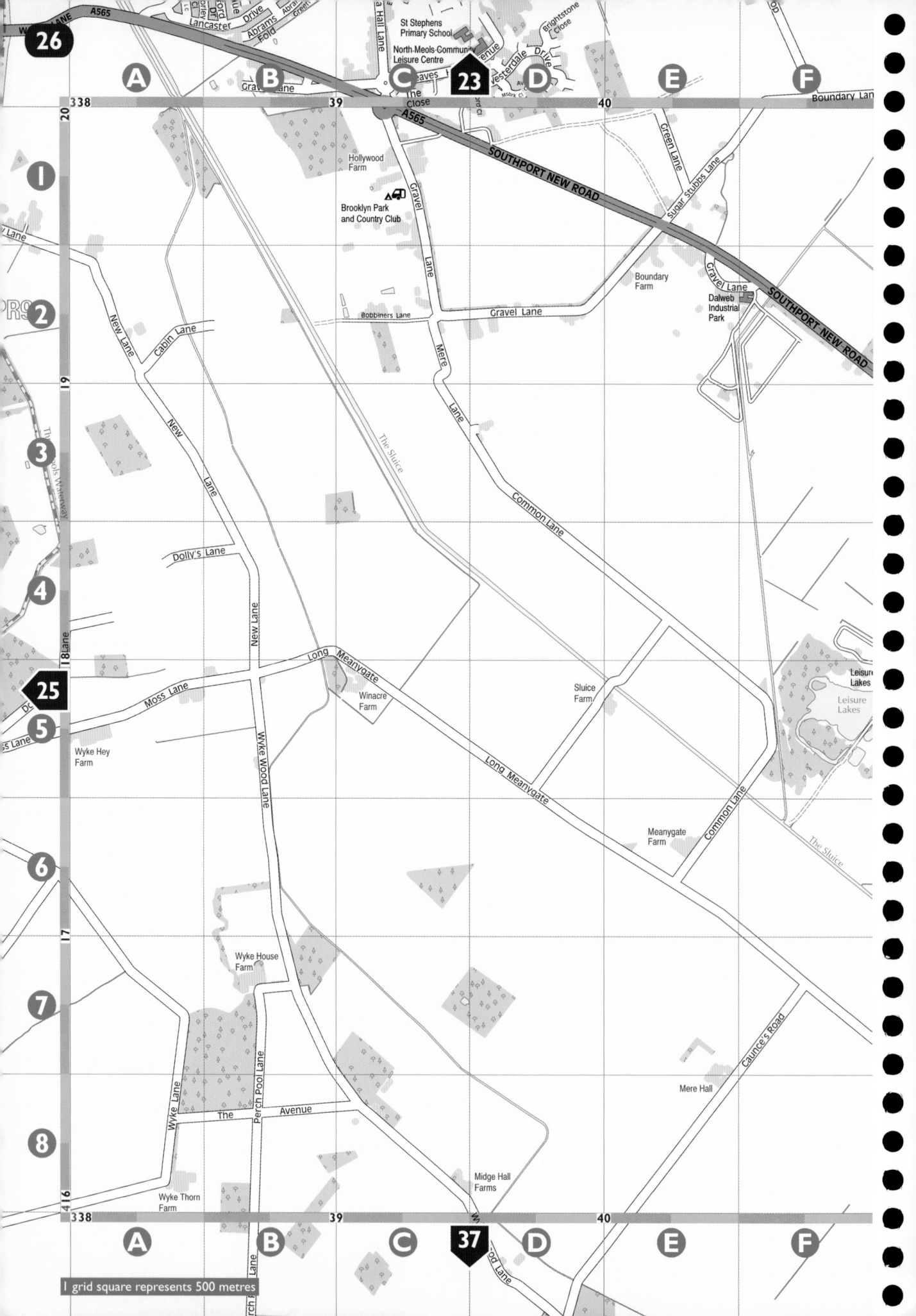

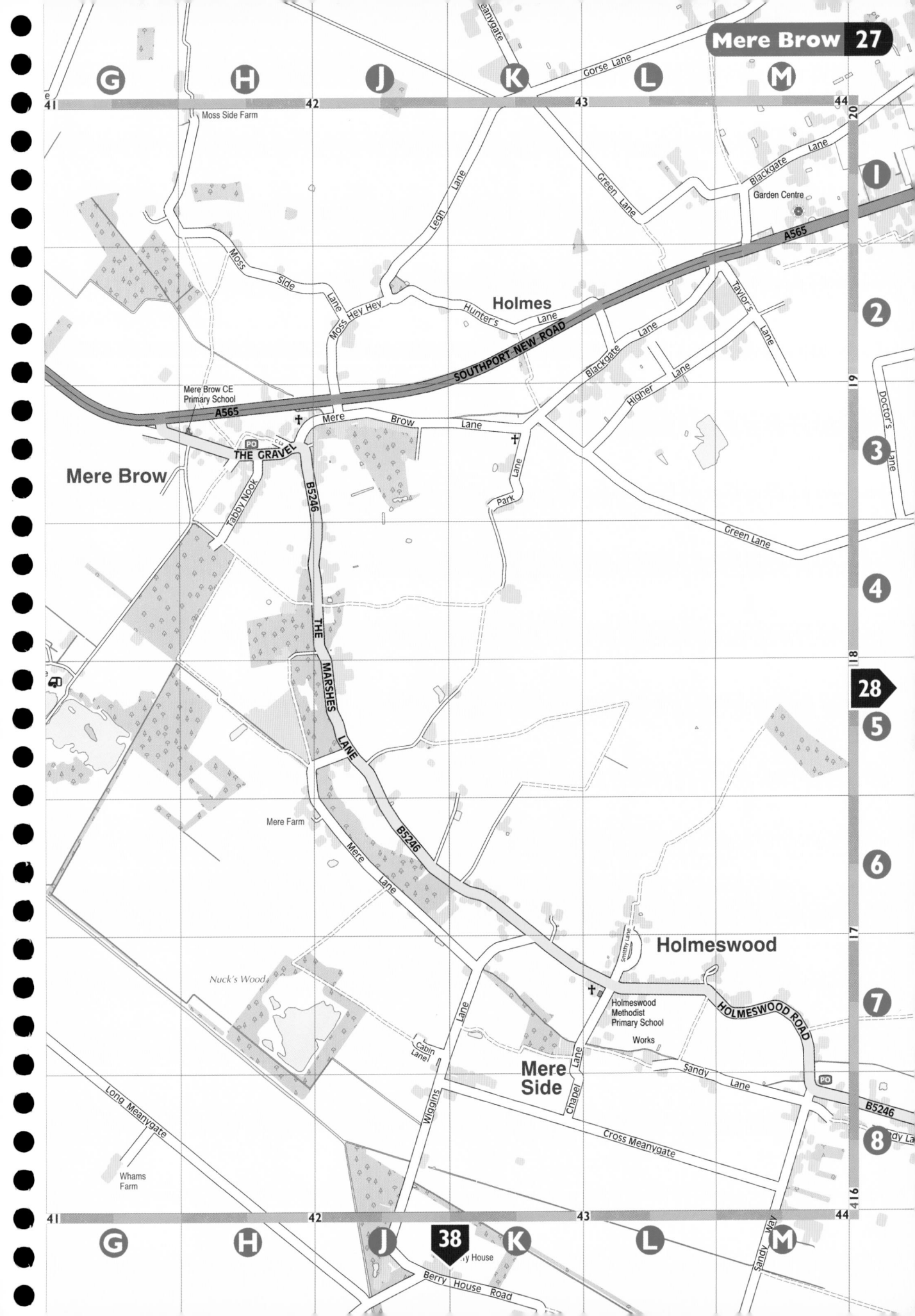

Moss Side Farm

G H J K L M

Gorse Lane

Green Lane

Blackgate Lane

Garden Centre

A565

Holmes

SOUTHPORT NEW ROAD

Moss Side Lane

Legh Lane

Hunter's Lane

Lane

Blackgate Lane

Higher Lane

Taylor's Lane

Doctor's Lane

Mere Brow CE Primary School

A565

PO

THE GRAVEL

CU

Mere Brow

Tabby Nook

B5246

Mere Brow Lane

Park Lane

Green Lane

THE MARSHES LANE

Mere Farm

B5246

Mere Lane

28

Nuck's Wood

Cabin Lane

Wiggins Lane

Lane

Chapel Lane

Smithy Lane

Holmeswood

Holmeswood Methodist Primary School

Works

HOLMESWOOD ROAD

Sandy Lane

PO

B5246

Sandy La

Mere Side

Long Meanygate

Whams Farm

Cross Meanygate

G H J 38 K L M

ry House

Berry House Road

Sandy Way

I 2 3 4 5 6 7 8

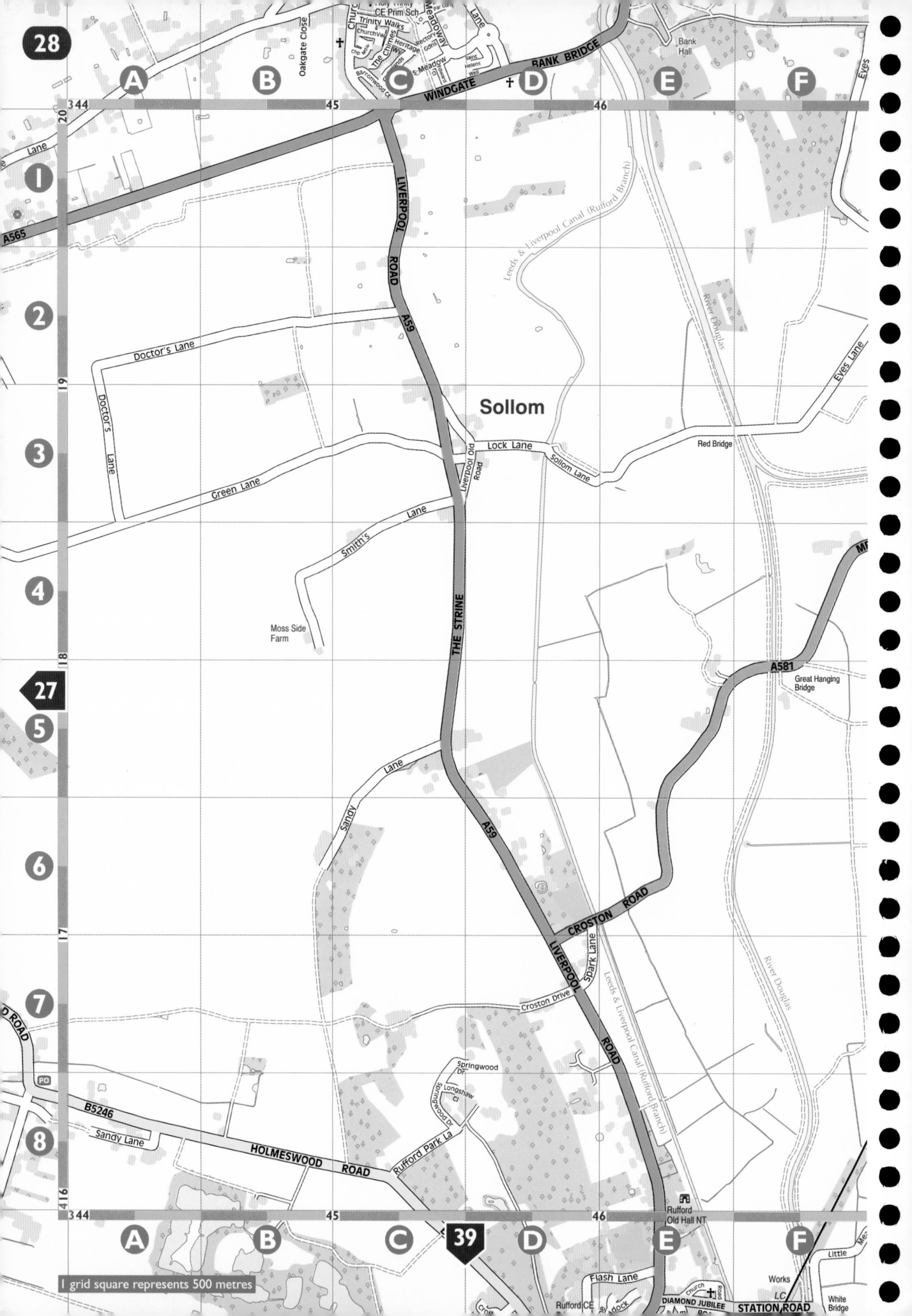

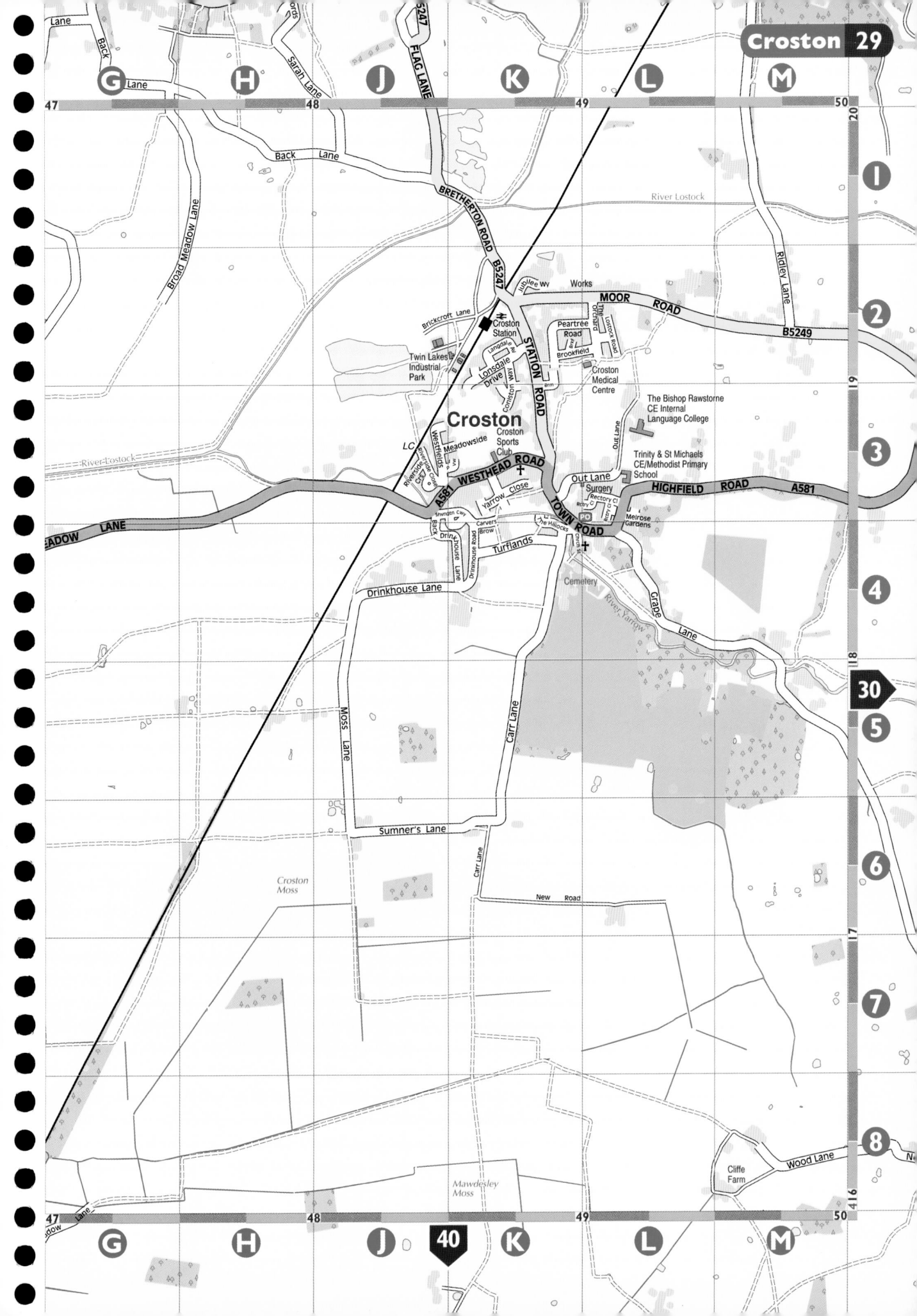

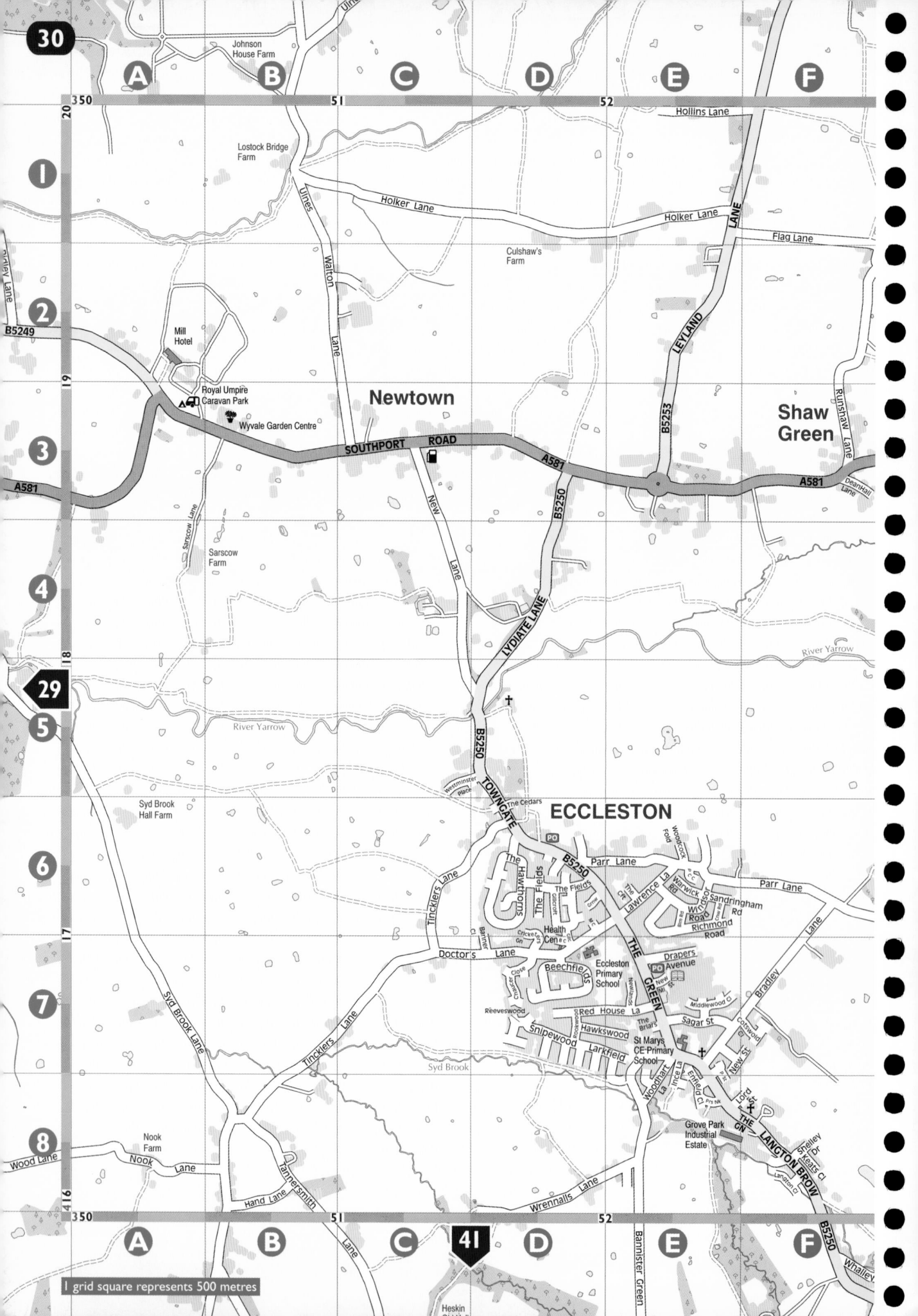

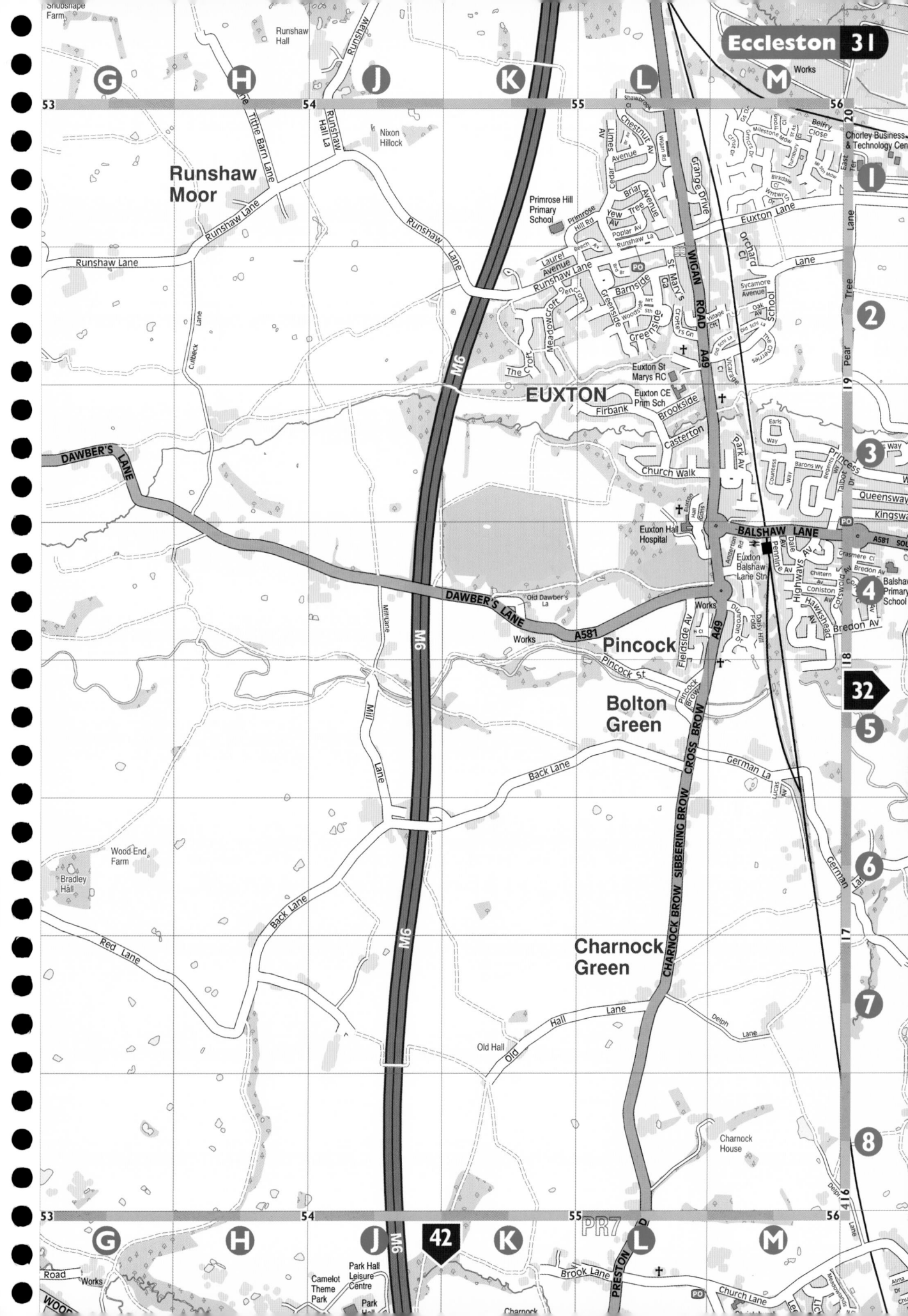

1 grid square represents 500 metres

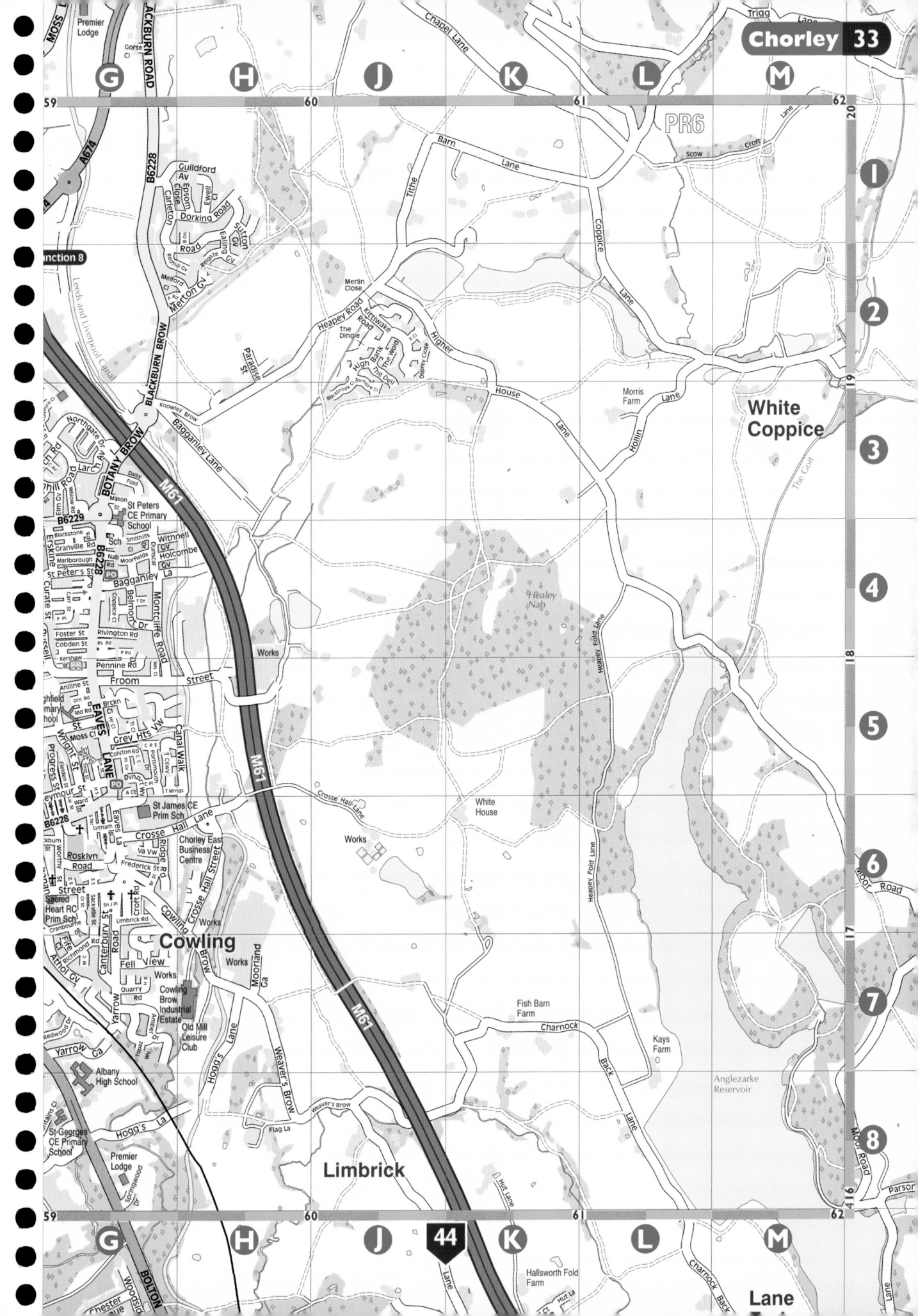

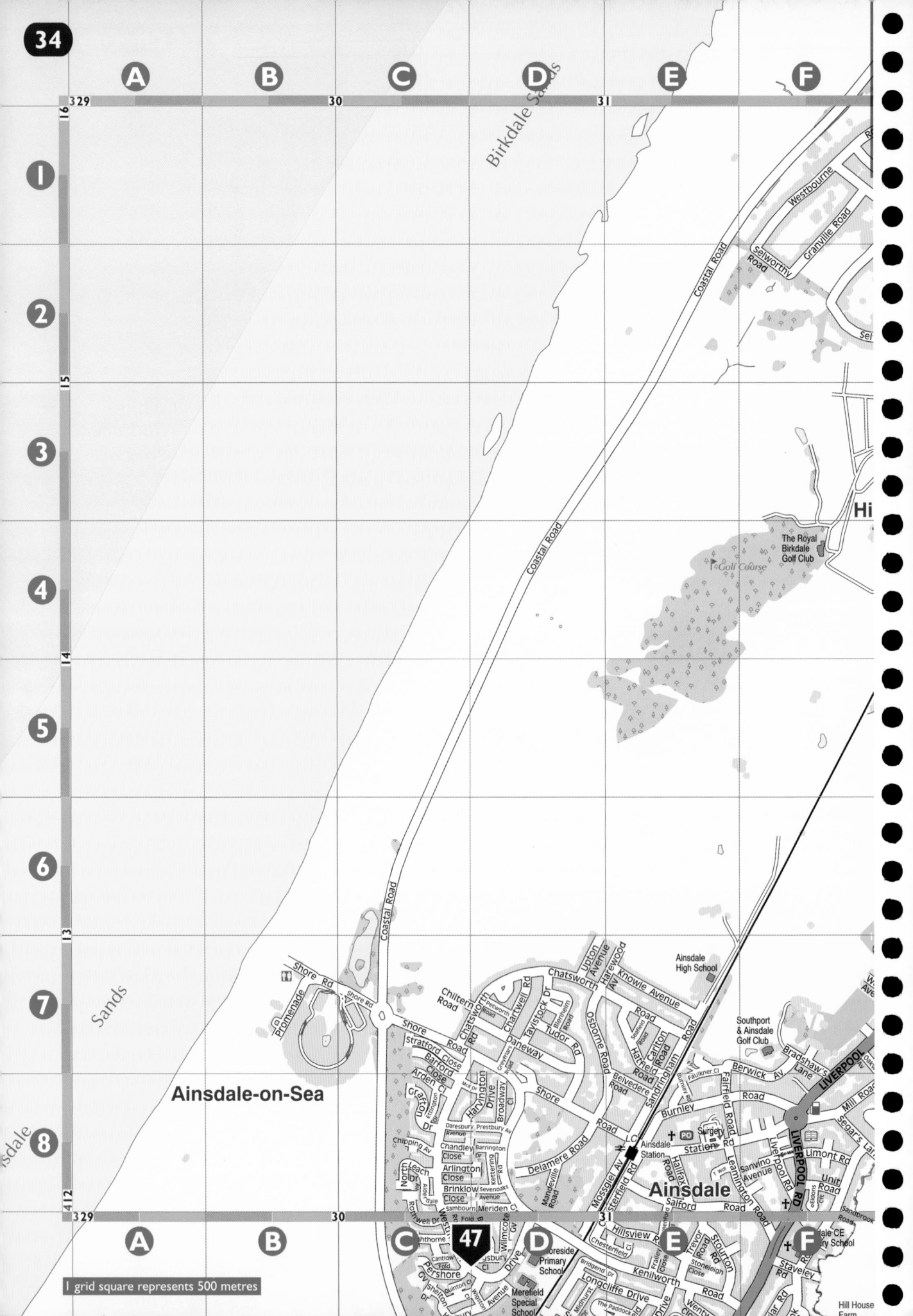

329 30 31

16

15

14

13

12

329 30 31

A B C D E F

Birkdale Sands

Westbourne

Granville Road

Selworthy Road

Coastal Road

Sel

Hi

The Royal Birkdale Golf Club

Golf Course

Coastal Road

Coastal Road

Sands

Shore Rd

Promenade

Shore Rd

Ainsdale-on-Sea

Shore Road

Stratford Av

Barford Close

Grefton Dr

Harrington Drive

Broadway

Shore

Chiltern Road

Chatsworth Rd

Petworth

Tavystock Dr

Tudor Rd

Daneway

Chartwell Rd

Upton Avenue

Chatsworth Road

Harewood

Knowle Avenue

Osborne Road

Hatfield Road

Carlton Road

Belvedere Road

Sandringham Road

Ainsdale High School

Ainsdale Station

Southport & Ainsdale Golf Club

Bradshaw's Lane

Berwick Av

LIVERPOOL

Chipping Av

Leach

Arden

Union

Daresbury Avenue

Prestbury Av

Chandley Close

Barrington

Kettering Av

Arlington Close

Brinklow Close

Sevenoaks Avenue

Delamere Road

Mandeville Road

Shore Road

Burnley Road

Surgery

PO

Mossley Av

Chesterfield Rd

Halifax Road

Leamington Road

Sanvino Avenue

Fairfield Road

Liverpool Rd

LIVERPOOL RD

Sedar's Lane

Limont Rd

Unit Road

Mill Road

Ainsdale

Salford Road

Coastal Road

Ainsdale CE Primary School

dale

dsdale

Cantlow Fold

Quinton

Sambourn

Meriden Avenue

Pershore

GV Shelton Dr

Wilmcote Cl

Weston Drive

Hillsview Rd

Chesterfield

Longcliffe Drive

Bridgend Dr

Stoneleigh Close

Staveley Rd

Foreside Primary School

Merefield Special School

The Paddock

Hill House Farm

47

Staley

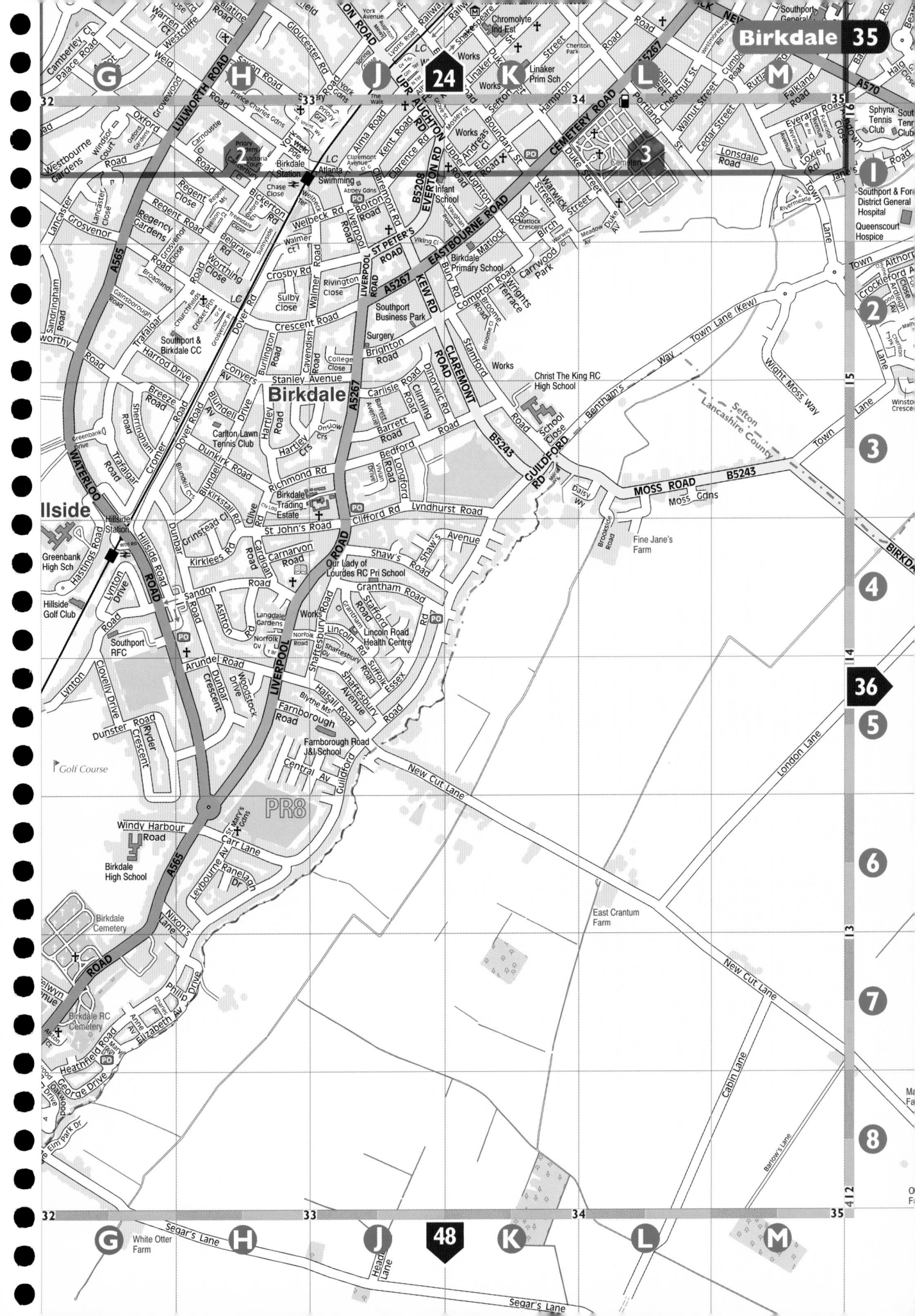

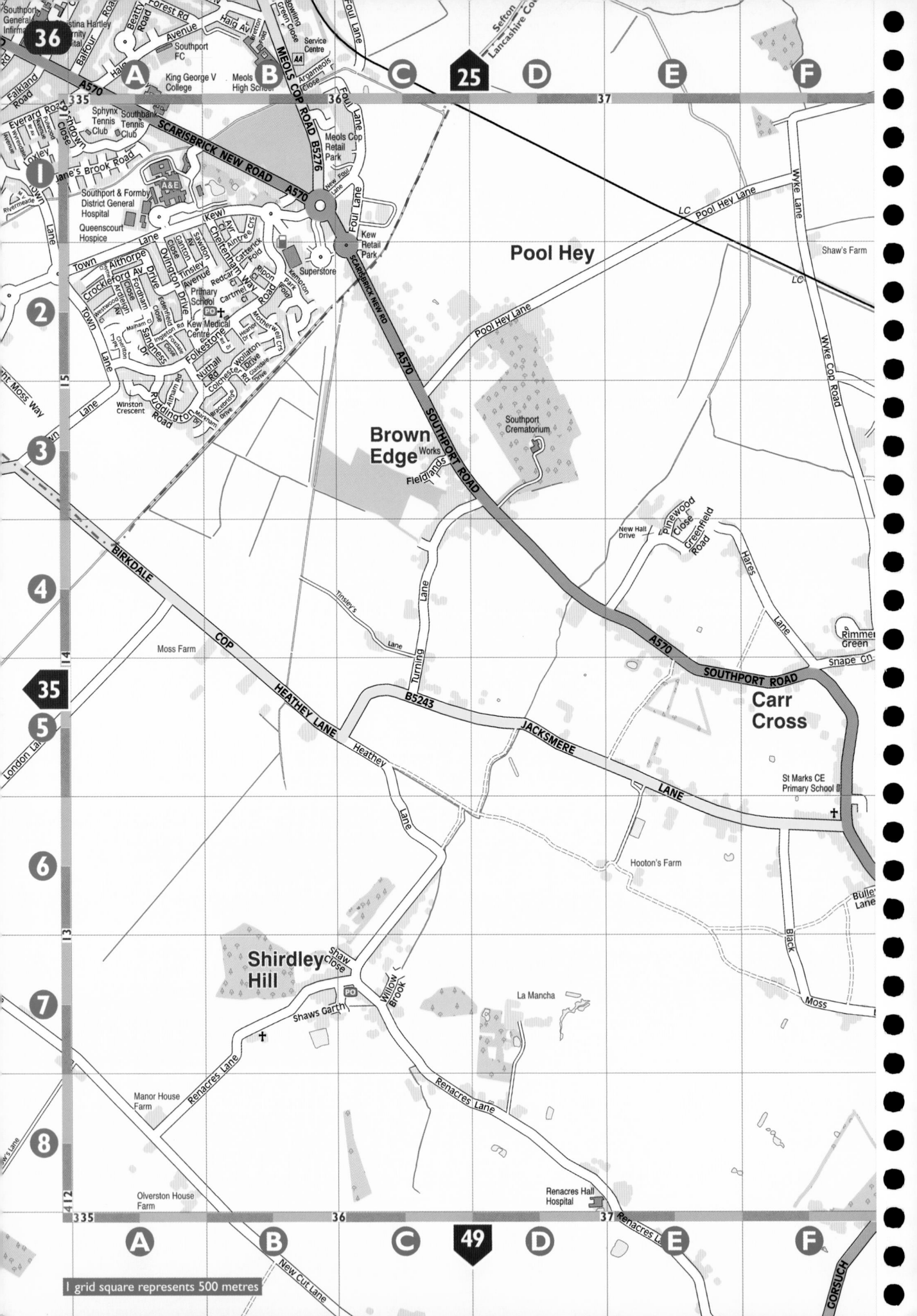

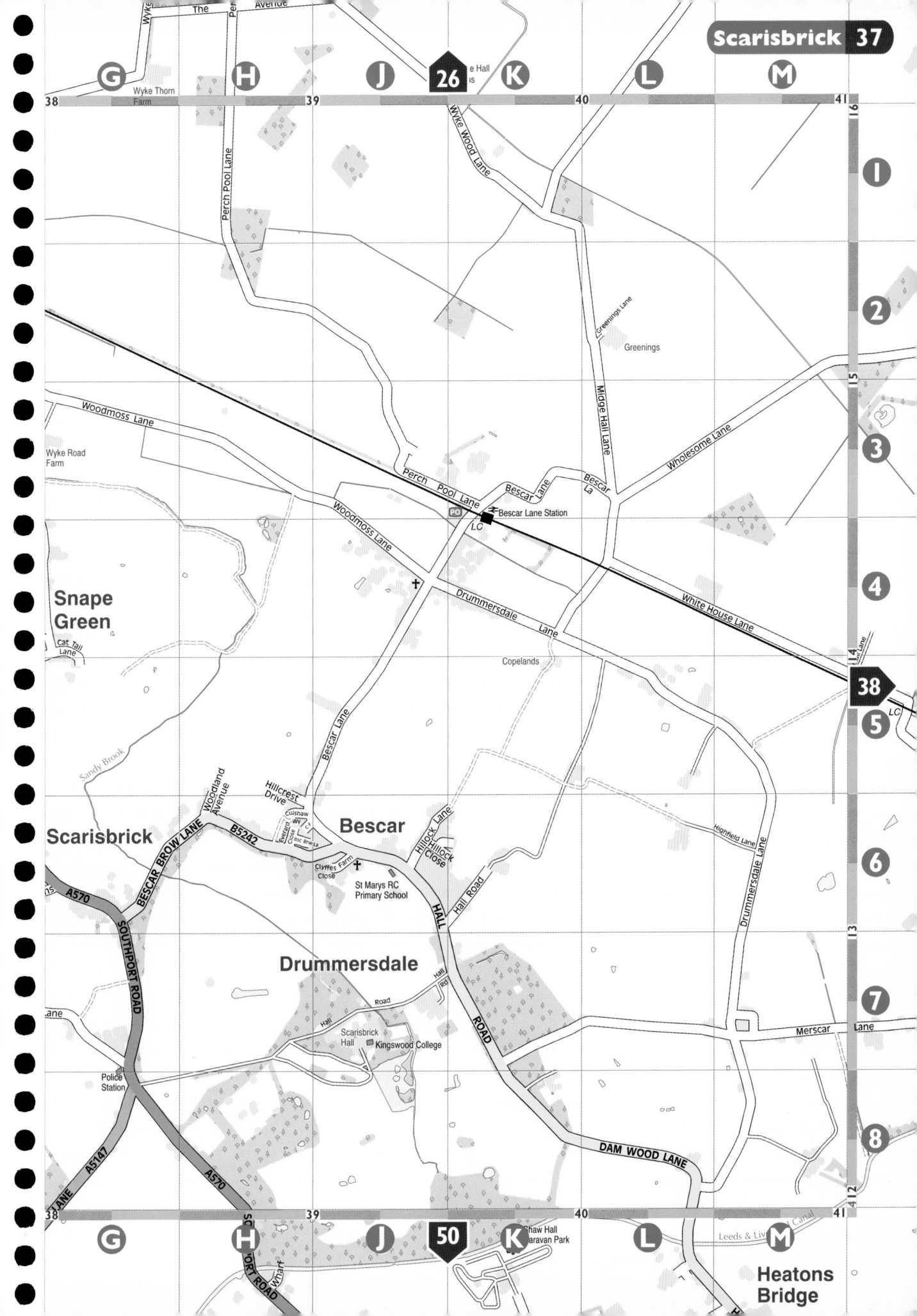

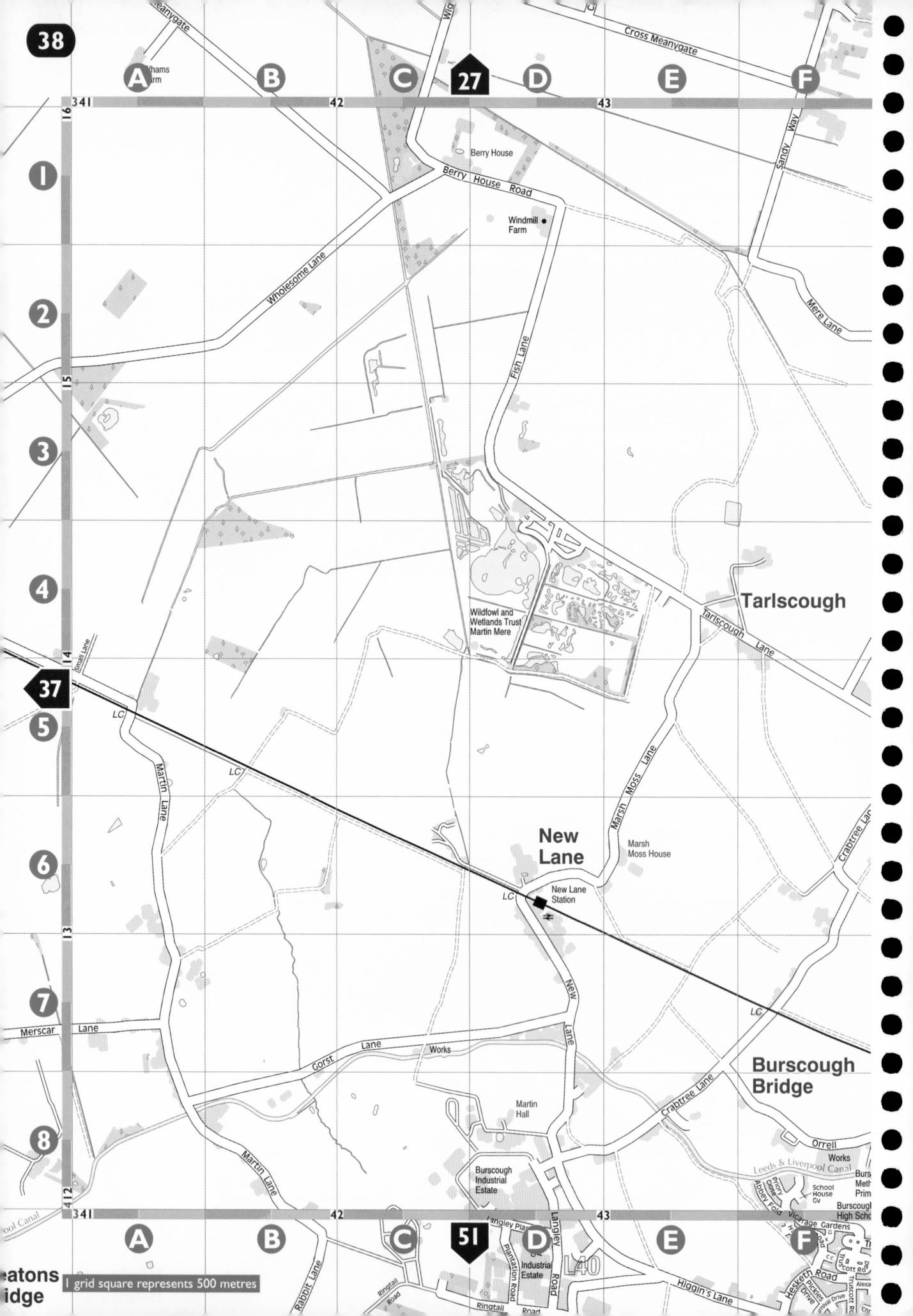

A B C 27 D E F

341 42 43

16

1

Whams Farm

2

15

3

4

14

37 5

6

13

7

8

412

341 42 43

A B C 51 D E F

L40

eatons
idge

1 grid square represents 500 metres

Cross Meanygate

Berry House

Berry House Road

Windmill Farm

Wholesome Lane

Fish Lane

Tarlscough

Wildfowl and Wetlands Trust Martin Mere

Tarlscough Lane

Mere Lane

Way

Sandy

Small Lane

LC

LC

Martin Lane

Marsh Moss Lane

Marsh Moss House

New Lane

New Lane Station

LC

New Lane

Crabtree Lane

LC

Merscar Lane

Gorst Lane

Works

Martin Hall

Burscough Bridge

Crabtree Lane

Orrell

Works

Martin Lane

Burscough Industrial Estate

Langley Pla

Plantation Road

Industrial Estate

Langley Road

Ringtail Road

Ringtail Road

Higgin's Lane

Hesketh Road

Leeds & Liverpool Canal

School House Cv

Burscough High School

Vicarage Gardens

ol Canal

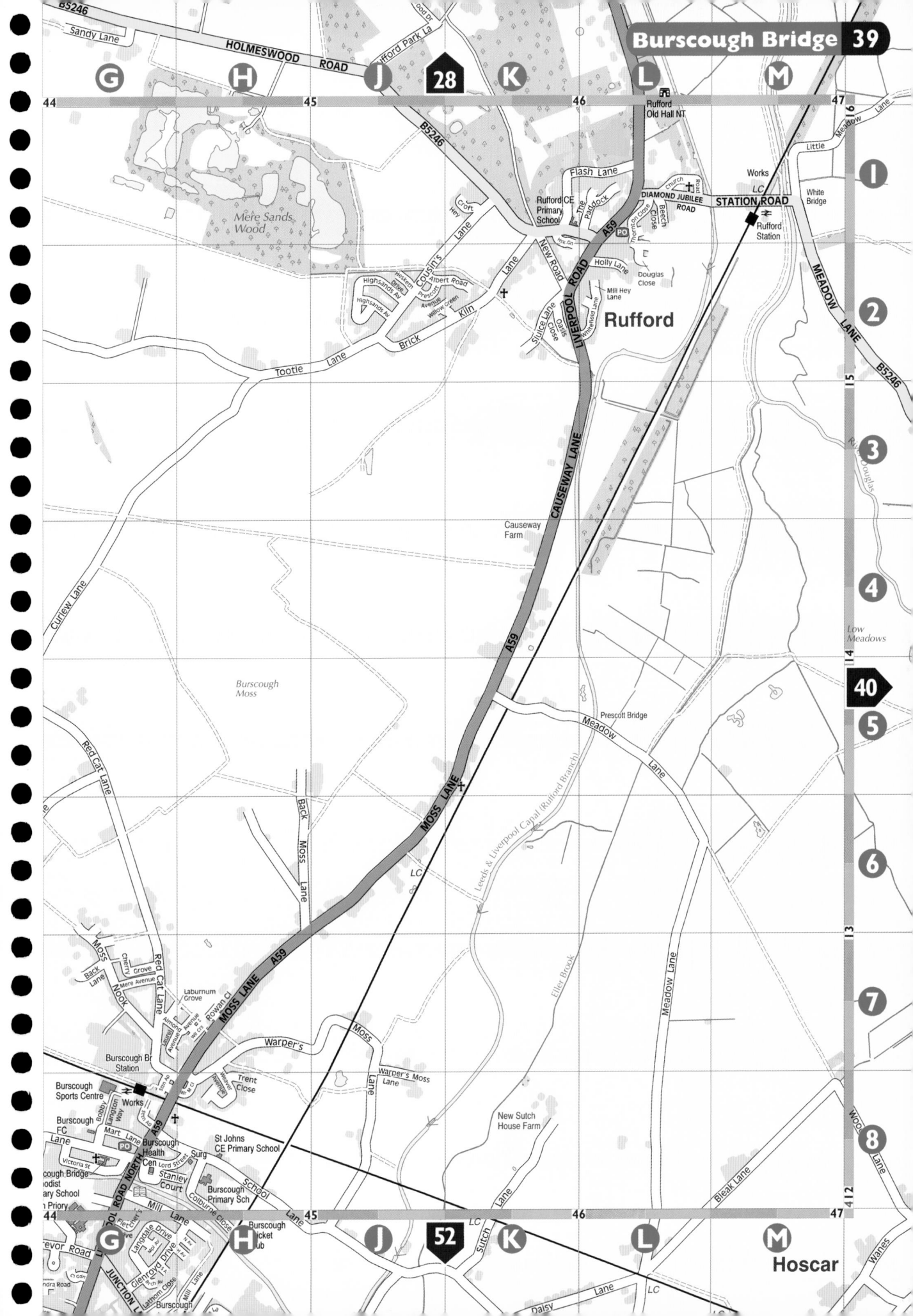

B5246

Sandy Lane

HOLMESWOOD ROAD

Rufford Park La

B5246

G **H** **J** **28** **K** **L** **M**

44 45 46 47

Rufford Old Hall NT

Little

Meadow Lane

Flash Lane

16

Works

LC

Station Road

White Bridge

I

The Paddock

Rufford CE Primary School

Church

DIAMOND JUBILEE ROAD

Beech Close

PO

Rufford Station

Croft Hey

Hey Gn

Holly Lane

Thornton Close

2

Willow Green

Mere Sands Wood

Highsands Av

Highsands Av

Prescott Avenue

Cousin's Lane

Albert Road

Kiln Lane

Brick Lane

Sluice Lane

Oasis Close

LIVERPOOL ROAD

New Road

Mill Hey Lane

Whytefield Lane

Douglas Close

Rufford

River Douglas

15

3

Tootle Lane

CAUSEWAY LANE

Curlew Lane

A59

Causeway Farm

4

Low Meadows

14

40

Burscough Moss

Red Cat Lane

Back Moss Lane

MOSS LANE

LC

Prescott Bridge

Meadow Lane

Leeds & Liverpool Canal (Rufford Branch)

5

Eller Brook

Meadow Lane

6

13

7

MOSS LANE A59

Moss Lane Nook

Back Lane

Cherry Grove

Mere Avenue

Laburnum Grove

Rowan Cl

Almond Avenue

Warper's

Moss Lane

Warper's Moss Lane

Trent Close

Woo Lane

8

Burscough Bge Station

Burscough Sports Centre

Burscough FC

Bobby Lane

Works

Langton Way

Langford Av

Mart Lane

PO

Burscough Health Cen

Lord Street

St Johns CE Primary School

School Lane

Burscough Primary Sch

Colburne Close

Stanley Court

New Sutch House Farm

Sutch Lane

Bleak Lane

LIVERPOOL ROAD NORTH

A59

412

Burscough Bridge Methodist Primary School

Priory

Victoria St

Mill Lane

Fletcher

Trevor Road

Langdale Drive

Glenroyd Drive

Llanthom Close

Burscough

Alexandra Road

JUNCTION L

G **H** **J** **52** **K** **L** **M**

44 45 46 47

LC

Daisy Lane

LC

Wanes

Hoscar

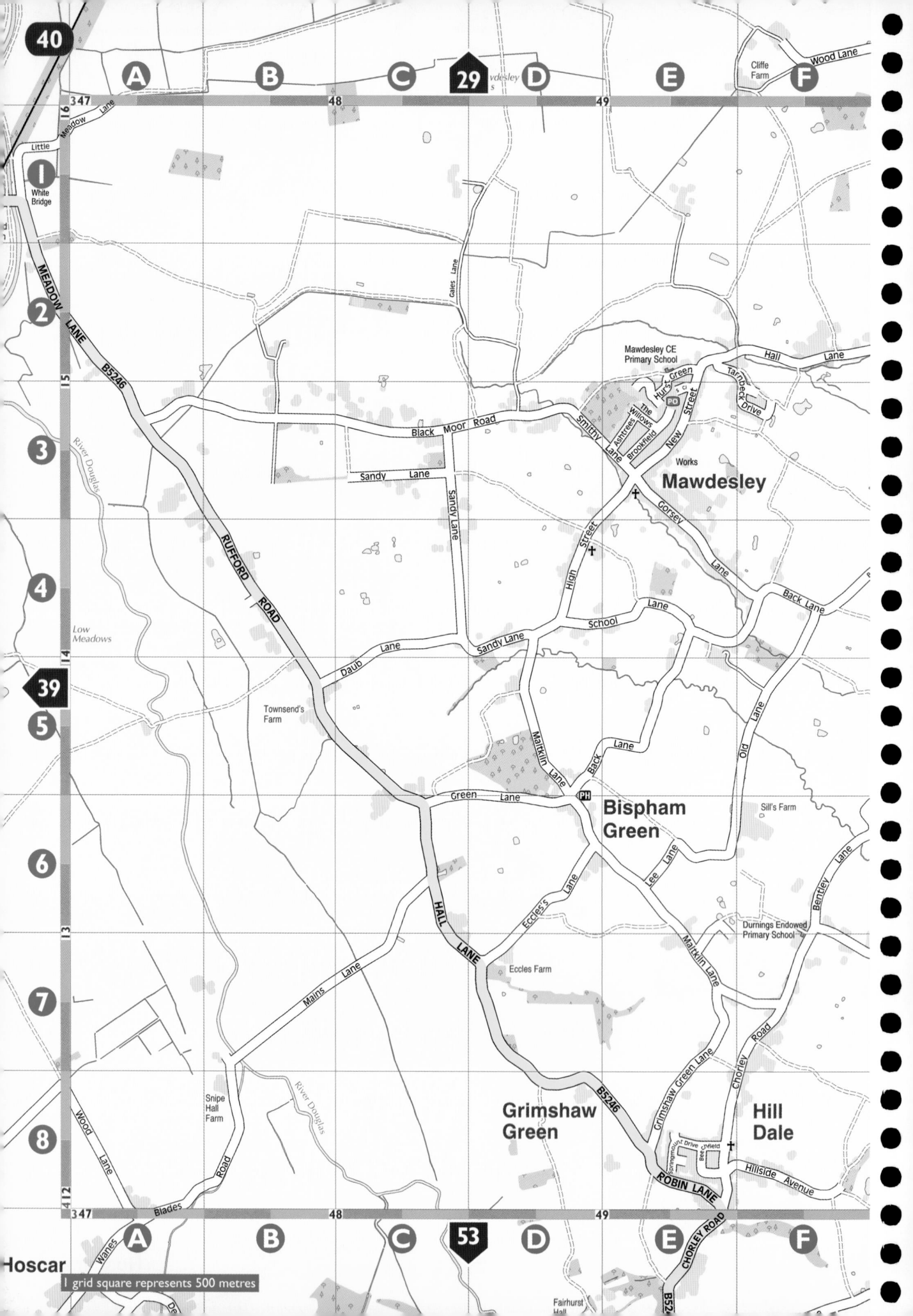

40

A   B   C   **29** vdesley s   D   E   F

347   48   49

Cliffe Farm   Wood Lane

Little   **I**

White Bridge

2   MEADOW LANE   B5246

Gales Lane

Mawdesley CE Primary School

Hall Lane

Tarnbeck Drive

The Willows   Ashtrees   Brookfield   New Street

Hurst Green   PO

River Douglas

3

Black Moor Road

Smithy Lane

Works

Mawdesley

Sandy Lane

Gorsey Lane

High Street

RUFFORD ROAD

4

Sandy Lane

School Lane

Back Lane

Low Meadows

Daub Lane

Sandy Lane

Old Lane

39

5

Townsend's Farm

Lane

Sill's Farm

Malkin Lane

Back Lane

Bispham Green

PH

6

Green Lane

Lee Lane

Eccles's Lane

Durnings Endowed Primary School

Bentley Lane

Mains Lane

HALL LANE

Eccles Farm

Maltkin Lane

Chorley Road

7

Snipe Hall Farm

River Douglas

Grimshaw Green

B5246

Grimshaw Green Lane

Hill Dale

Hillside Avenue

8

Wood Lane

Road

Springmount Drive   Bec field

ROBIN LANE

CHORLEY ROAD

347   48   49

Wanes   A   Blades   B   C   **53**   D   E   CHORLEY ROAD   F

B52

Hoscar

Fairhurst Hall

1 grid square represents 500 metres

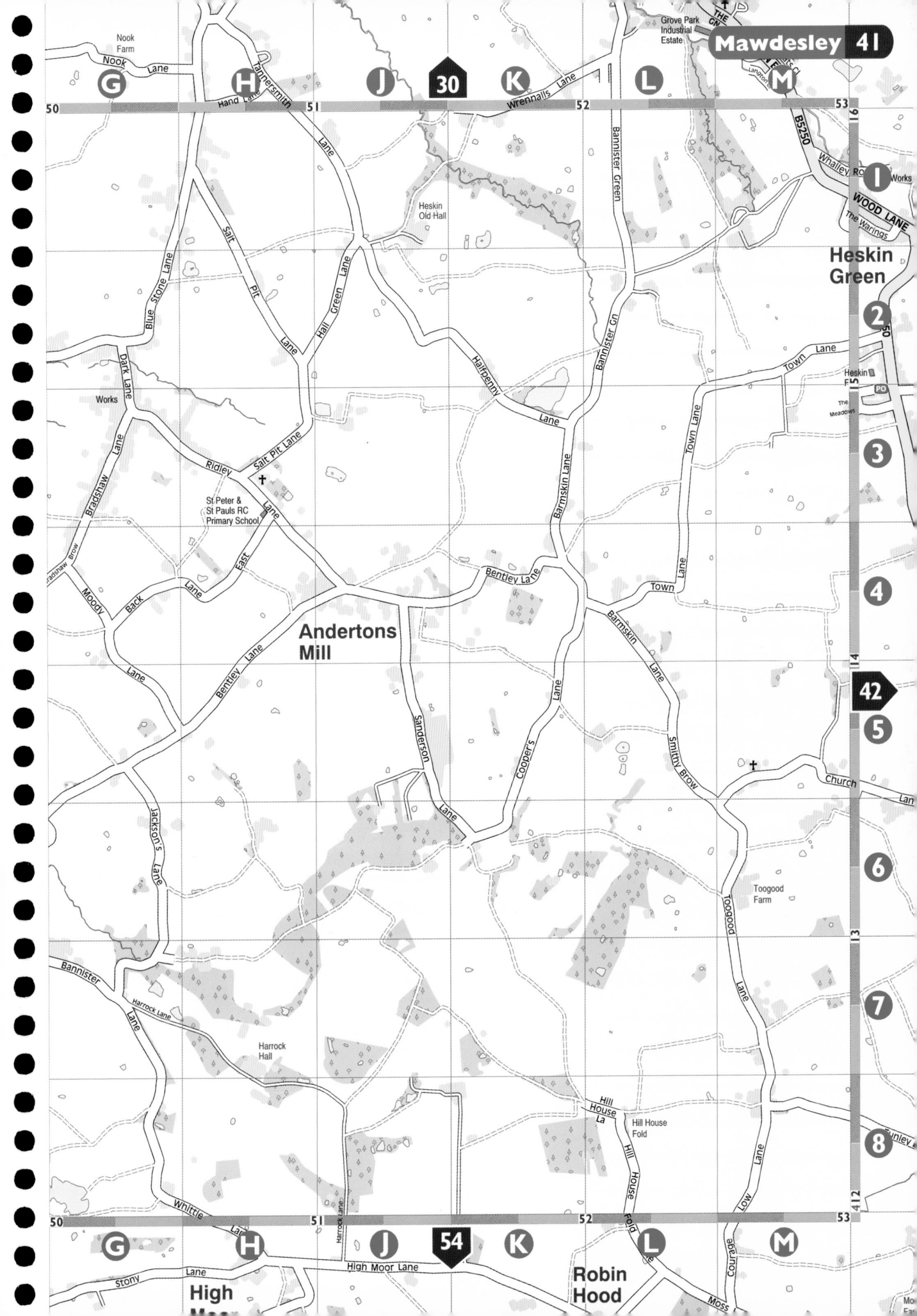

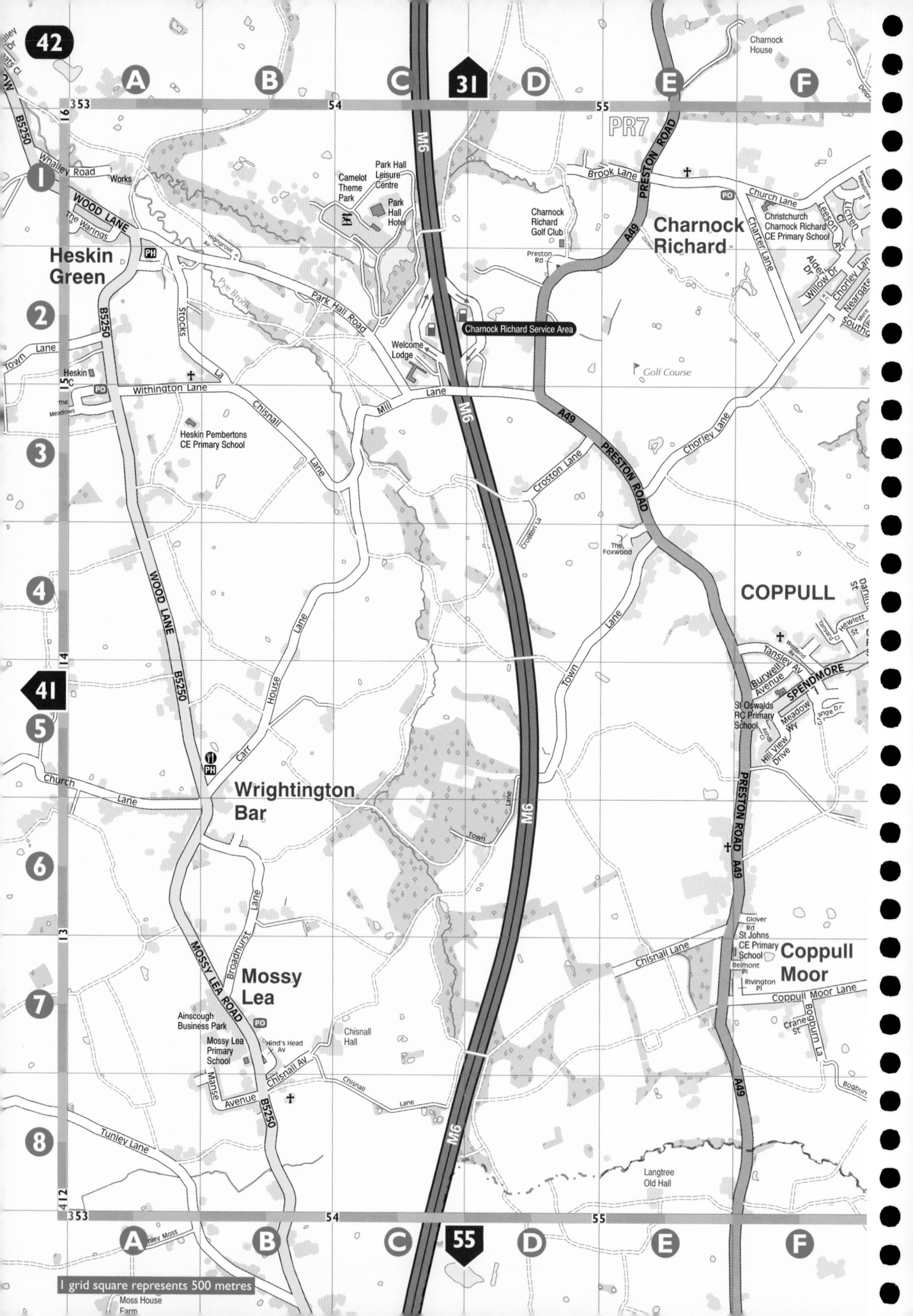

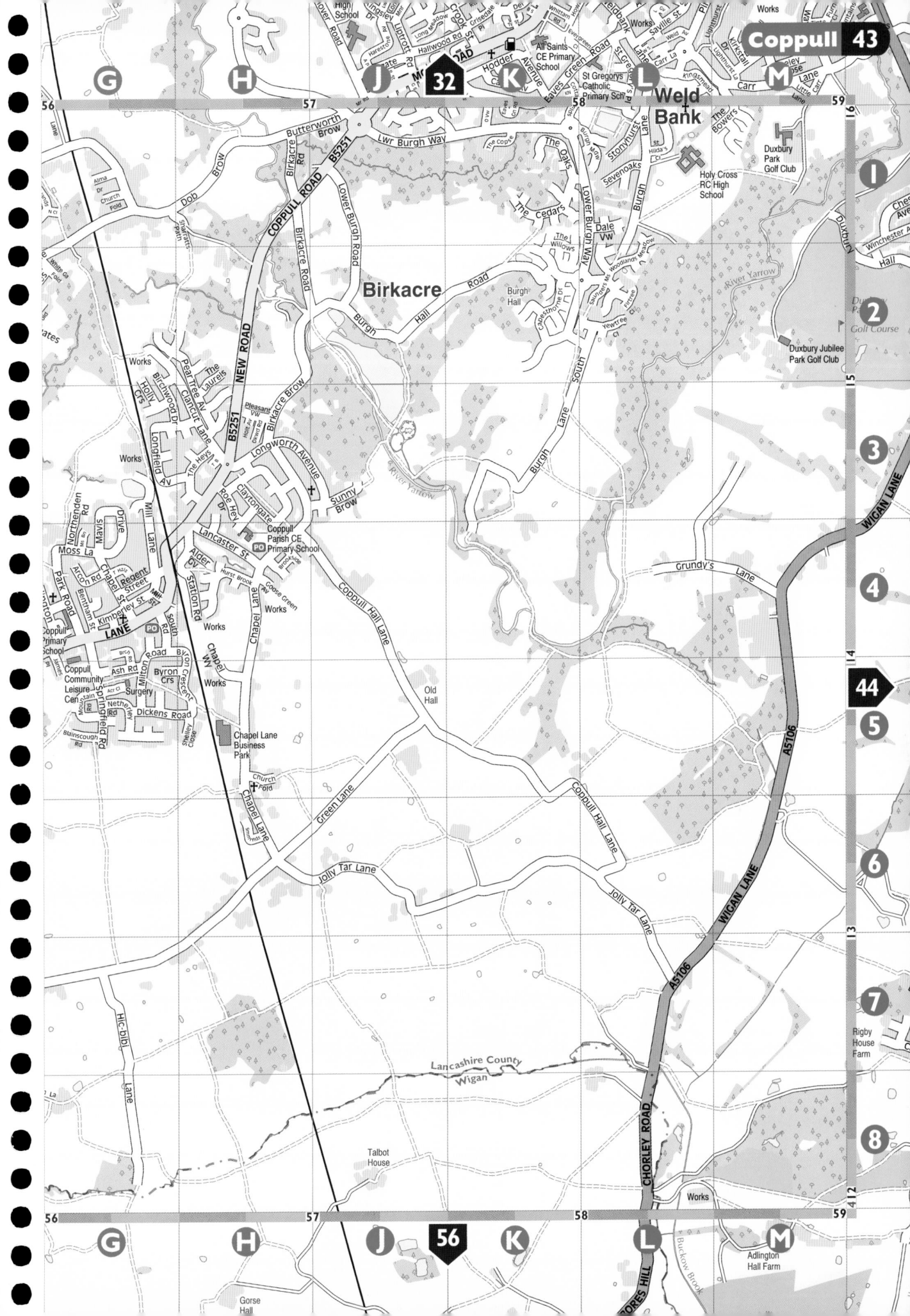

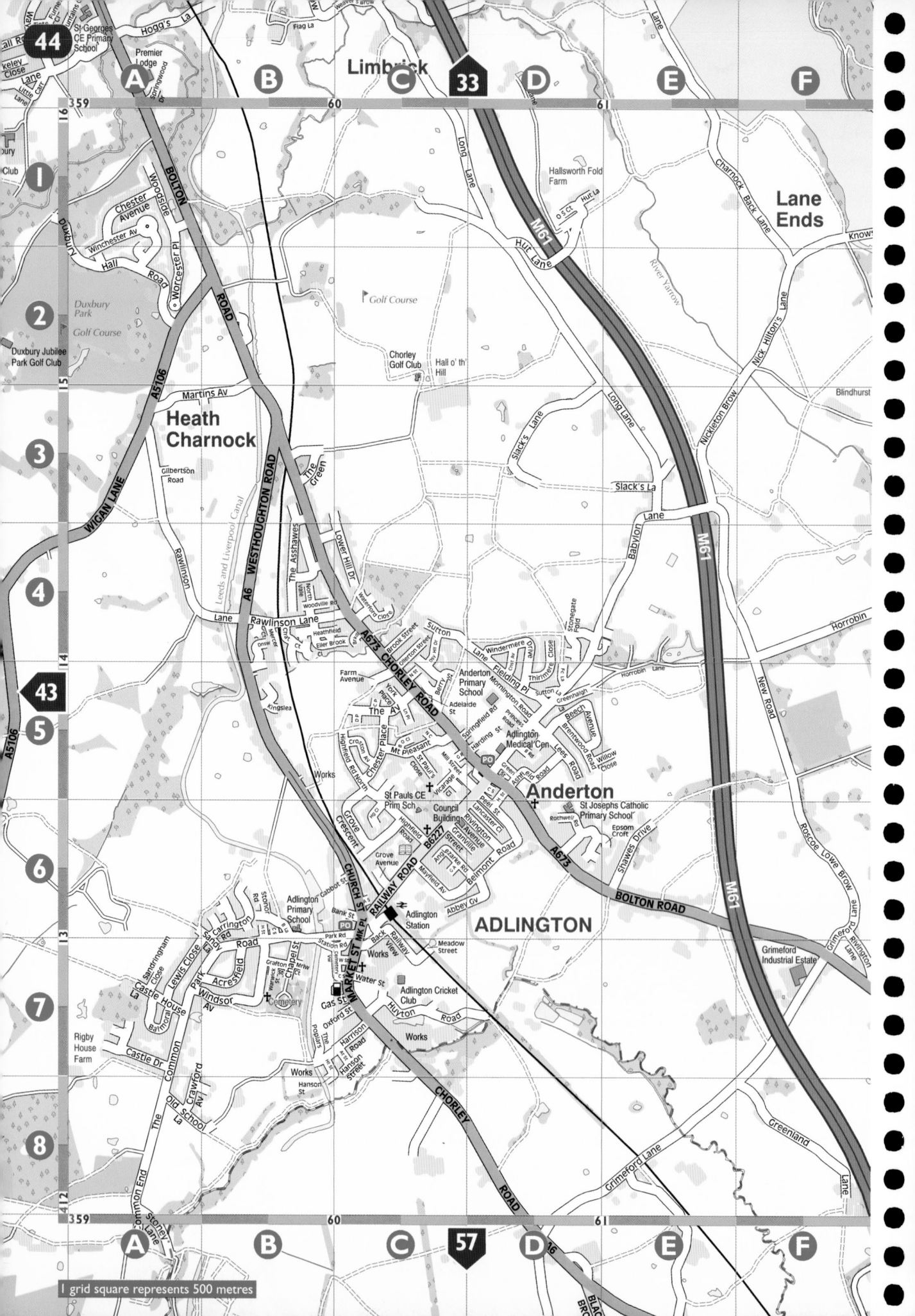

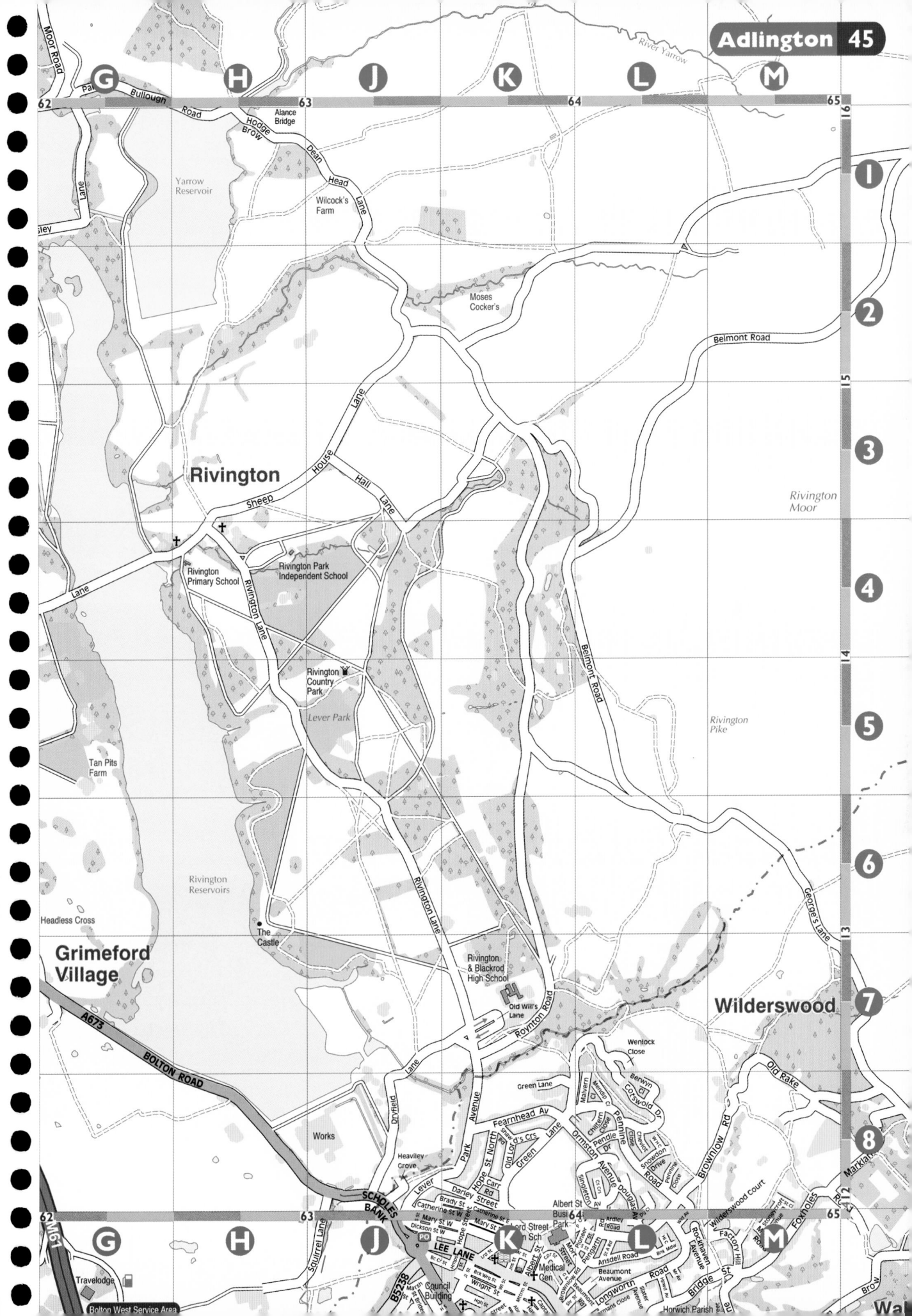

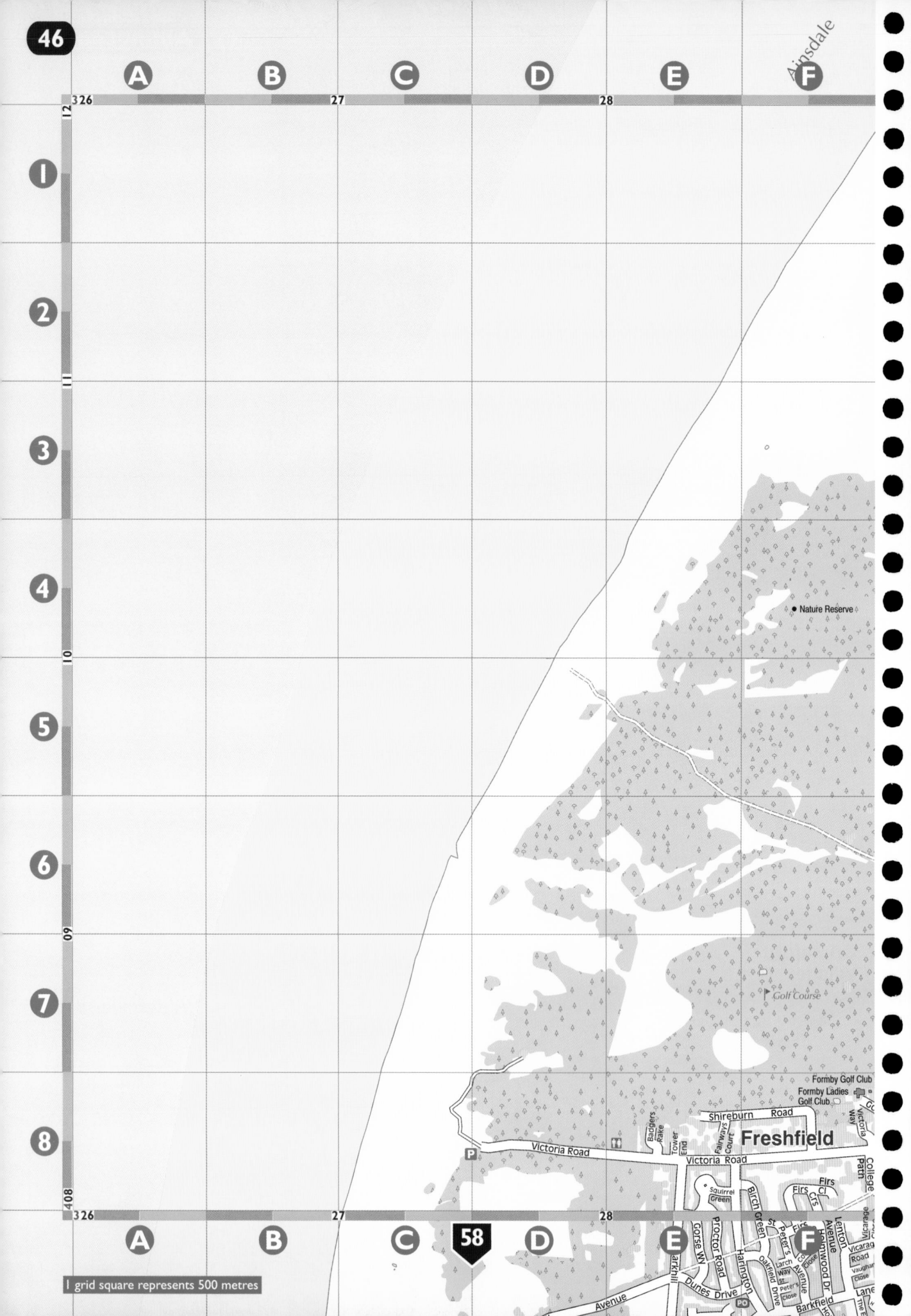

A   B   C   D   E   F

326   27   28

Ainsdale

I

2

3

4   ● Nature Reserve

5

6

09

7   ▶ Golf Course

Formby Golf Club
Formby Ladies
Golf Club

Shireburn   Road
Badgers
Rake
Tower
End   Fairways
Court   Freshfield
Victoria Road
Victoria Road   College
Path

8   P
Squirrel   Firs   Firs
Green   Cl   Cts
Birch Green   Lenton   Harwood Dr
St Peter's   Avenue
Close   Vicarage
Larch   Road
Close   Vaughan
St Peter's   Close
Proctor Road   Avenue   Lane
Oakfield Drive
Gorse Wy
Barkhill   Harrington   Barkfield
Dunes Drive   PO
Avenue

408
326   27   28

A   B   C   58 ▼   D   E   F

1 grid square represents 500 metres

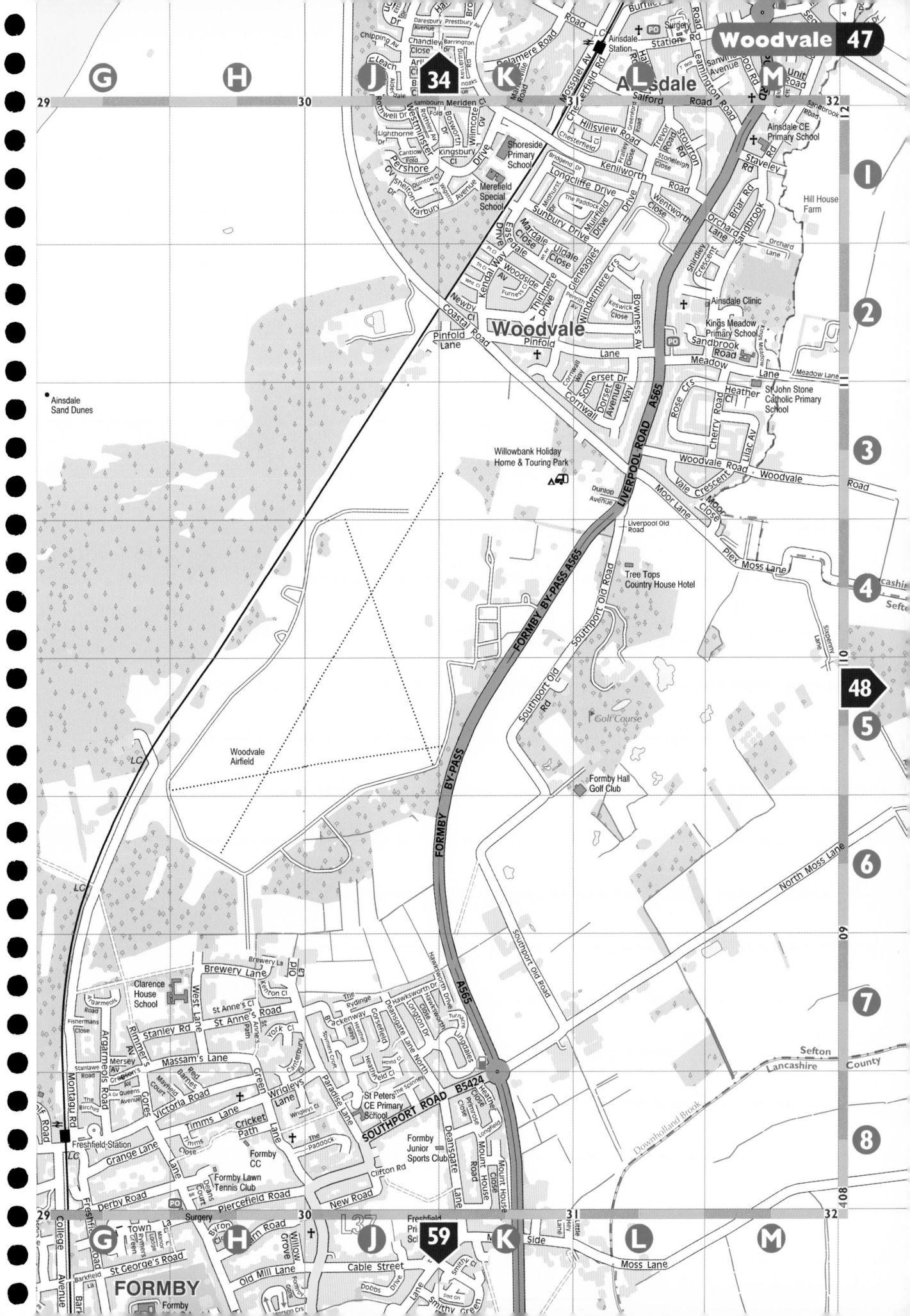

48

A B C 35 D E F

332 33 34

Segar's Lane

White Otter
Farm

Headbolt Lane

I

Hill House
Farm

Segar's Lane

2

Meadow L

John Stone
Catholic Primary
School

Spencer's La

Carr Moss Lane

Heather
Farm

3

odvale Road

Plex Moss

Carr Moss Lane

Lancashire County

4

Sefton

Plex Moss Lane

Gettern Farm

Plex Moss Lane

47

5

Heathy Lane

Alder Lane

Gorsey Lane

North Lane

6

Gorsey Lane

60

7

Shaw

Sefton

Lancashire County

Cheshire Lines Path

Moss Lane

8

Old Moss Lane

408

332 33 34

A B C 60 ownh Moss D E F

I grid square represents 500 metres

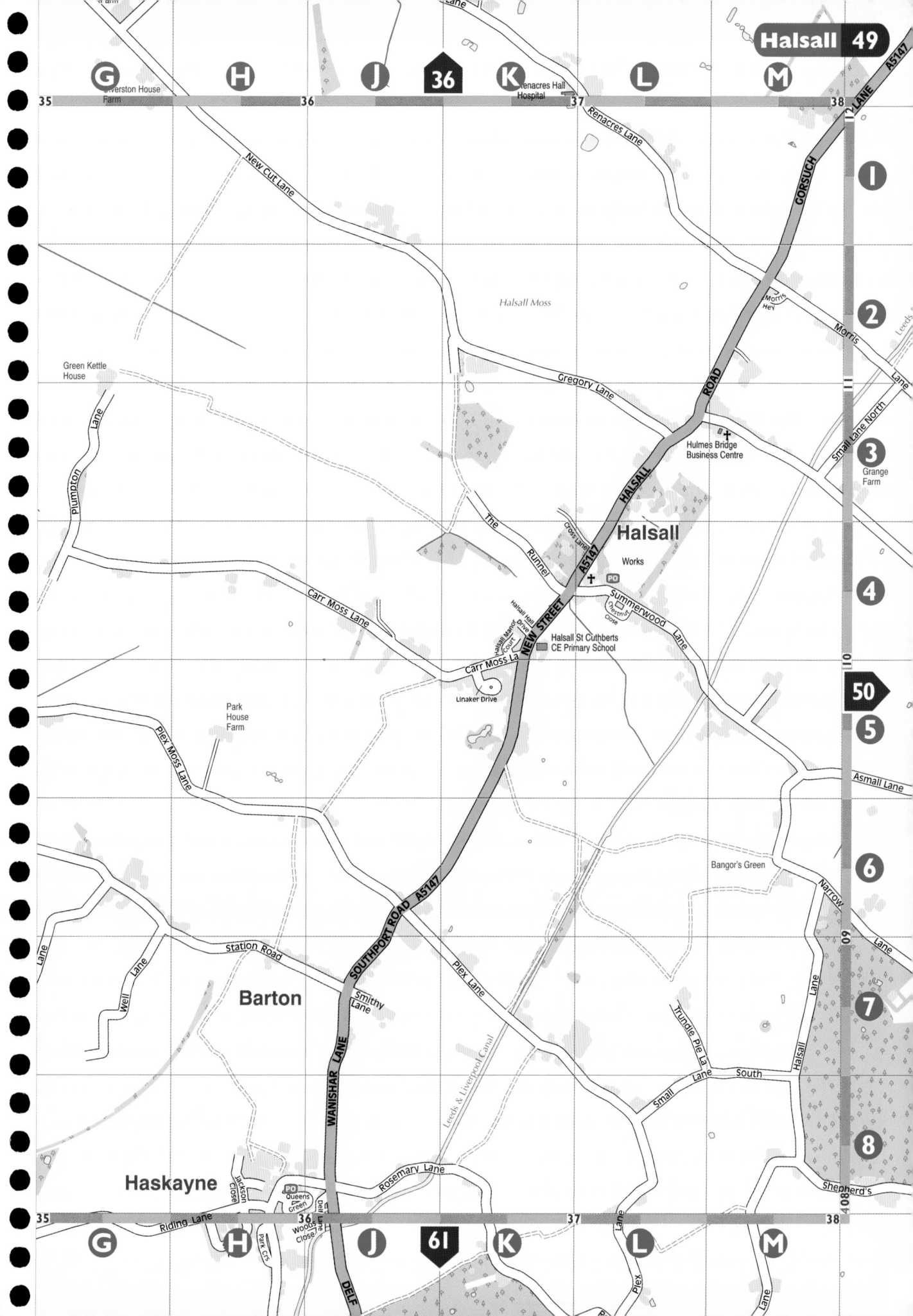

G H J **36** K L M

35   **36**   **37**   **38**

Ulverston House Farm

1

New Cut Lane

GORSUCH LANE

A5147

Renacres Hall Hospital

Renacres Lane

Morris Hey

2

Small Lane North

Morris Lane

Leeds

Green Kettle House

Halsall Moss

Gregory Lane

HALSALL ROAD

3

Grange Farm

Plumpton Lane

Hulmes Bridge Business Centre

The Runnel

Cross Lane

Halsall

Works

4

Carr Moss Lane

A5147

Summerwood Lane

Chestnut Close

PO

Halsall Hall

Halsall Manor Court

Carr Moss La

NEW STREET

Halsall St Cuthberts CE Primary School

50

Asmall Lane

5

Park House Farm

Piex Moss Lane

Linaker Drive

6

Bangor's Green

Narrow Lane

SOUTHPORT ROAD A5147

Station Road

Piex Lane

7

Well Lane

Lane

Barton

WANISHAR LANE

Smithy Lane

Trundle Pie La

Small Lane South

Halsall Lane

A408

8

Leeds & Liverpool Canal

Haskayne

Jackson Close

PO
Queens Green

Rosemary Lane

Woot Close

DELF

Riding Lane

Park Cts

Plex Lane

Lane

Shepherd's

35   **36**   **37**   **38**

G H J **61** K L M

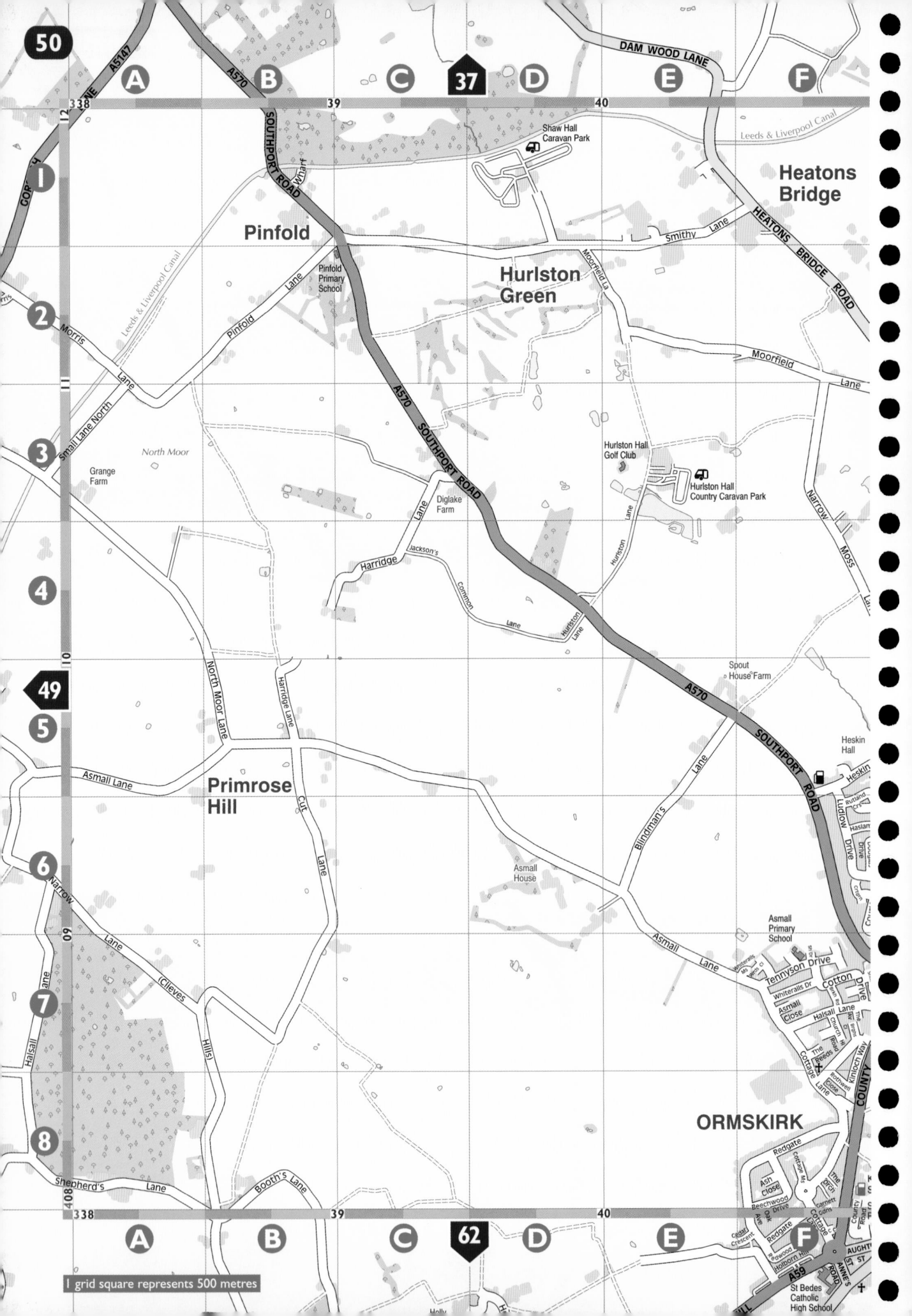

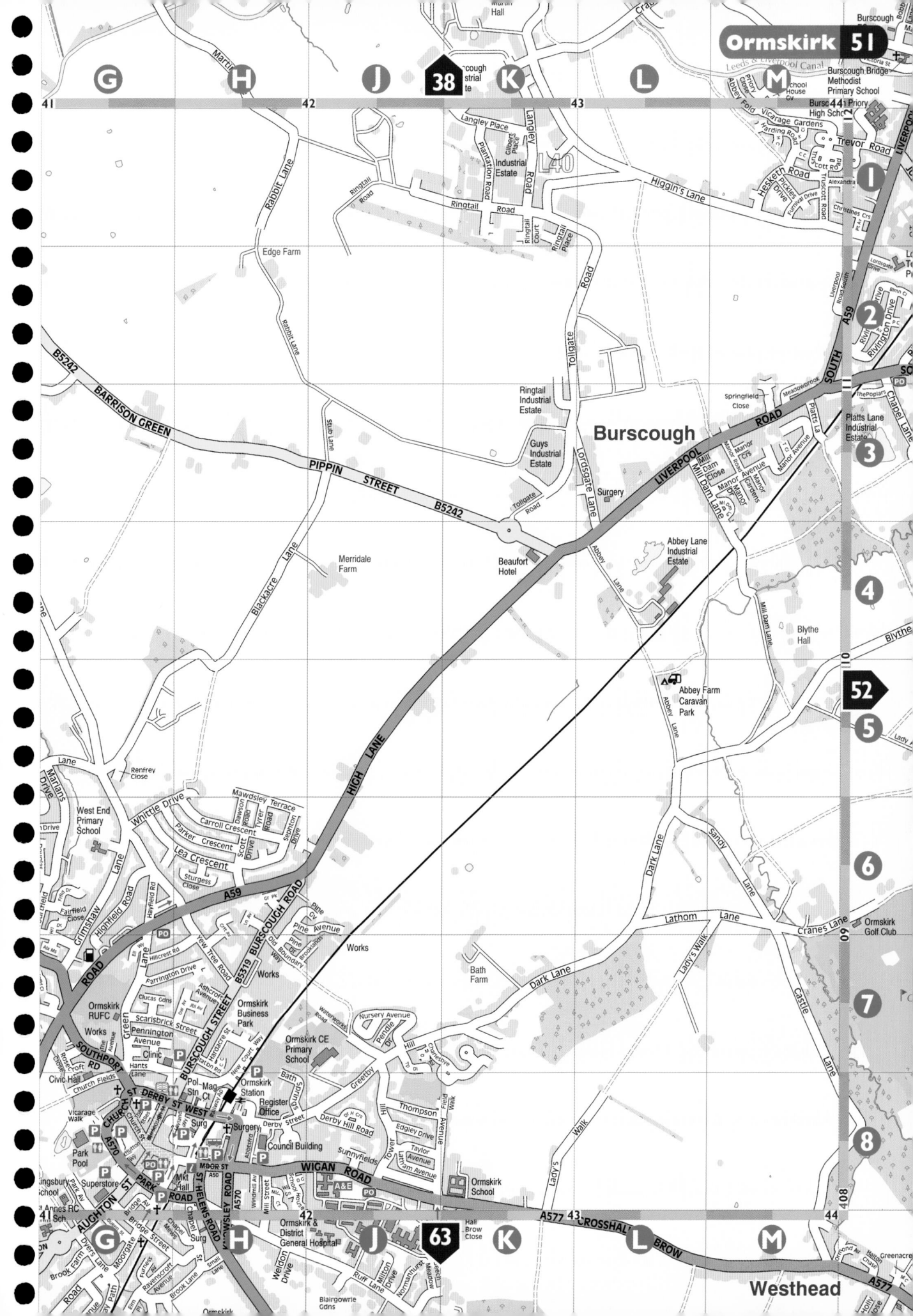

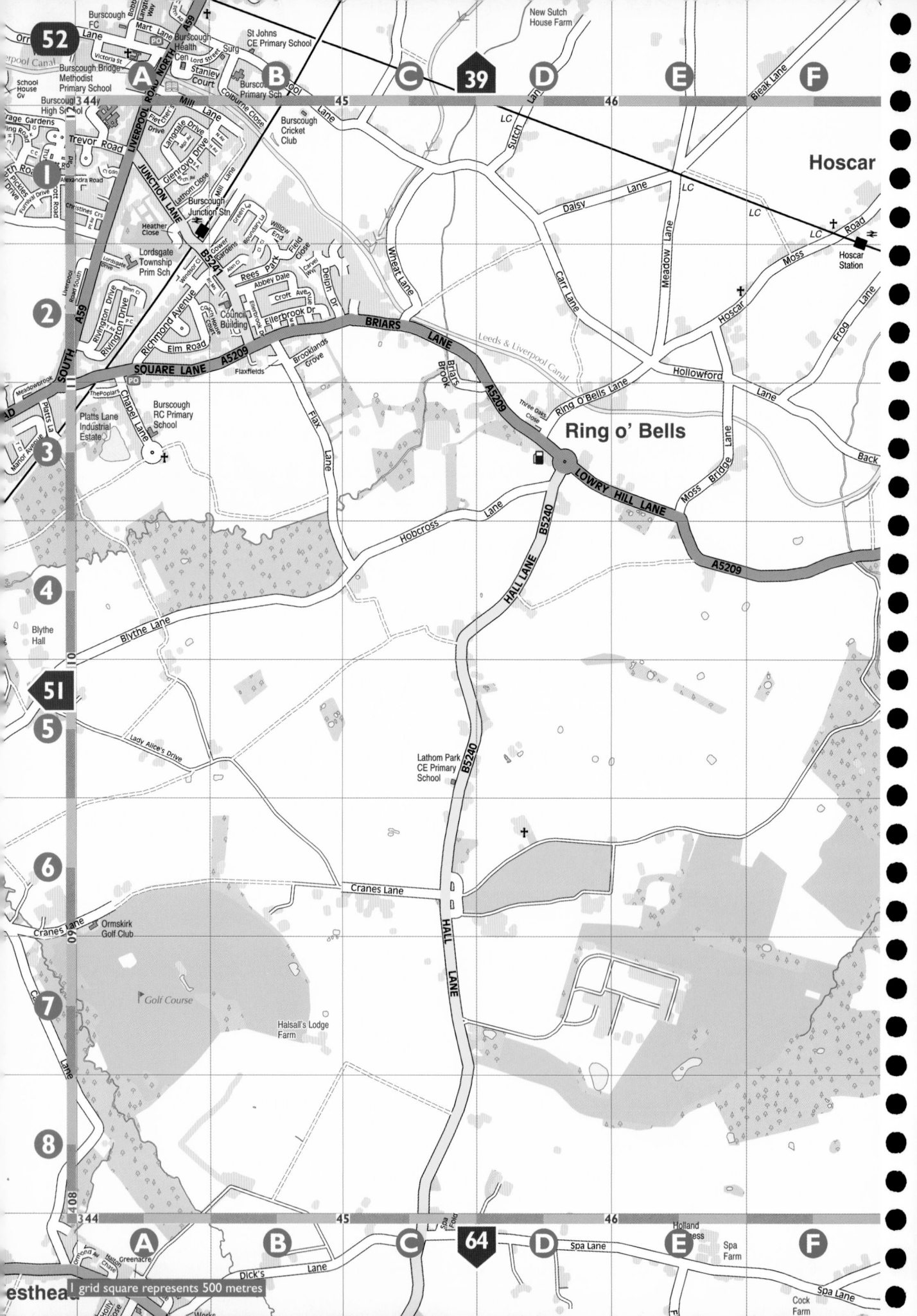

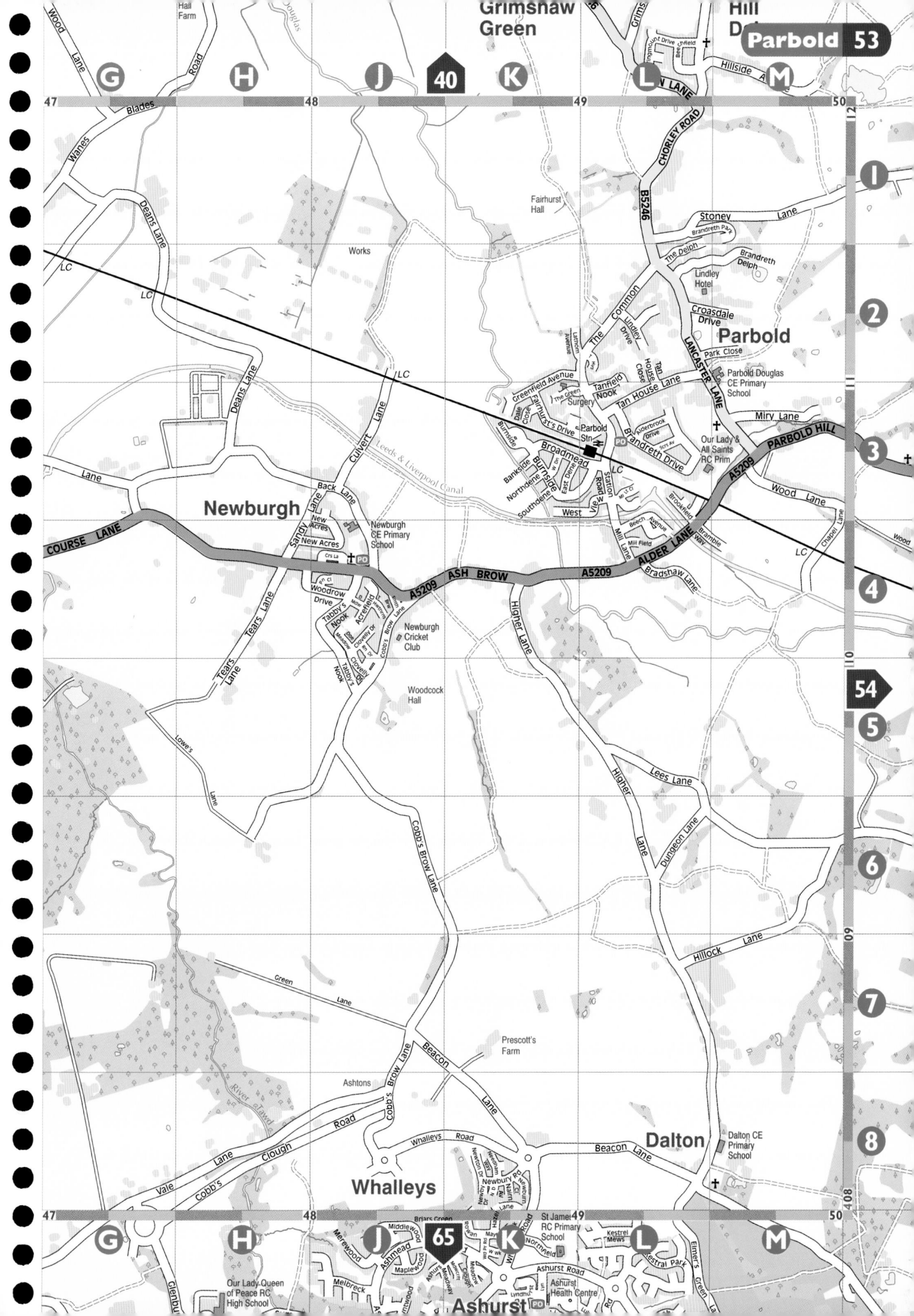

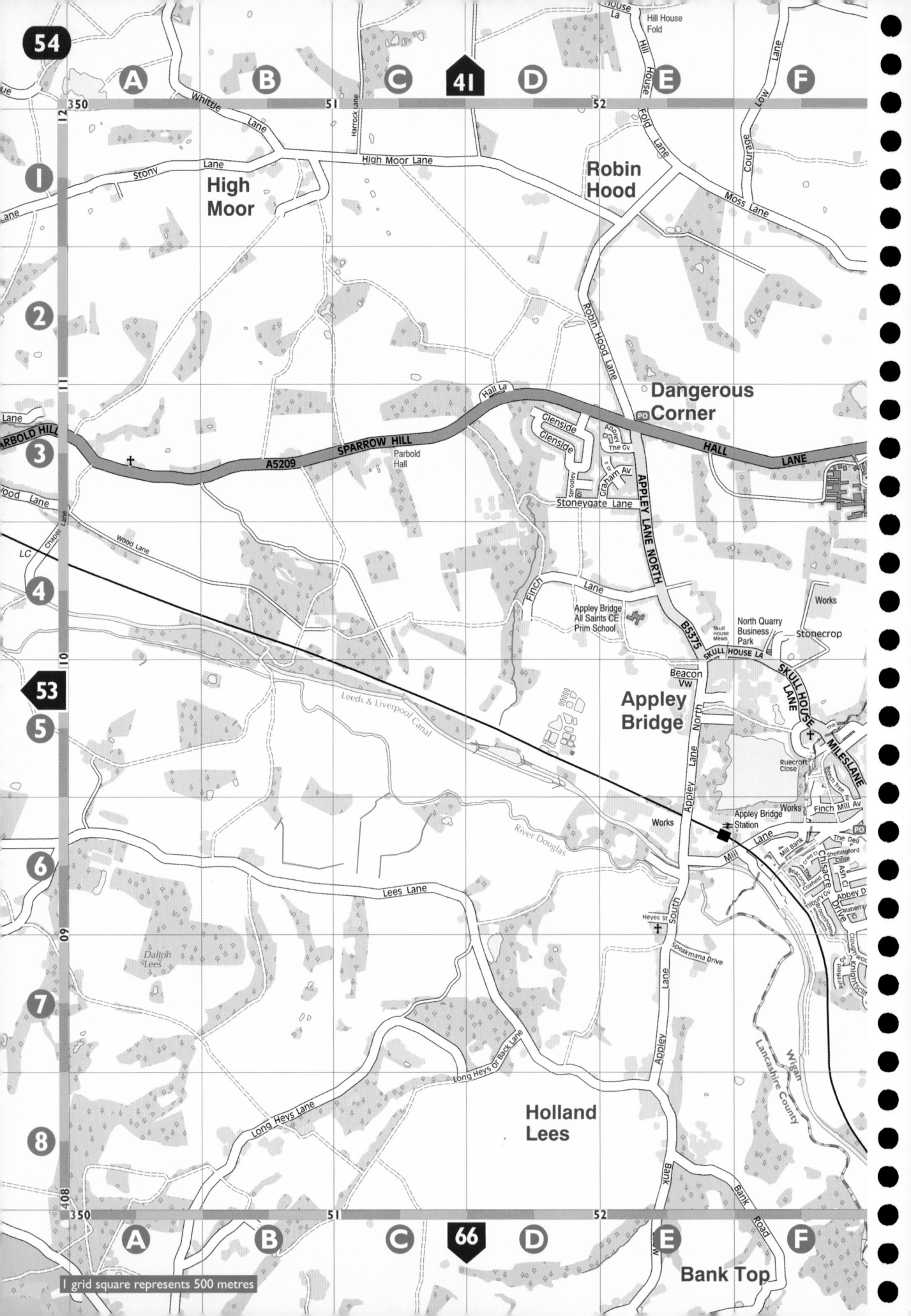

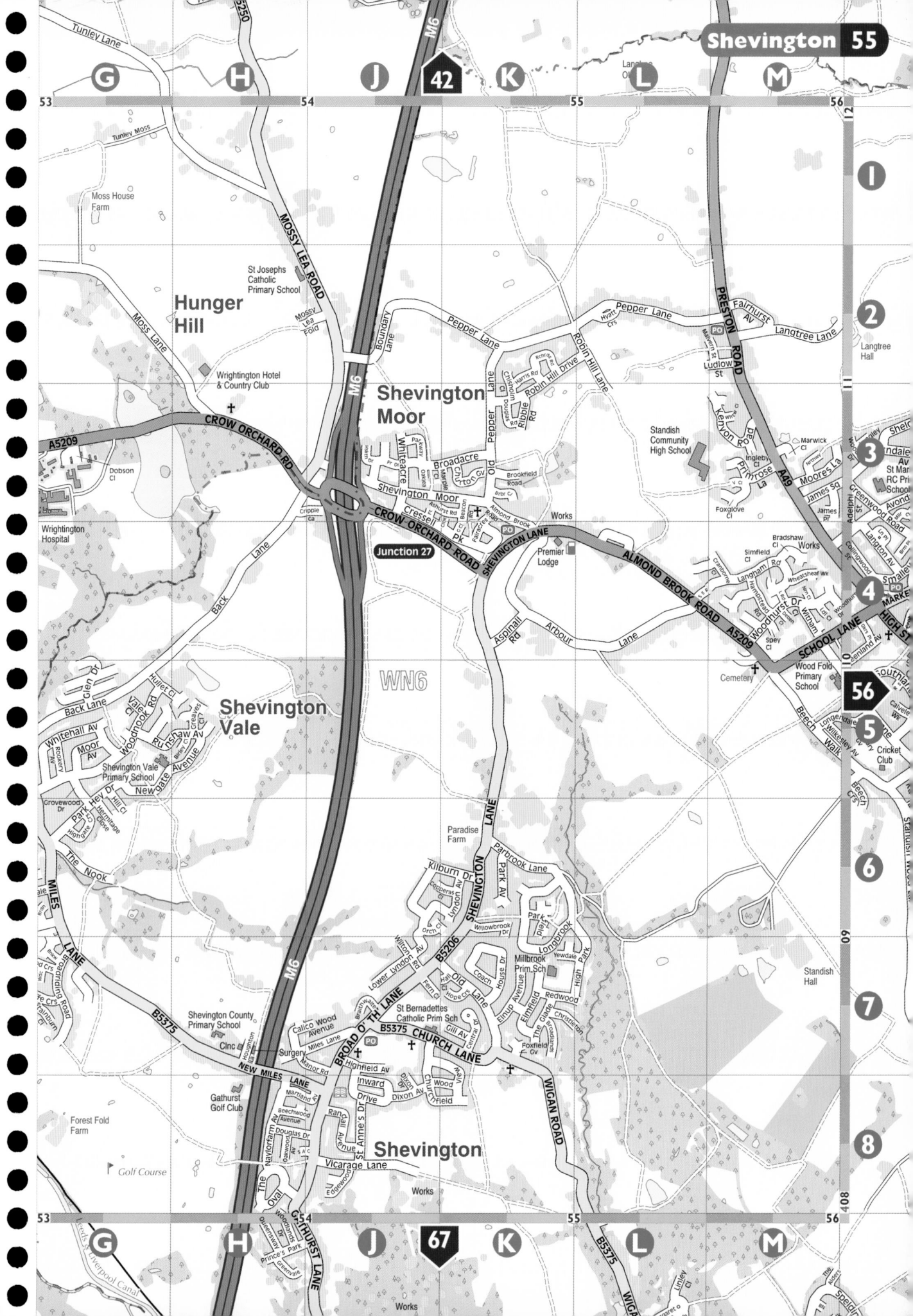

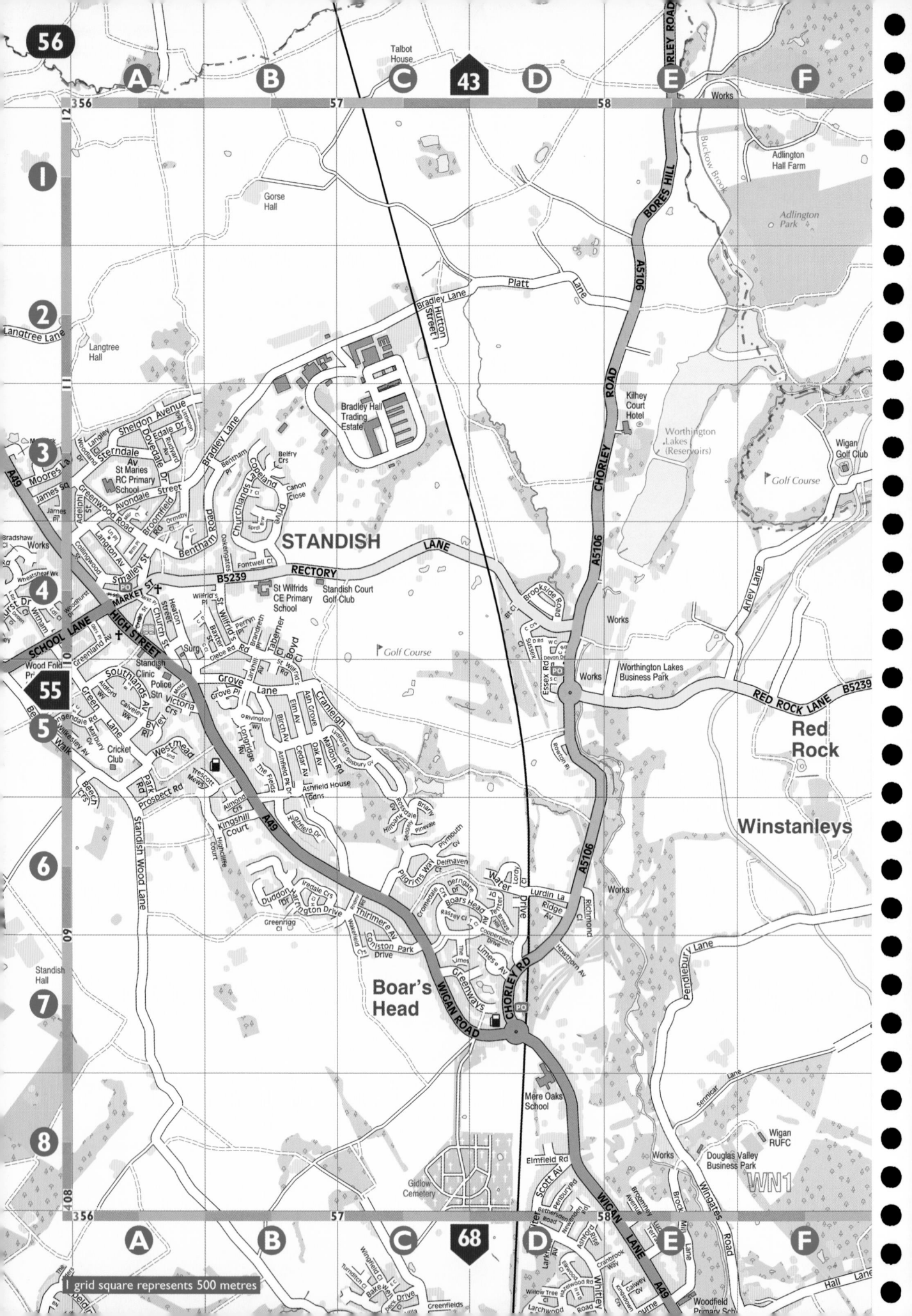

G H J 44 K L M

59 60 61 62

I

2

Blackrod

3

4 STATION

5

6

7

8

M61

Travelodge
Bolton

Lancashire County
Bolton

BS408
Greenbarn
Way

Hope

ESK

SCOT
LANE

ASPULL

Aberdeen
Farm

Crowshaw
Farm

CHORLEY ROAD

BLACKROD BROW

A6 CHORLEY ROAD

Dark Lane

Blundell Lane

Arley Lane

Little
Scotland

Bolton
Wigan

Bolton
Wigan

Scotland

Little

Copperas Lane

Tucker's
Hill Farm

Tucker's Hill Brow

Toddington Lane

Meadow Pit Lane

Willoughbys

Freezeland Farm

Gorses
Farm

Stanley Lane

SCHOOL LANE

Pennington La
Pennington Lane

MEADOW PIT LANE

BS239 RILEY LANE

Haigh

St Davids
CE Prim Sch

Copperas Lane

School Lane

New Road

Sennicar Lane

Haigh Hall Country Park

Leeds & Liverpool Canal

Leeds and Liverpool Canal

Church St

Henley Street

Victoria Cl

BS239 HAIGH ROAD

St Mary's Road

St John's Rd

St Elizabeth's Rd

St David's Crescent

Cncl Bldg

Our Lady
RC Prim
Sch

Holly Rd

Brayford

Manor Gv

Crawford Avenue

Balcarres Road

Ratcliffe Road

Parklands Dr

Stancliffe Grove

Ashfield
Drive

Aspull
Clinic

Belmont Ter

Stanmoor Dr

BS228

Harold Street

Lincoln Dr

Windsor Dr

Exeter Dr

Dundonald Old Fold Rd

Corfe Cl

Restormel Rd

Bolton Road

Conway Drive

Crawford Road

The Fields

BS239 BOLTON

Higher Lane

Nightingale Rd
Thirlmere Rd

Carlson Crs

Ainse Road

Clifton Dr

Hill Lane

BLACK HORSE ST

Surgery

Folds

Coniston
Road

Whitehall Lane

Carlton Close

CHURCH STREET

Council
Building

Vicarage Rd W

Ridgeway

Blackrod Church
School

Half Acre Lane

Vicarage Road

PO

Sibberings
Farm

Greenbarn Way

MANCHESTER RD

Castlecroft

Vauze House

Cemetery

Hillside
Avenue

Grimeford Lane

Anderson Lane

Factory Brow

59 60 61 62

G H J 69 K L M

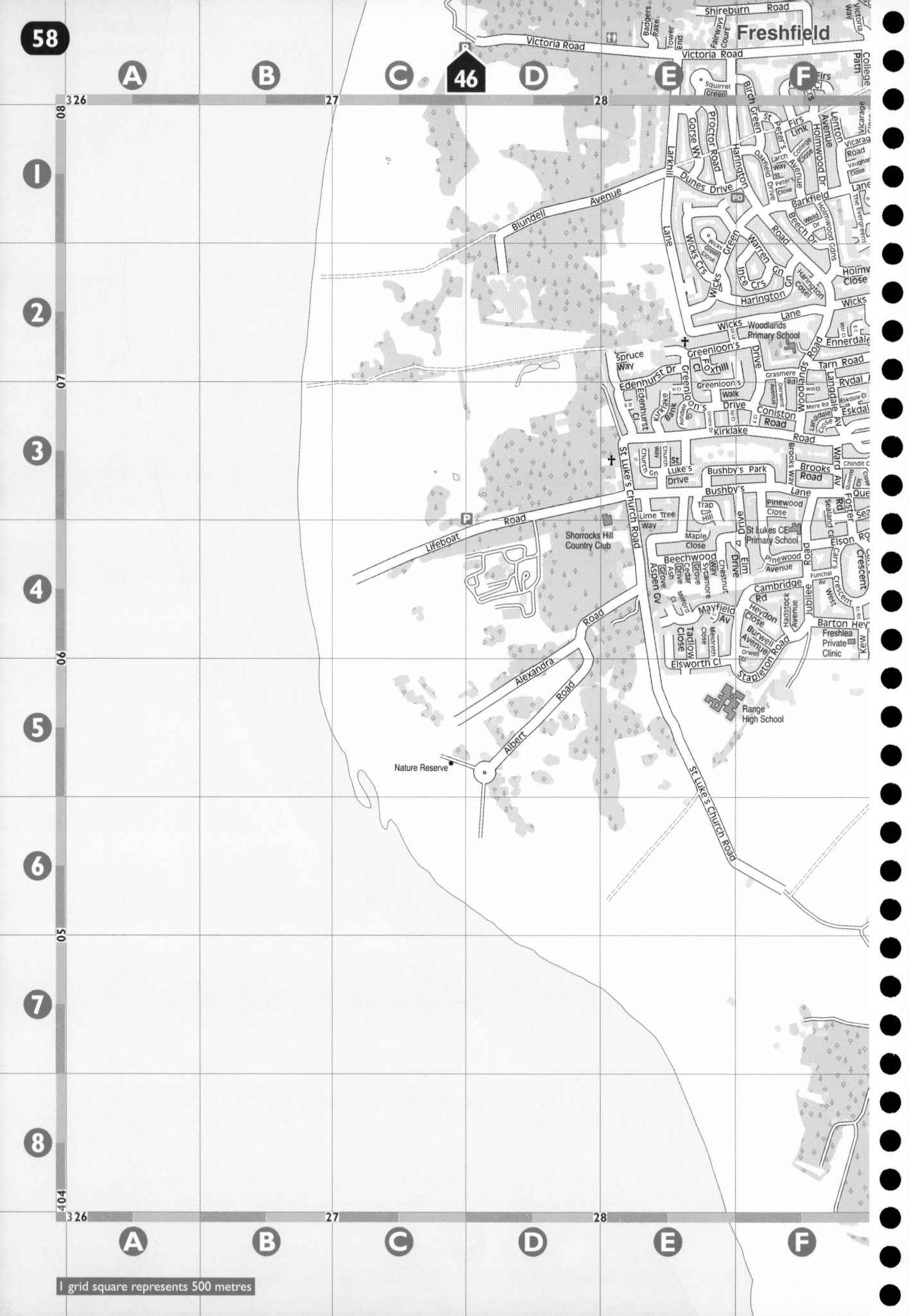

Freshfield

46

A   B   C   D   E   F

1 2 3 4 5 6 7 8

I grid square represents 500 metres

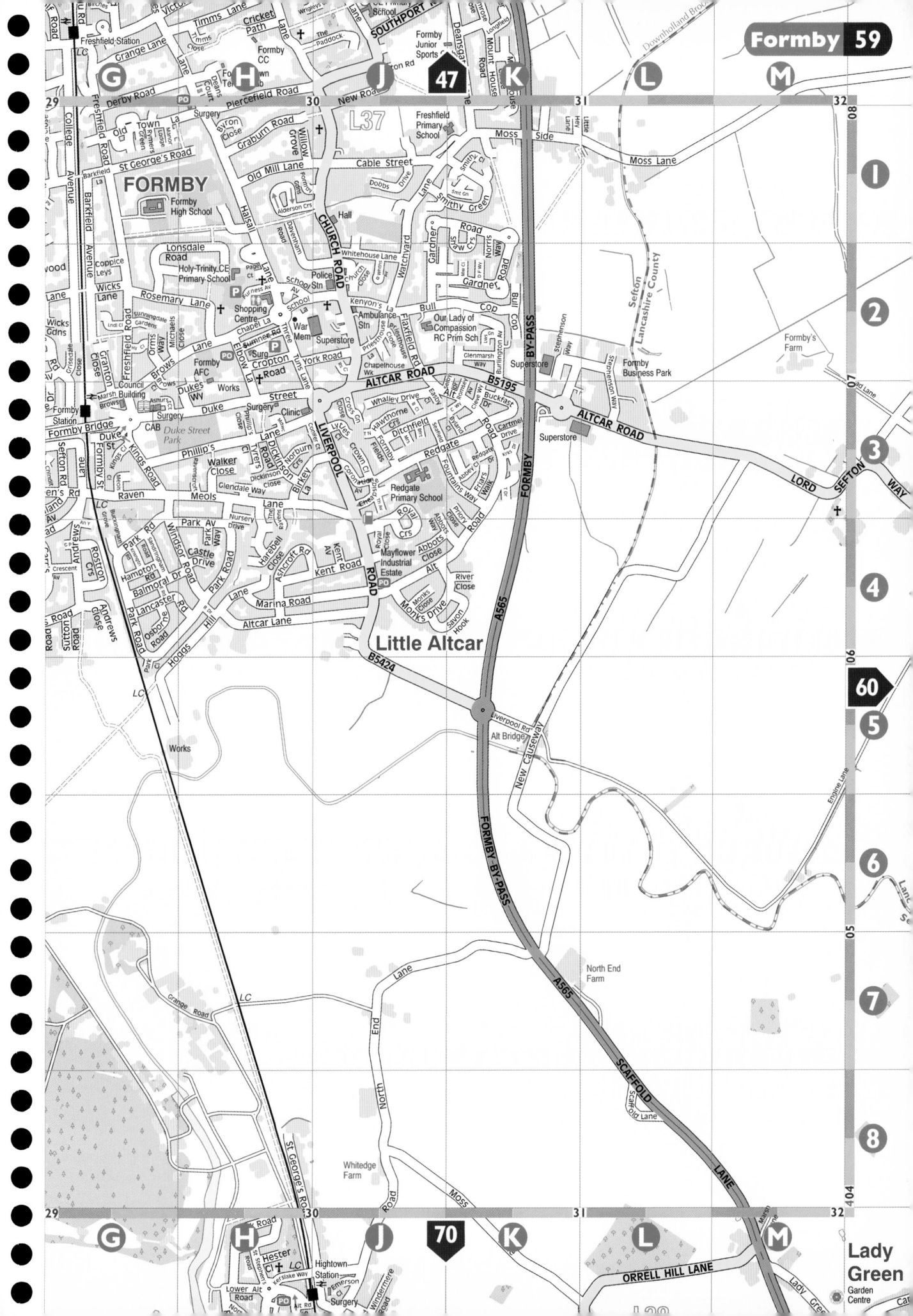

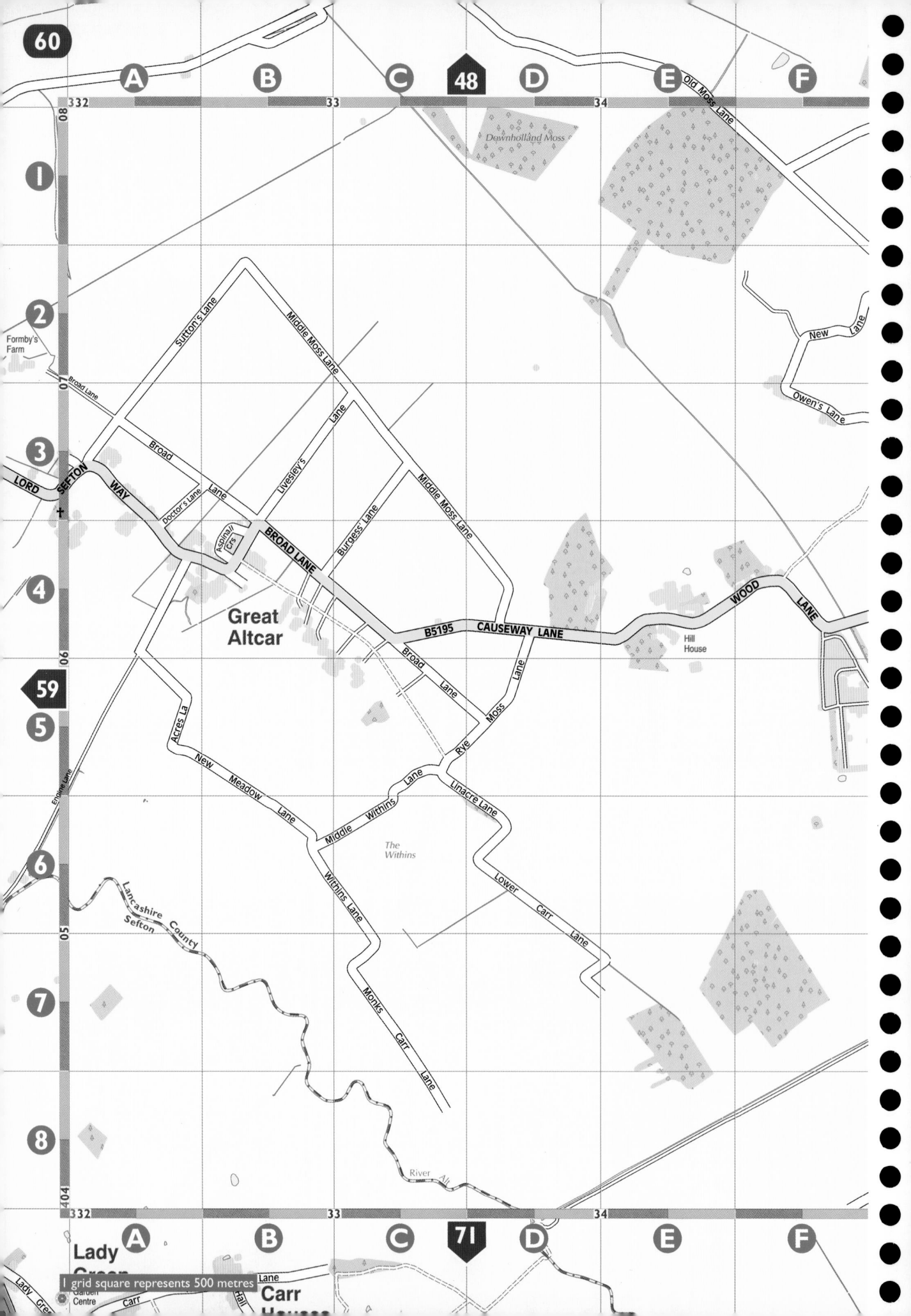

I

2

3

4

59

5

6

7

8

Formby's Farm

LORD

SEFTON WAY

Broad Lane

Broad Lane

Doctor's Lane

Aspinall Crs

Great Altcar

BROAD LANE

Sutton's Lane

Middle Moss Lane

Livesley's Lane

Burgess' Lane

Middle Moss Lane

B5195   CAUSEWAY LANE

Broad Lane

Moss Lane

Rye Lane

Acres La

New Meadow Lane

Middle Withins Lane

Withins Lane

Linacre Lane

Lower Carr Lane

The Withins

Monks Carr Lane

Lancashire County
Sefton

Enfield Lane

Downholland Moss

New Lane

Owen's Lane

WOOD LANE

Hill House

River Alt

Lady Green

Carr Houses

Lady Green

Garden Centre

Carr   Lane

Hall Lane

1 grid square represents 500 metres

Old Moss Lane

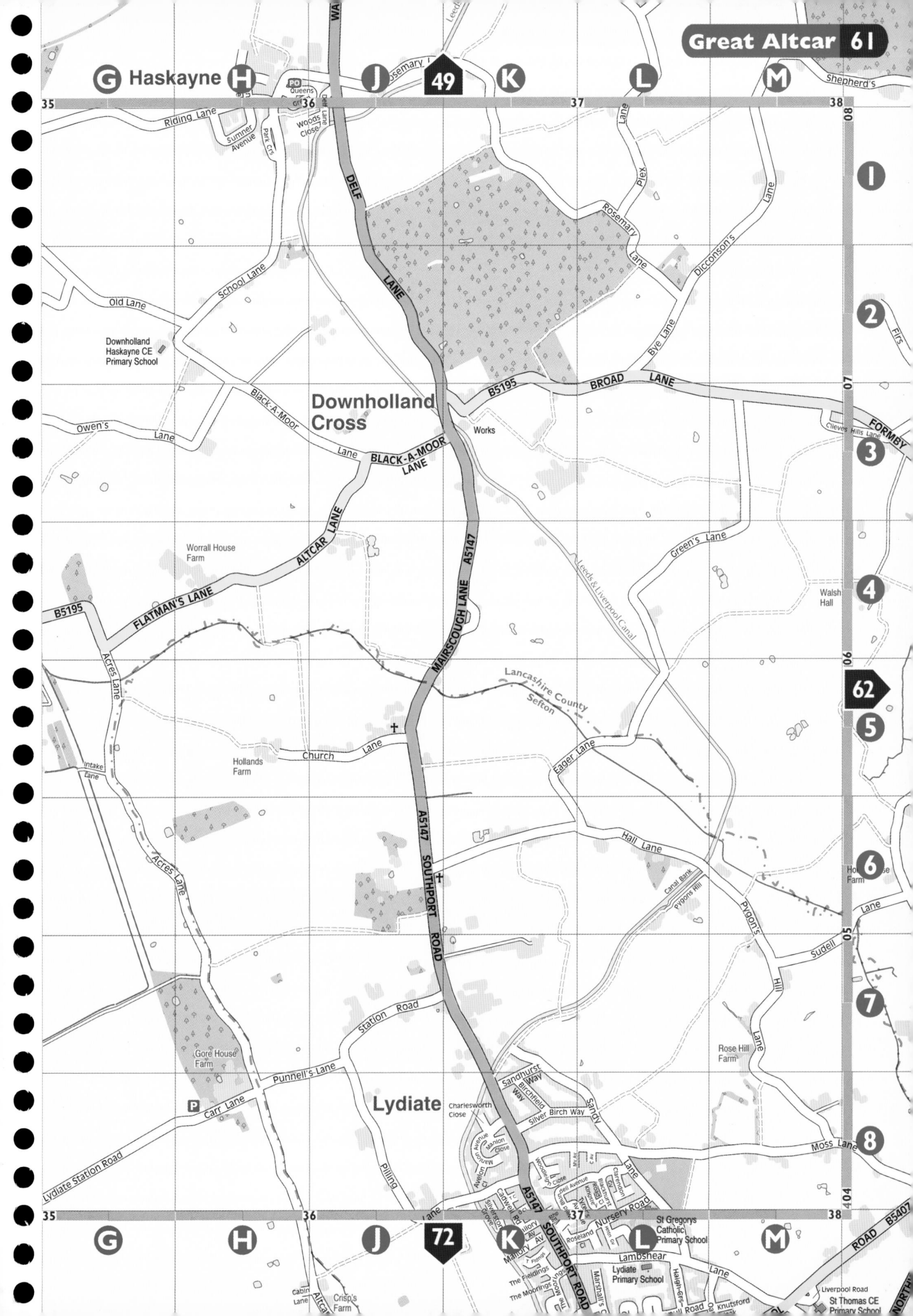

G **Haskayne** H J 49 K L M

I

2

3 FORMBY

4

62

5

6

7

8

G H J 72 K L M

Riding Lane

Sumner Avenue

Park Crs

Old Lane

School Lane

Downholland Haskayne CE Primary School

Black-A-Moor Lane

Downholland Cross

Owen's Lane

Worrall House Farm

ALTCAR LANE

FLATMAN'S LANE

B5195

Acres Lane

Intake Lane

Acres Lane

Gore House Farm

Punnell's Lane

P Carr Lane

Lydiate Station Road

DELF LANE

Queens PO

Delf Lane

Woods Close

B5195

BLACK-A-MOOR LANE

Works

MAIRSCOUGH LANE A5147

Church Lane

Hollands Farm

A5147 SOUTHPORT ROAD

Station Road

Pilling

Lydiate

Sandhurst Way

Charlesworth Close

Birchfield Way

Silver Birch Way

Sandy

A5147

Rosemary La

Rosemary Lane

Plex

Bye Lane

BROAD LANE

Green's Lane

Dicconson's Lane

Clieves Hills Lane

Walsh Hall

Leeds & Liverpool Canal

Lancashire County Sefton

Eager Lane

Hall Lane

Canal Bank

Pygons Hill

Pygon's Hill Lane

Sudell Lane

Rose Hill Farm

Hol... se Farm

Moss Lane

St Gregorys Catholic Primary School

Nursery Road

Lambshear Lane

Lydiate Primary School

The Fieldings

The Moorings

ROAD B5407

Liverpool Road

St Thomas CE Primary School

Shepherd's

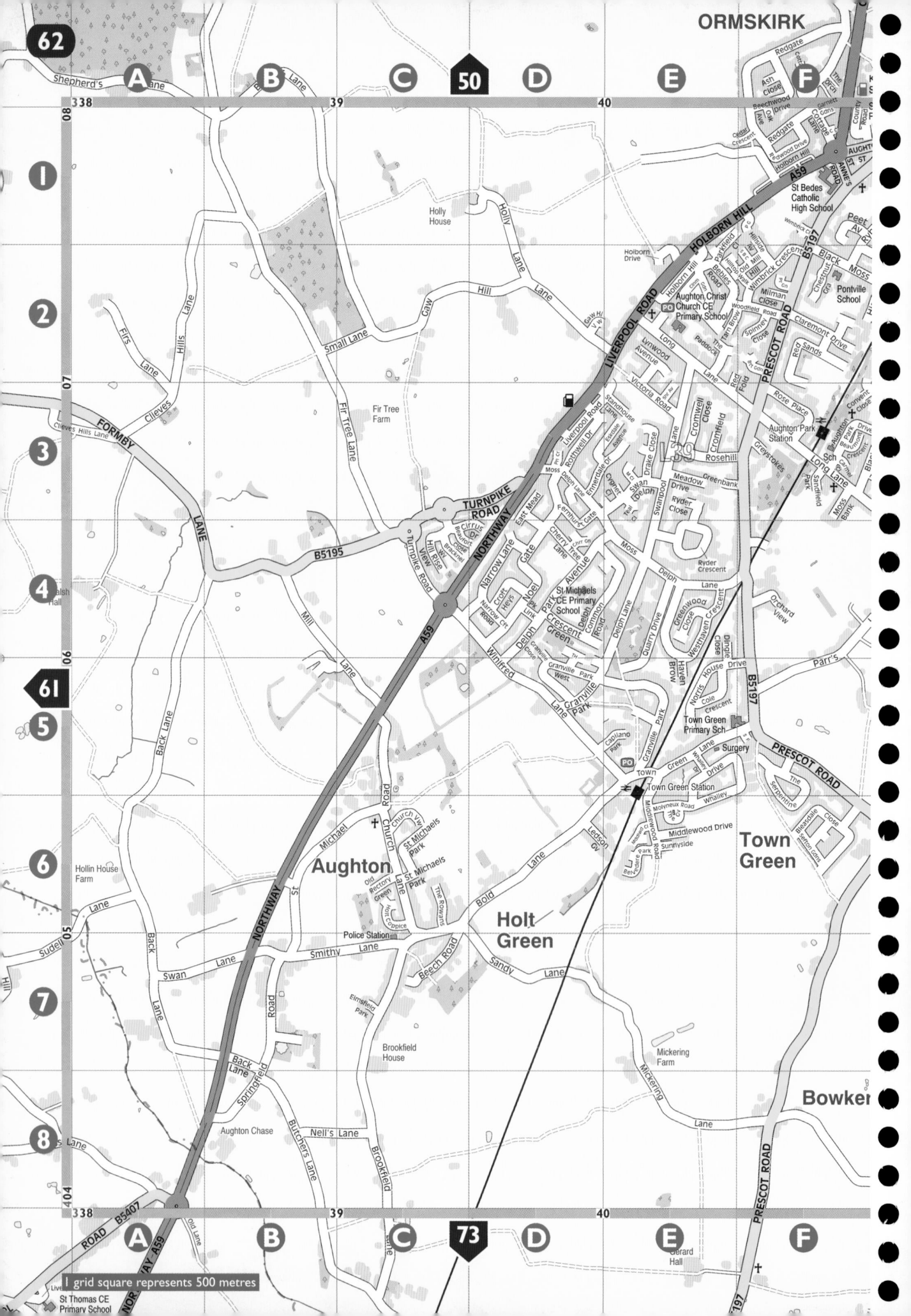

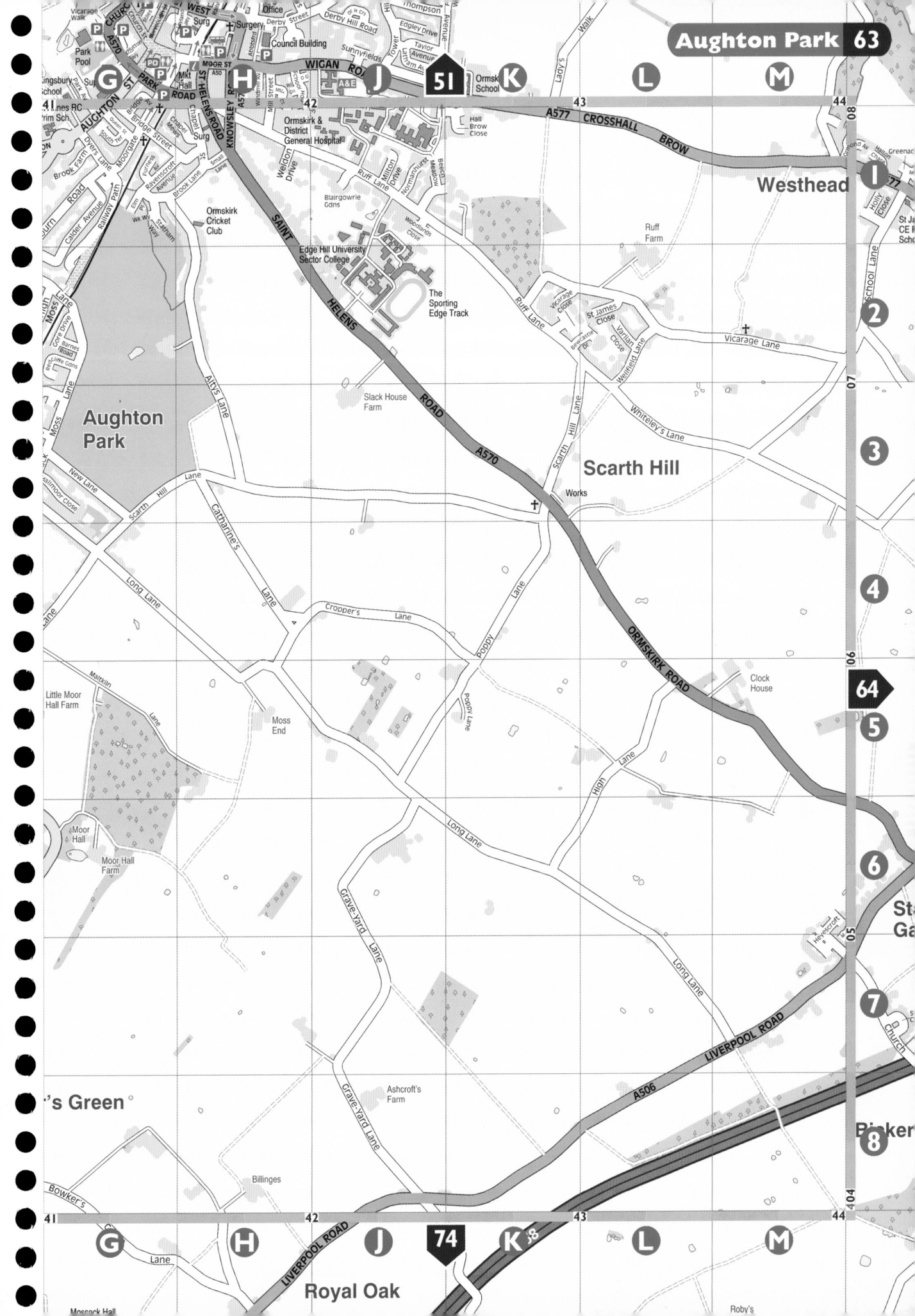

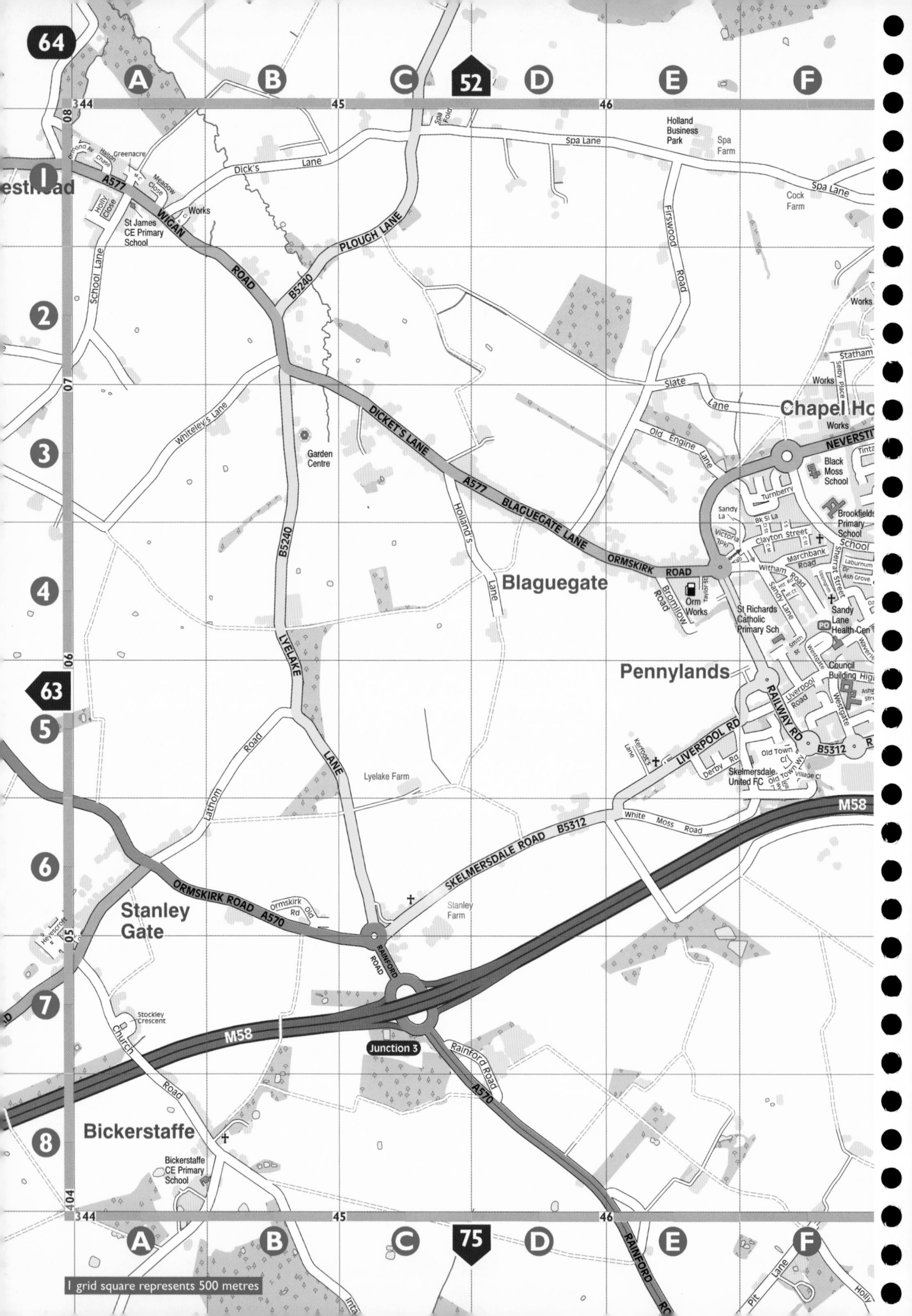

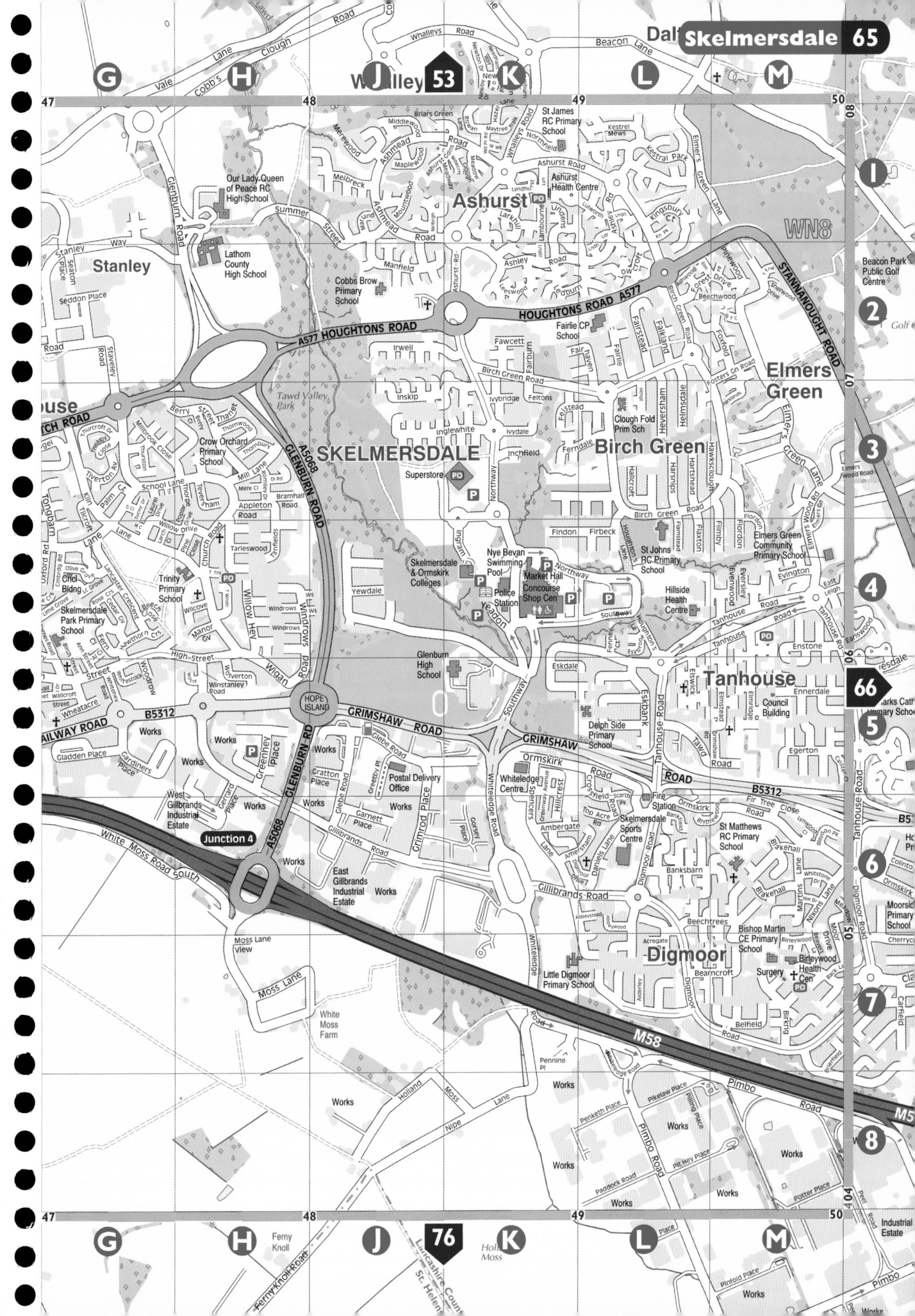

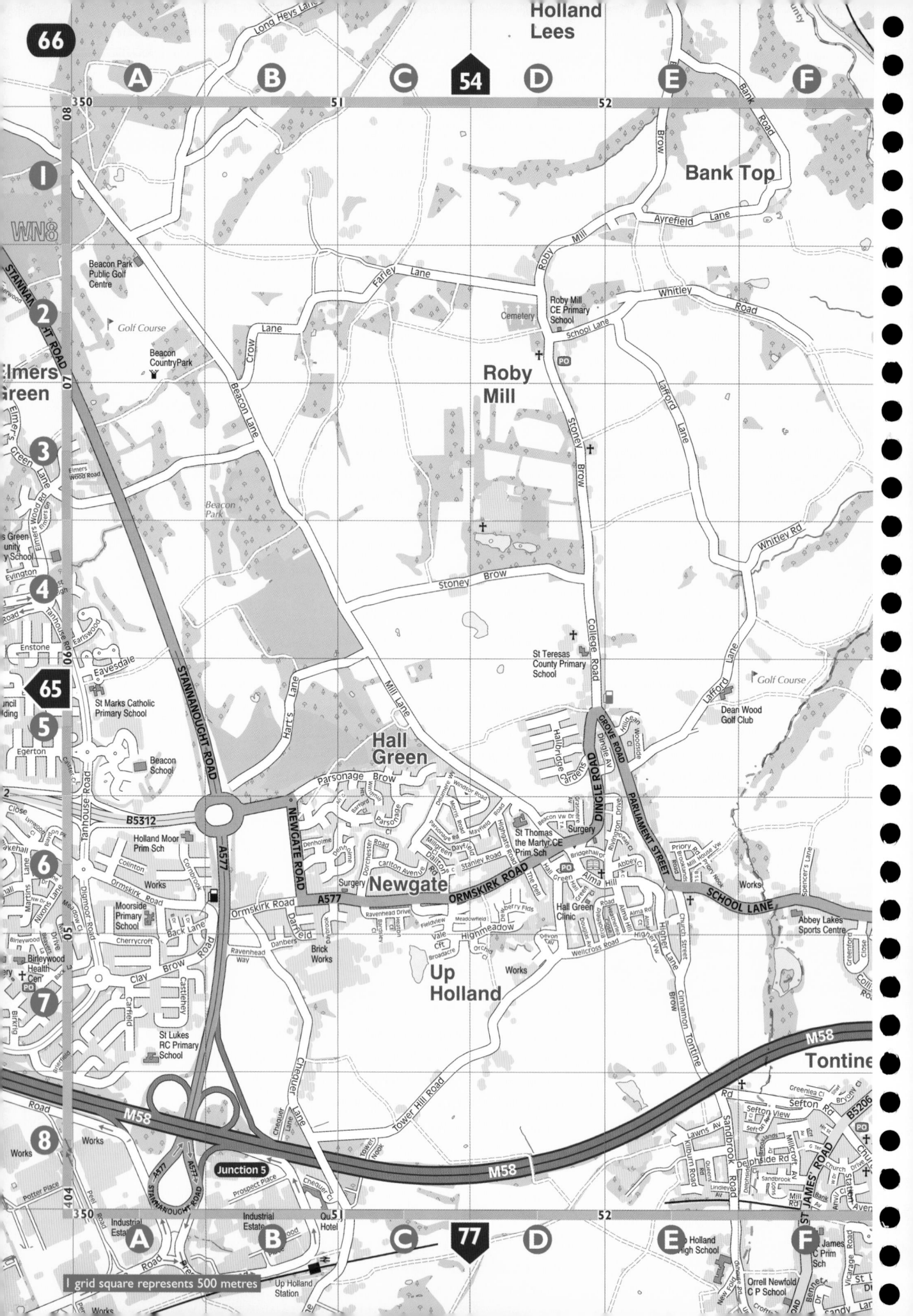

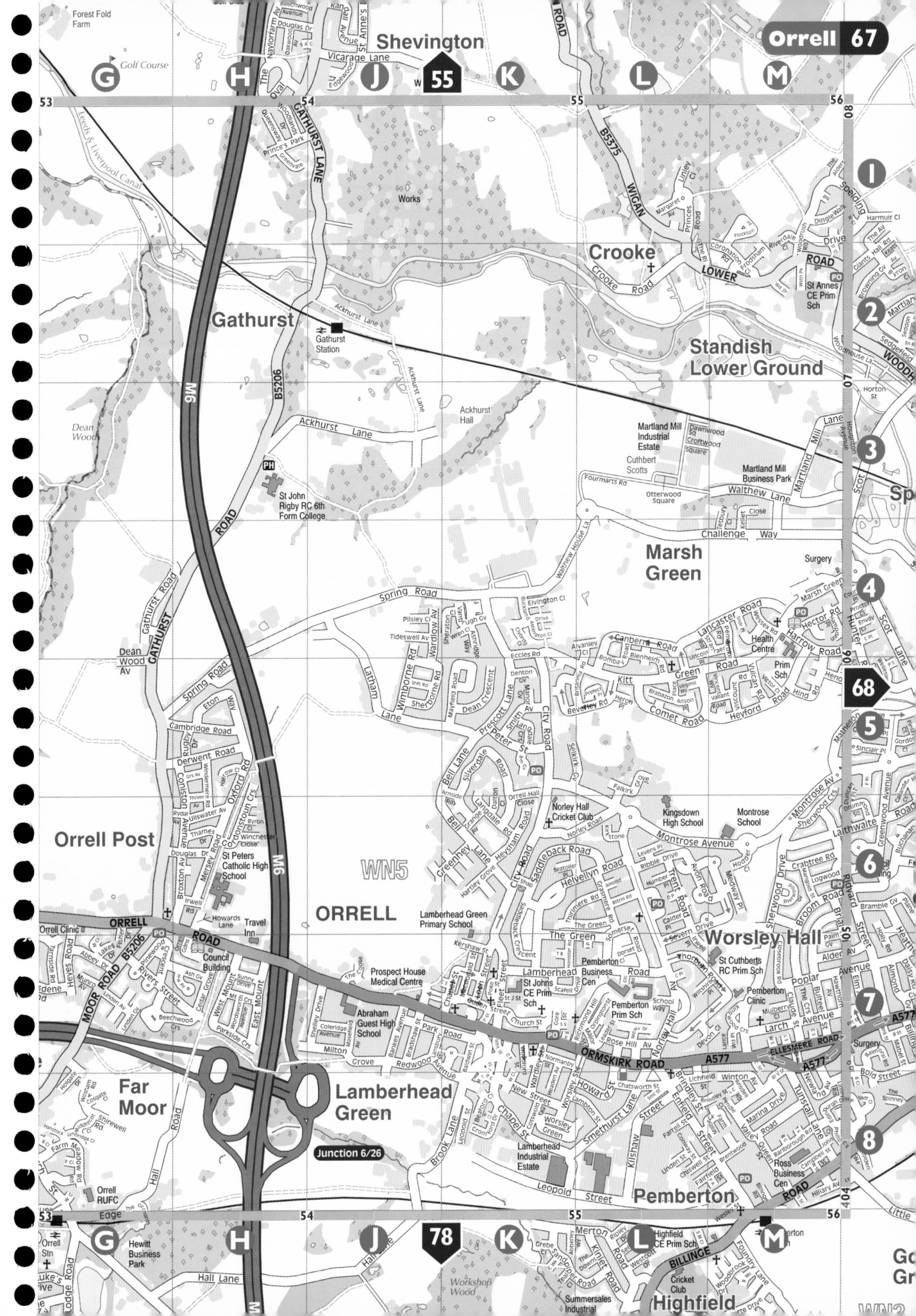

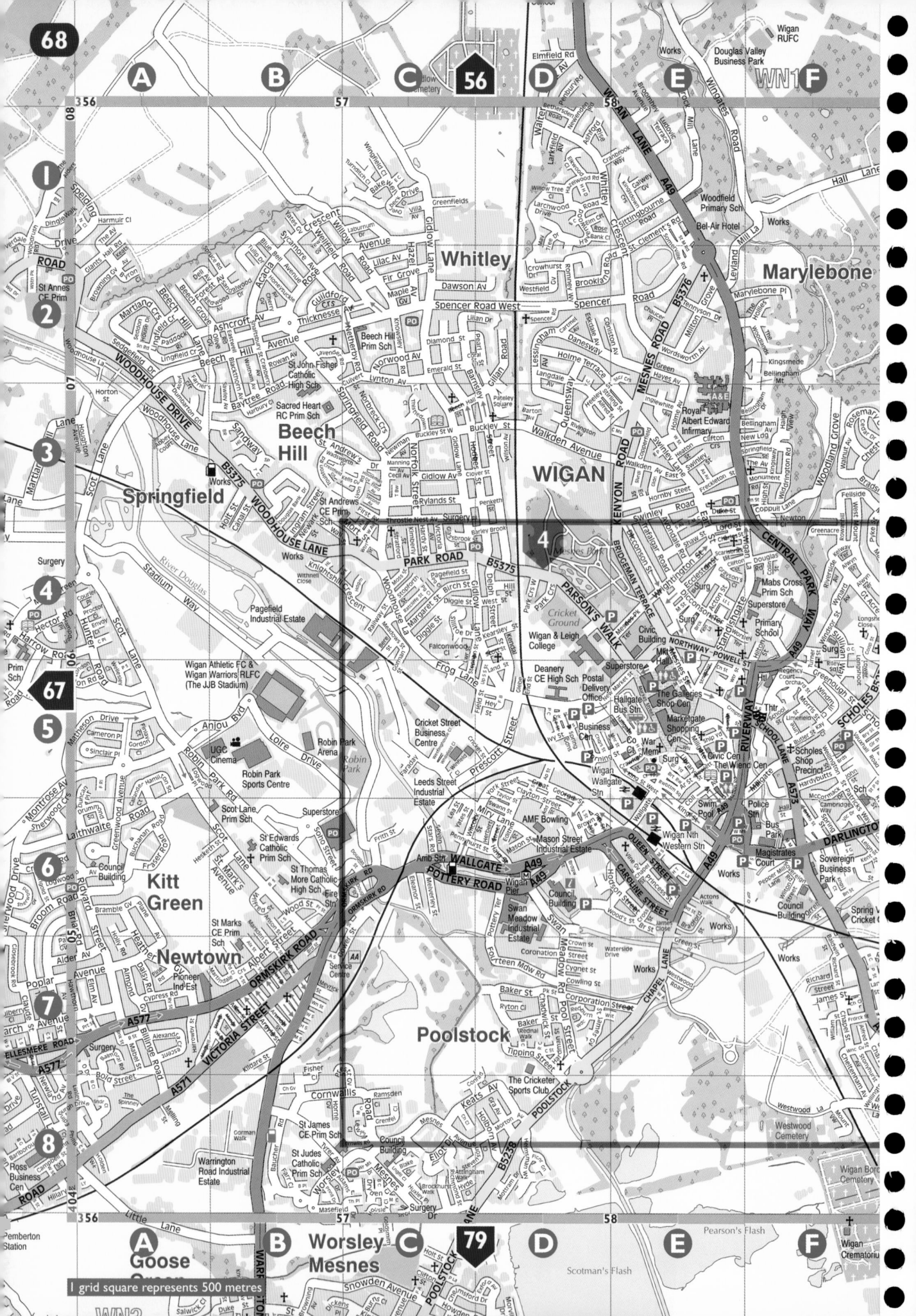

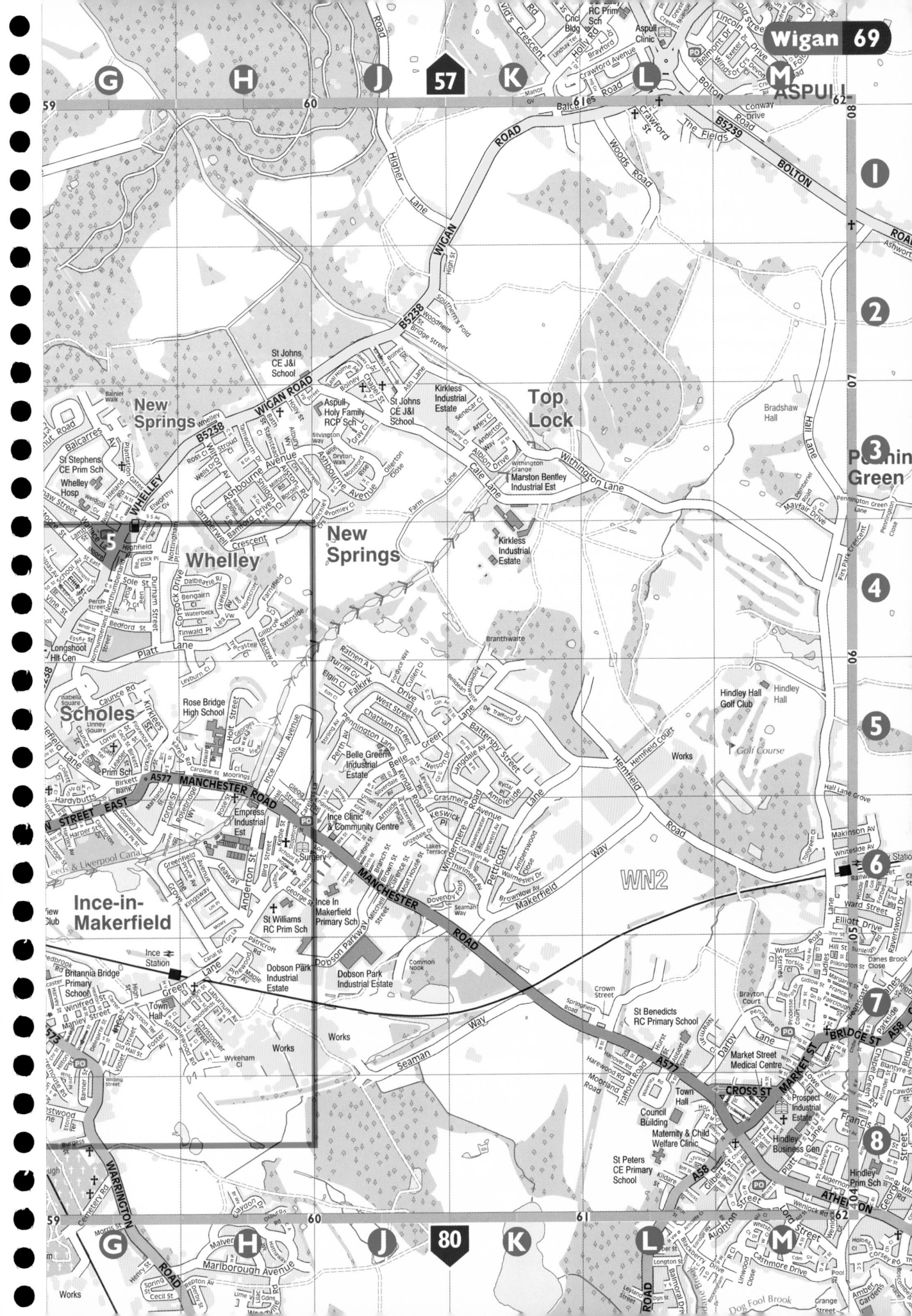

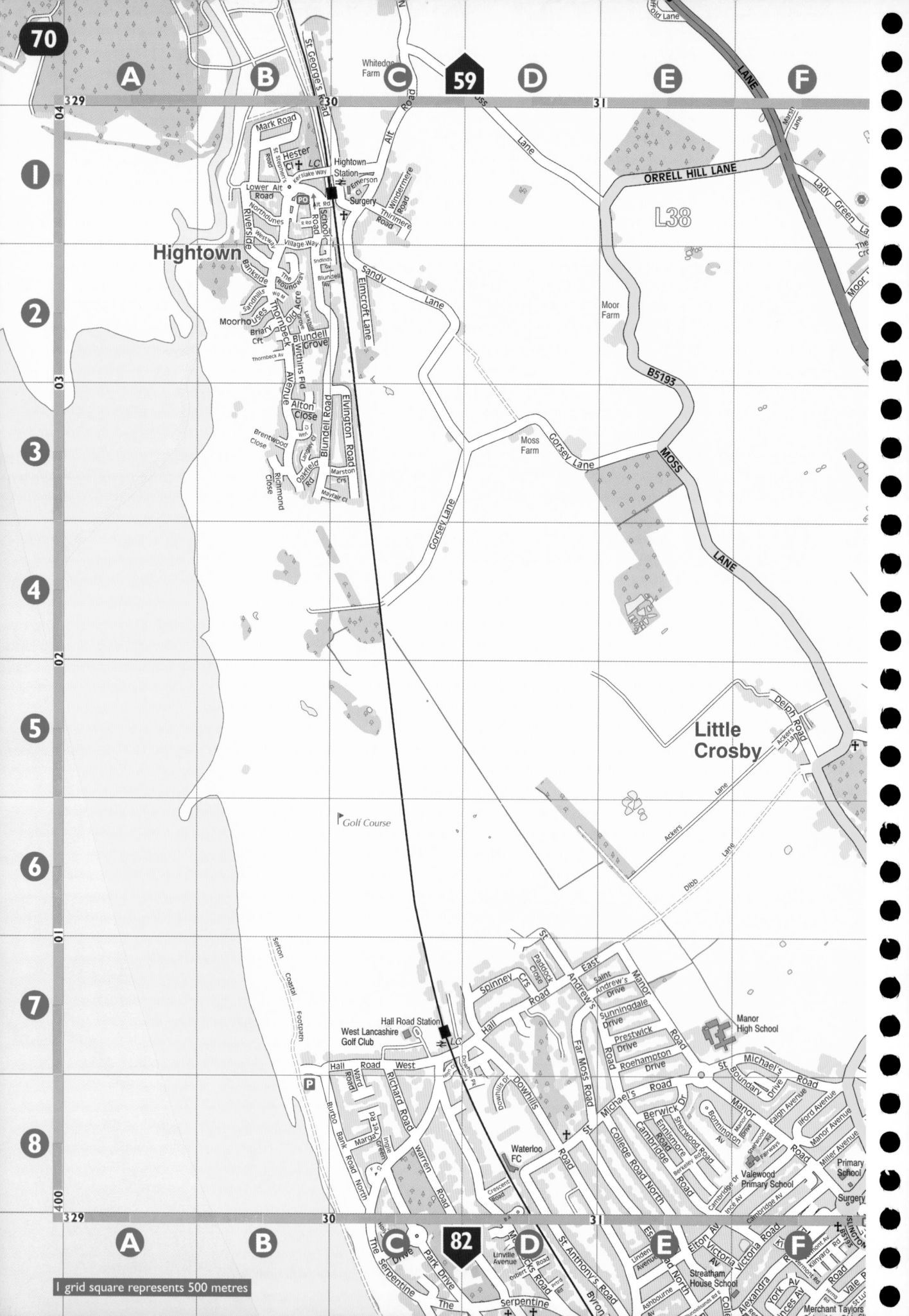

A   B   C   59   D   E   F

329   30   31

I

 I

2   Hightown

03

3

4

02

5

6

01

7

8

400

329   30   31

A   B   C   82   D   E   F

Mark Road

Hester Ct   LC
Hightown Station
Lower Alt Road   Emerson Cl   Surgery
Northdunes   Riverside   Windermere Road   Thirlmere Road
Westway   Village Way   Sndings   Blundell Av
Bankside   The Roundway   School Road   Elmcroft Lane   Alt Road
Sandhills   Blundell Grove
Moorhouses   Thornbeck Av   Withins Fld   sandy Lane
Briar Cft   Blundell Avenue
Alton Close   Elvington Road   Blundell Road
Brentwood Close   Langley   Oakfield Rd   Marston Crs
Richmond Close   Mayfair Cl

St George's Road

Alt Road   Lane   Whitedge Farm   Orrell Hill Lane

L38

Moor Farm

B5193

MOSS

Moss Farm   Gorsey Lane

LANE

Little Crosby

Ackers Lane

Delph Road

Gorsey Lane   Ackers Lane

Dibb Lane

Golf Course

Sefton   Coastal   Footpath

Hall Road Station
West Lancashire Golf Club

Spinney   Paddock Close   East
Hall Road Crs   St Andrew's   Saint Andrew's Drive   Manor
Hall Road West   Richard Road   Sunningdale Drive
Prestwick Drive   Far Moss Road   Manor High School
Roehampton Drive
Hall Ward Road   Dowhills   Michael's Road   St Michael's Road   Boundary Drive
Burbo Bank Road North   Marga   Ingle Green   Dowhills Dr   College Road North   Berwick Dr   Ennismore Road   Cambridge Road   Bonnington Av   Manor   Kalgh Avenue   Ilford Avenue
Warren Road   Crescent Road   St Anthony's Road   Cambridge Road   Fairway   Manor Avenue   Primary School
Waterloo FC   Byron Road   Sherwood Road   Valewood Primary School   Cambridge Av   Surgery
Linden Avenue   Eiton Av   Elton Victoria Road   Streatham House School
The Serpentine   Park Drive   Linville Avenue   Ashbourne   York Av   Alexandra   Vale Road
The Serpentine   Osbert   St Luke's   College   Merchant Taylors

1 grid square represents 500 metres

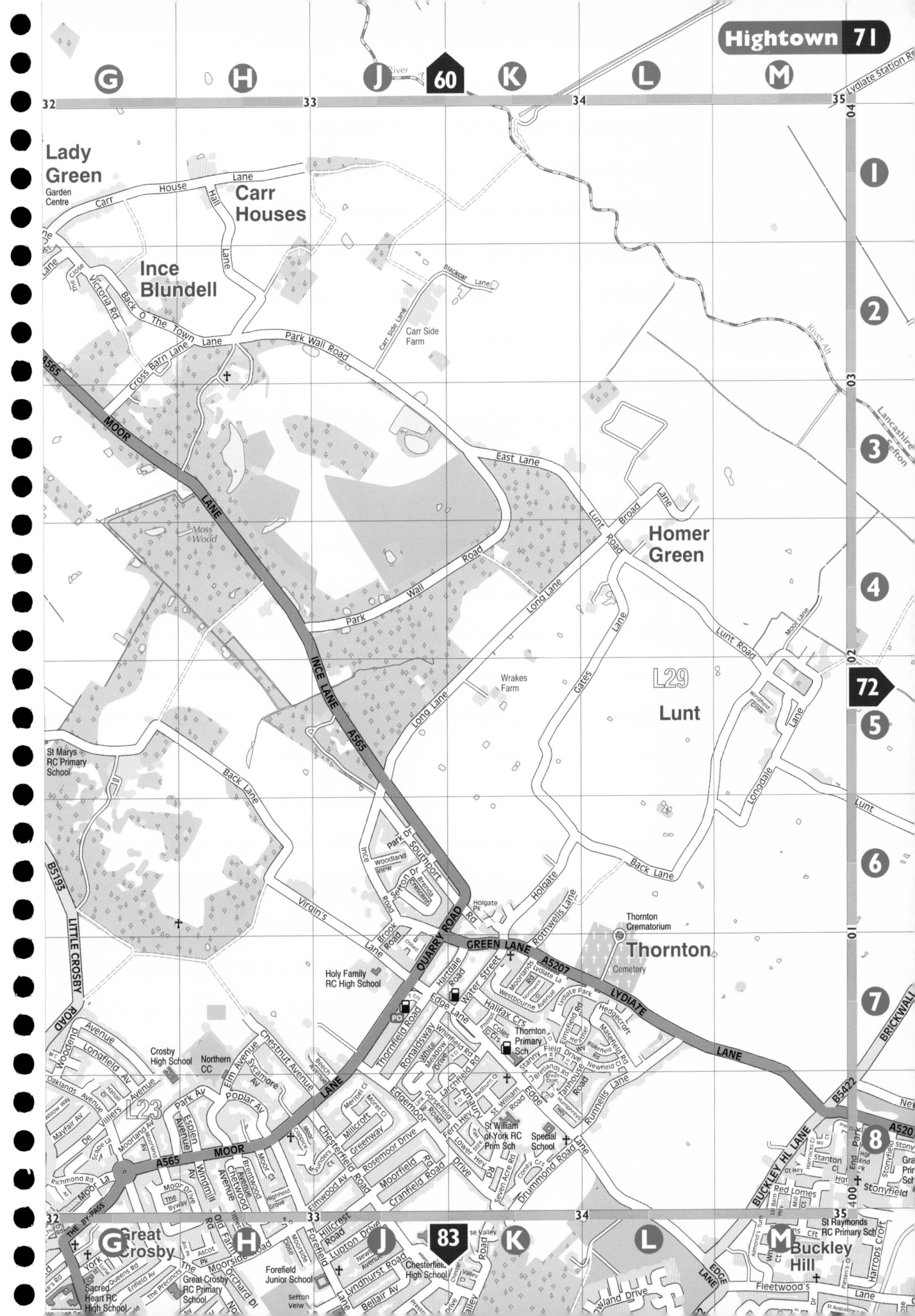

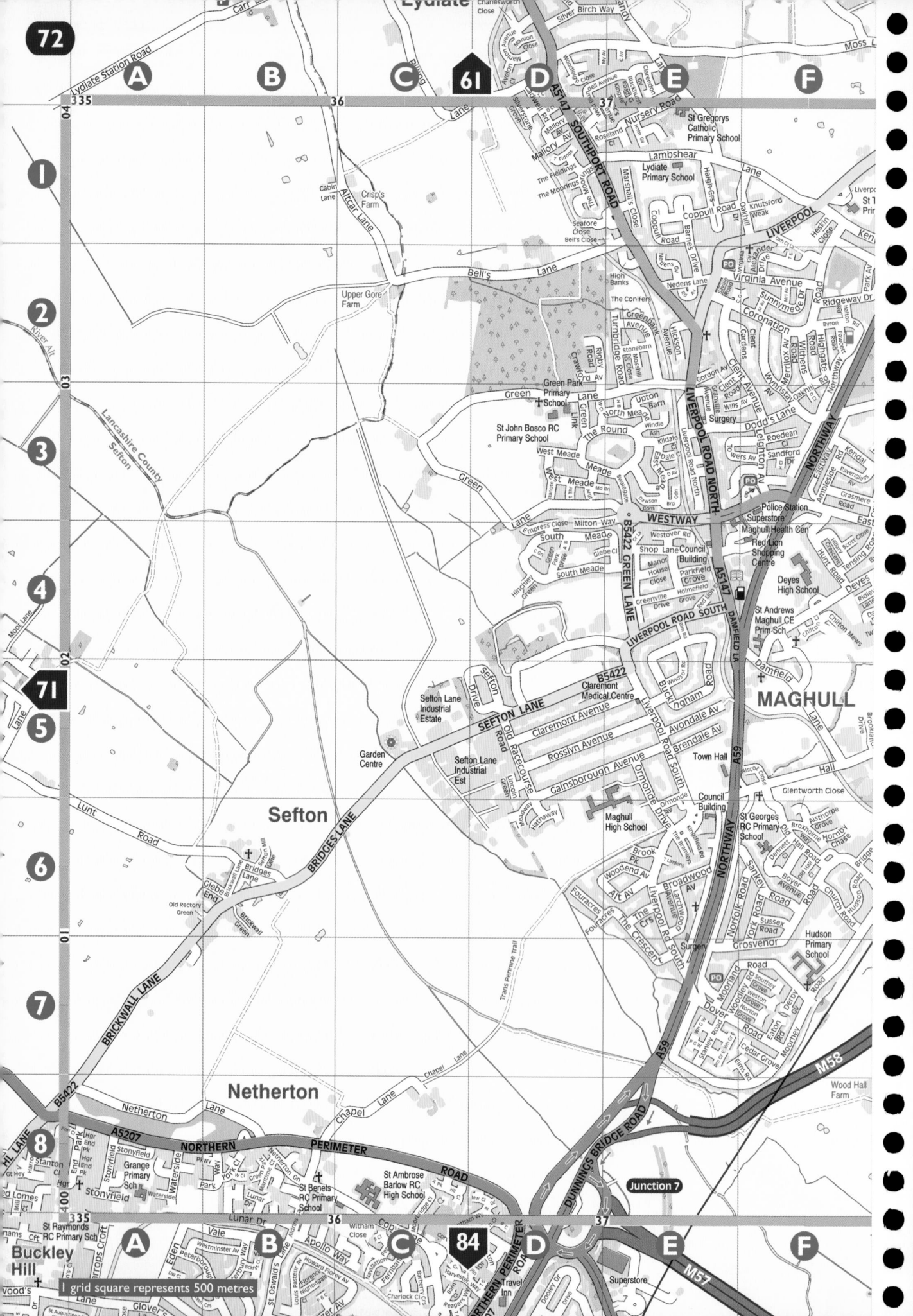

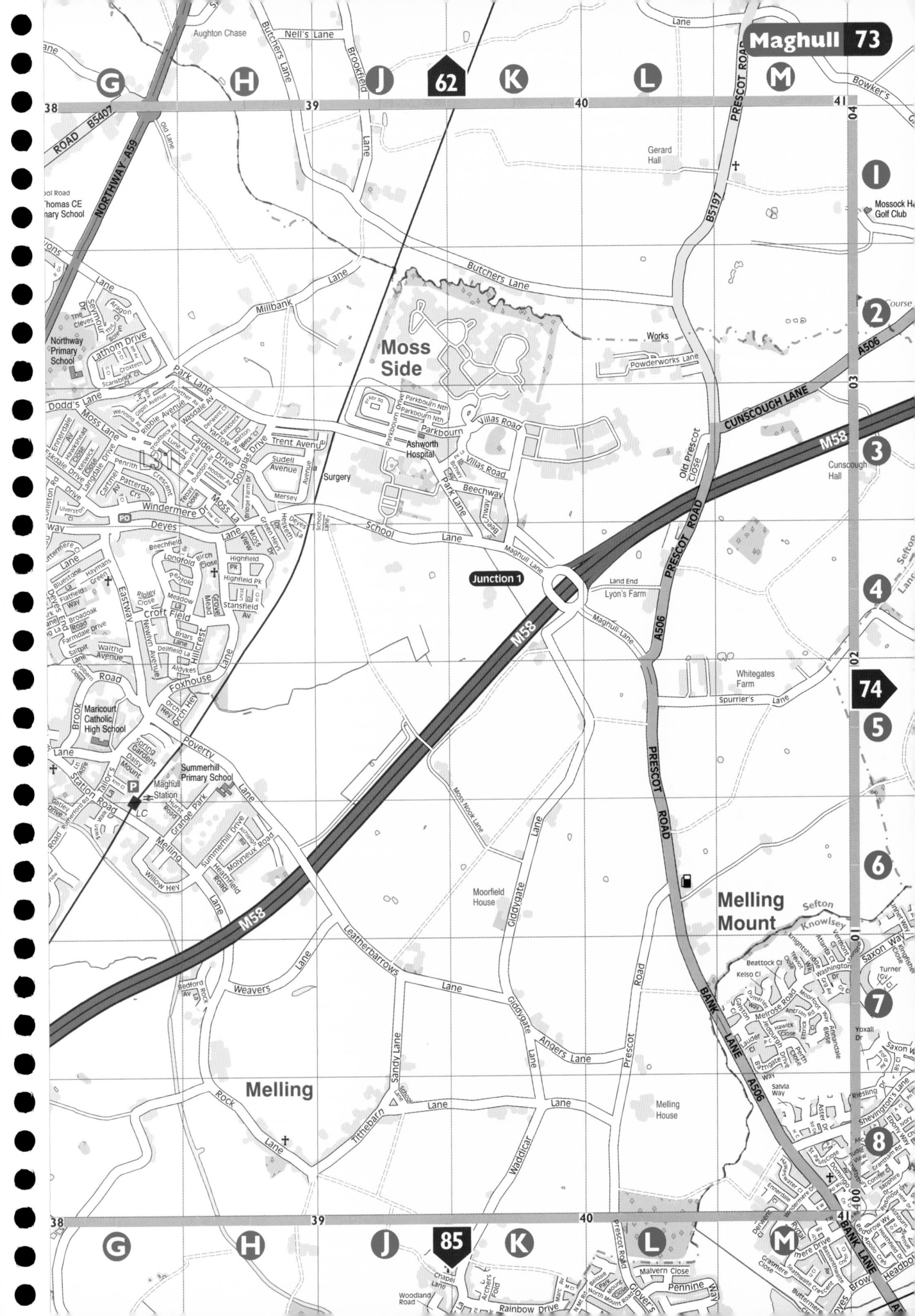

341
42
63
43

A   **B**   **C**   **D**   **E**   **F**

1

Bowker's

Green

Lane

LIVERPOOL ROAD

Mossock Hall
Golf Club

Royal Oak

Roby's
Farm

2

Golf Course

A506

New Way

04
03
'58

Mercer's Lane

Simonswood Lane

M58

Back   Lane

3

Cunscough
Hall

New Way

Bullens
Farm

Back Lane

Bickerstaffe
Moss

Outlet Lane

Hurst's Lane

Simonswood Lane

Outlet
Farm

Sefton
Lancashire County

Outlet   Lane

4

02

73

5

Hall Lane

6

Grayson's
Farm

Moss Lane

Hall Lane

Stopgate Lane

Sefton
Knowsley

01

Saxon Way

Tern Close

Swallow

Deca Lane

Weaver Avenue

Stopgate Lane

Simonswood
Industrial Park

7

Penda
Dr

Turner
Gv

Elwood
Cl

Hall Lane

Saxon
Rd

Redwood
Way

Whitebeam
Close

Greenham Avenue

Meadowside

Pingwood
Lane

Cart's Way

Yoxall
Dr

Shevington's Lane

PO

Moorfield

Shevington's Lane

Steeple View

Saints
Peter & Paul
Catholic Sch

Tower Hill
Health
Centre

Tower Hill

Ravenscroft
Primary
School

Eastcroft
Park CP
School

Eastcroft

Headbolt Lane

8

400
341
42

Bank Lane

Headbolt
Lane

A   **B**   **C**   **86**   **D**   **E**   **F**

43

Spencer's
House

Urban
Farm

Perimeter Road

Knowsley Northern
Prim Support Cen

Bramcote
Walk

Bramcote Road

Lanford Crescent

Roughwood Drive

Lane

Depot

1 grid square represents 500 metres

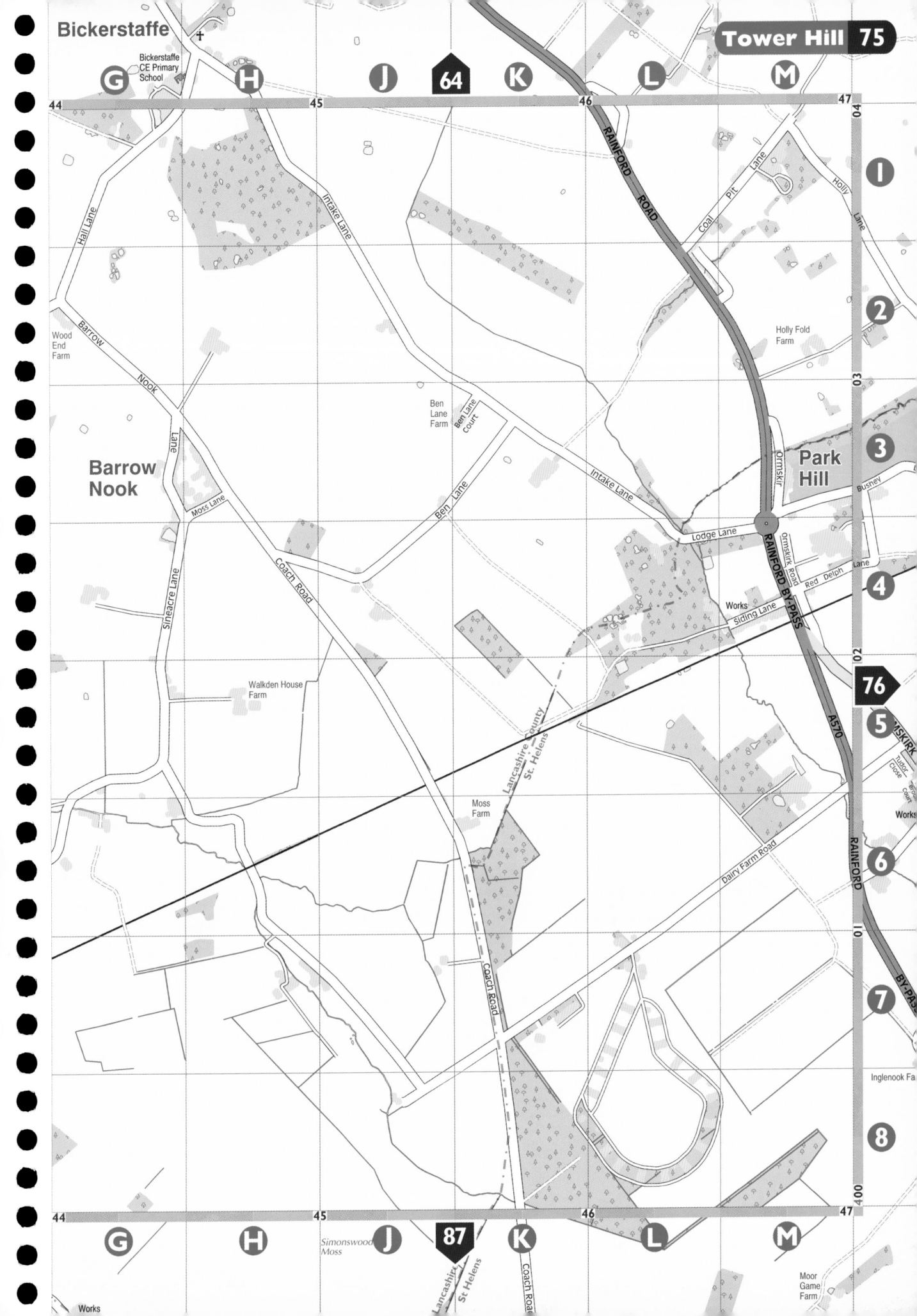

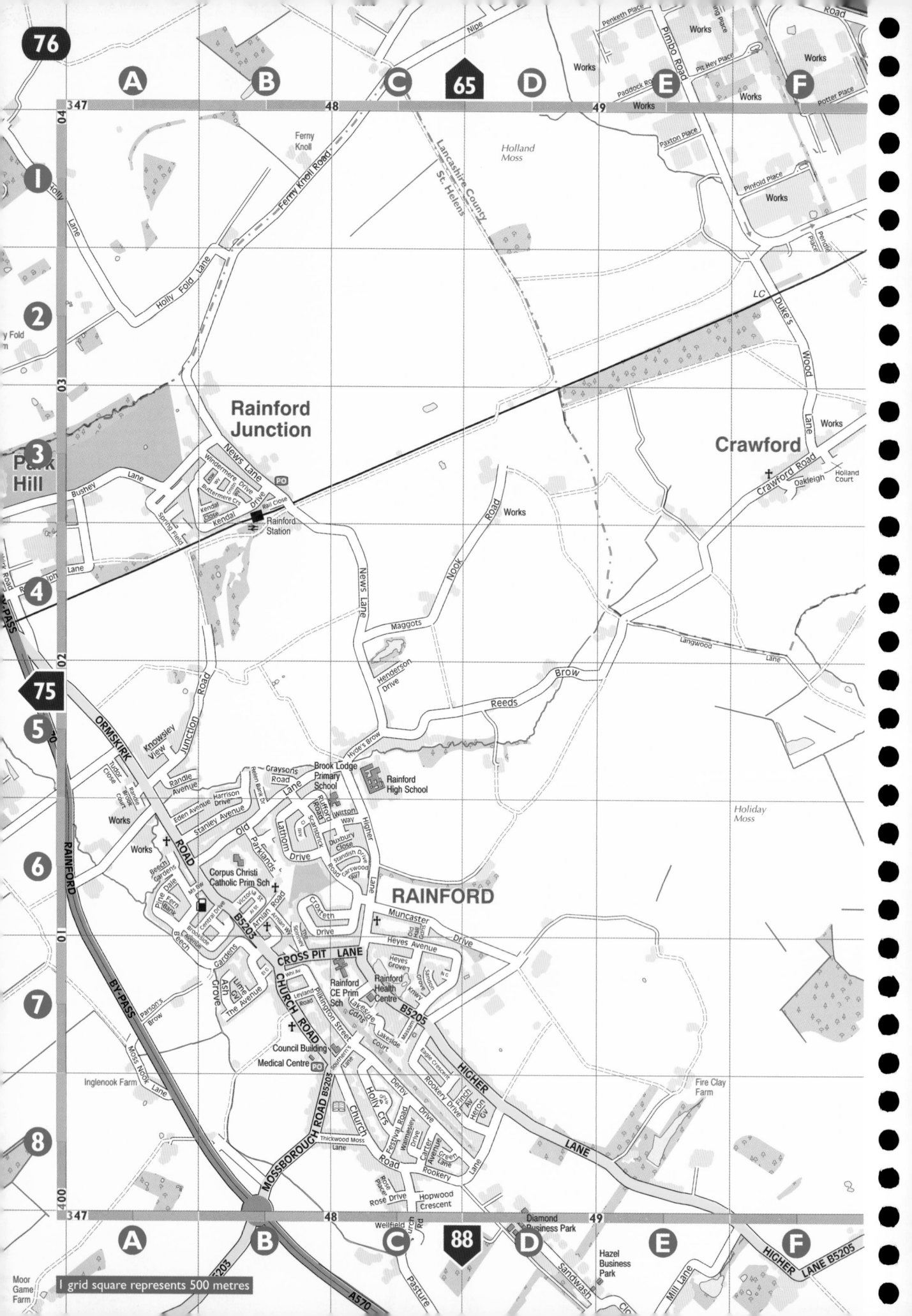

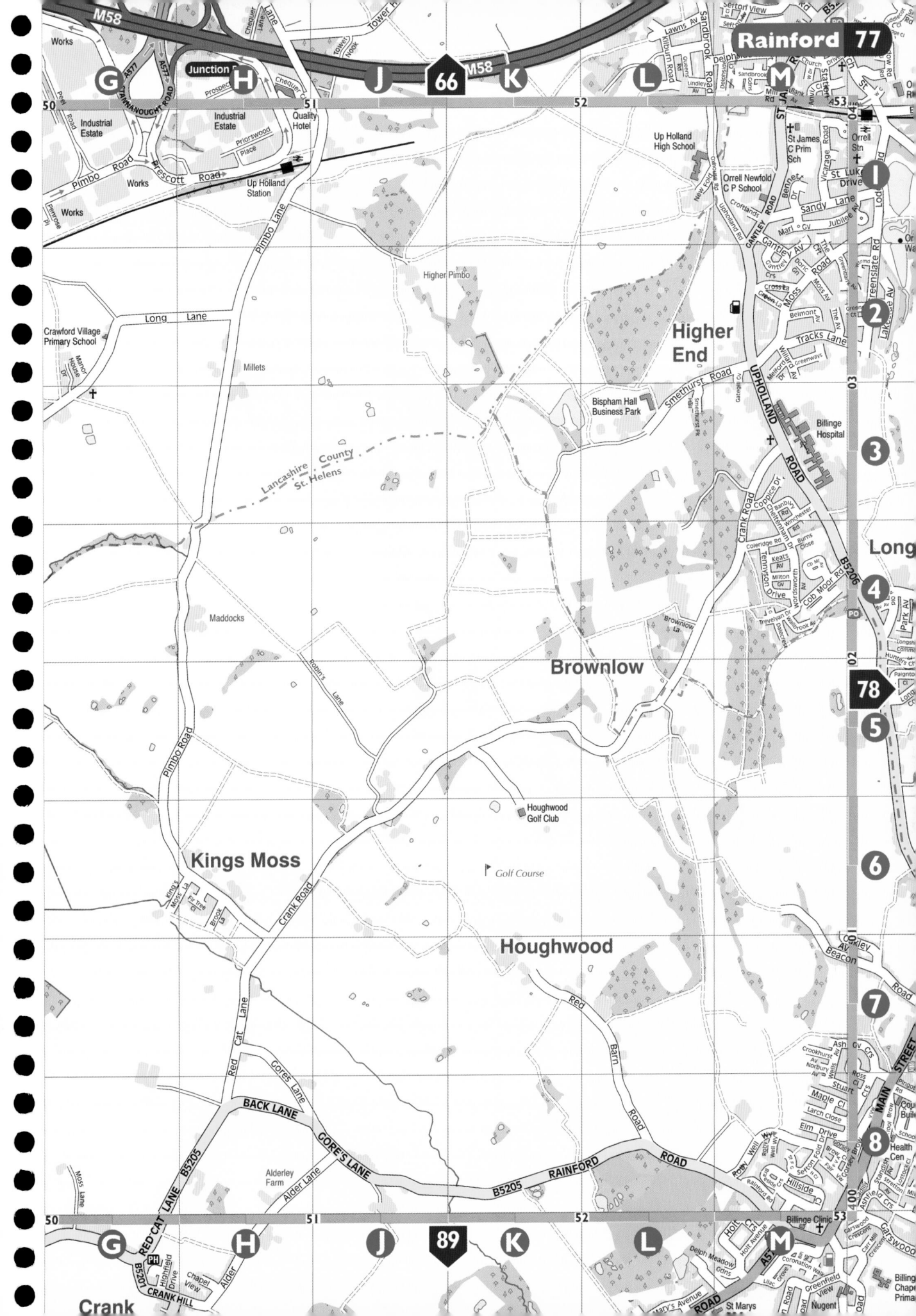

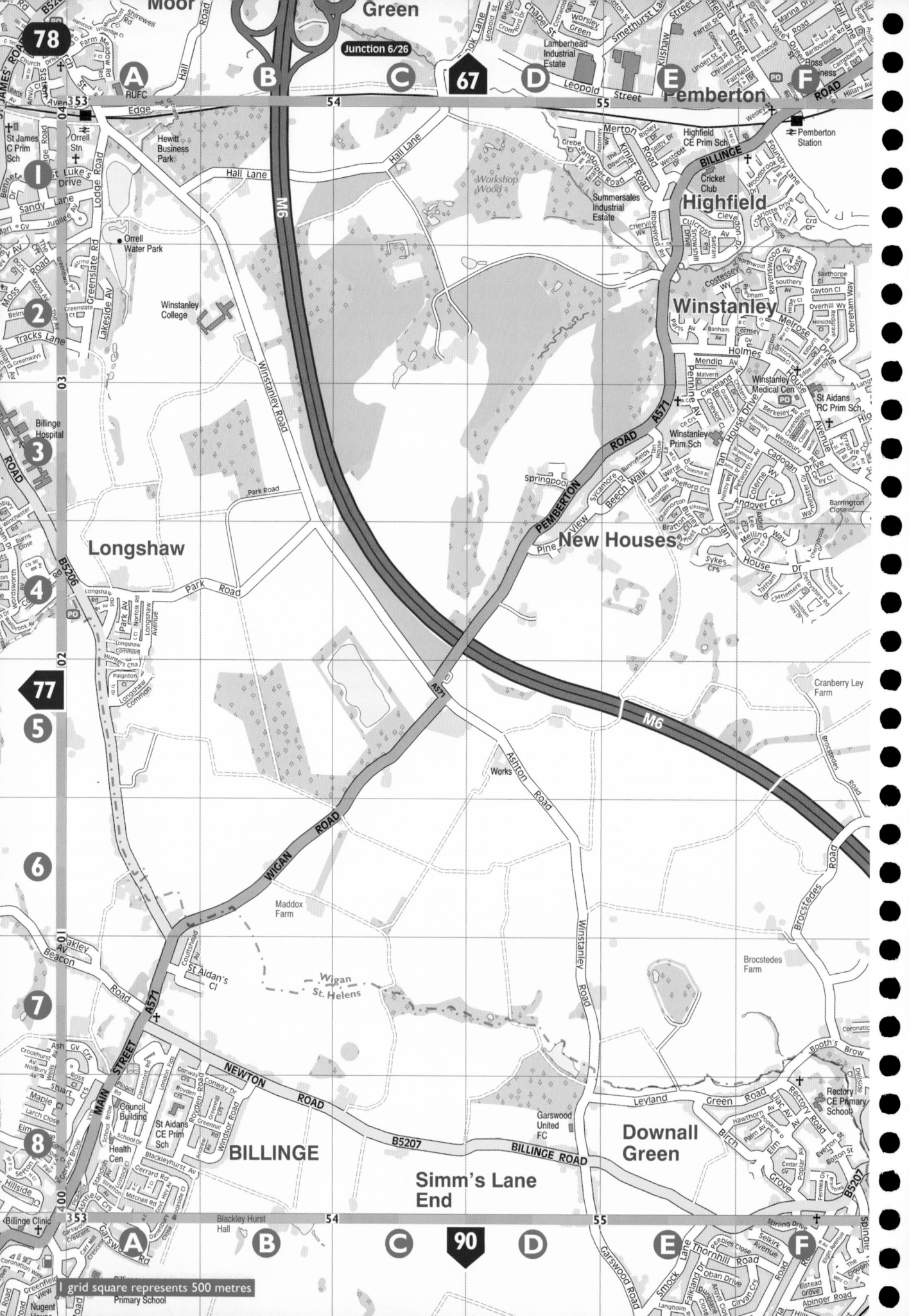

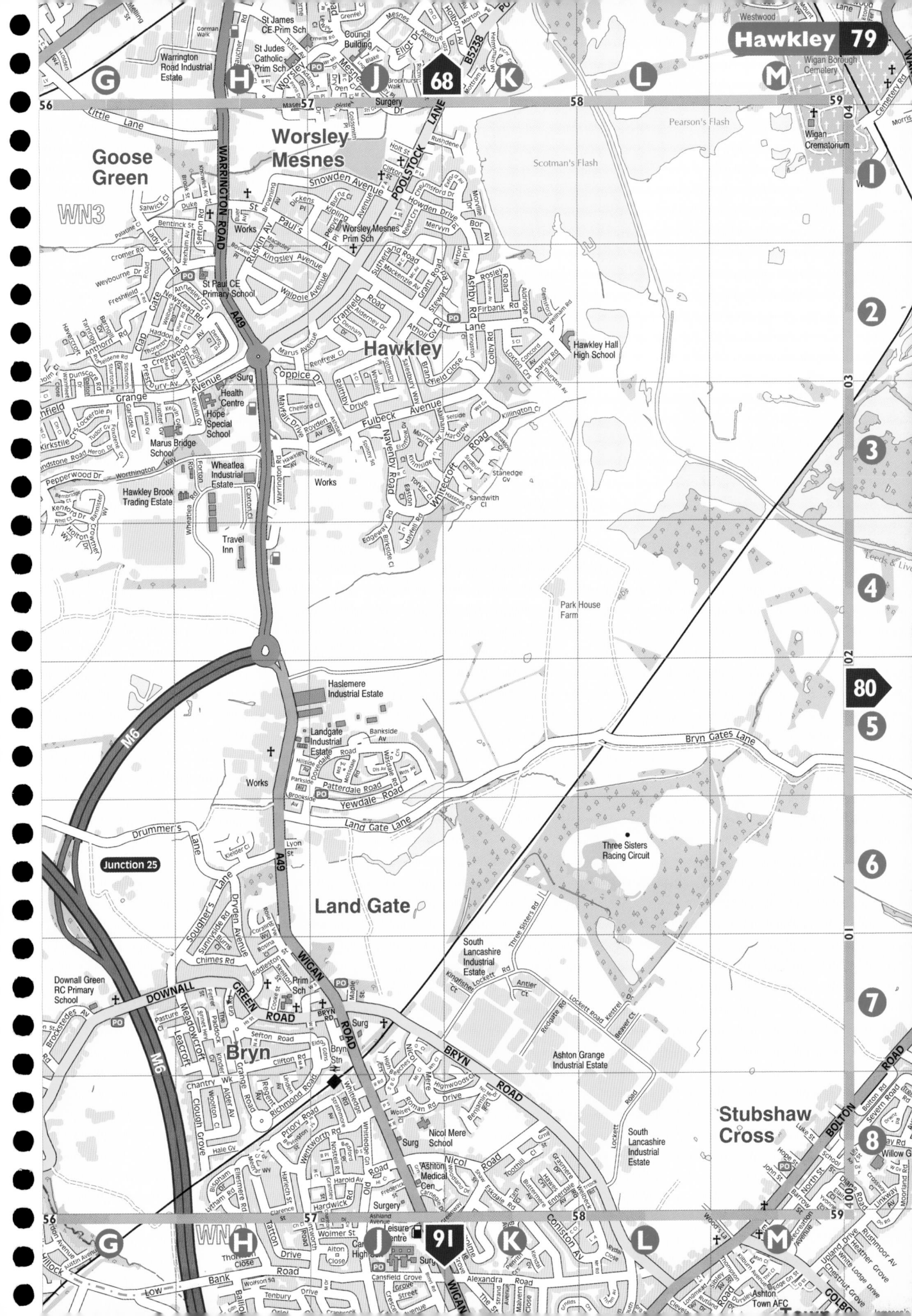

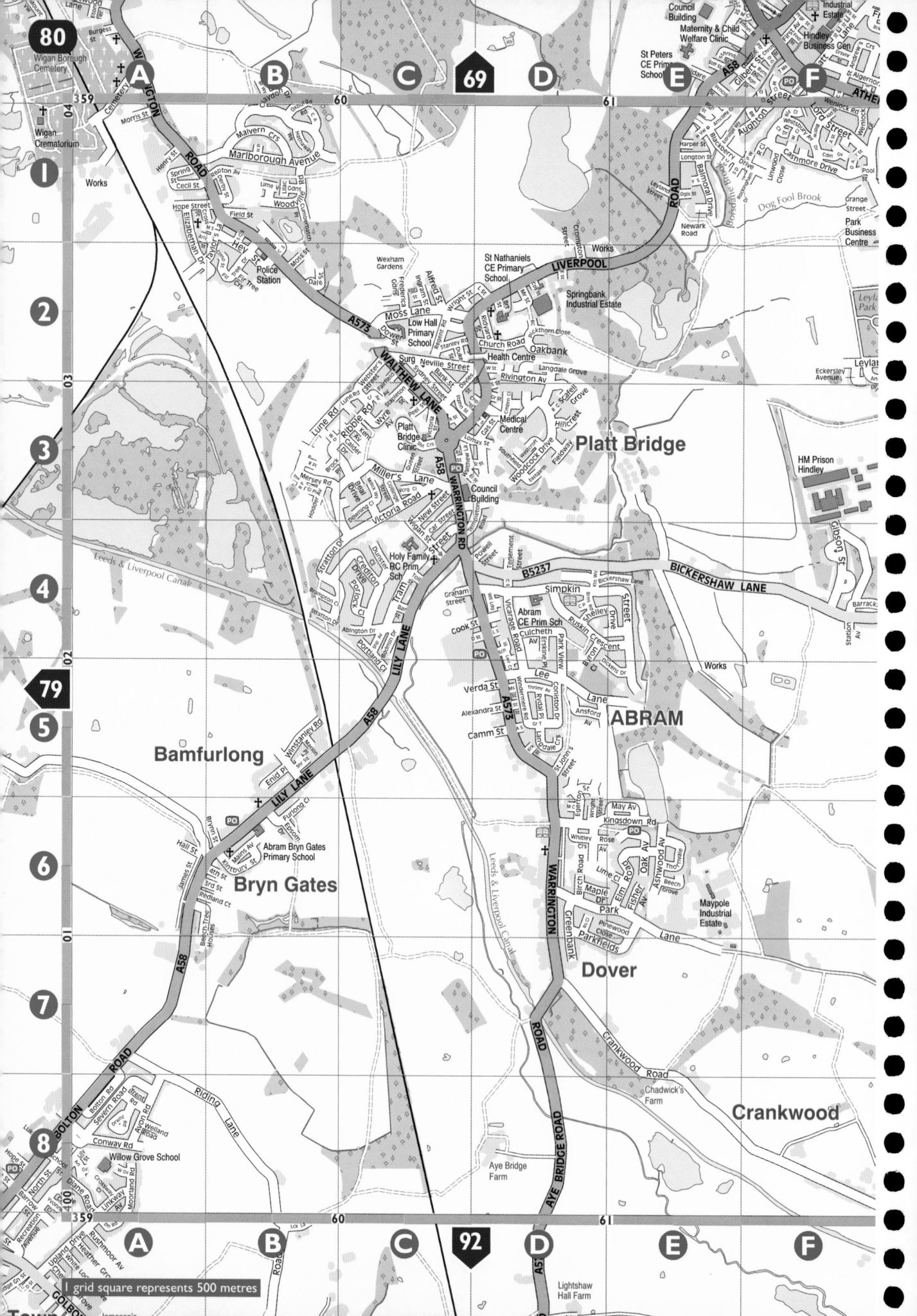

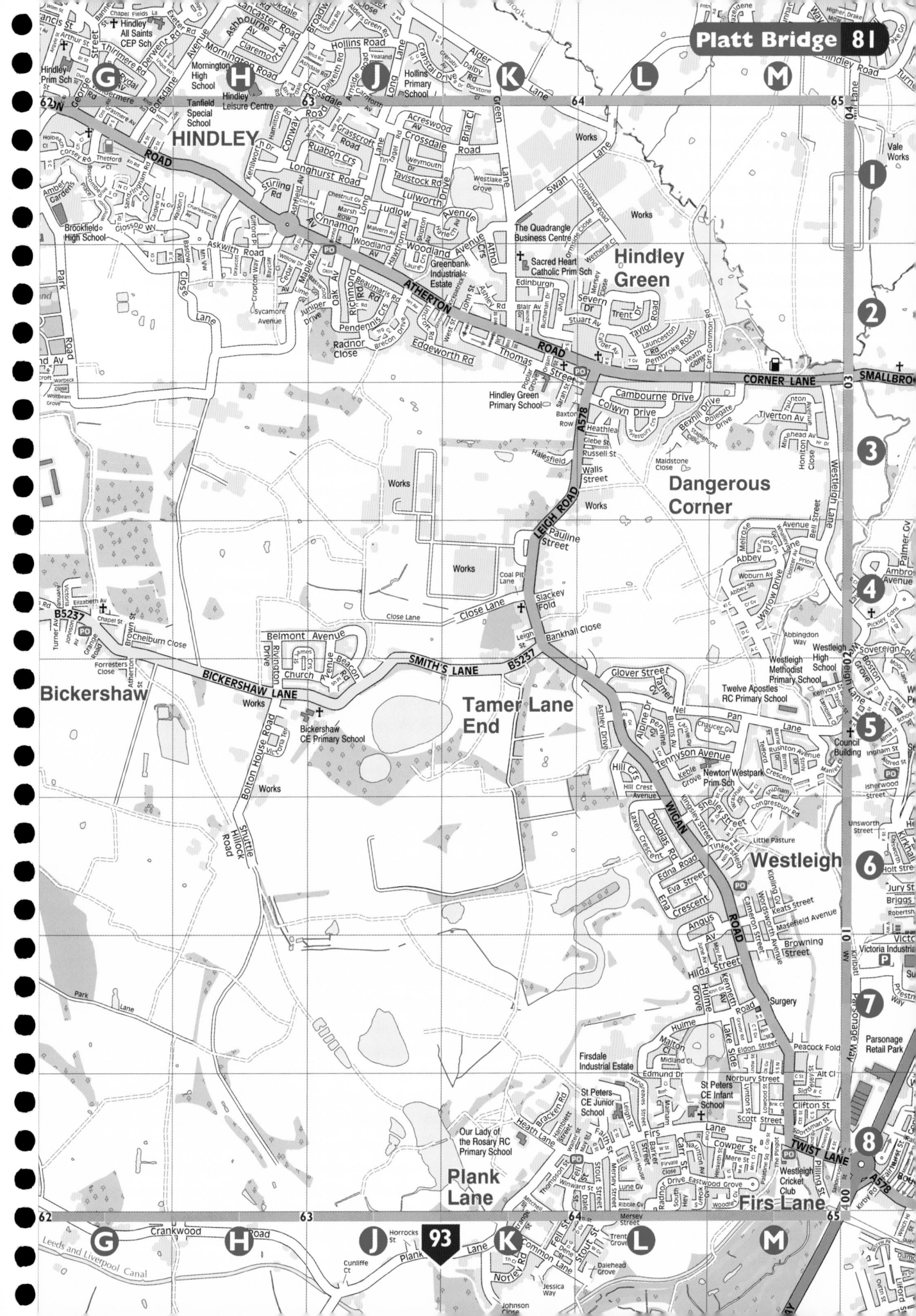

A · **B** · **C** · **70** · **D** · **E** · **F**

329 · 30 · 31

400

99

98

97

96

I · **2** · **3** · **4** · **5** · **6** · **7** · **8**

Blundellsands

Waterloo FC

Crescent Road

The Serpentine

serpentine

Park Drive

Park Drive

The Burbo Bank

Devon Cl

Channel Rd

Blundellsands Rd W

Nicholas Rd

Warren Road

Linville Avenue

Culbert's Road

St Anthony's Road

Byron Road

South Road

Blundellsands & Crosby Station

The Mount St Marys Prep Sch

Ursuline RC Primary Sch

PO

Streatham House School

College Rd

Ashbourne

Linden Avenue

Ivanhoe Rd

Esme Rd

Elton Av

Victoria Rd

Alexandra Rd

Princes Av

York Av

Kings Rd

Victoria Road

Coronation Rd

Cambridge Rd

Valewood Primary Sch

Primary School

Surgery

Merchant Taylors School for Girls

Atherton House School

Ever

Kimbe

Kingswood

Coronation Drive

St Nicholas CE Primary School

Agnes Road

Mersey Rd

Bridge Road

Weld Rd

Harlech Rd

Cavendish Rd

Abbotsford Gardens

Crossender Rd

Rossett Road

Jubilee Road

Sunnyside Road

Marine FC

Winchester Rd

Woodville Av

Brookfield Av

Myers Rd

College Av

Surgery

Brighton le Sands

PO

Mariners Rd

Riverslea Rd

Crosby Baths

Endsleigh Road

Holden Road

Warren House

Sudbury Rd

Leopold Road

Heathfield Rd

Mersey View

Pinehurst Avenue

Rosebery Rd

College Road East

Lancaster Av

Alder Rd

Park View

Waterloo

Brooke Road West

Oxford Drive

Brooke Road

Courtenay Av

Courtenay Rd

Manley Rd

Somerville Road

Lawton

CROSBY

Sandheys Av

Oxford Road

Burdett Rd

St Johns CE Primary School

St Edmunds & St Thomas CP Sch

Harbord Rd

Picton Rd

Beach Lawn

Blucher St

Wellington St

Brighton Road

John St

Lyra Rd

Works

L22

Adelaide Terrace

Marine Crs

East St

South

Marine Terrace

Dean Bath

Marine Lake

The Royal Hotel

Sefton Coastal Footpath

Works

DOUGLAS

DUBLIN

I grid square represents 500 metres

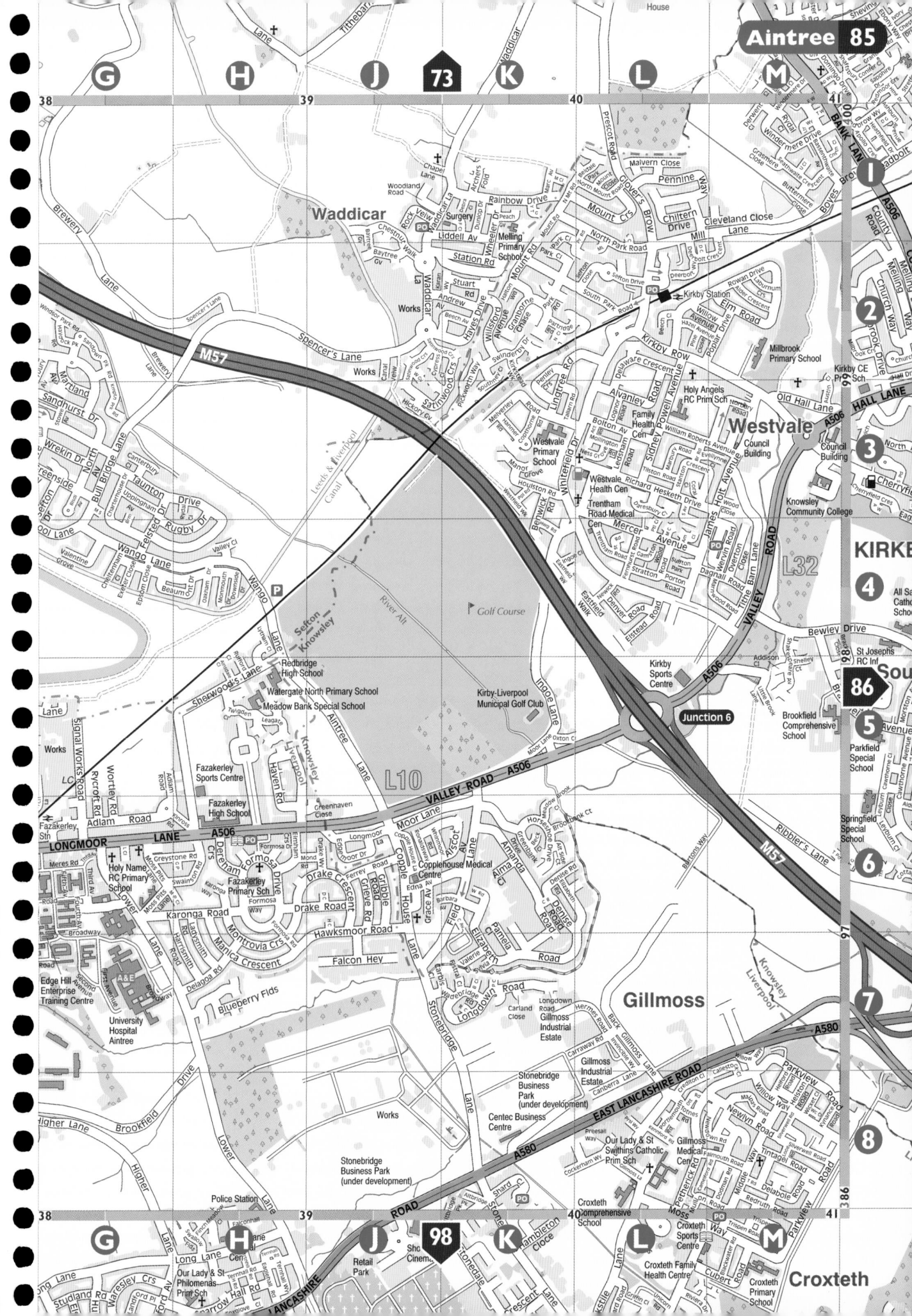

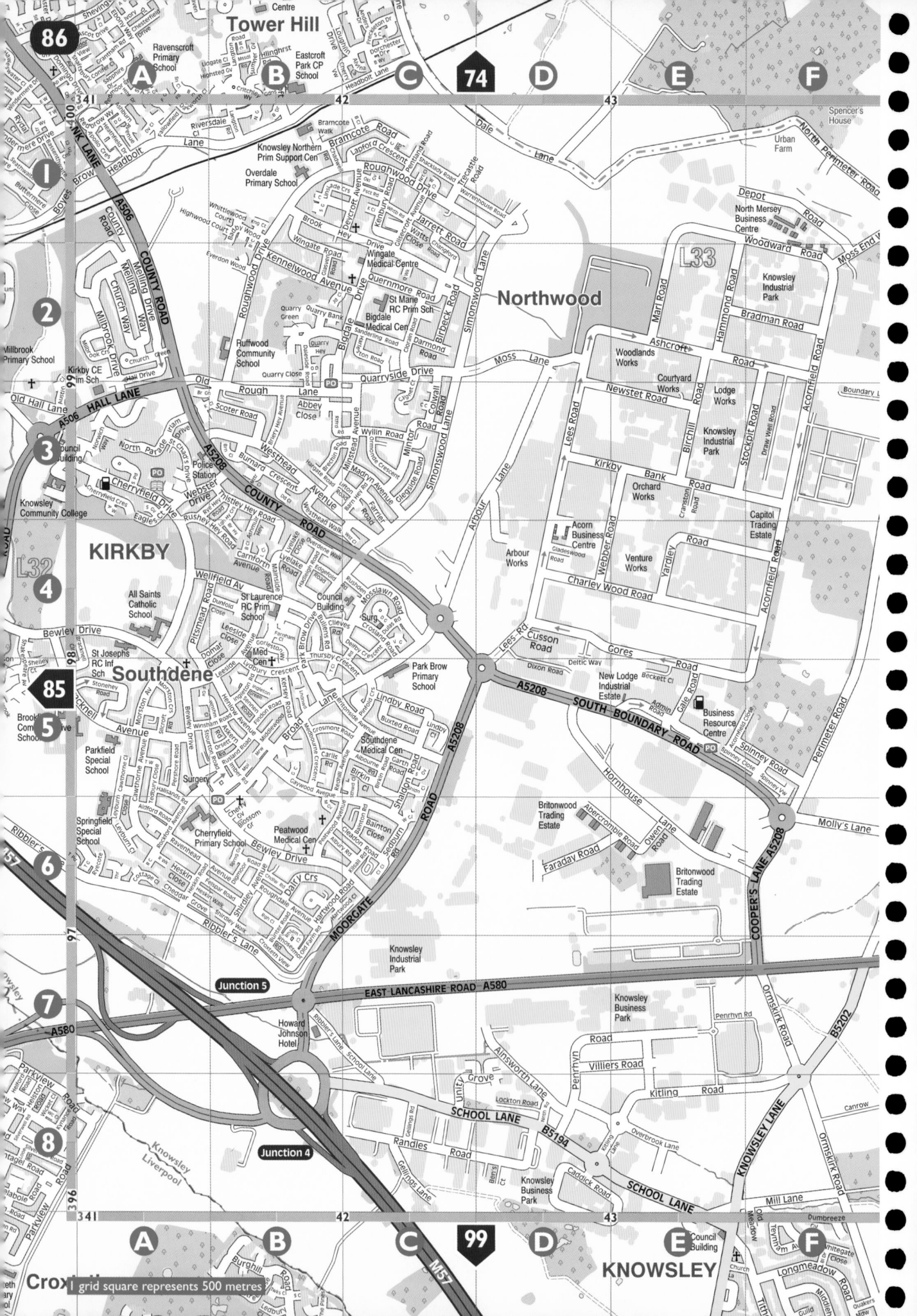

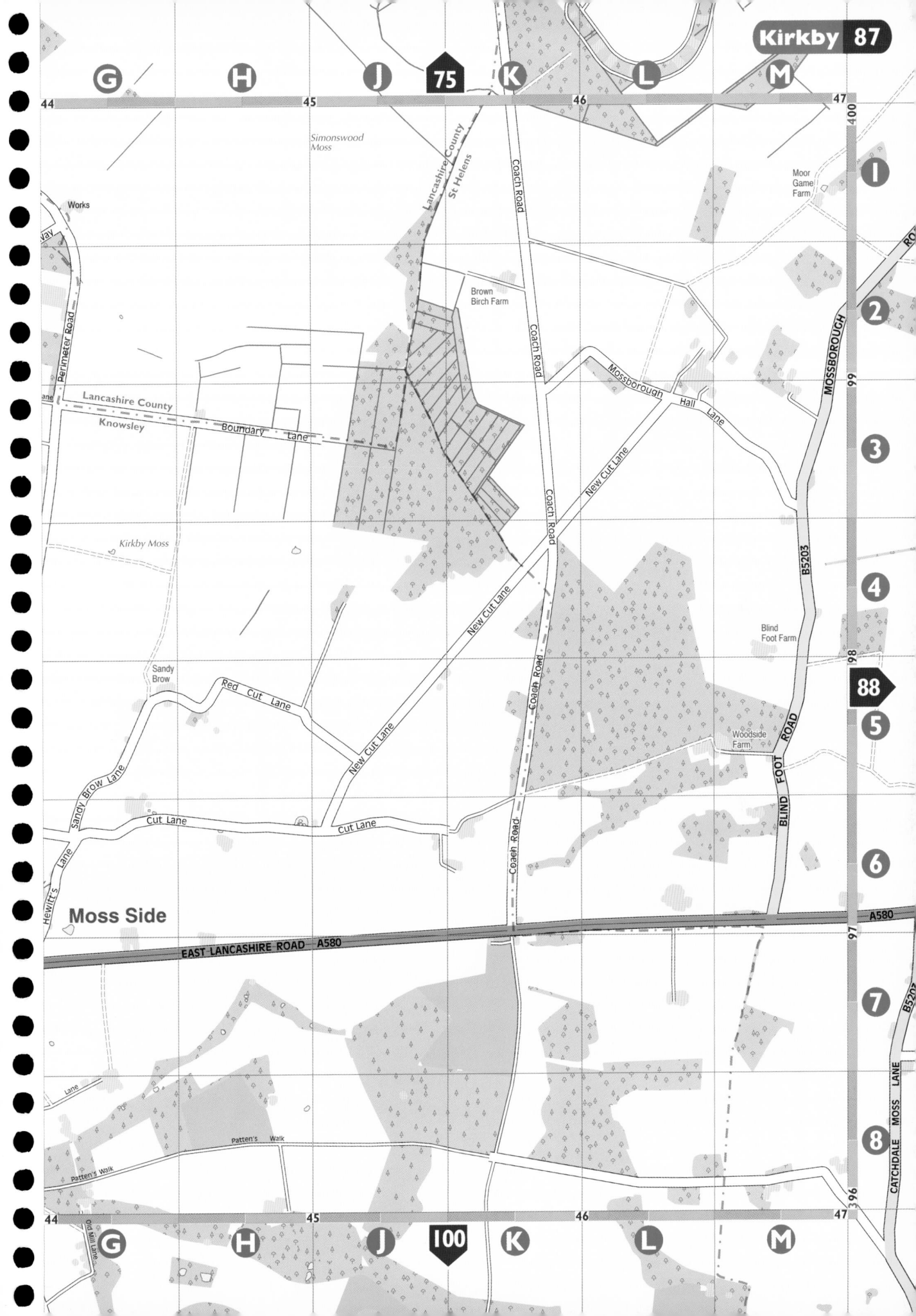

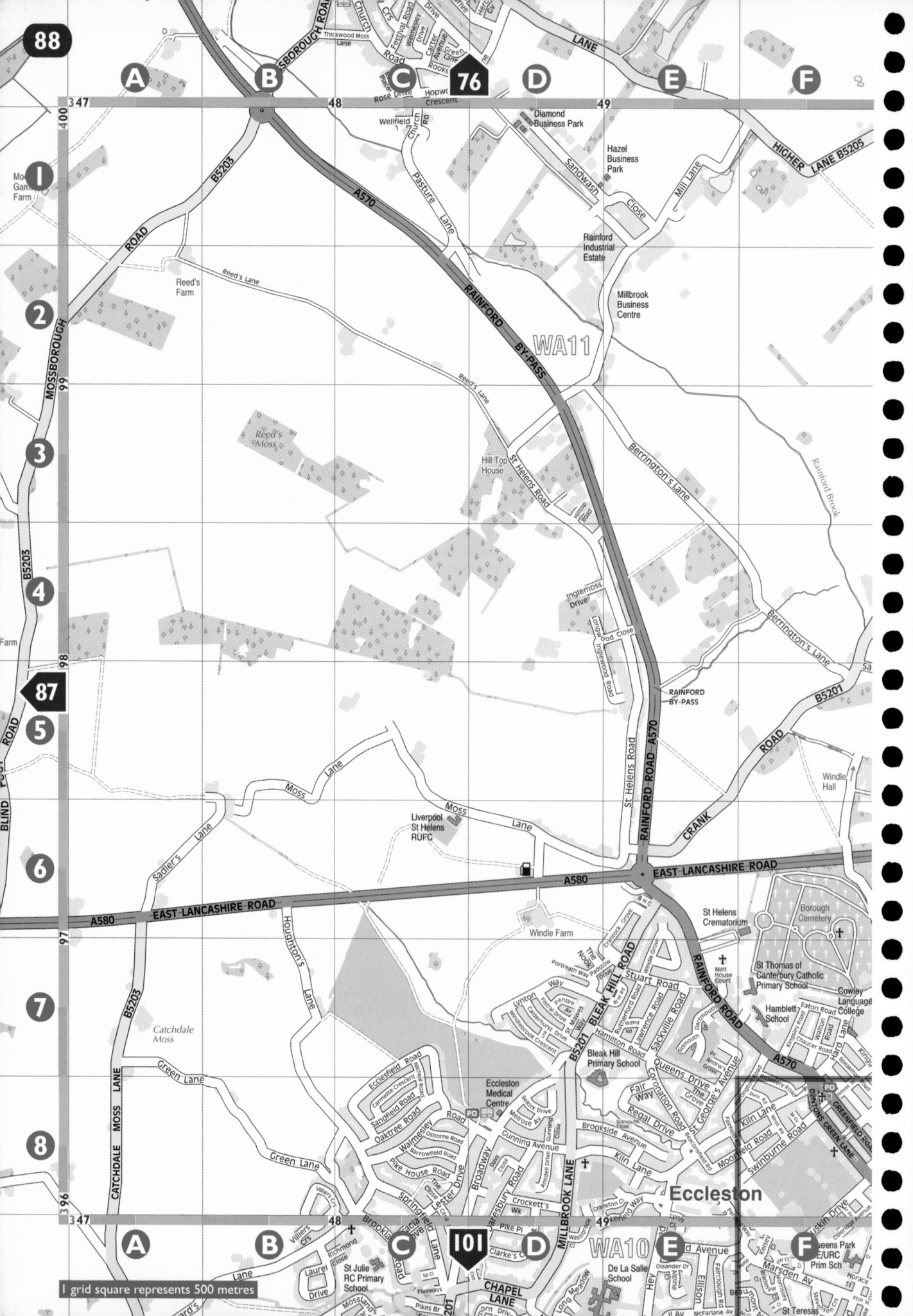

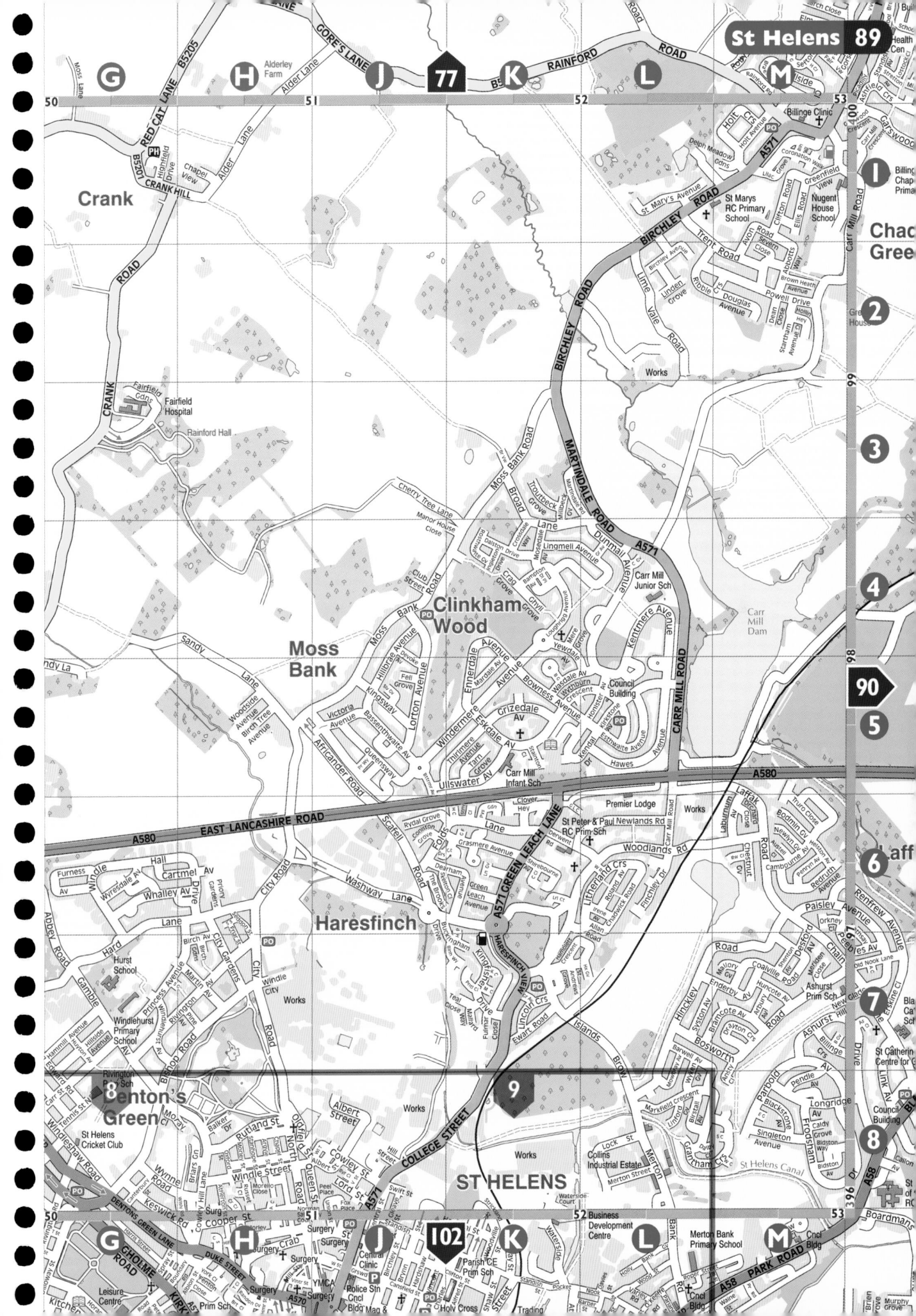

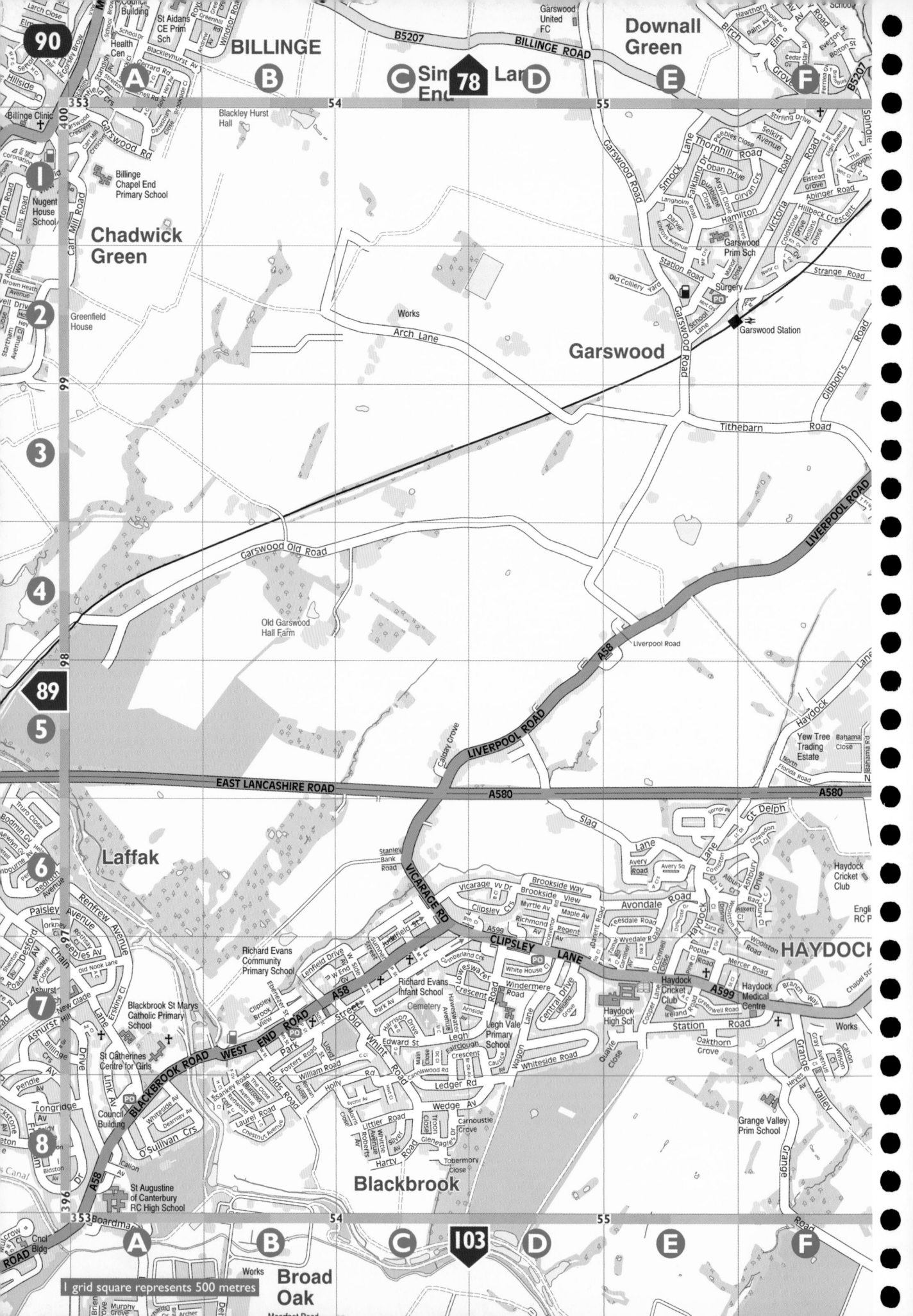

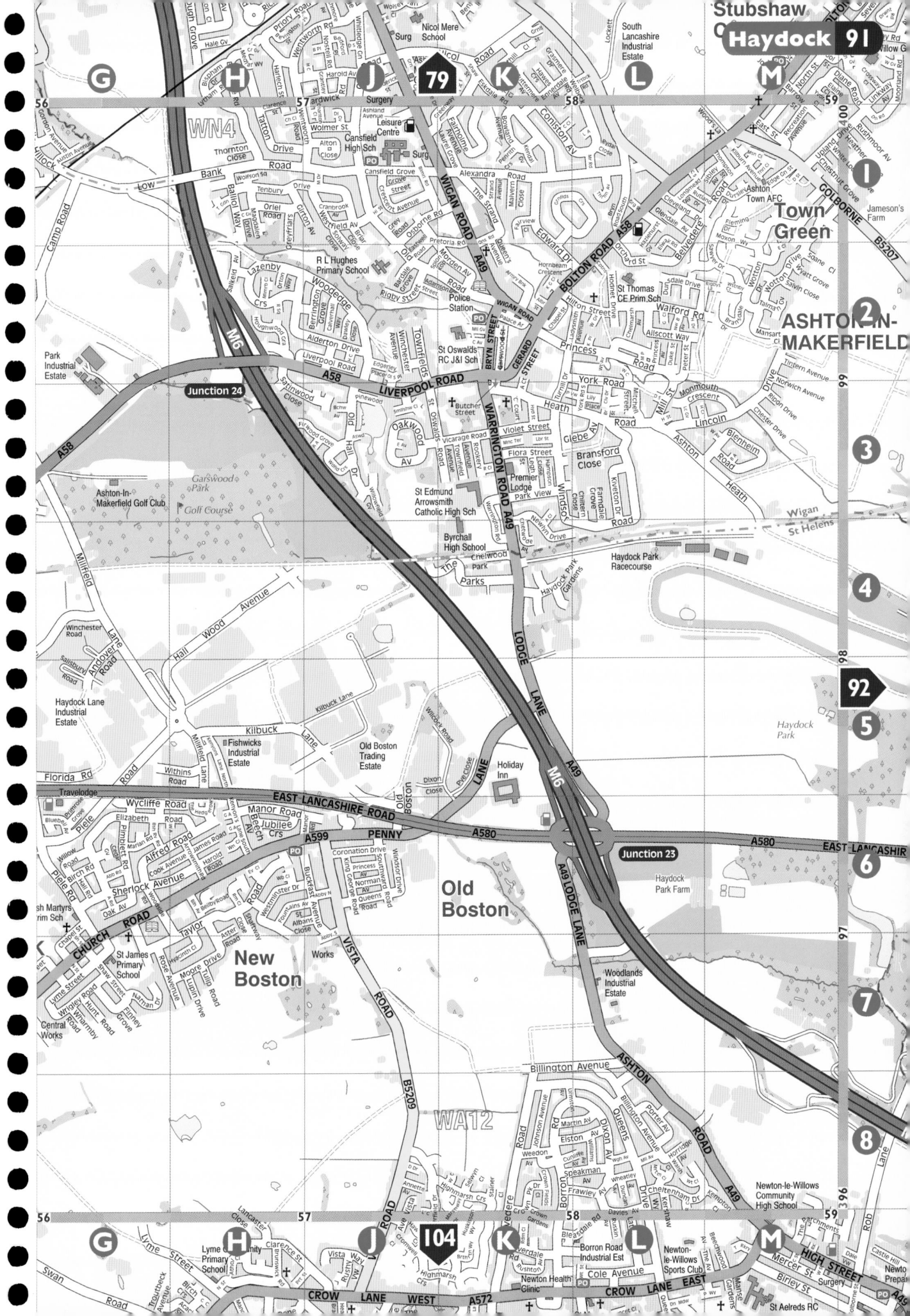

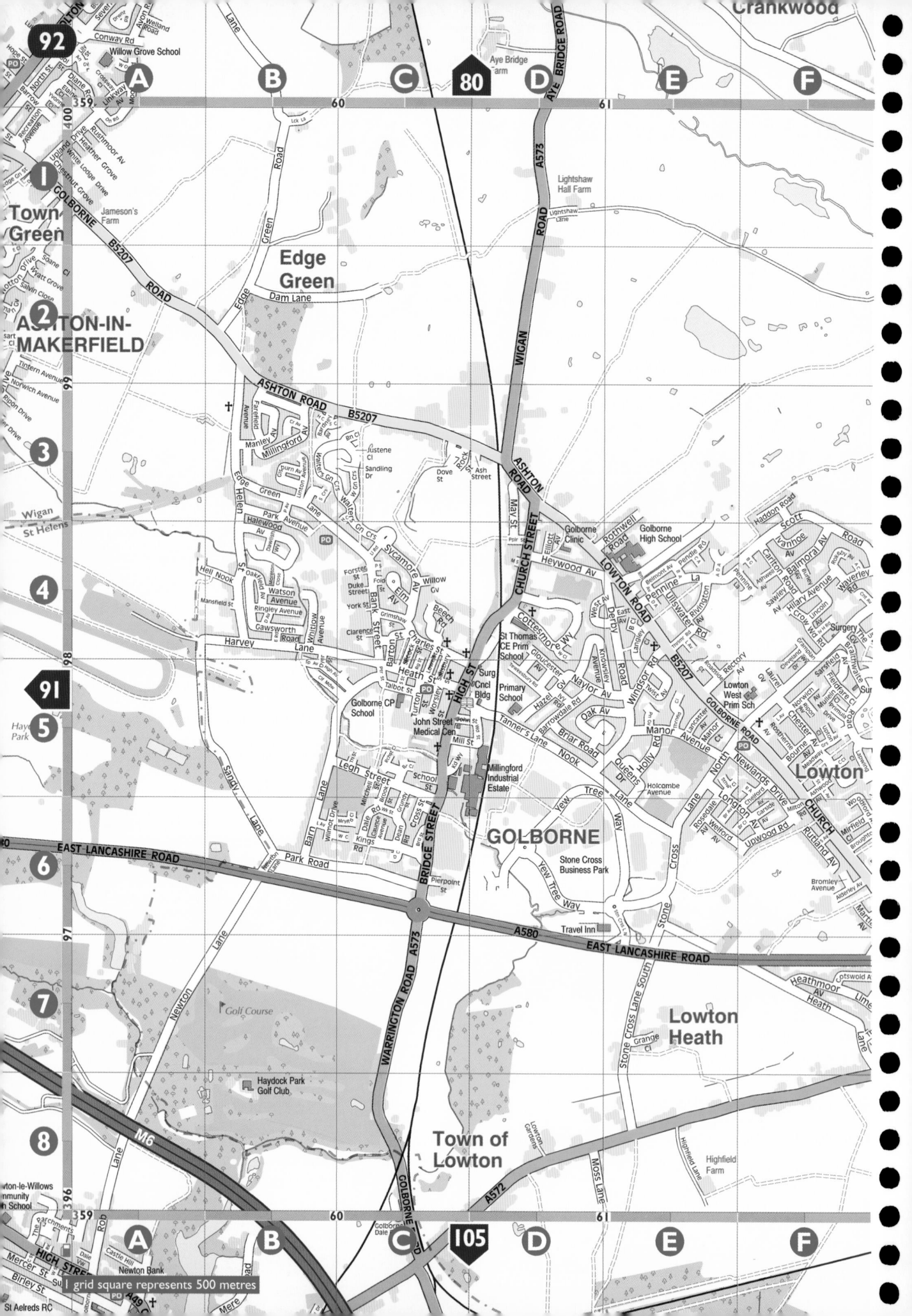

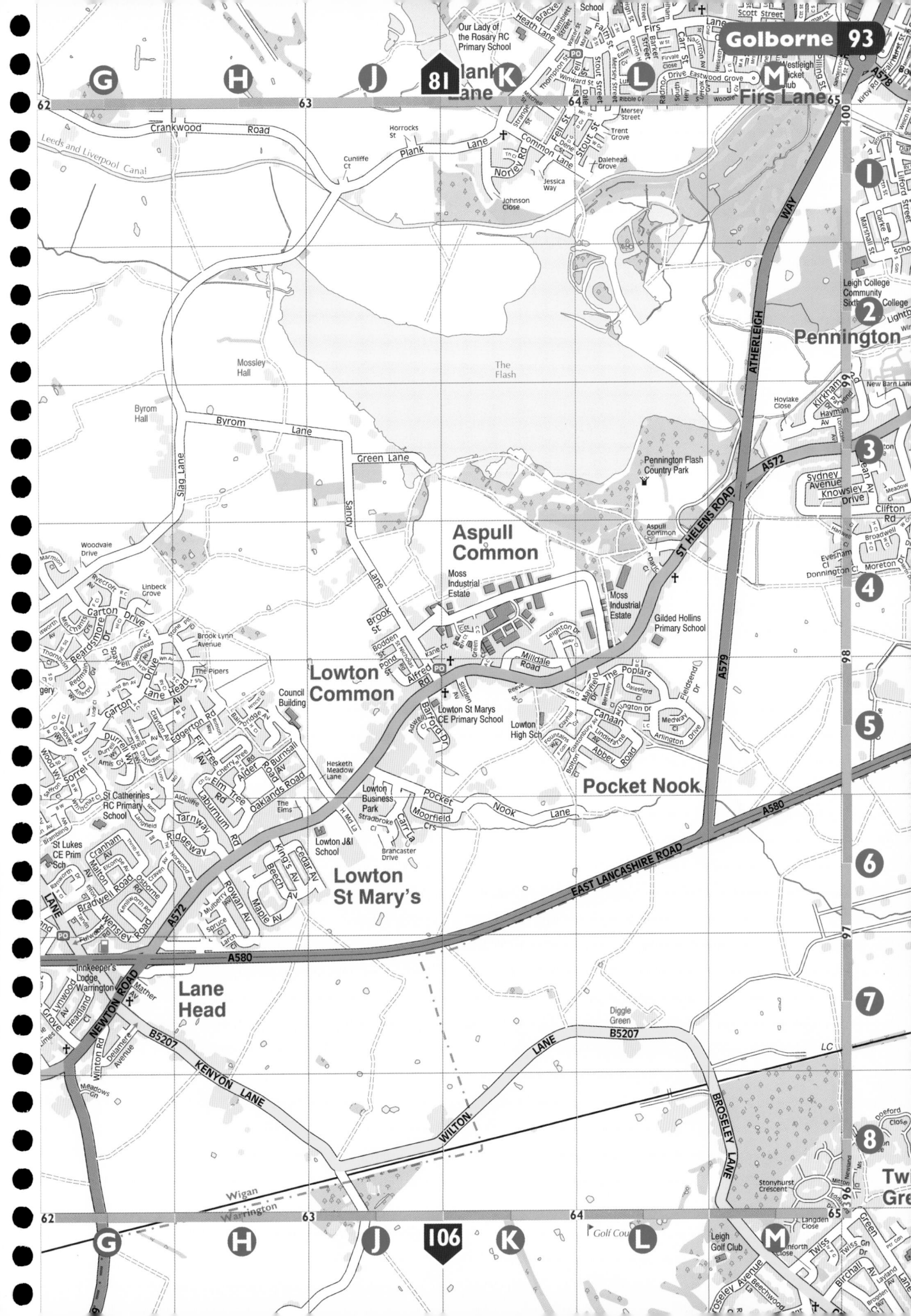

Our Lady of the Rosary RC Primary School

Plank Lane

Firs Lane

Pennington

Leigh College Community Sixth Form College

Crankwood Road

Leeds and Liverpool Canal

Cunliffe Ct

Horrocks St

Plank Lane

Norley Rd

Common Lane

Johnson Close

Jessica Way

Trent Grove

Dalehead Grove

Mersey Street

Mossley Hall

The Flash

New Barn Lane

Hoylake Close

Kirkham

Hayman Av

Byrom Hall

Byrom Lane

Green Lane

Pennington Flash Country Park

ATHERLEIGH WAY

A572

Sydney Avenue

Knowsley Drive

Clifton Rd

Broadwell

Woodvale Drive

Slag Lane

Sandy Lane

Aspull Common

Aspull Common

ST HELENS ROAD

Evesham Cl

Donnington Cl

Moreton

Linbeck Grove

Garton Drive

Beardsmore Drive

Brook Lynn Avenue

The Pipers

Brook St

Bodden St

Moss Industrial Estate

Moss Industrial Estate

Gilded Hollins Primary School

Leighton Dr

Milldale Road

A579

The Poplars

Dalesford

Fieldsend Dr

Lowton Common

Council Building

Alfred Rd

Pond

Lowton St Marys CE Primary School

Reeve

Lowton High Sch

Canaan

Lindisfarne

Medway Cl

Arlington Drive

St Catherines RC Primary School

Lane Head

Garton Av

Edgerton Rd

Fir Tree Av

Cherry Tree Rd

Elm Tree Rd

Burnsall Av

Ball Bridge

Barford Dr

Hesketh Meadow Lane

Lowton Business Park

Stradbroke Cl

Pocket Moorfield Crs

Carria

Pocket Nook

Nook Lane

Pocket Nook

Abbey Road

Fountains

St Lukes CE Prim Sch

Bradwell Road

Wensley Road

A572

Tarnway

Laburnum Rd

Oaklands Road

The Elms

Ridgeway

Cranham Av

Cedar Av

King's Av

Rowan Av

Beech Av

Maple Av

Mulberry

Spruce

Larch

Brancaster Drive

Lowton J&I School

Lowton St Mary's

A580

EAST LANCASHIRE ROAD

A580

Innkeeper's Lodge Warrington

Lane Head

Lynwood Av

Headland

NEWTON ROAD

Mather

Wilton Rd

Delamere Avenue

B5207

KENYON LANE

Meadows Gn

Diggle Green

WILTON LANE

B5207

BROSELEY LANE

LC

Stonyhurst Crescent

Langden Close

Twi Gre

Wigan

Warrington

Golf Cou

Leigh Golf Club

Roseley Avenue

Beechwood

Birchall

Twiss Gn

Twiss

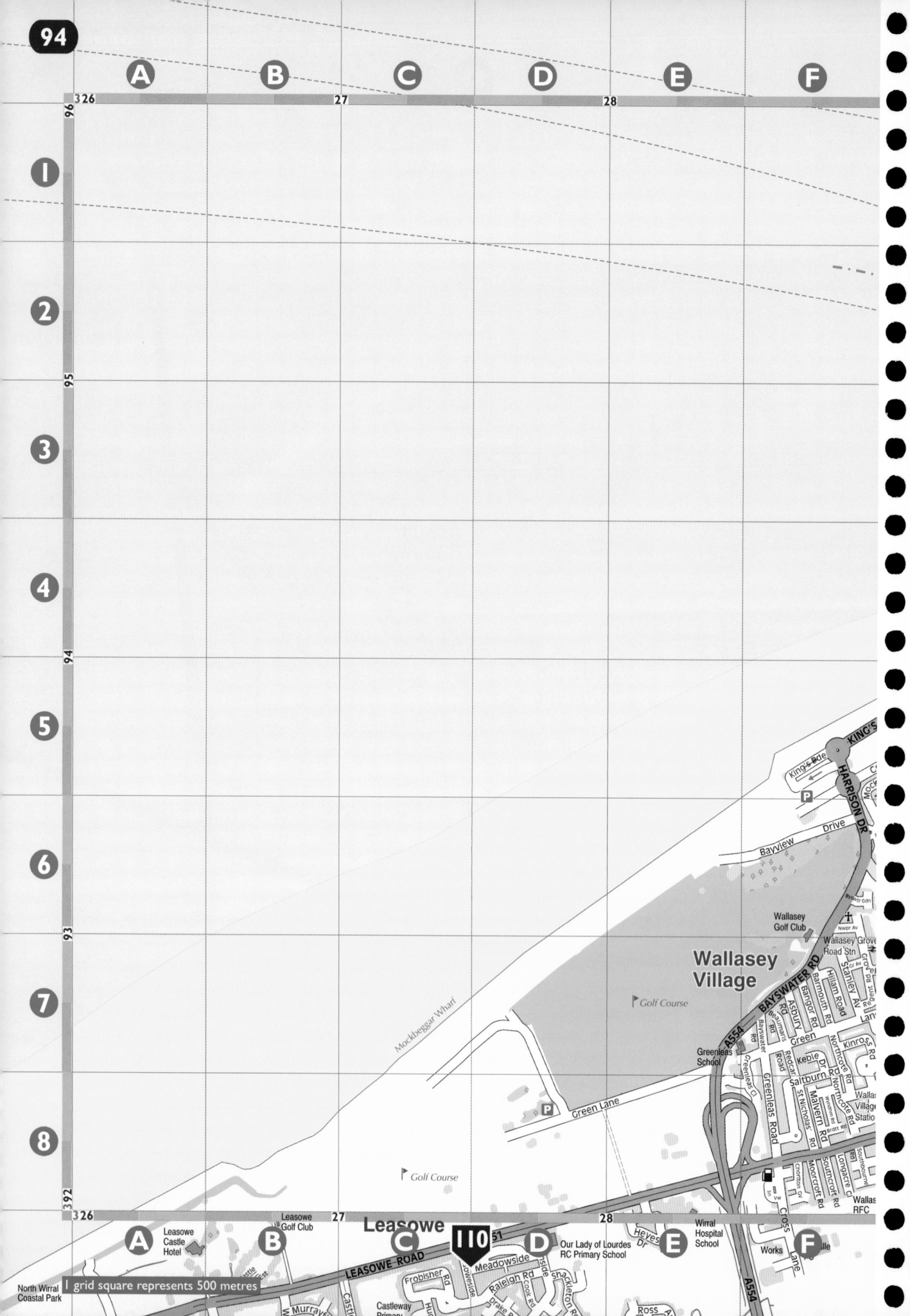

A B C D E F

326 27 28

I

95

2

3

94

4

5

6

93

7

Mockbeggar Wharf

Wallasey Golf Club

Wallasey Grove Road Stn

Wallasey Village

Golf Course

KING'S

HARRISON DR

King's Pde

Bayview Drive

Bayswtr Gdn

Nwpr Av

Wallasey Grove

BAYSWATER RD

A554

Greenleas School

Greenleas Cl

Greenleas Road

Bayswater Road

Asbury Rd

Barnor Rd

Barmouth Rd

Hillam Road

Stanley Av

Lang

Kinross Rd

Northcote Rd

Redcar Rd

Keble Dr

Saltburn Rd

St Nicholas

Malvern Rd

Wyndms Rd

Northcote Rd

Brott Rd

Wallas Village Statio

Green

8

392

326 27 Leasowe 28

A Leasowe Castle Hotel

B Leasowe Golf Club

C

110 51

LEASOWE ROAD

Meadowside

Jolyeside

Frobisher Rd

Raleigh Rd

Shackleton Rd

Cook Rd

Drake Rd

D Our Lady of Lourdes RC Primary School

E Wirral Hospital School

Heyes Dr

F Works ville

Wallas RFC

Southmrne

Moorcroft Rd

Longacre Rd

Scorton Dr

Crofton Rv

SW

Vw

A554

Cross Lane

North Wirral Coastal Park

1 grid square represents 500 metres

Castle

Castleway Primary

Murrayf

Ross

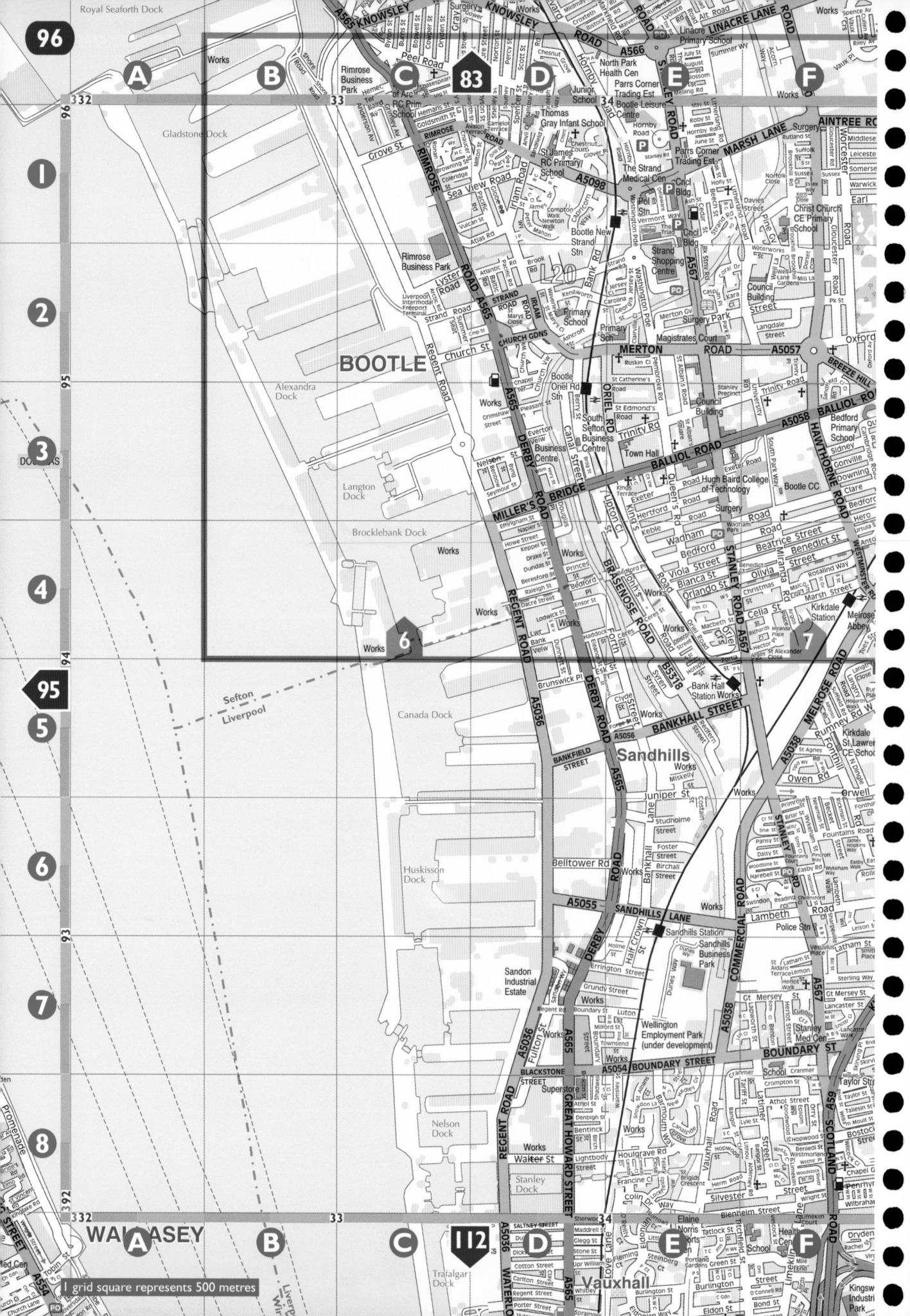

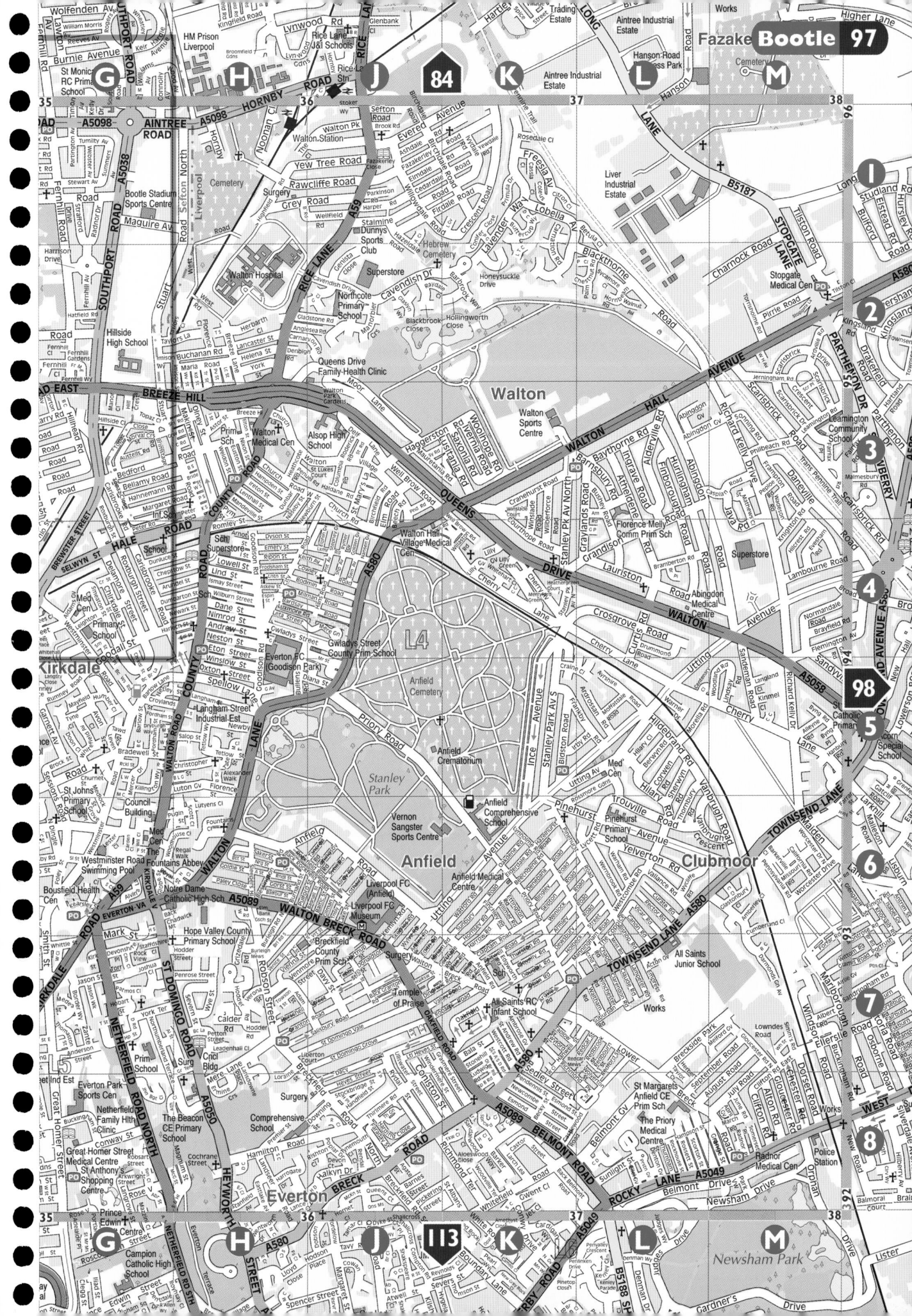

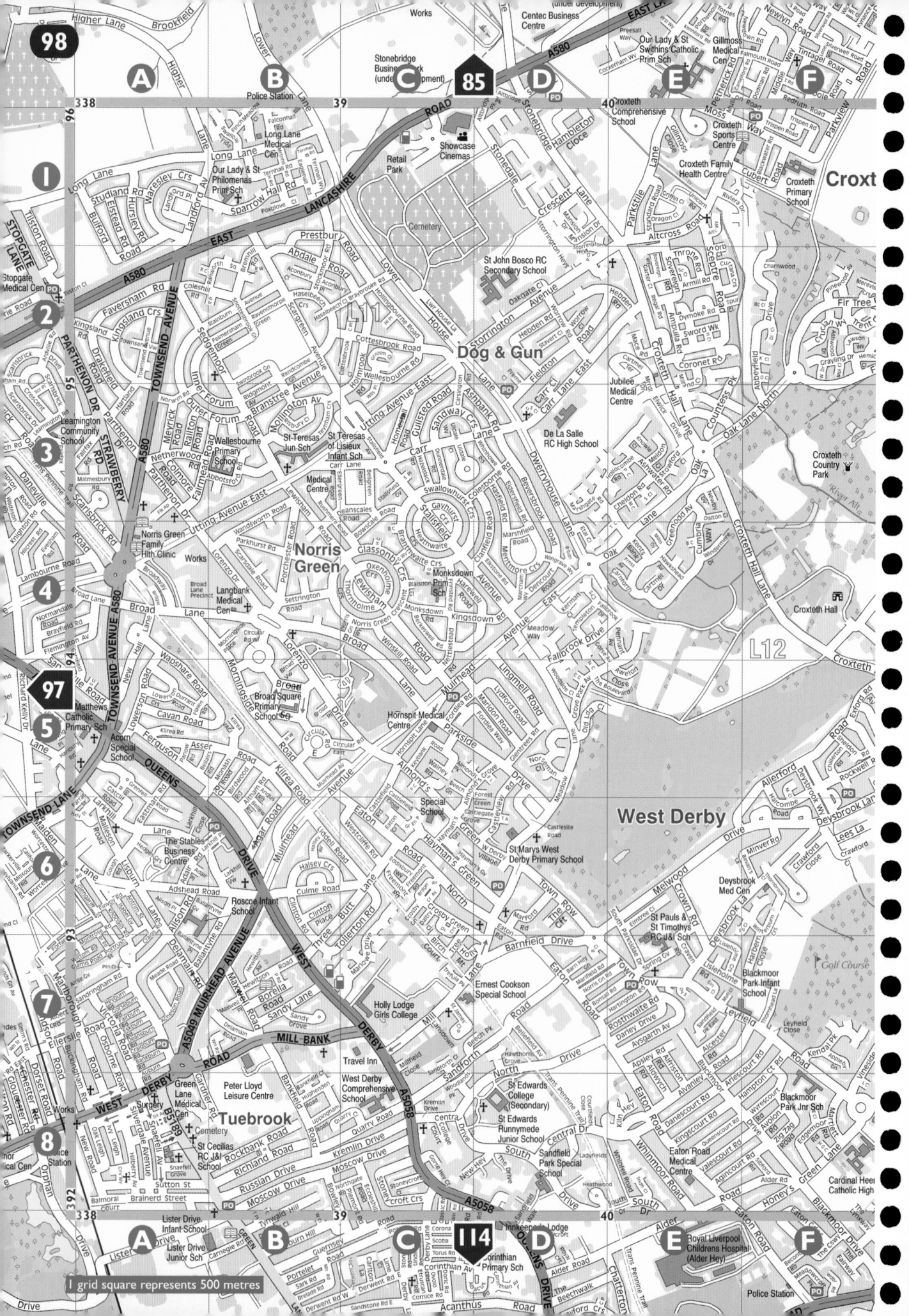

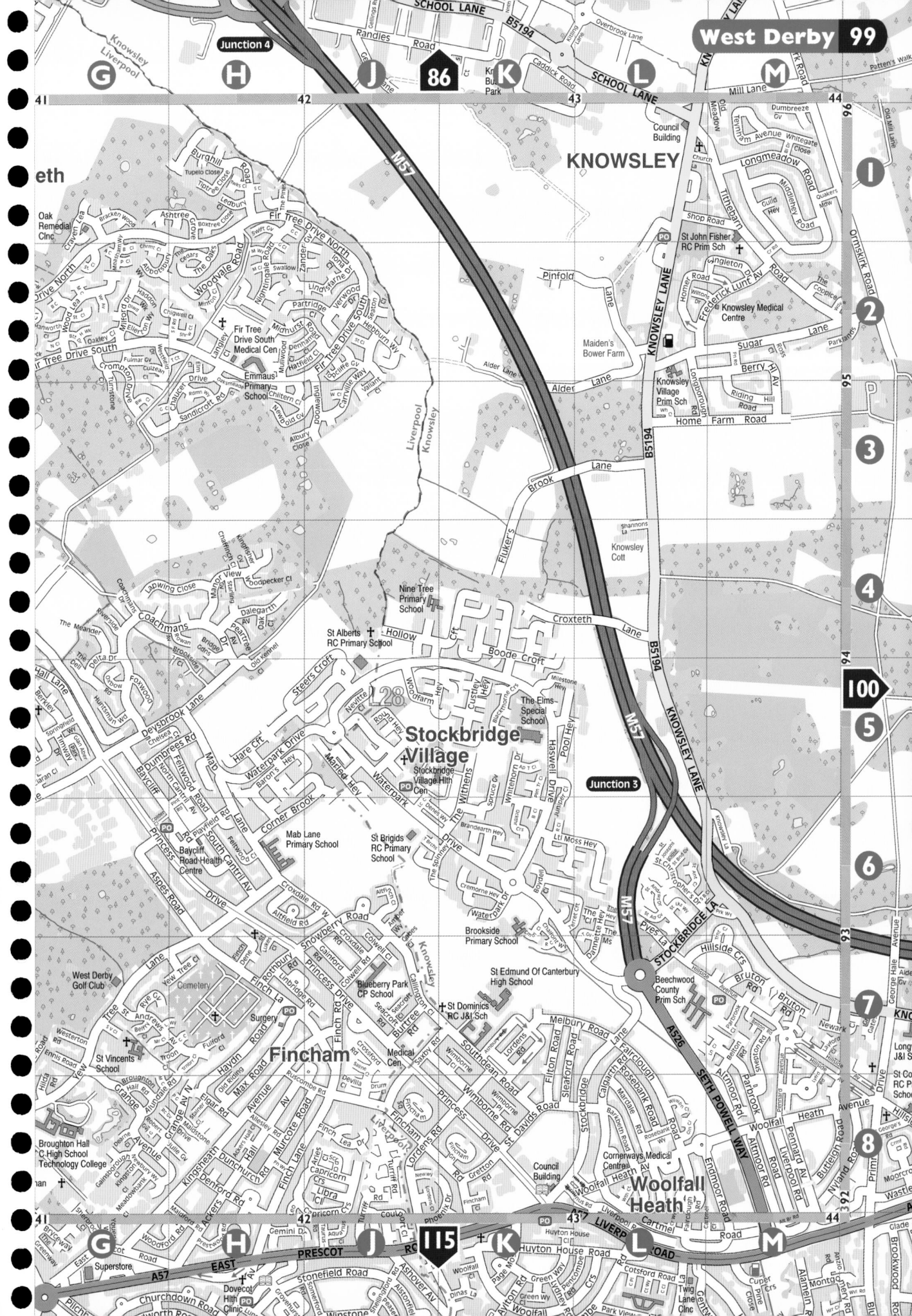

A   B   C   87   D   E   F

344   45   46

96

I

Dumbreeze
Gv
Whitegate
Close
eadow
Quakers
Mow
Middeley
Road

The
Coppice

2

Lane
Parklands

95

HI AV

Jack's

3

Brow

94

4

Entry

Park

L34

99

5

Knowsley
Hall

6

93

7

M57

Junction 2

PRESCOT

KNOWSLEY LANE   B5194

Longview J&I Sch

St Columbas RC Primary School

8

92

344   45   46

A   B   C   116   D   E   F

Longview

Alt Bridge Secondary
Support Centre
Knowsley Central Primary
Support Centre

Huyton & Prescot
Golf Club

Golf C

HUYTON

1 grid square represents 500 metres

Ormskirk Road

Knowsley Park

Knowsley Safari Park

White Man's Dam

No. 4 Reservoir

Works

St Helens
Knowsley

A58

Prescot School

Our Ladys RC Primary School

Prescot AFC

Police Station

Prescot Mus

Natural Hlth Clinic

Park House Medical Cen

Prescot Medical Cen

Council Building

Cemetery

Cables Retail Park

Prescot Station

Works

Liverpool Road A57   WEST STREET

LIVERPOOL ROAD

B5199

Kings Bus Pk

Carr Lane

Manchester Road

Central Avenue

Preston Avenue

KEMBLE ST   B5200

Steley

Station Road

ST HELENS ROAD

WARRINGTON

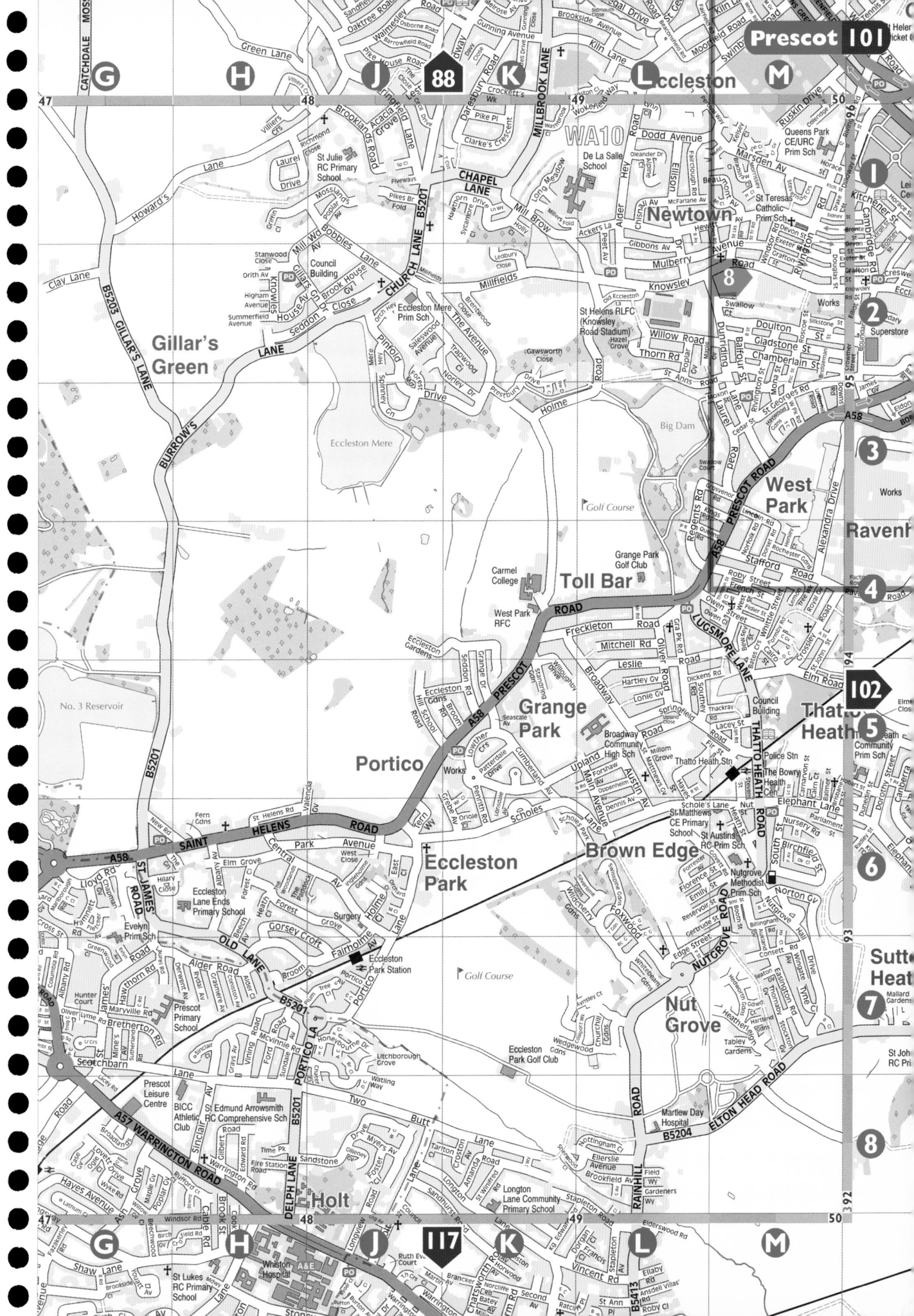

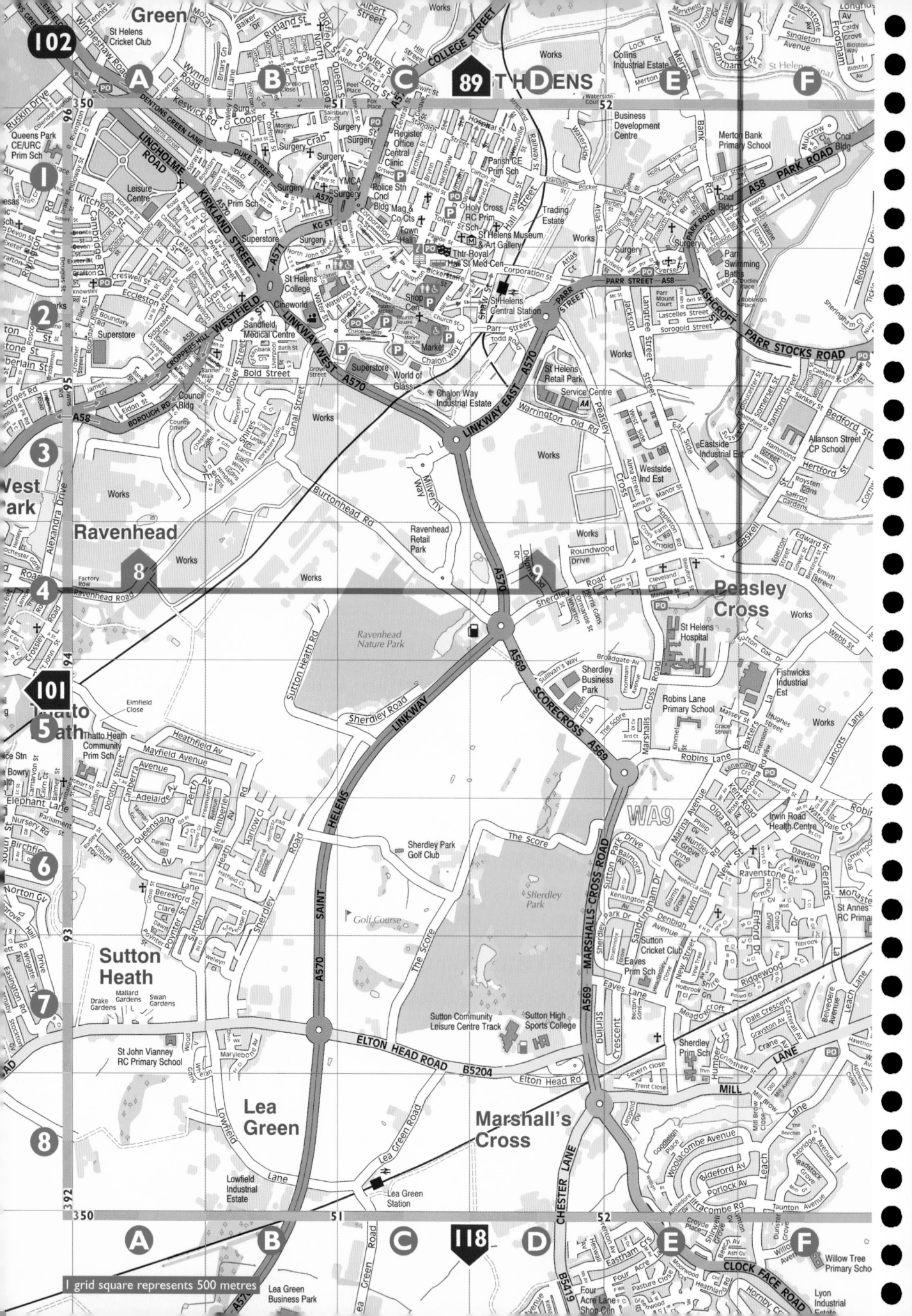

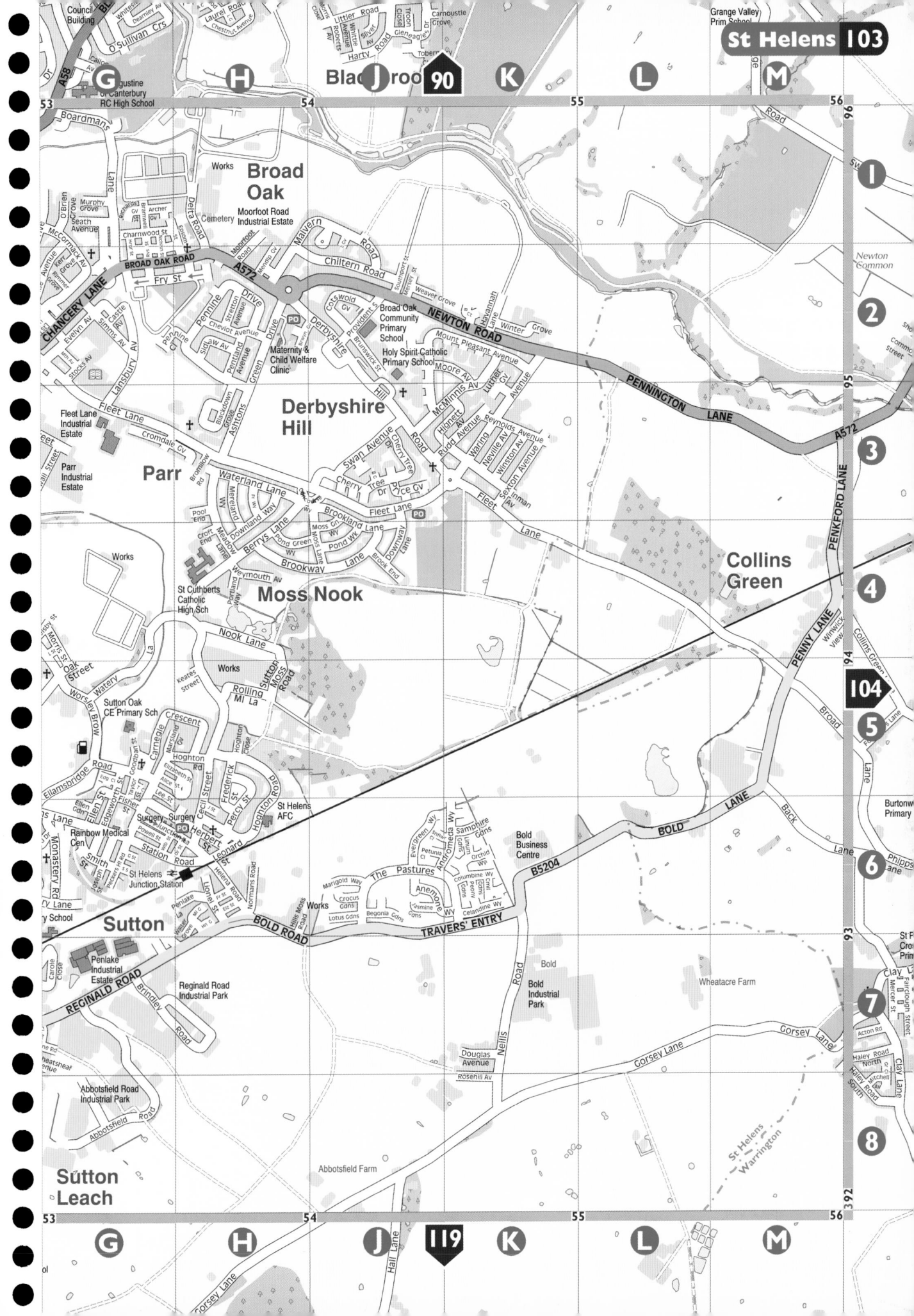

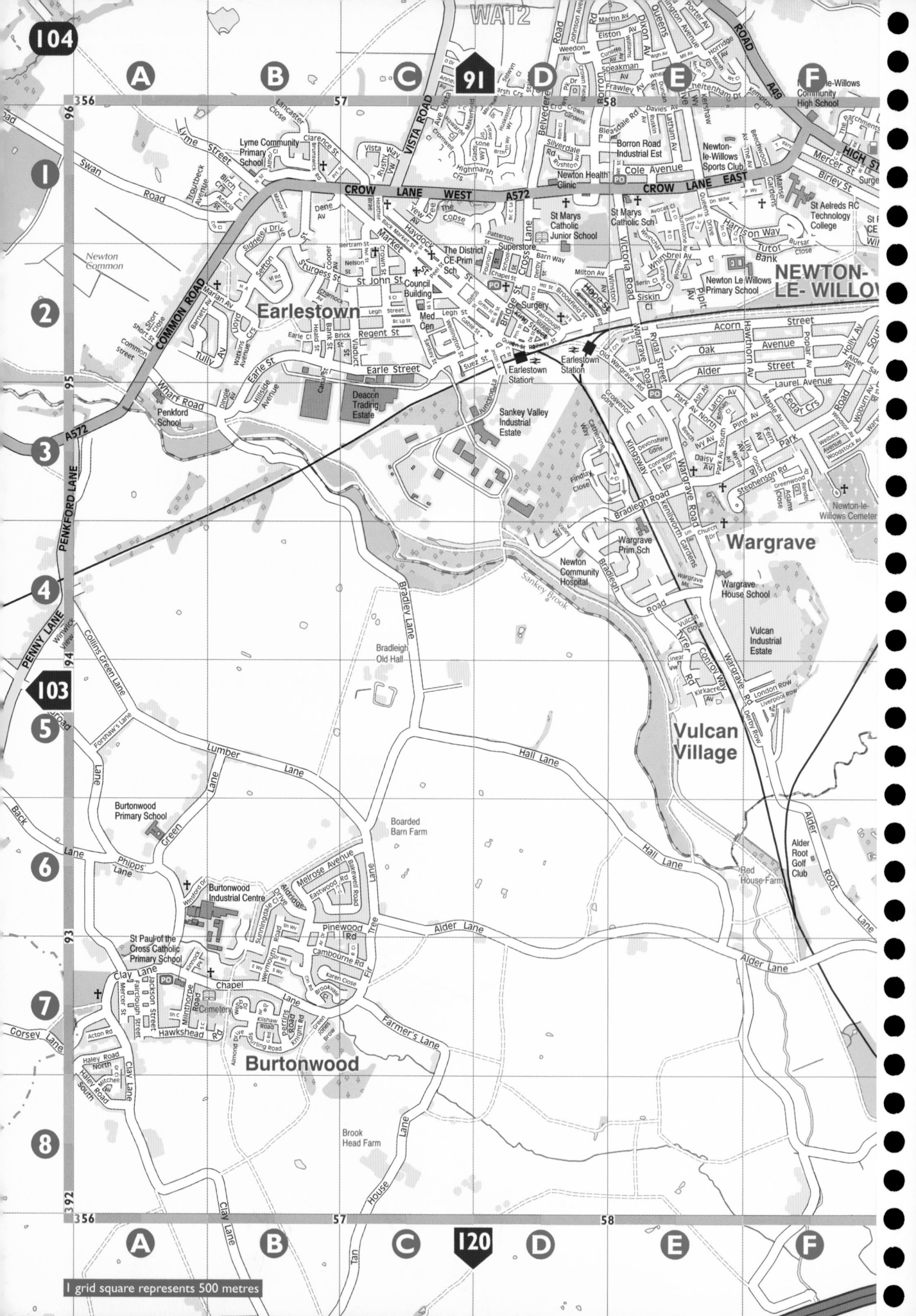

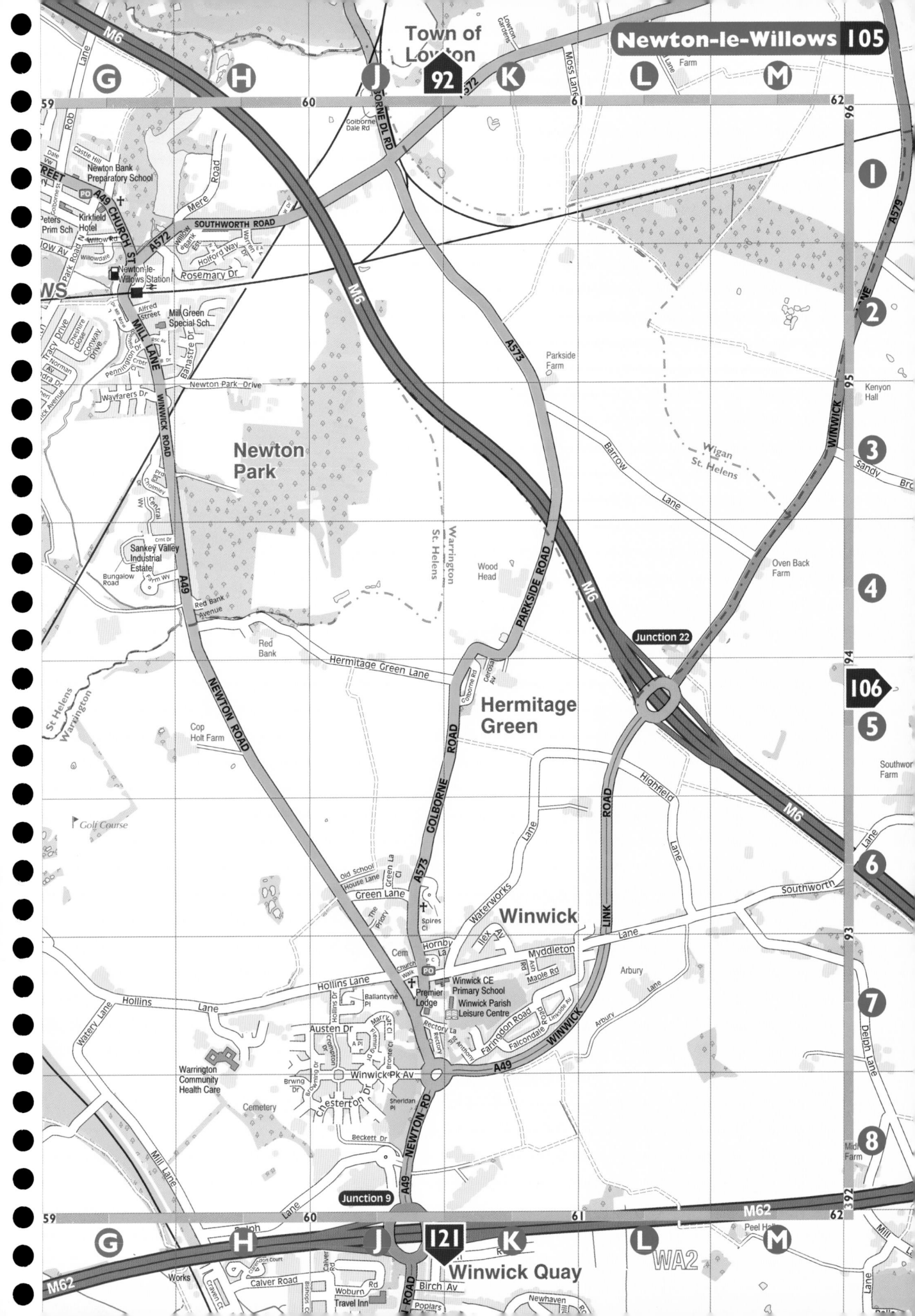

Town of Lowton

M6

G **H** **J** **92** **K** **L** **M**

59 60 61 62

I

96

Golborne Dale Rd

GOLBORNE DL RD

Moss Lane

Lowton Gardens

Farm

Castle Hill

Dale View

Newton Bank Preparatory School

PO

Kirkfield Hotel

Peters Prim Sch

Rob Lane

Mere Road

Park Road

Willowdale

Willowfield

A49 CHURCH ST

SOUTHWORTH ROAD

A572

Holford Way

Water La

Ashton Regent

95

WINWICK LANE

A579

2

Kenyon Hall

STREET

WS

Newton-le-Willows Station

Alfred Street

Mill Green Special Sch

Banastre Dr

Rosemary Dr

A572

Norman

Penningt

Cheshire Close

Conway Drive

Tracy Drive

Alexandra Avenue

Wayfarers Dr

MILL LANE

WINWICK ROAD

Cholmley Wy

Central Cr

Newton Park Drive

M6

A573

Parkside Farm

Wigan St. Helens

Barrow Lane

3

Sandy Bro

94

4

Oven Back Farm

Newton Park

Sankey Valley Industrial Estate

Bungalow Road

Prm Wy

Crnt Dr

Red Bank Avenue

A49

St Helens Warrington

Cop Holt Farm

NEWTON ROAD

Red Bank

Warrington St. Helens

Wood Head

PARKSIDE ROAD

Hermitage Green Lane

Junction 22

M6

106

5

Southwor Farm

Golf Course

Old School House Lane

Green Lane

Green La

The Priory

Cem

Spires Cl

Hermitage Green Lane

Geroge Av

Golborne Rd

GOLBORNE ROAD

A573

Hermitage Green

Waterworks Lane

Highfield Lane

LINK ROAD

M6

Southworth Lane

6

93

Hollins Lane

Watery Lane

Hollins Lane

Ballantyne Pl

Marr

Church walk

PO

Hornby La

Ilex Av

Winwick

Myddleton

Maple Rd

Arbury Lane

WINWICK LINK

Arbury

7

Austen Dr

Compton Dr

A Pl

Premier Lodge

Winwick CE Primary School

Winwick Parish Leisure Centre

Rectory La

Farringdon Road

Linwood Av

Falcondale rd

WINWICK

A49

Delph Lane

Warrington Community Health Care

Cemetery

Brwng Dr

Broome Dr

Chesterton

Winwick Pk Av

Sheridan Pl

Beckett Dr

NEWTON RD

A49

392

8

Mid Farm

Junction 9

M62

Peel Hall

G **H** **J** **121** **K** **L** **M**

59 60 61 WA2 62

M62

Winwick Quay

Works

Craven Cl

Calver Road

Birch Av

Woburn Travel Inn

Poplars

Newhaven

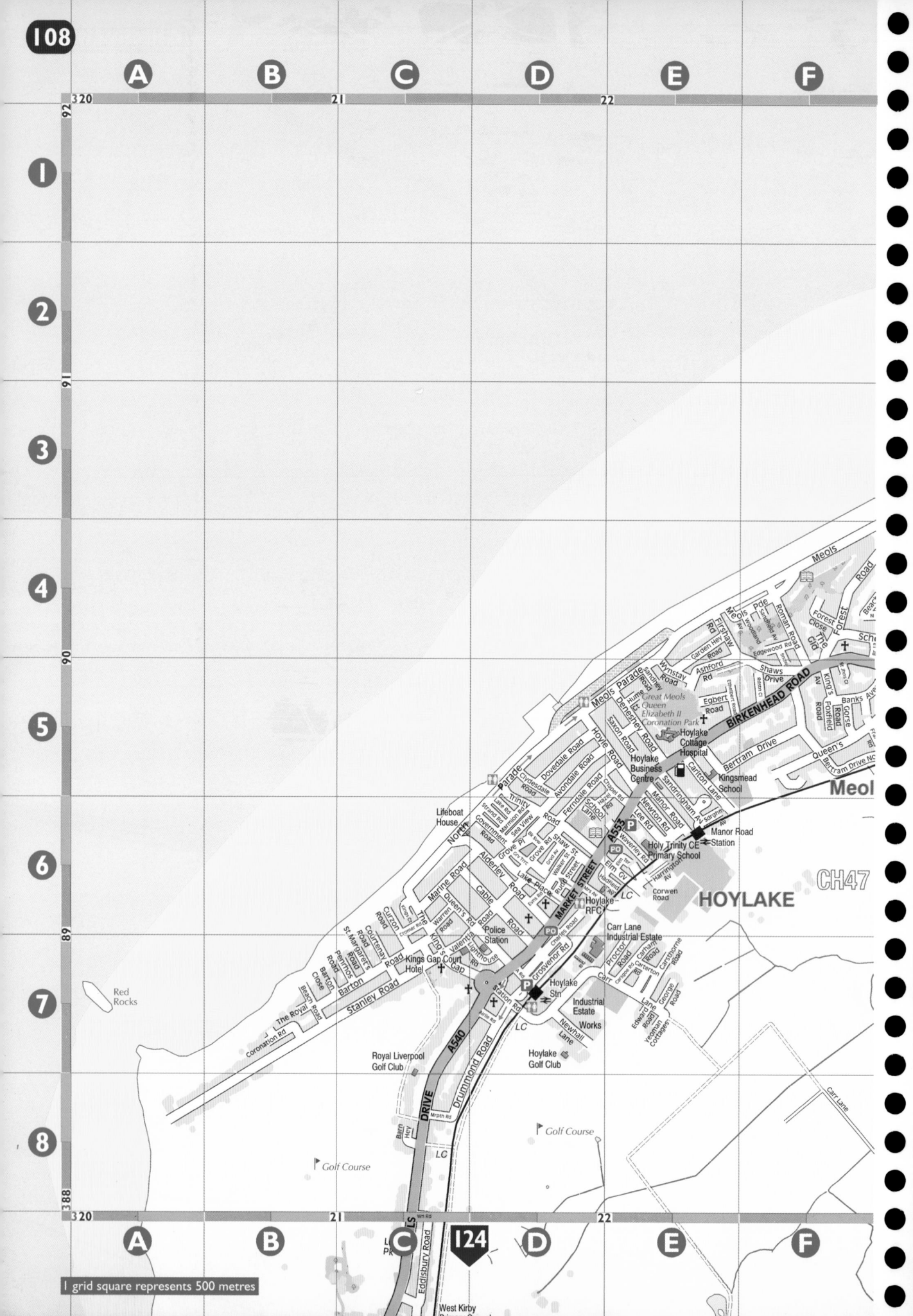

A   B   C   D   E   F

320   21   22

92

1

16

2

3

90

4

5

Meols Parade
Great Meols
Queen Elizabeth II
Coronation Park
Hoylake Cottage Hospital
BIRKENHEAD ROAD
Hoylake Business Centre
Kingsmead School
Meol

Parade
Clydesdale
Dovedale Road
Avondale Road
Ferndale Road
Trinity
Saxon Road
Carlton Lane
Sandringham Av
Newton Rd
Manor Rd
Bertram Drive
Queen's Road
Bertram Drive No

6

89

Lifeboat House
North
Government Road
Sea View
Grove
Marine Road
Alderley Road
Cable Road
Queen's Rd
Warren Rd
King's
MARKET STREET
A553
Holy Trinity CE Primary School
Manor Road Station
Corwen Road
HOYLAKE   CH47
Hoylake RFC
Police Station
Carr Lane Industrial Estate
Proctor
Carham Rd
Carsthorne Road

Curzon Road
Courtenay Road
St Margaret's Road
Penthos
Barton
Close
Beach Road
The Royal
Stanley Road
Kings Gap Court
Hotel
Valentia Rd
Lighthouse
Station Rd
Grosvenor Rd
Hoylake Stn
Industrial Estate
Works
Newhall Lane
Yeoman Cottages
Edward Road
George Road
Carr Lane

7

Red Rocks
Coronation Rd
Barn Hey
Mrpth Rd
Royal Liverpool Golf Club
DRIVE
A540
Drummond Road
Hoylake Golf Club
LC
Golf Course

388

8

Golf Course
LC
Wn Rd

320   21   22

A   B   C   D   E   F

124

Eddisbury Road
West Kirby

1 grid square represents 500 metres

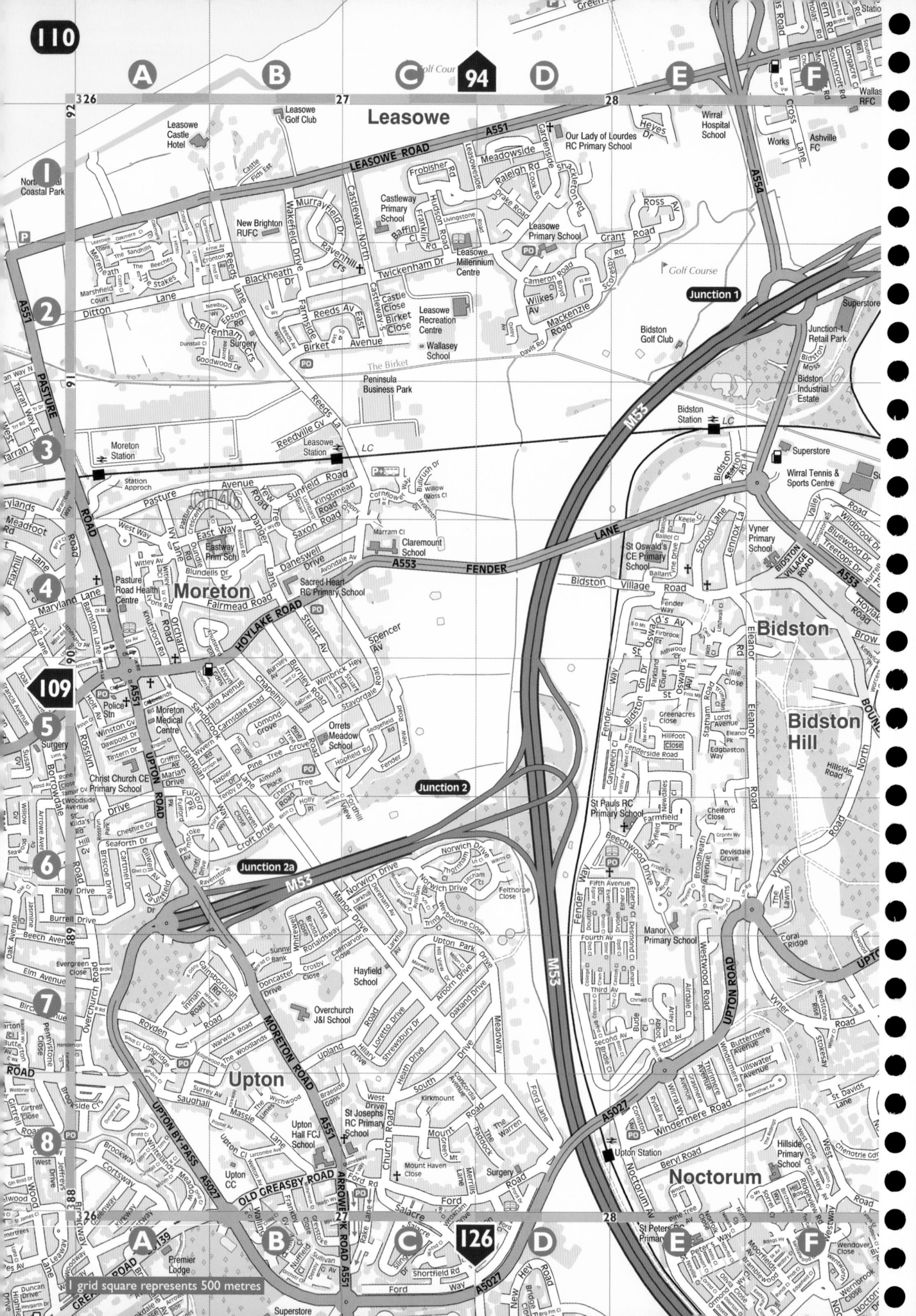

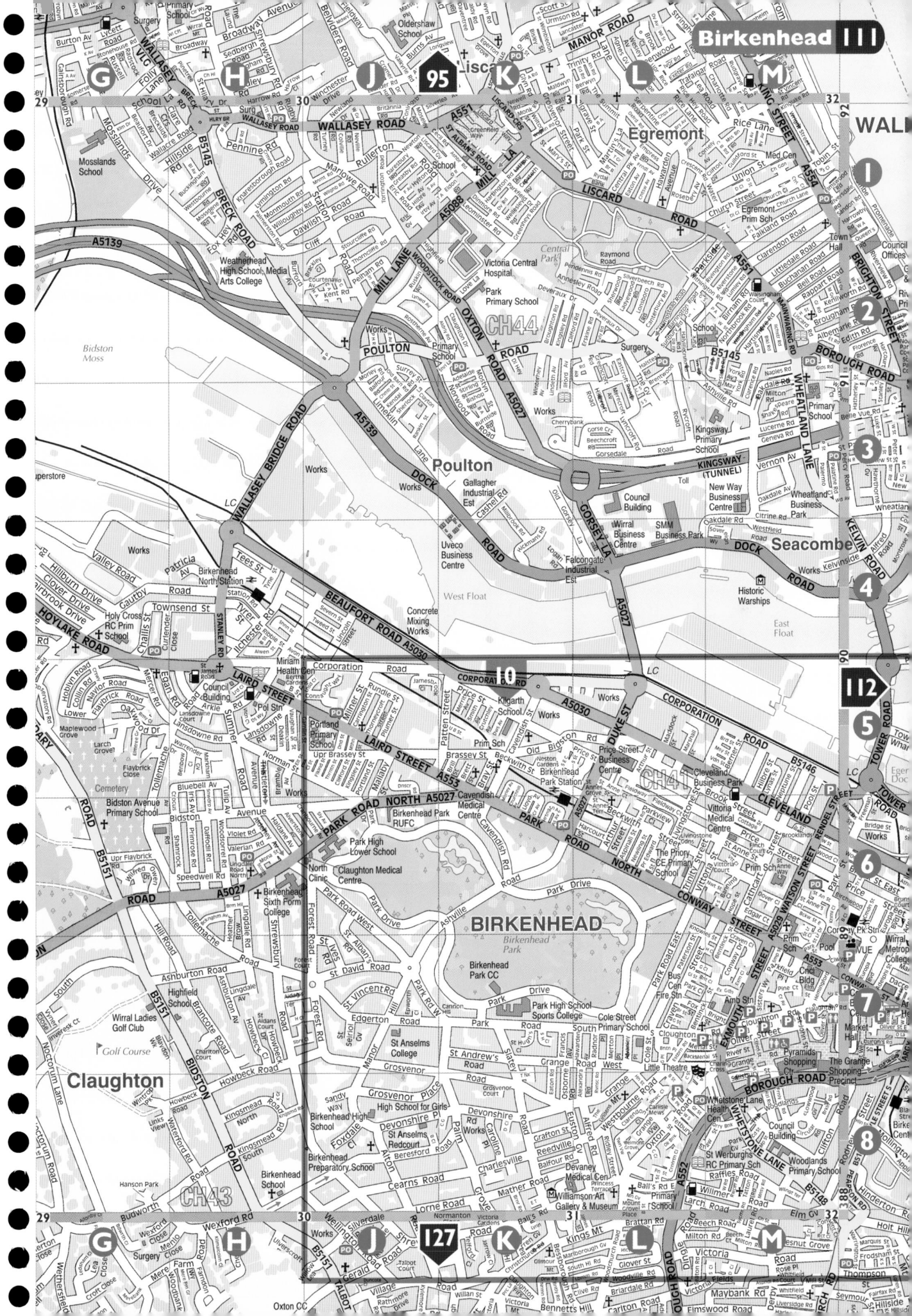

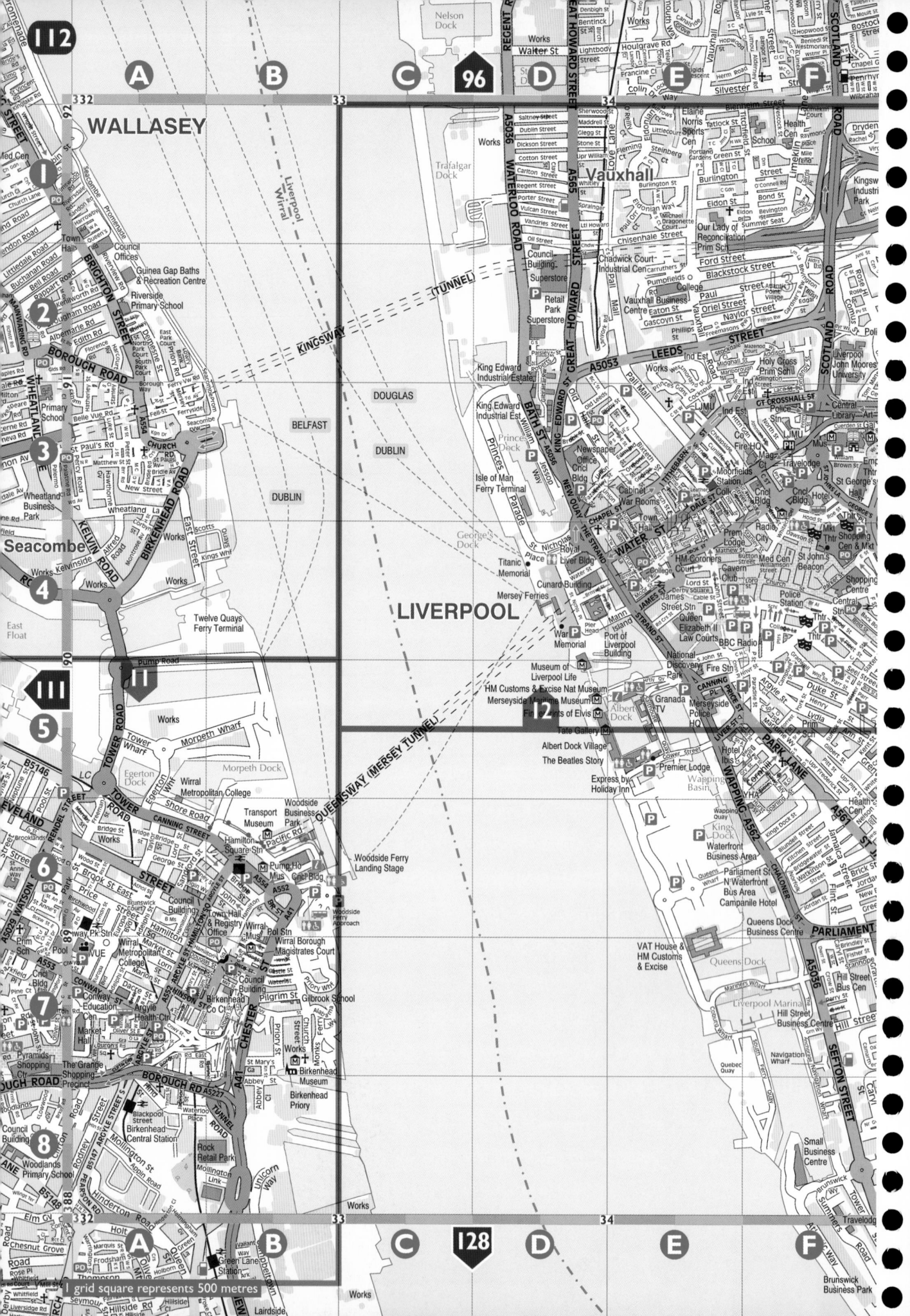

WALLASEY

A · B · C · 96 · D · E · F

Vauxhall

LIVERPOOL

Seacombe

III

Kingsway (Tunnel)

DOUGLAS

BELFAST

DUBLIN

DUBLIN

Twelve Quays Ferry Terminal

East Float

Morpeth Wharf

Egerton Dock

Morpeth Dock

Wirral Metropolitan College

Woodside Business Park

Transport Museum

Woodside Ferry Landing Stage

Queensway (Mersey Tunnel)

Woodside Ferry Approach

Museum of Liverpool Life
HM Customs & Excise Nat Museum
Merseyside Maritime Museum
Fingerprints of Elvis
Tate Gallery

Albert Dock Village
The Beatles Story

Express by Holiday Inn

Premier Lodge

Wapping Basin

Kings Dock Waterfront Business Area

Parliament St N Waterfront Bus Area
Campanile Hotel

Queens Dock Business Centre

VAT House & HM Customs & Excise

Queens Dock

Liverpool Marina

Hill Street Business Centre

Quebec Quay

Navigation Wharf

Small Business Centre

Brunswick Business Park

A · B · C · 128 · D · E · F

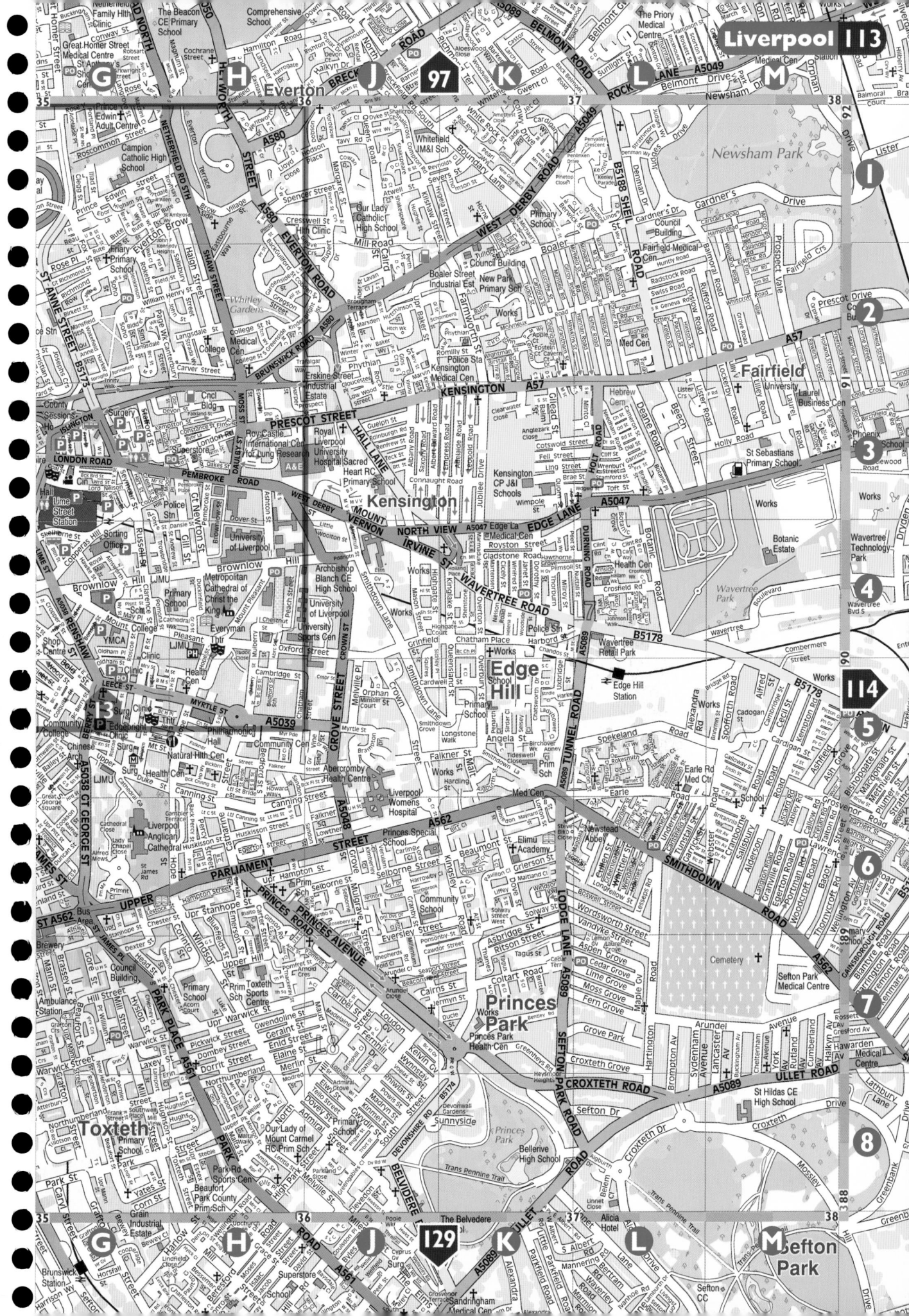

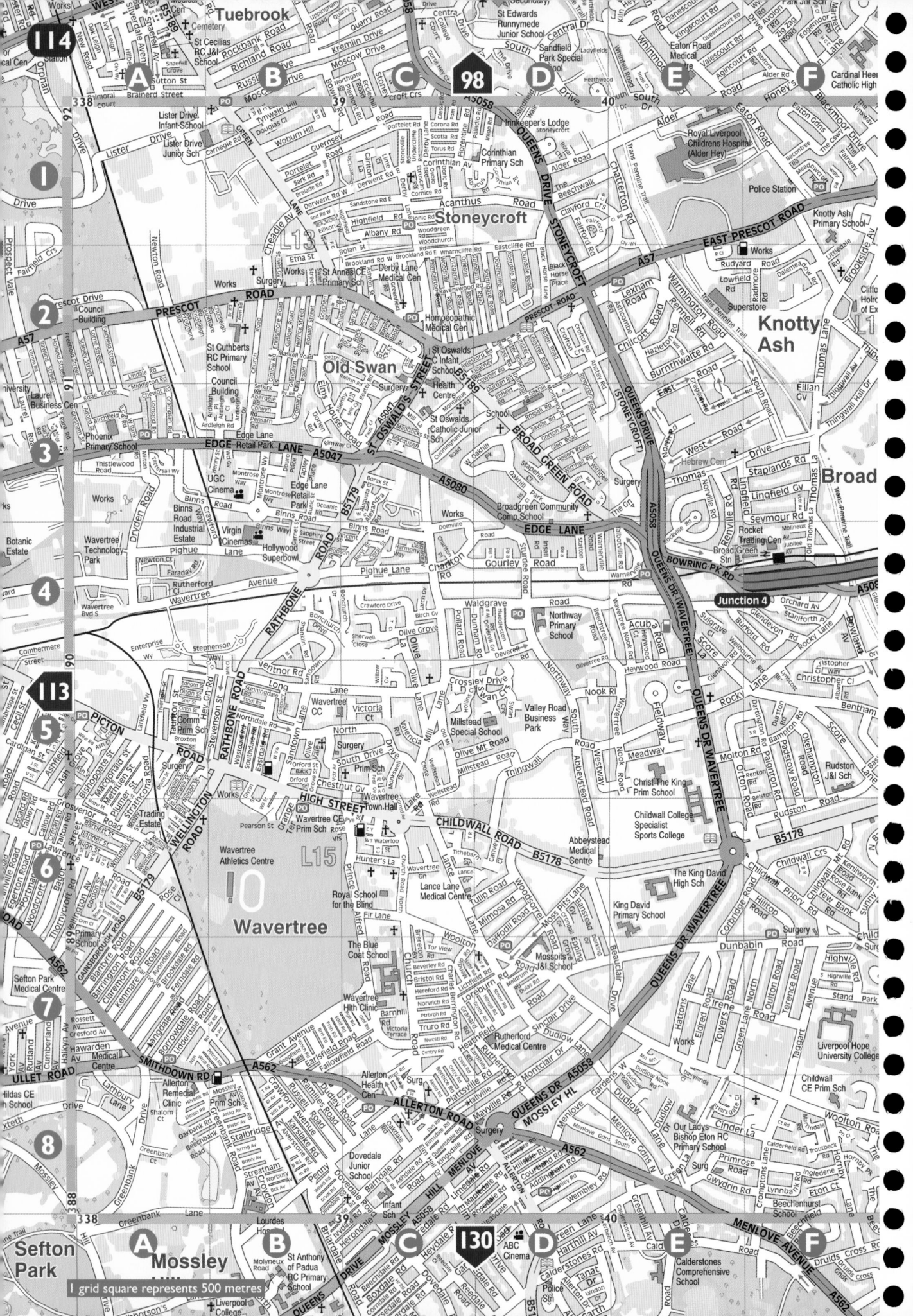

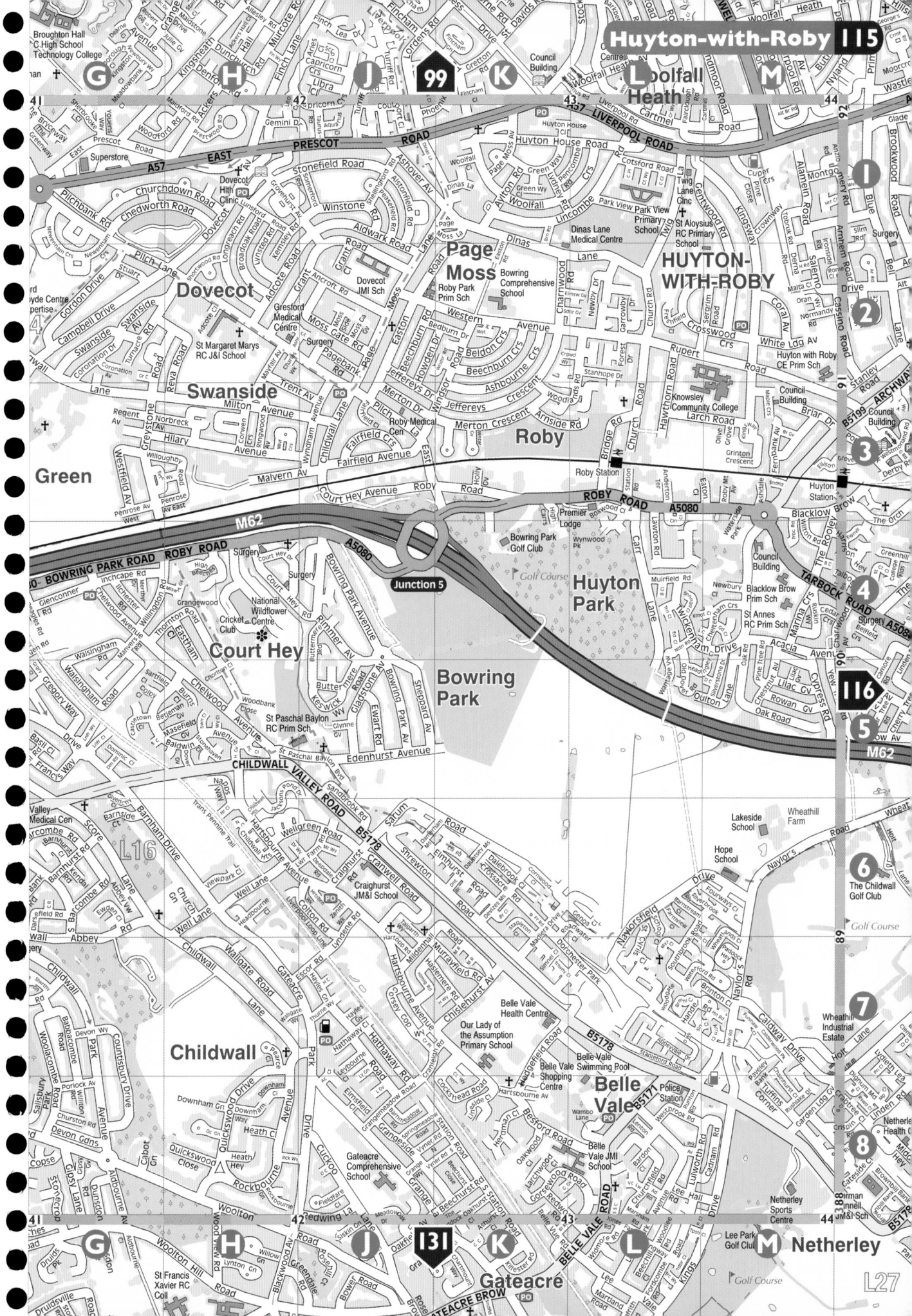

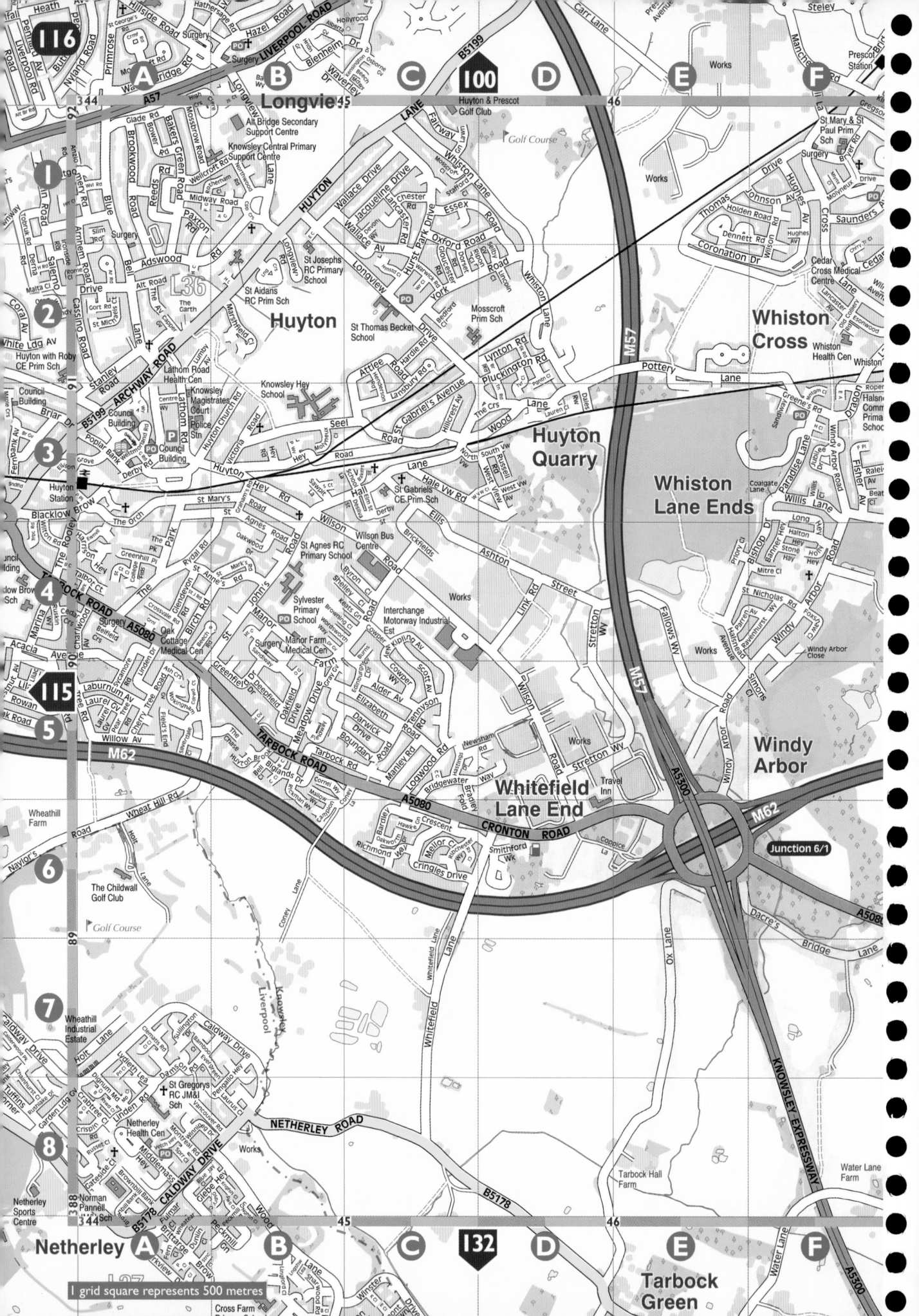

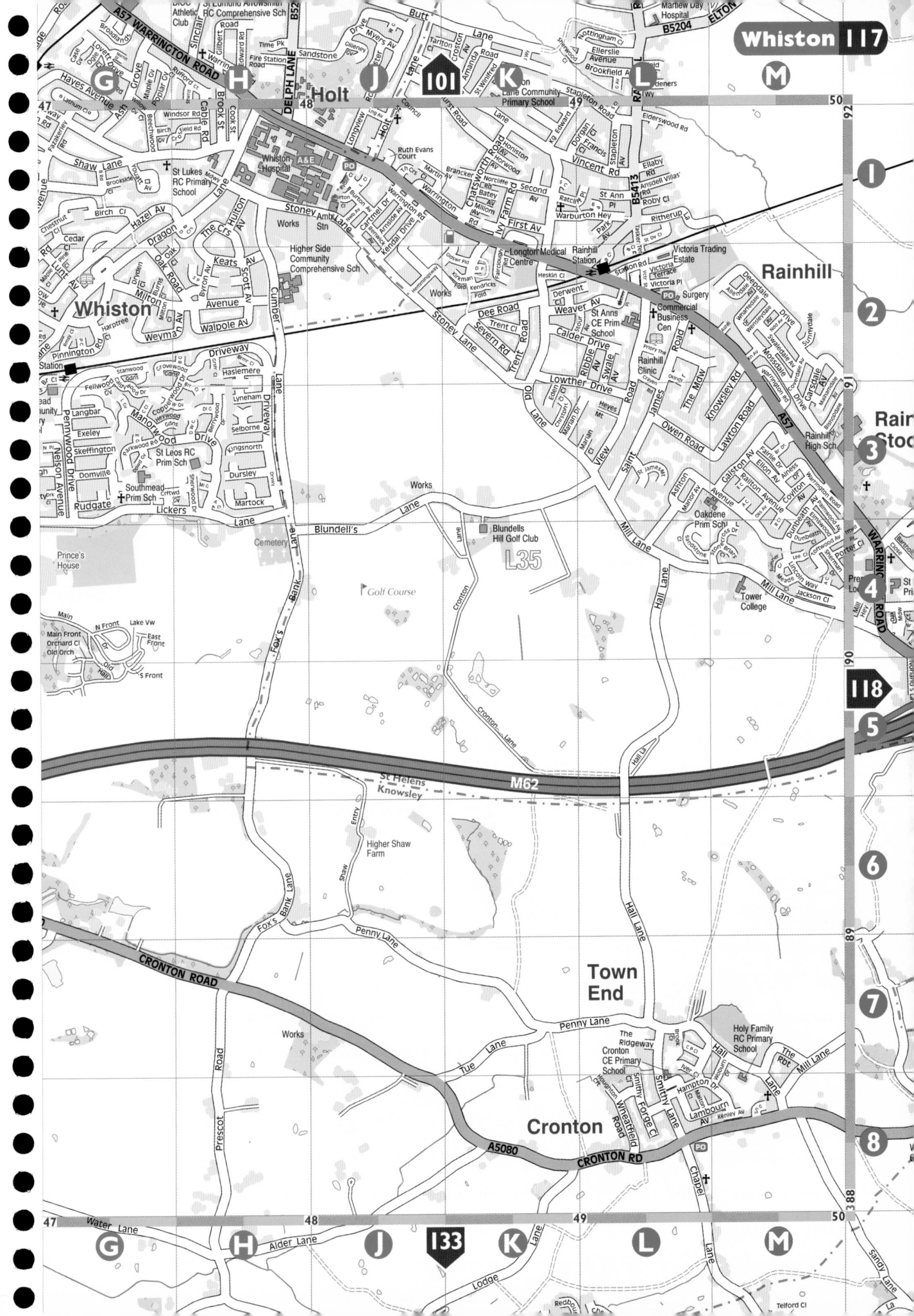

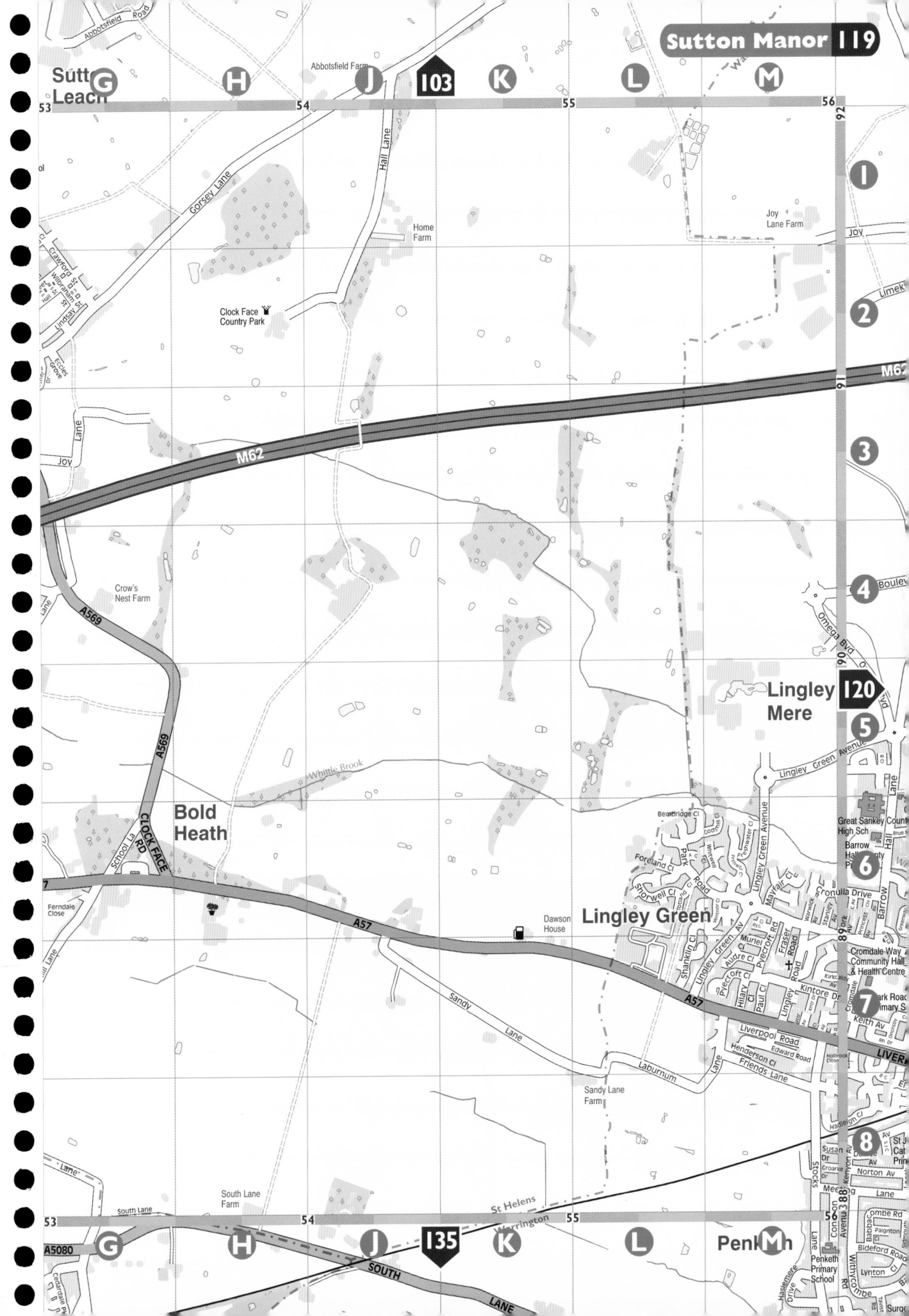

Sutt Leach

G   H   J   **103**   K   L   M

Abbotsfield Road

Abbotsfield Farm

Gorsey Lane

Hall Lane

Home Farm

Clock Face Country Park

Joy Lane Farm

I

Joy

Limek

2

M62

M62

3

Joy Lane

A569

Crow's Nest Farm

4   Bouley

Omega Blvd

Lingley Mere   **120**

5

Lingley Green Avenue

Whittle Brook

CLOCK FACE RD

Bold Heath

School La

Great Sankey Count High Sch

Bembridge Cl

Barrow Hall

6

Foreland Cl

Shorwell Cl

Cronulla Drive

Ferndale Close

A57

Dawson House

Lingley Green

Shanklin Cl

Lingley Green Av

Mayfair Cl

Muriel Cl

Fraser Road

Cromdale Way Community Hall & Health Centre

A57

Pyecroft Cl

Hilary Cl

Paul Cl

Kintore Dr

Cromdale

7   Keith Av

Liverpool Road

Sandy Lane

Edward Road

Laburnum

Friends Lane

Henderson Cl

LIVER

Sandy Lane Farm

Hadleigh Cl

8

Susan Dr

Kenyon Av

Norton Av

Lane

South Lane Farm

South Lane

St Helens

Warrington

Combe Rd

Paignton

Bideford Road

Lynton

A5080   G   H   J   **135**   K   L   Penk M h

SOUTH   LANE

Penketh Primary School

Haslemere Drive

Withycombe Rd

Conon Av

Avenue 388

53   54   55   56

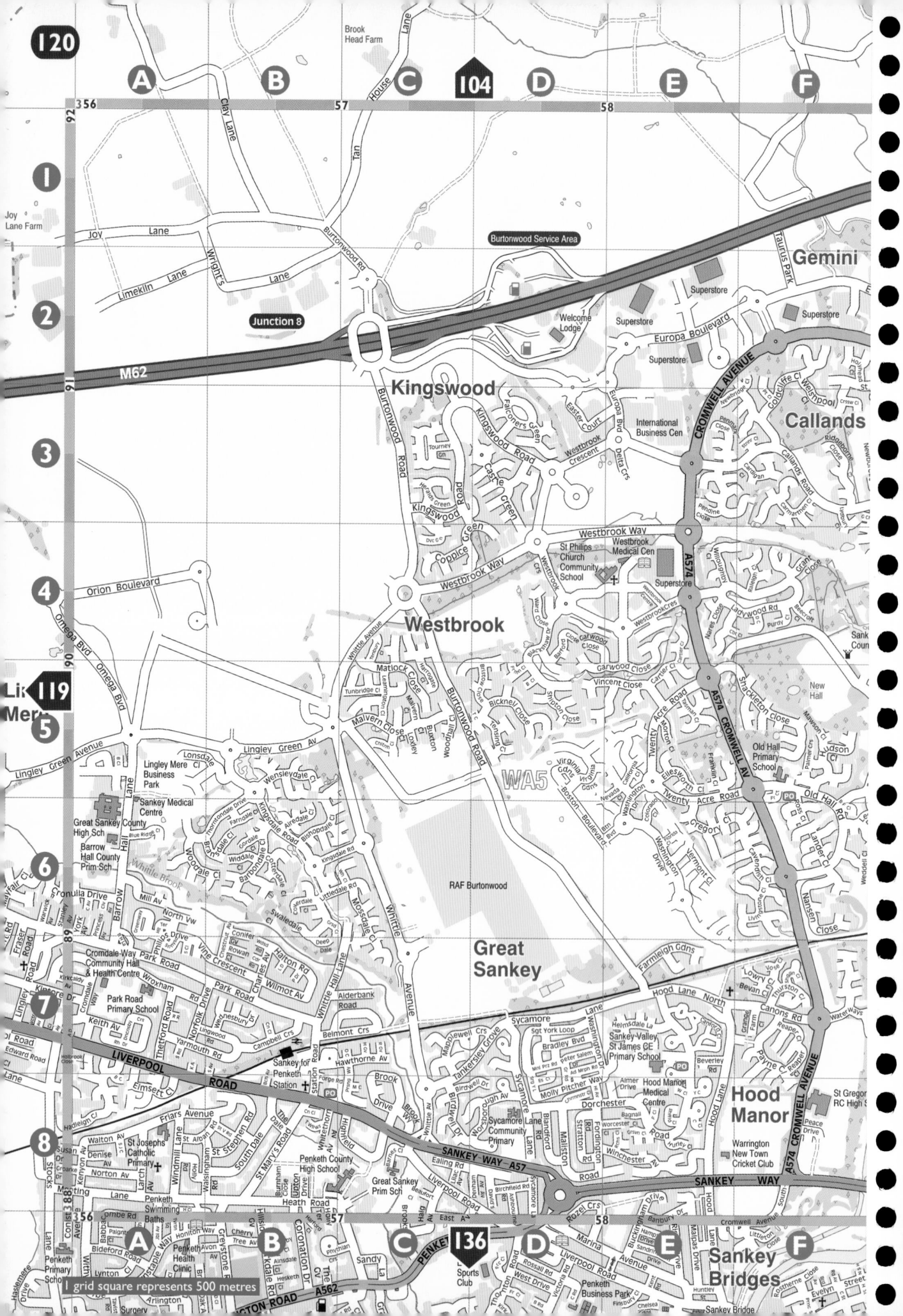

A B C 106 D E F

362 92 Houghton Green 63 Course 64

I

Cinnamon Brow

Poulton Park Golf Club

Locking Stumps

2

Blackbrook

3

Fearnhead

Longbarn

Padgate

Paddington

4

Birchwood Community High School

121

5

Bruche

Woolston CE Primary School

Woolston

6

Padgate Lane

New Manchester Road

Manchester Road

7

Cemetery

WA1

River Mersey

15

8

Cardinal Newman RC High School

Westy

The Eyes

Howley

362 WARRINGTON

River Mersey

A B C 138 D E F

3388 89 63 64

Victoria Park

I grid square represents 500 metres

P

108

A   B   C   D   E   F

WEST
KIRBY

Golf Course

Golf Course

MEOLS DR

Leas Pk

Eddisbury Road

West Kirby
Primary School

West Kirby
Girls Grammar
School

Pinfold
Lane

Bramerton
Court

West Kirby
Residential School

Lingdale Road

Riversdale Road

Dee Lane

Graham Road

Anglesey Road

Greenbank
Road

Greenbank
Avenue

Marine Avenue

Lang Lane

Boulton Avenue

Raeburn Avenue

Broxton Avenue

Grosvenor Avenue

Dorset Road

Essex Road

Sussex Road

PO

Gilroy Rd

Paton Close

Black Horse
Hill Junior School

Black Horse
Hill Infant School

FRANKBY

Belmont Road

Claremont Road

Leigh Road

War Memorial

Cemetery

Grange Hill

Black Horse Close

BLACK HORSE HILL

B5139

Simpson Rd

Douglas Road

Wirral Mount

Kingsbury

Queensbury

Grange Mount

Superstore

Salisbury Av

Cote Pk

Groveside

Victoria Drive

Shrewsbury Rd

Alexandra

Ashton Drive

Church Road

Eaton Rd

South Rd

Victoria Rd

Albert Rd

BANKS ROAD

Mostyn Avenue

Hydro Avenue

South Pde

Sailing Club

Tell's Tower

Beach Walk

Shelley Way

SANDY LANE

Macclona Drive

Riverside Drive

York Avenue

CALDY ROAD B5140

Fire Station

Health Cen
& Swimming
Pool

West Kirby
Station

North Road

Park Med Cen

Brook House
Business Centre

Corner House Clinic

Westbourne

Carpenters Lane

Wirral Way

Townfield

Brookfield

Grosvenor Dr

Egerton Dr

Princes Avenue

St Bridgets CE
Primary School

Rectory Road

The Oatlands

Village

A540

HILBRE VIEW

West Kirby Foot
Health Clinic

Abbey Road

Monk's Way

Priory Rd

Beacon Drive

Kingswalk

Croome Drive

Burlingham Avenue

Gourley's La

A540

CH48

Gran

Grammar Road

Bramall Close

COLUMN

Caldy Grange
Grammar School

Fleck Lane

Boundary Rd

Mount Road

Avalon School

Warwick Drive

Kirby Mount

Surrey Dr

Thorsway

King's Drive

Caldy

Mellongroft Dr

Croft Drive West

West Drive

Shore Road

Caldy Wood

The Green

Caldy Chase Dr

CALD

Croft Drive

Barton

Croft

Mill Hey Rd

Hey

Westward Ho

Badgers Set

The Steeple

Tanskey Rocks

Marine Lake

1 grid square represents 500 metres

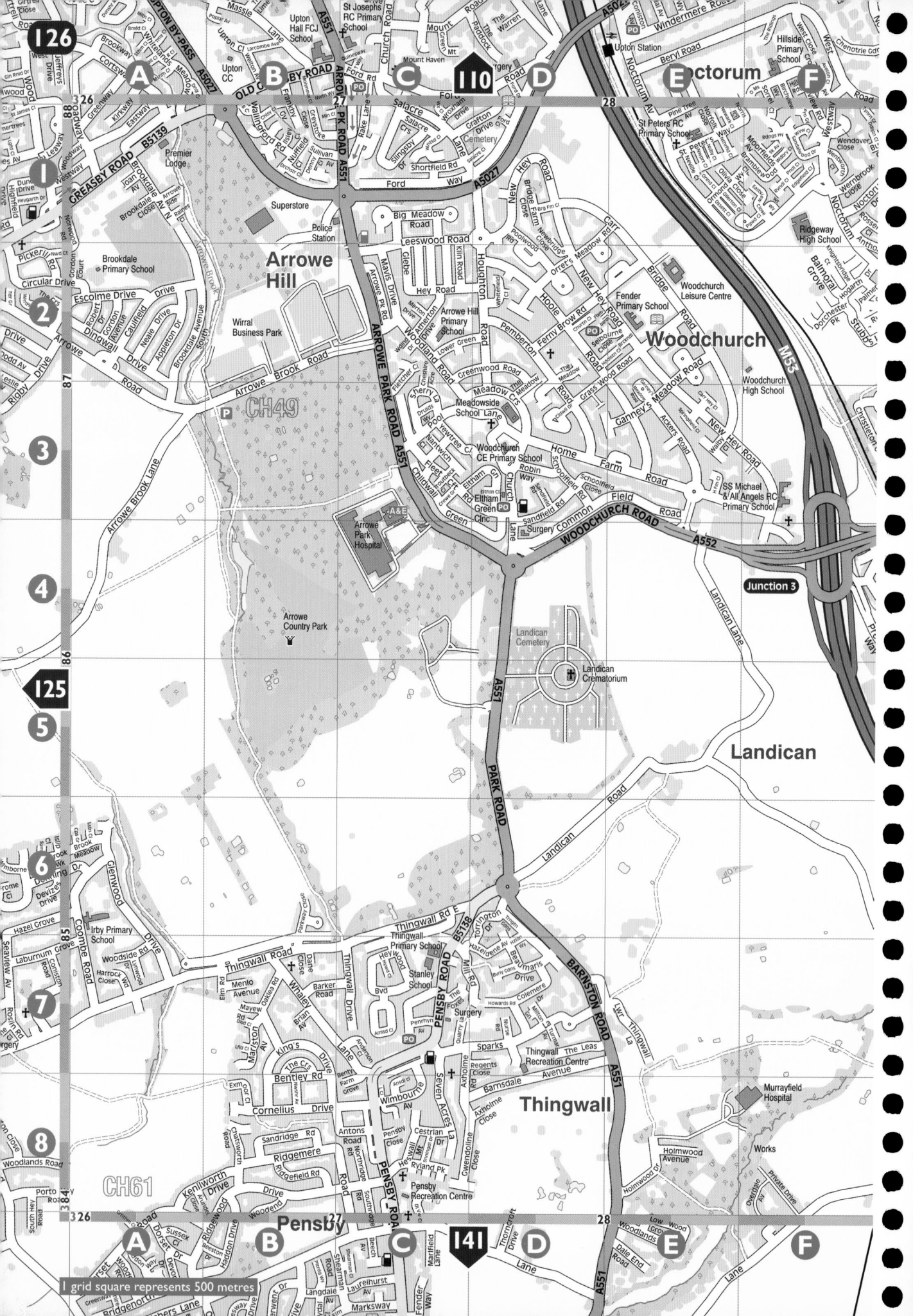

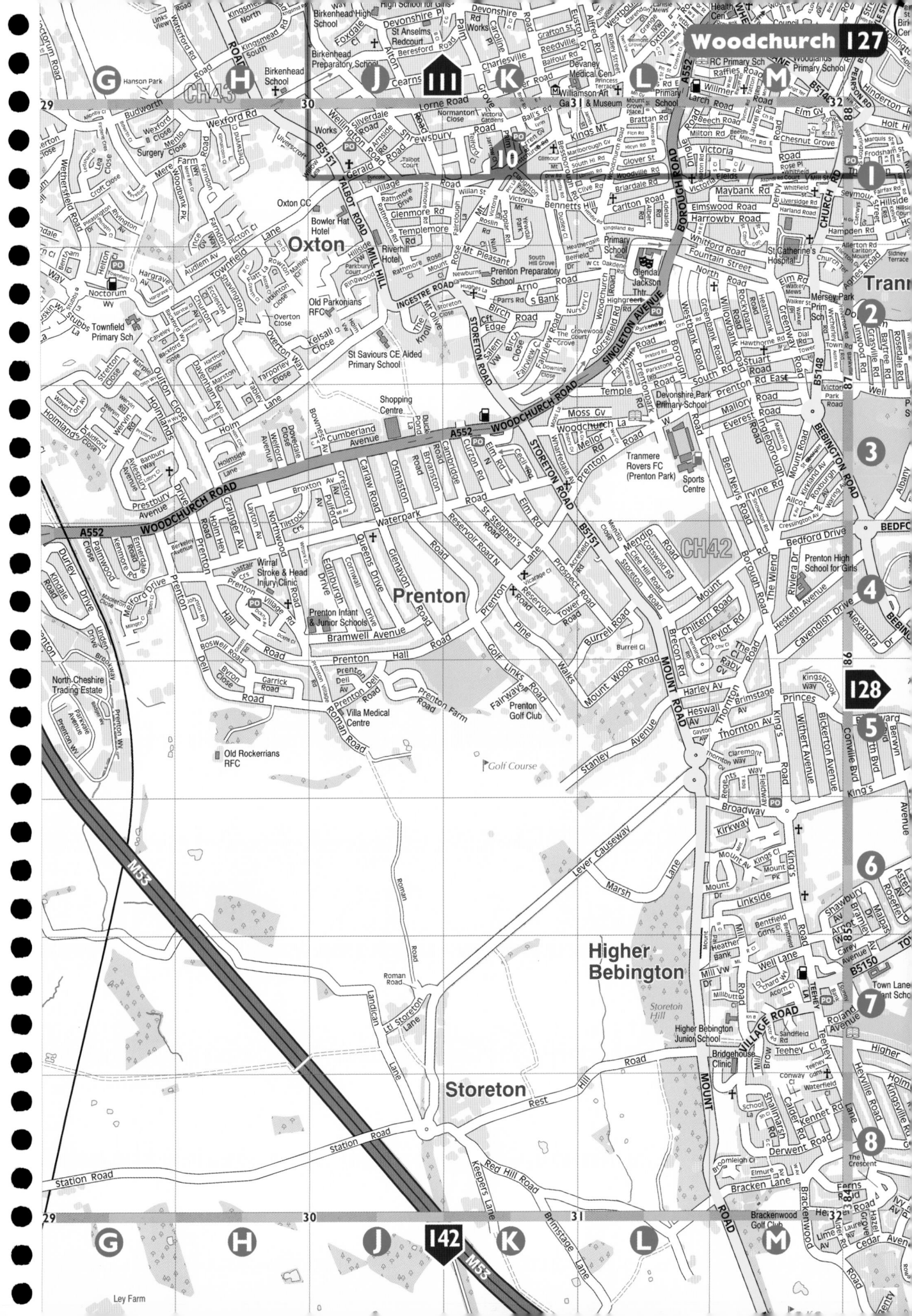

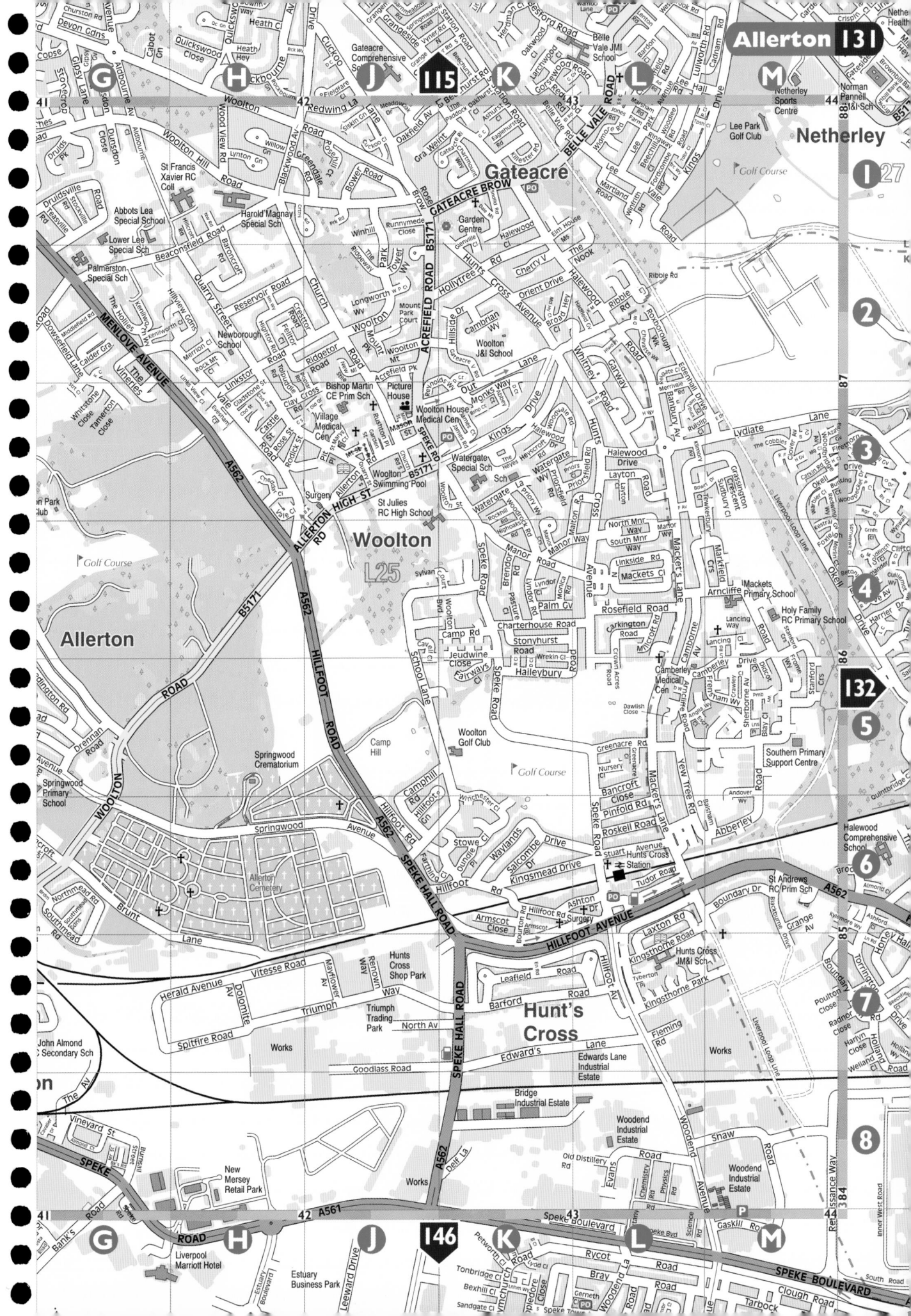

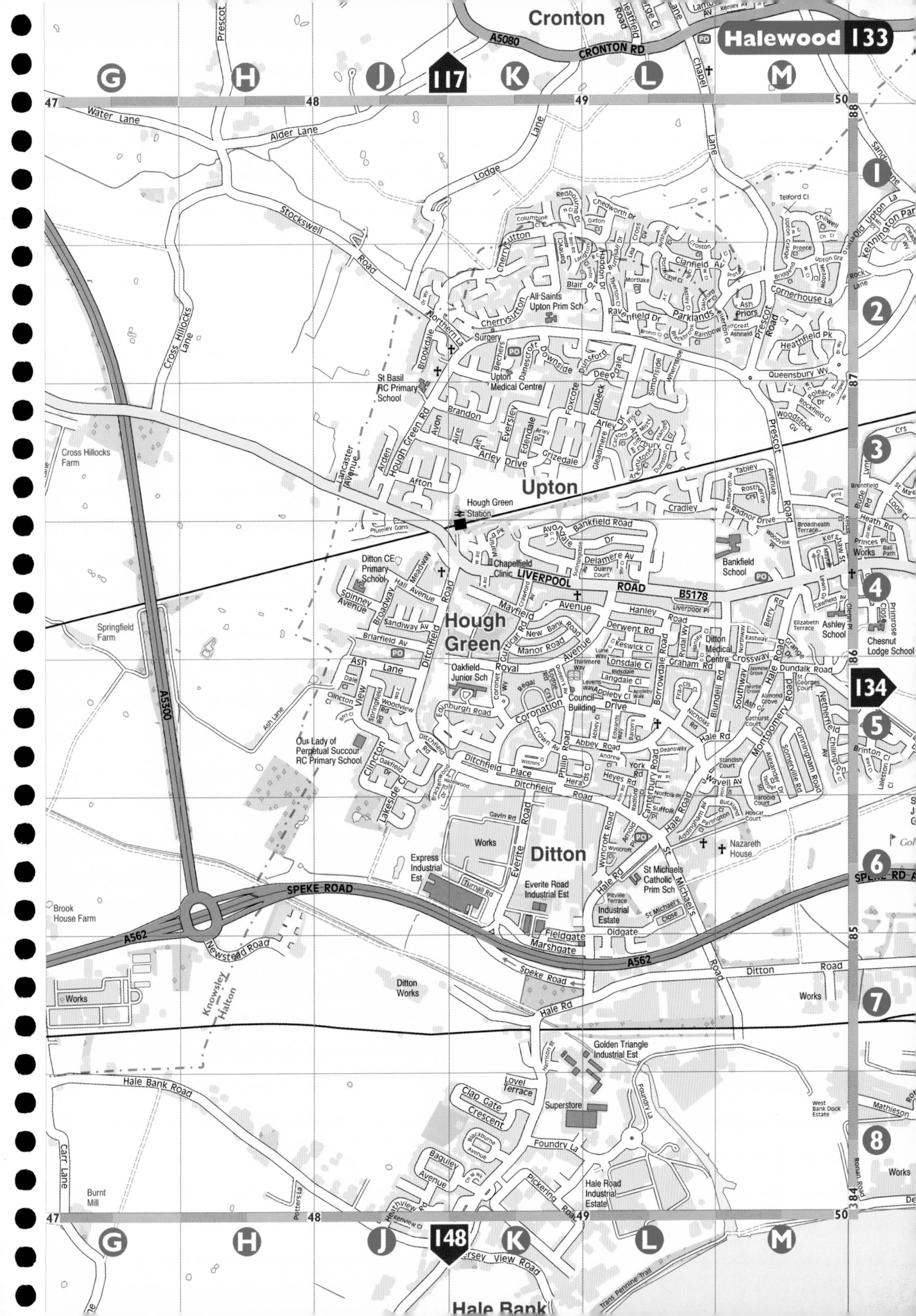

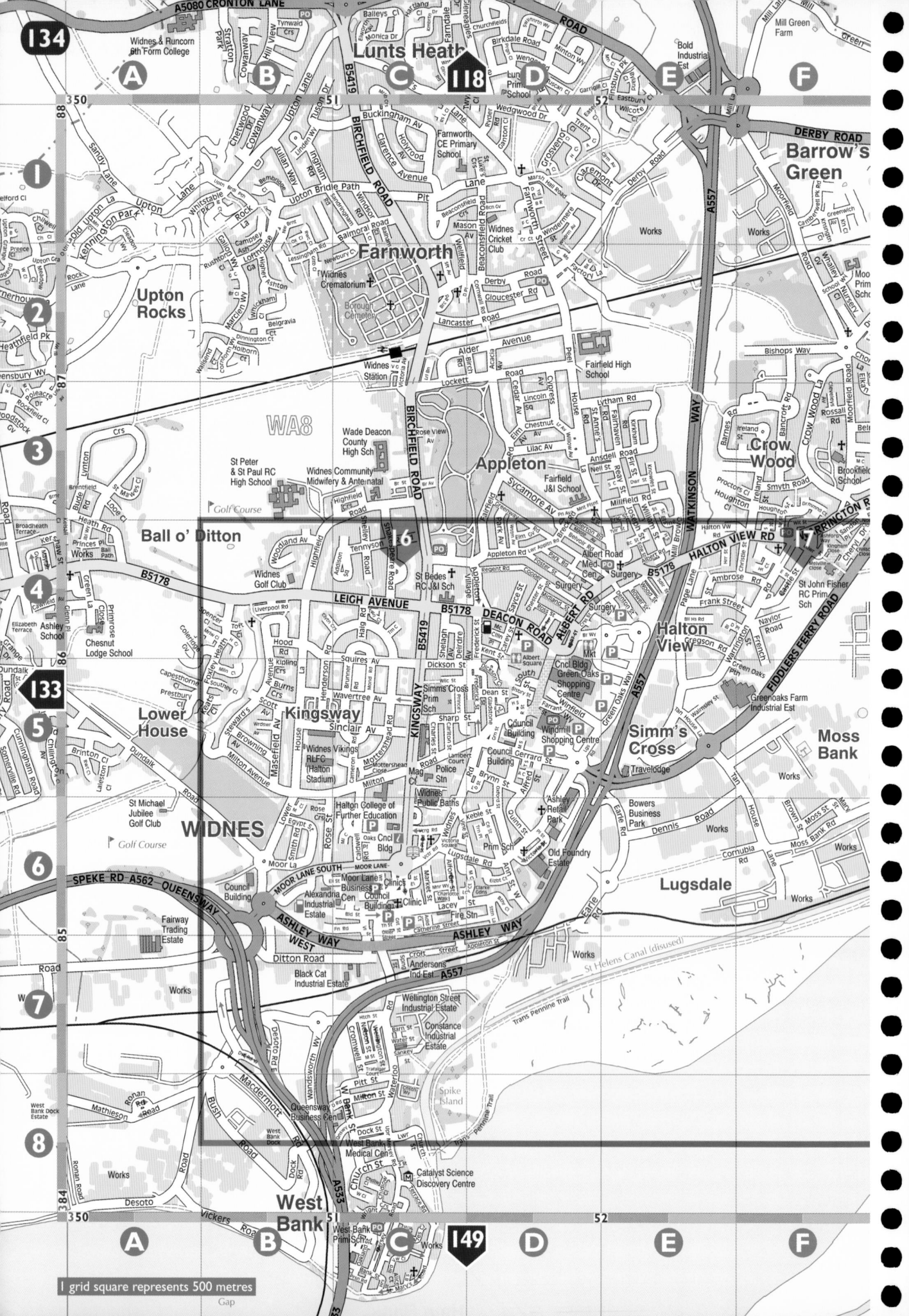

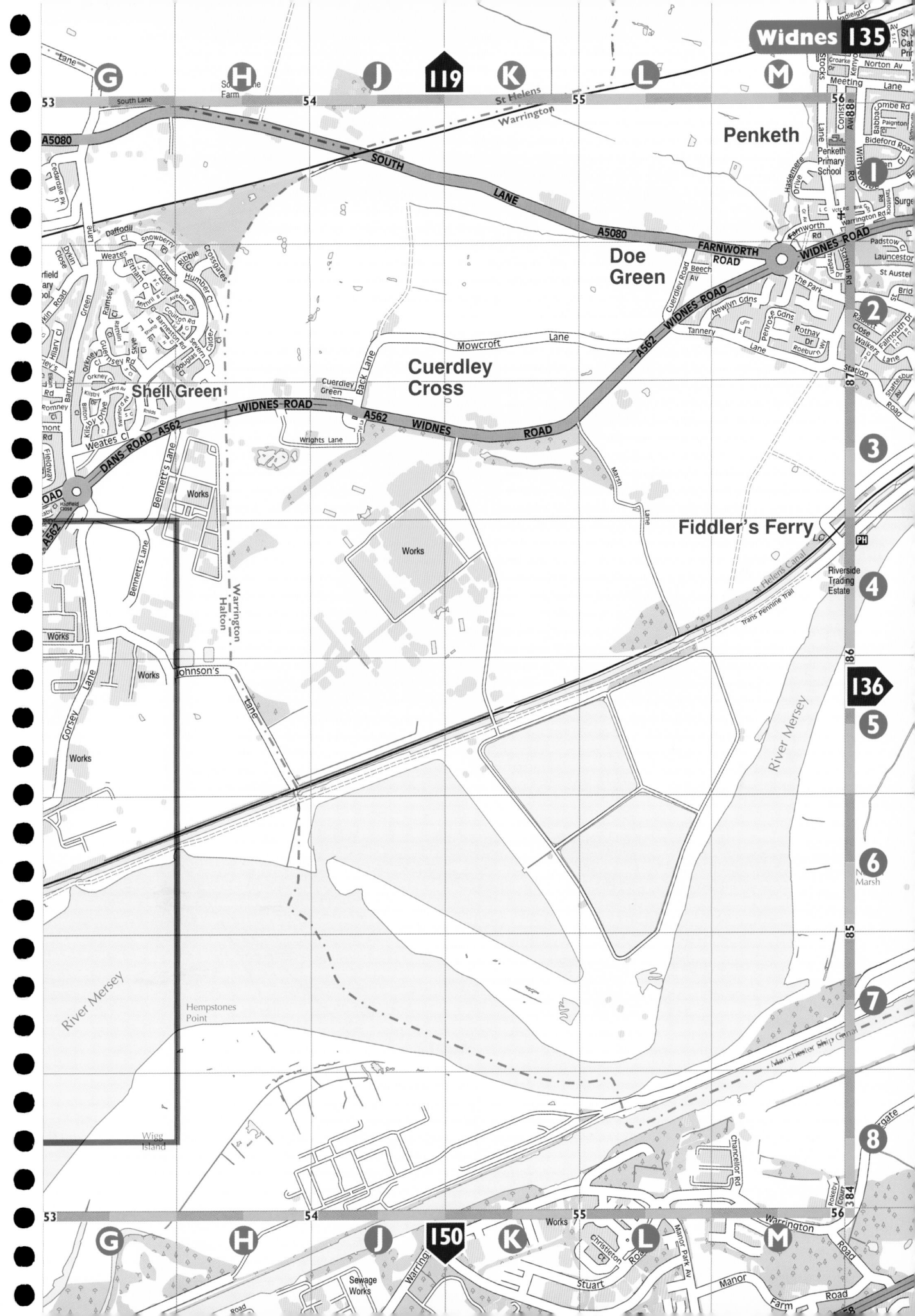

G H J 119 K L M

South Lane Farm

53 South Lane 54 St Helens 55 56
Warrington

A5080

Penketh

SOUTH

LANE

A5080 FARNWORTH ROAD

Doe Green

WIDNES ROAD WIDNES ROAD

Penketh Primary School

Farnworth Rd

I

2

Mowcroft Lane

Tannery

Cuerdley Cross

Cuerdley Green

Back Lane

A562 WIDNES ROAD

Shell Green

WIDNES ROAD

DANS ROAD A562 A562 WIDNES ROAD

Wrights Lane

3

Works

Bennett's Lane

Works

Fiddler's Ferry

St Helens Canal

Trans Pennine Trail

Riverside Trading Estate

PH

4

Works

Works

Warrington Halton

Johnson's

Lane

136

5

Gorsey Lane

Works

Works

River Mersey

6
Marsh

River Mersey

Hempstones Point

7

Manchester Ship Canal

Wigg Island

8

Chancellor Rd

53 54 55 56
Warrington Road

G H J 150 K L M

Sewage Works

Works

Stuart

Manor Park Av

Manor Farm Road

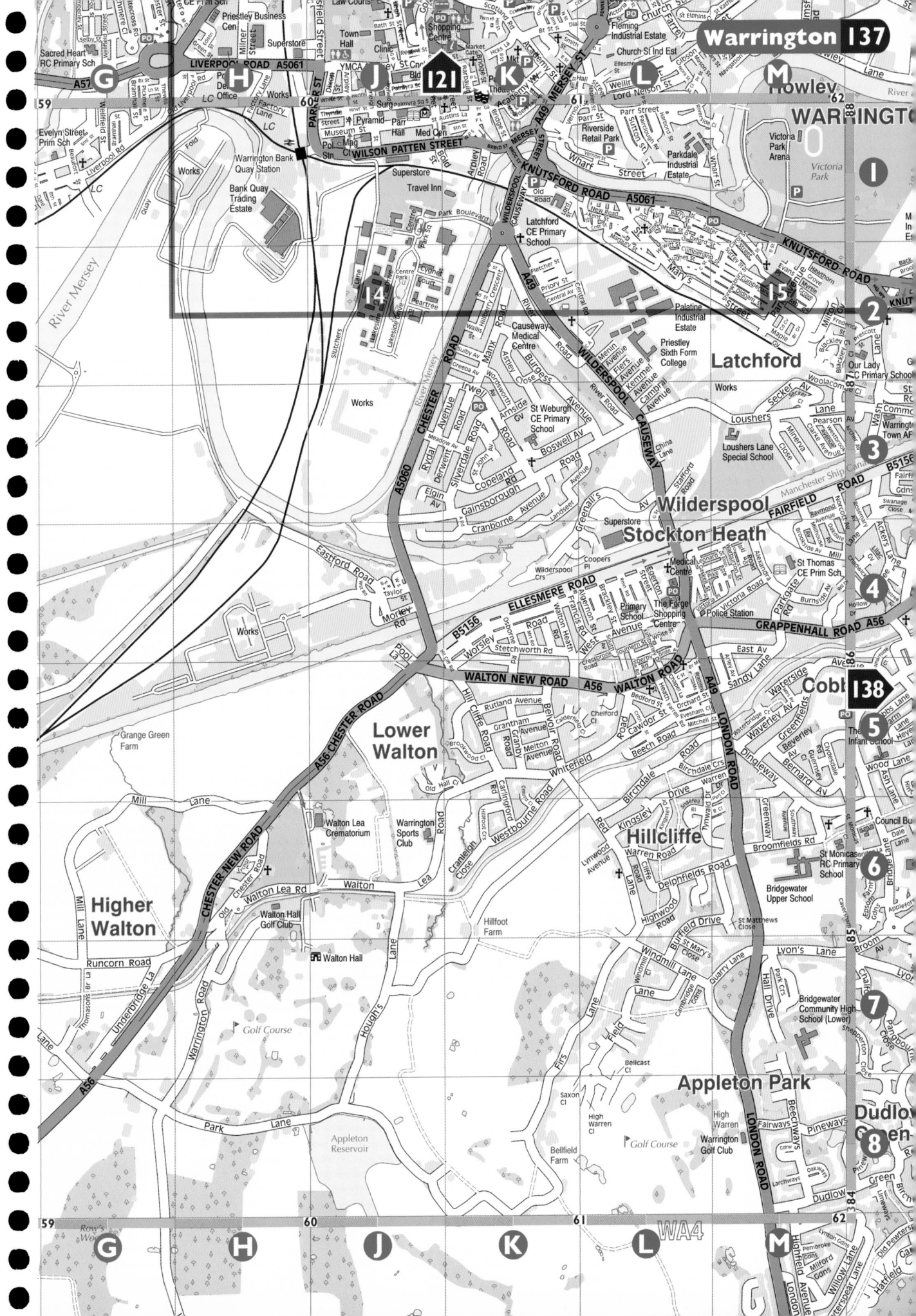

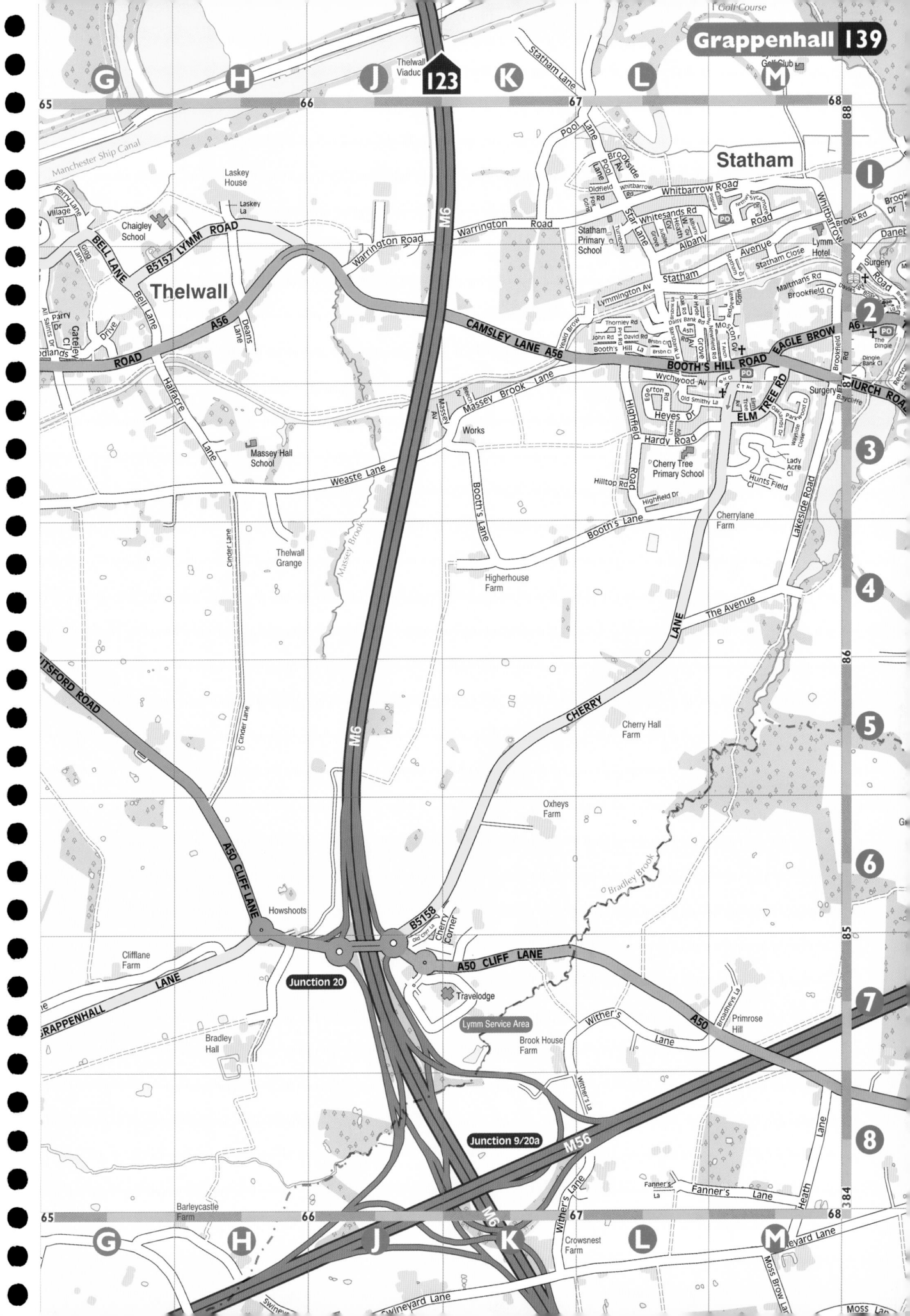

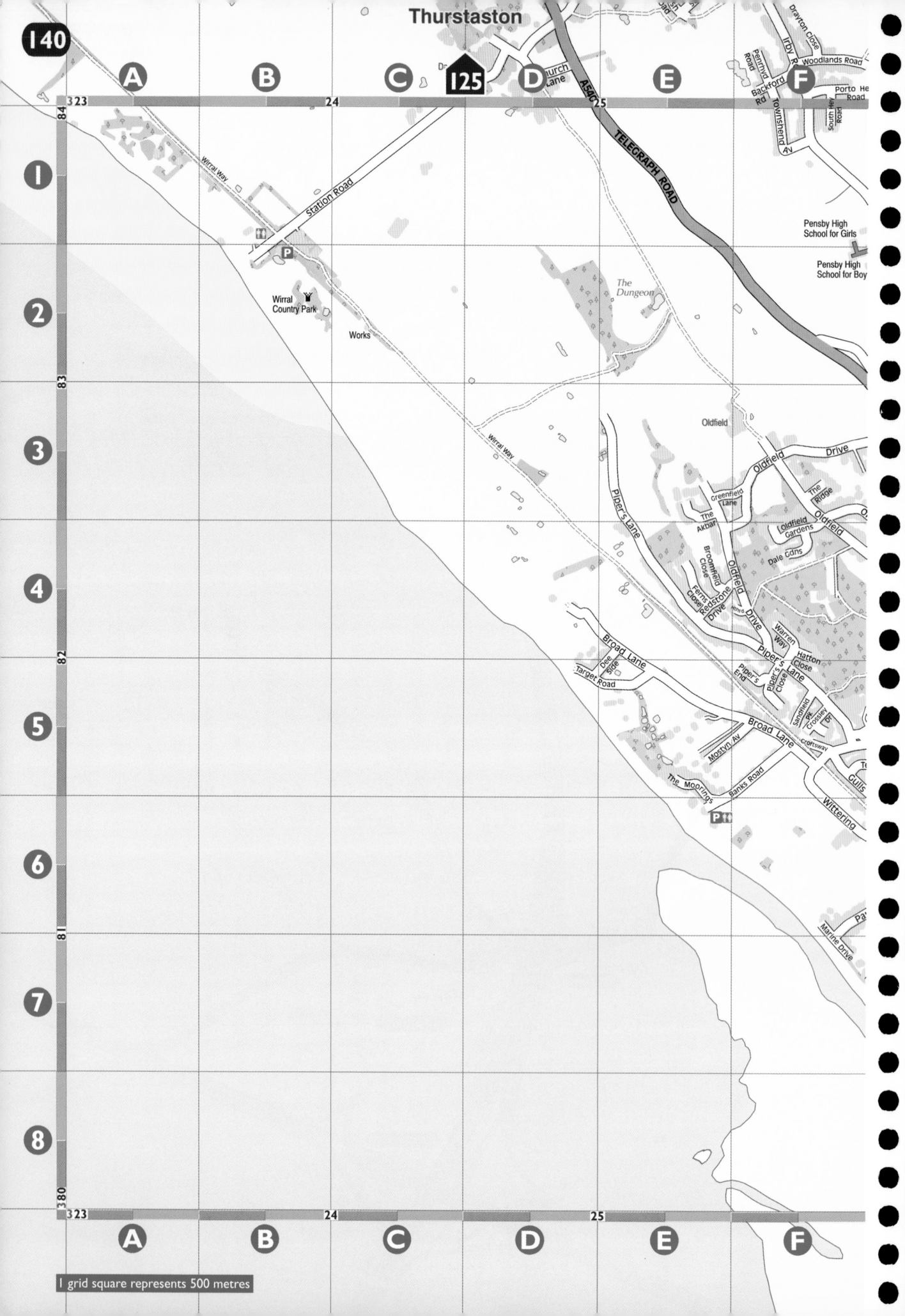

Thurstaston

125

TELEGRAPH ROAD

A54C

A B C D E F

Woodlands Road

Drayton Close

Perrys Road

Irby R

Backford Rd

Townshend

Porto He Road

South He Road

Av

Pensby High
School for Girls

Pensby High
School for Boy

The
Dungeon

Oldfield

Oldfield Drive

Wirral Way

The
Ridge

Station Road

Piper's Lane

Greenfield
Lane

The
Akbar

Oldfield
Gardens

Oldfield

O

Wirral Country Park

Dale Gdns

Works

Broomfield
Close

Oldfield Drive

Wirral Way

Ferns
Close

Redstone
Drive

Warren
Way

Hatton

Broad Lane

Item 6

Piper's Lane

Close

Target Road

Dee
Side

Piper's
End

Piper's
Close

Close

Sandfield

Crossley

Pk

Mostyn Av

Broad Lane

croftsway

The Moorings

Banks Road

Te

Gulls

Wittering

Marine Drive

Pa

P

1 grid square represents 500 metres

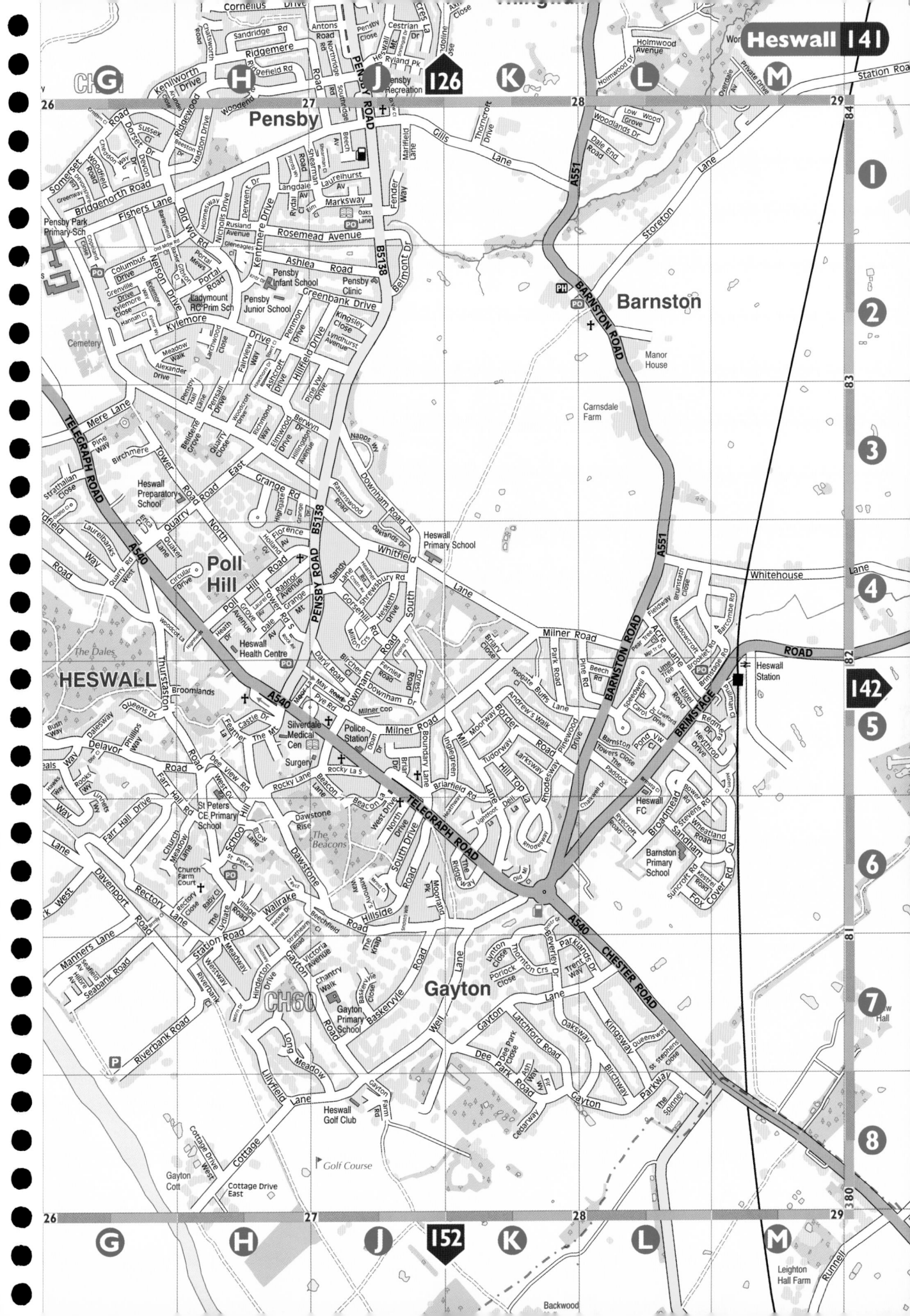

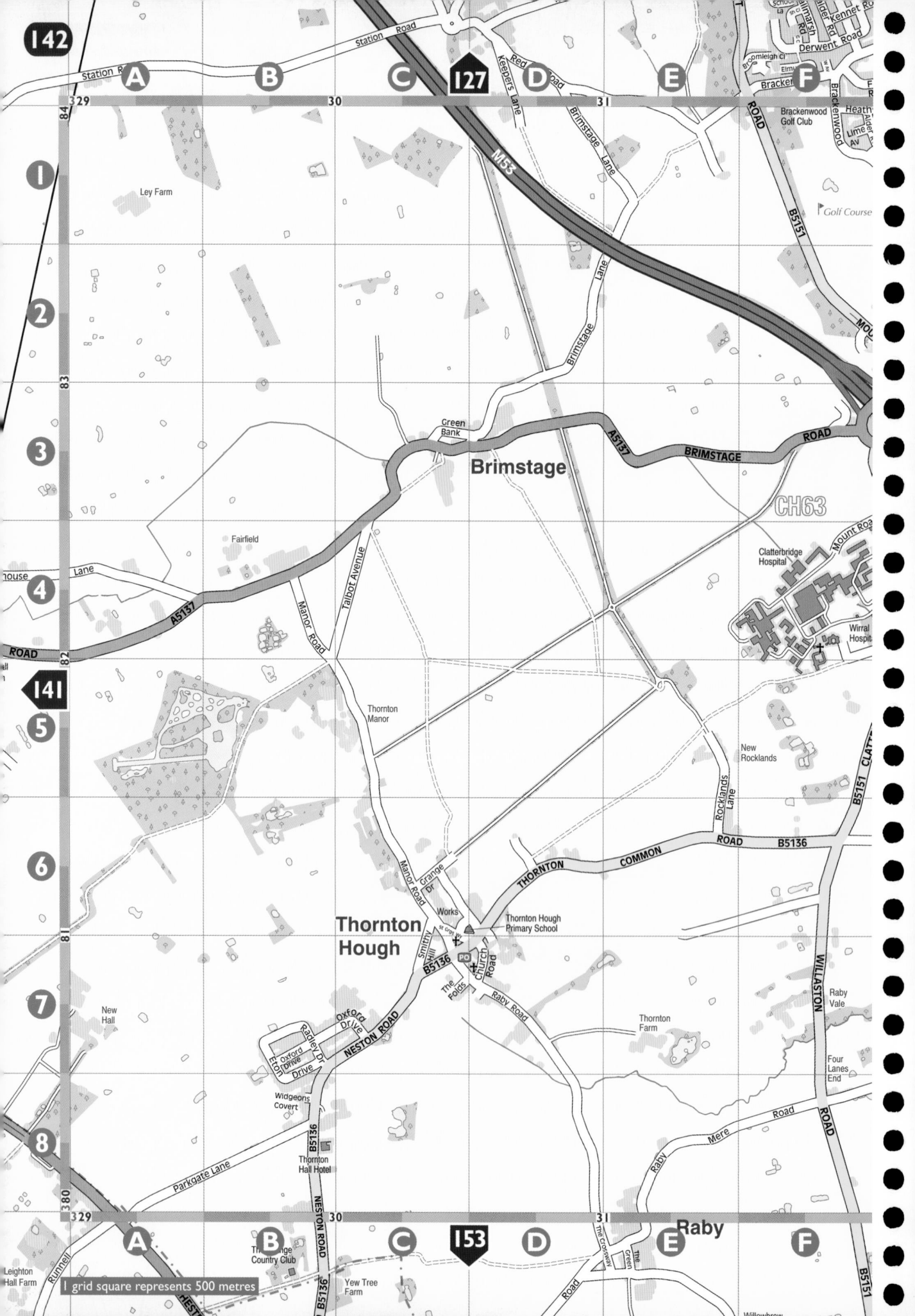

142

A **B** **C** **127** **D** **E** **F**

329   30   31

84

Station Road

Station Rd

1

Ley Farm

83

2

M53

3

Green Bank

Brimstage

A5137   BRIMSTAGE   ROAD

CH63

Fairfield

Lane

A5137

Talbot Avenue

Manor Road

Clatterbridge Hospital

Mount Road

Wirral Hospital

4

82

ROAD

141

5

Thornton Manor

New Rocklands

Rocklands Lane

B5151 Clatter

6

81

Manor Road

Grange Dr

Works

THORNTON   COMMON   ROAD   B5136

Thornton Hough Primary School

WILLASTON ROAD

Thornton Hough

Smithy

PO

Church Road

Raby Vale

7

New Hall

Oxford Drive

Radley Dr

Eton

B5136

The Folds

Raby Road

Thornton Farm

Four Lanes End

NESTON ROAD

Widgeons Covert

Oxford Drive

8

380

B5136

Thornton Hall Hotel

Parkgate Lane

Mere   Road

Raby

Raby

Leighton Hall Farm

Runnell

329   30   31

A **B** **C** **153** **D** **E** **F**

The Grange Country Club

NESTON ROAD

Yew Tree Farm

B5136

HEST

The Crossway

The Green

B5151

1 grid square represents 500 metres

Red Keepers Lane

Brimstage Lane

Brimstage Lane

Brackenwood Golf Club

Brackenwood

B5151

Golf Course

MOU

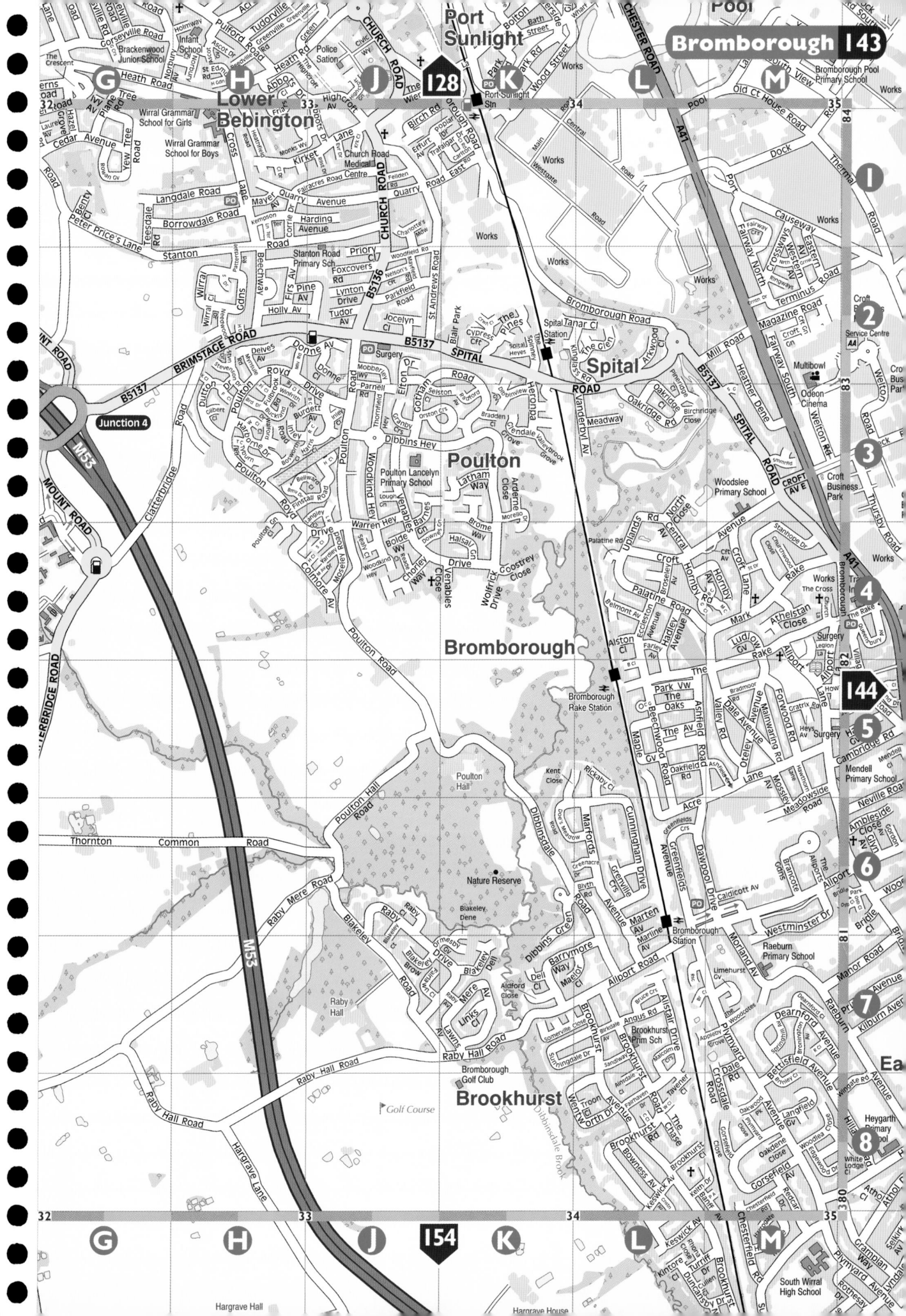

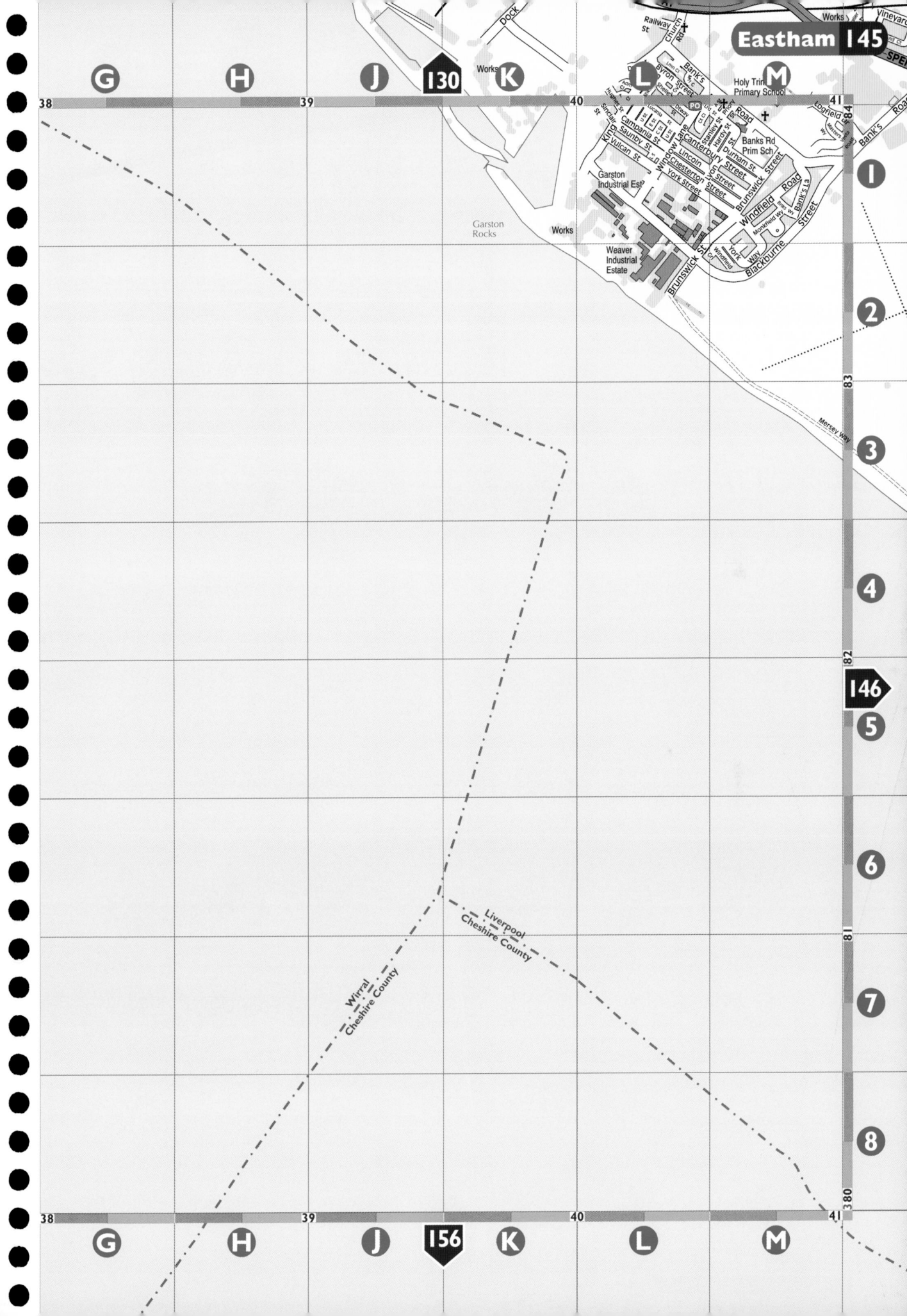

G   H   J   **130**   K   L   M

38   39   40   41

I

2

3

4

146

5

6

7

8

38   39   40   41

G   H   J   **156**   K   L   M

Garston
Rocks

Works

Weaver
Industrial
Estate

Garston
Industrial Est

Holy Trin
Primary School

Banks Rd
Prim Sch

Mersey Way

Liverpool
Cheshire County

Wirral
Cheshire County

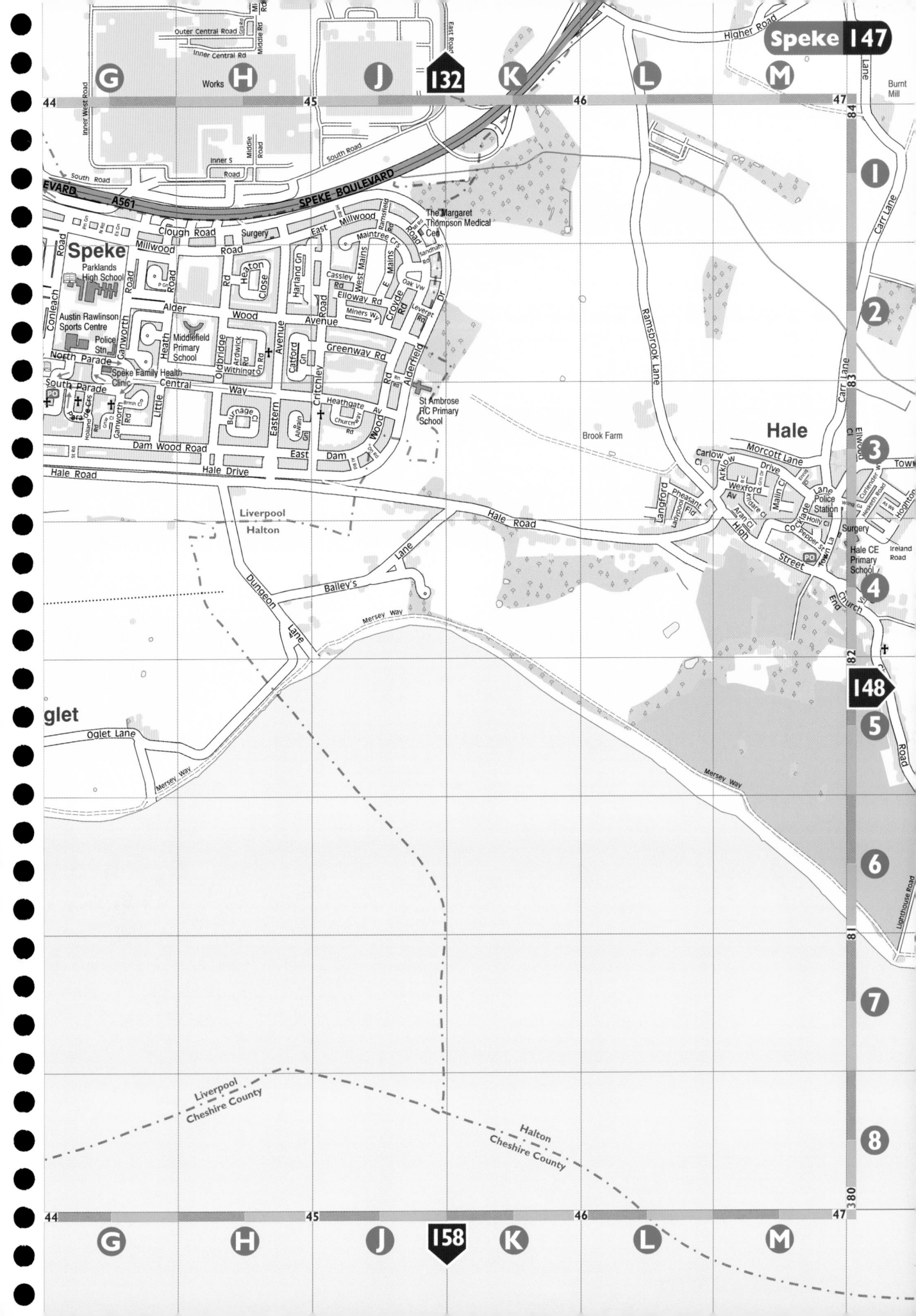

133

147

159

A B C D E F
1
2
3
4
5
6
7
8

Carr Lane
Burn Mill
347
84
83
82
81
380
347
48
48
49
49

Potter's La
Hale Gate Road
Hale Cate Road
Town Lane
Halegate Farm
Garnetts Lane
Trans Pennine Trail

Hexton View Rd
Kenview Cl
Mersey View Road

Hale Bank

Pickerings Pasture
Trans Pennine Trail

River Mersey

Crescent
Blackburne Avenue
Foundry La
Bag
Superstore
Pickering Road
Hale Road Industrial Estate

ale
Ellwood
Cullender Wy
Hesketh Road
Wong Gr
Hoghton Rd
Lane
Police Station
Surgery
Holly Cl
Pepper St La
Town
COCK
Street
PO
Church End
Within Way

Hale CE Primary School
Ireland Road
Vicarage Close

Church Road
Lighthouse Road

Mersey Way
Hale Head

Weston Point

Manchester Ship Canal
Salt Works Wharf
Works
Works
Works
Picow Farm Rd
Sandy Lane
South Parade
Baker Road
Leonard St
Sydney St
Mersey View Post Office
PO
Clarkes Terrace
Beacon Hill View
Weston Point Dock
West La
Mersey Vw St
Canal Side
Halton
Cheshire County

Bank Dock Estate

1 grid square represents 500 metres

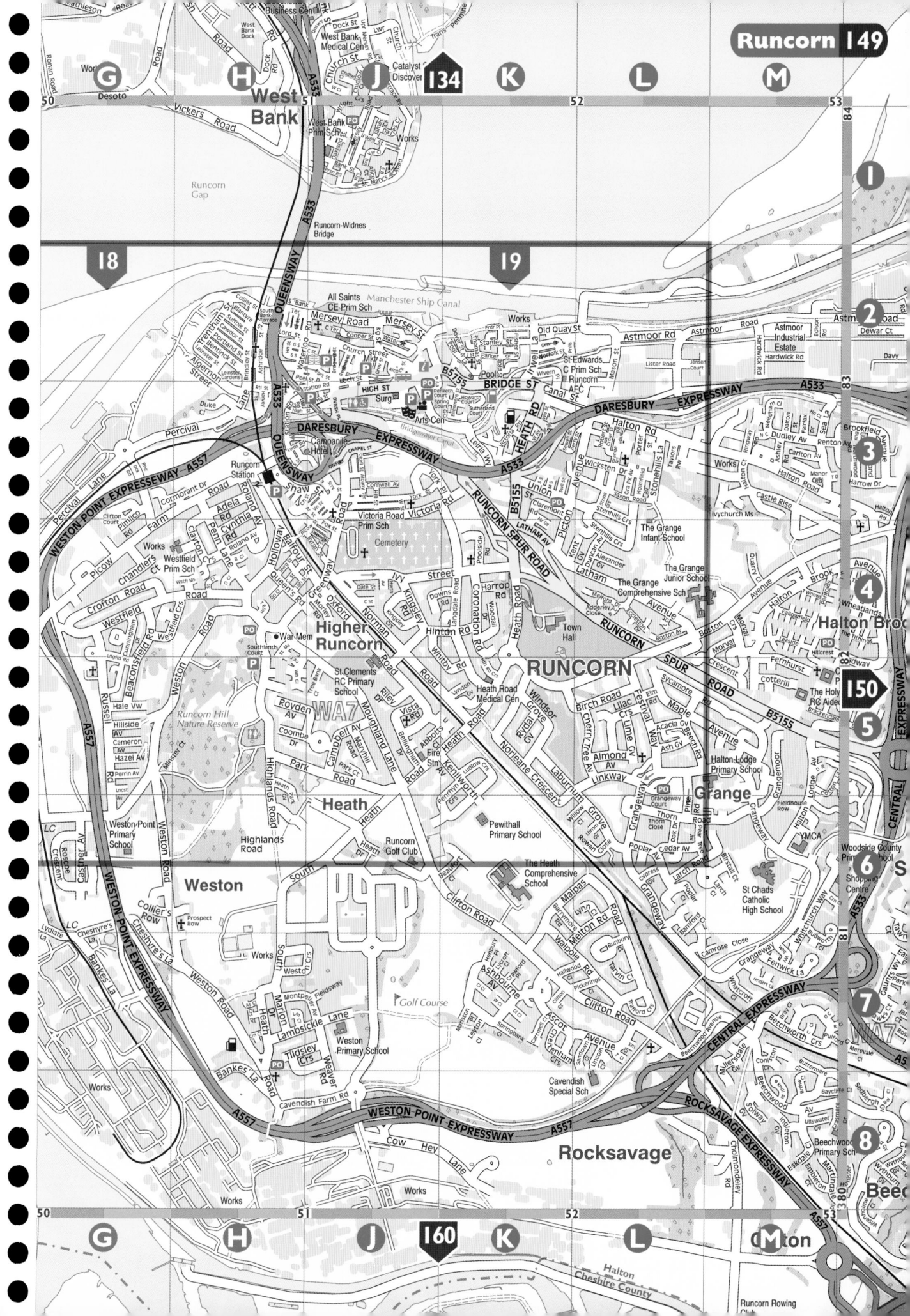

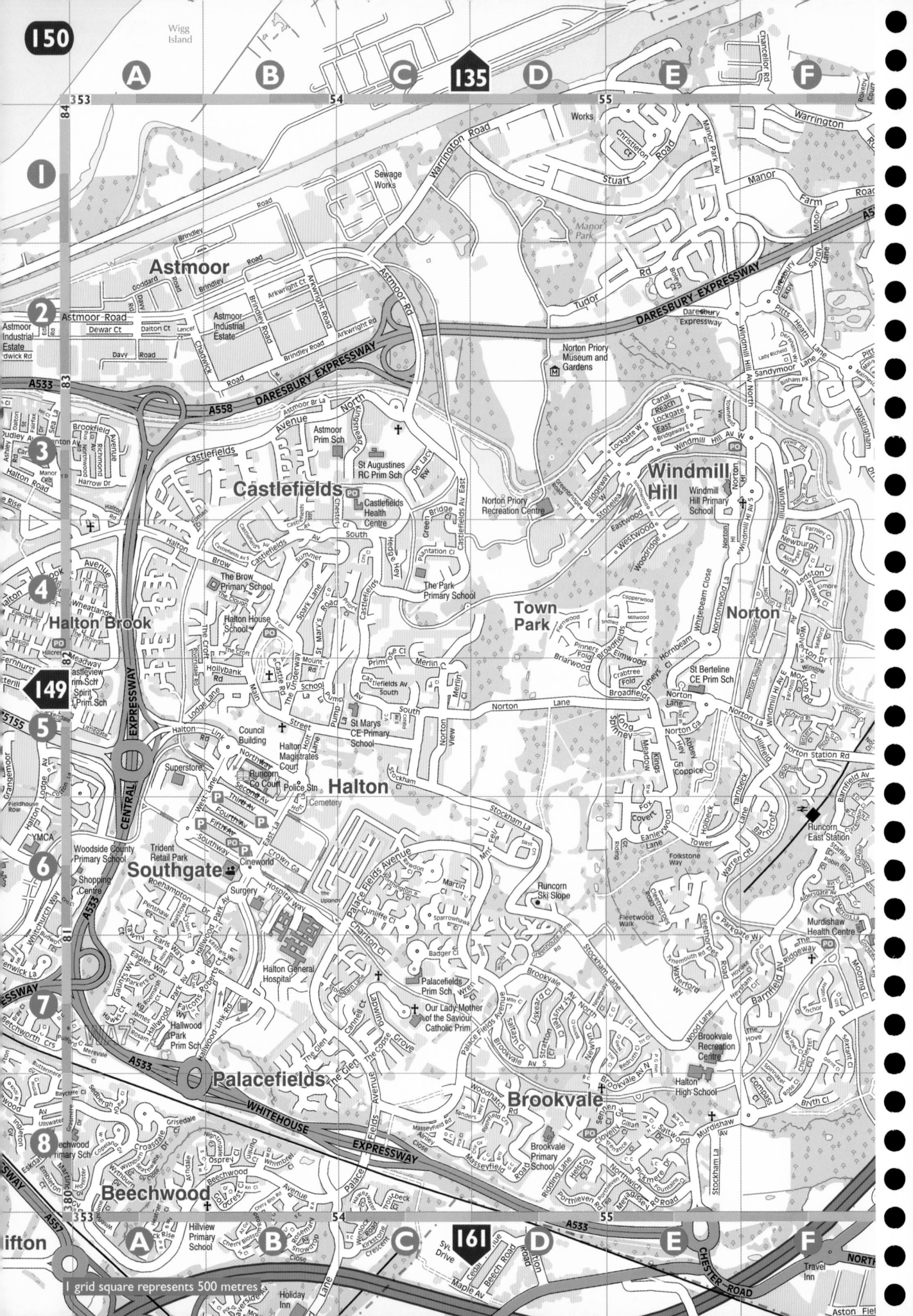

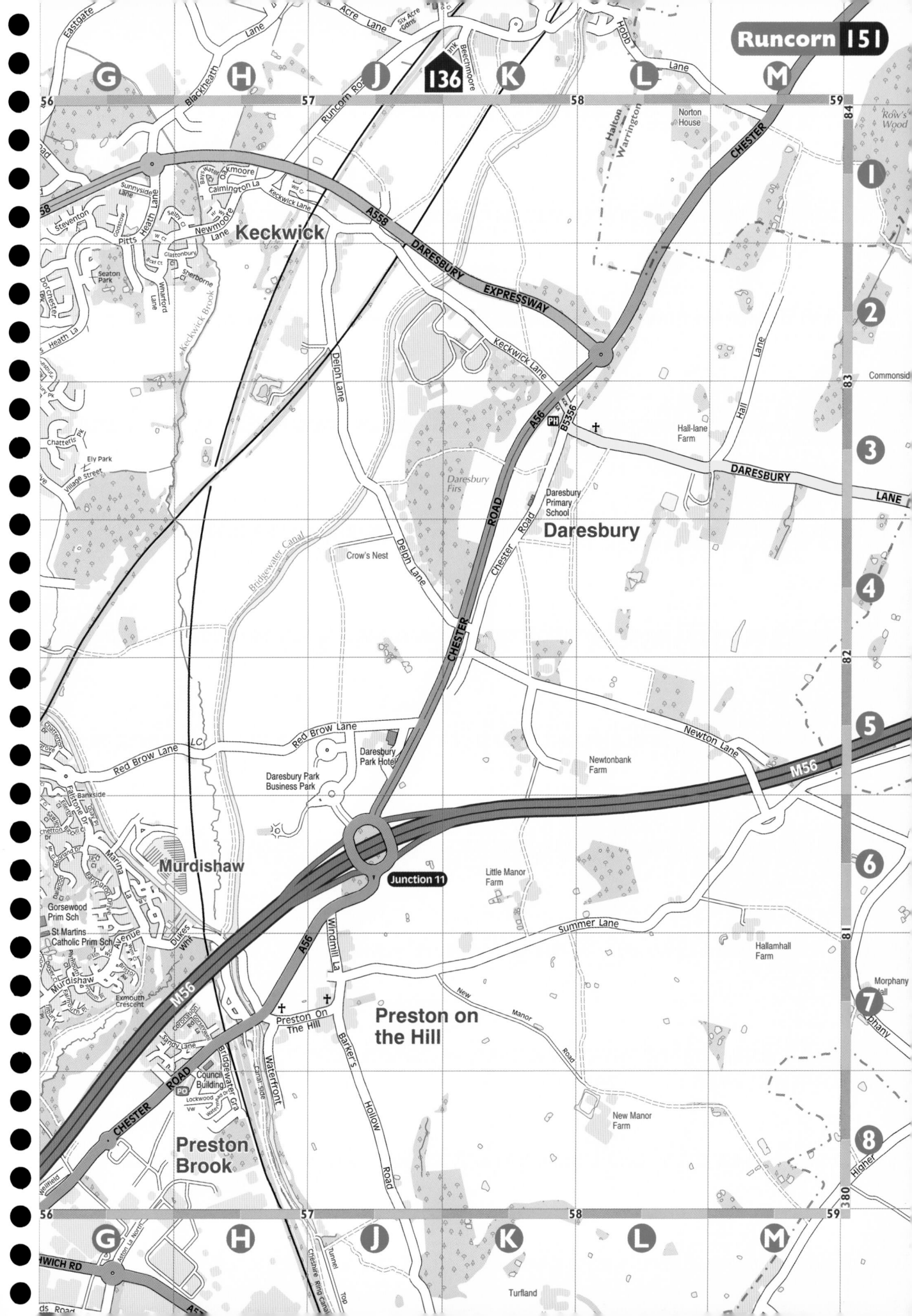

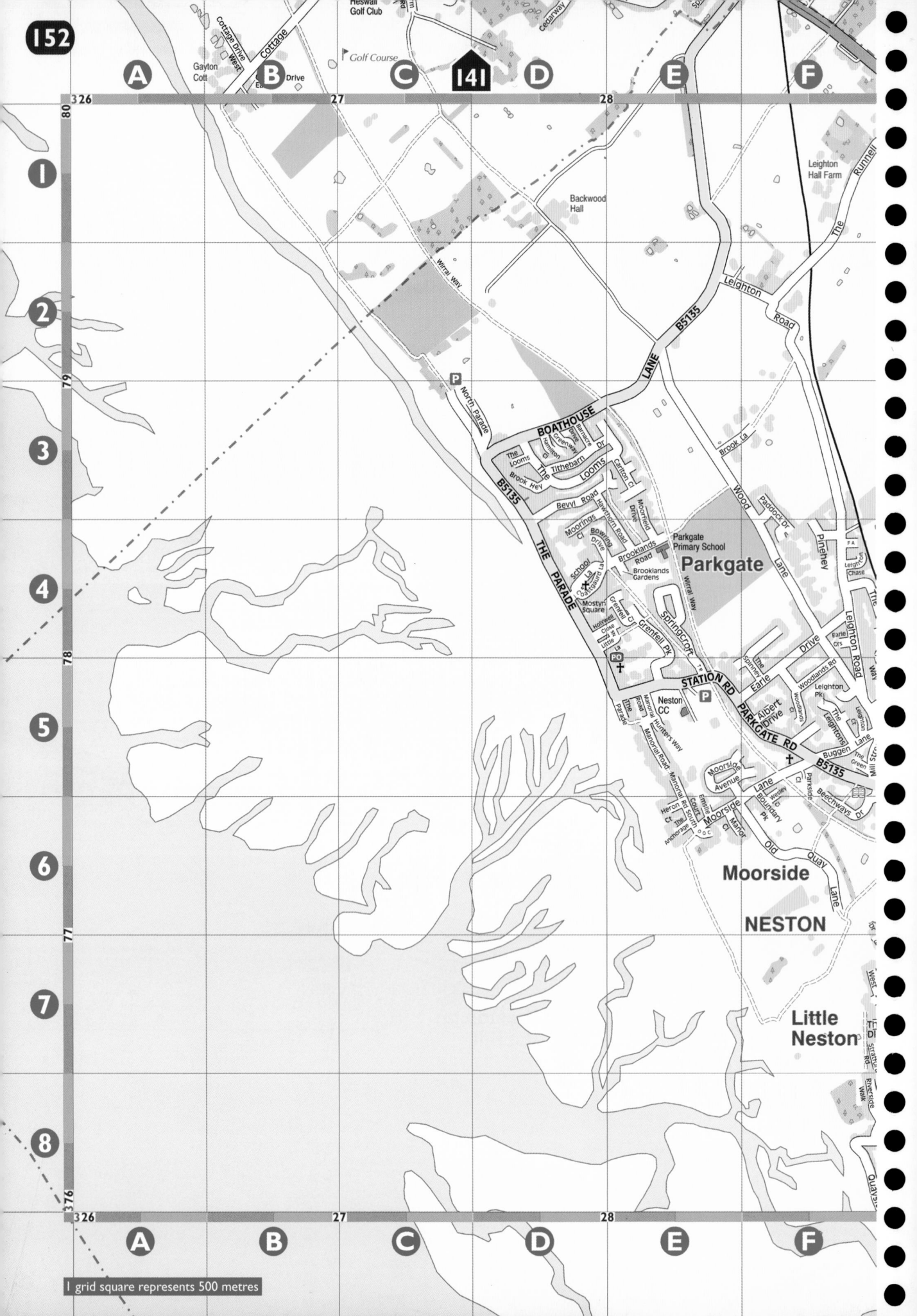

A B C **141** D E F

80 326 27 28

Heswall
Golf Club

Cottage Drive West

Cottage

Cedarway

Gayton
Cott

Drive

Golf Course

Leighton
Hall Farm

The Runnell

1

Backwood
Hall

2

79

Wirral Way

LANE

B5135

Leighton

Road

3

P

North Parade

BOATHOUSE

Barnacre

Greenway

Hamilton

The Looms

Tithebarn

The Looms

Brook La

Brook Hey

The Looms Dr

Cotton Dr

B5135

Moorland Drive

Bevyl Road

Hawthorn Road

THE PARADE

Wood Lane

Paddock Dr

4

78

Moorings Cl

Bowling

Brooklands Road

Brooklands Gardens

Parkgate
Primary School

Wirral Way

Parkgate

FA
Leighton
Chase

Pinehey

School

Mostyn Square

Grenfell Cl

Oakspare La

Springcroft

Earle Drive

Leighton Road

The Way

5

77

Holwell Close Little

PO

Grenfell Cl

STATION RD

Neston CC

P

The Parade

Manorial Road

PARKGATE RD

Albert Drive

Earle

Woodlands Rd

Leighton Pk

The Leighton

Buggen La

Wesley Cl

B5135

The Green

Mill Street

Beechways Dr

Parkside

6

Heron Ct

Hunter's Way

Manorial Road

Manorial Rd South

The Anchorage

Moorside Avenue

Moorside Lane

Manor

Emily St

Boundary Pk

Old Quay Lane

West...

Moorside

NESTON

7

**Little
Neston**

Riverside Walk

strath... Rd

8

376

Quay...

326 27 28

A B C D E F

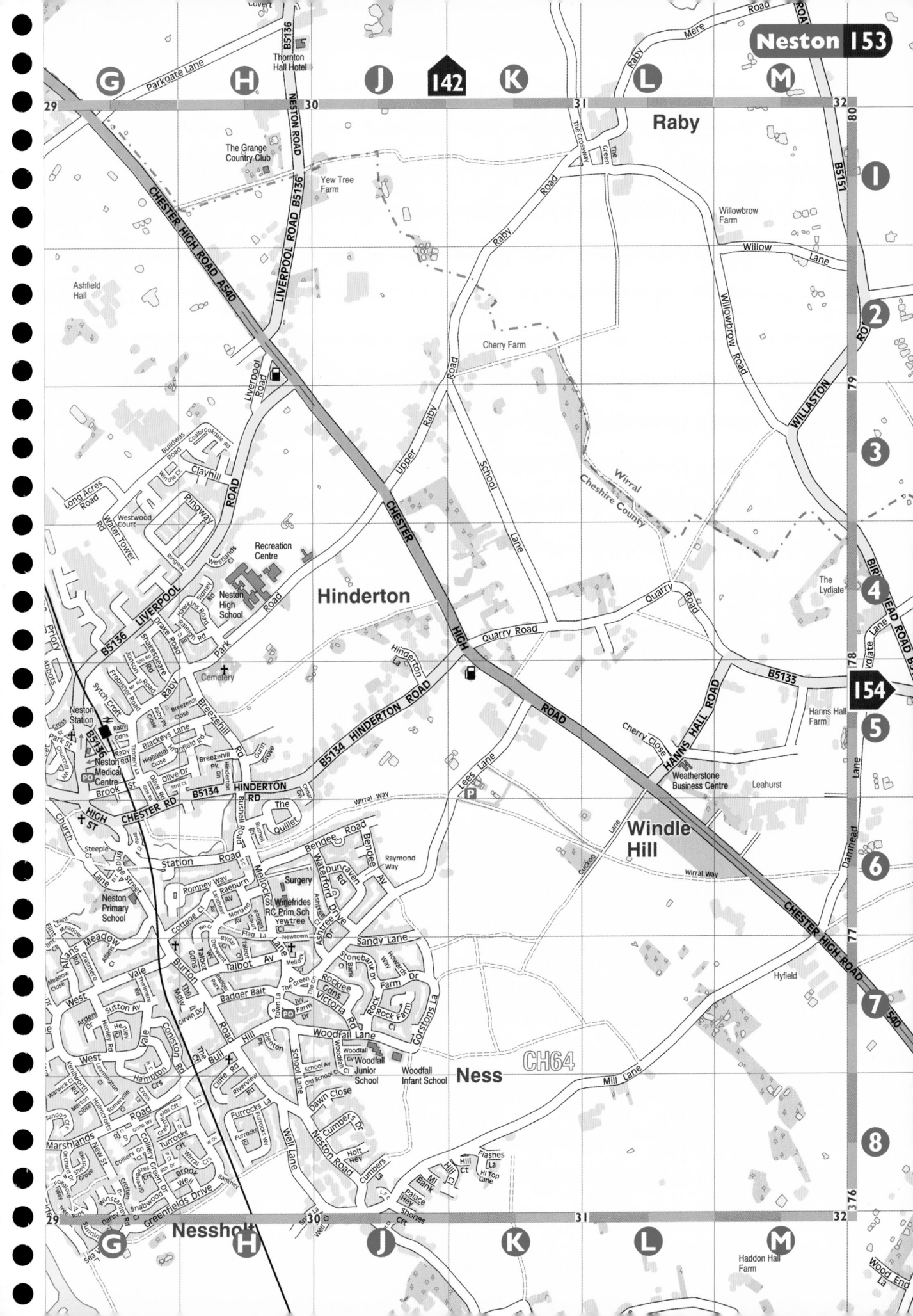

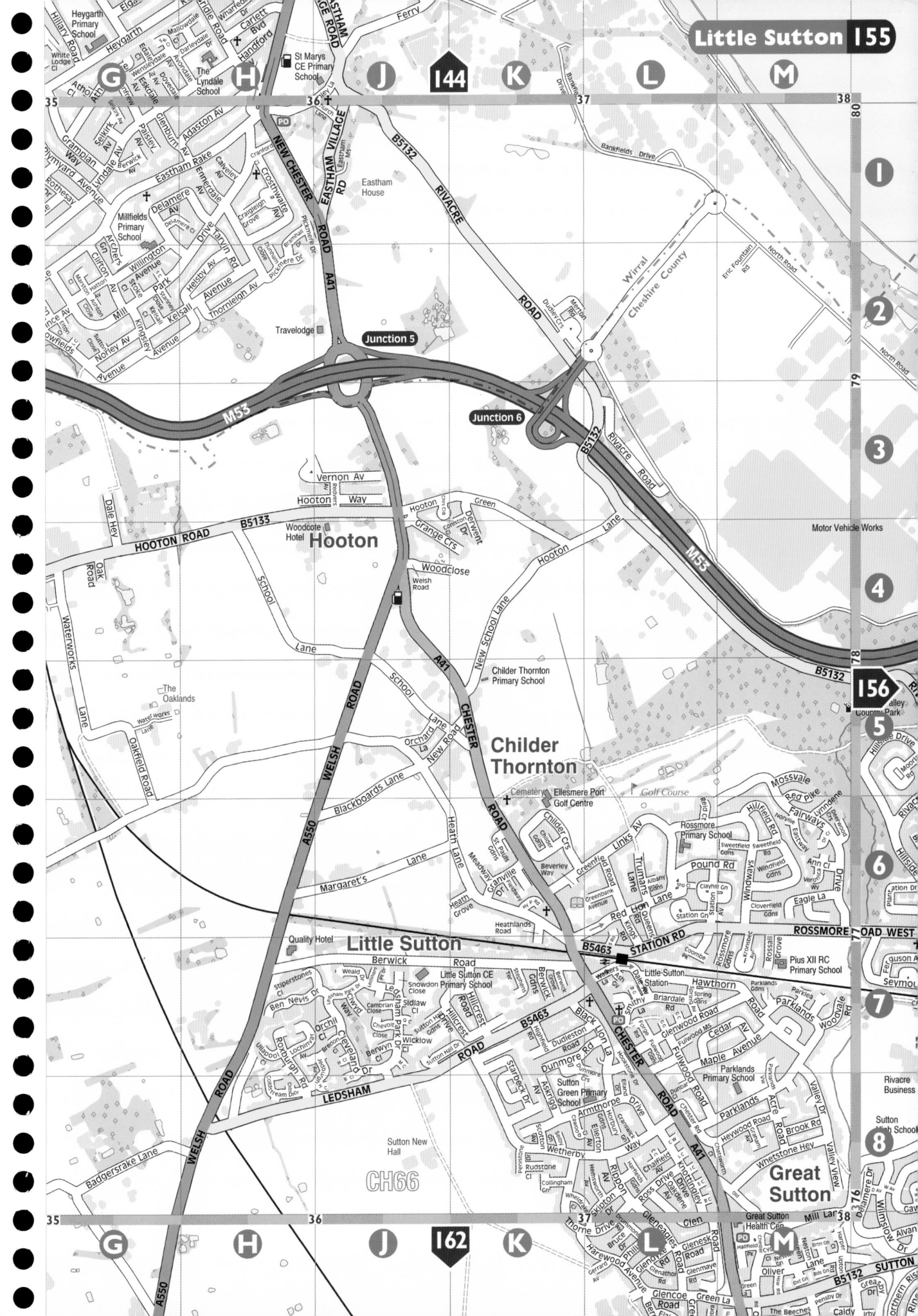

G H J **146** K L M

41 42 43 44 80

1

2

79

3

4

78

158

5

6

ERE

21

Manchester Ship Canal

Canalside
Industrial Estate

Stanlow
Point

77 Manchester

7

CH65

Works

Indigo Road

rd Road

Oil Sites Road

Corridor Road

Oil Sites Road

8

76

Chapterhouse
Cl

Cloister Way

Bridges Road

South Road

Stanlow

Lees

Telford

Burnett

New B

Stanlow 44 ornton
Station

41 42 43

G H J **164** K L M

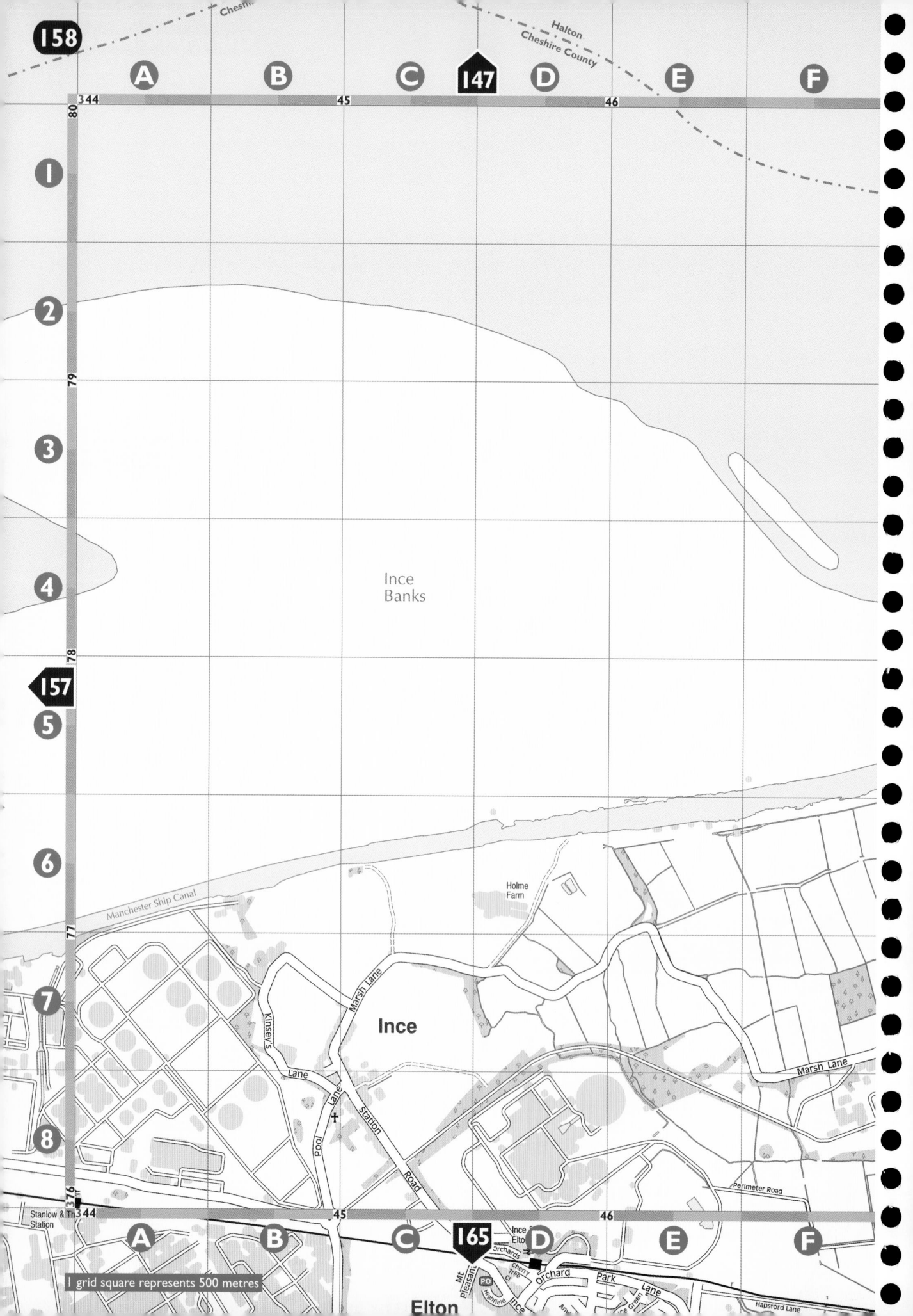

158

A   B   C   **147**   D   E   F

344   45   46

80

I

79

2

3

4

78

157

5

Ince
Banks

77

6

Manchester Ship Canal

Holme
Farm

7

Ince

Kinsey's
Lane

Marsh Lane

Marsh Lane

Pool Lane

Station Road

8

Perimeter Road

376

344   45   46

Stanlow & Th
Station

A   B   C   **165**   D   E   F

Ince
Elto
Orchards

Orchard   Park
Cherry
Tree
Ct.

Mt.
Pleasant

PO

Ince

Highfield

Lane

Hapsford Lane

I grid square represents 500 metres

Elton

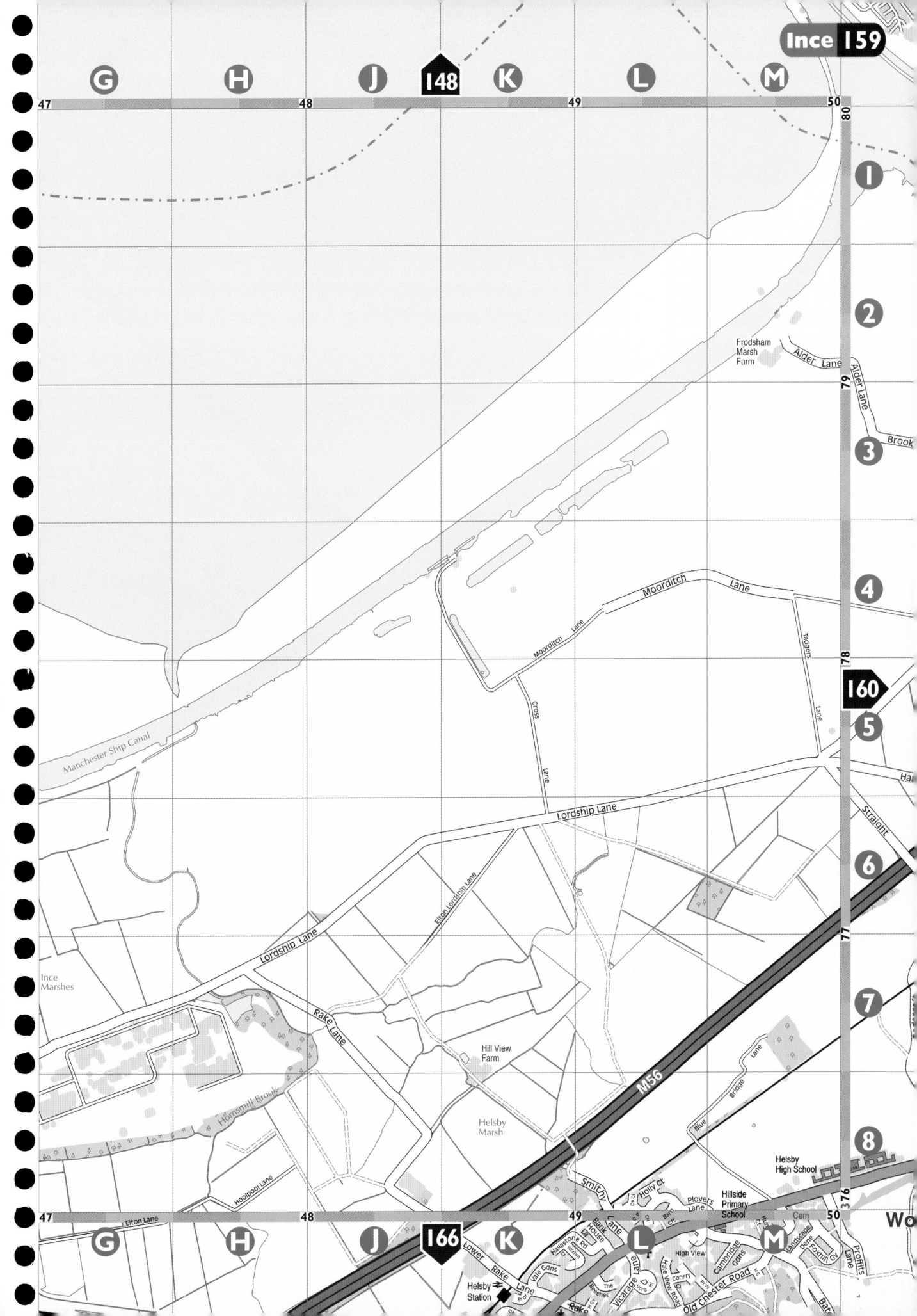

1

2

3

4

160

5

6

7

8

79

78

77

376

Frodsham
Marsh
Farm

Alder Lane

Alder Lane

Brook

Moorditch Lane

Moorditch Lane

Tadgers Lane

Cross Lane

Lordship Lane

Straight

Ha

Manchester Ship Canal

Lordship Lane

Elton Lordship Lane

Lordship Lane

Rake Lane

Ince
Marshes

Hornsmill Brook

Hill View
Farm

Helsby
Marsh

M56

Blue Bridge Lane

Helsby
High School

Hillside
Primary
School

Cem

Wo

Smithy

Holly Ct

Bank
House

Plovers
Lane

High View

Cambridge Gdns

Old Chester Road

Landscape

Foxhill Gv

Profits Lane

Lower Rake Lane

Hallastone Rd

Vale Gdns

Vicarage Lane

Hale View Road

The Beeches

Conery

Rake

Helsby
Station

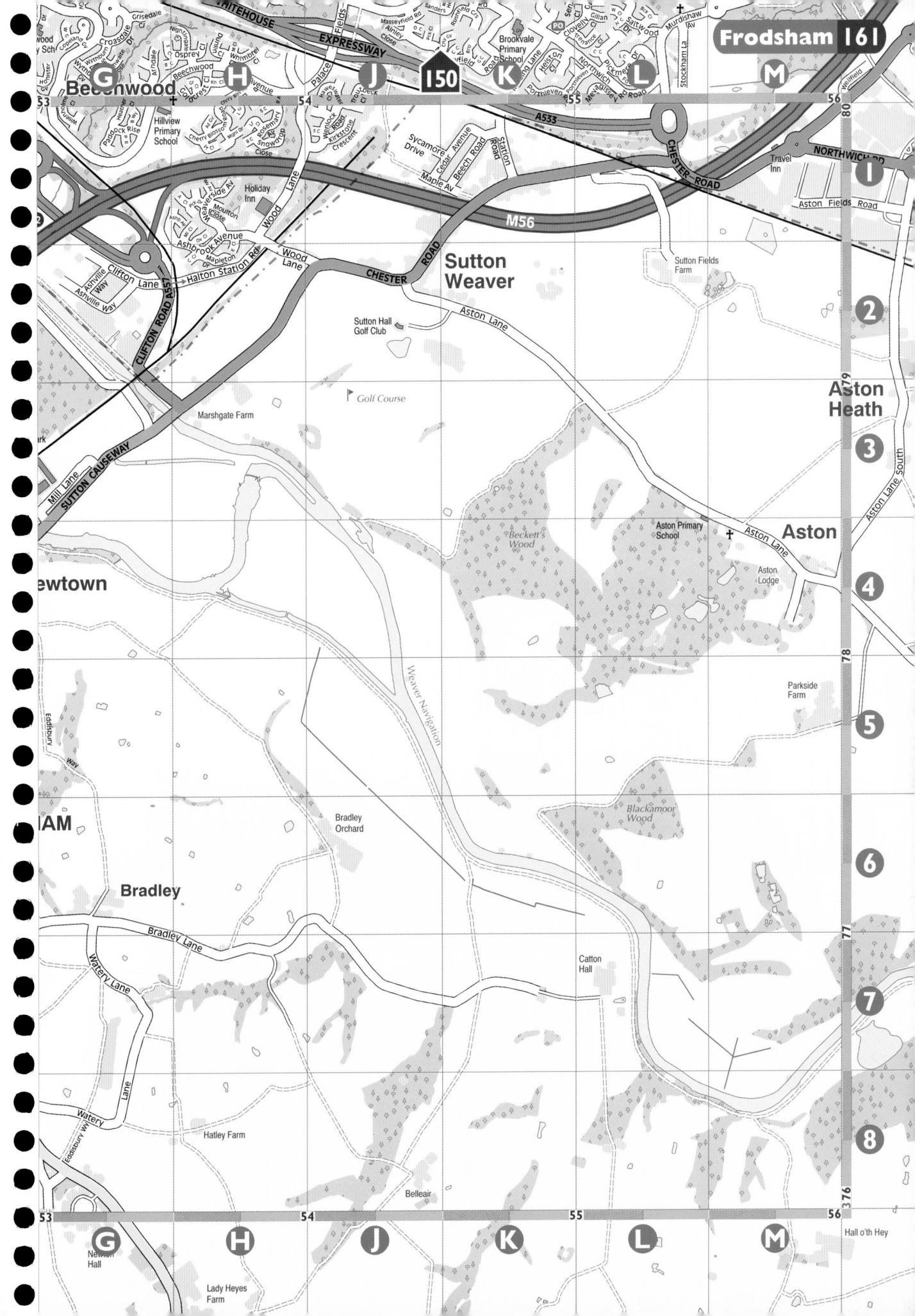

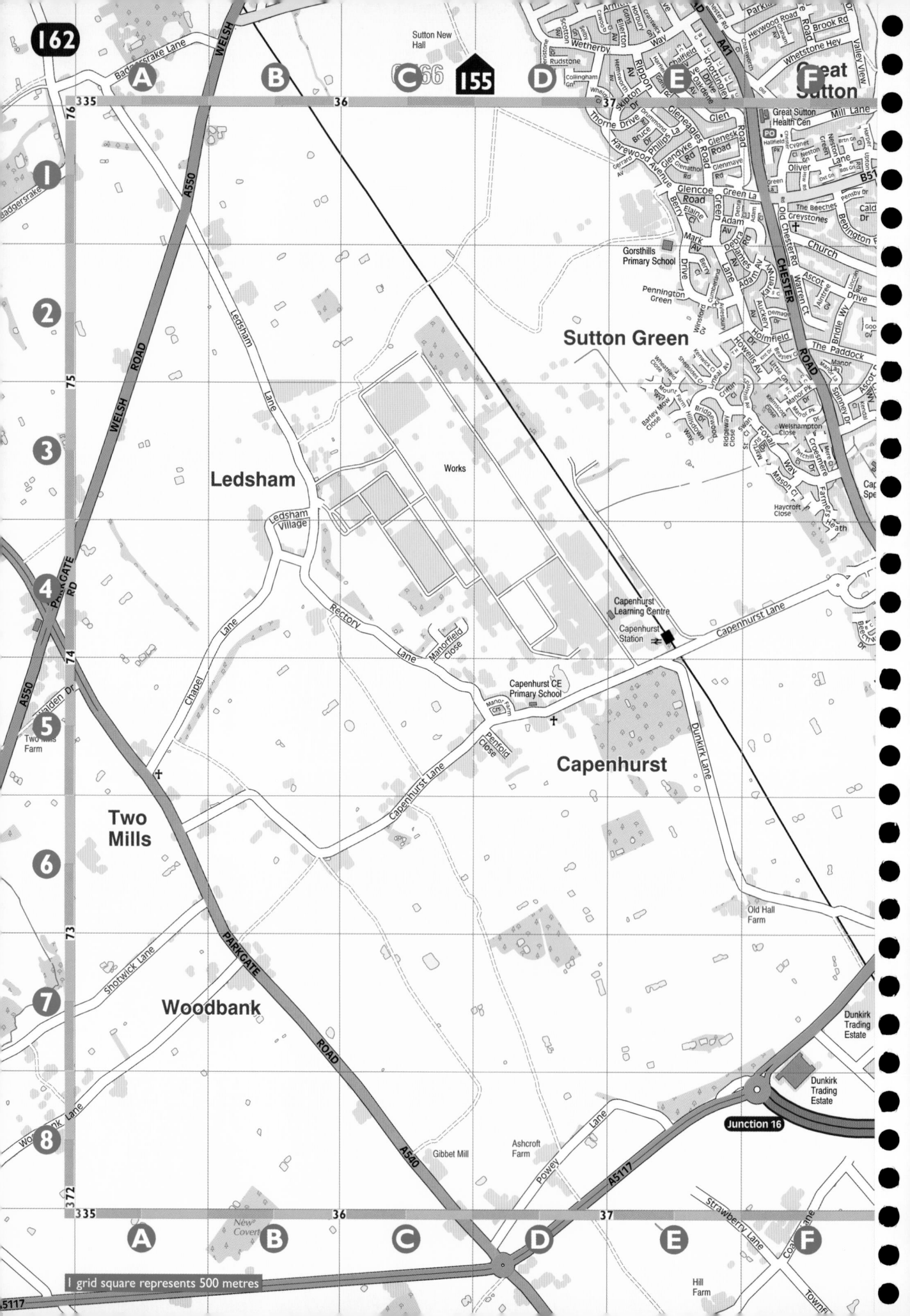

162

A   B   C 66   155   D   E   F eat Sutton

Sutton New Hall

Sutton Green

Ledsham

Works

Ledsham Village

Capenhurst Learning Centre

Capenhurst Station

Capenhurst Lane

Capenhurst CE Primary School

Capenhurst

Two Mills Farm

Two Mills

Woodbank

Old Hall Farm

Dunkirk Trading Estate

Dunkirk Trading Estate

Junction 16

Gibbet Mill

Ashcroft Farm

Hill Farm

Gorsthills Primary School

Pennington Green

Great Sutton Health Cen

The Beeches

Haycroft Close

Farmers Heath

I grid square represents 500 metres

5117

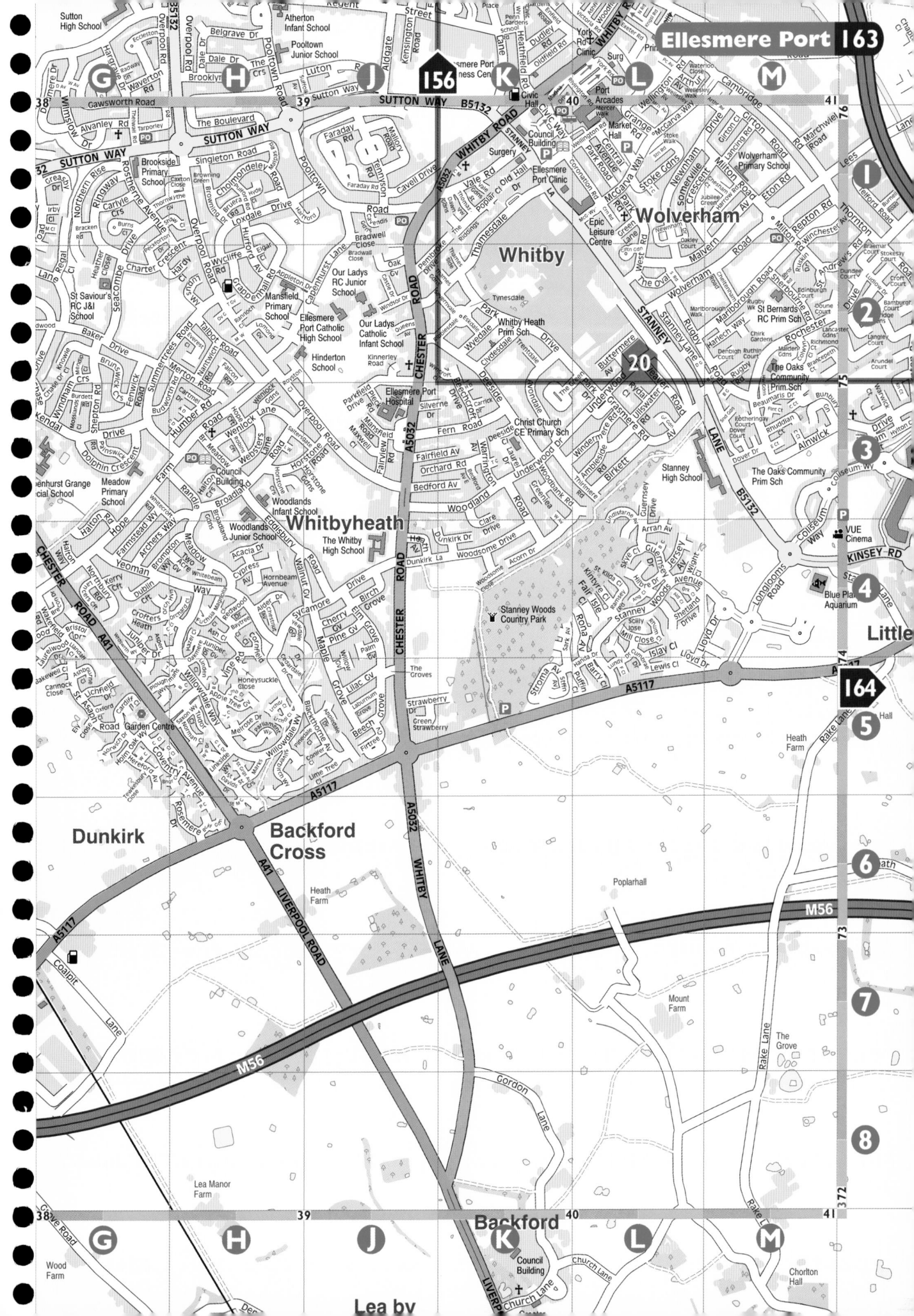

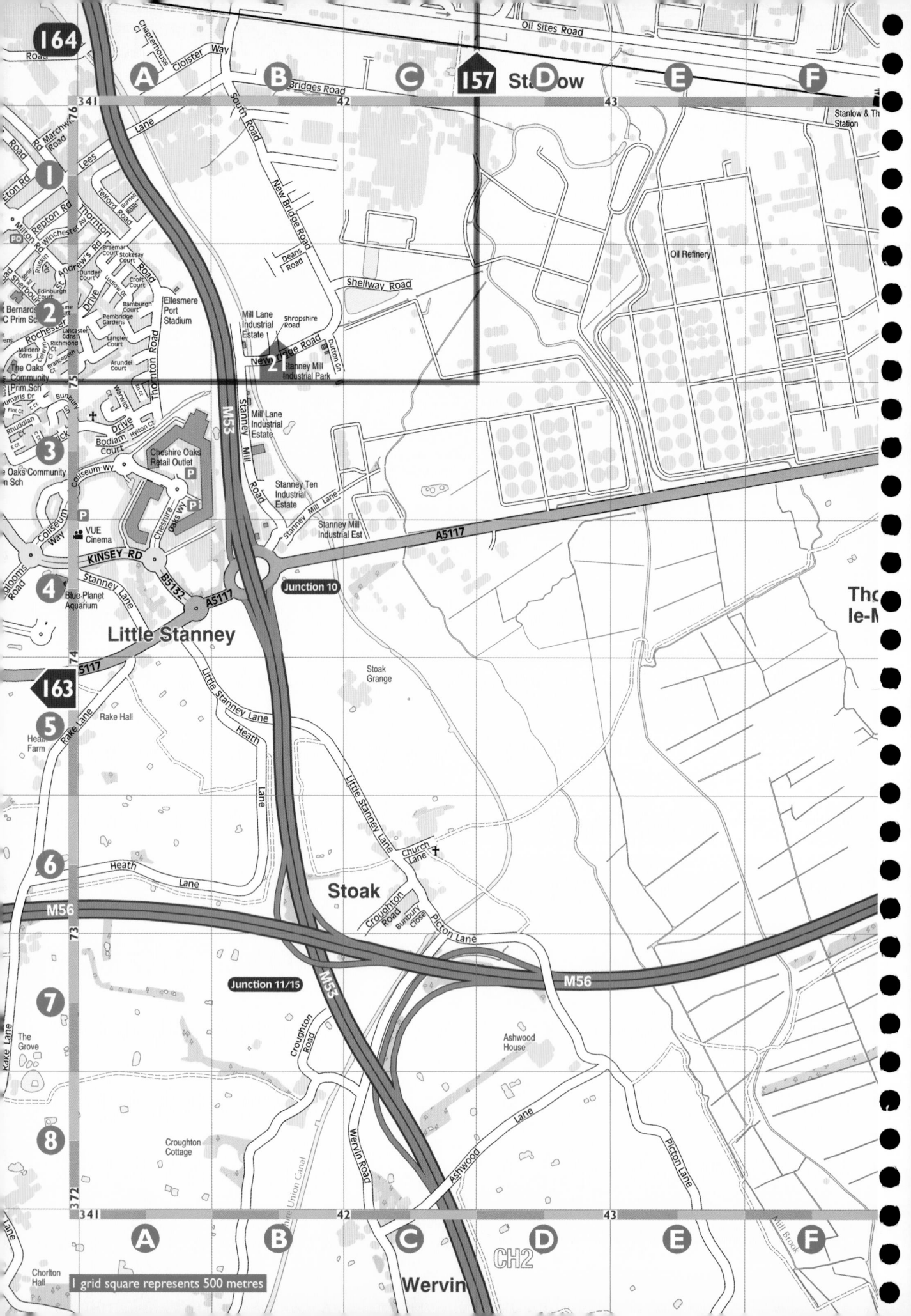

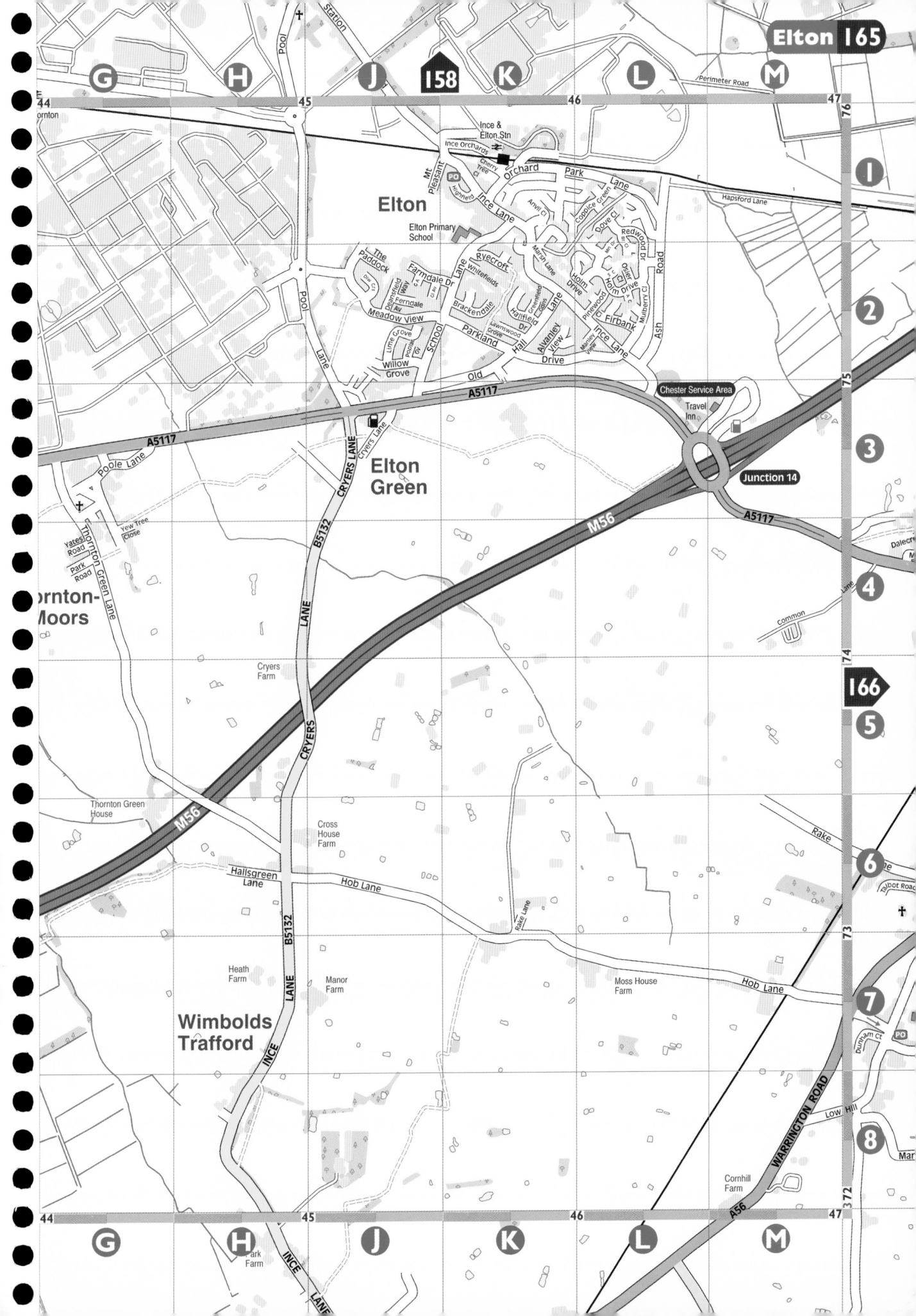

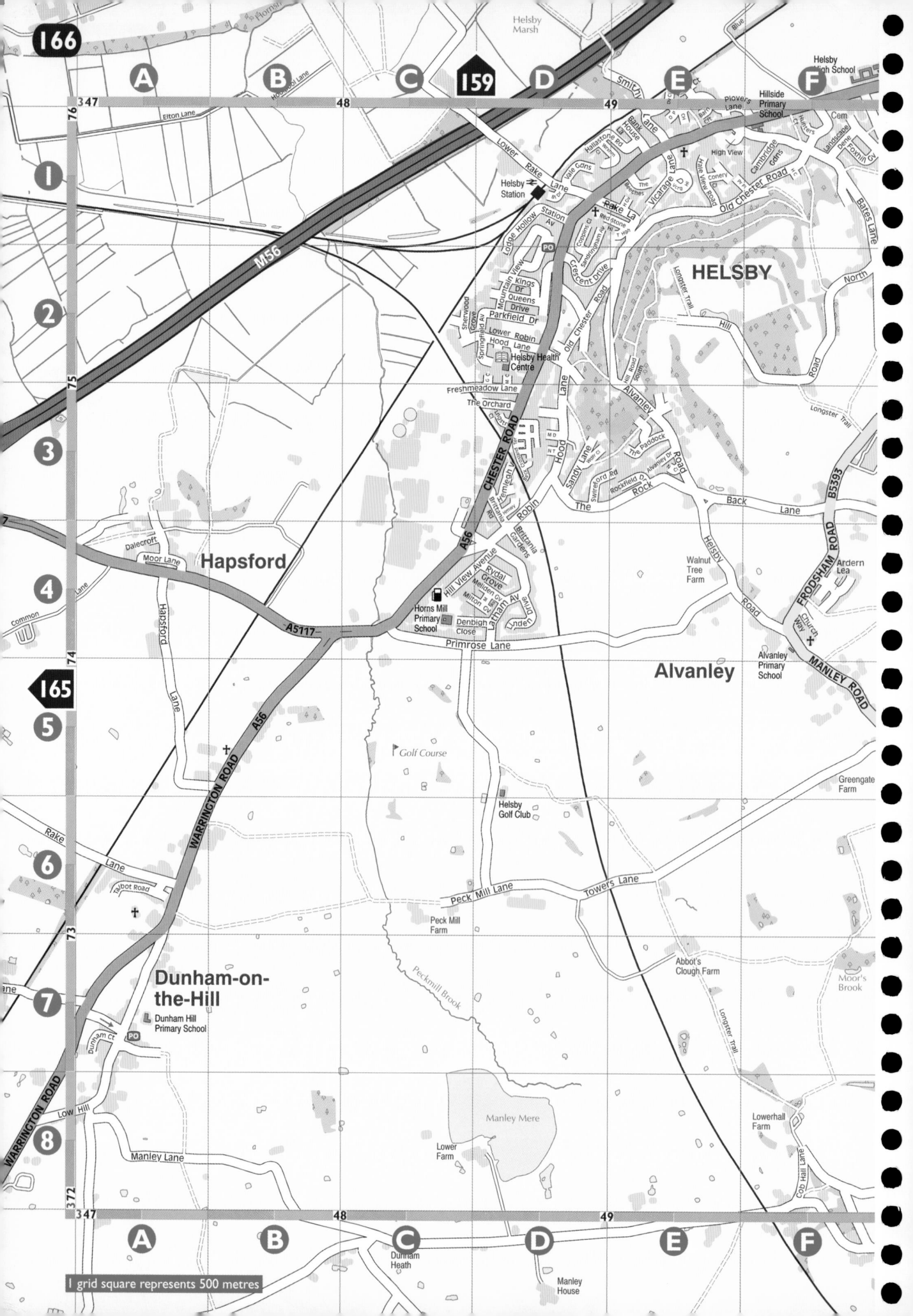

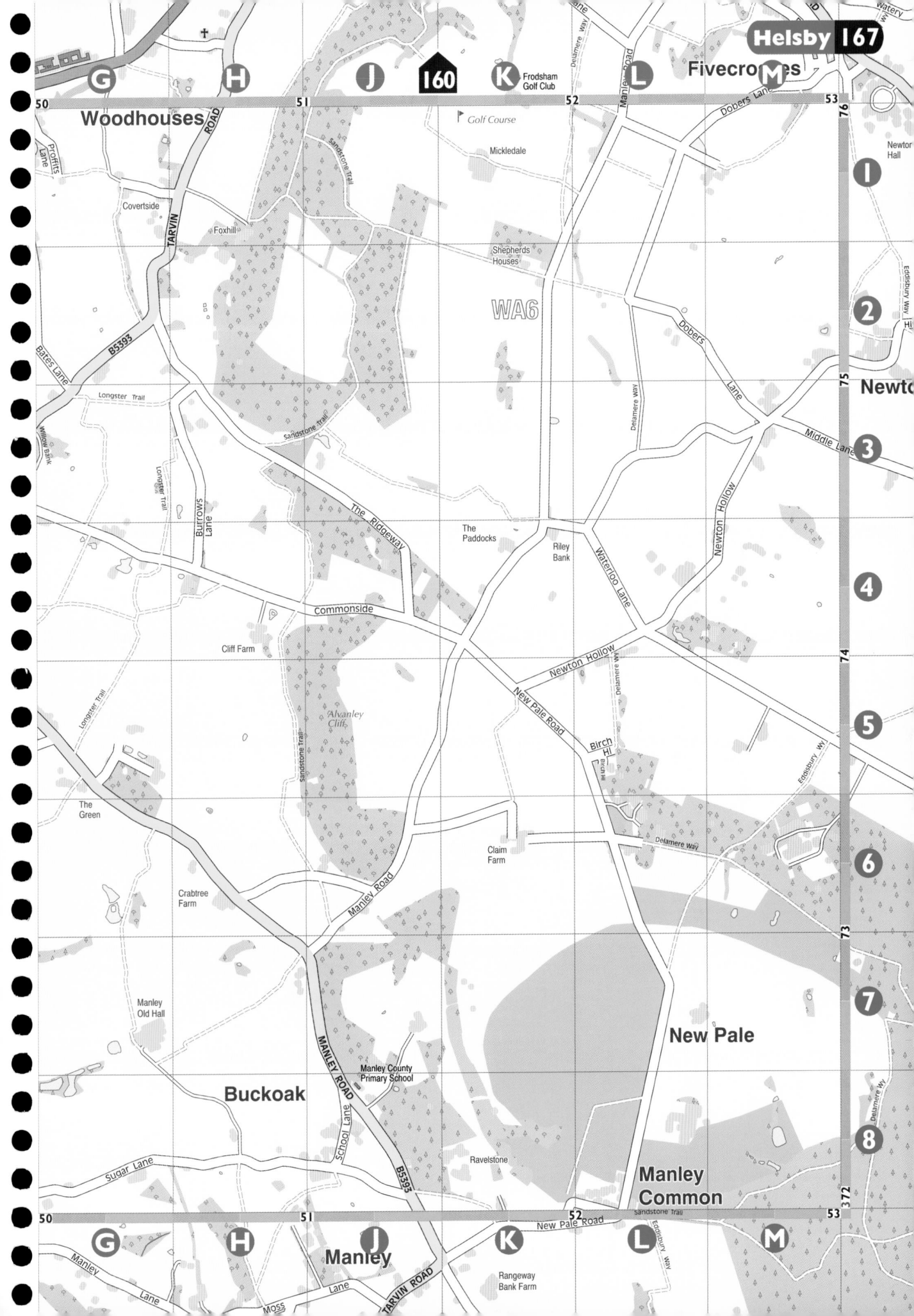

Fivecrosses

Frodsham
Golf Club

Newton
Hall

Newto

Middle Lane

Woodhouses

Profits
Lane

Covertside

Foxhill

TARVIN ROAD

Mickledale

Golf Course

160

WA6

Shepherds
Houses

Bates Lane

B5393

Longster Trail

Willow Bank

Longster Trail

Burrows Lane

Sandstone Trail

Sandstone Trail

The Ridgeway

Dobers Lane

Delamere Way

Delamere Way

Newton Hollow

Waterloo Lane

The Paddocks

Riley
Bank

Commonside

Cliff Farm

Alvanley
Cliff

Longster Trail

Sandstone Trail

Newton Hollow

New Pale Road

Birch
HI

Birch HI

Delamere Wy

Delamere Way

Eddisbury Wy

Eddisbury Way

The
Green

Claim
Farm

Manley Road

Crabtree
Farm

Manley
Old Hall

New Pale

Manley County
Primary School

Buckoak

MANLEY ROAD

School Lane

B5393

Ravelstone

Manley
Common

Sandstone Trail

Sugar Lane

Manley
Lane

Moss
Lane

TARVIN ROAD

Manley

New Pale Road

Rangeway
Bank Farm

G H J K L M

50 51 52 53

Abram	80	E5
Adlington	44	D6
Aigburth	130	B4
Ainsdale	34	A8
Ainsdale-on-Sea	34	A8
Aintree	84	A1
Allerton	131	G4
Alvanley	166	E5
Anderton	44	D5
Andertons Mill	41	H4
Anfield	97	J6
Appleton	134	D3
Appleton Park	137	L8
Appley Bridge	54	E5
Arrowe Hill	126	B2
Ashton-in-Makerfield	91	M2
Ashurst	65	K1
Aspull	57	M8
Aspull Common	93	K4
Astmoor	150	A2
Aston	161	M4
Aston Heath	161	M3
Aughton	62	B6
Aughton Park	63	G3
Backford Cross	163	H6
Ball o' Ditton	134	A4
Bamfurlong	80	A5
Banks	23	H7
Bank Top	66	E1
Barnston	141	L2
Barrow Nook	75	G3
Barrow's Green	134	F1
Barton	49	H7
Bebington	128	E6
Beech Hill	68	B3
Beechwood	150	A8
Belle Vale	115	L8
Bescar	37	J6
Bewsey	121	G5
Bickershaw	81	G5
Bickerstaffe	64	A8
Bidston	110	F4
Bidston Hill	110	F5
Billinge	78	B8
Birch Green	65	L3
Birchwood	123	C1
Birkacre	43	J2
Birkdale	35	H3
Birkenhead	10	D5
Bispham Green	40	E6
Blackbrook	90	C8
Blackbrook	122	A3
Blackford	57	L2
Blaguegate	64	D4
Blowick	25	G7
Blundellsands	82	C1
Boar's Head	56	C7
Bold Heath	119	G6
Bolton Green	31	L5
Bootle	6	C5
Bowker's Green	62	F8
Bowring Park	115	K5
Bradley	161	G6
Brighton le Sands	82	C2
Brimstage	142	D3
Broad Green	114	F3
Broad Oak	103	H1
Bromborough	143	K4
Bromborough Pool	128	F8
Brookhurst	143	K8
Brookvale	150	D8
Brown Edge	36	C3
Brown Edge	101	L6
Brownlow	77	K5
Bruche	122	B6
Bryn	79	H7
Bryn Gates	80	B6
Buckley Hill	83	M1
Buckoak	167	H8
Burscough	51	L3
Burscough Bridge	38	F7
Burtonwood	104	B7
Calderstones	130	E2
Caldy	124	F6
Callands	120	F3
Capenhurst	162	D5
Carr Cross	36	F5
Carr Houses	71	H1
Castlefields	150	B3
Chadwick Green	90	A1
Chapel House	64	F3
Charnock Green	31	K7
Charnock Richard	42	E1
Childer Thornton	155	K5
Childwall	115	H7
Chorley	32	D4
Churchtown	25	K4
Cinnamon Brow	122	C1
Claughton	111	G8
Clifton	160	F1
Clinkham Wood	89	J4
Clock Face	118	F2
Clubmoor	97	L6
Cobbs	137	M5
Collins Green	103	M4
Coppull	42	F4
Coppull Moor	42	F7
Court Hey	115	H4
Cowling	33	G7
Crank	89	G1
Crankwood	80	E8
Crawford	76	E3
Croft	106	D5
Cronton	117	K8
Crooke	67	L2
Crosby	82	D4
Crossens	25	K1
Croston	29	J3
Crow Wood	134	F3
Croxteth	98	F1
Cuerdley Cross	135	J2
Culcheth	107	J2
Dallam	121	H4
Dalton	53	L8
Dangerous Corner	54	E5
Dangerous Corner	81	L3
Daresbury	151	K4
Denton's Green	8	C1
Derbyshire Hill	103	H3
Digmoor	65	L7
Dingle	129	J2
Ditton	133	K6
Doe Green	135	L2
Dog & Gun	98	C2
Dovecot	115	H2
Dover	80	D7
Downall Green	78	B8
Downholland Cross	61	J3
Drummersdale	37	H7
Dudlows Green	138	A8
Dunham-On-The-Hill	166	A4
Dunkirk	163	G6
Earlestown	104	B2
Eastham	144	A7
Eastham Ferry	144	C5
Eccleston	30	D6
Eccleston	88	E8
Eccleston Park	101	J6
Edge Green	92	B2
Edge Hill	113	K5
Egremont	111	L1
Ellesmere Port	20	A3
Elmers Green	65	M2
Elton	165	J1
Elton Green	165	J3
Euxton	31	K3
Everton	97	H8
Fairfield	113	M2
Far Moor	67	G8
Farnworth	134	C2
Fazakerley	84	E8
Fearnhead	122	C3
Fiddler's Ferry	22	F7
Fiddler's Ferry	135	L4
Fincham	99	H7
Firs Lane	81	M8
Fivecrosses	160	E8
Ford	83	L3
Formby	59	G1
Frankby	125	J3
Freshfield	42	A1
Frodsham	160	F6
Garston	130	F8
Garswood	90	D2
Gateacre	131	K1
Gathurst	67	H2
Gayton	141	J7
Gemini	120	F2
Gillar's Green	101	G2
Gillmoss	85	L7
Golborne	92	D6
Goose Green	79	G1
Gorse Covert	107	K7
Grange	19	M9
Grange	124	F4
Grange Park	101	K6
Grappenhall	138	D3
Grassendale	130	C6
Greasby	125	L1
Great Altcar	60	B4
Great Crosby	83	G1
Great Meols	109	H3
Great Sankey	120	D7
Great Sutton	155	M8
Grimeford Village	45	G7
Grimshaw Green	40	D8
Haigh	57	K6
Hale	147	M3
Hale Bank	148	D1
Halewood	132	A5
Hall Green	66	C5
Halsall	49	L4
Halton	150	B5
Halton Brook	149	M4
Halton View	17	H2
Hapsford	166	A4
Haresfinch	89	J6
Hartwood	32	F3
Haskayne	49	G8
Hawkley	79	J2
Haydock	90	F7
Heath	19	G9
Heath Charnock	44	A3
Heaton's Bridge	50	F1
Helsby	166	E2
Hermitage Green	105	K5
Heskin Green	41	M2
Heswall	141	G5
Higher Bebington	127	L7
Higher End	77	L2
Higher Runcorn	19	C6
Higher Walton	137	G6
Highfield	78	E1
High Moor	54	B1
High Park	25	H5
Hightown	70	A2
Hillcliffe	137	L6
Hill Dale	40	F8
Hillside	34	F3
Hinderton	153	J4
Hindley	81	G1
Hindley Green	81	L2
Holland Lees	54	D8
Holmes	27	K2
Holmeswood	27	L7
Holt	101	J8
Holt Green	62	D6
Homer Green	71	L4
Hood Manor	120	E8
Hooton	155	H4
Hoscar	52	F1
Hough Green	133	J4
Houghton Green	106	A8
Houghwood	77	K7
Howley	15	K6
Hoylake	108	E6
Hulme	121	K2
Hunger Hill	55	H2
Hunt's Cross	131	K7
Hurlston Green	50	D2
Huyton	116	B2
Huyton Park	115	L4
Huyton Quarry	116	D3
Huyton-With-Roby	115	L2
Ince	158	C7
Ince Blundell	71	G2
Ince-in-Makerfield	5	K6
Keckwick	151	H1
Kensington	113	J3
Kenyon	106	C1
Kings Moss	77	H6
Kingsway	16	C3
Kingswood	120	C3
Kirkby	86	A4
Kirkdale	96	F5
Kitt Green	68	A6
Knotty Ash	114	F2
Knowsley	99	K1
Lady Green	71	G1
Laffak	90	A6
Lamberhead Green	67	J8
Land Gate	79	J6
Landican	126	E5
Lane Ends	44	F1
Lane Head	93	H7
Latchford	137	L2
Lea Green	102	B8
Leasowe	110	C1
Ledsham	162	B3
Limbrick	33	J8
Lingley Green	119	L6
Lingley Mere	119	M5
Liscard	95	K8
Litherland	83	L4
Little Altcar	59	J4
Little Crosby	70	E5
Little Neston	152	F7
Little Scotland	57	J3
Little Stanney	164	A4
Little Sutton	155	J7
Little Town	106	D3
Liverpool	12	B7
Locking Stumps	122	D1
Longbarn	122	E4
Longford	121	K4
Longshaw	78	A4
Longview	116	B1
Lower Bebington	128	B8
Lower House	134	A5
Lower Walton	137	J5
Lowton	92	F5
Lowton Common	93	J5
Lowton Heath	92	E7
Lowton St Mary's	93	J6
Lugsdale	17	G5
Lunt	71	L5
Lunts Heath	118	C8
Lydiate	61	J8
Maghull	72	F5
Manley Common	167	L8
Marshall's Cross	102	D8
Marsh Green	67	L4
Marsh Green	160	B5
Marshside	25	G2
Martinscroft	122	F6
Marylebone	68	F2
Mawdesley	40	E3
Melling	73	H8
Melling Mount	73	M6
Meols	108	F5
Mere Brow	27	G3
Mere Side	27	K8
Moore	136	C7
Moorside	152	E6
Moreton	110	A4
Moss Bank	17	K4
Moss Bank	89	H4
Mossley Hill	130	A1
Moss Nook	103	H4
Moss Side	73	J2
Moss Side	87	G6
Mossy Lea	42	B7
Murdishaw	151	G6
Ness	153	K8
Neston	152	F6
Netherley	131	M1
Netherton	72	B8
Netherton	160	B7
New Boston	91	H7
New Brighton	95	J5
Newburgh	53	H3
New Ferry	128	E5
Newgate	66	C6
New Houses	78	D4
New Lane	38	D6
New Lane End	106	C3
New Pale	167	L7
New Springs	69	G3
New Springs	69	J4
Newton	125	H3
Newton-le-Willows	104	F2
Newton Park	105	H3
Newtown	30	C3
Newtown	68	A7
Newtown	101	L1
Newtown	160	F4
Noctorum	110	E8
Norris Green	98	B4
Northwood	86	D2
Norton	150	E4
Nut Grove	101	L7
Oakwood	123	G2
Oglet	146	F5
Old Boston	91	K6
Old Swan	114	B2
Orford	121	M4
Ormskirk	50	E8
Orrell	67	J6
Orrell	83	M7
Orrell Post	67	G6
Otterspool	129	M4
Overpool	156	B6
Overton	160	D6
Oxton	127	H2
Paddington	122	D5
Padgate	122	B4
Page Moss	115	K2
Palacefields	150	B8
Parbold	53	M2
Parkgate	152	E4
Park Hill	75	M3
Parr	103	G3
Peasley Cross	102	E4
Pemberton	67	L8
Penketh	135	M1
Pennington	93	M2
Pennylands	64	E5
Pensby	141	H1
Pincock	31	L4
Pinfold	50	B1
Plank Lane	81	K8
Platt Bridge	80	D3
Pocket Nook	93	L5
Poll Hill	141	H4
Pool Hey	36	D2
Poolstock	4	B8
Portico	101	J5
Port Sunlight	128	D8
Poulton	111	J3
Poulton	143	K3
Prenton	127	J4
Prescot	100	D7
Preston Brook	151	H8
Preston on the Hill	151	J7
Primrose Hill	50	D5
Princes Park	113	K7
Raby	153	L1
Rainford	76	C6
Rainford Junction	76	B3
Rainhill	117	M2
Rainhill Stoops	118	A3
Ravenhead	8	C8
Red Rock	56	F5
Ring o' Bells	52	D3
Risley	107	G7
Rivington	45	H3
Robin Hood	54	D1
Roby	115	K3
Roby Mill	66	D2
Rock Ferry	128	C3
Rocksavage	149	K8
Royal Oak	74	B1
Rufford	39	L2
Runcorn	19	K6
Runshaw Moor	31	G1
St Helens	9	H2
St Michael's Hamlet	129	K3
Sandhills	96	E5
Sankey Bridges	136	E1
Saughall Massie	109	K7
Scarisbrick	37	G6
Scarth Hill	63	L3
Scholes	5	H4
Seacombe	111	M4
Seaforth	83	G6
Sefton	72	B6
Sefton Park	129	M1
Shaw Green	30	F3
Shell Green	135	G3
Shevington	55	J8
Shevington Moor	55	J3
Shevington Vale	55	H5
Shirdley Hill	36	B7
Simm's Cross	16	F4
Simm's Lane End	78	C8
Skelmersdale	65	J3
Snape Green	37	G4
Sollom	28	D3
Southdene	86	A5
Southgate	150	A6
Southport	2	C1
Speke	147	G2
Spital	143	L2
Springfield	68	A3
Standish	56	B4
Standish Lower Ground	67	L2
Stanley	65	G2
Stanley Gate	64	A6
Stanlow	157	K8
Statham	139	M1
Stoak	164	B6
Stockbridge Village	99	J5
Stockton Heath	137	L4
Stoneycroft	114	C1
Storeton	127	K8
Stubshaw Cross	79	M8
Sutton	103	G6
Sutton Green	162	D2
Sutton Heath	102	A7
Sutton Leach	103	G8
Sutton Manor	118	C3
Sutton Weaver	161	K2
Swanside	115	H3
Tamer Lane End	81	K5
Tanhouse	65	L5
Tarbock Green	132	E1
Tarlscough	38	F4
Thatto Heath	101	M5
Thelwall	139	G2
Thingwall	126	D8
Thornton	71	L7
Thornton Hough	142	C6
Thornton-le-Moors	164	F4
Thurstaston	125	J8
Toll Bar	101	K4
Tontine	66	F7
Top Lock	69	K3
Tower Hill	74	B8
Town End	117	L7
Town Green	62	F6
Town Green	91	M1
Town of Lowton	92	C8
Town Park	150	D4
Toxteth	113	G8
Tranmere	128	A2
Tuebrook	98	B8
Two Mills	162	A6
Up Holland	66	C7
Upton	110	B8
Upton	133	K3
Upton Rocks	134	A2
Vauxhall	12	D1
Vulcan Village	104	E5
Waddicar	85	J1
Wallasey	112	A1
Wallasey Village	94	E7
Walton	97	K3
Wargrave	104	E4
Warrington	14	C3
Waterloo	82	F3
Waterloo Park	83	H4
Wavertree	114	B6
Weld Bank	32	E8
West Bank	134	B8
Westbrook	120	C4
West Derby	98	E6
Westhead	63	M1
West Kirby	124	B3
Westleigh	81	H6
Weston	149	H6
Weston Point	18	A8
West Park	8	A7
Westvale	85	M3
Westy	122	B8
Whalleys	53	J8
Whelley	5	L1
Whiston	117	G2
Whiston Cross	116	F2
Whiston Lane Ends	116	E3
Whitby	20	B7
Whitbyheath	163	H4
White Coppice	33	M3
Whitefield Lane End	116	D5
Whitley	68	C2
Widnes	16	A5
Wigan	4	C2
Wilderspool	137	L3
Wilderswood	45	M7
Willaston	154	D5
Wimbolds Trafford	165	H7
Windle Hill	153	L6
Windmill Hill	150	E3
Windy Arbor	116	F5
Winstanley	78	E2
Winstanleys	56	E6
Winwick	105	K6
Winwick Quay	121	K1
Wolverham	20	D7
Woodbank	162	A7
Woodchurch	126	E2
Woodhey	128	B6
Woodhouses	167	G1
Woodvale	47	K2
Woolfall Heath	99	L8
Woolston	122	E6
Woolton	131	J4
Worsley Hall	67	L7
Worsley Mesnes	79	H1
Wrightington Bar	42	B5
Wright's Green	138	C8

USING THE STREET INDEX

Street names are listed alphabetically. Each street name is followed by its postal town or area locality, the Postcode District, the page number, and the reference to the square in which the name is found.

Standard index entries are shown as follows:

Abacus Rd *CLB/OSW/ST* L13 ....**114** C1

Street names and selected addresses not shown on the map due to scale restrictions are shown in the index with an asterisk:

Abbeyway North *RNFD/HAY* WA11 * **90** D5

GENERAL ABBREVIATIONS

ACC.....ACCESS	CTYD.....COURTYARD	HLS.....HILLS	MWY.....MOTORWAY	SE.....SOUTH EAST
ALY.....ALLEY	CUTT.....CUTTINGS	HO.....HOUSE	N.....NORTH	SER.....SERVICE AREA
AP.....APPROACH	CV.....COVE	HOL.....HOLLOW	NE.....NORTH EAST	SH.....SHORE
AR.....ARCADE	CYN.....CANYON	HOSP.....HOSPITAL	NW.....NORTH WEST	SHOP.....SHOPPING
ASS.....ASSOCIATION	DEPT.....DEPARTMENT	HRB.....HARBOUR	O/P.....OVERPASS	SKWY.....SKYWAY
AV.....AVENUE	DL.....DALE	HTH.....HEATH	OFF.....OFFICE	SMT.....SUMMIT
BCH.....BEACH	DM.....DAM	HTS.....HEIGHTS	ORCH.....ORCHARD	SOC.....SOCIETY
BLDS.....BUILDINGS	DR.....DRIVE	HVN.....HAVEN	OV.....OVAL	SP.....SPUR
BND.....BEND	DRO.....DROVE	HWY.....HIGHWAY	PAL.....PALACE	SPR.....SPRING
BNK.....BANK	DRY.....DRIVEWAY	IMP.....IMPERIAL	PAS.....PASSAGE	SQ.....SQUARE
BR.....BRIDGE	DWGS.....DWELLINGS	IN.....INLET	PAV.....PAVILION	ST.....STREET
BRK.....BROOK	E.....EAST	IND EST.....INDUSTRIAL ESTATE	PDE.....PARADE	STN.....STATION
BTM.....BOTTOM	EMB.....EMBANKMENT	INF.....INFIRMARY	PH.....PUBLIC HOUSE	STR.....STREAM
BUS.....BUSINESS	EMBY.....EMBASSY	INFO.....INFORMATION	PK.....PARK	STRD.....STRAND
BVD.....BOULEVARD	ESP.....ESPLANADE	INT.....INTERCHANGE	PKWY.....PARKWAY	SW.....SOUTH WEST
BY.....BYPASS	EST.....ESTATE	IS.....ISLAND	PL.....PLACE	TDG.....TRADING
CATH.....CATHEDRAL	EX.....EXCHANGE	JCT.....JUNCTION	PLN.....PLAIN	TER.....TERRACE
CEM.....CEMETERY	EXPY.....EXPRESSWAY	JTY.....JETTY	PLNS.....PLAINS	THWY.....THROUGHWAY
CEN.....CENTRE	EXT.....EXTENSION	KG.....KING	PLZ.....PLAZA	TNL.....TUNNEL
CFT.....CROFT	F/O.....FLYOVER	KNL.....KNOLL	POL.....POLICE STATION	TOLL.....TOLLWAY
CH.....CHURCH	FC.....FOOTBALL CLUB	L.....LAKE	PR.....PRINCE	TPK.....TURNPIKE
CHA.....CHASE	FK.....FORK	LA.....LANE	PREC.....PRECINCT	TR.....TRACK
CHYD.....CHURCHYARD	FLD.....FIELD	LDG.....LODGE	PREP.....PREPARATORY	TRL.....TRAIL
CIR.....CIRCLE	FLDS.....FIELDS	LGT.....LIGHT	PRIM.....PRIMARY	TWR.....TOWER
CIRC.....CIRCUS	FLS.....FALLS	LK.....LOCK	PROM.....PROMENADE	U/P.....UNDERPASS
CL.....CLOSE	FLS.....FLATS	LKS.....LAKES	PRS.....PRINCESS	UNI.....UNIVERSITY
CLFS.....CLIFFS	FM.....FARM	LNDG.....LANDING	PRT.....PORT	UPR.....UPPER
CMP.....CAMP	FT.....FORT	LTL.....LITTLE	PT.....POINT	V.....VALE
CNR.....CORNER	FWY.....FREEWAY	LWR.....LOWER	PTH.....PATH	VA.....VALLEY
CO.....COUNTY	FY.....FERRY	MAG.....MAGISTRATE	PZ.....PIAZZA	VIAD.....VIADUCT
COLL.....COLLEGE	GA.....GATE	MAN.....MANSIONS	QD.....QUADRANT	VIL.....VILLA
COM.....COMMON	GAL.....GALLERY	MD.....MEAD	QU.....QUEEN	VIS.....VISTA
COMM.....COMMISSION	GDN.....GARDEN	MDW.....MEADOWS	QY.....QUAY	VLG.....VILLAGE
CON.....CONVENT	GDNS.....GARDENS	MEM.....MEMORIAL	R.....RIVER	VLS.....VILLAS
COT.....COTTAGE	GLD.....GLADE	MKT.....MARKET	RBT.....ROUNDABOUT	VW.....VIEW
COTS.....COTTAGES	GLN.....GLEN	MKTS.....MARKETS	RD.....ROAD	W.....WEST
CP.....CAPE	GN.....GREEN	ML.....MALL	RDG.....RIDGE	WD.....WOOD
CPS.....COPSE	GND.....GROUND	ML.....MILL	REP.....REPUBLIC	WHF.....WHARF
CR.....CREEK	GRA.....GRANGE	MNR.....MANOR	RES.....RESERVOIR	WK.....WALK
CREM.....CREMATORIUM	GRG.....GARAGE	MS.....MEWS	RFC.....RUGBY FOOTBALL CLUB	WKS.....WALKS
CRS.....CRESCENT	GT.....GREAT	MSN.....MISSION	RI.....RISE	WLS.....WELLS
CSWY.....CAUSEWAY	GTWY.....GATEWAY	MT.....MOUNT	RM.....RAMP	WY.....WAY
CT.....COURT	GV.....GROVE	MTN.....MOUNTAIN	RW.....ROW	YD.....YARD
CTRL.....CENTRAL	HGR.....HIGHER	MTS.....MOUNTAINS	S.....SOUTH	YHA.....YOUTH HOSTEL
CTS.....COURTS	HL.....HILL	MUS.....MUSEUM	SCH.....SCHOOL	

POSTCODE TOWNS AND AREA ABBREVIATIONS

AIG/SPK.....Aigburth/Sefton Park
AIMK.....Ashton-in-Makerfield
AIN/FAZ.....Aintree/Fazakerley
ALL/GAR.....Allerton/Garston
ANF/KKDL.....Anfield/Kirkdale
BBR.....Bamber Bridge
BEB.....Bebington
BIRK.....Birkenhead
BRSC.....Burscough
BTL.....Bootle
CALD/MH.....Calderstones/Mossley Hill
CH/BCN.....Chester/Blacon
CHLDW.....Childwall
CHLY/EC.....Chorley/Eccleston
CHLYE.....Chorley east/
Adlington/Whittle-le-Woods
CHNE.....Chester northeast
CL/PREN.....Claughton/Prenton
CLB/OSW/ST.....Clubmoor/
Old Swan/Stoneycroft
CLVP.....Central Liverpool

CLVPS.....Central Liverpool south
CROS/BRETH.....Croston/Bretherton
CSBY/BLUN.....Crosby/Blundellsands
CSBY/WL.....Crosby/Waterloo
DV/KA/FCH.....Dovecot/
Knotty Ash/Fincham
ECCL.....Eccleston
EHL/KEN.....Edge Hill/Kensington
EP.....Ellesmere Port
EV.....Everton
FMBY.....Formby
FROD/HEL.....Frodsham/Helsby
GOL/RIS/CUL.....Golborne/
Risley/Culcheth
GR/UP/WCH.....Greasby/
Upton/Woodchurch
GTS/LS.....Great Sutton/Little Sutton
HES.....Heswall
HLWD.....Halewood
HOR/BR.....Horwich/Blackrod
HOY.....Hoylake

HTWN.....Hightown
HUY.....Huyton
KIRK/FR/WAR.....Kirkham/
Freckleton/Warton
KKBY.....Kirkby
KNUT.....Knutsford
LEIGH.....Leigh
LEYL.....Leyland
LITH.....Litherland
LYMM.....Lymm
MGHL.....Maghull
MOR/LEA.....Moreton/Leasowe
NEWLW.....Newton-le-Willows
NG/CROX.....Norris Green/Croxteth
NPK/KEN..Newsham Park/Kensington
NSTN.....Neston
NTHLY.....Netherley
NTHTN.....Netherton
NWD/KWIPK.....Northwood/
Knowsley Industrial Park
ORM.....Ormskirk

PEN/TH.....Pensby/Thingwall
PR/KW.....Prescot/Knowsley
PS/BROM.....Port Sunlight/
Bromborough
RAIN/WH.....Rainhill/Whiston
RF/TRAN.....Rock Ferry/Tranmere
RNFD/HAY.....Rainford/Haydock
RUNC.....Runcorn
SFTN.....Sefton
SKEL.....Skelmersdale
SPK/HALE.....Speke/Hale
STBRV.....Stockbridge Village
STHEL.....St Helens
STHP.....Southport
TOX.....Toxteth
VAUX/LVPD..Vauxhall/Liverpool Docks
WAL/EG.....Wallasey/Egremont
WAL/NB.....Wallasey/New Brighton
WARR.....Warrington
WARRN/WOL..Warrington north/
Wooliston

WARRS.....Warrington south
WARRW/BUR.....Warrington west/
Burtonwood
WAV.....Wavertree
WD/CROXPK.....West Derby/
Croxteth Park
WDN.....Widnes
WGN.....Wigan
WGNE/HIN.....Wigan east/Hindley
WGNNW/ST.....Wigan northwest/
Standish
WGNS/IIMK.....Wigan south/
Ince-in-Makerfield
WGNW/BIL/OR.....Wigan west/
Billinge/Orrell
WHTN.....Westhoughton
WKBY.....West Kirby
WLT/FAZ.....Walton/Fazakerley
WLTN.....Woolton

3rd St WGNE/HIN WN2.....80 A6
4th St WGNE/HIN WN2.....80 B6

A

Abacus Rd CLB/OSW/ST L13.....114 C1
Abberley Cl ECCL WA10.....8 E5
Abberley Rd WLTN L25.....131 M6
Abberley Wy WGNS/IIMK WN3.....78 D1
Abberton Pk NTHTN L30.....72 C8
Abbey Cl BIRK CH41.....11 L7
  FMBY L37.....59 K5
  GOL/RIS/CU WA3.....107 M6
  NWD/KWIPK L33.....86 B3
  SKEL WN8.....66 E6
  WDN WA8.....133 L5
Abbey Ct WGNNW/ST WN6.....68 A3
  WLTN L25.....131 K3
Abbey Dl BRSC L40.....52 B2
  WGNNW/ST WN6.....54 F6
Abbey Dr WGNW/BIL/O WN5.....67 G7
Abbeyfield Dr WD/CROXPK L12.....98 F3
Abbeyfields WGNNW/ST WN6.....68 A3
Abbey Fold BRSC L40.....38 F8
Abbey Gdns STHP PR8.....38 J1
Abbey Gv CHLYE PR6.....44 C6
Abbey Hey RUNC WA7.....150 E5
Abbey La BRSC L40.....51 L5
  LEIGH WN7.....81 M4
Abbey Rd ECCL WA10.....89 G6
  GOL/RIS/CU WA3.....93 L5
  RNFD/HAY WA11.....91 C6
  WDN WA8.....133 K5
  WKBY CH48.....124 D3
Abbey Sq LEIGH WN7.....81 M4
Abbeystead SKEL WN8.....65 K6
Abbeystead Av NTHTN L30.....84 C4
Abbeystead Rd WAV L15.....114 D5
Abbey St BIRK CH41.....11 L7
Abbeyvale Dr NTHLY L27.....115 L7
Abbey Vw CHLDW L16.....115 G6
Abbeyway North
  RNFD/HAY WA11 *.....90 D5
  RNFD/HAY WA11.....91 H6
Abbeyway South
  RNFD/HAY WA11.....91 J7
Abbeywood Gv RAIN/WH L35.....117 H3
Abbingdon Wy LEIGH WN7.....81 M4
Abbot Cl CL/PREN CH43.....110 E7
Abbotsbury Wy WD/CROXPK L12..99 G2
Abbots Cl FMBY L37.....59 J4
Abbots Dr BEB CH63.....128 B8
Abbotsfield Cl WARRS WA4.....138 A7

Abbotsfield Rd STHEL WA9.....103 G8
Abbotsford ORM L39.....51 H8
Abbotsford Rd GOL/RIS/CU WA3..92 F4
Abbotsford Gdns
  CSBY/BLUN L23.....82 E2
Abbotsford St CSBY/BLUN L23..82 E2
  NG/CROX L11.....98 A3
Abbotshey Av CALD/MH L18.....130 D2
  RUNC WA7.....19 H8
Abbots Hall Av STHEL WA9.....118 F2
Abbots Ms EP CH65.....20 B2
Abbott Dr BTL L20 *.....84 A8
Abbotts Cl CALD/MH L18.....130 D2
  RUNC WA7.....19 H8
Abbotts St WGNE/HIN WN2.....69 L7
Abbotts Wy WGNW/BIL/O WN5..89 M2
Abdale Rd NG/CROX L11.....98 B2
Abercrombie Rd
  NWD/KWIPK L33.....86 D6
Abercromby Sq EHL/KEN L7.....13 M8
Aberdale Rd CLB/OSW/ST L13..114 D2
Aberdare Cl WARRW/BUR WA5..121 G4
Aberdeen St BIRK CH41.....10 F4
Aberford Av WAL/NB CH45.....95 C8
Abergele Rd CLB/OSW/ST L13....114 B3
Aber St NPK/KEN L6.....113 J3
Abingdon Av WARR WA1.....123 C6
Abingdon Gv ANF/KKDL L4.....97 L3
  HLWD L26.....132 C4
Abingdon Rd ANF/KKDL L4.....97 L3
  GR/UP/WCH CH49.....125 K2
Abinger Rd AIMK WN4.....90 F1
Abington Dr CHTN/BK PR9.....23 J8
  WGNE/HIN WN2.....80 C4
Abney Cl EHL/KEN L7.....113 K5
Aboyne Cl WGNE/HIN WN2.....97 J1
Abrams Fold CHTN/BK PR9.....23 H8
Abrams Gn CHTN/BK PR9.....23 H8
Abram St EV L5.....96 F7
Abratio St BIRK CH41.....11 G6
Abstone Cl WARR WA1.....122 F4
Abyssinia Cl WAV L15 *.....114 A6
Acacia Av HUY L36.....115 M4
  WARR WA1.....122 F5
  WDN WA8.....134 D2
Acacia Cl CHNE CH2.....165 L2
  GTS/LS CH66.....165 H4
Acacia Crs WGNNW/ST WN6.....68 F3
Acacia Dr ECCL WA10.....101 J1
  RUNC WA7.....19 M8
  WAL/EG CH44.....112 A3
  WKBY CH48.....124 C3
  WLT/FAZ L9.....84 D7
Acacia Gv NEWLW WA12.....104 A1
Acacia St NEWLW WA12.....104 A1
Acacia Wy WARR WA1.....14 E7

Acanthus Rd CLB/OSW/ST L13.....114 C1
Access Rd WD/CROXPK L12 *.....98 F6
Acer Leigh ALL/SPK L17.....129 M4
Acheson Rd CLB/OSW/ST L13....98 A7
Achilles Av WARRN/WOL WA2....121 K3
Ackerley Cl WARRN/WOL WA2....122 B2
Ackers Hall Av DV/KA/FCH L14..115 H1
Ackers Hall Cl DV/KA/FCH L14...99 H8
Ackers La ECCL WA10.....101 L1
  HTWN L38.....70 E6
  WARRS WA4.....138 A4
Ackers Rd GR/UP/WCH CH49.....126 E3
  WARRS WA4.....138 A4
Acland Rd WAL/EG CH44 *.....111 K1
Aconbury Cl NG/CROX L11.....98 B2
Aconbury Pl NG/CROX L11.....98 B2
Acorn Cl BEB CH63.....127 M7
  STHEL WA9 *.....118 E1
Acorn Ct TOX L8.....113 H7
Acorn Dr EP CH65.....163 K4
Acornfield Cl NWD/KWIPK L33...86 E5
Acornfield Rd NWD/KWIPK L33...86 F4
Acorn St NEWLW WA12.....104 E2
Acorn Wy BTL L20.....5 M8
  VAUX/LVPD L3.....13 C4
  WGNS/IIMK WN3.....4 D5
Addison Cl KKBY L32.....85 M5
Addison Sq WDN WA8.....16 C1
Addison St BTL L20.....83 J8
  VAUX/LVPD L3.....13 G4
Addison Wy VAUX/LVPD L3.....13 G4
Adelaide Av STHEL WA9.....102 A6
Adelaide Pl EV L5.....13 J1
  WLTN L25.....131 J2
Adelaide Rd EHL/KEN L7.....113 L1
  LITH L21.....83 H6
  RF/TRAN CH42.....127 L1
Adelaide St CHLYE PR6.....44 C5
Adelaide Ter CSBY/WL L22.....82 E4
Adela Rd RUNC WA7.....18 E4
Adele Thompson Dr TOX L8.....113 J6
Adelphi St BIRK CH41.....11 K4
  WGNNW/ST WN6.....4 E2
Adfalent La NSTN CH64.....154 C6
Adkins St EV L5 *.....97 J7
Adlam Crs WLT/FAZ L9.....85 G6
Adlam Rd AIN/FAZ L10.....85 G6
Adlington Ct GOL/RIS/CU WA3..107 H8
Adlington Rd RUNC WA7.....150 E3
Adlington St VAUX/LVPD L3.....13 G4
Admin Rd NWD/KWIPK L33.....86 E5
Admiral Gv TOX L8.....113 J8
Admiral Rd CLB/OSW/ST L13.....98 A6
Admiral St TOX L8.....113 H8
Admiralty Cl BRSC L40 *.....51 L3
Adrian's Wy KKBY L32.....86 A3
Adshead Rd CLB/OSW/ST L13.....98 A6
Adstone Rd HUY L36.....116 A2
Adswood Rd HUY L36.....116 B8
Adwell Cl GOL/RIS/CU WA3.....93 J5
Africander Rd RNFD/HAY WA11..89 J5

Acuba Rd WAV L15.....114 E4
Adair Pl CLB/OSW/ST L13.....98 A6
Adair Rd CLB/OSW/ST L13.....98 A6
Adam Av GTS/LS CH66.....162 E2
Adam Cl ALL/GAR L19.....130 E8
  GTS/LS CH66.....162 F1
Adams Cl NEWLW WA12.....104 F3
Adams Dr WGNS/IIMK WN3.....4 B8
Adamson Ct WARRS WA4.....138 D3
Adamson St AIMK WN4.....91 J2
  EHL/KEN L7.....113 M5
  WARRS WA4.....14 E9
Adam St EV L5.....97 H7
  WARRN/WOL WA2.....15 C1
Adaston Av PS/BROM CH62.....155 H1
Ada St STHEL WA9.....9 L9
Adcote Cl DV/KA/FCH L14.....115 H2
Adcote Rd DV/KA/FCH L14.....115 H2
Adderley Cl RUNC WA7.....19 L6
Adderley St EHL/KEN L7.....113 K3
Addingham Av WDN WA8.....13 L8
Addingham Rd CALD/MH L18.....114 D8
Addington St WAL/EG CH44.....111 M2
Addison Av RNFD/HAY WA11....90 B2

Afton WDN WA8.....133 J3
Agar Rd NG/CROX L11.....98 B6
Agate St NPK/KEN L6.....97 J8
Agincourt Rd WD/CROXPK L12...98 E8
Agnes Gv WAL/EG CH44.....95 L8
Agnes Rd CSBY/BLUN L23.....82 E2
  RF/TRAN CH42.....127 M2
Agnes St STHEL WA9.....118 E2
Agnes Wy EHL/KEN L7.....113 K4
Aiden Long Gv PR/KW L34.....100 A7
Aigburth Dr AIG/SPK L17.....113 L8
Aigburth Hall Av ALL/GAR L19...130 C5
Aigburth Hall Rd ALL/GAR L19...130 C5
Aigburth Rd AIG/SPK L17.....129 K2
Aigburth St TOX L8.....113 K5
Aigburth V AIG/SPK L17.....130 A3
Ailsa Rd WAL/NB CH45.....95 J8
Ainley Cl RUNC WA7.....150 C8
Ainscough Rd GOL/RIS/CU WA3..123 G2
Ainsdale Cl AIN/FAZ L10.....85 H5
  BEB CH63.....143 L8
  PEN/TH CH61.....126 C8
  WARRW/BUR WA5.....136 B1
Ainsdale Rd BTL L20.....83 M8
Ainse Rd HOR/BR BL6.....57 K2
Ainsworth Av MOR/LEA CH46....109 L7
Ainsworth La PR/KW L34.....86 D7
Ainsworth Rd ECCL WA10.....8 B2
Ainsworth St VAUX/LVPD L3.....13 K7
Aintree Barracks WLT/FAZ L9 *..84 E8
Aintree Cl MOR/LEA CH46.....110 B2
Aintree Crs STHP PR8.....36 B2
Aintree Gv GTS/LS CH66.....162 E2
Aintree La AIN/FAZ L10.....84 E3
Aintree Rd BTL L20.....7 M2
  WLT/FAZ L9.....84 F3
Aintree Wy WLT/FAZ L9.....84 E3
Airdale Cl CL/PREN CH43.....110 E3
Airdale Rd WAV L15.....114 B7
Airdrie Cl PS/BROM CH62.....154 F1
Aire WDN WA8.....133 K3
Aire Cl EP CH65.....156 C3
Airedale Cl WARRW/BUR WA5..120 B6
Airegate MGHL L31.....72 D3
Airlie Gv CLB/OSW/ST L13.....98 M7
Airlie Rd HOY CH47.....108 D7
Airton Pl WGNS/IIMK WN3.....79 J3
Aisthorpe Gv MGHL L31.....72 F6
Ajax Av WARRN/WOL WA2.....121 J3
The Akbar HES CH60.....140 E4
Akenside Ct LITH L21 *.....83 J7
Akenside St BTL L20.....83 J7
Alabama Wy BIRK CH41.....11 M6
Alamein Crs WARRN/WOL WA2...14 F1
Alamein Rd HUY L36.....115 M1
Alance Br CHLYE PR6.....45 H1
Alastair Crs CL/PREN CH43.....127 H4
Alban Rd CHLDW L16.....114 F5
Albany Av PR/KW L34.....101 H6

Albany Ct CHLYE PR6 ...33 G5
Albany Crs LYMM WA13 * ...139 M1
Albany Gdns CLB/LS CH66 ...155 L6
Albany Gv LYMM WA13 ...139 L1
Albany Rd CLB/OSW/ST L13 ...114 C1
 EHL/KEN L7 ...113 J3
 LYMM WA13 ...139 L2
 PR/KW L34 ...101 G7
 RF/TRAN CH42 ...128 A3
 STHP PR8 ...2 D4
 WLT/FAZ L9 ...84 D6
Albany Ter RUNC WA7 ...19 G4
The Albany VAUX/LVPD L3 * ...12 E6
Albemarle Rd WAL/EC CH44 ...111 M2
Alberta Gv PR/KW L34 ...100 B8
Albert Colliery Est
 WGNE/HIN WN2 * ...81 H5
Albert Dr BTL L20 ...84 B7
 NSTN CH64 ...152 F6
 WARRW/BUR WA5 ...119 M7
Albert Edward Rd EHL/KEN L7 ...113 J3
Albert Gv CLB/OSW/ST L13 * ...82 F1
 WAV L15 ...113 J4
Alberton Cl WGNE/HIN WN2 ...57 L7
Albert Pk AIG/SPK L17 ...113 K8
Albert Pl STHP PR8 ...3 G2
Albert Rd BRSC L40 ...39 J2
 CHTN/BK PR9 ...3 K1
 CLB/OSW/ST L13 ...97 M7
 CSBY/WL L22 ...82 F4
 FMBY L37 ...58 D5
 HOY CH47 ...108 D7
 RF/TRAN CH42 ...127 L1
 WARRS WA4 ...138 C3
 WDN WA8 ...16 F2
 WKBY CH48 ...124 C4
Albert Schweitzer Av NTHTN L30..84 B2
Albert Sq WDN WA8 ...16 E3
Albert St AIMK WN4 ...91 K2
 CHLY/EC PR7 ...32 F6
 ECCL WA10 ...9 G2
 EHL/KEN L7 ...113 J4
 RUNC WA7 ...19 G4
 WGNE/HIN WN2 ...69 M8
 WGNW/BIL/O WN5 ...68 B7
Albert Ter STHP PR8 ...2 F8
Albion Dr WGNE/HIN WN2 * ...69 K3
Albion Pl WAL/NB CH45 ...95 K5
Albion St BIRK CH41 ...11 L6
 CHLY/EC PR7 ...32 E6
 ECCL WA10 ...8 E4
 EV L5 ...97 G5
 WAL/NB CH45 ...95 J5
 WGNE/HIN WN2 ...69 K3
 WGNW/BIL/O WN5 ...80 C5
Albourne Rd KKBY L32 ...86 C5
Albury Cl RNFD/HAY WA11 ...90 E6
 WD/CROXPK L12 ...99 H5
Albury Rd KKBY L32 ...86 B6
Albury Wy RNFD/HAY WA11 ...69 H3
Alcester Rd WD/CROXPK L12..98 E7
Alcock St RUNC WA7 ...19 H2
Alcott Pl WARRN/WOL WA2 ...105 J7
Aldams Gv ANF/KKDL L4 ...7 L9
Aldbourne Av CALD/MH L18 ...115 G8
Aldbourne Cl WLTN L25 ...131 G1
Aldcliffe GOL/RIS/CU WA3 ...93 H6
Alder Av WDN WA4 ...79 H8
 HUY L36 ...116 C5
 WDN WA8 ...134 C2
 WGNW/BIL/O WN5 ...67 M8
 WGNW/BIL/O WN5 * ...77 M8
Alderbank Rd
 WARRW/BUR WA5 ...120 C7
Alderbrook Dr SKEL WN8 ...53 L3
Alder Cl PR/KW L34 ...101 H7
Alder Crs KKBY L32 ...85 M2
Alderdale Av STHP PR8 ...34 C8
Alder Dr CHLY/EC PR7 ...42 F2
 GTS/LS CH66 ...163 H4
Alderfield Dr SPK/HALE L24..147 J3
Alder Gv CHLY/EC PR7 ...43 H4
 CSBY/WL L22 ...82 F3
Alder Hey Rd ECCL WA10 ...101 L1
Alder La FROD/HEL WA6 ...159 M2
 ORM L39 ...48 A5
 PR/KW L34 ...99 K3
 RNFD/HAY WA11 ...77 H8
 SKEL WN8 ...54 D1
 WARRN/WOL WA2 ...121 K5
 WARRW/BUR WA5 ...104 C6
 WDN WA8 ...118 D3
Alder Lee Cl WGNS/IIMK WN3 ...78 F3
Alderley SKEL WN8 ...64 B3
Alderley Av BIRK CH41 ...111 H6
 GOL/RIS/CU WA3 ...92 F6
Alderley Rd HOY CH47 ...108 D6
 WAL/EC CH44 ...111 K2
 WARRS WA4 ...138 F1
Alderney Cl EP CH65 ...163 L4
Alderney Dr WGNS/IIMK WN3 ...79 J2
Alderney Rd EV L5 ...96 F8
Alder Rd BEB CH63 ...142 F1
 GOL/RIS/CU WA3 ...93 H5
 PR/KW L34 ...101 H7
 WARR WA1 ...122 F6
 WD/CROXPK L12 ...114 D1
Alder Root La
 WARRN/WOL WA2 ...104 A4
Aldersey Rd RUNC WA7 ...150 F4
Aldersey St WLTN L25 ...13 H3
Aldersgate RF/TRAN CH42 ...128 D8
Aldersgate Av RUNC WA7 ...150 F6
Aldersgate Dr HLWD L26 ...132 C7
Alderson Crs FMBY L37 ...59 H1
Alderson Rd WAV L15 ...113 M6
The Alders WGNNW/ST WN6 ...67 M1
Alder St NEWLW WA12 ...104 F2
Alderton Dr AIMK WN4 ...91 J2
Alderville Rd ANF/KKDL L4 ...97 L3
Alder Wood Av SPK/HALE L24..147 J5
Alderwood Cl GOL/RIS/CU WA3 ...107 J7
Aldford Cl BEB CH63 ...143 K7
 CL/PREN CH43 ...127 G3
Aldford Rd KKBY L32 ...86 A6
Aldford Wy WGNNW/ST WN6 ...56 A5
Aldgate EP CH65 ...156 C8
Aldred St WGNE/HIN WN2 ...80 F1
Aldridge Cl WD/CROXPK L12 ...99 G2
 WGNS/IIMK WN3 ...79 K2
Aldridge Dr WARRW/BUR WA5 ...104 B6
Aldrins La NTHTN L30 ...84 B1
Aldwark Rd DV/KA/FCH L14..115 J1
Aldwych Rd WD/CROXPK L12 ...98 E7
Aldykes MGHL L31 ...73 G5
Alexander Cl BRSC L40 ...52 B2
Alexander Dr MGHL L31 ...72 F2
 PEN/TH CH61 ...141 G2
 WDN WA8 ...133 M5
Alexander Fleming Av
 NTHTN L30 ...84 B1
Alexander Gv RUNC WA7 ...19 G4
Alexander Wk ANF/KKDL L4 ...97 H5
Alexandra Cl NPK/KEN L6 ...113 K2
 SKEL WN8 ...65 G5
Alexandra Crs
 WGNW/BIL/O WN5 ...68 A7
Alexandra Dr AIG/SPK L17 ...129 K1

 BTL L20 ...84 A7
 ECCL WA10 ...8 B9
 RF/TRAN CH42 ...128 A4
Alexandra Gn AIG/SPK L17 ...129 K1
Alexandra Ms CHTN/BK PR9 ...3 K1
 ORM L39 ...51 G7
Alexandra Mt LITH L21 ...83 K5
Alexandra Pk AIG/SPK L17 ...129 K2
Alexandra Rd AIMK WN4 ...91 K1
 BRSC L40 ...51 M1
 CHTN/BK PR9 ...3 K1
 CL/PREN CH43 ...10 E7
 CLB/OSW/ST L13 ...97 M7
 CSBY/BLUN L23 ...82 F1
 CSBY/WL L22 ...83 G5
 EHL/KEN L7 ...113 L5
 FMBY L37 ...58 D5
 WAL/NB CH45 ...95 J3
 WARRS WA4 ...137 M4
 WDN WA8 ...124 C4
Alexandra St ECCL WA10 ...101 M4
 EP CH65 ...20 C1
 WARR WA1 ...15 L2
 WDN WA8 ...15 J3
 WGNE/HIN WN2 ...80 C5
 WGNW/BIL/O WN5 ...68 B7
Alexandria Rd ALL/GAR L19 ...130 E6
Alex Cl TOX L8 ...113 H7
Alfonso Rd ANF/KKDL L4 ...96 F5
Alford Av STHEL WA9 ...118 D1
Alforde St WDN WA8 ...16 D6
Alford St EHL/KEN L7 ...114 A3
Alfred Cl WDN WA8 ...16 E4
Alfred Ms CLVPS L1 ...113 G6
Alfred Rd CL/PREN CH43 ...127 J1
 GOL/RIS/CU WA3 ...93 J5
 RNFD/HAY WA11 ...91 G6
 WAL/EG CH44 ...112 A4
Alfred St ECCL WA10 ...9 J1
 NEWLW WA12 ...105 G2
 RNFD/HAY WA11 ...76 B7
 WAV L15 ...113 M5
 WDN WA8 ...16 E4
 WGN WN1 ...68 D3
 WGNE/HIN WN2 ...80 C2
 WGNS/IIMK WN3 ...79 J1
Alice Cl WDN WA8 ...149 J1
Alice St STHEL WA9 ...103 G5
Alison Av RF/TRAN CH42 ...128 B2
Alison Pl CLB/OSW/ST L13 ...98 A4
Alison Rd CLB/OSW/ST L13 ...98 A4
Alistair Dr BEB CH63 ...143 L7
Alker La CHLYE PR6 ...32 C2
Alker St CHLY/EC PR7 ...32 E6
 WGNW/BIL/O WN5 ...68 B7
Allangate Cl GR/UP/WCH CH49...125 L3
Allangate Rd ALL/GAR L19 ...130 D5
Allan Rd RNFD/HAY WA11 ...89 L6
Allans Cl NSTN CH64 ...153 G7
Allans Meadow NSTN CH64 ...153 G7
Allanson St STHEL WA9 ...102 F3
Allcard St WARRW/BUR WA5 ...14 B1
Allcot Av RF/TRAN CH42 ...127 M3
Allen Av GOL/RIS/CU WA3 ...107 L1
Allenby Av CSBY/WL L22 ...83 H3
Allenby Sq CLB/OSW/ST L13 ...114 B3
Allendale RUNC WA7 ...150 D7
Allendale Av RAIN/WH L35 ...117 M2
 WLT/FAZ L9 ...84 D6
Allengate CSBY/BLUN L23 ...71 G8
Allen Rd RUNC WA7 ...18 B9
Allerby Wy GOL/RIS/CU WA3 ...93 G5
Allerford Rd WD/CROXPK L12 ...98 F5
Allerton Beeches CALD/MH L18 ...130 A2
Allerton Dr CALD/MH L18 ...130 D1
Allerton Gv RF/TRAN CH42 ...127 M3
Allerton Rd CALD/MH L18 ...114 D8
 CALD/MH L18 ...130 D1
 CHTN/BK PR9 ...25 C4
 RF/TRAN CH42 ...127 M3
 WAL/NB CH45 ...95 J7
 WDN WA8 ...16 F1
Allesley Rd DV/KA/FCH L14..114 C1
Alleyne Rd ANF/KKDL L4 ...97 M5
Alliance St AIG/SPK L17 ...129 K2
Allington Cl WGN WN1 ...5 G5
Allonby Cl CL/PREN CH43 ...127 G1
Allport La PS/BROM CH62 ...143 M4
Allport Rd BEB CH63 ...143 L4
The Allports PS/BROM CH62 ...143 M6
All Saints Cl NTHTN L30 ...84 A2
All Saints Dr WARRS WA4 ...139 G2
All Saints Rd SPK/HALE L24 ...146 E2
Allscott Wy AIMK WN4 ...91 L2
Alma Cl AIN/FAZ L10 ...85 K6
 SKEL WN8 ...66 E6
Alma St BIRK CH41 ...11 K6
 NEWLW WA12 ...104 D2
 PS/BROM CH62 * ...143 L6
 STHEL WA9 ...9 L8
Alma Vale Ter BTL L20 * ...6 F5
Almeda Rd SPK/HALE L24..148 J8
Almer Dr WARRW/BUR WA5 ...120 E8
Almond Av BRSC L40 ...39 G7
 NTHTN L30 ...83 L2
 RUNC WA7 ...19 L8
Almond Brook Rd
 WGNNW/ST WN6 ...55 L4
Almond Cl HLWD L26 ...132 A6
 RNFD/HAY WA11 ...90 B8
Almond Ct CALD/MH L18 ...130 C8
Almond Crs WGNNW/ST WN6 ...56 B6
Almond Dr WARRW/BUR WA5 ...104 B8
 WDN WA8 ...133 M5
 WGNW/BIL/O WN5 ...68 A7
Almond Gv WARR WA1 ...122 D6
Almond Pl MOR/LEA CH46 ...110 B5
Almond's Gn WD/CROXPK L12 ...98 C5
Almond's Gv WD/CROXPK L12 ...98 C5
Almonds Pk WD/CROXPK L12 ...98 C5
Almond's Turn NTHTN L30 ...83 M1
Almond Wy GR/UP/WCH CH49 *..125 L3
Alness Dr RAIN/WH L35 ...117 M3
Alnwick Cl WGNE/HIN WN2 ...57 M8
Alnwick Dr EP CH65 ...163 M4
 MOR/LEA CH46 ...109 L5
Aloeswood Cl NPK/KEN L6 ...97 K8
Alpass Rd AIG/SPK L17 * ...129 K1
Alpha Dr RF/TRAN CH42 ...128 C4
Alpha St LITH L21 ...83 K8
Alpine Cl ECCL WA10 ...101 L1
Alpine Dr LEIGH WN7 ...81 L5

Alpine Rd CHLYE PR6 ...33 G2
Alpine St NEWLW WA12 ...104 C2
Alresford Rd ALL/GAR L19 ...130 D5
Alroy Rd ANF/KKDL L4 ...97 J6
Alscot Av AIN/FAZ L10 ...85 K6
Alscot Cl MGHL L31 ...72 F5
Alsop Ar VAUX/LVPD L3 * ...13 M7
Alsop Ct VAUX/LVPD L3 * ...13 M7
Alston Cl PS/BROM CH62 ...143 L4
Alston Ct STHP PR8 ...35 G7
Alstonfield Rd DV/KA/FCH L14..115 J1
Alston Rd AIG/SPK L17 ...130 A5
 WGNE/HIN WN2 ...69 H3
Alt WDN WA8 ...133 K3
Altair Cl EHL/KEN L7 ...113 K5
Altbridge Pk NG/CROX L11 ...85 K8
Alt Bridge Pk HUY L36 ...115 M1
Altcar Av WAV L15 ...113 M6
Altcar Dr MOR/LEA CH46 ...109 M6
Altcar La FMBY L37 ...59 H4
 MGHL L31 ...72 C1
Altcar Rd BTL L20 * ...83 J8
 FMBY L37 ...59 K3
Alt Cl LEIGH WN7 ...81 M8
Altcross Rd NG/CROX L11 ...98 E1
Altcross Wy NG/CROX L11 ...98 E1
Altfield Rd DV/KA/FCH L14..99 H6
Altfinch Cl DV/KA/FCH L14..99 J6
Altham Rd NG/CROX L11 ...98 B6
 STHP PR8 ...36 A3
Althorpe Dr STHP PR8 ...36 A2
Althorp St TOX L8 ...129 H2
Altmoor Rd HUY L36 ...99 M8
Alton Av LITH L21 ...83 J4
Alton Cl AIMK WN4 ...91 J1
 HTWN L38 ...70 B3
Alton Rd CL/PREN CH43 ...70 B8
 NPK/KEN L6 ...97 M8
Alt Rd BTL L20 ...83 L8
 FMBY L37 ...59 J4
 HTWN L38 ...70 C1
 HUY L36 ...116 A2
Alt Side Ct AIN/FAZ L10 ...85 K6
Alt St TOX L8 ...113 K6
Altway AIN/FAZ L10 ...84 E2
Altys La ORM L39 ...63 H2
Alundale Rd WD/CROXPK L12 ...99 G8
Alvanley Cl WGNW/BIL/O WN5 ...67 K4
Alvanley Pl CL/PREN CH43 ...10 E6
Alvanley Rd FROD/HEL WA6 ...166 B3
 GTS/LS CH66 ...163 G1
 KKBY L32 ...85 L3
 WD/CROXPK L12 ...98 E8
Alvanley Vw CHNE CH2 ...165 K2
Alvega Cl PS/BROM CH62 ...128 E6
Alverstone Av BIRK CH41 ...111 H4
Alverstone Cl
 WARRW/BUR WA5 ...119 L6
Alverstone Rd CALD/MH L18..114 B8
 WAL/EG CH44 ...111 M2
Alverton Cl WDN WA8 ...133 M5
Alvina La ANF/KKDL L4 ...97 G6
 NWD/KWIPK L33 ...74 D3
Alwain Gn SPK/HALE L24..147 H3
Alwen St BIRK CH41 ...111 H4
Alwyn Av LITH L21 ...83 K4
Alwyn Gdns MOR/LEA CH46 ...110 B5
Alwyn St AIG/SPK L17 ...129 K2
Alwyn St CLB/OSW/ST L13 ...98 A6
 WGN WN1 ...5 H1
Alwyn Ter WGN WN1 ...5 H1
Amanda Rd AIN/FAZ L10 ...85 K6
 RAIN/WH L35 ...101 K8
Amanda Wy MGHL L31 * ...85 K1
Amar St WGNE/HIN WN2 ...5 M6
Amathyst Cl WGNE/HIN WN2 ...69 J3
Amaury Cl CSBY/BLUN L23 ...71 K8
Amaury Rd CSBY/BLUN L23 ...71 K8
Ambassador Dr HLWD L26 ...132 C4
Amber Dr CHLYE PR6 ...33 G7
Amber Gdns WGNE/HIN WN2 ...4 C1
Ambergate SKEL WN8 ...65 K6
Ambergate St TOX L8 ...102 F6
Amberley Av MOR/LEA CH46 ...109 L6
Amberley Cl MOR/LEA CH46 ...109 L6
 NPK/KEN L6 ...97 M6
 WGNE/HIN WN2 ...69 H3
Amberswood Cl WGNE/HIN WN2 ...69 K6
Amber Wy DV/KA/FCH L14..99 J6
Ambleside Av MOR/LEA CH46 ...69 K5
 WGNW/BIL/O WN5 ...68 B7
Ambleside Av CHLY/EC PR7 * ...31 M4
 MOR/LEA CH46 ...109 M5
 PS/BROM CH62 ...144 A6
Ambleside Crs
 WARRN/WOL WA2 ...121 L2
Ambleside Cl CALD/MH L18 ...130 D4
 EP CH65 ...163 J3
 MGHL L31 ...72 F3
Amelia Cl NPK/KEN L6 ...13 M4
 WDN WA8 ...134 D1
Amelia St WARRN/WOL WA2 ...15 C1
Amersham SKEL WN8 ...65 K5
Amersham Rd ANF/KKDL L4 ...97 L3
Amery Gv RF/TRAN CH42 ...127 L3
Amesbury Dr WGNS/IIMK WN3 ...78 E3
Amethyst Cl NPK/KEN L6 ...113 K1
Amherst Rd AIG/SPK L17 ...129 K1
Amis Gv GOL/RIS/CU WA3 ...93 G5
Amity St TOX L8 ...113 H7
Amos Av LITH L21 ...83 L5
Ampleforth Cl KKBY L32 ...85 L4
Ampthill Rd AIG/SPK L17 ...129 L3
Ampulla Rd NG/CROX L11 ...85 L8
Ancaster Rd AIG/SPK L17 ...129 L3
Ancholme Cl RAIN/WH L35 ...101 J7
The Anchorage LYMM WA13 ...139 M2
 NSTN CH64 ...152 E6
 VAUX/LVPD L3 ...112 F7
Anchor Cl RUNC WA7 ...150 F7
Anchor St CHTN/BK PR9 ...3 H3
Ancient Mdw WLT/FAZ L9 ...84 D6
Ancroft Dr WGNE/HIN WN2 ...80 F2
Ancroft Rd DV/KA/FCH L14..115 J2
Ancrum Rd NWD/KWIPK L33 ...73 M7
Anders Dr NWD/KWIPK L33 ...74 C3
Anderson Av BTL L20 ...6 B1
Anderson Cl PEN/TH CH61 ...126 C7
 RAIN/WH L35 ...117 M4
 WARRN/WOL WA2 ...122 D3
Anderson Rd LITH L21 ...83 M4
Anderson St EV L5 ...97 G7
Anderton St HOR/BR BL6 * ...45 J3
Anderton St CHLY/EC PR7 ...31 M4
 CHLYE PR6 ...46 G
 WGNE/HIN WN2 ...69 K3
Anderton Ter HUY L36 ...115 L3
Andover Rd RNFD/HAY WA11 ...91 G5
Andover Wy WLTN L25 ...131 M5
Andreas Ct STHP PR8 ...3 G9
Andrew Av MGHL L31 ...85 J2
 GOL/RIS/CU WA3 ...78 A8

Andrew Cl WDN WA8 ...133 L5
Andrews Cl FMBY L37 ...59 G4
Andrews La CSBY/BLUN L23 ...71 G8
Andrew Dr ANF/KKDL L4 ...97 H4
Andrew's Wk HES CH60 ...141 K5
Andrews Yort FMBY L37 ...59 G4
Andromeda Wy STHEL WA9 ...103 J6
Anemone Wy STHEL WA9 ...103 J6
Anfield Rd ANF/KKDL L4 ...97 H6
Angela St EHL/KEN L7 ...113 K5
Angers La MGHL L31 ...73 K7
Anglesea Rd WLT/FAZ L9 ...97 H2
Anglesea Wy TOX L8 ...129 H1
Anglesey Cl EP CH65 ...163 L4
Anglesey Rd WAL/EC CH44 ...95 K8
 WKBY CH48 ...124 C2
Anglezark Cl EHL/KEN L7 ...113 K3
Anglezarke Rd CHLYE PR6 ...44 C6
Anglia Wy WLTN L25 ...131 C5
Anglican Ct TOX L8 * ...113 G6
Anglo Cl WLT/FAZ L9 ...84 E5
Angus Av LEIGH WN7 ...81 L7
Angus Rd BEB CH63 ...143 L7
 NG/CROX L11 ...98 B5
Anline St CHLYE PR6 ...33 G5
Annandale Cl NWD/KWIPK L33 ...73 M7
Annandale Gdns SKEL WN8 ...66 C6
Annan Gv AIMK WN4 ...80 A8
Ann Gv GTS/LS CH66 ...155 M6
Anne Av STHP PR8 ...35 G7
Anne Gv STHEL WA9 ...102 E6
Annerley St EHL/KEN L7 * ...9 L7
Annesley Crs WGNS/IIMK WN3 ...79 H2
Annesley Rd AIG/SPK L17 ...129 L3
 WAL/EG CH44 ...111 K2
Anne St WARRW/BUR WA5 * ...118 F2
Annette Av NEWLW WA12 ...91 J8
Annie Rd BTL L20 ...6 F2
Annie St WARRN/WOL WA2 ...15 G3
Ann St RUNC WA7 ...19 J8
 EP CH65 ...65 G4
Ann St West WDN WA8 ...16 E6
Anscot Av BEB CH63 ...128 B7
Ansdell Dr ECCL WA10 ...88 D8
Ansdell Gv CHTN/BK PR9 ...25 J1
Ansdell Rd WDN WA8 ...134 D3
Ansdell Villas' Rd RAIN/WH L35 ...117 L1
Ansford Av WGNE/HIN WN2 ...80 D5
Anson Cl WARRN/WOL WA2 ...122 A3
Anson Pl VAUX/LVPD L3 ...13 L3
Anson St VAUX/LVPD L3 ...13 L6
 WGNW/BIL/O WN5 ...68 B6
Anstey Cl MOR/LEA CH46 ...109 K4
Anstey Rd CLB/OSW/ST L13 ...114 D2
Ansty Cl RNFD/HAY WA11 ...89 H8
Anthony's Wy HES CH60 ...141 J6
Anthorn Cl CL/PREN CH43 ...126 F1
Anthorn Rd WGNS/IIMK WN3 ...79 G2
Antler Ct AIMK WN4 ...79 K7
Antonio St BTL L20 ...6 C1
Antons Cl HLWD L26 ...132 B7
Antons Rd HLWD L26 ...132 B7
 PEN/TH CH61 ...126 C8
Antony Rd WARRS WA4 ...137 K3
Antrim Cl RNFD/HAY WA11 ...90 E7
 WGNS/IIMK WN3 ...78 E3
Antrim Dr GTS/LS CH66 ...163 H3
Antrim Rd WARRN/WOL WA2 ...121 J3
Antrim St CLB/OSW/ST L13 ...98 A6
Anvil Cl BTL L20 ...6 F2
 CHNE CH2 ...165 K1
 WGNW/BIL/O WN5 ...66 F8
The Anzacs PS/BROM CH62 ...128 E7
Anzio Rd HUY L36 ...115 M1
Apex Ct PS/BROM CH62 * ...144 A4
Apollo Crs NWD/KWIPK L33 ...86 A1
Apollo Wy NPK/KEN L6 * ...97 K8
 NTHTN L30 ...84 B1
Apostles Wy NWD/KWIPK L33 ...73 M8
Appin Rd BIRK CH41 ...11 J8
Appleby Cl WDN WA8 ...133 L6
Appleby Dr NTHTN L30 ...83 L2
Appleby Gn WD/CROXPK L12 ...98 F7
Appleby Gv PS/BROM CH62 ...143 M7
Appleby Lawn NTHLY L27 ...132 C1
Appleby Rd NWD/KWIPK L33 ...86 A1
 WARRN/WOL WA2 ...121 L2
Appleby Wk WDN WA8 ...133 L6
Applecorn Cl STHEL WA9 ...102 F7
Apple Ct NPK/KEN L6 ...113 K2
Applecross Cl GOL/RIS/CU WA3 ...107 J7
Appledale Dr GTS/LS CH66 ...163 H5
Apple Dell Av GOL/RIS/CU WA3..92 G4
Appledore Ct SPK/HALE L24..146 D1
Appledore Gv STHEL WA9 ...118 E1
Appleford Cl WARRS WA4 ...138 A6
Applegarth MOR/LEA CH46 ...109 L7
Applethwaite WGNE/HIN WN2 ...69 K5
Appleton Dr EP CH65 ...163 H2
 GR/UP/WCH CH49 ...126 A2
Appleton Rd ANF/KKDL L4 ...97 L3
 LITH L21 ...83 J2
 SKEL WN8 ...65 H3
 STHEL WA9 ...9 H1
 WDN WA8 ...16 E7
Appleton St WDN WA8 ...16 E7
 WGNS/IIMK WN3 ...4 D4
Appleton Village WDN WA8 ...16 D7
Appletree Cl CALD/MH L18 ...130 E4
Apple Tree Gv STBRV L28 ...99 K5
Apple Tree Gv GTS/LS CH66 ...163 H5
Appletree Gv WARRN/WOL WA2..122 B3
Appley Cl WGNNW/ST WN6 ...54 C7
Appley La North
 WGNNW/ST WN6 ...54 E3
Appley La South SKEL WN8 ...54 E7
April Gv NPK/KEN L6 ...97 M8
April Ri WLTN L25 * ...84 A2
Apsley Av WAL/NB CH45 ...95 K7
Apsley Brow MGHL L31 ...72 D4
Apsley Gv BEB CH63 ...128 C3
Apsley Rd PS/BROM CH62 ...128 D5
 WD/CROXPK L12 ...98 E7
Aquarius Cl DV/KA/FCH L14..115 J1
Aragon Cl MGHL L31 ...73 G2
Aran Cl SPK/HALE L24..147 M3
Arborn Dr GR/UP/WCH CH49 ...110 C7
Arbour La NWD/KWIPK L33 ...86 C4
Arbour St STHP PR8 ...3 H6
Arbury Av RNFD/HAY WA11 ...89 M7
Arbury La WARRN/WOL WA2 ...105 L2
Arcade St WGN WN1 ...5 H4
Arcadia Av MGHL L31 ...72 C7
Archbishop Worlock Ct
 VAUX/LVPD L3 ...12 E2
Archbrook Ms CALD/MH L18 ...114 E7
Archer Av WARRS WA4 ...138 A3
Archer Cl ANF/KKDL L4 ...97 G6
Archerfield Rd CALD/MH L18..130 D4
Archer Gv STHEL WA9 ...103 G1
Archers Cft PS/BROM CH62 * ...143 M4
Archers Fold MGHL L31 ...85 K1
Archers Gn PS/BROM CH62 ...155 G5
Archer St ANF/KKDL L4 ...97 G6
Archers Wy GR/UP/WCH CH49 *..126 C3
Archer Wy GR/UP/WCH CH49 ...126 C3

The Arches PR/KW L34 * ...100 F7
Arch La AIMK WN4 ...90 C2
Archway Rd HUY L36 ...116 A3
Arcon Rd CL/PREN CH43 ...43 C4
Arctic Rd BTL L20 ...6 D4
Arden WDN WA8 ...133 J3
Arden Cl GOL/RIS/CU WA3 ...107 K3
 STHP PR8 ...34 C7
Arden Dr FROD/HEL WA6 ...153 G7
Ardennes Rd HUY L36 ...116 A3
Arderne Cl BEB CH63 ...143 K3
Ardleigh Av CLB/OSW/ST L13 ...114 B3
Ardleigh Cl BEB CH63 ...143 J7
Ardleigh Gv CLB/OSW/ST L13 ...114 B3
Ardleigh Pl CLB/OSW/ST L13 ...114 B3
Ardleigh Rd CLB/OSW/ST L13 ...114 B3
Ardmore Rd CALD/MH L18 ...130 C3
Ardrossan Rd ANF/KKDL L4 ...97 K3
Ardville Rd NG/CROX L11 ...97 M3
Ardwick Rd SPK/HALE L24..147 M3
Ardwick St STHEL WA9 ...9 K5
Argameols Cl STHP PR8 ...25 C8
Argameols Gv FMBY L37 ...47 G8
Argameols Rd FMBY L37 ...47 G7
Argo Rd CSBY/WL L22 ...82 F4
Argos Pl BTL L20 ...7 J9
Argos Rd BTL L20 ...7 J9
Argyle Rd ALL/GAR L19 ...130 E2
 ANF/KKDL L4 ...97 K7
 CHTN/BK PR9 ...24 F4
Argyle St BIRK CH41 ...11 H6
 BIRK CH41 ...11 K6
 CLVPS L1 ...13 G9
 ECCL WA10 ...8 F1
 WGNW/BIL/O WN5 ...68 B3
Argyle St South BIRK CH41 ...11 H8
Argyll Av PS/BROM CH62 ...154 F1
Argyll Cl AIMK WN4 ...90 E1
Aries Cl DV/KA/FCH L14..99 J8
Ariss Gv RAIN/WH L35 * ...101 J8
Arkenshaw Rd
 GOL/RIS/CU WA3 ...106 C6
Arkenstone Cl WDN WA8 ...133 L3
Arkle Rd CL/PREN CH43 ...111 H5
Arkles Rd ANF/KKDL L4 ...97 J7
Arklow Dr SPK/HALE L24..147 M3
Ark Royal Wy BIRK CH41 ...11 L9
Arkwood Cl PS/BROM CH62 ...143 L2
Arkwright Rd RUNC WA7 ...150 B2
Arkwright St EV L5 ...97 G8
Arlescourt Rd WD/CROXPK L12 ...98 E3
Arley Av WARRS WA4 ...137 M4
Arley Cl CL/PREN CH43 ...110 E7
 WGNE/HIN WN2 ...69 J3
Arley Dr WDN WA8 ...133 K3
Arley La CHLY/EC PR7 ...57 H3
 WGN WN1 ...56 F4
Arley St CHLY/EC PR7 ...32 F5
 WGN WN1 ...5 J4
Arlington Av CALD/MH L18 ...114 D8
Arlington Cl STHP PR8 ...34 C8
Arlington Dr GOL/RIS/CU WA3 ...93 L5
 WARRW/BUR WA5 ...136 A1
Arlington Rd WAL/NB CH45 ...95 G2
Armill Rd NG/CROX L11 ...98 E3
Armitage Gdns CALD/MH L18..130 D4
Armitstead St WGNE/HIN WN2 ...80 F1
Armley Rd ANF/KKDL L4 ...97 K6
Armour Av WARRN/WOL WA2 ...91 K2
Armoury Bank AIMK WN4 ...91 K2
The Armoury WD/CROXPK L12 ...98 D6
Armscot Cl WLTN L25 ...131 K6
Armscot Pl WLTN L25 ...131 K6
Armstrong Gv GOL/RIS/CU WA3..122 F7
Armstrong Quay VAUX/LVPD L3..129 J2
Armstrong St WGNNW/ST WN2 * ...69 J2
Armthorpe Dr GTS/LS CH66 ...155 K8
Arncliffe Cl WGNE/HIN WN2 ...80 C1
Arncliffe Dr WARRW/BUR WA5 ...104 B7
Arncliffe Rd WLTN L25 ...131 K4
Arndale RUNC WA7 ...150 A8
Arnhem Crs WARRN/WOL WA2 ...14 F1
Arnhem Rd HUY L36 ...115 M1
Arnian Rd RNFD/HAY WA11 ...76 B6
Arnian Wy RNFD/HAY WA11 ...76 B6
Arnold Av ECCL WA10 ...8 B2
Arnold Cl STHEL WA9 ...103 J6
 TOX L8 ...113 H7
Arnold Crs TOX L8 ...113 H7
Arnold Gv WAV L15 ...114 C6
Arnold Pl CHLY/EC PR7 ...32 C8
 WDN WA8 ...133 L6
Arnold St TOX L8 ...113 H7
 WAL/NB CH45 ...95 K8
 WARR WA1 ...15 K3
Arno Rd CL/PREN CH43 ...127 K2
Arnot St ECCL WA10 ...8 F2
Arnot Wy BEB CH63 ...143 J3
Arnside Av RAIN/WH L35 ...117 J1
 RNFD/HAY WA11 ...90 C7
Arnside Gv WARRS WA4 ...137 K3
Arnside Rd CHTN/BK PR9 ...3 J5
 CL/PREN CH43 ...10 B9
 EHL/KEN L7 ...113 L4
 HUY L36 ...115 K3
 WAL/NB CH45 ...95 K8
 WGNW/BIL/O WN5 ...67 J5
Arnside Ter CHTN/BK PR9 ...3 K3
Arpley Rd WARR WA1 ...14 C6
Arpley St WARR WA1 ...14 C6
Arrad St EHL/KEN L7 ...113 J5
Arran Av EP CH65 ...163 L4
Arran Cl RNFD/HAY WA11 ...90 A7
 WARRN/WOL WA2 ...122 C3
Arran Dr FROD/HEL WA6 ...160 E6
Arranmore Rd CALD/MH L18..130 C3
Arrowe Brook La
 GR/UP/WCH CH49 ...126 A4
Arrowe Brook Rd
 GR/UP/WCH CH49 ...126 B3
Arrowe Park Rd
 GR/UP/WCH CH49 ...110 B8
Arrowe Rd GR/UP/WCH CH49 ...125 M2
Arrowe Side GR/UP/WCH CH49 ...126 A3
Arrowe Vw GR/UP/WCH CH49 ...125 M2
Arrowsmith Rd RNFD/HAY WA11..91 H6
Arthur Av EP CH65 ...20 E5
Arthur St ALL/GAR L19 * ...130 F8
 BIRK CH41 ...11 G8
 RUNC WA7 ...19 J8
 WARRN/WOL WA2 ...14 C4
Arundel Av AIG/SPK L17 ...113 K7
 WAL/NB CH45 ...95 H7
 TOX L8 ...113 J7
Arundel Cl EP CH65 ...21 G9
Arundel Rd STHP PR8 ...35 H5
Arundel St ANF/KKDL L4 ...7 M8
 WGNW/BIL/O WN5 ...68 B7
Arvon St BTL L20 ...83 M7
Asbridge St TOX L8 ...113 J8
Asbury Cl CALD/MH L18 ...130 F2
Asbury Rd WAL/NB CH45 ...94 F7

Ascot Av LITH L21 83 J5
RUNC WA7 149 K7
Ascot Cl STHP PR8 2 A8
WARR WA1 123 G6
WARRS WA4 138 E3
Ascot Dr BEB CH63 128 B8
GTS/LS CH66 162 F2
NWD/KWIPK L33 74 A8
Ascot Gv BEB CH63 128 B8
Ascot Pk CSBY/BLUN L23 83 H1
Ascroft Rd WLT/FAZ L9 84 D5
Ascroft St WGN WN1 5 J5
Ash Av NEWLW WA12 104 E3
Ashbank Rd NG/CROX L11 98 C3
Ashberry Dr WARRS WA4 138 D8
Ashbourne Av CSBY/BLUN L23 82 E1
NTHTN L30 84 A3
RUNC WA7 149 K7
WGNE/HIN WN2 69 J3
Ashbourne Cl GTS/LS CH66 163 G5
LEIGH WN7 81 M4
Ashbourne Crs HUY L36 115 K3
Ashbourne Rd AIG/SPK L17 129 L4
WARRW/BUR WA5 120 D8
Ashbrook Av RUNC WA7 151 G2
Ashbrook Crs WARRN/WOL WA2 121 M5
Ashbrook Dr WLT/FAZ L9 84 E7
Ash Brow SKEL WN8 53 K4
Ashburn Av NWD/KWIPK L33 86 A1
Ashburton Av CL/PREN CH43 111 H7
Ashburton Rd CL/PREN CH43 111 G7
WAL/EG CH44 111 K1
WKBY CH48 124 D2
Ashbury Cl RUNC WA7 150 F3
Ashbury Dr RNFD/HAY WA11 90 F6
Ashbury Rd DV/KA/FCH L14 99 K7
Ashby Cl MOR/LEA CH46 109 K4
Ashby Gv LEIGH WN7 81 L5
Ashby Rd WGNS/IIMK WN3 79 K2
Ashby St CHLY/EC PR7 32 E7
Ash Cl GTS/LS CH66 163 H4
ORM L39 50 F8
WAV L15 114 A5
WGNNW/ST WN6 54 F6
Ashcombe Rd DV/KA/FCH L14 114 E2
Ash Crs HUY L36 116 A5
Ashcroft Av ORM L39 51 H7
WGNNW/ST WN6 68 B2
Ashcroft Dr PEN/TH CH61 141 H3
Ashcroft Rd FMBY L37 59 H4
NWD/KWIPK L33 86 E2
Ashcroft St BTL L20 6 F5
STHEL WA9 9 M5
WGNE/HIN WN2 81 G1
Ashdale HUY L36 115 M3
Ashdale Cl CHLY/EC PR7 42 F5
FMBY L37 58 E3
Ashdale Pk GR/UP/WCH CH49 125 K2
Ashdale Rd CALD/MH L18 114 C8
CSBY/WL L22 82 F3
WGNS/IIMK WN3 79 J3
WLT/FAZ L9 97 J1
Ashdown Crs STHEL WA9 118 E1
Ashdown Dr GR/UP/WCH CH49 125 L3
Ashdown Gv HLWD L26 132 C4
Ashdown La GOL/RIS/CU WA3 107 J8
Ashfarm Ct DV/KA/FCH L14 115 H2
Ashfield RAIN/WH L35 117 M2
WAV L15 113 M5
Ashfield Av WGNE/HIN WN2 81 H1
Ashfield Crs PS/BROM CH62 143 M5
WGNW/BIL/O WN5 78 A8
Ashfield Dr WGNE/HIN WN2 57 L8
Ashfield House Gdns
WGNNW/ST WN6 56 B5
Ashfield Park Dr
WGNNW/ST WN6 56 B5
Ashfield Rd AIG/SPK L17 129 M3
CHLY/EC PR7 32 D6
CHLYE PR6 44 D5
PS/BROM CH62 143 L5
Ashfield Rd North EP CH65 20 C4
Ashford Cl HLWD L26 132 A6
Ashford Ri WGN WN1 68 D1
Ashford Rd BIRK CH41 10 F9
HOY CH47 108 E5
Ashford Wy WDN WA8 17 K1
Ash Gv CHLY/EC PR7 32 E8
FMBY L37 58 E4
GTS/LS CH66 155 L7
LITH L21 83 J7
RAIN/WH L35 117 G1
RNFD/HAY WA11 76 B7
RUNC WA7 19 M8
SKEL WN8 64 F4
STHEL WA9 118 E1
WAL/NB CH45 95 L6
WARRS WA4 15 K9
WAV L15 113 M5
WDN WA8 133 M5
WGNNW/ST WN6 56 B5
WGNW/BIL/O WN5 67 H7
Ash Grove Crs
WGNW/BIL/O WN5 77 M7
Ashington Cl WGNW/BIL/O WN5 67 K4
Ashland Av AIMK WN4 91 J1
WGN WN1 68 E3
Ashlands FROD/HEL WA6 160 E6
Ash La WARRS WA4 138 A5
WDN WA8 133 J5
WGNE/HIN WN2 69 J3
Ashlar Gv AIG/SPK L17 130 A3
Ashlar Rd AIG/SPK L17 130 A3
CSBY/WL L22 83 G3
Ashlea Rd PEN/TH CH61 141 H2
Ashleigh Rd MGHL L31 73 H6
Ashley Av HOY CH47 109 H4
Ashley Cl NWD/KWIPK L33 74 A8
RAIN/WH L35 117 M3
WARRS WA4 138 E2
Ashley Dr LEIGH WN7 81 L5
Ashley Rd CHTN/BK PR9 3 K4
RUNC WA7 149 M3
SKEL WN8 65 L1
WGNE/HIN WN2 81 K2
Ashley St RF/TRAN CH42 128 B3
Ashley Wy WDN WA8 16 D7
Ashley Wy West WDN WA8 16 B6
Ashmead Rd SKEL WN8 65 J1
Ashmore Cl GOL/RIS/CU WA3 123 J2
Ashmuir Hey KKBY L32 86 B4
Ashover Av DV/KA/FCH L14 115 J1
Ash Priors WDN WA8 133 M2
Ashridge St RUNC WA7 18 F2
Ashridge Wy WGNW/BIL/O WN5 67 L7
Ash Rd BEB CH63 128 B6
CHLY/EC PR7 43 G5
CHNE CH2 165 L2
LITH L21 83 J6
LYMM WA13 139 L2
RF/TRAN CH42 11 G9
RNFD/HAY WA11 91 G6
WARRN/WOL WA2 105 K7
WARRW/BUR WA5 136 B1
Ash St BTL L20 7 H3
GOL/RIS/CU WA3 92 D3
STHP PR8 3 L6
Ashton Av RAIN/WH L35 117 L3
Ashton Cl FROD/HEL WA6 160 E4
PS/BROM CH62 155 G2
RUNC WA7 149 H7
Ashton Dr FROD/HEL WA6 160 E4
WKBY CH48 124 C4
WLTN L25 131 K6
Ashton Gallery WGN WN1 * 4 E3
Ashton Heath AIMK WN4 91 L3
Ashton Rd GOL/RIS/CU WA3 92 B3
NEWLW WA12 91 L7
STHP PR8 35 H4
WGNW/BIL/O WN5 78 D5
Ashtons Green Dr STHEL WA9 103 H3
Ashton St CLB/OSW/ST L13 114 C2
VAUX/LVPD L3 13 M6
WARRN/WOL WA2 14 E4
Ashtree Cl NSTN CH64 153 J6
Ashtree Cft NSTN CH64 154 C6
Ashtree Dr NSTN CH64 153 J7
Ashtree Farm Ct NSTN CH64 154 C5
Ashtree Gv WD/CROXPK L12 99 G1
Ashtrees BRSC L40 40 E3
Ashurst Cl RNFD/HAY WA11 90 A7
SKEL WN8 65 J4
WLTN L25 131 K1
Ashurst Ct FMBY L37 59 G3
Ashurst Dr RNFD/HAY WA11 89 M7
Ashurst Gdns SKEL WN8 65 J1
Ashurst Rd SKEL WN8 65 K2
WGNNW/ST WN6 55 J3
Ash V WAV L15 114 A5
Ash Vls WAL/EG CH44 * 111 M3
Ashville Rd BIRK CH41 10 B5
WAL/EG CH44 111 L3
Ashville Wy RUNC WA7 161 G2
Ashwall St SKEL WN8 64 F5
Ashwater Rd NG/CROX L11 98 E3
Ash Wy HES CH60 141 K8
Ashwell Av GOL/RIS/CU WA3 92 F4
Ashwell St TOX L8 113 G6
Ashwood SKEL WN8 65 L2
Ashwood Av AIMK WN4 91 J3
GOL/RIS/CU WA3 92 F5
WARR WA1 15 L1
WGNE/HIN WN2 80 E6
Ashwood Cl GTS/LS CH66 * 162 F4
NWD/KWIPK L33 74 A8
Ashwood Ct CL/PREN CH43 110 E4
Ashwood Dr WD/CROXPK L12 98 F2
Ashwood La CHNE CH2 164 C8
Askern Rd KKBY L32 86 B5
Askett Cl RNFD/HAY WA11 90 E6
Askew Cl WAL/EG CH44 111 M1
Askew St ANF/KKDL L4 97 H4
Askham Cl TOX L8 113 K6
Askrigg Av GTS/LS CH66 155 K8
Askwith Rd WGNE/HIN WN2 81 H2
Asland Gdns CHTN/BK PR9 25 L1
Asmall Cl ORM L39 50 F7
Asmall La ORM L39 50 A5
Aspen Cl GTS/LS CH66 163 G4
HES CH60 141 M5
NWD/KWIPK L33 74 B7
Aspendale Rd RF/TRAN CH42 127 M1
Aspen Gdns CHLY/EC PR7 32 D7
Aspen Gv FMBY L37 58 E4
TOX L8 113 L7
WARR WA1 122 C6
Aspen Wk WGNNW/ST WN6 * 68 C2
Aspenwood AIMK WN4 91 J3
Aspes Rd WD/CROXPK L12 99 G6
Aspinall Cl WARRN/WOL WA2 122 C2
Aspinall Crs FMBY L37 60 B4
Aspinall Rd WGNNW/ST WN6 55 K4
Aspinall St BIRK CH41 10 E3
WGNE/HIN WN2 80 C3
Aspinal St PR/KW L34 100 F7
Aspull Cl GOL/RIS/CU WA3 122 E1
Aspull Common LEIGH WN7 93 L4
Asquith Av BIRK CH41 10 D3
Asser Rd NG/CROX L11 98 A5
The Asshawes CHLYE PR6 44 B4
Assheton Wk SPK/HALE L24 148 A3
Assissian Crs NTHTN L30 84 A1
Astbury Cl GOL/RIS/CU WA3 93 K5
Aster Crs RUNC WA7 * 161 H1
Aster Dr NWD/KWIPK L33 73 M8
Asterfield Av BEB CH63 128 A6
Aster Rd RNFD/HAY WA11 91 H7
Astley Cl RNFD/HAY WA11 76 B6
WARRS WA4 137 K2
WDN WA8 133 L2
Astley Rd CHLY/EC PR7 32 D4
HUY L36 100 A7
Astley St CHLY/EC PR7 32 E4
Astmoor Bridge La RUNC WA7 150 B3
Astmoor Rd RUNC WA7 19 M2
Aston Av GOL/RIS/CU WA3 123 H1
Aston Cl CL/PREN CH43 125 M4
Aston Ct WARR WA1 122 E4
Aston Fields Rd RUNC WA7 161 M1
Aston Gn RUNC WA7 * 151 G7
Aston La RUNC WA7 151 K2
Aston St ALL/GAR L19 145 M1
Astonwood Rd RF/TRAN CH42 127 M2
Astor Dr WARRS WA4 138 B5
Astor St ANF/KKDL L4 97 H3
Atheldene Rd ANF/KKDL L4 97 L3
Athelstan Cl PS/BROM CH62 143 M4
Atherleigh Wy LEIGH WN7 93 M2
Atherton Cl EV L5 97 H8
Atherton Dr GR/UP/WCH CH49 126 A2
Atherton Rd EP CH65 156 B7
WGNE/HIN WN2 81 J2
WLT/FAZ L9 84 E8
Atherton Sq WGN WN1 * 4 E3
Atherton St CHLY/EC PR7 44 C7
ECCL WA10 8 E2
PR/KW L34 * 100 F7
WAL/NB CH45 95 J4
WGNE/HIN WN2 81 G5
WGNW/BIL/O WN5 68 B7
Athertons Yd WGN WN1 * 68 E1
Athlone Rd WARRN/WOL WA2 121 J4
Athol Cl NEWLW WA12 104 B1
PS/BROM CH62 144 A8
Athol Crs WGNE/HIN WN2 81 K1
Athol Dr PS/BROM CH62 144 A8
Athole Gv CHTN/BK PR9 25 H6
Athol Gv CHLYE PR6 33 G7
Atholl Crs AIN/FAZ L10 84 F3
Atholl Gv WGNS/IIMK WN3 79 J2
Athol St BIRK CH41 11 K4
EV L5 96 D8
Atkinson Gv HUY L36 116 B1
Atkinson St WGNE/HIN WN2 80 D5
Atlanta Ct NWD/KWIPK L33 73 M7
Atlantic Point Village
VAUX/LVPD L3 13 G3
Atlantic Rd BTL L20 6 E4
Atlantic Wy NTHTN L30 84 A5
VAUX/LVPD L3 128 F1
Atlas Ct STHEL WA9 9 K5
Atlas Rd BTL L20 6 D4
Atlas St STHEL WA9 9 K5
Atterbury Cl WDN WA8 133 L3
Atterbury St TOX L8 113 G8
Attingham Wk WGNS/IIMK WN3 68 C8
Attlee Av GOL/RIS/CU WA3 107 K1
Attlee Rd HUY L36 116 C2
Attwood St ANF/KKDL L4 97 H6
Atwell St NPK/KEN L6 113 J1
Aubourn Cl WDN WA8 133 L2
Aubrey Ct NPK/KEN L6 113 J1
Auburn Rd CLB/OSW/ST L13 98 A8
WAL/NB CH45 95 J6
The Aubynes WAL/NB CH45 95 G6
Auckery Av GTS/LS CH66 162 F2
Audie Murphy Rd
WARRW/BUR WA5 120 D7
Audlem Av CL/PREN CH43 127 H2
Audlem Cl RUNC WA7 161 H1
Audley St VAUX/LVPD L3 13 K5
Audre Cl WARRW/BUR WA5 119 M7
Aughton Cl WGNW/BIL/O WN5 90 A1
Aughton Ms STHP PR8 2 F8
Aughton Park Dr ORM L39 62 F3
Aughton Rd BTL L20 83 M8
STHP PR8 2 E7
Aughton St ORM L39 62 F1
WGNE/HIN WN2 80 E1
Augusta Cl CLB/OSW/ST L13 114 C3
August Rd NPK/KEN L6 97 L8
August St BTL L20 7 H1
Aukland Gv STHEL WA9 101 M6
Aukland Rd CALD/MH L18 114 C8
Aurorean Cl NTHLY L27 115 M7
Austell Cl RNFD/HAY WA11 89 M6
Austen Dr WARRN/WOL WA2 105 J7
Austin Av AIMK WN4 91 G1
ECCL WA10 101 L5
Austin Cl KKBY L32 85 M3
Austin St LEIGH WN7 * 81 M8
WAL/EG CH44 * 111 J3
Austral Av WARR WA1 122 D6
Australia La WARRS WA4 138 E4
Autumn Gv RF/TRAN CH42 128 A5
Avalon Ter BTL L20 6 D2
Avebury Cl GOL/RIS/CU WA3 93 G5
WDN WA8 135 G2
Aveley Cl WARR WA1 122 D6
Aveling Dr CHTN/BK PR9 23 J7
Avelon Cl CL/PREN CH43 110 F8
MGHL L31 61 K8
Avenham Cl CHTN/BK PR9 23 K8
Avenham Rd CHLY/EC PR7 32 E6
The Avenue ALL/GAR L19 131 G8
CHLYE PR6 44 C5
CHTN/BK PR9 23 H8
CHTN/BK PR9 26 B8
ECCL WA10 101 K2
HLWD L26 132 A6
HUY L36 116 A2
LYMM WA13 139 L4
NEWLW WA12 104 E1
ORM L39 50 F7
PS/BROM CH62 143 L5
RNFD/HAY WA11 76 B7
WGN WN1 68 F3
WGNNW/ST WN6 68 A1
WGNW/BIL/O WN5 77 M2
Averham Cl AIMK WN4 91 K4
Avery Cl WARRN/WOL WA2 122 A3
Avery Crs RNFD/HAY WA11 90 E6
Avery Rd RNFD/HAY WA11 90 E6
Avery Sq RNFD/HAY WA11 90 E6
Aviary Ct WLT/FAZ L9 * 84 B7
Aviemore Cl AIMK WN4 90 F1
Aviemore Dr WARRN/WOL WA2 122 C2
Aviemore Rd CLB/OSW/ST L13 114 B2
Avocet Cl NEWLW WA12 104 E1
WARRN/WOL WA2 121 M2
Avolon Rd WD/CROXPK L12 98 F8
Avon WDN WA8 133 J3
Avon Av WARRW/BUR WA5 136 B1
Avon Cl ANF/KKDL L4 97 G5
NWD/KWIPK L33 74 B7
Avondale EP CH65 20 B9
Avondale Av MGHL L31 72 E5
MOR/LEA CH46 110 B4
PS/BROM CH62 144 A8
Avondale Dr WDN WA8 133 K4
Avondale Rd CHLY/EC PR7 32 E6
CHTN/BK PR9 3 H1
HOY CH47 108 D6
RNFD/HAY WA11 90 E6
WAV L15 114 A7
WGN WN1 68 E3
Avondale Rd North
CHTN/BK PR9 24 E4
Avondale St WGNNW/ST WN6 56 A3
Avonmore Av CALD/MH L18 130 C2
Avon Rd AIMK WN4 80 A8
GOL/RIS/CU WA3 107 J3
WGNW/BIL/O WN5 67 L6
WGNW/BIL/O WN5 89 M2
Avon St BIRK CH41 111 H4
NPK/KEN L6 * 97 K8
Awelon Cl WD/CROXPK L12 98 E5
Axbridge Av STHEL WA9 102 F8
Axholme Cl PEN/TH CH61 126 D8
Axholme Rd PEN/TH CH61 126 C8
Ayala Cl BTL L20 84 B6
Aycliffe Rd STHEL WA9 * 101 M7
Aye Bridge Rd GOL/RIS/CU WA3 80 D8
Aylesbury Av CL/PREN CH43 127 G3
Aylesbury Cl GTS/LS CH66 162 E2
Aylesbury Crs WGNE/HIN WN2 81 L3
Aylesbury Rd WAL/NB CH45 95 L6
Aylesford Rd CLB/OSW/ST L13 114 C2
Aylsham Cl WDN WA8 133 L2
Aylsham Dr GR/UP/WCH CH49 110 C6
Aylton Rd HUY L36 115 K1
Aylward Pl BTL L20 * 6 F2
Aynsley Ct STHEL WA9 101 L7
Ayr Cl STHP PR8 36 B1
Ayrefield Gv WGNNW/ST WN6 54 F7
Ayrefield La SKEL WN8 66 E1
Ayres Ct STHEL WA9 102 A6
Ayrshire Gdns ECCL WA10 8 D7
Ayrshire Rd ANF/KKDL L4 97 L5
Aysgarth Av WD/CROXPK L12 98 E7
Aysgarth Rd WAL/NB CH45 95 H7
Azalea Gv HLWD L26 131 M3
RUNC WA7 161 H1

B

Babbacombe Rd CHLDW L16 115 G7
WARRW/BUR WA5 136 A1
Babylon La CHLYE PR6 44 E4
Back Ashby St CHLY/EC PR7 32 E7
Back Barlow La ANF/KKDL L4 97 G5
Back Bath St STHP PR8 3 G2
Back Beau St EV L5 * 13 J2
Back Bedford St EHL/KEN L7 13 M9
Back Belmont Rd NPK/KEN L6 97 K8
Back Berry St CLVPS L1 13 J9
Back Blackfield Ter ANF/KKDL L4 96 F6
Back Bold St CLVPS L1 13 H8
Back Boundary St EV L5 96 F7
Back Bridge St NEWLW WA12 104 D2
Back Bridport St VAUX/LVPD L3 13 J6
Back Brook Pl WARRS WA4 15 L9
Back Canning St TOX L8 113 H5
Back Catharine St TOX L8 113 H5
Back Chadwick Mt EV L5 97 G6
Back Chatham Pl EHL/KEN L7 113 K4
Back Colquitt St CLVPS L1 13 J9
Back Commutation St
VAUX/LVPD L3 13 J6
Back Crosland Ter
FROD/HEL WA6 166 D3
Back Cross La NEWLW WA12 104 D1
Back Drinkhouse La
CROS/BRETH PR26 29 J3
Back Eastford Rd WARRS WA4 137 J4
Back Egerton St North
TOX L8 * 113 H6
Back Falkner St South TOX L8 113 H5
Backford Cl CL/PREN CH43 127 G2
RUNC WA7 150 E8
Backford Gdns GTS/LS CH66 163 H6
Backford Rd PEN/TH CH61 125 M8
Backford Wy CL/PREN CH43 127 G2
Back Forest Rd STHP PR8 3 L6
Back Forshaw St
WARRN/WOL WA2 15 G2
Back Gillmoss La NG/CROX L11 85 L7
Back Granton Rd EV L5 97 J7
Back Guilford St NPK/KEN L6 13 M2
Back High St RUNC WA7 19 G3
Back Holland Pl EHL/KEN L7 113 K4
Back Hope Pl CLVPS L1 13 L9
Back Huskisson St TOX L8 * 113 H6
Back Kelvin Gv TOX L8 113 J7
Back Knight St CLVPS L1 113 G5
Back La BRSC L40 39 G7
BRSC L40 40 D5
BRSC L40 52 F3
CHLY/EC PR7 31 H6
CROS/BRETH PR26 29 H1
CSBY/BLUN L23 71 H5
FROD/HEL WA6 166 E3
ORM L39 62 A5
ORM L39 74 C2
RNFD/HAY WA11 77 H8
SKEL WN8 53 J3
SKEL WN8 65 M7
WARRW/BUR WA5 103 M6
WARRW/BUR WA5 135 J3
WGNNW/ST WN6 55 H4
Back La East BRSC L40 41 G4
Back Leeds St VAUX/LVPD L3 12 D4
Back Legh St NEWLW WA12 104 C2
Back Lime St CLVPS L1 13 H7
Back Little Canning St TOX L8 * 113 H6
Back Luton Gv ANF/KKDL L4 97 G5
Back Market St NEWLW WA12 104 C1
WGNE/HIN WN2 * 69 M8
Back Maryland St CLVPS L1 * 13 K9
Back Menai St CL/PREN CH43 10 F6
Back Mersey Vw CSBY/WL L22 82 E3
Back Mesnes St WGN WN1 4 F2
Back Moss La BRSC L40 39 H6
Back Mt CHLY/EC PR7 * 32 E5
Back Mount St CSBY/WL L22 * 82 F4
Back Mount Vernon Gn
EHL/KEN L7 * 113 J4
Back Mulberry St EHL/KEN L7 * 113 H5
Back Oliver St BIRK CH41 11 K6
Back Orford St WAV L15 114 B5
Back O the Town La HTWN L38 71 H2
Back Percy St TOX L8 113 H6
Back Pickop St VAUX/LVPD L3 12 F5
Back Railway Vw CHLY/EC PR7 44 C7
Back Renshaw St CLVPS L1 13 K9
Back Rockfield Rd ANF/KKDL L4 97 H6
Back Rw SKEL WN8 * 66 E6
Back St Bride St EHL/KEN L7 113 H5
Back Sandon St TOX L8 113 H6
Back Sandstone Rd
CLB/OSW/ST L13 114 B1
Back School La SKEL WN8 64 F4
SKEL WN8 66 E6
Back Seaview HOY CH47 108 D6
Back Seel St CLVPS L1 13 H9
Back Sir Howard St
EHL/KEN L7 * 113 H5
Back South Rd CSBY/WL L22 83 G4
Back Stanley Rd BTL L20 7 H4
Back Towerlands St
EHL/KEN L7 113 K4
Back Virginia St STHP PR8 3 H6
Back Wellesley Rd TOX L8 129 J1
Back Westminster Rd
ANF/KKDL L4 97 G5
Back Windsor Vw TOX L8 * 113 K6
Back Winstanley Rd
CSBY/WL L22 83 G3
Back York Ter EV L5 * 97 G7
Baclaw Cl WGN WN1 5 M2
Badbury Cl RNFD/HAY WA11 90 F6
Badby Wd NWD/KWIPK L33 86 B1
Baden Rd CLB/OSW/ST L13 114 D2
Bader Cl PEN/TH CH61 141 G2
Badger Bait NSTN CH64 153 H7
Badger Cl RUNC WA7 150 C7
Badgers Cl GTS/LS CH66 163 H5
Badgers Pk NSTN CH64 153 H7
Badgers Rake FMBY L37 46 E8
Badger's Set WKBY CH48 124 F7
Badgers Wk CHLY/EC PR7 32 D2
Badger Wy CL/PREN CH43 127 G5
Badminton St TOX L8 * 129 H2
Baffin Cl MOR/LEA CH46 110 C1
Bagganley La CHLYE PR6 33 G4
Bagnall Cl WARRW/BUR WA5 120 E8
Bagnall St ANF/KKDL L4 97 J6
Bagot Av WARRW/BUR WA5 121 H5
Bagot St WAV L15 113 M6
Baguley Av WDN WA8 133 J8
Bahama Cl RNFD/HAY WA11 90 F5
Bahama Rd RNFD/HAY WA11 90 F5
Bailey Av EP CH65 156 B7
Bailey Dr BTL L20 84 A7
Baileys Cl WDN WA8 118 C8
Baileys La HLWD L26 132 C5
SPK/HALE L24 147 J4
Bailey St CLVPS L1 113 G6
Bainbridge Av GOL/RIS/CU WA3 93 H5
Bainton Cl KKBY L32 86 C6
Bainton Rd KKBY L32 86 C6
Baird Av BTL L20 6 C2
Baker Dr GTS/LS CH66 163 G2
Baker Rd RUNC WA7 18 B9
Bakers Green Rd HUY L36 116 A1
Baker's La CHTN/BK PR9 25 J2
Bakers St HUY L36 116 C3
Baker St NPK/KEN L6 113 J2
STHEL WA9 9 M5
WGNS/IIMK WN3 4 C8
Baker Wy NPK/KEN L6 113 J2
Bakewell Cl GTS/LS CH66 163 G5
Bakewell Dr WGNNW/ST WN6 68 C1
Bakewell Gv WLT/FAZ L9 84 D6
Bakewell Rd WARRW/BUR WA5 104 C8
Bala Cl WARRW/BUR WA5 * 121 G3
Bala Gv WAL/EG CH44 * 111 J2
Bala St ANF/KKDL L4 97 K7
Balcarres Av CALD/MH L18 114 B8
WGN WN1 69 G3
Balcarres Rd CHLY/EC PR7 32 D8
WGNE/HIN WN2 69 K1
Baldock Cl WARRS WA4 138 E2
Baldwin Av CHLDW L16 115 H5
Baldwin St ECCL WA10 9 G4
WGN WN1 5 H3
WGNE/HIN WN2 81 K2
WGNW/BIL/O WN5 67 K8
The Bales NTHTN L30 84 C1
Balfe St LITH L21 83 J7
Balfour Av BTL L20 * 6 F1
Balfour Rd BTL L20 6 E1
CL/PREN CH43 10 D8
STHP PR8 25 G8
WAL/EG CH44 111 J3
Balfour St ANF/KKDL L4 97 H6
ECCL WA10 8 A6
RUNC WA7 18 F5
Balham Cl WDN WA8 134 C1
Balharry Av RNFD/HAY WA11 91 H6
Balker Dr ECCL WA10 8 E1
Ballantrae Rd CALD/MH L18 130 E2
Ballantyne Dr CL/PREN CH43 110 E4
Ballantyne Gv BTL L20 84 A7
CLB/OSW/ST L13 98 A6
Ballantyne Pl CLB/OSW/ST L13 98 A6
WARRN/WOL WA2 105 J7
Ballantyne Rd CLB/OSW/ST L13 98 A7
Ballantyne Wy GOL/RIS/CU WA3 93 G5
Ballard Rd WKBY CH48 125 G2
Ballater Dr WARRN/WOL WA2 122 A1
Ball Av WAL/NB CH45 95 J5
Balliol Cl CL/PREN CH43 110 E4
Balliol Gv CSBY/BLUN L23 82 D3
Balliol Rd BTL L20 7 H7
Balliol Rd East BTL L20 7 K6
Balliol Wy AIMK WN4 91 H1
Ball Pth WDN WA8 134 A4
Ball's Pl STHP PR8 3 G4
Ball's Rd CL/PREN CH43 10 E8
Ball's Rd East BIRK CH41 10 E8
Balmer St STHEL WA9 101 M6
Balmoral CHLY/EC PR7 44 A7
Balmoral Av CSBY/BLUN L23 83 G2
GOL/RIS/CU WA3 92 F4
STHEL WA9 102 E6
Balmoral Cl CHTN/BK PR9 25 K2
NWD/KWIPK L33 74 A8
Balmoral Ct CLB/OSW/ST L13 98 A8
Balmoral Dr CHTN/BK PR9 25 K2
FMBY L37 59 G4
FROD/HEL WA6 166 D1
WGNE/HIN WN2 80 E1
Balmoral Gdns CL/PREN CH43 * 127 H4
EP CH65 * 20 E9
Balmoral Gv CL/PREN CH43 126 F2
Balmoral Rd AIMK WN4 91 J1
CHLY/EC PR7 30 E6
CHLY/EC PR7 32 D6
MGHL L31 72 E4
NPK/KEN L6 113 L2
WAL/NB CH45 95 K4
WARRS WA4 138 B3
WDN WA8 134 C1
WGNW/BIL/O WN5 68 A7
WLT/FAZ L9 * 84 C7
Balmoral Wy HUY L36 100 B8
Balm St EHL/KEN L7 113 K3
Balniel Cl CHLY/EC PR7 32 D6
Balniel St STHEL WA9 118 F2
Balniel Wk WGN WN1 69 G3
Balsham Cl WLTN L25 131 L6
Balshaw La CHLY/EC PR7 31 M4
Baltic Rd BTL L20 6 E4
Baltic St ANF/KKDL L4 97 J6
Baltimore St CLVPS L1 13 K9
Bamber Gdns CHTN/BK PR9 25 K3
Bamber St CHLY/EC PR7 32 D8
Bamboo Cl NTHLY L27 116 A7
Bamburgh Ct EP CH65 21 G8
Bamburgh Pl AIMK WN4 79 J8
Bamford Cl RUNC WA7 149 L7
Bamford Dr WGNE/HIN WN2 5 L1
Bampton Av RNFD/HAY WA11 89 K4
Bampton Rd CHLDW L16 114 F5
Banastre CHLY/EC PR7 32 C3
Banastre Dr NEWLW WA12 105 H2
Banastre Rd STHP PR8 2 F8
Banbury Av WLTN L25 131 L3
Banbury Dr WARRW/BUR WA5 136 E1
Banbury Rd WGNW/BIL/O WN5 77 M3
Banbury Wy CL/PREN CH43 127 G3
Bancroft Cl WLTN L25 131 L6
Bancroft Rd WDN WA8 134 F3
Bandon Cl SPK/HALE L24 147 M3
Banff Av BEB CH63 143 L8
Bangor Cl GTS/LS CH66 163 G5
Bangor Rd WAL/NB CH45 94 F7
Bangor St EV L5 96 F8
Banham Av WGNS/IIMK WN3 78 E2
Bank Av WGNW/BIL/O WN5 66 F8
Bankbrook WGNNW/ST WN6 67 M1
Bank Brow SKEL WN8 54 E8
Bank Buildings
WGNE/HIN WN2 * 80 C3
Bankburn Rd CLB/OSW/ST L13 98 A7
Bank Cl NSTN CH64 153 J7
Bank Dene RF/TRAN CH42 128 C5
Bankes Av WGNW/BIL/O WN5 67 J7
Bankes' La RUNC WA7 149 H8
Bankfield SKEL WN8 65 L6
Bankfield Ct CLB/OSW/ST L13 98 B8
Bankfield La CHTN/BK PR9 25 K3
Bankfield Rd CLB/OSW/ST L13 98 B8
WDN WA8 133 K4
Bankfields Dr PS/BROM CH62 144 D8
Bankfield St BTL L20 96 D5
Bank Gdns WARRW/BUR WA5 136 A1
Bankhall Cl WGNE/HIN WN2 81 K4
Bankhall La BTL L20 96 E6
Bankhall St BTL L20 96 E5
Bankhey NSTN CH64 153 H8
Bank House La FROD/HEL WA6 166 E1
Bankland Rd CLB/OSW/ST L13 98 B8
Bank La MGHL L31 73 L7
Bank Ms FROD/HEL WA6 * 166 E1
Bank Nook CHTN/BK PR9 * 25 H2
Bank Pas GOL/RIS/CU WA3 * 92 C4
Bank Rd BTL L20 6 F4
SKEL WN8 54 E8
Banks Av HOY CH47 108 F5
Banksbarn SKEL WN8 65 L6
Banks Ct LEIGH WN7 81 M8
Banks Crs WARRS WA4 138 B1
Bankside HTWN L38 70 B2
RUNC WA7 151 G6
SKEL WN8 53 K3
Bankside Av AIMK WN4 79 J5
Bankside Rd RF/TRAN CH42 128 B5
Bank's La ALL/GAR L19 145 M1
SPK/HALE L24 146 B3
Bank Sq CHTN/BK PR9 3 G1
Bank's Rd ALL/GAR L19 130 E8
CHTN/BK PR9 22 F7
HES CH60 140 E5
WKBY CH48 124 C4
The Banks WAL/NB CH45 * 95 G6
Bank St BIRK CH41 11 K6
CHLY/EC PR7 32 E5
CHLY/EC PR7 44 B6

ECCL WA10 ....8 C6
GOL/RIS/CU WA3 ....92 C4
NEWLW WA12 ....104 B2
WARR WA1 ....14 F6
WDN WA8 ....149 J1
WGNE/HIN WN2
WGNW/BIL/O WN5 ....80 C2
Bank's Wy ALL/GAR L19 ....68 A7
Bankville Rd RF/TRAN CH42 ...128 A2
Bankwood WGNE/HIN WN2
Banner Cl CHLY/EC PR7 ....30 D6
Banner Hey RAIN/WH L35 .....116 F4
Bannerman Ter CHLYE PR6 ....32 F3
Banner St ECCL WA10 ....8 E6
WAV L15 ....114 A6
WGNS/IIMK WN3 ....5 J9
Banning Cl BIRK CH41 ....11 G4
Bannister Gn CHLY/EC PR7 .....41 L2
Bannister La BRSC L40 ....41 G7
Bannister St CHLY/EC PR7 .....32 E6
Bannister Wy WGNS/IIMK WN3 ..79 G3
Banstead Gv WAV L15 ....114 A6
Barbara Av ALL/FAZ L10 ....85 J6
Barbara St STHEL WA9 ....119 L2
Barbauld St WARR WA1 ....14 E7
Barberry Cl MOR/LEA CH46 ...109 K5
Barberry Crs NTHTN L30 ....84 C1
Barber St STHEL WA9 ....9 K4
Barbondale Cl
 WARRW/BUR WA5 ....120 B6
Barbrook Cl WARRN/WOL WA2 ..55 K3
Barbrook Wy WLT/FAZ L9 ....97 K2
Barchester Dr AIG/SPK L17 ...129 L1
Barclay St TOX L8 * 129 H1
Barcombe Rd HES CH60 ....141 M4
Bardale Gv AIMK WN4 ....91 J2
Bardley Crs RUNC WA7 ....116 C6
Bardney Av GOL/RIS/CU WA3 ...92 B3
Bardon Cl WLTN L25 ....115 L8
Bardsay Rd ANF/KKDL L4 ....97 H4
Bardsey Cl EP CH65 ....163 L4
Bardsley Av WARRW/BUR WA5 .121 H3
Bardsley Cl SKEL WN8 ....66 C6
Barford Cl CL/PREN CH43 .....110 D7
SKEL WN8 ....66 C6
STHP PR8 ....34 C7
WARRW/BUR WA5 ....120 D4
Barford Dr GOL/RIS/CU WA3 ...93 J5
Barford Gra NSTN CH64 ....94 D5
Barford Rd HUY L36 ....100 B3
SPK/HALE L24 ....131 K7
Barham Ct GOL/RIS/CU WA3 ...122 F1
Barholm Cl CL/PREN CH43 * 10 E2
Barington Dr RUNC WA7 ....151 G6
Barkbeth Rd HUY L36 ....99 J8
Barkeley Dr LITH L21 ....83 H7
Barker Cl HUY L36 ....116 B5
Barker La GR/UP/WCH CH49 ..125 M3
Barker Wy NPK/KEN L6 ....97 K8
Barker Rd PEN/TH CH61 ....126 D7
Barker's Hollow Rd
 WARRS WA4 ....151 J7
Barker St LEIGH WN7 ....81 L8
Barkerville Cl CLB/OSW/ST L13 .97 M6
Barker Wy NPK/KEN L6 ....97 K8
Barkfield Av FMBY L37 ....59 G1
Barkfield La FMBY L37 ....58 F1
Barkhill Ct AIG/SPK L17 * 130 B4
Barkhill Rd AIG/SPK L17 ....130 B4
Barkiss Cl TOX L8 ....113 H8
Bark Rd LITH L21 ....113 H8
Barlborough Rd
 WGNW/BIL/O WN5 ....67 M8
Barley Brook St
 WGNNW/ST WN6 ....4 B1
Barleycastle La WARRS WA4 ...138 F8
Barleyfield PEN/TH CH61 ......141 G1
Barley Mow Cl CH/BCN CH1 ...162 E3
Barley Rd WARRS WA4 ....138 E2
Barlow Av BEB CH63 ....128 C6
Barlow Cl STHEL WA9 ....103 J3
Barlow La ANF/KKDL L4 ....97 G5
Barlows Cl WLT/FAZ L9 ....84 F5
Barlow's La ORM L39 ....35 M8
 WLT/FAZ L9 ....84 F5
Barlow St ANF/KKDL L4 ....97 G5
Barmouth Cl WARRW/BUR WA5 .121 G3
Barmouth Rd WAL/NB CH45 ....94 F7
Barmouth Wy EV L5 ....96 F8
Barmskin La CHLY/EC PR7 ......41 L4
Barnack Cl WARR WA1 ....122 C5
Barnacre La WKBY CH48 ....148 A7
Barnacre La WKBY CH48 ....109 K7
Barnard Rd CL/PREN CH43 .....10 F3
Barnard St WARRW/BUR WA5 .136 F2
Barn Cft NTHTN L30 ....84 C1
Barncroft RUNC WA7 ....150 F6
Barn Croft Rd HLWD L26 .....132 C6
The Barncroft
 GR/UP/WCH CH49 * 125 M1
Barndale Rd CALD/MH L18 ....130 B1
Barnes Av WARRN/WOL WA2 ..122 D3
Barnes Cl NWD/KWIPK L33 ....74 A7
 WARRW/BUR WA5 ....120 C8
 WDN WA8 ....134 F3
Barnes Dr MGHL L31 ....72 E1
Barnes Gn BEB CH63 ....143 J4
Barnes Rd ORM L39 ....35 G2
 SKEL WN8 ....64 F4
 WDN WA8 ....134 E3
Barnes St NPK/KEN L6 ....97 J8
Barneston Rd WDN WA8 ....135 G2
Barnet Cl EHL/KEN L7 ....113 L5
Barnett Av NEWLW WA12 ......104 A2
Barnfield Cl GTS/LS CH66 .....162 E3
 HOY CH47 ....109 G4
 NTHTN L30 ....84 A3
 WD/CROXPK L12 ....98 D7
Barnfield Dr SKEL WN8 ....66 A6
 WD/CROXPK L12 ....98 D7
Barnfield Rd WARR WA1 ......122 E6
Barngill Gv WGNS/IIMK WN3 ...79 G2
Barnham Cl GOL/RIS/CU WA3 ...92 C5
 SPK/HALE L24 ....146 D1
Barn Hey HOY CH47 ....108 C8
Barn Hey Crs HOY CH47 ......109 H6
Barn Hey Rd NWD/KWIPK L33 ..86 C3
Barnhill Rd WAV L15 ....114 C7
Barnhurst Cl CHLDW L16 ......115 G6
Barnhurst Rd CHLDW L16 .....115 G6
Barn La GOL/RIS/CU WA3 ....92 B6
Barnmeadow Rd WLTN L25 ....115 J2
Barnsbury Rd ANF/KKDL L4 ....97 G1
Barnsdale Av PEN/TH CH61 ...126 D8
Barnside CHLY/EC PR7 ....31 L2
Barnside Ct CHLDW L16 ....115 G6
Barnsley St WGNNW/ST WN6 ..15 H3
Barnstaple Wy
 WARRW/BUR WA5 ....136 A1
Barnston Av EP CH65 ....156 B8
Barnston La MOR/LEA CH46 ...110 A5
Barnston Rd HES CH60 ....141 M5
 PEN/TH CH61 ....126 D7

WLT/FAZ L9 ....84 C6
Barnston Towers Cl HES CH60 ..141 L5
Barnstream Cl NTHLY L27 .....115 L6
Barn St WDN WA8 ....16 C8
Barnswood Cl WARRS WA4 ....138 E4
Barnton Cl GOL/RIS/CU WA3 ...92 F4
Barnwell Av GOL/RIS/CU WA3 ..104 D2
Barnwell Av GOL/RIS/CU WA3 ..106 F1
 WAL/EG CH44 ....95 K8
Barnwood Rd HUY L36 ....115 K1
Baron Cl WARR WA1 ....122 F6
Baroncroft Rd WLTN L25 ......131 H1
Baron's Cl WDN WA8 ....133 L5
Barons Great Outdoors
 CHLY/EC PR7 * 43 H5
Baron's Hey STBRV L28 ....99 H5
Barons Wy CHLY/EC PR7 ....31 M5
Barrack Sq WGN WN1 * 4 F4
Barracks Rd WGNE/HIN WN2 ...80 F4
Barracks Yd GOL/RIS/CU WN1 * .4 F4
Barren Gv CL/PREN CH43 ....10 D9
Barrett Av STHP PR8 ....35 J3
Barrett Rd STHP PR8 ....35 J3
Barrie St LEIGH WN7 ....81 M5
Barrington Cl WGNS/IIMK WN3 ..78 F3
Barrington Dr STHP PR8 ....34 D8
Barrington Rd WAL/EG CH44 ..111 L2
 WAV L15 ....114 A7
Barrison Gn BRSC L40 ....51 G3
Baron Meadow LEIGH WN7 .....81 M6
Barrow Av WARRN/WOL WA2 ..122 A3
Barrow Cl WD/CROXPK L12 .....98 E4
Barrowcroft Cl WGN WN1 ......56 D4
Barrowdale Rd
 GOL/RIS/CU WA3 ....92 D5
Barrowfield Rd ECCL WA10 ....88 C8
Barrow Hall La
 WARRW/BUR WA5 ....120 A6
Barrow La GOL/RIS/CU WA3 ...105 L3
Barrow Nook La ORM L39 ......75 G2
Barrow's Green La WDN WA8 ..135 G3
Barrow's Rw WDN WA8 ....135 G3
Barrow St AIMK WN4 ....79 M8
 ECCL WA10 ....9 G5
Barrule Cl WARRS WA4 ....137 M6
Barry Cl EP CH65 ....163 L5
Barrymore Av WARRS WA4 ....138 B1
Barrymore Rd CLB/OSW/ST L13 .114 B2
 RUNC WA7 ....149 K6
Barrymore Wy BEB CH63 ......143 K7
Barry St WARRS WA4 ....15 H8
Barsbank Cl LYMM WA13 ....139 L2
Barsbank La LYMM WA13 ......139 L2
Bar St WGNE/HIN WN2 ....80 C4
Bartholomew Cl RAIN/WH L35 .118 A4
Bartlegate RUNC WA7 ....150 D8
Bartlett St WAV L15 ....114 A6
Barton Av WARRS WA4 ....138 C3
 WGN WN1 ....68 D3
Barton Cl ECCL WA10 ....8 E4
 HOY CH47 ....108 B7
 LITH L21 ....83 J3
 RUNC WA7 ....150 F6
Barton Clough
 WGNW/BIL/O WN5 ....78 A8
Barton Hey Dr WKBY CH48 ...124 E7
Barton Heys Rd FMBY L37 .....58 F4
Barton Rd HOY CH47 ....108 C7
 WLT/FAZ L9 ....97 H1
Bartons Cl CHTN/BK PR9 ....22 F8
Barton St BIRK CH41 ....10 F7
 GOL/RIS/CU WA3 ....92 C5
 WGNE/HIN WN2 ....80 D2
 WGNW/BIL/O WN5 ....67 K8
Barwell Av RNFD/HAY WA11 ...89 L7
Barwell Cl GOL/RIS/CU WA3 ...92 E4
Basil Cl CHLDW L16 ....115 G5
Basildon Ct STHEL WA9 ....102 A7
Basil Rd CHLDW L16 ....114 F5
Basing St ALL/GAR L19 ....130 E7
Baskervyle Cl HES CH60 ......141 J7
Baskervyle Rd HES CH60 .....141 J7
Baslow Av WGNE/HIN WN2 .....81 H1
Basnett St CLVPS L1 ....13 G2
Bassendale Rd PS/BROM CH62 .144 A3
Bassenthwaite Av
 CL/PREN CH43 ....110 F8
 NWD/KWIPK L33 ....85 M1
 RNFD/HAY WA11 ....89 J5
Basset St WGNS/IIMK WN3 .....78 E3
Basswood Gn WGNE/HIN WN2 ..81 J1
Bates Crs ECCL WA10 ....101 M5
Bates La FROD/HEL WA6 ......166 F2
Batey Av RAIN/WH L35 ....117 K1
Batheaston Gv LEIGH WN7 .....81 M6
Batherton Cl WDN WA8 ....16 E6
Bathgate Wy NWD/KWIPK L33 ..73 M7
Bath Springs ORM L39 ....51 H8
Bath St CSBY/WL L22 ....82 F5
 ECCL WA10 ....8 F6
 PS/BROM CH62 ....128 D8
 STHP PR8 ....3 G2
 VAUX/LVPD L3 ....12 C5
 WARR WA1 ....14 D6
 WGNE/HIN WN2 ....69 H3
Bath St North CHTN/BK PR9 ....3 H1
Bathurst Rd ALL/GAR L19 .....130 F6
Bathwood Dr NSTN CH64 .....153 G8
Batley St CLB/OSW/ST L13 ...114 C2
Battenberg St EHL/KEN L7 ...113 J3
Battersby La WARRN/WOL WA2 ..15 L3
Battersby St WGNE/HIN WN2 ..69 K5
Battersea Ct WDN WA8 * 134 B2
Battery La WAV L15 ....114 A7
Battle Wy FMBY L37 * 59 K3
Baucher Dr BTL L20 ....84 A6
Baucher Rd WGNS/IIMK WN3 ..68 B8
Baumville Dr BEB CH63 ....143 H5
Baverstock Cl WGNS/IIMK WN3 ..5 H7
Bawtry Ct WARRN/WOL WA2 ..122 A4
Baxter Cl RUNC WA7 ....150 F6
Baxters La STHEL WA9 ....102 F5
Baxter's Rw WGNE/HIN WN2 ...81 K3
Baxter St WARRW/BUR WA5 ..121 G8
Baycliff Cl WGNE/HIN WN2 .....81 H2
Baycliffe LYMM WA13 ....139 M3
Baycliffe Cl RUNC WA7 ....149 M8
Bayfield Rd ALL/GAR L19 .....130 C6
Bayhorse La VAUX/LVPD L3 ....13 L1
Baysdale Cl TOX L8 ....129 J1
Bayswater Cl RUNC WA7 ....151 H1
Bayswater Gdns WAL/NB CH45 ..94 F6
Bayswater Rd WAL/NB CH45 ...94 F6
Baythorne Rd ANF/KKDL L4 ....97 L5
Baytree Cl CHTN/BK PR9 ....22 F8
 GTS/LS CH66 ....163 H4
Baytree Gv MGHL L31 ....85 J1
Baytree Rd RF/TRAN CH42 ...128 A2
 WGNNW/ST WN6 ....68 B3
Bayview Dr WAL/NB CH45 ......94 F6
Bayvil Cl RUNC WA7 ....151 G6
Beacham Rd STHP PR8 ....25 G6
Beach Bank CSBY/WL L22 .....82 E5
Beachcroft Rd HOY CH47 ....108 F4
Beach Gv WAL/NB CH45 ....95 L6

Beach Lawn CSBY/WL L22 ......82 E4
Beach Priory Gdns STHP PR8 ...2 E5
Beach Rd HOY CH47 ....108 B7
 LITH L21 ....83 J5
 STHP PR8 ....2 C6
Beach Wk WKBY CH48 ....124 D5
Beacon Crossing SKEL WN8 ...53 L3
Beacon Dr WKBY CH48 ....124 E3
Beacon Gv RNFD/HAY WA11 ...89 M7
Beacon Hl WGNW/BIL/O WN5 * .77 M6
Beacon Hill Vw RUNC WA7 * 8 A9
Beacon La BRSC L40 ....53 J7
 EV L5 ....97 H7
 HES CH60 ....141 J6
 SKEL WN8 ....66 B3
Beaconsfield Cl BIRK CH41 ...128 B2
Beaconsfield Crs WDN WA8 ...134 C1
Beaconsfield Gv WDN WA8 ....134 D1
Beaconsfield Rd CHTN/BK PR9 ..88 E8
 ECCL WA10 ....8 A3
 LITH L21 ....83 H6
 PS/BROM CH62 ....128 D6
 RUNC WA7 ....18 D7
 WLTN L25 ....131 G2
Beaconsfield St TOX L8 ....113 J7
Beaconsfield Ter ALL/GAR L7 * .130 D7
 CHLYE PR6 ....32 F3
Beacon Vw WGNNW/ST WN6 ..54 F5
Beacon View Dr SKEL WN8 .....66 D6
Beadnell Dr WARRW/BUR WA5 .136 A2
Beaford Cl WGNW/BIL/O WN5 ...67 K8
Beal Dr WGNE/HIN WN2 ....80 C3
Beames Cl EHL/KEN L7 ....113 L4
Beamont St WDN WA8 ....149 H1
Beardsmore Dr
 GOL/RIS/CU WA3 ....93 C3
Bearncroft SKEL WN8 ....65 L7
Beasley Cl GTS/LS CH66 ......162 F2
Beatrice Av BEB CH63 ....128 A6
Beatrice St BTL L20 ....7 J8
 WARRS WA4 ....15 J9
Beattock Cl NWD/KWIPK L33 ...73 M7
Beatty Av CHLY/EC PR7 ....32 D7
 WARRN/WOL WA2 ....121 L4
Beatty Cl RAIN/WH L35 ....116 F3
 WKBY CH48 ....124 E7
Beatty Rd CLB/OSW/ST L13 ...114 C3
 STHP PR8 ....25 G7
Beauclair Dr WAV L15 ....114 D7
Beaufort Cl ORM L39 ....62 C4
 RUNC WA7 ....149 K6
 WDN WA8 ....133 J7
Beaufort Dr WAL/EG CH44 ...111 G1
Beaufort Rd BIRK CH41 ....111 J4
Beaufort St STHEL WA9 ....9 M9
 TOX L8 ....113 G8
 WARRW/BUR WA5 ....137 G1
 WGNE/HIN WN2 * 69 M8
 WGNW/BIL/O WN5 ....67 L8
Beaumaris Cl WLTN L25 ....131 L1
Beaumaris Dr EP CH65 ....163 M3
Beaumaris Rd WAL/NB CH45 ...94 F7
Beaumaris St BTL L20 ....96 D5
Beaumont Av ECCL WA10 ....8 A4
Beaumont Crs ORM L39 ....62 F3
Beaumont Dr AIN/FAZ L10 .....85 G4
Beaumont Gv
 WGNW/BIL/O WN5 ....67 K5
Beaumont St TOX L8 ....113 K6
Beau St VAUX/LVPD L3 ....13 J1
Beauworth Av
 GR/UP/WCH CH49 * 125 L2
Beaverbrook Av
 GOL/RIS/CU WA3 ....107 K1
Beaver Ct AIMK WN4 ....79 L7
Beaver Gv WLT/FAZ L9 ....84 C7
Beavers La SKEL WN8 ....65 M7
Bebington Rd GTS/LS CH66 ...162 F1
 RF/TRAN CH42 ....127 M3
Bebles Rd ORM L39 ....62 E2
Bechers WDN WA8 ....133 K2
Bechers Dr WLT/FAZ L9 ....84 E3
Bechers Rw WLT/FAZ L9 ....84 D6
Beck Cl AIN/FAZ L10 ....85 K6
Beckenham Av CALD/MH L18 ..114 B8
Beckenham Rd WAL/NB CH45 ...95 K4
Becket St ANF/KKDL L4 ....96 F1
Beckett Cl NWD/KWIPK L33 ....86 E5
Beckett Dr WARRN/WOL WA2 ..105 J8
Beckett Gv BEB CH63 ....127 M6
Beck Gv RNFD/HAY WA11 ......89 K5
Beck Rd BTL L20 ....83 L8
Beckwith WGNE/HIN WN2 ....80 D2
Beckwith St BIRK CH41 ....10 E3
Beckwith St East BIRK CH41 ...11 H4
Becky St NPK/KEN L6 ....97 K8
Becontree Rd WD/CROXPK L12 .114 F1
Bedburn Dr HUY L36 ....115 J2
Bedford Av EP CH65 ....163 J3
 MGHL L31 ....73 H7
 RF/TRAN CH42 ....128 A4
Bedford Av East EP CH65 .....163 K5
Bedford Cl EHL/KEN L7 ....113 H5
 HUY L36 ....116 C2
Bedford Dr RF/TRAN CH42 ...127 M4
Bedford Gdns BIRK CH41 ....10 E4
Bedford Pl AIMK WN4 ....79 J8
 BTL L20 ....6 F8
 LITH L21 ....83 H6
 RF/TRAN CH42 ....128 B3
 STHP PR8 ....35 J3
 WAL/NB CH45 ....95 J4
Bedford Rd East RF/TRAN CH42 .128 C3
Bedford St STHEL WA9 ....102 F3
 WARRS WA4 ....137 L5
 WGN WN1 ....5 J2
 WGNW/BIL/O WN5 * 67 L8
Bedford St North EHL/KEN L7 ..13 H8
 EHL/KEN L7 ....13 M9
Bedford Wk EHL/KEN L7 * 113 H5
Beecham Cl HUY L36 ....115 M4
Beech Av AIG/SPK L17 ....131 K2
 CHLY/EC PR6 ....44 D5
 CSBY/BLUN L23 ....71 J7
 FROD/HEL WA6 ....160 E5
 GOL/RIS/CU WA3 ....93 H6
 GR/UP/WCH CH49 ....109 M7
 MGHL L31 ....85 K2
 PEN/TH CH61 ....101 J4
 PR/KW L34 ....101 H7
 RNFD/HAY WA11 ....91 H6
 SKEL WN8 ....53 L4
 STHEL WA9 ....118 E1

WARRS WA4 ....138 F2
 WARRW/BUR WA5 ....135 L2
Beechbank Rd AIG/SPK L17 ...114 A8
Beechburn Crs HUY L36 ......115 K3
Beechburn Rd HUY L36 ....115 K3
Beech Cl BRSC L40 ....39 L1
 KKBY L32 ....85 L2
 NEWLW WA12 ....104 E3
 SKEL WN8 ....65 G4
 WD/CROXPK L12 ....98 F2
Beech Crs WCNNW/ST WN6 ...56 A5
Beechcroft Dr EP CH65 ....20 A9
Beechcroft Rd WAL/CAR CH44 .111 L3
Beechdale Rd CALD/MH L18 ..130 C1
Beechdene ANF/KKDL L4 ....97 K6
Beech Dr FMBY L37 ....58 F7
Beeches CHLY/EC PR7 ....30 D7
The Beeches CALD/MH L18 ...114 F8
 FROD/HEL WA6 ....166 E1
 MOR/LEA CH46 ....162 F1
 RF/TRAN CH42 ....128 C4
 STHEL WA9 ....102 F8
Beechfield MGHL L31 ....78 G3
 SKEL WN8 ....40 E8
Beechfield Cl HES CH60 ......141 H6
 HLWD L26 ....132 A7
Beechfield Gdns STHP PR8 .....2 D5
Beechfield Rd CALD/MH L18 ..130 F1
 EP CH65 ....20 B4
 WARRS WA4 ....14 F6
Beechfields CHLY/EC PR7 ......30 D7
Beech Gdns STHEL WA9 ....103 L1
Beech Gn CL/PREN CH43 ......10 C5
 GTS/LS CH66 ....163 J5
 LITH L21 ....83 H7
 LYMM WA13 ....139 K3
 NTHTN L30 ....84 C3
 WARR WA1 ....122 C6
 WGNE/HIN WN2 ....80 E6
 WGNNW/ST WN6 ....55 K3
 WLT/FAZ L9 ....84 D7
Beech Hall St WGNNW/ST WN6 .68 A2
Beech Hey La WGNNW/ST WN6 .68 A2
Beech Hill La WGNNW/ST WN6 ..68 A2
Beechill Cl WLTN L25 ....131 L1
Beech Lawn ALL/GAR L19 .....130 B6
Beech Meadow ORM L39 ....63 J1
Beech Mdw PR/KW L34 ....100 C8
Beechmill Dr GOL/RIS/CU WA3 ..93 H5
Beechmoore WARRS WA4 .....136 D8
Beech Pk ANF/KKDL L4 ....97 J4
 BEB CH63 ....128 B6
 COL/RIS/CU WA3 ....92 C4
 HES CH60 ....141 L5
 HUY L36 ....116 A4
Beech Rd ANF/KKDL L4 ....97 J4
 RF/TRAN CH42 ....128 C4
 RUNC WA7 ....19 M8
 WARRS WA4 ....161 K1
 WDN WA8 ....137 L5
Beech St BTL L20 ....96 D5
 ECCL WA10 ....101 M5
 EHL/KEN L7 ....113 L3
Beech Ter EHL/KEN L7 * 113 L3
Beech Tree Av
 WGNNW/ST WN6 ....54 F5
Beech Tree Houses
 WGNE/HIN WN2 ....80 A7
Beechtree Rd WAV L15 ....114 D4
Beechtrees SKEL WN8 ....65 L6
Beechurst Cl WLTN L25 ....115 K8
Beechurst Rd WLTN L25 ....115 K8
Beech Wk WGNNW/ST WN6 ....55 M5
 WGNS/IIMK WN3 ....5 M5
Beechway BEB CH63 ....143 H2
 MGHL L31 ....73 K4
Beechway Av MGHL L31 ....73 K3
Beechways WARRS WA4 ......137 M8
Beechways Dr NSTN CH64 ...152 F5
Beechwood SKEL WN8 ....65 L2
Beechwood Av AIMK WN4 ......91 J3
 HLWD L26 ....132 A6
 NEWLW WA12 ....104 F1
 RUNC WA7 ....150 M8
 WAL/NB CH45 ....95 G8
 WARR WA1 ....122 A5
 WARRW/BUR WA5 ....120 B8
 WGNNW/ST WN6 ....56 A5
Beechwood Cl ALL/GAR L19 ...130 C6
 RAIN/WH L35 ....117 G1
Beechwood Ct CHLY/EC PR7 * ..43 H5
Beechwood Crs
 WGNW/BIL/O WN5 ....67 G7
Beechwood Dr CL/PREN CH43 .110 D6
 FMBY L37 ....58 E4
 GTS/LS CH66 ....162 F4
 ORM L39 ....62 F1
Beechwood Gdns ALL/GAR L19 .130 B6
Beechwood La
 GOL/RIS/CU WA3 ....106 F1
Beechwood Rd ALL/GAR L19 ..130 B6
 LITH L21 ....83 K7
 PS/BROM CH62 ....143 L5
Beechwood Rd South
 ALL/GAR L19 ....130 B7
Beecroft Cl WARRW/BUR WA5 .120 F4
Beesands Cl NTHLY L27 ....132 B1
Beesley Rd PR/KW L34 ....100 E7
Beeston Cl CL/PREN CH43 ...110 E7
 GOL/RIS/CU WA3 ....122 F1
 RUNC WA7 ....150 E1
Beeston Dr NTHTN L30 ....72 D8
 PEN/TH CH61 ....141 M1
Beeston Gn GTS/LS CH66 ....156 A8
Beeston Gv CALD/MH L18 ....130 C6
 WLTN L25 ....130 F1
Beeston St ANF/KKDL L4 ....97 G5
Begonia Gdns STHEL WA9 ....103 J3
Beilby Rd RNFD/HAY WA11 .....91 H6
Beidale Pk KKBY L32 ....72 C2
Beldon Crs HUY L36 ....115 K2
Belem Cl AIG/SPK L17 ....113 L8
Belfast Rd CLB/OSW/ST L13 ..114 D2
Belfield Crs HUY L36 ....116 A4
Belfield Dr CL/PREN CH43 ....127 K6
Belford Dr MOR/LEA CH46 ...109 K6
Belford Rd WLTN L25 ....131 K1
Belfry Cl CHLYE PR6 ....31 M1
Belfry Crs WGNNW/ST WN6 ....56 B3
Belgrave Av WAL/EG CH44 ....111 L1
 WARR WA1 ....122 B6
 WGNE/HIN WN2 ....79 G1
Belgrave Cl LEIGH WN7 ....93 J3
 WDN WA8 ....135 G2
Belgrave Dr EP CH65 ....156 B8
Belgrave Rd AIG/SPK L17 ....129 K2
 LITH L21 ....83 H7
 STHP PR8 ....35 H1
Belgrave St WAL/EG CH44 .....95 L1
Belgravia Ct WDN WA8 ....134 D2

Belhaven Rd CALD/MH L18 ....114 B8
Bellair Av CSBY/BLUN L23 .....83 J1
Bellairs Rd NG/CROX L11 ......98 A5
Bellamy Rd ANF/KKDL L4 ....7 M7
Bellcast Cl WARRS WA4 ....137 L2
Bell Cl HUY L36 ....116 B5
Belldean WGNE/HIN WN2 ....69 J5
Belldene Rd HES CH60 ....69 J5
Bellefield Av WD/CROXPK L12 ..98 D7
Bellemonte Rd FROD/HEL WA6 .160 A3
Belle Vale Rd WLTN L25 ......131 K1
Belle Vue Rd WAL/EG CH44 ...115 K8
 WLTN L25 ....115 K8
Belle Vue Ter WGNW/BIL/O WN5 .67 M8
Bellew Rd NG/CROX L11 ....98 B6
Bellfield Crs WAL/NB CH45 .....95 J5
Bellgreen Rd NG/CROX L11 ....98 C3
Bellhouse La WARRS WA4 ....136 F5
 WARRS WA4 ....138 E4
Bell House Rd WDN WA8 ....17 H2
Bellingham Av WAV L15 ....69 J3
Bellingham Dr RUNC WA7 .....19 H7
 WGN WN1 ....68 F7
Bellini Cl LITH L21 ....83 M8
Bellis Av CHTN/BK PR9 ....25 G3
Bellis Gv NWD/KWIPK L33 .....73 M8
Bell La RAIN/WH L35 ....118 C3
 WARRS WA4 ....139 G2
 WGNW/BIL/O WN5 ....67 K5
Bellmore St ALL/GAR L19 ....130 E6
Bell Rd WAL/EG CH44 ....111 M2
Bell's Cl CHLY/EC PR7 ....30 D7
Bell's La MGHL L31 ....72 C1
Bell St CLB/OSW/ST L13 ......114 C2
 LEIGH WN7 ....81 M4
Belltower Rd BTL L20 ....96 D6
Bellward Cl BEB CH63 ....143 H5
Belmont BIRK CH41 ....10 E8
Belmont Av GOL/RIS/CU WA3 ...92 E4
 PS/BROM CH62 ....138 B2
 WARRS WA4 ....138 B2
 WGNE/HIN WN2 ....69 J3
 WGNW/BIL/O WN5 ....77 M2
Belmont Cl BRSC L40 ....22 E2
Belmont Crs WARRW/BUR WA5 .120 B7
Belmont Dr CHLYE PR6 ....33 G4
 NPK/KEN L6 ....97 L8
 PEN/TH CH61 ....141 J2
Belmont Gv CL/PREN CH43 ....10 E8
 HOR/BR BL6 ....45 L4
 NPK/KEN L6 ....97 L8
 WAL/NB CH45 ....95 K4
 WDN WA8 ....134 F1
 WKBY CH48 ....124 D2
Belmont St ECCL WA10 ....8 A6
 STHP PR8 ....2 E6
Beloe St TOX L8 ....129 H1
Belper St ALL/GAR L19 ....130 D7
Belston Rd CHLDW L16 ....114 F6
Belton Rd HUY L36 ....99 M7
Belvedere Av STHEL WA9 ....102 F7
Belvedere Cl FROD/HEL WA6 ..160 E4
 PR/KW L34 ....101 G6
Belvedere Dr CHLY/EC PR7 ....44 D6
 FMBY L37 ....59 H4
Belvedere Pk ORM L39 ....62 G6
Belvedere Rd AIMK WN4 ....91 L2
 CHLYE PR6 ....44 D5
 NEWLW WA12 ....104 D1
 TOX L8 ....113 J8
 WAL/NB CH45 ....95 K4
Belvoir Rd CALD/MH L18 .....130 E5
 WARRS WA4 ....16 F1
Bembridge Cl
 WARRW/BUR WA5 ....119 L6
 WDN WA8 ....133 J8
Bembridge Ct WGNS/IIMK WN3 .79 G3
Bempton Rd AIG/SPK L17 ....129 K3
Benbow Cl BIRK CH41 ....111 H5
Benbow St BTL L20 ....7 G8
Bendee Av NSTN CH64 ....153 J6
Bendee Rd NSTN CH64 ....153 H6
Benedict Ct BTL L20 ....7 H8
Benedict St BTL L20 ....7 J8
Bengairn Cl WGN WN1 ....5 K2
Bengal St CHLY/EC PR7 ....32 F5
Bengarth Rd CHTN/BK PR9 ....25 H5
Bengel St EHL/KEN L7 ....113 J3
Benjamin Fold AIMK WN4 ......79 K8
Ben La RNFD/HAY WA11 ....75 K3
Ben Lane Ct ORM L39 ....75 K3
Benledi St EV L5 ....96 F8
Benmore Rd CALD/MH L18 ...130 C3
Bennet Cl NSTN CH64 ....153 J6
Bennet's La HOY CH47 ....109 G3
Bennett Av WARR WA1 ....15 M3
Bennett Dr WGNW/BIL/O WN5 .77 M1
Bennetts Hl CL/PREN CH43 ...127 K1
Bennett's La WDN WA8 ....17 M2
Bennett St ALL/GAR L19 ......14 F6
 WARR WA1 ....14 F6
Ben Nevis Dr GTS/LS CH66 ...155 H7
Ben Nevis Rd RF/TRAN CH42 .127 M3
Bennison Dr ALL/GAR L19 * ...130 C6
Ben's Ct PR/KW L34 ....5 J8
Benson Cl GR/UP/WCH CH49 .126 B1
Benson Rd GOL/RIS/CU WA3 ..122 F3
Benson St CLVPS L1 ....13 J8
Bentfield AIG/SPK L17 ....53 J8
Bentfield Cl BEB CH63 ....127 M6
Bentfield Gdns BEB CH63 ....127 M6
Bentham Av WARRN/WOL WA2 .121 L2
Bentham Cl CL/PREN CH43 ...114 F5
Bentham Dr CHLDW L16 ......114 F5
Bentham Pl WGNNW/ST WN6 ...56 B3
Bentham Rd GOL/RIS/CU WA3 .107 J3
 WGNNW/ST WN6 ....54 A4
Bentham's Wy STHP PR8 ....3 G7
Bentinck Cl BIRK CH41 ....10 F5
Bentinck Pl BIRK CH41 ....10 F6
Bentinck St BIRK CH41 ....10 F6
 EV L5 ....18 D2
 RUNC WA7 ....18 E2
 STHEL WA9 ....99 G1
Bentley Cl BRSC L40 ....40 F5
Bentley Rd CL/PREN CH43 ....127 K1
 PEN/TH CH61 ....126 B8
 TOX L8 ....113 K7
Bentley St STHEL WA9 ....99 G1
Benton Cl EV L5 ....96 F7
Bents La WGNE/HIN WN2 * 81 L4
Bentley St BEB CH63 ....143 L5
Benty Farm Gv PEN/TH CH61 .126 C8
Benty Heath La NSTN CH64 ...154 C2

Benwick Rd KKBY L32 85 K4
Berbice Rd WAV L15 114 C7
Beresford Av BEB CH63 128 C7
Beresford Cl CL/PREN CH43 10 B8
Beresford Dr CHTN/BK PR9 25 H4
Beresford Gdns CHTN/BK PR9 25 H3
Beresford Rd CL/PREN CH43 10 B8
TOX L8 129 H1
WAL/NB CH45 95 H6
Beresford St BTL L20 6 E8
EV L5 13 K2
STHEL WA9 102 A6
WARR WA1 15 L2
WGNNW/ST WN6 4 A2
Bergen Cl BTL L20 7 L6
Berkeley Av CL/PREN CH43 127 G4
WGNS/IIMK WN3 78 F3
Berkeley Cl CHLY/EC PR7 32 F8
LEIGH WN7 93 L5
Berkeley Dr WAL/NB CH45 95 L6
Berkeley Rd CSBY/BLUN L23 70 E8
Berkeswell Rd NG/CROX L11 98 C4
Berkley Av WD/CROXPK L12 98 F5
Berkley St TOX L8 113 H7
Berkshire Dr WARR WA1 122 F6
Berkshire Gdns ECCL WA10 8 E8
Bermuda Rd MOR/LEA CH46 109 L5
Bernard Av WAL/NB CH45 * 95 L6
WARRS WA4 137 M5
Berner's Rd ALL/GAR L19 130 D6
Berner St BIRK CH41 11 G2
Berrington Av WLTN L25 131 J3
Berrington Gv AIMK WN4 91 J2
Berrington's La
RNFD/HAY WA11 88 E3
Berry Cl GTS/LS CH66 162 E2
SKEL WN8 65 H3
Berry Dr GTS/LS CH66 162 E1
Berry Hill Av PR/KW L34 99 M2
Berry House Rd BRSC L40 38 C1
Berrylands Cl MOR/LEA CH46 109 M4
Berrylands Rd MOR/LEA CH46 109 M3
Berry Rd WDN WA8 133 M4
Berrys La STHEL WA9 103 H4
Berry St BTL L20 6 F5
CHLYE PR6 44 C5
CLVPS L1 113 G5
SKEL WN8 65 G3
Berrywood Dr RAIN/WH L35 117 H3
Bertha Gdns BIRK CH41 111 H5
Bertha St BIRK CH41 111 H5
Bertram Dr HOY CH47 108 E5
Bertram Dr North HOY CH47 108 F5
Bertram Rd AIG/SPK L17 129 L1
Bertram St NEWLW WA12 104 B2
Berwick Av PS/BROM CH62 155 G1
STHP PR8 34 E7
Berwick Cl CL/PREN CH43 * 110 E7
MOR/LEA CH46 109 K5
NPK/KEN L6 113 K1
WARR WA1 123 G7
Berwick Dr CSBY/BLUN L23 70 E8
Berwick Gdns GTS/LS CH66 155 K7
Berwick Gv GTS/LS CH66 155 K7
Berwick Pl WGN WN1 5 K1
Berwick Rd GTS/LS CH66 155 J7
Berwick St NPK/KEN L6 113 K1
Berwyn Av HOY CH47 * 108 E6
PEN/TH CH61 * 126 C7
Berwyn Bvd BEB CH63 128 A5
Berwyn Cl GTS/LS CH66 155 J7
HOR/BR BL6 45 L8
Berwyn Dr PEN/TH CH61 141 H3
Berwyn Gv STHEL WA9 103 H2
Berwyn Rd ANF/KKDL L4 97 L5
WAL/EG CH44 95 L8
Beryl Rd CL/PREN CH43 110 E8
Beryl St CLB/OSW/ST L13 114 C4
Bescar Brow La BRSC L40 37 H6
Bescar La BRSC L40 37 J5
Besford Rd WLTN L25 115 K8
Bessborough Rd CL/PREN CH43 10 D9
Bessbrook Rd AIG/SPK L17 129 M3
Bessemer St TOX L8 129 H1
Bessie's Well Pl
WGNNW/ST WN6 * 56 B5
Beta Cl PS/BROM CH62 128 C6
Betchworth Crs RUNC WA7 149 M7
Bethany Cl RNFD/HAY WA11 90 C6
Bethersden Rd WGN WN1 56 D8
Betjeman Cl WARRS WA4 138 B1
Betjeman Gv CHLDW L16 115 G5
Betony Cl HLWD L26 132 A4
Betsyfield Dr GOL/RIS/CU WA3 106 C6
Bettisfield Av PS/BROM CH62 143 M8
Betula Cl WLT/FAZ L9 97 L1
Beulah Av WGNW/BIL/O WN5 89 M1
Bevan Cl STHEL WA9 101 M7
WARRW/BUR WA5 120 F7
Bevan's La WD/CROXPK L12 98 F6
Beverley Av WARRS WA4 137 M5
WGNW/BIL/O WN5 78 A4
Beverley Cl CHTN/BK PR9 22 E8
Beverley Dr HES CH60 141 K6
Beverley Gdns PEN/TH CH61 126 D7
Beverley Rd PS/BROM CH62 128 D5
WAL/NB CH45 95 H7
WARRW/BUR WA5 120 F7
WAV L15 114 C7
WGNW/BIL/O WN5 67 K5
Beverley Wy GTS/LS CH66 155 K6
Beversbrook Rd NG/CROX L11 98 D3
Bevin Av GOL/RIS/CU WA3 107 K1
Bevington Bush VAUX/LVPD L3 13 G3
Bevington Hl VAUX/LVPD L3 13 H2
Bevington St AIMK WN4 79 H8
VAUX/LVPD L3 13 G2
Bevyl Rd NSTN CH64 152 D3
Bewcastle Dr BRSC L40 63 K2
Bewerley Cl WGNS/IIMK WN3 4 C8
Bewey Cl TOX L8 129 G1
Bewley Dr KKBY L32 85 M4
Bewsey Farm Cl
WARRW/BUR WA5 120 F5
Bewsey Park Cl
WARRW/BUR WA5 14 A1
Bewsey Rd WARRW/BUR WA5 14 A2
Bewsey St ECCL WA10 101 M4
WARR WA1 14 E5
Bexhill Av WARRN/WOL WA2 121 K1
Bexhill Cl SPK/HALE L24 146 D1
Bexhill Dr WGNE/HIN WN2 81 L3
Bexley St WGNE/HIN WN2 81 K2
Bianca St BTL L20 7 H8
Bibby Av WARR WA1 15 M3
Bibby Rd CHTN/BK PR9 25 J4
Bibby's La BTL L20 6 D1
Bibby St CLB/OSW/ST L13 114 B2
Bickershaw La WGNE/HIN WN2 80 E4
Bickerstaffe St ECCL WA10 9 H5
VAUX/LVPD L3 * 13 K3
Bickerton Av BEB CH63 127 M5
FROD/HEL WA6 160 F6
Bickerton Cl GOL/RIS/CU WA3 122 F1
Bickerton Rd STHP PR8 35 H1
Bickerton St AIG/SPK L17 129 L2
Bickley Cl RUNC WA7 19 L6
WARRN/WOL WA2 122 B2
Bicknell Cl WARRW/BUR WA5 120 D5
Bidder St VAUX/LVPD L3 13 K4
Bideford Av STHEL WA9 102 E8
Bideford Rd WARRW/BUR WA5 136 A1
Bidston Av BIRK CH41 111 H6
RNFD/HAY WA11 89 M8
WAL/NB CH45 95 G7
Bidston Gn GTS/LS CH66 162 F1
Bidston Green Ct
CL/PREN CH43 * 110 E5
Bidston Green Dr
CL/PREN CH43 110 E5
Bidston Moss WAL/EG CH44 110 F2
Bidston Rd ANF/KKDL L4 97 K5
CL/PREN CH43 111 H7
Bidston Station Ap
CL/PREN CH43 110 E3
Bidston Village Rd
CL/PREN CH43 110 D4
Bidston Wy RNFD/HAY WA11 89 M8
Bigdale Dr NWD/KWIPK L33 86 C2
Big Fold HOR/BR BL6 * 57 M3
Biggin Ct WARRN/WOL WA2 122 A4
Bigham Rd NPK/KEN L6 113 L2
Biglands Dr HUY L36 116 B5
Big Meadow Rd
GR/UP/WCH CH49 126 C1
Billinge Ar WGN WN1 * 4 E3
Billinge Crs RNFD/HAY WA11 89 M7
Billinge Rd AIMK WN4 78 D8
WGNS/IIMK WN3 78 E1
WGNW/BIL/O WN5 67 M8
Billingham Rd STHEL WA9 101 M6
Billings Cl EV L5 96 E7
Billington Av NEWLW WA12 91 L8
Billington Cl WARRW/BUR WA5 120 A5
Billington Rd WDN WA8 133 K1
Bilston Rd AIG/SPK L17 130 A5
Bilton Cl WDN WA8 135 G3
Binbrook Pl CHLY/EC PR7 32 C5
Bingley Rd ANF/KKDL L4 97 K6
Binns Rd CLB/OSW/ST L13 114 A3
Binns Wy CLB/OSW/ST L13 114 B4
Binsey Cl GR/UP/WCH CH49 109 M8
Birbeck Rd NWD/KWIPK L33 86 C2
Birchall Av GOL/RIS/CU WA3 106 F1
Birchall St BTL L20 96 E6
GOL/RIS/CU WA3 106 C6
Birch Av BRSC L40 52 A1
CHLY/EC PR7 31 L1
ECCL WA10 101 H5
GR/UP/WCH CH49 109 M7
WARRN/WOL WA2 121 J1
WGNNW/ST WN6 56 B5
WLT/FAZ L9 84 D7
Birchcliffe Rd RF/TRAN CH42 128 B3
Birch Cl CL/PREN CH43 127 K2
MGHL L31 73 H4
RAIN/WH L35 117 G1
Birch Crs NEWLW WA12 104 B1
Birchdale Cl GR/UP/WCH CH49 109 M8
Birchdale Crs WARRS WA4 137 L5
Birchdale Rd CSBY/WL L22 82 F3
WARR WA1 122 C6
WARRS WA4 137 L6
WLT/FAZ L9 84 C8
Birchen Rd HLWD L26 132 C6
Birches Cl HES CH60 141 J4
The Birches FMBY L37 47 G8
STBRV L28 99 J6
WAL/EG CH44 112 A3
Birchfield MOR/LEA CH46 109 L6
Birchfield Av WDN WA8 134 C3
Birchfield Cl EHL/KEN L7 114 A3
MOR/LEA CH46 109 L7
Birchfield Rd ANF/KKDL L4 97 J4
EHL/KEN L7 114 A3
WARRW/BUR WA5 120 D8
WDN WA8 16 D1
Birchfield St STHEL WA9 101 M6
VAUX/LVPD L3 13 K4
Birchfield Wy MGHL L31 61 K8
Birch Gdns ECCL WA10 89 H7
Birch Gn FMBY L37 46 F8
Birch Green Rd SKEL WN8 65 L3
Birch Gv AIMK WN4 78 E8
GTS/LS CH66 163 J4
HUY L36 115 M3
RAIN/WH L35 117 G1
WAL/NB CH45 95 L6
WARR WA1 122 B6
WARRS WA4 137 M2
WAV L15 114 C4
Birch Heys WKBY CH48 125 J4
Birch Hl FROD/HEL WA6 167 L5
Birchill Rd NWD/KWIPK L33 86 E3
Birchley Av WGNW/BIL/O WN5 89 L2
Birchley Rd RNFD/HAY WA11 89 K2
Birchley St ECCL WA10 9 H3
Birchley Vw RNFD/HAY WA11 89 K3
Birchmere HES CH60 141 G3
Birchmuir Hey KKBY L32 86 B4
Birchover Wk EHL/KEN L7 113 K5
Birchridge Cl PS/BROM CH62 143 L3
Birch Rd BEB CH63 143 J1
CHLY/EC PR7 43 G4
CHLYE PR6 32 F3
CL/PREN CH43 127 K2
HOY CH47 109 G5
HUY L36 116 A4
RNFD/HAY WA11 91 G6
RUNC WA7 19 K7
WDN WA8 134 C2
WGNE/HIN WN2 80 D6
Birch St EV L5 96 D8
SKEL WN8 65 G4
STHP PR8 35 K1
WGNE/HIN WN2 69 M8
WGNNW/ST WN6 4 B1
Birch Tree Av RNFD/HAY WA11 89 H5
Birch Tree Ct WD/CROXPK L12 98 C7
Birchtree Rd AIG/SPK L17 130 A2
Birch Tree Rd GOL/RIS/CU WA3 93 H5
Birchview Wy CL/PREN CH43 110 F8
Birchway HES CH60 141 L7
Birchways WARRS WA4 138 A8
Birchwood Av BIRK CH41 11 H4
Birchwood Bvd
GOL/RIS/CU WA3 122 F3
Birchwood Cl BIRK CH41 11 H4
CHNE CH2 165 L1
GTS/LS CH66 163 J5
WGNS/IIMK WN3 78 E4
Birchwood Dr CHLY/EC PR7 43 G2
Birchwood Park Av
GOL/RIS/CU WA3 106 F8
Birchwood Wy
GOL/RIS/CU WA3 107 H8
NWD/KWIPK L33 74 C8
WARRN/WOL WA2 122 A5
Bird St EHL/KEN L7 113 L6
WGNE/HIN WN2 5 M6
Birdwell Dr WARRW/BUR WA5 120 C8
Birdwood Rd NG/CROX L11 98 B5
Birkacre Brow CHLY/EC PR7 43 H3
Birkacre Rd CHLY/EC PR7 43 H1
Birkdale Av BEB CH63 143 L7
Birkdale Cl CHLYE PR6 31 M1
HUY L36 115 L4
NPK/KEN L6 97 M7
Birkdale Cop STHP PR8 36 A4
Birkdale Rd WARRW/BUR WA5 136 B1
WDN WA8 118 D8
Birkenhead Rd BIRK CH41 112 A4
HOY CH47 108 E5
NSTN CH64 154 A4
Birkenshaw Av CSBY/BLUN L23 82 D1
Birket Av MOR/LEA CH46 110 B2
Birket Cl MOR/LEA CH46 110 C2
Birket Sq MOR/LEA CH46 110 B2
Birkett Av EP CH65 163 L3
Birkett Bank WGN WN1 5 K4
Birkett Rd RF/TRAN CH42 128 A4
WKBY CH48 124 D1
Birkett St VAUX/LVPD L3 13 J4
WGN WN1 5 K4
Birkey La FMBY L37 59 H3
Birkin Cl KKBY L32 86 C5
Birkin Rd KKBY L32 86 C5
Birkrig SKEL WN8 65 M7
Birkside Cl WGNS/IIMK WN3 79 J4
Birley Cl WGNNW/ST WN6 55 H5
Birley Ct TOX L8 113 H6
Birley St NEWLW WA12 104 F1
Birleywood SKEL WN8 65 M7
Birnam Dr RAIN/WH L35 117 M3
Birnam Rd WAL/EG CH44 111 M2
Birstall Av RNFD/HAY WA11 91 M3
Birstall Ct RUNC WA7 149 M6
Birstall Rd NPK/KEN L6 113 K2
Birt Cl TOX L8 113 K6
Birtles Rd WARRN/WOL WA2 121 L4
Bisham Pk RUNC WA7 150 F3
Bishopdale Cl
WARRW/BUR WA5 120 B6
Bishopdale Dr RAIN/WH L35 117 M3
Bishop Dr RAIN/WH L35 116 F4
Bishopgate St WAV L15 114 A6
Bishop Reeves Rd
RNFD/HAY WA11 91 G6
Bishop Rd ECCL WA10 8 D2
NPK/KEN L6 97 L6
WAL/EG CH44 111 K3
Bishops Ct WARRN/WOL WA2 121 H1
WLTN L25 131 K3
Bishops Gdns EP CH65 156 C8
Bishop Sheppard Ct
VAUX/LVPD L3 12 E2
Bishops Wy WDN WA8 134 F2
Bisley St WAL/NB CH45 95 K8
WAV L15 114 A6
Bispham Dr AIMK WN4 79 H8
HOY CH47 109 G6
Bispham Rd CHTN/BK PR9 25 L6
WARRW/BUR WA5 136 D1
Bittern Cl RUNC WA7 150 F5
WARRN/WOL WA2 121 M2
Bixteth St VAUX/LVPD L3 12 E5
Blackacre La BRSC L40 51 H4
Black-a-Moor La ORM L39 61 J3
Blackberry Dr WGNE/HIN WN2 80 E1
Blackberry Gv HLWD L26 131 M3
Blackboards La GTS/LS CH66 155 J6
Blackbrook Av
WARRN/WOL WA2 122 B3
Blackbrook Cl CHLYE PR6 33 J3
WDN WA8 133 L2
WLT/FAZ L9 97 J2
Blackbrook Rd RNFD/HAY WA11 90 A8
Blackburn Brow CHLYE PR6 33 G3
Blackburn Cl GOL/RIS/CU WA3 93 H5
Blackburne Av WDN WA8 133 K8
Blackburne Cl
WARRN/WOL WA2 122 E3
Blackburne Dr WLTN L25 131 M6
Blackburne Pl TOX L8 113 H5
Blackburne St SPK/HALE L24 145 M2
Blackburne Ter CLVPS L1 * 113 H5
Blackburn St CHLYE PR6 32 F6
Blackcar La SFTN L29 71 J2
Black Denton's Pl WDN WA8 17 H2
Blackdown Cl GTS/LS CH66 155 J8
Blackdown Gv STHEL WA9 103 H3
Blackeys La NSTN CH64 153 M5
Blackfield St EV L5 96 F7
Blackgate La KIRK/FR/WA PR4 27 M1
Blackheath Dr MOR/LEA CH46 110 B2
Blackheath La RUNC WA7 151 H1
Blackhorse Av HOR/BR BL6 * 57 L3
Blackhorse Cl HOR/BR BL6 57 L2
Black Horse Cl WKBY CH48 124 E2
Black Horse Hl WKBY CH48 124 E3
Black Horse La
CLB/OSW/ST L13 114 D2
Black Horse Pl
CLB/OSW/ST L13 114 D2
Black Horse St CHLY/EC PR7 * 32 D7
HOR/BR BL6 57 L2
Blackhorse St STHEL WA9 9 M3
Blackhurst Rd MGHL L31 61 L8
Blackhurst St WARR WA1 14 F6
Blackledge Cl WARRN/WOL WA2 122 C2
WGNW/BIL/O WN5 67 G8
Blackley Cl WARRS WA4 137 M6
Blackley Gv NWD/KWIPK L33 * 74 C7
Blackleyhurst Av
WGNW/BIL/O WN5 78 A8
Black Lion La GTS/LS CH66 155 K7
Blacklock Hall Rd SPK/HALE L24 146 E2
Blacklow Brow HUY L36 115 M3
Blackmoor Dr WD/CROXPK L12 98 F8
Black Moor Rd BRSC L40 40 C3
Black Moss La BRSC L40 36 F6
ORM L39 62 F3
Blackpool St BIRK CH41 11 K7
Blackrod Av SPK/HALE L24 146 E2
Blackrod Brow HOR/BR BL6 57 K1
Blackshaw Dr
WARRW/BUR WA5 120 D4
Blackstock St VAUX/LVPD L3 12 F3
Blackstone Av RNFD/HAY WA11 89 M8
Blackstone Rd CHLYE PR6 33 G4
Blackstone St EV L5 96 D8
Blackthorn Av WGNNW/ST WN6 68 B2
Blackthorn Cl MOR/LEA CH46 110 B6
Blackthorne Av GTS/LS CH66 163 J5
Blackthorne Crs STBRV L28 99 K5
Blackthorne Rd WLT/FAZ L9 97 L2
Blackwater Rd NG/CROX L11 98 F1
Blackwood Av WLTN L25 131 H1
Blaguegate La SKEL WN8 64 D3
Blainscough Rd CHLY/EC PR7 43 G5
Blair Av WGNE/HIN WN2 81 K2
Blair Dr WDN WA8 133 K2
Blairgowrie Gdns ORM L39 63 J1
Blair Gv CHTN/BK PR9 25 H6
Blair Pk BEB CH63 143 K2
Blair St TOX L8 113 G6
Blaisdon Cl NG/CROX L11 98 C4
Blakeacre Cl HLWD L26 132 B7
Blakeacre Rd HLWD L26 132 B7
Blake Cl WGNS/IIMK WN3 68 C8
Blakefield Rd CSBY/BLUN L23 71 L7
Blakehall SKEL WN8 65 M6
Blakeley Brow BEB CH63 143 J7
Blakeley Ct BEB CH63 143 J7
Blakeley Dell BEB CH63 143 K5
Blakeley Dene BEB CH63 143 K6
Blakeley Rd BEB CH63 143 J6
Blakemere Ct EP CH65 20 C1
Blakeney Cl GR/UP/WCH CH49 110 C6
Blakenhall Wy GR/UP/WCH CH49 109 M7
Blaking Dr PR/KW L34 99 M1
Blandford Cl STHP PR8 2 B7
Blandford Rd WARRW/BUR WA5 120 B8
Blantyre Rd WAV L15 114 A7
Blantyre St RUNC WA7 18 E1
Blay Cl WLTN L25 131 M5
Blaydon Cl NTHTN L30 84 B4
WGNE/HIN WN2 57 M8
Blaydon Gv STHEL WA9 101 M6
Blaydon Pk SKEL WN8 65 M6
Blaydon Wk CL/PREN CH43 111 G7
Bleach St WGNE/HIN WN2 69 L8
Bleak Hill Cl ECCL WA10 88 E6
Bleak Hill Rd ECCL WA10 88 D7
Bleak La BRSC L40 39 M8
Bleaklow Cl WGNS/IIMK WN3 79 K3
Bleasdale Av AIN/FAZ L10 85 G3
Bleasdale Cl GR/UP/WCH CH49 110 A7
ORM L39 62 F6
Bleasdale Rd CALD/MH L18 130 D1
NEWLW WA12 104 D1
Blenheim Av LITH L21 83 L5
Blenheim Cl WARRN/WOL WA2 122 B3
Blenheim Dr HUY L36 100 B8
Blenheim Rd AIMK WN4 91 M3
CALD/MH L18 * 114 B8
STHP PR8 34 D7
WAL/EG CH44 95 M8
WGNW/BIL/O WN5 67 L5
Blenheim St EV L5 12 F1
Blenheim Wy RNFD/HAY WA11 89 K7
SPK/HALE L24 146 D2
Blessington Rd ANF/KKDL L4 97 H6
Bletchley Av WAL/EG CH44 111 H1
Bligh St WAV L15 114 A6
Blind Foot Rd RNFD/HAY WA11 87 M6
Blindman's La ORM L39 50 E6
Blissford Cl WGNE/HIN WN2 80 F1
Blisworth St LITH L21 83 K7
Blomfield Rd ALL/GAR L19 130 F5
Bloomsbury Wy WDN WA8 133 M2
Blossom Gv KKBY L32 86 B6
Blossom St BTL L20 7 H1
Blucher St CSBY/WL L22 82 E4
Bluebell Av BIRK CH41 111 H5
RNFD/HAY WA11 91 G6
WGNW/BIL/O WN5 * 67 K6
Blue Bell Av WGNNW/ST WN6 68 B1
Bluebell Cl CSBY/WL L22 83 C4
Bluebell Ct RUNC WA7 161 H1
Blue Bell La HUY L36 116 A1
Blueberry Flds AIN/FAZ L10 85 H7
Blue Bridge La FROD/HEL WA6 159 L8
Bluecoat Chambers CLVPS L1 * 13 G8
Bluecoat St WARRN/WOL WA2 14 E2
Bluefields St TOX L8 113 H6
Blue Hatch FROD/HEL WA6 160 E5
Blue Jay Cl NTHLY L27 116 A8
Blue Ridge Cl WARRW/BUR WA5 120 B8
Blue Stone La BRSC L40 41 G2
Bluestone La MGHL L31 73 G4
Bluewood Dr BIRK CH41 110 F4
Blundell Av FMBY L37 58 D1
HTWN L38 70 B2
STHP PR8 35 H3
Blundell Crs STHP PR8 35 H3
Blundell Dr STHP PR8 35 H3
Blundell Gv HTWN L38 70 B2
Blundell La CHTN/BK PR9 25 L3
HOR/BR BL6 57 J3
Blundell Ms WGNS/IIMK WN3 78 F1
Blundell Rd HTWN L38 70 B3
WDN WA8 133 M5
Blundellsands Rd East
CSBY/BLUN L23 82 E1
Blundellsands Rd West
CSBY/BLUN L23 82 D2
Blundells Dr MOR/LEA CH46 110 A4
Blundell's La RAIN/WH L35 117 J4
Blundell St CLVPS L1 112 F6
Blyth Cl RUNC WA7 150 F8
Blythe Av WDN WA8 134 D1
Blythe La BRSC L40 52 A4
Blythe Ms STHP PR8 35 H5
Blythewood SKEL WN8 65 L6
Blyth Hey NTHTN L30 83 M2
Blyth Rd BEB CH63 143 L6
Blythswood St AIG/SPK L17 129 K2
Boaler St NPK/KEN L6 113 K2
Boarded Barn CHLY/EC PR7 31 L2
Boardmans La STHEL WA9 103 G1
Boardman St HOR/BR BL6 57 M3
Boars Head Av WGNNW/ST WN6 56 C6
Boathouse La NSTN CH64 152 D3
Bobbies La ECCL WA10 101 J1
Bobbiners La CHTN/BK PR9 26 C2
Bobby Langton Wy BRSC L40 39 G8
Bodden St GOL/RIS/CU WA3 93 J4
STHEL WA9 118 F1
Bodiam Ct EP CH65 164 A3
Bodley St ANF/KKDL L4 * 97 K5
Bodmin Av CHTN/BK PR9 22 D8
Bodmin Cl RUNC WA7 150 D7
Bodmin Dr WGNE/HIN WN2 80 C4
Bodmin Gv RNFD/HAY WA11 89 M6
Bodmin Rd ANF/KKDL L4 97 H4
Bodmin Wy HLWD L26 132 A5
Bogburn La CHLY/EC PR7 42 F8
Bognor Cl SPK/HALE L24 146 D1
Bolan St CLB/OSW/ST L13 114 C2
Bolden Cl NTHTN L30 84 B4
Bolderwood Dr WGNE/HIN WN2 80 F1
Bolde Wy BEB CH63 143 J4
Bold La ORM L39 62 D6
WARRW/BUR WA5 103 L6
Bold Pl CLVPS L1 13 K9
Bold Rd STHEL WA9 103 H6
Bold St CHTN/BK PR9 3 G2
CLVPS L1 13 J9
ECCL WA10 8 E6
RUNC WA7 19 J2
WARR WA1 14 D7
WDN WA8 16 C6
WGNW/BIL/O WN5 68 A8
Boleyn Ct RUNC WA7 150 E2
The Boleyn MGHL L31 73 G2
Bollin Cl GOL/RIS/CU WA3 107 J3
Bollington Cl CL/PREN CH43 127 H2
Bolney St WGNE/HIN WN2 69 G6
Bolton Av KKBY L32 85 L3
WARRS WA4 138 B1
Bolton Cl FMBY L37 59 J3
GOL/RIS/CU WA3 93 K5
STHEL WA9 * 9 L4
Bolton House Rd
WGNE/HIN WN2 81 H6
Bolton Rd AIMK WN4 91 K2
CHLY/EC PR7 32 F7
CHLYE PR6 44 E6
PS/BROM CH62 128 E7
STHP PR8 35 J1
WGNE/HIN WN2 57 L8
Bolton Rd East PS/BROM CH62 128 E7
Bolton Sq WGN WN1 5 J2
Bolton St AIMK WN4 78 F8
CHLY/EC PR7 32 F7
STHEL WA9 9 L4
VAUX/LVPD L3 13 J7
Bombay Rd WGNW/BIL/O WN5 67 L5
Bonchurch Dr CLB/OSW/ST L13 114 B4
Bond Cl WARRW/BUR WA5 136 F1
Bond's La CHLY/EC PR7 44 B6
CHTN/BK PR9 23 J6
Bond St PR/KW L34 100 F7
VAUX/LVPD L3 13 G2
Bonnington Av CSBY/BLUN L23 70 E8
Bonsall Rd WD/CROXPK L12 98 D7
Boode Cft STBRV L28 99 K4
Booker Av CALD/MH L18 130 E4
Booth's Brow Rd AIMK WN4 78 F7
Booths Cl CHNE CH2 * 165 J3
Booths Hill Cl LYMM WA13 139 M3
Booth's Hill La LYMM WA13 139 L2
Booth's Hill Rd LYMM WA13 139 L2
Booth's La LYMM WA13 139 K3
ORM L39 50 B8
Booth St CHTN/BK PR9 3 G2
CLB/OSW/ST L13 114 C2
STHEL WA9 101 M6
WARRW/BUR WA5 137 G1
Boothwood Cl EHL/KEN L7 113 K4
Bor Av WGNS/IIMK WN3 79 K1
Borax St CLB/OSW/ST L13 114 C3
Borden Cl WGNE/HIN WN2 69 H3
Border Rd HES CH60 141 K5
Border Wy EV L5 97 G7
Borella Rd CLB/OSW/ST L13 98 B7
Bores Hl WGN WN1 56 E1
Borough Pl BIRK CH41 * 11 K6
Borough Rd ECCL WA10 8 D7
RF/TRAN CH42 10 F8
WAL/EG CH44 111 M2
Borough Rd East BIRK CH41 11 K6
WAL/EG CH44 112 A3
Borough Wy WAL/EG CH44 112 A3
Borron Rd NEWLW WA12 91 K8
Borrowdale FMBY L37 47 H8
Borrowdale Av
WARRN/WOL WA2 121 K2
Borrowdale Cl FROD/HEL WA6 160 F5
Borrowdale Rd BEB CH63 143 G1
ECCL WA10 101 K5
MOR/LEA CH46 109 M5
WAV L15 114 A7
WDN WA8 133 L5
WGNW/BIL/O WN5 * 67 K6
Borsdane Av WGNE/HIN WN2 81 G1
Boscombe Pl WGNE/HIN WN2 81 G1
Boscow Crs STHEL WA9 102 F6
Bosnia St TOX L8 129 J2
Bostock Gn EP CH65 156 B8
Bostock St EV L5 96 F8
WARRW/BUR WA5 121 G7
Boston Av RUNC WA7 19 K7
Boston Bvd WARRW/BUR WA5 120 D5
Boston Cl GOL/RIS/CU WA3 107 H1
Boswell Av WARRS WA4 137 K3
Boswell Pl WGNS/IIMK WN3 79 H1
Boswell Rd CL/PREN CH43 127 H4
Boswell St BTL L20 6 D1
TOX L8 113 L6
Bosworth Cl BEB CH63 143 H3
Bosworth Dr STHP PR8 47 K1
Bosworth Rd RNFD/HAY WA11 89 L7
Botanic Gv EHL/KEN L7 113 L3
Botanic Pl EHL/KEN L7 113 L3
Botanic Rd CHTN/BK PR9 25 K3
EHL/KEN L7 113 L4
Botany Brow CHLYE PR6 33 G3
Botany Cl WGNE/HIN WN2 69 J3
Botany Rd SPK/HALE L24 146 E1
Boteler Av WARRW/BUR WA5 14 A2
Botley Cl GR/UP/WCH CH49 * 109 M8
The Boulevard EP CH65 163 H1
WD/CROXPK L12 98 D5
Boulting Av WARRW/BUR WA5 121 H3
Boulton Av PS/BROM CH62 128 D5
WKBY CH48 124 D1
Boundary Cl CHLY/EC PR7 30 D7
Boundary Dr CSBY/BLUN L23 70 E7
WLTN L25 131 M6
Boundary Farm Rd HLWD L26 131 M7
Boundary La BRSC L40 52 B2
HES CH60 141 J5
NPK/KEN L6 113 K1
NWD/KWIPK L33 86 F3
WGNNW/ST WN6 55 J2
Boundary Pk NSTN CH64 152 F5
Boundary Rd CL/PREN CH43 110 F5
ECCL WA10 8 C6
HUY L36 116 B5
LITH L21 83 M4
PS/BROM CH62 128 D6
WKBY CH48 124 F5
Boundary St EV L5 96 E7
STHP PR8 3 G9
WARR WA1 15 M1
WGN WN1 5 H6
Boundary St East EV L5 96 F7
Bourchier Wy WARRS WA4 138 C5
Bourne Av GOL/RIS/CU WA3 92 F5
Bourne Gdns STHEL WA9 102 D4
Bournemouth Cl RUNC WA7 150 F7
Bourne St NPK/KEN L6 113 K2
Bourton Rd WLTN L25 131 K7
Bousfield St ANF/KKDL L4 * 97 G6
Bowden Cl ECCL WA10 101 K2
GOL/RIS/CU WA3 107 H1
WD/CROXPK L12 99 G3
Bowden Rd ALL/GAR L19 130 D7
Bowden St LITH L21 83 K7
Bowdon Cl WARR WA1 * 122 B5
Bowdon Rd WAL/NB CH45 95 J7
Bowen Cl WDN WA8 133 M1
Bower Gv LITH L21 83 H6
Bower Rd HES CH60 141 L5
HUY L36 116 A1
WLTN L25 131 J1
The Bowers CHLY/EC PR7 43 M1
Bower St WDN WA8 17 G1
Bowfell Cl BEB CH63 154 F2
Bowfield Rd ALL/GAR L19 130 D6
Bowgreen Cl CL/PREN CH43 110 E6
Bowker's Green La ORM L39 63 G8
Bowland Av AIMK WN4 91 K1
CHLDW L16 114 F4
CHLYE PR6 32 F5
GOL/RIS/CU WA3 92 E4
STHEL WA9 118 C2
Bowland Cl GOL/RIS/CU WA3 107 K8
PS/BROM CH62 143 M4
RUNC WA7 150 A8
Bowland Dr LITH L21 83 L1
Bowles St BTL L20 83 J8
Bowley Rd CLB/OSW/ST L13 98 B8
Bowling Green Cl STHP PR8 25 H8
The Bowlings WGNNW/ST WN6 68 C3
Bowman Av WARRS WA4 122 C8
Bowness Av BEB CH63 143 L8
CL/PREN CH43 127 J3
RNFD/HAY WA11 89 K5
STHP PR8 47 L2
WARRN/WOL WA2 121 L3
Bowness Pl WGNE/HIN WN2 69 K5
Bowood Ct WARRN/WOL WA2 121 J1
Bowood St TOX L8 129 H2

Bowring Cl TOX L8 * 129 J1
Bowring Dr NSTN CH64 ....152 D4
Bowring Park Av CHLDW L16 .....115 J1
Bowring Park Rd CHLDW L16 .....114 F4
Bowring St TOX L8 * 129 J1
Bowscale Cl
  GR/UP/WCH CH49 * 110 A8
Bowscale Rd CALD/MH L18 ....130 C1
Boxdale Rd CALD/MH L18 ....130 C1
Boxgrove Cl WDN WA8 ....134 D2
Boxmoor Rd CALD/MH L18 ....130 C3
Boxtree Cl WD/CROXPK L12 ......99 H1
Boxwood Cl HUY L36 ....115 L3
Boycott St EV L5 ....97 J7
Boyd Cl MOR/LEA CH46 ....110 D2
  WGNNW/ST WN6 ....56 B5
Boydell Av WARRS WA4 ....138 B1
Boydell Cl STBRV L28 ....99 K6
Boyer Av MGHL L31 ....72 F6
Boyes Brow NWD/KWIPK L33 .....85 M1
Boyle Av WARRN/WOL WA2 ....122 A8
Boyton Ct EHL/KEN L7 ....113 L5
Brabant Rd AIG/SPK L17 ....130 A4
Braby Rd LITH L21 ....83 L7
Bracebridge Dr STHP PR8 ....36 B3
Bracewell St WA9 ....102 E7
Bracken Cl CHLYE PR6 ....33 G5
  GOL/RIS/CU WA3 ....106 E3
Bracken Ct STHEL WA9 ....118 E1
Brackendale CHNE CH2 ....165 K2
  CR/UP/WCH CH49 ....110 C5
  RUNC WA7 ....149 M5
  WLT/FAZ L9 * 97 K6
Brackendale Av WLT/FAZ L9 ......84 D6
Bracken Dr WAL/NB CH45 ....95 L6
Brackenhurst Dr WAL/NB CH45 ...95 L6
Brackenhurst Gn
  NWD/KWIPK L33 ....86 A3
Bracken La BEB CH63 ....127 H8
  LEIGH WN7 ....81 K8
Brackenside HES CH60 * 141 H5
Brackenway FMBY L37 ....37 J7
Bracken Wy FROD/HEL WA6 ......160 E7
Bracken Wd WD/CROXPK L12 .....99 G1
Brackenwood Dr WDN WA8 ....133 J3
Brackenwood Gv BEB CH63 ......127 M8
Brackenwood Rd BEB CH63 ......127 M8
Brackley Cl WAL/EC CH44 ....111 J2
Brackley St RUNC WA7 ....18 E2
  WARRS WA4 ....137 L4
Bracknell Av KKBY L32 ....85 M5
Bracknell Cl KKBY L32 ....86 A4
Bracknell Wy ORM L39 ....62 C4
Bradbourne Cl WD/CROXPK L12 ...99 G2
Bradda Cl GR/UP/WCH CH49 .....110 B6
Braddan Av CLB/OSW/ST L13 * ...98 A8
Bradden Cl BEB CH63 ....143 K3
Brade St CHTN/BK PR9 ....25 L1
Bradewell St ANF/KKDL L4 ....97 G5
Bradfield Av AIN/FAZ L10 ....84 E2
Bradfield St EHL/KEN L7 ....113 L3
Bradford St WGNS/IIMK WN3 .....4 E6
Bradgate Cl MOR/LEA CH46 .....109 K4
Bradlegh Rd NEWLW WA12 ......104 E5
Bradley Bvd WARRW/BUR WA5 ...120 D7
Bradley Fold RAIN/WH L35 ......116 C5
Bradley La CHLY/EC PR7 ....30 F7
  FROD/HEL WA6 ....160 F7
  WARRW/BUR WA5 ....104 C4
  WGNNW/ST WN6 ....56 B3
Bradley Rd LITH L21 ....83 K4
Bradley St CHTN/BK PR9 ....3 K7
Bradley Wy WDN WA8 ....17 G2
Bradman Rd MOR/LEA CH46 .....109 L4
  NWD/KWIPK L33 ....86 B1
Bradmoor Rd PS/BROM CH62 ....143 M5
Bradshaw Brow BRSC L40 ....40 F4
Bradshaw Cl ECCL WA10 ....8 A3
  WGNNW/ST WN6 ....55 M4
Bradshawgate WGN WN1 ....5 G4
Bradshaw La BRSC L40 ....41 C3
  SKEL WN8 ....53 L4
  WARRS WA4 ....138 D2
Bradshaw's La STHP PR8 ....34 F7
Bradshaw St WDN WA8 ....134 C3
  WGN WN1 ....5 J1
  WGNW/BIL/O WN5 ....67 J7
Bradstone Cl NG/CROX L11 ......85 K7
Bradville Rd WLT/FAZ L9 ....84 E6
Bradwall Cl EP CH65 ....163 J2
Bradwell Cl EP CH65 ....163 J1
  WKBY CH48 ....124 F3
Bradwell Rd GOL/RIS/CU WA3 ....93 C6
Brady St HOR/BR BL6 ....45 J8
Braeburn Ct LEIGH WN7 ....81 M8
Braehaven Rd WAL/NB CH45 .....95 L6
Braemar Av CHTN/BK PR9 ....25 H3
  RAIN/WH L35 ....117 H2
  WARRN/WOL WA2 ....122 C2
Braemar Ct EP CH65 ....21 C8
Braemar St BTL L20 * 7 K8
Braemore Av WGNS/IIMK WN3 ....78 E3
Braemore Rd WAL/EC CH44 ......111 H1
Braeside Cl GTS/LS CH66 ....155 L8
Braeside Crs WGNW/BIL/O WN5 ..7 M8
Braeside Gdns
  GR/UP/WCH CH49 ....110 B8
Braeside La EHL/KEN L7 ....113 K3
Brahms Cl TOX L8 * 113 V7
Braidhaven WGNNW/ST WN6 .....55 J7
Braid St BIRK CH41 ....11 G2
Brainerd St CLB/OSW/ST L13 ....98 A3
Braithwaite Cl RAIN/WH L35 ....117 L2
  RUNC WA7 ....149 M8
Braithwaite Rd
  GOL/RIS/CU WA3 ....92 F4
Brakenwood Ms WARRS WA4 * ...138 A4
Bramberton Pl ANF/KKDL L4 .....97 L4
Bramberton Rd ANF/KKDL L4 ....97 L4
Bramble Av BIRK CH41 ....111 H5
Bramble Cl WARRW/BUR WA5 ....136 A2
Bramble Gv WGNW/BIL/O WN5 ...68 A4
The Brambles AIMK WN4 ....78 F8
  CHLY/EC PR7 ....43 H3
  NWD/KWIPK L33 * 86 D3
Bramble Wy MOR/LEA CH46 .....109 M3
  RUNC WA7 ....161 G1
  SKEL WN8 ....53 L4
Bramblewood
  CROS/BRETH PR26 ....29 K3
Bramblewood Cl
  CL/PREN CH43 ....126 E1
  NTHLY L27 ....116 A8
Brambling Cl RUNC WA7 ....150 A4
Brambling Pk HLWD L26 ....92 A8
Brambling Wy GOL/RIS/CU WA3 ...93 C6
Bramcote Av WARRN/HAY WA11 ..89 M7
Bramcote Cl NWD/KWIPK L33 ....86 C1
Bramcote Rd NWD/KWIPK L33 ....86 B1
Bramcote Wk NWD/KWIPK L33 ...86 B1

Bramhall Rd CSBY/WL L22 ....83 C5
  SKEL WN8 ....65 H3
Bramhall St WARRW/BUR WA5 ...121 C8
Bramley Av BEB CH63 ....128 A6
Bramley Cl GTS/LS CH66 ....163 H5
  NTHLY L27 ....116 A8
Bramley Ms WARRS WA4 ....137 L5
The Bramleys MGHL L31 ....72 E6
Brampton Cl WGNE/HIN WN2 .....80 B4
Brampton Ct STHEL WA9 ....103 K2
Brampton Dr TOX L8 ....113 J5
Bramshill Cl GOL/RIS/CU WA3 ....97 J6
Bramwell Av CL/PREN CH43 .....127 J4
Bramwell St STHEL WA9 ....102 B2
Brancaster Dr GOL/RIS/CU WA3 ..93 J6
Brancepeth Ct EP CH65 ....20 F9
Branch St WGNE/HIN WN2 ....69 J6
Branch Wy RNFD/HAY WA11 .....90 F7
Brancker Av RAIN/WH L35 ....117 K1
Brandon Cl CHLY/EC PR7 ....32 C8
Brancote Gdns PS/BROM CH62 ..143 H6
Brancote Mt CL/PREN CH43 * ...111 H7
Brancote Rd CL/PREN CH43 .....111 H7
Brandearth Hey STBRV L28 ......99 K6
Brandon WDN WA8 ....133 J3
Brandon Cl SKEL WN8 ....66 C6
Brandon St BIRK CH41 ....11 L5
Brandreth Cl RAIN/WH L35 ......117 L2
Brandreth Delph SKEL WN8 ......53 M2
Brandreth Dr SKEL WN8 ....53 L2
Brandreth Pk SKEL WN8 ....53 L2
Brandreth Pl WGNNW/ST WN6 ...56 B4
Brandwood Av
  WARRN/WOL WA2 ....121 K3
Branfield Cl WD/CROXPK L12 .....99 G2
Bransdale Cl WARRW/BUR WA5 ..120 A6
Bransdale Dr AIMK WN4 ....91 M4
Bransfield Cl WGNS/IIMK WN3 ...79 J2
Bransford St AIMK WN4 ....91 L3
Branson Cl GOL/RIS/CU WA3 .....92 F7
Branstree Av NG/CROX L11 ......98 B3
Brantfield Ct WARRN/WOL WA2 .122 A5
Branthwaite WGNE/HIN WN2 ....69 K4
Branthwaite Cl NG/CROX L11 ....98 C4
Branthwaite Crs NG/CROX L11 ...98 C4
Branthwaite Gv NG/CROX L11 ...98 C4
Brasenose Rd BTL L20 ....6 F3
  TOX L8 ....113 G7
Brassey St BIRK CH41 ....10 B2
Brathay Cl WARRN/WOL WA2 ...121 L2
Brattan Rd RF/TRAN CH42 ....10 D8
Bratton Cl WGNS/IIMK WN3 .....78 E4
Braunton Rd AIG/SPK L17 ....130 A5
  WAL/NB CH45 ....95 J7
Braybrooke Rd NG/CROX L11 ....98 C2
Bray Cl RUNC WA7 ....149 M7
Braydon Cl WLTN L25 * 131 L7
Brayfield Rd ANF/KKDL L4 ....97 M4
Brayford Dr WGNE/HIN WN2 .....57 L8
Bray Rd SPK/HALE L24 ....146 E1
Bray St BIRK CH41 ....10 C2
Brayton Ct WGNE/HIN WN2 .....69 M7
Breckfield Pl EV L5 * 97 H8
Breckfield Rd North EV L5 ....97 H8
Breckfield Rd South NPK/KEN L6 .97 J8
Breck Pl WAL/EC CH44 ....111 J2
Breck Rd NPK/KEN L6 ....97 J8
  WAL/EG CH44 ....111 J2
  WDN WA8 ....16 F1
Breckside Av WAL/EG CH44 .....111 J4
Breckside Pk NPK/KEN L6 ....97 L7
The Breck GTS/LS CH66 ....155 L8
Brecon Av NTHTN L30 ....84 B4
Brecon Ct WGNE/HIN WN2 ......80 D3
Brecon Dr GTS/LS CH66 ....163 G4
  WGNE/HIN WN2 ....80 C3
Brecon Rd RF/TRAN CH42 ......127 L4
Brecon St AIG/SPK L17 ....131 J7
Bredon Av CHLY/EC PR7 ....31 M4
Bredon Cl GTS/LS CH66 ....155 J7
Breeze Hl ANF/KKDL L4 ....7 M6
Breezehill Cl NSTN CH64 ....153 H5
Breezehill Pk NSTN CH64 ....153 H5
Breezehill Rd NSTN CH64 ....153 H5
Breeze La WLT/FAZ L9 ....97 H2
Breeze Rd STHP PR8 ....35 G3
Brelade Rd CLB/OSW/ST L13 ....116 C5
Bremhill Rd NG/CROX L11 ....98 B2
Bremner Cl ANF/KKDL L4 ....97 J8
Brenda Crs CSBY/BLUN L23 .....71 J6
Brendale Av MGHL L31 ....72 E5
Brendon Av LITH L21 ....84 A8
  WARRN/WOL WA2 ....121 J2
Brendon Gv STHEL WA9 * 103 J1
Brendor Rd WLTN L25 ....131 K4
Brenig St BIRK CH41 ....111 H4
Brenka Av WLT/FAZ L9 ....84 D4
Brentfield WDN WA8 ....133 M3
Brentnall Cl WARRW/BUR WA5 ..130 E8
Brent Wy HLWD L26 ....132 B7
Brentwood WCNW/BIL/O WN5 ...67 M8
Brentwood Av AIG/SPK L17 .....129 L2
  CSBY/BLUN L23 ....71 K8
Brentwood Cl ECCL WA10 ....101 K2
  HTWN L38 ....70 B3
Brentwood Ct CHTN/BK PR9 ....24 F4
Brentwood Rd CHLYE PR6 ....44 D5
Brentwood St WAL/EC CH44 ....111 J3
Brereton Av BEB CH63 ....128 C7
  WAV L15 ....114 C6
Brereton Cl RUNC WA7 ....150 C5
Bretherton Pl RAIN/WH L35 ....117 L1
Bretherton Rd
  CROS/BRETH PR26 ....29 J1
  PR/KW L34 ....101 V7
Bretherton Rw WGN WN1 * 4 E4
Bretherton St WGNE/HIN WN2 ..69 L7
Bretlands Rd CSBY/BLUN L23 ...71 K8
Bretton Fold STHP PR8 ....25 H8
Brett St BIRK CH41 ....10 C2
Brewery La FMBY L37 ....37 H7
Brewster Cl ANF/KKDL L4 ......7 L8
Brian Av PEN/TH CH61 ....126 B7
  WARRN/WOL WA2 ....121 M5
  WARRS WA4 ....138 A4
Briar Av CHLY/EC PR7 ....31 L1
  AIMK WN4 ....91 J1
  WGNE/HIN WN2 ....81 K1
Briardale Gdns GTS/LS CH66 ...155 L7
Briardale Rd BEB CH63 ....128 B6
  CALD/MH L18 ....130 B1
  NSTN CH64 ....154 C5
  RF/TRAN CH42 ....127 L1
Briar Dr HES CH60 ....141 J4
  HUY L36 ....115 M3
Briarfield Av WDN WA8 ....133 J4
Briarfield Rd EP CH65 ....20 B4
  HES CH60 ....141 J5
Briarly GOL/RIS/CU WA3 ....92 D5
Briar Rd GOL/RIS/CU WA3 ......92 D5
  WGNW/BIL/O WN5 ....67 M6
Briars Brook BRSC L40 ....52 C2
Briars Cl RAIN/WH L35 ....117 M4
Briars Gn ECCL WA10 ....8 E2

SKEL WN8 ....65 J1
Briars La BRSC L40 ....52 D3
  SKEL WN8 ....65 H3
Briary Cft HTWN L38 ....70 B2
Briar St ANF/KKDL L4 ....96 F6
Briarswood Cl RAIN/WH L35 ....117 H2
  RF/TRAN CH42 ....128 B5
Briarwood RUNC WA7 ....150 D4
Briarwood Av WARR WA1 ....15 L1
Briarwood Rd AIG/SPK L17 ......130 A2
Briary Cl HES CH60 ....141 K4
Brickcroft La
  CROS/BRETH PR26 ....29 J2
Brickfields HUY L36 ....115 M5
Brickhurst Wy WARR WA1 ......122 D5
Brick Kiln La BRSC L40 ....39 J2
  WGN WN1 ....4 F1
Brick St CLVPS L1 ....112 F6
  NEWLW WA12 ....104 B2
  WARR WA1 ....15 C5
Brickwall Gn SFTN L29 ....72 B6
Brickwall La SFTN L29 ....72 A7
Bride St ANF/KKDL L4 ....97 H3
  WARRS WA4 ....138 D2
Bridge Av ORM L39 ....63 G1
  WARRS WA4 ....138 A6
Bridge Ct NSTN CH64 ....153 G6
  STHEL WA9 * 118 F2
  WKBY CH48 ....124 C2
Bridge Cft LITH L21 ....83 L2
Bridgecroft Rd WAL/NB CH45 ...95 K7
Bridge Farm Cl
  GR/UP/WCH CH49 ....126 D1
Bridge Farm Dr MGHL L31 .....73 H3
Bridgefield Cl WLTN L25 ....115 K6
Bridgeford Av WD/CROXPK L12 .98 C6
Bridge Gdns WD/CROXPK L12 ...99 H4
Bridgehall Dr SKEL WN8 ....66 D6
Bridge La FROD/HEL WA6 ......160 E4
  NTHTN L30 ....84 A2
  WARR WA1 ....122 E7
  WARRS WA4 ....138 A6
Bridgeman St WARRN/WOL WA2 .8 B6
Bridgeman Ter WGN WN1 ....4 E1
Bridge Meadow GTS/LS CH66 ...163 H6
Bridgend Cl WDN WA8 ....133 M2
Bridgend Dr STHP PR8 ....47 L1
Bridgenorth Rd PEN/TH CH61 ..141 G1
Bridge Rd CALD/MH L18 ....130 C2
  CSBY/BLUN L23 ....82 E2
  EHL/KEN L7 ....113 M5
  HUY L36 ....115 L3
  LITH L21 ....85 K6
  MGHL L31 ....72 F6
  PR/KW L34 ....100 F8
  STHEL WA9 ....118 F3
  WARR WA1 ....14 C7
  WKBY CH48 ....124 C2
Bridges Rd EP CH65 ....21 J5
Bridge St BIRK CH41 ....11 J3
  BTL L20 ....6 F7
  CL/PREN CH43 ....9 G6
  GOL/RIS/CU WA3 ....92 C6
  NEWLW WA12 ....104 D2
  NSTN CH64 ....153 G6
  ORM L39 ....63 G1
  RUNC WA7 ....19 J3
  STHP PR8 ....3 H5
  WARR WA1 ....14 C7
  WGNE/HIN WN2 ....69 J2
  WGNE/HIN WN2 ....69 M7
  WGNS/IIMK WN3 ....4 E6
Bridgeview Cl WD/KWIPK L33 ...86 B1
Bridgewater Av WARRS WA4 ....138 B1
Bridgewater Cl LITH L21 ....83 J3
Bridgewater Gra RUNC WA7 ....151 H7
Bridgewater Ms STHEL WA9 ....137 L5
Bridgewater St CLVPS L1 ....112 F6
  RUNC WA7 ....19 G2
  WGNS/IIMK WN3 ....4 E6
  WGNW/BIL/O WN5 ....68 B7
Bridgeway WAL/NB CH45 ....95 K8
Bridgeway Cl STHP PR8 ....34 D8
Bridgeway East RUNC WA7 .....150 D3
Bridgeway West RUNC WA7 .....150 D3
Bridge Wills La CHTN/BK PR9 ...22 E8
Bridgewood Dr GTS/LS CH66 ...162 E3
Bridle Av WAL/EC CH44 ....112 A3
Bridle Cl CL/PREN CH43 ....110 D7
  PS/BROM CH62 ....144 A6
Bridle Ct STHEL WA9 ....102 E5
Bridlemere Ct WARR WA1 ......122 A5
Bridle Pk PS/BROM CH62 ......143 M6
Bridle Rd NTHTN L30 ....84 C5
  PS/BROM CH62 ....144 A6
  WAL/EC CH44 ....112 A3
Bridle Wy GTS/LS CH66 ....162 F2
  NTHTN L30 ....84 B5
Bridport St CLVPS L1 ....11 H4
Brierfield Rd WAV L15 ....114 B7
Brierley Cl NTHTN L30 ....84 D1
Brierley St WARRW/BUR WA5 ...14 B4
Briers Cl WARRN/WOL WA2 .....122 B2
Briery Hey Av NWD/KWIPK L33 .86 B3
Brightgate Cl EHL/KEN L7 * 113 K5
Brighton Rd CSBY/WL L22 ......82 F4
  HUY L36 ....116 D2
  STHP PR8 ....35 J2
Brighton St CHLYE PR6 * 33 C5
  WAL/EC CH44 ....112 A2
  WARRW/BUR WA5 ....121 C7
Brighton V CSBY/WL L22 ....82 E3
Brightstone Cl CHTN/BK PR9 ...23 K8
Bright St BIRK CH41 ....10 F6
  NPK/KEN L6 ....113 J2
Brightwell Cl
  GR/UP/WCH CH49 * 126 D1
  WARRW/BUR WA5 ....120 A8
Brignall Gv GOL/RIS/CU WA3 ...92 F4
Brill St BIRK CH41 ....10 C2
Brimelow Crs
  WARRW/BUR WA5 ....136 A2
Brimstage Av BEB CH63 ....128 B6
Brimstage Cl HES CH60 ....141 L5
Brimstage Gn HES CH60 * 141 M5
Brimstage La BEB CH63 ....142 D2
Brimstage Rd ANF/KKDL L4 ....97 M6
  BEB CH63 ....142 E3
  HES CH60 ....141 L5
Brimstage St BIRK CH41 ....10 F9
Brindle St CHLY/EC PR7 ....32 E7
Brindley Av WARRS WA4 ....138 B1
Brindley Cl LITH L21 ....83 J3
Brindley Rd KKBY L32 ....85 J2
  RUNC WA7 ....150 B2
Brindley St RUNC WA7 ....18 F2
  TOX L8 ....112 F7
  WGNW/BIL/O WN5 ....67 J7
Brinklow Cl STHP PR8 ....34 C8

Brinks Rw HOR/BR BL6 * 45 M8
Brinley Cl PS/BROM CH62 ......143 M8
Brinton Cl NTHLY L27 ....115 L7
  WDN WA8 ....134 A5
Brisbane Av WAL/NB CH45 ......95 J5
Brisbane St STHEL WA9 ....101 M6
Briscoe Dr MOR/LEA CH46 .....110 A6
Bristol Av RUNC WA7 ....151 G7
  WAL/EG CH44 ....111 L1
Bristol Dr GTS/LS CH66 ....163 G4
Bristol Rd WAV L15 ....114 C7
Bristow Cl WARRW/BUR WA5 ...120 D5
Britannia Crs TOX L8 ....129 H2
Britannia Rd WAL/NB CH45 ....111 J1
  WGNNW/ST WN6 ....67 C5
Britannic Buildings
  WAL/NB CH45 * 111 J1
Britannia Gdns FROD/HEL WA6 .166 D3
Britannia Rd FROD/HEL WA6 ...160 A6
Brittany Brow NTHLY L27 ......132 A1
Britten Cl TOX L8 ....113 K7
Broadacre SKEL WN8 ....66 C7
Broadbelt St ANF/KKDL L4 .....97 H3
Broadbent Av WARRS WA4 .....138 B2
Broadfield Av CL/PREN CH43 ...110 E5
Broadfield Cl CL/PREN CH43 * .110 D6
Broadfields RUNC WA7 ....150 E5
Broadgate Av STHEL WA9 ......102 A4
Broad Green Rd
  CLB/OSW/ST L13 ....114 D3
Broadheath Av CL/PREN CH43 ..110 D3
Broadheath Ter WDN WA8 ......133 M4
Broad Hey NTHTN L30 ....83 M2
Broad Hey Cl WLTN L25 ....131 K2
Broadheys La KNUT WA16 .....139 M7
Broadhurst Av
  GOL/RIS/CU WA3 ....107 H3
  WARRW/BUR WA5 ....136 F1
Broadhurst La WGNNW/ST WN6 .42 B7
Broadhurst St AIG/SPK L17 ....129 H7
Broadlake NSTN CH64 ....154 B5
Broadland Gdns GTS/LS CH66 ...163 H5
Broadland Rd GTS/LS CH66 ....163 H5
Broadlands RAIN/WH L35 ......101 G8
Broad La ANF/KKDL L4 ....97 M4
  FMBY L37 ....59 M2
  HES CH60 ....140 E4
  KKBY L32 ....86 B5
  ORM L39 ....61 J3
  RNFD/HAY WA11 ....89 K3
  SFTN L29 ....71 J2
  WARRS WA4 ....138 D5
  WARRW/BUR WA5 ....103 M5
Broad Lane Prec NG/CROX L11 ..98 A4
Broadley Av GOL/RIS/CU WA3 ...92 E6
Broadmead ALL/GAR L19 ......131 G6
  HES CH60 ....141 L4
  SKEL WN8 ....53 K3
Broad Meadow La
  CROS/BRETH PR26 ....29 C2
Broad Oak Av RNFD/HAY WA11 ..90 C7
  WARRW/BUR WA5 ....136 A1
Broad Oak Cl CHLYE PR6 ....44 C5
Broadoak Rd DV/KA/FCH L14 ...115 H2
  MGHL L31 ....73 C4
Broad Oak Rd STHEL WA9 ......103 C3
Broadoaks GR/UP/WCH CH49 ...110 A7
Broad O' Th' La WGNNW/ST WN6 .55 J7
Broad Pl NG/CROX L11 ....98 B5
Broadriding Rd WGNNW/ST WN6 .55 G7
Broad Sq NG/CROX L11 ....98 B5
Broadstone Dr BEB CH63 ......143 K4
Broad Vw NG/CROX L11 ....98 B5
Broadway BEB CH63 ....127 M6
  ECCL WA10 ....88 D8
  ECCL WA10 ....101 L5
  GR/UP/WCH CH49 ....109 M8
  NG/CROX L11 ....98 A4
  WAL/NB CH45 ....95 H4
  WDN WA8 ....133 J4
  WLT/FAZ L9 ....85 G7
Broadway Av WAL/NB CH45 ....95 H4
Broadway Cl STHP PR8 ....34 D8
Broadwood Av MGHL L31 ......73 C8
Broadwood St WAV L15 ....114 A6
Brockenhurst Rd WLT/FAZ L9 ...84 C7
Brockhall Cl STHEL WA9 * 101 J7
Brockholme Rd CALD/MH L18 ..130 A6
Brockhurst Wk WGNS/IIMK WN3 .68 C8
Brocklebank La ALL/GAR L19 ...130 F5
Brocklebank Rd CHTN/BK PR9 ..25 C4
Brock Mill La WGNE/HIN WN2 ...56 E8
Brock Pk WGNE/HIN WN2 ......80 A3
Brock Rd CHLYE PR6 ....32 F4
  GOL/RIS/CU WA3 ....122 F2
Brockstedes Av AIMK WN4 .....79 H4
Brock St ANF/KKDL L4 ....97 C5
  WGN WN1 ....5 K4
Brocstedes Rd AIMK WN4 ......78 F6
Brodie Av ALL/GAR L19 ....130 E5
  CALD/MH L18 ....130 C2
Brogden Av GOL/RIS/CU WA3 ..107 G1
Bromborough Rd BEB CH63 ....128 C8
Bromborough Village Rd
  PS/BROM CH62 ....143 M4
Brome Wy BEB CH63 ....143 K3
Bromilow Rd SKEL WN8 ....64 C4
  STHEL WA9 ....103 H3
Bromley Av CALD/MH L18 .....114 B8
  GOL/RIS/CU WA3 ....92 C6
Bromley Cl HES CH60 ....141 L5
  WARRN/WOL WA2 ....122 B2
  WGNE/HIN WN2 ....69 J3
Bromley Dr LEIGH WN7 ....81 M5
Bromley Rd WAL/NB CH45 .....95 J6
Brompton Av AIG/SPK L17 .....113 L8
  CSBY/BLUN L23 ....82 E2
  WAL/EG CH44 ....111 L1
Brompton Gdns
  WARRW/BUR WA5 ....121 C6
Brompton Rd STHP PR8 ....25 G6
Brompton Wy GTS/LS CH66 ....163 G4
Bromsgrove Rd
  GR/UP/WCH CH49 ....125 L1
Bromyard Cl BTL L20 * 6 E3
Bronington Av PS/BROM CH62 .143 M7
Bronte Cl CSBY/BLUN L23 ......82 D1
  WARRN/WOL WA2 ....105 J3
  WGNS/IIMK WN3 ....79 J2
Bronte St ECCL WA10 ....8 A4
  VAUX/LVPD L3 ....13 K6
Bronte Wy NSTN CH64 ....153 C8
Brook Av AIMK WN4 ....91 L3
  BIRK CH41 ....10 F2
  CHLYE PR6 ....44 A7
  CHTN/BK PR9 ....25 L1
  ECCL WA10 ....92 C6

Brookdale Av North
  GR/UP/WCH CH49 ....126 A1
Brookdale Av South
  GR/UP/WCH CH49 ....126 A2
Brookdale Cl GR/UP/WCH CH49 .126 A1
Brookdale Rd WAV L15 ....114 A7
Brook Dr WARRW/BUR WA5 .....122 C8
Brooke Cl CHTN/BK PR9 ....25 K6
Brook End STHEL WA9 ....118 A8
Brooke Rd East CSBY/WL L22 ...82 E3
Brooke Rd West CSBY/WL L22 ..82 E3
Brooke St EP CH65 ....2 F6
Brook Farm ORM L39 ....63 G1
Brookfield BRSC L40 ....40 E3
  CROS/BRETH PR26 ....29 K2
Brookfield Av CSBY/BLUN L23 ..82 F2
  CSBY/WL L22 ....82 E3
  RAIN/WH L35 ....101 L8
  RUNC WA7 ....150 A3
Brookfield Cl WARR WA13 .....139 M8
Brookfield Dr WLT/FAZ L9 .....84 E8
Brookfield Gdns WKBY CH48 ...124 C3
Brookfield La ORM L39 ....62 C8
  LYMM WA13 ....139 M1
  SKEL WN8 ....66 E7
  WGNNW/ST WN6 ....56 B7
  WKBY CH48 ....124 D3
Brookfields
  WGNW/BIL/O WN5 ....67 K8
Brookfield St NEWLW WA12 ...104 D2
Brook Furlong FROD/HEL WA6 ..160 A3
Brook Hey NSTN CH64 ....152 D3
Brook Hey Dr NWD/KWIPK L33 .86 B3
Brookhill Cl BTL L20 ....7 J4
Brookhill Rd BTL L20 ....7 J3
Brook House Gv ECCL WA10 ...101 J2
Brookhouse Rd ORM L39 ......50 F7
Brookhouse Ter WGN WN1 .....5 G5
Brookhurst Av BEB CH63 ......143 L8
Brookhurst Cl BEB CH63 ......143 L8
Brookhurst Rd BEB CH63 ......143 L8
Brookland Av WGNE/HIN WN2 ..69 M8
Brookland La STHEL WA9 ......103 J3
Brookland Rd BIRK CH41 ......11 H7
  BIRK CH41 ....68 D2
Brookland Rd East
  CLB/OSW/ST L13 ....114 C2
Brookland Rd West
  CLB/OSW/ST L13 ....114 C2
Brooklands BIRK CH41 ....51 H7
Brooklands Av AIMK WN4 ......91 M3
  CSBY/WL L22 ....82 G5
  WGNW/BIL/O WN5 ....66 F8
Brooklands Gdns NSTN CH64 ...152 E4
Brooklands Gv BRSC L40 ......52 B2
Brooklands Rd ECCL WA10 ....101 J1
  NSTN CH64 ....152 E4
  SKEL WN8 ....66 E6
The Brooklands HUY L36 ......116 A4
Brookland St WARR WA1 ....15 J2
Brook La CHLY/EC PR7 ....43 D1
  GOL/RIS/CU WA3 ....123 J3
  NSTN CH64 ....152 E4
  ORM L39 ....63 G1
  RNFD/HAY WA11 ....77 H6
  WGNW/BIL/O WN5 ....67 J7
Brooklet Rd HES CH60 ....141 L5
Brooklyn Dr EP CH65 ....156 B8
Brook Lynn Av GOL/RIS/CU WA3 .93 J4
Brook Meadow PEN/TH CH61 ..126 A6
Brook Rd BTL L20 ....72 E6
  CSBY/BLUN L23 ....71 J7
  GTS/LS CH66 ....155 M8
  LYMM WA13 ....139 M1
  MGHL L31 ....73 C8
  WLT/FAZ L9 ....97 J1
Brooks Aly CLVPS L1 ....13 H8
Brookside CHLY/EC PR7 ....31 L3
  CHLY/EC PR7 ....43 H4
  WGNS/IIMK WN3 * 68 C3
Brookside Av AIMK WN4 ....79 H5
  DV/KA/FCH L14 ....115 F2
  ECCL WA10 ....83 H3
  LYMM WA13 ....139 L1
  RNFD/HAY WA11 ....76 A3
  WARRS WA4 ....137 M4
  WARRW/BUR WA5 ....105 G8
Brookside Cl RAIN/WH L35 ....117 G1
  RNFD/HAY WA11 ....90 D6
  WD/CROXPK L12 ....99 H4
Brookside Crs GR/UP/WCH CH49 .109 M8
Brookside Dr
  GR/UP/WCH CH49 * 110 A8
Brookside Rd FROD/HEL WA6 ...160 C5
  RAIN/WH L35 ....117 G1
  STHP PR8 ....35 L4
Brookside Vw RNFD/HAY WA11 ..90 D6
Brookside Wy RNFD/HAY WA11 ..90 D6
Brooks Rd FMBY L37 ....58 F3
The Brooks RNFD/HAY WA11 ...90 D6
Brook St AIMK WN4 ....91 L3
  BIRK CH41 ....10 F2
  CHLYE PR6 ....44 A6
  CHTN/BK PR9 ....25 L1
  ECCL WA10 ....92 C6
  COL/RIS/CU WA3 ....92 C6
  COL/RIS/CU WA3 ....93 J4
  NSTN CH64 ....153 G6
  PS/BROM CH62 ....143 M6
  RAIN/WH L35 ....101 H8
  RUNC WA7 ....19 M3
  VAUX/LVPD L3 ....12 D5
  WGNE/HIN WN2 ....56 J6
  WGNW/BIL/O WN5 ....29 H1
Brook St East BIRK CH41 ......11 J4
Brooks Wy FMBY L37 ....58 F3
Brookthorpe Cl WAL/NB CH45 ..95 K8
Brook V CSBY/WL L22 ....82 F2
Brookvale Av North RUNC WA7 .150 D7
Brookvale Av South RUNC WA7 .150 D7
Brook Wy WARRW/BUR WA5 ....120 C8
Brookway LYMM WA13 ....139 H4
Brook Well NSTN CH64 ....153 G8
Brookwood Cl WARRS WA4 ....137 K5
Brookwood Rd HUY L36 ....116 A1
Broom Cl PR/KW L34 ....101 H7
Broome Cl STHP PR8 ....35 G2
Broome Ct RUNC WA7 ....150 D2
Broome Rd STHP PR8 ....35 G2
Broomfield Cl HES CH60 ......140 E4
Broomfield Gdns WLT/FAZ L9 ..84 B8

Broomfield Pl *WGNNW/ST* WN6 .....56 A4
Broomfield Rd *WCNNW/ST* WN6 ...56 A4
WLT/FAZ L9 .....84 B8
Broomfields Rd *WARRS* WA4 ...137 M6
Broomfield Ter *WGN* WN1 * 5 K5
Broomflat Cl *WGNNW/ST* WN6 ...56 A4
Broomhey Av *WGN* WN1 .....56 E8
Broomhey Ter *WGNE/HIN* WN2 ....5 K5
Broom Hl *CL/PREN* CH43 .....111 H6
Broomhill Cl *NTHLY* L27 .....115 L7
Broomholme *WGNNW/ST* WN6 ...54 F6
Broomlands *HES* CH60 .....141 G5
Broomleigh Cl *BEB* CH63 .....127 M8
Broom Rd *ECCL* WA10 .....101 K5
WGNW/BIL/O WN5 .....67 M6
Broomsgrove *AIN/FAZ* L10 .....85 G4
Broom Wy *HLWD* L26 .....131 M6
Broseley Av *GOL/RIS/CU* WA3 ...106 F1
PS/BROM CH62 .....143 L4
Broseley La *GOL/RIS/CU* WA3 ...93 M8
Broster Av *MOR/LEA* CH46 .....109 L5
Brosters La *HOY* CH47 .....108 F4
Brotherhood Dr *STHEL* WA9 .....102 F6
Brotherton Cl *PS/BROM* CH62 ...143 L5
Brotherton Wy *NEWLW* WA12 ...104 D1
Brougham Av *BIRK* CH41 .....128 B2
Brougham Rd *WAL/EG* CH44 ...111 M2
Brougham Ter *NPK/KEN* L6 .....113 J2
Broughton Cl *WGNE/HIN* WN2 ...81 C2
Broughton Av *GOL/RIS/CU* WA3 ..92 F6
STHP PR8 .....3 M9
WKBY CH48 .....124 C2
Broughton Cl *WARRS* WA4 ....138 B5
Broughton Dr *ALL/GAR* L19 .....130 C6
Broughton Hall Rd
WD/CROXPK L12 .....99 G8
Broughton Rd *WAL/EG* CH44 ...111 K2
Brow La *HES* CH60 .....141 H6
Browmere Dr *GOL/RIS/CU* WA3 ..106 C6
Brownbill Bank *NTHLY* L27 .....116 A8
Brown Heath Av
WGNW/BIL/O WN5 .....89 M2
Brownhill Dr *WARR* WA1 .....122 B5
Browning Av *RF/TRAN* CH42 ...128 B4
WDN WA8 .....16 A4
WGNS/IIMK WN3 .....79 H1
Browning Cl *HUY* L36 .....116 B4
Browning Dr *EP* CH65 .....163 H1
WARRN/WOL WA2 .....105 M8
Browning Gn *EP* CH65 .....163 H1
Browning Gv *WGNNW/ST* WN6 ...68 A2
Browning Rd *CSBY/WL* L22 .....82 F3
WAL/NB CH45 * 95 J1
Browning St *BTL* L20 .....6 D2
LEIGH WN7 .....81 M7
Brownley St *CHLYE* PR6 .....33 G6
Brownlow Ar *ECCL* WA10 * 9 H6
Brownlow Hl *VAUX/LVPD* L3 .....13 J1
Brownlow Rd *WGNE/HIN* WN2 ...69 K6
Brownlow Rd *HOR/BR* BL6 .....45 L8
PS/BROM CH62 .....128 D6
Brownmere *WGNNW/ST* WN6 ...68 B3
Brownmoor La *CSBY/BLUN* L23 *.83 J1
Brownmoor Pk *CSBY/BLUN* L23 ..83 H1
Browns Hey *CHLY/EC* PR7 .....32 C5
Brown's La *WTN* L38 .....84 C2
Brown St *CHLYE* PR6 .....32 F5
HOR/BR BL6 .....57 M3
WDN WA8 .....17 J5
WGNE/HIN WN2 .....69 J6
WGNE/HIN WN2 .....81 C4
WGNS/IIMK WN3 .....4 D5
Brownville Rd
CLB/OSW/ST L13 * 97 M7
Brow Rd *CL/PREN* CH43 .....110 F4
Brow Side *EV* L5 .....13 L2
Brows La *FMBY* L37 .....59 C2
Broxholme Wy *MGHL* L31 .....72 F6
Broxton Av *CL/PREN* CH43 .....127 H3
WGNW/BIL/O WN5 .....67 H6
WKBY CH48 .....124 D2
Broxton Cl *WDN* WA8 .....133 L2
Broxton Rd *CSBY/LS* CH66 .....156 A8
Broxton St *WAV* L15 .....114 A4
Bruce Av *WARRN/WOL* WA2 .....121 M4
Bruce Crs *BEB* CH63 .....143 L7
Bruce Dr *GTS/LS* CH66 .....162 E4
TOX L8 .....129 J1
Bruche Av *WARR* WA1 .....122 B5
Bruche Dr *WARR* WA1 .....122 B5
Bruera Rd *EP* CH65 .....163 H1
Brunel Dr *LITH* L21 .....83 J3
Brunner Rd *WDN* WA8 .....16 C5
Brunsborough Cl
PS/BROM CH62 .....143 L7
Brunsfield Rd *MOR/LEA* CH46 ...109 L6
Brunstath Cl *HES* CH60 .....141 L4
Brunswick Cl *BIRK* CH41 .....11 J4
Brunswick Ct *GTS/LS* CH66 .....163 G2
Brunswick Ms *BIRK* CH41 .....11 K4
CSBY/WL L22 .....83 G5
Brunswick Pde *CSBY/WL* L22 ...82 F5
Brunswick Pl *BTL* L20 .....96 D5
Brunswick Rd *NEWLW* WA12 ...103 K3
NPK/KEN L6 .....13 M4
Brunswick St *ALL/GAR* L19 .....145 M1
CHLY/EC PR7 .....32 F5
CLVP L2 .....12 D8
STHEL WA9 .....103 J2
Brunswick Wy *VAUX/LVPD* L3 ...112 F4
Brunt La *ALL/GAR* L19 .....131 C6
Bruntleigh Av *WARRS* WA4 .....138 C3
Bruton Rd *HUY* L36 .....99 M7
Bryanston Rd *AIG/SPK* L17 .....129 K2
RF/TRAN CH42 .....128 B1
Bryant Av *WARRS* WA4 .....138 B1
Bryant Rd *LITH* L21 .....83 K7
The Bryceway *WD/CROXPK* L12 ..114 F1
Brydges St *EHL/KEN* L7 .....113 J4
Bryer Rd *RAIN/WH* L35 .....116 F1
Bryham St *WGN* WN1 .....5 H4
Bryn Bank *WAL/EG* CH44 .....111 L4
Bryn Gates La *AIMK* WN4 .....79 L5
Brynmor Rd *CALD/MH* L18 .....130 C4
Brynmoss Av *WAL/EG* CH44 ...111 H1
Brynn St *ECCL* WA10 .....9 H3
WGNE/HIN WN2 .....80 B6
Bryn Rd *AIMK* WN4 .....79 J7
Bryn Rd South *AIMK* WN4 .....91 K5
Bryn St *AIMK* WN4 .....91 K2
WGNS/IIMK WN3 .....5 J8
Bryony Cl *WGNW/BIL/O* WN5 ...66 F8
Bryony Wy *RF/TRAN* CH42 .....128 B5
Brython Dr *CSBY/BLUN* L23 .....81 L1
Buchanan Dr *WGNE/HIN* WN2 ...81 K7
Buchanan Rd *WAL/EG* CH44 ...110 B5
WGNW/BIL/O WN5 .....67 H2
WLT/FAZ L9 .....83 L1
Buchanan St *CHLYE* PR6 .....32 F5
Buchan Cl *WARRW/BUR* WA5 ...120 D5
Buckfast Av *RNFD/HAY* WA11 ....91 H6
Buckfast Cl *NTHLY* L30 .....84 B1

WARRW/BUR WA5 .....136 A2
Buckfast Ct *RUNC* WA7 .....151 G2
Buckfast Dr *FMBY* L37 .....58 E8
Buckingham Av *AIG/SPK* L17 ...113 M8
BEB CH63 .....128 A6
CL/PREN CH43 .....111 H6
WDN WA8 .....134 C1
Buckingham Cl *ECCL* WA10 .....8 D8
WGNW/BIL/O WN5 .....68 A4
Buckingham Ct *NWD/KWIPK* L33 .86 B2
Buckingham Dr *RNFD/HAY* WA11.89 J6
WARRW/BUR WA5 .....136 E1
Buckingham Gdns *EP* CH65 ...163 M3
Buckingham Gv *FMBY* L37 .....59 C3
Buckingham Rd
CLB/OSW/ST L13 .....97 M7
MGHL L31 .....72 F5
WAL/EG CH44 .....111 H1
Buckingham St *CHLYE* PR6 .....32 F6
EV L5 .....97 C8
Buckland Cl *WDN* WA8 .....133 M6
Buckland Dr *BEB* CH63 .....143 H5
WGNW/BIL/O WN5 .....67 K4
Buckland St *AIG/SPK* L17 .....129 K2
Buckley Hill La *NTHTN* L30 .....71 M8
Buckley St *WARRN/WOL* WA2 ....14 D3
WGNNW/ST WN6 .....68 C3
Buckley St West
WGNNW/ST WN6 .....68 C3
Buckshaw Hall Cl *CHLY/EC* PR7 ..32 D5
Buckthorn Cl *STBRV* L28 .....99 K6
Buckthorn Gdns *STHEL* WA9 ...101 L7
Bude Cl *CL/PREN* CH43 .....110 F2
Budworth Av *WDN* WA8 .....134 A3
WARRS WA4 .....138 B1
Budworth Cl *CL/PREN* CH43 ...127 G1
RUNC WA7 .....149 M6
Budworth Dr *WLTN* L25 .....131 L3
Budworth Rd *CL/PREN* CH43 ...127 G1
GTS/LS CH66 .....163 G1
Buer Av *WGNS/IIMK* WN3 .....79 H1
Buerton Cl *CL/PREN* CH43 .....126 F1
Buffs La *HES* CH60 .....141 K5
Buggen La *NSTN* CH64 .....152 F5
Buildwas Rd *NSTN* CH64 .....153 C3
Bulford Rd *WLT/FAZ* L9 .....98 A1
Bulkeley Rd *WAL/EG* CH44 .....111 M2
Bull Bridge La *AIN/FAZ* L10 .....85 G3
Bull Cop *FMBY* L37 .....59 K2
Bullens La *BRSC* L40 .....56 F6
Bullens Rd *ANF/KKDL* L4 .....97 H5
KKBY L32 .....86 B4
Bullfinch Ct *HLWD* L26 .....132 A4
Bull HI *NSTN* CH64 .....153 H7
Bull La *WLT/FAZ* L9 .....84 D6
Bullrush Dr *MOR/LEA* CH46 ...110 C3
Bulteel St *WGNW/BIL/O* WN5 ...67 M7
Bulwer St *BTL* L20 .....6 E2
EV L5 * 97 J8
Bunbury Cl *CHNE* CH2 .....164 C6
Bunbury Dr *RUNC* WA7 .....149 L7
Bunbury Gn *EP* CH65 .....163 M3
Bundoran Rd *AIG/SPK* L17 .....130 A3
Bungalow Rd *NEWLW* WA12 ...105 C4
The Bungalows Red Bank
NEWLW WA12 * 105 L4
Bunter Av *KKBY* L32 .....86 B7
Bunting Cl *GOL/RIS/CU* WA3 ....93 C5
Bunting Ct *HLWD* L26 .....131 M3
Burbo Bank Rd *CSBY/BLUN* L23 ..82 C1
Burbo Bank Rd North
CSBY/BLUN L23 .....70 B8
Burbo Bank Rd South
CSBY/BLUN L23 .....82 D2
Burbo Crs *CSBY/BLUN* L23 .....82 D2
Burbo Wy *WAL/NB* CH45 .....95 C5
Burden Rd *MOR/LEA* CH46 .....109 L5
Burdett Av *BEB* CH63 .....143 H4
Burdett Cl *BEB* CH63 .....143 J3
Burdett Rd *CSBY/WL* L22 .....82 E4
GTS/LS CH66 .....163 C3
Burdett St *AIG/SPK* L17 .....129 K1
Burfield Dr *WARRS* WA4 .....137 L2
Burford Av *WAL/EG* CH44 .....111 H2
Burford Rd *CHLDW* L16 .....114 E4
Burgess Av *WARRS* WA4 .....137 M4
Burgess Gdns *MGHL* L31 .....72 E5
Burgess' La *FMBY* L37 .....60 C4
Burgess St *VAUX/LVPD* L3 .....13 K5
Burgh Hall Rd *CHLY/EC* PR7 .....43 J2
Burghill Rd *WD/CROXPK* L12 ...99 H1
Burgh La *CHLY/EC* PR7 .....43 L1
Burgh La South *CHLY/EC* PR7 ...43 L4
Burghley Av *WGNS/IIMK* WN3 ...69 H8
Burgh Mdw *CHLY/EC* PR7 .....43 L1
Burgundy Cl *AIG/SPK* L17 .....129 K2
Burkhardt Dr *NEWLW* WA12 ...105 G2
Burland Cl *RUNC* WA7 .....18 F5
Burland Rd *HLWD* L26 .....132 C7
Burland St *WGNW/BIL/O* WN5 ...68 B6
Burleigh Ms *EV* L5 .....97 H1
Burleigh Rd North *EV* L5 .....97 H1
Burleigh Rd South *EV* L5 .....97 H1
Burley Av *GOL/RIS/CU* WA3 .....92 F4
Burley Cl *KKBY* L32 .....86 B4
Burley Crs *WGNS/IIMK* WN3 .....78 E3
Burlingham Av *WKBY* CH48 ...124 E4
Burlington Av *FMBY* L37 .....59 K2
Burlington Rd *STHP* PR8 .....35 H7
WAL/NB CH45 .....95 K4
Burlington St *BIRK* CH41 .....11 H5
CHLY/EC PR7 .....32 F6
VAUX/LVPD L3 .....12 F2
Burton Gv *WGNE/HIN* WN2 .....69 J3
Burman Crs *ALL/GAR* L19 .....130 E6
Burman Rd *ALL/GAR* L19 .....130 E6
Burnage Av *RNFD/HAY* WA11 ...91 H6
Burnage Cl *SPK/HALE* L24 .....147 H3
Burnard Cl *NWD/KWIPK* L33 .....86 B3
Burnard Crs *NWD/KWIPK* L33 ...86 B3
Burnaston Gv *WGNW/BIL/O* WN5.67 M8
Burnell Cl *ECCL* WA10 .....8 E4
Burnell Rd *EP* CH65 .....21 C7
Burnet Cl *WARRN/WOL* WA2 ...122 D3
Burney Cl *GOL/RIS/CU* WA3 .....93 C6
Burnham Cl *GOL/RIS/CU* WA3 ...107 C5
WARRW/BUR WA5 .....120 B8
Burnham Gv *WGNE/HIN* WN2 ...69 J3
Burnham Rd *CALD/MH* L18 .....130 B2
Burnhill Cl *WGNNW/ST* WN6 * ...56 A5
Burnie Av *BTL* L20 .....7 L1
Burnley Av *MOR/LEA* CH46 .....110 C5
Burnley Cl *NPK/KEN* L6 .....13 M2
Burnley Rd *MOR/LEA* CH46 .....110 D5
STHP PR8 .....34 A8
Burnsall Av *GOL/RIS/CU* WA3 ...93 H5
Burnsall Dr *WDN* WA8 .....131 C3
Burnsall St *ALL/GAR* L19 .....131 G8

Burns Av *LEIGH* WN7 .....81 L5
WAL/NB CH45 .....95 J4
Burns Cl *AIMK* WN4 .....79 H7
CHLDW L16 .....115 H5
GTS/LS CH66 .....163 G1
WAV L15 .....117 G2
WGNS/IIMK WN3 .....79 J1
WGNW/BIL/O WN5 .....77 M4
Burns Crs *WDN* WA8 .....16 B3
Burns Gv *HUY* L36 .....116 C4
WARRN/WOL WA2 .....121 C4
Burnside *SKEL* WN8 .....53 K3
Burnside Av *WAL/EG* CH44 .....111 K3
WARRS WA4 .....137 M4
Burnside Rd *WAL/EG* CH44 .....111 K3
Burns Rd *STHEL* WA9 .....118 C2
Burns St *BTL* L20 .....6 C1
WGNE/HIN WN2 .....80 D4
Burnt Ash Cl *ALL/GAR* L19 .....130 B6
Burnthwaite Rd
DV/KA/FCH L14 .....114 E2
Burnvale *WGNS/IIMK* WN3 .....78 F3
Burrell Cl *RF/TRAN* CH42 .....127 L4
Burrell Dr *MOR/LEA* CH46 .....109 M6
Burrell Rd *RF/TRAN* CH42 .....127 L4
Burrell St *ANF/KKDL* L4 .....97 H5
Burrington Dr *LEIGH* WN7 .....81 M6
Burrough Cl *GOL/RIS/CU* WA3 ...123 H2
Burroughs Gdns *VAUX/LVPD* L3 ..13 C2
Burrows Av *RNFD/HAY* WA11 .....90 B8
Burrows Cl *VAUX/LVPD* L3 .....12 E1
Burrow's La *ECCL* WA10 .....101 G3
Burrows St *RNFD/HAY* WA11 .....90 C7
Bursar Cl *NEWLW* WA12 .....104 F1
Burscough Rd *ORM* L39 .....51 H7
Burscough St *ORM* L39 .....51 H8
Burton Av *WAL/NB* CH45 .....95 G8
Burton Cl *CLVPS* L1 .....112 F5
GOL/RIS/CU WA3 .....107 H2
RAIN/WH L35 .....117 J1
WDN WA8 .....134 B2
Burtonhead Rd *STHEL* WA9 .....9 G8
Burtonwood Rd *NSTN* CH64 ...153 C2
WARRN/WOL WA2 .....121 M3
Burton St *EV* L5 .....96 E7
Burtons Wy *NG/CROX* L11 .....85 L6
Burtonwood Rd
WARRW/BUR WA5 .....120 B1
Burtree Rd *DV/KA/FCH* L14 .....99 J7
Burwell Av *CHLY/EC* PR7 .....42 F5
FMBY L37 .....58 E4
Burwen Dr *WLT/FAZ* L9 .....84 B7
Bury Rd *STHP* PR8 .....14 E2
Busby's Cottages *WAL/NB* CH45 .95 K5
Bushby's La *FMBY* L37 .....58 E3
Bushby's Pk *FMBY* L37 .....58 E3
Bushell Cl *NSTN* CH64 .....153 H6
Bushell Rd *NSTN* CH64 .....153 H6
Bushel's Dr *STHEL* WA9 .....118 F3
Bushey La *RNFD/HAY* WA11 .....76 A3
Bushey Rd *ANF/KKDL* L4 .....97 L3
Bushley Cl *BTL* L20 .....6 F3
Bush Rd *WDN* WA8 .....16 A9
Bush Wy *HES* CH60 .....141 G5
Butchers La *ORM* L39 .....62 B8
Butcher St *AIMK* WN4 .....91 K4
Bute St *EV* L5 .....13 K3
Butleigh Rd *HUY* L36 .....99 M8
Butler Crs *NPK/KEN* L6 .....113 M3
Butler St *NPK/KEN* L6 .....113 K1
WGN WN1 .....5 G8
Buttercup Cl *CSBY/WL* L22 .....83 H4
MOR/LEA CH46 .....110 C3
Buttercup Wy *WLT/FAZ* L9 .....97 K1
Butterfield Av *AIMK* WN4 .....79 K8
Butterfield St *ANF/KKDL* L4 .....97 H6
Buttermarket St *WARR* WA1 * ...15 C3
Buttermere Av *AIMK* WN4 .....79 K8
CHLY/EC PR7 .....32 C7
CL/PREN CH43 .....110 E7
EP CH65 .....20 C9
RNFD/HAY WA11 .....89 J3
WARRN/WOL WA2 .....121 L2
Buttermere Cl *FMBY* L37 .....58 F2
FROD/HEL WA6 .....160 F5
MGHL L31 .....72 F4
NWD/KWIPK L33 .....85 M1
Buttermere Crs
RNFD/HAY WA11 .....76 B3
Buttermere Gdns
CSBY/BLUN L23 .....83 H3
Buttermere Gv *RUNC* WA7 .....149 M7
Buttermere Rd *CHLDW* L16 .....115 J5
TOX L8 .....67 L6
Buttermere St *TOX* L8 .....113 K6
Butterton Av
GR/UP/WCH L49 .....109 M7
Butterworth Dr *WD/CROXPK* L12 .99 G2
Butterworth Brow
CHLY/EC PR7 .....43 H1
Button St *CLVP* L2 .....13 G7
Butts La *STHP* PR8 .....25 H8
Buxted Rd *KKBY* L32 .....86 C5
Buxton Cl *WARRW/BUR* WA5 ...120 C5
Buxton La *WARR* WA1 .....122 C2
Exchange St West *CLVP* L2 * ...12 F7
Bye La *ORM* L39 .....61 L2
Byerley St *WAL/EG* CH44 .....112 A2
Byfleet Cl *WGNS/IIMK* WN3 .....78 E4
Byland Cl *FMBY* L37 .....59 K3
WDN WA8 .....118 A3
Byles St *TOX* L8 .....129 J1
Byley Ri *WGNNW/ST* WN6 .....56 A5
Byng Pl *ANF/KKDL* L4 .....97 M5
Byng Rd *ANF/KKDL* L4 .....97 M5
Byng St *BTL* L20 .....6 C1
The By-Pass *CSBY/BLUN* L23 .....83 G1
Byrom La *GOL/RIS/CU* WA3 .....93 H3
Byrom St *CHTN/BK* PR9 .....25 H7
VAUX/LVPD L3 .....13 H5
Byrom Wy *VAUX/LVPD* L3 .....13 H5
Byron Av *RAIN/WH* L35 .....117 J2
WGNE/HIN WN2 .....69 M8
Byron Cl *CL/PREN* CH43 .....110 F3
ECCL WA10 .....9 G2
FMBY L37 .....59 H1
HUY L36 .....116 C4
WDN WA8 .....16 D5
WGNNW/ST WN6 .....68 A2
WGNW/BIL/O WN5 .....67 H6
Byron Ct *WARRN/WOL* WA2 .....13 M8
BTL L20 .....6 C1
CHLY/EC PR7 .....32 E5
RUNC WA7 .....18 F5
The Byway *CSBY/BLUN* L23 .....71 C8

C

Cabes Cl *DV/KA/FCH* L14 .....99 J7
Cabin La *CHTN/BK* PR9 .....26 A7
KIRK/FR/WA PR4 .....27 J7
MGHL L31 .....72 B1
ORM L39 .....35 M8
Cable Rd *HOY* CH47 .....108 D6
RAIN/WH L35 .....101 H8
Cable St *CLVP* L2 .....12 F8
FMBY L37 .....59 J1
STHP PR8 .....3 G3
Cabot Cl *WARRW/BUR* WA5 .....120 E4
Cabot Gn *WLTN* L25 .....115 M4
Cabul Cl *WARRN/WOL* WA2 .....15 J1
Caddick Rd *PR/KW* L34 .....86 D8
Cadman Gv *WGNE/HIN* WN2 .....80 F7
Cadnam Rd *WLTN* L25 .....115 M8
Cadogan Dr *WGNS/IIMK* WN3 ...78 F3
Cadogan St *WAV* L15 .....113 M5
Cadshaw Cl *GOL/RIS/CU* WA3 ...106 F3
Cadwell Rd *MGHL* L31 .....61 K8
Caernarvon Cl
GR/UP/WCH L49 .....110 B7
Caernarvon Ct *EP* CH65 .....163 M3
Caernarvon Rd *WGNE/HIN* WN2 .81 J2
Caerwys Gv *RF/TRAN* CH42 .....128 A1
Caird St *NPK/KEN* L6 .....113 J2
Cairn Ct *STHEL* WA9 .....101 M6
Cairnmore Rd *CALD/MH* L18 ...130 C3
Cairns St *TOX* L8 .....113 J7
Cairo St *RF/TRAN* CH42 .....2 D6
ECCL WA10 .....101 M4
WARR WA1 .....14 E6
Caister Cl *SKEL* WN8 .....65 M5
Caithness Ct *RUNC* WA7 .....19 H3
Caithness Dr *CSBY/BLUN* L23 ...83 H2
WAL/NB CH45 .....95 L7
Caithness Gdns
CL/PREN CH43 .....127 H4
Caithness Rd *CALD/MH* L18 .....130 D4
Calday Grange Cl *WKBY* CH48 ..124 F4
Calday Gv *RNFD/HAY* WA11 .....90 C5
Caldbeck Av *WARRN/WOL* WA2 .121 M3
Caldbeck Cl *AIMK* WN4 .....91 K1
Caldbeck Gv *RNFD/HAY* WA11 ...89 L4
Caldbeck Rd *PS/BROM* CH62 ...144 A3
Calder Av *CHLY/EC* PR7 .....32 D7
CL/PREN CH43 .....127 J3
ORM L39 .....63 G1
WGNE/HIN WN2 .....81 L2
Calderbank St
WGNW/BIL/O WN5 .....68 A3
Calder Cl *NWD/KWIPK* L33 .....74 B7
WDN WA8 .....135 H2
Calder Dr *CALD/MH* L18 .....114 E8
MGHL L31 .....73 H3
RAIN/WH L35 .....117 K3
Calderfield Cl *WARRS* WA4 .....137 K5
Calderfield Rd *CALD/MH* L18 ...114 F8
Calder Gra *WLTN* L25 * 131 G2
Calderhurst Dr *ECCL* WA10 .....88 D7
Calder Pl *WGNW/BIL/O* WN5 ...67 L6
Calder Rd *BEB* CH63 .....127 M8
EV L5 .....97 H7
The Calders *CALD/MH* L18 .....130 E2
Calderstones Av *CALD/MH* L18 .114 E8
Calderstones Rd *CALD/MH* L18 .130 E1
Calder Wy *GTS/LS* CH66 .....155 L8
Calderwood Pk *NTHLY* L27 .....115 M7
Caldew Cl *WGNE/HIN* WN2 .....81 C1
Caldford Cl *WGNE/HIN* WN2 .....57 J7
Caldicott Av *PS/BROM* CH62 ...143 M6
Caldon Cl *LITH* L21 .....83 J4
Caldway Dr *NTHLY* L27 .....115 M7
Caldwell Av *WARRW/BUR* WA5 .121 H3
Caldwell Cl *NWD/KWIPK* L33 * ..74 B8
Caldwell Rd *ALL/GAR* L19 .....130 E5
WDN WA8 .....16 C5
Caldwell St *STHEL* WA9 .....102 F2
Caldy Chase Dr *WKBY* CH48 ...124 F6
Caldy Dr *GTS/LS* CH66 .....162 F1
Caldy Gv *RNFD/HAY* WA11 .....89 M4
Caldy Rd *WAL/NB* CH45 .....95 K8
WKBY CH48 .....124 F6
WLT/FAZ L9 .....84 C6
Caldy Wd *WKBY* CH48 .....124 F6
Caledonia Av *STHEL* WA9 .....102 A6
Caledonia La *NG/CROX* L11 .....85 L8
Caledonia St *EHL/KEN* L7 .....13 J3
Cale La *WGNE/HIN* WN2 .....69 K3
Caledonia St *EHL/KEN* L7 .....13 J3
Calgarth Rd *HUY* L36 .....99 L8
California Cl *WARRW/BUR* WA5 .120 E5
California Rd *CLB/OSW/ST* L13 ..97 M6
Callaghan Cl *EV* L5 .....96 F9
Callander Ct *WGNNW/ST* WN6 ...68 A6
Callander Rd *NPK/KEN* L6 .....113 M2
Callands Rd *WARRW/BUR* WA5 .120 F3
Callestock Cl *NG/CROX* L11 .....85 M8
Callington Cl *DV/KA/FCH* L14 ...99 J7
Callon Av *RNFD/HAY* WA11 .....90 A8
WGNE/HIN WN2 .....113 M6
Calmet Cl *EV* L5 .....97 G7
Calmington La *RUNC* WA7 .....151 H1
Calne Cl *PEN/TH* CH61 .....125 M6
Calstock Dr *WARRW/BUR* WA5 ..136 A2
Calthorpe St *ALL/GAR* L19 .....130 D7
Calthorpe Wy *CL/PREN* CH43 ...110 F7
Calton Av *CALD/MH* L18 * 114 C8
Calvados Cl *AIG/SPK* L17 .....129 L4
Calveley Av *PS/BROM* CH62 ...155 H1
Calveley Cl *CL/PREN* CH43 .....127 G2
Calveley Rd *HLWD* L26 .....132 C7
Calveley Wk *WGNNW/ST* WN6 ...56 A5
Calverhall Wy *AIMK* WN4 .....91 J2
Calverly Cl *RUNC* WA7 .....150 E8
Calver Rd *WARRN/WOL* WA2 ...121 J2
Camarthen Crs *TOX* L8 .....112 F7
Camberley Dr *WLTN* L25 .....131 L5
Camberley Dr *WLTN* L25 .....131 L5
Camberwell Crs
WGNE/HIN WN2 .....69 H3
Camberwell Park Rd *WDN* WA8 ..133 L5
Camborne Av *WLTN* L25 .....131 L5
Camborne Cl *RUNC* WA7 .....150 E7
Cambourne Av *RNFD/HAY* WA11.89 M6
Cambourne Dr *WGNE/HIN* WN2 .81 J3
Cambourne Rd
WARRW/BUR WA5 .....104 B7
Cambrai Av *WARRS* WA4 .....137 L3
Cambrian Cl *GTS/LS* CH66 .....162 F1
MOR/LEA CH46 .....109 K6
Cambrian Crs *WGNS/IIMK* WN3 ..78 E3
Cambrian Rd *MOR/LEA* CH46 ...109 L6
Cambria St *NPK/KEN* L6 .....113 M3
Cambria St North *NPK/KEN* L6 .113 M3
Cambridge Av *CHTN/BK* PR9 ...25 H3
CSBY/BLUN L23 .....82 F1
LITH L21 .....83 K5
Cambridge Dr *CSBY/BLUN* L23 ...70 E8

HLWD L26 .....132 B5
Cambridge Gdns *CHTN/BK* PR9 ..25 H3
FROD/HEL WA6 .....166 F1
WARRS WA4 .....137 L7
Cambridge Rd *BTL* L20 .....7 K6
CHTN/BK PR9 .....25 H3
CSBY/BLUN L23 .....70 E8
EP CH65 .....20 C5
FMBY L37 .....58 F4
LITH L21 .....83 G6
PS/BROM CH62 .....143 M5
RF/TRAN CH42 .....127 J3
SKEL WN8 .....65 C4
WAL/NB CH45 .....95 K6
WGNW/BIL/O WN5 .....67 C5
WLT/FAZ L9 .....83 L1
Cambridge St *CHLY/EC* PR7 .....32 E6
EHL/KEN L7 .....13 L9
PR/KW L34 .....100 F3
RUNC WA7 .....18 E8
WAV L15 .....113 M5
WDN WA8 .....19 G3
WGN WN1 .....5 H5
Cambridge Wks *STHP* PR8 .....3 H5
Cambridge Wy *WGN* WN1 .....5 H5
Camdale Cl *STBRV* L28 .....99 M6
Camden Cl *RUNC* WA7 .....150 F4
Camden Pl *BIRK* CH41 .....11 J5
Camden Rd *EP* CH65 .....156 C8
Camden St *BIRK* CH41 .....11 J4
VAUX/LVPD L3 .....13 G4
Camelford Rd *NG/CROX* L11 .....85 L8
Camelia Ct *AIG/SPK* L17 .....129 J3
Camelia Gdns *STHEL* WA9 .....103 K6
Camelot Cl *NEWLW* WA12 .....104 B1
Camelot Ter *BTL* L20 .....6 E2
Cameo Cl *NPK/KEN* L6 .....113 K1
Cameron Av *RUNC* WA7 .....18 D8
Cameron Ct *WARRN/WOL* WA2 .121 J3
Cameron Cft *PS/BROM* CH62 * ...1
Cameron Pl *WGNW/BIL/O* WN5 ..68 A5
Cameron Rd *MOR/LEA* CH46 ...110 D2
WDN WA8 .....16 C4
LEIGH WN7 .....81 M6
Camm St *WGNE/HIN* WN2 .....80 C5
Camomile Cl *CHLY/EC* PR7 * 32 C2
Campania Ct *ALL/GAR* L19 .....145 L1
Campania St *ORM* L39 .....63 G2
Campbell Av *RUNC* WA7 .....19 H7
Campbell Crs *WARRW/BUR* WA5.120 B7
Campbell Dr *DV/KA/FCH* L14 ...115 G2
Campbell St *BTL* L20 .....6 E2
CLVPS L1 .....13 G9
ECCL WA10 .....8 D4
RUNC WA7 .....18 F5
Campbeltown Rd *BIRK* CH41 .....11 L9
Camperdown St *BIRK* CH41 .....11 L8
Camphill Rd *WLTN* L25 .....131 J6
Campion Cl *GOL/RIS/CU* WA3 ...106 E8
RNFD/HAY WA11 .....89 K6
Campion Gv *AIMK* WN4 .....91 H1
Campion Wy *HUY* L36 .....116 B6
Camp Rd *AIMK* WN4 .....91 G2
WLTN L25 .....131 K4
Campsey Ash *WDN* WA8 .....134 B3
Camrose Cl *RUNC* WA7 .....149 L7
Camsley La *LYMM* WA13 .....139 L2
Cam St *WLTN* L25 * 131 J4
Canaan *GOL/RIS/CU* WA3 .....93 L5
Canada Cl *WARRN/WOL* WA2 ...122 C3
Canal Bank Pygons Hi *MGHL* L31.61 L5
Canal Reach *RUNC* WA7 .....150 E5
Canalside *EP* CH65 .....2 C9
Canal Side *RUNC* WA7 .....148 F6
WARRS WA4 .....136 C8
WARRS WA4 .....138 E4
WARRS WA4 .....151 H7
Canal St *BTL* L20 .....6 F5
CHLY/EC PR7 .....44 C7
ECCL WA10 .....8 F7
NEWLW WA12 .....104 B3
RUNC WA7 .....19 G5
WGNE/HIN WN2 .....5 L7
WGNNW/ST WN6 .....68 B4
Canal Ter *WGNE/HIN* WN2 .....5 K5
Canal Vw *LYMM* WA13 * 139 L2
MGHL L31 .....85 J3
Canal Wk *CHLYE* PR6 .....33 G5
Canberra Av *STHEL* WA9 .....102 A6
Canberra La *NG/CROX* L11 .....85 L8
Canberra Rd *WGNW/BIL/O* WN5 .67 C4
Canberra Sq *WARRN/WOL* WA2 .121 M3
Candleston Cl
WARRW/BUR WA5 .....121 G4
Canford Cl *WARRW/BUR* WA5 ...120 E7
Cannell Ct *RUNC* WA7 .....150 C7
Cannell St *WARRW/BUR* WA5 ...136 F1
Canning Pl *CLVPS* L1 .....12 F7
Canning Rd *CHTN/BK* PR9 .....25 J6
Canning St *BIRK* CH41 .....11 K3
CLVPS L1 .....113 H5
CSBY/WL L22 .....82 F5
Canniswood Rd
RNFD/HAY WA11 .....90 C4
Cann La North *WARRS* WA4 .....138 A7
Cannock Cl *GTS/LS* CH66 .....163 G5
Cannock Gn *MGHL* L31 .....72 D4
Cannon Hl *CL/PREN* CH43 .....10 C6
Cannon St *EP* CH65 .....156 C8
STHEL WA9 .....118 C2
Canon Cl *WGNNW/ST* WN6 .....56 B3
Canon Rd *NPK/KEN* L6 .....97 L6
Canons Rd *WARRW/BUR* WA5 ...120 C7
Canon St *RUNC* WA7 .....18 F2
Canon Wilson Cl
RNFD/HAY WA11 .....90 C7
Canrow La *PR/KW* L34 .....86 F8
Cansfield Gv *AIMK* WN4 .....91 J1
Cansfield St *ECCL* WA10 .....9 H4
Canterbury Av *CSBY/WL* L22 .....82 F2
GOL/RIS/CU WA3 .....93 L5
Canterbury Cl *AIN/FAZ* L10 .....85 G3
FMBY L37 .....47 H8
GTS/LS CH66 .....163 C5
PR/KW L34 .....101 C6
STHP PR8 .....2 C9
Canterbury Pk *CALD/MH* L18 ...130 E5
Canterbury Rd *RF/TRAN* CH42 ..128 C4
WAL/EG CH44 .....111 J2
WDN WA8 .....133 L6
Canterbury St *ALL/GAR* L19 .....145 L1
CHLYE PR6 .....33 G7
ECCL WA10 .....8 D3
VAUX/LVPD L3 .....13 K4
WARRS WA4 .....15 J4
Canterbury Wy *NTHTN* L30 .....84 B1
VAUX/LVPD L3 .....13 L4
Canter Cl *WLT/FAZ* L9 .....98 B1
Cantley Cl *RUNC* WA7 .....149 M7
Cantlow Fold *STHP* PR8 .....47 J1
Cantsfield St *EHL/KEN* L7 .....113 L6
Canvey Cl *WAV* L15 .....114 D6
Capenhurst Av
WARRN/WOL WA2 .....122 C3
Capenhurst La *CH/BCN* CH1 .....162 C6
EP CH65 .....163 J1

Cape Rd WLT/FAZ L9 * 84 E7
Capesthorne Cl WDN WA8 134 A5
Capesthorne Dr CHLY/EC PR7 43 K2
Capesthorne Rd
WARRN/WOL WA2 121 M4
Capilano Pk ORM L39 62 E5
Capper Gv HUY L36 116 A2
Capps St WGNE/HIN WN2 80 D2
Capricorn Crs DV/KA/FCH L14 99 J8
Capricorn Wy BTL L20 6 F3
Captain's La AIMK WN4 91 L2
NTHTN L30 83 M5
Caradoc Rd LITH L21 83 H7
Caraway Cl CSBY/BLUN L23 71 K8
Caraway Gv ECCL WA10 8 A3
Carawood Cl WGNNW/ST WN6 54 F6
Carbis Cl AIN/FAZ L10 85 J7
Carden Cl ANF/KKDL L4 97 G6
GOL/RIS/CU WA3 122 E1
Cardeston Cl RUNC WA7 161 H2
Cardiff Cl GTS/LS CH66 163 G5
Cardiff St SKEL WN8 64 F4
Cardigan Av BIRK CH41 11 H5
Cardigan Cl ECCL WA10 8 E7
WARRW/BUR WA5 120 F3
Cardigan Rd STHP PR8 35 H4
WAL/NB CH45 95 K6
Cardigan St WAV L15 113 M5
Cardigan Wy NPK/KEN L6 113 K1
NTHTN L30 * 84 D1
Cardus Cl MOR/LEA CH46 109 K5
Cardwell St EHL/KEN L7 113 J5
Careless La WGNE/HIN WN2 5 M5
Carey Av BEB CH63 127 M7
Carey Cl WGNS/IIMK WN3 78 F3
Carey St WDN WA8 16 E2
Carfax Rd NWD/KWIPK L33 86 C1
Carfield SKEL WN8 66 A7
Cargill Gv RF/TRAN CH42 128 D5
Carham Rd HOY CH47 108 E7
Carisbrooke Cl WKBY CH48 124 E5
Carisbrooke Dr CHTN/BK PR9 25 H4
Carisbrooke Pl ANF/KKDL L4 * 97 H4
Carisbrooke Rd ANF/KKDL L4 7 M8
Carkington Rd WLTN L25 131 L4
Carland Cl NG/CROX L11 85 K7
Carlaw Rd RF/TRAN CH42 127 J3
Carleen Cl AIG/SPK L17 129 K3
Carleton Rd CHLYE PR6 33 G1
Carlett Bvd PS/BROM CH62 144 B8
Carlile Wy NWD/KWIPK L33 74 B7
Carlingford Cl TOX L8 113 J6
Carlingford Rd WARRS WA4 137 K5
Carlisle Cl ANF/KKDL L4 97 M5
Carlisle Ms CL/PREN CH43 10 F7
Carlisle Pl CHLYE PR6 44 C5
Carlisle Rd STHP PR8 35 J3
Carlisle St WARRS WA4 137 L5
WGNW/BIL/O WN5 67 M7
Carlis Rd KKBY L32 86 B5
Carlow Cl SPK/HALE L24 147 L3
Carlow St ECCL WA10 101 M4
Carlsruhe Ct TOX L8 * 113 J8
Carl's Wy NWD/KWIPK L33 74 C7
Carlton Av RUNC WA7 149 M3
SKEL WN8 66 C6
Carlton Cl HOR/BR BL6 57 M3
NSTN CH64 152 E3
Carlton Crs GTS/LS CH66 156 A5
Carlton Gv WGNE/HIN WN2 81 H2
Carlton La CLB/OSW/ST L13 114 C1
HOY CH47 108 E5
Carlton Mt RF/TRAN CH42 128 A2
Carlton Rd BEB CH63 143 K1
GOL/RIS/CU WA3 92 F4
RF/TRAN CH42 127 L1
STHP PR8 34 E7
WAL/NB CH45 95 K5
Carlton St ECCL WA10 8 D6
PR/KW L34 100 F6
VAUX/LVPD L3 12 C1
WARRS WA4 137 L5
WDN WA8 16 D3
WGNS/IIMK WN3 4 D8
Carlton Ter CSBY/BLUN L23 * 82 F1
HOY CH47 * 108 E5
Carlyle Crs GTS/LS CH66 163 G1
Carlyle Gv LEIGH WN7 81 L5
Carlyon Wy HLWD L26 * 132 A5
Carmarthen Cl
WARRW/BUR WA5 120 F3
Carmel Cl ORM L39 62 F3
Carmel Ct WDN WA8 134 D1
Carmelite Crs ECCL WA10 88 C8
Carmichael Av
GR/UP/WCH CH49 125 M3
Carnaby Cl HUY L36 116 C5
Carnarvon Rd STHP PR8 35 H4
WLT/FAZ L9 97 H2
Carnarvon St STHEL WA9 101 M6
Carnatic Rd AIG/SPK L17 130 A2
Carnation Rd WLT/FAZ L9 97 K1
Carnegie Av CSBY/BLUN L23 82 F2
Carnegie Crs STHEL WA9 103 G5
Carnegie Dr AIMK WN4 79 J8
Carnegie Rd CLB/OSW/ST L13 114 B1
Carnforth Av KKBY L32 86 B4
Carnforth Cl BIRK CH41 10 F8
WD/CROXPK L12 98 E4
Carnforth Rd CALD/MH L18 130 E3
Carnoostie Dr CHLYE PR6 31 M1
Carno St WAV L15 * 114 A5
Carnoustie Cl MOR/LEA CH46 109 K4
STHP PR8 2 C9
WD/CROXPK L12 99 H7
Carnoustie Gv RNFD/HAY WA11 90 C8
Carnsdale Rd MOR/LEA CH46 110 B5
Carol Dr HES CH60 141 L5
Carole Cl STHEL WA9 103 G4
Carolina St BTL L20 7 G4
Caroline Pl CL/PREN CH43 10 E4
Caroline St WDN WA8 * 16 E6
WGN WN1 5 L4
WGNS/IIMK WN3 4 D5
Carol St WARRS WA4 15 J9
Caronia St ALL/GAR L19 * 145 L1
Carpathia St ALL/GAR L19 145 L1
Carpenter Gv WARRN/WOL WA2 122 C4
Carpenter's La WKBY CH48 124 D3
Carpenters Rw CLVPS L1 112 E5
Carradon Dr WGNNW/ST WN6 56 A4
Carraway Rd NG/CROX L11 85 K7
Carr Bridge Rd
GR/UP/WCH CH49 126 D1
Carr Cl NG/CROX L11 98 D3
Carr Common Rd
WGNE/HIN WN2 81 M2
Carr Cft LITH L21 83 J2
Carrfield Av CSBY/BLUN L23 83 J2
Carr Ga MOR/LEA CH46 109 K6
Carr Hey MOR/LEA CH46 109 K5
Carr Hey Cl GR/UP/WCH CH49 126 E3
Carr House La HTWN L38 71 G1
MOR/LEA CH46 109 K5
WGNNW/ST WN6 42 B5
Carriage Dr FROD/HEL WA6 160 C7
Carrick Dr EP CH65 163 K3
Carrickmore Av CALD/MH L18 130 C3
Carrington Cl GOL/RIS/CU WA3 122 E1
Carrington Rd CHLY/EC PR7 32 D6
CHLY/EC PR7 44 B6
WAL/NB CH45 95 K7
Carrington St BIRK CH41 10 A1
Carr La BRSC L40 52 D2
CHLY/EC PR7 32 F8
CROS/BRETH PR26 29 K6
GOL/RIS/CU WA3 93 J6
HOY CH47 108 D7
HOY CH47 109 J4
HUY L36 115 L4
MGHL L31 61 H8
NG/CROX L11 98 B3
PR/KW L34 100 D8
SPK/HALE L24 147 M3
STHP PR8 35 H6
WGNS/IIMK WN3 79 J2
Carr La East NG/CROX L11 98 D3
Carr Meadow Hey NTHTN L30 83 L3
Carr Mill Crs WGNW/BIL/O WN5 90 A1
Carr Mill Rd RNFD/HAY WA11 89 L6
WGNW/BIL/O WN5 90 A2
Carr Moss La ORM L39 48 E2
ORM L39 49 K5
Carrock Rd PS/BROM CH62 144 A3
Carroll Crs ORM L39 51 H6
Carrow Cl MOR/LEA CH46 109 K6
Carr Rd BTL L20 83 M6
HOR/BR BL6 45 K8
Carr's Crs FMBY L37 58 F4
Carr's Crs West FMBY L37 58 F4
Carr Side La HTWN L38 71 J2
Carr St CHLYE PR6 33 G4
ECCL WA10 8 C1
LEIGH WN7 81 L8
WGNE/HIN WN2 69 M7
Carruthers St VAUX/LVPD L3 12 E3
Carrville Wy WD/CROXPK L12 99 J3
Carrwood Cl RNFD/HAY WA11 90 C7
Carrwood Pk STHP PR8 35 K2
Carsdale Rd CALD/MH L18 114 C8
Carsgoe Rd HOY CH47 108 E7
Carsington Rd NG/CROX L11 98 C3
Carstairs Rd NPK/KEN L6 113 L1
Carsthorne Rd HOY CH47 108 E7
Car St WGNE/HIN WN2 80 C4
Cartbridge La HLWD L26 132 B4
Carter Av RNFD/HAY WA11 76 C8
The Carters GR/UP/WCH CH49 125 L1
NTHTN L30 84 C1
Carter St TOX L8 113 H7
WGNS/IIMK WN3 5 J7
Carterton Rd HOY CH47 108 E7
Cartier Cl WARRW/BUR WA5 120 E5
Cartmel Av ECCL WA10 89 G6
MGHL L31 73 G3
WARRN/WOL WA2 121 L2
WGN WN1 68 D2
Cartmel Cl BIRK CH41 * 10 F8
HUY L36 115 M1
STHP PR8 36 B2
WARRW/BUR WA5 121 G3
Cartmel Dr FMBY L37 59 K3
GTS/LS CH66 163 H3
MOR/LEA CH46 110 A6
RAIN/WH L35 117 J1
WD/CROXPK L12 98 E4
Cartmell Cl RUNC WA7 149 K7
Cartmel Rd HUY L36 115 M1
Cartmel Ter NG/CROX L11 98 E2
Cartmel Wy HUY L36 115 L1
Cartridge La WARRS WA4 138 F7
Cartwright's Gv LEIGH WN7 81 M4
Cartwright's Farm Rd
SPK/HALE L24 146 C2
Cartwright St RUNC WA7 19 L4
WARRW/BUR WA5 121 G7
Carvel Wy BRSC L40 52 B2
Carvers Brow
CROS/BRETH PR26 29 K4
Carver St VAUX/LVPD L3 13 L4
Caryl Gv TOX L8 129 G1
Caryl St TOX L8 112 F8
Cascades SKEL WN8 * 65 L6
Case Gv RAIN/WH L35 101 G8
Case Rd RNFD/HAY WA11 90 F7
Cashel Rd BIRK CH41 111 K3
Cashmore Dr WGNE/HIN WN2 80 F1
Caspian Pl BTL L20 7 H4
Caspian Rd ANF/KKDL L4 97 L3
Cassia Cl WLT/FAZ L9 97 K1
Cassino Rd HUY L36 115 M2
Cassio St BTL L20 * 7 L7
Cassley Rd SPK/HALE L24 147 J2
Cassville Rd CALD/MH L18 114 C7
Castell Gv ECCL WA10 8 E5
Casterton CHLY/EC PR7 31 L3
Casterton St EHL/KEN L7 * 113 L5
Castle Av STHEL WA9 103 G2
Castle Cl MOR/LEA CH46 110 C2
Castle Crs HOR/BR BL6 45 L8
Castlecroft Av HOR/BR BL6 57 M3
Castle Dr CHLY/EC PR7 44 A7
EP CH65 163 J2
FMBY L37 59 H4
HES CH60 141 H5
Castlefield Cl WD/CROXPK L12 98 C5
Castlefield Rd WD/CROXPK L12 98 C6
Castlefields Av East RUNC WA7 150 C4
Castlefields Av North
RUNC WA7 150 A3
Castlefields Av South
RUNC WA7 150 C5
Castle Fields Est
MOR/LEA CH46 110 B1
Castleford Ri MOR/LEA CH46 110 A2
Castleford St WAV L15 114 C6
Castlegate Gv WD/CROXPK L12 98 C6
Castlegrange Cl MOR/LEA CH46 110 A1
Castle Gn WARRW/BUR WA5 120 D3
Castleheath Cl MOR/LEA CH46 110 A2
Castlehey SKEL WN8 66 A7
Castle Hl CLVP L2 * 12 E7
NEWLW WA12 105 G1
Castle House La CHLY/EC PR7 44 A7
Castle La BRSC L40 51 M7
Castlemere Cl WGNS/IIMK WN3 78 F4
Castle Mt HES CH60 * 141 H5
Castle Ri RUNC WA7 149 M3
Castle Rd RUNC WA7 150 B5
WAL/NB CH45 95 J7
Castlesite Rd WD/CROXPK L12 98 D6
Castle St BIRK CH41 11 L5
CHLY/EC PR7 32 F6
CHTN/BK PR9 3 H3
CLVP L2 12 E7
WDN WA8 17 J2
WLTN L25 131 H3
Castleton Dr NTHTN L30 84 D1
Castleton Wy WGNS/IIMK WN3 78 E3
Castletown Cl CHLDW L16 115 G5
Castleview Rd WD/CROXPK L12 98 D6
Castle Wk STHP PR8 2 E6
Castleway North
MOR/LEA CH46 110 C1
Castleway South
MOR/LEA CH46 110 C2
Castlewood Rd NPK/KEN L6 97 K8
Castner Av RUNC WA7 18 C9
Castor St NPK/KEN L6 97 K8
Catchdale Moss La ECCL WA10 88 A8
Catford Cl WDN WA8 133 L3
Catford Gn SPK/HALE L24 147 H2
Catfoss Cl WARRN/WOL WA2 122 A4
Catharine's La ORM L39 63 H3
Catharine St TOX L8 113 H6
Cathcart Quay BIRK CH41 * 11 H2
Cathcart St BIRK CH41 11 G4
Cathedral Cl CLVPS L1 113 G6
Cathedral Ga CLVPS L1 113 G5
Cathedral Rd NPK/KEN L6 97 L7
Cathedral Wk VAUX/LVPD L3 13 K8
Catherine St BIRK CH41 11 G6
CHLY/EC PR7 * 32 E7
LITH L21 83 K7
WARRW/BUR WA5 14 C2
WDN WA8 16 D7
Catherine St East HOR/BR BL6 45 K8
Catherine St West HOR/BR BL6 45 J8
Catherine Ter WGN WN1 5 J4
Catherine Wy NEWLW WA12 104 D3
RNFD/HAY WA11 * 90 B7
Catkin Rd HLWD L26 131 M3
Caton Cl CHTN/BK PR9 25 H1
Catonfield Rd CALD/MH L18 114 F8
Cat Tail La STHP PR8 37 G4
Catterall Av STHEL WA9 102 F7
WARRN/WOL WA2 121 M3
Catterick Cl HLWD L26 132 B5
Catterick Fold STHP PR8 36 B2
Caulfield Dr GR/UP/WCH CH49 126 A2
Caunce Av CHTN/BK PR9 23 J7
GOL/RIS/CU WA3 92 C6
RNFD/HAY WA11 90 D7
Caunce Rd WGN WN1 5 J3
Caunce's Rd CHTN/BK PR9 26 F7
Caunce St WGN WN1 5 J3
Causeway Av WARRS WA4 137 L2
Causeway Cl PS/BROM CH62 128 D8
Causeway La BRSC L40 39 K4
FMBY L37 60 D4
The Causeway CHLYE PR6 33 G5
CHTN/BK PR9 22 E8
PS/BROM CH62 128 D8
WD/CROXPK L12 114 F1
Cavalier Dr ALL/GAR L19 131 G8
Cavan Rd NG/CROX L11 98 A5
Cavell Cl WLTN L25 131 J4
Cavell Dr EP CH65 163 J1
Cavendish Av GOL/RIS/CU WA3 107 G8
Cavendish Cl WARRW/BUR WA5 120 F6
Cavendish Dr RF/TRAN CH42 127 M4
WGNS/IIMK WN3 78 F3
WLT/FAZ L9 97 J2
Cavendish Farm Rd RUNC WA7 149 H8
Cavendish Gdns EP CH65 163 J1
TOX L8 * 113 J8
Cavendish Pl GOL/RIS/CU WA3 107 H8
Cavendish Rd BIRK CH41 10 C3
CSBY/BLUN L23 82 E2
STHP PR8 35 H2
WAL/NB CH45 95 K4
Cavendish St BIRK CH41 10 D2
CHLYE PR6 33 H3
RUNC WA7 18 F4
Cavendish Whf BIRK CH41 * 111 L4
Cavern Ct NPK/KEN L6 113 K2
Caversham Cl WARRS WA4 137 M6
Cawdor St RUNC WA7 18 E2
TOX L8 113 J7
WARRS WA4 137 L5
WGNW/BIL/O WN5 68 B7
Cawfield Av WDN WA8 133 M4
Cawley Av GOL/RIS/CU WA3 107 G1
Cawley St RUNC WA7 19 G6
Cawood Cl GTS/LS CH66 155 K8
Cawthorne Av KKBY L32 86 A6
WARRS WA4 138 C3
Cawthorne Cl KKBY L32 86 A5
Cawthorne Wk KKBY L32 * 86 A5
Caxton Cl CL/PREN CH43 110 E7
GTS/LS CH66 163 H1
WDN WA8 * 133 L2
WGNS/IIMK WN3 79 H3
Caxton Rd RAIN/WH L35 118 A4
Cazneau St VAUX/LVPD L3 13 H3
C Ct AIMK WN4 91 K3
Cearns Rd CL/PREN CH43 10 B8
Cecil Av WGNNW/ST WN6 68 C3
Cecil Dr ECCL WA10 88 C8
Cecil Rd LITH L21 83 K8
PS/BROM CH62 128 D5
RF/TRAN CH42 127 K3
WAL/EG CH44 111 J1
Cecil St STHEL WA9 103 H6
WAV L15 113 M5
WGN WN1 5 K4
WGNS/IIMK WN3 80 A1
Cedab Rd EP CH65 20 D3
Cedar Av BEB CH63 143 G1
CHLY/EC PR7 31 L1
GOL/RIS/CU WA3 93 H6
GTS/LS CH66 155 L7
RUNC WA7 19 M9
RUNC WA7 161 J1
WDN WA8 134 D2
WGNE/HIN WN2 81 H2
WGNNW/ST WN6 56 B5
Cedar Cl CALD/MH L18 130 F2
RAIN/WH L35 117 G1
Cedar Ct GOL/RIS/CU WA3 107 H3
Cedar Crs HUY L36 115 M4
NEWLW WA12 104 F3
ORM L39 62 E1
Cedardale Dr GTS/LS CH66 163 H4
Cedardale Pk WDN WA8 135 G1
Cedardale Rd WLT/FAZ L9 97 J1
Cedar Dr FMBY L37 58 E4
WGN WN1 68 D1
Cedar Gv AIMK WN4 78 F8
CSBY/WL L22 82 F3
MGHL L31 72 F7
NSTN CH64 153 H5
RNFD/HAY WA11 91 G6
SKEL WN8 65 G4
TOX L8 113 L7
WARR WA1 122 C6
WARRS WA4 137 M2
WGNW/BIL/O WN5 67 H7
Cedar Rd CHLYE PR6 32 F3
RAIN/WH L35 116 F2
WARRW/BUR WA5 120 B7
WLT/FAZ L9 84 D7
The Cedars CHLY/EC PR7 30 D6
CHLY/EC PR7 43 K1
MOR/LEA CH46 109 L6
WD/CROXPK L12 99 H2
Cedar St BIRK CH41 11 G7
BTL L20 7 H3
ECCL WA10 8 A7
NEWLW WA12 * 104 E3
STHP PR8 3 K9
Cedar Ter TOX L8 113 K7
Cedarway HES CH60 141 K8
Cedarways WARRS WA4 137 M8
Cedarwood Cl
GR/UP/WCH CH49 125 K1
Cedarwood Ct HUY L36 116 A5
Celandine Wk WGNS/IIMK WN3 78 D1
Celandine Wy STHEL WA9 103 K6
Celebration Dr NPK/KEN L6 97 L8
Celedine Cl WAV L15 114 A5
Celia St BTL L20 7 J9
Celtic Rd HOY CH47 109 G4
Celtic St TOX L8 113 J7
Celt St NPK/KEN L6 * 113 L1
Cemeas Cl EV L5 96 E8
Cemetery Rd STHP PR8 3 H9
WGNS/IIMK WN3 80 A1
Cemetery Vw CHLY/EC PR7 44 C7
Centenary Cl ANF/KKDL L4 97 L5
Central Av EP CH65 20 C6
PR/KW L34 100 E7
PR/KW L34 101 H6
PS/BROM CH62 143 L4
SPK/HALE L24 146 F2
STHP PR8 35 H5
WARRN/WOL WA2 121 L5
WARRS WA4 14 F9
Central Buildings
CSBY/BLUN L23 * 83 G1
Central Dr RNFD/HAY WA11 76 B6
RNFD/HAY WA11 90 D7
WD/CROXPK L12 98 D8
WGNNW/ST WN6 55 K7
Central Expy RUNC WA7 149 M7
Central Flats WGNE/HIN WN2 * 5 M5
Central Park Av WAL/EG CH44 111 L1
Central Park Wy WGN WN1 5 G1
Central Rd PS/BROM CH62 128 D6
WARRS WA4 15 G9
Central Sq MGHL L31 72 F3
Central St ECCL WA10 9 G3
Central Wy NEWLW WA12 105 G3
SPK/HALE L24 147 G3
WARRN/WOL WA2 14 E4
Centre Cl LEIGH WN7 93 K4
Centre Pk WARR WA1 14 D9
Centre Park Sq WARR WA1 14 D8
Centreville Rd CALD/MH L18 114 C7
Centre Wy HUY L36 116 A3
Centurion Cl GOL/RIS/CU WA3 * 106 F8
HOY CH47 109 G4
Centurion Dr HOY CH47 109 G4
Ceres St BTL L20 7 G9
Cestrian Dr PEN/TH CH61 126 C8
Chadlow Rd KKBY L32 86 B6
Chadwell Rd NWD/KWIPK L33 86 B1
Chadwick Av GOL/RIS/CU WA3 106 D6
WARRS WA4 138 A4
Chadwick Pl GOL/RIS/CU WA3 107 G8
Chadwick Rd RNFD/HAY WA11 89 L6
RUNC WA7 150 A2
Chadwick St MOR/LEA CH46 110 A5
VAUX/LVPD L3 12 D2
WGNS/IIMK WN3 4 C7
Chaffinch Cl GOL/RIS/CU WA3 123 H2
WD/CROXPK L12 99 H4
Chaffinch Gld HLWD L26 132 A4
Chainhurst Cl NTHLY L27 115 M7
Chain La RNFD/HAY WA11 89 M7
Chalbury Cl WGNE/HIN WN2 * 80 F1
Chalfield Av GTS/LS CH66 155 L8
Chalfield Cl GTS/LS CH66 155 L8
Chalfont Cl WARRS WA4 138 A7
Chalfont Rd CALD/MH L18 130 F4
Chalfont Wy STBRV L28 99 K6
Chalgrave Cl WDN WA8 135 G2
Chalkwell Dr HES CH60 141 L6
Challenge Wy
WGNW/BIL/O WN5 67 L4
Challis St BIRK CH41 11 G4
Challoner Cl HUY L36 116 B5
Chaloner Gv ALL/GAR L19 130 B6
Chaloner St VAUX/LVPD L3 112 F6
Chalon Wy ECCL WA10 9 H6
Chalon Wy West ECCL WA10 9 G6
Chamberlain St BIRK CH41 11 K9
ECCL WA10 8 A6
WAL/EG CH44 111 J3
Chambres Rd STHP PR8 3 L7
Chambres Rd North STHP PR8 3 M6
Chancellor Rd RUNC WA7 135 M8
Chancel St ANF/KKDL L4 97 G6
Chancery La STHEL WA9 103 G2
Chancery Rd CHLY/EC PR7 32 C4
Chandlers Ct RUNC WA7 18 D5
Chandler Wy GOL/RIS/CU WA3 93 G5
Chandley Cl STHP PR8 34 C8
Chandos St EHL/KEN L7 113 K4
Change La NSTN CH64 154 D5
Changford Rd NWD/KWIPK L33 86 C2
Channell Rd NPK/KEN L6 113 L2
Channel Rd CSBY/BLUN L23 82 D2
The Channel WAL/NB CH45 * 95 G5
Chantler Av WARRS WA4 15 M7
Chantrell Rd WKBY CH48 125 G3
Chantry Cl CL/PREN CH43 110 E7
Chantry Wk AIMK WN4 79 H8
HES CH60 141 J7
Chapel Av WLT/FAZ L9 84 C8
Chapel Cl EP CH65 20 C1
WGNS/IIMK WN3 5 H8
Chapel Cross Rd
WARRN/WOL WA2 122 C3
Chapelfields FROD/HEL WA6 160 C5
Chapel Gdns EV L5 96 F8
Chapelhill Rd MOR/LEA CH46 110 B5
Chapelhouse Wk FMBY L37 59 J2
Chapel La BRSC L40 52 A3
CH/BCN CH1 162 A5
CHLY/EC PR7 43 H5
CHTN/BK PR9 23 K7
ECCL WA10 101 K1
FMBY L37 59 H2
KIRK/FR/WA PR4 27 K8
MGHL L31 85 J1
NTHTN L30 72 C8
RAIN/WH L35 118 B3
SKEL WN8 53 M4
WARRS WA4 137 L5
WARRW/BUR WA5 104 B7
WDN WA8 117 L8
WGNS/IIMK WN3 4 E7
Chapel Ms EP CH65 20 A6
ORM L39 63 G1
Chapel Pl AIMK WN4 * 91 K2
ALL/GAR L19 130 E7
Chapel Rd ALL/GAR L19 130 E7
HOY CH47 108 D5
NPK/KEN L6 97 L7
WARRW/BUR WA5 136 A2
Chapel St AIMK WN4 91 K2
CHLY/EC PR7 32 E5
CHLY/EC PR7 43 G4
CHLY/EC PR7 44 B7
ECCL WA10 8 F1
HOR/BR BL6 57 M3
NEWLW WA12 104 D2
ORM L39 51 H8
PR/KW L34 * 100 F7
RNFD/HAY WA11 90 F8
RUNC WA7 19 G3
STHP PR8 3 G4
VAUX/LVPD L3 12 D7
WDN WA8 16 C6
WGNE/HIN WN2 69 J2
WGNE/HIN WN2 69 M8
WGNE/HIN WN2 80 C3
WGNE/HIN WN2 81 G4
WGNS/IIMK WN3 4 E6
WGNS/IIMK WN3 5 H8
WGNW/BIL/O WN5 67 K8
Chapel Ter BTL L20 6 E6
Chapel Vw RNFD/HAY WA11 89 H1
Chapel Wy CHLY/EC PR7 43 H4
Chapel Yd WAV L15 114 C6
Chapman Cl TOX L8 * 113 G8
WDN WA8 133 M1
Chapman Gv PR/KW L34 101 G6
Chapterhouse Cl EP CH65 21 H4
Chardstock Dr WLTN L25 * 131 L1
Charing Cross BIRK CH41 11 G6
Charity St LEIGH WN7 81 L8
Charlecombe St RF/TRAN CH42 11 G9
Charlecote St TOX L8 129 H2
Charles Av STHP PR8 35 G7
WARRW/BUR WA5 120 E5
Charles Berrington Rd WAV L15 114 C7
Charlesbye Av ORM L39 51 J7
Charles Price Gdns EP CH65 20 C3
Charles Rd HOY CH47 108 D7
Charles St BIRK CH41 11 G3
ECCL WA10 9 H4
GOL/RIS/CU WA3 92 C4
WDN WA8 16 D3
WGN WN1 4 F1
WGNE/HIN WN2 * 69 J6
Charleston Cl GTS/LS CH66 162 F2
Charleston Rd TOX L8 129 H1
Charlesville CL/PREN CH43 10 C8
Charles Wk DV/KA/FCH L14 115 H2
Charlesworth Av WGNE/HIN WN2 81 H1
Charlesworth Cl MGHL L31 61 K8
Charley Wood Rd
NWD/KWIPK L33 86 D4
Charlock Cl NTHTN L30 84 C1
Charlotte Dr WGNS/IIMK WN3 78 F1
Charlotte Rd WAL/EG CH44 95 M8
Charlotte's Meadow BEB CH63 143 J1
Charlotte Wk WDN WA8 16 E6
Charlton Cl AIMK WN4 79 J8
RUNC WA7 150 C6
Charlton Ct CL/PREN CH43 111 H7
Charlton Pl CLB/OSW/ST L13 114 C4
Charlton Rd CLB/OSW/ST L13 114 C4
Charlton St WARRS WA4 138 B2
Charlwood Av HUY L36 116 A4
Charlwood Cl CL/PREN CH43 110 E7
Charminster Cl
WARRW/BUR WA5 120 D8
Charmouth Cl WD/CROXPK L12 99 G2
Charnley's La CHTN/BK PR9 23 G5
Charnock Av NEWLW WA12 104 B2
Charnock Back La CHLYE PR6 33 K7
Charnock Brow Preston Rd
CHLY/EC PR7 31 L7
Charnock Rd GOL/RIS/CU WA3 107 H2
WLT/FAZ L9 97 M2
Charnock St CHLYE PR6 32 F6
WGNE/HIN WN2 80 D4
Charnwood Cl GOL/RIS/CU WA3 107 K6
WD/CROXPK L12 98 F2
Charnwood Rd HUY L36 115 K2
Charnwood St STHEL WA9 103 G1
Charter Av WARRW/BUR WA5 121 J5
Charter Crs GTS/LS CH66 163 G2
Charterhouse Dr AIN/FAZ L10 85 G3
Charterhouse Rd
WGNS/IIMK WN3 5 H8
WLTN L25 131 K4
Charter La CHLY/EC PR7 42 F1
Chartmount Wy WLTN L25 131 K1
Chartwell Gv HLWD L26 132 C4
Chartwell Rd STHP PR8 34 D7
Chase Cl STHP PR8 2 D9
Chase Dr GTS/LS CH66 163 G3
Chase Heys CHTN/BK PR9 25 H4
Chaser Cl WLT/FAZ L9 84 E5
The Chase BEB CH63 143 L8
HUY L36 116 B5
Chase Wy EV L5 13 K2
GTS/LS CH66 162 F3
Chatburn Av GOL/RIS/CU WA3 92 E4
Chatburn Ct GOL/RIS/CU WA3 107 G3
Chatburn Wk TOX L8 * 129 H1
Chater Cl RAIN/WH L35 101 J7
Chatfield Dr GOL/RIS/CU WA3 123 G2
Chatham Cl LITH L21 83 H6
Chatham Pl CHLYE PR6 33 G5
EHL/KEN L7 113 K4
Chatham Rd RF/TRAN CH42 128 C3
Chatham St EHL/KEN L7 113 H5
Chatsworth Av
GOL/RIS/CU WA3 107 H1
WAL/EG CH44 111 L1
WGNS/IIMK WN3 80 B1
WLT/FAZ L9 84 B8
Chatsworth Cl AIMK WN4 91 H1
CHLY/EC PR7 32 D5
GTS/LS CH66 155 L8
Chatsworth Ct CHLYE PR6 44 B4
Chatsworth Dr EHL/KEN L7 113 K5
WDN WA8 * 133 L2
Chatsworth Rd PEN/TH CH61 126 B8
RAIN/WH L35 117 K1
RF/TRAN CH42 128 C3
STHP PR8 34 D7
Chatsworth St WGNW/BIL/O WN5 67 L8
Chatteris Cl WGNE/HIN WN2 81 G1
Chatteris Pk RUNC WA7 151 G3
Chatterton Dr RUNC WA7 151 G5
Chatterton Rd DV/KA/FCH L14 114 E1
Chatwell Gdns WARRS WA4 138 B8
Chaucer Cl CHLY/EC PR7 30 D7
Chaucer Dr WD/CROXPK L12 99 H3
Chaucer Gv LEIGH WN7 81 L5
Chaucer Pl WARRS WA4 138 B1
WGN WN1 68 E2
WGNE/HIN WN2 80 D4
Chaucer Rd ECCL WA10 88 F7
Chaucer St BTL L20 6 D2
RUNC WA7 19 G5
VAUX/LVPD L3 13 H3
Cheadle Av CLB/OSW/ST L13 114 B2
Cheam Av CHLY/EC PR7 32 F7
Cheapside CHLY/EC PR7 32 E6
CLVP L2 12 F5
FMBY L37 59 J3
Cheapside Aly CLVP L2 * 12 F6
Cheddar Cl WLTN L25 131 H3
Cheddar Gv KKBY L32 86 A6
WARRW/BUR WA5 104 B6
Cheddon Wy PEN/TH CH61 141 G1
Chedworth Dr WDN WA8 133 L1
Chedworth Rd DV/KA/FCH L14 115 G1
Cheetham Gv WGNS/IIMK WN3 68 B8
Chelburn Cl WGNE/HIN WN2 81 G4
Cheldon Rd NG/CROX L11 98 E3
Chelford Av GOL/RIS/CU WA3 92 F6
Chelford Cl CL/PREN CH43 110 E6
WARRS WA4 137 L5
WGNS/IIMK WN3 79 H3
Chellowdene CSBY/BLUN L23 71 J7

Chelmarsh Av AIMK WN4 ....91 L2
Chelmorton Gv WCNS/IIMK WN3 ..78 E3
Chelmsford St EV L5 ....96 F6
Chelmsford Gv WGNS/IIMK WN3 ..79 J1
Chelmsford Dr NEWLW WA12 ..32 D6
Chelmsford Pl CHLY/EC PR7 ....32 D6
Chelmsford Ms WGN WN1 ....68 E3
Chelmsford Ct WD/CROXPK L12 ..99 G5
Chelsea Gdns
    WARRW/BUR WA5 ....136 E1
Chelsea Rd LITH L21 ....83 K7
    WLT/FAZ L9 ....84 C7
Cheltenham Av AIG/SPK L17 ..113 M8
    WGNS/IIMK WN3 ....5 H8
Cheltenham Cl
    WARRW/BUR WA5 ....120 C5
    WLT/FAZ L9 ....85 G4
Cheltenham Crs HUY L36 ....115 M4
    MOR/LEA CH46 ....110 A2
    RUNC WA7 ....149 K7
Cheltenham Dr NEWLW WA12 ....91 L8
    WGNW/BIL/O WN5 ....77 M3
Cheltenham Rd EP CH65 ....20 E8
    WAL/NB CH45 ....95 C7
Cheltenham Wy WGNE/HIN WN2 ..69 H3
Cheltenham Wy STHP PR8 ....36 B1
Chelwood Av CHLDW L16 ....115 H5
Chelwood Pk RNFD/HAY WA11 ....91 K4
Chemical St NEWLW WA12 ....104 D2
Chemistry Rd SPK/HALE L24 ....131 L8
Chenotrie Gdns CL/PREN CH43 ..110 F8
Chepstow Av WAL/EG CH44 ....111 L1
Chepstow Cl WARRW/BUR WA5 ..121 G2
Chepstow St ANF/KKDL L4 ....7 M8
Chequer Cl SKEL WN8 ....66 B8
Chequer La SKEL WN8 ....66 B8
Chequers Gdns ALL/GAR L19 ..130 B5
Chequers St WGN WN1 ....4 D4
Cheriton Av WKBY CH48 ....124 F3
Cheriton Cl HLWD L26 ....132 A5
Cheriton Pk STHP PR8 ....3 H8
    STHP PR8 ....36 A2
Chernside Rd AIG/SPK L17 ..130 A4
The Cherries CHLY/EC PR7 ....44 D5
Cherry Av WAL/EG CH44 ....97 K4
Cherrybank WAL/EG CH44 ....111 K3
Cherry Blossom Rd RUNC WA7 ..150 B8
Cherrybrook Dr
    WCNS/IIMK WN3 ....78 F4
Cherry Cl ANF/KKDL L4 ....97 K4
    NEWLW WA12 ....104 B1
    NSTN CH64 ....153 L5
Cherry Cnr LYMM WA13 ....139 J3
Cherrycroft SKEL WN8 ....66 A7
Cherrydale Rd CALD/MH L18 ..130 C1
Cherryfield Crs KKBY L32 ....86 A3
Cherryfield Dr KKBY L32 ....86 A3
Cherry Gn ORM L39 ....62 D4
Cherry Gv BRSC L40 ....39 G7
    GTS/LS CH66 ....163 J4
    KKBY L32 ....86 B6
    WGNW/ST WN6 ....68 B2
Cherry La ANF/KKDL L4 ....97 L4
    LYMM WA13 ....139 K5
Cherry Rd STHP PR8 ....47 M3
Cherrysutton WDN WA8 ....133 K2
Cherrysutton Ms WDN WA8 * ..133 K1
Cherry Tree Av LYMM WA13 ....139 M3
    RUNC WA7 ....19 L7
    WARRW/BUR WA5 ....136 B1
Cherry Tree Cl CHNE CH2 ....165 K1
    RAIN/WH L35 ....116 F2
    RNFD/HAY WA11 * 90 C8
Cherry Tree Dr STHEL WA9 ....103 J3
Cherry Tree Gv CHLYE PR6 ....32 E2
    LEIGH WN7 ....81 M7
Cherry Tree La ORM L39 ....62 D4
    RNFD/HAY WA11 ....89 J3
Cherry Tree Rd GOL/RIS/CU WA3 ..93 H5
    HUY L36 ....116 A5
    MOR/LEA CH46 ....110 B6
Cherry V WLTN L25 ....131 K2
Cherry Vw NWD/KWIPK L33 ....74 B8
Chervil Wk WGNS/IIMK WN3 ....78 E1
Cherwell Cl WARRW/WOL WA2 ..121 M3
    WGNE/HIN WN2 ....57 L7
Cheryl Dr WDN WA8 ....17 K1
Chesford Gra WARR WA1 ....123 G6
Chesham Ct EP CH65 ....20 E7
Cheshire Acre
    GR/UP/WCH CH49 ....126 C3
Cheshire Av AIN/FAZ L10 ....85 K6
Cheshire Cl NEWLW WA12 ....105 G2
Cheshire Gdns ECCL WA10 ....8 D7
Cheshire Gv MOR/LEA CH46 ....110 A6
Cheshire Lines Pth FMBY L37 ....48 B3
Cheshire Oaks Wy EP CH65 ....164 A4
Cheshire Ring Canal Wk
    WARRS WA4 ....136 E7
Cheshyre Dr RUNC WA7 ....150 B4
Cheshyre's La RUNC WA7 ....149 G7
Chesnell Gv NWD/KWIPK L33 ..74 B8
Chesney Cl TOX L8 ....113 G7
Chesnut Gv BTL L20 ....6 F2
    RF/TRAN CH42 ....11 G3
Chessington Cl WARRS WA4 ..138 B7
Chester Av CHLY/EC PR7 ....44 A1
    CHTN/BK PR9 ....25 H5
    GOL/RIS/CU WA3 ....92 F5
    NTHTN L30 ....84 B4
Chester Cl CSBY/BLUN L23 ....83 K1
    RUNC WA7 ....150 B3
Chester Dr AIMK WN4 ....91 M3
Chesterfield Cl STHP PR8 ....47 L1
Chesterfield Dr NWD/KWIPK L33 ..74 A8
Chesterfield Rd CSBY/BLUN L23 ..71 J8
    PS/BROM CH62 ....154 F1
    STHP PR8 ....47 K1
Chesterfield St TOX L8 ....113 G6
Chester High Rd NSTN CH64 ..153 G1
    NSTN CH64 ....153 M6
Chester La STHEL WA9 ....118 D1
Chester New Rd WARRS WA4 ..137 H6
Chester Pl CHLYE PR6 ....44 C5
Chester Rd CHTN/BK PR9 ....25 H5
    EP CH65 ....163 G4
    FROD/HEL WA6 ....160 B7
    FROD/HEL WA6 ....166 D3
    GTS/LS CH66 ....163 G4
    HES CH60 ....141 C7
    HUY L36 ....116 C1
    NPK/KEN L6 ....97 M7
    NSTN CH64 ....153 G6
    RUNC WA7 ....161 J2
    WARRS WA4 ....137 J5
    WARRS WA4 ....151 K4
Chester St BIRK CH41 ....11 J5
    PR/KW L34 ....100 F7
    TOX L8 ....113 G6
    WAL/EG CH44 * 111 G1
    WDN WA8 ....16 E2
Chesterton Cl WGNS/IIMK WN3 ....4 B1
Chesterton Dr
    WARRW/WOL WA2 ....105 J8
Chesterton St ALL/GAR L19 ..145 L1
Chestnut Av CHLY/EC PR7 ....33 G3
    CHLYE PR6 ....33 G3
    CSBY/BLUN L23 ....71 H7
    GTS/LS CH66 ....163 H4

HUY L36 ....115 M5
RNFD/HAY WA11 ....90 B8
WARRW/BUR WA5 ....120 D3
WDN WA8 ....134 D3
Chestnut Ct BTL L20 * 6 D6
    ORM L39 ....49 L4
    RAIN/WH L35 ....117 C1
Chestnut Gra ORM L39 ....51 H7
Chestnut Gra ORM L39 ....62 F2
Chestnut Gv AIMK WN4 ....91 M1
    GOL/RIS/CU WA3 ....93 H5
    PS/BROM CH62 ....143 L5
    RNFD/HAY WA11 ....89 M6
    WAV L15 ....114 B5
    WGNE/HIN WN2 ....81 J1
Chestnut Rd LITH L21 ....83 H6
    WAV L15 ....114 B5
    WLT/FAZ L9 ....97 K2
Chestnut St EHL/KEN L7 ....13 M8
    STHP PR8 ....13 M8
Chestnut Wk MGHL L31 ....85 J1
Chestnut Wy FMBY L37 ....58 E4
Cheswood Cl RAIN/WH L35 ..117 G3
Chetham Ct WARRN/WOL WA2 ..121 J2
Chetton Dr RUNC WA7 ....151 G6
Chetwode Av AIMK WN4 ....91 K3
Chetwood Av CSBY/BLUN L23 ..71 H8
Chetwood Dr WDN WA8 ....134 B1
Chetwynd Cl CL/PREN CH43 ..127 H1
Chetwynd Rd CL/PREN CH43 ..10 A8
Chetwynd St AIG/SPK L17 ....129 K2
Chevasse Wk WLTN L25 ....131 L2
Cheverton Cl GR/UP/WCH CH49 ..126 D2
Cheviot Av STHEL WA9 ....103 F1
    WARRN/WOL WA2 ....121 J2
Cheviot Cl HOR/BR BL6 ....45 L8
    RF/TRAN CH42 ....127 M4
    WGNS/IIMK WN3 ....78 E3
Cheviot Rd EHL/KEN L7 ....114 A3
    RF/TRAN CH42 ....127 M4
Cheviot Wy NWD/KWIPK L33 ..74 B7
Cheviot Cl GTS/LS CH66 ....155 J7
Cheyne Cl CSBY/BLUN L23 ....82 C2
Cheyne Gdns ALL/GAR L19 ..130 B5
Cheyne Wk STHEL WA9 ....102 B7
Chichester Cl RUNC WA7 ..150 F7
    WARRS WA4 ....138 C6
    WAV L15 ....113 M5
Chidden Cl GR/UP/WCH CH49 ..125 J1
Chidlow Cl WDN WA8 ....134 C8
Chigwell Cl WD/CROXPK L12 ....99 G2
Chilcott Rd CLB/OSW/ST L13 ..114 E2
Childer Cl GTS/LS CH66 ....155 K6
Childer Gdns GTS/LS CH66 ..155 K6
Childers St CLB/OSW/ST L13 ..114 C2
Childwall Abbey Rd CHLDW L16 ..114 F7
Childwall Av MOR/LEA CH46 ..109 M6
    WAV L15 ....113 M6
Childwall Bank Rd CHLDW L16 ..114 F6
Childwall Cl GR/UP/WCH CH49 ..109 M6
Childwall Crs CHLDW L16 ....114 F6
Childwall Gdns CHLDW L16 ..114 F6
Childwall Gn GR/UP/WCH CH49 ..126 C3
Childwall Hts WLTN L25 ....115 H6
Childwall La DV/KA/FCH L14 ..115 J5
    WLTN L25 ....115 H7
Childwall Mount Rd CHLDW L16 ..114 F7
Childwall Park Av CHLDW L16 ..115 G7
Childwall Priory Rd CHLDW L16 ..114 F7
Childwall Rd GTS/LS CH66 ..156 B5
    WAV L15 ....114 C6
Childwall Valley Rd CHLDW L16 ..114 F8
    WLTN L25 ....115 H5
Chilgrove Av HOR/BR BL6 ....57 M4
Chilham St WGNW/BIL/O WN5 ....67 J7
Chilham Cl TOX L8 ....132 A1
Chilington Av WDN WA8 ....133 M5
Chillerton Rd WD/CROXPK L12 ..98 F5
Chillingham St TOX L8 ....129 J1
Chiltern Av CHLY/EC PR7 ....31 M4
    WARRN/WOL WA2 ....121 J2
Chiltern Cl AIMK WN4 ....91 L3
    HOR/BR BL6 ....45 L8
    WD/CROXPK L12 ....99 H3
Chiltern Crs WARRN/WOL WA2 ..121 J2
Chiltern Dr KKBY L32 ....85 L1
Chiltern Pl RF/TRAN CH42 ..127 L4
    STHEL WA9 ....103 J2
    WARRN/WOL WA2 ....121 J2
Chiltern Rd GOL/RIS/CU WA3 ..107 C5
    RF/TRAN CH42 ....127 L4
    STHEL WA9 ....103 J2
    WARRN/WOL WA2 ....121 J2
Churchmeadow Cl
    WAL/EG CH44 ....111 M1
Chilton Cl MGHL L31 ....72 F5
Chilton Dr GTS/LS CH66 ....163 G3
Chilton Ms MGHL L31 ....72 F4
Chilwell Cl WDN WA8 ....133 M1
Chimes Rd AIMK WN4 ....79 H7
China Farm La WKBY CH48 ..125 C1
China La WARRS WA4 ....137 L3
Chindit Cl FMBY L37 ....58 F3
Chippenham Av
    GR/UP/WCH CH49 ....125 L1
Chipping Gv STHP PR8 ....23 J7
Chippingdall Cl
    WARRW/BUR WA5 ....120 E8
Chirkdale St ANF/KKDL L4 ....7 M9
Chirk Gdns EP CH65 ....20 E9
Chirk Wy MOR/LEA CH46 ....110 B6
Chirton Cl RNFD/HAY WA11 ....90 F6
Chisacre Dr WGNNW/ST WN6 ..54 F6
Chisenhale St VAUX/LVPD L3 ..12 E2
Chisholm Cl WGNNW/ST WN6 ..55 K2
Chisledon Cl RNFD/HAY WA11 ..90 F7
Chislehurst Av WLTN L25 ..115 K7
Chislett Cl BRSC L40 * 51 M1
Chisnall Av ECCL WA10 ....101 L1
Chisnall La CHLY/EC PR7 ....42 B8
    CHLY/EC PR7 ....42 C8
Chiswell St EHL/KEN L7 ....113 L3
    WGNW/BIL/O WN5 ....67 J7
Chiswick Cl RUNC WA7 * ..150 F6
Chiswick Gdns WARRS WA4 ..138 B7
Cholmley Dr NEWLW WA12 ..105 G1
Cholmondeley Rd EP CH65 ..163 H1
    RUNC WA7 ....149 M8
    WKBY CH48 ....126 C5
Cholmondeley St WDN WA8 * ..149 J1
Cholsey Cl GR/UP/WCH CH49 ..126 B1
Chorley Rd CHTN/BK PR9 ....23 G8
Chorley Hall Rd CHLY/EC PR7 ..32 E3
Chorley La CHLY/EC PR7 ....42 E3
Chorley Rd CHLY/EC PR7 ....44 C4
    CHLYE PR6 ....44 C4
    HOR/BR BL6 ....57 J2
    PR/KW L34 * 100 D7
    SKEL WN8 ....40 F4
    WGN WN1 ....43 L8
    WGN WN1 ....56 D1
Chorley's La WDN WA8 ....134 F2
Chorley St CHLYE PR6 ....44 D5
    ECCL WA10 ....8 E3
    WARRN/WOL WA2 ....14 C1
Chorley Wy BEB CH63 ....143 J4
Chorlton Cl CHLDW L16 ....115 H5
    RUNC WA7 ....150 F6
Chorlton Gv WAL/NB CH45 ..94 F3

Christchurch Rd CL/PREN CH43 ..10 D9
Christian St VAUX/LVPD L3 ....13 H4
Christie Cl GTS/LS CH66 ....155 J3
Christie St WDN WA8 ....17 J1
Christleton Cl CL/PREN CH43 ..126 F3
Christleton Ct RUNC WA7 ....156 A7
Christleton Dr GTS/LS CH66 ..156 A7
Christmas St BTL L20 ....6 F1
Christopher Cl CHLDW L16 ....114 F5
    RAIN/WH L35 ....116 C6
Christopher Dr PS/BROM CH62 ..144 C8
Christophers Cl PEN/TH CH61 * ..125 K8
Christopher St ANF/KKDL L4 ..97 H5
Christopher Wy CHLDW L16 ..114 F5
Chris Ward Cl EHL/KEN L7 ..113 L4
Chudleigh Cl HLWD L26 ....132 A4
Chudleigh Rd CLB/OSW/ST L13 ..114 D2
Church Av WGNE/HIN WN2 ....81 H5
    WLT/FAZ L9 ....84 D6
Church Cl CHTN/BK PR9 ....25 J2
    FMBY L37 ....59 J2
    WAL/EG CH44 ....111 M1
Church Close Ct FMBY L37 * 59 J2
Church Crs WAL/EG CH44 ....112 A3
Churchdown Gv
    DV/KA/FCH L14 * 115 G1
Churchdown Rd
    DV/KA/FCH L14 ....115 G1
Church Dr NEWLW WA12 ....104 E4
    PS/BROM CH62 ....128 D7
    WARRN/WOL WA2 ....122 C4
    WGNW/BIL/O WN5 ....66 F8
Church End RAIN/WH L35 ....147 M4
Church Farm Ct HES CH60 ..141 H6
Churchfield Rd FROD/HEL WA6 ..160 E6
Churchfield Rd GOL/RIS/CU WA3 ..106 D6
Churchfields STHEL WA9 ....118 L5
    STHP PR8 ....35 H2
Church Flds BRSC L40 ....51 L8
    ORM L39 ....51 L8
Churchgate CHTN/BK PR9 ....25 J4
Churchgate Ms CHTN/BK PR9 ..25 J4
Church Gates WGN WN1 ....4 E4
Church Gn CHLDW L16 ....115 H6
    FMBY L37 ....58 E3
    KKBY L32 ....86 A2
Church Gv LITH L21 ....83 H7
    WGN WN1 * 5 J4
Church HI WAL/EG CH44 ....95 M8
Churchhill Av BIRK CH41 ....10 D3
Church Hill Rd ORM L39 ....50 F7
Churchill Av CHTN/BK PR9 ....25 H5
    GOL/RIS/CU WA3 ....107 K1
Churchill Gdns STHEL WA9 ..103 G5
Churchill Gv WAL/EG CH44 * ..95 L8
Churchill Wy NSTN CH64 ....153 G5
Churchill Wy (Elevated Rd)
    CLVPS L1 ....13 G5
Churchlands La WGNNW/ST WN6 ..56 B4
Church La AIG/SPK L17 ....130 A4
    ANF/KKDL L4 ....97 H3
    CHLY/EC PR7 ....42 F1
    CHNE CH2 ....164 C6
    ECCL WA10 ....101 J2
    GOL/RIS/CU WA3 ....107 H2
    GR/UP/WCH CH49 ....125 G3
    GTS/LS CH66 ....162 F1
    NSTN CH64 ....153 G6
    ORM L39 ....61 H5
    PEN/TH CH61 ....125 K8
    PS/BROM CH62 ....143 M4
    PS/BROM CH62 ....155 J1
    WAL/EG CH44 ....111 M1
    WARRS WA4 ....138 D4
    WGNNW/ST WN6 ....55 J7
    WGNNW/ST WN6 ....55 J7
Churchmeadow Cl
    WAL/EG CH44 ....111 M1
Church Meadow La HES CH60 ..141 G6
Church Meadow Wk WDN WA8 ..133 K8
Church Mt EHL/KEN L7 ....113 K4
Church Pde EP CH65 * 20 D7
Church Rd ALL/GAR L19 ....150 E8
    ANF/KKDL L4 ....97 H3
    BEB CH63 ....142 D7
    BEB CH63 ....143 J1
    BRSC L40 ....39 L1
    BTL L20 ....83 M7
    CHLY/EC PR7 ....32 F6
    CLB/OSW/ST L13 ....114 B2
    CSBY/BLUN L23 ....83 G1
    CSBY/WL L22 ....83 G5
    FMBY L37 ....59 J1
    FROD/HEL WA6 ....160 E6
    GR/UP/WCH CH49 ....125 L1
    HUY L36 ....115 L3
    LITH L21 ....83 M5
    LITH L21 ....83 M5
    LYMM WA13 ....139 M3
    MGHL L31 ....72 F6
    ORM L39 ....61 H5
    RF/TRAN CH42 ....127 M1
    RNFD/HAY WA11 ....76 C8
    RNFD/HAY WA11 ....88 C1
    RNFD/HAY WA11 ....91 G7
    SKEL WN8 ....64 D8
    SPK/HALE L24 ....148 A5
    WAL/EG CH44 ....112 A3
    WAV L15 ....114 C2
    WGNE/HIN WN2 ....80 D2
    WKBY CH48 ....124 C4
    WLTN L25 ....131 J2
Church Rd North WAV L15 ....114 C6
Church Rd South WLTN L25 ..131 J3
Church Rd West ANF/KKDL L4 ..97 H3
Church Sq ECCL WA10 ....9 G5
Church St BIRK CH41 ....11 M6
    BTL L20 ....6 D5
    CHLY/EC PR7 ....44 D6
    CHLYE PR6 ....44 D6
    CHTN/BK PR9 ....3 J3
    CLVPS L1 ....13 G3
    CROS/BRETH PR26 ....29 K4
    ECCL WA10 ....9 H6
    EP CH65 ....20 D2
    FROD/HEL WA6 ....160 D5
    GOL/RIS/CU WA3 ....92 D4
    HOR/BR BL6 ....57 L3
    NEWLW WA12 ....104 E1
    ORM L39 ....51 L8
    PR/KW L34 * 100 F7
    RUNC WA7 ....19 G2
    SKEL WN8 ....66 C6

WAL/EG CH44 ....111 M1
WARR WA1 ....15 G5
WDN WA8 ....134 C8
WGN WN1 ....4 F3
WGNE/HIN WN2 ....57 M7
WGNE/HIN WN2 ....69 M8
WGNNW/ST WN6 ....56 A4
WGNS/IIMK WN3 ....5 L7
WGNW/BIL/O WN5 ....66 F8
Church Ter RF/TRAN CH42 ..127 M2
Church Vw BTL L20 ....6 C5
    ORM L39 ....62 C6
Churchview Rd BIRK CH41 ....10 D2
Church Wk BTL L20 ....6 C5
    CHLY/EC PR7 ....31 L3
    EP CH65 ....20 D2
    WARRN/WOL WA2 ....105 J7
Church Wy FMBY L37 ....58 E3
    FROD/HEL WA6 ....166 F4
    KKBY L32 ....86 A2
Churchway Rd SPK/HALE L24 ..147 J3
Churchwood Cl PS/BROM CH62 ..143 M4
Churnet St ANF/KKDL L4 ....97 G5
Churn Wy GR/UP/WCH CH49 ..125 M1
Churston Rd CHLDW L16 ....115 G8
Churton Av CL/PREN CH43 ..127 H2
Churton Ct NPK/KEN L6 * 113 J2
Churton Gv WGNNW/ST WN6 ..55 K5
Ciaran Cl WD/CROXPK L12 ....98 F5
Cicely St EHL/KEN L7 ....113 K4
Cinder La BTL L20 ....83 M6
    CALD/MH L18 ....114 E8
    KIRK/FR/WA PR4 ....27 H3
    WARRS WA4 ....139 M1
Cinnamon Av WGNE/HIN WN2 ..81 J1
Cinnamon Brow SKEL WN8 ....66 E7
Cinnamon La WARRN/WOL WA2 ..122 B2
Cinnamon La North
    WARRN/WOL WA2 * 122 B1
Cinnamon Pk
    WARRN/WOL WA2 * 122 A1
Circular Dr GR/UP/WCH CH49 ..125 M2
    HES CH60 ....141 G4
    PS/BROM CH62 ....128 D6
Circular Rd BIRK CH41 ....11 H7
Circular Rd East NG/CROX L11 ..98 B3
Circular Rd West NG/CROX L11 ..98 B4
Cirencester Av
    GR/UP/WCH CH49 ....125 L1
Cirrus Dr ORM L39 ....62 C4
Citrine Rd WAL/EG CH44 ....111 M3
Citron Cl WLT/FAZ L9 ....97 K1
City Gdns ECCL WA10 ....89 H7
City Rd ANF/KKDL L4 ....97 H4
    ECCL WA10 ....89 H7
    WGNW/BIL/O WN5 ....67 K6
Civic Wy BEB CH63 ....128 C8
    EP CH65 ....20 B4
    HUY L36 ....116 A3
Clairville Cl BTL L20 ....7 G5
Clairville Wy CLB/OSW/ST L13 ..114 A1
Clancut La CHLY/EC PR7 ....43 H5
Clandon Rd CALD/MH L18 ..130 F4
Clanfield Av WDN WA8 ....133 L2
Clanfield Rd NG/CROX L11 ....98 D4
Clanwood Cl WGNS/IIMK WN3 ..79 G3
Clap Gate Crs WDN WA8 ....133 L8
Clap Gate La WGNS/IIMK WN3 ..79 G2
Clap Gates Rd
    WARRW/BUR WA5 ....121 G6
Clapham Rd ANF/KKDL L4 ....97 K3
Clare Cl STHEL WA9 ....102 A6
Clare Crs WAL/EG CH44 ....111 G1
Clare Dr EP CH65 ....163 K4
Claremont Av CHLY/EC PR7 ....32 D6
    MGHL L31 ....72 E5
    STHP PR8 ....3 E2
    WDN WA8 ....134 D1
Claremont Cl LITH L21 ....83 H6
Claremont Dr ORM L39 ....62 F2
    WDN WA8 ....134 D1
Claremont Gdns STHP PR8 ....3 E2
Claremont Rd CHLY/EC PR7 ....32 D8
    CSBY/BLUN L23 ....82 F1
    GOL/RIS/CU WA3 ....106 F1
    LITH L21 ....83 H6
    RUNC WA7 ....19 K4
    STHP PR8 ....3 E3
    WAV L15 ....114 A7
    WCNW/BIL/O WN5 ....67 K6
    WKBY CH48 ....124 C2
Claremont Ter CSBY/BLUN L23 * ..70 F8
Claremont Wy BEB CH63 ....127 M5
Claremount Dr BEB CH63 ....143 H1
Claremount Rd WAL/NB CH45 ..95 H7
Clarence Av WARRW/BUR WA5 ..119 M7
    WDN WA8 ....134 C1
Clarence Cl STHEL WA9 ....9 J5
Clarence Rd RF/TRAN CH42 ..127 L2
    STHP PR8 ....35 J1
    WAL/EG CH44 ....111 H1
    WARRS WA4 ....138 D3
Clarence St AIMK WN4 ....91 H1
    CLVPS L1 ....13 J4
    ECCL WA10 ....9 G4
    PR/KW L34 * 100 F7
    RUNC WA7 ....19 G2
    SKEL WN8 ....66 C6

Claybridge Cl
    WGNW/BIL/O WN5 ....67 K4
Clay Brow Rd SKEL WN8 ....66 A7
Clayburn Cl CHLYE PR6 ....33 G3
Clay Cross Rd WLTN L25 ....131 H3
Claydon Ct HLWD L26 ....132 C4
Claydon Dr WGNS/IIMK WN3 ..80 D1
Clayfield Cl BTL L20 ....6 F7
Clayford Crs DV/KA/FCH L14 ..114 C1
Clayford Pl DV/KA/FCH L14 ..114 D1
Clayford Rd DV/KA/FCH L14 ..114 C1
Clayford Wy DV/KA/FCH L14 ..114 L1
Clayhill NSTN CH64 ....153 H3
Clayhill Gn GTS/LS CH66 ....155 K6
Clayhill Gv GOL/RIS/CU WA3 ..93 K5
Clay La GOL/RIS/CU WA3 ....101 G2
    WARRW/BUR WA5 ....104 J7
Claypole Cl EHL/KEN L7 ....113 L5
Clay St VAUX/LVPD L3 ....12 D1
Clayton Av GOL/RIS/CU WA3 ..93 G5
    WDN WA8 ....16 B3
Clayton Crs RUNC WA7 ....18 C5
Clayton Gdns BRSC L40 ....52 A1
Clayton House LEIGH WN7 ....81 L8
Clayton Ms WAL/EG CH44 ....111 J3
Clayton Pl CL/PREN CH43 ....10 F7
Clayton Rd GOL/RIS/CU WA3 ..10 F7
Clayton Sq CL/PREN CH43 ....10 F7
    SKEL WN8 ....64 F7
    WGNS/IIMK WN3 ....4 C4
Cleadon Cl KKBY L32 ....86 A6
Cleadon Rd KKBY L32 ....86 B6
Cleadon Wy WDN WA8 ....134 A1
Clearwater Cl EHL/KEN L7 ..113 K3
Cleary St BTL L20 ....6 C1
Clee Hill Rd RF/TRAN CH42 ..127 L4
Cleethorpes Rd RUNC WA7 ..150 E6
Cleeves Cl WARR WA1 ....15 H6
Clegge St WARRN/WOL WA2 ..15 J1
Clegg St EV L5 ....13 J1
    SKEL WN8 ....64 F4
Clelland St WARRS WA4 ....15 H5
Clematis Cl CHLY/EC PR7 ....32 C2
Clematis Rd NTHLY L27 ....116 A7
Clement Gdns VAUX/LVPD L3 ..12 F2
Clementina Rd CSBY/BLUN L23 ..82 D1
Clemmey Dr BTL L20 ....84 A7
Clengers Brow CHTN/BK PR9 ..25 J1
Clent Av MGHL L31 ....72 E2
Clent Gdns MGHL L31 ....72 E3
Clent Rd MGHL L31 ....72 E3
Cleopas St TOX L8 ....129 H1
Clevedon Dr WGNS/IIMK WN3 ..78 E3
Clevedon St TOX L8 ....129 J1
Cleveland Av WGNS/IIMK WN3 ..78 E3
Cleveland Buildings CLVPS L1 ..13 G9
Cleveland Cl KKBY L32 ....85 L1
Cleveland Dr AIMK WN4 ....91 L1
    GOL/RIS/CU WA3 ....92 F5
    GTS/LS CH66 ....155 J7
Cleveland Sq CLVPS L1 ....13 G6
Cleveland St BIRK CH41 ....10 E1
    CHLY/EC PR7 ....32 E5
    CHLY/EC PR7 * 43 G4
    STHEL WA9 ....9 L9
Cleveley Pk CALD/MH L18 ..130 F4
Cleveley Rd CALD/MH L18 ..130 F4
    HOY CH47 ....109 G5
Cleveleys Av CHTN/BK PR9 ....25 J1
    WDN WA8 ....134 F2
Cleveleys Rd CHTN/BK PR9 ....25 J2
    WARRW/BUR WA5 ....121 G7
The Cleves MGHL L31 ....75 G2
Cleve Wy FMBY L37 ....59 K3
Clieves Hills La ORM L39 ....61 M3
Clieves Rd KKBY L32 ....86 B3
Cliff Dr WAL/EG CH44 ....95 M8
Cliffe Rd NSTN CH64 ....153 H4
    WARRS WA4 ....137 L6
Cliffe St WARR WA1 ....14 B5
    WDN WA8 ....17 G1
Clifford Rd STHP PR8 ....35 J4
    WAL/EG CH44 ....111 K2
    WARRW/BUR WA5 ....136 C1
Clifford St BIRK CH41 ....10 A2
    CHLY/EC PR7 ....32 F5
    VAUX/LVPD L3 ....13 K5
Cliff Rd CHTN/BK PR9 ....24 F3
    WAL/EG CH44 ....111 J2
Cliff St EHL/KEN L7 ....113 L3
Clifton Av GOL/RIS/CU WA3 ..106 C4
    HLWD L26 ....132 A4
    PS/BROM CH62 ....155 G2
Clifton Cl WARR WA1 ....122 E6
Clifton Cl RUNC WA7 ....18 C5
Clifton Crs BIRK CH41 ....11 J6
    FROD/HEL WA6 ....160 E4
    WGN WN1 ....68 B7
Clifton Dr AIN/FAZ L10 ....84 F7
    HOR/BR BL6 ....57 K2
Clifton Gdns EP CH65 ....20 C8
Clifton Gv CHLY/EC PR7 ....32 D6
    EV L5 ....13 K2
    WAL/EG CH44 ....111 M1
Clifton La RUNC WA7 ....161 G2
Cliftonmill Mdw
    GOL/RIS/CU WA3 ....92 B5
Clifton Rd AIMK WN4 ....79 H3
    BIRK CH41 ....11 H8
    FMBY L37 ....47 J8
    NPK/KEN L6 ....97 M8
    RUNC WA7 ....19 H4
    STHP PR8 ....25 H7
    WGNW/BIL/O WN5 ....89 M1
    WGNS/IIMK WN3 ....79 J1
Clifton Rd East NPK/KEN L6 ..97 M8
Clifton St ALL/GAR L19 ....130 E2
    ECCL WA10 ....9 H3
    LEIGH WN7 ....81 M8
    WARRS WA4 ....15 H8
    WGN WN1 ....4 F1
    WGNS/IIMK WN3 ....79 J1
Clifton Vls EP CH65 * 163 G4
Cliftonville Rd PR/KW L34 ..101 K2
    WARR WA1 ....122 E7
Clilmarsh Cl WDN WA8 ....133 J5
Clinkard Crs ECCL WA10 ....8 F4
Clinning Rd STHP PR8 ....35 J5
Clinton Pl WD/CROXPK L12 ....98 B6
Clinton Rd WD/CROXPK L12 ....98 B6
Clint Rd EHL/KEN L7 ....113 L4
Clint Wy EHL/KEN L7 ....113 L4
Clipper Vw PS/BROM CH62 ..128 C7
Clipsley Brook Vw
    RNFD/HAY WA11 ....90 B7
Clipsley Crs RNFD/HAY WA11 ..90 D6
Clipsley La RNFD/HAY WA11 ..90 D7
Clive Av WARRW/WOL WA2 ..121 L4
Clive Ldg STHP PR8 ....35 H5
Clive Rd CL/PREN CH43 ....127 L1
    STHP PR8 ....35 H4
Clock Face Rd STHEL WA9 ..118 E1
    WDN WA8 ....119 G4
Clocktower St ECCL WA10 ....8 F5

Cloister Av LEIGH WN7 81 M4
The Cloisters CSBY/BLUN L23 82 F2
ECCL WA10 101 K1
FMBY L37 * 59 H2
Cloister Wy EP CH65 21 H5
Clorain Rd NWD/KWIPK L33 86 C2
Closebrook Rd
WGNW/BIL/O WN5 67 M7
Closeburn Av HES CH60 * 141 G7
Close La WGNE/HIN WN2 81 H2
WGNE/HIN WN2 81 K4
The Close, Red Bank School
NEWLW WA12 * 105 G4
Close St STHEL WA9 102 A6
The Close CHTN/BK PR9 23 J8
CSBY/BLUN L23 82 F2
ECCL WA10 88 C8
GR/UP/WCH CH49 125 M3
HTWN L38 71 G2
PEN/TH CH61 125 M7
RF/TRAN CH42 127 M4
RNFD/HAY WA11 90 B8
STBRV L28 99 L6
WLT/FAZ L9 97 H1
Cloudberry Cl NTHLY L27 116 A7
Clough Acre CHLY/EC PR7 32 C3
Clough Av WARRN/WOL WA2 121 K3
Clough Gv AIMK WN4 79 H8
Clough Rd SPK/HALE L24 146 F1
The Clough AIMK WN4 90 F1
RUNC WA7 150 B4
Cloughton Rd BIRK CH41 11 G6
Cloughwood Crs
WGNNW/ST WN6 54 F6
Clovelly Av STHEL WA9 102 F7
WARRW/BUR WA5 120 A6
Clovelly Dr SKEL WN8 53 J5
STHP PR8 35 C5
Clovelly Gv RUNC WA7 150 D8
Clovelly Rd ANF/KKDL L4 97 K7
Clover Av FROD/HEL WA6 160 F6
HLWD L26 131 M3
Clover Ct RUNC WA7 150 D8
Cloverdale Dr AIMK WN4 91 L3
Cloverdale Rd WLTN L25 115 K6
Clover Dr BIRK CH41 111 G4
Cloverfield RUNC WA7 * 150 E6
Cloverfield Gdns GTS/LS CH66 155 M6
Clover Hey RNFD/HAY WA11 89 K6
Clover Rd CHLY/EC PR7 32 C8
Clover St WGNNW/ST WN6 68 C3
Club St RNFD/HAY WA11 89 J4
Clucas Gdns ORM L39 51 G7
Clwyd Gv WD/CROXPK L12 98 D5
Clwyd St BIRK CH41 11 J5
WAL/NB CH45 95 J6
Clwyd Wy GTS/LS CH66 155 J7
Clyde Rd CLB/OSW/ST L13 114 A3
Clydesdale EP CH65 20 A9
Clydesdale Rd HOY CH47 108 D5
WAL/EG CH44 95 M8
WARRS WA4 137 M5
Clyde St BTL L20 96 E5
RF/TRAN CH42 128 B3
Clyffes Farm Cl BRSC L40 37 J6
Coach House Ct BRSC L40 52 A2
Coach House Dr
WGNNW/ST WN6 55 K7
Coachmans Dr WD/CROXPK L12 99 G4
Coach Rd ORM L39 75 H4
PR/KW L34 87 K6
Coalbrookdale Rd NSTN CH64 153 H3
Coalgate La RAIN/WH L35 116 F3
Coalpit La CH/BCN CH1 163 G8
Coal Pit La ORM L39 75 L1
WGNE/HIN WN2 81 K4
Coalport Wk STHEL WA9 101 L7
Coal St CLVPS L1 13 J6
Coalville Rd RNFD/HAY WA11 89 M7
Coastal Dr WAL/NB CH45 94 F5
Coastal Rd STHP PR8 34 C7
Coastguard La NSTN CH64 152 D4
Coastline Ms CHTN/BK PR9 * 25 J1
Cobb Av LITH L21 83 K7
The Cobbles HLWD L26 131 M3
Cobblestone Cnr ALL/GAR L19 130 C6
Cobb's Brow La SKEL WN8 53 J4
Cobb's Clough Rd BRSC L40 53 H8
Cobbs La WARRS WA4 138 A5
Cobden Av BIRK CH41 128 B2
Cobden Ct BIRK CH41 128 B2
Cobden Pl RF/TRAN CH42 128 B2
Cobden Rd CHTN/BK PR9 25 H7
Cobden St CHLYE PR6 33 G4
NEWLW WA12 104 F1
NPK/KEN L6 13 M3
WARRN/WOL WA2 14 F2
WLTN L25 131 H3
Cobden Vw WLTN L25 131 H3
Cob Hall La FROD/HEL WA6 166 F8
Cobham Av WLT/FAZ L9 84 B7
Cobham Rd MOR/LEA CH46 109 M5
Cob Moor Av WGNW/BIL/O WN5 77 M4
Cob Moor Rd WGNW/BIL/O WN5 77 M4
Coburg Whf VAUX/LVPD L3 112 E7
Cochrane St EV L5 97 H8
Cockburn St TOX L8 129 H1
Cockerell Cl ANF/KKDL L4 * 97 H6
Cockerham Wy NG/CROX L11 85 K8
Cockhedge La WARR WA1 14 F5
Cockhedge Wy WARR WA1 14 F5
Cocklade La SPK/HALE L24 147 M4
Cock Lane Ends WDN WA8 * 133 K8
Cockle Dick's La CHTN/BK PR9 25 G3
Cockshead Rd WLTN L25 115 K8
Cockshead Wy WLTN L25 115 K7
Cockspur St VAUX/LVPD L3 12 F5
Cockspur St West VAUX/LVPD L3 12 E5
Coerton Rd WLT/FAZ L9 84 D6
The Cokers BEB CH63 128 A5
Colbern Cl MGHL L31 73 G5
Colbrooke Rd AIG/SPK L17 129 K2
Colburn Cl WGNS/IIMK WN3 79 J3
Colburne Cl BRSC L40 39 H8
Colby Cl CHLDW L16 115 G5
Colby Rd WGNS/IIMK WN3 79 K2
Colchester Rd STHP PR8 36 B3
Colden Cl WD/CROXPK L12 99 G6
Coldstone Dr AIMK WN4 90 F1
Coldstream Cl
WARRN/WOL WA2 122 A1
Coldstream Dr GTS/LS CH66 155 H8
Cole Av NEWLW WA12 104 E1
Colebrook Cl GOL/RIS/CU WA3 123 J1
Coleclough Pl GOL/RIS/CU WA3 107 H1
Cole Crs ORM L39 62 E5
Coleman Dr GR/UP/WCH CH49 125 K2
Colemere Cl WARR WA1 122 D4
Colemere Ct EP CH65 20 B1
Colemere Dr PEN/TH CH61 126 D7
Coleridge Av ECCL WA10 8 B3
WGNW/BIL/O WN5 67 J7
Coleridge Dr PS/BROM CH62 128 C6
Coleridge Gv WDN WA8 134 A4
Coleridge Rd WGNW/BIL/O WN5 77 M4
Coleridge St BTL L20 6 D3
NPK/KEN L6 113 K2
Colerne Wy WGNS/IIMK WN3 78 F3
Colesborne Rd NG/CROX L11 98 C3
Coles Crs CSBY/BLUN L23 71 K7
Coleshill Ri WGNS/IIMK WN3 78 E3
Coleshill Rd NG/CROX L11 98 A2
Cole St CL/PREN CH43 10 F6
Colette Rd AIN/FAZ L10 85 K6
Coleus Cl WLT/FAZ L9 97 K1
Colin Cl HUY L36 115 L4
Colindale Rd CHLDW L16 115 G6
Colin Dr VAUX/LVPD L3 96 E8
Colinmander Gdns ORM L39 62 E2
Colin St WGN WN1 5 G1
Colinton SKEL WN8 66 A6
Colinton St WAV L15 114 A5
Coliseum Wy EP CH65 163 M4
College Av CSBY/BLUN L23 82 F2
FMBY L37 59 G1
WGN WN1 4 F5
College Cl CL/PREN CH43 110 D7
FMBY L37 58 F1
STHP PR8 35 J2
WAL/NB CH45 95 G7
WARR WA1 15 J5
WARRN/WOL WA2 122 C3
College Ct WD/CROXPK L12 98 C8
College Dr BEB CH63 128 C6
College Flds HUY L36 116 A4
College La CLVPS L1 13 G8
College Pth FMBY L37 46 F8
College Rd CSBY/BLUN L23 82 E1
SKEL WN8 66 D4
College Rd North
CSBY/BLUN L23 70 E8
College St ECCL WA10 9 G4
College St North NPK/KEN L6 13 L4
College St South NPK/KEN L6 13 M4
College Vw BTL L20 7 G7
Collett Cl WGN WN1 5 J4
Collier's Rw RUNC WA7 149 G6
Collier St RUNC WA7 18 E1
WGNE/HIN WN2 69 M7
Colliery Green Cl NSTN CH64 153 G8
Colliery Green Ct NSTN CH64 153 G8
Colliery Green Dr NSTN CH64 153 G8
Collinge St WGNE/HIN WN2 80 C3
Collingham Gn GTS/LS CH66 155 K8
Collingwood Rd BEB CH63 143 K1
CHLY/EC PR7 32 C6
NEWLW WA12 104 D2
Collingwood St
WGNNW/ST WN6 56 A4
Collin Rd CL/PREN CH43 111 G5
Collins Cl BTL L20 83 K8
Collins Green La
WARRW/BUR WA5 104 A4
Collin St WARRW/BUR WA5 121 G8
Collisdene Rd
WGNW/BIL/O WN5 66 F7
Collison Av CHLY/EC PR7 32 D5
Colmore Av BEB CH63 143 H4
Colmore Rd NG/CROX L11 98 A3
Colnbrook WGNNW/ST WN6 55 K4
Colne Dr STHEL WA9 102 F6
Colne Rd WARRW/BUR WA5 104 B7
Colorado Cl WARRW/BUR WA5 120 E6
Colquitt St CLVPS L1 13 J9
Coltart Rd TOX L8 113 K7
Colton Rd WLTN L25 115 H6
Coltsfoot Dr CHLYE PR6 32 F3
Columban Cl NTHTN L30 84 A2
Columbia Rd ANF/KKDL L4 97 J3
CL/PREN CH43 10 C9
PR/KW L34 101 G7
Columbine Cl CHLY/EC PR7 * 32 C2
WDN WA8 133 K1
Columbine Wy STHEL WA9 103 K6
Columbus Dr PEN/TH CH61 141 G2
Columbus Quay VAUX/LVPD L3 129 G2
Columbus Wy LITH L21 * 83 K6
Column Rd WKBY CH48 124 F4
Colville Ct WARRN/WOL WA2 121 J2
Colville Rd WAL/EG CH44 111 J1
Colville St WAV L15 114 A5
Colwall Cl NWD/KWIPK L33 86 C3
Colwall Rd NWD/KWIPK L33 86 C3
Colwell Cl DV/KA/FCH L14 99 J6
Colwell Rd DV/KA/FCH L14 99 J7
Colworth Rd SPK/HALE L24 146 D1
Colwyn Cl EP CH65 20 F9
WARRW/BUR WA5 121 G3
Colwyn Dr WGNE/HIN WN2 81 L3
Colwyn Rd CLB/OSW/ST L13 114 B3
Colwyn St BIRK CH41 10 A2
Colyton Av STHEL WA9 102 F8
Colyton Cl CHLYE PR6 33 G5
Colyton Rd CHLYE PR6 33 G5
Colyton Rd East CHLYE PR6 33 G5
Combermere St TOX L8 * 113 H7
WAV L15 113 M4
Comely Av WAL/EG CH44 111 L1
Comely Bank Rd WAL/EG CH44 111 M1
Comer Gdns MGHL L31 72 E2
Comet Rd WGNW/BIL/O WN5 67 L5
Comfrey Gv HLWD L26 132 A3
Commercial Rd CHLY/EC PR7 32 E4
EV L5 96 E7
PS/BROM CH62 144 A2
Commodore Pl
WGNW/BIL/O WN5 68 A4
Common Bank La CHLY/EC PR7 32 A6
Common End CHLY/EC PR7 57 G1
Common Field Rd
GR/UP/WCH CH49 126 D4
Common La CHTN/BK PR9 26 D3
FROD/HEL WA6 165 M4
GOL/RIS/CU WA3 106 F1
LEIGH WN7 93 K1
WARRS WA4 138 A3
Common Nook WGNE/HIN WN2 69 J7
Common Rd NEWLW WA12 104 A2
Commonside FROD/HEL WA6 167 J4
Common St NEWLW WA12 104 A2
STHEL WA9 * 101 M6
The Common CHLY/EC PR7 44 A8
SKEL WN8 53 L2
Commutation Rw VAUX/LVPD L3 13 G5
Company's Cl RUNC WA7 149 H7
Compass Cl RUNC WA7 150 F8
Compton Cl RNFD/HAY WA11 90 E6
Compton Pl EP CH65 20 B4
Compton Rd BIRK CH41 110 F4
NPK/KEN L6 113 J1
STHP PR8 35 K2
Compton Wk BTL L20 6 F3
Compton Wy HLWD L26 132 A7
Comus St VAUX/LVPD L3 13 H3
Concert St CLVPS L1 13 H9
Concord Av WGNS/IIMK WN3 79 K2
Concorde Pl WARRN/WOL WA2 121 M3
Concordia Av
GR/UP/WCH CH49 110 C8
The Concourse WKBY CH48 * 124 C2
Concourse Wy STHEL WA9 103 H3
Condor Cl ALL/GAR L19 130 F7
Condron Rd North LITH L21 83 L4
Condron Rd South LITH L21 83 L4
Conery Cl FROD/HEL WA6 166 E1
Coney Crs CSBY/BLUN L23 71 K8
Coney Gv RUNC WA7 150 D8
Coney La HUY L36 116 B6
Coney Wk GR/UP/WCH CH49 109 M7
Congresbury Rd LEIGH WN7 81 M6
Congress St CHLY/EC PR7 32 E4
Conifer Cl GTS/LS CH66 163 J5
NWD/KWIPK L33 74 A8
WLT/FAZ L9 97 K2
Conifer Ct FMBY L37 59 H3
Conifer Gv WARRW/BUR WA5 120 B6
The Conifers MGHL L31 72 E2
Coningsby Dr WAL/NB CH45 111 J1
Coningsby Rd ANF/KKDL L4 97 J6
Coniston Av AIMK WN4 91 K1
BEB CH63 143 L8
CHLY/EC PR7 31 M4
CHLYE PR6 44 D5
CL/PREN CH43 110 E8
PR/KW L34 101 H7
WAL/NB CH45 95 G6
WARRW/BUR WA5 135 M1
WGN WN1 68 D2
WGNE/HIN WN2 69 K6
WGNW/BIL/O WN5 67 H5
Coniston Cl GTS/LS CH66 155 J4
NWD/KWIPK L33 85 M1
RUNC WA7 149 M7
WLT/FAZ L9 84 D6
Coniston Dr FROD/HEL WA6 160 F5
WGNE/HIN WN2 80 D5
Coniston Gv RNFD/HAY WA11 89 J6
Coniston Park Dr
WGNNW/ST WN6 56 C6
Coniston Rd CHLY/EC PR7 32 D7
FMBY L37 58 F3
HOR/BR BL6 57 M2
MGHL L31 73 G3
NSTN CH64 153 G7
PEN/TH CH61 125 M7
WGNE/HIN WN2 81 G1
Coniston St EV L5 97 J7
Coniston Wy CROS/BRETH PR26 29 K3
RNFD/HAY WA11 76 B3
Conleach Rd SPK/HALE L24 147 G2
Connaught Av WARR WA1 15 M1
Connaught Cl BIRK CH41 10 A1
Connaught Dr NEWLW WA12 104 E3
Connaught Rd EHL/KEN L7 113 J3
Connaught Wy BIRK CH41 10 A1
Connolly Av BTL L20 7 M2
Conrad Cl WGNS/IIMK WN3 4 B9
Conroy Wy NEWLW WA12 104 E4
Consett Rd STHEL WA9 101 M7
Constables Cl RUNC WA7 150 C4
Constance St ECCL WA10 8 A7
VAUX/LVPD L3 13 L5
Constance Wy WDN WA8 16 C9
Constantia St WGNS/IIMK WN3 80 B2
Constantine Av HES CH60 141 J4
Convent Cl ALL/GAR L19 130 C6
ORM L39 62 F3
RF/TRAN CH42 11 H9
Conville Bvd BEB CH63 128 A5
Conway Av WARRW/BUR WA5 121 H3
Conway Cl BEB CH63 127 M8
CHLY/EC PR7 32 A4
NWD/KWIPK L33 73 M8
WARRW/BUR WA5 120 B7
Conway Crs WGNW/BIL/O WN5 78 A7
Conway Dr BIRK CH41 11 G5
NEWLW WA12 105 G2
WGNE/HIN WN2 69 M1
WGNW/BIL/O WN5 78 B8
Conway Rd AIMK WN4 80 A8
CHLY/EC PR7 30 E6
WGNE/HIN WN2 81 H1
Conway St BIRK CH41 10 F4
BIRK CH41 11 J5
EV L5 97 G8
WGNW/BIL/O WN5 67 L8
Conwy Dr NPK/KEN L6 97 K8
Conyers Av STHP PR8 35 H2
Coogee Av WARRW/BUR WA5 120 A6
Cook Av RNFD/HAY WA11 91 G6
Cooke St AIMK WN4 79 H7
Cook Rd MOR/LEA CH46 110 D1
Cooks Ct CSBY/BLUN L23 * 70 E8
Cookson Rd LITH L21 83 J7
Cookson St CLVPS L1 113 G6
Cook St BIRK CH41 11 G7
CLVP L2 12 F7
EP CH65 20 D3
RAIN/WH L35 101 H8
WGNE/HIN WN2 80 C4
Coombe Dr RUNC WA7 18 F8
Coombe Pk GTS/LS CH66 155 L7
Coombe Rd PEN/TH CH61 126 A6
Cooperage Cl TOX L8 129 G1
Co-operative St LEIGH WN7 81 M8
Cooper Av NEWLW WA12 104 B2
WARRN/WOL WA2 121 K3
Cooper Av North CALD/MH L18 130 C4
Cooper Av South CALD/MH L18 130 C4
Cooper Cl ALL/GAR L19 130 C5
Cooper La RNFD/HAY WA11 90 E7
Coopers Gln WGNE/HIN WN2 69 J5
Cooper's La CHLY/EC PR7 41 K5
NWD/KWIPK L33 86 F7
Coopers Pl WARRS WA4 137 L4
Cooper St ECCL WA10 8 F3
RUNC WA7 19 G2
WDN WA8 16 E1
Coop St WGN WN1 5 H2
Copeland Cl PEN/TH CH61 141 G1
Copeland Dr WGNNW/ST WN6 56 B3
Copeland Gv RUNC WA7 150 A8
Copeland Rd WARRS WA4 137 K3
Copesthorne Cl WGNE/HIN WN2 57 L7
Coplow Dl WGNE/HIN WN2 81 G2
Copperas Cl WGNNW/ST WN6 55 J6
Copperas Hl VAUX/LVPD L3 13 K6
Copperas La WGNE/HIN WN2 57 J7
Copperas St ECCL WA10 8 F6
Copperbeech Dr
WGNNW/ST WN6 56 D6
Copperfield WGN WN1 68 E3
Copperfield Cl GOL/RIS/CU WA3 106 E8
TOX L8 113 H8
Copperwood RUNC WA7 150 E4
Copperwood Dr RAIN/WH L35 117 G3
Copperwood Wy CHLY/EC PR7 32 B4
Coppice Cl CHLYE PR6 33 G4
CL/PREN CH43 110 D7
Coppice Crs HUY L36 116 B1
Coppice Dr WGNS/IIMK WN3 79 H2
WGNW/BIL/O WN5 77 M3
Coppice Gra MOR/LEA CH46 109 L6
Coppice Gn CHNE CH2 165 L1
WARRW/BUR WA5 120 C4
Coppice Gv GR/UP/WCH CH49 * 125 L3
Coppice La CHLYE PR6 33 L1
RAIN/WH L35 116 D6
Coppice Leys FMBY L37 59 G2
The Coppice NPK/KEN L6 97 L7
PR/KW L34 99 M2
WAL/NB CH45 95 J6
Coppins Cl FROD/HEL WA6 166 D2
The Coppins WARRN/WOL WA2 121 J3
Copple House La AIN/FAZ L10 85 J6
Coppull Hall La CHLY/EC PR7 43 J4
Coppull La WGN WN1 68 F3
Coppull Moor La CHLY/EC PR7 42 F7
Coppull Rd CHLY/EC PR7 43 H1
MGHL L31 72 E1
Copse Gv PEN/TH CH61 126 A6
The Copse CALD/MH L18 114 F8
CHLY/EC PR7 43 K1
NEWLW WA12 104 C1
RUNC WA7 150 C7
WGNW/BIL/O WN5 67 J7
Copthorne Rd KKBY L32 85 K3
Copy La NTHTN L30 84 C1
Coral Av HUY L36 115 M2
STHEL WA9 102 B6
Coral Cl KKBY L32 85 L3
Coral Dr BTL L20 7 H4
Coralin Wy AIMK WN4 79 H6
Coral Rdg CL/PREN CH43 110 F7
Coral St CLB/OSW/ST L13 114 C4
WGNNW/ST WN6 68 C2
Corbet Av WARRN/WOL WA2 121 K5
Corbet St WARRN/WOL WA2 * 121 K5
Corbridge Rd CHLDW L16 114 E7
Corbyn St WAL/EG CH44 112 A4
Corfe Cl WGNE/HIN WN2 57 M8
Corfu St BIRK CH41 * 10 F6
Corinthian Av CLB/OSW/ST L13 114 D1
Corinthian St LITH L21 83 H6
RF/TRAN CH42 * 128 B3
Corinto St TOX L8 113 H6
Cormorant Dr RUNC WA7 18 D4
Cornbrook SKEL WN8 66 A6
Corncroft Rd PR/KW L34 99 M2
Corndale Rd CALD/MH L18 130 C1
Cornelian Gv AIMK WN4 79 H8
Cornelius Dr PEN/TH CH61 126 B8
Cornel Wy HUY L36 116 B5
Corner Brook STBRV L28 99 H6
Cornerhouse La WDN WA8 133 M2
Corner La WGNE/HIN WN2 81 M3
Cornett Rd WLT/FAZ L9 84 D6
Corney St EHL/KEN L7 113 L6
Cornfield Cl GTS/LS CH66 163 H4
Cornfields Cl ALL/GAR L19 130 E7
Cornflower Cl CHLYE PR6 32 F3
Cornflower Wy MOR/LEA CH46 110 C3
Cornforth Wy WDN WA8 134 B2
Cornhill CLVPS L1 112 F5
Cornice Rd CLB/OSW/ST L13 114 C1
Corniche Rd PS/BROM CH62 128 D7
Cornmill Ct GOL/RIS/CU WA3 * 106 C5
Corn St LEIGH WN7 81 M8
TOX L8 113 G8
Cornubia Rd WDN WA8 17 H5
Cornwall Av RUNC WA7 19 G4
Cornwall Cl PS/BROM CH62 128 D5
Cornwall Crs WGN WN1 56 D4
Cornwall Dr CL/PREN CH43 127 J4
Cornwallis Rd WGNS/IIMK WN3 68 C8
Cornwallis St CLVPS L1 112 F5
Cornwall Pl WGNW/BIL/O WN5 67 L7
Cornwall Rd WDN WA8 134 D2
Cornwall St STHEL WA9 102 F3
WARR WA1 15 L2
Cornwall Wy STHP PR8 47 K3
Cornwood Cl HUY L36 115 K6
Corona Av MGHL L31 61 L8
Corona Rd CLB/OSW/ST L13 114 C1
CSBY/WL L22 82 F4
PS/BROM CH62 128 E7
Coronation Av DV/KA/FCH L14 115 G2
FMBY L37 59 J3
WAL/NB CH45 95 K6
WARRS WA4 138 D3
Coronation Buildings
WAL/NB CH45 * 95 K8
Coronation Dr CSBY/BLUN L23 82 F2
DV/KA/FCH L14 115 G2
FROD/HEL WA6 160 F4
NEWLW WA12 105 G4
PS/BROM CH62 143 M2
RAIN/WH L35 116 E2
RNFD/HAY WA11 91 J6
WARRW/BUR WA5 136 B1
WDN WA8 133 K5
Coronation Rd CSBY/BLUN L23 82 F2
ECCL WA10 88 E7
EP CH65 20 C7
HOY CH47 108 B7
MGHL L31 72 F2
RUNC WA7 19 J5
RUNC WA7 151 H7
WGNNW/ST WN6 67 M2
Coronation St AIMK WN4 78 F7
WGNS/IIMK WN3 4 D7
Coronation Vls
WD/CROXPK L12 * 98 F6
Coronation Wk STHP PR8 2 E4
WGNW/BIL/O WN5 89 M1
Coroner's La WDN WA8 118 C8
Coronet Rd NG/CROX L11 98 E2
Coronet Wy WDN WA8 133 K5
Corporation Rd BIRK CH41 10 C1
Corporation St CHLYE PR6 32 F4
ECCL WA10 9 G4
WGNS/IIMK WN3 4 D7
Corridor Rd EP CH65 157 K8
Corrie Dr BEB CH63 143 H1
Corsewall St EHL/KEN L7 113 M5
Corsey Rd WGNE/HIN WN2 81 G1
Corsican Gdns STHEL WA9 101 L7
Corsock Dr WGN WN1 5 K1
Corston Gv HOR/BR BL6 57 M4
Cortsway GR/UP/WCH CH49 110 A8
Cortsway West
GR/UP/WCH CH49 109 M8
Corwen Cl CL/PREN CH43 110 D7
MOR/LEA CH46 110 B6
WARRW/BUR WA5 121 G4
Corwen Crs DV/KA/FCH L14 115 H3
Corwen Dr NTHTN L30 84 C1
Corwen Rd ANF/KKDL L4 97 L5
HOY CH47 108 E6
Cosgate Cl WGNW/BIL/O WN5 67 G8
Cosgrove Cl NPK/KEN L6 97 M6
Cossack Av WARRN/WOL WA2 121 K4
Costain St BTL L20 96 E5
Costessey Wy WGNS/IIMK WN3 78 E2
Cote Lea Ct RUNC WA7 * 150 B7
Cotham St ECCL WA10 9 G5
Cotsford Cl HUY L36 115 L1
Cotsford Pl HUY L36 115 L1
Cotsford Rd HUY L36 115 L1
Cotsford Wy HUY L36 115 L1
Cotswold Av CHLY/EC PR7 31 M4
GOL/RIS/CU WA3 92 F7
WGNW/BIL/O WN5 67 K8
Cotswold Cl CHLY/EC PR7 30 E7
Cotswold Dr HOR/BR BL6 45 L8
Cotswold Gv STHEL WA9 103 J2
Cotswold Rd CHLY/EC PR7 32 E7
RF/TRAN CH42 127 L4
WARRN/WOL WA2 121 K2
Cotswolds Crs HLWD L26 * 132 A6
Cotswold St EHL/KEN L7 113 K3
Cottage Cl BEB CH63 143 L8
KKBY L32 86 A6
NSTN CH64 153 G6
ORM L39 62 F1
Cottage Dr East HES CH60 141 H8
Cottage Dr West HES CH60 141 H8
Cottage Flds CHLY/EC PR7 32 D8
Cottage La HES CH60 141 H8
ORM L39 50 F7
Cottage Ms ORM L39 50 F8
Cottage Pl STHEL WA9 * 118 E1
Cottage St BIRK CH41 11 G3
Cottam Dr WARRN/WOL WA2 122 C2
Cottam St CHLY/EC PR7 32 E7
Cottenham St NPK/KEN L6 113 K2
Cotterdale Cl STHEL WA9 102 E7
WARRW/BUR WA5 120 B6
Cotterill RUNC WA7 149 M5
Cotterill Dr WARR WA1 122 E6
Cottesbrook Cl NG/CROX L11 98 C2
Cottesbrook Pl NG/CROX L11 98 C2
Cottesbrook Rd NG/CROX L11 98 C2
Cottesmore Dr HES CH60 * 141 M5
Cottesmore Wy
GOL/RIS/CU WA3 92 D4
Cotton Dr ORM L39 50 F7
Cotton La RUNC WA7 149 M5
Cotton St LEIGH WN7 81 M8
VAUX/LVPD L3 12 C1
Cottonwood AIG/SPK L17 129 H2
Cottrell Cl ALL/GAR L19 145 L1
Cotty's Brow CHTN/BK PR9 25 H2
Coudray Rd CHTN/BK PR9 25 G4
Coulport Cl DV/KA/FCH L14 115 J1
Coulsdon Pl TOX L8 129 J1
Coulthard Rd RF/TRAN CH42 128 C5
Coulton Rd WDN WA8 135 G2
Coultshead Av WGNW/BIL/O WN5 78 A7
Council Av AIMK WN4 91 K2
Council St RAIN/WH L35 101 J8
Countess Pk NG/CROX L11 98 E3
Countess Wy CHLY/EC PR7 31 M3
Countisbury Dr CHLDW L16 115 G7
County Dr ECCL WA10 8 D7
County Police St WGNE/HIN WN2 5 M5
County Rd ANF/KKDL L4 97 H5
KKBY L32 86 A1
ORM L39 50 F8
Coupland Rd WGNE/HIN WN2 81 K1
Courage Low La
WGNNW/ST WN6 54 F1
Courier Pl WGNW/BIL/O WN5 68 A4
Course La BRSC L40 53 G4
Court Av HLWD L26 132 C4
Courtenay Av CSBY/WL L22 82 E3
WAL/EG CH44 111 J2
Courtenay Rd CSBY/WL L22 82 E3
HOY CH47 108 C6
WLTN L25 131 H1
Courtfield ORM L39 50 F6
Courtfields Cl WD/CROXPK L12 98 D8
Courtgreen ORM L39 50 F6
Court Hey Av DV/KA/FCH L14 115 J3
Court Hey Dr CHLDW L16 115 H4
Court Hey Rd CHLDW L16 115 H4
Courthope Rd ANF/KKDL L4 97 K4
Courtland Rd CALD/MH L18 114 D8
Court Ms CHTN/BK PR9 * 25 J4
Courtney Av WAL/EG CH44 111 J2
Courtney Rd RF/TRAN CH42 128 C5
Court Rd CHTN/BK PR9 3 K1
The Court BEB CH63 * 143 J1
NSTN CH64 153 H7
STBRV L28 * 99 L6
Cousin's La BRSC L40 39 J2
Covent Gdn CLVP L2 12 E7
Coventry Av GTS/LS CH66 163 G5
Coventry Rd WAV L15 114 C7
Coventry St BIRK CH41 11 H6
CHLY/EC PR7 * 32 E7
Coverdale Av RAIN/WH L35 117 M3
Coverdale Cl WARRW/BUR WA5 120 B6
Covertside WKBY CH48 124 F3
The Coverts WGNNW/ST WN6 68 B3
Cowan Dr NPK/KEN L6 113 J1
Cowanway WDN WA8 118 B8
Cowburn St LEIGH WN7 81 M8
Cowdell St WARRN/WOL WA2 14 F1
Cowdrey Av CL/PREN CH43 110 E4
Cow Hey La RUNC WA7 149 J8
Cowley Cl GR/UP/WCH CH49 * 109 M8
Cowley Ct ECCL WA10 * 8 E3
Cowley Hill La ECCL WA10 8 D1
Cowley Rd ANF/KKDL L4 97 H4
Cowley St ECCL WA10 9 G2
Cowling Brow CHLYE PR6 33 G6
Cowling St WGNS/IIMK WN3 4 D7
Cowper Rd CLB/OSW/ST L13 114 D3
Cowper St BTL L20 6 D1
LEIGH WN7 81 M8
Cowper Wy HUY L36 116 C5
Cowslip Wy CHLYE PR6 32 F3
Coxfield WGNNW/ST WN6 54 F6
Coyford Dr CHTN/BK PR9 25 J1
Coylton Av RAIN/WH L35 117 M3
Crab La WARRN/WOL WA2 122 D2
Crab St ECCL WA10 8 F3
Crabtree Cl BRSC L40 51 M1
NEWLW WA12 105 G2
NTHLY L27 115 M8
Crabtree Fold RUNC WA7 150 E5
Crabtree La BRSC L40 38 E8
Crabtree Rd WGNW/BIL/O WN5 67 M6
Cradley WDN WA8 133 L3
Crag Gv RNFD/HAY WA11 89 K4
Craigburn Rd CLB/OSW/ST L13 98 A7
Craig Gdns GTS/LS CH66 156 A6
Craighurst Rd WLTN L25 115 J6
Craigleigh Gv PS/BROM CH62 155 H1
Craigmore Rd CALD/MH L18 130 C4
Craigside Av WD/CROXPK L12 98 C6
Craig Rd CLB/OSW/ST L13 98 A7
Craigwood Wy HUY L36 115 K2
Craine Cl ANF/KKDL L4 97 K5
Cramond Av CALD/MH L18 114 C8
Cramond Cl WGNS/IIMK WN3 78 F1
Cranage Cl RUNC WA7 149 M6
Cranberry Av WGNNW/ST WN6 68 B2
Cranberry Cl ECCL WA10 8 E2
Cranborne Av HOY CH47 109 G4
WARRS WA4 137 K4
Cranborne Cl WGNNW/ST WN6 55 M4
Cranborne Rd WAV L15 113 M6
Cranbourne Av BIRK CH41 111 H6
MOR/LEA CH46 109 M6
Cranbourne Dr CHLYE PR6 33 G6
Cranbourne St CHLYE PR6 32 F6
Cranbrook Av AIMK WN4 91 J1
Cranbrook Wy WGN WN1 68 D1
Cranby St WGNE/HIN WN2 69 M8
Crane Av STHEL WA9 102 F7
Cranehurst Rd ANF/KKDL L4 97 K3
Cranes La BRSC L40 51 M6
Crane St CHLY/EC PR7 42 F7
Cranfield Rd CSBY/BLUN L23 71 J8
WGNS/IIMK WN3 79 J2
Cranford Cl PS/BROM CH62 155 H1
Cranford Ct WARR WA1 * 123 G5
Cranford Rd ALL/GAR L19 130 D5
Cranford St WAL/EG CH44 111 L3
Cranham Av GOL/RIS/CU WA3 93 G6
Crank Hl RNFD/HAY WA11 89 G1
Crank Rd RNFD/HAY WA11 77 H6
RNFD/HAY WA11 88 E6

Crankwood Rd WGNE/HIN WN2....80 D7
Cranleigh WGNNW/ST WN6..........56 B5
Cranleigh Cl HOR/BR BL6............57 M4
WARRS WA4..............................137 K6
Cranleigh Pl WLTN L25..............115 J7
Cranleigh Rd WLTN L25..............115 J8
Cranmer St EV L5.......................96 F7
Cranmore Av CSBY/BLUN L23.......83 G3
Cranshaw Av STHEL WA9............118 F2
Cranshaw La WDN WA8..............118 D8
Cranston Cl ECCL WA10...............88 D8
Cranston Rd NWD/KWIPK L33.......86 E3
Cranswick Gn GTS/LS CH66.........155 L8
Crantock Cl HLWD L26................132 B5
NG/CROX L11 *...........................98 E1
Crantock Gv ECCL WA10..............88 E7
Cranwell Av GOL/RIS/CU WA3......107 H1
Cranwell Cl AIN/FAZ L10..............84 E3
Cranwell Rd GR/UP/WCH CH49....125 K2
WLTN L25..................................115 J6
Craven Av GOL/RIS/CU WA3.........93 G6
Craven Cl BIRK CH41...................11 G5
Craven Ct WARRN/WOL WA2........121 H1
Craven Lea WD/CROXPK L12........99 G2
Craven Rd RAIN/WH L35.............117 L2
WD/CROXPK L12........................98 E7
Craven St BIRK CH41...................10 F6
VAUX/LVPD L3............................13 K5
Cravenwood Rd HLWD L26..........132 B6
Crawford Av CALD/MH L18..........114 B8
CHLY/EC PR7.............................32 D6
CHLY/EC PR7.............................44 A8
MGHL L31...................................72 D2
WDN WA8..................................133 K4
WGNE/HIN WN2..........................57 L8
Crawford Cl STHEL WA9.............118 F1
WD/CROXPK L12........................98 F6
Crawford Dr WAV L15.................114 C4
Crawford Pk CALD/MH L18..........130 B2
Crawford Pl RUNC WA7..............149 K7
WGN WN1 *...............................68 F2
Crawford Rd SKEL WN8...............76 F3
Crawford St STHEL WA9.............119 G1
WGN WN1....................................4 E4
WGNE/HIN WN2..........................69 M8
Crawford Wy CLB/OSW/ST L13.....114 A3
Crawley Av WARRN/WOL WA2 * ..121 J2
Crawley Cl WLTN L25.................131 M5
Crediton Av CHTN/BK PR9...........22 D8
Crediton Cl NG/CROX L11.............85 L8
Crediton Dr WGNE/HIN WN2........80 C4
The Creek WAL/NB CH45..............95 G5
Cremorne Hey STBRV L28.............99 K6
Crescent Av AIMK WN4...............91 J1
FMBY L37...................................59 G4
Crescent Ct LITH L21..................83 J7
Crescent Dr FROD/HEL WA6........166 D2
Crescent Gn ORM L39.................62 D4
Crescent Rd CSBY/BLUN L23........70 D8
EP CH65.....................................20 E3
LITH L21....................................83 J7
STHP PR8...................................35 H2
WAL/EG CH44............................111 L1
WLT/FAZ L9................................97 K1
The Crescent BEB CH63.............128 A8
CHLY/EC PR7.............................32 E3
CHTN/BK PR9.............................25 L2
CSBY/BLUN L23..........................71 J7
CSBY/WL L22..............................83 G4
EP CH65...................................156 B8
GR/UP/WCH CH49......................125 M2
HUY L36...................................116 C3
MGHL L31..................................72 E6
PEN/TH CH61............................126 B7
RAIN/WH L35.............................117 H1
WGNE/HIN WN2 *........................69 K6
WGNW/BIL/O WN5........................67 M7
WKBY CH48...............................124 C3
The Cresents RAIN/WH L35.........117 J1
Cressbrook Rd WARRS WA4.........137 L5
Cressell Pk WGNNW/ST WN6.........55 J3
Cressingham Rd WAL/NB CH45......95 K5
Cressington Av RF/TRAN CH42....127 M4
Cressington Esp ALL/GAR L19.......130 B7
Cressington Gdns EP CH65...........20 C2
Cresswell Cl HLWD L26...............132 C4
WARRW/BUR WA5.......................120 F3
Cresswell St NPK/KEN L6..............13 M2
Cresta Dr RUNC WA7..................149 H7
Crestfield Gv WGNNW/ST WN6......68 B3
Crestor Rd WLTN L25..................131 H2
Crestwood Av WGNS/IIMK WN3......79 G2
Creswell St ECCL WA10..................8 C5
Creswick Cl WGNE/HIN WN2.........80 E1
Cretan Rd WAV L15.....................113 M6
Crewe Gn GR/UP/WCH CH49........126 C3
Criccieth Av WGNE/HIN WN2.........57 M8
Criccieth Ct EP CH65..................163 M3
Cricketers Gn CHLY/EC PR7..........30 D6
Cricket Pth FMBY L37...................47 H8
STHP PR8...................................35 H2
Cricket St WGNNW/ST WN6.............4 C4
Cricklade Cl BTL L20......................6 E3
Criftin Cl GTS/LS CH66...............162 E3
Cringles Dr RAIN/WH L35............116 C6
Cripple Ga WGNNW/ST WN6...........55 H3
Crispin Rd NTHLY L27.................115 M8
Crispin St ECCL WA10....................8 D6
Critchley Rd SPK/HALE L24..........147 J3
Critchley Wy NWD/KWIPK L33.......74 B8
Croal Av WGNE/HIN WN2...............80 C3
Croasdale Dr RUNC WA7.............150 A8
SKEL WN8..................................53 L2
Crockett's Wk ECCL WA10.............88 D8
Crockleford Av STHP PR8..............36 A2
Crocus Av BIRK CH41..................111 H5
Crocus Gdns STHEL WA9..............103 J6
Crocus St EV L5...........................96 F6
Croesmere Dr GTS/LS CH66.........162 F3
Croft Av BRSC L40........................52 B2
GOL/RIS/CU WA3..........................92 B3
PS/BROM CH62..........................143 M4
WGNW/BIL/O WN5........................66 F8
Croft Av East PS/BROM CH62.......143 M3
Croft Cl CL/PREN CH43...............127 G1
Croft Ct EP CH65..........................21 G8
Croft Dr GR/UP/WCH CH49...........110 A6
WKBY CH48...............................124 E7
Croft Dr East WKBY CH48............124 F7
Croft Dr West WKBY CH48............124 E6
Croft Edge CL/PREN CH43............127 K2
Croft End STHEL WA9..................103 H4
Croften Dr NSTN CH64.................153 G8
Crofters Cl GTS/LS CH66..............163 G4
Crofters Gn CHLY/EC PR7..............31 L2
Crofters Heath GTS/LS CH66........163 G4
The Crofters GR/UP/WCH CH49...125 M3
Croft Fld MGHL L31.......................73 G4
Croft Gdns WARRS WA4...............138 C6
Croft Gn PS/BROM CH62...............143 M2
Croft Heath Gdns
GOL/RIS/CU WA3........................106 C5
Croft Hey BRSC L40.......................39 K1
Croft Heys ORM L39......................62 D4
Croftlands WGNW/BIL/O WN5.........77 M1
Croft La PS/BROM CH62...............143 M4
WLT/FAZ L9.................................84 F6
Crofton Cl WARRS WA4................138 E8
Crofton Crs CLB/OSW/ST L13.......114 D2
Crofton Gdns GOL/RIS/CU WA3 ..107 G2
Crofton Rd CLB/OSW/ST L13........114 D2
RF/TRAN CH42...........................128 A2
RUNC WA7...................................18 C6
Croft Rd CHLYE PR6......................33 G6
Croftside WARR WA1...................123 H6
Croftson Av ORM L39.....................51 H6
Croft St GOL/RIS/CU WA3 *...........92 C5
WDN WA8...................................133 M5
Croftsway HES CH60....................140 F5
The Croft CHLY/EC PR7.................30 E6
CHLY/EC PR7..............................31 K2
GR/UP/WCH CH49.......................125 M3
MGHL L31....................................61 K8
RUNC WA7..................................150 B4
STBRV L28 *.................................99 J5
WD/CROXPK L12..........................98 D6
WGNW/BIL/O WN5........................77 M1
Croftwood Gv RAIN/WH L35.........117 G3
Croftwood Sq
WGNW/BIL/O WN5........................67 L3
Cromarty Rd CLB/OSW/ST L13 ....114 B3
WAL/EG CH44..............................111 H1
Cromdale Gv STHEL WA9..............103 G3
Cromdale Wy
WARRW/BUR WA5.......................120 A7
Cromedale Crs WGNNW/ST WN6 ..56 C6
Cromer Dr WAL/NB CH45...............95 J8
Cromer Rd AIG/SPK L17...............130 A4
HOY CH47...................................108 C7
STHP PR8.....................................35 G3
WGNS/IIMK WN3............................79 G2
Cromer Wy HLWD L26..................132 B7
Cromfield ORM L39.........................62 E3
Cromford Dr WGNW/BIL/O WN5.....67 K8
Cromford Rd HUY L36...................100 A8
Crompton Dr WARRN/WOL WA2 ..105 J7
WD/CROXPK L12...........................99 G2
Cromptons La CALD/MH L18.........114 F8
Crompton St EV L5.........................96 F8
WGN WN1......................................4 F3
WGNS/IIMK WN3............................80 B2
Cromwell Av WARRW/BUR WA5 ..120 E3
Cromwell Av South
WARRW/BUR WA5.......................136 E1
Cromwell Cl NEWLW WA12............104 C1
ORM L39.......................................62 E3
Cromwell Ct WARR WA1.................14 C6
Cromwell Rd ANF/KKDL L4............97 H3
EP CH65.......................................20 D4
Cromwell St WDN WA8..................16 C8
Crondall Gv WAV L15...................114 D6
Cronton Av MOR/LEA CH46...........110 A2
Cronton La RAIN/WH L35.............117 K4
WDN WA8....................................118 B8
Cronton Park Cl WDN WA8...........117 L7
Cronton Rd RAIN/WH L35.............116 D6
WAV L15.....................................114 C8
Cronulla Dr WARRW/BUR WA5 ....119 M6
Crookall St AIMK WN4....................91 L1
Crooke Rd WGNNW/ST WN6............67 L2
Crookhurst Av
WGNW/BIL/O WN5........................77 M7
Crook St CHLY/EC PR7...................32 D8
CHLY/EC PR7...............................44 B6
WGN WN1.......................................4 D3
WGNE/HIN WN2 *..........................80 F1
Croome Dr WKBY CH48.................124 E3
Croppers Hl ECCL WA10...................8 D6
Cropper's La ORM L39....................63 J4
Croppers Rd WARRN/WOL WA2 ..122 B2
Cropper St CLVPS L1......................13 J8
Cropton Rd FMBY L37....................59 H2
Cropton Wy WGNE/HIN WN2..........81 H2
Crosby Av WARRW/BUR WA5.........121 J5
Crosby Cl GR/UP/WCH CH49..........110 B7
Crosby Gn WD/CROXPK L12...........98 C6
Crosby Gv ECCL WA10...................101 M4
NSTN CH64..................................154 D4
Crosby Rd STHP PR8.......................35 H2
Crosby Rd North CSBY/WL L22.......83 G4
Crosby Rd South CSBY/WL L22.......83 G5
Crosender Rd CSBY/BLUN L23.........82 E1
Crosfield Cl EHL/KEN L7...............113 L4
Crosfield Rd EHL/KEN L7...............113 L4
RAIN/WH L35................................117 H1
WAL/EG CH44................................111 L2
Crosfield St WARR WA1...................14 C5
Crosfield Wk EHL/KEN L7...............113 L4
Crosgrove Rd ANF/KKDL L4..............97 L4
Crosland Rd KKBY L32.....................86 C4
Crossacre Rd WLTN L25.................115 K6
Cross Barn La HTWN L38.................71 G3
Cross Brow Preston Rd
CHLY/EC PR7.................................31 L5
Crossdale Rd CSBY/BLUN L23.........82 E2
PS/BROM CH62............................143 M7
WGNE/HIN WN2..............................81 J1
Crossdale Wy RNFD/HAY WA11........89 K4
Crosse Hall La CHLYE PR6...............33 G6
Crosse Hall St CHLYE PR6...............33 H6
Crossens Wy CHTN/BK PR9..............22 E7
Cross Farm Rd STHEL WA9................9 L9
Crossfield Av GOL/RIS/CU WA3....107 H3
Crossfield Rd SKEL WN8..................65 L5
Crossfield St STHEL WA9..................9 J5
Crossford Cl WGNS/IIMK WN3.........78 F1
Crossford Rd DV/KA/FCH L14..........99 J7
Crossgates WDN WA8....................115 M8
Cross Green Cl FMBY L37.................59 J3
Crosshall Brow BRSC L40.................63 L1
Crosshall St CLVPS L1.....................13 G6
Cross Hey LITH L21..........................83 K3
MGHL L31 *...................................73 G6
Cross Hey Av CL/PREN CH43..........110 F8
Cross Hillocks La RAIN/WH L35......133 G2
The Crossings NEWLW WA12..........104 E2
Cross La BEB CH63.........................143 H1
FROD/HEL WA6..............................159 K5
GOL/RIS/CU WA3...........................106 F6
NEWLW WA12.................................104 D2
NSTN CH64.....................................153 G8
ORM L39...49 K4
RAIN/WH L35...................................116 F1
WAL/NB CH45....................................94 F8
WARRS WA4.....................................138 C3
WGNW/BIL/O WN5..............................77 M2
Cross La South
GOL/RIS/CU WA3............................106 F7
Crossley Av GTS/LS CH66.................156 A7
Crossley Dr HES CH60.....................140 F5
WAV L15..114 C5
Crossley Rd ECCL WA10...................101 M5
Crossley St WARR WA1......................15 G4
Cross Meanygate
KIRK/FR/WA PR4...............................27 L8
Cross Pit La RNFD/HAY WA11.............76 B7
Cross St BIRK CH41.............................11 L5
CHLY/EC PR7 *..................................32 E4
CSBY/WL L22......................................82 F5
ECCL WA10..9 G5
GOL/RIS/CU WA3.................................92 C6
NSTN CH64..153 G5
PR/KW L34...100 F6
PS/BROM CH62 *...............................128 D8
RUNC WA7 *...19 G2
STHP PR8...3 G6
WARRN/WOL WA2.................................14 F1
WDN WA8..16 F2
WGNE/HIN WN2..................................69 M8
WGNNW/ST WN6....................................56 A4
WGNS/IIMK WN3..4 E6
WGNW/BIL/O WN5 *...........................67 K7
The Cross HTWN L38............................70 F2
MOR/LEA CH46 *...............................110 A5
PS/BROM CH62...................................143 M4
Crossvale Rd HUY L36.........................116 A4
Crossway CL/PREN CH43.....................111 G5
WDN WA8...133 M5
Crossway Cl AIMK WN4..........................80 A8
Crossways PS/BROM CH62...................143 M2
The Crossway BEB CH63.....................153 K1
Crosswood Crs HUY L36......................115 L2
Crosthwaite Av PS/BROM CH62 ..155 H1
Croston Av CHLYE PR6..........................44 C5
RAIN/WH L35.......................................101 K8
Croston Cl WDN WA8............................133 L1
Croston Dr BRSC L40...............................28 D7
Croston La CHLY/EC PR7.........................42 D4
Croston Rd BRSC L40..............................28 D7
Croston's Brow CHTN/BK PR9...............25 H2
Croston St WGNE/HIN WN2.....................69 L7
Crouch St EV L5.......................................97 J7
STHEL WA9 *...102 F5
Croughton Rd CHNE CH2........................164 C6
GTS/LS CH66..156 B5
Crowe Av WARRN/WOL WA2................121 K2
Crowhurst Dr WGN WN1.........................68 D2
Crowland Cl CHTN/BK PR9......................25 J7
Crowland St CHTN/BK PR9......................25 J7
Crowland Wy FMBY L37...........................59 K3
Crow La SKEL WN8...................................66 B2
Crow La East NEWLW WA12..................104 E1
Crow La West NEWLW WA12................104 D1
Crowmarsh Cl
GR/UP/WCH CH49 *..............................126 B1
Crown Acres Rd WLTN L25......................131 L4
Crown Av WDN WA8................................133 K5
Crown Cl FMBY L37..................................59 J3
Crown Fields Cl NEWLW WA12.................91 K8
Crown Gdns NEWLW WA12....................104 D1
Crown Ga RUNC WA7..............................150 B6
Crown Park Dr NEWLW WA12................104 D1
Crown Rd WD/CROXPK L12.......................98 E6
Crown St CHLY/EC PR7.............................32 E5
EHL/KEN L7..13 M6
NEWLW WA12..104 C2
STHEL WA9 *...101 M6
TOX L8...113 J6
WARR WA1..14 E5
WGNE/HIN WN2..69 L7
WGNS/IIMK WN3...4 D7
Crownway HUY L36..................................115 M1
Crow Orchard Rd
WGNNW/ST WN6.......................................55 J3
Crow St TOX L8..112 F7
Crowther Dr WGNS/IIMK WN3.................79 G4
Crowther St ECCL WA10...............................8 C6
Crow Wood La WDN WA8........................134 F3
Crow Wood Pl WDN WA8 *......................134 F2
Crow Wood Rd
GOL/RIS/CU WA3.....................................92 F4
Croxdale Rd DV/KA/FCH L14....................99 J6
Croxdale Rd West
DV/KA/FCH L14.......................................99 H6
Croxteth Av LITH L21.................................83 H6
WAL/EG CH44...111 K1
Croxteth Cl MGHL L31................................73 G2
Croxteth Dr AIG/SPK L17.........................113 M8
RNFD/HAY WA11.......................................76 B6
Croxteth Gv TOX L8..................................113 K7
Croxteth Hall La NG/CROX L11..................98 E2
Croxteth La STBRV L28..............................99 K4
Croxteth Rd BTL L20...................................83 K8
TOX L8..113 K8
Croxteth Vw KKBY L32.................................86 B7
Croyde Cl CHTN/BK PR9.............................22 D8
Croyde Pl STHEL WA9................................118 E1
Croyde Rd SPK/HALE L24..........................147 J2
Croydon Av CALD/MH L18.........................114 B8
Croylands St ANF/KKDL L4.........................97 G5
Crucian Wy WD/CROXPK L12.....................98 F2
Crummock Dr WGNS/IIMK WN3..................79 H2
Crump St CLVPS L1.....................................113 G6
Crutchley Av BIRK CH41............................110 F6
Cryers La CHNE CH2...................................165 H5
Cubbin Crs EV L5..96 F7
Cubert Rd NG/CROX L11...............................98 E1
Cuckoo Cl WLTN L25..................................131 J1
Cuckoo La NSTN CH64................................153 K6
WLTN L25...115 J8
Cuerden St CHLYE PR6..................................33 G6
VAUX/LVPD L3..13 H5
Cuerdley Gn WDN WA8................................135 J3
Cuerdley Rd WARRW/BUR WA5 ..135 L2
Cuerdon Dr WARRS WA4............................138 F4
Culbeck La CHLY/EC PR7................................31 H2
Culbin Cl GOL/RIS/CU WA3........................107 J7
Culcheth Av WGNE/HIN WN2........................80 D4
Culcheth Hall Dr
GOL/RIS/CU WA3.......................................107 H1
Culcross Av WGNS/IIMK WN3.........................78 E1
Culford Cl RUNC WA7.................................150 F4
Cullen Av BTL L20..83 M8
Cullen Cl BEB CH63.......................................154 E1
WGNE/HIN WN2..69 J5
Cullen Rd RUNC WA7.......................................18 B9
Cullen St TOX L8..113 L6
Culme Rd WD/CROXPK L12............................98 B6
Culraven WGNE/HIN WN2 *..............................57 K6
Culshaw Wy BRSC L40.....................................37 H6
Culvert La SKEL WN8.......................................53 J3
Culvert St WGNNW/ST WN6.............................68 B1
Culzean Cl WD/CROXPK L12.............................99 G2
Cumberbatch Pl
WGNS/IIMK WN3..80 B1
Cumberland Av AIG/SPK L17........................113 M7
CL/PREN CH43...127 J3
ECCL WA10...101 K5
NTHTN L30...83 L2
Cumberland Cl NPK/KEN L6..............................97 M7
Cumberland Crs
RNFD/HAY WA11...90 C7
Cumberland Ga NTHTN L30.................................84 C1
Cumberland Gv GTS/LS CH66...........................162 E2
Cumberland Rd STHP PR8.....................................3 L8
WAL/NB CH45...95 L6
Cumberland St CLVPS L1 *...................................12 F6
WARRS WA4..15 J9
WGN WN1..5 J1
Cumber La RAIN/WH L35..................................117 H2
Cumbers Dr NSTN CH64....................................153 J8
Cumbers La NSTN CH64.....................................153 J8
Cumbrae Dr EP CH65...163 L4
Cumbrian Cl WGNE/HIN WN2..............................80 D3
Cumbria Wy WD/CROXPK L12.............................98 E4
Cummings St CLVPS L1......................................113 G5
Cumpsty Rd LITH L21...83 L4
Cunard Av WAL/EG CH44......................................95 M8
Cunard Cl CL/PREN CH43...................................110 E7
Cunard Rd LITH L21...83 K6
Cunliffe Av NEWLW WA12....................................91 K8
Cunliffe Cl RUNC WA7...150 C6
Cunliffe Ct LEIGH WN7..93 J1
Cunliffe St CHLY/EC PR7..32 E6
CLVP L2..12 F5
LEIGH WN7..81 L8
Cunningham Av CHLY/EC PR7..............................32 C7
Cunningham Cl
WARRW/BUR WA5...120 B8
WKBY CH48 *..124 E7
Cunningham Dr BEB CH63...................................143 L6
RUNC WA7...18 D7
Cunningham Rd
CLB/OSW/ST L13...114 C3
WDN WA8...133 M5
Cunscough La MGHL L31..73 M3
Cuper Crs HUY L36..115 M1
Curate Rd NPK/KEN L6..97 L6
Curate St CHLYE PR6...33 G4
Curlender Cl BIRK CH41...111 G4
Curlender Wy SPK/HALE L24....................................148 A3
Curlew Av GR/UP/WCH CH49....................................109 M7
Curlew Cl GOL/RIS/CU WA3.......................................92 F5
GR/UP/WCH CH49...109 M7
Curlew Ct MOR/LEA CH46...109 L4
Curlew Gv GOL/RIS/CU WA3....................................123 G2
Curlew La BRSC L40...39 G4
Curlew Wy MOR/LEA CH46..109 L4
Currans Rd WARRN/WOL WA2...................................121 J3
Curtana Crs NG/CROX L11..98 E2
Curtis Rd ANF/KKDL L4...97 L4
Curtis St WGNW/BIL/O WN5..67 M7
Curwell Cl BEB CH63..143 K2
Curzon Av BIRK CH41...10 D3
WAL/NB CH45...95 K5
Curzon Dr WARRS WA4...138 C6
Curzon Rd CSBY/WL L22..83 G4
HOY CH47..108 C6
RF/TRAN CH42...127 K3
STHP PR8..3 M7
Curzon St RUNC WA7...18 F5
Cusson Rd NWD/KWIPK L33..86 D4
Custley Hey STBRV L28..99 K5
Custom House La CLVPS L1 *..12 F8
Cuthbert St WGNW/BIL/O WN5.......................................67 M7
Cut La BRSC L40..50 B5
NWD/KWIPK L33...87 G6
Cygnet Cl GTS/LS CH66...162 F1
ORM L39...62 E3
Cygnet Ct NWD/KWIPK L33...86 C3
WARR WA1...14 D9
Cygnet St WGNS/IIMK WN3..4 D7
Cynthia Av WARR WA1..122 D6
Cynthia Rd RUNC WA7...18 E5
Cypress Av GTS/LS CH66..163 H4
WDN WA8...134 D2
Cypress Cl MGHL L31...85 J2
WARR WA1..123 G6
Cypress Cft BEB CH63...143 K2
Cypress Gdns STHEL WA9...101 L6
Cypress Gv RUNC WA7...149 L6
Cypress Rd HUY L36...115 M5
STHP PR8...25 G7
WGNW/BIL/O WN5..68 A7
Cyprus Gv TOX L8..129 J1
Cyprus St PR/KW L34...100 F7
Cyprus Ter WAL/NB CH45 *..95 K6
Cyril Gv AIG/SPK L17...130 A3
Cyril St WARRN/WOL WA2...14 F2

D

Dacre's Bridge La RAIN/WH L35 ..116 F6
Dacre St BIRK CH41.....................11 J5
BTL L20......................................6 E9
Dacy Rd EV L5..............................97 J8
Daffodil Cl WDN WA8.................135 G1
Daffodil Rd BIRK CH41...............111 H6
WAV L15....................................114 D7
Dagnall Av WARRW/BUR WA5 ....121 H3
Dagnall Rd KKBY L32.....................85 L4
Dahlia Cl WLT/FAZ L9....................97 K1
Dailton Rd SKEL WN8......................66 C6
Dairy Farm Rd RNFD/HAY WA11.....75 M6
Dairylands Cl CALD/MH L18..........114 E7
Daisy Av NEWLW WA12..................104 E3
Daisybank Cl WGNE/HIN WN2..........69 M8
Daisy Bank Mill Cl
GOL/RIS/CU WA3.........................107 G2
Daisy Bank Rd LYMM WA13............139 L2
WARRW/BUR WA5 *......................136 B1
Daisy Fold CHLYE PR6.....................33 G3
Daisy Hill Dr CHLYE PR6..................44 C5
Daisy Hill Fold CHLY/EC PR7...........31 M4
Daisy La BRSC L40...........................52 D1
Daisy Ms LITH L21...........................83 K7
Daisy Mt MGHL L31..........................73 G5
Daisy Rd WGNW/BIL/O WN5.............68 A7
Daisy St EV L5...................................96 F6
Daisy Wy STHP PR8...........................35 K3
Dalbeatie Ri WGN WN1......................5 L1
Dalby Cl GOL/RIS/CU WA3..............107 K8
RNFD/HAY WA11.................................9 M2
Dale Acre Dr NTHTN L30...................83 L2
Dale Av CHLY/EC PR7.......................31 M4
GTS/LS CH66...................................155 L7
HES CH60...141 H4
PS/BROM CH62................................143 M5
Dalebrook Cl WLTN L25...................115 K6
Dale Cl MGHL L31..............................72 E3
SKEL WN8..53 K3
WARRW/BUR WA5............................136 F1
WDN WA8..133 J5
Dale Crs STHEL WA9........................102 F7
Dalecrest WGNW/BIL/O WN5.............77 M4
Dalecroft FROD/HEL WA6.................166 A4
Dale Dr EP CH65..............................156 B8
Dale End Rd PEN/TH CH61...............141 L1
Dale Farm RAIN/WH L35 *...............132 D1
Dale Gdns HES CH60.......................140 F4
Dalegarth Av WD/CROXPK L12..........99 H4
Dale Gv LEIGH WN7...........................93 L1
Dalehead Gv LEIGH WN7...................93 L1
Dalehead Pl RNFD/HAY WA11.............89 K4
Dale Hey GTS/LS CH66.....................155 G3
WAL/EG CH44...................................111 K2
Dalehurst Cl WAL/EG CH44...............111 M1
Dale La NWD/KWIPK L33.....................86 C1
WARRS WA4.......................................138 A6
Dalemeadow Rd
DV/KA/FCH L14...................................114 F2
Dale Ms WLTN L25.............................131 K1
Dale Rd GOL/RIS/CU WA3....................92 C6
PS/BROM CH62...................................143 M8
Dalesford Cl LEIGH WN7.......................93 L5
Daleside Av AIMK WN4..........................79 J5
Daleside Cl PEN/TH CH61...................126 B7
Daleside Rd NWD/KWIPK L33................86 B2
Dales Rw HUY L36................................116 D3
Dale St ALL/GAR L19............................130 E8
CLVP L2...12 F6
LEIGH WN7...81 L8
RUNC WA7..19 G6
WGNS/IIMK WN3.......................................80 B2
Daleswey HES CH60.............................141 G5
The Dale NSTN CH64............................152 F7
WARRW/BUR WA5.................................120 B8
Dale Vw CHLY/EC PR7............................43 L1
NEWLW WA12..105 G1
Dale View Cl PEN/TH CH61...................126 C8
Dalewood WD/CROXPK L12......................99 G2
Dalewood Cl WARRN/WOL WA2 ....14 C4
Dalewood Crs CHNE CH2...............165 J2
Dalewood Gdns RAIN/WH L35 ...117 H3
Daley Pl BTL L20............................84 A6
Daley Rd LITH L21...........................83 L4
Dallam Ct WARRN/WOL WA2 *........14 D2
Dallam La WARRN/WOL WA2...........14 D4
Dallas Gv WLT/FAZ L9......................84 C7
Dalmeny St AIG/SPK L17................129 K2
Dalmorton Rd WAL/NB CH45..............95 L5
Dalry Crs KKBY L32...........................86 B6
Dalrymple St EV L5............................96 F8
Dalston Dr RNFD/HAY WA11...............89 K4
Dalston Gv WGNS/IIMK WN3...............78 F2
Dalton Av WARRW/BUR WA5..............14 B1
Dalton Bank WARR WA1.....................15 H4
Dalton Cl WD/CROXPK L12..................98 E3
WGNW/BIL/O WN5...............................67 K6
Dalton Ct RUNC WA7.........................150 A2
Dalton Dr WGNS/IIMK WN3.................79 G2
Dalton Gv AIMK WN4..........................91 J1
Dalton Rd WAL/NB CH45.....................95 L6
Dalton St GOL/RIS/CU WA3...............107 G8
RUNC WA7..149 M3
Daltry Cl WD/CROXPK L12...................98 C6
Dalwood Cl RUNC WA7......................151 G6
Damerham Ms WLTN L25....................115 J6
Damfield La MGHL L31..........................72 E4
Damhead La NSTN CH64....................154 A6
Damian Dr NEWLW WA12.......................91 J8
Dam La GOL/RIS/CU WA3......................92 B2
GOL/RIS/CU WA3................................106 B6
WARR WA1..122 F6
Damson Rd NTHLY L27.........................116 A8
Dam Wood La BRSC L40.........................37 L8
Dam Wood Rd SPK/HALE L24 ....146 F3
Danbers SKEL WN8................................66 B7
Danby Cl EV L5......................................97 H8
RUNC WA7..149 M7
WARRW/BUR WA5...............................121 G6
Danby Fold RAIN/WH L35....................117 K2
Danebury Cl WGNE/HIN WN2 *..............80 F1
Dane Cl GR/UP/WCH CH49..................126 B7
Danefield Pl ALL/GAR L19....................130 F5
Danefield Rd ALL/GAR L19...................130 F5
GR/UP/WCH CH49...............................125 L3
Danehurst Rd WAL/NB CH45..................95 H6
WLT/FAZ L9...84 D6
Danesbury Cl WGNW/BIL/O WN5 ..90 A1
Danescourt Rd BIRK CH41...................110 B2
WD/CROXPK L12.................................98 E8
Danescroft WDN WA8..........................133 K2
Dane St ANF/KKDL L4............................97 H4
Danesway CHLY/EC PR7.........................44 B4
WGN WN1...68 D2
Daneswell Dr MOR/LEA CH46...............110 B4
Daneswell Rd SPK/HALE L24................147 J3
Daneville Rd ANF/KKDL L4.....................97 M3
Daneway STHP PR8.................................34 D7
Danger La MOR/LEA CH46....................110 B3
Daniel Cl GOL/RIS/CU WA3..................123 J1
LITH L21..83 J7
Daniel Davies Dr TOX L8.......................113 J6
Daniels La SKEL WN8..............................65 L6
Dannette Hey STBRV L28.........................99 L7
Dansie St VAUX/LVPD L3..........................13 L7
Dans Rd WDN WA8.................................135 G3
Dante Cl WLT/FAZ L9...............................84 E5
Danube St TOX L8 *................................113 L6
Darby Gv ALL/GAR L19..........................130 D7
Darby La WGNE/HIN WN2........................69 M7
Darby Rd ALL/GAR L19...........................130 C5
Darent Rd RNFD/HAY WA11.....................90 D7
Daresbury Av STHP PR8..........................34 C8
Daresbury Cl KKBY L32............................85 L3
Daresbury Expy RUNC WA7......................18 F3
WARRS WA4..151 J2
Daresbury La WARRS WA4.....................151 M3
Daresbury Rd ECCL WA10......................101 K1
WAL/EG CH44.......................................111 J1
Darfield SKEL WN8..................................66 B6
Daric Cl LEIGH WN7..................................93 L4
Dark Entry PR/KW L34............................100 A4
Dark La BRSC L40......................................41 G2
BRSC L40...51 K7
HOR/BR BL6...57 K1
MGHL L31...72 F4
Darley Av WARRN/WOL WA2...................122 A2
Darley Cl WDN WA8................................133 K2
Darleydale Dr PS/BROM CH62 ....144 B8
Darley Dr WD/CROXPK L12.......................98 F7
Darley Rd WGNS/IIMK WN3......................79 K2
Darley St HOR/BR BL6..............................45 K8
Darlington Cl WAL/EG CH44...................111 M1
Darlington St CHLY/EC PR7......................42 F4
WAL/EG CH44...111 M1
WGNE/HIN WN2.......................................69 J6
Darlington St East WGN WN1..................5 H5
Darmond Rd NWD/KWIPK L33.................86 C2
Darmond's Gn WKBY CH48.....................124 D2
Darmonds Green Av
NPK/KEN L6...97 M7
Darnaway Cl GOL/RIS/CU WA3 ....107 K7
Darnhall St WGNS/IIMK WN3 *................80 B1
Darnley St TOX L8...................................113 G8
Darran Av WGNS/IIMK WN3.....................79 H2
Darrel Dr EHL/KEN L7............................113 L6
Darsefield Rd CHLDW L16.......................115 G6
Dartington Rd CHLDW L16.......................114 F5
Dartmouth Av AIN/FAZ L10......................84 E3
Dartmouth Dr ECCL WA10........................88 E7
NTHTN L30...83 L1
Darvel Av AIMK WN4.................................90 E1
Darwall Rd ALL/GAR L19..........................130 F5
Darwen St EV L5 *......................................96 E8
Darwick Dr HUY L36..................................116 C5
Darwin Gv STHEL WA9..............................102 A6
Daryl Rd HES CH60...................................141 J4
Dashwood Cl WARRS WA4.......................138 C6
Daten Av GOL/RIS/CU WA3......................107 H7
Daub La BRSC L40......................................40 C5
Daulby St VAUX/LVPD L3...........................13 M6
Dauntsey Brow WLTN L25........................115 K6
Dauntsey Ms WLTN L25...........................115 K6
Davenham Av CL/PREN CH43...................127 H2
WARR WA1...122 A5
Davenham Cl CL/PREN CH43....................127 H3
Davenham Rd FMBY L37............................59 H1
Davenhill Pk WLT/FAZ L9..........................84 E3
Davenport Av WARRS WA4.......................122 B8
Davenport Cl WKBY CH48........................124 E7
Davenport Gv NWD/KWIPK L33 ....86 A1
Davenport Rd HES CH60..........................141 G6
Davenport Rw RUNC WA7........................149 M5
Daventree Rd WAL/NB CH45.....................95 K8
Daventry Rd AIG/SPK L17.......................130 A3
David Rd LYMM WA13..............................139 L2
David's Av WARRW/BUR WA5 ....120 D8
Davidson Rd CLB/OSW/ST L13................114 B2
David St TOX L8.......................................129 H1
Davids Wk WLTN L25...............................131 L2
Davies Av NEWLW WA12..........................104 E1
WARRS WA4..138 B1
Davies Cl WDN WA8................................149 J1
Davies St BTL L20...7 J3
CLVPS L1 *...12 F6
STHEL WA9...9 L4
WGNE/HIN WN2......................................80 C3
Davies Wy LYMM WA13...........................139 M2

Davis Rd MOR/LEA CH46 110 D2
Davy Av GOL/RIS/CU WA3 107 G8
Davy Cl ECCL WA10 88 D8
Davy Rd RUNC WA7 150 A2
Davy St EV L5 97 J7
Dawber Cl NPK/KEN L6 113 J1
Dawber's La CHLY/EC PR7 31 G3
Dawber St AIMK WN4 91 M1
Dawley Cl AIMK WN4 91 J2
Dawlish Cl WLTN L25 131 L5
Dawlish Dr CHTN/BK PR9 22 C8
Dawlish Rd PEN/TH CH61 125 L8
WAL/EG CH44 111 H1
Dawlish Wy GOL/RIS/CU WA3 92 B4
Dawn Cl NSTN CH64 153 H8
STHEL WA9 102 A6
Dawn Gdns EP CH65 20 A7
Dawnwood Sq
WGNW/BIL/O WN5 67 L3
Dawpool Dr MOR/LEA CH46 110 A5
PS/BROM CH62 143 L6
Dawpool Farm PEN/TH CH61 * 125 K8
Dawson Av BIRK CH41 10 C2
CHTN/BK PR9 22 E8
STHEL WA9 102 F6
WGNNW/ST WN6 68 C2
Dawson Gdns MGHL L31 72 E3
Dawson Rd ORM L39 51 H6
Dawson St CLVPS L1 13 G7
Dawstone Ri HES CH60 141 H6
Dawstone Rd HES CH60 141 H6
Daybrook SKEL WN8 66 B7
Dayfield SKEL WN8 66 C6
Days Meadow
GR/UP/WCH CH49 125 L2
Day St CLB/OSW/ST L13 114 C2
Deacon Cl CSBY/WL L22 82 F5
GOL/RIS/CU WA3 106 C5
Deacon Ct CSBY/WL L22 82 F5
WLTN L25 131 K3
Deacon Rd WDN WA8 16 E2
Deakin St BIRK CH41 111 H5
WGNS/IIMK WN3 5 J9
Dean Av WAL/NB CH45 95 G7
Dean Cl SKEL WN8 66 E6
WDN WA8 16 E3
WGNW/BIL/O WN5 89 M2
Dean Ct GOL/RIS/CU WA3 92 C6
Dean Crs WARRN/WOL WA2 121 K3
WGNW/BIL/O WN5 67 K5
Deane Rd EHL/KEN L7 113 L3
Deanhall La CHLY/EC PR7 30 F3
Dean Head La CHLYE PR6 45 J1
Dean Meadow NEWLW WA12 104 E1
Dean Rd GOL/RIS/CU WA3 92 C6
Deansburn Rd CLB/OSW/ST L13 98 A7
Deanscales Rd NG/CROX L11 98 B3
Deans Ct FMBY L37 47 H8
Deansfield Wy CHNE CH2 165 J2
Deansgate EP CH65 156 C8
Deansgate La FMBY L37 47 K8
Deansgate La North FMBY L37 47 J7
Deans La BRSC L40 53 G1
WARRS WA4 139 H2
Deans Rd EP CH65 21 K8
Dean St CSBY/WL L22 82 F5
WDN WA8 16 E3
Deans Wy CL/PREN CH43 111 H5
Deansway WDN WA8 133 L5
Deanwater Cl GOL/RIS/CU WA3 122 F1
Dean Wy STHEL WA9 118 D2
Dean Wood Av
WGNW/BIL/O WN5 67 G4
Dean Wood Cl RAIN/WH L35 117 H3
Dearham Av RNFD/HAY WA11 89 J6
Dearne Cl WD/CROXPK L12 99 G8
Dearnford Av PS/BROM CH62 143 M7
Dearnford Cl PS/BROM CH62 143 M7
Dearnley Av RNFD/HAY WA11 90 A8
Deauville Rd WLT/FAZ L9 84 E6
Deben Cl WGNNW/ST WN6 55 M4
Debra Cl GTS/LS CH66 162 E1
MGHL L31 85 K1
Debra Rd GTS/LS CH66 162 E2
Dee Cl NWD/KWIPK L33 74 B7
Dee La WKBY CH48 124 C3
Deeley Cl EHL/KEN L7 113 L4
Dee Park Cl HES CH60 141 K7
Dee Park Rd HES CH60 141 K7
Deep Dl WARRW/BUR WA5 120 B7
Deepdale WDN WA8 133 L2
Deepdale Av BTL L20 83 J8
RNFD/HAY WA11 * 89 L4
Deepdale Cl CL/PREN CH43 110 E7
Deepdale Dr RAIN/WH L35 117 M2
Deepdale Rd WLTN L25 115 J6
Deepfield Dr HUY L36 116 B5
Deepfield Rd WAV L15 114 B7
Deepwood Gv RAIN/WH L35 117 G3
Deerbarn Dr NTHTN L30 84 D2
Deerbolt Cl KKBY L32 85 L2
Deerbolt Crs KKBY L32 85 L2
Deerbolt Wy KKBY L32 85 L2
Deerfold CHLY/EC PR7 32 D3
Dee Rd RAIN/WH L35 117 K2
Deer Park Ct RUNC WA7 150 B7
Deerwood Cl GTS/LS CH66 155 M6
Deerwood Crs GTS/LS CH66 155 M6
Deeside EP CH65 20 A9
Dee Side HES CH60 140 E5
Deeside Cl CL/PREN CH43 110 D7
EP CH65 163 K3
Dee View Rd HES CH60 141 H5
De Grouchy St WKBY CH48 * 124 D2
Deighton Rd CHLY/EC PR7 32 D7
Deirdre Av WDN WA8 16 D2
Delabole Rd NG/CROX L11 85 M8
De Lacy Rw RUNC WA7 150 C3
Delafield Cl WARRN/WOL WA2 122 B2
Delagoa Rd AIN/FAZ L10 85 H7
Delamain Rd CLB/OSW/ST L13 98 B7
Delamere Av GOL/RIS/CU WA3 93 G7
GTS/LS CH66 156 A8
PS/BROM CH62 155 G1
STHEL WA9 118 C2
WDN WA8 133 L4
Delamere Cl CL/PREN CH43 110 D7
PS/BROM CH62 155 G1
WD/CROXPK L12 98 F2
Delamere Dr GTS/LS CH66 163 G1
Delamere Gv WAL/EG CH44 * 112 A3
Delamere Pl CHLYE PR6 32 F5
Delamere Rd SKEL WN8 65 H3
STHP PR8 34 D8
Delamere St WARRW/BUR WA5 121 G8
Delamere Wy FROD/HEL WA6 160 E8
SKEL WN8 66 C6
Delamore Pl ANF/KKDL L4 7 L8
Delamore's Acre NSTN CH64 154 C5
Delamore St ANF/KKDL L4 7 M8
Delavor Cl HES CH60 141 G5
Delavor Rd HES CH60 141 G5
Delaware Crs KKBY L32 85 L2
Delaware Rd BTL L20 7 G3
Delegarte St WGNS/IIMK WN3 5 J8
Delenty Dr GOL/RIS/CU WA3 122 F1
Delery Dr WARR WA1 122 A5
Delfby Crs KKBY L32 86 C4
Delfhaven Ct WGNNW/ST WN6 56 C6
Delf La ANF/KKDL L4 97 J3
ORM L39 49 J8
SPK/HALE L24 131 K8
Dell Av WGNNW/ST WN6 68 A2
Dell Cl BEB CH63 143 K7
Dell Dr WARRN/WOL WA2 122 C3
Dellfield La MGHL L31 73 G4
Dell Gv RF/TRAN CH42 128 C5
Dell La HES CH60 141 K6
Dellside Cl AIMK WN4 78 F7
Dellside Gv STHEL WA9 102 E5
Dell St EHL/KEN L7 113 L3
The Dell CHLYE PR6 33 J2
RF/TRAN CH42 128 D4
SKEL WN8 66 D6
WD/CROXPK L12 99 G4
WGNNW/ST WN6 54 F6
Delph Common Rd ORM L39 62 D4
Delph Dr BRSC L40 52 B2
Delphfields Rd WARRS WA4 137 L6
Delph Gv LEIGH WN7 81 M4
Delphield RUNC WA7 150 F5
Delph La CHLY/EC PR7 31 M7
FMBY L37 58 E2
ORM L39 62 E4
RAIN/WH L35 117 H1
WARRN/WOL WA2 106 A7
WARRS WA4 151 J2
Delph Meadow Gdns
WGNW/BIL/O WN5 89 L1
Delph Park Av ORM L39 62 D4
Delph Rd HTWN L38 70 F5
Delphside Cl WGNW/BIL/O WN5 66 F8
Delphside Rd WGNW/BIL/O WN5 66 E8
Delph St WGNNW/ST WN6 4 C1
The Delph SKEL WN8 53 L2
Delphwood Dr STHEL WA9 9 J9
Delta Crs WARRW/BUR WA5 120 E3
Delta Dr WD/CROXPK L12 99 G5
Delta Rd LITH L21 83 K6
STHEL WA9 103 H1
Delta Rd East RF/TRAN CH42 128 D4
Delta Rd West RF/TRAN CH42 * 128 D4
Deltic Wy NTHTN L30 84 C5
NWD/KWIPK L33 86 D5
Delves Av BEB CH63 143 H2
WARRW/BUR WA5 14 A1
Delyn Cl RF/TRAN CH42 128 A4
Demage Dr GTS/LS CH66 162 F2
Demesne St WAL/EG CH44 112 A2
Denbigh Av CHTN/BK PR9 25 H2
STHEL WA9 102 E6
Denbigh Cl FROD/HEL WA6 166 C4
Denbigh Ct EP CH65 20 E9
Denbigh Gdns EP CH65 * 20 D9
Denbigh Rd WLT/FAZ L9 97 H2
Denbigh St EV L5 96 D8
Denbury Av WARRS WA4 138 B3
Dencourt Rd NG/CROX L11 98 D4
Dene Av NEWLW WA12 104 B1
Denebank Rd ANF/KKDL L4 97 K6
Dene Gv LEIGH WN7 93 K1
Denehurst Cl WARRW/BUR WA5 136 B1
Deneshey Rd HOY CH47 108 E5
Dene St LEIGH WN7 93 K1
Denes Wy STBRV L28 99 J6
Denford Cl WGNS/IIMK WN3 79 H2
Denford Rd DV/KA/FCH L14 99 H8
Denham Av WARRW/BUR WA5 120 D8
Denham Cl WD/CROXPK L12 99 H2
Denham Dr WGNS/IIMK WN3 79 J2
Denholme SKEL WN8 66 B6
Denise Av WARRW/BUR WA5 120 A8
Denise Rd AIN/FAZ L10 85 K6
Denison Gv STHEL WA9 * 102 A6
Denman Dr NPK/KEN L6 113 L1
Denman Gv WAL/EG CH44 * 112 A2
Denman St NPK/KEN L6 113 K2
Denman Wy NPK/KEN L6 113 L1
Denmark Rd CHTN/BK PR9 25 J3
Denmark St CSBY/WL L22 82 F4
Dennett Cl MGHL L31 72 F6
WARR WA1 123 G7
Dennett Rd RAIN/WH L35 116 E1
Denning Dr PEN/TH CH61 125 M6
Dennis Av ECCL WA10 101 L6
Dennis Rd WDN WA8 17 G5
Denny Cl GR/UP/WCH CH49 126 B1
Densham Av WARRN/WOL WA2 121 K3
Denston Cl CL/PREN CH43 110 D6
Denstone Av AIN/FAZ L10 84 F3
Denstone Cl WLTN L25 131 K5
Dentdale Dr EV L5 13 K2
Denton Dr WAL/NB CH45 95 L7
Denton Gv NPK/KEN L6 97 L8
WGNW/BIL/O WN5 67 K5
Dentons Green La ECCL WA10 8 B2
Denton St TOX L8 129 H1
WDN WA8 17 G2
Dentwood St TOX L8 129 J1
Denver Rd KKBY L32 85 L4
WARRS WA4 138 C2
Depot Rd NWD/KWIPK L33 86 E1
Derby Cl NEWLW WA12 104 D2
Derby Dr RNFD/HAY WA11 76 C8
WARR WA1 15 M1
Derby Gv MGHL L31 72 F7
Derby Hill Crs ORM L39 51 J8
Derby Hill Rd ORM L39 51 J8
Derby La CLB/OSW/ST L13 114 C2
Derby Pl CHLYE PR6 44 C5
Derby Rd BTL L20 6 E6
CHTN/BK PR9 3 J4
FMBY L37 59 G1
GOL/RIS/CU WA3 92 E4
HUY L36 116 A3
RF/TRAN CH42 127 M1
SKEL WN8 64 E5
WAL/NB CH45 95 J7
WARRS WA4 137 L5
WDN WA8 134 E1
Derby Rw NEWLW WA12 104 E5
Derbyshire Hill Rd STHEL WA9 103 J2
Derbyshire Rd WGNS/IIMK WN3 78 F4
Derby Sq CLVP L2 12 F8
PR/KW L34 101 G7
Derby St CLB/OSW/ST L13 * 114 B2
HUY L36 116 C3
NEWLW WA12 104 D2
ORM L39 51 H8
WGNS/IIMK WN3 80 B1
Derby St West ORM L39 51 G8
Dereham Av GR/UP/WCH CH49 110 C6
Dereham Crs AIN/FAZ L10 85 H6
Dereham Wy RUNC WA7 150 F2
WGNS/IIMK WN3 78 F2
Derek Av WARRN/WOL WA2 121 M4
Derna Rd HUY L36 115 M2
Derngate Dr WGNNW/ST WN6 56 C6
Derringstone Cl ECCL WA10 101 M4
Derwent Av CHTN/BK PR9 25 H4
FMBY L37 58 F3
GOL/RIS/CU WA3 92 E4
PR/KW L34 101 H7
WGNE/HIN WN2 69 K6
Derwent Cl BEB CH63 * 127 M8
GOL/RIS/CU WA3 107 J3
MGHL L31 73 H3
NWD/KWIPK L33 85 M1
RAIN/WH L35 117 K2
Derwent Dr GTS/LS CH66 155 K3
LITH L21 83 M5
PEN/TH CH61 141 H1
WAL/NB CH45 95 J7
Derwent Pl WGNW/BIL/O WN5 67 L6
Derwent Rd AIMK WN4 80 A8
BEB CH63 127 M8
CHLY/EC PR7 32 D8
CL/PREN CH43 127 K1
CSBY/BLUN L23 83 H3
HOY CH47 109 G5
RNFD/HAY WA11 89 K6
WARRS WA4 137 J3
WDN WA8 133 L4
WGNW/BIL/O WN5 67 H5
Derwent Rd East
CLB/OSW/ST L13 114 C1
Derwent Rd West
CLB/OSW/ST L13 114 B1
Derwent Sq CLB/OSW/ST L13 114 C1
Derwent Wy NSTN CH64 153 H7
Desborough Crs
WD/CROXPK L12 98 C6
Desford Av RNFD/HAY WA11 89 M7
Desford Cl MOR/LEA CH46 109 K4
Desford Rd ALL/GAR L19 130 A5
Desilva St HUY L36 116 C3
Desmond Cl CL/PREN CH43 110 E6
Desmond Gv CSBY/BLUN L23 83 H2
Desoto Rd WDN WA8 134 A8
Desoto Rd East WDN WA8 16 A8
De Trafford Dr WGNE/HIN WN2 69 K5
Deva Cl NWD/KWIPK L33 74 A6
Deva Rd WKBY CH48 124 C3
Deveraux Dr WAL/EG CH44 111 K2
Deverell Gv WAV L15 114 D4
Deverell Rd WAV L15 114 D4
Deverill Rd RF/TRAN CH42 128 A4
Devilla Cl DV/KA/FCH L14 99 J8
De Villiers Av CSBY/BLUN L23 71 G8
Devisdale Gv CL/PREN CH43 110 E6
Devizes Dr PEN/TH CH61 125 M6
Devizes Ms WLTN L25 115 K6
Devoke Av RNFD/HAY WA11 89 J4
Devon Av SKEL WN8 66 D7
WAL/EG CH44 95 L8
Devon Cl CSBY/BLUN L23 82 C1
WGNE/HIN WN2 57 M8
WGNW/BIL/O WN5 67 L7
Devon Ct EV L5 97 J8
Devondale Rd CALD/MH L18 114 C8
Devon Dr PEN/TH CH61 141 G1
WGN WN1 56 D4
Devon Farm Wy FMBY L37 59 K2
Devonfield Rd WLT/FAZ L9 84 B8
Devon Gdns CHLDW L16 115 G8
RF/TRAN CH42 128 B4
Devon Pl WDN WA8 134 C2
Devonport St TOX L8 113 H8
Devonport Wy CHLYE PR6 33 G5
Devonshire Cl CL/PREN CH43 10 C8
NWD/KWIPK L33 86 A1
Devonshire Ct CHLY/EC PR7 * 32 E5
Devonshire Gdns NEWLW WA12 104 E3
Devonshire Pl CL/PREN CH43 10 B7
EV L5 97 G7
RUNC WA7 19 G3
Devonshire Rd CHLY/EC PR7 32 E6
CHTN/BK PR9 25 J6
CL/PREN CH43 10 C7
CSBY/WL L22 82 E3
ECCL WA10 8 A1
GR/UP/WCH CH49 110 A8
PEN/TH CH61 141 G1
TOX L8 113 J8
WAL/EG CH44 111 K1
WARR WA1 122 B5
WKBY CH48 124 E4
Devonshire Rd West TOX L8 113 J8
Devon St ECCL WA10 8 B4
VAUX/LVPD L3 13 L5
Devonwall Gdns TOX L8 113 K8
Devon Wy CHLDW L16 115 G7
HUY L36 116 C1
Dewar Ct RUNC WA7 150 A2
Dewar St GOL/RIS/CU WA3 107 G8
Dewberry Cl RF/TRAN CH42 * 11 G9
Dewberry Flds SKEL WN8 66 D6
Dewey Av WLT/FAZ L9 84 D5
Dewhurst Rd GOL/RIS/CU WA3 122 F3
Dewlands Rd LITH L21 83 H5
Dewsbury Rd ANF/KKDL L4 97 K7
Dexter St TOX L8 113 G7
Deycroft Av NWD/KWIPK L33 86 C1
Deyes End MGHL L31 73 G4
Deyes La MGHL L31 72 F4
Deysbrook La WD/CROXPK L12 98 E7
Deysbrook Side WD/CROXPK L12 98 E7
Deysbrook Wy WD/CROXPK L12 98 F5
Dial Rd RF/TRAN CH42 127 M2
Dial St EHL/KEN L7 113 L3
WARR WA1 14 F5
Diamond Jubilee Rd BRSC L40 39 L1
Diamond St EV L5 13 G1
WGNNW/ST WN6 68 C2
Diana Rd BTL L20 83 M6
Diana St ANF/KKDL L4 97 H5
Diane Rd AIMK WN4 79 M8
Dibbinsdale Rd BEB CH63 143 K6
Dibbins Gn BEB CH63 143 K7
Dibbins Hey BEB CH63 143 J3
Dibbinview Gv BEB CH63 143 K3
Dibb La CSBY/BLUN L23 70 E6
Dicconson Crs WGN WN1 4 F2
Dicconson's La ORM L39 61 L2
Dicconson St ECCL WA10 * 9 G3
WGN WN1 4 E1
Dicconson Ter WGN WN1 4 E1
Dicconson Wy ORM L39 * 63 J1
Dickens Av CL/PREN CH43 127 H4
Dickens Cl CL/PREN CH43 127 H4
Dickens Dr WGNE/HIN WN2 80 D5
Dickenson St CLVPS L1 112 F5
WARRN/WOL WA2 15 G2
WGNE/HIN WN2 81 G1
Dickens Pl WGNS/IIMK WN3 79 H1
Dickens Rd CHLY/EC PR7 43 G5
ECCL WA10 101 L5
Dickens St TOX L8 * 113 H7
Dicket's La SKEL WN8 64 C3
Dickinson Cl FMBY L37 59 H3
RNFD/HAY WA11 90 C7
Dickinson Rd FMBY L37 59 H3
Dick's La BRSC L40 64 B1
Dickson Cl WDN WA8 16 E3
Dickson St VAUX/LVPD L3 12 C1
WDN WA8 16 D3
Didcot Cl WLTN L25 131 M5
Didsbury Cl NWD/KWIPK L33 86 B3
Didsbury Gv WGNE/HIN WN2 69 M8
Digg La MOR/LEA CH46 109 M4
Diggle St WGNNW/ST WN6 4 B2
Dig La FROD/HEL WA6 160 C6
WARRN/WOL WA2 122 C1
Digmoor Dr SKEL WN8 65 K6
Digmoor Rd KKBY L32 86 B6
SKEL WN8 65 L7
Dignum Md NTHLY L27 116 A7
Dilloway St ECCL WA10 8 C3
Dinas La DV/KA/FCH L14 115 J1
Dinesen Rd ALL/GAR L19 130 E6
Dingle Av NEWLW WA12 104 B3
SKEL WN8 66 D5
Dingle Brow TOX L8 129 J2
Dingle Cl ORM L39 62 E4
Dingle Gv TOX L8 129 J1
Dingle La TOX L8 129 J2
WARRS WA4 138 B7
Dingle Mt TOX L8 129 J2
Dingle Rd RF/TRAN CH42 10 F9
SKEL WN8 66 D6
TOX L8 129 H2
The Dingle CHLYE PR6 33 J2
Dingle V TOX L8 129 J2
Dingle Wk WGNNW/ST WN6 67 M1
Dingleway WARRS WA4 137 M5
Dingley Av WLT/FAZ L9 84 B7
Dingwall Dr GR/UP/WCH CH49 126 A2
Dinmore Rd WAL/EG CH44 111 K1
Dinnington Ct WDN WA8 134 B2
Dinorwic Rd ANF/KKDL L4 97 J7
STHP PR8 35 J2
Ditchfield FMBY L37 59 J3
Ditchfield Pl WDN WA8 133 K5
Ditchfield Rd WARRW/BUR WA5 136 A2
WDN WA8 133 K5
Ditton La MOR/LEA CH46 110 A2
Ditton Rd WDN WA8 16 B7
Dixon Av NEWLW WA12 91 L8
WGNNW/ST WN6 55 J8
Dixon Cl RNFD/HAY WA11 91 J5
Dixon Dr WGNNW/ST WN6 55 J8
Dixon Rd NWD/KWIPK L33 86 D5
Dixon St WARR WA1 14 C6
Dob Brow CHLY/EC PR7 43 H1
Dobbs Dr FMBY L37 59 J1
Dobers La FROD/HEL WA6 167 M1
Dobson Cl WGNNW/ST WN6 55 G3
Dobson Pkwy WGNE/HIN WN2 5 M7
Dobson St NPK/KEN L6 113 J1
Dock Rd ALL/GAR L19 130 D8
BIRK CH41 111 J3
WDN WA8 16 B9
Dock Rd North PS/BROM CH62 128 E7
Dock Rd South PS/BROM CH62 143 M1
Dock St EP CH65 20 D1
WDN WA8 16 C9
Dock Yard Rd EP CH65 20 F3
Doctor's La CHLY/EC PR7 30 C7
FMBY L37 60 A4
KIRK/FR/WA PR4 28 A3
Dodd Av ECCL WA10 101 L1
GR/UP/WCH CH49 125 M2
Doddridge Rd TOX L8 113 G8
Dodd's La MGHL L31 72 F3
WARRS WA4 138 C8
Dodleston Cl CL/PREN CH43 126 F1
Dodman Rd NG/CROX L11 85 M8
Dodworth Av STHP PR8 25 G8
Doe Meadow SKEL WN8 53 J4
Doe Park Ctyd WLTN L25 * 131 K5
Doe's Meadow Rd BEB CH63 143 K6
Dole La CHLY/EC PR7 32 E5
Dolly's La CHTN/BK PR9 25 M5
Dolomite Av ALL/GAR L19 131 H7
Dolphin Crs GTS/LS CH66 163 G3
Domar Cl KKBY L32 86 A5
Dombey St TOX L8 113 H7
Domingo Dr NWD/KWIPK L33 73 M8
Dominic Cl CHLDW L16 115 G5
Dominic Rd CHLDW L16 115 G5
Dominion St NPK/KEN L6 * 97 L8
Domville RAIN/WH L35 117 G3
Domville Rd CLB/OSW/ST L13 114 C4
Donaldson St EV L5 97 J7
Donalds Wy AIG/SPK L17 130 A4
Doncaster Dr
GR/UP/WCH CH49 110 B7
Donegal Rd CLB/OSW/ST L13 114 D2
Donne Av BEB CH63 143 H2
Donne Cl BEB CH63 143 J2
Donnington Cl HUY L36 115 M5
LEIGH WN7 93 M4
Donsby Rd WLT/FAZ L9 84 D7
Don Wk EP CH65 156 C6
Dooley Dr NTHTN L30 84 D1
Doon Cl ANF/KKDL L4 97 G5
Dootson St WGNE/HIN WN2 80 C4
Dorbett Dr CSBY/BLUN L23 83 H3
Dorchester Cl
GR/UP/WCH CH49 126 B1
Dorchester Dr NWD/KWIPK L33 74 C8
Dorchester Pk CL/PREN CH43 126 F2
RUNC WA7 150 F2
WLTN L25 115 K7
Dorchester Rd SKEL WN8 66 C6
WARRW/BUR WA5 120 D8
Dorchester Wy
WARRW/BUR WA5 104 B7
Doreen Av MOR/LEA CH46 109 M5
Dorgan Cl RAIN/WH L35 117 K1
Doric Av FROD/HEL WA6 160 E6
Doric Gn WGNW/BIL/O WN5 77 M2
Doric Rd CLB/OSW/ST L13 114 C1
Doric St LITH L21 83 H6
RF/TRAN CH42 * 128 B3
Dorien Rd CLB/OSW/ST L13 114 B3
Doris St CHLYE PR6 32 F4
Dorking Gv WAV L15 114 D6
Dorking Rd CHLYE PR6 33 H1
Dorney Cl WARRS WA4 138 A7
Dorning St WGN WN1 4 D3
Dorothea St WARRN/WOL WA2 15 G1
Dorothy St EHL/KEN L7 113 K4
STHEL WA9 102 A6
Dorrington Cl RUNC WA7 150 F5
Dorrit St TOX L8 113 H7
Dorset Av STHP PR8 47 L3
WAV L15 113 M6
Dorset Cl BTL L20 7 K4
WGNW/BIL/O WN5 67 L7
Dorset Dr PEN/TH CH61 141 G1
Dorset Rd ECCL WA10 8 A9
HUY L36 116 C2
NPK/KEN L6 97 M7
WAL/NB CH45 95 J6
WGN WN1 56 D4
WKBY CH48 124 E2
Dorset Wy WARR WA1 122 D5
Douglas Av HOR/BR BL6 45 L8
SKEL WN8 66 D6
STHEL WA9 103 K7
WGNW/BIL/O WN5 89 M2
Douglas Bank Dr
WGNNW/ST WN6 68 B4
Douglas Cl BRSC L40 39 L2
CLB/OSW/ST L13 114 B1
WDN WA8 135 H2
Douglas Dr MGHL L31 73 H3
MOR/LEA CH46 109 L5
ORM L39 50 F6
WGNNW/ST WN6 55 H8
WGNW/BIL/O WN5 67 G6
Douglas Pl BTL L20 6 F7
Douglas Rd ANF/KKDL L4 97 K7
CHTN/BK PR9 25 L1
LEIGH WN7 81 L6
WGN WN1 5 G1
WGNNW/ST WN6 55 K3
WKBY CH48 124 F2
Douglas St BIRK CH41 11 K5
ECCL WA10 8 B5
WGNE/HIN WN2 80 E1
WGNW/BIL/O WN5 4 A6
Douglas Wy NWD/KWIPK L33 74 B7
Doulton Cl CL/PREN CH43 110 D6
Doulton St ECCL WA10 8 A6
Doune Ct EP CH65 20 F9
Dounrey Cl WARRN/WOL WA2 122 C3
Douro Pl CLB/OSW/ST L13 114 B3
Douro St EV L5 13 J2
Dove Cl CHNE CH2 165 L1
EP CH65 156 B6
FROD/HEL WA6 159 L8
GOL/RIS/CU WA3 123 H1
Dovecot Av DV/KA/FCH L14 115 H1
Dovecote Dr RNFD/HAY WA11 90 E6
Dovecote Gn WARRW/BUR WA5 120 C4
Dove Ct WLTN L25 131 K3
Dovedale Av MGHL L31 72 E3
PS/BROM CH62 144 A8
Dovedale Cl CL/PREN CH43 127 H3
WARRN/WOL WA2 122 A2
Dovedale Crs AIMK WN4 79 J5
Dovedale Dr WGNNW/ST WN6 56 A3
Dovedale Rd AIMK WN4 79 J5
CALD/MH L18 114 B8
HOY CH47 108 D5
WAL/NB CH45 95 J6
Dovenby Fold WGNE/HIN WN2 69 J6
Dovepoint Rd HOY CH47 109 G5
Dovercliffe Rd CLB/OSW/ST L13 114 D2
Dover Cl BIRK CH41 11 G4
RUNC WA7 151 G7
Dover Ct EP CH65 163 M3
Dover Dr EP CH65 163 M3
Dover Gv CHLDW L16 115 H5
Dove Rd WLT/FAZ L9 84 B7
Dover Rd MGHL L31 72 E7
STHP PR8 35 H3
WARRS WA4 138 C2
WLT/FAZ L9 84 B7
Dover St RUNC WA7 19 J2
VAUX/LVPD L3 13 L7
Dovesmead Rd HES CH60 * 141 L6
Dovestone Cl EHL/KEN L7 113 K5
Dove St GOL/RIS/CU WA3 92 C3
TOX L8 113 K6
Dovey St TOX L8 113 H8
Doward St WDN WA8 134 E3
Dower St WGNE/HIN WN2 80 C2
Dowhills Dr CSBY/BLUN L23 70 D8
Dowhills Pk CSBY/BLUN L23 70 D7
Dowhills Rd CSBY/BLUN L23 70 D8
Dowling Cl WGNNW/ST WN6 67 M2
Downall Green Rd AIMK WN4 79 G7
Downes Gn BEB CH63 143 J4
Downham Av GOL/RIS/CU WA3 107 H3
Downham Cl WLTN L25 115 H8
Downham Dr HES CH60 141 J5
Downham Gn WLTN L25 115 H8
Downham Rd RF/TRAN CH42 128 A2
Downham Rd North
PEN/TH CH61 141 J3
Downham Rd South HES CH60 141 J5
Downham Wy WLTN L25 115 H8
Downing Cl CL/PREN CH43 127 K2
WGNE/HIN WN2 80 C4
Downing Rd BTL L20 7 K7
Downing St EV L5 97 J8
Downland Wy STHEL WA9 103 H4
Downside WDN WA8 133 K2
Downside Cl NTHTN L30 84 A1
Downside Dr AIN/FAZ L10 85 H4
Downs Rd ECCL WA10 8 B7
RUNC WA7 19 H6
The Downs WGNS/IIMK WN3 78 E1
Downton Av WGNE/HIN WN2 80 F1
Downway La STHEL WA9 103 J4
Dowsefield La CALD/MH L18 131 G2
Dragon Cl NG/CROX L11 98 E1
Dragon Crs RAIN/WH L35 117 H1
Dragon La RAIN/WH L35 116 F3
Dragon Yd WDN WA8 134 D1
Drake Cl AIN/FAZ L10 85 J6
ORM L39 62 E3
RAIN/WH L35 117 G3
WARRW/BUR WA5 120 F4
Drake Crs AIN/FAZ L10 85 J6
Drakefield Rd NG/CROX L11 98 A2
Drake Gdns STHEL WA9 102 A7
Drake Pl AIN/FAZ L10 * 85 H6
Drake Rd AIN/FAZ L10 85 H6
MOR/LEA CH46 110 D1
NSTN CH64 153 G4
Drake St BTL L20 6 E8
ECCL WA10 8 B4
Drake Wy AIN/FAZ L10 85 J6
Drapers Av CHLY/EC PR7 30 E7
Draw Well Rd NWD/KWIPK L33 86 F3
Draycott Cl WGNE/HIN WN2 81 H2
Draycott St TOX L8 129 H2
Drayton Cl PEN/TH CH61 125 M8
RUNC WA7 18 E5
Drayton Crs RNFD/HAY WA11 89 M7
Drayton Rd ANF/KKDL L4 * 97 J3
WAL/EG CH44 111 M2
Drennan Rd ALL/GAR L19 131 G5
Drewell Rd CALD/MH L18 130 B2
Drewitt Crs CHTN/BK PR9 25 L1
Driffield Rd PR/KW L34 100 E7
Drinkhouse La
CROS/BRETH PR26 29 J4
Drinkhouse Rd
CROS/BRETH PR26 29 K4
Drinkwater Gdns
VAUX/LVPD L3 * 13 J3
The Drive WD/CROXPK L12 98 D8
Driveway RAIN/WH L35 117 H3
Droitwich Av GR/UP/WCH CH49 125 L1
Dromore Av CALD/MH L18 130 C2
Dronfield Wy WLTN L25 115 H6
Druids Cross Gdns
CALD/MH L18 130 F1
Druids Cross Rd CALD/MH L18 130 F1
Druids Pk CALD/MH L18 131 G1
Druid St AIMK WN4 91 L3
Druidsville Rd CALD/MH L18 131 G1
Druids Wy GR/UP/WCH CH49 126 C3
Drum Cl DV/KA/FCH L14 99 J8
Drumhead Rd CHLYE PR6 32 F3
Drummersdale La BRSC L40 37 K4
Drummer's La AIMK WN4 79 G6
Drummond Av GTS/LS CH66 162 E1
Drummond Ct WDN WA8 134 F3
Drummond Rd ANF/KKDL L4 97 L4
CSBY/BLUN L23 71 K8
HOY CH47 108 C8
Drummond Sq
WGNW/BIL/O WN5 68 A6
Druridge Dr WARRW/BUR WA5 136 B1
Drury La CLVP L2 12 E7
Dryburgh Wy ANF/KKDL L4 97 G5
Dryden Av AIMK WN4 79 H6
Dryden Cl CL/PREN CH43 110 E6
RAIN/WH L35 117 G2

WGNS/IIMK WN3 ....68 C8
Dryden Gv HUY L36 ....116 B4
Dryden Pl WARRN/WOL WA2 ...121 L3
Dryden Rd EHL/KEN L7 ....114 A4
Dryden St BTL L20 ....6 D1
EV L5 ....13 H1
Dryebeck Gv STHEL WA9 ....102 F7
Dryfield Cl GR/UP/WCH CH49 *..123 M1
Dryfield La HOR/BR BL6 ....45 J8
Drysdale St TOX L8 ....129 J1
Drysdale Wk TOX L8 ....129 J1
Dryton Wk WDN WA2.................69 G3
Dublin Cft GTS/LS CH66 ....155 G4
Dublin St VAUX/LVPD L3 ....12 C1
Ducie St TOX L8 ....113 K7
Duckinfield St EHL/KEN L7 ....13 L7
Duck Pond La RF/TRAN CH42 ....127 J7
Duckworth Gv
  WARRN/WOL WA2 ....122 C4
Duddingston Av CALD/MH L18 * 114 E8
  CSBY/BLUN L23 ....83 G3
Duddon Av MGHL L31 ....73 H5
Duddon Cl CL/PREN CH43 ....127 H1
Duddon Dr WGNNW/ST WN6 ....56 B6
Dudlestone Rd GTS/LS CH66 .....155 G4
Dudley Av RUNC WA7 ....149 M3
Dudley Cl CL/PREN CH43 ....127 K1
Dudley Crs PS/BROM CH62 ....155 K2
Dudley Gv CSBY/BLUN L23 ....83 G3
Dudley Pl STHEL WA9 ....9 M5
Dudley Rd CALD/MH L18 ....114 B8
  EP CH65 ....20 B5
  WAL/NB CH45 ....95 J5
Dudley St AIMK WN4 ....79 J8
  WARRN/WOL WA2 ....14 F1
Dudlow Dr CALD/MH L18 ....114 E8
Dudlow Gdns CALD/MH L18 ......114 E7
Dudlow Green Rd WARRS WA4 ...137 M8
Dudlow La CALD/MH L18 ....114 E8
Dudlow Nook Rd CALD/MH L18 ..114 E8
Dugdale Cl ALL/GAR L19 ....130 C6
Duke Av STHP PR8 ....35 L1
Duke Cl RUNC WA7 ....149 J8
Dukes Rd EV L5 ....97 G7
Duke St AIMK WN4 ....91 L2
  ALL/GAR L19 ....130 F4
  BIRK CH41 ....10 C2
  CHLY/EC PR7 ....32 E7
  CLVPS L1 ....13 H9
  CSBY/WL L22 ....82 F5
  ECCL WA10 ....8 E5
  FMBY L37 ....59 G3
  GOL/RIS/CU WA3 ....92 C4
  NEWLW WA12 ....104 D2
  PR/KW L34 ....100 F6
  STHP PR8 ....2 D7
  STHP PR8 ....3 H9
  WAL/NB CH45 ....95 K5
  WGN WN1 ....68 E3
  WGNE/HIN WN2 ....80 C2
  WGNS/IIMK WN3 ....79 H1
Duke's Wood La SKEL WN8 ....76 F2
Dulas Gn KKBY L32 ....86 C4
Dulas Rd KKBY L32 ....86 C4
  WAV L15 ....114 D7
Dulverton Rd AIG/SPK L17 ....130 A5
Dumbarton Gn WGNNW/ST WN6 ..68 A4
Dumbarton St ANF/KKDL L4 ....7 M9
Dumbrees Rd WD/CROXPK L12 ....99 G5
Dumbreeze Gv PR/KW L34 ....99 H1
Dumfries St NWD/KWIPK L33 .....73 M9
Dunacre Wy HLWD L26 ....132 B6
Dunbabin Rd CHLDW L16 ....114 E7
Dunbar Cl GTS/LS CH66 ....155 H5
Dunbar Crs STHP PR8 ....35 H5
Dunbar Rd STHP PR8 ....35 G4
Dunbar St ANF/KKDL L4 ....97 H3
Dunbeath Av RAIN/WH L35 ....117 M4
Dunbeath Cl RAIN/WH L35 ....117 M4
Dunblane Cl AIMK WN4 ....90 F1
  RUNC WA7 ....19 L5
Duncan Av NEWLW WA12 ....91 J8
Duncan Cl ECCL WA10 ....8 E7
Duncan Dr GR/UP/WCH CH49 ....125 M1
Duncan Pl WGNW/BIL/O WN5 ......68 A6
Duncansby Crs
  WARRN/BUR WA5 ....120 A7
Duncansby Dr BEB CH63 ....154 E1
Duncan St BIRK CH41 ....11 L5
  CLVPS L1 ....113 G6
  ECCL WA10 ....8 D6
  WARRN/WOL WA2 ....15 H1
Dunchurch Rd DV/KA/FCH L14 ....99 H8
Duncombe Rd North
  ALL/GAR L19 ....130 D6
Duncombe Rd South
  ALL/GAR L19 ....130 D6
  RAIN/WH L35 ....101 H8
Duncote Cl CL/PREN CH43 ....10 D7
Dundale Rd CLB/OSW/ST L13 ...114 D4
Dundalk Rd WAV L15 ....133 M5
Dundas St BTL L20 ....6 A8
Dundee Cl WARRN/WOL WA2 .....122 A4
Dundee Gv EP CH65 ....21 D9
Dundee Gv WAL/EC CH44 ....111 J2
Dundonald Av WARRS WA4 ....137 L4
Dundonald Rd AIG/SPK L17 ......130 A4
Dundonald St BIRK CH41 ....10 A2
Dunedin St STHEL WA9 ....102 A6
Dunes Dr FMBY L37 ....58 F1
Dunes Wy EV L5 ....96 F3
Dunfold Cl KKBY L32 ....86 B4
Dungeon La SKEL WN8 ....53 L6
  SPK/HALE L24 ....147 H4
Dunham Av GOL/RIS/CU WA3 .....92 B4
Dunham Cl PS/BROM CH62 ....155 H1
Dunham Ct FROD/HEL WA6 ....166 A4
Dunham Rd WAV L15 ....114 C4
Dunkeld Cl NPK/KEN L6 ....113 J2
Dunkirk Dr EP CH65 ....163 J4
Dunkirk La CH/BCN CH1 ....162 E5
  GTS/LS CH66 ....163 J4
Dunkirk Rd STHP PR8 ....35 H3
Dunley Cl GOL/RIS/CU WA3 ....107 J3
Dunlin Av NEWLW WA12 ....104 C2
Dunlin Cl NTHLY L27 ....116 B8
  RUNC WA7 ....150 B8
  WARRN/WOL WA2 ....122 A4
Dunlop Av STHP PR8 ....47 L3
Dunlop Dr MGHL L31 ....63 K1
Dunlop Rd SPK/HALE L24 ....146 D3
Dunlop St WARRS WA4 ....14 E9
Dunluce St ANF/KKDL L4 ....7 M8
Dunmail Av RNFD/HAY WA11 ......89 G4
Dunmail Gv RUNC WA7 ....160 F1
Dunmore Crs GTS/LS CH66 ....155 H3
Dunmore Rd CLB/OSW/ST L13 ..114 A2
  GTS/LS CH66 ....155 K7
Dunmow Rd WARRS WA4 ....138 G2
Dunmow Wy WLTN L25 ....131 L5
Dunnerdale Rd NG/CROX L11 .....98 C5
Dunnett St BTL L20 ....6 F9
Dunning Cl GR/UP/WCH CH49...110 D9
Dunnings Bridge Rd NTHTN L30..72 D8
  NTHTN L30 ....84 A4

Dunnock Cl WARRN/WOL WA2 ...122 A2
  WLTN L25 ....115 J8
Dunnock Gv GOL/RIS/CU WA3 ...123 G1
Dunoon Rd WGNE/HIN WN2 ....57 M8
Dunraven Rd CH64 ....153 J6
  WKBY CH48 ....124 C3
Dunriding La ECCL WA10 ....8 A6
Dunrobin Dr CHLY/EC PR7 ....31 M4
Dunscar Cl COL/RIS/CU WA3 ....106 F3
Dunscar Dr CHLYE PR6 ....33 G4
Dunscroft STHEL WA9 ....102 F6
Dunsdon Cl CALD/MH L18 ....131 G1
Dunsdon Rd CALD/MH L18 ....115 G8
Dunsford WDN WA8 ....88 A1
Dunsop Av STHEL WA9 ....118 F1
Dunstall Cl MOR/LEA CH46 ....110 A2
Dunstan La EHL/KEN L7 ....113 L5
Dunstan St WAV L15 ....114 A5
Dunster Cl WGNE/HIN WN2 ....80 C4
Dunster Gv HES CH60 ....141 K6
  STHEL WA9 ....118 F1
Dunster Rd STHP PR8 ....35 G5
Durban Rd CLB/OSW/ST L13 ....114 D3
  WAL/NB CH45 ....95 K7
Durden St EHL/KEN L7 ....113 L6
Durham Av NTHTN L30 ....84 C4
  WARR WA1 ....123 G6
Durham Ms East NTHTN L30 * 84 C4
Durham Ms West NTHTN L30 * 84 C4
Durham Rd LITH L21 ....83 G6
  WDN WA8 ....134 D2
  WDN WA8 * 145 M1
Durham St ALL/GAR L19 ....145 M1
  WGN WN1 ....5 L1
Durley Dr CL/PREN CH43 ....127 G4
Durley Rd WLT/FAZ L9 ....84 D7
Durleston Cl WDN WA8 ....133 L3
Durning Rd EHL/KEN L7 ....113 L4
Durrant Rd NG/CROX L11 ....98 A4
Durrell Wy GOL/RIS/CU WA3 ....93 C5
Dursley RAIN/WH L35 ....117 H3
Dursley Dr WARR WA1 ....91 M1
Durston Rd CHLDW L16 ....114 F5
Durweston Wk NTHLY L27 ....115 L7
Dutch Barn Cl CHLY/EC PR7 ....32 D2
Dutton Dr BEB CH63 ....143 H5
Dutton Gn EP CH65 ....21 K9
Dutton St WARR WA1 ....15 G6
Duxbury Cl NTHLY L27 ....116 B8
  RNFD/HAY WA11 ....76 B6
Duxbury Hall Rd CHLY/EC PR7 ....43 M1
Duxford Ct WARRN/WOL WA2 ....122 A4
Dwerryhouse La NG/CROX L11 ....98 D3
Dwerryhouse St TOX L8 ....112 F7
Dyers La ORM L39 ....63 G1
Dyer St GOL/RIS/CU WA3 ....92 B5
Dyke St NPK/KEN L6 ....113 J1
Dykin Cl WDN WA8 ....135 G2
Dykin Rd WDN WA8 ....134 F2
Dymchurch Rd SPK/HALE L24 ...146 D1
Dymoke Rd NG/CROX L11 ....98 E2
Dyson Hall Dr WLT/FAZ L9 ....84 F8
Dyson St ANF/KKDL L4 ....97 H4

E

Eager La MGHL L31 ....61 K5
Eagle Brow LYMM WA13 ....139 M2
Eagle Crs RNFD/HAY WA11 ....76 J3
Eaglehall Rd WLT/FAZ L9 ....98 B1
Eaglehurst Rd WLTN L25 ....131 K1
Eagle La GTS/LS CH66 ....155 M6
Eagle Park Dr
  WARRN/WOL WA2 ....121 J4
Eagles Ct KKBY L32 ....86 A3
Eaglesfield Cl STHEL WA9 * 102 E6
Eagles Wy RUNC WA7 ....150 A7
Ealing Cv CHLYE PR6 ....33 H1
Ealing Rd WARRN/BUR WA5 .....120 C8
  WLT/FAZ L9 ....84 D6
Eamont Av CHTN/BK PR9 ....22 D8
Eanleywood La RUNC WA7 ....150 B6
Eardisley Rd WAV L15 ....114 C7
Earle Cl NEWLW WA12 ....104 E3
Earle Crs NSTN CH64 ....152 F4
Earle Dr NSTN CH64 ....152 F5
Earle Rd EHL/KEN L7 ....113 L5
  WDN WA8 ....16 F9
Earle St NEWLW WA12 ....104 B3
  VAUX/LVPD L3 ....12 C5
Earl Rd BTL L20 ....6 C7
Earl's Cl CSBY/BLUN L23 ....82 F2
Earlsfield Rd WAV L15 ....114 B7
Earls Gdns EP CH65 ....20 A4
Earlston Rd WAL/NB CH45 ....95 J3
Earl St NEWLW WA12 ....104 B3
  STHEL WA9 ....9 M7
  WARRN/WOL WA2 ....14 F1
  WGN WN1 ....68 A3
Earlswood SKEL WN8 ....66 A4
Earlswood Cl MOR/LEA CH46 ....109 K6
Earlwood Gdns RAIN/WH L35 ...117 G3
Earp St ALL/GAR L19 ....130 E4
Easby Cl FMBY L37 ....59 J3
  RUNC WA7 ....19 L4
Easby Rd ANF/KKDL L4 ....96 F6
Easby Wk ANF/KKDL L4 ....96 F6
Easedale Dr STHP PR8 ....47 K1
Easedale Wk NWD/KWIPK L33 ....73 M8
Easenhall Cl STHEL WA9 ....134 D1
Easington Rd STHEL WA9 ....101 M7
East Albert Rd AIG/SPK L17 ......129 K1
East Av GOL/RIS/CU WA3 ....92 D1
  WARRN/WOL WA2 ....121 L5
  WARRS WA4 ....137 M4
  WARRW/BUR WA5 ....136 C1
Eastbank St STHP PR8 ....3 G4
Eastbourne Rd CL/PREN CH43 ...10 C1
  CSBY/WL L22 ....82 D3
  STHP PR8 ....35 J2
  WLT/FAZ L9 ....84 D6
Eastbourne Wk NPK/KEN L6 ....113 J1
Eastbury Cl WDN WA8 ....118 F8
Eastcliffe Rd CLB/OSW/ST L13 ..114 D2
Eastcote Rd AIG/SPK L17 ....130 A5
Eastcott Cl GR/UP/WCH CH49 ...125 L3
Eastcroft NWD/KWIPK L33 ....74 B8
Eastcroft Rd WAL/EC CH44 ....111 J2
Eastdale Rd WARR WA1 ....122 C6
  WAV L15 ....114 B5
East Dam Wood Rd
  SPK/HALE L24 ....147 H4
East Dene SKEL WN8 ....53 K3
Easter St WARRW/BUR WA5 ....120 D3
Eastern Av PS/BROM CH62 ....143 M1
  SPK/HALE L24 ....147 H3
Eastern Dr ALL/GAR L19 ....130 C4

Eastfield Dr AIG/SPK L17 ....129 L2
Eastfield Wk KKBY L32 ....85 L4
East Float BIRK CH41 * 111 H4
Eastford Rd WARRS WA4 ....137 J4
East Front RAIN/WH L35 ....117 G4
Eastgate Rd RUNC WA7 ....136 A8
Eastham Cl CHLDW L16 ....115 H4
Eastham Crs STHEL WA9 ....118 E1
Eastham Gn SPK/HALE L24 ....147 J1
Eastham Ms PS/BROM CH62 .....155 J1
Eastham Rake GTS/LS CH66 .....154 E3
Eastham Village Rd
  PS/BROM CH62 ....144 C8
Eastlake Av EV L5 ....97 H8
East Lancashire Rd ECCL WA10...89 H6
  GOL/RIS/CU WA3 ....92 D7
  NG/CROX L11 ....85 K9
  NG/CROX L11 ....86 B2
  NWD/KWIPK L33 ....86 C7
  RNFD/HAY WA11 ....89 M5
East La RUNC WA7 ....150 B6
  SFTN L29 ....71 K3
East Leigh SKEL WN8 ....65 H3
Eastleigh Dr PEN/TH CH61 ....125 M6
East Mains SPK/HALE L24 ....147 J2
Eastman Rd CLB/OSW/ST L13 ....98 D4
East Md ORM L39 ....62 D4
East Meade MGHL L31 ....72 E3
East Millwood Rd
  SPK/HALE L24 ....147 J1
East Mt WCNW/BIL/O WN5 ....67 H7
East Orchard La WLT/FAZ L9 ......84 F4
East Park Ct WAL/EC CH44 ....112 A2
East Prescot Rd
  DV/KA/FCH L14 ....115 H1
East Rd DV/KA/FCH L14 ....114 E3
  SPK/HALE L24 ....138 D3
East Side STHEL WA9 ....9 M7
East St AIMK WN4 ....91 M1
  BIRK CH41 ....112 A3
  CHTN/BK PR9 ....3 J3
  CSBY/WL L22 ....82 F4
  PR/KW L34 ....101 J2
  VAUX/LVPD L3 ....12 E5
  WDN WA8 ....17 J1
East Ter CHLYE PR6 ....32 A1
East Vw WARRS WA4 ....138 D3
Eastview Cl CL/PREN CH43 ....126 F1
East Wy CHLYE PR6 ....32 F5
Eastway GR/UP/WCH CH49 ......110 A4
  GTS/LS CH66 ....155 M6
  MGHL L31 ....72 F3
  MOR/LEA CH46 ....110 A4
  WDN WA8 ....133 M4
Eastwell Rd AIMK WN4 ....91 J2
  WARRW/ST WN6 ....68 B2
Eastwood AIG/SPK L17 ....129 J2
  RUNC WA7 ....19 L5
Eastwood Av NEWLW WA12 ......105 H2
Eastwood Gv LEIGH WN7 ....81 L8
Eastwood Rd
  WARRW/BUR WA5 ....104 B6
  WGNS/IIMK WN3 ....4 C5
Eaton Av LITH L21 ....83 K6
  WAL/EC CH44 ....111 J4
Eaton Cl HUY L36 ....115 L3
  WD/CROXPK L12 ....98 C6
Eaton Gdns WD/CROXPK L12 .....98 C6
Eaton Rd ALL/GAR L19 ....130 C2
  CL/PREN CH43 ....10 D7
  ECCL WA10 ....8 C3
  MGHL L31 ....72 F7
  WD/CROXPK L12 ....98 C6
  WKBY CH48 ....124 C4
Eaton Rd North
  WD/CROXPK L12 ....98 C6
Eaton St PR/KW L34 ....100 F7
  RUNC WA7 ....19 G4
  VAUX/LVPD L3 ....12 D3
  WAL/EC CH44 ....111 K1
Eaves Brow Rd
  WARRW/BUR WA5 ....106 D6
Eavesdale SKEL WN8 ....66 A5
Eaves Green Rd CHLY/EC PR7 ....32 D8
Eaves La CHLYE PR6 ....33 G6
  STHEL WA9 ....102 F7
Ebenezer Howard Rd LITH L21....83 L7
Ebenezer Rd EHL/KEN L7 ....113 L3
Ebenezer St RF/TRAN CH42 .....128 C3
  RNFD/HAY WA11 ....90 B7
Eberle St CLVP L2 ....12 F7
Ebony Cl WARR CH46 * 109 K5
Ebony Wy NWD/KWIPK L33 ....74 A8
Ebor La EV L5 ....13 J2
Ebrington St ALL/GAR L19 ....130 E7
Eccesall Av LITH L21 ....83 L5
Eccles Dr WLTN L25 ....115 K6
Ecclesfield Rd ECCL WA10 ....88 C5
Ecclesfield Rd CLB/OSW/ST L13 ..98 E7
Eccles Gn FMBY L37 ....58 F4
Eccleshall Rd PS/BROM CH62 ...128 E7
Eccles Rd FMBY L37 ....58 F4
  PS/BROM CH62 ....128 D6
  WLTN L25 ....113 M6
Eccles's La ORM L39 * 63 L8
Eccleston Av CTS/LS CH66 ....156 A8
  PS/BROM CH62 ....143 L4
Eccleston Cl CL/PREN CH43 .....127 H2
  GOL/RIS/CU WA3 ....122 K1
Eccleston Dr RUNC WA7 ....19 M6
Eccleston Gdns WLT/FAZ L9 ......84 B7
Eccleston Rd WLT/FAZ L9 ....84 B7
Eccleston St ECCL WA10 ....8 C5
  PR/KW L34 ....100 F7
Eccleston St EP CH65 ....20 C2
  RUNC WA7 ....18 F2
  STHEL WA9 ....102 F4
  TOX L8 ....113 H6
  WAL/NB CH45 ....95 K5
  WARR WA1 ....137 H5
  WARRS WA4 ....137 H5
  WGNE/HIN WN2 ....80 D6
Egerton Whf BIRK CH41 ....11 K3
Eglington Av RAIN/WH L35 ....116 F3
Egremont Cl NTHLY L27 ....132 C1
Egremont Lawn NTHLY L27 ....132 C1
Egremont Prom WAL/EC CH44 ....95 M7
Egypt St WARR WA1 ....14 C4
  WDN WA8 ....16 B5
Eighth Av WLT/FAZ L9 ....84 B7
Eilian Gv DV/KA/FCH L14 ....114 F3
Eisenhower Cl
  WARRW/BUR WA5 ....120 D8
Elaine Cl AIMK WN4 ....91 J3
  GTS/LS CH66 ....162 E1
  WDN WA8 ....133 K3
Elaine St TOX L8 ....13 H7
  WARR WA1 ....15 K2
Elbow La FMBY L37 ....59 H2
Elbow St CHLY/EC PR7 ....32 E6
Elcombe Av GOL/RIS/CU WA3 .....93 C6
Elderberry Cl WGN WN1 ....68 C2
Elderdale Rd ANF/KKDL L4 ....97 K6
Elder Gdns ALL/GAR L19 ....130 D5
Elder Gv WKBY CH48 ....124 D3
Eldersfield Rd NG/CROX L11 .....98 D5
Elderswood Rd RAIN/WH L35 ...117 L3
Elderwood Rd RF/TRAN CH42 ...128 F2
Eldon Cl ECCL WA10 ....8 C7
Eldon Gdns AIMK WN4 ....79 J7
Eldonian Wy VAUX/LVPD L3 ....12 C2
Eldon Pl VAUX/LVPD L3 ....12 C2
Eldon Rd RF/TRAN CH42 ....128 B3
  WAL/EC CH44 ....111 K1

Eldons Cft STHP PR8 ....34 F8
Eldon St CHLYE PR6 ....32 F6
  ECCL WA10 ....8 C7
  LEIGH WN7 ....81 M7
  VAUX/LVPD L3 ....12 C2
  WARR WA1 ....15 H5
Eldon Ter NSTN CH64 ....153 G6
Eldred Rd CHLDW L16 ....114 F7
Eleanor Pk CL/PREN CH43 ....110 E5
Eleanor Rd BTL L20 ....83 M7
  CL/PREN CH43 ....110 E5
  MOR/LEA CH46 ....109 L4
Eleanor St BTL L20 ....6 F9
  EP CH65 ....20 D2
  WDN WA8 ....16 D6
  WGNS/IIMK WN3 ....4 D9
Elephant La STHEL WA9 ....101 M6
Elfet St BIRK CH41 ....111 H5
Elgar Av PS/BROM CH62 ....144 A8
Elgar Cl EP CH65 ....163 H2
Elgar Rd DV/KA/FCH L14 ....99 H8
Elgin Av AIMK WN4 ....90 F1
  WARRS WA4 ....137 J3
Elgin Cl WGNE/HIN WN2 ....69 J5
Elgin Ct RAIN/WH L35 * 117 M3
Elgin Dr WAL/NB CH45 ....95 L7
Elgin Wy BIRK CH41 ....11 K4
Eliot Cl PS/BROM CH62 ....128 C6
Eliot Dr WGNS/IIMK WN3 ....68 C3
Eliot St BTL L20 ....83 K8
Elizabethan Dr WGNS/IIMK WN3 .80 A3
Elizabeth Av STHP PR8 ....35 G7
  WGNE/HIN WN2 ....81 G4
Elizabeth Ct WDN WA8 ....16 E6
Elizabeth Dr WARR WA1 ....122 C6
Elizabeth Rd AIN/FAZ L10 ....85 K6
  BTL L20 ....83 M7
  HUY L36 ....116 C4
  RNFD/HAY WA11 ....91 J6
Elizabeth St CL/PREN CH43 ....105 G5
  STHEL WA9 ....118 F2
  VAUX/LVPD L3 * 13 L4
  WGNE/HIN WN2 ....69 J5
Elizabeth Ter WDN WA8 ....133 M4
Eliza St STHEL WA9 ....103 H6
Elkan Cl WDN WA8 ....135 G4
Elkan Rd WDN WA8 ....134 F2
Elkstone Cl WGNS/IIMK WN3 .....78 E3
Elkstone Rd NG/CROX L11 ....98 D4
Elkwood Cl WKBY CH48 ....88 D1
Ellaby Rd RAIN/WH L35 ....117 L1
Ellamsbridge Rd STHEL WA9 .....103 G6
Elland Dr GTS/LS CH66 ....155 L6
Ellel Gv NPK/KEN L6 ....97 L8
Ellen Gdn STHEL WA9 ....103 G6
Ellen's La BEB CH63 ....128 C8
Ellen St STHEL WA9 ....103 G6
  WARRW/BUR WA5 ....14 B2
  WGN WN1 ....5 J5
Elleray Dr TOX L8 ....129 H1
Elleray Park Rd WAL/NB CH45 ....95 J6
Eller Brook Cl CHLYE PR6 ....44 B4
Ellerbrook Dr BRSC L40 ....42 D2
Ellerbrook Wy ORM L39 ....51 G7
Ellerby Cl RUNC WA7 ....151 G6
Ellergreen Rd NG/CROX L11 ....98 D3
Ellerman Rd VAUX/LVPD L3 ......129 H2
Ellerslie Av RAIN/WH L35 ....101 L4
Ellerslie Rd CLB/OSW/ST L13 .....97 M7
Ellerton Cl GTS/LS CH66 ....155 L8
Ellerton Cl WDN WA8 ....133 M2
Ellerton Wy WD/CROXPK L12 .....99 G5
Ellesmere Av AIN/FAZ L10 ....84 G3
Ellesmere Gv WAL/NB CH45 ....95 K7
Ellesmere Rd AIMK WN4 ....79 J5
  GOL/RIS/CU WA3 ....107 G1
  WGNW/BIL/O WN5 ....67 M7
Ellesmere St RUNC WA7 ....19 J3
  WARR WA1 ....15 H6
Ellesworth Cl
  WARRW/BUR WA5 ....120 E5
Elliot St CLVPS L1 ....13 H7
  ECCL WA10 ....8 C5
  WDN WA8 ....16 E3
Elliott Av GOL/RIS/CU WA3 ....92 D4
  WARR WA1 ....15 L2
Elliott Dr WGNE/HIN WN2 ....69 M6
Ellis Ashton St HUY L36 ....116 C3
Ellis La FROD/HEL WA6 ....160 F4
Ellison Dr ECCL WA10 ....101 L1
Ellison Gv HUY L36 ....115 M3
Ellison St CLB/OSW/ST L13 ......114 B1
  WARRS WA4 ....137 M4
Ellis Pl TOX L8 ....113 H8
Ellis Rd WGNW/BIL/O WN5 ....89 M1
Ellis St WDN WA8 ....16 B6
  WGN WN1 ....5 J5
Elon Av RAIN/WH L35 ....117 M3
Elloway Rd SPK/HALE L24 ....147 J2
Ellwood Cl SPK/HALE L24 ....148 A5
Elmar Rd AIG/SPK L17 ....130 A3
Elm Av AIMK WN4 ....78 E4
  CSBY/BLUN L23 ....71 L8
  GOL/RIS/CU WA3 ....92 C4
  GR/UP/WCH CH49 ....109 M7
  WDN WA8 ....134 D3
  WGNNW/ST WN6 ....56 A7
  WGNW/BIL/O WN5 ....68 A7
Elm Bank EV L5 ....97 H6
Elmbank Rd CALD/MH L18 ....114 A8
  PS/BROM CH62 ....128 D7
Elmbank St WAL/EC CH44 * 111 L2
Elm Cl PEN/TH CH61 ....141 H1
  WD/CROXPK L12 ....99 H2
Elm Cft WGN WN1 ....68 D1
Elmcroft Cl WLT/FAZ L9 ....84 F6
Elmcroft La HTWN L38 ....70 C2
Elmdale Cl FMBY L37 ....58 F3
Elmdale Rd WLT/FAZ L9 ....97 J1
Elmdene Ct
  GR/UP/WCH CH49 * 125 L3
Elm Dr FMBY L37 ....58 F4
  GR/UP/WCH CH49 ....125 L2
  LITH L21 ....83 H7
  WGNW/BIL/O WN5 ....77 M8
Elmers Gn SKEL WN8 ....65 M4
Elmer's Green La SKEL WN8 ....65 L1
Elmers Wood Rd SKEL WN8 ....65 M4
Elmfield WGNNW/ST WN6 ....56 A3
Elmfield Cl STHEL WA9 ....102 A5
  WLT/FAZ L9 ....84 D8
Elm Gdns LITH L21 * 83 J7
  RNFD/HAY WA11 ....76 B7
Elm Gv CHLYE PR6 ....33 G2
  EHL/KEN L7 ....113 J4
  GTS/LS CH66 ....163 J4
  HOY CH47 ....108 D2
  PR/KW L34 ....101 J6
  RF/TRAN CH42 ....11 H9
  SKEL WN8 ....65 G4
  WARR WA1 ....82 B6
  WDN WA8 ....16 E1
Elm Hall Dr CALD/MH L18 ....114 C8
Elmham Crs AIN/FAZ L10 ....85 H6
Elm House Ms WLTN L25 ....131 K1
Elmhow Gv WGNS/IIMK WN3 ......79 J3
Elmhurst Rd WLTN L25 ....115 J6

Elmore Cl EV L5 97 H8
RUNC WA7 150 F4
Elm Park Dr STHP PR8 35 G8
Elm Park Rd WAL/NB CH45 95 J6
Elm Pl ORM L39 63 G1
Elmridge SKEL WN8 65 M5
Elm Ri FROD/HEL WA6 160 E6
Elm Rd ANF/KKDL L4 97 J4
BEB CH63 128 B6
BRSC L40 52 A2
ECCL WA10 101 M5
KKBY L32 85 M2
LITH L21 83 H7
NSTN CH64 154 B5
PEN/TH CH61 126 B7
RF/TRAN CH42 127 M2
RNFD/HAY WA11 * 91 G6
RUNC WA7 19 M7
STHP PR8 3 G9
WARRN/WOL WA2 121 K1
WARRW/BUR WA5 136 B2
WGNE/HIN WN2 80 E6
Elm Rd North RF/TRAN CH42 127 K5
Elmsbury St AIMK WN4 79 H8
Elmsdale Rd CALD/MH L18 114 C8
Elmsett Cl WARRW/BUR WA5 120 A8
Elmsfield Cl WLTN L25 115 J8
Elmsfield Pk ORM L39 62 C7
Elmsfield Rd CSBY/BLUN L23 71 K7
Elms House Rd
CLB/OSW/ST L13 114 B2
Elmsley Rd CALD/MH L18 130 B2
Elms Rd MGHL L31 72 E7
Elm St EP CH65 156 E6
Elmstead SKEL WN8 65 M5
The Elms GOL/RIS/CU WA3 93 H6
MGHL L31 72 F2
RUNC WA7 18 F6
TOX L8 129 J1
Elm St BIRK CH41 11 H5
HUY L36 116 C3
WGNE/HIN WN2 80 C3
Elmswood Av RAIN/WH L35 117 M3
Elmswood Ct CALD/MH L18 * 130 B2
Elmswood Gv HUY L36 115 K2
Elmswood Rd AIG/SPK L17 130 A3
RF/TRAN CH42 127 L1
WAL/EG CH44 111 M1
Elm Ter EHL/KEN L7 * 113 L3
HOY CH47 108 E6
Elm Tree Av LYMM WA13 139 M3
WARR WA1 122 B5
Elmtree Cl WD/CROXPK L12 98 E6
Elmtree Gv CL/PREN CH43 111 M8
Elm Tree Rd GOL/RIS/CU WA3 93 H6
LYMM WA13 139 M3
Elmure Av BEB CH63 127 M8
Elm V NPK/KEN L6 113 M2
Elmway Cl CLB/OSW/ST L13 114 B3
Elmwood CHLY/EC PR7 32 D4
RUNC WA7 150 E4
SKEL WN8 65 L2
Elmwood Av AIMK WN4 91 J3
CSBY/BLUN L23 83 H1
WARR WA1 15 L2
Elmwood Dr PEN/TH CH61 141 H3
Elnup Av WGNNW/ST WN6 55 K7
Elphin Gv ANF/KKDL L4 97 J4
Elsbeck Gv STHEL WA9 102 F7
Elsie Rd ANF/KKDL L4 97 K7
Elsmere Av AIG/SPK L17 129 L2
Elson Rd FMBY L37 58 F4
Elstead Gv AIMK WN4 90 F1
Elstead Rd KKBY L32 85 L4
WLT/FAZ L9 98 A1
Elston Av NEWLW WA12 91 K8
Elstow St EV L5 96 F6
Elstree Rd NPK/KEN L6 113 M2
Elswick SKEL WN8 65 L5
Elswick Rd CHTN/BK PR9 25 H1
Elswick St TOX L8 129 H2
Elsworth Cl FMBY L37 58 E5
Eltham Av LITH L21 83 K4
Eltham Cl AIMK WN4 91 M2
GR/UP/WCH CH49 126 D3
WDN WA8 135 G2
Eltham Gn GR/UP/WCH CH49 126 C3
Eltham St EHL/KEN L7 113 M3
Elton Av CSBY/BLUN L23 82 E1
NTHTN L30 84 A2
Elton Cl GOL/RIS/CU WA3 93 G6
GOL/RIS/CU WA3 122 E1
PS/BROM CH62 155 G2
Elton Dr BEB CH63 143 J3
Elton Head Rd STHEL WA9 101 M8
Elton La FROD/HEL WA6 166 A1
Elton Lordship La
FROD/HEL WA6 159 J6
Elton St ANF/KKDL L4 97 H3
Elvington Cl RUNC WA7 161 H2
WGNW/BIL/O WN5 67 K4
Elvington Rd HTWN L38 70 C3
Elway Rd AIMK WN4 91 L2
Elwick Dr NG/CROX L11 98 E3
Elwood Cl NWD/KWIPK L33 74 A7
Elworth Av WDN WA8 118 C8
Elworthy Av HLWD L26 132 B4
Elworthy Gv WGN WN1 69 G3
Elwyn Dr HLWD L26 132 C5
Elwyn Rd HOY CH47 109 G4
Elwy St TOX L8 113 J8
Ely Av MOR/LEA CH46 109 L5
Ely Cl GTS/LS CH66 163 G5
NTHTN L30 84 B4
Ely Ms CHTN/BK PR9 25 J3
Ely Pk RUNC WA7 151 G3
Ember Crs NPK/KEN L6 13 M1
Embledon St TOX L8 113 K6
Embleton Ct RUNC WA7 149 M8
Emerald Cl NTHTN L30 84 D2
Emerald St TOX L8 129 H2
WGNNW/ST WN6 68 C2
Emerson Cl HTWN L38 70 C1
Emerson St TOX L8 113 H6
Emery St ANF/KKDL L4 97 H4
Emily St STHEL WA9 101 L6
WDN WA8 16 D5
Emlyn St STHEL WA9 102 F4
WGNE/HIN WN2 69 L8
Emmanuel Rd CHTN/BK PR9 25 H3
Emmett St STHEL WA9 102 E4
Empire Rd LITH L21 83 K7
Empress Cl MGHL L31 72 D4
Empress Rd EHL/KEN L7 113 K3
NPK/KEN L6 97 L7
WAL/EG CH44 111 L1
Empress Wy CHLY/EC PR7 32 A3
Emslie Ct NSTN CH64 152 E5
Ena Crs LEIGH WN7 81 L6
Endborne Rd WLT/FAZ L9 84 C7
Endbutt La CSBY/BLUN L23 83 G2
Enderby Av RNFD/HAY WA11 89 L7
Endfield Pk ALL/GAR L19 130 D5
Endmoor Rd HUY L36 99 L8
Endsleigh Rd CLB/OSW/ST L13 114 A2
CSBY/WL L22 82 D3
Enerby Cl CL/PREN CH43 110 E6
Enfield Av CSBY/BLUN L23 83 G1
Enfield Cl CHLY/EC PR7 30 E7
Enfield Park Rd
WARRN/WOL WA2 122 A1
Enfield Rd CLB/OSW/ST L13 114 D3
EP CH65 20 B4
Enfield St ECCL WA10 8 C7
WGNW/BIL/O WN5 67 L8
Enfield Ter CL/PREN CH43 10 D8
Enford Dr STHEL WA9 102 F6
Engineer St WGNE/HIN WN2 69 J6
Engine La FMBY L37 59 M6
Enid Pl WGNE/HIN WN2 80 B5
Enid St TOX L8 113 H7
Ennerdale SKEL WN8 65 M5
Ennerdale Av AIMK WN4 79 K8
MGHL L31 73 G3
PS/BROM CH62 155 H1
RNFD/HAY WA11 89 K5
WARRN/WOL WA2 121 K2
Ennerdale Cl FMBY L37 58 F2
NWD/KWIPK L33 73 M8
Ennerdale Dr FROD/HEL WA6 160 E5
NTHTN L30 83 M5
ORM L39 62 D3
Ennerdale Pl WGNE/HIN WN2 69 K5
Ennerdale Rd CHLY/EC PR7 32 C7
CL/PREN CH43 127 G4
FMBY L37 58 F2
WAL/NB CH45 95 H5
WLT/FAZ L9 84 F7
Ennerdale St VAUX/LVPD L3 13 G2
Ennis Cl SPK/HALE L24 147 M3
Ennisdale Dr WKBY CH48 124 F3
Ennismore Rd CLB/OSW/ST L13 114 B2
CSBY/BLUN L23 70 E8
Ennis Rd WD/CROXPK L12 99 G7
Ensor St BTL L20 6 F9
Enstone SKEL WN8 65 M4
Enstone Av LITH L21 83 J4
Enstone Rd WLTN L25 131 K7
Ensworth Rd CALD/MH L18 114 D8
Enterprise Wy WAV L15 114 A4
Enville St WARRS WA4 15 G8
Envoy Cl WGNW/BIL/O WN5 68 A4
Ephraim's Fold WGNE/HIN WN2 57 M7
Epping Av STHEL WA9 118 D2
Epping Cl RAIN/WH L35 117 M3
Epping Ct HES CH60 141 J4
Epping Dr WARR WA1 122 F5
Epping Gv WAV L15 114 D7
Epping Pl CHLYE PR6 32 F5
Epsom Cl CHLYE PR6 33 H1
WLT/FAZ L9 85 G4
Epsom Cft CHLYE PR6 44 E6
Epsom Dr WGNE/HIN WN2 80 B6
Epsom Gdns WARRS WA4 138 A6
Epsom Gv NWD/KWIPK L33 74 C7
Epsom Rd MOR/LEA CH46 110 B2
Epsom St STHEL WA9 103 H1
Epsom Wy EV L5 96 F8
Epstein Ct NPK/KEN L6 113 K2
Epworth Cl CL/PREN CH43 10 B6
Epworth Gra CL/PREN CH43 * 10 B6
Epworth St NPK/KEN L6 13 M5
Eremon Cl WLT/FAZ L9 84 F5
Erfurt Av BEB CH63 143 J1
Erica Ct HES CH60 141 H6
Eric Av WARR WA1 122 A5
Eric Fountain Rd EP CH65 155 M2
Eric Gv WAL/EG CH44 111 J1
Eric Rd WAL/EG CH44 111 J1
Eric St WDN WA8 17 G1
Eridge St TOX L8 129 J1
Erin Cl TOX L8 113 G8
Erindale Crs FROD/HEL WA6 160 C7
Erl St WLT/FAZ L9 84 E8
Ermine Crs EV L5 97 H8
Erradale Crs WGNS/IIMK WN3 78 F3
Errington Av EP CH65 20 C2
Errington Ct AIG/SPK L17 130 A5
Errington St EV L5 96 D7
Errol St AIG/SPK L17 129 K2
Erskine Cl RNFD/HAY WA11 90 A7
Erskine Pl WGNE/HIN WN2 80 D4
Erskine Rd CHLYE PR6 33 G4
WAL/EG CH44 111 L2
Erskine St NPK/KEN L6 13 M5
Erwood St WARRN/WOL WA2 14 D3
Erylmore Rd CALD/MH L18 130 C4
Escolme Dr GR/UP/WCH CH49 126 A2
Escor Rd WLTN L25 115 H7
Escort Cl WLTN L25 131 L5
Eshelby Cl CSBY/WL L22 83 G4
Esher Cl CL/PREN CH43 110 E6
Eshe Rd CSBY/BLUN L23 82 E1
Eshe Rd North CSBY/BLUN L23 82 E1
Esher Rd NPK/KEN L6 113 L2
PS/BROM CH62 128 D5
Eskbank SKEL WN8 65 L5
Eskbrook SKEL WN8 65 L4
Eskburn Rd CLB/OSW/ST L13 98 A7
Eskdale EP CH65 20 A9
SKEL WN8 65 K5
Eskdale Av ORM L39 62 E3
PS/BROM CH62 144 A8
RNFD/HAY WA11 89 K5
WGN WN1 68 D2
Eskdale Cl FMBY L37 58 F3
RUNC WA7 149 M8
Eskdale Dr FMBY L37 58 F3
MGHL L31 72 F3
Eskdale Rd AIMK WN4 79 K8
WLT/FAZ L9 84 C7
Esk St BTL L20 96 D5
Eslington St ALL/GAR L19 130 C6
Esmond St NPK/KEN L6 97 K8
Esonwood Rd RAIN/WH L35 116 F2
Espin St ANF/KKDL L4 97 H4
Esplanade STHP PR8 2 B6
Esplen Av CSBY/BLUN L23 71 H8
Essex Rd HUY L36 116 C1
STHP PR8 35 J5
WGN WN1 56 D5
WKBY CH48 124 E2
Essex St TOX L8 113 H8
WGN WN1 5 J2
Essex Wy BTL L20 7 J3
Esther St WDN WA8 16 F2
Esthwaite Av RNFD/HAY WA11 89 L5
Estuary Banks SPK/HALE L24 146 B1
Estuary Bvd SPK/HALE L24 146 B1
Etal Cl NG/CROX L11 98 D4
Ethelbert Rd HOY CH47 108 E5
Ethel Rd WAL/EG CH44 111 M2
Etna St CLB/OSW/ST L13 114 B2
Eton Ct CALD/MH L18 114 F8
Eton Dr AIN/FAZ L10 84 E3
BEB CH63 142 B7
Eton Hall Dr STHEL WA9 102 E6
Eton Rd EP CH65 20 E7
Eton St ANF/KKDL L4 97 H4
Eton Ter WGNS/IIMK WN3 5 J9
Eton Wy WGNW/BIL/O WN5 67 H5
Etruria St ALL/GAR L19 145 L1
Etruscan Rd CLB/OSW/ST L13 114 C1
Ettington Dr STHP PR8 34 C8
Ettington Rd ANF/KKDL L4 97 K6
Ettrick Cl NWD/KWIPK L33 73 M7
Euclid Av WARRS WA4 138 D3
Eurolink STHEL WA9 118 B1
Europa Bvd BIRK CH41 11 J5
WARRW/BUR WA5 120 F2
Europa Wy EP CH65 20 D3
Eustace St WARRN/WOL WA2 14 C4
Euston Gv CL/PREN CH43 10 E8
Euston St ANF/KKDL L4 97 H3
Euxton Hall Gdns CHLY/EC PR7 31 L3
Euxton La CHLY/EC PR7 31 M1
Evans Cl RNFD/HAY WA11 91 H6
Evans Pl WARRS WA4 15 K9
Evans Rd HOY CH47 108 D6
SPK/HALE L24 131 L8
Evans St PR/KW L34 100 F6
Eva St LEIGH WN7 81 L6
Evellynne Cl KKBY L32 85 L3
Evelyn Av PR/KW L34 101 G7
STHEL WA9 103 G2
Evelyn Rd WAL/EG CH44 111 L2
Evelyn St WARRW/BUR WA5 136 F1
Evenwood SKEL WN8 65 M4
STHEL WA9 102 E7
Evenwood Ct SKEL WN8 * 65 L4
Everard Cl BRSC L40 37 H6
Everard Rd STHP PR8 3 M9
Everdon Wd NWD/KWIPK L33 86 A2
Evered Av WLT/FAZ L9 97 J1
Everest Cl GTS/LS CH66 163 H2
Everest Pl WGN WN1 68 E3
Everest Rd CSBY/BLUN L23 82 F1
RF/TRAN CH42 127 M3
Evergreen Cl CHLY/EC PR7 32 D8
GR/UP/WCH CH49 109 M7
NTHLY L27 116 A7
The Evergreens FMBY L37 58 F1
Evergreen Wy STHEL WA9 103 J6
Everite Rd WDN WA8 133 K6
Everleigh Cl CL/PREN CH43 110 D6
Eversham Cl CHTN/BK PR9 23 J8
Eversleigh Dr BEB CH63 143 J1
Eversley SKEL WN8 65 M4
WDN WA8 133 K3
Eversley Cl FROD/HEL WA6 160 E7
WARRS WA4 138 B8
Eversley Pk CL/PREN CH43 * 127 K2
Eversley St TOX L8 113 J7
Everton Brow VAUX/LVPD L3 13 K3
Everton Gv RNFD/HAY WA11 89 M8
Everton Rd NPK/KEN L6 13 M2
STHP PR8 35 J1
Everton St AIMK WN4 78 F8
Everton Ter EV L5 13 L1
Everton Va ANF/KKDL L4 97 G6
Everton Vw BTL L20 6 E6
Every St NPK/KEN L6 113 K1
Evesham Cl LEIGH WN7 93 M4
WARRS WA4 137 L5
WLTN L25 131 H3
Evesham Rd ANF/KKDL L4 97 M4
WAL/NB CH45 95 H7
Evington SKEL WN8 65 M4
Ewanville HUY L36 116 A4
Ewart Rd CHLDW L16 115 J5
LITH L21 83 H6
RNFD/HAY WA11 89 K7
Ewden Cl CHLDW L16 115 G6
Ewell Cl CHLYE PR6 33 H1
Ewloe Ct EP CH65 163 M3
Exchange Pas West CLVP L2 * 12 E6
Exchange Pl RAIN/WH L35 117 L2
Exchange St ECCL WA10 9 G6
Exchange St East CLVP L2 12 E6
Exeley RAIN/WH L35 117 G3
Exeter Cl WLT/FAZ L9 85 G4
Exeter Dr WGNE/HIN WN2 57 M8
Exeter Rd BTL L20 7 G7
EP CH65 20 C4
WAL/EG CH44 95 L8
Exeter St ECCL WA10 8 B5
Exford Av WGNS/IIMK WN3 79 K1
Exford Rd WD/CROXPK L12 98 F5
Exmoor Cl CHTN/BK PR9 22 D7
PEN/TH CH61 126 B8
Exmouth Cl BIRK CH41 11 G5
Exmouth Crs RUNC WA7 151 G7
Exmouth Gdns BIRK CH41 11 G5
Exmouth St BIRK CH41 11 G6
Exmouth Wy BIRK CH41 11 G5
WARRW/BUR WA5 104 B7
Extension Vw STHEL WA9 102 F5
Eyes La CROS/BRETH PR26 28 F2

F

Factory Brow HOR/BR BL6 57 M2
Factory Fold WGNE/HIN WN2 * 69 J6
Factory La CHLYE PR6 44 D5
WARR WA1 14 C7
WDN WA8 134 D2
Factory Rw ECCL WA10 8 C9
Faggy La WGNS/IIMK WN3 4 F6
Fairacre Rd ALL/GAR L19 130 C6
Fairacres WGNNW/ST WN6 55 K4
Fairacres Rd BEB CH63 143 H1
Fairbairn Rd CSBY/WL L22 83 G4
Fairbank St WAV L15 114 A6
Fairbeech Ct CL/PREN CH43 110 E6
Fairbeech Ms CL/PREN CH43 * 110 E6
Fairbourne Av WGNS/IIMK WN3 79 J1
Fairbourne Cl
WARRW/BUR WA5 121 G2
Fairbrook Dr BIRK CH41 110 F4
Fairbrother Crs
WARRN/WOL WA2 121 M3
Fairburn SKEL WN8 65 K2
Fairburn Cl WDN WA8 135 G2
Fairburn Rd CLB/OSW/ST L13 98 A7
Fairclough Av WARR WA1 15 G7
Fairclough Crs RNFD/HAY WA11 90 C7
Fairclough La CL/PREN CH43 127 K1
Fairclough Rd ECCL WA10 101 L1
HUY L36 115 L1
RAIN/WH L35 117 K2
Fairclough St CLVPS L1 13 H8
NEWLW WA12 104 D2
WARRW/BUR WA5 104 A7
WGN WN1 5 G5
WGNE/HIN WN2 69 M7
Fairfax Dr RUNC WA7 149 M3
Fairfax Pl NG/CROX L11 97 M3
Fairfax Rd NG/CROX L11 98 A3
RF/TRAN CH42 128 A1
Fairfield CSBY/BLUN L23 83 G1
Fairfield Av DV/KA/FCH L14 115 J3
EP CH65 163 J3
WGNE/HIN WN2 80 C3
WGNW/BIL/O WN5 67 M8
Fairfield Cl HUY L36 115 J3
ORM L39 51 G6
Fairfield Crs HUY L36 115 J3
MOR/LEA CH46 109 M5
NPK/KEN L6 113 M2
Fairfield Dr ORM L39 51 G6
WKBY CH48 125 G2
Fairfield Gdns RNFD/HAY WA11 89 G3
WARRS WA4 138 A3
Fairfield Rd ECCL WA10 89 E8
RF/TRAN CH42 128 A3
STHP PR8 34 E7
WARRS WA4 137 M3
WDN WA8 16 E1
Fairfield St EHL/KEN L7 114 A2
WARR WA1 15 H3
WGNW/BIL/O WN5 67 L8
Fairford Crs DV/KA/FCH L14 114 D1
Fairford Rd DV/KA/FCH L14 114 D1
Fairhaven NWD/KWIPK L33 74 A8
SKEL WN8 65 K2
Fairhaven Cl RF/TRAN CH42 128 B3
WARRW/BUR WA5 136 D1
Fairhaven Dr BEB CH63 143 L8
Fairhaven Rd CHTN/BK PR9 25 K1
WDN WA8 134 E3
Fairholme Av AIMK WN4 91 K1
NSTN CH64 152 F4
PR/KW L34 101 J7
Fairholme Cl WD/CROXPK L12 98 C5
Fairholme Rd CSBY/BLUN L23 83 G1
Fairhurst Av WGNNW/ST WN6 55 M2
Fairhurst's Dr SKEL WN8 53 K3
Fairhurst St WGNS/IIMK WN3 4 C4
Fairhurst Ter PR/KW L34 * 101 G7
Fair Isle Cl EP CH65 163 L4
Fairlawn Cl BEB CH63 143 J7
Fairlawne Cl NWD/KWIPK L33 74 A8
Fairlie SKEL WN8 65 L2
Fairlie Crs BTL L20 83 M6
Fairlie Dr RAIN/WH L35 117 M3
Fairmead Rd MOR/LEA CH46 110 A4
NG/CROX L11 98 A3
Fairoak Cl CL/PREN CH43 110 E6
Fairoak Ms CL/PREN CH43 * 110 E6
Fairstead SKEL WN8 65 L2
Fairview BIRK CH41 128 A1
Fair Vw WGNW/BIL/O WN5 77 M8
Fairview Av WAL/NB CH45 95 J8
Fair View Av WGNW/BIL/O WN5 77 M8
Fairview Cl AIMK WN4 91 K1
CL/PREN CH43 127 K2
Fair View Pl TOX L8 * 129 J1
Fairview Rd CL/PREN CH43 127 K2
GTS/LS CH66 163 J3
Fairview Wy PEN/TH CH61 141 H2
Fairway CHLY/EC PR7 32 E3
CHTN/BK PR9 24 E3
Fair Wy ECCL WA10 88 D8
Fairway HUY L36 116 C1
Fairway Crs PS/BROM CH62 143 M1
Fairway North PS/BROM CH62 143 M1
Fairways CL/PREN CH43 127 K5
CSBY/BLUN L23 70 F8
FROD/HEL WA6 160 C7
WARRS WA4 137 M8
Fairways Cl WLTN L25 131 K5
Fairways Ct FMBY L37 46 E8
Fairways Dr GTS/LS CH66 155 M6
Fairway South PS/BROM CH62 143 M2
The Fairways AIMK WN4 90 F3
SKEL WN8 65 M2
The Fairway WD/CROXPK L12 114 F1
Faith St LEIGH WN7 81 L8
Falcondale Rd
WARRN/WOL WA2 105 K7
Falconers Gn
WARRW/BUR WA5 120 D3
WGNS/IIMK WN3 68 D8
Falconer St BTL L20 83 J7
Falconhall Rd WLT/FAZ L9 98 B1
Falcon Hey AIN/FAZ L10 85 J7
Falcon Rd GTS/LS CH66 163 H2
RF/TRAN CH42 110 E8
Falcons Wy RUNC WA7 150 A7
Falconwood Cl WGNNW/ST WN6 4 B2
Falkirk Dr WGNE/HIN WN2 69 J5
Falkirk Gv WGNW/BIL/O WN5 67 L6
Falkland SKEL WN8 65 L2
Falkland Dr AIMK WN4 90 E1
Falkland Rd STHP PR8 3 L9
WAL/EG CH44 111 M1
Falklands Ap NG/CROX L11 98 A3
Falkland St BIRK CH41 10 A2
VAUX/LVPD L3 13 L5
Falkner Sq TOX L8 113 J6
Falkner St TOX L8 113 H5
Fallbrook Dr WD/CROXPK L12 98 D5
Fallow Cl STHEL WA9 118 E1
Fallowfield NWD/KWIPK L33 74 A8
RUNC WA7 149 M4
Fallowfield Gv
WARRN/WOL WA2 122 D4
Fallowfield Rd WAV L15 114 B7
Fallows Wy RAIN/WH L35 116 E4
Falmouth Dr WARRW/BUR WA5 136 A2
Falmouth Pl RUNC WA7 151 G7
Falmouth Rd NG/CROX L11 85 L8
Falstaff St BTL L20 96 E5
Falstone Cl GOL/RIS/CU WA3 107 K7
WGNS/IIMK WN3 78 F3
Falstone Dr RUNC WA7 151 G5
Fanner's La KNUT WA16 139 L8
Faraday Cl WGNNW/ST WN6 4 A4
Faraday Rd CLB/OSW/ST L13 114 A4
EP CH65 163 J1
NWD/KWIPK L33 86 D6
Faraday St EV L5 97 J8
GOL/RIS/CU WA3 107 G8
Fardon Cl WGNS/IIMK WN3 79 H2
Farefield Av GOL/RIS/CU WA3 92 B3
Fareham Cl GR/UP/WCH CH49 109 M7
Fareham Dr CHTN/BK PR9 23 J8
Fareham Rd EHL/KEN L7 113 M3
Faringdon Cl WLTN L25 * 131 K7
Faringdon Rd
WARRN/WOL WA2 105 K7
Farley Av PS/BROM CH62 143 L4
Farley La SKEL WN8 66 C2
Farlow Rd RF/TRAN CH42 128 B4
Farm Av CHLYE PR6 44 C5
Farmbrook Rd WLTN L25 115 K6
Farm Cl CHTN/BK PR9 25 J5
GR/UP/WCH CH49 125 L1
Farmdale Cl CALD/MH L18 130 D3
Farmdale Dr CHNE CH2 165 J2
MGHL L31 73 G4
Far Meadow La PEN/TH CH61 125 L7
Farmer Pl BTL L20 84 A6
Farmers Heath GTS/LS CH66 162 F3
Farmer's La WARRW/BUR WA5 104 C7
Farmfield Dr CL/PREN CH43 110 E6
Farm La WARRS WA4 138 A5
WGNE/HIN WN2 69 J3
Farmleigh Gdns
WARRW/BUR WA5 120 E7
Farm Meadow Rd
WGNW/BIL/O WN5 67 G8
Far Moss Rd CSBY/BLUN L23 70 D7
Farm Rd STHEL WA9 118 F2
Farmside MOR/LEA CH46 110 B2
Farmside Cl WARRW/BUR WA5 121 G6
Farmstead Wy GTS/LS CH66 163 G4
Farm Vw LITH L21 83 K3
Farmview Cl NTHLY L27 115 L6
Farm Wy NEWLW WA12 105 G4
Farmworth St NPK/KEN L6 113 K2
Farnborough Gv HLWD L26 132 B4
Farnborough Rd STHP PR8 35 H5
Farndale WDN WA8 118 C8
Farndale Cl WARRW/BUR WA5 120 B6
Farndale Gv AIMK WN4 91 L3
Farndon Av STHEL WA9 118 D1
WAL/NB CH45 95 G7
Farndon Dr WKBY CH48 125 G2
Farndon Rd GTS/LS CH66 156 A7
Farndon Wy CL/PREN CH43 127 H1
Farne Cl EP CH65 163 L5
Farnham Cl KKBY L32 86 B4
WARRS WA4 138 A6
Farnhill Cl RUNC WA7 150 F5
Farnley Cl RUNC WA7 150 F4
Farnsfield WGN WN1 5 M2
Farnworth Av MOR/LEA CH46 110 A2
Farnworth Cl WDN WA8 134 D1
Farnworth Gv NWD/KWIPK L33 74 A8
Farnworth Rd
WARRW/BUR WA5 135 M1
Farnworth St STHEL WA9 9 L4
WDN WA8 134 D1
Farrant St WDN WA8 16 F3
Farrar St CLB/OSW/ST L13 97 M6
Farr Cl WGNS/IIMK WN3 68 B8
Farrell Cl MGHL L31 85 K1
Farrell Rd WARRS WA4 137 L5
Farrell St WARR WA1 15 J5
WGNW/BIL/O WN5 67 L8
Farr Hall Dr HES CH60 141 G6
Farr Hall Rd HES CH60 141 G5
Farrier Rd NWD/KWIPK L33 86 C3
Farrier's Cft WGNNW/ST WN6 68 A2
Farriers Wy NTHTN L30 84 B5
WKBY CH48 125 K3
Farrier Wk STHEL WA9 118 E1
Farringdon Cl STHEL WA9 102 B8
Farrington Dr ORM L39 51 G7
Farrington St CHLY/EC PR7 32 E5
Farthing Cl WLTN L25 131 J6
The Farthings CHLY/EC PR7 32 B4
Farthingstone Cl RAIN/WH L35 101 J7
Fatherside Dr NTHTN L30 * 83 L2
Faulkner Cl STHP PR8 34 E8
Faulkner Gdns STHP PR8 34 E7
Faversham Rd NG/CROX L11 98 A2
Fawcett SKEL WN8 65 K2
Fawcett Rd MGHL L31 72 F2
Fawley Rd CALD/MH L18 130 E3
RAIN/WH L35 118 A4
Fazakerley Cl WLT/FAZ L9 97 J1
Fazakerley Rd RAIN/WH L35 117 G1
WLT/FAZ L9 97 J1
Fazakerley St CHLY/EC PR7 32 E5
VAUX/LVPD L3 12 E6
Fearnhead Av HOR/BR BL6 45 K8
Fearnhead Cross
WARRN/WOL WA2 * 122 A4
Fearnhead La
WARRN/WOL WA2 122 C3
Fearnley Rd BIRK CH41 11 H7
Fearnside St EHL/KEN L7 113 L5
Feather La HES CH60 141 H5
Feeny St STHEL WA9 * 118 D3
Feilden Rd BEB CH63 143 J1
Felicity Gv MOR/LEA CH46 109 M4
Fellery St CHLY/EC PR7 32 E5
Fell Gv RNFD/HAY WA11 89 J5
Fellside WGN WN1 68 F3
Fell St EHL/KEN L7 113 K3
LEIGH WN7 81 L8
WAL/EG CH44 112 A3
Felltor Cl WLTN L25 131 H2
Fell Vw CHLYE PR6 33 G7
Fellview CHTN/BK PR9 22 F7
Fellwood Gv RAIN/WH L35 117 G3
Felmersham Gn NG/CROX L11 98 B2
Felspar Rd KKBY L32 86 A6
Felstead SKEL WN8 65 K3
Felsted Av WLTN L25 131 L3
Felsted Dr AIN/FAZ L10 85 G4
Felthorpe Cl GR/UP/WCH CH49 110 D6
Felton Gv CLB/OSW/ST L13 114 B1
Feltons SKEL WN8 65 K3
Feltwell Rd ANF/KKDL L4 97 K7
Feltwood Cl WD/CROXPK L12 99 H6
Feltwood Rd WD/CROXPK L12 99 H5
Fender La MOR/LEA CH46 110 C4
Fenderside Rd CL/PREN CH43 110 E5
Fender View Rd MOR/LEA CH46 110 C5
Fender Wy CL/PREN CH43 110 D6
PEN/TH CH61 141 J1
Fenham Dr WARRW/BUR WA5 136 A1
Fennel St WARR WA1 15 G5
Fenney Ct SKEL WN8 65 L4
Fenton Cl ECCL WA10 8 E3
NTHTN L30 84 D5
SPK/HALE L24 146 F2
WDN WA8 133 L2
Fenton Gn SPK/HALE L24 146 F3
Fenwick La RUNC WA7 149 M7
Fenwick Rd GTS/LS CH66 163 G3
Fenwick St CLVP L2 12 E7
Ferguson Av GR/UP/WCH CH49 125 L2
GTS/LS CH66 156 A7
Ferguson Dr WARRN/WOL WA2 121 M4
Ferguson Ri WGNW/BIL/O WN5 68 A5
Ferguson Rd LITH L21 83 L4
NG/CROX L11 98 A5
Fern Av NEWLW WA12 104 F3
Fern Bank CHLYE PR6 32 F2
RNFD/HAY WA11 76 A6
Fernbank Av HUY L36 115 M3
Fernbank Cl GOL/RIS/CU WA3 123 G1
Fernbank Dr NTHTN L30 84 C1
Fern Cl GOL/RIS/CU WA3 122 F1
NTHLY L27 132 A1
SKEL WN8 65 G4
WGNNW/ST WN6 55 J7
Ferndale SKEL WN8 65 K3
Ferndale Av CHNE CH2 165 J2
WAL/EG CH44 111 L1
WKBY CH48 125 K4
Ferndale Cl WARR WA1 122 E6
WDN WA8 119 G6
WLT/FAZ L9 84 C6
Ferndale Rd CSBY/WL L22 82 F3
HOY CH47 108 D6
WAV L15 114 A7
Fern Gdns PR/KW L34 101 H6
Fern Gv BTL L20 7 H3
CL/PREN CH43 110 F8
TOX L8 113 L7
Fern Hey CSBY/BLUN L23 71 J8
Fern Hl WAL/NB CH45 95 K5
Fernhill Av BTL L20 7 L4
Fernhill Cl BTL L20 7 L5
Fernhill Dr TOX L8 113 J7
Fernhill Gdns BTL L20 7 L5
Fernhill Ms East BTL L20 7 L5
Fernhill Ms West BTL L20 * 7 L5
Fernhill Rd BTL L20 83 M8
Fernhill Wy BTL L20 7 L5
Fernhurst RUNC WA7 149 M5
Fernhurst Cl WGNS/IIMK WN3 5 L8
Fernhurst Ga ORM L39 62 D3
Fernhurst Rd KKBY L32 85 L4
Fernlea Av STHEL WA9 101 M6

Fernlea Gv AIMK WN4 .....78 F8
Fernlea Ms CL/PREN CH43 .....110 E5
Fernlea Rd HES CH60 .....141 E5
Fernleigh Rd CLB/OSW/ST L13 *..114 D2
Fernley Rd STHP PR8 .....2 F1
Fern Rd EP CH65 .....163 H4
Ferns Cl HES CH60 .....140 E4
Fernside Gv WGNS/IIMK WN3 .....78 H3
Ferns Rd BEB CH63 .....127 M8
Fern Vls WAL/EG CH44 * 112 A3
Fernwood Rd WAV 150 D4
Fernwood Dr HLWD L26 .....132 A5
Fernwood Rd AIG/SPK L17 .....130 A3
Ferny Brow Rd
.....GR/UP/WCH CH49 .....126 D2
Ferny Knoll Rd RNFD/HAY WA11 ..76 B1
Ferrer St AIMK WN4 .....79 H7
Ferrey Rd AIN/FAZ L10 .....85 J6
Ferries Cl RF/TRAN CH42 .....128 C5
Ferry La WARRS WA4 .....139 G1
Ferry PS/BROM CH62 .....144 C5
Ferryside WAL/EG CH44 .....112 A3
Ferry Side La CHTN/BK PR9 .....2 E1
Ferry View Rd WAL/EG CH44 .....112 A3
Festival Av WAL/NB CH45 .....95 G5
Festival Ct NG/CROX L11 * 98 D2
Festival Crs WARRN/WOL WA2 .....121 M3
Festival Rd EP CH65 .....156 B8
.....RNFD/HAY WA11 .....76 C8
Festival Wy RUNC WA7 .....19 L2
Ffrancon Dr BEB CH63 .....128 B6
Fiddlers Ferry Rd WDN WA8 .....17 J3
Fidler St ECCL WA10 .....101 M4
Field Av LITH L21 .....83 J5
Field Cl BRSC L40 .....52 B2
.....PS/BROM CH62 .....128 D5
Fielden St CHLYE PR6 .....33 L4
Fieldfare Cl GOL/RIS/CU WA3 .....92 F5
.....GOL/RIS/CU WA3 .....123 H1
.....WLTN L25 .....115 J3
Fieldgate WDN WA8 .....133 K7
Field Hey La NSTN CH64 .....154 D4
Fieldhouse Rw RUNC WA7 .....149 M6
Fielding Pl CHLYE PR6 .....44 D5
The Fieldings MGHL L31 .....72 D1
Fielding St NPK/KEN L6 * 113 J2
Fieldlands STHP PR8 .....25 H7
Field La AIN/FAZ L10 .....85 K6
.....LITH L21 .....83 J4
.....WARRS WA4 .....137 L7
Field Rd STHEL WA9 .....118 F2
.....WAL/NB CH45 .....95 K6
Field's End HUY L36 .....116 A5
Fieldsend Cl NTHLY L27 .....132 A1
Fieldsend Dr LEIGH WN7 .....93 L5
Fieldside Av CHLY/EC PR7 .....31 L5
Fieldside Rd RF/TRAN CH42 .....128 A3
The Fields CHLY/EC PR7 .....30 D6
.....WGNE/HIN WN2 .....69 L1
.....WGNNW/ST WN6 .....56 B5
Field St VAUX/LVPD L3 .....13 K3
.....WGNE/HIN WN2 .....81 G1
.....WGNNW/ST WN6 .....4 E3
.....WGNS/IIMK WN3 .....80 B1
Fieldsway RUNC WA7 .....149 J7
Fieldton Rd NG/CROX L11 .....98 D2
Field Vw LITH L21 .....83 J4
Fieldview SKEL WN8 .....64 F7
Fieldview Dr WARRN/WOL WA2 ...121 L4
Fieldview SKEL WN8 .....88 C3
Field Wk ORM L39 .....51 K8
Field Wy RAIN/WH L35 .....101 L8
Fieldway BEB CH63 .....127 M5
.....FROD/HEL WA6 .....160 E6
.....GTS/LS CH66 .....155 K6
.....HES CH60 .....141 L4
.....HOY CH47 .....109 H6
.....HUY L36 .....116 B5
.....MGHL L31 .....73 G6
.....WAL/NB CH45 .....95 J8
.....WAV L15 .....114 E5
.....WDN WA8 .....135 G3
.....WGNE/HIN WN2 .....80 D3
Fieldway Ct BIRK CH41 .....10 C1
Fife Cl CHLYE PR6 .....33 G7
Fife Rd WARR WA1 .....15 L2
Fifth Av CL/PREN CH43 .....110 D6
.....RUNC WA7 .....150 B6
.....WLT/FAZ L9 .....84 F6
Filbert Cl NWD/KWIPK L33 .....74 A7
Fildes Cl WARRW/BUR WA5 .....120 D8
File St CHLY/EC PR7 .....32 E6
Filton Rd DV/KA/FCH L14 .....99 K8
Finborough Rd ANF/KKDL L4 .....97 L3
Fincham Cl DV/KA/FCH L14 .....99 K8
Fincham Gn DV/KA/FCH L14 .....99 K8
Fincham Rd DV/KA/FCH L14 .....99 J8
Fincham Sq DV/KA/FCH L14 .....99 J8
Finch Av RNFD/HAY WA11 .....76 D5
Finch Cl DV/KA/FCH L14 * 99 H7
.....STHEL WA9 .....118 E4
Finch Ct BIRK CH41 .....11 G3
Finchdale Gdns
.....GOL/RIS/CU WA3 .....93 K5
Finchdean Cl
.....GR/UP/WCH CH49 .....125 L1
Finch Dene DV/KA/FCH L14 .....99 H7
Finch La DV/KA/FCH L14 .....99 H7
.....HLWD L26 .....132 D7
.....WGNNW/ST WN6 .....54 D4
Finch Lea Rd DV/KA/FCH L14 .....99 J8
Finchley Crs WGNE/HIN WN2 .....69 J4
Finchley Dr RNFD/HAY WA11 .....89 L6
Finch Meadow Cl ANF/KKDL L4 ...97 K6
Finch Meadow Cl WLT/FAZ L9 ....98 B1
Finch Mill Av WGNNW/ST WN6 ...54 D4
Finch PI VAUX/LVPD L3 .....13 L5
Finch Rd DV/KA/FCH L14 .....99 J7
Finch Wy DV/KA/FCH L14 .....99 H8
Findlay Cl WARR WA12 .....104 E3
Findley Dr MOR/LEA CH46 .....110 D2
Findon SKEL WN8 .....65 K4
Findon Rd KKBY L32 .....86 B5
Fine Jane's Wy CHTN/BK PR9 .....25 K5
Fingall Rd WAV L15 .....114 D7
Finger House La WDN WA8 .....118 F4
Fingland Rd WAV L15 .....114 A6
Finlan Rd WDN WA8 .....16 B6
Finlay Av WARRW/BUR WA5 .....136 A2
Finlay Ct WGNW/BIL/O WN5 .....68 A5
Finlay St NPK/KEN L6 .....113 L2
Finney Gv RNFD/HAY WA11 .....91 G7
The Finney WKBY CH48 * 124 F7
Finningley Ct WARRN/WOL WA2...122 A5
Finsbury Cl WARRW/BUR WA5 ...136 E1
Finsbury Pk WDN WA8 .....118 E8
Finstall Rd BEB CH63 .....143 H3
Finvoy Rd CLB/OSW/ST L13 .....98 D5
Fir Avenue HLWD L26 .....131 C5
Firbank CHLY/EC PR7 .....31 C5
.....CHNE CH2 .....165 L1
Firbank Cl RUNC WA7 .....150 H4
Firbank Rd WGNS/IIMK WN3 .....79 K2
Firbeck SKEL WN8 .....65 L4
Firbrook Ct CL/PREN CH43 .....110 E5
Fir Cl HLWD L26 .....132 C5
Firdale Rd WLT/FAZ L9 .....97 J1
Firdene Crs CL/PREN CH43 * 127 C1
Firecrest Ct WARR WA1 .....14 D9

Fire Station Rd RAIN/WH L35 .....101 H8
Firethorne Rd HLWD L26 .....131 M3
Fir Gv WARR WA1 .....122 B6
.....WGNNW/ST WN6 .....68 C2
.....WLT/FAZ L9 .....84 E5
Firman Cl WARRW/BUR WA5 .....120 D5
Fir Rd CSBY/WL L22 .....83 C3
Firs Av BEB CH63 .....143 H2
Firs Cl FMBY L37 .....46 F8
Firshaw Rd HOY CH47 .....108 E4
Firs La LEIGH WN7 .....81 J8
.....ORM L39 .....62 A2
.....WARRS WA4 .....137 K7
Firs Link FMBY L37 .....58 F1
Firs Park Crs WGNE/HIN WN2 .....69 M4
First Av CL/PREN CH43 .....110 E7
.....CSBY/BLUN L23 * 82 F1
.....RAIN/WH L35 .....117 K1
.....WGNE/HIN WN2 .....69 M8
.....WGNS/IIMK WN3 .....80 B2
.....WLT/FAZ L9 .....84 E6
Firstone Gv KKBY L32 .....86 A5
Fir St ECCL WA10 .....101 L5
.....STHP PR8 .....25 H7
.....WDN WA8 .....134 E3
Firswood Rd BRSC L40 .....64 E1
Firthland Wy WARR WA1 .....103 H3
Fir Tree Av GOL/RIS/CU WA3 .....93 H5
Fir Tree Av WARR WA1 .....122 C5
Firtree Cl CHLY/EC PR7 .....43 C2
Fir Tree Cl RNFD/HAY WA11 .....77 H6
.....SKEL WN8 .....65 M6
Fir Tree Crs WGNS/IIMK WN3 .....80 B2
Fir Tree Dr WGNS/IIMK WN3 .....80 B2
Fir Tree Dr North
.....WD/CROXPK L12 .....98 F2
Fir Tree Dr South
.....WD/CROXPK L12 .....98 F2
Firtree Gv GTS/LS CH66 .....163 J5
Fir Tree La ORM L39 .....62 C3
.....WARRW/BUR WA5 .....104 C7
Firvale Cl LEIGH WN7 .....81 L8
Fir Wy HES CH60 .....141 K8
Firwood Gv AIMK WN4 .....91 H5
Firwood SKEL WN8 .....65 M2
Fisher Av RAIN/WH L35 .....116 F3
.....WARRN/WOL WA2 .....121 K4
Fisher Cl WGNS/IIMK WN3 .....68 B7
Fisher Dr CHTN/BK PR9 .....25 H6
.....WGNW/BIL/O WN5 .....67 G7
Fisherfield Dr GOL/RIS/CU WA3 ...93 H5
Fishermans Cl FMBY L37 .....47 G7
Fisher PI RAIN/WH L35 .....116 F3
Fishers La PEN/TH CH61 .....141 G1
Fisher St RUNC WA7 .....19 K2
.....STHEL WA9 .....103 G6
.....TOX L8 .....112 F7
Fishguard Cl NPK/KEN L6 * 113 M1
Fish La BRSC L40 .....38 D1
Fistral Av AIN/FAZ L10 .....85 K7
Fistral Dr ECCL WA10 .....88 C3
Fitzadam St WGN WN1 .....5 H5
Fitzclarence Wy NPK/KEN L6 .....113 M2
Fitzgerald Rd CLB/OSW/ST L13 ...114 C2
Fitzherbert St WARRN/WOL WA2 ...14 C1
Fitzpatrick Ct VAUX/LVPD L3 .....12 E1
Fitzroy Wy NPK/KEN L6 .....113 J2
Fitzwalter Rd WARR WA1 .....122 F6
Fiveways ECCL WA10 .....101 J1
Flag La CHLYE PR6 .....33 H4
.....CROS/BRETH PR26 .....30 F1
.....NSTN CH64 .....153 H6
Flail Cl GR/UP/WCH CH49 .....125 L1
Flambards GR/UP/WCH CH49 .....126 D2
Flamstead SKEL WN8 .....65 L4
Flander Cl AIN/FAZ L10 .....85 J6
Flashes La NSTN CH64 .....153 K8
Flash La BRSC L40 .....39 K1
Flatfield Wy MGHL L31 .....73 G3
Flatman's La ORM L39 .....61 G4
Flatt La CL/PREN CH43 .....127 H2
.....EP CH65 .....20 A4
Flawn Rd NG/CROX L11 .....98 A5
Flaxfield Rd FMBY L37 .....59 J2
Flaxfields BRSC L40 .....52 B3
Flaxhill MOR/LEA CH46 .....109 M4
Flax La BRSC L40 .....52 B3
Flaxley Cl GOL/RIS/CU WA3 .....107 G3
Flaxman St EHL/KEN L7 * 113 L3
Flaxton SKEL WN8 .....65 L4
Flaybrick Cl CL/PREN CH43 .....111 G5
Fleck La WKBY CH48 .....124 F4
Fleet Croft Rd
.....GR/UP/WCH CH49 .....126 C3
Fleet La STHEL WA9 .....103 G3
Fleet St CHLY/EC PR7 .....32 E6
.....CLVPS L1 .....13 G5
.....EP CH65 .....156 C8
.....WGNW/BIL/O WN5 .....67 K7
Fleetwood Cl CHTN/BK PR9 * 23 J7
.....WARRW/BUR WA5 .....136 D1
Fleetwood Crs CHTN/BK PR9 .....24 E4
Fleetwood Dr CHTN/BK PR9 .....23 J7
Fleetwood La NTHTN L30 .....83 M1
Fleetwood Wk RUNC WA7 .....150 E6
Fleming Cl VAUX/LVPD L3 .....12 E1
.....WARRN/WOL WA2 .....105 J7
Fleming Rd SPK/HALE L24 .....131 L2
Fleming St EP CH65 .....20 D2
Flemington Av ANF/KKDL L4 * 97 M4
Flers Av WARRS WA4 .....137 L5
Fletcher Av CL/PREN CH43 .....110 E7
.....RF/TRAN CH42 .....128 A3
Fletcher Cl GR/UP/WCH CH49 ...126 C3
Fletcher Dr ALL/GAR L19 .....130 C6
Fletcher's Dr BRSC L40 .....52 A1
Fletcher St WARRS WA4 .....114 A6
Flimby SKEL WN8 .....65 M4
Flint Cl NSTN CH64 .....152 F1
Flint Ct EP CH65 .....163 M3
Flint St NSTN CH64 .....153 G6
Flint Meadow NSTN CH64 .....153 G6
Flint St CLVPS L1 .....112 F6
Flockton Av WGNNW/ST WN6 ...67 M1
Floral Wd AIG/SPK L17 .....130 C1
Florence Av HES CH60 .....141 K3
Flordon SKEL WN8 .....65 M4
Florence Rd WAL/EG CH44 .....112 A3
Florence St ANF/KKDL L4 .....11 H5
.....BIRK CH41 .....11 H5
.....STHEL WA9 .....101 L6
.....WARRS WA4 .....15 K3
Florentine Rd CLB/OSW/ST L13 ..114 C1
Florida Cl WARRW/BUR WA5 .....120 E6

Florida Ct ALL/GAR L19 .....130 D5
Flowermead Cl HOY CH47 .....109 H4
Fluin La FROD/HEL WA6 .....160 E5
Fluker's Brook La PR/KW L34 .....99 K4
Foinavon Cl WLT/FAZ L9 * 84 B6
Folds HOR/BR BL6 .....57 L2
Folds La RNFD/HAY WA11 .....89 J6
Folds Rd RNFD/HAY WA11 .....90 B7
Fold St EP CH65 .....22 C4
Fold St CHLY/EC PR7 .....32 D3
Foley St ANF/KKDL L4 .....97 G6
.....WGNE/HIN WN2 .....69 M8
Folkestone Rd STHP PR8 .....36 A2
Folkstone Wy RUNC WA7 .....150 B6
Folly La WAL/EG CH44 .....95 G8
.....WARRW/BUR WA5 .....14 B1
Fontenoy St CLVP L2 .....13 G5
Fonthill Cl ANF/KKDL L4 .....96 F6
Fonthill Rd ANF/KKDL L4 .....96 F5
Fontwell Cl WARRW/BUR WA5 ...56 D4
Forbes Cl GOL/RIS/CU WA3 .....107 L7
Ford Av NWD/KWIPK L33 .....74 A7
Ford Cl BTL L20 .....84 A6
.....GR/UP/WCH CH49 .....126 D1
.....LITH L21 .....83 K3
Fordcombe Rd WLTN L25 .....131 L1
Ford Dr GR/UP/WCH CH49 .....110 D8
Fordham St STHP PR8 .....36 A2
Fordham St ANF/KKDL L4 .....97 C5
Fordhill Vw MOR/LEA CH46 .....110 C5
Fordington Rd
.....WARRW/BUR WA5 .....120 D8
Fordland Cl GOL/RIS/CU WA3 .....93 C4
Ford La GR/UP/WCH CH49 .....110 D8
.....LITH L21 .....83 K2
Fordlea Rd WD/CROXPK L12 .....98 C5
Fordlea Wy WD/CROXPK L12 .....98 C5
Ford Rd GR/UP/WCH CH49 .....110 C8
.....RAIN/WH L35 .....101 H3
Ford St VAUX/LVPD L3 .....12 F3
.....WARR WA1 .....15 J3
Ford Vw LITH L21 .....83 K2
Ford Wy GR/UP/WCH CH49 .....126 C1
Fordyce Wy WGNE/HIN WN2 .....69 J4
Forefield La CSBY/BLUN L23 .....83 H1
Foreland Cl WARRW/BUR WA5 ...119 L6
Forest Cl HOY CH47 .....108 F4
.....PR/KW L34 .....101 H6
Forest Ct CL/PREN CH43 .....111 H7
Forest Dr HUY L36 .....115 L2
.....SKEL WN8 .....65 L2
.....WCNNW/ST WN6 .....55 J3
Forest Gn WD/CROXPK L12 .....98 D5
Forest Gv PR/KW L34 .....101 L6
Forest Lawn WD/CROXPK L12 ...98 D5
Forest Mdl ECCL WA10 .....101 J2
Forest Rd CL/PREN CH43 .....156 A6
.....GTS/LS CH66 .....141 J5
.....HES CH60 .....141 J5
.....HOY CH47 .....108 F4
.....STHEL WA9 .....118 C2
.....STHP PR8 .....3 G1
Forest Wk RUNC WA7 * 150 B6
Forfar Av CLB/OSW/ST L13 .....97 M7
Forge Cl BRSC L40 .....64 A1
.....WDN WA8 .....117 L8
Forge Rd GTS/LS CH66 .....155 L7
.....WARRW/BUR WA5 .....120 B8
Forge St BTL L20 .....96 E5
.....WGNE/HIN WN2 .....5 G5
Formby Br FMBY L37 .....59 G3
Formby By-Pass FMBY L37 .....47 K4
Formby Flds FMBY L37 .....59 J3
Formby Gdns FMBY L37 .....59 H1
Formby La ORM L39 .....62 A3
Formby Rd ECCL WA10 .....100 E2
Formby St FMBY L37 .....59 G3
Formosa Dr AIN/FAZ L10 .....85 H6
Formosa Wy AIN/FAZ L10 .....85 H6
Fornalls Green La HOY CH47 .....109 G6
Forres Gv WLT/FAZ L9 .....90 E1
Forrester Av STHEL WA9 .....101 C5
Forresters Cl WGNE/HIN WN2 .....81 C5
Forrest St CLVPS L1 .....13 G9
Forrest Wy WARRW/BUR WA5 ...136 F2
Forshaw Av ANF/KKDL L4 .....97 M6
Forshaw's La
.....WARRW/BUR WA5 .....104 A5
Forshaw St WARRN/WOL WA2 .....15 C2
Forster St GOL/RIS/CU WA3 .....92 C4
.....WARRN/WOL WA2 .....14 F2
Forsythia Cl WLT/FAZ L9 * 97 L2
Forthlin Rd CALD/MH L18 .....130 E4
Forth St BTL L20 .....7 G9
Forton Lodge Flats
.....CSBY/BLUN L23 * 82 E1
.....CLVPS L1 .....12 F9
Forton Rd WGNS/IIMK WN3 .....79 H3
Fort St WAL/NB CH45 .....95 L6
Forwood Rd PS/BROM CH62 .....143 M5
Foscote Rd NWD/KWIPK L33 .....86 C1
Foster Av WGNS/IIMK WN3 .....5 K8
Foster Cl RAIN/WH L35 .....101 J8
Fosterfield CHLYE PR6 .....33 C4
Foster Rd FMBY L37 .....58 F3
Fosters Buildings
.....WGNNW/ST WN6 .....4 C3
Fosters Cl CHTN/BK PR9 .....25 K5
Fosters Green Rd SKEL WN8 .....65 L3
Fosters Rd RNFD/HAY WA11 .....90 B7
Fosters Rd RNFD/HAY WA11 .....90 B7
Foster St BTL L20 .....96 E6
.....CHLYE PR6 .....33 C4
.....WDN WA8 .....16 F1
.....WGNNW/ST WN6 .....4 A2
Fotherby Pl WGNS/IIMK WN3 .....79 J3
Fothergill St WARR WA1 .....15 L6
Fotheringay Ct EP CH65 .....163 M3
Foul La STHP PR8 .....25 J8
Foundry La WDN WA8 .....133 K8
Foundry St CHLY/EC PR7 * 32 E5
.....ECCL WA10 .....104 D2
.....NEWLW WA12 .....104 D2
.....WARRN/WOL WA2 .....14 C4
.....WGNE/HIN WN2 .....69 M8
Fountain Ct CSBY/BLUN L23 .....70 C5
Fountain La FROD/HEL WA6 .....160 C5
Fountain Rd PR/KW L34 .....99 M2
.....WAL/NB CH45 .....95 K6
Fountains Av RNFD/HAY WA11 .....91 H6
Fountains Cl ANF/KKDL L4 .....97 H1
.....CHLY/EC PR7 .....32 F6
.....RUNC WA7 .....188 B4
Fountains Rd ANF/KKDL L4 .....96 F6
Fountain St RF/TRAN CH42 .....127 L2
.....STHEL WA9 .....118 C2
Fountains Wk GOL/RIS/CU WA3 ...93 K5
Fountains Wy FMBY L37 .....59 H1
Four Acre Dr LITH L21 .....83 K3
Four Acre La STHEL WA9 .....118 E1
Fouracres MGHL L31 .....72 D6
Fouracarts Rd
.....WCNW/BIL/O WN5 .....67 L3
Fourteen Meadows Rd
.....WGNS/IIMK WN3 .....4 C7

Fourth Av CL/PREN CH43 .....110 D7
.....RUNC WA7 .....150 B6
.....WLT/FAZ L9 .....84 F6
Fourways Cl NTHLY L27 .....115 M6
Fowell Rd WAL/NB CH45 .....95 K5
Fowler Cl EHL/KEN L7 .....113 L4
Foxall Wy GTS/LS CH66 .....162 F3
Foxcote CHLY/EC PR7 .....32 D3
.....WDN WA8 .....133 K3
Fox Cover Rd HES CH60 .....141 L6
Foxcovers Rd BEB CH63 .....143 J2
Fox Covert RUNC WA7 .....150 B6
Foxdale Cl WAV L15 .....114 B7
Foxdale Rd WAV L15 .....114 B7
Foxdell Cl CLB/OSW/ST L13 .....114 C3
Foxdene Gv WGNS/IIMK WN3 .....79 C3
Foxes Cl GR/UP/WCH CH49 .....126 C7
The Foxes PEN/TH CH61 .....126 C7
Foxfield Cl WARRW/BUR WA5 ...120 A2
Foxfield Gv WGNNW/ST WN6 .....55 M5
Foxfield Rd HOY CH47 .....108 F4
Foxfold SKEL WN8 .....65 M2
Fox Gdns LYMM WA13 .....139 L1
Foxglove Av HLWD L26 .....132 A4
Foxglove Cl WGNNW/ST WN6 .....55 M5
.....WLT/FAZ L9 .....98 B1
Foxglove Ct FROD/HEL WA6 .....160 E6
Foxglove Rd BIRK CH41 * 111 H6
Foxglove Wy NSTN CH64 .....153 G8
Fox Hey Rd WAL/EG CH44 .....111 H2
Foxhill Cl FMBY L37 .....58 F4
.....TOX L8 .....113 J8
Foxhill Gv FROD/HEL WA6 .....166 F1
Foxhill La HLWD L26 .....132 B3
Foxhole Rd CHLY/EC PR7 .....32 E5
Foxhouse La MGHL L31 .....73 G5
Foxhunter Dr WLT/FAZ L9 .....84 E5
Foxleigh HLWD L26 .....131 M3
Foxley Heath WDN WA8 .....16 A3
Fox PI ECCL WA10 .....9 L7
Fox's Bank La WDN WA8 .....117 H4
Foxshaw Cl RAIN/WH L35 .....116 F4
Fox St BIRK CH41 .....10 E5
.....RUNC WA7 .....19 G5
.....VAUX/LVPD L3 .....13 J2
.....WARRW/BUR WA5 .....121 G8
Foxton Cl MOR/LEA CH46 .....109 K4
.....WKBY CH48 .....125 G2
Foxwood STHEL WA9 .....101 L6
Foxwood Cl WGNW/BIL/O WN5 ...67 G8
The Foxwood CHLY/EC PR7 .....42 E4
Foy St AIMK WN4 * 91 K2
Frailey Cl STHP PR8 .....4 B1
Frampton Rd ANF/KKDL L4 .....97 M1
France St WGNE/HIN WN2 .....69 M7
.....WGNW/BIL/O WN5 .....68 D4
Franceys St VAUX/LVPD L3 * 13 K7
Francine Cl EV L5 .....96 E3
Francis Av CL/PREN CH43 .....110 D6
.....MOR/LEA CH46 .....109 M3
Francis Cl RAIN/WH L35 .....117 L1
.....WDN WA8 .....133 L5
Francis Rd FROD/HEL WA6 .....166 F3
.....WARRS WA4 .....137 K4
Francis St STHEL WA9 .....103 H6
.....WGNE/HIN WN2 .....69 M8
Francis Wy CHLDW L16 .....115 G5
Frankby Av WAL/EG CH44 .....111 J1
Frankby Cl GR/UP/WCH CH49 ...125 K2
Frankby Gv GR/UP/WCH CH49 ...110 D8
Frankby Rd ANF/KKDL L4 .....97 K5
.....GR/UP/WCH CH49 .....125 G2
.....HOY CH47 .....108 F5
.....WKBY CH48 .....125 H1
Franklin Rd MOR/LEA CH46 .....110 C1
Franklin PI NPK/KEN L6 * 97 M8
Frank Rd TOX L8 .....113 G8
Frank St WDN WA8 .....17 H2
Fraser Rd WARRW/BUR WA5 .....119 M7
.....WGNW/BIL/O WN5 .....68 A4
Fraser St VAUX/LVPD L3 .....13 J5
Frawley Av NEWLW WA12 .....91 K8
Freckleton Cl WARRW/BUR WA5 ...136 D1
Freckleton Dr NWD/KWIPK L33 ...74 C8
Freckleton Rd CHTN/BK PR9 .....25 H1
.....ECCL WA10 .....101 J1
Freckleton St WGN WN1 .....68 E3
Freda Av STHEL WA9 * 102 F7
Frederica Ter WGNE/HIN WN2 ....5 G6
Frederick Banting Cl NTHTN L30 ..84 D1
Frederick Gv WAV L15 .....114 C5
Frederick Lunt Av PR/KW L34 .....99 L3
Frederick St WDN WA8 .....17 J2
Frederic St WGN WN1 * 5 H6
Fredric Pl RUNC WA7 .....19 J2
Freedom Cl EHL/KEN L7 .....113 L3
Freehold St EHL/KEN L7 .....113 M2
Freeland St ANF/KKDL L4 .....96 F4
Freeman St BIRK CH41 .....11 J3
.....EHL/KEN L7 .....113 L5
Freemantle Av STHEL WA9 .....104 A1
Freemasons Rw VAUX/LVPD L3 ...2 F4
Freemont Rd WD/CROXPK L12 ...98 C5
Freeport Gv WLT/FAZ L9 .....84 D6
Freesia Av WLT/FAZ L9 .....97 K1
Freme Cl NG/CROX L11 .....98 D2
French St ECCL WA10 .....101 M4
.....WDN WA8 .....17 J2
Frenchwood Ct WGNE/HIN WN2 ..69 L1
Frensham Cl BEB CH63 .....143 H3
Frensham Wy WLTN L25 .....131 M5
Freshfield Cl HUY L36 .....115 L2
Freshfield Rd FMBY L37 .....59 G2
.....WAV L15 .....114 B7
.....WGNS/IIMK WN3 .....79 G2
Freshfields Dr
.....WARRN/WOL WA2 .....122 D4
Freshford STHEL WA9 .....102 F7
Freshmeadow La
.....FROD/HEL WA6 .....166 C3
Freshwater Cl WARRW/BUR WA5 ...119 M6
Friars Av WARRW/BUR WA5 .....120 A8
Friars Cl BEB CH63 .....143 H1
Friars Ga WARR WA1 .....14 E1
Friarsgate Cl CALD/MH L18 .....114 E8
Friars La WARR WA1 .....14 E1
Friar St ECCL WA10 .....89 H1
.....EV L5 .....97 J8
Friars Wk FMBY L37 .....59 H1
Friday St CHLYE PR6 .....32 F5
Friends La WARRW/BUR WA5 ...104 A5
Frinsted Rd NG/CROX L11 .....98 C2
Frith St WGNNW/ST WN6 .....4 A5
Frobisher Dr WARRW/BUR WA5 ...120 F1
Frobisher Rd MOR/LEA CH46 .....110 C1

Froda Av FROD/HEL WA6 .....160 D6
Frodsham Cl WGNNW/ST WN6 ...67 M2
Frodsham Dr RNFD/HAY WA11 ...91 G6
Frodsham Rd FROD/HEL WA6 ...166 F4
Frodsham St ANF/KKDL L4 .....97 H4
.....BIRK CH41 .....11 K9
Frogmore Rd CLB/OSW/ST L13 ..114 A2
Frome Cl PEN/TH CH61 .....125 M6
Frome Ct EP CH65 .....156 C6
Frome Wy WLTN L25 .....131 M4
Froom St CHLYE PR6 .....33 G5
Frost Dr PEN/TH CH61 .....125 L6
Frosts Ms EP CH65 .....20 B2
Frost St EHL/KEN L7 .....113 L3
Fryent Cl HOR/BR BL6 .....57 M3
Fry St STHEL WA9 .....103 C5
Fuchsia Cl GTS/LS CH66 .....163 H4
Fuchsia Wk GR/UP/WCH CH49 ...126 C1
Fulbeck WDN WA8 .....133 L3
Fulbeck Av WGNS/IIMK WN3 .....79 J3
Fulbrook Cl BEB CH63 .....143 H3
Fulbrook Rd BEB CH63 .....143 H3
Fulford Cl DV/KA/FCH L14 .....99 H7
Fulford Pk MOR/LEA CH46 .....110 A6
Fullerton Gv HUY L36 .....116 A1
Fulmar Cl NTHLY L27 .....132 A1
Fulmar Gv WD/CROXPK L12 .....99 G2
Fulshaw Cl NTHLY L27 .....115 M7
Fulton Av WKBY CH48 .....124 F2
Fulton St EV L5 .....96 E8
Fulwood Av WLT/FAZ L9 * 84 F6
Fulwood Cl AIG/SPK L17 .....129 M3
Fulwood Dr AIG/SPK L17 .....129 L3
Fulwood Gdns GTS/LS CH66 .....155 L7
Fulwood Ms AIG/SPK L17 .....129 L3
Fulwood Pk AIG/SPK L17 .....129 L4
Fulwood Rd AIG/SPK L17 .....129 L3
.....GTS/LS CH66 .....93 C7
.....GTS/LS CH66 .....155 L7
Funchal Av FMBY L37 .....58 F4
Furlong Cl WGNE/HIN WN2 .....80 B6
.....WLT/FAZ L9 .....84 F5
Furness Av ECCL WA10 .....101 H3
.....FMBY L37 .....59 H2
.....ORM L39 .....63 G1
.....WD/CROXPK L12 .....98 E4
Furness Cl CHLY/EC PR7 .....43 K2
.....STHP PR8 .....47 K2
Furness Crs LEIGH WN7 .....81 M4
Furness St ANF/KKDL L4 .....97 C6
Furnival Dr BRSC L40 .....51 M1
Furrocks Cl NSTN CH64 .....153 H8
Furrocks La NSTN CH64 .....153 H8
Furrocks Wy NSTN CH64 .....153 H8
The Furrows GTS/LS CH66 .....163 C5
Fylde Rd CHTN/BK PR9 .....22 D8

G

Gabbot St CHLY/EC PR7 .....44 B6
Gable Ct NG/CROX L11 * 98 A2
Gables Cl WARRN/WOL WA2 .....122 B2
The Gables MGHL L31 * 73 C6
Gable St NEWLW WA12 .....104 C2
Gable Vw NG/CROX L11 * 98 A2
Gabriel Cl MOR/LEA CH46 .....110 B5
Gainford Cl WDN WA8 .....133 L2
Gainford Rd DV/KA/FCH L14 .....99 H7
Gainsborough Av MGHL L31 .....72 D5
Gainsborough Cl
.....WD/CROXPK L12 .....99 G3
.....WGNS/IIMK WN3 .....78 F3
Gainsborough Ct WDN WA8 .....133 K4
Gainsborough Rd
.....GR/UP/WCH CH49 .....110 A7
.....STHP PR8 .....35 C1
.....WAL/NB CH45 .....95 C8
.....WARRS WA4 .....137 K3
.....WAV L15 .....114 A7
Gairloch Cl WARRN/WOL WA2 ...122 B1
Gaisgill Ct WDN WA8 .....133 L4
Galbraith Cl AIG/SPK L17 .....129 L3
Gale Av WARRW/BUR WA5 .....121 L4
Galemeade NG/CROX L11 * 98 D2
Gale Rd LITH L21 .....83 L4
.....NWD/KWIPK L33 .....86 E5
Gales La BRSC L40 .....40 C5
Galion Wy WDN WA8 .....134 B1
Galloway Rd CSBY/WL L22 .....83 C3
Galloway St EHL/KEN L7 .....113 M5
Galston Av RAIN/WH L35 .....117 H3
Galston Ct NWD/KWIPK L33 .....73 M7
Galsworthy Av NTHTN L30 .....84 A5
Galsworthy PI NTHTN L30 .....84 A5
Galton St VAUX/LVPD L3 .....12 C4
Galtres Pk BEB CH63 .....128 A3
Galwey Gv WGN WN1 .....68 E1
Gambier Ter CLVPS L1 .....113 G6
Gamble Av ECCL WA10 .....89 G7
Gamlin St BIRK CH41 .....111 H5
Gamston Wd KKBY L32 .....85 L4
Ganney's Meadow Rd
.....GR/UP/WCH CH49 .....126 E2
Gannock St EHL/KEN L7 .....113 L4
Gantley Av WGNW/BIL/O WN5 ...77 M1
Gantley Crs WGNW/BIL/O WN5 ...77 M1
Gantley Rd WGNW/BIL/O WN5 ...77 M2
Ganton Cl STHP PR8 .....36 A1
.....WDN WA8 .....134 D1
Ganworth Cl SPK/HALE L24 .....147 C3
Ganworth Rd SPK/HALE L24 .....147 C3
Garage Rd SPK/HALE L24 .....148 A1
Gardeners Vw NWD/KWIPK L33 ...74 B7
Gardeners Wy RAIN/WH L35 .....101 L8
Garden Hey Rd HOY CH47 .....108 C5
.....MOR/LEA CH46 .....109 K6
Gardenia Gv AIG/SPK L17 .....129 C3
Garden La MOR/LEA CH46 .....110 A4
.....VAUX/LVPD L3 * 13 C2
.....WLT/FAZ L9 .....84 F6
Garden Lodge Gv NTHLY L27 .....115 M8
Garden PI BTL L20 * 7 H4
Gardenside MOR/LEA CH46 .....110 D1
Gardenside St NPK/KEN L6 .....13 M3
Gardens Rd BEB CH63 .....128 D8
Garden St WLTN L25 .....131 J3
Garden Ter CHLY/EC PR7 .....32 C6
Garden Wk PR/KW L34 .....100 F8
Gardiner Av RNFD/HAY WA11 .....90 F4
Gardiners PI SKEL WN8 .....65 C6
Gardner Av BTL L20 .....83 M6
Gardner Rd CLB/OSW/ST L13 .....98 A8
.....FMBY L37 .....59 J2
Gardner's Dr NPK/KEN L6 .....113 L1
Gardner's Rw VAUX/LVPD L3 .....13 G3
Garden Av RNFD/HAY WA11 .....90 F4
Garfield Ter CHLYE PR6 .....32 F3
.....GR/UP/WCH CH49 .....110 C8
Garforth Cl ALL/GAR L19 .....130 F6
Garforth Rd ALL/GAR L19 .....130 F6

Garmoyle Cl WAV L15 114 A6
Garmoyle Rd WAV L15 114 A7
Garner St WARRN/WOL WA2 15 H1
Garnet St CLB/OSW/ST L13 114 B4
STHEL WA9 102 F6
Garnett Av ANF/KKDL L4 97 G5
WARRS WA4 138 B1
Garnett Gdns ORM L39 62 F1
Garnett Pl SKEL WN8 65 J6
Garnetts La RAIN/WH L35 132 F4
WDN WA8 148 C2
Garrett Fld GOL/RIS/CU WA3 106 F8
Garrick Av MOR/LEA CH46 109 L5
Garrick Pde STHP PR8 2 E5
Garrick Rd CL/PREN CH43 127 H5
Garrick St EHL/KEN L7 113 L6
Garrigill Cl WDN WA8 118 D8
Garrowby Dr HUY L36 115 L2
Garsdale Av RAIN/WH L35 117 M3
Garsdale Cl WARRW/BUR WA5 120 B6
Garsfield Rd ANF/KKDL L4 97 M4
Garside Av GOL/RIS/CU WA3 92 F6
Garside Gv WGNS/IIMK WN3 79 G3
Garstang Rd CHTN/BK PR9 25 H1
Garston Old Rd ALL/GAR L19 130 E6
Garston Wy ALL/GAR L19 130 E8
Garswood Av RNFD/HAY WA11 76 C6
Garswood Cl MGHL L31 73 G2
MOR/LEA CH46 110 A1
Garswood Crs
WGNW/BIL/O WN5 89 M1
Garswood Old Rd AIMK WN4 90 B4
Garswood Rd AIMK WN4 90 E2
WGNW/BIL/O WN5 90 A1
Garswood St AIMK WN4 91 K2
ECCL WA10 9 G3
TOX L8 129 H2
Garter Cl NG/CROX L11 98 E2
Garth Bvd BEB CH63 128 A5
Garthdale Rd CALD/MH L18 130 C1
Garth Dr CALD/MH L18 130 D1
Garthowen Rd EHL/KEN L7 113 M3
Garth Rd KKBY L32 86 C5
The Garth HUY L36 116 A2
Garton Dr GOL/RIS/CU WA3 93 G4
Gartons La STHEL WA9 118 E2
Garven Pl WARR WA1 14 D6
Garway WLTN L25 131 L2
Garwood Cl WARRW/BUR WA5 120 D5
Gascoyne St VAUX/LVPD L3 12 E4
Gaskell Av WARRS WA4 138 C2
Gaskell St CHLYE PR6 33 G5
STHEL WA9 102 F4
WARRS WA4 137 L4
Gaskill Rd SPK/HALE L24 146 F1
Gas St CHLY/EC PR7 44 B7
WGNE/HIN WN2 80 D3
Gatclif Rd CLB/OSW/ST L13 98 A5
Gateacre Brow WLTN L25 131 J1
Gateacre Ct GTS/LS CH66 156 B5
Gateacre Park Dr WLTN L25 115 H7
Gateacre Ri WLTN L25 131 K1
Gateacre Vale Rd WLTN L25 131 K2
Gategill Gv WGNW/BIL/O WN5 77 M3
Gateley Cl WARRS WA4 139 G2
Gateside Cl NTHLY L27 116 A8
Gates La SFTN L29 71 K5
Gate Warth St
WARRW/BUR WA5 * 136 F2
Gathurst Ct WDN WA8 133 M5
Gathurst Hall WGNNW/ST WN6 * 67 H2
Gathurst La WGNNW/ST WN6 55 H8
Gathurst Rd WGNW/BIL/O WN5 67 G5
Gatley Dr MGHL L31 73 G5
Gaunts Wy RUNC WA7 150 A7
Gautby Rd BIRK CH41 111 G4
Gavin Rd WDN WA8 133 K6
Gaw Hill La ORM L39 62 C2
Gaw Hill Vw ORM L39 62 D2
Gawsworth Cl CL/PREN CH43 127 H2
ECCL WA10 101 K2
Gawsworth Ct
GOL/RIS/CU WA3 * 107 H7
Gawsworth Rd
GOL/RIS/CU WA3 92 B4
GTS/LS CH66 163 G1
Gaybeech Cl CL/PREN CH43 110 E5
Gayhurst Av
WARRN/WOL WA2 * 122 B3
Gayhurst Crs NG/CROX L11 98 C3
Gaynor Av RNFD/HAY WA11 91 H6
Gayton Av BEB CH63 127 L5
WAL/NB CH45 95 K5
Gayton Cl WGNS/IIMK WN3 78 F2
Gayton Farm Rd HES CH60 141 J8
Gayton La HES CH60 141 K7
Gayton Mill Cl HES CH60 * 141 K6
Gayton Pkwy HES CH60 141 K8
Gayton Rd HES CH60 141 H7
Gaywood Av KKBY L32 86 B5
Gaywood Cl CL/PREN CH43 * 110 E6
KKBY L32 86 B5
Gellings La PR/KW L34 86 C8
Gellings Rd PR/KW L34 86 C8
Gelling St TOX L8 113 H8
Gemini Cl BTL L20 6 F3
Gemini Dr DV/KA/FCH L14 115 H1
General St WARR WA1 15 G5
Geneva Rd NPK/KEN L6 113 L2
WAL/EC CH44 111 M3
Genista Cl WLT/FAZ L9 97 J2
Genoa Cl WLTN L25 115 L6
Gentwood Rd HUY L36 115 L1
Geoffrey St CHLYE PR6 32 F4
George Dr STHP PR8 35 G8
George Hale Av PR/KW L34 100 A7
George Harrison Cl
NPK/KEN L6 113 K2
George Moore Ct
CSBY/BLUN L23 * 71 L7
George Rd HOY CH47 108 E7
WARRW/BUR WA5 136 E1
Georges Crs WARRS WA4 138 D3
George's Dock Gates
VAUX/LVPD L3 12 D6
Georges Dockway
VAUX/LVPD L3 12 D8
George's La CHTN/BK PR9 23 H5
HOR/BR BL6 45 M6
WGN WN1 5 L4
Georges Pierhead
VAUX/LVPD L3 12 D8
George's Ter WGNW/BIL/O WN5 66 F8
George St AIMK WN4 91 L1
BIRK CH41 11 K3
CHLY/EC PR7 32 E6
ECCL WA10 9 H5
EP CH65 20 C1
NEWLW WA12 * 104 C1
VAUX/LVPD L3 12 E6
WGNE/HIN WN2 5 M6
WGNE/HIN WN2 81 G1
Georgia Av NWD/KWIPK L33 73 M7
PS/BROM CH62 144 A2
Georgian Cl HLWD L26 132 B7
RAIN/WH L35 101 J7
Georgian Pl FMBY L37 59 G4
Georgia St BTL L20 7 G4
Geraint St TOX L8 113 H7
Gerald Rd CL/PREN CH43 10 A9
Gerard Av WAL/NB CH45 95 J6
Gerard Rd WAL/NB CH45 95 J7
WKBY CH48 124 D2
Gerards Ct RNFD/HAY WA11 * 89 L5
Gerards La STHEL WA9 102 F6
Gerard St AIMK WN4 91 K2
VAUX/LVPD L3 13 H5
Germander Cl HLWD L26 132 A4
German La CHLY/EC PR7 31 M5
Gerneth Cl SPK/HALE L24 146 E1
Gerneth Rd SPK/HALE L24 146 D2
Gerosa Av WARRN/WOL WA2 105 K5
Gerrard Av GTS/LS CH66 162 E1
WARRW/BUR WA5 14 A1
Gerrard Cl WGNE/HIN WN2 69 M3
Gerrard Pl SKEL WN8 65 H6
Gerrard Rd GOL/RIS/CU WA3 106 C6
WGNW/BIL/O WN5 78 A8
Gerrard's La HLWD L26 132 A3
Gerrard St WDN WA8 16 E4
Gertrude Rd ANF/KKDL L4 97 J7
Gertrude St BIRK CH41 11 L5
STHEL WA9 101 L7
Geves Gdns CSBY/WL L22 83 G4
Ghyll Gv RNFD/HAY WA11 89 K4
Giants Hall Rd WGNNW/ST WN6 68 A2
Gibbons Av ECCL WA10 101 L2
Gibbon's Rd AIMK WN4 90 F3
Gibraltar Rw VAUX/LVPD L3 12 D5
Gibson Cl PEN/TH CH61 141 H2
Gibson Ct EP CH65 * 156 D5
Gibson Rd TOX L8 113 H6
Gibson St TOX L8 113 H6
WARR WA1 15 H6
WARRS WA4 137 M4
WGNE/HIN WN2 80 F3
Giddygate La MGHL L31 73 K7
Gidlow Av CHLYE PR6 44 C6
WGNNW/ST WN6 68 C3
Gidlow La WGNNW/ST WN6 4 B2
Gidlow Rd CLB/OSW/ST L13 114 B2
Gidlow Rd South
CLB/OSW/ST L13 114 B2
Gidlow St WGNE/HIN WN2 69 J5
Gifford Pl WGNE/HIN WN2 81 H1
Gigg La WARRS WA4 136 D8
WARRS WA4 139 G1
Gig La WARR WA1 122 F5
Gilbert Cl BEB CH63 143 H3
Gilbert Pl BRSC L40 51 K1
Gilbert Rd RAIN/WH L35 101 H8
Gilbertson Rd CHLY/EC PR7 44 A3
Gilbert St CHLY/EC PR7 * 32 E7
CLVPS L1 13 G9
WGNE/HIN WN2 69 L8
Gilbrook Sq BIRK CH41 111 H5
Gildarts Gdns VAUX/LVPD L3 12 F2
Gildart St VAUX/LVPD L3 13 L5
Gilderdale Cl GOL/RIS/CU WA3 107 K8
Gilead St EHL/KEN L7 113 K3
Gillan Cl RUNC WA7 150 E8
Gillan Rd WGNNW/ST WN6 68 D3
Gillars Green Dr ECCL WA10 101 H2
Gillar's La ECCL WA10 101 G2
Gill Av WGNNW/ST WN6 55 K7
Gillbrow Crs WGN WN1 5 M2
Gillcroft CHLY/EC PR7 30 D6
Gilleney Gv RAIN/WH L35 101 J8
Gillibrands Rd SKEL WN8 65 K6
Gillibrand St CHLY/EC PR7 32 E6
Gillibrand Wks CHLY/EC PR7 32 E7
Gillmoss Cl NG/CROX L11 98 E1
Gillmoss La NG/CROX L11 85 L8
Gills La PEN/TH CH61 141 J1
Gill St VAUX/LVPD L3 13 L6
Gilman St ANF/KKDL L4 97 J6
Gilmour Mt CL/PREN CH43 10 D9
Gilpin Av MGHL L31 73 G3
Gilpin Pl WGNE/HIN WN2 80 B3
Gilroy Rd NPK/KEN L6 113 K1
WKBY CH48 124 F2
Gilroy St WGN WN1 5 H4
Gilsecroft Av NWD/KWIPK L33 86 C2
Giltbrook Cl WDN WA8 133 M4
Gilwell Av MOR/LEA CH46 110 A6
Gilwell Cl MOR/LEA CH46 110 A6
WARRS WA4 138 E3
Gin Bow CHLY/EC PR7 32 F7
The Ginnel PS/BROM CH62 128 D8
Gipsy Gv CALD/MH L18 115 G8
Gipsy La CALD/MH L18 115 G8
Girton Av AIMK WN4 91 H1
BTL L20 7 L6
Girton Cl EP CH65 20 E6
Girton Rd EP CH65 20 E6
Girtrell Cl GR/UP/WCH CH49 109 M8
Girtrell Rd GR/UP/WCH CH49 109 M8
Girvan Crs AIMK WN4 90 E1
Girvin Dr NSTN CH64 153 G7
Gisburn Av GOL/RIS/CU WA3 92 B3
Givenchy Cl CHLDW L16 115 G5
Gladden Hey Dr
WGNS/IIMK WN3 78 F4
Gladden Pl SKEL WN8 65 G5
Glade Rd HUY L36 116 A1
Gladeswood Rd
NWD/KWIPK L33 86 D4
The Glade HOY CH47 108 F4
WGNNW/ST WN6 55 K7
Gladeville Rd AIG/SPK L17 130 A3
Gladstone Av CHLDW L16 115 J3
LITH L21 83 H6
Gladstone Cl BIRK CH41 10 F5
Gladstone Hall Rd
PS/BROM CH62 * 143 K1
Gladstone Rd ALL/GAR L19 130 E7
CHTN/BK PR9 25 H7
EHL/KEN L7 113 K4
LITH L21 83 H6
NSTN CH64 153 G5
RF/TRAN CH42 128 B2
WAL/EG CH44 111 M2
WLT/FAZ L9 97 H2
Gladstone St BIRK CH41 * 10 F5
ECCL WA10 8 A6
VAUX/LVPD L3 12 F4
WARRN/WOL WA2 14 C4
WDN WA8 16 E3
WLTN L25 131 H3
Gladstone Wy NEWLW WA12 104 D1
Glaisdale Cl AIMK WN4 91 L2
Glaisdale Dr STHP PR8 36 B2
Glaisher St EV L5 97 J7
Glamis Dr CHLY/EC PR7 32 D5
CHTN/BK PR9 25 K5
Glamis Gv STHEL WA9 102 F5
Glamis Rd CLB/OSW/ST L13 97 M7
Glamorgan Cl ECCL WA10 8 E7
Glan Aber Pk WD/CROXPK L12 99 G5
Glasier Rd MOR/LEA CH46 109 L4
Glaslyn Wy WLT/FAZ L9 97 J2
Glassbrook St WGNNW/ST WN6 4 B1
Glassonby Crs NG/CROX L11 98 C4
Glassonby Wy NG/CROX L11 98 C4
Glastonbury Av GOL/RIS/CU WA3 93 K5
Glastonbury Cl NPK/KEN L6 97 M6
RUNC WA7 151 G2
Glasven Rd NWD/KWIPK L33 86 B2
Glazebrook St WARR WA1 15 J4
Glaziers La GOL/RIS/CU WA3 106 F3
Gleadmere WDN WA8 133 L3
Gleaston Cl PS/BROM CH62 143 L4
Gleave Crs NPK/KEN L6 13 M2
Gleave Rd WARRW/BUR WA5 104 B7
Gleave St ECCL WA10 9 H3
Glebe Av AIMK WN4 91 K3
WARRS WA4 138 E4
Glebe Cl MGHL L31 72 D4
WGNNW/ST WN6 56 A4
Glebecroft Av CHNE CH2 165 J2
Glebe End SFTN L29 72 A6
Glebe End St WGNNW/ST WN6 4 C3
Glebe Hey NTHLY L27 116 A8
Glebe Hey Rd
GR/UP/WCH CH49 126 C2
Glebeland GOL/RIS/CU WA3 107 G2
Glebelands Rd MOR/LEA CH46 110 A5
Glebe La CHTN/BK PR9 23 J6
WDN WA8 118 C8
Glebe Pl STHP PR8 3 G3
Glebe Rd SKEL WN8 65 J6
WAL/NB CH45 95 J7
WGNNW/ST WN6 56 B5
Glebe St WGNE/HIN WN2 81 L3
The Glebe RUNC WA7 150 A4
Gleggside WKBY CH48 124 E3
Glegg St VAUX/LVPD L3 12 D1
WGNE/HIN WN2 5 M4
Glegside Rd NWD/KWIPK L33 86 C3
Glemsford Cl WGNS/IIMK WN3 79 K2
Glenacres WLTN L25 * 131 J2
Glenalmond Rd WAL/EG CH44 * 111 M1
Glenathol Rd CALD/MH L18 130 E3
GTS/LS CH66 162 E1
Glenavon Rd CHLDW L16 114 E5
CL/PREN CH43 127 J4
Glenbank CSBY/WL L22 82 E3
Glenbank Cl WLT/FAZ L9 84 C8
Glenbranter Av WGNE/HIN WN2 69 J5
Glenburn Av PS/BROM CH62 155 G1
Glenburn Rd SKEL WN8 65 G1
SKEL WN8 65 H6
WAL/EG CH44 111 M2
Glenby Av CSBY/BLUN L23 83 H3
Glencairn Rd CLB/OSW/ST L13 114 B3
Glencoe Rd GTS/LS CH66 162 E1
WAL/NB CH45 95 K7
Glenconner Rd CHLDW L16 115 G4
Glencourse Rd WDN WA8 118 C8
Glencoyne Dr CHTN/BK PR9 22 D7
Glencroft CHLY/EC PR7 31 K2
Glencroft Cl HUY L36 99 L8
Glendale Av AIMK WN4 91 L1
CHNE CH2 165 J2
Glendale Cl TOX L8 129 H2
Glendale Gv BEB CH63 143 K3
Glendale Wy FMBY L37 59 H3
Glendevon Cl WGNE/HIN WN2 69 J5
Glendevon Rd CHLDW L16 114 F4
HUY L36 116 A4
Glendower Rd CSBY/WL L22 83 G4
Glendower St BTL L20 7 H9
Glen Dr WGNNW/ST WN6 55 G5
Glendyke Rd CALD/MH L18 130 E3
GTS/LS CH66 162 E1
Gleneagles Cl NWD/KWIPK L33 73 M7
PEN/TH CH61 141 H2
Gleneagles Dr CHLYE PR6 31 M1
RNFD/HAY WA11 90 C8
STHP PR8 47 K2
WDN WA8 118 C8
Gleneagles Rd CHLDW L16 114 F4
GTS/LS CH66 162 E1
Glenesk Rd GTS/LS CH66 162 E1
Glenfield Cl CL/PREN CH43 110 E5
MOR/LEA CH46 109 K4
Glenfield Rd WAV L15 114 C7
Glengariff St CLB/OSW/ST L13 98 A6
Glenham Cl HOY CH47 109 G5
Glenhead Rd ALL/GAR L19 130 D5
Glenholm Rd MGHL L31 * 72 E6
Glenluce Rd ALL/GAR L19 130 D5
Glenmarsh Cl BEB CH63 127 M8
WD/CROXPK L12 98 E7
Glenmarsh Wy FMBY L37 59 K2
Glenmaye Cl WD/CROXPK L12 99 G3
Glenmaye Rd GTS/LS CH66 162 E1
Glenmore Av CALD/MH L18 130 B2
Glenmore Rd CL/PREN CH43 127 J1
Glenn Pl WDN WA8 133 M4
Glenpark Dr CHTN/BK PR9 25 K1
Glen Park Rd WAL/NB CH45 95 J6
Glen Rd CLB/OSW/ST L13 114 D3
GTS/LS CH66 162 E1
Glen Ronald Dr
GR/UP/WCH CH49 109 M8
Glenrose Ter STHP PR8 2 F8
Glenroyd Dr BRSC L40 52 A1
Glenside CALD/MH L18 130 E3
WGNNW/ST WN6 54 D3
The Glen CALD/MH L18 130 E2
PS/BROM CH62 143 L2
RUNC WA7 150 B8
Glenton Pk NSTN CH64 153 H7
Glentrees Cl GR/UP/WCH CH49 109 M8
Glentrees Rd WD/CROXPK L12 98 D5
Glentworth Cl MGHL L31 72 F5
Glenville Cl RUNC WA7 149 K7
WLTN L25 131 K2
Glen Vine Cl CHLDW L16 * 115 H5
Glenway NWD/KWIPK L33 74 B7
Glenwood Cl GTS/LS CH66 155 L7
Glenwood Dr PEN/TH CH61 126 A6
Glenwood Gdns GTS/LS CH66 155 L7
Glenwood Rd GTS/LS CH66 155 L7
Glenwyllin Rd CSBY/WL L22 83 G3
Globe Rd BTL L20 6 E3
Globe St ANF/KKDL L4 97 G6
Glossop Wy WGNE/HIN WN2 81 G1
Gloucester Av GOL/RIS/CU WA3 92 D4
Gloucester Cl GTS/LS CH66 163 G5
WARR WA1 122 F6
Gloucester Ct NPK/KEN L6 113 J2
Gloucester Pl NPK/KEN L6 113 J3
Gloucester Rd BTL L20 7 K3
CHLY/EC PR7 32 E8
HUY L36 116 C2
NPK/KEN L6 97 M8
STHP PR8 2 D7
WAL/NB CH45 95 G7
WDN WA8 134 D2
WGNW/BIL/O WN5 67 L7
Gloucester Rd North
NPK/KEN L6 97 M7
Gloucester St STHEL WA9 102 F3
Gloucestor Ct NPK/KEN L6 113 J2
Glover Pl BTL L20 6 F2
Glover Rd CHLY/EC PR7 42 F6
GOL/RIS/CU WA3 106 E8
Glover's Brow KKBY L32 85 L1
Glover's La NTHTN L30 84 A1
Glover St ECCL WA10 8 E7
LEIGH WN7 81 L5
NEWLW WA12 104 E2
RF/TRAN CH42 10 E9
Glyn Av PS/BROM CH62 144 A6
Glynne Gv CHLDW L16 115 J5
Glynne St BTL L20 83 M7
Glynn St WAV L15 114 B6
Glyn Rd WAL/EG CH44 95 K8
Goddard Rd RUNC WA7 150 A2
Godetia Cl WLT/FAZ L9 * 98 B1
Godfrey St WARRN/WOL WA2 15 J2
Godscroft La FROD/HEL WA6 160 A7
Godshill Cl WARRW/BUR WA5 119 M6
Godstow RUNC WA7 151 G1
Golborne Dale Rd NEWLW WA12 92 C8
Golborne Gallery WGN WN1 * 4 E3
Golborne Pl WGN WN1 * 5 J3
Golborne Rd AIMK WN4 91 M1
GOL/RIS/CU WA3 92 E5
WARRN/WOL WA2 105 K5
Golborne St NEWLW WA12 105 G1
WARR WA1 14 D5
Goldcliffe Cl WARRW/BUR WA5 120 F3
Goldcrest Cl RUNC WA7 150 B8
WD/CROXPK L12 99 H1
Goldcrest Ms HLWD L26 132 A4
Golden Gv ANF/KKDL L4 97 J4
Goldenways WGN WN1 68 E3
Goldfinch Cl HLWD L26 132 A4
Goldfinch Farm Rd
SPK/HALE L24 146 E2
Goldfinch La GOL/RIS/CU WA3 123 G1
Goldie St ANF/KKDL L4 97 H6
Goldsmith Pl WGNS/IIMK WN3 79 J4
Goldsmith Rd CL/PREN CH43 127 H4
Goldsmith St BTL L20 6 D2
NPK/KEN L6 * 113 K2
Goldsworth Wy CL/PREN CH43 * 127 J2
Goldsworth Fold RAIN/WH L35 117 K2
Golf Links Rd RF/TRAN CH42 127 K4
Golf Rd FMBY L37 46 F8
Gondover Av WLT/FAZ L9 84 B7
Gonville Rd BTL L20 7 K7
Gooch Dr NEWLW WA12 104 F3
Goodacre Rd WLT/FAZ L9 84 D6
Goodaker's Meadow
GR/UP/WCH CH49 * 126 C3
Goodall Pl ANF/KKDL L4 7 L9
Goodall St ANF/KKDL L4 7 M9
Goodban St STHEL WA9 103 G5
Goodison Av ANF/KKDL L4 97 H5
Goodison Pl ANF/KKDL L4 97 H4
Goodison Rd ANF/KKDL L4 97 H5
Goodlass Rd SPK/HALE L24 131 J8
Goodleigh Pl STHEL WA9 102 E8
Good Shepherd Cl
NG/CROX L11 98 D3
Goodwood Cl HUY L36 115 M4
Goodwood Ct STHEL WA9 101 M7
Goodwood Dr MOR/LEA CH46 110 A2
Goodwood Gv GTS/LS CH66 162 F2
Goodwood St EV L5 96 F8
Gooseberry La RUNC WA7 150 F4
Goose Green Av CHLY/EC PR7 43 H4
Goostrey Cl BEB CH63 143 K4
Gordale Cl WARRW/BUR WA5 120 B6
Gordon Av AIMK WN4 91 G1
CHTN/BK PR9 24 E4
CSBY/WL L22 82 E3
GR/UP/WCH CH49 126 A2
MGHL L31 72 E2
PS/BROM CH62 144 A6
RNFD/HAY WA11 91 H6
WARR WA1 122 D6
Gordon Cl WGNW/BIL/O WN5 68 A5
Gordon Ct GR/UP/WCH CH49 126 A2
Gordon Dr ALL/GAR L19 130 C6
DV/KA/FCH L14 115 G2
Gordon La CHNE CH2 163 K8
Gordon Rd LITH L21 83 H7
WAL/NB CH45 95 K6
Gordonstoun Crs
WGNW/BIL/O WN5 67 H6
Gordon St BIRK CH41 10 F6
CHLYE PR6 32 F6
CHTN/BK PR9 3 J1
WAV L15 114 A6
WGN WN1 5 K5
Gore Dr ORM L39 63 G2
Goree Piazza CLVP L2 * 12 E7
Gores La FMBY L37 47 G8
RNFD/HAY WA11 77 J8
Gores Rd NWD/KWIPK L33 86 D4
Gore St TOX L8 113 G7
WGNW/BIL/O WN5 67 K7
Goring St CHLY/EC PR7 32 F6
Gorleston Wy KKBY L32 86 B4
Gorman St WGNNW/ST WN6 4 A3
Gorman Wk WGNS/IIMK WN3 68 B8
Gorse Av WD/CROXPK L12 98 D4
Gorsebank Rd CALD/MH L18 * 114 A8
Gorsebank St WAL/EG CH44 111 L2
Gorseburn Rd CLB/OSW/ST L13 98 A7
Gorse Covert Rd
GOL/RIS/CU WA3 107 K7
Gorse Crs WAL/EG CH44 111 L3
Gorsedale Pk WAL/EG CH44 * 111 M3
Gorsedale Rd CALD/MH L18 130 C1
WAL/EG CH44 111 L3
Gorsefield FMBY L37 47 J7
STHEL WA9 101 M6
Gorsefield Av PS/BROM CH62 143 M8
Gorsefield Cl PS/BROM CH62 143 M8
Gorsefield Rd CSBY/BLUN L23 71 J8
RF/TRAN CH42 127 L2
Gorse Hey Ct WD/CROXPK L12 98 C8
Gorsehill Rd HES CH60 141 J4
WAL/NB CH45 95 J6
Gorse La WKBY CH48 125 G4
Gorse Rd HOY CH47 108 F5
Gorses Dr WGNE/HIN WN2 57 L7
Gorse Wy FMBY L37 58 E1
Gorsewood Gv WLTN L25 115 K8
Gorsewood Rd RUNC WA7 150 F7
WLTN L25 115 K8
Gorsey Av NTHTN L30 83 L2
Gorsey Brow
WGNW/BIL/O WN5 77 M8
Gorsey Brow Cl
WGNW/BIL/O WN5 77 M8
Gorsey Cop Wy WLTN L25 115 J7
Gorsey Cft PR/KW L34 101 H6
Gorsey La BRSC L40 40 E3
HTWN L38 70 C4
LITH L21 83 K3
ORM L39 48 C6
STHEL WA9 119 H1
WAL/EG CH44 110 F2
WARRN/WOL WA2 15 J1
WDN WA8 17 L4
Gorsey Pl SKEL WN8 65 K6
Gorseyville Crs BEB CH63 128 A8
Gorseyville Rd BEB CH63 128 A8
Gorseywell La RUNC WA7 151 H7
Gorst La CHTN/BK PR9 38 B7
Gorstons La NSTN CH64 153 J7
Gorst St ANF/KKDL L4 97 H6
Gorsuch La BRSC L40 49 M1
Gorton Rd CLB/OSW/ST L13 114 D3
Gort Rd HUY L36 116 A2
Goschen St CLB/OSW/ST L13 114 B2
EV L5 97 H6
Gosford St TOX L8 129 H1
Gosforth Rd CHTN/BK PR9 25 H5
Gosling Rd GOL/RIS/CU WA3 106 D6
Gosport Cl WARRN/WOL WA2 122 A4
Goswell St WAV L15 114 A6
Gotham Rd BEB CH63 143 J3
Gothic St RF/TRAN CH42 128 B3
Gough Av WARRN/WOL WA2 121 K3
Gough Rd CLB/OSW/ST L13 98 A6
Goulden St WARRW/BUR WA5 121 G7
Goulders Ct RUNC WA7 150 D8
Goulding St CHLY/EC PR7 32 F7
Gourley Rd CLB/OSW/ST L13 114 D4
Gourley's La WKBY CH48 124 F4
Government Rd HOY CH47 108 D6
Govett Rd STHEL WA9 101 L6
Gower Gdns BRSC L40 52 B2
Gower St BTL L20 83 J8
STHEL WA9 102 F4
VAUX/LVPD L3 112 E5
WGNW/BIL/O WN5 68 B7
Gowrie Gv LITH L21 83 J6
Gowy Ct GTS/LS CH66 156 A5
Goyt Hey Av WGNW/BIL/O WN5 90 A1
Graburn Rd FMBY L37 59 H1
Grace Av AIN/FAZ L10 85 J6
WARRN/WOL WA2 121 K5
Grace Cl WAL/NB CH45 95 K8
Grace Rd EP CH65 20 C2
WLT/FAZ L9 84 C7
Grace St LEIGH WN7 81 L8
STHEL WA9 102 E5
TOX L8 129 H1
Gradwell St CLVPS L1 13 G8
Grafton Ct CHLY/EC PR7 32 D8
Grafton Crs TOX L8 113 G7
Grafton Dr GR/UP/WCH CH49 126 C1
STHP PR8 34 C8
Grafton Gv TOX L8 129 G1
Grafton Rd EP CH65 20 C1
WAL/NB CH45 95 K6
Grafton St CHLY/EC PR7 44 B7
CL/PREN CH43 10 D7
ECCL WA10 8 B5
NEWLW WA12 104 D2
TOX L8 112 F7
WARRW/BUR WA5 121 G7
Grafton Wk WKBY CH48 124 E3
Graham Av GTS/LS CH66 155 M8
WGNNW/ST WN6 54 E3
Graham Cl WDN WA8 133 L5
Graham Dr HLWD L26 132 C5
Graham Rd WDN WA8 133 L5
WKBY CH48 124 C2
Graham's Rd HUY L36 116 B3
Graham St STHEL WA9 9 L5
WGNE/HIN WN2 80 C4
Grainger Av BTL L20 84 A7
CL/PREN CH43 127 H3
WKBY CH48 124 D1
Graley Cl HLWD L26 132 B7
Grammar School Ct
WARRS WA4 * 138 B2
Grammar School La
WKBY CH48 124 F4
Grammar School Rd
WARRS WA4 138 B2
Grampian Av MOR/LEA CH46 110 A5
Grampian Rd EHL/KEN L7 114 A3
Grampian Wy GOL/RIS/CU WA3 92 F4
MOR/LEA CH46 110 A5
NSTN CH64 153 G8
PS/BROM CH62 155 G1
Granams Cft NTHTN L30 83 M1
Granard Rd WAV L15 114 C7
Granary Wy VAUX/LVPD L3 112 F7
Granborne Cha KKBY L32 85 K2
Granby Cl CHTN/BK PR9 25 H2
RUNC WA7 * 150 E8
Granby Crs BEB CH63 143 J5
Granby Rd WARRS WA4 137 K5
Granby St TOX L8 113 J6
Grandison Rd ANF/KKDL L4 97 L4
Grand National Av WLT/FAZ L9 84 D4
Grange Av CHTN/BK PR9 25 G5
WAL/NB CH45 95 K7
WARRS WA4 15 M8
WD/CROXPK L12 99 G8
WGNS/IIMK WN3 4 C9
WGNW/BIL/O WN5 67 K6
WLTN L25 131 M6
Grange Av North
WD/CROXPK L12 99 H8
Grange Cl GOL/RIS/CU WA3 92 E7
Grange Crs GTS/LS CH66 155 J4
Grange Cross Cl WKBY CH48 125 G4
Grange Cross Hey WKBY CH48 125 G4
Grange Cross La WKBY CH48 125 G4
Grange Dr BEB CH63 142 C6
CHLY/EC PR7 42 F5
CHLYE PR6 31 L1
ECCL WA10 101 K4
HES CH60 141 H4
WARRW/BUR WA5 136 C1
WDN WA8 133 M4
Grange Farm Cl
WARRW/BUR WA5 120 F7
Grange Farm Crs WKBY CH48 125 G2
Grange Green Mnr
WARRS WA4 * 137 G6
Grangehurst Ct WLTN L25 131 K1
Grange La FMBY L37 47 G8
WLTN L25 115 J8
Grangemeadow Rd WLTN L25 115 J8
Grange Ms WLTN L25 * 131 K1
Grangemoor RUNC WA7 149 M6
Grange Mt CL/PREN CH43 10 E7
HES CH60 141 H4
WKBY CH48 124 F3
Grange Old Rd WKBY CH48 124 E3
Grange Pk MGHL L31 73 G6
Grange Park Av RUNC WA7 19 L4
Grange Park Rd ECCL WA10 101 L4
RUNC WA7 19 L4
Grange Pl CL/PREN CH43 10 F6
Grange Rd AIMK WN4 79 H7
BIRK CH41 11 G6
CHTN/BK PR9 25 G6
EP CH65 20 C5
HES CH60 141 H3
HTWN L38 59 G7
NTHTN L30 84 D3
RNFD/HAY WA11 90 F8
RUNC WA7 19 L4
WGNE/HIN WN2 81 G4
WKBY CH48 124 D3
Grange Rd North RUNC WA7 19 L3
Grange Rd West CL/PREN CH43 10 E6
Grangeside WLTN L25 115 J8
Grange St NPK/KEN L6 97 M8
WGNE/HIN WN2 80 F1
Grange Ter WAV L15 114 B6
The Grange WAL/EC CH44 111 L1
Grange V RF/TRAN CH42 128 C4
Grange Va RNFD/HAY WA11 90 F7
Grange Vw CL/PREN CH43 10 E7
Grangeway RUNC WA7 19 L9
Grange Wy WLTN L25 115 J8
Grangeway Ct RUNC WA7 19 M9
Grange Weint WLTN L25 131 J1
Grangewood CHLDW L16 115 H4

Granston Cl WARRW/BUR WA5 ...121 G3
Grant Av WAV L15 ...114 B7
Grant Cl DV/KA/FCH L14 ...115 J2
  ECCL WA10 ...8 D4
  WARRW/BUR WA5 ...120 F4
Grantham Av WARR WA1 ...15 M1
  WARRS WA4 ...137 K5
Grantham Cl PEN/TH CH61 ...141 G1
  STHP PR8 ...35 U4
Grantham Gv WGNE/HIN WN2 ...69 H3
Grantham Rd NWD/KWIPK L33 ...74 A8
  STHP PR8 ...35 J4
Grantham St NPK/KEN L6 ...113 K2
Grantham Wy NTHTN L30 ...84 C1
Grantley Rd WAV L15 ...114 C7
Grantley St AIMK WN4 ...79 J8
Granton Cl FMBY L37 ...59 G2
Granton Rd EV L5 ...97 H7
Grant Rd DV/KA/FCH L14 ...115 H2
  MOR/LEA CH46 ...110 D1
  WARRW/BUR WA5 ...120 D7
  WGNS/IIMK WN3 ...79 J2
Grantwood AIMK WN4 ...79 J8
Granville Av MGHL L31 ...72 E3
Granville Cl ORM L39 ...62 D4
  WAL/NB CH45 ...95 G7
Granville Dr GTS/LS CH66 ...155 K6
Granville Pk WAV L15 ...62 E5
Granville Pk West ORM L39 ...62 D5
Granville Rd ALL/GAR L19 * ...130 E7
  CHLYE PR6 ...33 F2
  STHP PR8 ...34 F2
  WAV L15 ...113 M6
Granville St CHLYE PR6 ...44 C6
  RUNC WA7 ...19 H2
  STHEL WA9 ...102 A2
  WARR WA1 ...15 J3
Grape La CROS/BRETH PR26 ...29 L4
Grappenhall La WARR WA4 ...138 F8
Grappenhall Rd EP CH65 ...163 F2
  WARRS WA4 ...137 M4
Grappenhall Wy CL/PREN CH43 ...110 E6
Grasmere Av CL/PREN CH43 ...110 E6
  PR/KW L34 ...101 H7
  RNFD/HAY WA11 ...89 K6
  SKEL WN8 ...66 D5
  WARRN/WOL WA2 ...121 M2
  WGNE/HIN WN2 ...69 J6
  WGNW/BIL/O WN5 ...67 H5
Grasmere Cl CHLY/EC PR7 ...31 M4
  NWD/KWIPK L33 ...85 M1
  RNFD/HAY WA11 ...89 J6
Grasmere Ct AIMK WN4 ...79 K8
Grasmere Dr AIMK WN4 ...79 K8
  LITH L21 ...84 A4
  RUNC WA7 ...149 M8
  WAL/NB CH45 ...95 J8
Grasmere Fold RNFD/HAY WA11 ...89 K6
Grasmere Gdns CSBY/BLUN L23 ...83 H2
Grasmere Rd EP CH65 ...163 F3
  FMBY L37 ...58 F2
  FROD/HEL WA6 ...160 E6
  MGHL L31 ...72 F3
  NSTN CH64 ...153 G7
  WGNW/BIL/O WN5 ...67 H5
Grasmere St EV L5 ...97 J7
Grasmere Ter CHLY/EC PR7 ...32 D8
  WGNE/HIN WN2 ...80 D5
Grasscroft Rd WGNE/HIN WN2 ...81 J1
Grassendale Esp ALL/GAR L19 ...130 B7
Grassendale La ALL/GAR L19 ...130 C6
Grassendale Rd ALL/GAR L19 ...130 C6
Grassington Crs WLTN L25 ...131 M3
Grassmoor Cl PS/BROM CH62 ...144 A5
Grass Wood Rd
  GR/UP/WCH CH49 ...126 D3
Grasville Rd RF/TRAN CH42 ...128 D2
Gratrix Rd PS/BROM CH62 ...143 M5
Gratton Pl SKEL WN8 ...65 J5
Gravel La CHLY/EC PR9 ...23 H8
Grave-Yard La ORM L39 ...63 J6
The Gravel KIRK/FR/WA PR4 ...27 H3
Gray Av RNFD/HAY WA11 ...90 F7
Gray Cl WGNE/HIN WN2 ...69 J3
Gray Gv HUY L36 ...116 B8
Graylag Cl RUNC WA7 ...150 B8
Graylands Pl ANF/KKDL L4 ...97 L4
Graylands Rd ANF/KKDL L4 ...97 L4
  PS/BROM CH62 ...128 E7
Grayling Dr WD/CROXPK L12 ...98 F2
Grays Av WD/HAY WL35 ...101 H7
Grayson's Cl WGN WN1 ...4 F1
Graysons Rd RNFD/HAY WA11 ...76 B5
Grayson St CLVPS L1 ...112 E5
Grayston Av STHEL WA9 ...102 F7
Gray St BTL L20 ...83 J8
Greasby Dr GTS/LS CH66 ...155 K4
Greasby Rd GR/UP/WCH CH49 ...125 M2
  WAL/EG CH44 ...111 J1
Great Acre WGN WN1 ...5 L1
Great Ashfield WDN WA8 ...133 H2
Great Charlotte St CLVPS L1 ...13 H7
Great Crosshall St
  VAUX/LVPD L3 ...12 F5
Great Delph RNFD/HAY WA11 ...90 F6
Great George Pl CLVPS L1 ...113 G6
Great George Sq CLVPS L1 ...113 G6
Great George's Rd
  CSBY/WL L22 ...82 F5
Great George St CLVPS L1 ...113 G5
  WGNS/IIMK WN3 ...4 C4
Great Hanging Br
  CROS/BRETH PR26 ...28 F5
Great Hey NTHTN L30 ...71 M8
Great Homer St EV L5 ...97 G8
Great Howard St EV L5 ...96 D8
  VAUX/LVPD L3 ...12 D4
Great Meadow CHLY/EC PR7 ...32 C5
Great Mersey St EV L5 ...96 F7
Great Nelson St VAUX/LVPD L3 ...13 L6
Great Newton St VAUX/LVPD L3 ...13 L6
Great Orford St VAUX/LVPD L3 ...13 L8
Great Richmond St
  VAUX/LVPD L3 ...13 J3
Great Riding RUNC WA7 ...150 E6
Greaves Cl CHTN/BK PR9 ...23 J8
  WCNNW/ST WN6 ...55 H5
Greaves Hall Av CHTN/BK PR9 ...23 J3
Greaves St TOX L8 * ...113 H8
Grebe Av ECCL WA10 ...101 J5
Grebe Cl WGNS/IIMK WN3 ...78 D5
Grecian St EV L5 ...97 H7
Gredington St TOX L8 ...129 J2
Greeba Av WARRS WA4 ...137 K2
Greek St RUNC WA7 ...18 F2
  VAUX/LVPD L3 ...13 K6
Greenacre BRSC L40 ...64 A1
  WGN WN1 ...5 H1
Greenacre Cl WLTN L25 ...131 H5
Greenacre Dr BEB CH63 ...143 K6
Greenacre Rd WLTN L25 ...131 L5
Greenacres FROD/HEL WA6 ...160 E2
Greenacres Cl CL/PREN CH43 ...127 H8
  GOL/RIS/CU WA3 ...93 K5
Greenacres Dr CHLYE PR6 ...31 M1
Greenall Av WARRW/BUR WA5 ...135 M1

Greenall's Av WARRS WA4 ...137 L4
Greenall St AIMK WN4 ...79 K8
  WN4 ...8 B3
Green Bank BEB CH63 ...142 C3
Greenbank CSBY/WL L22 ...83 G5
  ORM L39 ...62 E5
  WGNE/HIN WN2 ...80 D6
  WGNE/HIN WN2 ...81 J2
Greenbank Av GTS/LS CH66 ...155 L6
  MGHL L31 ...72 E2
  WAL/NB CH45 ...95 K6
  WGNW/BIL/O WN5 ...77 M2
Greenbank Ct AIG/SPK L17 ...114 A8
Greenbank Crs ECCL WA10 ...8 E6
Greenbank Dr AIG/SPK L17 ...114 A8
  AIN/FAZ L10 ...85 K6
  PEN/TH CH61 ...141 H2
  STHP PR8 ...35 G3
Greenbank Gdns WARRS WA4 ...138 E3
Greenbank La AIG/SPK L17 ...130 A1
Greenbank Rd CALD/MH L18 ...130 B1
  RF/TRAN CH42 ...127 L2
  WARRS WA4 ...138 B3
  WKBY CH48 ...124 D1
Greenbank St WARRS WA4 ...137 L4
Green Bridge Cl RUNC WA7 ...150 C4
Greenbridge Rd RUNC WA7 ...150 C4
Greenburn Av RNFD/HAY WA11 ...89 L4
Green Ct COL/RIS/CU WA3 ...93 K4
Green Cft CSBY/BLUN L23 ...71 K8
Greencroft Rd WAL/EG CH44 ...111 L2
Greendale Rd PS/BROM CH62 ...128 C7
  WLTN L25 ...131 H1
Green End La STHEL WA9 ...103 J5
Green End Pk WD/CROXPK L12 ...98 C6
Greene's Rd RAIN/WH L35 ...116 F3
Greenfield Av SKEL WN8 ...53 K3
  WGNE/HIN WN2 ...5 L6
Greenfield Dr HUY L36 ...116 B5
Greenfield Gdns CHNE CH2 ...165 K2
Greenfield Gv HUY L36 ...116 B5
Greenfield La FROD/HEL WA6 ...160 D4
  HES CH60 ...141 G8
  LITH L21 ...83 J4
Greenfield Rd CHLYE PR6 ...33 G5
  CHLYE PR6 ...44 C5
  CLB/OSW/ST L13 ...114 E3
  ECCL WA10 ...8 B1
  GTS/LS CH66 ...155 K6
  STHP PR8 ...36 E4
Greenfields WGNNW/ST WN6 ...67 H1
Greenfields Av PS/BROM CH62 ...143 L6
  WARRS WA4 ...137 M5
Greenfields Cl NEWLW WA12 ...104 E1
  NSTN CH64 ...153 H8
  WARR WA1 ...122 E6
Greenfields Crs AIMK WN4 ...91 K1
  PS/BROM CH62 ...143 L6
Greenfields Cft NSTN CH64 ...153 G8
Greenfield Vw
  WGNW/BIL/O WN5 ...89 M1
Greenfield Wy CALD/MH L18 ...130 E4
  WAL/EG CH44 ...111 K1
Greenfinch Cl HLWD L26 ...132 A4
  WD/CROXPK L12 ...99 H2
Greenford Cl WGNNW/BIL/O WN5 ...66 F7
Greenford Rd WLTN L25 ...131 J1
Greengables Cl TOX L8 ...113 J8
Green Gates HUY L36 ...100 A7
Greengates Crs NSTN CH64 ...153 G8
Greenhalgh La CHLYE PR6 ...44 D5
Greenham Av NWD/KWIPK L33 ...74 B7
Greenhaven Cl AIN/FAZ L10 ...85 J6
Green Hayes Av WGN WN1 ...68 E2
Greenheath Wy MOR/LEA CH46 ...110 D2
Greenhey WGNW/BIL/O WN5 ...67 J6
Green Hey Dr NTHTN L30 ...83 L3
Green Heys Dr MGHL L31 ...73 H3
Greenheys Gdns TOX L8 * ...113 K7
Greenheys Rd PEN/TH CH61 ...125 L8
  TOX L8 ...113 J8
  WAL/EG CH44 ...111 K1
Greenhill Av CALD/MH L18 ...114 E8
Greenhill Cl CALD/MH L18 ...130 D3
Greenhill Crs WGNW/BIL/O WN5 ...78 B8
Greenhill Pl HUY L36 ...116 A4
Greenhill Rd CALD/MH L18 ...130 D2
  WGNW/BIL/O WN5 ...67 G7
Greenholme Cl NG/CROX L11 ...98 C2
Greenhouse Farm Rd
  RUNC WA7 ...150 D7
Greenhow Av WKBY CH48 ...124 D2
Greenings La CHTN/BK PR9 ...37 L2
Green Jones Brow
  WARRW/BUR WA5 ...104 B7
Greenlake Rd CALD/MH L18 ...130 D3
Greenland Av WGNNW/ST WN6 ...56 A5
Greenland La CHLYE PR6 ...44 B8
Greenlands HUY L36 ...116 C1
Greenland St CLVPS L1 ...112 F6
Green La BEB CH63 ...128 B8
  BIRK CH41 ...11 L3
  BRSC L40 ...40 C6
  BRSC L40 ...52 B1
  CALD/MH L18 ...130 D1
  CHLY/EC PR7 ...43 J6
  CHTN/BK PR9 ...26 E1
  CLB/OSW/ST L13 ...114 B1
  CSBY/BLUN L23 ...71 K7
  CSBY/WL L22 ...82 E3
  ECCL WA10 ...20 C7
  EP CH65 ...6 C3
  FMBY L37 ...48 E7
  GOL/RIS/CU WA3 ...93 J3
  GTS/LS CH66 ...162 F1
  HOR/BR BL6 ...45 K8
  KIRK/FR/WA PR4 ...21 L1
  LITH L21 ...83 L6
  MGHL L31 ...72 C3
  ORM L39 ...51 D7
  RNFD/HAY WA11 ...76 D3
  VAUX/LVPD L3 ...13 K8
  WAL/NB CH45 ...95 J4
  WARR WA1 ...122 C5
  WARRN/WOL WA2 ...105 J4
  WARRS WA4 ...137 L5
  WARRW/BUR WA5 ...104 A6
  WDN WA8 ...134 A4
  WGNNW/ST WN6 ...56 A5
  WGNW/BIL/O WN5 ...77 M2
Green Lane Av ORM L39 * ...51 D7
Green Lane North WARRN/WOL WA2 ...105 J3
Green La North CHLDW L16 ...114 C1
Green Lawn HUY L36 ...116 C1
  RF/TRAN CH42 ...128 C3
Green Lawn Gv RF/TRAN CH42 * ...128 B3
Green Lawns GTS/LS CH66 ...163 H5
Green Leach Av RNFD/HAY WA11 ...89 K6
Green Leach Ct RNFD/HAY WA11 ...89 K6
Green Leach La RNFD/HAY WA11 ...89 K6
Greenlea Cl BEB CH63 ...128 D7
  EP CH65 ...6 D5
  WGNW/BIL/O WN5 ...66 F8
Greenleaf St TOX L8 ...113 L6
Greenleas Cl WAL/NB CH45 ...94 F7

Greenleas Rd WAL/NB CH45 ...94 F7
Greenleigh Rd CALD/MH L18 ...130 D3
Green Link WAL/NB CH45 ...72 D5
Greenloon's Dr FMBY L37 ...58 E5
Greenloon's Wk FMBY L37 ...58 E5
Green Mt GR/UP/WCH CH49 ...110 C8
Green Oaks Pth WDN WA8 ...17 H4
Green Oaks Wy WDN WA8 ...17 G5
Greenock St VAUX/LVPD L3 ...12 C4
Greenodd Av WD/CROXPK L12 ...98 E4
Greenore Dr SPK/HALE L24 ...147 M3
Greenough Av RAIN/WH L35 ...101 L8
Greenough St WGN WN1 ...5 H3
  WLTN L25 ...131 H3
Green Pk NTHTN L30 ...72 B8
Green Park Dr MGHL L31 ...72 B8
Greenrigg Cl WGNNW/ST WN6 ...56 B6
Green Rd PR/KW L34 ...100 D1
Greensbridge La HLWD L26 ...132 D4
Greenshank Cl NEWLW WA12 ...104 E1
Greenside CHLY/EC PR7 ...31 L2
  NPK/KEN L6 ...13 M4
Greenside Av AIN/FAZ L10 ...84 F3
  FROD/HEL WA6 ...160 F6
  WAV L15 ...114 C6
Greenside Cl NWD/KWIPK L33 ...74 D7
Green's La RAIN/WH L35 ...61 L4
Greenslate Ct
  WGNW/BIL/O WN5 ...77 M2
Greenslate Rd
  WGNW/BIL/O WN5 ...78 A2
Green Strawberry EP CH65 ...163 J5
Green St CHLY/EC PR7 ...32 C7
  CHLYE PR6 ...44 D5
  EV L5 ...12 F1
  WARRW/BUR WA5 ...14 A4
  WGNE/HIN WN2 ...80 D3
Greensward Cl WCNNW/ST WN6 ...55 K4
The Green BEB CH63 ...128 L1
  CHLY/EC PR7 ...30 E8
  CHLYE PR6 ...44 C5
  CLB/OSW/ST L13 ...114 E3
  EP CH65 ...163 K3
  NSTN CH64 ...152 F5
  NSTN CH64 ...153 H7
  PR/KW L34 ...101 G6
  PS/BROM CH62 ...143 M2
  RUNC WA7 ...150 B4
  SKEL WN8 ...53 K3
  WGNW/BIL/O WN5 ...67 H7
  WKBY CH48 ...124 F6
Greenvale WGNNW/ST WN6 ...67 H1
Greenville Cl BEB CH63 ...128 B8
Greenville Dr MGHL L31 ...72 A6
Greenville Rd BEB CH63 ...128 B8
  NSTN CH64 ...153 H4
Green Wk STHP PR8 ...34 F8
Green Wy HUY L36 ...115 G3
Greenway AIMK WN4 ...91 J1
  CHLY/EC PR7 ...30 D6
  CSBY/BLUN L23 ...71 J8
  GR/UP/WCH CH49 ...126 A1
  NSTN CH64 ...153 H7
  PEN/TH CH61 ...141 G1
  PS/BROM CH62 ...143 M2
  WARR WA1 ...122 B6
  WARRS WA4 ...137 M6
  WARRW/BUR WA5 ...120 A6
Greenway Av SKEL WN8 ...65 K6
Green Way Cl HUY L36 ...115 K1
Greenway Cl FROD/HEL WA6 ...166 C3
  SKEL WN8 ...65 G3
Greenway Rd RF/TRAN CH42 ...18 F6
  SPK/HALE L24 ...147 J2
  WDN WA8 ...134 D3
Greenways WGNNW/ST WN6 ...56 C7
  WGNW/BIL/O WN5 ...77 M2
The Greenway WD/CROXPK L12 ...115 G1
Greenwell Rd RNFD/HAY WA11 ...90 E7
Greenwich Av WDN WA8 ...134 F1
Greenwich Ct WLT/FAZ L9 ...84 D5
Greenwich Rd WLT/FAZ L9 ...84 D5
Greenwood Av
  WGNW/BIL/O WN5 ...68 A6
Greenwood Cl COL/RIS/CU WA3 ...107 H3
  ORM L39 ...62 E4
  PR/KW L34 ...101 G7
Greenwood Ct STHEL WA9 ...118 F3
Greenwood Crs
  WARR/WOL WA2 ...121 M3
Greenwood Dr NEWLW WA12 ...104 F3
Greenwood La WAL/EG CH44 ...95 L8
Greenwood Rd CALD/MH L18 ...130 D4
  GR/UP/WCH CH49 ...126 C2
  HOY CH47 ...109 G5
  WGNW/BIL/O WN5 ...68 A7
Greetby Hl ORM L39 ...51 J8
Greetby Pl SKEL WN8 ...65 J5
Greetham St CLVPS L1 ...112 F5
Gregory Cl CHLDW L16 ...115 G5
  WARRN/BUR WA5 ...120 B4
Gregory La ORM L39 ...49 K2
Gregory St WGNE/HIN WN2 * ...69 L7
Gregory Wy CHLDW L16 ...115 G5
Gregson Ct WAL/NB CH45 ...95 L5
Gregson Rd DV/KA/FCH L14 ...114 F2
  RAIN/WH L35 ...100 F8
  WDN WA8 ...17 H2
Gregson's Av FMBY L37 ...47 G8
Gregson St NPK/KEN L6 ...13 M3
Grenfell Cl NSTN CH64 ...152 F5
Grenfell Pk NSTN CH64 ...152 K4
Grenfell Rd CLB/OSW/ST L13 ...98 B5
Grenfell St WDN WA8 ...16 A4
Grennan Ct WAL/NB CH45 * ...95 K5
The Grennan WAL/NB CH45 * ...95 K5
Grenville Crs BEB CH63 ...143 L6
Grenville Dr PEN/TH CH61 ...141 G2
Grenville Rd RF/TRAN CH42 ...128 B2
Grenville St South CLVPS L1 ...112 F5
Grenville Wy RF/TRAN CH42 ...128 B2
Gresford Av AIG/SPK L17 ...113 M7
  CL/PREN CH43 ...127 J3
  WKBY CH48 ...124 D1
Gresford Cl WARRN/WOL WA2 ...117 K2
  WARRW/BUR WA5 ...120 C4
Gresham St EHL/KEN L7 * ...113 M4
Gresley Cl EHL/KEN L7 * ...113 L4
Gressingham Rd CALD/MH L18 ...130 D2
Gretton Rd DV/KA/FCH L14 ...99 K8
Greyfriars AIMK WN4 ...91 H2
Greyfriars Rd STHP PR8 ...34 F7
Grey Heights Vw CHLYE PR6 ...33 G5
Greyhound Farm Rd
  SPK/HALE L24 ...146 E2
Greymist Av WARR WA1 ...122 E6
Grey Rd AIMK WN4 ...91 J1
  WLT/FAZ L9 ...97 G2
Greys St WARR WA1 * ...122 E4
Greystoke Cl GR/UP/WCH CH49 ...126 F1
Greystokes ORM L39 ...62 F3
Greystone Av WGNE/HIN WN2 ...57 L8
Greystone Crs DV/KA/FCH L14 ...115 G2
Greystone Pl AIN/FAZ L10 ...85 H6
Greystone Rd AIN/FAZ L10 ...85 G5

  DV/KA/FCH L14 ...115 G3
  WARRW/BUR WA5 ...136 B1
Greystones GTS/LS CH66 ...162 F1
Grey St TOX L8 ...113 H7
Gribble Rd AIN/FAZ L10 ...85 J6
Grice Cl WARRS WA4 ...137 L4
Grierson St TOX L8 ...113 K6
Grieve Rd AIN/FAZ L10 ...85 J6
Griffin Av MOR/LEA CH46 ...110 A5
  NG/CROX L11 ...98 E1
Griffin Cl ECCL WA10 ...101 H1
  WARRN/BUR WA5 ...104 A7
Griffin Ms WDN WA8 ...134 D2
Griffin St STHEL WA9 ...2 A5
Griffith Av GOL/RIS/CU WA3 ...107 G8
Griffiths Cl GR/UP/WCH CH49 ...125 L7
Griffiths Dr CHTN/BK PR9 ...25 H5
Griffith's Rd HUY L36 ...116 A3
Griffiths St CLVPS L1 ...113 G5
Grimeford La CHLYE PR6 ...44 F3
Grime St CHLY/EC PR7 ...32 F7
Grimley Av BTL L20 ...6 C4
Grimrod Pl SKEL WN8 ...65 J6
Grimshaw Green La SKEL WN8 ...40 E8
Grimshaw La ORM L39 ...51 G7
Grimshaw Rd SKEL WN8 ...65 K5
Grimshaw St BTL L20 ...6 E6
  GOL/RIS/CU WA3 ...92 C4
  STHEL WA9 ...102 E7
Grindley Gdns EP CH65 ...163 L5
Grinfield St EHL/KEN L7 ...113 L4
Grinshill Cl TOX L8 ...113 J7
Grinstead Cl STHP PR8 ...35 H4
Grinton Crs HUY L36 ...115 M3
Grisedale Cl FMBY L37 ...58 E2
  RUNC WA7 ...150 A8
Grisedale Pl CHLY/EC PR7 ...32 D8
Grisedale Rd PS/BROM CH62 ...144 A5
Grizedale WDN WA8 ...133 K3
Grizedale Av RNFD/HAY WA11 ...89 K5
Grizedale Cl WGNE/HIN WN2 ...69 J3
Grizedale Rd EV L5 ...97 H7
Groarke Dr WARRW/BUR WA5 ...119 M8
Groes Cl ALL/GAR L19 ...130 C6
Grogan Sq BTL L20 ...83 M7
Gronow Pl BTL L20 * ...84 A7
Grosmont Rd KKBY L32 ...86 B5
Grosvenor Av CSBY/BLUN L23 ...83 G3
  COL/RIS/CU WA3 ...92 F4
  WARR WA1 ...15 M1
  WKBY CH48 ...124 D3
Grosvenor Cl STHP PR8 ...35 G2
  WARRS WA4 ...120 E8
Grosvenor Ct CL/PREN CH43 ...10 C3
  WAV L15 * ...114 C6
Grosvenor Dr WAL/NB CH45 ...95 K5
Grosvenor Gdns WALLW12 ...104 D3
  STHP PR8 ...35 H2
Grosvenor Gra WARR WA1 ...122 D4
Grosvenor Pl CL/PREN CH43 ...10 C3
  STHP PR8 ...35 H2
Grosvenor Rd ALL/GAR L19 ...130 C7
  ANF/KKDL L4 ...7 M6
  CHLY/EC PR7 ...32 C7
  CL/PREN CH43 ...10 A3
  ECCL WA10 ...101 L3
  HOY CH47 ...108 D7
  LEIGH WN7 ...81 M7
  MGHL L31 ...72 E7
  PR/KW L34 ...100 F7
  RNFD/HAY WA11 ...89 K6
  STHP PR8 ...35 G1
  WAL/NB CH45 ...95 K5
  WAV L15 ...113 M6
  WDN WA8 ...134 D1
Grosvenor St RUNC WA7 ...19 H4
  VAUX/LVPD L3 ...13 H3
  WAL/EG CH44 ...95 K8
  WGNE/HIN WN2 ...69 M8
  WGNW/BIL/O WN5 ...68 B7
Grove Av CHLYE PR6 ...44 C6
  HES CH60 ...141 H4
  LYMM WA13 ...139 L2
Grovedale Rd CALD/MH L18 ...114 D8
Grovehurst Av DV/KA/FCH L14 ...115 H1
Groveland Av HOY CH47 ...108 D6
  WAL/NB CH45 ...94 F7
Groveland Rd WAL/NB CH45 ...94 F7
Grovelands EHL/KEN L7 * ...113 J5
Groves La WGNNW/ST WN6 ...56 B5
Grove Md MGHL L31 ...72 A6
Grovenor Ct NTHTN L30 ...84 B2
Grove Pk CHTN/BK PR9 ...25 H4
  TOX L8 ...113 J8
Grove Park Av WD/CROXPK L12 ...98 D5
Grove Pl ANF/KKDL L4 ...97 G6
  HOY CH47 ...108 D6
  WGNNW/ST WN6 ...56 B5
Grove Rd CH/BCN L7 ...163 G6
  HOY CH47 ...108 D6
  NPK/KEN L6 ...113 M2
  RF/TRAN CH42 ...128 B3
  SKEL WN8 ...65 G3
  WAL/NB CH45 ...95 H4
Grove Side EHL/KEN L7 ...113 J5
Groveside WKBY CH48 ...124 C3
Grove Sq PS/BROM CH62 ...128 C6
The Groves EHL/KEN L7 * ...113 J5
  EP CH65 ...163 J5
  KKBY L32 ...86 A5
Grove St AIMK WN4 ...91 J1
  BTL L20 ...6 C2
  ECCL WA10 ...101 L3
  PS/BROM CH62 ...128 C6
  RUNC WA7 ...18 D7
  TOX L8 ...113 J5
  WARRS WA4 ...15 G4
  WAV L15 ...114 B6
Grove Ter HOY CH47 ...108 D6
  STHP PR8 ...2 D1
Grove Wy EHL/KEN L7 ...113 J4
Grovewood STHP PR8 ...2 B2
Grovewood Cl CL/PREN CH43 ...127 K2
Grovewood Dr WGNNW/ST WN6 ...56 F5
Grovewood Gdns RAIN/WH L35 ...117 G2
Grundy Cl STHP PR8 ...2 B2
  WDN WA8 ...134 D2
Grundy's La CHLY/EC PR7 ...43 L4
Grundy St EV L5 ...96 E7

  GOL/RIS/CU WA3 ...92 C6
Guardian St WARRW/BUR WA5 ...8 B4
Guelph St EHL/KEN L7 ...113 J3
Guernsey Cl WARRS WA4 ...137 M5
Guernsey Dr EP CH65 ...163 L4
  WDN WA8 ...135 G2
Guest St WAL/NB CH45 ...16 C6
Guffitts Cl HOY CH47 ...109 G4
Guffitt's Rake HOY CH47 ...109 G4
Guildford Av CSBY/BLUN L23 ...33 H1
  WARRN/WOL WA2 ...122 C3
Guildford Crs WGNNW/ST WN6 ...68 J5
Guildford Rd STHP PR8 ...35 J5
Guildford St WAL/EG CH44 ...111 H1
Guildhall Rd WLT/FAZ L9 ...84 D7
Guild Hey PR/KW L34 ...99 H1
Guillemot Wy HLWD L26 ...132 A4
Guilsted Rd NG/CROX L11 ...98 F2
Guinea Hall La CHTN/BK PR9 ...23 J8
Guion Rd LITH L21 ...83 K6
Guion St NPK/KEN L6 ...113 K1
Gulls Wy HES CH60 ...140 F5
Gunn Gv NSTN CH64 ...153 H5
Gunning Av ECCL WA10 ...88 D8
Gunning Cl ECCL WA10 ...88 D8
Gurnall St ANF/KKDL L4 ...97 H6
Gutticar Rd WDN WA8 ...133 K3
Gwendoline Cl PEN/TH CH61 ...126 C8
Gwendoline St TOX L8 ...113 H7
Gwenfron Rd NPK/KEN L6 ...113 K2
Gwent Cl NPK/KEN L6 ...113 K1
Gwent St TOX L8 ...113 J7
Gwladys St ANF/KKDL L4 ...97 H4
Gwydir St TOX L8 ...113 J8
Gwydrin Rd CALD/MH L18 ...114 E8

H

Hackett Av BTL L20 ...83 M7
Hackins Hey CLVP L2 ...12 E6
Hackthorpe St EV L5 ...97 G6
Hadassah Gv AIG/SPK L17 ...129 L3
Hadden Cl RAIN/WH L35 ...117 J3
Haddock St BTL L20 ...6 F9
Haddon Av WLT/FAZ L9 ...84 D7
Haddon Dr PEN/TH CH61 ...141 H1
  WDN WA8 ...133 L2
Haddon Rd GOL/RIS/CU WA3 ...92 F4
  RF/TRAN CH42 ...128 C3
  WGNS/IIMK WN3 ...79 G2
Hadfield Av HOY CH47 ...108 D6
Hadfield Cl WDN WA8 ...135 G3
Hadfield Gv WLTN L25 ...131 J3
Hadleigh Cl WARRW/BUR WA5 ...119 M8
Hadleigh Rd KKBY L32 ...86 B4
Hadley Av PS/BROM CH62 ...143 L4
Hadlow Gdns RF/TRAN CH42 ...128 C3
Hadlow La NSTN CH64 ...154 B6
Hadlow Rd NSTN CH64 ...154 B7
Hadstock Av FMBY L37 ...58 F4
Haggerston Rd ANF/KKDL L4 ...97 J3
Hague Bush Cl
  GOL/RIS/CU WA3 ...93 G4
Hahnemann Rd ANF/KKDL L4 ...7 M7
Haig Av MOR/LEA CH46 ...110 A5
  STHP PR8 ...25 H8
  WARRW/BUR WA5 ...136 C1
Haigh Cl CHLY/EC PR7 ...32 C6
Haigh Crs CHLY/EC PR7 ...32 C6
  MGHL L31 ...72 E1
Haigh Rd CSBY/WL L22 ...83 G3
  WGNE/HIN WN2 ...69 M2
High St VAUX/LVPD L3 ...13 L4
Haigh Vw WGN WN3 ...68 J5
  WGNS/IIMK WN3 ...5 K7
Haig Rd WDN WA8 ...16 C2
Haigh St WGNS/IIMK WN3 ...4 C5
Haileybury Av AIN/FAZ L10 ...84 F3
Haileybury Rd WLTN L25 ...131 K5
Hailsham Rd ALL/GAR L19 ...130 A5
Halby Rd WLT/FAZ L9 ...84 D7
Halcombe Rd WD/CROXPK L12 ...98 C5
Halcyon Rd RF/TRAN CH42 ...10 E3
Haldane Av BIRK CH41 ...111 H6
Haldane Rd ANF/KKDL L4 ...97 J3
Hale Bank Rd WDN WA8 ...133 H5
Hale Dr SPK/HALE L24 ...147 H3
Halefield St ECCL WA10 ...8 E3
Hale Gate Rd WDN WA8 ...148 B3
Hale Gv AIMK WN4 ...79 H8
  WARRW/BUR WA5 ...120 C4
Hale Rd ANF/KKDL L4 ...7 M8
  SPK/HALE L24 ...146 E2
  WAL/NB CH45 ...95 L7
  WDN WA8 ...133 K7
Halesfield WGNE/HIN WN2 ...81 K3
Hale St CLVP L2 ...12 F6
  WARRN/WOL WA2 ...12 E2
Hale Vw RUNC WA7 ...18 D7
Hale View Rd FROD/HEL WA6 ...166 C1
  HUY L36 ...116 C3
Halewood Av GOL/RIS/CU WA3 ...92 B4
Halewood Dr WLTN L25 ...131 K3
Halewood Pl WLTN L25 ...131 K3
Halewood Rd WLTN L25 ...131 K2
Halewood Wy WLTN L25 ...131 K2
Haley Rd North
  WARRW/BUR WA5 ...104 A7
Haley Rd South
  WARRW/BUR WA5 ...104 A7
Half Acre La HOR/BR BL6 ...57 L4
Halfacre La WARRS WA4 ...139 G2
Half Crown St EV L5 ...96 E7
Halfpenny Cl ALL/GAR L19 ...130 D7
Halfpenny La CHLY/EC PR7 ...41 K2
Halidon Ct BTL L20 ...6 D2
Halifax Cl WARRN/WOL WA2 ...121 M3
Halifax Crs CSBY/BLUN L23 ...71 K7
Halifax Rd STHP PR8 ...34 E8
Halkirk Rd CALD/MH L18 ...114 D8
Halkyn Av AIG/SPK L17 ...113 M7
Halkyn Dr EV L5 ...97 J8
Hallam Wk EHL/KEN L7 ...113 L4
Hallastone Rd FROD/HEL WA6 ...166 D1
Hall Av WDN WA8 ...133 J4
Hall-way WARRS WA4 ...
Hall Brow Cl BRSC L40 ...
Hall Cl WGNNW/ST WN6 ...55 K7
Hallcroft SKEL WN8 ...
Hallcroft Pl WARRS WA4 ...138 C3
Hall Dr CALD/MH L18 ...
  GR/UP/WCH CH49 ...125 L2
  KKBY L32 ...86 A5
  WARRS WA4 ...137 M7
Hallfield Dr CHNE CH2 ...165 K2
Hallfields Rd WARRN/WOL WA2 ...105 M4
Hall Ga CHLY/EC PR7 ...32 C4
Hallgate WGN WN1 ...4 E4
Hall Gn SKEL WN8 ...66 D6

Hall Green Cl SKEL WN8 ...66 D6
Hall Green La CHLY/EC PR7 ...41 J2
Halliday Rd GOL/RIS/CU WA3 ...123 H2
Halliwell La CHLYE PR6 ...32 E1
Halliwell Pl CHLY/EC PR7 *...32 E6
Halliwell St CHLY/EC PR7 ...32 E6
Hall La BRSC L40 ...40 C6
  BRSC L40 ...40 F2
  EHL/KEN L7 ...113 J5
  HOR/BR BL6 ...45 J3
  HTWN L38 ...71 H1
  HUY L36 ...116 C3
  KKBY L32 ...86 A3
  MGHL L31 ...61 G6
  MGHL L31 ...72 F5
  NWD/KWIPK L33 ...74 B7
  ORM L39 ...75 G1
  PR/KW L34 ...100 F9
  RAIN/WH L35 ...117 L4
  STHEL WA9 ...119 J1
  WARRS WA4 ...138 D5
  WARRS WA4 ...151 M3
  WARRW/BUR WA5 ...104 D5
  WGN WN1 ...68 F1
  WGNE/HIN WN2 ...69 M3
  WGNNW/ST WN6 ...54 E3
  WGNW/BIL/O WN5 ...78 B1
  WLT/FAZ L9 ...84 D6
Hall Lane Gv WGNE/HIN WN2 ...69 M5
Hallinoor Cl ORM L39 ...62 F3
Hall Nook WARRW/WOL WA5 ...136 B1
Hallows Av WARRN/WOL WA2 ...121 M5
Hall Rd BRSC L40 ...37 K6
  RNFD/HAY WA11 ...91 G6
  WARR WA1 ...122 F6
Hall Rd East CSBY/BLUN L23 ...70 D7
Hall Rd West CSBY/BLUN L23 ...70 C7
Hallsands Rd KKBY L32 ...86 A5
Hallsgreen La CHNE CH2 ...165 H6
Hallside Rd ALL/GAR L19 ...130 A5
Hall St CHTN/BK PR9 ...3 K4
  ECCL WA10 ...9 J4
  STHEL WA9 ...119 G2
  WARR WA1 ...5 C5
  WGN WN1 ...5 J5
  WGNE/HIN WN2 ...5 M5
  WGNE/HIN WN2 ...80 A6
Hall Ter WARRW/BUR WA5 ...120 A6
Halltine Cl CSBY/BLUN L23 ...70 D7
Hallville Rd CALD/MH L18 ...114 C8
Hallwood Cl RUNC WA7 ...149 K7
Hallwood Link Rd RUNC WA7 ...150 A7
Hallwood Park Av RUNC WA7 ...150 A7
Hallwood Rd CHLY/EC PR7 ...32 C8
Hallworthy Cl LEIGH WN7 ...93 K4
Halsall Av WARRN/WOL WA2 ...112 A2
Halsall Buildings CHTN/BK PR9 *...3 K2
  RUNC WA7 ...150 E8
Halsall Gn BEB CH63 ...143 K4
Halsall Hall Dr ORM L39 ...49 K4
Halsall La FMBY L37 ...59 H1
  ORM L39 ...49 M7
  ORM L39 ...50 A4
Halsall Manor Ct ORM L39 ...49 M4
Halsall Rd BTL L20 ...83 L8
  ORM L39 ...49 L3
  STHP PR8 ...35 J5
Halsall St PR/KW L34 ...100 F6
  RUNC WA7 ...19 K3
  WAL/NB CH45 ...95 J7
  WARRW/BUR WA5 ...120 B7
Halsbury Rd NPK/KEN L6 ...113 L2
  WAL/NB CH45 ...95 K7
Halsey Av WD/CROXPK L12 ...98 B6
Halsey Crs WD/CROXPK L12 ...98 B6
Halsnead Av RAIN/WH L35 ...116 E4
Halstead Rd WAL/EG CH44 ...111 L2
  WLT/FAZ L9 ...84 B7
Halton Brook Av RUNC WA7 ...149 M4
Halton Brow RUNC WA7 ...150 A4
Halton Cha BRSC L40 ...64 A1
Halton Crt RUNC WA7 ...149 M3
Halton Crs GR/UP/WCH CH49 ...125 K2
  GTS/LS CH66 ...163 H5
Halton Hey RAIN/WH L35 ...116 F4
Halton Link Rd RUNC WA7 ...150 A5
Halton Lodge Av RUNC WA7 ...149 M6
Halton Rd GTS/LS CH66 ...163 G4
  MGHL L31 ...72 F7
  RUNC WA7 ...19 K3
  WAL/NB CH45 ...95 J7
  WARRW/BUR WA5 ...120 B7
Halton Station Rd RUNC WA7 ...161 H2
Halton View Rd WDN WA8 ...17 H1
Halton Wy GTS/LS CH66 ...163 H4
Halton Wd WAL/EG CH44 ...85 K2
Halville Rd WAL/EG CH44 ...111 L4
Hambledon Cl GTS/LS CH66 ...155 J7
Hambledon Dr
  GR/UP/WCH CH49 ...125 L1
Hamble Dr WARRW/BUR WA5 ...136 B2
Hambleton Cl NG/CROX L11 ...98 D1
  WDN WA8 *...133 L2
Hamblett Crs RNFD/HAY WA11 ...89 K7
Hamblett St LEIGH WN7 ...81 K8
Hamer St ECCL WA10 ...8 A1
Hamil Cl HOY CH47 ...109 G4
Hamilton La BIRK CH41 ...11 K4
Hamilton Rd AIMK WN4 ...79 H7
  CHLY/EC PR7 ...32 D6
  ECCL WA10 ...8 D7
  EV L5 ...97 H8
  WAL/NB CH45 ...95 J5
  WGNE/HIN WN2 ...81 H1
Hamilton Sq BIRK CH41 ...11 L4
  WGNW/BIL/O WN5 ...68 A5
Hamilton St BIRK CH41 ...11 L6
  LEIGH WN7 ...81 M7
Hamlet St WAL/NB CH45 ...95 H7
The Hamlet CHLY/EC PR7 *...44 B4
Hammersley Av STHEL WA9 ...118 C2
Hammersley St STHEL WA9 *...118 C2
Hammill Av ECCL WA10 ...89 C7
Hammill St ECCL WA10 ...8 A1
Hammond Rd NWD/KWIPK L33 ...86 E2
Hammond St STHEL WA9 ...102 F3
Hamnett Ct GOL/RIS/CU WA3 ...123 G2
Hamnett Rd PR/KW L34 ...101 G6
Hampden Gv RF/TRAN CH42 ...128 A1
Hampden Pl WGNW/BIL/O WN5 ...67 M4
Hampden Rd RF/TRAN CH42 ...127 M1
Hampden St ANF/KKDL L4 ...97 H1
Hampshire Av RNTHLN L30 ...83 L2
Hampshire Gdns ECCL WA10 ...8 E8
Hampson Av GOL/RIS/CU WA3 ...107 H2
Hampson Cl AIMK WN4 ...79 K3
Hampson St NPK/KEN L6 ...113 L4
  WAL/EG CH44 ...111 L2
  WGNNW/ST WN6 ...55 M4
Hampton Cl CHLY/EC PR7 ...32 D5
  NSTN CH64 ...153 G7
  WDN WA8 ...117 L8
Hampton Court Rd WD/CROXPK L12 ...98 E2
Hampton Crs NSTN CH64 ...153 G8
Hampton Dr WARRW/BUR WA5 ...136 E1
  WDN WA8 ...117 L8

Hampton Gdns EP CH65 ...156 C8
Hampton Pl RNFD/HAY WA11 ...89 K7
Hampton Rd FMBY L37 ...59 G4
  STHP PR8 ...3 H9
Hampton St TOX L8 ...113 H6
Hamsterley St GOL/RIS/CU WA3 ...107 K3
Hanbury Rd ANF/KKDL L4 ...97 M5
Handa Dr EP CH65 ...163 L5
Handel Cl TOX L8 *...113 K7
Handel Rd RNFD/HAY WA11 ...115 M7
Handfield Pl EV L5 ...97 J8
Handfield Rd CSBY/WL L22 ...82 F4
Handfield St EV L5 ...97 J8
Handforth Av PS/BROM CH62 ...144 B8
Handforth La WARRS WA4 ...138 E1
Handforth La RUNC WA7 ...149 M7
Hand La CHLY/EC PR7 ...30 B8
Handley Ct ALL/GAR L19 ...130 B5
Hands St LITH L21 ...85 K7
Hanford Av WLT/FAZ L9 ...84 B7
Hankey Dr BTL L20 ...84 D1
Hankey St RUNC WA7 ...18 F3
Hankin St EV L5 ...96 F8
Hanley Cl WDN WA8 ...133 L4
Hanley Rd WDN WA8 ...133 L4
Hanlon Av BTL L20 ...83 M7
Hanmer Rd KKBY L32 ...85 K3
Hanmer St WGNE/HIN WN2 ...69 M8
Hannah Cl PEN/TH CH61 ...141 G2
Hannan Rd NPK/KEN L6 ...113 L2
Hanns Hall Rd NSTN CH64 ...155 L5
Hanover Av GOL/RIS/CU WA3 ...123 G2
Hanover Ct WD/CROXPK L12 ...111 H7
Hanover St WGNE/HIN WN2 ...69 L7
  WARR WA1 ...14 C1
Hanover Pk CL/PREN CH43 ...111 G8
Hanson Av WLT/FAZ L9 ...84 E8
Hanson St CHLY/EC PR7 ...44 C7
Hans Rd ANF/KKDL L4 ...97 J4
Hanstock WGNW/BIL/O WN5 ...67 G8
Hants La ORM L39 ...51 G7
Hanwell Cl LEIGH WN7 ...93 J4
Hanwell St NPK/KEN L6 ...97 K7
Hanworth Cl WD/CROXPK L12 ...98 F2
Hapsford Cl GOL/RIS/CU WA3 ...122 E1
Hapsford La CHNE CH2 ...165 M1
  FROD/HEL WA6 ...166 A4
Hapton St LITH L21 ...83 K7
Hapton St EV L5 ...97 G7
Harbern Cl WD/CROXPK L12 ...98 F7
Harbord Dr LEIGH WN7 ...81 M3
Harbord Rd CSBY/WL L22 ...82 E4
Harbord St EHL/KEN L7 ...113 K4
  WARR WA1 ...14 E5
Harborne Dr BEB CH63 ...143 H3
Harbury Av HOY CH47 ...127 J7
Harbury Rd WGNNW/ST WN6 ...68 B3
Harcourt Av WAL/EG CH44 ...112 A2
Harcourt Rd GOL/RIS/CU WA3 ...123 G2
Harcourt St ANF/KKDL L4 ...96 F6
  BIRK CH41 ...10 E3
Hardacre St ORM L39 ...51 H7
  WGNS/IIMK WN3 ...5 H8
Hardie Av MOR/LEA CH46 ...109 L4
Hardie St STHEL WA9 ...118 C2
Hardie Rd HUY L36 ...116 C2
Harding Av BEB CH63 ...143 H1
  WARRN/WOL WA2 ...121 M4
Harding Cl EV L5 ...97 J8
Hardinge Rd ALL/GAR L19 ...130 E5
Harding Rd BRSC L40 ...51 M1
  CHLYE PR6 ...44 D5
  TOX L8 ...113 K5
Hardknott Rd PS/BROM CH62 ...144 A4
Hard La ECCL WA10 ...88 F7
Hardman St CLVPS L1 ...13 K9
  WGNS/IIMK WN3 ...79 K3
Hardrow Cl WGNS/IIMK WN3 ...79 K3
Hardshaw St ECCL WA10 ...9 H4
Hardwick Gra WARR WA1 ...122 F5
Hardwick Rd AIMK WN4 ...79 J8
  RUNC WA7 ...149 M2
Hardybutts WGN WN1 ...5 G4
Hardy Cl GTS/LS CH66 ...163 H2
Hardy Dr CHLY/EC PR7 ...32 C6
Hardy Rd LYMM WA13 ...139 L3
Hardy St ALL/GAR L19 ...145 M1
  CLVPS L1 ...112 F6
  WARRW/WOL WA2 ...13 K9
  WGNW/ST WN6 ...4 B1
Harebell Cl FMBY L37 ...59 H4
Harebell St EV L5 ...96 F6
Hare Cft STBRV L28 ...99 H5
Harefield Gdns STHEL WA9 ...155 L8
Harefield Rd SPK/HALE L24 ...146 F2
Harefinch Rd RNFD/HAY WA11 ...9 J1
Harefinch Vw RNFD/HAY WA11 ...89 K7
Hare's La FROD/HEL WA6 ...160 A5
Harestone Av CHLY/EC PR7 ...32 C8
Harewell Rd NG/CROX L11 ...98 C4
Harewood Av CTS/LS CH66 ...162 F1
  STHP PR8 ...34 E7
Harewood Cl HUY L36 ...116 A2
Harewood Rd WAL/NB CH45 ...95 J6
  WGNE/HIN WN2 ...69 L7
Harewood St NPK/KEN L6 *...113 J7
Harford Cl WARRW/BUR WA5 ...136 B1
Hargate Rd NWD/KWIPK L33 ...86 B3
Hargrave Av CL/PREN CH43 ...127 G2
Hargrave Cl CL/PREN CH43 ...127 G2
Hargrave Dr GTS/LS CH66 ...156 A8
Hargrave La BEB CH63 ...143 H8
Hargreaves Ct WDN WA8 ...17 J1
Hargreaves Rd AIG/SPK L17 ...129 L2
Hargreaves St STHEL WA9 ...103 G1
Harington Cl FMBY L37 ...58 F2
Harington Gn FMBY L37 ...58 F2
Harington Rd FMBY L37 ...58 E1
Harker St VAUX/LVPD L3 ...13 K5
Harland av AIMK WN4 ...79 J7
Harland Dr RF/TRAN CH42 ...127 M1
Harlea Av WGNE/HIN WN2 ...81 J2
Harlech Cl WARRW/BUR WA5 ...121 G3
Harlech Rd CSBY/BLUN L23 ...82 E2
Harlech St AIMK WN4 ...79 J6
  ANF/KKDL L4 ...97 L4
  WAL/EG CH44 ...112 A4
Harlech Wy EP CH65 ...156 B2
Harleston Rd NWD/KWIPK L33 ...86 C2
Harley Av BEB CH63 ...127 L5
Harley St WLT/FAZ L9 ...84 C8
Harlian Av MOR/LEA CH46 ...109 M6
Harlow Cl STHEL WA9 ...102 B6
  WARRS WA4 ...138 C3
Harlyn Cl HLWD L26 ...132 A7
Harlyn Gdns WARRW/BUR WA5 ...135 M2
Harmony Wy CLB/OSW/ST L13 ...114 C4
Harmsworth St WGNNW/ST WN6 ...68 B1
The Harn GTS/LS CH66 ...162 E2
Harold Av AIMK WN4 ...79 J8
Haroldene Gv HUY L36 ...100 D8
Harold Rd RNFD/HAY WA11 ...91 H6

Harold St WGNE/HIN WN2 ...57 M8
Harper Cl GTS/LS CH66 ...162 F1
Harperley CHLY/EC PR7 ...32 D3
Harper Rd WLT/FAZ L9 ...84 C8
Harper's La CHLY/EC PR7 ...32 E1
Harper St WGN WN1 ...5 J5
  WGNE/HIN WN2 ...80 A1
Harp's Cft NTHTN L30 ...83 L2
Harptree Cl RAIN/WH L35 ...117 G2
Harptree Gv LEIGH WN7 ...81 M6
Harradon Rd WLT/FAZ L9 ...84 D6
Harridge La BRSC L40 ...50 C4
Harrier Dr HLWD L26 ...132 A4
Harrier Rd WARRN/WOL WA2 ...122 B3
Harringay Av CALD/MH L18 ...114 B8
Harrington Rd CHLY/EC PR7 ...32 D5
  CSBY/BLUN L23 ...82 F1
  LITH L21 ...83 M4
  VAUX/LVPD L3 ...129 G1
Harrington St CLVP L2 ...12 F7
Harris Cl BEB CH63 ...143 H3
Harris Dr BTL L20 ...83 M6
Harrismith Rd AIN/FAZ L10 ...85 G6
Harrison Crs HOR/BR BL6 ...57 L2
Harrison Dr BTL L20 ...7 L4
  RNFD/HAY WA11 ...76 B6
  RNFD/HAY WA11 ...90 C7
  WAL/NB CH45 ...94 F5
Harrison Hey HUY L36 ...115 M4
Harrison Rd CHLY/EC PR7 ...32 E7
  CHLY/EC PR7 ...44 C7
Harrison St WDN WA8 ...133 K7
  WGNE/HIN WN2 ...81 K2
  WGNW/BIL/O WN5 *...68 B6
Harrisons Yd PS/BROM CH62 *...144 B7
Harrison Wy NEWLW WA12 ...104 D3
  VAUX/LVPD L3 ...129 G1
Harris Rd WGNNW/ST WN6 ...55 K3
Harris St WDN WA8 ...17 H1
Harrock Av BRSC L40 ...41 C7
  WGNNW/ST WN6 ...51 M8
Harrock Cl NTHTN L30 ...71 M8
Harrock Vw CHLY/EC PR7 ...41 L4
Harrock Wood Cl PEN/TH CH61 ...126 A7
Harrod Dr STHP PR8 ...35 G2
Harrogate Cl PS/BROM CH62 ...154 F1
  WARRW/BUR WA5 ...120 C5
Harrogate Dr EV L5 ...97 H8
Harrogate Rd PS/BROM CH62 ...154 F1
  RF/TRAN CH42 ...128 C5
Harrop Rd RUNC WA7 ...19 J6
Harrops Cft NTHTN L30 ...84 A1
Harrowby Cl TOX L8 ...113 J6
Harrowby Rd LITH L21 ...83 L7
  RF/TRAN CH42 ...127 L1
  WAL/EG CH44 ...112 A3
Harrowby Rd South
  RF/TRAN CH42 ...127 L1
Harrowby St TOX L8 *...113 J6
Harrow Cl NTHTN L30 ...68 A7
Harrow Dr AIN/FAZ L10 ...84 F3
  RUNC WA7 ...150 A3
Harrow Gv PS/BROM CH62 ...144 A4
Harrow Pl WGNS/IIMK WN3 ...80 B1
Harrow Rd ANF/KKDL L4 ...97 J7
  EP CH65 ...20 E7
  WAL/EG CH44 ...95 H8
  WGNW/BIL/O WN5 ...67 M4
Harsnips SKEL WN8 ...65 L3
Hartdale Rd CALD/MH L18 ...130 C1
  CSBY/BLUN L23 ...71 J7
Hartford Cl CL/PREN CH43 ...127 H2
Hartford Dr EP CH65 ...163 H1
Harthill Av CALD/MH L18 ...130 D1
Harthill Rd CALD/MH L18 ...130 D1
Hartington Dr WCNNW/ST WN6 ...56 B6
Hartington Rd ALL/GAR L19 ...130 E7
  ECCL WA10 ...88 B3
  TOX L8 ...113 L7
  WAL/EG CH44 ...111 K1
  WD/CROXPK L12 ...98 E7
Hartismere Rd WAL/EG CH44 ...111 M2
Hartland Av CHTN/BK PR9 ...22 D8
Hartland Cl WDN WA8 ...118 C8
Hartland Gdns STHEL WA9 ...101 M7
Hartland Rd NG/CROX L11 ...98 A3
Hartley Av WGN WN1 ...5 J5
  WLT/FAZ L9 ...84 D8
Hartley Cl ANF/KKDL L4 ...97 H6
  CTS STHP PR8 ...35 H3
Hartley Gv EV L5 ...101 L5
  WGNW/BIL/O WN5 ...67 K6
Hartley Quay VAUX/LVPD L3 ...12 D9
Hartley St STHP PR8 ...35 H3
Hartleys Village WLT/FAZ L9 ...84 D8
Hartley Ter WGNS/IIMK WN3 ...4 B6
Hartnup St EV L5 ...97 J7
Hartopp Rd CLB/OSW/ST L13 ...115 J7
Hartsbourne Av WLTN L25 ...115 H6
Hartsbourne Cl WLTN L25 ...115 H6
Hartsbourne Wk WLTN L25 ...115 J6
Hartshead WDN WA8 ...65 L3
Hart's La WDN WA8 ...66 B5
Hart St STHP PR8 ...3 M5
  VAUX/LVPD L3 ...13 K6
Hart Street Br STHP PR8 ...3 M5
Hartswell Ct SKEL WN8 ...65 J3
Hartwell St LITH L21 ...83 K7
Hartwood Cl KKBY L32 ...86 B6
Hartwood Gn CHLYE PR6 ...32 E2
Hartwood Rd CHLYE PR6 ...32 E2
  KKBY L32 ...86 B6
Hartwood Sq KKBY L32 *...86 B6
Harty Rd RNFD/HAY WA11 ...90 F3
Harvard Cl RUNC WA7 ...150 F3
Harvard Ct WARRN/WOL WA2 ...122 A4
Harvard Gv PR/KW L34 ...100 F6
Harvester Wy
  GR/UP/WCH CH49 *...125 L1
  NTHTN L30 ...84 C1
Harvest La MOR/LEA CH46 ...109 M4
Harvey Av GR/UP/WCH CH49 ...125 M2
  NEWLW WA12 ...104 B2
Harvey Cl GOL/RIS/CU WA3 ...93 K4
Harvey La GOL/RIS/CU WA3 ...92 B4
Harvey Rd WAL/NB CH45 ...95 J7
Harvey St WGNS/IIMK WN3 ...5 H7
Harvington Dr STHP PR8 ...34 D7
Harwood Gdns WARRS WA4 ...138 C3
Harwood Rd CHLDW L16 ...139 M2
Haryngton Av
  WARRW/BUR WA5 ...14 A1
Haselbeech Cl NG/CROX L11 ...98 B2
Haselbeech Crs NG/CROX L11 ...98 B2

Haseldine St AIMK WN4 ...79 H7
Hasfield Rd NG/CROX L11 ...98 D3
Haslam Dr ORM L39 ...50 F6
Haslemere RAIN/WH L35 ...117 H2
Haslemere Dr
  WARRW/BUR WA5 ...135 M1
Haslemere Rd WLTN L25 ...115 J7
Haslemere Wy WLTN L25 ...115 K7
Haslingden Cl CLB/OSW/ST L13 ...114 D3
Haslington Gv HLWD L26 ...132 C7
Hassal Rd RF/TRAN CH42 ...128 C5
Hassnes Ct WGNS/IIMK WN3 ...79 K3
Hastings Av WARRN/WOL WA2 ...121 K1
Hastings Dr HUY L36 ...116 C5
Hastings Rd CSBY/WL L22 ...82 D5
  STHP PR8 ...35 G4
Haswell Dr STBRV L28 ...99 H5
Hatchmere Cl CL/PREN CH43 ...127 H2
  WARRW/BUR WA5 ...121 G8
Hatfield Cl STHEL WA9 ...102 B6
  WD/CROXPK L12 ...99 H1
Hatfield Gdns WLTN L25 ...116 B4
Hatfield Rd BTL L20 ...84 E7
  STHP PR8 ...34 E7
Hathaway MGHL L31 ...72 D6
Hathaway Cl WLTN L25 ...115 J7
Hathaway Rd WLTN L25 ...115 J7
Hathaway Wk WGNS/IIMK WN3 ...80 B1
Hatherley Av CSBY/WL L22 ...83 G3
Hatherley Cl TOX L8 ...113 J4
Hatherley St TOX L8 ...113 J7
  WAL/EG CH44 ...112 A3
Hathersage Rd HUY L36 ...116 A4
Hatley La FROD/HEL WA6 ...160 B6
Hatters Rw WARR WA1 *...14 E5
Hatton Av WGNW/BIL/O WN5 ...68 B1
Hatton Cl HES CH60 ...140 F4
Hatton Gdn VAUX/LVPD L3 ...12 F5
Hatton Hill Rd LITH L21 ...83 J5
Hattons La CHLDW L16 ...114 E7
Hatton St CHLY/EC PR7 ...44 B7
Hauxwell Gv RNFD/HAY WA11 ...89 C7
Havannah La STHEL WA9 ...103 K3
Havelock Cl ECCL WA10 ...101 M3
Haven Brow ORM L39 ...62 F5
Haven Rd AIN/FAZ L10 ...85 H5
Havenwood Rd WGNW/BIL/O WN5 ...68 D1
Havergal St RUNC WA7 ...18 F5
Haverstock Rd NPK/KEN L6 ...113 M2
Haverton Wk WD/CROXPK L12 *...99 G2
Havisham Cl GOL/RIS/CU WA3 ...106 F3
Hawarde Cl ANF/KKDL L4 ...104 C1
Hawarden Av CSBY/WL L22 ...82 F2
  CL/PREN CH43 ...10 E6
  WAL/EG CH44 ...112 A4
Hawarden Gdns EP CH65 ...20 E9
Hawarden Gv LITH L21 ...83 J7
Hawdon Ct EHL/KEN L7 ...113 L5
Hawes Av RNFD/HAY WA11 ...89 L5
Hawes Crs AIMK WN4 ...79 K8
Haweside St CHTN/BK PR9 ...3 H4
Haweswater Av CHLY/EC PR7 ...32 D7
  RNFD/HAY WA11 ...90 C7
  WGNE/HIN WN2 ...69 K6
Haweswater Cl NWD/KWIPK L33 ...73 M8
  WD/CROXPK L12 ...98 E7
Haweswater Gn WD/CROXPK L12 *...98 E7
Hawick Cl GTS/LS CH66 ...155 J8
  NWD/KWIPK L33 ...73 M7
Hawke Gn HUY L36 ...116 C6
Hawke St VAUX/LVPD L3 ...13 L6
Hawkesworth St ANF/KKDL L4 ...97 J7
Hawkhurst Cl TOX L8 ...129 H1
Hawkins St NSTN CH64 ...153 H4
Hawkins St NPK/KEN L6 ...113 K2
Hawkley Av WGNS/IIMK WN3 ...79 H3
Hawkrigg Cl WGNNW/ST WN6 ...66 G6
Hawksclough SKEL WN8 ...65 G6
Hawks Ct RUNC WA7 ...150 A7
Hawkshaw Cl GOL/RIS/CU WA3 ...122 E1
  WGNE/HIN WN2 ...69 J2
Hawkshead Av CHLY/EC PR7 ...31 M4
  WD/CROXPK L12 ...98 E4
Hawkshead Cl MGHL L31 ...73 G3
  RUNC WA7 ...150 C8
Hawkshead Dr LITH L21 ...83 M5
Hawkshead Rd PS/BROM CH62 ...144 A4
Hawksmoor Cl AIN/FAZ L10 ...85 K7
Hawksmoor Rd AIN/FAZ L10 ...85 K7
Hawksmore Cl
  GR/UP/WCH CH49 ...109 M7
Hawkstone Gv FROD/HEL WA6 ...166 E1
Hawkstone St TOX L8 ...113 J8
Hawkstone Wk TOX L8 *...129 J1
Hawks Wy HES CH60 ...141 G5
Hawkswood Cl CHLY/EC PR7 ...30 C7
Hawksworth Cl FMBY L37 ...47 J7
Hawksworth Dr FMBY L37 ...47 J7
Hawley's La WARRN/WOL WA2 ...121 J4
Haworth Dr BTL L20 ...83 M6
Haworth St WGNE/HIN WN2 *...69 M7
Hawthorn Av WCNW/BIL/O WN5 ...67 M8
Hawthorn Crs SKEL WN8 ...65 G4
Hawthorn Dr ECCL WA10 ...101 K1
  PEN/TH CH61 ...141 H3
  WKBY CH48 ...125 G3
Hawthorne Av HLWD L26 ...132 A7
  WARR WA1 ...122 B6
  WARRW/BUR WA5 ...120 B7
Hawthorne Cl RNFD/HAY WA11 ...90 C8
Hawthorne Crs WDN WA8 ...59 J3
Hawthorne Dr NSTN CH64 ...154 D4
Hawthorne Gv CHTN/BK PR9 ...23 H6
  EHL/KEN L7 ...113 K4
  WAL/EG CH44 ...112 A3
  WARR WA1 ...122 B6
Hawthorne Rd BTL L20 ...7 K6
  FROD/HEL WA6 ...160 D4
  LITH L21 ...83 K6
  RF/TRAN CH42 ...127 M2
  STHEL WA9 ...102 F7
  WARR WA1 ...122 B6
  WARRW/WOL WA2 ...121 M5
The Hawthornes NTHLY L27 *...115 G7
Hawthorne St
  WARRW/BUR WA5 ...121 J5
Hawthorn Gv EHL/KEN L7 ...113 K4
  WARRS WA4 ...15 G3
Hawthorn La PS/BROM CH62 ...143 M5
Hawthorn Rd GTS/LS CH66 ...155 L7
  HUY L36 ...115 L8
  LYMM WA13 ...139 M2
  NSTN CH64 ...152 D3
  PR/KW L34 ...101 G7

Haycroft Cl GTS/LS CH66 ...162 F3
Haydn Rd DV/KA/FCH L14 ...99 H8
Haydock La RNFD/HAY WA11 ...90 E7
Haydock Park Gdns
  NEWLW WA12 ...91 K4
Haydock Park Rd AIN/FAZ L10 ...85 G2
Haydock Rd WAL/NB CH45 ...95 K3
Haydock St AIMK WN4 ...91 K3
  ECCL WA10 ...9 J5
  WARRN/WOL WA2 ...14 E4
Hayes Av RAIN/WH L35 ...101 G8
Hayes Crs FROD/HEL WA6 ...160 E4
Hayes Dr MGHL L31 ...85 K2
Hayes St ECCL WA10 ...101 L5
Hayfield Rd WGNS/IIMK WN3 ...79 J4
Hayfield St ANF/KKDL L4 *...97 H6
Hayfield Wy GTS/LS CH66 ...132 C4
Hayles Cl WLTN L25 ...115 J7
Hayles Gn WLTN L25 ...115 J7
Hayles Gv WLTN L25 ...115 J7
Haylock Cl TOX L8 ...129 H1
Hayman's Cl WD/CROXPK L12 *...98 C6
Hayman's Gn MGHL L31 ...73 G4
  WD/CROXPK L12 ...98 C6
Hayman's Gv WD/CROXPK L12 ...98 C6
Hayscastle Cl
  WARRW/BUR WA5 ...121 G4
Haywood Cl GOL/RIS/CU WA3 ...93 G4
Haywood Crs RUNC WA7 ...150 F3
Haywood Gdns ECCL WA10 ...8 A7
Hazel Av KKBY L32 ...85 L2
  RAIN/WH L35 ...117 G1
  RUNC WA7 ...18 D8
Hazelbank Gdns FMBY L37 ...47 G8
Hazelborough Cl
  GOL/RIS/CU WA3 ...107 K7
Hazel Cl GTS/LS CH66 ...163 H4
Hazeldale Rd WLT/FAZ L9 ...97 J1
Hazeldene Av PEN/TH CH61 ...126 D7
  WAL/NB CH45 ...95 J8
Hazeldene Wy PEN/TH CH61 ...126 D7
Hazelfield Ct STHEL WA9 *...118 C1
Hazel Gv BEB CH63 ...143 G1
  CHLYE PR6 ...32 E2
  CSBY/BLUN L23 ...83 H2
  GOL/RIS/CU WA3 ...101 L2
  GOL/RIS/CU WA3 ...92 D5
  PEN/TH CH61 ...125 M6
  STHP PR8 ...25 G6
  WARR WA1 ...122 C5
Hazelhurst Rd ANF/KKDL L4 ...97 K6
Hazel La SKEL WN8 ...63 H2
Hazelmere Gdns WGNE/HIN WN2 ...81 G1
Hazel Ms MGHL L31 *...85 K2
Hazel Rd BIRK CH41 ...11 G7
  HOY CH47 ...108 D6
  HUY L36 ...100 B8
Hazelslack Rd NG/CROX L11 ...98 C3
The Hazels CHLY/EC PR7 ...43 G4
Hazel St WARR WA1 ...15 L1
Hazelwood GR/UP/WCH CH49 ...125 M1
  WDN WA8 ...133 J5
Hazelwood Cl BRSC L40 ...52 A1
  STHEL WA9 ...118 C2
Hazelwood Gv HLWD L26 ...131 M3
  WDN WA8 ...133 J5
Hazelwood Ms WARRS WA4 ...138 E4
Hazelwood Rd WGN WN1 ...68 D1
Hazlehurst Cl FMBY L37 ...58 E5
Hazlehurst Gv AIMK WN4 ...91 L2
Hazlehurst Rd FROD/HEL WA6 ...160 E8
Hazleton Rd DV/KA/FCH L14 ...114 E2
Headbolt La NWD/KWIPK L33 ...86 A1
  STHP PR8 ...49 C1
Headbourne Ct WLTN L25 ...115 H6
Headingley Cl HUY L36 ...115 L5
  STHEL WA9 ...102 E7
Headington Rd
  GR/UP/WCH CH49 ...109 M8
Headland Cl GOL/RIS/CU WA3 ...93 G2
  WKBY CH48 ...124 D5
Headley Cl ECCL WA10 ...9 M6
Head St TOX L8 ...113 G7
Heald St ALL/GAR L19 ...130 E2
  CHLYE PR6 ...33 L6
  NEWLW WA12 ...104 B2
Heanor Dr STHP PR8 ...36 B2
Heapey Fold La CHLYE PR6 ...33 L6
Heapey Rd CHLYE PR6 ...33 J2
Heardman Av WGNNW/ST WN6 ...4 A1
Hearne Rd ECCL WA10 ...101 L1
Heartwood Cl WLT/FAZ L9 ...84 C6
Heath Av GTS/LS CH66 ...163 J4
Heathbank Av PEN/TH CH61 ...125 L6
  WAL/EG CH44 ...111 J2
Heathbank Rd RF/TRAN CH42 ...127 M2
Heath Cl PR/KW L34 ...101 H6
  WKBY CH48 ...124 D5
  WLTN L25 ...115 H8
Heathcote Cl EHL/KEN L7 *...113 L5
Heathcote Gdns BEB CH63 ...128 B8
Heathcote Rd ANF/KKDL L4 ...97 H3
Heath Dl BEB CH63 ...143 H2
Heath Dr GR/UP/WCH CH49 ...110 C8
  HES CH60 ...141 H4
  RUNC WA7 ...19 G9
Heather Bank BEB CH63 ...127 M7
Heather Brae NEWLW WA12 ...104 C1
Heather Brow CL/PREN CH43 ...111 H7
Heather Cl ANF/KKDL L4 *...97 H5
  BRSC L40 ...52 A1
  CHLYE PR6 ...33 G5
  FMBY L37 ...47 K8
  GOL/RIS/CU WA3 ...106 A3
  GTS/LS CH66 ...163 G2
  RUNC WA7 ...161 G1
  STHP PR8 ...47 M3
Heatherdale Rd CALD/MH L18 ...114 B5
Heatherdale Rd CALD/MH L18 ...130 D2
Heather Dene PS/BROM CH62 ...143 M2
Heatherden Rd WKBY CH48 ...124 D2
Heathergreen Ct ANF/KKDL L4 ...97 K4
  WGNW/BIL/O WN5 ...67 M4
Heatherlea Cl SKEL WN8 ...66 G6
Heatherleigh STHEL WA9 ...101 M7
  WKBY CH48 ...124 D5
Heatherleigh Cl WLT/FAZ L9 ...84 C6
Heather Rd BEB CH63 ...142 F1
Heathers Cft NTHTN L30 ...84 A2
Heather Wy CSBY/BLUN L23 ...71 J7
Heatherways FMBY L37 ...47 J7
Heathey La STHP PR8 ...36 C5
Heathfield CHLYE PR6 ...44 B4
  FMBY L37 ...47 J7
Heathfield Av STHEL WA9 ...102 A5
  LITH L21 ...83 L7
Heathfield Dr NWD/KWIPK L33 ...74 A8
Heathfield Pk WARRS WA4 ...138 C3
  WDN WA8 ...133 M2
Heathfield Rd BEB CH63 ...143 H1
  CL/PREN CH43 ...127 L1

CSBY/WL L22 ....82 E3
EP CH65 ....20 B4
MGHL L31 ....73 H6
STHP PR8 ....35 G8
WAV L15 ....114 C7
Heathfield St CLVPS L1 ....13 H1
Heath Gdns WGNE/HIN WN2 ....81 L2
Heathgate SKEL WN8 ....J9
Heathgate Av SPK/HALE L24 ....147 J3
Heath Gv GTS/LS L36 ....155 K6
Heathland Rd STHEL WA9 ....118 L1
Heathlands Rd GTS/LS CH66 ....155 H6
The Heathlands CALD/MH L46 ....110 A4
Heath La CHNE CH2 ....164 A6
GOL/RIS/CU WA3 ....92 F7
GOL/RIS/CU WA3 ....106 C3
GTS/LS CH66 ....155 J6
LEIGH WN7 ....81 K8
NSTN CH64 ....154 E5
Heathlea WGNE/HIN WN2 ....81 L3
Heathmoor Av GOL/RIS/CU WA3 ....92 F7
Heathmoor Rd MOR/LEA CH46 ....109 M4
Heath Park Gv RUNC WA7 ....18 F5
Heath Rd AIMK WN4 ....91 K3
ALL/GAR L19 ....130 F5
BEB CH63 ....128 A8
HUY L36 ....99 K8
RUNC WA7 ....19 J8
WARRW/BUR WA5 ....120 B8
WDN WA8 ....134 A4
Heath Road Crs RUNC WA7 ....19 J6
Heathrow Pl CHLY/EC PR7 ....32 C6
Heathside HES CH60 ....140 E4
Heath St AIMK WN4 ....91 L3
GOL/RIS/CU WA3 ....92 C5
STHEL WA9 ....101 M6
WARRS WA4 ....137 J5
The Heath RUNC WA7 * 19 H9
Heath Vw LITH L21 ....2 C1
Heathview Rd WDN WA8 ....148 C1
Heathwaite Crs NG/CROX L11 ....98 C4
Heathway HES CH60 ....141 K6
Heathwood GV/CROXPK L12 ....98 D8
Heathwood Gv WARR WA1 ....122 D3
Heathy La ORM L39 ....48 C5
Heatley Cl CL/PREN CH43 ....110 E4
Heaton Cl BRSC L40 ....51 M1
SKEL WN8 ....66 C6
SPK/HALE L24 ....147 H2
Heaton Gv GOL/RIS/CU WA3 ....107 H7
Heatons Bridge Rd BRSC L40 ....50 F1
Heaton St WGN WN1 ....5 K1
WGNE/HIN WN2 ....57 M7
WGNNW/ST WN6 ....56 A4
WGNS/IIMK WN3 ....5 J7
Heaviley Gv HOR/BR BL6 ....45 J8
Hebburn Wy WD/CROXPK L12 ....99 J2
Hebden Av GOL/RIS/CU WA3 ....107 K1
Hebden Rd NG/CROX L11 ....98 C2
Hebdon Cl AIMK WN4 ....79 J8
Heber St WGNE/HIN WN2 ....5 M6
Hector Rd WCNW/BIL/O WN5 ....67 M4
Hedgebank Cl WLT/FAZ L9 ....5 J1
Hedgecroft CSBY/BLUN L23 ....71 L7
Hedgefield Rd WLTN L25 ....115 K8
Hedge Hey RUNC WA7 ....150 C4
Hedgemead WGNNW/ST WN6 ....4 D1
The Hedgerows
RNFD/HAY WA11 ....91 H6
Hedges Crs CLB/OSW/ST L13 ....98 A6
Hedingham Cl HLWD L26 ....132 C4
Hedworth Gdns STHEL 101 M7
Heeley St WAV L15 ....68 C5
The Heights FROD/HEL WA6 ....105 H6
Helena Rd STHEL WA9 ....105 H5
Helena St BIRK CH41 ....11 J7
EHL/KEN L7 ....113 K4
WLT/FAZ L9 ....97 H2
Helen Bank Dr RNFD/HAY WA11 ....76 B5
Helen St AIMK WN4 ....91 J1
GOL/RIS/CU WA3 ....92 B3
Helford Cl RAIN/WH L35 ....101 J7
Helford Rd NG/CROX L11 ....85 M8
Heliers Rd CLB/OSW/ST L13 ....114 D3
Hell Nook GOL/RIS/CU WA3 ....92 A4
Helmdon Cl NG/CROX L11 ....98 C4
Helmingham Gv BIRK CH41 ....11 K9
Helmsdale SKEL WN8 ....65 L3
Helmsdale La
WARRW/BUR WA5 ....120 E7
Helmsley Cl WARRW/BUR WA5 ....121 G6
Helmsley Rd HLWD L26 ....132 B6
Helmsman Wy WGNS/IIMK WN3 ....4 D9
Helsby Av PS/BROM CH62 ....155 H6
Helsby Rd FROD/HEL WA6 ....166 E4
WLT/FAZ L9 ....84 D6
Helsby St EHL/KEN L7 ....113 J4
STHEL WA9 ....102 F4
WARR WA1 ....15 L3
Helsby Wy WGNS/IIMK WN3 ....78 C3
Helston Av NG/CROX L11 ....85 M8
Helston Cl CHTN/BK PR9 ....22 D8
RUNC WA7 ....150 D8
WARRW/BUR WA5 ....120 A8
Helston Rd NG/CROX L11 ....85 M8
Helton Cl CL/PREN CH43 ....127 G2
Helvelyn Rd WCNW/BIL/O WN5 ....67 K6
Hemans St BTL L20 ....6 D2
Hemer Ter BTL L20 ....7 J6
Hemfield Ct WGNE/HIN WN2 ....69 L5
Hemfield Rd WGNE/HIN WN2 ....69 L5
Hemingford Cl GTS/LS CH66 ....162 F3
Hemingford St BIRK CH41 ....11 H5
Hemlegh Vw FROD/HEL WA6 ....166 D3
Hemlock Cl WD/CROXPK L12 ....98 F2
Hemmingsway RAIN/WH L35 ....117 J2
Hempstead Cl STHEL WA9 ....102 B6
Hemsworth Av GTS/LS CH66 ....155 L8
Henbury Pl RUNC WA7 ....149 K7
Henderson Cl
GR/UP/WCH CH49 ....109 M7
WARRW/BUR WA5 ....119 M7
Henderson Rd RNFD/HAY WA11 ....76 A5
Henderson Rd HUY L36 ....116 C2
WDN WA8 ....16 B3
Hendon Rd NPK/KEN L6 ....113 M1
WGNW/BIL/O WN5 ....67 M4
Hendon Wk GR/UP/WCH CH49 ....125 G2
Hengers La NPK/KEN L6 * 113 J2
Henglers Av LITH L21 ....2 E5
Henley Cl BEB CH63 ....143 J3
NSTN CH64 ....153 G2
WARRS WA4 ....138 A7
Henley Ct ECCL WA10 ....8 F7
RUNC WA7 ....149 M3
Henley Dr CHTN/BK PR9 ....25 G4
Henley Rd CALD/MH L18 ....114 D7
NSTN CH64 ....153 G2
Henley St WGNE/HIN WN2 ....57 K7
Henllan Gdns STHEL WA9 ....103 H6
Henlow Av KKBY L32 ....86 B5
Hennawood Cl NPK/KEN L6 ....97 K8
Henry Edward St
VAUX/LVPD L3 * 13 G4
Henry Park St WGN WN1 ....5 K5
Henry St BIRK CH41 ....11 K6

CLB/OSW/ST L13 ....114 B3
CLVPS L1 ....13 G9
ECCL WA10 ....8 A7
WARR WA1 ....14 C6
WDN WA8 ....17 H1
WGNS/IIMK WN3 ....A1
Henshall Av WARRS WA4 ....138 A1
Henthorne Rd PS/BROM CH62 ....128 D5
Henthorne St CL/PREN CH43 ....10 E6
Hepherd St WARRW/BUR WA5 ....136 F1
Hepworth Cl GOL/RIS/CU WA3 ....92 B3
Herald Av ALL/GAR L19 ....131 G2
Herald Cl NG/CROX L11 ....98 E2
Heralds Cl WDN WA8 ....133 K5
Heralds Cn WARRW/BUR WA5 ....120 C3
Herbarth Cl WLT/FAZ L9 ....83 G4
Herbert St STHEL WA9 ....103 H6
WARRW/BUR WA5 * 104 A7
WGNS/IIMK WN3 ....4 F5
Herbert Taylor Ct NPK/KEN L6 * 97 L7
Herculaneum Rd TOX L8 ....129 H2
Herculaneum Rd TOX L8 ....129 G1
Herdman Cl WLTN L25 ....115 K8
Hereford Av GOL/RIS/CU WA3 * 92 D5
GR/UP/WCH CH49 ....110 A7
GTS/LS CH66 ....163 G5
Hereford Cl AIMK WN4 ....91 L3
WARR WA1 ....122 F6
Hereford Dr NTHTN L30 ....84 B4
Hereford Rd CHTN/BK PR9 ....23 H6
LITH L21 ....83 G6
WAV L15 ....114 C7
Heriot St EV L5 ....96 F7
Heriot Wk EV L5 ....96 F7
Hermes Cl NTHTN L30 ....84 A5
Hermes Rd NG/CROX L11 ....98 E2
Hermitage Cl WGNNW/ST WN6 ....55 G6
Hermitage Green La
WARRN/WOL WA2 ....105 J5
Hermitage Gv BTL L20 ....83 H6
Heron Rd EV L5 ....96 E8
Heron Cl RUNC WA7 * 150 F5
Heron Ct HLWD L26 ....132 A4
Herondale Rd CALD/MH L18 ....130 F1
Heron Dr WGNS/IIMK WN3 ....79 G3
Heron Gv RNFD/HAY WA11 ....76 D3
Heronhall Rd WLT/FAZ L9 ....98 B1
Heronpark Wy BEB CH63 ....143 K2
Heron Pl WGNW/BIL/O WN5 ....67 L5
Heron Rd WKBY CH48 ....109 J7
Herons Wy RUNC WA7 ....151 H1
Hero St BTL L20 ....7 K7
Herrick St CLB/OSW/ST L13 ....114 B2
Herschell St EV L5 ....97 H1
Hertford Cl HLWD L26 ....132 B6
WARR WA1 ....123 G6
Hertford Dr WAL/NB CH45 ....95 L7
Hertford St STHEL WA9 ....102 F3
RF/TRAN CH42 ....127 M4
Hesketh Av CHTN/BK PR9 ....23 G2
Hesketh Dr BRSC L40 ....25 G3
CHTN/BK PR9 ....25 G3
HES CH60 ....141 J4
MGHL L31 ....73 H3
WGNNW/ST WN6 ....55 J3
Hesketh Gn BRSC L40 ....39 K1
Hesketh Meadow La
GOL/RIS/CU WA3 ....93 J6
Hesketh Rd BRSC L40 ....51 M1
CHTN/BK PR9 ....24 F2
SPK/HALE L24 ....148 A3
Hesketh St North
WARRW/BUR WA5 ....136 F1
Hesketh St AIG/SPK L17 * 129 L1
LEIGH WN7 ....81 M8
WARRW/BUR WA5 ....136 F1
WGNW/BIL/O WN5 ....68 A6
Heskin Cl KKBY L32 ....86 A6
MGHL L31 ....72 F1
Heskin La ORM L39 ....50 F5
Heskin Rd KKBY L32 ....86 A6
Heskin Wk KKBY L32 ....86 A6
Hessle Dr HES CH60 ....141 H6
Hester Cl HTWN L38 ....70 B1
Heswall Av BEB CH63 ....127 L5
GOL/RIS/CU WA3 ....107 G2
STHEL WA9 ....118 D1
Heswall Mt PEN/TH CH61 ....126 C8
Heswall Rd GTS/LS CH66 ....162 F1
WLT/FAZ L9 ....84 D6
Hever Dr HLWD L26 ....132 C4
Heversham SKEL WN8 ....65 L3
Heward Av STHEL WA9 * 102 F7
Hewitson Av CLB/OSW/ST L13 ....98 B7
Hewitson Rd CLB/OSW/ST L13 ....98 B7
Hewitt Av ECCL WA10 ....101 L1
Hewitt's La PR/KW L34 ....87 G6
Hewitts Pl CLVP L2 * 12 F6
Hewitt St WARRS WA4 ....15 H9
Hewlett St CHLY/EC PR7 ....42 F4
WGN WN1 ....4 F4
The Heyes WLTN L25 ....131 K3
Heyfield Park Rd GTS/LS CH66 ....155 H6
Heyford Rd RNFD/HAY WA11 ....67 M5
Heygarth Dr GR/UP/WCH CH49 ....125 M1
Heygarth Rd PS/BROM CH62 ....144 A8
Hey Green Rd WAV L15 ....114 A5
Hey Lock Cl NEWLW WA12 * 104 E5
Hey Rd HUY L36 ....116 F1
Heys Av PS/BROM CH62 ....143 M5
Heyscroft Rd WLTN L25 ....131 K3
Heysham Cl RUNC WA7 ....150 F7
Heysham Lawn NTHLY L27 ....132 C1
Heysham Rd CHTN/BK PR9 ....25 H6
NTHTN L30 ....84 C3
WGNW/BIL/O WN5 ....67 J6
Heysmoor Hts TOX L8 ....113 K8
The Heys STBRV L28 ....99 L6
Heythrop Dr HES CH60 ....141 L5
Heyville Rd BEB CH63 ....128 A7
Heywood Av GOL/RIS/CU WA3 ....92 D4
Heywood Bvd PEN/TH CH61 ....141 G5

Heywood Cl FMBY L37 ....59 G2
Hey Wood Cl NEWLW WA12 * 104 E5
Heywood Ct WGNE/HIN WN2 ....126 C7
Heywood Ct WAV L15 ....114 C4
Heywood Gdns RAIN/WH L35 ....117 G5
Heywood Rd GTS/LS CH66 ....155 M8
WAV L15 ....114 C6
Heyworth St EV L5 ....97 H1
NPK/KEN L6 ....13 M1
Hibbert St WDN WA8 ....16 E3
Hic-bibi La CHLY/EC PR7 ....43 C7
Hickmans Rd CH41 ....111 K4
Hickory Cl WARR WA1 ....123 G4
Hickory Gv MGHL L31 ....85 J3
Hicks Rd CSBY/WL L22 ....83 G4
Hieland Rd WCN WN1 ....69 G3
Higgin's La BRSC L40 ....51 L1
Higham Av ECCL WA10 ....101 H2
WARRW/BUR WA5 ....121 H4
Higham Sq EV L5 * 13 K2
High Bank CHLY PR6 ....33 J2
High Bank Cl CL/PREN CH43 * 110 F8
Highbank Dr ALL/GAR L19 ....130 F7
High Banks MGHL L31 ....72 E2
High Beeches CHLDW L16 ....115 H4
High Beeches Crs AIMK WN4 * 79 G7
High Carrs HUY L36 ....115 K3
High Clere Crs HUY L36 ....100 A8
Highcliffe Ct WGNNW/ST WN6 ....56 B6
Highcroft Av BEB CH63 ....128 C8
Highcroft Gn BEB CH63 ....128 C8
The Highcroft BEB CH63 ....128 C8
Higher Ashton WDN WA8 ....134 B2
Higher Bebington Rd
BEB CH63 ....128 A7
Higher End Pk NTHTN L30 ....71 M8
Higher Highfield Ct
WGNE/HIN WN2 ....57 K7
Higher House La CHLYE PR6 ....33 J2
Higher La KIRK/FR/WA PR4 ....27 L3
RNFD/HAY WA11 ....76 C7
SKEL WN8 ....53 L5
SKEL WN8 ....66 J1
WLT/FAZ L9 ....84 E6
Higher Parr St STHEL WA9 ....9 L5
Higher Rd HLWD L26 ....132 A6
Higher Vw SKEL WN8 ....66 E7
Highfield CHNE CH2 ....165 K1
NWD/KWIPK L33 ....74 B7
Highfield Av GOL/RIS/CU WA3 ....92 B5
WARRW/BUR WA5 ....120 C8
WGN WN1 ....5 K1
WGNNW/ST WN6 ....56 B6
Highfield Cl CHLYE PR6 ....44 C6
NSTN CH64 ....153 G5
WAL/EG CH44 ....111 J2
Highfield Crs RF/TRAN CH42 ....128 B4
WDN WA8 ....134 C3
Highfield Dr GR/UP/WCH CH49 ....125 M1
LYMM WA13 ....139 L3
RNFD/HAY WA11 ....89 G1
WGNNW/ST WN6 ....56 B6
Highfield Grange Av
WGNS/IIMK WN3 ....78 F3
Highfield Gv CSBY/BLUN L23 ....71 J7
RF/TRAN CH42 ....128 B4
WGNE/HIN WN2 ....57 L8
Highfield La BRSC L40 ....37 L6
GOL/RIS/CU WA3 ....92 E8
WARRN/WOL WA2 ....105 L5
Highfield Pk MGHL L31 ....73 H4
Highfield Pl CHLYE PR6 ....44 C6
Highfield Rd CHLYE PR6 ....44 C6
CHTN/BK PR9 ....25 K2
CLB/OSW/ST L13 ....114 C1
CROS/BRETH PR26 ....29 L3
GTS/LS CH66 ....155 K7
LITH L21 ....83 J5
LYMM WA13 ....139 L3
NSTN CH64 ....153 G5
ORM L39 ....51 G7
RF/TRAN CH42 ....128 B4
WDN WA8 ....16 B9
WLT/FAZ L9 ....97 H1
Highfield Rd North CHLY/EC 32 E3
CHLYE PR6 ....44 C5
EP CH65 ....20 C7
Highfield Rd South CHLY/EC PR7 ....32 E4
Highfields HES CH60 ....141 H6
PR/KW L34 ....100 F1
Highfield South RF/TRAN CH42 ....128 B4
Highfield St STHEL WA9 ....102 F5
VAUX/LVPD L3 ....12 F5
Highfield Ter CLB/OSW/ST L13 ....114 B1
Highgate Cl HES CH60 ....141 H4
RUNC WA7 ....150 F4
Highgate St EHL/KEN L7 ....113 J4
Highgate Crs WGNNW/ST WN6 ....55 G6
Highgate Rd MGHL L31 ....73 G4
SKEL WN8 ....66 D6
High Gates Cl
WARRW/BUR WA5 ....121 G6
Highgate St EHL/KEN L7 ....113 J4
Highgreen Rd RF/TRAN CH42 ....127 L5
Highgrove CHLY/EC PR7 ....42 A7
Highgrove Pk ALL/GAR L19 ....130 C5
Highlands Rd RUNC WA7 ....18 F9
High La BRSC L40 ....51 J5
ORM L39 ....63 L5
Highmarsh Crs NEWLW WA12 ....91 K8
Highmeadow SKEL WN8 ....66 C7
High Moor La WGNNW/ST WN6 ....54 C1
High Moss ORM L39 ....63 G2
Highoaks Rd WLTN L25 ....131 K4
High Pk WGNNW/ST WN6 ....55 L7
High Park Pl CHTN/BK PR9 ....25 J5
High Park Rd CHTN/BK PR9 ....25 J5
Highpark Rd RF/TRAN CH42 * 127 L2
High Park St TOX L8 ....113 H8
Highsands Av BRSC L40 ....39 J2
Highsted Gv NWD/KWIPK L33 ....74 A8
High St BRSC L40 ....40 D4
CHLY/EC PR7 ....32 E5
CLVP L2 ....12 E6
FROD/HEL WA6 ....160 D4
GOL/RIS/CU WA3 ....92 C5
NEWLW WA12 ....104 E1
NSTN CH64 ....153 G6
PR/KW L34 ....100 F1
PS/BROM CH62 * 144 A4
RUNC WA7 ....18 F4
SKEL WN8 ....64 F5
SPK/HALE L24 ....147 M4
WARR WA1 ....14 E5
WGNE/HIN WN2 ....69 M7
WGNNW/ST WN6 ....C1
WGNS/IIMK WN3 ....K7
WLTN L25 ....131 J5
Hightor Rd WLTN L25 ....131 J5
High Vw FROD/HEL WA6 ....166 E1
Highville Rd CHLDW L16 ....114 F4
High Warren Cl WARRS WA4 ....137 L8
Highways Av CHLY/EC PR7 ....31 M4
Highwood Ct NWD/KWIPK L33 ....86 A1

Highwood Rd WARRS WA4 ....137 L6
Highwoods Cl AIMK WN4 ....79 J8
Hignett Av STHEL WA9 ....103 J3
Hilary Av DV/KA/FCH L14 ....115 C3
GOL/RIS/CU WA3 ....92 C5
Hilary Cl ANF/KKDL L4 ....97 L6
PR/KW L34 ....101 G6
WARRW/BUR WA5 ....119 M7
WDN WA8 ....135 G2
Hilary Dr GR/UP/WCH CH49 ....110 C7
Hilary Rd ANF/KKDL L4 ....97 L6
Hilberry Av CLB/OSW/ST L13 ....98 A3
Hilbre Av HES CH60 ....141 G7
WAL/EG CH44 ....111 J1
Hilbre Cl CHTN/BK PR9 ....25 G4
Hilbre Dr EP CH65 ....163 L4
Hilbre Rd WKBY CH48 ....124 D4
Hilbre St BIRK CH41 ....11 G2
VAUX/LVPD L3 ....13 J7
Hilbre Vw WKBY CH48 ....124 D3
Hilcrest Av ANF/KKDL L4 ....97 M4
Hilda Rd WD/CROXPK L12 ....99 C8
Hilda St LEIGH WN7 ....81 L7
Hildebrand Cl ANF/KKDL L4 ....97 L5
Hilden Rd WARRN/WOL WA2 ....122 A4
Hildyard St WGNW/BIL/O WN5 ....68 B7
Higay Cl WGNS/IIMK WN3 ....5 J8
Hillaby Cl TOX L8 * 113 J7
Hillam Rd WAL/NB CH45 ....94 F7
Hillary Av WCNW/BIL/O WN5 ....67 M4
Hillary Crs MGHL L31 ....72 F4
Hillary Dr CSBY/BLUN L23 ....83 J1
Hillary Rd PS/BROM CH62 ....144 A8
Hillary Wk CSBY/BLUN L23 * 83 J1
Hillbank Rd WKBY CH48 ....56 C6
Hillbark WGNNW/ST WN6 ....56 C6
Hillbeck Crs AIMK WN4 ....90 F1
Hillberry Crs WARRS WA4 ....137 J5
Hillbrae Av RNFD/HAY WA11 ....89 H5
Hillburn Dr BIRK CH41 ....111 G4
Hill Cliffe Rd WARRS WA4 ....137 K5
Hill Cl NSTN CH64 ....153 H8
WGNNW/ST WN6 ....55 G6
Hill Ct NSTN CH64 ....153 H8
Hill Crs LEIGH WN7 ....81 L5
Hill Crest ANF/KKDL L4 * 7 M6
Hillcrest MGHL L31 ....73 H5
RUNC WA7 ....149 M4
SKEL WN8 ....65 K6
WGNE/HIN WN2 ....58 B5
Hillcrest Av HUY L36 ....116 C3
Hill Crest Av LEIGH WN7 ....81 L5
Hillcrest Dr BRSC L40 ....37 H5
GR/UP/WCH CH49 ....125 G2
GTS/LS CH66 ....155 J7
Hillcrest Rd CSBY/BLUN L23 ....83 J1
GTS/LS CH66 ....155 K7
ORM L39 ....51 G2
Hillcroft Rd WAL/EG CH44 ....111 L3
WLTN L25 ....131 H1
Hilldean SKEL WN8 ....66 C7
Hillerton Cl WD/CROX L11 * 98 E3
Hillfield FROD/HEL WA6 ....160 D6
RUNC WA7 ....150 F5
Hillfield Dr PEN/TH CH61 ....141 H4
Hillfield Rd GTS/LS CH66 ....155 M6
Hillfoot Av WLTN L25 ....131 K4
Hillfoot Cl CL/PREN CH43 ....110 E5
Hillfoot Crs WARRS WA4 ....137 K6
Hillfoot Gn WLTN L25 ....131 J6
Hillfoot Rd WLTN L25 ....131 J4
Hill Gv WD/MOR/LEA CH46 ....110 A6
Hillhead Rd BTL L20 ....7 L6
Hill House Fold La
WGNNW/ST WN6 ....41 J8
Hill House La WGNNW/ST WN6 ....41 J8
Hillingdon Av PEN/TH CH61 ....141 H4
Hillingdon Rd WAV L15 ....114 D7
Hill La HOR/BR BL6 ....57 K2
Hillock La BRSC L40 ....37 J6
Hillock La BRSC L40 ....37 J6
RF/TRAN CH42 ....128 B4
The Hillocks CROS/BRETH PR26 ....29 K3
Hillreed WGNNW/ST WN6 ....68 B4
Hill Rdg CHLY PR6 ....110 F8
Hill Rise Vw ORM L39 ....62 C4
Hill Rd CL/PREN CH43 ....111 G6
Hill Rd North FROD/HEL WA6 ....166 C2
Hill Rd South FROD/HEL WA6 ....166 C6
Hillsboro Av FROD/HEL WA6 ....160 B6
Hill School Rd ECCL WA10 ....101 H3
Hillsdown Wy GTS/LS CH66 ....162 E3
Hillside Av AIMK WN4 ....79 H5
ECCL WA10 ....99 M1
HUY L36 ....99 M7
NEWLW WA12 ....104 B3
RUNC WA7 ....18 D7
SKEL WN8 ....40 F8
Hillside Cl BIRK CH41 ....128 A1
BTL L20 ....7 L6
CHLY/EC PR7 ....31 L4
FROD/HEL WA6 ....166 F1
WGNS/IIMK WN3 ....78 F2
WGNW/BIL/O WN5 ....67 G3
Hillside Crs HUY L36 ....99 M7
WLTN L25 ....131 K2
Hillside Dr GTS/LS CH66 ....156 A6
Hillside Gv WARRW/BUR WA5 ....120 B8
Hillside Rd BIRK CH41 ....128 A1
CALD/MH L18 ....114 D8
CL/PREN CH43 ....110 F5
FROD/HEL WA6 ....160 E6
HES CH60 ....141 H6
Hillside St NPK/KEN L6 ....13 M1
Hillside Vw CL/PREN CH43 ....127 J2
Hills Moss STHEL WA9 ....103 H6
Hills Pl WAV L15 * 114 C6
Hill St CHTN/BK PR9 ....3 H2
CSBY/BLUN L23 ....83 H7
ECCL WA10 ....9 L1
RUNC WA7 ....19 H4
STHP PR8 ....11 F7
WARR WA1 ....14 E5
WGNE/HIN WN2 ....69 M7
WGNNW/ST WN6 ....C1
Hillswood Av
WARRW/BUR WA5 * C1
Hilltop La HES CH60 ....141 H6
NSTN CH64 ....153 H5
Hilltop Rd WARR WA1 ....115 J8
LYMM WA13 ....139 L3
RNFD/HAY WA11 ....88 D3
Hill Top Rd WARR WA1 ....138 B3
Hilltop Wk ORM L39 ....62 C2
Hillview AIG/SPK L17 ....130 A3
Hill Vw WDN WA8 ....118 D4
Hill View Av FROD/HEL WA6 ....166 C4
Hillview Av WKBY CH48 ....124 D3
Hillview Ct FROD/HEL WA6 ....160 E6
Hill View Dr CHLY/EC PR7 ....42 F5

GR/UP/WCH CH49 ....110 C7
Hillview Gdns WLTN L25 ....131 G2
Hillview Rd PEN/TH CH61 ....125 L7
Hillwood Cl BEB CH63 ....143 J4
Hilton Av WARRW/BUR WA5 ....120 D8
Hilton Cl BIRK CH41 ....11 G5
Hilton Gv WKBY CH48 ....124 C2
Hilton Pl AIMK WN4 ....57 L7
Hilton St AIMK WN4 ....91 K2
WGN WN1 ....5 J1
WGNS/IIMK WN3 ....5 J8
Hinchley Gv NSTN CH64 ....72 D4
Hinckley Rd RNFD/HAY WA11 ....89 L7
Hinderton Cl BIRK CH41 ....73 H3
Hinderton Dr HES CH60 ....141 H7
WKBY CH48 ....125 G4
Hinderton Gn NSTN CH64 ....153 H5
Hinderton La NSTN CH64 ....153 J4
Hinderton Rd BIRK CH41 ....11 J8
NSTN CH64 ....153 J5
Hindle Av WARRW/BUR WA5 ....121 H4
Hindley Beech MGHL L31 ....72 E3
Hindley St CHLY/EC PR7 ....32 C5
Hindley Wk WGN WN1 ....5 J4
Hindlip St TOX L8 ....129 J2
Hind Rd WGNW/BIL/O WN5 ....67 M5
Hind's Head Av WGNNW/ST WN6 ....62 B7
Hind St BIRK CH41 ....11 K7
Hinson St BIRK CH41 ....11 J6
Hinton Crs WARRS WA4 ....138 A5
Hinton Rd RUNC WA7 ....19 H6
Hinton St LITH L21 ....83 K7
NPK/KEN L6 ....113 L2
Hitchen's Cl RUNC WA7 ....150 F6
Hobart Dr NWD/KWIPK L33 ....74 A7
Hobart St STHEL WA9 ....101 M5
Hobb La WARRS WA4 ....136 E8
Hobby Ct RUNC WA7 ....150 A7
Hobcross La BRSC L40 ....52 C4
Hob Hey La GOL/RIS/CU WA3 ....106 C1
Hobhouse Ct CL/PREN CH43 * 10 D6
Hob La CHNE CH2 ....165 A4
Hoblyn Rd CL/PREN CH43 ....111 G5
Hockenhall Aly CLVP L2 ....12 F5
Hockenhull Cl BEB CH63 * 143 J3
Hockery Vw WGNE/HIN WN2 ....80 E1
Hodder Av CHLY/EC PR7 ....32 D8
MGHL L31 ....73 H5
WGNE/HIN WN2 ....80 B3
Hodder Cl RNFD/HAY WA11 ....89 K6
WGNW/BIL/O WN5 ....67 M6
Hodder Rd EV L5 ....97 H7
Hodder St EV L5 ....97 H7
Hodge Brow CHLYE PR6 ....45 H1
Hodges St WGNNW/ST WN6 ....68 C3
Hodge St STHP PR8 ....3 F2
Hodgkinson Av
WARRW/BUR WA5 ....121 H4
Hodnet Av WKBY CH48 ....91 L2
Hodson Pl NPK/KEN L6 ....13 M1
Hodson St STHP PR8 ....3 K5
WGNS/IIMK WN3 ....4 E5
Hogarth Dr CL/PREN CH43 ....126 F2
Hogarth St LITH L21 ....83 J7
Hogarth Wk ANF/KKDL L4 ....96 F5
Hoggs Hill La FMBY L37 ....59 G5
Hogg's La CHLYE PR6 ....33 H8
Hoghton Cl STHEL WA9 ....103 H5
Hoghton Gv CHTN/BK PR9 ....3 J2
Hoghton Rd SPK/HALE L24 ....148 A4
STHEL WA9 ....103 H6
Hoghton St CHTN/BK PR9 ....3 H3
Holbeach Cl WGNE/HIN WN2 ....81 G1
Holbeck RUNC WA7 ....150 E6
Holbeck Av ANF/KKDL L4 ....97 K7
Holborn Av WGNS/IIMK WN3 ....4 C9
Holborn Ct WDN WA8 ....134 D7
Holborn Dr ORM L39 ....62 C2
Holborn Hl BIRK CH41 ....11 K9
ORM L39 ....62 F1
Holborn Sq BIRK CH41 ....128 A1
Holborn St EHL/KEN L7 ....113 J2
Holbrook Cl STHEL WA9 ....102 F7
WARRW/BUR WA5 ....121 M7
Holcombe Cl
GR/UP/WCH CH49 * 125 M1
Holcombe Gv CHLYE PR6 ....33 G4
Holcroft La GOL/RIS/CU WA3 ....107 L2
Holden Gv CSBY/WL L22 ....82 E3
Holden Rd CSBY/WL L22 ....82 D3
RAIN/WH L35 ....116 E1
Holden Rd East CSBY/WL L22 * 82 E3
Holden St CHLY/EC PR7 ....32 C5
Holden Ter CSBY/WL L22 ....82 E3
Holden Wk WGNW/BIL/O WN5 ....68 A4
Holding St WGNE/HIN WN2 ....69 M7
Holdsworth St EHL/KEN L7 ....113 K3
Holes La WARR WA1 ....122 D6
Holford Av WARRW/BUR WA5 ....121 H5
Holford Wy NEWLW WA12 ....105 H2
Holgate CSBY/BLUN L23 ....71 K6
Holgate Dr WGNW/BIL/O WN5 ....67 G3
Holgate Pk CSBY/BLUN L23 ....71 K6
Holker La CROS/BRETH PR26 ....30 C1
Holkham Cl WDN WA8 ....16 A2
Holland Ct SKEL WN8 ....76 F3
Holland Gv HES CH60 ....141 H4
Holland Moss SKEL WN8 ....65 J8
Holland Pl EHL/KEN L7 ....113 K4
Holland Rd HLWD L26 ....132 A2
SPK/HALE L24 ....147 G3
WAL/NB CH45 ....95 L6
Holland's La SKEL WN8 ....64 C3
Holland St EHL/KEN L7 ....113 L4
Holland Wy HLWD L26 ....132 A7
Hollies Rd HLWD L26 ....132 D6
The Hollies RUNC WA7 * 149 M5
WGN WN1 ....C1
WGNE/HIN WN2 * 57 L8
WLTN L25 ....131 G2
Hollinbrook WGNNW/ST WN6 ....68 B3
Hollingbourne Pl NG/CROX L11 ....98 C2
Hollingbourne Rd NG/CROX L11 ....98 C2
Hollinghurst Rd NWD/KWIPK L33 ....74 B8
Hollingwood Cl AIMK WN4 ....91 J3
Hollingworth Cl WLT/FAZ L9 ....97 K2
Hollinhey Cl NTHTN L30 ....72 C8
Hollins Cl WGNE/HIN WN2 ....80 M2
Hollins Hey La CHLYE PR6 ....89 M3
Hollins Cl AIMK WN4 ....90 F1
WAV L15 ....114 C6
Hollins Dr WARRN/WOL WA2 ....105 J7
Hollinshead St CHLY/EC PR7 ....32 C5
Hollins La CROS/BRETH PR26 ....30 E1
WARRN/WOL WA2 ....105 G7
Holloway RUNC WA7 ....18 F6
Hollow Cft STBRV L28 ....99 J4
Hollow Dr WARRS WA4 ....138 A4
Holloword La BRSC L40 ....51 J8
Holly Av BEB CH63 ....143 H2
NEWLW WA12 ....104 F2
Holly Bank LYMM WA13 ....139 M3
Hollybank WARRS WA4 ....136 C8
Hollybank Ct WDN WA8 ....16 B1
Holly Bank Gv STHEL WA9 ....9 J8
Hollybank Rd BIRK CH41 ....11 G7

CALD/MH L18 ... 114 A8
RUNC WA7 ... 150 B5
Hollybrook Rd STHP PR8 ... 2 E7
Holly Bush La GOL/RIS/CU WA3 .. 123 L4
Hollybush Sq GOL/RIS/CU WA3 ... 93 G4
Holly Cl BRSC L40 ... 64 A1
ECCL WA10 ... 101 K1
SKEL WN8 ... 65 G4
SPK/HALE L24 ... 147 M4
Holly Ct FROD/HEL WA6 ... 159 L8
Holly Crs CHLY/EC PR7 ... 43 G2
RNFD/HAY WA11 ... 76 C8
Hollydale Rd CALD/MH L18 ... 114 C8
Hollydene WGNE/HIN WN2 * ... 57 K8
Holly Farm Rd ALL/GAR L19 ... 130 F7
Hollyfield Rd EP CH65 ... 20 B4
WLT/FAZ L9 ... 84 B8
Holly Fold La RNFD/HAY WA11 ... 76 A2
Holly Gv BIRK CH41 ... 128 A1
HUY L36 ... 115 K3
LITH L21 ... 83 H7
WARR WA1 ... 122 C6
Holly Heath Dr WGN WN1 ... 68 D1
Holly Hedge La WARRS WA4 ... 136 F7
Holly House RAIN/WH L35 ... 116 F4
Holly La BRSC L40 ... 39 L2
ORM L39 ... 62 D1
SKEL WN8 ... 75 M1
Holly Mt WD/CROXPK L12 ... 98 C7
Holly Pl MOR/LEA CH46 ... 110 B6
Holly Rd EHL/KEN L7 ... 113 M3
EP CH65 ... 20 D4
GOL/RIS/CU WA3 ... 92 E5
RNFD/HAY WA11 ... 90 B8
WARRW/BUR WA5 ... 120 A8
WGNE/HIN WN2 ... 57 K8
WGNW/BIL/O WN5 ... 68 A6
Hollyrood PR/KW L34 ... 100 B8
Holly St BTL L20 ... 7 H3
WGNE/HIN WN2 ... 69 H3
Holly Ter WARRW/BUR WA5 ... 120 B8
Hollytree Rd WLTN L25 ... 131 K2
Hollywood Rd AIG/SPK L17 ... 130 A2
Holman Rd ALL/GAR L19 ... 130 F7
Holm Cottages CL/PREN CH43 ... 127 H3
Holmcrofts NSTN CH64 ... 153 G8
Holmdale Av CHTN/BK PR9 ... 25 L1
Holm Dr CHNE CH2 ... 165 L2
Holme Av WGN WN1 ... 68 E3
Holme Cl PR/KW L34 ... 101 J6
Holme Ct WGN WN1 ... 68 E3
Holmefield Av ALL/GAR L19 ... 130 C5
Holmefield Gv MGHL L31 ... 72 E4
Holmefield Rd ALL/GAR L19 ... 130 B4
Holme Rd ECCL WA10 ... 101 K3
Holmes Ct GOL/RIS/CU WA3 ... 122 E1
Holmes House Av
WGNS/IIMK WN3 ... 78 E2
Holmes La LITH L21 * ... 83 J6
Holmes St TOX L8 ... 113 L6
Holme St EV L5 ... 96 E7
Holmesway PEN/TH CH61 ... 141 H1
Holmeswood Rd
KIRK/FR/WA PR4 ... 27 M7
Holme Ter WGN WN1 ... 68 D2
Holmfield CL/PREN CH43 ... 127 J3
Holmfield Av RUNC WA7 ... 19 L4
Holmfield Dr GTS/LS CH66 ... 162 F2
Holmfield Gv HUY L36 ... 116 B5
Holmfield Pk FMBY L37 ... 58 F1
Holm Hey Rd CL/PREN CH43 ... 127 H3
Holm Hl WKBY CH48 ... 124 E4
Holmlands Crs CL/PREN CH43 * .. 127 G3
Holmlands Dr CL/PREN CH43 ... 127 G3
Holmlands Wy CL/PREN CH43 ... 127 G3
Holm La CL/PREN CH43 ... 127 H3
Holmleigh Rd WLTN L25 ... 115 J7
Holm Oak Wy GTS/LS CH66 ... 163 G5
Holmrook Rd NG/CROX L11 ... 98 C3
Holmsfield Cl WGNE/HIN WN2 ... 69 J3
Holmsfield Rd WARR WA1 ... 15 K6
Holmside Cl MOR/LEA CH46 ... 110 B5
Holmside La CL/PREN CH43 ... 127 H3
Holm View Cl CL/PREN CH43 ... 127 J2
Holmville Rd BEB CH63 ... 128 A8
Holmway BEB CH63 ... 128 B8
Holmwood Av PEN/TH CH61 ... 126 E8
Holmwood Cl AIMK WN4 ... 79 J8
FMBY L37 ... 58 F2
Holmwood Dr EP CH65 ... 163 K3
FMBY L37 ... 58 F1
PEN/TH CH61 ... 126 E8
Holmwood Gdns FMBY L37 ... 58 F1
Holt Av CHLY/EC PR7 ... 43 H3
MOR/LEA CH46 ... 110 A5
WGNW/BIL/O WN5 ... 89 M1
Holt Coppice ORM L39 ... 62 C6
Holt Crs WGNW/BIL/O WN5 ... 89 M1
Holt Hey NSTN CH64 ... 153 J8
Holt Hl BIRK CH41 ... 11 J9
Holt Hill Ter BIRK CH41 ... 11 H8
Holt La NTHLY L27 ... 115 M7
RAIN/WH L35 ... 117 J1
RUNC WA7 ... 150 B6
Holton Wy WGNS/IIMK WN3 ... 79 G4
Holt Rd BIRK CH41 ... 128 A1
EHL/KEN L7 ... 113 L3
Holt St WGN WN1 ... 5 L4
WGNE/HIN WN2 ... 69 L8
WGNNW/ST WN6 ... 68 B4
WGNS/IIMK WN3 ... 79 J1
WGNW/BIL/O WN5 ... 66 F8
Holtswell Cl GOL/RIS/CU WA3 ... 93 G4
Holyhead Cl WARRW/BUR WA5 ... 120 F2
Holyrood CSBY/BLUN L23 ... 82 C1
Holyrood Av WDN WA8 ... 134 C1
Holywell Cl NSTN CH64 ... 152 D4
STHEL WA9 ... 102 F7
Home Farm Cl
GR/UP/WCH CH49 ... 126 E3
Home Farm Rd
GR/UP/WCH CH49 ... 126 D3
PR/KW L34 ... 99 L3
Homer Rd PR/KW L34 ... 99 L2
Homerton Rd NPK/KEN L6 ... 113 M2
Homestall Rd NG/CROX L11 ... 98 C3
Homestead Av NTHTN L30 ... 84 D2
RNFD/HAY WA11 * ... 91 G6
Homestead Cl HUY L36 ... 116 C2
Homestead Ms WKBY CH48 * ... 124 D3
Homeway FROD/HEL WA6 ... 166 D3
Honeybourne Dr RAIN/WH L35 ... 101 J7
Honey Hall Rd HLWD L26 ... 132 A7
Honeys Green Cl
WD/CROXPK L12 ... 98 F8
Honey's Green La
WD/CROXPK L12 ... 98 F8
Honey St STHEL WA9 * ... 101 L6
Honeysuckle Av
WGNNW/ST WN6 ... 68 B2
Honeysuckle Cl GTS/LS CH66 ... 163 H5
HLWD L26 ... 131 M3
WDN WA8 ... 134 D1
Honeysuckle Dr WLT/FAZ L9 ... 97 K2
Honister Av RNFD/HAY WA11 ... 89 L5
WARRN/WOL WA2 ... 121 L3
Honister Gv RUNC WA7 ... 150 A8
Honister Rd WGNW/BIL/O WN5 ... 67 K7
Honister Wk NTHLY L27 ... 132 C2
Honiston Av RAIN/WH L35 ... 117 K1
Honiton Cl LEIGH WN7 ... 81 M3
Honiton Rd AIG/SPK L17 ... 130 A5
Honiton Wy WARRW/BUR WA5 ... 136 A1
Hood La WARRW/BUR WA5 ... 120 E8
Hood La North
WARRW/BUR WA5 ... 120 E7
Hood Rd WDN WA8 ... 16 B2
Hood St BTL L20 ... 6 D1
CLVPS L1 ... 13 G6
WAL/EG CH44 ... 111 M2
Hookstone Dr GTS/LS CH66 ... 155 L7
Hook St WGNE/HIN WN2 ... 5 M5
Hoole La CHTN/BK PR9 ... 23 J7
Hoole Rd GR/UP/WCH CH49 ... 126 D2
Hoolpool La FROD/HEL WA6 ... 159 H8
Hooton Gn GTS/LS CH66 ... 155 J3
Hooton La GTS/LS CH66 ... 155 K4
Hooton Rd NSTN CH64 ... 154 D4
WLT/FAZ L9 ... 84 D6
WGNS/IIMK WN3 ... 79 J1
Hooton Wy GTS/LS CH66 ... 155 H3
Hope Cl ECCL WA10 ... 8 D4
Hope Crs WGNNW/ST WN6 ... 55 K7
Hope Cft GTS/LS CH66 ... 163 H3
Hope Farm Rd GTS/LS CH66 ... 163 G4
Hope Island SKEL WN8 ... 65 H5
Hope Pl CLVPS L1 * ... 13 K9
Hope Sq CHTN/BK PR9 ... 3 K3
Hope St AIMK WN4 ... 79 M8
BIRK CH41 ... 11 G4
CHLY/EC PR7 ... 32 E4
CHLYE PR6 ... 44 D6
CHTN/BK PR9 ... 3 K3
NEWLW WA12 ... 104 D2
PR/KW L34 ... 100 F7
TOX L8 ... 113 H5
WAL/NB CH45 ... 95 K5
WGN WN1 * ... 4 E3
WGNS/IIMK WN3 ... 80 A1
Hope St North HOR/BR BL6 ... 45 K8
Hope Wy TOX L8 ... 113 H5
Hopfield Rd MOR/LEA CH46 ... 110 B5
Hopkins Cl ECCL WA10 ... 8 A4
Hopwood Cl GOL/RIS/CU WA3 ... 93 H5
Hopwood Crs RNFD/HAY WA11 ... 76 C8
Hopwood St EV L5 ... 96 F8
WARR WA1 ... 15 G4
Horace Black Gdns EP CH65 ... 20 C3
Horace St ECCL WA10 ... 8 C4
Horbury Gdns GTS/LS CH66 ... 155 L8
Hornbeam Av GTS/LS CH66 ... 163 H4
Hornbeam Cl MOR/LEA CH46 * ... 109 K5
RNFD/HAY WA11 ... 90 B8
RUNC WA7 ... 150 E5
Hornbeam Crs AIMK WN4 ... 91 K2
Hornbeam Rd HLWD L26 ... 132 C6
WLT/FAZ L9 ... 97 L2
Hornby Av BTL L20 ... 6 F1
PS/BROM CH62 ... 143 M4
Hornby Bvd LITH L21 ... 83 K7
Hornby Cha MGHL L31 ... 72 F6
Hornby Cl WLT/FAZ L9 ... 97 H1
Hornby Crs STHEL WA9 ... 118 F1
Hornby Flats LITH L21 * ... 83 K7
Hornby La CALD/MH L18 ... 114 F8
WARRN/WOL WA2 ... 105 J7
Hornby Pk CALD/MH L18 ... 114 F8
Hornby Pl WLT/FAZ L9 ... 84 E8
Hornby Rd BTL L20 ... 7 H2
CHLYE PR6 ... 33 G7
CHTN/BK PR9 ... 25 J1
PS/BROM CH62 ... 143 L4
WLT/FAZ L9 ... 97 H1
Hornby Steet WGN WN1 ... 68 E3
Hornby St BIRK CH41 ... 11 L5
CSBY/BLUN L23 * ... 83 G1
LITH L21 ... 83 J7
Hornby Wk EV L5 ... 12 F1
Horncastle Cl GOL/RIS/CU WA3 ... 93 H5
Hornchurch Dr CHLY/EC PR7 ... 32 C5
Horne Gv WGNS/IIMK WN3 ... 68 B8
Horne St NPK/KEN L6 ... 113 K1
Hornet Cl NPK/KEN L6 ... 113 J1
Hornhouse La NWD/KWIPK L33 ... 86 D5
Hornsey Gv WGNS/IIMK WN3 ... 78 F2
Hornsey Rd ANF/KKDL L4 ... 97 K7
Hornspit La WD/CROXPK L12 ... 98 C5
Horridge Av NEWLW WA12 ... 91 L8
Horringford Rd ALL/GAR L19 ... 130 B5
Horrobin La CHLYE PR6 * ... 44 F4
Horrocks Av ALL/GAR L19 ... 130 F4
Horrocks Cl HUY L36 ... 115 M1
Horrocks La WARR WA1 ... 14 E6
Horrocks Rd HUY L36 ... 115 M2
Horrocks St LEIGH WN7 ... 93 J1
Horseman Pl WAL/EG CH44 ... 112 A3
Horseshoe Crs
WARRN/WOL WA2 ... 122 A2
Horseshoe Dr AIN/FAZ L10 ... 85 K6
Horsfall Gv TOX L8 ... 129 G1
Horsfall St TOX L8 ... 129 G1
Horsham Gv WGNE/HIN WN2 ... 69 H3
Horstone Crs GTS/LS CH66 ... 163 H3
Horstone Gdns GTS/LS CH66 ... 163 H3
Horstone Rd GTS/LS CH66 ... 163 H3
Horton St WGNNW/ST WN6 ... 68 A3
Horwood Av RAIN/WH L35 ... 117 K1
Horwood Cl NG/CROX L11 * ... 98 E3
Hoscar Ct WDN WA8 ... 133 M6
Hoscar Moss Rd BRSC L40 ... 52 E2
Hoscote Pk WKBY CH48 ... 124 C3
Hose Side Rd WAL/NB CH45 ... 95 J7
Hospital St ECCL WA10 ... 9 H3
Hospital Wy RUNC WA7 ... 150 B6
Hosta Cl NWD/KWIPK L33 ... 73 M8
Hostock Cl RAIN/WH L35 ... 116 F3
Hotel St NEWLW WA12 ... 104 D2
Hotham St VAUX/LVPD L3 ... 13 J6
Hothfield Rd WAL/EG CH44 * ... 111 M2
Hotspur St BTL L20 ... 96 E5
Hough Green Rd WDN WA8 ... 133 J3
Hough's La WARRS WA4 ... 137 J7
Houghton Av WGNW/BIL/O WN5 .. 68 A3
Houghton Cl NEWLW WA12 * ... 104 D2
WDN WA8 ... 134 E3
Houghton Cft WDN WA8 ... 117 L8
Houghton La CLVPS L1 * ... 13 H7
WGNNW/ST WN6 ... 55 H7
Houghton Rd
GR/UP/WCH CH49 ... 126 D2
Houghton's La ECCL WA10 ... 88 B6
SKEL WN8 ... 65 J2
Houghtons Rd SKEL WN8 ... 65 J2
Houghton St CHLYE PR6 ... 32 F5
CLVPS L1 ... 13 H7
NEWLW WA12 ... 104 D2
PR/KW L34 ... 100 F7
RAIN/WH L35 * ... 117 L2
WARRN/WOL WA2 ... 14 E3
WDN WA8 ... 134 F3
Houghwood Gra AIMK WN4 ... 91 H2
Hougoumont Av CSBY/WL L22 ... 83 G4
Hougoumont Gv CSBY/WL L22 ... 83 G3
Houlding St ANF/KKDL L4 * ... 97 J7
Houlgrave Rd EV L5 ... 96 E8
Houlston Rd KKBY L32 ... 85 K3
Houlton St EHL/KEN L7 ... 113 L3
Houseman Gv WGNNW/ST WN6 ... 68 C3
Housley Cl WGNS/IIMK WN3 ... 79 J1
The Hove RUNC WA7 ... 150 F7
Howard Av PS/BROM CH62 ... 143 M5
Howard Cl LITH L21 ... 83 L3
MGHL L31 ... 73 H4
Howard Dr ALL/GAR L19 ... 130 C6
Howard Florey Av NTHTN L30 ... 84 B1
Howard Rd CHLY/EC PR7 ... 32 D8
GOL/RIS/CU WA3 ... 107 J3
Howard's La ECCL WA10 ... 101 G1
WGNW/BIL/O WN5 ... 67 H6
Howards Rd PEN/TH CH61 ... 126 D7
Howard St ECCL WA10 * ... 101 L5
WGNW/BIL/O WN5 ... 67 L8
Howards Wy NSTN CH64 ... 153 J7
Howarth Ct RUNC WA7 ... 19 J3
Howbeck Cl CL/PREN CH43 ... 111 H7
Howbeck Dr CL/PREN CH43 ... 111 H7
Howbeck Rd CL/PREN CH43 ... 111 H8
Howden Dr HUY L36 ... 115 J3
WGNS/IIMK WN3 ... 79 J1
Howe Gv CHLY/EC PR7 ... 32 C6
Howell Dr GR/UP/WCH CH49 ... 125 M3
Howell Rd PS/BROM CH62 ... 128 C6
Howells Av GTS/LS CH66 ... 162 E2
Howells Cl MGHL L31 ... 72 F3
Howe St BTL L20 ... 6 E8
Howey La FROD/HEL WA6 ... 160 D6
Howey Ri FROD/HEL WA6 ... 160 C6
Howley La WARR WA1 ... 15 J6
Howley Quay WARR WA1 * ... 15 J6
Howson Rd WARRN/WOL WA2 ... 121 L3
Howson St RF/TRAN CH42 ... 128 B3
Hoylake Cl LEIGH WN7 ... 93 M3
RUNC WA7 ... 150 E7
Hoylake Gv STHEL WA9 ... 118 E1
Hoylake Rd BIRK CH41 ... 110 F4
CL/PREN CH43 ... 110 F4
MOR/LEA CH46 ... 110 B4
Hoyle Rd HOY CH47 ... 108 D5
Hoyle St WARRW/BUR WA5 ... 14 B2
Huddleston Cl
GR/UP/WCH CH49 ... 126 D2
Huddleston Rd WAV L15 ... 114 D4
Hudson Cl WARRW/BUR WA5 ... 120 F5
Hudson Rd MGHL L31 ... 72 F6
MOR/LEA CH46 ... 110 C1
Hudswell Cl NTHTN L30 ... 84 D4
Hughenden Rd CLB/OSW/ST L13 .. 98 B8
Hughes Av RAIN/WH L35 ... 116 F1
WARRN/WOL WA2 ... 121 M3
Hughes Cl EHL/KEN L7 ... 113 L4
Hughes Dr BTL L20 ... 84 A7
Hughes La CL/PREN CH43 ... 127 K2
Hughes Pl WARRN/WOL WA2 ... 121 M3
Hughes St ALL/GAR L19 ... 130 E8
NPK/KEN L6 ... 113 J2
STHEL WA9 ... 102 F5
WARRS WA4 ... 15 H9
Hughestead Gv ALL/GAR L19 ... 130 D7
Hughson St TOX L8 ... 113 H8
Hullet Cl WGNNW/ST WN6 ... 55 G5
Hulme Gv LEIGH WN7 ... 81 L7
Hulme Rd LEIGH WN7 ... 81 L7
Hulme St STHP PR8 ... 2 F4
Hulmewood BEB CH63 ... 128 C6
Hulton Av RAIN/WH L35 ... 117 H1
Humber Cl ANF/KKDL L4 ... 97 G5
WDN WA8 ... 135 H2
Humber Crs STHEL WA9 ... 102 E8
Humber Pl WGNW/BIL/O WN5 ... 67 L6
Humber Rd GTS/LS CH66 ... 163 H3
WARRN/WOL WA2 ... 122 A3
Hume Ct HOY CH47 ... 108 E5
Hume St WARR WA1 ... 15 J3
Humphrey's Cl RUNC WA7 * ... 150 F6
Humphreys Hey CSBY/BLUN L23 .. 71 K8
Humphrey St BTL L20 ... 83 L7
Huncote Av RNFD/HAY WA11 ... 89 M7
Hunslett Rd WLT/FAZ L9 ... 84 D7
Hunstanton Cl
GR/UP/WCH CH49 ... 110 C6
Hunt Cl WARRW/BUR WA5 * ... 120 D5
Hunter Av WARRN/WOL WA2 ... 121 K3
Hunter Ct PR/KW L34 ... 101 G7
Hunter Rd WGNW/BIL/O WN5 ... 68 A4
Hunters Cha WGNW/BIL/O WN5 ... 78 A4
Hunters Ct FROD/HEL WA6 ... 166 F1
RUNC WA7 ... 150 A7
Hunter's La KIRK/FR/WA PR4 ... 27 K2
WAV L15 ... 114 C6
Hunter St STHEL WA9 ... 9 L8
VAUX/LVPD L3 ... 13 J5
Hunters Wy NSTN CH64 ... 152 E5
Huntingdon Cl MOR/LEA CH46 ... 109 K5
Huntingdon Ct CHTN/BK PR9 * ... 25 J3
Huntingdon Gv MGHL L31 ... 72 E1
Huntley Gv STHEL WA9 ... 102 E6
Huntley St WARRW/BUR WA5 ... 136 E1
Huntly Rd NPK/KEN L6 ... 113 L2
Hunt Rd MGHL L31 ... 72 F4
RNFD/HAY WA11 ... 91 G7
Hunts Cross Av WLTN L25 ... 131 K2
Hunts Field Cl LYMM WA13 ... 139 M3
Hunts La WARRS WA4 ... 138 B3
Huntsman Wd WD/CROXPK L12 .. 99 G5
Hunt St WGN WN1 ... 5 J5
Hurford Av EP CH65 ... 163 H1
Hurley Cl WARRW/BUR WA5 ... 120 E8
Hurlingham Rd ANF/KKDL L4 ... 97 L3
Hurlston Av SKEL WN8 * ... 65 L5
Hurlston Dr ORM L39 ... 51 G6
Hurlston La BRSC L40 ... 50 E4
Hurn Gv CHLY/EC PR7 ... 32 C6
Hurrell Rd BIRK CH41 ... 110 F4
Hursley Rd WLT/FAZ L9 ... 98 A1
Hurst Bank RF/TRAN CH42 ... 128 B5
Hurst Brook CHLY/EC PR7 ... 43 H4
Hurst Gn BRSC L40 ... 40 E3
Hurstlyn Rd CALD/MH L18 ... 130 E4
Hurst Park Cl HUY L36 * ... 116 C1
Hurst Park Dr HUY L36 ... 116 C2
Hurst Rd MGHL L31 ... 73 G6
Hurst's La ORM L39 ... 74 C3
Hurst St CLVPS L1 ... 112 F6
WDN WA8 ... 149 J1
WGNE/HIN WN2 ... 69 L7
Huskisson St TOX L8 ... 113 H6
Huskisson Wy NEWLW WA12 ... 104 D1
Hutchinson St NPK/KEN L6 ... 113 J2
WDN WA8 ... 16 C8
Hutchinson Wk NPK/KEN L6 ... 113 J2
Hut La CHLYE PR6 ... 33 K8
Huttfield Rd SPK/HALE L24 ... 147 J1
Hutton Ct SKEL WN8 ... 64 F4
Hutton Rd SKEL WN8 ... 64 F4
Hutton St WGN WN1 ... 56 C2
Hutton Wy ORM L39 ... 51 G8
Huxley Cl MOR/LEA CH46 ... 109 K5
Huxley Ct GTS/LS CH66 ... 156 B5
Huxley Pl WGNS/IIMK WN3 ... 68 E8
Huxley St CLB/OSW/ST L13 ... 97 M6
Huyton Av ECCL WA10 ... 89 G7
Huyton Brook HUY L36 ... 116 B5
Huyton Church Rd HUY L36 ... 116 A3
Huyton Hall Crs HUY L36 * ... 116 A3
Huyton Hey Rd HUY L36 ... 116 B3
Huyton House Cl HUY L36 ... 115 K1
Huyton House Rd HUY L36 ... 115 K1
Huyton La HUY L36 ... 116 B2
Huyton Rd CHLY/EC PR7 ... 44 C7
Hyacinth Cl RNFD/HAY WA11 ... 91 H7
Hyacinth Gv MOR/LEA CH46 ... 110 C3
Hyatt Crs WGNNW/ST WN6 ... 55 L2
Hyde Cl EP CH65 ... 163 H1
RUNC WA7 * ... 149 M7
WGNS/IIMK WN3 ... 68 C8
Hyde Rd CSBY/WL L22 ... 82 F4
Hyde's Brow RNFD/HAY WA11 ... 76 C5
Hydro Av WKBY CH48 ... 124 D4
Hygeia St NPK/KEN L6 ... 113 J1
Hylton Av WAL/EG CH44 ... 111 J1
Hylton Ct EP CH65 ... 164 A3
Hylton Rd ALL/GAR L19 ... 130 F5
Hyslop St TOX L8 ... 113 G7
Hythe Av LITH L21 ... 83 L5
Hythe Cl STHP PR8 ... 36 A2
Hythedale Cl AIG/SPK L17 ... 129 L3

I

Ibbotson's La AIG/SPK L17 ... 130 A1
Ibis Ct WARR WA1 ... 14 C9
Ibstock Rd BTL L20 ... 83 K8
Iffley Cl GR/UP/WCH CH49 ... 109 M8
Ikin Cl CL/PREN CH43 ... 110 E4
Ilchester Rd BIRK CH41 ... 111 H4
CHLDW L16 ... 115 G4
WAL/EG CH44 ... 111 M2
Ilex Av WARRN/WOL WA2 ... 105 K7
Ilford Av CSBY/BLUN L23 ... 70 F8
WAL/EG CH44 ... 111 K3
Ilford St VAUX/LVPD L3 ... 13 K5
Ilfracombe Rd STHEL WA9 ... 102 E8
Iliad St EV L5 ... 13 J2
Ilkley Av CHTN/BK PR9 ... 22 E7
Ilsley Cl GR/UP/WCH CH49 ... 126 B1
Imber Rd KKBY L32 ... 86 B5
Imison St WLT/FAZ L9 ... 97 H2
Imison Wy WLT/FAZ L9 ... 7 M5
Imperial Av WAL/NB CH45 ... 95 L7
Imperial Ms EP CH65 ... 20 B2
Imrie St ANF/KKDL L4 ... 97 H3
Ince Av ANF/KKDL L4 ... 97 K5
CSBY/BLUN L23 ... 70 E8
LITH L21 ... 83 K6
PS/BROM CH62 ... 155 G2
Ince Cl CL/PREN CH43 * ... 127 H1
Ince Crs FMBY L37 ... 58 F2
Ince Green La WGNE/HIN WN2 ... 5 L7
Ince Gv CL/PREN CH43 ... 127 H1
Ince Hall Av WGNE/HIN WN2 ... 5 M4
Ince La CHLY/EC PR7 ... 30 E8
CHNE CH2 ... 165 K1
CSBY/BLUN L23 ... 71 H4
Incemore Rd CALD/MH L18 ... 130 D4
Ince Orchards CHNE CH2 ... 165 K1
Ince Rd CSBY/BLUN L23 ... 71 J6
Inchcape Rd CHLDW L16 ... 115 G4
NEWLW WA12 * ... 94 F8
Inchfield SKEL WN8 ... 65 K3
Index St ANF/KKDL L4 ... 97 H4
Indigo Rd EP CH65 ... 21 K4
Ingestre Rd CL/PREN CH43 ... 127 J2
Ingham Rd WDN WA8 ... 134 B1
Ingleborough Rd
RF/TRAN CH42 ... 127 M3
Ingleby Cl WGNNW/ST WN6 ... 55 M3
Ingleby Rd PS/BROM CH62 ... 128 D5
WAL/EG CH44 ... 111 J2
Ingle Cl CHLYE PR6 ... 32 F4
Ingledene Rd CALD/MH L18 ... 114 F8
Ingle Gn CSBY/BLUN L23 ... 70 C8
Inglegreen HES CH60 ... 141 J5
Ingleholme Gdns PR/KW L34 ... 101 J6
Ingleholme Rd CALD/MH L18 ... 130 C4
Inglemere Rd RF/TRAN CH42 ... 128 A3
Inglemoss Dr RNFD/HAY WA11 ... 88 D4
Inglenook Rd
WARRW/BUR WA5 ... 136 B1
Ingleton Cl GR/UP/WCH CH49 * .. 125 M1
NEWLW WA12 * ... 104 D1
Ingleton Dr RNFD/HAY WA11 ... 89 K4
Ingleton Gn KKBY L32 ... 86 B5
Ingleton Gv RUNC WA7 ... 149 M8
Ingleton Rd CALD/MH L18 ... 114 B8
KKBY L32 ... 86 B5
STHP PR8 ... 36 A2
Inglewhite SKEL WN8 ... 65 J3
Inglewhite Av WGN WN1 ... 68 E3
Inglewhite Crs WGN WN1 * ... 68 E3
Inglewood WD/CROXPK L12 ... 99 J3
Inglewood Av MOR/LEA CH46 ... 109 M6
WGN WN1 ... 5 J5
Inglewood Cl GOL/RIS/CU WA3 ... 107 K7
Inglewood Rd RNFD/HAY WA11 ... 88 D4
Inglis Rd WLT/FAZ L9 ... 84 D6
Ingoe Cl KKBY L32 ... 85 K4
Ingoe La KKBY L32 ... 85 K5
Ingram SKEL WN8 ... 65 K4
Ingram St WGNE/HIN WN2 ... 80 C2
WGNNW/ST WN6 ... 68 B4
Ingrave Rd ANF/KKDL L4 ... 97 L3
Ingrow Rd NPK/KEN L6 ... 113 K2
Inigo Rd CLB/OSW/ST L13 ... 114 D1
Inley Cl BEB CH63 ... 143 J3
Inley Rd BEB CH63 ... 143 H3
Inman Av STHEL WA9 ... 103 K3
Inman Rd GR/UP/WCH CH49 ... 110 A7
LITH L21 ... 83 K6
Inner Central Rd SPK/HALE L24 .. 132 B8
Inner Forum NG/CROX L11 ... 98 A2
Inner South Rd SPK/HALE L24 ... 147 H1
Inner West Rd SPK/HALE L24 ... 147 G1
Innisfree Cl GTS/LS CH66 ... 155 L8
Insall Rd CLB/OSW/ST L13 ... 114 D4
WARRN/WOL WA2 ... 122 B3
Inskip SKEL WN8 ... 65 J3
Inskip Rd CHTN/BK PR9 ... 25 J1
Intake Cl NSTN CH64 ... 154 C6
Intake La ORM L39 ... 61 G5
ORM L39 ... 75 J1
Inveresk Ct CL/PREN CH43 ... 111 G7
Invincible Cl NTHTN L30 ... 84 A5
Invincible Wy NG/CROX L11 ... 85 L7
Inward Dr WGNNW/ST WN6 ... 55 J8
Inward Wy EP CH65 ... 156 D6
Inwood Rd ALL/GAR L19 ... 130 E6
Iona Cl WD/CROXPK L12 ... 99 J2
Ionic Rd CLB/OSW/ST L13 ... 114 C1
Ionic St LITH L21 * ... 83 H6
RF/TRAN CH42 ... 128 B3
Irby Av WAL/EG CH44 ... 111 J1
Irby Cl GTS/LS CH66 ... 163 G1
Irby Rd ANF/KKDL L4 ... 97 K5
PEN/TH CH61 ... 125 M8
Irbyside Rd WKBY CH48 ... 125 K4
Iredale Crs WGNNW/ST WN6 ... 56 B6
Ireland Rd RNFD/HAY WA11 ... 90 E7
SPK/HALE L24 ... 148 A4
Ireland St WARRN/WOL WA2 ... 121 K5
WDN WA8 ... 134 F3
Irene Av RNFD/HAY WA11 ... 89 L6
Irene Rd CHLDW L16 ... 114 E7
Ireton St ANF/KKDL L4 ... 97 H3
Iris Av BIRK CH41 ... 111 H5
Iris Cl WDN WA8 ... 133 L3
Irlam Dr KKBY L32 ... 86 A3
Irlam Pl BTL L20 ... 6 E3
Irlam Rd BTL L20 ... 6 E4
Ironbridge Vw TOX L8 ... 129 G1
Ironmonger La
WGNS/IIMK WN3 ... 4 E6
Ironside Rd HUY L36 ... 115 M1
Irton Rd CHTN/BK PR9 ... 25 G5
Irvin Av CHTN/BK PR9 ... 22 E8
Irvine Rd RF/TRAN CH42 ... 127 M3
Irvine St EHL/KEN L7 ... 113 J4
Irving St CHTN/BK PR9 ... 24 D4
Irwell SKEL WN8 ... 65 J2
Irwell Cl AIG/SPK L17 ... 130 A2
Irwell La AIG/SPK L17 ... 130 A2
RUNC WA7 ... 19 K2
Irwell Pl WGNW/BIL/O WN5 ... 67 L7
Irwell Rd WARRS WA4 ... 137 K3
WGNW/BIL/O WN5 ... 67 H6
Irwell St WDN WA8 ... 149 J1
Irwin Rd STHEL WA9 ... 102 E6
Isaac St TOX L8 ... 129 H1
Isabel Gv CLB/OSW/ST L13 ... 98 A6
Isabella Sq WGN WN1 ... 5 J3
Isherwood Cl WARRN/WOL WA2 .. 122 B2
Island Pl ALL/GAR L19 * ... 130 E7
Island Rd ALL/GAR L19 ... 130 E7
Island Rd South ALL/GAR L19 ... 130 E7
Islands Brow RNFD/HAY WA11 ... 89 K7
Islay Cl EP CH65 ... 163 L5
Isleham Cl CALD/MH L18 ... 130 E5
Isleworth Dr CHLY/EC PR7 ... 32 D6
Islington CSBY/BLUN L23 ... 70 F8
VAUX/LVPD L3 ... 13 K5
Islip Cl PEN/TH CH61 ... 125 M6
Ismay Dr WAL/EG CH44 ... 95 M8
Ismay Rd LITH L21 ... 83 K6
Ismay St ANF/KKDL L4 ... 97 H4
Ivanhoe Av GOL/RIS/CU WA3 ... 92 F4
Ivanhoe Rd AIG/SPK L17 ... 129 L1
CSBY/BLUN L23 ... 82 E2
Ivatt Wy EHL/KEN L7 ... 113 L4
Iveagh Cl RUNC WA7 ... 150 C6
Iver Cl WDN WA8 ... 117 L7
Ivernia Rd ANF/KKDL L4 ... 97 K3
Ivor Rd WAL/EG CH44 ... 95 L8
Ivory Dr NWD/KWIPK L33 ... 74 A8
Ivy Av ALL/GAR L19 ... 130 C6
BEB CH63 ... 128 A8
NEWLW WA12 ... 104 E3
Ivybridge SKEL WN8 ... 65 K3
Ivychurch Ms RUNC WA7 ... 149 M3
Ivy Ct STHEL WA9 ... 9 L5
Ivydale SKEL WN8 ... 65 K3
Ivydale Rd CALD/MH L18 ... 130 B1
RF/TRAN CH42 ... 128 A2
WLT/FAZ L9 ... 97 K1
Ivy Farm Dr NSTN CH64 ... 153 H7
Ivy Farm Gdns GOL/RIS/CU WA3 .. 106 F1
Ivy Farm Rd RAIN/WH L35 ... 117 K1
Ivy House Rd GOL/RIS/CU WA3 ... 92 F4
Ivyhurst Cl ALL/GAR L19 ... 130 B5
Ivy La MOR/LEA CH46 ... 110 A4
Ivy Leigh CLB/OSW/ST L13 ... 98 A8
Ivy Rd GOL/RIS/CU WA3 ... 92 D5
WARR WA1 ... 123 G6
Ivy St BIRK CH41 ... 11 L6
RUNC WA7 ... 19 H5
STHP PR8 ... 3 M6
WGNNW/ST WN6 ... 4 D4

J

Jack McBain Ct VAUX/LVPD L3 ... 12 E2
Jack's Brow PR/KW L34 ... 100 A3
Jacksfield Wy ALL/GAR L19 ... 130 B6
Jacksmere La BRSC L40 ... 36 D5
Jackson Av GOL/RIS/CU WA3 ... 107 G2
WARR WA1 ... 122 B6
Jackson Cl BEB CH63 ... 128 B5
ORM L39 ... 49 H8
RAIN/WH L35 ... 117 M4
Jackson Rd CHLY/EC PR7 * ... 32 C8
Jackson's Common La BRSC L40 .. 50 C4
Jackson's La BRSC L40 ... 41 G6
Jacksons Pond Dr WLTN L25 ... 115 H6
Jackson St ALL/GAR L19 ... 130 E6
BIRK CH41 ... 11 K7
CHLY/EC PR7 ... 32 F7
RNFD/HAY WA11 * ... 90 C6
STHEL WA9 ... 9 L5
WARRW/BUR WA5 ... 104 A7
WGNE/HIN WN2 ... 69 J6
Jacobs Cl LITH L21 ... 83 K7
Jacob St TOX L8 ... 129 H1
WGNW/BIL/O WN5 ... 69 M7
Jacqueline Dr HUY L36 ... 116 C1
Jade Cl NWD/KWIPK L33 ... 86 B2
Jade Rd NPK/KEN L6 ... 113 K1
Jamaica St CLVPS L1 ... 112 F6
James Av GTS/LS CH66 ... 162 E2
Jamesbrook Cl BIRK CH41 ... 10 B1
James Clarke St EV L5 ... 12 F1
James Cl WDN WA8 ... 149 J1
WGNS/IIMK WN3 ... 4 E6
James Ct WLTN L25 ... 131 K3
James Gv ECCL WA10 ... 8 C7
James Holt Av KKBY L32 ... 85 M4
James Hopkins Wy ANF/KKDL L4 .. 96 F6
James Larkin Wy ANF/KKDL L4 ... 96 F6
James Pl CHLY/EC PR7 ... 43 G4
WGNNW/ST WN6 ... 55 M3
James Rd RNFD/HAY WA11 ... 91 H6
WLTN L25 ... 131 K3
James Sq WGNNW/ST WN6 ... 55 M3
James St ALL/GAR L19 ... 130 E8
CL/PREN CH43 ... 10 E8
CLVPS L1 ... 12 E6
STHEL WA9 ... 118 F2
WAL/EG CH44 ... 112 A3
WARR WA1 ... 14 F5
WGNE/HIN WN2 ... 80 A6
WGNS/IIMK WN3 ... 5 H7
Jamieson Av CSBY/BLUN L23 ... 83 J1
Jamieson Rd WAV L15 ... 114 A6
Jane's Brook Rd STHP PR8 ... 35 M1
Jane St STHEL WA9 ... 103 H6
Janet St EHL/KEN L7 ... 113 K4
Jarrett Rd NWD/KWIPK L33 ... 86 C1
Jarrow Cl CL/PREN CH43 ... 10 C9
Jasmine Cl EV L5 ... 13 L1
MOR/LEA CH46 ... 109 M6
Jasmine Ct HUY L36 ... 100 B8
Jasmine Gdns STHEL WA9 ... 103 J6
Jasmine Gv WDN WA8 ... 133 M5
Jasmine Ms AIG/SPK L17 ... 129 J2
Jasmine Rd WGNW/BIL/O WN5 * .. 67 M6
Jason St EV L5 ... 97 G7
Jason Wk EV L5 ... 97 G7
Java Rd ANF/KKDL L4 ... 97 M3
Jay Cl GOL/RIS/CU WA3 ... 123 J1

Jays Cl RUNC WA7 151 G6
Jedburgh Av GTS/LS CH66 155 J7
Jedburgh Dr NWD/KWIPK L33 73 M7
Jeffereys Crs HUY L36 115 K3
Jeffereys Dr HUY L36 115 J2
Jeffreys Dr GR/UP/WCH CH49 109 M8
Jeffrey St WGNE/HIN WN2 69 J5
Jellicoe Cl WKBY CH48 * 124 F7
Jenkinson St VAUX/LVPD L3 13 K3
WGNE/HIN WN2 69 M7
Jennet Hey AIMK WN4 79 H7
Jensen Ct RUNC WA7 149 L2
Jericho Cl AIG/SPK L17 129 M3
Jericho Ct AIG/SPK L17 * 129 M3
Jericho Farm Cl AIG/SPK L17 129 M4
Jericho La AIG/SPK L17 129 M4
Jermyn St TOX L8 113 J7
Jerningham Rd NG/CROX L11 97 M2
Jersey Av EP CH65 163 L4
LITH L21 83 K4
Jersey Cl BTL L20 7 G4
Jersey St BTL L20 7 G4
STHEL WA9 118 E2
Jervis Cl WARRN/WOL WA2 122 C2
Jesmond St WAV L15 113 M5
Jessamine Rd RF/TRAN CH42 128 A2
Jessica Wy LEIGH WN7 93 K1
Jet Cl NPK/KEN L6 113 K1
Jeudwine Cl WLTN L25 131 K5
Joan Av GR/UP/WCH CH49 126 A1
MOR/LEA CH46 109 M5
Jocelyn Cl BEB CH63 143 J2
Jockey St WARRN/WOL WA2 14 E1
John Bagot Cl EV L5 97 G8
John F Kennedy Hts
VAUX/LVPD L3 13 K2
John Hunter Wy NTHTN L30 84 B2
John Lennon Dr NPK/KEN L6 113 K2
John Moores Cl EHL/KEN L7 * 113 J5
John Nicholas Crs EP CH65 20 D3
John Rd LYMM WA13 139 L2
Johns Av RUNC WA7 18 F6
Johnson Av NEWLW WA12 91 K8
RAIN/WH L35 116 E1
WGNE/HIN WN2 81 G4
Johnson Cl LEIGH WN7 93 K1
Johnson Gv WD/CROXPK L12 99 G8
Johnson Rd CL/PREN CH43 127 H4
Johnson's La WDN WA8 17 M2
Johnson St STHEL WA9 9 M4
VAUX/LVPD L3 13 G5
WGNW/BIL/O WN5 67 K7
Johnson Wk EHL/KEN L7 113 L4
Johnston Av BTL L20 84 A7
John St AIMK WN4 79 M8
BIRK CH41 11 L4
CHLY/EC PR7 * 43 G4
ECCL WA10 * 9 G4
EP CH65 20 B2
GOL/RIS/CU WA3 92 C5
VAUX/LVPD L3 13 K3
WARRN/WOL WA2 14 F4
WGN WN1 5 H4
WGNE/HIN WN2 81 K2
WGNW/BIL/O WN5 67 M8
Jolly Tar La CHLY/EC PR7 43 J6
Jones Farm Rd WLTN L25 131 L1
Jonson Rd NSTN CH64 153 G4
Jonville Rd WLT/FAZ L9 84 E6
Jordan St CLVPS L1 112 F6
Joseph Gardner Wy BTL L20 6 F2
Joseph Groome Towers EP CH65 20 C3
Joseph Lister Cl NTHTN L30 84 B2
Joseph St STHEL WA9 103 G6
WDN WA8 134 E3
Joshua Cl EV L5 97 G7
Joule St GOL/RIS/CU WA3 107 H8
Joy La STHEL WA9 119 G3
WARRW/BUR WA5 120 A1
Jubilee Av DV/KA/FCH L14 114 F4
ORM L39 51 H7
WARR WA1 122 B5
WARRW/BUR WA5 136 A1
WGNW/BIL/O WN5 77 M1
Jubilee Crs PS/BROM CH62 128 D8
RNFD/HAY WA11 91 H6
Jubilee Dr EHL/KEN L7 113 K3
NTHTN L30 84 C4
RAIN/WH L35 116 F3
SKEL WN8 65 G5
WKBY CH48 124 C1
Jubilee Gn EP CH65 20 E7
Jubilee Gv LYMM WA13 139 L1
Jubilee Pl CHLYE PR6 32 F4
Jubilee Rd CSBY/BLUN L23 82 E2
FMBY L37 58 F4
LITH L21 83 K6
Jubilee Wy CROS/BRETH PR26 29 K2
WDN WA8 134 A4
Jubits La WDN WA8 118 C5
Juddfield St RNFD/HAY WA11 90 C7
Judeland CHLY/EC PR7 32 C3
Judges Dr NPK/KEN L6 113 L1
Judges Wy NPK/KEN L6 113 L1
Julian Wy WDN WA8 134 B1
Julie Gv WD/CROXPK L12 99 G8
Juliet Av BEB CH63 128 A6
Juliet Gdns BEB CH63 * 128 A6
July Rd NPK/KEN L6 97 M8
July St BTL L20 7 H1
Junction La BRSC L40 52 A1
NEWLW WA12 104 D3
STHEL WA9 103 G6
Junction Rd RNFD/HAY WA11 76 A5
Junction Ter WGNS/IIMK WN3 5 K8
June Av LEIGH WN7 81 L7
PS/BROM CH62 144 A5
June Rd NPK/KEN L6 97 M8
June St BTL L20 7 H2
Juniper Cl ECCL WA10 8 A3
GR/UP/WCH CH49 125 L3
STBRV L28 99 K6
Juniper Dr GTS/LS CH66 163 G4
WGNE/HIN WN2 81 H2
Juniper Gdns CSBY/BLUN L23 71 K7
Juniper Gv GTS/LS CH66 163 H4
Juniper La GOL/RIS/CU WA3 123 J5
Juniper St BTL L20 96 E6
Jupiter Gv WGNS/IIMK WN3 79 G3
Jurby Ct WARRN/WOL WA2 122 B4
Justene Cl GOL/RIS/CU WA3 92 C3
Justin Wy RAIN/WH L35 101 K8
Juvenal Pl VAUX/LVPD L3 13 J2
Juvenal St VAUX/LVPD L3 13 H3

K

Kaigh Av CSBY/BLUN L23 70 F8
Kale Cl WKBY CH48 124 D4
Kale Gv NWD/KWIPK L33 74 C8
Kane Ct GOL/RIS/CU WA3 93 J4
Kara Cl BTL L20 7 H4
Karan Wy MGHL L31 85 J2
Karen Cl WARRW/BUR WA5 104 B7
Karen Rd WGN WN1 5 K4
Karen Wy GTS/LS CH66 162 F2
Karonga Rd AIN/FAZ L10 85 G6
Karonga Wy AIN/FAZ L10 85 H6
Karslake Rd CALD/MH L18 114 B8
WAL/EG CH44 111 M3
Kay Cl WGN WN1 5 H4
Kaye Av GOL/RIS/CU WA3 107 H2
Kearsley Cl ANF/KKDL L4 * 97 G6
Kearsley St ANF/KKDL L4 97 G6
LEIGH WN7 81 M8
WGNNW/ST WN6 4 C2
Keates St STHEL WA9 103 H5
Keats Av RAIN/WH L35 117 H2
WGNNW/ST WN6 68 A2
WGNS/IIMK WN3 4 B9
WGNW/BIL/O WN5 77 M4
Keats Cl CHLY/EC PR7 30 F8
GTS/LS CH66 * 163 G5
WDN WA8 16 A3
Keats Gn HUY L36 116 B4
Keats Gv WARRN/WOL WA2 121 L3
Keats St BTL L20 6 E1
LEIGH WN7 81 M6
Keats Ter STHP PR8 25 H7
Keats Wy WGNE/HIN WN2 80 D4
Keble Dr AIN/FAZ L10 84 E2
WAL/NB CH45 94 F7
Keble Gv LEIGH WN7 81 L5
Keble Rd BTL L20 7 G8
Keble St NPK/KEN L6 113 J2
WDN WA8 16 E5
WGNE/HIN WN2 5 M5
Keckwick La RUNC WA7 151 H1
Kedleston St TOX L8 129 J1
Keegan Dr WAL/EG CH44 112 A3
Keele Cl CL/PREN CH43 110 E4
Keel Hey NSTN CH64 154 D4
Keenan Dr BTL L20 84 A8
Keepers La BEB CH63 127 K8
Keeper's Rd WARRS WA4 138 C6
Keighley Av WAL/NB CH45 95 G8
Keightley St BIRK CH41 11 G4
Keir Hardie Av BTL L20 7 M1
Keith Av ANF/KKDL L4 97 H4
WARRW/BUR WA5 120 A7
Keith Dr BEB CH63 143 L8
Kelbrook Cl STHEL WA9 102 F7
Kelburn Ct GOL/RIS/CU WA3 107 H7
Kelby Cl TOX L8 * 129 J1
Kelday Cl NWD/KWIPK L33 86 A3
Kelkbeck Cl MGHL L31 73 H3
Kellaton Cl WGNS/IIMK WN3 5 J7
Kellbank Rd WGNS/IIMK WN3 79 G2
Kellet Cl WGNW/BIL/O WN5 67 M4
Kellett Rd MOR/LEA CH46 110 D2
Kellett St CHLY/EC PR7 * 32 E5
Kellitt Rd WAV L15 114 A6
Kells Gv WGNNW/ST WN6 68 B3
Kelly Dr BTL L20 7 L2
Kelly St PR/KW L34 100 F7
Kelmscott Cl GTS/LS CH66 162 F3
Kelmscott Dr WAL/EG CH44 111 G1
Kelsall Av PS/BROM CH62 155 G2
STHEL WA9 118 D1
Kelsall Cl CL/PREN CH43 127 J2
GOL/RIS/CU WA3 122 E2
PS/BROM CH62 155 G2
WDN WA8 133 M3
Kelsey Cl ECCL WA10 8 A3
Kelso Cl NWD/KWIPK L33 73 M7
Kelso Rd NPK/KEN L6 113 L2
Kelton Gv AIG/SPK L17 130 A3
Kelvin Cl AIMK WN4 * 90 F1
GOL/RIS/CU WA3 106 F7
Kelvin Gv TOX L8 113 J7
WGNS/IIMK WN3 79 H3
Kelvin Pk BIRK CH41 * 112 A4
Kelvin Rd BIRK CH41 128 A1
WAL/EG CH44 112 A4
Kelvinside CSBY/BLUN L23 83 H3
WAL/EG CH44 111 M4
Kelvin St GOL/RIS/CU WA3 107 G7
Kelway Ter WGN WN1 5 H1
Kemberton Dr WDN WA8 118 C8
Kemble St EHL/KEN L7 * 113 K3
PR/KW L34 100 F7
Kemlyn Rd ANF/KKDL L4 97 J7
Kemmel Av WARRS WA4 137 L3
Kempsell Wy HLWD L26 132 C6
Kempsey Gv STHEL WA9 102 A6
Kempson Ter BEB CH63 143 H1
Kempston St VAUX/LVPD L3 13 K5
Kempton Cl HUY L36 115 L4
NEWLW WA12 91 M8
RUNC WA7 149 L7
Kempton Park Fold STHP PR8 36 B2
Kempton Park Rd AIN/FAZ L10 85 G3
Kempton Rd PS/BROM CH62 128 D5
WAV L15 113 M5
Kemsley Rd DV/KA/FCH L14 115 H2
Kenbury Cl NWD/KWIPK L33 86 C1
Kenbury Rd NWD/KWIPK L33 86 C1
Kendal Av WARRN/WOL WA2 121 L3
Kendal Cl BEB CH63 128 B7
GTS/LS CH66 162 F3
RNFD/HAY WA11 76 B3
Kendal Dr GTS/LS CH66 162 F3
MGHL L31 72 F3
RAIN/WH L35 117 J2
RNFD/HAY WA11 76 B4
RNFD/HAY WA11 89 L5
Kendal Gv AIMK WN4 91 K1
LEIGH WN7 81 M8
Kendal Pk WD/CROXPK L12 98 F7
Kendal Ri RUNC WA7 149 M8
Kendal Rd CHLDW L16 115 G6
WAL/EG CH44 111 J3
WDN WA8 * 133 L4
WGNE/HIN WN2 69 J5
Kendal St BIRK CH41 * 11 J6
WGNNW/ST WN6 4 C2
Kendal Wy STHP PR8 47 K2
Kendrick Pl WGN WN1 5 J3
Kendricks Fold RAIN/WH L35 117 K2
Kendrick St WARR WA1 14 C5
Kenford Dr WGNS/IIMK WN3 79 G3
Kenilworth Av RUNC WA7 19 H8
Kenilworth Cl WLTN L25 131 G2
Kenilworth Ct EP CH65 164 A3
Kenilworth Dr PEN/TH CH61 126 A8
WARR WA1 122 B5
WGNE/HIN WN2 81 H1
Kenilworth Gdns
GR/UP/WCH CH49 110 A7
NEWLW WA12 104 E3
Kenilworth Rd CHLDW L16 114 F6
CSBY/BLUN L23 82 E2
GOL/RIS/CU WA3 93 G6
NSTN CH64 153 G7
STHP PR8 47 L1
WAL/EG CH44 111 M2
Kenilworth St BTL L20 6 F4
Kenilworth Wy WLTN L25 131 G2
Kenley Av WDN WA8 117 M8
Kenley Cl NPK/KEN L6 113 L1
Kenley Pde NPK/KEN L6 113 L1
Kenmare Rd WAV L15 114 A7
Kenmore Gv AIMK WN4 90 F2
Kenmore Rd CL/PREN CH43 127 G4
Kennelwood Av
NWD/KWIPK L33 86 B2
Kennessee Cl MGHL L31 73 G5
Kenneth Av LEIGH WN7 81 M7
Kenneth Cl NTHTN L30 84 A2
Kenneth Gv LEIGH WN7 81 M7
Kenneth Rd WDN WA8 133 L6
Kennet Rd BEB CH63 127 M8
RNFD/HAY WA11 90 E7
Kennford Rd NG/CROX L11 85 L8
Kennington Pk WDN WA8 134 A2
Kensington EHL/KEN L7 113 K3
Kensington Av STHEL WA9 102 E6
WARRS WA4 138 E3
Kensington Cl WDN WA8 134 F1
Kensington Dr HUY L36 100 C8
Kensington Gdns
MOR/LEA CH46 110 A5
Kensington Rd CHLY/EC PR7 32 D6
CHTN/BK PR9 3 K4
EP CH65 156 C8
FMBY L37 59 G4
WGNW/BIL/O WN5 * 67 M8
Kensington St NPK/KEN L6 113 J2
Kent Av FMBY L37 59 J4
LITH L21 83 L5
WGNE/HIN WN2 80 C3
Kent Cl BEB CH63 143 K5
BTL L20 7 J3
Kent Gv RUNC WA7 19 K5
Kentmere Av RNFD/HAY WA11 89 L4
Kentmere Dr PEN/TH CH61 141 H2
Kentmere Pl WARRN/WOL WA2 121 J2
Kenton Cl FMBY L37 47 H7
Kenton Rd HLWD L26 132 B6
Kentridge Dr GTS/LS CH66 162 F2
Kent Rd FMBY L37 59 J4
STHEL WA9 102 E5
STHP PR8 2 F9
WAL/EG CH44 111 J2
WARRW/BUR WA5 136 E1
Kents Bank WD/CROXPK L12 98 E4
Kent St CL/PREN CH43 10 B9
CLVPS L1 112 F5
WARRS WA4 15 G8
WDN WA8 16 E2
WGN WN1 5 H5
Kenview Cl WDN WA8 148 C1
Kenway RNFD/HAY WA11 76 C7
Kenwick Cl GTS/LS CH66 162 E2
Kenworthys Flats
CHTN/BK PR9 3 G2
Kenwright Crs STHEL WA9 102 E5
Kenwyn Rd WAL/NB CH45 95 K8
Kenyon Av WARRW/BUR WA5 120 A8
Kenyon Cl NWD/KWIPK L33 74 B7
Kenyon La GOL/RIS/CU WA3 93 H7
GOL/RIS/CU WA3 106 B2
Kenyon Rd WAV L15 114 C8
WGNNW/ST WN6 55 M3
Kenyon's La FMBY L37 59 J2
MGHL L31 72 F1
Kenyons La North
RNFD/HAY WA11 91 H5
Kenyon's La South
RNFD/HAY WA11 91 H5
Kenyon St LEIGH WN7 81 M5
Kepler St LITH L21 83 J7
Keppel St BTL L20 6 E8
Kerfoot's La SKEL WN8 64 E5
Kerfoot St WARRN/WOL WA2 14 D1
Kerman Cl WD/CROXPK L12 98 D4
Kerr Gv STHEL WA9 103 G2
Kerris Cl AIG/SPK L17 129 L3
Kerry Cft GTS/LS CH66 163 G4
Kerrysdale Cl STHEL WA9 102 F6
Kersey Rd KKBY L32 86 B5
Kershaw Av CSBY/BLUN L23 83 H2
Kershaw St CHLYE PR6 33 G5
WDN WA8 133 M4
WGNW/BIL/O WN5 67 K7
Kershaw Wy NEWLW WA12 91 L8
Kerslake Wy HTWN L38 70 B1
Kerswell Cl STHEL WA9 102 F7
Kerton Rw STHP PR8 * 35 H1
Kestral Gv HLWD L26 131 M4
Kestral Pk SKEL WN8 65 L1
Kestrel Av GR/UP/WCH CH49 109 M7
Kestrel Cl CHLYE PR6 33 J2
GR/UP/WCH CH49 109 M7
RNFD/HAY WA11 89 K7
Kestrel Dr AIMK WN4 79 L7
Kestrel La GOL/RIS/CU WA3 123 G1
Kestrel Ms SKEL WN8 65 L1
Kestrel Rd HES CH60 141 L6
MOR/LEA CH46 109 L5
Kestrels Wy RUNC WA7 150 B7
Keswick Av BEB CH63 143 L8
WARRN/WOL WA2 121 L3
Keswick Cl MGHL L31 73 G3
STHP PR8 47 L2
WDN WA8 133 L4
Keswick Crs WARRN/WOL WA2 121 L3
Keswick Dr FROD/HEL WA6 160 F5
LITH L21 84 A5
Keswick Pl CL/PREN CH43 110 F4
WGNE/HIN WN2 69 J6
Keswick Rd CALD/MH L18 130 E3
ECCL WA10 8 D2
WAL/NB CH45 95 H6
Keswick Vls CHLDW L16 * 115 J5
Keswick Wy CHLDW L16 115 J5
RNFD/HAY WA11 76 B3
Kettering Rd STHP PR8 34 D8
Kevelioc Cl BEB CH63 143 H2
Kew Rd FMBY L37 58 F4
STHP PR8 35 K3
Keybank Rd WD/CROXPK L12 98 C5
Keyes Cl GOL/RIS/CU WA3 123 H1
Keyes Gdns GOL/RIS/CU WA3 123 H1
Kiddman St WLT/FAZ L9 97 H2
Kidstone Cl STHEL WA9 102 F6
Kielder Cl AIMK WN4 79 H6
Kilbuck La RNFD/HAY WA11 91 J5
Kilburn Av AIMK WN4 91 M1
PS/BROM CH62 144 A7
Kilburn Clqse LEIGH WN7 81 M4
Kilburn Dr WGNNW/ST WN6 55 J6
Kilburn Gv STHEL WA9 102 A6
WGNS/IIMK WN3 78 F2
Kilburn Rd SKEL WN8 66 E8
Kilburn St LITH L21 83 K7
Kildale Cl MGHL L31 72 E3
Kildare Cl SPK/HALE L24 147 M3
Kildare St WGNE/HIN WN2 69 L8
WGNW/BIL/O WN5 68 B7
Kildonan Rd AIG/SPK L17 129 M3
WARRS WA4 138 C3
Kilford Cl WARRW/BUR WA5 121 G3
Kilgraston Gdns AIG/SPK L17 130 B4
Kilkerran Cl CHLYE PR6 32 F5
Killarney Gv WAL/EG CH44 * 111 J2
Killarney Rd CLB/OSW/ST L13 114 C2
Killester Rd WLTN L25 131 K1
Killingbeck Cl BRSC L40 51 M1
Killington Cl WGNS/IIMK WN3 79 K3
Killington Wy ANF/KKDL L4 97 G5
Killingworth La
GOL/RIS/CU WA3 107 K8
Kilmalcolm Cl CL/PREN CH43 127 H1
Kilmore Cl WLT/FAZ L9 84 E5
Kilmory Av WLTN L25 131 L3
Kilncroft RUNC WA7 * 150 D8
Kiln Hey WD/CROXPK L12 98 E8
Kiln La ECCL WA10 88 E8
SKEL WN8 65 G3
Kiln Rd GR/UP/WCH CH49 126 C2
Kilnyard Rd CSBY/BLUN L23 82 F1
Kilrea Cl NG/CROX L11 98 B5
Kilrea Rd NG/CROX L11 98 B5
Kilsail Rd KKBY L32 86 C6
Kilsby Dr WDN WA8 135 G3
Kilshaw Rd WARRW/BUR WA5 104 B7
Kilshaw St NPK/KEN L6 113 J1
WGNW/BIL/O WN5 67 L8
Kilsyth Cl WARRN/WOL WA2 122 B1
Kimberley Av CSBY/BLUN L23 * 82 F2
STHEL WA9 102 B6
Kimberley Cl TOX L8 113 J6
Kimberley Dr CSBY/BLUN L23 82 F2
WARRS WA4 137 L4
Kimberley Pl AIMK WN4 91 L2
Kimberley Rd WAL/NB CH45 95 K7
Kimberley St CHLY/EC PR7 43 G4
WARRW/BUR WA5 121 G8
Kimberly St WGNNW/ST WN6 4 A1
Kindale Rd CL/PREN CH43 127 G4
Kinder Gv AIMK WN4 79 H7
Kinder St NPK/KEN L6 13 M4
King Av BTL L20 84 A7
King Edward Rd ECCL WA10 88 F7
RAIN/WH L35 117 K1
King Edward's Dr
PS/BROM CH62 128 D7
King Edward St VAUX/LVPD L3 12 D5
WARR WA1 15 M2
Kingfield Rd WLT/FAZ L9 84 B8
Kingfisher Cl GOL/RIS/CU WA3 123 H1
NTHLY L27 116 B8
NWD/KWIPK L33 74 A7
RUNC WA7 150 B8
Kingfisher Ct AIMK WN4 79 K7
CHTN/BK PR9 3 M2
Kingfisher Dr RNFD/HAY WA11 89 K7
Kingfisher Gv WD/CROXPK L12 99 H4
Kingfisher Pk SKEL WN8 65 L1
Kingfisher Wy
GR/UP/WCH CH49 109 M7
King George Cl AIMK WN4 91 K2
King George Crs WARR WA1 15 L2
King George Dr WAL/NB CH45 95 L8
King George Rd RNFD/HAY WA11 91 J6
King George's Dr PS/BROM CH62 128 D7
Kingham Cl WDN WA8 17 K1
WLTN L25 131 L3
King James Ct RUNC WA7 150 A7
Kinglake Rd WAL/EG CH44 111 M1
Kinglake St EHL/KEN L7 113 K4
Kinglass Rd PS/BROM CH62 143 K2
King's Av GOL/RIS/CU WA3 93 H6
HOY CH47 108 F5
Kingsbrook Wy BEB CH63 127 M5
King's Brow BEB CH63 127 M7
Kingsbury WKBY CH48 124 F2
Kingsbury Cl STHP PR8 47 J1
Kingsbury Ct SKEL WN8 65 L1
Kings Cl AIG/SPK L17 129 L3
BEB CH63 127 M6
FMBY L37 59 G3
Kings Ct HOY CH47 108 C6
LITH L21 83 H6
RUNC WA7 * 150 F1
Kingscourt Rd WD/CROXPK L12 98 E8
Kingscroft Ct WGN WN1 5 H5
Kingsdale Av RAIN/WH L35 117 M2
RF/TRAN CH42 127 M3
Kingsdale Rd CALD/MH L18 114 C8
WARRW/BUR WA5 120 B6
Kings Dock St CLVPS L1 112 F6
Kingsdown Crs WGN WN1 68 E1
Kingsdown Rd NG/CROX L11 98 C4
WGNE/HIN WN2 80 D6
Kingsdown St BIRK CH41 * 11 J9
Kings Dr FROD/HEL WA6 166 D2
PEN/TH CH61 126 B7
WKBY CH48 124 F5
WLTN L25 131 K3
Kingsfield Rd MGHL L31 72 E6
The King's Gap HOY CH47 108 C6
Kingshead Cl RUNC WA7 150 C3
Kingsheath Av DV/KA/FCH L14 99 H8
Kings Hey Dr CHTN/BK PR9 25 H4
Kingshill Ct WGNNW/ST WN6 56 B6
Kingsland Crs NG/CROX L11 98 A2
Kingsland Gra WARR WA1 122 F4
Kingsland Rd NG/CROX L11 97 M2
RF/TRAN CH42 127 L1
King's La BEB CH63 128 A6
Kingslea CHLY/EC PR7 44 B5
Kingsley Av PS/BROM CH62 155 G2
WGNS/IIMK WN3 79 H2
Kingsley Cl MGHL L31 61 L8
PEN/TH CH61 141 J2
Kingsley Crs RUNC WA7 19 H6
Kingsley Dr CHLY/EC PR7 32 C8
WARRS WA4 137 L6
Kingsley Rd ECCL WA10 88 F7
EP CH65 20 D4
FROD/HEL WA6 160 F7
RUNC WA7 19 H5
TOX L8 113 K6
WAL/EG CH44 111 K2
Kingsley St BIRK CH41 10 A2
LEIGH WN7 81 L6
Kingsmead CHLY/EC PR7 32 E8
Kingsmead Ct GOL/RIS/CU WA3 106 C5
Kingsmead Dr WLTN L25 131 K6
Kingsmead Gv CL/PREN CH43 111 H8
Kings Meadow RUNC WA7 150 E5
STHP PR8 47 M2
Kingsmead Rd CL/PREN CH43 111 H8
MOR/LEA CH46 110 B3
Kingsmead Rd North
CL/PREN CH43 111 H8
Kingsmead Rd South
CL/PREN CH43 111 H8
Kingsmede WGN WN1 68 F2
Kings Ms WARRS WA4 * 137 L5
King's Moss La RNFD/HAY WA11 77 G6
Kings Mt CL/PREN CH43 10 E9
Kingsnorth RAIN/WH L35 117 H3
Kingsoak Cl WGN WN1 5 G3
Kings Pde VAUX/LVPD L3 * 112 E7
WAL/NB CH45 94 F5
Kings Pk LITH L21 83 H6
King's Rd AIMK WN4 79 J8
BEB CH63 127 M6
BTL L20 7 G8
CSBY/BLUN L23 82 F1
ECCL WA10 101 L3
FMBY L37 59 G3
GOL/RIS/CU WA3 92 C6
GTS/LS CH66 155 L6
WARRN/WOL WA2 122 C3
Kings Ter BTL L20 7 G7
Kingsthorne Pk SPK/HALE L24 131 L7
Kingsthorne Rd WLTN L25 131 L7
Kingston Av WARRW/BUR WA5 120 A7
Kingston Cl MOR/LEA CH46 110 A5
RUNC WA7 150 A3
WD/CROXPK L12 99 G8
WGNS/IIMK WN3 79 K2
Kingston Crs CHTN/BK PR9 22 E8
King St ALL/GAR L19 145 L1
CHLY/EC PR7 32 F7
CSBY/WL L22 82 F4
ECCL WA10 8 F5
EP CH65 20 D2
NEWLW WA12 104 D2
RF/TRAN CH42 128 C4
RUNC WA7 19 H2
STHP PR8 2 F5
WAL/EG CH44 95 M8
WGN WN1 4 F5
WGNE/HIN WN2 69 J6
WGNE/HIN WN2 69 M7
King St West WGN WN1 4 E4
Kings Vw HOY CH47 * 108 B7
Kingsville Rd BEB CH63 128 A8
Kingswalk WKBY CH48 124 E3
Kingsway CHLY/EC PR7 32 A3
CSBY/WL L22 83 G3
FROD/HEL WA6 160 D6
HES CH60 141 L7
HUY L36 115 M1
NEWLW WA12 104 E3
RAIN/WH L35 100 F8
RNFD/HAY WA11 89 J5
STHP PR8 2 E4
WAL/NB CH45 95 J7
WDN WA8 16 D3
WGN WN1 68 F3
WGNE/HIN WN2 5 L6
Kingsway Ct VAUX/LVPD L3 13 G2
Kingsway North WARR WA1 15 M3
Kingsway Pk VAUX/LVPD L3 * 13 H2
Kingsway South WARRS WA4 138 B1
Kingsway (Tunnel)
WAL/EG CH44 111 L3
Kingswell Cl EHL/KEN L7 113 K5
Kings Whf BIRK CH41 112 A4
Kingswood CHLY/EC PR7 32 D8
Kingswood Av CSBY/WL L22 83 H4
WLT/FAZ L9 84 D6
Kingswood Bvd BEB CH63 128 A5
Kingswood Ct NWD/KWIPK L33 86 B1
Kingswood Dr CSBY/BLUN L23 82 F2
Kingswood Pk STHP PR8 2 C6
Kingswood Rd WAL/EG CH44 95 L8
WARRW/BUR WA5 120 D3
Kington Rd WKBY CH48 124 C2
Kingwood Crs
WGNW/BIL/O WN5 67 M7
Kinlet Rd WGNS/IIMK WN3 78 E1
Kinley Gdns BTL L20 * 84 A8
Kinloch Cl HLWD L26 132 C6
Kinloch Wy ORM L39 50 F8
Kinloss Rd GR/UP/WCH CH49 125 L2
Kinmel Cl ANF/KKDL L4 97 M5
BIRK CH41 11 H4
Kinmel St STHEL WA9 102 E5
TOX L8 113 J8
Kinnaird Rd WAL/NB CH45 95 J7
Kinnaird St TOX L8 129 J2
Kinnerley Rd EP CH65 163 J2
Kinnerton Cl MOR/LEA CH46 109 K5
Kinnington Wy GTS/LS CH66 * 163 H6
Kinniside Cl WGNS/IIMK WN3 79 J3
Kinnock Pk WARRW/BUR WA5 104 A7
Kinross Av AIMK WN4 90 E1
Kinross Cl WARRN/WOL WA2 122 B1
Kinross Rd AIN/FAZ L10 85 G6
CSBY/WL L22 83 G5
WAL/NB CH45 94 F7
Kinsale Dr GOL/RIS/CU WA3 122 E1
Kinsey Rd EP CH65 164 A4
Kinsey's La EP CH65 158 B7
Kintbury St WGNE/HIN WN2 80 B6
Kintore Cl BEB CH63 154 E1
Kintore Dr WARRW/BUR WA5 119 M7
Kintore Rd ALL/GAR L19 130 D6
Kintyre Cl EP CH65 163 L4
Kipling Av HUY L36 116 C4
RF/TRAN CH42 128 B4
WARRN/WOL WA2 121 L4
WGNS/IIMK WN3 79 J1
Kipling Crs WDN WA8 16 B3
Kipling Gv LEIGH WN7 81 M6
STHEL WA9 118 C2
Kipling St BTL L20 83 J8
Kirby Cl WKBY CH48 124 D4
Kirby Mt WKBY CH48 124 E5
Kirby Pk WKBY CH48 124 D4
Kirby Park Man WKBY CH48 * 124 D4
Kirby Rd BTL L20 83 M7
Kirkacre Av NEWLW WA12 104 E5
Kirkbride Cl NTHLY L27 132 C1
Kirkburn Cl TOX L8 * 129 H1
Kirkby Bank Rd
NWD/KWIPK L33 86 D3
Kirkby Rd GOL/RIS/CU WA3 107 H2
Kirkby Rw KKBY L32 85 L2
Kirkcaldy Av WARRW/BUR WA5 119 M7
Kirkdale Gdns SKEL WN8 * 66 B6
Kirkdale Rd EV L5 96 F7
Kirkdale V ANF/KKDL L4 97 G6
Kirket Cl BEB CH63 143 J1
Kirket La BEB CH63 143 H1
Kirkfield Gv RF/TRAN CH42 128 C4
Kirkham Av GOL/RIS/CU WA3 * 93 G7
Kirkham Cl WARRW/BUR WA5 136 D1
Kirkham Rd CHTN/BK PR9 25 J1
LEIGH WN7 93 M3
WDN WA8 134 E3
Kirkham St WGNE/HIN WN2 80 D5
Kirklake Bank FMBY L37 58 E3
Kirklake Rd FMBY L37 58 E3
Kirkland Av RF/TRAN CH42 127 M3
Kirkland Cl WLT/FAZ L9 * 84 B6
Kirkland Rd WAL/NB CH45 95 L5
The Kirklands WKBY CH48 124 E3
Kirkland St ECCL WA10 8 E4
Kirklees Rd STHP PR8 35 H4
Kirklees St WGN WN1 5 K4
Kirkless St WGNE/HIN WN2 69 J2
Kirkless Vls WGNE/HIN WN2 * 69 J3
Kirkmaiden Rd ALL/GAR L19 130 D5
Kirkman Fold RAIN/WH L35 117 K2
Kirkmore Rd CALD/MH L18 130 C3
Kirkmount GR/UP/WCH CH49 110 C8
Kirkpatrick St WGNE/HIN WN2 81 K2
Kirk Rd BTL L20 83 L7
Kirkside Cl WD/CROXPK L12 98 F2
Kirkstall Cl CHLY/EC PR7 32 F8
Kirkstall Dr CHLY/EC PR7 32 F8
FMBY L37 59 K3
Kirkstall Rd CHLY/EC PR7 32 F8
STHP PR8 35 H3
Kirkstead Wk KKBY L32 85 K2
Kirkstead Wy GOL/RIS/CU WA3 92 C5
Kirkstile Crs WGNS/IIMK WN3 79 G3
Kirkstone WGNW/BIL/O WN5 67 L6
Kirkstone Av RNFD/HAY WA11 89 L5
WARRN/WOL WA2 121 L2
Kirkstone Crs RUNC WA7 161 J1
Kirkstone Rd North LITH L21 83 L4

Kirkstone Rd South LITH L21 83 M5
Kirk Stone Rd West LITH L21 83 K5
Kirk St EV L5 97 G7
Kirkwall Dr WARRW/BUR WA5 136 C2
Kirkway BEB CH63 127 M6
GR/UP/WCH CH49 126 A1
WAL/NB CH45 95 K6
Kitchener Dr WLT/FAZ L9 84 B7
Kitchener St ECCL WA10 8 C4
Kitchen St CLVPS L1 112 F6
Kitling La PR/KW L34 86 E8
Kitling Rd PR/KW L34 86 E8
Kitt Green Rd WGNW/BIL/O WN5 67 L5
Kittiwake Rd CHLYE PR6 33 J2
Kiverley Cl WLTN L25 131 G2
Kiveton Dr AIMK WN4 91 L3
The Knap HES CH60 141 J7
Knaresborough Rd
WAL/EG CH44 111 H1
WGNE/HIN WN2 81 G1
Knighton Rd ANF/KKDL L4 97 M4
Knight Rd WARRW/BUR WA5 104 B7
Knightsbridge Av WARRS WA4 138 E2
Knightsbridge Cl WDN WA8 134 F1
Knightsbridge Ct
CL/PREN CH43 126 F1
WARR WA1 * 14 D6
Knightsbridge Wk
NWD/KWIPK L33 73 M7
Knightscliffe Crs
WGNNW/ST WN6 54 F7
Knights Gra STHEL WA9 9 M4
Knightshill Crs WGNNW/ST WN6 68 B4
Knight St CLVPS L1 113 G5
Knightsway CSBY/WL L22 83 H3
Knob Hall Gdns CHTN/BK PR9 25 H2
Knob Hall La CHTN/BK PR9 25 H2
Knoclaid Rd CLB/OSW/ST L13 98 A6
The Knoll CL/PREN CH43 127 J2
Knottingley Dr GTS/LS CH66 155 L8
Knotty Ms WLTN L25 131 L2
The Knowe NSTN CH64 154 C5
Knowle Av STHP PR8 34 E7
Knowle Cl GTS/LS CH66 163 G2
NG/CROX L11 98 E3
Knowles Av WGNS/IIMK WN3 79 H1
Knowles House Av ECCL WA10 101 H2
Knowles Pl WGN WN1 5 K3
Knowles St BIRK CH41 10 F4
CHLY/EC PR7 32 E7
WDN WA8 134 E3
WGNS/IIMK WN3 5 H8
Knowley Brow CHLYE PR6 33 G3
Knowl Hey Rd HLWD L26 132 C7
Knowsley Av GOL/RIS/CU WA3 92 D4
Knowsley Cl RF/TRAN CH42 128 E4
Knowsley Dr LEIGH WN7 93 M3
Knowsley Expy RAIN/WH L35 116 F7
WDN WA8 133 G5
Knowsley La CHLYE PR6 44 F1
PR/KW L34 88 A4
Knowsley Park La PR/KW L34 100 E6
Knowsley Rd ALL/GAR L19 130 F7
BTL L20 83 K8
CHTN/BK PR9 24 D4
ECCL WA10 101 L2
ORM L39 63 H1
RAIN/WH L35 117 M3
RF/TRAN CH42 128 C4
WAL/NB CH45 95 J7
WGNNW/ST WN6 68 C2
Knowsley St ANF/KKDL L4 97 H3
LEIGH WN7 81 M8
Knowsley Vw RNFD/HAY WA11 76 A5
Knox Cl PS/BROM CH62 128 D7
Knox St BIRK CH41 11 L6
Knutsford Cl ECCL WA10 101 K3
Knutsford Gn MOR/LEA CH46 110 A4
Knutsford Old Rd WARRS WA4 138 C3
Knutsford Rd MOR/LEA CH46 110 A4
WARRS WA4 15 G8
Knutsford Wk MGHL L31 72 F1
Kremlin Dr CLB/OSW/ST L13 98 B8
Kronsbec Av GTS/LS CH66 155 M7
Kylemore Av CALD/MH L18 130 B2
Kylemore Cl PEN/TH CH61 141 G2
Kylemore Dr PEN/TH CH61 141 G2
Kylemore Rd CL/PREN CH43 127 J1
Kylemore Wy HLWD L26 131 M6
PEN/TH CH61 141 G2
Kynance Rd NG/CROX L11 85 M8

L

Laburnum Av HUY L36 116 A5
RNFD/HAY WA11 89 M6
WARR WA1 122 E6
WGNS/IIMK WN3 5 L7
Laburnum Crs KKBY L32 85 M2
Laburnum Dr SKEL WN8 64 F4
WGNNW/ST WN6 68 C1
Laburnum Farm Cl NSTN CH64 153 J8
Laburnum Gv BRSC L40 39 H7
GTS/LS CH66 163 J5
MGHL L31 73 H4
PEN/TH CH61 125 M7
RUNC WA7 19 L9
STHP PR8 25 H6
Laburnum La
WARRW/BUR WA5 119 L7
Laburnum Pl BTL L20 7 J4
Laburnum Rd CHLYE PR6 32 F2
CL/PREN CH43 127 L1
EHL/KEN L7 113 M2
GOL/RIS/CU WA3 93 H5
WAL/NB CH45 95 K6
Laburnum St AIMK WN4 91 K3
Laburnum Ter ALL/GAR L19 * 130 E7
Lace St VAUX/LVPD L3 13 G5
Lacey Ct WDN WA8 16 E6
Lacey Rd PR/KW L34 101 G8
Lacey St ECCL WA10 101 M5
WDN WA8 16 D6
Ladies La WGNE/HIN WN2 69 M7
Lad La VAUX/LVPD L3 * 12 D5
Lady Acre Cl LYMM WA13 139 M3
Lady Alice's Dr BRSC L40 52 A5
Ladybarn Av GOL/RIS/CU WA3 92 B6
Ladybower Cl EHL/KEN L7 113 K5
Lady Chapel Cl CLVPS L1 113 G6
Ladycroft Cl WARR WA1 123 G6
Ladyewood Rd WAL/EG CH44 111 L2
Ladyfield CL/PREN CH43 110 E6
Ladyfields WD/CROXPK L12 98 D8
Lady Green Cl HTWN L38 * 71 G2
Lady Green La HTWN L38 70 F1
Lady La GOL/RIS/CU WA3 106 E4
WGNS/IIMK WN3 79 G1
Ladypool SPK/HALE L24 147 L4
Lady Richeld Cl RUNC WA7 150 F2
Ladysmith Av AIMK WN4 91 L2
Ladysmith Rd AIN/FAZ L10 85 H6
Lady's Wk BRSC L40 51 L7
Ladywood Rd
WARRW/BUR WA5 120 E4
Laffak Rd RNFD/HAY WA11 89 M5
Lafford La SKEL WN8 66 E2
Laggan St EHL/KEN L7 * 113 K3
Lagrange Ar ECCL WA10 * 9 G5
Laira Ct WARRN/WOL WA2 * 15 G2
Laira St WARRN/WOL WA2 15 G2
Laird Cl CL/PREN CH43 111 H5
Lairds Pl VAUX/LVPD L3 13 G2
Laird St BIRK CH41 10 A2
CL/PREN CH43 111 H5
Laithwaite Cl STHEL WA9 118 D2
Laithwaite Rd WGNW/BIL/O WN5 67 M6
Lakeland Av AIMK WN4 91 L1
Lakeland Cl CLVPS L1 13 G9
Lakeland Gdns CHLY/EC PR7 32 C8
Lakemoor Cl STHEL WA9 102 F6
Lakenheath Rd HLWD L26 132 A7
Lake Pl HOY CH47 108 D6
Lake Rd HOY CH47 108 D6
WAV L15 114 C6
Lakes Dr WGNW/BIL/O WN5 67 G7
Lake Side LEIGH WN7 81 M7
Lakeside Av WGNW/BIL/O WN5 78 A2
Lakeside Cl WDN WA8 133 J6
Lakeside Ct RNFD/HAY WA11 76 C7
STHP PR8 * 3 G2
WAL/NB CH45 95 L5
Lakeside Dr WARR WA1 137 J2
Lakeside Gdns RNFD/HAY WA11 76 C7
Lakeside Rd LYMM WA13 139 M4
Lakeside Vw CSBY/WL L22 * 82 F5
Lakes Rd WLT/FAZ L9 84 F6
Lakes Ter WGNE/HIN WN2 69 J6
Lake St ANF/KKDL L4 97 J6
Lake Vw RAIN/WH L35 117 G4
Laleston Cl WDN WA8 134 A5
Lamberhead Rd
WGNW/BIL/O WN5 67 K7
Lambert Ct WDN WA8 16 E4
Lambert St VAUX/LVPD L3 13 K5
Lambert Wy VAUX/LVPD L3 13 K5
Lambeth Rd EV L5 96 F6
Lambeth Wk ANF/KKDL L4 96 F6
Lambley Cl LEIGH WN7 81 M5
Lambourn Av WDN WA8 117 L8
Lambourne SKEL WN8 65 K1
Lambourne Cl GTS/LS CH66 163 H5
Lambourne Gv STHEL WA9 103 J2
Lambourne Rd ANF/KKDL L4 97 M4
Lambshear La MGHL L31 72 E1
Lambsickle Cl RUNC WA7 149 H7
Lambsickle La RUNC WA7 149 H7
Lambs La WARR WA1 122 C5
Lamb St WGN WN1 5 J1
Lambton Rd AIG/SPK L17 129 K2
Lambton St WGNW/BIL/O WN5 67 K8
Lamburth Dr AIG/SPK L17 129 L1
Lamerton Cl WARRW/BUR WA5 135 M1
Lammermoor Rd CALD/MH L18 130 C3
Lampeter Cl
WARRW/BUR WA5 * 121 G3
Lampeter Rd NPK/KEN L6 97 L7
Lamport Cl WDN WA8 135 G2
Lamport St TOX L8 113 G7
Lanark Cl ECCL WA10 8 E7
Lancashire Gdns ECCL WA10 8 E7
Lancaster Av AIG/SPK L17 113 M8
CSBY/BLUN L23 82 F2
GOL/RIS/CU WA3 92 E5
RAIN/WH L35 116 F2
RAIN/WH L35 133 J3
RUNC WA7 18 D8
WAL/NB CH45 95 K8
Lancaster Cl CHLYE PR6 44 D6
EV L5 96 F7
MGHL L31 73 H4
NEWLW WA12 91 H8
PS/BROM CH62 128 D7
STHP PR8 35 G1
WARRN/WOL WA2 * 122 B3
Lancaster Ct WARRS WA4 * 138 A4
Lancaster Crs SKEL WN8 65 G4
Lancaster Dr CHTN/BK PR9 23 G3
Lancaster Gdns EP CH65 20 F9
Lancaster Ga CHTN/BK PR9 23 H8
Lancaster La SKEL WN8 53 L2
Lancaster Pl CHLYE PR6 44 C5
Lancaster Rd FMBY L37 59 G4
HUY L36 116 C1
STHP PR8 35 G1
WDN WA8 134 C2
WGNW/BIL/O WN5 67 L4
Lancaster St CHLY/EC PR7 43 H4
EV L5 96 F7
WARRW/BUR WA5 121 G8
WGNS/IIMK WN3 5 H7
WLT/FAZ L9 97 H2
Lancaster Ter PR/KW L34 * 101 G7
Lancaster Wk EV L5 96 F7
Lance Cl EV L5 97 H8
Lancefield Rd WLT/FAZ L9 * 84 B8
Lance Gv WAV L15 114 C6
Lance La WAV L15 114 C6
Lancelyn Prec BEB CH63 * 143 J2
Lancelyn Ter BEB CH63 143 H1
Lancer Ct RUNC WA7 150 A2
Lancers Cft GTS/LS CH66 163 G4
Lance Wood Pl WGNW/BIL/O WN5 67 M7
Lancing Av WARRN/WOL WA2 121 J1
Lancing Cl WLTN L25 131 M4
Lancing Dr AIN/FAZ L10 84 F3
Lancing Rd EP CH65 20 E6
WLTN L25 131 M5
Lancing Wy WLTN L25 131 M4
Lancots La STHEL WA9 102 F5
Land Cut La GOL/RIS/CU WA3 122 F2
Land End MGHL L31 73 L4
Lander Cl WARRW/BUR WA5 120 F6
Lander Rd LITH L21 83 K7
Landford Av WLT/FAZ L9 98 A1
Landford Pl WLT/FAZ L9 98 A1
Land Gate La AIMK WN4 79 J6
Landican La BEB CH63 127 J7
GR/UP/WCH CH49 126 E4
Landican Rd GR/UP/WCH CH49 126 D6
Land La CHTN/BK PR9 25 L1
Landor Cl EV L5 96 E8
Landor St EV L5 * 97 G8
GOL/RIS/CU WA3 93 G5
Landscape Dene
FROD/HEL WA6 166 F1
Landseer Av NSTN CH64 153 H6
WARRS WA4 137 K4
Landseer Rd EV L5 97 H8
Land St WGNNW/ST WN6 4 C3
Lane Head Av GOL/RIS/CU WA3 93 G5
Lanfranc Cl CHLDW L16 115 G5
Lanfranc Wy CHLDW L16 115 G5
Langbar RAIN/WH L35 117 G4
Langcliffe Cl GOL/RIS/CU WA3 * 107 G2
Langdale Av CROS/BRETH PR26 29 K2
FMBY L37 58 F2
GOL/RIS/CU WA3 92 E4
PEN/TH CH61 141 H1
WGN WN1 68 D2
WGNE/HIN WN2 69 K5
Langdale Cl FMBY L37 58 F3
KKBY L32 86 B4
WARRN/WOL WA2 122 A3
WDN WA8 133 L5
Langdale Crs WGNE/HIN WN2 80 D5
Langdale Ct WGNW/BIL/O WN5 67 K5
Langdale Dr BRSC L40 52 A1
MGHL L31 73 G3
Langdale Gdns STHP PR8 35 H4
Langdale Gv RNFD/HAY WA11 89 K6
WGNE/HIN WN2 80 D2
Langdale Rd BEB CH63 143 G1
RUNC WA7 19 J5
WAL/NB CH45 95 J6
WAV L15 114 A7
WGNW/BIL/O WN5 67 K6
Langdale St BTL L20 7 J5
Langdale Wy FROD/HEL WA6 160 E4
Langden Cl GOL/RIS/CU WA3 106 F1
Langfield GOL/RIS/CU WA3 93 G6
Langfield Gv PS/BROM CH62 143 M8
Langford SPK/HALE L24 147 L4
Langford Rd ALL/GAR L19 130 B5
Langham Av AIG/SPK L17 129 L2
Langham Rd WGNNW/ST WN6 55 M4
Langham St ANF/KKDL L4 97 H5
Langholm Cl WGNS/IIMK WN3 78 F3
Langholm Rd AIMK WN4 90 E1
Langland Cl ANF/KKDL L4 97 M5
WARRW/BUR WA5 121 G3
Lang La WKBY CH48 124 D2
Lang La South WKBY CH48 124 E2
Langley Cl BEB CH63 143 J4
GOL/RIS/CU WA3 92 E4
HTWN L38 70 B3
WD/CROXPK L12 99 H2
WGNNW/ST WN6 56 A3
Langley Ct EP CH65 21 G9
Langley Pl BRSC L40 51 K1
Langley Rd BEB CH63 143 J3
BRSC L40 51 K1
Langley St TOX L8 * 113 G7
WGNW/BIL/O WN5 67 M7
Langrove St EV L5 97 G8
Langsdale St VAUX/LVPD L3 13 L4
Langset Av WGNE/HIN WN2 69 M7
Langshaw Lea NTHLY L27 132 B1
Langstone Av
GR/UP/WCH CH49 125 K3
Langton Av WGNNW/ST WN6 56 A4
Langton Brow CHLY/EC PR7 30 F8
Langton Cl CHLY/EC PR7 30 F8
NEWLW WA12 104 C1
WDN WA8 133 K2
Langton Gn WARR WA1 122 F6
Langton Pl WGNNW/ST WN6 56 A4
Langton Rd NWD/KWIPK L33 74 B8
WAV L15 113 M6
Langtree SKEL WN8 65 K2
Langtree La WGNNW/ST WN6 55 M2
Langtree St STHEL WA9 9 L5
Langtry Cl ANF/KKDL L4 96 F5
Langtry Rd ANF/KKDL L4 96 F5
Langwell Cl GOL/RIS/CU WA3 107 J8
Langwood La RNFD/HAY WA11 76 E4
Lansbrook Ct RUNC WA7 * 19 L4
Lansbury Av STHEL WA9 103 G3
Lansbury Rd HUY L36 116 C3
Lansbury St WGNW/BIL/O WN5 67 J7
Lansdown WD/CROXPK L12 98 C7
Lansdowne FROD/HEL WA6 160 F7
GOL/RIS/CU WA3 107 G3
Lansdowne Cl BIRK CH41 10 A1
Lansdowne Ct CL/PREN CH43 111 H5
Lansdowne Pl EV L5 97 H7
Lansdowne Rd BIRK CH41 111 H5
STHP PR8 25 G7
WAL/NB CH45 95 H5
Lanville Rd ALL/GAR L19 130 D4
Lanyork Rd VAUX/LVPD L3 12 D4
Lapford Crs NWD/KWIPK L33 86 C1
Lapwing Cl GOL/RIS/CU WA3 92 F5
WD/CROXPK L12 99 G4
Lapwing Ct HLWD L26 132 A4
Lapwing Gv RUNC WA7 150 C7
Lapwing La WARRS WA4 136 B6
Lapworth Cl MOR/LEA CH46 109 K5
Lapworth St EV L5 96 F7
Larch Av CHLYE PR6 33 G3
NEWLW WA12 104 E3
WARRW/BUR WA5 120 A8
WDN WA8 134 D3
WGNW/BIL/O WN5 67 M7
Larch Cl ALL/GAR L19 130 B6
GOL/RIS/CU WA3 93 H7
RUNC WA7 19 M9
SKEL WN8 65 G4
WGNW/BIL/O WN5 77 M8
Larchdale Cl GTS/LS CH66 163 H5
Larchdale Gv WLT/FAZ L9 97 K1
Larchfield Rd CSBY/BLUN L23 71 J8
Larch Gv CL/PREN CH43 111 G5
WAV L15 114 C4
Larch Lea NPK/KEN L6 97 K8
Larch Rd HUY L36 115 L3
RF/TRAN CH42 10 F8
RNFD/HAY WA11 * 91 G6
RUNC WA7 149 L6
Larch St STHP PR8 25 G8
Larch Wy FMBY L37 58 F1
Larchways WARRS WA4 137 M8
Larchwood Av MGHL L31 72 E6
Larchwood Cl PEN/TH CH61 141 H2
WLTN L25 115 K8
Larchwood Dr BEB CH63 128 B6
WGN WN1 68 D1
Larcombe Av
GR/UP/WCH CH49 110 B8
Larkfield CHLY/EC PR7 30 D7
Larkfield Av WARR WA1 122 B6
WGN WN1 68 D1
Larkfield Cl AIG/SPK L17 129 L3
Larkfield Gv AIG/SPK L17 129 L3
Larkfield La CHTN/BK PR9 25 J2
Larkfield Rd AIG/SPK L17 129 L3
Larkfield Vw WAV L15 114 A5
Larkhill SKEL WN8 65 K1
Larkhill Av GR/UP/WCH CH49 110 C7
WGNNW/ST WN6 56 B5
Larkhill Cl CLB/OSW/ST L13 98 A6
Larkhill Gv HTWN L38 70 B2
Larkhill La CLB/OSW/ST L13 98 A6
FMBY L37 58 E1
Larkhill Pl CLB/OSW/ST L13 98 A6
Larkhill Vw CLB/OSW/ST L13 98 B6
Larkhill Wy GR/UP/WCH CH49 110 C6
Larkin Cl PS/BROM CH62 128 C6
Lark La AIG/SPK L17 129 L2
Larkspur Cl RUNC WA7 161 H1
STHP PR8 3 L6
Larkstoke Cl WARRS WA4 138 A7
Larksway HES CH60 141 K5
Lark Wy AIG/SPK L17 129 K2
Larton Farm Cl WKBY CH48 125 G2
Larton Rd WKBY CH48 124 F2
Lartonwood WKBY CH48 125 G3
Lascelles Rd ALL/GAR L19 130 F6
Lascelles St STHEL WA9 9 M5
Laskey La WARRS WA4 139 H1
Latchford Rd HES CH60 141 K7
Latchford St WARRS WA4 138 C2
Late Moffatt Rd West
WLT/FAZ L9 * 84 D6
Latham Av FROD/HEL WA6 166 D4
NEWLW WA12 104 E1
ORM L39 51 J8
RUNC WA7 19 L5
Latham La WGNW/BIL/O WN5 67 J5
Latham Rd HOR/BR BL6 57 L2
Latham St EV L5 96 F7
Latham Wy BEB CH63 143 K3
Lathbury La AIG/SPK L17 114 A8
Lathom Av LITH L21 83 H7
SKEL WN8 53 K3
WAL/EG CH44 111 K1
WARRN/WOL WA2 121 K5
Lathom Cl BRSC L40 52 A1
Lathom Dr MGHL L31 73 G2
RNFD/HAY WA11 76 B6
Lathom La BRSC L40 51 L6
Lathom Rd BTL L20 83 L8
CHTN/BK PR9 24 E4
HUY L36 116 A3
ORM L39 64 B6
Lathum Cl RAIN/WH L35 101 G8
Latimer Cl WGNW/BIL/O WN5 * 67 M7
Latimer St EV L5 96 F8
Latrigg Rd AIG/SPK L17 130 A3
Lauder Cl NWD/KWIPK L33 73 M7
Launceston Cl RUNC WA7 150 E7
Launceston Dr
WARRW/BUR WA5 136 A2
Launceston Rd WGNE/HIN WN2 81 L2
The Laund WAL/NB CH45 95 H8
Laurel Av BEB CH63 143 G1
BRSC L40 39 G7
CHLY/EC PR7 31 K2
HES CH60 141 H4
NEWLW WA12 104 F3
WARR WA1 * 122 F6
Laurel Bank WARRS WA4 138 E4
WDN WA8 134 C2
Laurelbanks HES CH60 141 G4
Laurel Ct RNFD/HAY WA11 89 K6
Laurel Crs WGNE/HIN WN2 81 J2
Laurel Dr ECCL WA10 101 H1
EP CH65 163 K3
NSTN CH64 154 D4
SKEL WN8 65 G3
Laurel Gv AIMK WN4 91 K1
CHTN/BK PR9 25 G6
CSBY/WL L22 82 F3
GOL/RIS/CU WA3 92 F5
HUY L36 116 A5
TOX L8 113 L7
Laurelhurst Av PEN/TH CH61 141 J1
Laurel Rd ECCL WA10 8 A7
EHL/KEN L7 113 M3
PR/KW L34 101 G7
RF/TRAN CH42 11 G9
RNFD/HAY WA11 90 B8
Laurels Farm Ct CHNE CH2 * 165 K2
The Laurels CHLY/EC PR7 43 H2
Laurel Wy ECCL WA10 * 8 A8
Laurelwood Dr GTS/LS CH66 163 G5
Laurence Deacon Ct
BIRK CH41 * 11 G3
Lauren Cl HUY L36 116 D3
Lauriston Rd ANF/KKDL L4 97 L4
Laurus Cl NTHLY L27 116 B8
Lavan Cl NPK/KEN L6 113 J2
Lavan St NPK/KEN L6 113 J2
Lavender Cl RUNC WA7 19 M6
Lavender Crs PR/KW L34 101 G7
Lavender Gv CHLY/EC PR7 32 E8
Lavender Rd WGNNW/ST WN6 68 B2
Lavender Wy WLT/FAZ L9 97 K2
Lavrock Bank TOX L8 129 G1
Lawford Dr HES CH60 141 L5
Lawler St LITH L21 83 K7
Lawn Av WARR WA1 122 B5
Lawns Av BEB CH63 143 K7
SKEL WN8 66 E8
Lawnside Cl RF/TRAN CH42 128 B4
The Lawns CHTN/BK PR9 25 H3
CL/PREN CH43 110 F6
Lawnswood Gv CHNE CH2 165 K2
Lawnwood Av CHLY/EC PR7 32 C8
Lawrence Cl ALL/GAR L19 130 C6
Lawrence Ct WGNE/HIN WN2 80 D4
Lawrence Gv WAV L15 114 A6
Lawrence La CHLY/EC PR7 30 E6
Lawrence Rd CHLY/EC PR7 32 D6
ECCL WA10 88 E7
WAV L15 113 M6
Lawrenson St ECCL WA10 8 D6
Lawson Cl WARR WA1 123 G6
Lawson St CHLYE PR6 33 G5
CHTN/BK PR9 25 J6
Lawson Wk WD/CROXPK L12 98 F2
Lawton Av BTL L20 84 A8
Lawton Cl GOL/RIS/CU WA3 * 107 G2
Lawton Rd CSBY/WL L22 82 F3
HUY L36 115 L3
RAIN/WH L35 117 M3
Lawton St CLVPS L1 13 J8
Laxey Av WARR WA1 122 F7
Laxey Crs LEIGH WN7 81 L6
Laxey St TOX L8 113 G7
Laxton Cl GTS/LS CH66 163 H5
Laxton Rd WLTN L25 131 L7
Layford Cl HUY L36 99 M7
Layford Rd HUY L36 99 M8
Layland Av GOL/RIS/CU WA3 107 G1
Layton Av CL/PREN CH43 127 H3
Layton Cl GOL/RIS/CU WA3 123 G2
WGNW/BIL/O WN5 67 M8
WLTN L25 131 L3
Layton Rd WLTN L25 131 L3
Lazenby Crs AIMK WN4 91 H2
Leach Cft STBRV L28 99 J6
Leach La STHEL WA9 102 F8
Leach St ECCL WA10 8 F4
Leach Vw RNFD/HAY WA11 * 89 K6
Leach Wy PEN/TH CH61 125 L7
Lea Cl CL/PREN CH43 127 G1
Lea Crs ORM L39 51 G8
Leacroft AIMK WN4 79 G7
Leacroft Rd GOL/RIS/CU WA3 107 J7
Lea Cross Gv WDN WA8 133 L2
Leadale Cl WGNNW/ST WN6 55 M4
Leadenhall Cl EV L5 97 H7
Leader St WGN WN1 5 K4
WGNW/BIL/O WN5 67 L7
Leafield Cl PEN/TH CH61 126 B7
Leafield Rd WLTN L25 131 K7
Leagate AIN/FAZ L10 85 H5
Lea Gate Cl WGNS/IIMK WN3 * 79 G2
Lea Green Rd STHEL WA9 102 C8
Leal Holme Av WGNE/HIN WN2 69 J3
Leamington Av NEWLW WA12 104 E4
Leamington Cl NSTN CH64 153 G7
WARRW/BUR WA5 120 C5
Leamington Rd NG/CROX L11 97 M3
STHP PR8 34 E8
Leander Rd WAL/NB CH45 95 J8
Lea Rd WAL/EG CH44 95 J8
Leas Cl GTS/LS CH66 155 L8
Leaside RUNC WA7 149 M4
Leasowe Av WAL/NB CH45 95 G7
Leasowe Gdns MOR/LEA CH46 110 A2
Leasowe Rd MOR/LEA CH46 110 C1
WLT/FAZ L9 84 D6
Leasoweside MOR/LEA CH46 110 C1
Leas Pk HOY CH47 124 C1
The Leas PEN/TH CH61 126 D7
WAL/NB CH45 95 G6
Lea St WGNS/IIMK WN3 4 B5
Leatham Cl GOL/RIS/CU WA3 123 G2
Leatherbarrows La MGHL L31 73 J6
Leather La CLVP L2 12 F6
Leather's La HLWD L26 132 B6
Leathwood MGHL L31 * 73 G5
Lea Vw WGN WN1 5 L2
Leaway GR/UP/WCH CH49 125 M1
WGNE/HIN WN2 5 L5
Leawood Gv MOR/LEA CH46 110 B5
Leckwith Rd NTHTN L30 84 D3
Ledburn SKEL WN8 65 K2
Ledbury Cl CL/PREN CH43 127 G3
ECCL WA10 101 K2
WD/CROXPK L12 99 H1
Ledger Rd RNFD/HAY WA11 90 C8
Ledmore Gv AIMK WN4 90 F2
Ledsham Cl CL/PREN CH43 127 G1
GOL/RIS/CU WA3 122 E2
Ledsham La GTS/LS CH66 162 B2
Ledsham Park Dr GTS/LS CH66 155 J7
Ledsham Rd GTS/LS CH66 155 J8
KKBY L32 85 L3
Ledsham Village GTS/LS CH66 162 B4
Ledson Gv ORM L39 62 D6
Ledston Cl RUNC WA7 150 F4
Ledyard Cl WARRW/BUR WA5 120 F6
Leece St CLVPS L1 13 J9
Lee Cl RAIN/WH L35 117 M4
Lee Ct WARRN/WOL WA2 121 L3
Leecourt Cl WD/CROXPK L12 98 F8
Leeds St VAUX/LVPD L3 12 E4
WGNS/IIMK WN3 4 C5
Lee Hall Rd WLTN L25 115 L8
Lee La BRSC L40 40 E6
WGNE/HIN WN2 80 D5
Leeming Cl ALL/GAR L19 130 E8
Lee Park Av WLTN L25 115 L8
Lee Rd HOY CH47 108 E6
WARRW/BUR WA5 * 120 D7
Lees Av RF/TRAN CH42 128 B3
Leeside Av KKBY L32 86 B5
Leeside Cl KKBY L32 86 B4
Lees La EP CH65 20 F7
NSTN CH64 153 K5
SKEL WN8 53 L5
SKEL WN8 54 C6
WD/CROXPK L12 98 F6
Leeson Av CHLY/EC PR7 42 F1
Lees Rd CHLYE PR6 44 D5
NWD/KWIPK L33 86 D4
Lee St STHEL WA9 103 G5
Leeswood SKEL WN8 65 K2
Leeswood Rd GR/UP/WCH CH49 126 C2
Lee Vale Rd WLTN L25 131 L1
Leeward Dr SPK/HALE L24 146 C1
Legh La KIRK/FR/WA PR4 27 J1
Legh Rd PS/BROM CH62 128 D6
RNFD/HAY WA11 90 C7
Legh St AIMK WN4 91 K3
GOL/RIS/CU WA3 92 C5
NEWLW WA12 104 C2
WARR WA1 14 D5
Legion La PS/BROM CH62 143 M4
Legion Rd ECCL WA10 101 M5
Leicester Av CSBY/WL L22 82 F3
Leicester Rd BTL L20 7 K2
Leicester St CHTN/BK PR9 3 H1
STHEL WA9 101 M5
WARRW/BUR WA5 121 G8
Leigh Ar WGN WN1 * 4 E5
Leigh Av WDN WA8 16 C2
Leigh Pl CLVPS L1 * 13 H7
Leigh Rd WGNE/HIN WN2 81 K4
WKBY CH48 124 D2
Leigh Rw CHLY/EC PR7 32 E6
Leighs Hey Crs KKBY L32 86 B4
Leigh St CLVPS L1 13 H7
LEIGH WN7 81 L8
WGN WN1 5 H5
WGNE/HIN WN2 81 K4
Leighton Av HOY CH47 109 G5
MGHL L31 72 F3
Leighton Cha NSTN CH64 152 F4
Leighton Ct NSTN CH64 152 F5
Leighton Dr LEIGH WN7 93 K4
Leighton Pk NSTN CH64 152 F5
Leighton Rd BIRK CH41 11 J9
NSTN CH64 152 E2
The Leightons NSTN CH64 152 F5
Leighton St ANF/KKDL L4 7 L9
Leinster Gdns RUNC WA7 18 E2
Leinster Rd CLB/OSW/ST L13 114 D2
Leinster St RUNC WA7 18 E2
Leison St ANF/KKDL L4 96 F6
Leiston Cl PEN/TH CH61 126 A6
Lemon Cl EHL/KEN L7 113 L4
Lemon Gv TOX L8 113 L7
Lemon St EV L5 96 F7
Lemon Tree Wk ECCL WA10 101 M4
Lendel Cl FMBY L37 59 G2
Lenfield Dr RNFD/HAY WA11 90 B7
Lenham Wy SPK/HALE L24 146 D1
Lennon St CHLY/EC PR7 32 E6
Lennox Av WAL/NB CH45 * 95 K6
Lennox La CL/PREN CH43 110 E4
Lenthall St ANF/KKDL L4 97 H3
Lenton Av FMBY L37 58 F1
Lenton Rd WLTN L25 115 L8
Leo Cl DV/KA/FCH L14 115 H1
Leominster Rd WAL/EG CH44 111 K1
Leonard Cheshire Dr
NTHTN L30 84 B2
Leonards Cl HUY L36 99 M7
Leonard St RUNC WA7 148 F6
STHEL WA9 103 H6
WARRN/WOL WA2 15 G2
WARRS WA4 137 L4
Leon Cl WARRW/BUR WA5 * 119 M6
Leonora St TOX L8 * 129 J1
Leopold Gv STHEL WA9 102 E8
Leopold Rd CSBY/WL L22 82 E3
EHL/KEN L7 113 K3
Leopold St WAL/EG CH44 * 112 A2
WGNW/BIL/O WN5 67 K8
Lesley Rd STHP PR8 25 G6
Leslie Av GR/UP/WCH CH49 125 M2
Leslie Rd ECCL WA10 101 L5
Lesseps Rd TOX L8 113 L6
Lessingham Av WGN WN1 68 D2
Lessingham Rd WDN WA8 134 B2
Lester Cl ANF/KKDL L4 97 G6
Lester Dr ECCL WA10 88 C8
PEN/TH CH61 125 L6
Lester Gv HUY L36 * 116 B1
Lestock St TOX L8 113 G6
Leta St ANF/KKDL L4 97 H4
Letchworth Dr CHLY/EC PR7 32 D7
Letchworth St NPK/KEN L6 97 L8
Letchworth Wks CHLY/EC PR7 32 D7
Lethbridge Cl EV L5 96 E7
Lethbridge Rd STHP PR8 3 M7

Letitia St *TOX* L8 ....113 H8
Levens Cl *CHTN/BK* PR9 ....23 J8
Levens Hey *MOR/LEA* CH46 ....109 M5
Levens Pl *WGNE/HIN* WN2 ....69 J5
　　WGNW/BIL/O WN5 ....67 L6
Leven Cl *ANF/KKDL* L4 ....97 G5
Levens Wy *WDN* WA8 ....133 L5
Levens Wk *EP* CH65 ....156 C5
Lever Av *WAL/EG* CH44 ....113 A3
Lever Cswy *BEB* CH63 ....127 K6
Lever Park Av *HOR/BR* BL6 ....45 J8
Lever St *STHEL* WA9 ....118 F1
Lever Ter *RF/TRAN* CH42 ....128 A2
Leveson Rd *CLB/OSW/ST* L13 ...114 D4
Levisham Gdns
　　WARRW/BUR WA5 ....121 G6
Lewis Av *WARRW/BUR* WA5 ......121 H3
Lewis Cl *CHLY/EC* PR7 ....44 A7
　　CHNE CH2 ....163 L5
　　WCNS/IIMK WN3 ....4 C5
Lewis Crs *WDN* WA8 ....16 C5
Lewis Gv *WDN* WA8 ....133 M4
Lewisham Rd *NG/CROX* L11 ....98 B3
　　PS/BROM CH62 ....128 E7
Lewis St *ECCL* WA10 ....8 D5
Lexden Cl *WARRW/BUR* WA5 ....121 G7
Lexham Rd *DV/KA/FCH* L14 ....114 E2
Lexington Wy *NWD/KWIPK* L33 ...73 M7
Lexton Dr *CHTN/BK* PR9 ....25 K2
Leybourne Av *STHP* PR8 ....25 K1
Leybourne Cl *WLTN* L25 ....115 J7
Leybourne Gn *WLTN* L25 ....115 J8
Leybourne Gv *WLTN* L25 ....115 J8
Leyburn Cl *KKBY* L32 ....86 A6
　　WGN WN1 ....5 L2
Leyburn Rd *WAL/NB* CH45 ....95 H6
Ley Cl *STHEL* WA9 ....118 E1
Leyfield Cl *WD/CROXPK* L12 ....98 F7
Leyfield Rd *WD/CROXPK* L12 ......98 F7
Leyland Av *WGNE/HIN* WN2 ....80 F2
Leyland Cl *WGNE/HIN* WN2 ....80 F2
Leyland Green Rd *AIMK* WN4 ......78 M8
Leyland Gv *RNFD/HAY* WA11 ....90 D7
Leyland La *CROS/BRETH* PR26 ...30 D7
Leyland Mill La *WGN* WN1 ....68 E2
Leyland Rd *CHTN/BK* PR9 ....3 L1
　　RNFD/HAY WA11 ....76 B7
Leyland St *PR/KW* L34 ....100 F7
　　WGNE/HIN WN2 ....80 D4
Leyland Wy *ORM* L39 ....51 M8
Leyton Cl *RUNC* WA7 ....149 K7
Liberton Ct *EV* L5 ....97 H7
Liberty St *WAV* L15 ....114 A6
Libra Cl *DV/KA/FCH* L14 ....99 J8
Library St *CHLY/EC* PR7 ....32 E6
　　WGN WN1 ....4 F4
Libson Cl *WARRN/WOL* WA2 .....122 C2
Lichen Cl *CHLY/EC* PR7 ....42 F1
Lichfield Av *CSBY/WL* L22 ....82 F2
　　GOL/RIS/CU WA3 ....92 F5
　　WARRS WA4 ....138 C6
Lichfield Cl *NTHTN* L30 ....84 C4
Lichfield Dr *GTS/LS* CH66 ....161 L5
Lichfield Gv *AIMK* WN4 ....91 L5
Lichfield Rd *CHLY/EC* PR7 ....32 E7
　　HLWD L26 ....132 A7
　　WAV L15 ....114 C7
Lichfield St *WAL/NB* CH45 ....95 J1
　　WGNW/BIL/O WN5 ....67 J8
Lickers La *RAIN/WH* L35 ....117 G3
Liddell Av *MGHL* L31 ....85 J1
Liddell Rd *WD/CROXPK* L12 ....98 B6
Lidderdale Rd *WAV* L15 ....114 A7
Liddesdale Rd *NWD/KWIPK* L33 ...78 M8
　　WGNS/IIMK WN3 ....4 E6
Liebig St *WDN* WA8 ....16 E4
Lifeboat Rd *FMBY* L37 ....58 C4
Liffey St *TOX* L8 ....113 K6
Lifton Rd *NWD/KWIPK* L33 ....86 B3
Lightbody St *EV* L5 ....96 D8
Lightburn St *RUNC* WA7 ....18 E4
Lightfoot Cl *HES* CH60 ....141 K6
Lightfoot La *HES* CH60 ....141 K6
Lighthorne Dr *STHP* PR8 ....47 J1
Lighthouse Rd *HOY* CH47 ....108 C7
　　SPK/HALE L24 ....148 A5
Lighthurst Av *CHLY/EC* PR7 ....32 E8
Lighthurst La *CHLY/EC* PR7 ....32 E8
Lightshaw La *GOL/RIS/CU* WA3 ...92 D1
Lightwood Dr *EHL/KEN* L7 ....113 L5
Lightwood St *EHL/KEN* L7 ....113 L5
Lilac Av *AIMK* WN4 ....78 F8
　　STHP PR8 ....47 M3
　　WARRW/BUR WA5 ....120 C8
　　WDN WA8 ....134 D3
　　WGNW/BIL/O WN5 ....89 M1
Lilac Crs *RUNC* WA7 ....19 L7
Lilac Gdns *WGNS/IIMK* WN3 ....80 B1
Lilac Gv *GTS/LS* CH66 ....163 K5
　　HUY L36 ....115 M5
　　RNFD/HAY WA11 ....90 B8
　　SKEL WN8 ....65 G4
　　WARRS WA4 ....138 A4
　　WGNW/BIL/O WN5 ....89 M1
Lilac Rd *GOL/RIS/CU* WA3 ....92 G4
Lilford Av *WARRW/BUR* WA5 .....121 H5
　　WLT/FAZ L9 ....84 B7
Lilford Dr *WARRW/BUR* WA5 ....14 B2
Lilford St *WARRW/BUR* WA5 ....14 B2
Lilian Dr *WGNNW/ST* WN6 ....68 C2
Lilley Rd *EHL/KEN* L7 ....113 M2
Lillian Rd *ANF/KKDL* L4 ....97 K7
Lillie Cl *CL/PREN* CH43 ....110 E5
Lillyfield *HES* CH60 ....141 M6
Lilly Gn *ANF/KKDL* L4 ....97 K4
Lilly Gv *ANF/KKDL* L4 ....97 K4
Lily Cl *EHL/KEN* L7 ....113 M2
Lily La *WGNE/HIN* WN2 ....80 C5
Lily Pl *AIMK* WN4 ....91 J3
Lily Rd *LITH* L21 ....83 K7
Lily St *WDN* WA8 ....80 A8
Limbrick St *CHLYE* PR6 ....33 G6
Lime Av *BEB* CH63 ....142 F1
　　FROD/HEL WA6 ....160 E5
　　WDN WA8 ....134 D3
Lime Cl *CLB/OSW/ST* L13 ....114 C1
　　WGNE/HIN WN2 ....80 D6
Limedale Rd *CALD/MH* L18 ....130 C1
Limefield *WGN* WN1 ....5 J1
Limefield Dr *SKEL* WN8 ....58 A6
Lime Gv *CHLY/EC* PR7 ....32 E8
　　CHNE CH2 ....165 J2
　　GOL/RIS/CU WA3 ....92 F7
　　LITH L21 ....83 J7
　　RNFD/HAY WA11 ....76 B3
　　RUNC WA7 ....19 L7
　　SKEL WN8 ....65 G4
　　TOX L8 ....113 J7
　　WGNE/HIN WN2 ....81 M7
Limehurst Cv *PS/BROM* CH62 ...143 M7
Limekiln Ct *EV* L5 ....13 G1
Limekiln La *EV* L5 ....13 G1
　　VAUX/LVPD L3 ....13 G3
　　WAL/EG CH44 ....111 J3
　　WARRW/BUR WA5 ....120 A3
Limes Av *CHLY/EC* PR7 ....31 L1

WGNNW/ST WN6 ....56 D7
The Limes *GOL/RIS/CU* WA3 ....92 F7
　　WGNW/BIL/O WN5 ....106 F1
　　GR/UP/WCH CH49 ....110 B3
　　WGNNW/ST WN6 ....56 C7
Lime St *CLVPS* L1 ....13 H7
　　NEWLW WA12 ....5 C1
　　STHP PR8 ....25 C7
　　WGN WN1 ....5 G3
Limetree Av *WARR* WA1 ....122 B6
　　WARRS WA4 ....138 A4
Lime Tree Cl *GTS/LS* CH66 ....163 J5
　　WLT/FAZ L9 ....97 K2
Lime Tree Gv *HES* CH60 ....141 L5
Lime Tree Wy *FMBY* L37 ....58 E3
Lime V *WGNS/IIMK* WN3 ....80 B1
Limeways *WARRS* WA4 ....138 A8
Limont Rd *STHP* PR8 ....54 F8
Linacre La *BTL* L20 ....83 M8
　　LITH L21 ....60 C5
Linacre Rd *LITH* L21 ....83 K7
Linaker Dr *ORM* L39 ....49 K5
Linaker St *STHP* PR8 ....3 H5
Linbeck Gv *GOL/RIS/CU* WA3 ......94 H5
Linbridge Rd *WGNE/HIN* WN2 .....81 J5
Lincoln Av *GOL/RIS/CU* WA3 ....92 F4
Lincoln Cl *GOL/RIS/CU* WA3 ....93 L5
　　HUY L36 ....116 D2
　　RUNC WA7 ....18 C7
　　WARR WA1 ....123 G7
Lincoln Crs *RNFD/HAY* WA11 ......89 K7
Lincoln Dr *AIMK* WN4 ....91 L3
　　AIN/FAZ L10 ....84 F2
　　WAL/NB CH45 ....95 L7
　　WGNE/HIN WN2 ....57 M8
Lincoln Gdns *BIRK* CH41 * 10 A1
Lincoln Pl *WGNE/HIN* WN2 ....72 D5
Lincoln Rd *ECCL* WA10 ....8 A8
　　GTS/LS CH66 ....163 J2
　　STHP PR8 ....35 J4
Lincoln Sq *WDN* WA8 ....134 D3
Lincoln St *ALL/GAR* L19 ....145 L1
　　BIRK CH41 ....10 A1
Lincoln Wy *RAIN/WH* L35 ....117 M4
Lincombe Rd *HUY* L36 ....115 K1
Lincroft Rd *WGNE/HIN* WN2 ....81 J5
Lindale Dr *STHEL* WA9 ....118 E1
Lindale Rd *EHL/KEN* L7 ....114 A2
Lindby Cl *KKBY* L32 ....86 C5
Lindby Rd *KKBY* L32 ....86 C5
Linden Av *AIMK* WN4 ....79 H8
　　CSBY/BLUN L23 ....82 E1
　　NTHTN L30 ....84 B3
　　WGNW/BIL/O WN5 ....67 C7
Linden Cl *GTS/LS* CH66 ....163 H5
　　WARR WA1 ....122 F6
Linden Ct *WDN* WA8 * 134 B1
Linden Dr *CL/PREN* CH43 ....127 G4
　　FROD/HEL WA6 ....166 D4
　　HUY L36 ....116 A5
Linden Gv *CHLYE* PR6 ....32 F2
　　RNFD/HAY WA11 ....90 B8
　　WAL/NB CH45 ....95 K6
　　WGNW/BIL/O WN5 ....67 C7
Linden Rd *NTHLY* L27 ....116 A8
Lindens *SKEL* WN8 ....65 K1
The Lindens *CL/PREN* CH43 ....10 E7
　　MGHL L31 ....72 E6
Linden St *WGNW/BIL/O* WN5 ....67 L8
Linden Wy *ECCL* WA10 ....101 K1
Lindenwood *KKBY* L32 ....86 B5
Lindeth Av *WAL/EG* CH44 ....111 K3
Lindfield Cl *TOX* L8 ....113 C1
　　WARRS WA4 ....136 A1
Lindholme *SKEL* WN8 ....65 L2
Lindi Av *WARRS* WA4 ....138 D4
Lindisfarne Av *EP* CH65 ....163 L4
　　GOL/RIS/CU WA3 ....93 L5
Lindisfarne Dr *WD/CROXPK* L12 ...99 M6
Lindley Av *WARRW/BUR* WA5 ...138 B1
　　WGNW/BIL/O WN5 ....66 B8
Lindley Cl *RAIN/WH* L35 ....117 J1
Lindley Dr *SKEL* WN8 ....53 L2
Lindley St *EHL/KEN* L7 ....113 M2
Lindow St *LEIGH* WN7 ....81 M8
Lindrick Cl *RAIN/WH* L35 ....117 J1
Lindsay Dr *CHLY/EC* PR7 ....32 C6
Lindsay Rd *ANF/KKDL* L4 ....97 M5
Lindsay St *STHEL* WA9 ....119 G2
Lindsay Ter *WGNE/HIN* WN2 ....57 K8
Lind St *ANF/KKDL* L4 ....97 M3
Lindsworth Cl
　　WARRW/BUR WA5 * 120 E7
Lindwall Cl *CL/PREN* CH43 ....110 E4
Linear Dr *MOR/LEA* CH46 ....109 L4
Linear Vw *NEWLW* WA12 ....104 E5
Lineside Cl *WLTN* L25 ....115 K8
Linford Gv *RNFD/HAY* WA11 ....9 M1
Lingdale Av *CL/PREN* CH43 ....111 H7
Lingdale Rd *CL/PREN* CH43 ......111 H6
　　WKBY CH48 ....124 C2
Lingdale Rd North *BIRK* CH41 ....111 H6
Lingdales *FMBY* L37 ....47 K7
Lingfield Av *CHLY/EC* PR7 ....43 G5
　　CSBY/BLUN L23 ....71 C7
　　FMBY L37 ....59 J3
　　HUY L36 ....99 L8
　　KIRK/FR/WA PR4 ....28 C1
　　MGHL L31 ....72 F1
　　NSTN CH64 ....153 H3
　　ORM L39 ....62 E2
Lingfield Crs *WGNNW/ST* WN6 ....68 A2
Lingfield Gv *DV/KA/FCH* L14 ......114 F3
Lingfield Rd *RF/TRAN* CH42 ....128 E3
　　RUNC WA7 ....18 D7
Lingford Cl *NTHLY* L27 ....132 B1
Lingham Cl *MOR/LEA* CH46 ....109 M4
Lingham La *MOR/LEA* CH46 ....109 L3
Lingholme Rd *ECCL* WA10 ....8 D3
Lingley Green Av
　　WARRW/BUR WA5 ....119 C7
Lingley Rd *WARRW/BUR* WA5 ...119 M7
Lingmell Av *RNFD/HAY* WA11 ......89 K4
Lingmell Rd *WD/CROXPK* L12 .....98 D5
Lingmoor Cl *WGNS/IIMK* WN3 .....79 J4
Ling St *EHL/KEN* L7 ....113 K3
Lingtree Rd *KKBY* L32 ....85 K3
Lingwell Av *WDN* WA8 ....133 M3
Lingwood Rd
　　WARRW/BUR WA5 ....120 A7
Linhope Wy *AIG/SPK* L17 ....129 L2
Link Av *CSBY/BLUN* L23 ....71 J8
　　RNFD/HAY WA11 ....90 A8
Link Rd *HUY* L36 ....116 D4
Links Av *CHTN/BK* PR9 ....25 J3
Links Cl *BEB* CH63 ....155 L6
　　WAL/NB CH45 ....95 H5
Links Hey Rd *WKBY* CH48 ....125 C9
Linkside *BEB* CH63 ....127 M6
Linkside Av *WARRN/WOL* WA2 ...105 K4
Linkside Wy *GTS/LS* CH66 ....163 H5
Links Rd *KKBY* L32 ....86 C5
The Links *GOL/RIS/CU* WA3 * 106 F1
Linkstor Rd *WLTN* L25 ....131 H5
Links Vw *CL/PREN* CH43 ....111 C8
Links View Cl *WLTN* L25 ....131 H5
Linksway *WAL/NB* CH45 ....95 H6
Linkway *ECCL* WA10 ....19 C8
　　RUNC WA7 ....19 L8
Linkway Av *AIMK* WN4 ....80 A8
Linkway East *STHEL* WA9 ....91 J7

Linkway West *ECCL* WA10 ....8 F6
Linley Cl *WGNNW/ST* WN6 ....67 L1
Linley Rd *WGNNW/ST* WN6 ....67 M8
Linner Rd *SPK/HALE* L24 ....146 F2
Linnet Cl *AIG/SPK* L17 ....113 L8
　　NEWLW WA12 ....104 D2
Linnet Gv *GOL/RIS/CU* WA3 ....93 L2
Linnet La *AIG/SPK* L17 ....113 K8
Linnets Wy *HES* CH60 ....141 G5
Linney Sq *WGN* WN1 ....5 J3
Linosa Cl *NPK/KEN* L6 ....113 L1
Linslade Cl *NWD/KWIPK* L33 ....86 B1
Linslade Crs *NWD/KWIPK* L33 .....86 B1
Linton Av *GOL/RIS/CU* WA3 ....93 B3
Linton St *ANF/KKDL* L4 ....97 L4
Linum Gdns *STHEL* WA9 ....103 K6
Linville Av *CSBY/BLUN* L23 ....82 D1
Linwood Cl *RUNC* WA7 ....150 B8
　　WGNE/HIN WN2 ....80 F1
Linwood Gv *RAIN/WH* L35 ....117 G3
Linwood Rd *RF/TRAN* CH42 ....128 A2
Lionel St *STHEL* WA9 ....103 H6
Lion Hotel Yd *WARR* WA1 * 57 L3
Lion La *HOR/BR* BL6 ....57 L3
Lipton Cl *BTL* L20 ....96 A7
Liptrot St *WGNW/BIL/O* WN5 ....68 B6
Liptrot Rd *AIMK* WN4 ....32 C8
Lisburn La *CLB/OSW/ST* L13 ....82 D1
Lisburn Rd *AIG/SPK* L17 ....130 A3
Liscard Gv *WAL/EG* CH44 ....111 K8
Liscard Rd *WAL/EG* CH44 ....111 M2
　　WAV L15 ....113 M6
Liscard Village *WAL/NB* CH45 .....95 K8
Liscard Crs *WAL/EG* CH44 ....111 K1
Liskeard Cl *RUNC* WA7 ....150 D7
Lisleholme Crs *WD/CROXPK* L12 ...98 F3
Lisleholme Rd *WD/CROXPK* L12 ...98 F7
Lismore Rd *CALD/MH* L18 ....130 C4
Lister Crs *EHL/KEN* L7 ....113 L3
Lister Dr *CLB/OSW/ST* L13 ....114 A1
Lister Rd *EHL/KEN* L7 ....113 L3
Liston St *ANF/KKDL* L4 * 97 H3
Litcham Cl *CR/UP/WCH* CH49 ....110 C6
Litchborough Gv *RAIN/WH* L35 ...101 J3
Litherland Av *MOR/LEA* CH46 ....109 M5
Litherland Crs *RNFD/HAY* WA11 ...89 L6
Litherland Pk *LITH* L21 ....83 K5
Litherland Rd *BTL* L20 ....7 H5
Lithou Cl *EV* L5 ....96 F8
Little Acre *MGHL* L31 ....73 C5
Little Barn Hey *NTHTN* L30 ....83 M1
Little Brook La *KKBY* L32 ....85 M5
Little Canning St *TOX* L8 ....113 H6
Little Carr La *CHLY/EC* PR7 ....32 F8
Little Catharine St *TOX* L8 ....113 H6
Littlecote Cl *WARRS* WA4 ....118 E1
Littlecourt *VAUX/LVPD* L3 ....12 E1
Little Crosby Rd *CSBY/BLUN* L23 ...71 G6
Little Dl *DV/KA/FCH* L14 * 114 F2
Littledale Rd *DV/KA/FCH* L14 .....114 F2
　　WAL/EG CH44 ....111 M2
　　WARRW/BUR WA5 ....120 B6
Little Delph *RNFD/HAY* WA11 ......90 E6
Littlegate *RUNC* WA7 ....150 A5
Little Gn *GTS/LS* CH66 ....162 F2
Little Hardman St *CLVPS* L1 * 13 K9
Little Heath Rd *SPK/HALE* L24 ...147 G3
Little Heyes St *EV* L5 ....97 J7
Little Hey La *FMBY* L37 ....59 J1
Little Howard St *VAUX/LVPD* L3 ...12 D2
Little Huskisson St *TOX* L8 ....113 H6
Little La *CHTN/BK* PR9 ....25 K4
　　NSTN CH64 ....152 D4
　　WGNS/IIMK WN3 ....79 C1
Little London *WGN* WN1 ....4 F2
Little Meadow La *BRSC* L40 ....39 M1
Littlemore St *GR/UP/WCH* CH49 ...109 M8
Little Moss Hey *STBRV* L28 ....99 K6
Little Parkfield Rd *AIG/SPK* L17 ...129 K1
Little Pasture *LEIGH* WN7 ....81 M6
Littler Rd *RNFD/HAY* WA11 ....90 C8
Little St Bride St *TOX* L8 ....113 H5
Little Scotland *HOR/BR* BL6 ....57 K3
Little Stanney La *CHNE* CH2 ......164 A5
Littlestone Cl *WDN* WA8 ....134 C1
Little Storeton La *BEB* CH63 ......127 J7
Little St *STHEL* WA9 ....103 G1
Littleton Cl *CL/PREN* CH43 * 127 G1
Littleton Gv *WGNNW/ST* WN6 .....56 A3
Little Wissage *GTS/LS* CH66 .....163 H3
Little Woolton St *EHL/KEN* L7 ....113 J4
Liverpool Loop Line *WLTN* L25 ...115 H6
Liverpool Old Rd
　　KIRK/FR/WA PR4 ....28 C3
　　STHP PR8 ....47 L4
Liverpool Pl *WDN* WA8 ....133 L4
Liverpool Rd *AIMK* WN4 ....91 J3
　　BRSC L40 ....28 D7
　　CH/BCN CH1 ....163 H6
　　CSBY/BLUN L23 ....71 C7
　　FMBY L37 ....59 J3
　　HUY L36 ....99 L8
　　KIRK/FR/WA PR4 ....28 C1
　　MGHL L31 ....72 F1
　　NSTN CH64 ....153 H3
　　ORM L39 ....62 E2
　　PR/KW L34 ....100 D7
　　RNFD/HAY WA11 ....90 E4
　　SKEL WN8 ....64 F5
　　STHP PR8 ....34 F8
　　WARRW/BUR WA5 ....14 B6
　　WARRW/BUR WA5 ....119 M7
　　WDN WA8 ....133 L4
　　WGNE/HIN WN2 ....80 D2
Liverpool Rd North *BRSC* L40 ......52 A1
Liverpool Rd South *BRSC* L40 .....51 M2
　　MGHL L31 ....72 B2
Liverpool Rw *NEWLW* WA12 ....104 F5
Liverpool St *ECCL* WA10 ....8 F6
Liversedge Rd *RF/TRAN* CH42 ...122 M1
Liver St *VAUX/LVPD* L3 ....113 C5
Livesley's Ct *STHEL* WA9 ....60 B3
Livingston Av *AIG/SPK* L17 ....129 L1
Livingston Dr *AIG/SPK* L17 ....129 L1
Livingston Dr North
　　AIG/SPK L17 ....129 L2
Livingston Dr South
　　AIG/SPK L17 ....129 L2
Livingstone Cl
　　WARRW/BUR WA5 ....120 F6
Livingstone Gdns *BIRK* CH41 ....10 C1
Livingstone Rd *EP* CH65 ....20 C1
　　MOR/LEA CH46 ....110 C1
　　RF/TRAN CH42 ....128 B3
Livingstone St *BIRK* CH41 ....10 F3
Llandaff Cl *GTS/LS* CH66 ....163 G4
Llanrwst Cl *TOX* L8 ....113 G8
Lloyd Cl *NPK/KEN* L6 ....13 M1
Lloyd Crs *NEWLW* WA12 ....104 B2
Lloyd Dr *EP* CH65 ....163 L4

GR/UP/WCH CH49 ....125 M2
Lloyd Rd *PR/KW* L34 ....101 G6
Lloyd St *RNFD/HAY* WA11 ....90 B7
Lobelia Av *WLT/FAZ* L9 ....97 K1
Lobelia Gv *RUNC* WA7 ....161 H1
Local Board St *WCNE/HIN* WN2 * ...5 M6
Lochinvar Av *GTS/LS* CH66 ....159 L4
Lochinvar St *WLT/FAZ* L9 ....97 H2
Lochmore Rd *CALD/MH* L18 ......130 C3
Lochryan Rd *ALL/GAR* L19 ....130 D5
Loch St *RUNC* WA7 ....19 G3
　　WGNW/BIL/O WN5 ....67 K7
Locker Av *WARRN/WOL* WA2 .....121 G4
Lockerbie Cl *WARRN/WOL* WA2 ...122 A1
Lockerbie Pl *WGNS/IIMK* WN3 .....79 G3
Lockerby Rd *EHL/KEN* L7 ....113 M2
Locker La *AIMK* WN4 ....92 B1
Locker Pk *GR/UP/WCH* CH49 .....125 L1
Locke St *ALL/GAR* L19 ....145 L1
Lockett Rd *AIMK* WN4 ....79 L8
　　WDN WA8 ....134 C3
Lockfields Vw *VAUX/LVPD* L3 ......96 E8
Lockgate East *RUNC* WA7 ....150 B5
Lockgate West *RUNC* WA7 ....150 B5
Locking Stumps La
　　WARRN/WOL WA2 ....122 D2
Lockington Cl *TOX* L8 ....129 J1
Lock Kd *KIRK/FR/WA* PR4 ....28 D3
Lock Rd *PS/BROM* CH62 ....144 D6
　　WARR WA1 ....122 B6
Lock St *WGN* WN1 ....9 L2
Lockton La *WARRW/BUR* WA5 ...121 G6
Lockton Rd *PR/KW* L34 ....86 D9
Lock Vls *WARR* WA1 * 138 D2
Lockwood Vw *RUNC* WA7 ....151 H4
Loddon Cl *GR/UP/WCH* CH49 ....110 C6
Lodge Dr *GOL/RIS/CU* WA3 ....107 H2
Lodge Hollow *FROD/HEL* WA6 ...166 D4
Lodge La *NEWLW* WA12 ....91 K4
　　PS/BROM CH62 ....128 D7
　　RNFD/HAY WA11 ....75 L4
　　RUNC WA7 ....150 A5
　　TOX L8 ....113 K6
　　WARRW/BUR WA5 ....121 G6
　　WDN WA8 ....133 L4
Lodge Rd *WDN* WA8 ....133 K5
Lodwick St *BTL* L20 ....6 F7
Loeminster Pl *WGNE/HIN* WN2 .....5 M5
Lofthouse Gate *WDN* WA8 ....134 B2
Logan Rd *BIRK* CH41 ....111 K4
Logfield Dr *ALL/GAR* L19 ....130 F8
Lognor Rd *KKBY* L32 ....85 J3
Logwood Av *WGNW/BIL/O* WN5 ...67 M6
Logwood Pl *WGNW/BIL/O* WN5 ...68 A5
Logwood Rd *HUY* L36 ....116 C5
Loire Dr *WGNW/BIL/O* WN5 ....68 B5
Lomax St *WGNE/HIN* WN2 ....80 C3
Lombard Rd *MOR/LEA* CH46 .....110 B3
Lombardy Av
　　GR/UP/WCH CH49 ....125 K3
Lomond Gv *EP* CH65 ....163 K3
　　MOR/LEA CH46 ....110 B5
Lomond Rd *EHL/KEN* L7 ....114 A3
London Cl *WGNW/BIL/O* WN5 ......68 A5
Londonderry Rd
　　CLB/OSW/ST L13 ....97 M6
London Flds *WGNW/BIL/O* WN5 ...78 A9
London La *STHP* PR8 ....35 M5
London Rd *FROD/HEL* WA6 ....2 F4
　　VAUX/LVPD L3 ....13 L6
　　WARRS WA4 ....137 M5
London Rw *NEWLW* WA12 ....104 C3
London Sq *STHP* PR8 ....3 G3
Longacre *CHTN/BK* PR9 ....3 H4
Longacre Cl *WAL/NB* CH45 ....94 F8
Long Acres *GR/UP/WCH* CH49 ....109 M8
Long Acres Rd *NSTN* CH64 ....153 G3
Long Av *WLT/FAZ* L9 ....84 D7
Longbarn Bvd
　　WARRN/WOL WA2 ....122 D3
Long Barn La *WARRN/WOL* WA2 ...122 D3
Longborough Rd *PR/KW* L34 ....99 L2
Longbrook *WGNNW/ST* WN6 ....55 K7
Longcliffe Dr *STHP* PR8 ....47 L1
Long Copse *CHLY/EC* PR7 ....32 B4
Longcroft Sq *ALL/GAR* L19 ....130 F6
Long Croft Meadow
　　CHLY/EC PR7 ....32 D3
Longcroft St *BTL* L20 ....6 D7
Longdale La *SFTN* L29 ....71 M6
Longdin St *WARRS* WA4 ....15 M9
Longdown Rd *NG/CROX* L11 ....85 K7
Longendale Av *RAIN/WH* L35 .....117 M3
Longfellow Cl *WGNS/IIMK* WN3 ...68 C8
Longfellow St *BTL* L20 ....6 D7
　　TOX L8 ....113 L6
Longfield Av *FMBY* L37 ....47 K8
　　CSBY/BLUN L23 ....71 C7
Longfield Cl *GR/UP/WCH* CH49 ...125 M1
Longfield Mnr *CHLY/EC* PR7 ....32 C8
Longfield Rd *LITH* L21 ....83 K7
　　KIRK/FR/WA PR4 ....28 C1
Longfold *MGHL* L31 ....73 G4
Longford Rd *STHP* PR8 ....35 J3
Longford St *WARRN/WOL* WA2 ....14 E1
Long Hey *RAIN/WH* L35 ....116 F3
Long Hey Rd *WKBY* CH48 ....125 G6
Long Heys La *SKEL* WN8 ....54 B8
Long Heys or Back La *SKEL* WN8 ...54 C8
Longhurst La *WGNE/HIN* WN2 .....81 J4
Longland Rd *WAL/NB* CH45 ....95 K7
Long La *ALL/GAR* L19 ....130 C8
　　CHLYE PR6 ....40 C1
　　CHTN/BK PR9 ....23 K7
　　ORM L39 ....62 F3
　　SFTN L29 ....71 J5
　　SKEL WN8 ....77 C2
　　WARRN/WOL WA2 ....114 B5
　　WAV L15 ....114 B5
　　WGNE/HIN WN2 ....81 J1
　　WLT/FAZ L9 ....84 B5
Longlooms Rd *EP* CH65 ....163 M4
Longmead Av *AIMK* WN4 ....91 L1
Long Meadow *CHLY/EC* PR7 ....32 D3
　　ECCL WA10 ....101 K1
　　HES CH60 ....141 M7
Longmeadow Rd *PR/KW* L34 ....99 M3
Longmoor Cl *AIN/FAZ* L10 ....84 D5
Longmoor Gv *WLT/FAZ* L9 ....84 D7
Longmoor La *AIN/FAZ* L10 ....84 D7
Longreach Rd *DV/KA/FCH* L14 ...115 H2
Longridge
　　GR/UP/WCH CH49 ....110 A7
Longridge Wk *ANF/KKDL* L4 ....97 C5
Longshaw Av *WGNW/BIL/O* WN5 ...78 A4
Longshaw Cl *BRSC* L40 ....28 C8

Longshaw Common
　　WGNW/BIL/O WN5 ....78 A5
Longshaw Old Rd
　　WGNW/BIL/O WN5 ....78 A4
Longshaw St *WARRW/BUR* WA5 ...121 H3
Longshoot Cl *WGN* WN1 ....5 H2
Long Spinney *RUNC* WA7 ....150 E5
Longster Cl *FROD/HEL* WA6 ......166 D3
Longstone Wk *EHL/KEN* L7 ....113 K5
Longton Av *GOL/RIS/CU* WA3 .....92 E5
Longton Dr *FMBY* L37 ....47 J7
Longton La *RAIN/WH* L35 ....101 K8
Longton St *CHLYE* PR6 ....33 G5
　　WGNE/HIN WN2 ....80 E1
Longview Crs *HUY* L36 ....116 B2
Longview Dr *HUY* L36 ....116 C2
Longview La *HUY* L36 ....100 B8
Longview Rd *HUY* L36 ....116 B1
　　RAIN/WH L35 ....117 J1
Longville St *TOX* L8 ....113 G8
Longwood Rd *WARRS* WA4 ....138 A8
Longworth Av *CHLY/EC* PR7 ....43 H3
Longworth Rd *CHLYE* PR6 ....57 L2
Longworth St *CHLY/EC* PR7 ....32 D7
Longworth Wy *WLTN* L25 ....131 L2
Lonie Cl *ECCL* WA10 ....101 L5
Lonsboro Rd *WAL/EG* CH44 ......111 L2
Lonsdale Cl *LITH* L21 ....83 K3
　　WARRW/BUR WA5 ....120 A5
　　WDN WA8 ....133 L5
Lonsdale Dr *CROS/BRETH* PR26 ...29 K3
Lonsdale Ms *LITH* L21 ....83 K3
Lonsdale Rd *FMBY* L37 ....59 C2
　　HLWD L26 ....132 A7
　　LITH L21 ....83 K3
　　STHP PR8 ....3 L9
Lonsdale Vls *WAL/NB* CH45 * 95 J7
Looe Cl *WDN* WA8 ....134 A3
Looe Rd *NG/CROX* L11 ....85 M8
The Looms *CHTN/CH64 ....152 D3
Loomsway *PEN/TH* CH61 ....125 L7
Loraine St *EV* L5 ....97 H8
Lord Av *DV/KA/FCH* L14 ....99 J1
Lordens Cl *DV/KA/FCH* L14 ....99 K7
Lordens Rd *DV/KA/FCH* L14 ....99 K7
Lord Nelson St *CLVPS* L1 ....13 C6
Lords Av *CL/PREN* CH43 ....110 E5
Lord Sefton Wy *FMBY* L37 ....59 M3
Lordsgate Dr *BRSC* L40 ....52 A2
Lordsgate La *BRSC* L40 ....51 K3
Lordship La *FROD/HEL* WA6 ......159 H7
Lords La *GOL/RIS/CU* WA3 ....122 E1
Lord St *AIMK* WN4 * 91 M1
　　ALL/GAR L19 ....145 L1
　　BIRK CH41 ....11 K4
　　BRSC L40 ....39 C8
　　CHLY/EC PR7 ....30 E8
　　CHLYE PR6 ....32 F6
　　CLVP L2 ....12 F7
　　ECCL WA10 ....8 F2
　　GOL/RIS/CU WA3 ....106 C5
　　NEWLW WA12 ....104 C2
　　RUNC WA7 ....18 F2
　　STHP PR8 ....2 F4
　　WARRS WA4 ....14 F8
　　WGNE/HIN WN2 ....69 J6
Lord St Boulevards *STHP* PR8 ....2 F4
Lord St West *STHP* PR8 ....2 E6
Lordy Cl *WGNNW/ST* WN6 ....56 D6
Loreburn Rd *WAV* L15 ....114 C7
Lorenzo Dr *NG/CROX* L11 ....98 B4
Loretto Dr *GR/UP/WCH* CH49 ....110 C7
Loretto Rd *WAL/EG* CH44 ....95 H8
Lorn Ct *BIRK* CH41 * 11 K5
Lorne Ct *CL/PREN* CH43 ....10 C8
Lorne Rd *CL/PREN* CH43 ....82 F4
　　CSBY/WL L22 ....82 E2
Lorne St *CHLY/EC* PR7 ....32 E6
　　EHL/KEN L7 ....114 A2
　　WGN WN1 ....5 J4
Lorn St *BIRK* CH41 ....11 K5
Lorton Av *RNFD/HAY* WA11 ....89 J5
Lorton St *TOX* L8 ....113 K6
Lostock Av *WARRW/BUR* WA5 * ...121 H5
Lostock Cl *WGNW/BIL/O* WN5 .....78 A4
Lostock Rd *CROS/BRETH* PR26 ...29 L2
Lothair Rd *ANF/KKDL* L4 ....97 J6
Lothian St *TOX* L8 ....113 J8
Lotus Gdns *STHEL* WA9 ....103 J6
Loudon Gv *TOX* L8 ....113 J7
Lough Gn *BEB* CH63 ....143 J3
Loughlin Dr *NWD/KWIPK* L33 ....74 D4
Loughrigg Av *RNFD/HAY* WA11 ...89 K4
Louis Braille Cl *NTHTN* L30 ....84 A1
Louis Pasteur Av *NTHTN* L30 ......84 B1
Loushers La *WARRS* WA4 ....137 M3
Lovage Cl *WARRW/BUR* WA5 ....122 E3
Lovelace Rd *ALL/GAR* L19 ....130 D6
Love La *VAUX/LVPD* L3 ....12 E1
　　WAL/EG CH44 ....111 K2
Lovel Rd *SPK/HALE* L24 ....146 F2
Lovel Ter *WDN* WA8 ....133 K8
Lovel Wy *SPK/HALE* L24 ....146 F2
Lovely La *WARRW/BUR* WA5 .....121 G7
Lovett Dr *RAIN/WH* L35 ....101 G8
Low Bank Rd *AIMK* WN4 ....91 G1
Lowcroft *SKEL* WN8 ....65 L2
Lowden Av *LITH* L21 ....83 K3
Lowe Av *WARRS* WA4 ....138 B1
Lowell St *ANF/KKDL* L4 ....97 H4
Lowe Mill La *WGNE/HIN* WN2 ....81 J3
Lower Alt Rd *HTWN* L38 ....70 B1
Lower Appleton Rd *WDN* WA8 ......16 F1
Lower Bank Vw *BTL* L20 ....6 E9
Lower Breck Rd *NPK/KEN* L6 ....97 M7
Lower Burgh Rd *CHLY/EC* PR7 ....43 J1
Lower Burgh Wy *CHLY/EC* PR7 ....43 J1
Lower Carr La *HTWN* L38 ....60 E9
Lower Castle St *CLVP* L2 ....12 E7
Lower Church St *WDN* WA8 ....16 C1
Lower Cl *HLWD* L26 ....132 C5
Lower Farm Rd *WLTN* L25 ....115 H6
Lower Flaybrick Rd
　　CL/PREN CH43 ....111 G5
Lower Gn *GR/UP/WCH* CH49 .....126 C2
Lower Hey *CSBY/BLUN* L23 ....71 K8
Lower Hill Dr *CHLYE* PR6 ....44 J1
Lower House La *WGNE/HIN* WN2 ...2 G5
　　WDN WA8 ....16 B5
Lower La *WLT/FAZ* L9 ....85 G1
Lower Longshoot *WGN* WN1 ....5 H1
Lower Lyndon Av
　　WGNNW/ST WN6 ....55 J7
Lower Mersey St *EP* CH65 ....156 E6
Lower Mersey Vw *BTL* L20 ....6 B5
Lower Milk St *VAUX/LVPD* L3 * 12 F5
Lower Prom *STHP* PR8 ....2 E3
Lower Rake La *FROD/HEL* WA6 ...166 D1
Lower Rd *HLWD* L26 ....132 D5
　　PS/BROM CH62 ....128 D7

Lower Robin Hood La
 FROD/HEL WA6 ....166 D2
Lower St Stephen St
 WGNNW/ST WN6 ....4 B3
Lowerson Crs NG/CROX L11 ...98 A5
Lowerson Rd NG/CROX L11 ...98 A5
Lower Thingwall La
 PEN/TH CH61 ....126 E7
Lower Wash La WARRS WA4 ...15 M9
Lowes Gn FMBY L37 ....59 K2
Lowe's La SKEL WN8 ....53 C5
Lowe St ECCL WA10 ....8 F4
 GOL/RIS/CU WA3 ....92 C5
Lowe St South ECCL WA10 ...8 F5
Loweswater Cl
 WARRN/WOL WA2 ....121 K2
Loweswater Crs
 RNFD/HAY WA11 ....90 C7
Loweswater Wy
 NWD/KWIPK L33 * 73 M8
Lowfield La BRSC L40 ......102 B8
Lowfield Rd DV/KA/FCH L14 ...114 C2
Lowfields Av WARRW/BUR WA5 ...154 F2
Lowfields Cl PS/BROM CH62 ...155 G2
Low Hl FROD/HEL WA6 .....165 M8
Lowlands Rd RUNC WA7 ....18 F4
Lowndes Rd NPK/KEN L6 ....97 M7
Lowood St LEIGH WN7 .....81 M8
Lowry Bank WAL/EG WA4 ...112 A2
Lowry Ct NWD/KWIPK L33 ...74 A2
 WARRW/BUR WA5 ....120 F7
Lowry Hill La BRSC L40 .....52 D3
Lowther Av AIN/FAZ L10 ....84 F3
 GOL/RIS/CU WA3 ....107 H1
 MGHL L31 ....73 G3
Lowther Crs ECCL WA10 ...101 K5
Lowther Dr RAIN/WH L35 ...117 K2
Lowther St TOX L8 ....113 J6
Lowton Gdns GOL/RIS/CU WA3 ...92 DB
Lowton Rd GOL/RIS/CU WA3 ...92 D4
Lowwood Gv BIRK CH41 ....11 H5
Low Wood Gv PEN/TH CH61 ...141 L1
Lowwood Rd BIRK CH41 ....11 H5
Low Wood St NPK/KEN L6 ...113 J5
Loxdale Cl TOX L8 ....113 J6
Loxdale Dr EP CH65 ....163 H1
Loxley Cl WARRW/BUR WA5 ...120 C5
Loxley Rd STHP PR8 ....3 M9
Loxton Crs WGNS/IIMK WN3 ...79 K2
Loyola Hey RAIN/WH L35 ...118 A3
Lucania St ALL/GAR L19 ....145 L1
Lucan Rd AIG/SPK L17 .....130 A3
Lucas Av CHLY/EC PR7 .....31 M6
Lucerne Rd WAL/EG WA4 ...111 M3
Lucerne St AIG/SPK L17 ....129 L2
Lucius Ct WLT/FAZ L9 ......84 B6
Lucknow St AIG/SPK L17 * ...129 L1
Ludlow SKEL WN8 ....65 L1
Ludlow Av WGNE/HIN WN2 ...81 J1
Ludlow Cl WARR WA1 ......122 D5
Ludlow Crs RUNC WA7 .....19 J8
Ludlow Dr EP CH65 ....21 G8
 ORM L39 ....50 F6
 WKBY CH48 ....124 D4
Ludlow Gv PS/BROM CH62 ...143 M4
Ludlow St ANF/KKDL L4 ....97 H4
 WGNNW/ST WN6 ....55 L2
Ludovic Ter WGN WN1 .....68 E1
Ludwig Rd ANF/KKDL L4 ....97 K8
Lugard Rd AIG/SPK L17 ....130 A3
Lugsdale Rd WDN WA8 .....16 D5
Lugsmore La ECCL WA10 ...101 L4
Luke St AIMK WN4 ....79 M8
 TOX L8 ....113 H7
 WAL/EG WA4 ....112 A3
Lulworth SKEL WN8 ....65 L1
Lulworth Av CSBY/WL L22 ...82 E4
Lulworth Dr WGNE/HIN WN2 ...81 J1
Lulworth Rd STHP PR8 ....2 C8
 WLTN L25 ....115 L8
Lumb Brook Rd WARRS WA4 ...138 A5
Lumber La WARRW/BUR WA5 ...146 A5
Lumby Av HUY L36 ....116 A2
Lumley St ALL/GAR L19 ....130 D7
Lunar Dr NTHTN L30 ....72 B8
Lunar Rd WLT/FAZ L9 ....84 D7
Lundy Dr EP CH65 ....163 L5
Lune Av MGHL L31 ....73 G3
Lune Gv LEIGH WN7 ....81 L8
Lunehurst GOL/RIS/CU WA3 ...93 G5
Lune Rd WGNE/HIN WN2 ...80 C3
Lunesdale Av WLT/FAZ L9 ...84 D6
Lune St CSBY/BLUN L23 ....83 G1
Lune Wy WDN WA8 ....133 L4
Lunsford Rd RAIN/WH L35 ...115 H1
Lunt Av NTHTN L30 ....84 C3
 RAIN/WH L35 ....117 G2
Lunt Rd BTL L20 ....83 L8
 SFTN L29 ....73 M1
 SFTN L29 ....72 A6
Lunt's Heath Rd WDN WA8 ...118 D8
Lupin Dr RNFD/HAY WA11 ...91 H7
Lupton Dr CSBY/BLUN L23 ...83 J1
Lupton St CHLY/EC PR7 ....32 E7
Lupus Wy GTS/LS CH66 ....163 H2
Lurdin La WGN WN1 ....56 D6
Luscombe Cl HLWD L26 ....132 C5
Lusitania Rd ANF/KKDL L4 ...97 J3
Luther Gv STHEL WA9 ......103 K3
Luton Gv ANF/KKDL L4 .....97 H5
Luton Rd EP CH65 ....156 E2
Luton St EV L5 ....96 F8
 WDN WA8 * 16 D6
Lutyens Cl ANF/KKDL L4 ...97 H6
Luxmore Rd ANF/KKDL L4 ...97 J4
Lycett Rd ANF/KKDL L4 ....97 G8
 WAL/EG WA4 ....95 G8
Lychgate WARRS WA4 .....137 H6
 WGNW/BIL/O WN5 .....68 A8
Lycroft Cl RUNC WA7 ......149 K7
Lydbrook Cl RF/TRAN CH42 ...128 B2
Lydbury Cl WARRW/BUR WA5 ...120 F3
Lydbury Crs KKBY L32 .....86 B5
Lydd Cl SPK/HALE L24 .....146 D1
Lydden Rd EP CH65 ....32 C6
Lydford Gn WGNNW/ST WN6 ...68 A6
Lydgate CHLY/EC PR7 ....32 E6
Lydia Ann St CLVPS L1 .....13 H9
Lydiate La CHLY/EC PR7 ....30 D4
 CSBY/BLUN L23 ....71 L7
 NSTN CH64 ....154 A5
 RUNC WA7 ....150 C6
 WLTN L25 ....131 M3
Lydiate Pk CSBY/BLUN L23 ...71 K7
Lydiate Rd BTL L20 ....83 L8
Lydiate Station Rd MGHL L31 ...61 G8
The Lydiate HES CH60 .....141 H6
Lydieth Lea NTHLY L27 ....116 A7
Lydney Rd HUY L36 ....115 K1
Lydstep Ct WARRW/BUR WA5 * ...5 L2
Lyefield Av WGN WN1 ......5 L2
Lyelake Cl KKBY L32 ....86 B4
Lyelake La BRSC L40 ....86 B4
Lyelake Rd KKBY L32 ......86 B4
Lyle St EV L5 ....96 F8
Lymbridge Dr HOR/BR BL6 ...57 M3

Lyme Cl HUY L36 ....100 C7
Lyme Cross Rd HUY L36 ...100 B7
Lyme Gv HUY L36 ....100 B8
 LYMM WA13 ....139 L3
Lyme St NEWLW WA12 ....104 A1
 RNFD/HAY WA11 ....91 G7
Lymington Gv WGNE/HIN WN2 ...84 B2
Lymington Av LYMM WA13 ...139 L2
Lymm Rd CL/PREN CH43 ...110 E6
 WARRS WA4 ....139 H2
Lymm St WGNE/HIN WN2 ...84 B2
Lynas Gdns ALL/GAR L19 ...130 D5
Lyncroft Rd WAL/EG WA4 ...84 D5
Lyndale Av WAL/EG WA4 ...111 L3
Lyndene Rd WLK PS/BROM CH62 ...115 J7
Lyndhurst SKEL WN8 ....65 K1
Lyndhurst Av CALD/MH L18 ...130 B2
 PEN/TH CH61 ....141 J2
Lyndhurst Cl PEN/TH CH61 ...141 J2
Lyndhurst Rd CALD/MH L18 ...130 B1
 CSBY/BLUN L23 ....83 J1
 HOY CH47 ....109 G4
 PEN/TH CH61 ....35 J3
 STHP PR8 ....35 J3
 WAL/NB CH45 ....95 H7
Lyndhurst Wy HUY L36 ...116 A3
Lyndon Av WGNNW/ST WN6 ...55 K6
Lyndon Dr CALD/MH L18 ...130 D1
Lyndon Gv RUNC WA7 ....19 J7
Lyndor Cl WLTN L25 ......131 K4
Lyndor Rd WLTN L25 .....131 K4
Lyneal Av GTS/LS CH66 ....162 E3
Lyneham RAIN/WH L35 ....117 H3
Lynham Av WGNNW/ST WN6 * ...120 D8
Lynholme Rd ANF/KKDL L4 ...97 K6
Lynmouth Cl WGNNW/ST WN6 ...68 C3
Lynmouth Rd AIG/SPK L17 ...129 L2
Lynnbank CL/PREN CH43 ...10 D9
Lynnbank Rd CALD/MH L18 ...114 F4
Lynn Cl ECCL WA10 ....101 L1
 RUNC WA7 ....149 L6
Lynndene GTS/LS CH66 ....155 M6
Lynscott Pl CHLDW L16 ....114 F1
Lynsted Rd DV/KA/FCH L14 ...115 H2
Lynton Av WGNNW/ST WN6 ...68 C3
Lynton Cl ALL/GAR L19 ....130 D5
 HES CH60 ....141 K7
 WARRW/BUR WA5 ....136 A3
Lynton Crs WDN WA8 ......134 A3
Lynton Dr BEB CH63 ....143 J2
 STHP PR8 ....35 G4
Lynton Gn WLTN L25 ......131 H1
Lynton Rd STHEL WA9 .....102 E8
Lynton Wy ECCL WA10 .....88 D7
Lynwood Av WAL/EG WA4 ...84 D5
 ORM L39 ....62 E2
 WAL/EG WA4 ....111 J2
 WARRS WA4 ....137 L6
Lynwood Cl SKEL WN8 .....81 M8
Lynwood Dr PEN/TH CH61 ...126 A7
Lynwood End ORM L39 * ...62 E2
Lynwood Gdns WLT/FAZ L9 ...84 B8
Lynwood Rd WLT/FAZ L9 ...84 M8
The Lynxway WD/CROXPK L12 ...98 F8
Lyon Cl ECCL WA10 ....10 F8
Lyon Rd ANF/KKDL L4 .....97 K7
Lyons Cl MOR/LEA CH46 ...110 A4
Lyons La CHLY/EC PR7 .....32 F6
 WARRS WA4 ....137 M7
Lyons La South CHLY/EC PR7 ...32 J1
Lyons Pl WLTN L25 ....131 M5
Lyons Rd MOR/LEA CH46 ...110 A4
 STHP PR8 ....2 F8
 WARRW/BUR WA5 ....136 B1
Lyon St AIMK WN4 ....79 H6
 ALL/GAR L19 ....145 L1
 ECCL WA10 ....8 C6
 WARRS WA4 ....138 B2
 WGNS/IIMK WN3 ......4 D5
Lyra Rd CSBY/WL L22 ......82 F4
Lyster Cl GOL/RIS/CU WA3 ...123 H2
Lyster Rd BTL L20 ....4 D4
Lytham Cl WLT/FAZ L9 .....85 H4
 WARRN/WOL WA2 ....121 M2
 WD/CROXPK L12 ....99 G7
Lytham Ct TKBY L32 ......85 K1
Lytham St CHLYE PR6 .....33 J8
 WDN WA8 ....134 D3
Lytham Wy WD/CROXPK L12 ...99 G7
Lythgoes La WARRN/WOL WA2 ...14 F4
Lytles St FMBY L37 ....59 J3
Lyttelton Rd AIG/SPK L17 ...130 A3
Lytton Av RF/TRAN CH42 ...128 B4
Lytton Gv LITH L21 ....83 J7
Lytton St NPK/KEN L6 .....13 M3

M

Mabel St WGNW/BIL/O WN5 ...68 A7
Maberry Cl WGNNW/ST WN6 ...54 F6
Mab La WD/CROXPK L12 ....99 H5
Macalpine Cl GR/UP/WCH CH49 ...110 C7
Macarthur Rd
 WARRW/BUR WA5 * 120 D7
Macauley Pl WGNS/IIMK WN3 ...79 H1
Macbeth St BTL L20 ....7 H9
Macclesfield Cl WGNE/HIN WN2 ...69 L8
Macdermott Rd WDN WA8 ...16 E6
Macdona Dr WKBY CH48 ...124 D5
Macdonald Av
 RNFD/HAY WA11 * 90 A8
 WGNS/IIMK WN3 ......79 J2
Macdonald Dr
 GR/UP/WCH CH49 .....125 M2
Macdonald Rd MOR/LEA CH46 ...109 L3
Macdonald St WAV L15 ...114 A5
 WGNW/BIL/O WN5 .....67 K7
Mace Rd NG/CROX L11 * ...99 J1
Macfarren St CLB/OSW/ST L13 ...114 C2
Mackay Cft CHLYE PR6 ....32 F5
Mackenzie Av WGNS/IIMK WN3 ...79 J2
Mackenzie Rd MOR/LEA CH46 ...110 D2
Mackenzie St NPK/KEN L6 ...97 J8
Mackenzie Cl CHLYE PR6 ...32 F5
Mackets Cl WLTN L25 .....131 L4
Macket's La WLTN L25 ....131 L4
Mack Gv NTHTN L30 ......72 B8
Macqueen St CLB/OSW/ST L13 ...114 C3
Maddock St CLB/OSW/ST L13 ...114 C3
Maddocks St BIRK CH41 ...10 F1
Maddrell St VAUX/LVPD L3 ...12 D1
Madelaine St TOX L8 ....113 J7

Madeley Cl WGNS/IIMK WN3 ...79 G2
 WKBY CH48 ....124 D4
Madeley Dr WKBY CH48 ...124 D4
Madeley St NPK/KEN L6 ...113 L1
Madeline McKenna Ct
 WDN WA8 * 133 L2
Madingley Ct CHTN/BK PR9 * ...25 H1
Madryn Av NWD/KWIPK L33 ...86 C5
Madryn St TOX L8 ....113 J8
Maelor Cl BEB CH63 ......143 K7
Maesbrook Cl CHTN/BK PR9 ...23 K8
Mafeking Cl WAV L15 .....114 B4
Mafeking Pl AIMK WN4 ...91 L2
Magazine Av WAL/NB CH45 ...95 K6
Magazine Brow WAL/NB CH45 ...95 L6
Magazine La PS/BROM CH62 ...144 A2
 WAL/NB CH45 ....95 K6
Magazine Rd PS/BROM CH62 ...143 M2
Magazines Prom WAL/NB CH45 ...95 L5
Magazine Wk PS/BROM CH62 * ...143 M2
Magdala St TOX L8 ....113 L6
Magdalen Dr AIMK WN4 ...91 H1
Magdalene Sq NTHTN L30 * ...84 B1
Maggots Nook Rd
 RNFD/HAY WA11 ....76 A3
Maghull La MGHL L31 ......73 L4
Maghull St CLVPS L1 * 112 F8
Magnolia Cl GTS/LS CH66 ...163 H4
Magnolia Dr RUNC WA7 ....18 F4
Magnolia Wk
 GR/UP/WCH CH49 .....125 L3
Magnum St EV L5 ....97 G8
Maguire Av BTL L20 ....7 J1
Mahon Av BTL L20 ....83 M7
Mahon Ct TOX L8 * 113 H6
Maiden Gdns EP CH65 .....20 F9
Maiden La CLB/OSW/ST L13 ...97 M6
Maidford Rd DV/KA/FCH L14 ...99 H8
Maidstone Cl WGNE/HIN WN2 ...81 L3
Maidstone Dr DV/KA/FCH L14 ...99 H8
Main Av ECCL WA10 ....101 L5
Main Cl RNFD/HAY WA11 ...90 C7
Main Dr AIN/FAZ L10 ......117 G4
Main Front RAIN/WH L35 ...117 G4
Main La GOL/RIS/CU WA3 ...106 A2
Main Rd PS/BROM CH62 ...143 K1
Mains Av WGNE/HIN WN2 ...80 B6
Mainside Rd KKBY L32 ....86 B4
Mains La BRSC L40 ....40 B7
Main St FROD/HEL WA6 ...160 C5
 RUNC WA7 ....150 B5
 WGNW/BIL/O WN5 .....78 A8
Maintree Crs SPK/HALE L24 ...147 J1
Mainwaring Rd PS/BROM CH62 ...143 M5
 WAL/EG WA4 ....111 M2
Mairesfield Av WARRS WA4 ...138 D3
Mairscough La ORM L39 ...61 J5
Maitland Cl TOX L8 ....113 K6
Maitland Rd WAL/NB CH45 ...95 L5
Maitland St TOX L8 ....113 K6
Major Cross St WDN WA8 ...16 D5
Major St EV L5 ....96 F7
 WGNW/BIL/O WN5 .....67 G8
Makerfield Dr NEWLW WA12 ...104 C1
Makerfield Wy NEWLW WA12 ...69 K6
Makinson Ar WGN WN1 ...4 E3
Makinson Av WGNE/HIN WN2 ...69 M6
Makin St ANF/KKDL L4 ....97 H3
Malcolm Av WARRN/WOL WA2 ...121 M4
Malcolm Crs BEB CH63 ...143 L7
Malcolm Gv EV L5 * 7 J9
Malcolm Pl WAV L15 ......114 B4
Malcolm St RUNC WA7 ....19 K4
Malden Rd NPK/KEN L6 ...113 L2
Maldon Cl HLWD L26 ......132 B7
 WGNE/HIN WN2 ....69 H3
Maldon Rd WGNNW/ST WN6 ...56 B5
Maldwyn Rd WAL/EG WA4 ...95 K8
Maley Cl TOX L8 ....129 J1
Malham Av WGNS/IIMK WN3 ...79 J3
Malham Cl LEIGH WN7 ....81 L8
Malhamdale Av RAIN/WH L35 ...117 M3
Malilia Pl AIMK WN4 * 79 G7
Malin Cl SPK/HALE L24 ...147 M3
Maliston Rd WARRW/BUR WA5 ...120 D8
Mallaby St BIRK CH41 .....10 B2
Mallard Cl HLWD L26 .....132 A4
 ORM L39 ....62 E3
 RUNC WA7 ....150 B8
 WARRN/WOL WA2 ....121 M2
 WD/CROXPK L12 ....99 G7
Mallard Gdns STHEL WA9 ...102 A7
Mallard Gv GOL/RIS/CU WA3 ...123 H2
The Mallards CHTN/BK PR9 ...25 L2
Mallard Wy MOR/LEA CH46 ...109 K7
 RNFD/HAY WA11 ....91 H7
Mallee Av CHTN/BK PR9 ...25 J2
Mallee Crs CHTN/BK PR9 ...25 J2
Malleson Rd CLB/OSW/ST L13 ...98 A6
Mallins Cl TOX L8 ....129 J1
Mallom Av CHLY/EC PR7 ...32 A4
Mallory Av MGHL L31 ....72 D1
Mallory Gv RNFD/HAY WA11 ...89 M7
Mallory Rd EP CH65 ......163 J1
 RF/TRAN CH42 ....127 M3
Mallowdale Cl PS/BROM CH62 ...144 A8
Mallow Rd NPK/KEN L6 ...113 L1
Mallow Wy HUY L36 ......116 B5
The Mall NPK/KEN L6 * 97 J8
Malmesbury Cl
 GR/UP/WCH CH49 .....125 L3
Malmesbury Pk RUNC WA7 ...150 F2
Malmesbury Rd NG/CROX L11 ...98 A3
Malpas Av CL/PREN CH43 ...127 J3
 WGN WN1 ....5 H1
Malpas Dr BEB CH63 ......128 A6
 WARRW/BUR WA5 ......136 E1
Malpas Gv WAL/NB CH45 ...95 H5
Malpas Rd EP CH65 ....163 H1
 NG/CROX L11 ....85 M8
 RUNC WA7 ....149 K6
 WAL/NB CH45 ....95 H5
Malpas Wy WARRW/BUR WA5 * ...136 E1
Malta Cl HUY L36 ....115 M2
Malta St TOX L8 ....113 H8
Malta Wk TOX L8 ....113 H8
Malt House Ct WAL/EG WA4 * ...88 E7
Maitkin La BRSC L40 ......40 D5
Maltmans Rd LYMM WA13 ...139 M2
Malton Av GOL/RIS/CU WA3 ...93 G6
Malton Cl LEIGH WN7 .....81 L7
 WDN WA8 ....117 J3
Malton Rd WLTN L25 .....131 L4
Malt St TOX L8 ....113 K5
Malvern Av DV/KA/FCH L14 ...115 H3
 EP CH65 ....20 D7
 HUY L36 ....116 A3
Malvern Cl AIMK WN4 ....91 K1
 HOR/BR BL6 ....45 J8
 KKBY L32 ....85 H1
 WARRW/BUR WA5 ......120 C5
 WGNS/IIMK WN3 ......78 E2
Malvern Crs DV/KA/FCH L14 ...115 H3

 WGNS/IIMK WN3 ....80 B1
 WGNW/BIL/O WN5 .....77 M8
Malvern Gv RF/TRAN CH42 ...127 M3
 WLT/FAZ L9 ....84 E3
Malvern Rd BTL L20 ....83 L8
 NPK/KEN L6 ....113 L2
 STHEL WA9 ....103 H2
Manfield SKEL WN8 ....65 J2
Manica Crs AIN/FAZ L10 ...85 H7
Manion Av BTL L20 ....61 K8
Manion Cl MGHL L31 .....61 K8
Manley Av PS/BROM CH62 ...92 B3
Manley Cl CL/PREN CH43 ...127 K2
Manley Gdns WARRW/BUR WA5 ...14 A5
Manley La FROD/HEL WA6 ...166 A8
Manley Pl STHEL WA9 .....102 A6
Manley Rd CSBY/WL L22 ...82 E3
 FROD/HEL WA6 ....166 F5
 HUY L36 ....116 C5
Manley Vw WGNS/IIMK WN3 ...5 L2
Manna Dr CHNE CH2 ......165 L2
Mannering Rd AIG/SPK L17 ...129 K1
Manners La HES CH60 ....141 G7
Manning Av WGNNW/ST WN6 ...68 B4
Manningham Rd NPK/KEN L6 ...97 K7
Manning Rd STHP PR8 .....35 M3
Manning St ECCL WA10 ...8 E6
Mannington Cl HOY CH47 ...109 G5
Manns Av WGNE/HIN WN2 ...80 F5
Mann Island VAUX/LVPD L3 ...12 D8
Mann St TOX L8 ....113 G7
Manorbier Crs WLT/FAZ L9 ...97 J2
Manor Av BRSC L40 ....51 M3
 CSBY/BLUN L23 ....70 F8
 GOL/RIS/CU WA3 ....92 E5
 NEWLW WA12 ....104 B1
 RAIN/WH L35 ....117 M3
Manor Ct AIMK WN4 ......90 A2
 BTL L20 ....7 M6
 NSTN CH64 ....152 E6
 WARR WA1 ....122 F6
Manor Crs BRSC L40 ......51 M3
 WLTN L25 ....131 K4
Manor Dr BRSC L40 ....51 M3
 CSBY/BLUN L23 ....70 F8
 GR/UP/WCH CH49 .....125 J3
 NTHTN L30 ....84 D2
Manor Farm Ct CH/BCN CH1 ...162 D5
Manor Farm Rd HUY L36 ...116 B4
Manor Fell RUNC WA7 ....150 D6
Manor Gdns BRSC L40 ....51 M3
 SKEL WN8 ....65 H4
 WGNW/BIL/O WN5 .....67 K5
Manor Gv CL/PREN CH43 ...10 B6
 RNFD/HAY WA11 ....89 J3
 SKEL WN8 ....65 H4
Manor Hl CL/PREN CH43 ...10 B6
Manor House Cl MGHL L31 ...72 E4
 RNFD/HAY WA11 ....77 G2
Manor House Dr SKEL WN8 ...65 L8
Manorial Rd North NSTN CH64 ...152 E5
Manorial Rd South NSTN CH64 ...152 E5
Manor La GTS/LS CH66 ...162 F2
 RF/TRAN CH42 ....128 C3
 WAL/NB CH45 ....95 L8
Manor Ldg FMBY L37 ....59 G1
Manor Ms WAL/NB CH45 * ...95 L8
Manor Park Av RUNC WA7 ...150 E1
Manor Park Dr GTS/LS CH66 ...162 F3
Manor Pl PS/BROM CH62 ...128 F8
Manor Rd BEB CH63 ....142 B4
 BRSC L40 ....51 M3
 CHTN/BK PR9 ....25 J3
 CSBY/BLUN L23 ....70 E8
 FROD/HEL WA6 ....160 E4
 HOY CH47 ....108 E5
 PEN/TH CH61 ....125 M7
 PS/BROM CH62 ....144 A7
 RNFD/HAY WA11 ....91 J3
 RUNC WA7 ....149 M5
 WAL/EG WA4 ....95 K8
 WDN WA8 ....133 K4
 WGNNW/ST WN6 ....55 H7
 WLTN L25 ....131 K4
Manorside Cl
 GR/UP/WCH CH49 .....110 B7
Manor St GOL/RIS/CU WA3 ...92 D4
 STHEL WA9 ....9 L8
 WGN WN1 ....5 H1
 WGNW/BIL/O WN5 .....67 K5
Manor Vw WD/CROXPK L12 ...99 H4
Manor Wy WLTN L25 ......131 K4
Manorwood Dr RAIN/WH L35 ...117 G3
Mansart Cl AIMK WN4 ....91 M2
Manse Av WGNNW/ST WN6 ...42 B7
Manse Gdns NEWLW WA12 ...104 F1
Mansell Cl WDN WA8 .....118 E6
Mansell Dr HLWD L26 ....132 A7
Mansell Rd NPK/KEN L6 ...113 K2
Mansfield Cl GOL/RIS/CU WA3 ...123 J1
Mansfield Rd EP CH65 ....163 J4
 VAUX/LVPD L3 ....13 J4
Mansion Dr NG/CROX L11 ...98 D1
Manston Cl CHLY/EC PR7 ...32 A4
Manston Rd WARRW/BUR WA5 ...136 B2
Manton Rd NPK/KEN L6 ...113 L2
Manuel Perez Rd
 WARRW/BUR WA5 .....120 D7
Manvers Rd CHLDW L16 ...115 G4
Manville Rd WAL/NB CH45 ...95 K6
Manville St STHEL WA9 ...102 E4
Manx Jane's La CHTN/BK PR9 ...25 J1
Manx Rd WARRS WA4 ....137 K2
Maori Dr FROD/HEL WA6 ...160 E4
Maple Av BRSC L40 ....51 M3
 GOL/RIS/CU WA3 ....93 H6
 GTS/LS CH66 ....155 L7
 NEWLW WA12 ....104 F3
 RNFD/HAY WA11 ....90 D2
 RUNC WA7 ....19 M7
 WARR WA1 ....161 J1
 WDN WA8 * 16 F1

 WD/CROXPK L12 ....98 F2
 WGNW/BIL/O WN5 .....77 M8
Maple Crs HUY L36 ....116 B3
 WARRW/BUR WA5 .....136 B1
Mapledale Rd CALD/MH L18 ...114 C8
Maple Dr NPK/KEN L6 * ...80 D6
Maple Gv CHLYE PR6 .....32 F2
 EP CH65 ....101 L2
 GTS/LS CH66 ....163 J4
 PS/BROM CH62 ....143 L5
 RAIN/WH L35 ....101 G4
 TOX L8 ....137 M2
Maple Rd WARR WA1 .....123 G6
 WARRN/WOL WA2 ....105 K7
Maple St AIMK WN4 ......79 J7
 BIRK CH41 ....3 M6
 STHP PR8 ....3 M6
Mapleton Cl CL/PREN CH43 ...127 J2
Mapleton Dr RUNC WA7 ...161 H2
Maple Tree Gv HES CH60 ...141 L4
Maplewood GTS/LS CH66 ...86 B5
Maplewood Cl NTHLY L27 ...116 A8
 SKEL WN8 ....65 J1
Maplewood Gv CL/PREN CH43 ...111 G5
Mapplewell Crs
 WARRW/BUR WA5 .....120 C7
Marathon Cl NPK/KEN L6 ...13 M2
Marble Cl BTL L20 ....7 G7
Marbury Gdns EP CH65 ...156 B7
Marbury Gv WGNNW/ST WN6 ...56 A5
Marbury Rd KKBY L32 ....85 L3
Marbury St WARRS WA4 ...15 G8
Marc Av MGHL L31 ....85 K1
Marcham Wy NG/CROX L11 ...98 D4
Marchant St NTHTN L30 ...84 C5
Marchbank WGNE/HIN WN2 ...69 J3
Marchfield Rd WLT/FAZ L9 ...84 B8
March Rd NPK/KEN L6 ....97 M8
Marchwiel Rd EP CH65 ....156 B7
Marchwood Wy WLTN L25 ...115 M1
Marcien Wy WDN WA8 ...134 B2
Marcot Rd NPK/KEN L6 ...113 M1
Marcross Cl WARRW/BUR WA5 ...121 G4
Marcus St BIRK CH41 .....3 G2
Mardale Av RNFD/HAY WA11 ...89 K5
 WARRN/WOL WA2 ....121 L2
Mardale Cl NTHLY L27 ....132 C2
 STHP PR8 ....47 K1
Mardale Lawn NTHLY L27 ...132 C2
Mardale Rd HUY L36 .....116 B2
Mareth Cl CALD/MH L18 ...114 F6
Marewood CHLY/EC PR7 ...32 D3
Marford Rd WD/CROXPK L12 ...98 D6
Marfords Av BEB CH63 ....143 L6
Margaret Av BTL L20 .....83 M8
 STHEL WA9 ....102 E6
 WARR WA1 ....14 C1
 WGNNW/ST WN6 ....67 L1
Margaret Ct WDN WA8 * ...16 E6
Margaret Rd ANF/KKDL L4 ...97 M7
 CSBY/BLUN L23 ....83 G8
Margaret's La GTS/LS CH66 ...155 J6
Margaret St NPK/KEN L6 ...113 L1
 STHEL WA9 * 9 J4
 WGNE/HIN WN2 ....69 M7
 EV L5 ....7 J9
Margery Rd ECCL WA10 ...101 L4
Marian Av NEWLW WA12 ...104 A2
Marian Cl RAIN/WH L35 ...117 L3
The Marian Cl NTHTN L30 ...84 A1
 RAIN/WH L35 ....117 K3
Marian Dr MOR/LEA CH46 ...110 A5
 RAIN/WH L35 ....117 K3
Marian Rd RNFD/HAY WA11 ...91 G6
Marians Dr ORM L39 .....51 G5
The Marian Sq NTHTN L30 ...84 A2
The Marian Wy NTHTN L30 ...84 A2
Maria Rd WLT/FAZ L9 .....97 H2
Marie Curie Av NTHTN L30 ...84 B1
Marie Dr WARRS WA4 ....138 F3
Marigold Cl WGNW/BIL/O WN5 * ...67 M6
Marigold Wy STHEL WA9 ...103 J6
Marina Av LITH L21 ....83 K6
 STHEL WA9 ....103 H5
 WARRW/BUR WA5 ......136 D1
Marina Crs HUY L36 .....115 M4
 NTHTN L30 ....84 C4
Marina Dr EP CH65 ....20 C5
 WARRN/WOL WA2 ....121 L4
 WGNW/BIL/O WN5 .....67 M8
Marina Gv RUNC WA7 ....19 K4
Marina La RUNC WA7 ....151 G6
Marina Rd CHTN/BK PR9 ...22 E7
The Marina CSBY/WL L22 * ...82 E3
Marina Village RUNC WA7 ...151 G6
Marine Crs CSBY/WL L22 ...82 F4
Marine Dr CHTN/BK PR9 ...22 E7
 HES CH60 ....140 F6
Marine Gate Man CHTN/BK PR9 * ...3 H1
Marine House VAUX/LVPD L3 * ...112 F7
Marine Pde STHP PR8 ....2 E1
Marine Pk WKBY CH48 ...124 D1
Marine Prom WAL/NB CH45 ...95 K4
Mariner Cl RUNC WA7 ....150 F7
Mariners Rd CSBY/BLUN L23 ...82 E8
 WAL/NB CH45 ....95 K4
Mariners Whf VAUX/LVPD L3 ...112 E7
Marine Ter CSBY/WL L22 ...82 E2
Marion Dr RUNC WA7 ....149 H7
Marion Gv CALD/MH L18 ...114 E5
Marion Pl WGNE/HIN WN2 ...80 B5
Marion Rd BTL L20 ....7 K5
Marion St BIRK CH41 .....11 K5
Maritime Cl NEWLW WA12 ...104 F1
 STHP PR8 ....2 F7
Maritime Ct NTHTN L30 ...72 B8
Maritime Pk BIRK CH41 * ...10 F7
Maritime Pl VAUX/LVPD L3 * ...13 J4
Maritime Vw RF/TRAN CH42 ...127 M2
Maritime Wy CLVPS L1 ...13 G9
Mariton Cl CALD/MH L18 ...130 F3
Mark Av GTS/LS CH66 ....162 E1
Market Ap AIMK WN4 * ...91 K2
Market Ga WARR WA1 ....14 E6
Market Pl BIRK CH41 .....11 K5
 CHLY/EC PR7 ....44 C7
 PR/KW L34 ....100 F7
 WGN WN1 ....4 E4
 WGNNW/ST WN6 ....56 A4
Market St BIRK CH41 .....11 K5
 CHLY/EC PR7 ....32 E5
 CHLY/EC PR7 ....44 C7
 ECCL WA10 ....8 G6
 EP CH65 ....6 D6
 HOY CH47 ....108 D6
 NEWLW WA12 ....104 F2
 STHP PR8 ....2 F4
 WDN WA8 ....20 B1
 WGNE/HIN WN2 ....69 M8
 WGNE/HIN WN2 ....69 M8
 WGNNW/ST WN6 ....56 A4
Markfield Crs RNFD/HAY WA11 ...9 M1

Mar - Mid 193

WLTN L25 131 M4
Markfield Rd BTL L20 83 K8
Markham Dr STHP PR8 36 A3
Markham Gv BIRK CH41 111 H5
Markland St WGN WN1 5 K5
Mark Rake PS/BROM CH62 143 M4
Mark Rd HTWN L38 70 B1
Mark St EV L5 97 G7
Marksway PEN/TH CH61 141 J1
Marland SKEL WN8 65 J1
Marlborough SKEL WN8 65 J1
Marlborough Av MGHL L31 72 F2
NTHTN L30 84 C3
WGNS/IIMK WN3 80 B1
Marlborough Crs WARRS WA4 138 B3
WDN WA8 118 C8
Marlborough Dr
FROD/HEL WA6 166 D3
Marlborough Gv CL/PREN CH43 10 D9
Marlborough Pl VAUX/LVPD L3 * 12 F4
Marlborough Rd CHTN/BK PR9 3 K3
CLB/OSW/ST L13 97 M7
CSBY/WL L22 83 G5
EP CH65 20 E9
PR/KW L34 101 G6
Marlborough St CHLYE PR6 33 G4
VAUX/LVPD L3 12 F4
Marlborough Wk EP CH65 20 D9
Marlbrook Rd WLTN L25 115 K7
Marldon Av CSBY/BLUN L23 83 G3
Marldon Rd WD/CROXPK L12 98 D5
Marled Hey STBRV L28 99 J5
Marley Cl RAIN/WH L35 118 A4
Marlfield La PEN/TH CH61 141 J1
Marlfield Rd WARRS WA4 138 C3
WD/CROXPK L12 98 D7
Marl Gv WGNW/BIL/O WN5 77 M1
Marline Av BEB CH63 143 L7
Marling Cl FROD/HEL WA6 160 F7
Marling Pk WDN WA8 133 K4
Marlow Cl GOL/RIS/CU WA3 106 E8
Marlow Ct CHLY/EC PR7 44 B7
Marlowe Cl ALL/GAR L19 130 E8
WDN WA8 16 A2
WGNS/IIMK WN3 68 C8
Marlowe Dr WD/CROXPK L12 98 C7
Marlowe Rd NSTN CH64 153 G5
WAL/EG CH44 111 J1
Marl Rd NTHTN L30 84 D2
NWD/KWIPK L33 86 E2
Marlsford St NPK/KEN L6 113 L2
Marlston Av PEN/TH CH61 126 B7
Marlston Pl RUNC WA7 149 K7
Marlwood Av WAL/EG CH44 95 G8
Marmaduke St EHL/KEN L7 113 K4
Marmion Av BTL L20 84 A6
Marmion Cl GOL/RIS/CU WA3 93 G4
Marmion Rd AIG/SPK L17 129 K1
HOY CH47 108 D6
Marmonde St ANF/KKDL L4 97 G5
Marnwood Rd KKBY L32 85 M4
Marple Cl CL/PREN CH43 127 G2
WGNNW/ST WN6 55 J3
Marquis St BIRK CH41 11 J9
PS/BROM CH62 128 D6
VAUX/LVPD L3 13 K6
Marram Cl MOR/LEA CH46 110 C4
Marrick Cl WGNS/IIMK WN3 79 J3
Marron Av WARRN/WOL WA2 121 K3
Marryat Cl WARRN/WOL WA2 105 J7
Marsden Av ECCL WA10 8 A3
WARRS WA4 138 C1
Marsden Cl CHLY/EC PR7 30 D6
WAL/EG CH44 95 M8
Marsden Ct WDN WA8 134 A1
Marsden Rd CHTN/BK PR9 25 G6
HLWD L26 132 B7
Marsden St NPK/KEN L6 113 J2
WGN WN1 4 F3
WGNS/IIMK WN3 80 A1
WGNW/BIL/O WN5 68 B6
Marsden Wy NPK/KEN L6 * 113 J2
Marshall Av STHEL WA9 * 102 E5
WARRW/BUR WA5 121 H3
Marshall Pl VAUX/LVPD L3 * 12 F2
Marshall Rd WARR WA1 122 F6
Marshallsay FMBY L37 59 J3
Marshall's Cl MGHL L31 72 E1
Marshalls Cross Rd STHEL WA9 102 D7
Marshall St BIRK CH41 10 F2
Marsham Cl
GR/UP/WCH CH49 * 110 C6
Marsham Rd WLTN L25 115 L8
Marsh Av BTL L20 84 A7
Marsh Brows FMBY L37 59 G3
The Marshes La
KIRK/FR/WA PR4 27 J4
Marshfield Cl HUY L36 116 B2
Marshfield Ct MOR/LEA CH46 110 A2
Marshfield Rd NG/CROX L11 98 D4
Marshgate WDN WA8 133 K7
Marshgate Pl FROD/HEL WA6 160 E3
Marshgate Rd NG/CROX L11 98 D3
Marsh Gn WGNW/BIL/O WN5 67 M4
Marsh Hall Rd WDN WA8 134 D1
Marsh House La
WARRN/WOL WA2 15 H2
Marshlands Rd NSTN CH64 153 G8
WAL/NB CH45 95 G7
Marsh La BEB CH63 127 L6
BTL L20 6 E2
CHNE CH2 158 C7
CHNE CH2 165 K2
FROD/HEL WA6 160 C5
HTWN L38 70 F1
RUNC WA7 150 B2
WARRW/BUR WA5 135 L3
WGN WN1 4 F3
Marsh Moss La BRSC L40 38 E6
Marsh Rd CHTN/BK PR9 23 J4
Marsh Rw WGNE/HIN WN2 81 J1
Marshside Cl TOX L8 113 H8
Marshside Rd CHTN/BK PR9 22 A8
CHTN/BK PR9 25 J2
Marsh St BTL L20 7 J9
STHEL WA9 9 M4
WARR WA1 15 K2
WDN WA8 16 C8
Marshway Dr NEWLW WA12 104 D1
Marsland Gv STHEL WA9 103 G5
Marson St WARRN/WOL WA2 14 D4
Marston Cl CL/PREN CH43 127 H3
PS/BROM CH62 155 G2
Marston Crs HTWN L38 70 C3
Marston Gdns EP CH65 156 B7
Marten Av BEB CH63 143 L6
Martensen St EHL/KEN L7 113 K4
Martham Cl WARRS WA4 138 C2
Martin Av ECCL WA10 89 H7
NEWLW WA12 91 K8
WARRN/WOL WA2 121 M4
Martin Cl CALD/MH L18 130 C4
PEN/TH CH61 125 L7
RAIN/WH L35 117 J1
RUNC WA7 150 C6
Martindale Crs
WGNW/BIL/O WN5 68 A7
Martindale Gv RUNC WA7 149 M8
Martindale Rd CALD/MH L18 114 F8
PS/BROM CH62 144 A4
RNFD/HAY WA11 89 K3
Martine Cl MGHL L31 85 K1
Martin Gv RAIN/WH L35 101 G8
Martinhall Rd WLT/FAZ L9 98 B1
Martin La BRSC L40 38 A5
Martin Rd CALD/MH L18 130 C4
FROD/HEL WA6 160 D5
Martins Av CHLY/EC PR7 44 A3
Martins La SKEL WN8 65 M6
WAL/EG CH44 111 L1
Martland Av AIN/FAZ L10 85 G2
GOL/RIS/CU WA3 92 F6
WGNNW/ST WN6 55 H8
Martland Crs WGNNW/ST WN6 68 A2
Martland Mill La
WGNW/BIL/O WN5 67 M3
Martland Rd WLTN L25 131 L1
Mart La BRSC L40 39 G8
Martlesham Crs
GR/UP/WCH CH49 125 K2
Martlett Rd WD/CROXPK L12 98 F8
Martock RAIN/WH L35 117 H3
Marton Cl GOL/RIS/CU WA3 107 G1
SPK/HALE L24 146 F3
Marton Gn SPK/HALE L24 * 146 F3
Marton Rd HUY L36 100 A7
Marton St WGN WN1 4 E2
Marus Av WGNS/IIMK WN3 79 H2
Marvin St NPK/KEN L6 113 J2
Marwick Cl WGNNW/ST WN6 55 M3
Mary Av STHP PR8 35 G7
Marybone VAUX/LVPD L3 12 F5
Maryfield Cl GOL/RIS/CU WA3 92 C6
Maryhill Rd RUNC WA7 19 G8
Maryland La MOR/LEA CH46 109 M4
Maryland St CLVPS L1 13 K9
Marylebone Av STHEL WA9 102 B7
Marylebone Pl WGN WN1 68 F2
Mary Rd BTL L20 83 M7
Mary Stockton Ct LITH L21 * 83 J7
Mary St STHEL WA9 119 G2
WDN WA8 17 K5
Maryton Gra CALD/MH L18 130 F3
Maryville Cl EP CH65 20 D1
Maryville Rd PR/KW L34 101 G7
Marywell Cl STHEL WA9 102 F6
Masefield Av LEIGH WN7 81 M6
WDN WA8 16 B4
WGNW/BIL/O WN5 67 J7
Masefield Cl PS/BROM CH62 128 C6
Masefield Crs NTHTN L30 83 M5
Masefield Dr WGNS/IIMK WN3 79 H1
Masefield Gv CHLDW L16 115 H5
ECCL WA10 8 A1
Masefield Pl NTHTN L30 84 A5
Masefield Rd CSBY/BLUN L23 71 L7
Maskell Rd CLB/OSW/ST L13 114 B2
Mason Av WARR WA1 122 A5
WDN WA8 134 C1
Mason Cl AIMK WN4 91 M1
GTS/LS CH66 162 F3
Mason St CHLYE PR6 33 G3
CSBY/WL L22 82 F4
EHL/KEN L7 113 J4
RUNC WA7 19 L2
WAL/NB CH45 95 K5
WARR WA1 15 H6
WGNE/HIN WN2 80 D5
WGNS/IIMK WN3 4 C5
WLTN L25 131 J3
Massam Cl RNFD/HAY WA11 76 C7
Massam's La FMBY L37 47 G7
Massey Av LYMM WA13 139 J3
WARRW/BUR WA5 121 H3
Massey Brook La LYMM WA13 139 K3
Masseyfield Rd RUNC WA7 150 C8
Massey Pk WAL/NB CH45 95 J8
Massey St BIRK CH41 11 G2
STHEL WA9 102 E5
Masters Wy ALL/GAR L19 145 M1
Mather Av CALD/MH L18 130 D1
GOL/RIS/CU WA3 93 G7
RUNC WA7 18 B9
STHEL WA9 103 G2
Mather Rd CL/PREN CH43 10 C8
Mathers Cl WARRN/WOL WA2 122 C1
Matheson Dr WGNW/BIL/O WN5 67 M5
Mathew St CLVP L2 12 F7
Mathieson Rd WDN WA8 134 A8
Matlock Av WLT/FAZ L9 84 C7
Matlock Cl WARRW/BUR WA5 120 C5
Matlock Crs STHP PR8 35 K1
Matlock Rd STHP PR8 35 K2
Matterdale Cl FROD/HEL WA6 160 F6
Matthew Cl WAL/EG CH44 112 A3
Matthews St WARR WA1 15 J2
Matthew St WAL/EG CH44 112 A3
Matty's La FROD/HEL WA6 160 C6
Maud St CHLY/EC PR7 32 D7
TOX L8 113 J7
Maunders Ct CSBY/BLUN L23 71 H8
Mauretania Rd ANF/KKDL L4 97 J3
Mavis Dr CHLY/EC PR7 43 G4
GR/UP/WCH CH49 126 C2
Mawdsley Av WARR WA1 123 G6
Mawdsley Cl FMBY L37 59 K2
Mawdsley Ter ORM L39 51 H5
Mawson Cl WARRW/BUR WA5 120 F5
Max Rd DV/KA/FCH L14 99 H8
Maxton Rd NPK/KEN L6 113 L2
Maxwell Cl EP CH65 163 J3
GR/UP/WCH CH49 110 C7
Maxwell Pl CLB/OSW/ST L13 98 B7
Maxwell Rd CLB/OSW/ST L13 98 B7
Maxwell St ECCL WA10 8 D6
GOL/RIS/CU WA3 107 G7
May Av LEIGH WN7 81 M7
WAL/EG CH44 111 M3
WGNE/HIN WN2 80 E6
Maybank Cl CHTN/BK PR9 25 J4
Maybank Gv AIG/SPK L17 130 B4
Maybank Rd RF/TRAN CH42 127 M1
Mayberry Gv WARRN/WOL WA2 122 C4
Maybury Wy AIG/SPK L17 129 L3
May Cl LITH L21 83 K7
Mayer Av BEB CH63 143 H1
Mayew Rd PEN/TH CH61 126 B7
Mayfair Av CSBY/BLUN L23 71 G8
DV/KA/FCH L14 115 H2
Mayfair Cl HTWN L38 70 B3
NPK/KEN L6 113 K1
WARRW/BUR WA5 119 M6
Mayfair Dr WGNE/HIN WN2 69 M3
WGNS/IIMK WN3 79 H3
Mayfair Gv WDN WA8 133 M4
Mayfayre Av MGHL L31 61 K8
Mayfield ANF/KKDL L4 97 G5
Mayfield Av CHLYE PR6 44 C6
FMBY L37 58 E4
STHEL WA9 102 A5
WDN WA8 133 K4
Mayfield Cl WD/CROXPK L12 98 E7
Mayfield Ct FMBY L37 47 G8
Mayfield Dr GOL/RIS/CU WA3 93 L5
PS/BROM CH62 144 D7
Mayfield Gdns ALL/GAR L19 130 C6
Mayfield Rd ALL/GAR L19 130 C6
BEB CH63 143 J2
CHLYE PR6 32 F4
SKEL WN8 66 C6
WAL/NB CH45 95 G8
WARRS WA4 138 C3
WGNW/BIL/O WN5 67 K5
Mayfields North
PS/BROM CH62 128 D6
Mayfields South
PS/BROM CH62 128 D6
Mayfield St AIMK WN4 * 91 J2
Mayflower Av SPK/HALE L24 131 J7
Maynard St TOX L8 113 K6
May Pl VAUX/LVPD L3 13 K8
Maypole Ct NTHTN L30 71 M8
May Rd HES CH60 141 J5
May St BTL L20 7 H2
GOL/RIS/CU WA3 92 D3
LEIGH WN7 81 L8
VAUX/LVPD L3 13 K8
Maythorn Av GOL/RIS/CU WA3 106 C6
Maytree Cl NTHLY L27 115 L7
May Tree Dr WGN WN1 68 D2
Maytree Wk SKEL WN8 65 K1
Mayville Rd CALD/MH L18 114 D8
Mazenod Ct VAUX/LVPD L3 13 G4
Mazzini Cl EV L5 97 G8
McBride St ALL/GAR L19 130 E7
McCarthy Cl GOL/RIS/CU WA3 123 J2
Mc Clellan Pl WDN WA8 16 E2
McCormack Av STHEL WA9 103 G1
McCormack Dr WGN WN1 5 H4
McCulloch St STHEL WA9 9 K5
McFarlane Av ECCL WA10 101 L1
McGarva Wy EP CH65 20 D6
McGough Cl STHEL WA9 118 C2
McGregor St EV L5 97 G8
McKee Av WARRN/WOL WA2 121 K3
McKeown Cl EV L5 96 F8
McMinnis Av STHEL WA9 103 J3
McVinnie Rd RAIN/WH L35 101 H7
Mead Av LITH L21 83 L5
Meade Cl RAIN/WH L35 117 M4
Meade Rd CLB/OSW/ST L13 98 A7
Meadfoot Rd MOR/LEA CH46 109 M4
Meadow Av STHEL WA9 118 F2
STHP PR8 35 L1
WARRS WA4 137 J3
Meadow Bank MGHL L31 72 D3
ORM L39 * 51 H8
Meadowbank Cl WD/CROXPK L12 99 G8
Meadowbridge Cl BRSC L40 64 A1
Meadowbrook BRSC L40 51 M3
Meadow Brook Cl AIN/FAZ L10 85 K6
Meadowbrook Rd
MOR/LEA CH46 109 M6
Meadow Brow CHTN/BK PR9 22 F8
Meadow Cl BRSC L40 64 A1
FROD/HEL WA6 166 D3
NSTN CH64 153 G7
NSTN CH64 154 B5
SKEL WN8 65 M6
WDN WA8 133 M2
Meadow Clough SKEL WN8 65 K1
Meadow Crs GR/UP/WCH CH49 126 D3
Meadow Cft NSTN CH64 154 A5
Meadowcroft AIMK WN4 79 H7
CHLY/EC PR7 31 K2
FMBY L37 59 H3
HES CH60 141 L4
SKEL WN8 65 K1
STHEL WA9 102 E7
Meadowcroft Pk
WD/CROXPK L12 114 F1
Meadowcroft Rd HOY CH47 109 G4
Meadow Dr HUY L36 116 B5
ORM L39 62 E3
Meadowfield SKEL WN8 66 C6
Meadowfield Cl RF/TRAN CH42 128 B3
WLT/FAZ L9 84 C6
Meadow Hey BTL L20 83 J8
Meadow Hey Cl WLTN L25 131 K2
Meadowlands CHLY/EC PR7 42 F1
Meadow La BRSC L40 39 L5
BRSC L40 39 M2
BRSC L40 52 E2
CROS/BRETH PR26 28 F4
EP CH65 20 E3
MGHL L31 73 G4
NSTN CH64 154 A4
RF/TRAN CH42 128 B3
STHEL WA9 103 H4
STHP PR8 47 M2
WARRN/WOL WA2 122 C3
WD/CROXPK L12 98 D6
Meadow Oak Dr WLTN L25 131 J1
Meadow Pk RF/TRAN CH42 128 B3
Meadow Pit La WGNE/HIN WN2 57 K5
Meadow Rd WKBY CH48 125 H2
Meadows Cl WGNE/HIN WN2 69 M8
Meadows Gn GOL/RIS/CU WA3 93 G8
Meadowside CROS/BRETH PR26 29 J3
MOR/LEA CH46 110 D1
Meadowside Av AIMK WN4 79 J5
Meadowside Dr
NWD/KWIPK L33 74 B7
Meadowside Rd
PS/BROM CH62 143 M6
WGNE/HIN WN2 81 J1
Meadows St WGNNW/ST WN6 4 A2
The Meadows CHLY/EC PR7 41 M3
NSTN CH64 153 H7
RAIN/WH L35 117 L3
STHP PR8 * 47 M1
Meadow St CHLYE PR6 44 C7
WAL/NB CH45 95 J5
The Meadow
GR/UP/WCH CH49 126 D2
Meadowvale Dr
WGNW/BIL/O WN5 67 L7
Meadow Vw CHNE CH2 165 J2
LITH L21 83 K2
STHP PR8 35 M1
Meadow View Dr
FROD/HEL WA6 160 C6
Meadow Wk PEN/TH CH61 141 G2
RUNC WA7 * 150 B6
Meadow Wy CHLY/EC PR7 42 F5
WD/CROXPK L12 98 D4
Mead Rd WARR WA1 122 C5
Meadway GOL/RIS/CU WA3 92 F5
GR/UP/WCH CH49 110 D7
GTS/LS CH66 155 K6
HES CH60 141 H7
MGHL L31 72 D6
NTHTN L30 84 B3
PS/BROM CH62 143 L3
RAIN/WH L35 117 H1
RUNC WA7 149 M4
SKEL WN8 65 J1
WAL/NB CH45 95 J8
WAV L15 114 E5
WDN WA8 133 J4
WGNE/HIN WN2 5 L6
Mealhouse La CHLY/EC PR7 32 E5
The Meander WD/CROXPK L12 99 G4
Measham Cl RNFD/HAY WA11 9 L1
Measham Wy WD/CROXPK L12 99 G2
Medbourne Crs KKBY L32 86 B5
Medea St EV L5 97 G7
Medlar Wy AIMK WN4 79 H8
Medlock St ANF/KKDL L4 97 G5
Medlock Wy WGNE/HIN WN2 80 C3
Medway Cl AIMK WN4 * 79 H7
LEIGH WN7 93 L5
WARRN/WOL WA2 122 A3
Medway Pl WGNW/BIL/O WN5 67 M6
Medway Rd GOL/RIS/CU WA3 107 J3
RF/TRAN CH42 128 C3
Meeting La WARRW/BUR WA5 119 M8
Melbreck SKEL WN8 65 J1
Melbreck Rd CALD/MH L18 130 D4
Melbury Ct GOL/RIS/CU WA3 107 H7
Melbury Rd DV/KA/FCH L14 99 K7
Melda Cl NPK/KEN L6 13 M4
Meldon Cl NG/CROX L11 98 E3
Meldreth Cl FMBY L37 58 E4
Meldrum Rd WAV L15 114 D7
Melford Cl CHLYE PR6 33 G2
Melford Ct WARR WA1 * 122 F5
Melford Dr AIMK WN4 91 J1
CL/PREN CH43 127 G4
RUNC WA7 19 L6
WGNW/BIL/O WN5 77 M2
Melford Gv NPK/KEN L6 97 M7
Meliden Gdns STHEL WA9 103 H6
Meliden Gv FROD/HEL WA6 166 C4
Melksham Dr PEN/TH CH61 125 M6
Melling Av WLT/FAZ L9 84 D6
Melling Cl CHLYE PR6 * 44 C4
Melling Dr KKBY L32 86 A2
Melling La MGHL L31 73 G6
Melling Rd BTL L20 7 H1
CHTN/BK PR9 25 G5
WAL/NB CH45 95 L6
WLT/FAZ L9 84 E4
Mellings Av WGNW/BIL/O WN5 * 78 A4
Melling St WGNW/BIL/O WN5 68 A8
Melling Wy KKBY L32 86 A2
WGNS/IIMK WN3 78 F4
Mellock Cl NSTN CH64 153 H7
Mellock La NSTN CH64 153 H6
Melloncroft Dr WKBY CH48 124 D5
Melloncroft Dr West
WKBY CH48 124 E6
Mellor Brook Dr
WGNE/HIN WN2 * 80 C3
Mellor Cl RAIN/WH L35 116 C6
RUNC WA7 150 F5
WGNNW/ST WN6 56 A3
Mellor Rd RF/TRAN CH42 127 L3
Melly Rd AIG/SPK L17 129 K2
Melmerby Cl AIMK WN4 91 H2
Melrose Av CHTN/BK PR9 22 D8
CSBY/BLUN L23 83 G2
ECCL WA10 88 D8
HOY CH47 108 D6
LEIGH WN7 81 M4
WARRS WA4 137 M5
WARRW/BUR WA5 104 B6
Melrose Crs AIMK WN4 90 E2
Melrose Dr GTS/LS CH66 163 H5
WGNS/IIMK WN3 78 F2
Melrose Gdns CL/PREN CH43 * 127 H4
CROS/BRETH PR26 29 L3
Melrose Rd ANF/KKDL L4 96 F5
CSBY/WL L22 83 G5
NWD/KWIPK L33 73 M7
Melrose Wy CHLY/EC PR7 32 F7
Melton Av WARRS WA4 137 K5
Melton Cl GR/UP/WCH CH49 110 A8
Melton Rd RUNC WA7 149 K7
Melverley Rd KKBY L32 85 K3
Melverley St WGNS/IIMK WN3 4 B6
Melville Av RF/TRAN CH42 128 C4
Melville Cl ECCL WA10 8 A4
WARRN/WOL WA2 14 E2
WDN WA8 17 K1
Melville Pl EHL/KEN L7 113 J5
Melville Rd BEB CH63 128 A8
BTL L20 83 L6
Melville St TOX L8 113 H8
Melwood Dr WD/CROXPK L12 98 E6
Menai Ms PR/KW L34 * 101 G7
Menai Rd BTL L20 83 M7
Menai St BIRK CH41 10 F6
Mendell Cl PS/BROM CH62 144 A5
Mendip Av WARRN/WOL WA2 121 K2
WGNS/IIMK WN3 78 E2
Mendip Cl GTS/LS CH66 163 G2
HLWD L26 132 A6
HOR/BR BL6 45 L8
RF/TRAN CH42 127 L4
Mendip Gv STHEL WA9 103 H2
Mendip Rd RF/TRAN CH42 127 L4
WAV L15 114 C7
Menin Av WARRS WA4 137 L2
Menivale Cl CHTN/BK PR9 22 C7
Menlo Av PEN/TH CH61 126 B7
Menlo Cl CL/PREN CH43 127 G1
Menlove Av CALD/MH L18 114 C8
Menlove Gdns North
CALD/MH L18 114 D8
Menlove Gdns South
CALD/MH L18 114 D8
Menlove Gdns West
CALD/MH L18 114 D8
Menlove Man CALD/MH L18 114 E7
Menlow Cl WARRS WA4 138 E4
Menstone Rd CLB/OSW/ST L13 114 B1
Mentmore Crs NG/CROX L11 98 D4
Mentmore Gdns WARRS WA4 138 B8
Mentmore Rd CALD/MH L18 130 B4
Menzies St TOX L8 129 J1
Meols Cl FMBY L37 59 G3
GTS/LS CH66 163 G1
Meols Cop Rd STHP PR8 25 H8
Meols Dr HOY CH47 124 C1
Meols Pde HOY CH47 108 E4
Mercer Av KKBY L32 85 L4
Mercer Ct CHLY/EC PR7 44 B4
WD/CROXPK L12 99 G8
Mercer Dr ANF/KKDL L4 97 G5
Mercer Rd CL/PREN CH43 111 G5
RNFD/HAY WA11 90 E7
Mercer's La ORM L39 74 D1
Mercer St ALL/GAR L19 * 130 E8
NEWLW WA12 104 F1
WARRW/BUR WA5 104 A7
Mercer Wk EP CH65 20 C5
Merchants Crs GOL/RIS/CU WA3 93 G4
Mere Av BEB CH63 143 K7
BRSC L40 39 G7
LEIGH WN7 81 M8
Merebank CL/PREN CH43 127 G1
Merebrook Gv NWD/KWIPK L33 74 B8
Mere Brow La KIRK/FR/WA PR4 27 J3
Mere Cl GTS/LS CH66 162 F3
SKEL WN8 65 H3
Merecroft Av WAL/EG CH44 111 L3
Meredale Rd CALD/MH L18 130 C1
Meredith Av WARRS WA4 138 D3
Meredith St ALL/GAR L19 131 G8
Mere Farm Gv CL/PREN CH43 127 H1
Mere Farm Rd CL/PREN CH43 127 G1
Merefield CHLY/EC PR7 32 C4
Mere Fld CL/PREN CH43 * 127 H1
Mere Fold CHLY/EC PR7 42 F2
Mere Gn ANF/KKDL L4 97 J4
Mere Gv RNFD/HAY WA11 89 K4
Mereheath MOR/LEA CH46 110 A2
Mere Hey ECCL WA10 101 J2
Mereland Cl WGNW/BIL/O WN5 67 G7
Mereland Wy STHEL WA9 103 H3
Mere La BRSC L40 38 F2
CHTN/BK PR9 26 C2
EV L5 97 H8
HES CH60 141 G3
KIRK/FR/WA PR4 27 J6
WAL/NB CH45 95 G6
Merepark Dr CHTN/BK PR9 25 K1
Mere Park Rd GR/UP/WCH CH49 125 L2
Mere Rd AIMK WN4 91 L1
FMBY L37 58 F3
NEWLW WA12 105 H1
WARRN/WOL WA2 122 C3
Meres Rd WLT/FAZ L9 85 G6
Mere St LEIGH WN7 81 M8
WGNW/BIL/O WN5 68 B7
Meres Wy STHP PR8 35 K3
Merevale Cl RUNC WA7 150 A7
Mereview Crs WD/CROXPK L12 98 F2
Merewood KKBY L32 86 B5
SKEL WN8 65 J1
Merewood Cl WARRN/WOL WA2 121 M2
Mereworth WKBY CH48 124 F7
Meribel Cl CSBY/BLUN L23 71 J8
Meriden Av BEB CH63 143 J4
Meriden Cl RNFD/HAY WA11 89 M7
STHP PR8 34 D8
Meriden Rd WLTN L25 115 K7
Merlewood Av CHTN/BK PR9 25 K2
Merlin Av GR/UP/WCH CH49 109 M7
Merlin Cl CHLYE PR6 33 J2
GR/UP/WCH CH49 109 L7
RNFD/HAY WA11 89 K7
RUNC WA7 150 C5
Merlin Ct HLWD L26 131 M4
Merlin St TOX L8 113 H7
Merrick Cl WARRN/WOL WA2 122 A3
Merrills La GR/UP/WCH CH49 110 C8
Merrilocks Rd CSBY/BLUN L23 82 D1
Merrilox Av MGHL L31 72 F3
Merrion Cl WLTN L25 131 H2
Merritt Av BIRK CH41 10 C1
Merrivale Rd WLTN L25 131 L3
Merrydale Dr NG/CROX L11 98 E2
Merryford Gn ANF/KKDL L4 97 K4
Merscar La BRSC L40 37 M7
Mersey Av ALL/GAR L19 130 B5
FMBY L37 47 G7
MGHL L31 73 H3
Merseybank Rd
PS/BROM CH62 128 D5
Mersey Cl WGNE/HIN WN2 81 L2
Mersey La South
RF/TRAN CH42 128 C3
Mersey Mt RF/TRAN CH42 128 A2
Mersey Rd AIG/SPK L17 130 A5
CSBY/BLUN L23 82 E2
RF/TRAN CH42 128 C2
RUNC WA7 18 F1
WDN WA8 149 J1
WGNE/HIN WN2 80 B3
WGNW/BIL/O WN5 67 H6
Mersey St LEIGH WN7 81 L8
STHEL WA9 103 J2
WAL/EG CH44 112 A3
WARR WA1 14 F7
Merseyton Rd EP CH65 156 E6
Mersey Vw ALL/GAR L19 130 E7
CSBY/WL L22 82 E3
RUNC WA7 18 A9
Mersey View Rd WDN WA8 148 D1
Mersey View South Rd
RUNC WA7 18 A9
Mersey Wk WARRS WA4 122 B8
Mersey Wy SPK/HALE L24 145 M3
WARRW/BUR WA5 136 E1
Mersham Ct WDN WA8 134 B1
Merstone Cl HLWD L26 132 B6
Merthyr Gv CHLDW L16 115 G4
Merton Bank Rd STHEL WA9 9 M2
Merton Cl NSTN CH64 153 G8
Merton Crs HUY L36 115 K3
Merton Dr GR/UP/WCH CH49 126 C2
HUY L36 115 J3
Merton Gv BTL L20 7 G5
CHLYE PR6 33 G2
CSBY/BLUN L23 82 E2
Merton Pl CL/PREN CH43 10 E6
Merton Rd BTL L20 7 G5
GTS/LS CH66 163 G2
PS/BROM CH62 155 K2
WAL/NB CH45 95 J8
WGNS/IIMK WN3 78 D1
Merton St STHEL WA9 9 L2
Mertoun Rd WARRS WA4 137 K4
Mervyn Pl WGNS/IIMK WN3 79 J1
Mesham Cl GR/UP/WCH CH49 110 A8
Mesnes Av WGNS/IIMK WN3 4 A9
Mesnes Park Ter WGN WN1 4 E2
Mesnes Rd WGN WN1 68 E3
Mesnes St WGN WN1 4 E2
Mesnes Ter WGN WN1 4 E3
Meteor Crs WARRN/WOL WA2 121 M3
Methuen St BIRK CH41 10 A2
WAV L15 114 A6
Mevagissey Rd RUNC WA7 150 E8
The Mews AIG/SPK L17 130 B4
STBRV L28 99 L6
STHP PR8 2 F7
WARRW/BUR WA5 * 104 A7
WGNE/HIN WN2 69 M8
Meyrick Rd NG/CROX L11 98 A3
Meyrick St WGNW/BIL/O WN5 68 B7
Micawber Cl TOX L8 113 H8
Michael Dragonette Ct
VAUX/LVPD L3 12 E2
Michaels Cl FMBY L37 59 G2
Mickering La ORM L39 62 E7
Micklefield Rd WAV L15 * 114 B7
Micklegate RUNC WA7 150 F6
Mickleton Dr STHP PR8 34 C8
Middlecot Cl WGNW/BIL/O WN5 67 G8
Middlefield Rd CALD/MH L18 131 G2
Middleham Cl KKBY L32 85 L4
Middlehey Rd PR/KW L34 99 M1
Middlehurst Av ECCL WA10 8 F3
Middlehurst Cl PR/KW L34 101 J6
Middlehurst Rd WARRS WA4 138 C3
Middle La FROD/HEL WA6 167 M3
Middlemass Hey NTHLY L27 116 A8
Middle Moss La FMBY L37 60 B2
Middle Rd SPK/HALE L24 132 B8
Middlesex Rd BTL L20 7 K2
Middleton Rd CSBY/WL L22 83 H3
EHL/KEN L7 114 A3
Middle Wk FROD/HEL WA6 160 D6
Middle Wy NG/CROX L11 85 M8
Middle Withins La HTWN L38 60 B6
Middlewood GOL/RIS/CU WA3 93 G5
KKBY L32 86 B5
SKEL WN8 65 J1
Middlewood Cl CHLY/EC PR7 30 E7
ORM L39 62 E6
Middlewood Dr ORM L39 62 E6
Middlewood Rd ORM L39 62 E6

Midge Hall La CHTN/BK PR9 37 L3
Midghall St VAUX/LVPD L3 12 F4
Midhurst Dr STHP PR8 47 K1
Midhurst Rd WD/CROXPK L12 99 H2
Midland Cl LEIGH WN7 81 L7
Midland St BIRK CH41 * 10 F7
WDN WA8 16 F2
Midland Ter CSBY/WL L22 82 F4
Midland Wy WARR WA1 14 C5
Midlothian Dr CSBY/BLUN L23 82 E2
Midway Rd HUY L36 116 A1
Midwood St WDN WA8 16 E4
Milbrook Crs KKBY L32 86 A2
Milbrook Dr KKBY L32 86 A2
Mildenhall Rd WLTN L25 115 J7
Mildmay Rd BTL L20 83 K8
NG/CROX L11 * 98 A3
Mile End EV L5 13 G1
Miles Cl GOL/RIS/CU WA3 123 H2
GR/UP/WCH CH49 125 L3
Miles La GR/UP/WCH CH49 125 L3
WGNNW/ST WN6 54 F5
Miles St TOX L8 129 J1
Milestone Hey STBRV L28 99 K5
Mile Stone Meadow CHLYE PR6 31 M1
Milford Cl FMBY L37 58 E4
Milford Dr WD/CROXPK L12 99 G2
Milford Rd WGNE/HIN WN2 69 H3
Milford St EV L5 96 D7
WGNS/IIMK WN3 5 J7
Milk St ECCL WA10 9 G5
WGNS/IIMK WN3 4 E5
Milland Cl NG/CROX L11 98 E2
Millar Crs WDN WA8 16 C5
Millar's Pace CHTN/BK PR9 22 D8
Mill Av WARRW/BUR WA5 120 A6
Mill Bank CLB/OSW/ST L13 98 B7
NSTN CH64 153 J8
WGNNW/ST WN6 54 F6
Millbank Brow BRSC L40 52 B2
Millbank Ct FROD/HEL WA6 160 C5
Millbank La MGHL L31 73 H2
Millbank Rd WAL/EG CH44 * 111 J2
Millbeck Farm
WGNW/BIL/O WN5 67 M8
Millbeck Gv RNFD/HAY WA11 89 K4
Millbrook Cl SKEL WN8 65 G3
Millbrook La ECCL WA10 101 K1
Millbrook Rd BIRK CH41 111 K3
Mill Brow BEB CH63 127 M7
ECCL WA10 101 K1
STHEL WA9 102 F8
WDN WA8 17 H1
Mill Brow Cl STHEL WA9 102 F8
Millbutt Cl BEB CH63 127 M7
Mill Cl CSBY/BLUN L23 71 G7
EP CH65 163 L4
WARRN/WOL WA2 122 A1
Mill Ct NTHTN L30 71 M8
Millcroft CSBY/BLUN L23 71 J8
Millcroft Av WGNW/BIL/O WN5 66 F8
Millcroft Pk GR/UP/WCH CH49 125 K2
Millcroft Rd WLTN L25 131 L4
Milldale Rd LEIGH WN7 93 K4
Mill Dam Cl BRSC L40 51 L3
Mill Dam La BRSC L40 51 M4
Millenium Rd TOX L8 113 J7
Miller Av CSBY/BLUN L23 70 F8
Miller Cl TOX L8 129 H1
Miller's Br BTL L20 6 F7
Millers Cl MOR/LEA CH46 109 K6
Millers Ct ORM L39 51 H8
Millerscroft KKBY L32 85 L2
Millersdale STHEL WA9 118 E1
Millersdale Av WLT/FAZ L9 84 D6
Millersdale Cl PS/BROM CH62 144 B8
Millersdale Gv RUNC WA7 149 M8
Millersdale Rd CALD/MH L18 130 C1
Millers Fold ECCL WA10 101 K1
Miller's La WGNE/HIN WN2 80 C3
Miller St WARRS WA4 15 H8
Millers Wy MOR/LEA CH46 * 109 L5
Mill Farm Cl WARRN/WOL WA2 122 A2
Mill Fld SKEL WN8 53 L4
Millfield Cl CLB/OSW/ST L13 98 C7
Millfield La RNFD/HAY WA11 91 H5
Millfield Rd CHLY/EC PR7 32 D4
WDN WA8 134 E3
Millfields ECCL WA10 101 K2
Millgate WGN WN1 4 F3
Mill Gn NSTN CH64 154 B5
Millgreen Cl SKEL WN8 66 C6
WD/CROXPK L12 99 G2
Mill Green La WDN WA8 118 F8
Mill Hey RAIN/WH L35 118 A4
Mill Hey La BRSC L40 39 L2
Mill Hey Rd WKBY CH48 124 F7
Mill Hl CL/PREN CH43 127 J2
Mill Hill Rd PEN/TH CH61 125 L6
Millhouse Av WARRS WA4 137 M4
Millhouse Cl MOR/LEA CH46 109 K4
Millhouse La GOL/RIS/CU WA3 106 C7
MOR/LEA CH46 109 K5
Mill House Vw SKEL WN8 66 E6
Millingford Av GOL/RIS/CU WA3 92 B3
Millingford Gv AIMK WN4 91 K2
Millington Cl CL/PREN CH43 127 G4
RUNC WA7 161 H1
WDN WA8 16 A3
Mill La BRSC L40 39 G8
BTL L20 7 J4
CHLY/EC PR7 31 J5
CHLY/EC PR7 42 C3
CHTN/BK PR9 25 J4
CLB/OSW/ST L13 114 C3
FROD/HEL WA6 161 G3
GR/UP/WCH CH49 125 L4
GTS/LS CH66 162 F1
HES CH60 141 K5
KKBY L32 85 L1
NEWLW WA12 105 G2
NSTN CH64 153 L8
NSTN CH64 154 A4
ORM L39 62 B4
PR/KW L34 86 F8
RAIN/WH L35 117 L4
RNFD/HAY WA11 88 E1
SKEL WN8 53 L4
SKEL WN8 65 H3
SKEL WN8 66 C5
STHEL WA9 102 E8
VAUX/LVPD L3 13 H5
WAL/EG CH44 111 K1
WARRN/WOL WA2 105 G8
WARRS WA4 137 G6
WARRS WA4 137 M4
WD/CROXPK L12 98 C7
WDN WA8 117 M8
WDN WA8 134 E1
WGNNW/ST WN6 54 E6
Mill Leat Cl SKEL WN8 53 L3
Mill Meadow NEWLW WA12 105 G2
WGN WN1 5 G5
Millom Av RAIN/WH L35 117 K1
Millom Gv ECCL WA10 101 L5
WD/CROXPK L12 98 E4
Mill Park Dr PS/BROM CH62 155 G2
Mill Rd BEB CH63 127 M6
NPK/KEN L6 13 M2
PEN/TH CH61 126 C7
PS/BROM CH62 143 M2
STHP PR8 34 F8
WGNW/BIL/O WN5 66 F8
Mill Sq AIN/FAZ L10 85 G3
Millstead Rd WAV L15 114 C5
Mill St AIMK WN4 91 L3
CHLY/EC PR7 43 G4
CHLYE PR6 44 C5
ECCL WA10 8 F3
GOL/RIS/CU WA3 92 C5
NSTN CH64 153 G5
ORM L39 63 H1
PR/KW L34 100 F7
RF/TRAN CH42 11 H9
STHP PR8 3 K5
TOX L8 113 G8
WGNE/HIN WN2 69 M8
WGNS/IIMK WN3 4 D5
WLTN L25 131 J3
Mill Ter BEB CH63 * 127 M8
Millthwaite Rd WAL/EG CH44 111 H1
Millvale St NPK/KEN L6 113 L2
Mill Vw TOX L8 113 G8
Mill View Ct ORM L39 63 M7
Mill View Dr BEB CH63 127 L7
Millway Rd SPK/HALE L24 147 J1
Millwood BEB CH63 127 M7
RUNC WA7 150 E4
Mill Wood Av ECCL WA10 101 H2
Millwood Cl AIMK WN4 79 J8
Millwood Ct SPK/HALE L24 * 147 J1
Millwood Gdns RAIN/WH L35 117 H3
Millwood Gld CHLY/EC PR7 32 D4
Millwood Rd SPK/HALE L24 147 G2
Milman Cl GR/UP/WCH CH49 126 B1
ORM L39 62 F2
Milman Rd ANF/KKDL L4 97 H4
Milner Cop HES CH60 141 J5
Milne Rd CLB/OSW/ST L13 98 A5
Milner Rd AIG/SPK L17 130 A4
HES CH60 141 J5
Milner St BIRK CH41 10 A1
WARRW/BUR WA5 14 B6
Milnthorpe Cl ANF/KKDL L4 97 G5
Milnthorpe Rd
WARRW/BUR WA5 104 A7
Milnthorpe St ALL/GAR L19 130 E7
Milroy St EHL/KEN L7 113 K4
Milton Av DV/KA/FCH L14 115 H3
NEWLW WA12 104 D2
RAIN/WH L35 117 G2
WDN WA8 16 A4
Milton Cl RAIN/WH L35 117 G2
Milton Crs HES CH60 141 J4
Milton Dr ORM L39 63 J1
Milton Gn PEN/TH CH61 126 D7
Milton Gv FROD/HEL WA6 166 C4
WARRS WA4 137 M2
WGN WN1 68 E2
WGNW/BIL/O WN5 67 J7
WGNW/BIL/O WN5 77 M4
Milton Rd ANF/KKDL L4 7 M6
CHLY/EC PR7 43 G5
CSBY/WL L22 83 G3
EHL/KEN L7 114 A3
EP CH65 20 F7
GOL/RIS/CU WA3 92 F6
RF/TRAN CH42 10 F9
WAL/EG CH44 111 M3
WDN WA8 16 C4
WKBY CH48 124 C2
Milton Rd East RF/TRAN CH42 11 G9
Milton St BTL L20 6 E2
CHTN/BK PR9 25 J6
STHEL WA9 118 C3
WDN WA8 16 C9
Milton Ter CHLYE PR6 32 F3
Milton Wy MGHL L31 72 D4
Milvain Dr WARRN/WOL WA2 121 L4
Milverny Wy STHEL WA9 9 H8
Milverton St NPK/KEN L6 113 L1
Mimosa Cl CHLY/EC PR7 32 C2
Mimosa Rd WAV L15 114 D6
Minehead Av LEIGH WN7 81 M3
Minehead Gv STHEL WA9 102 F8
Minehead Rd AIG/SPK L17 130 A4
Miners Wy SPK/HALE L24 147 J2
WDN WA8 16 D6
Minerva Cl WARRS WA4 137 M3
Mines Av AIG/SPK L17 130 B6
PR/KW L34 101 G7
Mine Wy RNFD/HAY WA11 * 91 H6
Minshull St EHL/KEN L7 113 J4
Minstead Av NWD/KWIPK L33 86 C3
Minster Ct EHL/KEN L7 113 J5
RUNC WA7 18 D8
Minstrel Cl WGNE/HIN WN2 80 D6
Minto Cl EHL/KEN L7 113 L3
Minton Cl WD/CROXPK L12 99 H2
Minton Wy WDN WA8 118 D8
Mintor Rd NWD/KWIPK L33 86 C3
Minto St EHL/KEN L7 113 K3
Minver Rd WD/CROXPK L12 98 F6
Miranda Pl BTL L20 7 J9
Miranda Rd BTL L20 7 J7
Mirfield Cl GOL/RIS/CU WA3 92 F6
HLWD L26 132 B7
Mirfield St NPK/KEN L6 113 K2
Miriam Rd ANF/KKDL L4 97 J7
Miry La SKEL WN8 53 M3
WGNNW/ST WN6 4 B4
Miskelly St BTL L20 96 E5
Mission Wk NPK/KEN L6 113 K2
Missouri Rd CLB/OSW/ST L13 97 M6
Mistlethrush Wy
WD/CROXPK L12 99 H2
Misty Cl WDN WA8 133 L3
Mitchell Av WARRW/BUR WA5 104 A8
Mitchell Crs LITH L21 83 K5
Mitchell Rd ECCL WA10 101 L4
PR/KW L34 100 E7
WGNW/BIL/O WN5 78 A8
Mitchell St AIMK WN4 91 L3
GOL/RIS/CU WA3 92 C6
LEIGH WN7 81 K8
WARRS WA4 137 L5
WGNE/HIN WN2 69 J6
WGNW/BIL/O WN5 68 A7
Mithril Cl WDN WA8 135 G2
Mitre Cl RAIN/WH L35 116 F4
Mitton Cl GOL/RIS/CU WA3 93 M8
Mitylene St EV L5 * 97 G7
Moat House St WGNE/HIN WN2 69 J6
Mobberley Cl WARRS WA4 138 F2
Mobberley Wy BEB CH63 143 J2
Mockbeggar Dr WAL/NB CH45 94 F6
Mockbeggar Whf
WAL/NB CH45 94 F6
Modred St TOX L8 113 H8
Moel Famau Vw AIG/SPK L17 129 K3
Moffatdale Rd ANF/KKDL L4 97 L5
Moffat Rd WLT/FAZ L9 * 84 E6
Moffatt Rd WLT/FAZ L9 84 D6
Molesworth Gv CHLDW L16 115 H4
Molineux Av DV/KA/FCH L14 114 F4
Molland Cl WD/CROXPK L12 98 F5
Mollington Av NG/CROX L11 98 B3
Mollington Link BIRK CH41 11 K8
Mollington Rd KKBY L32 85 L3
WAL/EG CH44 111 L2
Mollington St BIRK CH41 11 J7
Molly Pitcher Wy
WARRW/BUR WA5 120 D8
Molly's La NWD/KWIPK L33 86 F6
Molton Rd CHLDW L16 114 E5
Molyneux Av WARRW/BUR WA5 121 H5
Molyneux Cl GR/UP/WCH CH49 110 B8
HUY L36 116 B3
RAIN/WH L35 116 F1
Molyneux Ct NG/CROX L11 * 98 D2
Molyneux Dr RAIN/WH L35 116 F1
WAL/NB CH45 95 K5
Molyneux Rd CALD/MH L18 130 B1
CSBY/WL L22 83 G3
MGHL L31 73 H6
NPK/KEN L6 113 K2
ORM L39 62 E6
Molyneux St WGN WN1 5 H3
Molyneux Wy AIN/FAZ L10 84 E2
Monaghan Cl WLT/FAZ L9 84 B6
Monash Rd NG/CROX L11 98 B5
Monastery La STHEL WA9 102 F6
Monastery Rd NPK/KEN L6 97 L7
STHEL WA9 103 G6
Mona St BIRK CH41 111 H6
BTL L20 83 M7
ECCL WA10 8 A6
WGN WN1 4 D3
Mond Rd AIN/FAZ L10 85 H6
WDN WA8 16 C4
Monfa Rd BTL L20 83 M7
Monica Dr WDN WA8 118 C8
Monica Rd WLTN L25 131 K4
Monica Ter AIMK WN4 91 K3
Monkfield Wy ALL/GAR L19 145 M1
Monk Rd WAL/EG CH44 111 K1
Monks Carr La HTWN L38 60 C7
Monks Cl FMBY L37 59 J4
Monksdown Rd NG/CROX L11 98 C4
Monks Dr FMBY L37 59 J4
Monks Ferry BIRK CH41 11 M6
Monksferry Wk ALL/GAR L19 130 B6
Monks Gv EP CH65 20 B3
Monks St WARRW/BUR WA5 * 121 G7
Monk St EV L5 * 97 H7
Monks Wy BEB CH63 143 H1
WKBY CH48 124 D3
WLTN L25 131 K3
Monkswell Dr WAV L15 114 C5
Monkswell St TOX L8 129 J2
Monkswood Cl
WARRW/BUR WA5 121 G3
Monmouth Cl WARR WA1 123 G6
Monmouth Crs AIMK WN4 91 L3
Monmouth Dr AIN/FAZ L10 85 H4
Monmouth Gv STHEL WA9 102 F3
Monmouth Rd WAL/EG CH44 111 J1
Monro Cl TOX L8 * 129 H1
Monroe Cl WARR WA1 122 D6
WGNS/IIMK WN3 79 J2
Monro St TOX L8 129 H1
Montague Rd CLB/OSW/ST L13 114 C3
Montagu Rd FMBY L37 47 G8
Montclair Dr CALD/MH L18 114 D8
Montclare Crs WARRS WA4 138 A4
Montcliffe Cl GOL/RIS/CU WA3 106 E8
Montcliffe Rd CHLYE PR6 33 G4
Monterey Rd CLB/OSW/ST L13 114 D3
Montford Ri WGNE/HIN WN2 69 J3
Montfort Dr ALL/GAR L19 130 C6
Montgomery Av CHTN/BK PR9 25 J7
Montgomery Cl RAIN/WH L35 116 F3
Montgomery Hl WKBY CH48 125 J5
Montgomery Rd HUY L36 115 M1
WDN WA8 133 M5
WLT/FAZ L9 84 C7
Montgomery Wy NPK/KEN L6 113 K1
Montpelier Av RUNC WA7 149 H7
Montpelier Dr TOX L8 129 H1
Montpellier Crs WAL/NB CH45 95 J5
Montreal Rd NTHLY L27 116 A8
Montrey Crs AIMK WN4 90 E2
Montrose Av WAL/EG CH44 112 A4
WGNW/BIL/O WN5 67 M6
Montrose Cl CHLYE PR6 33 G7
WARRN/WOL WA2 122 B1
Montrose Dr CHTN/BK PR9 25 H4
Montrose Rd CLB/OSW/ST L13 98 A7
Montrose Wy CLB/OSW/ST L13 114 B3
Montrovia Crs AIN/FAZ L10 85 H6
Monument Man WGN WN1 * 68 E3
Monument Rd WGN WN1 68 F3
Monville Rd WLT/FAZ L9 84 E6
Monyash Vw WGNE/HIN WN2 81 H2
Moody La BRSC L40 41 G4
Moody St WGNNW/ST WN6 * 56 A4
Moor Av WGNNW/ST WN6 55 G5
Moorbridge Cl NTHTN L30 84 C1
Moor Cl CSBY/BLUN L23 71 H8
STHP PR8 47 L3
Moor Coppice CSBY/BLUN L23 71 H8
Moorcroft Rd CALD/MH L18 130 E4
HUY L36 100 A8
WAL/NB CH45 94 F8
Moorditch La FROD/HEL WA6 159 L4
Moor Dr CSBY/BLUN L23 71 G8
SKEL WN8 65 M6
Moore Av RF/TRAN CH42 128 A3
STHEL WA9 103 J2
WARRS WA4 138 F2
Moore Cl WDN WA8 134 F3
Moore Dr RNFD/HAY WA11 91 H7
Moore La WARRS WA4 136 D6
Moores La WGNNW/ST WN6 55 M3
Moore St BTL L20 6 E1
WGN WN1 68 F3
Moore St East WGN WN1 5 J1
Mooreway RAIN/WH L35 118 A4
Moorfield NWD/KWIPK L33 74 B8
Moorfield Crs GOL/RIS/CU WA3 93 J6
Moorfield Dr NSTN CH64 152 E3
Moorfield La BRSC L40 50 D2
Moorfield Rd CSBY/BLUN L23 71 J8
ECCL WA10 88 E8
WDN WA8 134 F1
Moorfields CHLYE PR6 33 G4
CLVP L2 12 F6
Moorfields Av CL/PREN CH43 126 F1
Moorfield St WGNE/HIN WN2 80 D2
Moorfoot Rd STHEL WA9 103 H2
Moorfoot Wy NWD/KWIPK L33 73 M7
Moorgate ORM L39 63 G1
Moorgate Av CSBY/BLUN L23 83 G2
Moorgate Rd NWD/KWIPK L33 86 B7
Moorgate St EHL/KEN L7 113 K4
Moorhey Rd MGHL L31 72 F7
Moorhouses HTWN L38 70 B2
Mooring Cl RUNC WA7 150 F7
Moorings Cl NSTN CH64 152 D4
WGN WN1 5 L4
The Moorings BIRK CH41 * 11 H7
CHLYE PR6 33 G5
HES CH60 140 E5
MGHL L31 72 D1
Moorland Av CSBY/BLUN L23 71 G8
Moorland Cl HES CH60 141 J6
Moorland Dr RUNC WA7 151 G6
Moorland Ga CHLYE PR6 33 H7
Moorland Pk HES CH60 141 J6
Moorland Rd AIMK WN4 80 A8
GTS/LS CH66 156 A5
MGHL L31 72 E7
RF/TRAN CH42 128 A2
WGNE/HIN WN2 69 L8
Moorlands Rd CSBY/BLUN L23 71 K7
Moor La AIN/FAZ L10 85 J6
ANF/KKDL L4 97 J2
CSBY/BLUN L23 71 H8
FROD/HEL WA6 160 D5
FROD/HEL WA6 166 A4
HES CH60 141 H5
HTWN L38 70 F2
SFTN L29 71 M4
STHP PR8 47 L3
WDN WA8 16 C6
Moor La South WDN WA8 16 B6
Moor Pl VAUX/LVPD L3 13 K6
Moor Rd CHLY/EC PR7 32 C8
CROS/BRETH PR26 29 L2
WGNW/BIL/O WN5 67 G7
Moorside Av NSTN CH64 152 E5
Moorside Cl CSBY/BLUN L23 83 H1
Moorside Ct WDN WA8 16 B5
Moorside La NSTN CH64 152 E6
Moorside Rd CSBY/BLUN L23 83 H1
Moor St CLVP L2 12 E8
ORM L39 51 H8
Moorway HES CH60 141 K5
Moorwood Crs STHEL WA9 118 E1
Moray Cl ECCL WA10 8 D1
Morcott La SPK/HALE L24 147 M3
Morden Av AIMK WN4 91 K2
Morden St NPK/KEN L6 113 L2
Morecambe St NPK/KEN L6 * 97 L8
Morecroft Rd RF/TRAN CH42 128 C3
Morella Rd ANF/KKDL L4 97 L5
Morello Cl ECCL WA10 8 F2
Morello Dr BEB CH63 143 K3
Moresby Cl LEIGH WN7 81 M8
RUNC WA7 151 G6
Moret Cl CSBY/BLUN L23 71 J8
Moreton Av STHEL WA9 118 E1
Moreton Cl GOL/RIS/CU WA3 92 B4
Moreton Gv WAL/NB CH45 95 G7
Moreton Rd GR/UP/WCH CH49 110 B7
Morgan Av WARRN/WOL WA2 121 L3
Morgan Ms NTHTN L30 83 M2
Morgan St STHEL WA9 102 F3
Morland Av NSTN CH64 153 H6
PS/BROM CH62 143 M6
Morley Av BIRK CH41 10 C3
Morley Rd CHTN/BK PR9 25 G5
RUNC WA7 19 G6
WAL/EG CH44 111 J2
WARRS WA4 137 J4
Morley St ANF/KKDL L4 * 97 G6
ECCL WA10 8 E1
WARR WA1 15 H4
Morley Wy ECCL WA10 8 F3
Morningside CSBY/BLUN L23 83 H2
Morningside Pl NG/CROX L11 98 B4
Morningside Rd NG/CROX L11 98 B5
Morningside Wy NG/CROX L11 98 B5
Mornington Av CSBY/BLUN L23 83 G3
EP CH65 20 D5
Mornington Rd CHLYE PR6 44 D5
CHTN/BK PR9 3 J3
WAL/NB CH45 95 K7
Mornington St TOX L8 113 G8
Morpeth Cl MOR/LEA CH46 109 K5
Morpeth Rd HOY CH47 108 C8
Morpeth St TOX L8 113 H6
Morpeth Whf BIRK CH41 11 K2
Morris Av WARRS WA4 138 B1
Morris Cl RNFD/HAY WA11 90 C8
Morris Hey ORM L39 49 M2
Morris La ORM L39 49 M2
Morrison Cl WARRW/BUR WA5 120 C8
Morrison St CHLYE PR6 32 F3
Morris Rd CHLYE PR6 * 33 G4
SKEL WN8 66 C6
Morrissey Cl ECCL WA10 8 A3
Morris St STHEL WA9 103 G4
WGN WN1 5 G3
WGNE/HIN WN2 69 M8
WGNS/IIMK WN3 80 A1
Morston Av KKBY L32 86 A5
Morston Crs KKBY L32 86 A5
Mort Av WARRS WA4 138 C1
Mortimer Av WARRN/WOL WA2 121 K5
Mortimer St BIRK CH41 11 L5
Mortlake Cl WDN WA8 133 L2
Morton Av FROD/HEL WA6 166 D4
WGNS/IIMK WN3 4 C9
Morton Cl WARRW/BUR WA5 120 E5
WGNS/IIMK WN3 78 E3
Morton Rd RUNC WA7 150 F5
Morton St TOX L8 113 H8
Mort St WGNNW/ST WN6 4 A1
Morvah Cl NG/CROX L11 98 E3
Morval Crs ANF/KKDL L4 7 M6
RUNC WA7 19 M6
Morven Cl WARRN/WOL WA2 122 A2
Morven Gv STHP PR8 25 G6
Morville Dr WGNS/IIMK WN3 79 K1
Moscow Dr CLB/OSW/ST L13 98 B8
Mosedale Av RNFD/HAY WA11 89 K4
Mosedale Gv RUNC WA7 * 150 A8
Mosedale Rd PS/BROM CH62 144 A3
WLT/FAZ L9 84 C8
Moseley Av WAL/NB CH45 111 J1
WARRS WA4 138 C1
Moseley Rd BEB CH63 143 J4
Moses St TOX L8 129 H1
Mosley St STHP PR8 3 G9
Moss Av WGNW/BIL/O WN5 77 M2
Moss Bank CHLY/EC PR7 43 G4
ORM L39 62 F3
Moss Bank Pk LITH L21 83 J5
Moss Bank Rd RNFD/HAY WA11 89 J4
WDN WA8 17 J5
Mossborough Hall La
RNFD/HAY WA11 87 L2
Mossborough Rd
RNFD/HAY WA11 76 B8
RNFD/HAY WA11 87 M3
Moss Bridge La BRSC L40 52 E3
Moss Brow RNFD/HAY WA11 76 A6
Mossbrow Rd HUY L36 116 A1
Moss Cl CHLYE PR6 33 G5
NSTN CH64 154 C5
WARRS WA4 138 A3
Mosscroft Cl HUY L36 116 C1
Mossdale Cl WARRW/BUR WA5 120 C6
Mossdale Dr RAIN/WH L35 117 M2
Mossdale Rd AIMK WN4 79 J5
NWD/KWIPK L33 74 B8
Moss Delph La ORM L39 62 E4
Mossdene Rd WAL/EG CH44 111 H1
Moss End Wy NWD/KWIPK L33 86 F2
Mossfield Rd CHLYE PR6 33 G5
WLT/FAZ L9 84 B7
Moss Gdns STHP PR8 35 L3
Moss Ga GOL/RIS/CU WA3 107 J8
Moss Gate Gv DV/KA/FCH L14 115 J2
Moss Gate Rd DV/KA/FCH L14 115 J2
Mossgiel Av STHP PR8 34 D8
Moss Green Wy STHEL WA9 103 J4
Moss Gv RF/TRAN CH42 127 K3
TOX L8 113 L7
WGNNW/ST WN6 56 A5
Moss Hey Hey KIRK/FR/WA PR4 27 J2
Mosshill Cl MGHL L31 72 E2
Mosslands ECCL WA10 101 J1
Mosslands Cl GTS/LS CH66 163 G3
Mosslands Dr WAL/EG CH44 111 G1
Moss La BRSC L40 39 J6
BTL L20 84 A7
CHLY/EC PR7 43 G4
CHTN/BK PR9 25 K5
CROS/BRETH PR26 29 J5
FMBY L37 59 L1
GOL/RIS/CU WA3 92 D8
HTWN L38 59 K8
HTWN L38 70 E3
LITH L21 83 M4
MGHL L31 61 M8
MGHL L31 73 G3
NWD/KWIPK L33 74 B5
NWD/KWIPK L33 86 D2
ORM L39 75 H3
RF/TRAN CH42 127 K3
RNFD/HAY WA11 77 G8
RNFD/HAY WA11 88 C6
SKEL WN8 65 H7
STHEL WA9 103 J4
WARRS WA4 136 C7
WGNE/HIN WN2 80 C2
WGNNW/ST WN6 54 E1
Moss Lane Vw SKEL WN8 65 H7
Mosslawn Rd KKBY L32 86 C4
Mosslea Pk CALD/MH L18 130 B1
Mossley Av CALD/MH L18 114 B8
PS/BROM CH62 143 M5
Mossley Hill Dr AIG/SPK L17 113 M8
Mossley Hill Rd CALD/MH L18 130 B3
Mossley Rd RF/TRAN CH42 128 A2
Moss Nook BRSC L40 39 G7
ORM L39 * 62 E3
Moss Nook La MGHL L31 73 K5
RNFD/HAY WA11 76 A7
Moss Pits Cl AIN/FAZ L10 85 G6
Moss Pits La AIN/FAZ L10 85 G6
WAV L15 114 D6
Moss Rd STHP PR8 35 L3
WARRS WA4 138 C2
WGNW/BIL/O WN5 77 M2
Moss Side DV/KA/FCH L14 115 J2
FMBY L37 59 K1
Moss Side La KIRK/FR/WA PR4 27 H2
WARRS WA4 136 A6
Moss St ALL/GAR L19 130 E7
NPK/KEN L6 13 M5
PR/KW L34 100 F6
WDN WA8 17 K5
WGNNW/ST WN6 4 A1
WGNS/IIMK WN3 80 B2
WGNW/BIL/O WN5 * 67 K7
Moss Ter WGNW/BIL/O WN5 67 K8
Mossvale GTS/LS CH66 155 M5
Moss Vw LITH L21 83 L5
MGHL L31 73 H4
Mossville Cl CALD/MH L18 130 C3
Mossville Rd CALD/MH L18 130 D3
Moss Wy NG/CROX L11 98 E1
Mossy Bank Rd WAL/EG CH44 111 M1
Mossy Lea Fold
WGNNW/ST WN6 55 H2
Mossy Lea Rd WGNNW/ST WN6 42 A7
Moston Gv LYMM WA13 139 M2
Moston Wy GTS/LS CH66 163 H2
Mostyn Av AIN/FAZ L10 84 E3
ALL/GAR L19 130 F5
HES CH60 140 E5
WKBY CH48 124 D4
Mostyn Cl ANF/KKDL L4 * 97 G6
Mostyn Sq NSTN CH64 152 D4
Mostyn St WAL/EG CH44 111 K2
Motherwell Crs STHP PR8 36 B2
Mottershead Cl WDN WA8 16 C4
Mottershead Rd WDN WA8 16 C4
Mottram Cl NWD/KWIPK L33 86 B3
WARRS WA4 138 D2
Mottram Dr WGNS/IIMK WN3 68 D8
Moughland La RUNC WA7 19 G7
Moulders La WARR WA1 14 F7
Mould St EV L5 96 F8
Moulton Cl RUNC WA7 161 H1
Mounsey Rd RF/TRAN CH42 11 G8
Mountain Rd CHLY/EC PR7 43 G5
Mountain Vw FROD/HEL WA6 166 D2
Mount Av BEB CH63 127 M6
BTL L20 83 M7
HES CH60 * 141 H5
Mountbatten Rd CHLY/EC PR7 32 C7
Mount Cl KKBY L32 85 L1
Mount Ct HES CH60 * 141 H5
Mount Crs KKBY L32 85 L1
WGNW/BIL/O WN5 67 H7
Mount Dr BEB CH63 127 L6
Mount Farm Wy GTS/LS CH66 162 E3
Mount Gv BIRK CH41 10 F8
Mount Grove Pl BIRK CH41 10 E8
Mount Haven Cl
GR/UP/WCH CH49 110 C8
Mount House Cl FMBY L37 47 K8
Mount House Rd FMBY L37 47 K8
Mount Ms HES CH60 * 141 H5
Mount Olive CL/PREN CH43 127 J2
Mount Pk BEB CH63 127 M6
WLTN L25 131 J2
Mount Park Ct WLTN L25 131 J2
Mount Pleasant CHLYE PR6 44 C5
CHNE CH2 165 J1
CL/PREN CH43 127 K2
CSBY/WL L22 82 F4
VAUX/LVPD L3 13 M8
WDN WA8 134 D3
Mount Pleasant Av STHEL WA9 103 J2
Mount Pleasant Rd
WAL/NB CH45 95 J6
Mount Rd BEB CH63 127 L7
BEB CH63 142 F2
GR/UP/WCH CH49 110 C8
KKBY L32 85 K1
RF/TRAN CH42 127 M3
RUNC WA7 150 B5
WAL/NB CH45 95 J5
WKBY CH48 124 E4
Mount St CHTN/BK PR9 3 L3
CLVPS L1 113 G5
CSBY/WL L22 82 F4
LEIGH WN7 93 L1
WDN WA8 16 F1
WLTN L25 131 J3
Mount Ter CHTN/BK PR9 3 L3
The Mount HES CH60 141 H5
SKEL WN8 * 65 K5
WAL/EG CH44 111 L1
Mount Vernon EHL/KEN L7 113 J3
Mount Vernon St EHL/KEN L7 113 J3
Mount Vernon Vw EHL/KEN L7 113 J3
Mount Vw WGNS/IIMK WN3 5 H9
Mountview Cl TOX L8 113 J8
Mountway BEB CH63 127 M6

Mountwood SKEL WN8 65 J1
Mount Wood Rd RF/TRAN CH42 127 L5
Mourne Cl GTS/LS CH66 155 J7
Mowbray Av RNFD/HAY WA11 9 M1
Mowbray Gv CLB/OSW/ST L13 114 C4
Mowcroft La WARRW/BUR WA5 135 K2
Moxon Av WARRS WA4 122 B8
Moxon St ECCL WA10 101 L3
Moxon Wy AIMK WN4 91 M1
Moyles Cl WDN WA8 133 M3
Mozart Cl TOX L8 113 K7
Muirfield Cl WARRN/WOL WA2 122 C2
WD/CROXPK L12 99 G7
Muirfield Dr STHP PR8 47 L1
Muirfield Rd HUY L36 115 L4
Muirhead Av CLB/OSW/ST L13 98 B6
Muirhead Av East
WD/CROXPK L12 98 C5
Mulberry Av ECCL WA10 101 L2
GOL/RIS/CU WA3 93 H6
Mulberry Cl CHNE CH2 165 L2
NWD/KWIPK L33 74 B7
WARR WA1 123 G6
WGNW/BIL/O WN5 67 M7
Mulberry Ct WARRS WA4 * 137 M4
Mulberry Gv WAL/EG CH44 111 M2
Mulberry Pl EHL/KEN L7 * 13 M9
Mulberry Rd RF/TRAN CH42 128 B3
Mulberry St EHL/KEN L7 13 M9
Mulcrow Cl STHEL WA9 102 F1
Mulgrave St TOX L8 113 J6
Mullein Cl GOL/RIS/CU WA3 92 F5
Mullen Cl WARRW/BUR WA5 * 14 A4
Mulliner St EHL/KEN L7 113 L6
Mullins Av NEWLW WA12 91 L8
Mullion Cl CHTN/BK PR9 22 D8
HLWD L26 132 A5
RUNC WA7 150 D7
Mullion Gv WARRN/WOL WA2 122 C4
Mullion Rd NG/CROX L11 98 E1
Mullion Wk NG/CROX L11 * 85 L8
Mullwood Cl WD/CROXPK L12 99 H2
Mulveton Rd BEB CH63 143 H2
Mumfords La HOY CH47 108 F4
Muncaster Cl PS/BROM CH62 143 M4
Muncaster Dr RNFD/HAY WA11 76 C6
Munro Av WGNW/BIL/O WN5 67 G7
Munster Rd CLB/OSW/ST L13 114 D2
Murat Gv CSBY/WL L22 82 E4
Murat St CSBY/WL L22 82 E4
Murcote Rd DV/KA/FCH L14 99 H8
Murdishaw Av RUNC WA7 150 E8
Muriel Cl WARRW/BUR WA5 119 M7
Muriel St ANF/KKDL L4 97 J5
Murphy Cl WGNS/IIMK WN3 4 A9
Murphy Gv STHEL WA9 103 G1
Murrayfield Dr MOR/LEA CH46 110 B1
Murrayfield Rd WLTN L25 115 J7
Murray Gv WKBY CH48 124 C2
Museum St WARR WA1 14 C7
Musker Dr NTHTN L30 83 L2
Musker St CSBY/BLUN L23 83 H2
Muspratt Rd LITH L21 83 J8
Mustard La GOL/RIS/CU WA3 106 D5
Myddleton La
WARRN/WOL WA2 105 K7
Myers Av RAIN/WH L35 101 J8
Myerscough Av BTL L20 7 M1
Myers Rd East CSBY/BLUN L23 83 G2
Myers Rd West CSBY/BLUN L23 82 F2
Mynsule Rd BEB CH63 143 H2
Myrtle Av AIMK WN4 79 H7
NEWLW WA12 104 E3
RNFD/HAY WA11 90 D6
Myrtle Gv CHTN/BK PR9 3 M5
CSBY/WL L22 82 F3
STHP PR8 25 G7
WAL/EG CH44 111 M2
WARRS WA4 15 K9
WDN WA8 133 M5
WGNW/BIL/O WN5 * 89 M1
Myrtle Pde EHL/KEN L7 113 H5
Myrtle St EHL/KEN L7 13 L9
EP CH65 156 E6
WGN WN1 4 D3

N

Nab Rd CHLYE PR6 33 G4
Nairn Av SKEL WN8 53 K8
Nairn Cl BEB CH63 154 F1
WARRN/WOL WA2 122 C2
WGNNW/ST WN6 55 M4
Nangreaves St LEIGH WN7 81 L8
Nansen Cl WARRW/BUR WA5 120 F6
Nansen Gv ANF/KKDL L4 97 J4
Nant Park Ct WAL/NB CH45 95 L5
Nantwich Cl GR/UP/WCH CH49 126 C3
Nantwich Rd GTS/LS CH66 163 H2
Napier Cl ECCL WA10 8 D5
Napier Dr MOR/LEA CH46 110 B5
Napier Rd PS/BROM CH62 128 D5
Napier St BTL L20 6 E8
ECCL WA10 8 D5
WARR WA1 15 G6
Napier Ter STHP PR8 2 F8
Naples Rd WAL/EG CH44 111 M2
Napps Cl WLTN L25 115 H6
Napps Wy PEN/TH CH61 141 J3
WLTN L25 115 H5
Narborough Cl WGNE/HIN WN2 81 G1
Nares Cl WARRW/BUR WA5 120 E4
Narrow Croft Rd ORM L39 62 D4
Narrow La ORM L39 62 D4
Narrow La (Clieves Hills)
ORM L39 49 M6
Narrow Moss La BRSC L40 50 F3
Naseby Cl CL/PREN CH43 126 E1
Naseby St ANF/KKDL L4 97 H3
Natal Rd WLT/FAZ L9 84 D7
Nathan Dr RNFD/HAY WA11 91 G7
Nathan Gv NWD/KWIPK L33 86 B1
Naunton Av LEIGH WN7 81 L8
Navenby Rd WGNS/IIMK WN3 79 J3
Navigation Cl NTHTN L30 84 C1
RUNC WA7 150 F7
Navigation St WARR WA1 15 J6
Navigation Whf VAUX/LVPD L3 112 F7
Naylor Av GOL/RIS/CU WA3 92 D5
Naylor Crs GTS/LS CH66 156 B5
Naylorfarm Av
WGNNW/ST WN6 55 H8
Naylor Rd CL/PREN CH43 111 G5
WDN WA8 17 J2
Naylorsfield Dr NTHLY L27 115 L7
Naylor's Rd NTHLY L27 115 M7
Naylor St VAUX/LVPD L3 12 F4
WARR WA1 14 F5
Nazeby Av CSBY/BLUN L23 83 H2
Neale Dr GR/UP/WCH CH49 126 A2
Neales Fold CHTN/BK PR9 22 F8
Neargates CHLY/EC PR7 42 F2
Neasham Cl HLWD L26 132 B6
Nedens Gv MGHL L31 72 E2
Nedens La MGHL L31 72 E2
Needham Cl RUNC WA7 149 M3
Needham Rd EHL/KEN L7 113 L3
Needham Wy SKEL WN8 53 K8
Needwood Dr BEB CH63 143 H2
Neills Rd STHEL WA9 103 K7
Neilson Rd AIG/SPK L17 129 K2
Neil St WDN WA8 134 D3
Nell's La ORM L39 62 B8
Nel Pan La LEIGH WN7 81 L5
Nelson Av RAIN/WH L35 117 G3
Nelson Ct STHP PR8 35 H1
Nelson Dr PEN/TH CH61 141 G2
WGNE/HIN WN2 69 J5
Nelson Pl RAIN/WH L35 117 G3
Nelson Rd CHLY/EC PR7 32 E6
EHL/KEN L7 113 K4
EP CH65 20 C1
GOL/RIS/CU WA3 122 F1
LITH L21 * 83 K6
RF/TRAN CH42 128 C4
Nelson's Cft BEB CH63 143 J2
Nelson St BTL L20 6 E7
CLVPS L1 113 G5
NEWLW WA12 104 C2
STHP PR8 2 F5
WAL/NB CH45 95 L6
WAV L15 114 A6
WDN WA8 16 C8
WGNE/HIN WN2 69 M7
Nelville Rd WLT/FAZ L9 84 E6
Nemos Cl FROD/HEL WA6 166 E3
Nene Gv WGNE/HIN WN2 81 G1
Neptune Cl RUNC WA7 150 F6
Neptune St BIRK CH41 11 H3
Ness Gv KKBY L32 85 L3
Neston Av STHEL WA9 118 D1
Neston Gdns BIRK CH41 10 D2
Neston Gn GTS/LS CH66 162 F1
Neston Rd BEB CH63 142 C7
NSTN CH64 153 H8
NSTN CH64 154 A5
Neston St ANF/KKDL L4 97 H4
Netherby Rd WGNNW/ST WN6 68 C2
Netherby St TOX L8 129 H2
Netherfield WDN WA8 133 M5
Netherfield Cl CL/PREN CH43 126 E1
Netherfield Rd North EV L5 97 G8
Netherfield Rd South EV L5 13 K1
Netherfields LEIGH WN7 81 M6
Netherley Rd CHLY/EC PR7 43 G5
RAIN/WH L35 116 B8
Netherpool Rd GTS/LS CH66 156 B5
Netherton Dr FROD/HEL WA6 160 C6
Netherton Gra NTHTN L30 84 D2
Netherton Gn NTHTN L30 72 B8
Netherton La NTHTN L30 72 A8
Netherton Park Rd LITH L21 83 M5
Netherton Rd BTL L20 83 M7
CALD/MH L18 130 C4
MOR/LEA CH46 110 A5
Netherton Wy NTHTN L30 84 A5
Netherwood Rd NG/CROX L11 98 A3
Netley St ANF/KKDL L4 97 G5
Nettlestead Rd NG/CROX L11 98 C5
Neva Av MOR/LEA CH46 109 M5
Nevada Cl WARRW/BUR WA5 120 D6
Neverstitch Cl SKEL WN8 * 65 H3
Neverstitch Rd SKEL WN8 64 F3
Neville Av STHEL WA9 103 K3
WARRN/WOL WA2 121 M4
Neville Cl CL/PREN CH43 126 E1
Neville Crs WARRW/BUR WA5 136 C2
Neville Rd CSBY/WL L22 83 G4
PS/BROM CH62 144 A6
WAL/EG CH44 111 J1
Neville St NEWLW WA12 104 C2
WGNE/HIN WN2 80 C2
Nevill St STHP PR8 3 G2
Nevin St NPK/KEN L6 113 J2
Nevison St EHL/KEN L7 113 K4
Nevitte Cl STBRV L28 99 J5
New Acres SKEL WN8 53 J3
New Acres Cl CL/PREN CH43 110 E5
Newark Cl CL/PREN CH43 126 E1
HUY L36 99 M7
NTHTN L30 72 D8
Newark Rd WGNE/HIN WN2 80 E1
Newark St ANF/KKDL L4 7 M9
WGNNW/ST WN6 68 B4
New Bank Rd WDN WA8 133 K4
New Barn Av AIMK WN4 91 L2
New Barnet WDN WA8 134 B1
New Bird St CLVPS L1 112 F6
Newbold Crs WKBY CH48 125 G2
Newbold Gv WD/CROXPK L12 99 H3
Newborough Av CALD/MH L18 114 B8
CSBY/BLUN L23 83 J1
Newborough Cl
WARRW/BUR WA5 120 F3
Newbridge Cl AIMK WN4 90 F2
GR/UP/WCH CH49 126 D1
RUNC WA7 150 E7
WARRW/BUR WA5 120 E3
New Bridge Rd EP CH65 21 J7
Newbridge Rd EP CH65 21 J9
Newburgh Cl RUNC WA7 150 F4
Newburn Cl SKEL WN8 53 K8
WGNS/IIMK WN3 79 G1
Newburns La CL/PREN CH43 127 K2
Newburn St ANF/KKDL L4 97 H4
Newbury Cl HUY L36 115 M4
WDN WA8 134 B2
Newbury Dr SKEL WN8 53 K8
Newbury Rd SKEL WN8 53 K8
Newbury Wy MOR/LEA CH46 110 A2
WD/CROXPK L12 99 G8
Newby Av RAIN/WH L35 117 J1
Newby Cl STHP PR8 47 K2
Newby Dr HUY L36 115 L2
SKEL WN8 53 K8
Newby Gv WD/CROXPK L12 98 E3
Newby Sq WGNW/BIL/O WN5 * 67 K8
Newby St ANF/KKDL L4 97 H5
Newcastle Rd WAV L15 114 C7
New Cswy HTWN L38 59 K5
New Chester Rd BIRK CH41 11 L7
PS/BROM CH62 155 J2
RF/TRAN CH42 128 C4
Newchurch La
GOL/RIS/CU WA3 107 H3
Newcombe Av
WARRN/WOL WA2 121 M5
Newcombe St NPK/KEN L6 97 K8
New Court Wy ORM L39 51 H8
Newcroft Rd WLTN L25 131 H1
New Cross St ECCL WA10 8 F5
PR/KW L34 * 100 F6
New Cut La NWD/KWIPK L33 87 J5
STHP PR8 35 J5
WARR WA1 122 D7
Newdales Cl CL/PREN CH43 110 E6
Newdown Rd NG/CROX L11 85 M8
Newell Rd WAL/EG CH44 111 K1
Newenden Rd WGN WN1 68 D1
Newenham Crs DV/KA/FCH L14 115 G2
New Ferry By-Pass
PS/BROM CH62 128 D6
New Ferry Rd PS/BROM CH62 128 D6
Newfield Cl CSBY/BLUN L23 71 L7
Newfield Rd LYMM WA13 139 M2
Newfields ECCL WA10 101 L1
Newfield Ter FROD/HEL WA6 166 D3
New Fold WGNW/BIL/O WN5 77 L1
New Fort Wy BTL L20 83 J7
New Foul La STHP PR8 36 B1
Newgate Av WGNNW/ST WN6 55 G5
Newgate Rd SKEL WN8 66 B6
New Glade Hl RNFD/HAY WA11 89 M7
New Grey Rock Cl NPK/KEN L6 113 K1
New Grosvenor Rd EP CH65 20 B1
New Hall Dr STHP PR8 36 E4
New Hall La GOL/RIS/CU WA3 107 G4
NG/CROX L11 98 A5
Newhall La HOY CH47 108 D7
Newhall St CLVPS L1 * 113 G6
Newhaven Rd WAL/NB CH45 95 L6
WARRN/WOL WA2 121 K1
New Hedley Gv EV L5 96 E8
New Henderson St TOX L8 113 G7
New Hey WD/CROXPK L12 98 C8
New Hey La NSTN CH64 154 C6
New Hey Rd GR/UP/WCH CH49 126 D2
Newholme Cl WD/CROXPK L12 99 G2
Newhope Rd BIRK CH41 10 E3
Newhouse Dr WGNS/IIMK WN3 78 F4
Newhouse Rd WAV L15 * 113 M6
New Hutte La HLWD L26 132 B7
Newick Rd KKBY L32 85 L4
Newington CLVPS L1 13 J8
New Islington VAUX/LVPD L3 13 K5
Newland Av WGNW/BIL/O WN5 67 M8
Newland Cl WDN WA8 133 L2
Newland Ct AIG/SPK L17 129 L2
Newland Dr WAL/EG CH44 111 J1
Newlands CHLY/EC PR7 30 E7
Newlands Av BRSC L40 52 B1
Newlands Cl FROD/HEL WA6 160 E7
Newlands Dr GOL/RIS/CU WA3 92 E5
Newlands Rd BEB CH63 * 143 J1
RNFD/HAY WA11 89 L6
WARRS WA4 138 B3
New La BRSC L40 38 D7
CHTN/BK PR9 25 M1
CHTN/BK PR9 26 B4
CROS/BRETH PR26 30 C3
GOL/RIS/CU WA3 106 C6
ORM L39 60 F2
ORM L39 63 G3
WARRS WA4 138 D8
New La Pace CHTN/BK PR9 23 K5
Newling St BIRK CH41 10 E4
New Ldg WGN WN1 68 E3
Newlyn Av LITH L21 83 J4
MGHL L31 73 G4
Newlyn Cl HOY CH47 109 G3
RUNC WA7 150 D7
Newlyn Dr AIMK WN4 91 K3
SKEL WN8 65 M6
Newlyn Gdns
WARRW/BUR WA5 135 M2
Newlyn Gv RNFD/HAY WA11 89 M6
Newlyn Rd HOY CH47 109 G4
NG/CROX L11 85 M8
Newlyn Wk NG/CROX L11 * 85 M8
Newman Av WGNNW/ST WN6 68 C3
New Manchester Rd
WARR WA1 122 C6
Newman Cl WGNE/HIN WN2 69 L7
New Manor Rd WARRS WA4 151 K7
Newman St ANF/KKDL L4 96 F5
WARRS WA4 138 B2
WGN WN1 69 G3
New Market Rd LITH L21 83 K5
New Market St CHLY/EC PR7 32 E5
WGN WN1 4 E3
New Meadow La FMBY L37 60 A5
New Miles La WGNNW/ST WN6 55 H7
New Mill Stile WLTN L25 131 J2
New Mill St CHLY/EC PR7 30 E7
Newmoore La RUNC WA7 151 H1
Newmorn Ct AIG/SPK L17 129 L3
Newnham Dr EP CH65 20 D7
New Pale Rd FROD/HEL WA6 167 K5
Newport Av WAL/NB CH45 94 F6
Newport Cl CL/PREN CH43 126 E1
Newport Ct EV L5 96 E8
New Quay VAUX/LVPD L3 12 D6
Newquay Cl RUNC WA7 150 D7
New Rd BRSC L40 39 K1
CHLY/EC PR7 43 H2
CHLYE PR6 44 F5
CLB/OSW/ST L13 98 A8
CROS/BRETH PR26 29 K6
FMBY L37 47 J8
GTS/LS CH66 155 J5
PR/KW L34 101 G6
WARRS WA4 14 F8
WGNE/HIN WN2 57 J7
New School La GTS/LS CH66 155 K5
Newsham Cl WDN WA8 133 K1
Newsham Dr NPK/KEN L6 97 L8
Newsham Rd HUY L36 116 C5
Newsham St EV L5 96 F8
Newsham Wk
WGNNW/ST WN6 * 68 B4
Newsholme Cl
GOL/RIS/CU WA3 107 H2
News La RNFD/HAY WA11 76 B3
Newstead Av CSBY/BLUN L23 82 D2
Newstead Rd TOX L8 * 113 L6
WDN WA8 133 H7
WGNS/IIMK WN3 79 G2
Newstet Rd NWD/KWIPK L33 86 D3
New St BRSC L40 40 E3
CHLY/EC PR7 30 E7
NSTN CH64 153 G8
ORM L39 49 K4
RUNC WA7 19 G4
STHEL WA9 102 E7
WAL/EG CH44 112 A3
WGNE/HIN WN2 80 C4
WGNW/BIL/O WN5 67 K8
Newton Av GOL/RIS/CU WA3 107 G8
Newton Cl WD/CROXPK L12 98 D5
WGN WN1 68 F3
Newton Ct CLB/OSW/ST L13 114 A4
Newton Cross La WKBY CH48 125 G3
Newton Dr SKEL WN8 53 K8
WKBY CH48 125 G3
Newton Gv WARRN/WOL WA2 122 B2
Newton Hollow FROD/HEL WA6 167 K5
Newton La NEWLW WA12 92 B6
WARRS WA4 151 L5
Newton Park Dr NEWLW WA12 105 H3
Newton Park Rd WKBY CH48 125 G3
Newton Rd CLB/OSW/ST L13 114 A1
EP CH65 20 D4
GOL/RIS/CU WA3 92 D8
HOY CH47 108 E6
STHEL WA9 103 J2
WAL/EG CH44 111 J1
WARRN/WOL WA2 105 H5
WGNW/BIL/O WN5 78 B7
Newton St BIRK CH41 10 F4
CHTN/BK PR9 25 J6
Newton Wk BTL L20 6 F3
Newton Wy GR/UP/WCH CH49 110 B8
VAUX/LVPD L3 13 L7
New Tower Ct WAL/NB CH45 95 L5
Newtown NSTN CH64 153 H7
Newway DV/KA/FCH L14 99 J8
New Wy ORM L39 74 D3
Nicander Rd CALD/MH L18 114 B8
Nicholas Rd CSBY/BLUN L23 82 D1
WDN WA8 133 L5
Nicholas St VAUX/LVPD L3 13 G3
Nicholford Hall Dr WDN WA8 118 B7
Nicholl Rd ECCL WA10 88 C7
Nicholls Dr PEN/TH CH61 141 H1
Nicholls St WARRS WA4 138 D3
Nicholson St STHEL WA9 103 G1
WARR WA1 14 B5
Nichol St CHLY/EC PR7 * 32 E4
Nick Hilton's La CHLYE PR6 44 F2
Nickleby Cl TOX L8 113 H8
Nickleton Brow CHLYE PR6 44 E3
Nicol Av GOL/RIS/CU WA3 123 H4
Nicol Mere Dr AIMK WN4 79 K8
Nicol Rd AIMK WN4 79 J8
Nidderdale Av RAIN/WH L35 117 M2
Nigel Rd HES CH60 141 L5
Nightingale Cl
GOL/RIS/CU WA3 123 H1
KKBY L32 85 K2
NTHLY L27 116 B8
RUNC WA7 150 A8
Nightingale Rd HOR/BR BL6 57 L2
WD/CROXPK L12 99 H2
Nightingale St CHLYE PR6 44 C5
Nimrod St ANF/KKDL L4 97 H4
Ninth Av WLT/FAZ L9 84 F6
Nipe La SKEL WN8 65 K8
Nithsdale Rd WAV L15 114 A7
Nixons La SKEL WN8 65 M6
STHP PR8 35 G6
Nixon St ANF/KKDL L4 97 H3
Noble Cl GOL/RIS/CU WA3 123 G2
Noctorum Av
GR/UP/WCH CH49 110 E8
Noctorum Dell CL/PREN CH43 126 F1
Noctorum La CL/PREN CH43 111 G7
Noctorum Rd CL/PREN CH43 110 F8
Noctorum Wy CL/PREN CH43 126 F1
Noel Ga ORM L39 62 D4
Noel St TOX L8 113 K6
Nolan St STHP PR8 3 K8
Nook La BRSC L40 30 A8
GOL/RIS/CU WA3 92 D5
STHEL WA9 103 H4
WARRN/WOL WA2 122 D3
WARRS WA4 138 C2
Nook Ri WAV L15 114 D5
The Nook CL/PREN CH43 10 D7
ECCL WA10 88 D7
WGNNW/ST WN6 55 G6
WKBY CH48 125 K3
WLTN L25 131 K2
Noonan Cl WLT/FAZ L9 97 H1
Nora St WARR WA1 15 H6
Norbreck Av DV/KA/FCH L14 115 G3
Norbreck Cl WARRW/BUR WA5 136 C1
Norbreck Crs
WARRW/BUR WA5 136 C1
WGNNW/ST WN6 68 C3
Norburn Crs FMBY L37 59 H3
Norbury Av BEB CH63 128 A8
CALD/MH L18 114 B8
WARRN/WOL WA2 121 M5
WGNW/BIL/O WN5 77 M7
Norbury Cl BEB CH63 128 B8
CHTN/BK PR9 22 E8
WDN WA8 17 K1
Norbury Fold RAIN/WH L35 118 A4
Norbury Rd KKBY L32 85 M3
Norbury St LEIGH WN7 81 M8
Norcliffe Rd RAIN/WH L35 117 K1
Norcott Av WARRS WA4 137 M3
Norcott Dr WARRW/BUR WA5 104 B7
Norden Cl GOL/RIS/CU WA3 106 E8
Norfolk Cl BTL L20 7 J3
CL/PREN CH43 110 E8
Norfolk Dr WARRW/BUR WA5 120 A7
WKBY CH48 124 E4
Norfolk Gv STHP PR8 35 H4
Norfolk Pl LITH L21 * 83 J6
WDN WA8 133 L5
Norfolk Rd ECCL WA10 8 A9
EP CH65 20 C5
MGHL L31 72 E6
STHP PR8 35 H4
WGNW/BIL/O WN5 78 A4
Norfolk St CLVPS L1 112 F6
RUNC WA7 19 K2
WGNNW/ST WN6 68 C3
WGNW/BIL/O WN5 68 B7
Norgate St ANF/KKDL L4 97 H6
Norgrove Cl RUNC WA7 150 F5
Norland's La RAIN/WH L35 118 A5
Norland St WDN WA8 17 J1
Norleane Crs RUNC WA7 19 J8
Norley Av EP CH65 156 B7
PS/BROM CH62 155 G2
Norley Dr ECCL WA10 101 J2
Norley Hall Av
WGNW/BIL/O WN5 67 L7
Norley Pl HLWD L26 132 A7
Norley Rd LEIGH WN7 93 K1
WGNW/BIL/O WN5 67 K6
Norman Av NEWLW WA12 105 G2
RNFD/HAY WA11 91 J6
Normanby Cl
WARRW/BUR WA5 121 G6
Normanby St
WGNW/BIL/O WN5 67 K7
Norman Cl GTS/LS CH66 163 H5
Normandale Rd ANF/KKDL L4 97 M4
Normandy Rd HUY L36 115 M2
Normanhurst ORM L39 63 J1
Norman Rd BTL L20 83 L6
CSBY/BLUN L23 82 F2
RUNC WA7 19 G6
WAL/EG CH44 112 A3
Norman Salisbury Ct
ECCL WA10 8 F3
Normans Rd STHEL WA9 103 H6
Normanston Cl CL/PREN CH43 10 D9
Normanston Rd CL/PREN CH43 127 K1
Norman St BIRK CH41 111 H5
VAUX/LVPD L3 13 L6
WARRN/WOL WA2 14 F3
Normanton Av AIG/SPK L17 129 L2
Normanton Cl WGNNW/ST WN6 68 A1
Norma Rd CSBY/WL L22 83 G4
Norreys Av WARRW/BUR WA5 121 H5
Norric Ct SPK/HALE L24 * 131 K8
Norris Cl CL/PREN CH43 110 E8
Norris Green Crs NG/CROX L11 98 C4
Norris Green Rd
WD/CROXPK L12 98 D7
Norris Green Wy NG/CROX L11 98 C4
Norris House Dr ORM L39 62 E5
Norris Rd PR/KW L34 100 E7
Norris St CHLY/EC PR7 32 E7
WARRN/WOL WA2 121 L5
Norris Wy FMBY L37 59 K2
Norseman Cl WD/CROXPK L12 98 D5
North Alfred Dock BIRK CH41 * 112 B4
Northam Cl CHTN/BK PR9 22 C8
North Av AIN/FAZ L10 85 G3
SPK/HALE L24 131 J7
WARRN/WOL WA2 121 K5
North Barcombe Rd CHLDW L16 114 F6
Northbrook Cl TOX L8 113 J6
Northbrook Rd WAL/EG CH44 111 M2
Northbrook St TOX L8 113 J6
Northbury Rd GTS/LS CH66 163 G4
North Cantril Av
WD/CROXPK L12 99 G5
North Cl PS/BROM CH62 143 L3
Northcote Cl EV L5 * 13 M1
Northcote Rd WAL/NB CH45 94 F8
WLT/FAZ L9 * 97 H2
Northcroft WGN WN1 5 M2
Northdale Rd WARR WA1 122 C5
WAV L15 114 B5
Northdene SKEL WN8 53 K3
North Dingle ANF/KKDL L4 96 F5
North Dr HES CH60 141 J6
WAV L15 114 B5
WD/CROXPK L12 98 D8
Northdunes HTWN L38 70 B1
Northenden Rd CHLY/EC PR7 43 G4
North End La HLWD L26 132 A2
HTWN L38 59 J8
Northern La RAIN/WH L35 133 J2
Northern Perimeter Rd
NTHTN L30 72 A8
Northern Ri GTS/LS CH66 163 G1
Northern Rd SPK/HALE L24 147 G1
The Northern Rd
CSBY/BLUN L23 83 G1
Northfield SKEL WN8 65 K1
Northfield Cl NWD/KWIPK L33 86 C1
STHEL WA9 118 F2
Northfield Rd BTL L20 84 A7
North Florida Rd
RNFD/HAY WA11 90 F5
North Front RAIN/WH L35 117 G4
Northgate Dr CHLYE PR6 33 G3
Northgate Rd CLB/OSW/ST L13 98 B8
North Gv CALD/MH L18 130 E4
North Hill St TOX L8 113 H8
North John St CLVP L2 12 F7
ECCL WA10 8 F5
North Leach Dr STHP PR8 34 C8
North Linkside Rd WLTN L25 131 L4
North Manor Wy WLTN L25 131 L4
North Meade MGHL L31 72 D3
Northmead Rd ALL/GAR L19 131 G6
North Moor La ORM L39 50 B5
North Moss La FMBY L37 47 M6
North Mossley Hill Rd
CALD/MH L18 130 B1
North Mount Rd KKBY L32 85 L1
Northolt Ct WARRN/WOL WA2 122 A4
North Pde HOY CH47 108 C6
KKBY L32 86 A3
NSTN CH64 152 C3
SPK/HALE L24 147 G2
North Park Brook Rd
WARRW/BUR WA5 121 G4
North Park Ct WAL/EG CH44 112 A2
North Park Rd KKBY L32 85 L1
North Perimeter Rd
NWD/KWIPK L33 86 F1
Northridge Rd PEN/TH CH61 126 C8
North Rd ALL/GAR L19 130 B7
CHTN/BK PR9 25 K1
DV/KA/FCH L14 114 E3
ECCL WA10 8 F1
EP CH65 155 M2
RF/TRAN CH42 127 L2
SPK/HALE L24 132 B8
WKBY CH48 124 C3
Northside CHLY/EC PR7 31 L2
North St AIMK WN4 79 M8
CHLYE PR6 32 E3
CHTN/BK PR9 3 J1
NEWLW WA12 104 B1
RNFD/HAY WA11 91 G7
VAUX/LVPD L3 13 G5
North Sudley Rd AIG/SPK L17 130 A3
Northumberland Gv TOX L8 112 F8
Northumberland St
CHLY/EC PR7 32 F6
TOX L8 113 H8
WGN WN1 5 J2
Northumberland Ter EV L5 97 G7
Northumberland Wy NTHTN L30 83 L2
North V CHLYE PR6 44 B4
North Vw EHL/KEN L7 113 K4
HUY L36 116 C3
WARRW/BUR WA5 120 A6
Northway HES CH60 * 141 M4
LYMM WA13 139 M1
MGHL L31 72 E6
RUNC WA7 150 B5
SKEL WN8 65 K4
WARRN/WOL WA2 121 K3
WAV L15 114 D5
WDN WA8 133 M4
WGN WN1 4 E2
Northways PS/BROM CH62 143 M2
WGNNW/ST WN6 55 M3
Northwich Cl CSBY/BLUN L23 71 K7
Northwich Rd RUNC WA7 150 E8
North William St
WAL/EG CH44 * 112 A3
Northwold Cl WGNS/IIMK WN3 78 E2
Northwood Av NEWLW WA12 105 H1
Northwood Rd CL/PREN CH43 127 H3
HUY L36 116 B1
RUNC WA7 150 A3
Norton Av WARRW/BUR WA5 120 A8
Norton Dr PEN/TH CH61 125 L6
Norton Ga RUNC WA7 150 E5
Norton Gv MGHL L31 72 F7
STHEL WA9 101 M6
Norton Hl RUNC WA7 150 E4
Norton La RUNC WA7 150 D5
Norton Rd WKBY CH48 124 C2
Norton Station Rd RUNC WA7 150 F5
Norton St BTL L20 6 E1
VAUX/LVPD L3 13 J5
Norton Vw RUNC WA7 150 C5
Norton Village RUNC WA7 150 F5
Nortonwood La RUNC WA7 150 E4
Norville GTS/LS CH66 155 M6
Norville Rd DV/KA/FCH L14 114 E3
Norwich Av AIMK WN4 91 M3
GOL/RIS/CU WA3 92 F5
Norwich Dr GR/UP/WCH CH49 110 C6
GTS/LS CH66 163 G5
Norwich Rd WAV L15 114 C7
Norwich Wy KKBY L32 86 A3
Norwood Av AIMK WN4 79 H7
CHTN/BK PR9 25 G5
GOL/RIS/CU WA3 93 G6
LITH L21 83 K4
WGNNW/ST WN6 68 C2
Norwood Cl CHLYE PR6 44 C5
Norwood Ct GR/UP/WCH CH49 125 M2
Norwood Crs CHTN/BK PR9 25 G5
Norwood Gv NPK/KEN L6 113 K1
RNFD/HAY WA11 76 C7

Norwood Rd GR/UP/WCH CH49 125 M1
STHP PR8 25 H6
WAL/EG CH44 111 K3
Norwyn Rd NG/CROX L11 98 A3
Nostell Rd AIMK WN4 79 J8
Nottingham Cl RAIN/WH L35 101 L8
WARR WA1 122 F7
Nottingham Pl WGN WN1 5 K1
Nottingham Rd HUY L36 115 L4
Nowshera Av PEN/TH CH61 126 B8
Nuffield Cl GR/UP/WCH CH49 126 B1
Nun Cl CL/PREN CH43 127 K1
Nunn St STHEL WA9 102 F2
Nunsford Cl LITH L21 83 M3
Nunthorpe Rd PR/KW L34 86 D8
The Nurseries FMBY L37 59 J3
Nurse Rd PEN/TH CH61 126 D7
Nursery Av ORM L39 51 J7
Nursery Cl CHLY/EC PR7 43 G1
CL/PREN CH43 127 K2
WDN WA8 134 F2
WLTN L25 131 L5
Nursery Dr FMBY L37 59 H3
Nursery La ALL/GAR L19 130 E6
Nursery Rd MGHL L31 72 E1
STHEL WA9 101 M6
Nutgrove Av STHEL WA9 * 101 M6
Nutgrove Hall Dr STHEL WA9 101 M6
Nutgrove Rd STHEL WA9 101 L7
Nuthall Rd STHP PR8 36 A2
Nut St STHEL WA9 101 M6
Nuttall Ct GOL/RIS/CU WA3 122 E1
Nuttall St EHL/KEN L7 113 L4
Nutt St WGN WN1 5 J1
Nyland Rd HUY L36 99 M8

O

Oak Av CHLY/EC PR7 31 M2
GOL/RIS/CU WA3 92 D5
GR/UP/WCH CH49 109 M7
NEWLW WA12 104 E2
ORM L39 62 F1
RNFD/HAY WA11 91 G6
WGNE/HIN WN2 80 E6
WGNE/HIN WN2 81 J2
WGNNW/ST WN6 56 B5
WLT/FAZ L9 84 D7
Oak Bank BIRK CH41 10 F7
Oakbank WGNE/HIN WN2 80 D2
Oakbank Rd AIG/SPK L17 114 A8
Oakbank St WAL/EG CH44 111 L2
Oakbourne Cl AIG/SPK L17 129 L3
Oak Cl MOR/LEA CH46 109 M6
RAIN/WH L35 117 G2
WD/CROXPK L12 99 H4
Oak Crs SKEL WN8 64 F4
Oakdale Av FROD/HEL WA6 160 F7
WAL/EG CH44 111 M3
WARRS WA4 137 M4
Oakdale Dr GR/UP/WCH CH49 125 L3
Oakdale Rd CALD/MH L18 114 C8
CSBY/WL L22 82 F3
WAL/EG CH44 111 M4
Oakdene Av GTS/LS CH66 155 L8
WARR WA1 122 E6
Oakdene Cl PS/BROM CH62 143 M8
Oakdene Rd ANF/KKDL L4 97 K6
RF/TRAN CH42 127 L2
Oak Dr CHLYE PR6 32 E2
RUNC WA7 19 M9
Oakenden Cl AIMK WN4 79 J7
Oakengates WGNNW/ST WN6 56 B4
Oakenholt Rd MOR/LEA CH46 110 A5
Oakes St VAUX/LVPD L3 13 L6
Oakfield ANF/KKDL L4 97 K7
Oakfield Av GOL/RIS/CU WA3 92 B4
WLTN L25 131 J1
Oakfield Cl STHEL WA9 101 M6
Oakfield Crs WGNE/HIN WN2 57 L8
Oakfield Dr FMBY L37 58 F1
HUY L36 116 B5
WDN WA8 133 J5
Oakfield Gv HUY L36 116 B5
Oakfield Rd ANF/KKDL L4 97 J7
GTS/LS CH66 155 G5
HTWN L38 70 B3
PS/BROM CH62 143 L5
Oakford Cl CHTN/BK PR9 23 K8
Oakgate Cl NG/CROX L11 98 D2
Oak Gn ORM L39 51 H8
Oak Gv EP CH65 163 J2
Oakham Ct CHTN/BK PR9 * 3 K2
Oakham Dr AIN/FAZ L10 85 H4
MOR/LEA CH46 109 K4
Oakham St TOX L8 112 F7
Oakhill Cl MGHL L31 72 F3
WD/CROXPK L12 98 F2
Oak Hill Cl WGN WN1 * 68 D2
Oakhill Cottage La MGHL L31 72 F1
Oakhill Dr MGHL L31 72 E1
Oakhill Pk CLB/OSW/ST L13 114 D3
Oakhill Rd CLB/OSW/ST L13 114 D3
MGHL L31 72 F3
Oakhurst Cl WLTN L25 131 K1
Oakland Cl LITH L21 83 L7
Oakland Dr GR/UP/WCH CH49 110 C7
Oakland Rd ALL/GAR L19 130 B5
Oaklands RAIN/WH L35 117 L2
Oaklands Av CSBY/BLUN L23 71 G8
Oaklands Ct STHEL WA9 118 E1
Oaklands Dr BEB CH63 128 C7
HES CH60 141 J4
LYMM WA13 139 M3
Oaklands Rd GOL/RIS/CU WA3 93 H6
Oaklands Ter PEN/TH CH61 * 141 J3
Oakland St WARR WA1 15 M1
WDN WA8 149 J1
Oak La WD/CROXPK L12 98 E3
Oak La North WD/CROXPK L12 98 E3
Oaklea WGNNW/ST WN6 55 J3
Oakleaf Ms CL/PREN CH43 110 F8
Oaklea Rd PEN/TH CH61 126 B7
Oaklee Gv NWD/KWIPK L33 86 C1
Oak Leigh CLB/OSW/ST L13 98 A8
Oakleigh SKEL WN8 76 F3
Oakleigh Gv BEB CH63 128 B7
Oakley Av WGNW/BIL/O WN5 77 M7
Oakley Cl WD/CROXPK L12 99 G2
Oakley Ct EP CH65 20 D8
Oakley Dr WGNW/BIL/O WN5 68 A7
The Oaklings WGNE/HIN WN2 81 J2
Oak Meadows Ct RAIN/WH L35 118 A4
Oakmere Cl MOR/LEA CH46 110 A1
WLT/FAZ L9 84 C6
Oakmere Dr GR/UP/WCH CH49 125 L1
GTS/LS CH66 163 H5
WARRW/BUR WA5 136 B2
Oakmere St RUNC WA7 19 G4
Oakmoore RUNC WA7 151 H1
Oakridge Cl PS/BROM CH62 143 L3
Oakridge Rd PS/BROM CH62 143 L3
Oak Rd BEB CH63 128 B6
GTS/LS CH66 155 G4
HUY L36 115 M5
LYMM WA13 139 L2
RAIN/WH L35 117 G2
WARRW/BUR WA5 136 B2
Oaks Cl STHEL WA9 118 F2
Oaks La PEN/TH CH61 141 J1
Oaksmeade Cl WD/CROXPK L12 99 H2
Oaks Pl WDN WA8 16 C5
The Oaks CHLY/EC PR7 43 K1
PS/BROM CH62 143 L5
WD/CROXPK L12 99 H2
WKBY CH48 * 124 E4
Oakston Av RAIN/WH L35 117 M3
Oak St BTL L20 7 H2
EP CH65 156 E6
GOL/RIS/CU WA3 106 C6
STHEL WA9 103 G5
STHP PR8 25 G7
WGN WN1 5 J4
Oaksway HES CH60 141 K7
Oak Ter EHL/KEN L7 * 113 L3
Oakthorn Gv RNFD/HAY WA11 90 E7
Oak Tree Ct SKEL WN8 65 M2
Oaktree Pl RF/TRAN CH42 128 B2
Oaktree Rd ECCL WA10 88 C8
Oak V CLB/OSW/ST L13 114 D3
Oak Vw SPK/HALE L24 147 J2
Oakways WARRS WA4 137 M8
Oak Wharf Ms WARRS WA4 * 137 L5
Oakwood SKEL WN8 * 65 M2
Oakwood Av AIMK WN4 91 J3
STHP PR8 34 F7
WARR WA1 15 K2
WGNNW/ST WN6 55 H8
Oakwood Cl WLTN L25 115 K8
Oakwood Dr CL/PREN CH43 111 G5
HUY L36 116 B4
STHP PR8 35 G8
Oakwood Ga GOL/RIS/CU WA3 122 F1
Oakwood Pk PS/BROM CH62 143 M8
Oakwood Rd CHLY/EC PR7 32 D7
CHLY/EC PR7 43 H3
HLWD L26 132 A6
Oakwood Vw CHLY/EC PR7 43 K1
Oakworth Cl NWD/KWIPK L33 86 A1
Oakworth Dr HUY L36 116 C6
PS/BROM CH62 128 E6
Oarside Dr WAL/NB CH45 95 J7
Oasis Cl BRSC L40 39 K2
Oatfield La LITH L21 83 K3
Oatlands Rd KKBY L32 * 85 L3
The Oatlands WKBY CH48 124 E4
Oban Dr AIMK WN4 90 E1
HES CH60 141 J5
Oban Gv WARRN/WOL WA2 122 C2
Oban Rd ANF/KKDL L4 97 K7
Oban Wy WGNE/HIN WN2 * 57 M8
Oberon St BTL L20 7 H9
O'Brien Gv STHEL WA9 103 G1
Observatory Rd CL/PREN CH43 110 F5
Oceanic Rd CLB/OSW/ST L13 114 B3
Ocean Rd LITH L21 83 K6
O'Connell Cl RNFD/HAY WA11 90 E7
O'Connell Rd VAUX/LVPD L3 13 G2
Octavia Ct HUY L36 * 116 B4
Octavia Hill Rd LITH L21 83 L4
Odsey St EHL/KEN L7 113 L3
Off Botanic Rd CHTN/BK PR9 25 J4
Ogle Cl RAIN/WH L35 101 G8
Oglet La SPK/HALE L24 146 E3
Oil Sites Rd EP CH65 20 E2
Oil St VAUX/LVPD L3 12 C2
O'Keeffe Rd STHEL WA9 9 M4
Okehampton Rd CHLDW L16 114 F5
Okell Dr HLWD L26 131 M4
Okell Gv LEIGH WN7 81 M8
Okell St RUNC WA7 19 G4
Old Acre HTWN L38 70 B2
Old Barn Rd ANF/KKDL L4 97 K7
WAL/EG CH44 111 J2
Old Bidston Rd BIRK CH41 10 E2
Old Boston RNFD/HAY WA11 91 J6
Old Boundary Wy ORM L39 51 H7
Oldbridge Dr WGNE/HIN WN2 69 M7
Oldbridge Rd SPK/HALE L24 147 H2
Old Bridge Wy CHLYE PR6 32 F4
Old Chapel Ct CHLYE PR6 * 44 C6
Old Cherry La LYMM WA13 139 J7
Old Chester Rd FROD/HEL WA6 166 D2
GTS/LS CH66 155 M8
RF/TRAN CH42 128 B3
WARRS WA4 137 H6
Old Church Cl EP CH65 * 20 D1
Old Church Yd CLVP L2 12 E7
Old Colliery Rd RAIN/WH L35 116 F2
Old Colliery Yd AIMK WN4 90 E2
Old Court House Rd
PS/BROM CH62 128 F8
Old Dawber's La CHLY/EC PR7 31 K4
Old Distillery Rd SPK/HALE L24 131 K8
Old Dover Rd HUY L36 115 L5
Old Eccleston La ECCL WA10 101 L2
Old Engine La SKEL WN8 64 E3
Olde Stoneheath Ct CHLYE PR6 44 D1
Old Farm Cl NSTN CH64 154 C5
Old Farm Rd CSBY/BLUN L23 83 H1
KKBY L32 86 B7
Oldfield Cl HES CH60 141 G3
Oldfield Dr HES CH60 140 E4
Oldfield Gdns HES CH60 140 F4
Oldfield La WKBY CH48 109 J8
Oldfield Rd ALL/GAR L19 130 C4
EP CH65 20 B5
HES CH60 140 F3
LYMM WA13 139 L1
Oldfield St ECCL WA10 8 F1
Oldfield Wy HES CH60 140 F3
Old Fold WGNW/BIL/O WN5 67 K7
Old Fold Rd WGNE/HIN WN2 57 M8
Oldgate WDN WA8 133 L7
Old Gorsey La WAL/EG CH44 111 K3
Old Greasby Rd
GR/UP/WCH CH49 110 B8
Old Hall RAIN/WH L35 117 G5
Old Hall Cl MGHL L31 72 F6
WARRS WA4 137 J5
Old Hall Dr AIMK WN4 91 J3
EP CH65 20 B7
Old Hall Gdns RNFD/HAY WA11 76 C7
Old Hall La CHLY/EC PR7 31 K7
CHNE CH2 165 K2
KKBY L32 85 M3
Old Hall Rd MGHL L31 72 F6
PS/BROM CH62 144 B4
WARRW/BUR WA5 120 F5
Old Hall St VAUX/LVPD L3 12 D5
WGNS/IIMK WN3 5 K8
Oldham Pl CLVPS L1 13 J8
Oldham St CLVPS L1 13 J9
WARRS WA4 15 H9
Old Haymarket CLVPS L1 13 H6
Old Higher Rd WDN WA8 132 F8
Old Hutte La SPK/HALE L24 132 C8
Old Kennel Cl STBRV L28 99 H5
Old La BRSC L40 40 F5
FMBY L37 47 H7
MGHL L31 73 G1
ORM L39 61 G2
PR/KW L34 101 H7
RAIN/WH L35 117 K3
RNFD/HAY WA11 76 B6
WGNNW/ST WN6 55 K7
Old Leeds St VAUX/LVPD L3 12 D5
Old Links Cl CHTN/BK PR9 25 K5
Old Liverpool Rd
WARRW/BUR WA5 14 A7
Old Lodge Cl WD/CROXPK L12 98 D5
Old Lord's Crs HOR/BR BL6 45 K8
Old Market Pl WARR WA1 14 D5
Old Maryland La
MOR/LEA CH46 110 A4
Old Meadow PR/KW L34 86 F8
Old Meadow Rd PEN/TH CH61 141 G2
Old Mill Av STHEL WA9 102 F8
Old Mill Cl HES CH60 141 K6
Old Mill Hl ORM L39 62 F2
Old Mill La FMBY L37 59 H1
PR/KW L34 100 A1
WAV L15 114 C5
Old Moss La ORM L39 48 E8
Old Nook La RNFD/HAY WA11 90 A7
Old Orch RAIN/WH L35 117 G4
Old Park La CHTN/BK PR9 25 J6
Old Pepper La WGNNW/ST WN6 55 K3
Old Post Office Pl CLVPS L1 * 13 G8
Old Prescot Cl MGHL L31 73 L3
Old Pump La GR/UP/WCH CH49 125 L2
The Old Quarry WLTN L25 131 J3
Old Quay Cl NSTN CH64 152 E6
Old Quay La NSTN CH64 152 F6
Old Quay St RUNC WA7 19 K2
Old Racecourse Rd MGHL L31 72 D5
Old Rake HOR/BR BL6 45 M7
Old Rectory Gn ORM L39 62 C6
SFTN L29 72 A6
Old Riding DV/KA/FCH L14 99 H8
Old Rd AIMK WN4 79 J8
WARRS WA4 14 F8
Old Ropery CLVP L2 * 12 E7
Old Rough La NWD/KWIPK L33 86 A3
Old School Cl NSTN CH64 153 H8
Old School House La
WARRN/WOL WA2 105 J6
Old School La CHLY/EC PR7 31 M2
CHLY/EC PR7 44 A8
Old School Pl AIMK WN4 91 J2
Old School Wy CL/PREN CH43 * 111 G6
Old Smithy La LYMM WA13 139 L3
Old Thomas La DV/KA/FCH L14 114 F4
Old Town Cl SKEL WN8 64 F5
Old Town La FMBY L37 59 G1
Old Town Wy SKEL WN8 64 F5
Old Upton La WDN WA8 133 M2
Old Vicarage Rd NSTN CH64 154 C5
Old Wargrave Rd NEWLW WA12 104 D2
Old Whint Rd RNFD/HAY WA11 90 C7
Old Will's La HOR/BR BL6 45 K7
Old Wood Rd PEN/TH CH61 141 H1
Oleander Dr ECCL WA10 101 L1
O'Leary St WARRN/WOL WA2 15 H1
Olga Rd STHEL WA9 102 E6
Olinda St PS/BROM CH62 128 D6
Olive Cl MGHL L31 * 85 J3
Olive Crs BIRK CH41 11 K9
Olivedale Rd CALD/MH L18 130 B1
Olive Dr NSTN CH64 153 G5
Olive Gv HUY L36 115 M3
NTHTN L30 84 C4
SKEL WN8 65 G4
STHP PR8 25 G6
WAV L15 114 C4
WGNNW/ST WN6 68 B2
Olive La WAV L15 114 C5
Olive Mt BIRK CH41 11 K9
Olive Mount Rd WAV L15 114 C5
Oliver La BIRK CH41 11 J6
GTS/LS CH66 162 F1
Oliver Lyme Rd PR/KW L34 101 G7
Olive Rd CSBY/WL L22 83 G5
NSTN CH64 153 G5
Oliver Rd ECCL WA10 101 L4
Oliver St BIRK CH41 11 H6
WARRN/WOL WA2 14 E3
Oliver St East BIRK CH41 11 J6
Olivetree Rd WAV L15 114 D5
Olive V WAV L15 114 B5
Olivia Cl CL/PREN CH43 126 E1
Olivia St BTL L20 7 J8
Ollerton Cl CL/PREN CH43 126 E1
WARRS WA4 138 D2
WGNE/HIN WN2 69 J3
Ollerton St CHLYE PR6 44 C5
Ollery Gn NTHTN L30 84 D1
Ollier St WDN WA8 16 C6
Olney St ANF/KKDL L4 97 H3
Olton St WAV L15 114 A5
Olympia St NPK/KEN L6 113 J2
Olympic Wy WLT/FAZ L9 84 C5
Omega Bvd WARRW/BUR WA5 119 M4
O'Neill St BTL L20 6 E2
Onslow Crs STHP PR8 35 J3
Onslow Rd NPK/KEN L6 113 L2
PS/BROM CH62 128 D5
WAL/NB CH45 95 K5
Opal Cl LITH L21 83 L5
NPK/KEN L6 113 K1
Openfields Cl HLWD L26 132 A3
Oppenheim Av ECCL WA10 101 L5
Orange Gv TOX L8 113 L7
WARRN/WOL WA2 122 A3
Orange Tree Cl STBRV L28 * 99 K5
Oran Wy HUY L36 115 M2
Orb Cl NG/CROX L11 98 E2
Orchard Av CHLDW L16 114 F4
Orchard Cl CHLY/EC PR7 31 M1
FROD/HEL WA6 160 C7
GTS/LS CH66 163 H4
PR/KW L34 101 J6
RAIN/WH L35 117 G4
RNFD/HAY WA11 89 M6
WGNNW/ST WN6 55 J6
Orchard Ct BIRK CH41 128 B2
Orchard Dl CSBY/BLUN L23 83 H1
Orchard Dr NSTN CH64 153 G8
Orchard Gra MOR/LEA CH46 109 L6
Orchard Hvn GTS/LS CH66 163 G4
Orchard Hey ECCL WA10 101 J2
MGHL L31 73 G5
NTHTN L30 84 D2
Orchard La GTS/LS CH66 155 J5
STHP PR8 47 M1
Orchard Park La CHNE CH2 165 K1
Orchard Pl FROD/HEL WA6 166 E1
Orchard Rd EP CH65 163 J3
MOR/LEA CH46 110 A4
The Orchards WGNW/BIL/O WN5 67 G8
Orchard St AIMK WN4 91 L2
WARR WA1 15 G5
WARRN/WOL WA2 122 C3
WARRS WA4 137 L5
WGN WN1 5 G3
The Orchard AIG/SPK L17 130 B4
CROS/BRETH PR26 29 L2
FROD/HEL WA6 166 C3
HUY L36 116 A4
ORM L39 50 F8
WAL/NB CH45 95 J6
Orchard Vw ORM L39 62 F4
Orchard Wk RUNC WA7 * 150 B6
Orchard Wy BEB CH63 127 M7
WDN WA8 133 J2
Orchid Cl SKEL WN8 66 D7
Orchid Gv AIG/SPK L17 129 H2
Orchid Wy STHEL WA9 103 K6
Orchil Cl GTS/LS CH66 155 J7
Ordnance Av GOL/RIS/CU WA3 123 H1
O'Reilly Ct VAUX/LVPD L3 12 E1
Orford Av WARRN/WOL WA2 15 G1
Orford Gn WARRN/WOL WA2 121 M4
Orford La WARRN/WOL WA2 14 F2
Orford Rd WARRN/WOL WA2 121 M5
Orford St WARR WA1 14 F5
WAV L15 114 B5
Organ St WGNE/HIN WN2 81 K2
Oriel Cl AIN/FAZ L10 84 F2
Oriel Crs BTL L20 7 H9
Oriel Dr AIN/FAZ L10 84 F2
Oriel Rd AIMK WN4 91 H1
BTL L20 6 F6
RF/TRAN CH42 128 A2
Oriel St VAUX/LVPD L3 12 F3
Orient Dr WLTN L25 131 K2
Origen Rd CHLDW L16 114 F4
Oriole Cl ECCL WA10 101 K6
Orion Bvd WARRW/BUR WA5 120 A4
Orith Av ECCL WA10 101 H2
Orkney Cl EP CH65 163 L4
RNFD/HAY WA11 89 M6
WDN WA8 135 G2
Orlando Cl CL/PREN CH43 126 E1
Orlando St BTL L20 7 H9
Orleans Rd CLB/OSW/ST L13 114 C2
Ormande St STHEL WA9 102 D4
Ormesby Gv BEB CH63 143 J7
Ormiston Rd WAL/NB CH45 95 K6
Ormond Av BRSC L40 63 M1
Ormonde Av MGHL L31 72 E6
Ormonde Crs NWD/KWIPK L33 86 C3
Ormonde Dr MGHL L31 72 E5
Ormond St VAUX/LVPD L3 12 E6
WAL/NB CH45 95 K8
Ormond Wy CL/PREN CH43 126 E1
Ormsby Cl WGNNW/ST WN6 56 A4
Ormsby St WAV L15 114 A6
Ormside Cl WGNE/HIN WN2 81 K2
Ormside Gv STHEL WA9 102 F6
Ormskirk Old Rd ORM L39 64 B6
Ormskirk Rd ORM L39 63 L4
PR/KW L34 86 F8
RNFD/HAY WA11 75 M4
SKEL WN8 64 A6
SKEL WN8 64 E4
SKEL WN8 65 L6
SKEL WN8 66 A6
WGNW/BIL/O WN5 4 A6
WLT/FAZ L9 84 D3
Ormskirk St ECCL WA10 8 F4
Ormston Av HOR/BR BL6 45 K8
Orms Wy FMBY L37 59 G2
Orphan Dr NPK/KEN L6 97 M8
Orphan St EHL/KEN L7 113 J5
Orpington St WGNW/BIL/O WN5 67 L7
Orrell Ar WGN WN1 4 E3
Orrell Cl WARRW/BUR WA5 120 C7
Orrell Gdns WGNW/BIL/O WN5 67 H7
Orrell Hall Cl WGNW/BIL/O WN5 67 K6
Orrell Hey BTL L20 83 M6
Orrell Hill La HTWN L38 70 E1
Orrell La BRSC L40 38 F8
BTL L20 84 B6
Orrell Ms BRSC L40 * 39 G8
Orrell Mt BTL L20 83 L6
Orrell Rd BTL L20 83 L6
WAL/NB CH45 95 L6
WGNW/BIL/O WN5 67 G6
Orrell St STHEL WA9 9 M5
WGN WN1 5 G6
Orret's Meadow Rd
GR/UP/WCH CH49 126 D2
Orrysdale Rd WKBY CH48 124 C2
Orry St EV L5 96 F8
Orsett Rd KKBY L32 86 B5
Orston Crs BEB CH63 143 J3
Ortega Cl PS/BROM CH62 128 E6
Orthes St VAUX/LVPD L3 13 L8
Orton Rd CHLDW L16 114 E5
Orton Wy AIMK WN4 91 H2
Orville St STHEL WA9 103 H6
Orwell Cl FMBY L37 58 F4
STHEL WA9 118 C2
Orwell Rd ANF/KKDL L4 96 F5
Osbert Rd CSBY/BLUN L23 82 D1
Osborne Av WAL/NB CH45 95 K6
WARRN/WOL WA2 121 M4
Osborne Ct PS/BROM CH62 128 D6
Osborne Gv PR/KW L34 100 C8
WAL/NB CH45 95 K7
Osborne Rd AIMK WN4 91 J1
CL/PREN CH43 10 D7
CLB/OSW/ST L13 98 A7
ECCL WA10 88 C8
FMBY L37 59 G4
GOL/RIS/CU WA3 93 G6
LITH L21 83 L4
STHP PR8 34 D7
WAL/NB CH45 95 L6
WARRS WA4 137 K4
Osborne Wd AIG/SPK L17 129 M4
Osbourne Cl PS/BROM CH62 144 A6
Osier Cl CHNE CH2 165 L2
Osmaston Rd RF/TRAN CH42 127 J3
Osprey Cl CHLYE PR6 33 J2
NTHLY L27 116 B8
RUNC WA7 150 B8
WARRN/WOL WA2 122 A2
The Ospreys WGNS/IIMK WN3 78 E2
Ossett Cl CL/PREN CH43 126 E1
RUNC WA7 150 F5
Osterley Gdns WLT/FAZ L9 84 B7
O'Sullivan Crs RNFD/HAY WA11 90 A8
Oteley Av PS/BROM CH62 143 M5
Othello Cl BTL L20 7 H9
Otterburn Cl MOR/LEA CH46 109 K5
Otterspool Dr AIG/SPK L17 129 M5
Otterspool Rd AIG/SPK L17 129 M4
Otterton Rd NG/CROX L11 85 L8
Otterwood Sq
WGNW/BIL/O WN5 67 L3
Ottery Cl CHTN/BK PR9 22 C8
Ottley St NPK/KEN L6 113 L2
Otway St ALL/GAR L19 145 L1
Oueenswood Av BEB CH63 128 A5
Oulton Cl CL/PREN CH43 127 G2
MGHL L31 72 D1
Oulton La HUY L36 115 L5
Oulton Rd CHLDW L16 114 F7
Oulton Wy CL/PREN CH43 127 G3
Oundle Dr AIN/FAZ L10 84 E2
Oundle Pl WLTN L25 131 K6
Oundle Rd MOR/LEA CH46 110 A4
Outer Central Rd SPK/HALE L24 132 A8
Outer Forum NG/CROX L11 98 A3
Out La CROS/BRETH PR26 29 L3
WLTN L25 131 K3
Outlet La MGHL L31 74 A4
The Oval EP CH65 20 D8
WAL/NB CH45 95 H7
WGNNW/ST WN6 55 H8
Overbeck Cl WGNNW/ST WN6 68 C1
Overbrook La PR/KW L34 86 E8
Overbury St EHL/KEN L7 113 K4
Overchurch Rd
GR/UP/WCH CH49 110 A7
Overdale Av PEN/TH CH61 126 F8
Overdale Rd NSTN CH64 154 C4
Overdene Wk KKBY L32 86 B4
Overgreen Gv MOR/LEA CH46 109 M4
Overhill Wy WGNS/IIMK WN3 78 F2
Overpool Gdns GTS/LS CH66 163 H2
Overpool Rd GTS/LS CH66 156 A8
Overton Av LITH L21 83 K4
Overton Cl CL/PREN CH43 127 H2
KKBY L32 85 M4
Overton Dr FROD/HEL WA6 160 E7
Overton Rd WAL/EG CH44 111 K1
Overton St EHL/KEN L7 113 K4
Overton Wy CL/PREN CH43 127 H2
Ovington Cl RUNC WA7 161 H1
Ovington Dr STHP PR8 36 A2
Ovolo Rd CLB/OSW/ST L13 114 C1
Owen Av ORM L39 51 H7
Owen Cl ECCL WA10 101 L4
Owen Dr SPK/HALE L24 146 D3
Owen Rd ANF/KKDL L4 96 F5
NWD/KWIPK L33 86 E6
RAIN/WH L35 117 L3
Owen's La ORM L39 60 F3
Owens St CHLYE PR6 * 33 G6
Owen St ECCL WA10 101 L4
LEIGH WN7 * 81 M8
WARRN/WOL WA2 14 D2
Owlsfield NEWLW WA12 105 G2
Oxborough Cl WDN WA8 134 B2
Oxbow Rd WD/CROXPK L12 99 G5
Oxburgh Rd WGNS/IIMK WN3 80 B1
Oxendale Cl TOX L8 113 K6
Oxenham Rd WARRN/WOL WA2 121 J2
Oxenholme Crs NG/CROX L11 98 C4
Oxford Av BTL L20 7 L5
LITH L21 83 K5
Oxford Cl AIG/SPK L17 129 L3
GTS/LS CH66 163 G5
Oxford Ct STHP PR8 35 H1
WGN WN1 5 H2
Oxford Dr BEB CH63 142 C7
CSBY/WL L22 82 E4
HLWD L26 132 B5
Oxford Gdns STHP PR8 2 B9
Oxford Rd BTL L20 7 K5
CSBY/WL L22 82 E3
HUY L36 116 C1
RUNC WA7 19 G6
SKEL WN8 65 G4
STHP PR8 2 A8
WAL/EG CH44 111 L1
WGNW/BIL/O WN5 67 H6
WLT/FAZ L9 84 D5
Oxford St CHLY/EC PR7 32 E6
CHLY/EC PR7 44 B7
ECCL WA10 8 E3
EHL/KEN L7 13 L8
NEWLW WA12 104 C2
WARRS WA4 15 H8
WDN WA8 16 E5
Oxheys RUNC WA7 150 E5
Oxhouse Rd WGNW/BIL/O WN5 77 L1
Ox La RAIN/WH L35 116 E7
Oxley Av MOR/LEA CH46 110 D2
Oxley St STHEL WA9 102 F6
Oxmead Cl WARRN/WOL WA2 122 D4
Oxmoor Cl RUNC WA7 150 C8
Oxton Cl AIG/SPK L17 129 L3
KKBY L32 85 K5
WDN WA8 133 L1
Oxton Gn GTS/LS CH66 162 F1
Oxton Rd BIRK CH41 10 F8
WAL/EG CH44 111 K2
Oxton St ANF/KKDL L4 97 H5

P

Pacific Rd BIRK CH41 11 L3
BTL L20 6 E4
Packenham Rd CLB/OSW/ST L13 98 B7
Paddington EHL/KEN L7 113 J4
Paddington Bank WARR WA1 122 B7
Paddock Cl CSBY/BLUN L23 70 D7
Paddock Dr NSTN CH64 152 F3
Paddock Gv STHEL WA9 118 F2
Paddock Hey NTHLY L27 115 M7
Paddock Ri RUNC WA7 161 G1
WGNNW/ST WN6 68 A2
Paddock Rd SKEL WN8 65 L8
The Paddock AIMK WN4 79 H7
BRSC L40 39 L1
CHNE CH2 165 J2
FMBY L37 47 J8
FROD/HEL WA6 166 E3
GR/UP/WCH CH49 110 D8
GTS/LS CH66 162 F2
HES CH60 141 L5
KKBY L32 85 M6
MOR/LEA CH46 109 L6
ORM L39 62 E2
PR/KW L34 101 H6
STHP PR8 47 K1
WLTN L25 131 K1
Padeswood Cl STHEL WA9 102 E7
Padgate La WARR WA1 15 L2
Padstow Cl CHTN/BK PR9 22 C8
HLWD L26 132 A5
WARRW/BUR WA5 136 A2
Padstow Dr ECCL WA10 88 D7
Padstow Rd CHLDW L16 114 F5
GR/UP/WCH CH49 125 L3
Pagebank Rd DV/KA/FCH L14 115 J2
Page Ct FMBY L37 59 H2
Pagefield Cl WGNNW/ST WN6 4 B1
Pagefield Rd WAV L15 114 C7
Pagefield St WGNNW/ST WN6 4 B1
Page La WDN WA8 17 H2
Page Moss Av HUY L36 115 K1
Page Moss La HUY L36 115 K1
Page Wk VAUX/LVPD L3 13 K4
Pagewood Cl CL/PREN CH43 126 F1
Paignton Cl HUY L36 116 D3
WARRW/BUR WA5 136 A1
WGNW/BIL/O WN5 78 A5
Paignton Rd CHLDW L16 114 F5
WAL/NB CH45 95 G7
Painswick Rd GTS/LS CH66 163 G3
Paisley Av PS/BROM CH62 155 G1
RNFD/HAY WA11 89 M6
Paisley St VAUX/LVPD L3 12 D4
Palace Ar AIMK WN4 91 K2
Palace Fields Av RUNC WA7 150 C6
Palace Hey NSTN CH64 153 J8
Palace Rd STHP PR8 2 A8
WLT/FAZ L9 84 C7
Palatine Ar ECCL WA10 * 9 G5
Palatine Cl WGNS/IIMK WN3 79 G1
Palatine Rd PS/BROM CH62 143 L4

STHP PR8 2 C7
WAL/EG CH44 111 M3
Palatine Sq LEIGH WN7 81 M8
Palermo Cl WAL/EG CH44 111 M3
Palewood Cl WGN WN1 5 J1
Paley Cl WGN WN1 97 H6
Palin Dr WARRW/BUR WA5 120 B7
Palin St WGNE/HIN WN2 81 K2
Palladio Rd CLB/OSW/ST L13 114 C1
Palliser Cl GOL/RIS/CU WA3 123 J2
Pall Ml CHLY/EC PR7 32 E7
  HOR/BR BL6 45 J6
  VAUX/LVPD L3 12 C5
Palm Av AIMK WN4 78 F8
Palm Cl WLT/FAZ L9 97 L2
Palm Ct SKEL WN8 65 G3
Palmer Cl CL/PREN CH43 126 F2
  ECCL WA10 8 E4
Palmer Crs WARRW/BUR WA5 120 F5
Palmerston Av LITH L21 83 J6
Palmerston Cl CALD/MH L18 130 B2
Palmerston Crs ALL/GAR L19 130 E7
Palmerston Dr LITH L21 83 K7
Palmerston Rd ALL/GAR L19 130 E7
  CALD/MH L18 130 B2
  CHTN/BK PR9 25 H7
  WAL/EG CH44 111 H1
Palmerston St RF/TRAN CH42 128 B3
Palm Gv CHTN/BK PR9 3 M5
  CL/PREN CH43 10 C9
  GTS/LS CH66 163 J4
  STHP PR8 25 C7
  WGNW/BIL/O WN5 M7
  WLTN L25 131 K4
Palm Hl CL/PREN CH43 10 C9
Palmwood Av RAIN/WH L35 117 M3
Palmwood Cl CL/PREN CH43 127 G4
Palmyra Sq North WARR WA1 14 D6
Palmyra Sq South WARR WA1 14 C7
Paltridge Wy PEN/TH CH61 141 H1
Pamela Cl AIN/FAZ L10 85 K6
Pampas Gv WLT/FAZ L9 97 K1
Pangbourne Cl WARRS WA4 138 D3
Pankhurst Rd LITH L21 83 L4
Pansy St EV L5 96 D8
Parade Crs SPK/HALE L24 147 G3
Parade St ECCL WA10 9 H4
The Parade GOL/RIS/CU WA3 * 107 G2
  NSTN L64 152 E5
Paradise La FMBY L37 47 J8
  RAIN/WH L35 116 F3
Paradise Rw CHLYE PR6 33 H2
  CLVPS L1 13 G7
Paragon Cl WDN WA8 118 D8
Parbold Av RNFD/HAY WA11 89 M8
Parbold Cl BRSC L40 52 A2
Parbold Ct WDN WA8 133 M6
Parbold Hl SKEL WN8 53 M3
Parbrook Cl HUY L36 99 H1
Parbrook La WGNNW/ST WN6 55 L5
Parbrook Rd HUY L36 99 M8
The Parchments NEWLW WA12 104 F1
Paris Av WGNS/IIMK WN3 78 D2
Park Av CALD/MH L18 130 A2
  CHLY/EC PR7 31 M3
  CHTN/BK PR9 25 J5
  CSBY/BLUN L23 71 G8
  FMBY L37 59 H4
  GOL/RIS/CU WA3 92 B3
  MGHL L31 72 F2
  ORM L39 51 J8
  PR/KW L34 101 H6
  RAIN/WH L35 117 L1
  RNFD/HAY WA11 90 C7
  WAL/EG CH44 111 M2
  WARRS WA4 137 M2
  WDN WA8 18 A8
  WGNNW/ST WN6 55 K6
  WGNW/BIL/O WN5 78 A4
  WLT/FAZ L9 84 F7
Park Av North NEWLW WA12 104 F1
Park Av South NEWLW WA12 104 F1
Park Bvd WARR WA1 14 E8
Parkbourn MGHL L31 73 J3
Parkbourn Dr MGHL L31 73 J3
Parkbourn North MGHL L31 73 J3
Parkbridge Rd RF/TRAN CH42 128 E3
Park Brow Dr KKBY L32 86 B5
Parkbury Ct CL/PREN CH43 127 J2
Park Cl BIRK CH41 10 F5
  FMBY L37 59 G5
  KKBY L32 85 K2
  SKEL WN8 53 L2
Park Ct CSBY/WL L22 83 G4
  RUNC WA7 19 G8
Park Crs CHTN/BK PR9 24 F7
  ORM L39 61 H1
  WARRS WA4 137 M7
  WGN WN1 4 C2
Park Crs West WGN WN1 4 C2
Parkdale WKBY CH48 124 F7
Parkdale Av WLT/FAZ L9 84 C6
Parkdale Rd WARR WA1 122 C6
Park Dr BIRK CH41 10 A3
  CSBY/BLUN L23 71 J6
  CSBY/BLUN L23 82 C1
  EP CH65 20 A3
Parkend Dr LEIGH WN7 93 M3
Parkend Rd RF/TRAN CH42 127 L2
Parker Av LITH L21 83 H6
Parker Cl NTHTN L30 72 A6
Parker Crs ORM L39 51 H6
Parkers Ct RUNC WA7 150 A7
Parker St CHLY/EC PR7 32 E5
  CLVPS L1 13 H4
  RUNC WA7 19 J2
  WARR WA1 14 C7
Parkfield WGNNW/ST WN6 55 K6
Parkfield Av BIRK CH41 11 H5
  NTHTN L30 84 C4
  WARRS WA4 138 C1
Parkfield Cl ORM L39 62 E2
Parkfield Dr EP CH65 3 J3
  FROD/HEL WA6 166 D2
  WAL/EG CH44 111 K1
Parkfield Pl BIRK CH41 11 H5
Parkfield Rd AIG/SPK L17 129 K1
  BEB CH63 143 H6
  CSBY/WL L22 83 G3
Parkfields WGNE/HIN WN2 80 D6
Parkfields La WARRW/WOL WA2 122 B3
Parkgate Cl AIG/SPK L17 130 A4
Parkgate La NSTN L64 142 A8
Parkgate Rd AIG/BCN L60 162 B7
  NSTN L64 152 E7
  WARRS WA4 137 M4
Parkgate Wy RUNC WA7 150 E6

Parkland Cl TOX L8 113 J8
Parkland Ct CL/PREN CH43 110 E5
Parkland Dr CHNE CH2 165 K2
Parklands CHTN/BK PR9 25 G5
  PR/KW L34 99 M2
  RNFD/HAY WA11 76 B6
  SKEL WN8 155 M8
  WDN WA8 133 L2
Parklands Dr HES CH60 141 K7
  WGNE/HIN WN2 57 L7
Parklands Gdns GTS/LS CH66 155 M7
Parklands Vw GTS/LS CH66 155 M7
Parklands Wy CSBY/WL L22 83 H4
Park La BTL L20 84 A6
  CLVPS L1 13 G9
  FROD/HEL WA6 160 D5
  HOY L47 109 J3
  KIRK/FR/WA PR4 27 K3
  MGHL L31 73 G2
  NTHTN L30 84 C4
  WARRS WA4 137 H8
  WDN WA8 80 D6
Park Lane Dr MGHL L31 73 J3
Park La West NTHTN L30 84 B2
Parklea GTS/LS CH66 155 M7
Park Link ORM L39 62 D4
Park Pl BTL L20 7 H5
  TOX L8 113 H7
Park Rd CHLY/EC PR7 32 E5
  CHLY/EC PR7 43 G4
  CHNE CH2 165 G4
  CSBY/WL L22 83 G4
  EP CH65 20 C7
  HES CH60 141 H4
  HOY L47 109 G4
  KKBY L32 85 L2
  NEWLW WA12 92 B6
  NSTN L64 154 D5
  ORM L39 51 J8
  PS/BROM CH62 128 D8
  RF/TRAN CH42 128 B7
  RUNC WA7 18 F8
  STHEL WA9 9 M4
  TOX L8 113 H8
  WAL/EG CH44 111 L1
  WARRN/WOL WA2 121 M4
  WARRW/BUR WA5 119 L6
  WDN WA8 16 F1
  WGNE/HIN WN2 81 G2
  WGNNW/ST WN6 4 B1
  WGNNW/ST WN6 56 A5
  WGNW/BIL/O WN5 67 J7
  WGNW/BIL/O WN5 78 B3
  WKBY CH48 124 C3
Park Rd East BIRK CH41 10 F6
  NEWLW WA12 105 G6
Park Rd North BIRK CH41 10 A3
  NEWLW WA12 104 F3
Park Rd South CL/PREN CH43 10 E6
  NEWLW WA12 104 F3
Park Rd West CL/PREN CH43 10 B5
Parkside WAL/EG CH44 111 L2
  CHLY/EC PR7 32 E5
  STHEL WA9 118 D7
Parkside Av AIMK WN4 79 H5
  CHLY/EC PR7 32 E5
  STHEL WA9 118 D7
Parkside Cl BEB CH63 128 C7
  NSTN L64 152 F5
Parkside Crs WGNW/BIL/O WN5 67 H7
Parkside Dr WD/CROXPK L12 98 C5
Parkside Rd BEB CH63 128 C7
  NEWLW WA12 105 G6
  RF/TRAN CH42 128 A2
Parkside St NPK/KEN L6 13 M3
The Parks RNFD/HAY WA11 91 K4
Parkstile La NG/CROX L11 98 E1
Parkstone Rd RF/TRAN CH42 127 L2
Park St BIRK CH41 11 H5
  BTL L20 7 K4
  CHLY/EC PR7 30 E7
  CHLY/EC PR7 32 E5
  NSTN L64 153 G5
  RNFD/HAY WA11 90 B7
  STHEL WA9 9 M4
  TOX L8 113 C8
  WAL/EG CH44 111 L1
Parksway WARR WA1 122 D6
Park Ter CSBY/WL L22 83 G5
The Park HUY L36 116 A4
  WARRW/BUR WA5 135 M2
Parkvale Av CL/PREN CH43 127 G5
Park Vale Rd WLT/FAZ L9 84 C7
Park Vw AIMK WN4 91 K3
  CSBY/WL L22 82 F5
  HUY L36 115 L1
  NPK/KEN L6 97 M8
  PS/BROM CH62 143 L5
  WARRN/WOL WA2 122 A2
  WGNE/HIN WN2 80 D4
  WGNW/BIL/O WN5 67 K8
Parkview Dr NTHLY L27 132 A1
Park View Flats LITH L21 * 83 J5
Parkview Rd NG/CROX L11 98 E1
Park Wall Rd HTWN L38 71 H2
Park Wy HEY 59 H4
  HOY L47 109 M6
  TOX L8 113 H7
Parkway GTS/LS CH66 163 H5
  NTHTN L30 72 B6
  WAL/NB CH45 95 C6
  WGNNW/ST WN6 55 J3
Parkway GR/UP/WCH CH49 126 C5
Park Wy West KKBY L32 * 85 K2
Park West HES CH60 140 F6
Parkwood Cl LYMM WA13 139 M3
  PS/BROM CH62 144 A4
  WGNW/BIL/O WN5 * 67 K8
Parkwood Rd RAIN/WH L35 117 L3
  WLTN L25 131 L2
Park Works SPK/HALE L24 * 131 K7
Parlane St STHEL WA9 9 H4
Parliament Cl CLVPS L1 113 C6
Parliament Pl TOX L8 113 H6
Parliament St SKEL WN8 66 B5
  TOX L8 113 H5
  WGNS/IIMK WN3 5 H7
Parliament Wy GTS/LS CH66 163 H5
Parlington Cl WDN WA8 133 L6
Parlow Rd NG/CROX L11 98 A5
Parnell Rd BEB CH63 143 J3
Parr Cottage Cl CHLY/EC PR7 30 E6
Parren Av RAIN/WH L35 116 E4
  RNFD/HAY WA11 90 C7
Parr La CHTN/BK PR9 25 J4
Parr Mount Ct STHEL WA9 9 L5
Parr Mount St STHEL WA9 9 M5
Parr's La ORM L39 62 F5
Parrs Rd CL/PREN CH43 127 K2

Parr Stocks Rd STHEL WA9 102 F2
Parr St CLVPS L1 13 H9
  LITH L21 83 K4
  STHEL WA9 9 J6
  WARR WA1 4 F7
  WDN WA8 17 G7
Parrs Wood View WARRS WA4 138 C4
Parry Dr WARRS WA4 139 G2
Parry St WAL/EG CH44 111 M3
Parsonage Brow SKEL WN8 66 B5
Parsonage Cl SKEL WN8 66 C6
Parsonage Rd SKEL WN8 66 C6
  WDN WA8 149 J1
Parsonage Wy WARRW/BUR WA5 120 C8
Parson's Brow CHLY/EC PR7 32 E6
Parson's Wk WGN WN1 4 D2
Parthenon Dr NG/CROX L11 97 M2
Parthington Av BTL L20 7 J3
Parthington St WGNW/BIL/O WN5 68 A5
Parton St NPK/KEN L6 113 L2
Partridge Cl GOL/RIS/CU WA3 123 J2
Partridge Rd CSBY/BLUN L23 82 D1
  KKBY L32 85 K2
Pasture Av MOR/LEA CH46 110 A3
Pasture Cl AIMK WN4 79 G7
  STHEL WA9 118 E1
Pasture Crs MOR/LEA CH46 110 A3
Pasture Dr GOL/RIS/CU WA3 106 C4
Pasture La RNFD/HAY WA11 88 C1
  WARRN/WOL WA2 122 D4
Pasture Rd MOR/LEA CH46 110 A3
The Pastures CHTN/BK PR9 22 F8
  STHEL WA9 103 J6
  WKBY CH48 125 H3
Pateley Cl KKBY L32 85 L4
Pateley Sq WGNNW/ST WN6 68 D3
Paterson St BIRK CH41 10 F6
Patmos Cl EV L5 97 G7
Paton Cl WKBY CH48 124 E2
Patricia Av BIRK CH41 11 J4
Patricia Gv BTL L20 83 M7
Patricroft Rd WGNE/HIN WN2 5 L7
Patrivale Cl WARR WA1 122 B6
Patten La WARR WA1 14 E6
Patten's Cl NTHTN L30 83 M1
Patten St BIRK CH41 10 C2
Patten's Wk PR/KW L34 87 G8
Patterdale Av
  WARRW/WOL WA2 121 L3
Patterdale Crs MGHL L31 73 G3
Patterdale Pl WGNE/HIN WN2 69 J4
Patterdale Rd AIMK WN4 79 J5
  BEB CH63 143 H2
  WAV L15 114 A7
Patterson Cl GOL/RIS/CU WA3 123 J2
Patterson St NEWLW WA12 104 D1
Pauline Cl WARR WA1 119 M7
Pauline St WGNE/HIN WN2 81 K4
Paul McCartney Wy
  NPK/KEN L6 113 K2
Paul Orr Ct VAUX/LVPD L3 12 F3
Paulsfield Dr MOR/LEA CH46 110 A6
Paul's La CHTN/BK PR9 25 H2
Paul St VAUX/LVPD L3 12 F3
Paulton Cl TOX L8 129 H1
Paveley Bank NTHLY L27 115 M8
Pavilion Cl TOX L8 129 H1
Pavilion Vw CROS/BRETH PR26 29 J5
Paxton Pl SKEL WN8 66 C6
Paxton Rd HUY L36 116 A1
Payne Cl WARRW/BUR WA5 120 F7
Paythorne Cl GOL/RIS/CU WA3 107 H2
Peace Dr WARRW/BUR WA5 120 F8
Peacehaven Cl CHLDW L16 115 H5
Peach Gv MGHL L31 85 K1
  RNFD/HAY WA11 91 G6
Peach St EHL/KEN L7 13 M8
Peacock Av WARR WA1 15 M3
Peacock Fold LEIGH WN7 81 M7
Pearce Cl WLTN L25 115 H7
Pear Gv NPK/KEN L6 113 K2
Pearl St WGNNW/ST WN6 68 D2
Pearl Wy NPK/KEN L6 113 K1
Pearson Av WARRS WA4 137 M3
Pearson Ct WAV L15 114 C7
Pearson Dr BTL L20 84 A6
Pearson Rd BIRK CH41 11 J8
Pearson St WAV L15 114 B6
Pear Tree Av CHLY/EC PR7 43 H2
  RUNC WA7 19 G4
Peartree Cl FROD/HEL WA6 160 F4
Pear Tree Cl HES CH60 141 L4
Pear Tree La CHLY/EC PR7 32 A2
  WD/CROXPK L12 99 H2
Peartree Rd CROS/BRETH PR26 29 K2
Pear Tree Rd HUY L36 116 A5
Pear Tree Wy GTS/LS CH66 * 163 G2
Peasefield Rd DV/KA/FCH L14 115 J1
Peasley Cl WARRN/WOL WA2 122 D4
Peasley Cross La STHEL WA9 9 H6
Peatwood Av KKBY L32 86 B6
Peckers Hill Rd STHEL WA9 103 G6
Peckfield Cl RUNC WA7 150 C8
Peckforton Cl CLB/OSW/ST L13 98 A7
Peckforton Dr GTS/LS CH66 163 G2
  RUNC WA7 161 H1
Peckmill Gn NTHLY L27 132 B1
Peck Mill La FROD/HEL WA6 166 C6
Pecksniff Cl TOX L8 113 H8
Peebles Av RNFD/HAY WA11 89 M7
Peebles Cl AIMK WN4 90 E1
  GTS/LS CH66 155 H7
  NWD/KWIPK L33 73 M7
Peel Av BIRK CH41 128 B2
  RAIN/WH L35 117 G2
Peel Cl RAIN/WH L35 117 G2
Peel House La WDN WA8 134 D2
Peel Pl ECCL WA10 9 G2
  TOX L8 113 H6
Peel Rd BTL L20 6 D8
  SKEL WN8 66 A8
Peel St CHLY/EC PR7 32 E6
  CHLYE 44 D7
  NEWLW WA12 104 D2
  RUNC WA7 18 F2
  STHP PR8 25 H7
  TOX L8 113 H6
  WGNE/HIN WN2 80 D7
Peerswood Ct NSTN L64 153 G8
Peet Av ECCL WA10 101 L1
Peet's La CHTN/BK PR9 25 J4
Peet St WAV L15 114 B6
Pelham Gv AIG/SPK L17 129 L1
Pelham Rd WAL/EG CH44 111 J4
Pemberlei Rd WGNE/HIN WN2 69 M3
Pemberton Cl NSTN L64 154 C5

Pemberton Rd
  CLB/OSW/ST L13 114 C2
  GR/UP/WCH CH49 126 D2
  WGNW/BIL/O WN5 78 D4
Pembertons Ct ECCL WA10 * 8 D1
Pembrey Wy WLTN L25 131 J3
Pembridge Gdns EP CH65 21 G9
Pembroke Av MOR/LEA CH46 110 A6
Pembroke Dr EP CH65 163 J2
Pembroke Gdns VAUX/LVPD L3 13 L6
Pembroke Pl CHLY/EC PR7 32 D7
  VAUX/LVPD L3 13 M6
Pembroke St EV L5 81 L2
  VAUX/LVPD L3 13 M6
  WGNW/BIL/O WN5 67 M4
Pembury Cl WD/CROXPK L12 99 G2
Penare Gorran Hvn RUNC WA7 150 E7
Penarth Cl EHL/KEN L7 113 K5
Penbury Rd WGN WN1 56 D8
Pencombe Rd HUY L36 115 K1
Penda Dr NWD/KWIPK L33 74 A7
Pendennis Crs WAL/EG CH44 111 K2
Pendennis Rd WAL/EG CH44 111 K2
Pendennis St NPK/KEN L6 97 K8
Pendine Cl NPK/KEN L6 113 L1
  WARRW/BUR WA5 120 F3
Pendlebury Cl WGN WN1 56 E7
Pendlebury St STHEL WA9 118 E1
  WARRS WA4 138 B1
Pendle Cl GR/UP/WCH CH49 * 110 A7
  LITH L21 83 J1
  ORM L39 51 J7
Pendle Dr HOR/BR BL6 45 J8
Pendle Gdns GOL/RIS/CU WA3 107 G2
Pendle Hl SKEL WN8 76 F1
Pendle Rd GOL/RIS/CU WA3 92 E4
Pendleton Gn HLWD L26 132 A6
Pendleton Rd ANF/KKDL L4 97 J3
Penfold MGHL L31 73 G4
Penfold Cl CALD/MH L18 114 F8
  CH/BCN L37 162 D5
Penfolds RUNC WA7 149 M4
Pengallo Hey NTHLY L27 116 B8
Pengwern Gv WAV L15 113 M5
Pengwern St TOX L8 113 H5
Penhale Cl AIG/SPK L17 129 K3
Peninsula Cl WAL/NB CH45 95 G5
Penistone Dr GTS/LS CH66 155 J7
Penketh Av WARRW/BUR WA5 121 H5
Penketh Ct RUNC WA7 19 H3
Penketh Gn SPK/HALE L24 147 G1
Penketh Pl SKEL WN8 65 L8
Penketh Rd WARRW/BUR WA5 136 D1
Penketh's La RUNC WA7 19 H2
Penkett Gv WAL/NB CH45 95 K7
Penkett Rd WAL/NB CH45 95 K7
Penkford La WARRW/BUR WA5 103 M4
Penkford St NEWLW WA12 104 A1
Penlake La STHEL WA9 103 G6
Penlinken Dr NPK/KEN L6 113 K1
Penmann Cl HLWD L26 132 B6
Penmann Crs HLWD L26 132 B6
Penmark Cl WARRW/BUR WA5 120 E3
Penmon Dr PEN/TH CH61 141 H2
Pennant Av WD/CROXPK L12 98 E4
Pennant Cl GOL/RIS/CU WA3 123 J2
Pennard Av HUY L36 99 M8
Pennell Dr WGNS/IIMK WN3 68 B8
Penn Gdns EP CH65 20 C8
Pennine Av CHLY/EC PR7 31 M4
  WGNS/IIMK WN3 78 E2
Pennine Dr STHEL WA9 103 H2
Pennine Gv LEIGH WN7 81 L5
Pennine La GOL/RIS/CU WA3 92 E4
Pennine Pl SKEL WN8 65 K7
Pennine Rd CHLYE PR6 33 G5
  HOR/BR BL6 45 L8
  RF/TRAN CH42 127 L4
  WAL/EG CH44 111 H1
  WARRN/WOL WA2 122 A3
Pennine Wy KKBY L32 85 L1
Pennington Av BTL L20 84 A6
Pennington Cl FROD/HEL WA6 160 E4
Pennington Dr NEWLW WA12 105 G2
Pennington Gn GTS/LS CH66 162 E2
Pennington Green La
  WGNE/HIN WN2 69 M3
Pennington La
  WARRW/BUR WA5 103 J2
  WGNE/HIN WN2 57 J4
  WGNE/HIN WN2 69 J3
Pennington Rd LITH L21 83 L7
  WGNE/HIN WN2 69 M3
Penn La RUNC WA7 18 C5
Pennsylvania Rd
  CLB/OSW/ST L13 97 M6
Pennyford Dr CALD/MH L18 130 A2
Pennygate Cl WGNE/HIN WN2 69 M7
Pennyhurst St WGNS/IIMK WN3 4 B5
Penny La CALD/MH L18 114 B8
  RAIN/WH L35 117 J6
  RNFD/HAY WA11 91 J6
  WARRW/BUR WA5 103 M5
Pennystone Cl
  WARRW/BUR WA5 120 F3
Pennywood Dr RAIN/WH L35 117 G3
Penrhos Rd HOY L47 108 B7
Penrhyd Rd PEN/TH CH61 125 M8
Penrhyn Av LITH L21 83 K6
  PEN/TH CH61 126 C7
Penrhyn Crs RUNC WA7 19 M4
Penrhyn Rd PR/KW L34 86 D8
Penrhyn St EV L5 96 F6
Penrith Av STHP PR8 47 L2
  WARRN/WOL WA2 122 A2
Penrith Cl FROD/HEL WA6 160 F5
Penrith Crs AIMK WN4 91 K1
  MGHL L31 73 G3
Penrith Rd ECCL WA10 101 K5
Penrith St BIRK CH41 10 F8

Pensby Rd PEN/TH CH61 126 C7
Penshaw Av WGNS/IIMK WN3 79 K2
Penshaw Ct RUNC WA7 150 A6
Penson St WGN WN1 68 F3
Pentire Av ECCL WA10 88 D7
Pentire Cl NG/CROX L11 85 K7
Pentland Av ANF/KKDL L4 97 H3
  STHEL WA9 103 H2
Pentland Pl WARRN/WOL WA2 121 K2
Pentland Rd NWD/KWIPK L33 86 A1
Penuel Rd ANF/KKDL L4 97 H3
Penvalley Crs NPK/KEN L6 113 L1
Peony Gdns STHEL WA9 103 K6
Peover St VAUX/LVPD L3 13 H3
Peploe Rd ANF/KKDL L4 97 H3
Peplow Rd KKBY L32 85 K3
Pepper La WGNNW/ST WN6 55 K2
Pepper Mill La WGN WN1 5 G6
Pepper St SPK/HALE L24 147 M4
Pepperwood Dr
  WGNS/IIMK WN3 79 G3
Pepys Pl WGNS/IIMK WN3 79 J1
Pera Cl NPK/KEN L6 113 J2
Perch Pool La CHTN/BK PR9 26 B8
Perch St WGN WN1 5 J2
Percival Rd EP CH65 20 B3
Percival St WARR WA1 15 J5
Percival Wy ECCL WA10 88 E3
  WGNE/HIN WN2 80 F1
Percy Rd WAL/EG CH44 112 A3
  CHLY/EC PR7 32 F6
  STHEL WA9 103 H6
  TOX L8 113 H6
  WARRW/BUR WA5 * 121 G8
Percy Vls WLT/FAZ L9 * 97 J3
Perimeter Rd CHNE CH2 158 E8
Perran St WGNS/IIMK WN3 86 F3
Perrey St RUNC WA7 19 K3
Perriam Rd ALL/GAR L19 130 F5
Perrin Av RUNC WA7 18 D8
Perrin Rd WAL/NB CH45 94 F7
Perrins Rd WARRW/BUR WA5 104 B7
Perrygate Cl EHL/KEN L7 113 K5
Perryn Pl WGNNW/ST WN6 55 B4
Perry St TOX L8 112 F7
Pershore Gv STHP PR8 47 J1
Pershore Rd KKBY L32 86 A5
Perth Av STHEL WA9 102 A6
Perth Cl NWD/KWIPK L33 73 M7
  WARRN/WOL WA2 122 B1
Perth St NPK/KEN L6 113 J1
Peterborough Cl GTS/LS CH66 163 H6
Peterborough Dr NTHTN L30 84 A1
Peterborough Rd WAV L15 114 C2
Peterlee Cl STHEL WA9 102 B6
Peter Mahon Wy BTL L20 6 E3
Peter Price's La BEB CH63 143 G1
Peter Salem Dr
  WARRW/BUR WA5 120 D7
Peters Av BRSC L40 52 A1
Petersfield Cl NTHTN L30 84 B4
Petersfield Gdns
  GOL/RIS/CU WA3 107 G1
Petersgate RUNC WA7 150 F6
Petersham Dr WARRS WA4 138 A8
Peter's La CLVPS L1 13 G3
Peterstone Cl
  WARRW/BUR WA5 120 F3
Peter St AIMK WN4 91 J2
  CHLY/EC PR7 32 E5
  CLVPS L1 13 G6
  ECCL WA10 8 D4
  WAL/EG CH44 92 C5
  WGNE/HIN WN2 69 M8
  WGNW/BIL/O WN5 67 K5
Peterwood RF/TRAN CH42 128 C4
Petherick Rd NG/CROX L11 85 L5
Petticoat La WGNE/HIN WN2 69 K6
Petton St EV L5 97 H7
Petunia Cl DV/KA/FCH L14 * 115 J1
  STHEL WA9 103 H4
Petworth Av WARRN/WOL WA2 121 K2
  WGNS/IIMK WN3 78 F3
Petworth Cl SPK/HALE L24 146 D1
Petworth Rd STHP PR8 34 D7
Peveril Cl WARRS WA4 137 M6
Peveril St WLT/FAZ L9 97 L2
Pheasant Cl GOL/RIS/CU WA3 123 J2
Pheasant Fld SPK/HALE L24 147 L3
Pheasant Gv HLWD L26 132 A4
Philbeach Rd ANF/KKDL L4 97 M3
Philip Cl WGNW/BIL/O WN5 67 K6
Philip Dr STHP PR8 35 G7
Philip Gv STHEL WA9 102 E6
Philip Rd WDN WA8 133 K5
Philips Dr WARRW/BUR WA5 120 A7
Philips La GTS/LS CH66 162 E1
Phillimore Rd NPK/KEN L6 113 L2
Phillips Cl CSBY/BLUN L23 71 K7
  FMBY L37 59 J3
Phillip's La FMBY L37 59 H3
Phillips St VAUX/LVPD L3 12 F4
Phipps' La WARRW/BUR WA5 104 A6
Phoenix Dr DV/KA/FCH L14 115 J1
Physics Rd SPK/HALE L24 131 K8
Phythian Cl NPK/KEN L6 113 K2
Phythian Crs WARRW/BUR WA5 136 A3
Phythian St NPK/KEN L6 113 J2
  RNFD/HAY WA11 90 B7
Picadilly WGNW/BIL/O WN5 78 A4
Pichael Nook WARRS WA4 138 C1
Pickerill Rd GR/UP/WCH CH49 125 M2
Pickering Crs WARRS WA4 137 M5
Pickering Rd WAL/NB CH45 95 K5
  WDN WA8 133 K8
Pickerings Cl RUNC WA7 149 L7
Pickering St NPK/KEN L6 97 J8
Pickles Dr BRSC L40 51 M1
Pickmere Dr PS/BROM CH62 155 H2
  RUNC WA7 150 F8
Pickmere St WARRW/BUR WA5 121 G8
Pickop St VAUX/LVPD L3 12 F5
Pickthorn Cl WGNE/HIN WN2 80 D2
Pickup St WGNE/HIN WN2 80 D2
Pickwick St TOX L8 113 H7
Pickworth Wy KKBY L32 85 K3
Picow Farm Rd RUNC WA7 18 C2
Picow St RUNC WA7 18 D2
Picton Av EP CH65 20 B3
  RUNC WA7 19 K5
Picton Cl CL/PREN CH43 127 J2
  GOL/RIS/CU WA3 123 J2
  PS/BROM CH62 154 F2
Picton Crs WAV L15 114 A3
Picton Gv WAV L15 114 A3
Picton La CHNE CH2 160 C6
Picton Rd CSBY/WL L22 82 F4
  WAV L15 114 A5
Piele Rd RNFD/HAY WA11 91 G6
Piercefield Rd FMBY L37 59 H1

Pier Head VAUX/LVPD L3 ... 12 D8
Pierpoint St NEWLW WA12 ... 92 C6
WARRW/BUR WA5 ... 14 B2
Pighue La CLB/OSW/ST L13 ... 114 A4
Pigot Pl WARRS WA4 ... 122 B8
Pigot St ECCL WA10 ... 8 D5
WGNW/BIL/O WN5 ... 67 K7
Pike House Rd ECCL WA10 ... 88 C8
Pikelaw Pl SKEL WN8 ... 65 L8
Pike Pl ECCL WA10 ... 101 K1
Pikes Bridge Fold ECCL WA10 ... 101 J1
Pikes Hey Rd WKBY CH48 ... 125 H6
Pike St WARRS WA4 ... 137 L4
Pilchbank Rd DV/KA/FCH L14 ... 115 G1
Pilch La DV/KA/FCH L14 ... 115 G2
Pilch La East HUY L36 ... 115 J3
Pilgrim Cl WARRN/WOL WA2 ... 105 J7
Pilgrim St BIRK CH41 ... 11 L5
CLVPS L1 ... 113 G5
Pilgrims Wy WGNNW/ST WN6 ... 56 C6
Pilkington Rd STHP PR8 ... 3 M7
Pilkington St RNFD/HAY WA11 ... 76 B7
WGNE/HIN WN2 ... 69 M7
Pilling Cl CHLY/EC PR7 ... 32 F7
CHTN/BK PR9 ... 22 B8
Pilling La CHLY/EC PR7 ... 32 E8
MGHL L31 ... 61 J8
Pilling Pl SKEL WN8 ... 65 L8
Pilling St LEIGH WN7 ... 81 M8
Pilot Gv WAV L15 ... 113 M5
Pilsley Cl WGNW/BIL/O WN5 ... 67 J4
Pimblett Rd RNFD/HAY WA11 ... 91 G6
Pimblett St GOL/RIS/CU WA3 * ... 92 C6
Pimbley Gv East MGHL L31 ... 72 E7
Pimbley Gv West MGHL L31 ... 72 E7
Pimbo La SKEL WN8 ... 77 H2
Pimbo Rd RNFD/HAY WA11 ... 77 G5
SKEL WN8 ... 65 M8
SKEL WN8 ... 77 G1
Pimhill Cl TOX L8 ... 113 J7
Pimlico Rd RUNC WA7 ... 18 D5
Pincock Brow CHLY/EC PR7 ... 31 L5
Pincock St CHLY/EC PR7 ... 31 L5
Pincroft Wy ANF/KKDL L4 ... 96 F6
Pine Av BEB CH63 ... 143 H2
ECCL WA10 ... 89 H7
NEWLW WA12 ... 104 E3
ORM L39 ... 51 H6
WDN WA8 ... 134 D3
Pine Cl HUY L36 ... 115 M1
KKBY L32 ... 85 L2
RAIN/WH L35 ... 117 G2
RNFD/HAY WA11 ... 90 E7
SKEL WN8 ... 53 J4
SKEL WN8 ... 65 H4
Pine Ct BIRK CH41 ... 11 H5
Pine Crest ORM L39 ... 62 D3
Pine Dl RNFD/HAY WA11 ... 76 A6
Pinedale Cl CL/PREN CH43 ... 126 F1
GTS/LS CH66 ... 163 H5
Pine Dr ORM L39 ... 51 H7
Pine Gv BTL L20 ... 7 J3
CHLYE PR6 ... 32 F2
CHTN/BK PR9 ... 3 M5
CSBY/WL L22 ... 82 F3
GOL/RIS/CU WA3 ... 92 E5
GTS/LS CH66 ... 163 J4
ORM L39 ... 51 J6
WARR WA1 ... 122 C6
Pinehey NSTN CH64 ... 152 F4
Pinehurst Av ANF/KKDL L4 ... 97 K6
CSBY/WL L22 ... 82 E2
Pinehurst Rd ANF/KKDL L4 ... 97 K6
Pinellas RUNC WA7 ... 19 K2
Pine Ms CLVPS L1 ... 113 G6
Pinemore Rd CALD/MH L18 ... 130 C3
Pineridge Cl PS/BROM CH62 ... 143 L2
Pine Rd HES CH60 ... 141 L4
RUNC WA7 ... 19 M9
WGNW/BIL/O WN5 ... 68 A7
The Pines BEB CH63 ... 143 K2
WD/CROXPK L12 ... 99 H1
Pinetop Cl NPK/KEN L6 ... 113 K1
Pine Tree Av CL/PREN CH43 ... 126 E1
Pine Tree Cl MOR/LEA CH46 ... 110 B5
Pinetree Cl NTHTN L30 ... 84 B2
Pinetree Ct WAL/EG CH44 ... 95 H8
Pinetree Dr WKBY CH48 ... 124 F4
Pine Tree Gv MOR/LEA CH46 ... 110 B5
Pine Tree Rd HUY L36 ... 115 M5
Pinevale WGNNW/ST WN6 ... 56 C6
Pine Vw WGNS/IIMK WN3 ... 78 D4
Pine View Dr PEN/TH CH61 ... 141 H3
Pine Wks RF/TRAN CH42 ... 127 K4
Pine Wy HES CH60 ... 141 G3
Pineways WARRS WA4 ... 137 M8
Pinewood AIMK WN4 ... 91 J3
SKEL WN8 ... 65 M2
Pinewood Av FMBY L37 ... 58 F4
WARR WA1 ... 15 L1
WD/CROXPK L12 ... 98 F2
Pinewood Cl CHNE CH2 ... 165 L2
FMBY L37 ... 58 F3
NTHLY L27 ... 116 A7
STHP PR8 ... 36 E4
WGNE/HIN WN2 ... 80 D6
Pinewood Crs WGNE/HIN WN2 ... 5 L7
WGNW/BIL/O WN5 ... 67 G7
Pinewood Dr HES CH60 ... 141 K5
Pinewood Gdns
NWD/KWIPK L33 ... 74 A8
Pinewood Rd
WARRW/BUR WA5 ... 104 B6
Pinfold Cl NTHTN L30 ... 71 M8
Pinfold Crs KKBY L32 ... 86 C5
Pinfold Dr ECCL WA10 ... 101 J2
Pinfold La BRSC L40 ... 50 B2
PR/KW L34 ... 99 K2
STHP PR8 ... 47 K2
WKBY CH48 ... 124 C1
Pinfold Pl SKEL WN8 ... 76 F1
Pinfold Rd WLTN L25 ... 131 L6
Pinfold St WGNE/HIN WN2 ... 69 J6
Pingot Rd WGNW/BIL/O WN5 ... 78 A8
The Pingot LEIGH WN7 ... 81 M8
Pingwood La NWD/KWIPK L33 ... 74 C7
Pinmill Brow FROD/HEL WA6 ... 160 D6
Pinmill Cl FROD/HEL WA6 ... 160 D6
Pinners Brow
WARRN/WOL WA2 ... 14 E3
Pinners Fold RUNC WA7 ... 150 D4
Pinnington Pl HUY L36 ... 115 M3
Pinnington Rd RAIN/WH L35 ... 117 G2
Pintail Cl RNFD/HAY WA11 ... 89 K7
Piper's Cl HES CH60 ... 140 F5
Piper's End HES CH60 ... 140 F5
Piper's La HES CH60 ... 140 E3
The Pipers GOL/RIS/CU WA3 ... 93 H5
Pipit Av NEWLW WA12 ... 104 E2
Pipit Cl HLWD L26 ... 132 A3
Pipit La GOL/RIS/CU WA3 ... 123 G2
Pippin St BRSC L40 ... 51 J3
Pippits Rw RUNC WA7 ... 161 G1
Pirrie Rd WLT/FAZ L9 ... 97 M2
Pitch Cl GR/UP/WCH CH49 * ... 125 M1
Pit Hey Pl SKEL WN8 ... 65 L8
Pit La WDN WA8 ... 134 C1
Pit Pl WLTN L25 ... 131 J3
Pitsmead Rd KKBY L32 ... 86 A4
Pitts Heath La RUNC WA7 ... 150 F2
Pitts House La CHTN/BK PR9 ... 25 K5
Pitt St CHTN/BK PR9 ... 25 H7
CLVPS L1 ... 112 F5
STHEL WA9 ... 9 L5
WARRW/BUR WA5 ... 14 B3
WDN WA8 ... 16 C9
WGNS/IIMK WN3 ... 4 D5
WGNS/IIMK WN3 * ... 5 H7
Pitville Av CALD/MH L18 ... 130 C2
Pitville Cl CALD/MH L18 ... 130 C3
Pitville Gv CALD/MH L18 ... 130 C2
Pitville Rd CALD/MH L18 ... 130 C2
Pitville Ter WDN WA8 ... 133 L6
Plaistow Ct RUNC WA7 ... 150 B6
Plane Av WGNW/BIL/O WN5 ... 68 A6
Plane Cl WLT/FAZ L9 ... 97 L2
Plane Tree Gv RNFD/HAY WA11 * ... 91 J6
Plane Tree Rd BEB CH63 ... 143 G1
Planetree Rd WD/CROXPK L12 ... 99 H6
Plank La LEIGH WN7 ... 93 J1
Plantation Cl RUNC WA7 ... 150 C4
Plantation Dr GTS/LS CH66 ... 156 A6
Plantation Gates WGN WN1 ... 69 G6
Plantation Rd BRSC L40 ... 51 K1
PS/BROM CH62 ... 144 B4
The Planters GR/UP/WCH CH49 ... 125 L1
NTHTN L30 ... 84 C1
Platt Gv RF/TRAN CH42 ... 128 C5
Platt La WGN WN1 ... 5 J3
WGN WN1 ... 56 D2
WGNE/HIN WN2 ... 69 M8
Platts La BRSC L40 ... 51 M3
Platts St RNFD/HAY WA11 ... 90 E7
Platt St WGNE/HIN WN2 ... 80 C3
Plattsville Rd CALD/MH L18 ... 114 C8
Playfield Rd WD/CROXPK L12 ... 99 H6
Pleasance Wy NEWLW WA12 ... 104 E1
Pleasant Hill St TOX L8 ... 112 F7
Pleasant St BTL L20 ... 6 E6
VAUX/LVPD L3 ... 13 K8
WAL/NB CH45 ... 95 K6
Pleasant Vw BTL L20 ... 6 E6
CHLY/EC PR7 ... 43 H3
Pleasington Cl CL/PREN CH43 ... 127 G1
Pleasington Dr CL/PREN CH43 ... 127 G1
Pleck Rd EP CH65 ... 163 J3
Plemont Rd CLB/OSW/ST L13 ... 98 C8
Plemston Ct GTS/LS CH66 ... 156 B5
Plex La ORM L39 ... 49 K7
Plex Moss La ORM L39 ... 48 C5
STHP PR8 ... 47 M4
Plimsoll St EHL/KEN L7 ... 113 K4
Plinston Av WARRS WA4 ... 138 B1
Plough La BRSC L40 ... 64 C2
Ploughmans Wy GTS/LS CH66 ... 163 G5
Plover Cl NEWLW WA12 ... 104 E2
Plover Dr RUNC WA7 ... 150 F5
Plovers La FROD/HEL WA6 ... 159 L8
Plover Wy GOL/RIS/CU WA3 ... 93 G5
Pluckington Rd HUY L36 ... 116 D3
Plumbers Wy HUY L36 ... 116 B3
Plumer St BIRK CH41 ... 10 B2
WAV L15 ... 114 A6
Plumley Gdns RAIN/WH L35 ... 133 J4
Plumpstons La FROD/HEL WA6 ... 160 D4
Plumpton La ORM L39 ... 49 G3
Plumpton St NPK/KEN L6 ... 13 M2
Plumtre Av WARRW/BUR WA5 ... 121 H5
Plum Tree Cl RAIN/WH L35 ... 101 H7
STBRV L28 ... 99 K6
Plymouth Cl RUNC WA7 ... 151 G7
Plymouth Gv CHLYE PR6 ... 33 G5
WGNNW/ST WN6 ... 56 C6
Plymyard Av PS/BROM CH62 ... 143 M7
Plymyard Cl PS/BROM CH62 ... 143 M8
Poachers' La WARRS WA4 ... 138 B2
Pochard Ri RUNC WA7 ... 150 F5
Pocket Nook La
GOL/RIS/CU WA3 ... 93 J5
Pocket Nook St STHEL WA9 ... 9 K4
Pocklington Ct
WARRN/WOL WA2 ... 122 B4
Podium Rd CLB/OSW/ST L13 ... 114 C1
Poets Cnr PS/BROM CH62 * ... 128 D8
Poke St WGNW/BIL/O WN5 ... 67 K7
Poleacre Dr WDN WA8 ... 133 M3
Polegate Dr WGNE/HIN WN2 ... 81 L3
Pole St WGNNW/ST WN6 ... 56 A4
Pollard Rd WAV L15 ... 114 C4
Poll Hill Rd HES CH60 ... 141 H4
Pollitt Crs STHEL WA9 ... 118 E2
Pollitt Sq PS/BROM CH62 ... 128 E5
Polperro Cl WARRW/BUR WA5 ... 136 A2
Pomfret St TOX L8 ... 113 H7
Pomona St VAUX/LVPD L3 ... 13 K8
Pond Green Wy STHEL WA9 ... 103 H4
Pond St GOL/RIS/CU WA3 ... 93 J5
Pond View Cl HES CH60 ... 141 L5
Pond Wk STHEL WA9 ... 103 J4
Ponsonby Rd WAL/NB CH45 ... 95 G8
Ponsonby St TOX L8 ... 113 J7
Pool Bank PS/BROM CH62 ... 128 D6
Poolbank Rd PS/BROM CH62 ... 128 D6
Poole Av WARRN/WOL WA2 ... 121 K3
Poole Crs WARRN/WOL WA2 ... 121 K3
Poole Hall La GTS/LS CH66 ... 156 A5
Poole Hall Rd EP CH65 ... 156 B5
Poole La CHNE CH2 ... 165 G3
Pool End STHEL WA9 ... 103 H3
Poole Rd WAL/EG CH44 ... 95 M8
Poole Wk TOX L8 ... 129 J1
Pool Hey STBRV L28 ... 99 K5
Pool Hey La STHP PR8 ... 36 D2
Pool La CHNE CH2 ... 158 B8
CHNE CH2 ... 165 H2
GR/UP/WCH CH49 ... 126 C3
LYMM WA13 ... 139 L1
PS/BROM CH62 ... 143 L2
RUNC WA7 ... 19 J2
WARRS WA4 ... 137 J4
Poolside Rd RUNC WA7 ... 19 J5
Poolside Wk CHTN/BK PR9 ... 25 K1
Poolstock WGNS/IIMK WN3 ... 4 D8
Poolstock La WGNS/IIMK WN3 ... 79 J1
Pool St BIRK CH41 ... 11 H3
CHTN/BK PR9 ... 25 L1
WDN WA8 ... 16 F5
WGNE/HIN WN2 ... 80 F1
WGNS/IIMK WN3 ... 4 D8
Pooltown Rd EP CH65 ... 156 B8
Poolwood Rd
GR/UP/WCH CH49 ... 126 D1
Pope St BTL L20 ... 83 H7
Poplar Av AIMK WN4 ... 78 F8
CHLY/EC PR7 ... 31 L1
CSBY/BLUN L23 ... 71 H8
ECCL WA10 ... 101 J1
GOL/RIS/CU WA3 ... 107 H2
GR/UP/WCH CH49 ... 110 B8
NEWLW WA12 ... 104 F2
RUNC WA7 ... 19 M9
WARRW/BUR WA5 ... 121 K3
WGNW/BIL/O WN5 ... 67 M7
Poplar Bank HUY L36 ... 116 A3
Poplar Cl EP CH65 ... 20 A7
RUNC WA7 ... 149 L6
Poplar Dr BEB CH63 ... 143 H3
EV L5 ... 97 J8
KKBY L32 ... 85 M2
SKEL WN8 ... 65 H4
Poplar Farm Cl MOR/LEA CH46 ... 109 L7
Poplar Gv CHNE CH2 ... 165 J2
ECCL WA10 ... 101 L2
LITH L21 ... 83 H7
RAIN/WH L35 ... 101 G8
RNFD/HAY WA11 ... 90 E7
WGNE/HIN WN2 ... 81 K3
Poplar Rd CL/PREN CH43 ... 127 K1
RNFD/HAY WA11 ... 90 E7
WLTN L25 ... 131 H2
Poplars Av WARRN/WOL WA2 ... 121 K1
The Poplars BRSC L40 ... 52 A3
CHLY/EC PR7 ... 44 B7
LEIGH WN7 ... 93 L5
LYMM WA13 ... 139 M1
Poplar St CHLY/EC PR7 ... 32 F7
GOL/RIS/CU WA3 ... 92 D4
STHP PR8 ... 25 H7
Poplar Vw WARRS WA4 * ... 136 C6
Poplar Wy ANF/KKDL L4 ... 96 F5
Poppleford Cl WLTN L25 ... 131 L1
Poppy Av CHLYE PR6 ... 32 F3
Poppy Cl MOR/LEA CH46 ... 110 C3
Poppy La ORM L39 ... 63 K5
Porchester Rd NG/CROX L11 ... 98 B4
Porchfield Cl NG/CROX L11 ... 98 D2
Porlock Av CHLDW L16 ... 115 G8
STHEL WA9 ... 102 E8
Porlock Cl HES CH60 ... 141 K7
WARRW/BUR WA5 ... 136 A1
WGNE/HIN WN2 ... 80 C4
Portal Ms PEN/TH CH61 ... 141 H2
Portal Rd PEN/TH CH61 ... 141 H2
Portbury Cl PS/BROM CH62 ... 128 E7
Port Cswy PS/BROM CH62 ... 143 M1
Portelet Rd CLB/OSW/ST L13 ... 114 B1
Porter Av NEWLW WA12 ... 91 L8
Porter Cl RAIN/WH L35 ... 117 M4
Porter St RUNC WA7 ... 19 M3
VAUX/LVPD L3 ... 12 C2
Porters Wood Cl
WGNW/BIL/O WN5 * ... 67 K6
Portgate Cl NG/CROX L11 ... 98 E3
Porthcawl Cl WDN WA8 ... 133 L2
Porthleven Rd RUNC WA7 ... 150 D8
Portia Av BEB CH63 ... 128 A6
Portia Gdns BEB CH63 * ... 128 A6
Portia St BTL L20 ... 96 E5
Portico Av RAIN/WH L35 ... 101 J7
Portico La RAIN/WH L35 ... 101 J7
Portland Av CSBY/WL L22 ... 82 E3
Portland Cl WGNE/HIN WN2 ... 80 C4
Portland Gdns EV L5 ... 12 F1
Portland Pl EV L5 ... 13 J1
FROD/HEL WA6 ... 166 E1
Portland St BIRK CH41 ... 10 A2
CHLY/EC PR7 ... 32 F5
EV L5 * ... 12 F1
NEWLW WA12 ... 104 B1
RUNC WA7 ... 18 E2
STHP PR8 ... 2 F5
STHP PR8 ... 3 J9
WAL/NB CH45 ... 95 J4
WGNW/BIL/O WN5 ... 68 A7
Portland Wy STHEL WA9 ... 103 H4
Portlemouth Rd NG/CROX L11 ... 85 L8
Portloe Av HLWD L26 ... 132 B4
Portman Rd WAV L15 ... 113 M6
Porto Hey Rd PEN/TH CH61 ... 125 M8
Portola Cl WARRS WA4 ... 138 E3
Porton Rd KKBY L32 ... 85 L4
Portreath Wy ECCL WA10 ... 88 D7
Portree Av BEB CH63 ... 143 M8
Portree Cl WLT/FAZ L9 ... 84 C8
Portrush St CLB/OSW/ST L13 ... 98 A7
Portside North EP CH65 ... 156 D5
Portsmouth Dr CHLYE PR6 ... 33 G5
Portsmouth Pl RUNC WA7 ... 151 G7
Portwood Cl TOX L8 * ... 113 K5
Post Office Av CHTN/BK PR9 ... 3 H3
Post Office La RUNC WA7 ... 18 A9
Potter Pl SKEL WN8 ... 65 M8
Potters La WDN WA8 ... 148 B1
Pottery Flds PR/KW L34 ... 100 F7
Pottery La RAIN/WH L35 ... 116 E2
Pottery Rd WGNS/IIMK WN3 ... 4 B6
Pottery Ter WGNS/IIMK WN3 ... 4 C6
Poulsom Dr NTHTN L30 ... 83 L3
Poulter Rd WLT/FAZ L9 ... 84 D6
Poulton Cl HLWD L26 ... 131 M7
Poulton Crs WARR WA1 ... 122 F5
Poulton Dr AIMK WN4 * ... 91 H1
WDN WA8 ... 133 M6
Poulton Green Cl BEB CH63 ... 143 H4
Poulton Hall Rd BEB CH63 ... 143 J6
WAL/EG CH44 ... 111 J2
Poulton Rd BEB CH63 ... 143 J4
CHTN/BK PR9 ... 25 H6
WAL/EG CH44 ... 111 J2
Poulton Royd Dr BEB CH63 ... 143 H3
Pound Rd GTS/LS CH66 ... 155 L6
Poverty La MGHL L31 ... 73 H5
Povey Rd WARRN/WOL WA2 ... 121 L4
Powderworks La MGHL L31 ... 73 L2
Powell Av GOL/RIS/CU WA3 ... 123 G1
Powell Dr WGNW/BIL/O WN5 ... 89 M2
Powell St STHEL WA9 ... 103 G6
WARRS WA4 ... 138 B2
WGN WN1 ... 4 F2
WGNE/HIN WN2 ... 80 D4
Power Rd PS/BROM CH62 ... 144 B4
RF/TRAN CH42 ... 128 C5
Powey La CH/BCN CH1 ... 162 D8
Powis St TOX L8 ... 113 J8
Pownall St CLVPS L1 ... 12 F9
Powys St WARRW/BUR WA5 ... 14 A6
Poynter St STHEL WA9 ... 102 A7
Poynton Cl WARRS WA4 ... 138 D2
Pratt Rd PR/KW L34 ... 100 E7
The Precincts CSBY/BLUN L23 ... 83 G1
Preece Cl WDN WA8 ... 133 M2
Preesall Cl CHTN/BK PR9 ... 22 B8
Preesall Wy NG/CROX L11 ... 85 L8
Prefect Pl WGNW/BIL/O WN5 ... 67 L5
Premier St EV L5 ... 97 H8
Prentice Rd RF/TRAN CH42 ... 128 A4
Prenton Av STHEL WA9 ... 118 D1
Prenton Dell Av CL/PREN CH43 ... 127 J5
Prenton Dell Rd CL/PREN CH43 ... 127 G4
Prenton Farm Rd
CL/PREN CH43 ... 127 J5
Prenton Gn SPK/HALE L24 ... 147 G2
Prenton Hall Rd CL/PREN CH43 ... 127 J5
Prenton La RF/TRAN CH42 ... 127 K4
Prentonpark Rd RF/TRAN CH42 ... 127 L2
Prenton Rd East RF/TRAN CH42 ... 127 M3
Prenton Rd West
RF/TRAN CH42 ... 127 L3
Prenton Village Rd
CL/PREN CH43 ... 127 J5
Prenton Wy CL/PREN CH43 ... 126 F4
Presbyterian Fold
WGNE/HIN WN2 ... 69 M7
Prescot Dr NPK/KEN L6 ... 113 M2
Prescot Gn ORM L39 ... 62 F2
Prescot Rd CLB/OSW/ST L13 ... 114 A2
ECCL WA10 ... 101 K5
MGHL L31 ... 73 L7
ORM L39 ... 73 M1
WDN WA8 ... 117 H8
Prescot St EHL/KEN L7 ... 13 M5
WAL/NB CH45 ... 95 J5
Prescott Av BRSC L40 ... 39 J2
GOL/RIS/CU WA3 ... 92 B3
Prescott Br BRSC L40 ... 39 L5
Prescott La WGNW/BIL/O WN5 ... 67 K5
Prescott Rd SKEL WN8 ... 66 A8
Prescott St GOL/RIS/CU WA3 ... 92 C4
WARRS WA4 ... 138 A2
WGNE/HIN WN2 ... 69 M8
WGNNW/ST WN6 ... 4 B4
Preseland Rd CSBY/BLUN L23 ... 83 G2
Prestbury Av CL/PREN CH43 ... 127 G3
STHP PR8 ... 34 D8
WGNS/IIMK WN3 ... 79 G2
Prestbury Cl CL/PREN CH43 ... 127 G3
WDN WA8 ... 134 A5
Prestbury Dr ECCL WA10 ... 101 K3
WARRS WA4 ... 138 F2
Prestbury Rd NG/CROX L11 ... 98 B1
Preston Av PR/KW L34 ... 100 E8
Preston Gv NPK/KEN L6 ... 97 L8
Preston New Rd CHTN/BK PR9 ... 25 J2
Preston Nook CHLY/EC PR7 ... 30 E8
Preston on the Hl WARRS WA4 ... 151 H7
Preston Rd CHLY/EC PR7 ... 42 D3
CHLYE PR6 ... 32 E1
CHTN/BK PR9 ... 25 G5
Preston St CHLYE PR6 ... 32 E3
CLVPS L1 ... 13 G6
STHEL WA9 ... 118 D3
Preston Wy CSBY/BLUN L23 ... 83 J1
Prestt Gv WGNS/IIMK WN3 ... 4 A8
Prestwich Av GOL/RIS/CU WA3 ... 107 G2
Prestwick Dr CSBY/BLUN L23 ... 70 E7
Prestwood Rd DV/KA/FCH L14 ... 115 H1
Pretoria Rd AIMK WN4 ... 91 J1
WLT/FAZ L9 ... 84 D7
Price Gv STHEL WA9 ... 103 J3
Price's La CL/PREN CH43 ... 127 K1
Price St BIRK CH41 ... 10 C1
BIRK CH41 ... 11 J4
CLVPS L1 * ... 13 G9
Pride Cl NEWLW WA12 ... 105 G3
Priestfield Rd EP CH65 ... 20 B4
Priesthouse Cl FMBY L37 ... 59 J2
Priesthouse La FMBY L37 ... 59 J2
Priestley St WARRW/BUR WA5 ... 14 A5
Primrose Cl CHTN/BK PR9 ... 22 E7
FMBY L37 ... 47 K8
RUNC WA7 ... 150 C5
WARRN/WOL WA2 ... 121 L4
WDN WA8 ... 134 A4
Primrose Dr HUY L36 ... 100 A8
Primrose Gv RNFD/HAY WA11 ... 91 G6
WAL/EG CH44 * ... 112 A3
WGNW/BIL/O WN5 * ... 68 A6
Primrose Hl PS/BROM CH62 ... 128 D7
VAUX/LVPD L3 ... 13 G5
Primrose Hill Rd CHLY/EC PR7 ... 31 K1
Primrose La FROD/HEL WA6 ... 166 C4
WGNNW/ST WN6 ... 55 M3
Primrose Rd BIRK CH41 ... 111 H6
CALD/MH L18 ... 114 E8
Primrose St ANF/KKDL L4 ... 96 F6
CHLYE PR6 ... 32 F5
LEIGH WN7 * ... 81 M8
Primrose Vw AIMK WN4 ... 91 K3
Primula Dr GOL/RIS/CU WA3 ... 92 F5
WLT/FAZ L9 ... 97 K1
Prince Albert Ms CLVPS L1 ... 113 G6
Prince Alfred Rd WAV L15 ... 114 C6
Prince Andrew's Gv ECCL WA10 ... 88 E7
Prince Charles Gdns STHP PR8 ... 2 D8
Prince Edward St BIRK CH41 ... 10 F4
Prince Edwin St EV L5 ... 13 J2
Princes Av CSBY/BLUN L23 ... 82 F1
PS/BROM CH62 ... 144 A7
TOX L8 ... 113 H6
WKBY CH48 ... 124 D3
Princes Bvd BEB CH63 ... 127 M5
Princes Gdns VAUX/LVPD L3 ... 12 F5
Princes Ga West TOX L8 ... 113 K7
Princes Pde VAUX/LVPD L3 ... 12 C5
Prince's Pk WGNNW/ST WN6 ... 67 H1
Princes Pl WDN WA8 ... 134 A4
Princes Rd ECCL WA10 ... 101 L4
EP CH65 ... 156 B7
TOX L8 ... 113 H6
Princess Av AIMK WN4 ... 91 L2
ECCL WA10 ... 89 G7
RNFD/HAY WA11 ... 91 J6
WARR WA1 ... 122 B7
WARRW/BUR WA5 ... 120 A7
Princess Crs WARR WA1 ... 122 B7
Princess Dr DV/KA/FCH L14 ... 99 H7
Princess Rd AIMK WN4 ... 91 K2
CHLYE PR6 ... 44 D5
LYMM WA13 ... 139 M2
WAL/NB CH45 ... 95 K6
WGNNW/ST WN6 ... 67 L1
Princess St CHLY/EC PR7 ... 32 F7
CLVP L2 ... 12 F7
RUNC WA7 ... 19 G2
WARRW/BUR WA5 ... 136 F1
WGNE/HIN WN2 ... 69 L8
WGNS/IIMK WN3 ... 4 E6
Princess Ter CL/PREN CH43 ... 10 E8
Princes St BTL L20 ... 6 F8
CLVP L2 ... 12 F6
NEWLW WA12 ... 104 D2
STHP PR8 ... 2 F5
WDN WA8 ... 16 D3
Princess Wy CHLY/EC PR7 ... 31 M3
LITH L21 ... 83 J6
Prince Streeet CLVPS L1 ... 12 F9
Prince St AIMK WN4 ... 79 J8
CSBY/WL L22 ... 82 F5
Princes Wy RNFD/HAY WA11 ... 89 J5
Princesway WAL/NB CH45 ... 95 J7
Princeway FROD/HEL WA6 ... 160 D5
Prince William St TOX L8 ... 113 G7
Prior Farm Cl ALL/GAR L19 ... 130 C6
Priors Cl WLTN L25 ... 131 K3
Priorsfield MOR/LEA CH46 ... 110 A5
Priorsfield Rd WLTN L25 ... 131 K3
Prior St BTL L20 ... 83 J7
Priorswood Pl SKEL WN8 ... 77 H1
Priory Av LEIGH WN7 ... 81 M4
Priory Cl AIG/SPK L17 ... 129 K3
BEB CH63 ... 143 J2
BRSC L40 ... 38 F8
FMBY L37 ... 59 K3
RAIN/WH L35 ... 116 E4
RUNC WA7 ... 150 C4
WGNW/BIL/O WN5 ... 67 K8
Priory Ct HUY L36 * ... 116 A3
RUNC WA7 * ... 151 G8
Priory Gdns ECCL WA10 ... 89 H6
STHP PR8 ... 2 C9
Priory Gra STHP PR8 ... 2 E9
Priory Gv ORM L39 ... 62 F1
Priory Ms BIRK CH41 * ... 11 M6
STHP PR8 ... 2 D5
Priory Nook SKEL WN8 ... 66 E6
Priory Rd AIMK WN4 ... 79 H8
ANF/KKDL L4 ... 97 J5
RUNC WA7 * ... 150 E3
SKEL WN8 ... 66 E6
WAL/EG CH44 ... 112 A2
WKBY CH48 ... 124 D3
Priory St ALL/GAR L19 ... 145 M1
BIRK CH41 ... 11 M6
WARRS WA4 ... 14 F9
The Priory NSTN CH64 ... 152 F4
RAIN/WH L35 ... 117 L2
WARRN/WOL WA2 ... 105 J6
Priory Wy WLTN L25 ... 131 K3
Priory Whf BIRK CH41 ... 11 M5
Pritchard Av LITH L21 ... 83 H6
Pritt St VAUX/LVPD L3 ... 13 J3
Private Dr PEN/TH CH61 ... 126 F8
Prizett Rd ALL/GAR L19 ... 130 D6
Probyn Rd WAL/NB CH45 ... 95 G8
Procter Rd RF/TRAN CH42 ... 128 C4
Proctor Cl WGNW/BIL/O WN5 ... 68 A4
Proctor Rd FMBY L37 ... 58 E1
HOY CH47 ... 108 E7
Proctors Cl WDN WA8 ... 134 E3
Prodesse Ct WGNE/HIN WN2 ... 69 M7
Proffits La FROD/HEL WA6 ... 167 G1
Progress St CHLYE PR6 ... 33 G5
WGNE/HIN WN2 ... 69 M8
Promenade STHP PR8 ... 2 F3
STHP PR8 ... 34 B7
Promenade Gdns AIG/SPK L17 ... 129 J2
The Promenade WARRS WA4 * ... 136 C6
Prospect Ct NPK/KEN L6 * ... 113 M2
Prospect La GOL/RIS/CU WA3 ... 123 L2
Prospect Pl SKEL WN8 ... 66 B8
Prospect Rd RF/TRAN CH42 ... 127 K4
STHEL WA9 ... 102 F1
WGNNW/ST WN6 ... 56 A6
Prospect Rw RUNC WA7 ... 149 H6
Prospect St NPK/KEN L6 ... 113 H3
WGNE/HIN WN2 ... 69 M8
Prospect V NPK/KEN L6 ... 113 M1
WAL/NB CH45 ... 95 H8
Prospect Wy NTHTN L30 ... 84 D2
Providence Crs TOX L8 ... 113 G7
Provident St STHEL WA9 ... 103 J2
Province Rd BTL L20 ... 83 M7
Prussia St VAUX/LVPD L3 * ... 12 E5
Pryce Av WGNE/HIN WN2 ... 5 L5
Public Hall St RUNC WA7 ... 19 H2
Pudsey St CLVPS L1 ... 13 J6
Puffin Cl EP CH65 ... 163 L5
Pugin St ANF/KKDL L4 ... 97 G6
Pulford Av CL/PREN CH43 ... 127 J3
Pulford Cl RUNC WA7 ... 149 M7
Pulford Rd BEB CH63 ... 128 B8
EP CH65 ... 163 H1
Pulford St ANF/KKDL L4 ... 97 H6
Pullman Cl HES CH60 ... 141 M5
Pumpfields Rd VAUX/LVPD L3 ... 12 E3
Pump La RUNC WA7 ... 150 B5
WKBY CH48 ... 125 K1
Pump Rd BIRK CH41 ... 11 K1
Pump St WGNE/HIN WN2 ... 69 M8
Punnell's La MGHL L31 ... 61 H8
Purbeck Dr PEN/TH CH61 ... 125 M6
Purdy Cl WARRW/BUR WA5 ... 120 F4
Purley Gv CALD/MH L18 ... 130 C3
Purley Rd CSBY/WL L22 * ... 82 E3
Purser Gv WAV L15 ... 113 M5
Putney Ct RUNC WA7 * ... 150 A6
Pye Cl RNFD/HAY WA11 ... 91 K5
Pyecroft Cl WARRW/BUR WA5 ... 119 M7
Pyecroft Rd WARRW/BUR WA5 ... 119 M7
Pye Rd HES CH60 ... 141 J5
Pyes Gdns RNFD/HAY WA11 ... 89 K6
Pyes La HUY L36 ... 99 L6
Pye St WAV L15 ... 114 C6
Pygon's Hill La MGHL L31 ... 61 M6
Pyke St WGN WN1 ... 5 H1
Pym St ANF/KKDL L4 ... 97 H3
The Pyramids BIRK CH41 * ... 11 H6
Pyrus Gv FROD/HEL WA6 * ... 166 E1

Q

Quadrangle VAUX/LVPD L3 * ... 13 M7
The Quadrangle CALD/MH L18 * ... 130 D1
Quadrant Cl RUNC WA7 ... 150 F7
Quail Cl WARRN/WOL WA2 ... 121 M2
Quaker La HES CH60 ... 141 G4
Quakers Meadow PR/KW L34 ... 99 M1
Quakers' Pl WGNNW/ST WN6 ... 56 A4
Quantock Cl GTS/LS CH66 ... 155 J7
WGNS/IIMK WN3 ... 78 E3
Quarry Av BEB CH63 ... 143 H1
Quarry Bank BIRK CH41 ... 11 G7
NWD/KWIPK L33 ... 86 B2
WAL/NB CH45 ... 95 K7
Quarrybank St BIRK CH41 ... 10 F7
Quarry Cl CLB/OSW/ST L13 ... 98 B8
HES CH60 ... 141 H3
NWD/KWIPK L33 ... 86 B2
RUNC WA7 ... 149 M4
Quarry Ct HES CH60 * ... 141 G4
WDN WA8 ... 133 L4
Quarry Dl NWD/KWIPK L33 ... 86 B2
Quarry Dr ORM L39 ... 62 E4
Quarry Gn NWD/KWIPK L33 ... 86 B2
Quarry Hey NWD/KWIPK L33 ... 86 B2
Quarry La PEN/TH CH61 ... 126 C7
WARRS WA4 ... 137 M7
Quarry Mt ORM L39 ... 51 J7
Quarry Pl WGN WN1 ... 5 J3
Quarry Rd BTL L20 ... 7 K6
CHLYE PR6 ... 33 G7
CLB/OSW/ST L13 ... 98 C8
CSBY/BLUN L23 ... 71 J7
NSTN CH64 ... 153 L4
Quarry Rd East BEB CH63 ... 143 J1
HES CH60 ... 141 G4
Quarry Rd West HES CH60 ... 141 G4
Quarryside Dr NWD/KWIPK L33 ... 86 C3
Quarry St WLTN L25 ... 131 H2
Quarry St South WLTN L25 ... 131 J3
Quartz Wy LITH L21 ... 83 L5
Quay Fold WARRS WA4 ... 137 G1
Quayle Cl RNFD/HAY WA11 ... 90 D7
Quay Pl RUNC WA7 ... 151 G6
Quay Side FROD/HEL WA6 ... 160 F4
Quayside NSTN CH64 ... 152 F8
The Quay FROD/HEL WA6 ... 160 F3
Quebec Quay VAUX/LVPD L3 ... 112 E7
Quebec Rd WARRN/WOL WA2 ... 15 J1
Queen Anne St STHP PR8 ... 3 G4
VAUX/LVPD L3 ... 13 J4
Queen Av CLVP L2 * ... 12 F7
Queen Mary's Dr PS/BROM CH62 ... 128 D7
Queen's Av AIMK WN4 ... 91 K1
EP CH65 ... 163 J2
FMBY L37 ... 47 G8
HOY CH47 ... 108 F5
WARR WA1 ... 15 M1
WDN WA8 ... 133 K5
Queensberry St TOX L8 ... 113 H8

Queensbury WKBY CH48 124 F2
Queensbury Av PS/BROM CH62 144 A4
Queensbury Wy WDN WA8 133 M2
Queen's Cl RUNC WA7 18 F6
Queens Ct NPK/KEN L6 97 J8
Queenscourt Rd
WD/CROXPK L12 98 E8
Queens Crs WARR WA1 * 122 C5
Queens Cft FMBY L37 58 F3
Queensdale Rd CALD/MH L18 114 C8
Queens Dr CL/PREN CH43 127 J4
ECCL WA10 88 E7
FROD/HEL WA6 166 D2
GOL/RIS/CU WA3 92 E5
HES CH60 141 G5
NEWLW WA12 91 L8
WARRS WA4 138 B3
Queens Drive Mossley Hl
CALD/MH L18 130 B1
Queens Drive Stoneycroft
CLB/OSW/ST L13 114 D1
CLB/OSW/ST L13 114 E3
Queens Drive Walton
ANF/KKDL L4 97 J3
Queens Drive Wavertree
DV/KA/FCH L14 114 E4
WAV L15 114 E7
Queens Drive West Derby
CLB/OSW/ST L13 98 A5
Queens Gdns EP CH65 20 A4
Queensgate CHLY/EC PR7 32 D6
Queens Gn ORM L39 49 H8
Queen's Gv CHLY/EC PR7 32 E5
Queens Hall Pas WGN WN1 * 4 E4
Queensland Av STHEL WA9 102 A6
Queensland Pl STHEL WA9 102 A6
Queensland St EHL/KEN L7 113 K4
Queens Ms NPK/KEN L6 97 J8
Queen Sq CLVPS L1 13 H6
Queen's Rd AIMK WN4 91 K2
BTL L20 7 G7
CHLY/EC PR7 32 D5
CHTN/BK PR9 3 K2
CSBY/BLUN L23 83 G1
ECCL WA10 101 L4
FMBY L37 58 F3
GTS/LS CH66 155 L6
HOY CH47 108 C6
NPK/KEN L6 113 J1
PR/KW L34 101 G7
RF/TRAN CH42 128 C4
RNFD/HAY WA11 91 J6
RUNC WA7 18 F5
WAL/EG CH44 112 A2
WGNW/BIL/O WN5 66 E8
Queen St ALL/GAR L19 130 E8
BIRK CH41 11 K9
CSBY/WL L22 82 F5
ECCL WA10 8 F2
EP CH65 20 D1
GOL/RIS/CU WA3 * 92 D5
NEWLW WA12 104 D2
ORM L39 63 G1
RUNC WA7 19 G2
WAL/NB CH45 95 K8
WGNE/HIN WN2 69 M7
WGNE/HIN WN2 80 C3
WGNS/IIMK WN3 4 E5
WGNW/BIL/O WN5 67 K7
Queen St East CHLY/EC PR7 32 F7
Queensway CHLY/EC PR7 32 A3
CSBY/WL L22 83 H3
FROD/HEL WA6 160 D6
HES CH60 141 L7
RNFD/HAY WA11 76 C8
RNFD/HAY WA11 89 J5
RUNC WA7 18 F2
WAL/NB CH45 95 J7
WDN WA8 134 A6
WGN WN1 68 D3
WGNE/HIN WN2 69 J5
WGNNW/ST WN6 67 H1
Queensway (Mersey Tunnel)
BIRK CH41 11 J3
VAUX/LVPD L3 12 D6
Queens Whf VAUX/LVPD L3 112 E6
Quernmore Rd NWD/KWIPK L33 86 C2
Quernmore Wk NWD/KWIPK L33 86 C2
Quickswood Cl WLTN L25 115 H8
Quickswood Dr WLTN L25 115 H8
Quickswood Gn WLTN L25 115 H8
Quickthorn Crs STBRV L28 99 K6
Quigley Av NTHTN L30 84 C4
Quigley St BIRK CH41 128 A1
The Quillet NSTN CH64 153 H6
Quinesway GR/UP/WCH CH49 110 C8
Quinn St WDN WA8 16 E5
Quintbridge Cl HLWD L26 132 A6
Quinton Cl STHP PR8 47 J1
Quorn St EHL/KEN L7 113 K3

R

Rabbit La BRSC L40 51 H2
Raby Av BEB CH63 143 K7
Raby Cl BEB CH63 143 J6
HES CH60 141 H6
WDN WA8 134 F3
Raby Dr BEB CH63 143 J6
MOR/LEA CH46 109 M6
Raby Gdns NSTN CH64 153 G5
Raby Gv RF/TRAN CH42 127 M5
Raby Hall Rd BEB CH63 143 G8
Raby Mere Rd BEB CH63 142 E8
Raby Park Cl NSTN CH64 153 G5
Raby Park Rd NSTN CH64 153 G5
Raby Rd BEB CH63 142 D7
NSTN CH64 153 G5
Rachel St EV L5 13 H1
Radburn Cl CSBY/BLUN L23 71 K8
Radcliffe Av GOL/RIS/CU WA3 107 G2
Raddon Pl WARRS WA4 15 M9
Radford Av BEB CH63 143 K3
Radford Cl WDN WA8 133 L6
Radlett Cl WARRW/BUR WA5 136 A2
Radley Dr AIN/FAZ L10 84 E2
BEB CH63 142 B7
Radley La WARRN/WOL WA2 121 M2
Radley Rd WAL/EG CH44 95 H8
Radleys Ct TOX L8 * 113 H7
Radley St STHEL WA9 102 A6
Radmore Rd DV/KA/FCH L14 114 F2
Radnor Av HES CH60 141 H4
Radnor Cl HLWD L26 131 M7
WGNE/HIN WN2 81 J2
Radnor Dr BTL L20 7 L4
CHTN/BK PR9 25 H2
LEIGH WN7 81 L8
WAL/NB CH45 95 L7
WDN WA8 133 M3
Radnor Pl CL/PREN CH43 10 E6
NPK/KEN L6 97 M8
Radnor St WARRW/BUR WA5 121 G7
Radstock Gv STHEL WA9 102 F8
Radstock Rd NPK/KEN L6 113 L2
WAL/EG CH44 95 G8
Radway Gn GTS/LS CH66 156 A8
Radway Rd HUY L36 100 B8
Raeburn Av NSTN CH64 153 H6
PS/BROM CH62 143 M7
WKBY CH48 124 E2
Raffles Rd RF/TRAN CH42 11 G8
Raffles St CLVPS L1 113 G6
Rafter Av BTL L20 84 A7
Raglan Ct GOL/RIS/CU WA3 107 H7
Rail Cl RNFD/HAY WA11 76 B3
Railside Ct EV L5 * 96 E8
Railton Av RAIN/WH L35 117 M3
Railton Cl RAIN/WH L35 117 M4
Railton Rd NG/CROX L11 98 A3
Railway Ap ORM L39 51 H8
Railway Pth ORM L39 63 G1
Railway Rd CHLYE PR6 32 F4
CHLYE PR6 44 C6
GOL/RIS/CU WA3 * 92 D5
RF/TRAN CH42 128 B3
SKEL WN8 64 F5
Railway St ALL/GAR L19 130 E8
CHLY/EC PR7 32 F6
NEWLW WA12 104 D2
STHEL WA9 9 J3
STHP PR8 3 G7
WGNNW/ST WN6 4 A2
Railway Ter STHP PR8 2 F7
Rainbow Cl WDN WA8 133 L2
Rainbow Dr HLWD L26 132 A5
MGHL L31 85 K1
Raines Cl GR/UP/WCH CH49 126 A1
Rainford Av BTL L20 84 A8
Rainford By-pass
RNFD/HAY WA11 75 M6
Rainford Rd ORM L39 64 C7
RNFD/HAY WA11 88 E6
WGNW/BIL/O WN5 77 K8
Rainham Cl ALL/GAR L19 130 E5
Rainhill Rd RAIN/WH L35 101 L8
Raithby Dr WGNS/IIMK WN3 79 J2
Rake Hey MOR/LEA CH46 109 K5
Rake Hey Cl MOR/LEA CH46 109 L5
Rake La CHNE CH2 163 M8
FROD/HEL WA6 159 J7
FROD/HEL WA6 165 K6
GR/UP/WCH CH49 126 C1
WAL/NB CH45 95 K7
Rakersfield Ct WAL/NB CH45 95 L5
Rakersfield Rd WAL/NB CH45 95 L5
The Rake PS/BROM CH62 144 A4
Raleigh Av RAIN/WH L35 116 F3
Raleigh Cl WARRW/BUR WA5 120 F4
Raleigh Rd MOR/LEA CH46 110 D1
NSTN CH64 153 G4
Raleigh St BTL L20 6 E9
Ralph's Wife's La CHTN/BK PR9 23 H7
Rame Cl NG/CROX L11 85 K7
Ramford St STHEL WA9 102 F3
Ramilies Rd CALD/MH L18 114 B8
Ramleh Cl CSBY/BLUN L23 82 D2
Rampit Cl RNFD/HAY WA11 91 H6
Ramsay Cl GOL/RIS/CU WA3 123 G2
Ramsbrook Cl SPK/HALE L24 146 E1
Ramsbrook La SPK/HALE L24 147 L2
Ramsbrook Rd SPK/HALE L24 146 E1
Ramsden Cl WGNS/IIMK WN3 4 A9
Ramsey Cl AIMK WN4 91 K3
ALL/GAR L19 130 F5
RAIN/WH L35 117 G2
WDN WA8 135 G2
Ramsey Ct WKBY CH48 124 D4
Ramsey Rd ALL/GAR L19 130 F5
EP CH65 163 L4
Ramsfield Rd SPK/HALE L24 147 J1
Ramsons Cl HLWD L26 132 A4
Randall Av WGNNW/ST WN6 55 J8
Randall Dr NTHTN L30 83 L3
Randle Av RNFD/HAY WA11 76 A5
Randle Brook Ct
RNFD/HAY WA11 76 A5
Randle Cl BEB CH63 143 J3
Randle Meadow GTS/LS CH66 163 H3
Randles Rd PR/KW L34 86 C8
Randolph St ANF/KKDL L4 97 H6
Randon Gv ECCL WA10 8 E4
Ranelagh Av LITH L21 83 J5
Ranelagh Dr STHP PR8 35 H6
Ranelagh Dr North
ALL/GAR L19 130 C5
Ranelagh Dr South
ALL/GAR L19 130 C6
Ranelagh St CLVPS L1 13 H8
Ranfurly Rd ALL/GAR L19 130 D6
Rangemoor Cl GOL/RIS/CU WA3 107 J7
Rangemore Rd CALD/MH L18 130 C4
Rangletts Av CHLY/EC PR7 32 E7
Ranicar Steet WGNE/HIN WN2 81 L2
Rankin St WAL/EG CH44 111 J3
Ranleigh Dr SKEL WN8 53 J4
Ranmore Av AIMK WN4 90 F1
Rannoch Cl GTS/LS CH66 163 H2
Ranulph Ct FROD/HEL WA6 160 E6
Ranworth Cl NG/CROX L11 98 A2
Ranworth Dr GOL/RIS/CU WA3 93 G6
Ranworth Pl NG/CROX L11 98 B2
Ranworth Rd
WARRW/BUR WA5 120 A7
Ranworth Sq NG/CROX L11 98 B2
Ranworth Wy NG/CROX L11 98 B2
Rappart Rd WAL/EG CH44 111 M2
Rassey Cl WGNNW/ST WN6 56 C6
Ratcliffe Rd WGNE/HIN WN2 57 L7
Ratcliffe St WGNNW/ST WN6 4 A2
Ratcliff Pl RAIN/WH L35 117 K1
Rathbone Rd HTWN L38 70 B1
WAV L15 114 B5
Rathen Av WGNE/HIN WN2 69 J4
Rathlin Cl WDN WA8 135 G2
Rathmell Cl GOL/RIS/CU WA3 107 G2
Rathmore Av CALD/MH L18 130 C2
Rathmore Cl CL/PREN CH43 127 J2
Rathmore Crs CHTN/BK PR9 25 K2
Rathmore Dr CL/PREN CH43 127 J1
Rathmore Rd CL/PREN CH43 127 J1
Raven Cl NPK/KEN L6 * 113 J2
Ravendale Cl CL/PREN CH43 126 F1
Ravenfield Cl HLWD L26 132 A5
Ravenfield Dr WDN WA8 133 L2
Ravenglass Av MGHL L31 72 F3
Ravenhead Av KKBY L32 86 A6
Ravenhead Colliery Yd
STHEL WA9 * 9 H9
Ravenhead Dr SKEL WN8 66 C6
Ravenhead Rd ECCL WA10 8 D9
Ravenhead Rw ECCL WA10 * 102 A4
Ravenhead Wy SKEL WN8 66 B7
Ravenhill Crs MOR/LEA CH46 110 B2
Ravenhill Dr CHLY/EC PR7 32 E4
Ravenhurst Ct GOL/RIS/CU WA3 107 H8
Ravenhurst Wy RAIN/WH L35 116 E4
Raven Meols La FMBY L37 59 G3
Ravenna Rd ALL/GAR L19 130 F5
Ravenscourt HLWD L26 * 132 B6
Ravenscroft FMBY L37 59 H3
Ravenscroft Av ORM L39 63 G1
Ravenscroft Rd CL/PREN CH43 10 E7
Ravensdale Cl
WARRN/WOL WA2 121 M2
The Ravens FMBY L37 59 H4
Ravensthorpe Gn NG/CROX L11 98 B2
Ravenstone Cl
GR/UP/WCH CH49 110 A6
Ravenstone Dr STHEL WA9 102 F6
Ravenstone Rd ALL/GAR L19 130 D5
Ravenswood Av RF/TRAN CH42 128 B5
WGNS/IIMK WN3 78 F2
Ravenswood Rd
CLB/OSW/ST L13 114 C2
PEN/TH CH61 141 J3
Rawcliffe Cl WDN WA8 134 B1
Rawcliffe Rd CHLY/EC PR7 32 E6
RF/TRAN CH42 11 G8
WLT/FAZ L9 97 H1
Rawdon Cl RUNC WA7 150 C6
Rawlings Cl GOL/RIS/CU WA3 123 H2
Rawlinson Ct CHTN/BK PR9 * 3 M1
Rawlinson Crs HLWD L26 132 D5
Rawlinson Gv CHTN/BK PR9 25 G4
Rawlinson La CHLY/EC PR7 44 B4
Rawlinson Rd CHTN/BK PR9 25 G4
CLB/OSW/ST L13 114 B2
Rawlins St EHL/KEN L7 113 M2
Rawson Cl LITH L21 83 H6
Rawson Rd LITH L21 83 H6
Rawthey Pl WGNE/HIN WN2 80 B3
Raydale Cl GOL/RIS/CU WA3 93 G4
WLT/FAZ L9 97 J2
Raymond Av NTHTN L30 84 C4
WARRS WA4 137 M3
Raymond Pl EV L5 13 G1
Raymond Rd WAL/EG CH44 111 L2
Raymond Wy NSTN CH64 153 J6
Rayner Av WGNE/HIN WN2 81 G2
Raynham Rd CLB/OSW/ST L13 114 B3
Reade Cl BEB CH63 143 J4
Reading Cl EV L5 96 F6
Reads Ct WLT/FAZ L9 84 B7
Reaper Cl WARRW/BUR WA5 120 F7
Reapers Wy NTHTN L30 84 C1
Reay St WDN WA8 134 E3
Rebecca Gdns STHEL WA9 102 E6
Recreation Av AIMK WN4 91 M1
Recreation Dr
WGNW/BIL/O WN5 * 78 A8
Rector Rd NPK/KEN L6 97 L6
Rectory Av GOL/RIS/CU WA3 92 E5
Rectory Cl CHLY/EC PR7 32 E4
CROS/BRETH PR26 29 L4
HES CH60 141 H6
RF/TRAN CH42 11 H9
WARRN/WOL WA2 105 J7
Rectory Dr HLWD L26 132 B4
Rectory Gdns STHEL WA9 102 E7
Rectory La CH/BCN CH1 162 B4
HES CH60 141 G6
WARRN/WOL WA2 105 J7
WGNNW/ST WN6 56 B4
Rectory Rd AIMK WN4 78 F8
CHTN/BK PR9 25 H4
WKBY CH48 124 D4
Red Bank Av NEWLW WA12 105 H4
Red Barnes FMBY L37 47 H7
Red Barn Rd WGNW/BIL/O WN5 77 K7
Redbourne Av HLWD L26 132 B7
Redbourne Dr WDN WA8 133 K1
Redbourn St NPK/KEN L6 97 L7
Red Br CROS/BRETH PR26 28 E3
Redbrook Cl PS/BROM CH62 143 M7
Redbrook Rd WGNS/IIMK WN3 5 J7
Redbrook St NPK/KEN L6 97 L7
Red Brow La RUNC WA7 151 G5
Redbrow Wy NWD/KWIPK L33 86 A1
Redburn Cl TOX L8 129 J1
WGNS/IIMK WN3 4 D8
Redcap Cl WAL/NB CH45 95 G5
Redcar Cl STHP PR8 36 B2
Redcar Dr PS/BROM CH62 143 M8
Redcar Ms NPK/KEN L6 97 K7
Redcar Rd WAL/NB CH45 94 F7
Redcar St NPK/KEN L6 97 L7
Red Cat La BRSC L40 39 G5
RNFD/HAY WA11 89 G1
Redcliffe Gdns ORM L39 63 G2
Redcroft GR/UP/WCH CH49 * 125 L2
Red Cross St CLVPS L1 12 E8
Red Cut La NWD/KWIPK L33 87 H5
Red Delph La RNFD/HAY WA11 75 M4
Redditch Cl GR/UP/WCH CH49 125 L1
Redesdale Cl WARRN/WOL WA2 122 A3
Redfern St BTL L20 96 E5
Redfield Cl WAL/EG CH44 111 M1
Red Fold ORM L39 62 E3
Redford Cl GR/UP/WCH CH49 125 L1
Redford St NPK/KEN L6 97 L8
Redgate FMBY L37 59 J3
ORM L39 62 F1
Redgate Av CSBY/BLUN L23 83 J1
Redgate Dr FMBY L37 59 K3
STHEL WA9 102 F2
Redgate Rd AIMK WN4 79 K7
Redgrave Ri WGNS/IIMK WN3 78 F2
Redgrave St EHL/KEN L7 113 L3
Redhill Av KKBY L32 86 B5
Redhill Gv CHLYE PR6 33 G2
Redhill Ms EP CH65 20 B2
Red Hill Rd BEB CH63 127 K8
Redhills Dr STHP PR8 36 B2
Red Hill Wy WGNE/HIN WN2 * 69 M7
Redhouse Bank WKBY CH48 124 C2
Red House La CHLY/EC PR7 30 D7
Redhouse La WKBY CH48 124 C2
Redington Rd ALL/GAR L19 130 F5
Redland Ct WGNE/HIN WN2 80 A6
Redland Rd WLT/FAZ L9 84 D5
Red La CHLY/EC PR7 31 G7
FROD/HEL WA6 160 E5
WARRS WA4 137 L6
Red Lion Cl MGHL L31 72 E4
Red Lion La GTS/LS CH66 155 L6
Red Lomes NTHTN L30 71 M8
Redmain Gv GOL/RIS/CU WA3 93 G5
Redmain Wy WD/CROXPK L12 99 H3
Redmayne Cl NEWLW WA12 104 D1
Redmere Dr HES CH60 141 L5
Redmires Cl EHL/KEN L7 * 113 K5
Redmond St BIRK CH41 * 11 J9
Redmoor Crs NWD/KWIPK L33 86 A1
Rednal Wk WGNS/IIMK WN3 4 C8
Red Pike GTS/LS CH66 155 M6
Redpoll Gv HLWD L26 132 A3
Redpoll La GOL/RIS/CU WA3 123 G1
Red Rock La WGNE/HIN WN2 56 F5
Red Rock St NPK/KEN L6 113 K1
Red Rum Cl WLT/FAZ L9 84 F5
Redruth Av RNFD/HAY WA11 89 M6
Redruth Cl RUNC WA7 150 E7
Redruth Rd NG/CROX L11 85 M8
Red Sands ORM L39 62 F2
Redshank Cl NEWLW WA12 104 E1
Redshank La GOL/RIS/CU WA3 123 H1
Redstart Cl GOL/RIS/CU WA3 93 G5
Redstone Cl HOY CH47 108 F5
Redstone Dr HES CH60 140 E4
Red Stone Hl FROD/HEL WA6 166 D1
Redstone Pk WAL/NB CH45 * 95 J5
Redstone Ri CL/PREN CH43 110 F7
Redvales Ct GOL/RIS/CU WA3 122 E1
Redvers Av GTS/LS CH66 155 J3
Redvers Dr WLT/FAZ L9 84 B7
Redwald Cl NWD/KWIPK L33 74 B7
Redwing La WLTN L25 131 J1
Redwing Wy HLWD L26 131 M3
Redwood WGNNW/ST WN6 55 K7
Redwood Av MGHL L31 72 E2
WGNNW/ST WN6 68 B2
WGNW/BIL/O WN5 67 J7
Redwood Cl CL/PREN CH43 * 127 H3
WARR WA1 123 G7
Redwood Dr CHLY/EC PR7 33 G7
CHNE CH2 165 L1
GTS/LS CH66 163 H4
ORM L39 62 F1
RNFD/HAY WA11 90 B8
Redwood Gv BTL L20 * 7 H3
Redwood Rd WLTN L25 115 K8
Redwood Wy NWD/KWIPK L33 74 A7
Reedale Cl CALD/MH L18 130 C1
Reedale Rd CALD/MH L18 130 C1
Reed Crs WGNS/IIMK WN3 79 J1
Reeds Av East MOR/LEA CH46 110 B2
Reeds Av West MOR/LEA CH46 110 B2
Reeds Brow RNFD/HAY WA11 76 D5
Reeds La MOR/LEA CH46 110 B2
RNFD/HAY WA11 88 B2
Reedsmere Cl WARRS WA4 138 A3
WGNW/BIL/O WN5 68 B7
Reeds Rd HUY L36 116 A1
The Reeds ORM L39 50 F7
Reedville CL/PREN CH43 10 D8
Reedville Gv MOR/LEA CH46 110 B3
Reedville Rd BEB CH63 128 B8
Reepham Cl WGNS/IIMK WN3 78 F2
Rees Pk BRSC L40 52 B2
Reeves Av BTL L20 7 L1
Reeves St STHEL WA9 103 G2
Reeve St GOL/RIS/CU WA3 93 K5
Reeveswood CHLY/EC PR7 30 D7
Regal Cl GTS/LS CH66 163 G2
Regal Crs WDN WA8 133 K5
Regal Dr ECCL WA10 88 E8
Regal Rd NG/CROX L11 98 E2
Regal Wk ANF/KKDL L4 97 H6
Regency Ct WGN WN1 5 G3
Regency Gdns STHP PR8 35 G1
Regent Av AIMK WN4 79 H8
DV/KA/FCH L14 115 G3
NTHTN L30 84 B2
RNFD/HAY WA11 90 D6
WARR WA1 122 C5
Regent Cl STHP PR8 35 H1
Regent Ms STHP PR8 35 H1
Regent Rd BTL L20 6 B2
CHLY/EC PR7 32 D6
CSBY/BLUN L23 82 F1
STHP PR8 35 G1
WAL/NB CH45 94 F7
WDN WA8 16 E1
WGNE/HIN WN2 80 C2
Regents Cl PEN/TH CH61 126 D7
Regents Fld FMBY L37 * 46 F8
Regents Rd ECCL WA10 101 L4
Regent St CHLY/EC PR7 43 G4
EP CH65 156 C8
NEWLW WA12 104 C2
RUNC WA7 19 G2
VAUX/LVPD L3 12 C2
WARR WA1 14 D6
WGNE/HIN WN2 69 M8
Regents Wy BEB CH63 127 M6
CHLY/EC PR7 31 M3
Regina Av CSBY/WL L22 82 E3
Reginald Rd STHEL WA9 103 G7
Regina Rd WLT/FAZ L9 84 C7
Reid Av WARRW/BUR WA5 121 H5
Reid Ct GTS/LS CH66 155 L6
Reigate CHLYE PR6 33 H2
Reigate Cl WLTN L25 131 L3
Renacres La ORM L39 36 A8
Renaissance Wy SPK/HALE L24 146 F1
Rendal Cl EV L5 97 J8
Rendcombe Gn NG/CROX L11 98 B2
Rendel Cl NEWLW WA12 104 F3
Rendelsham Cl
GR/UP/WCH CH49 110 A8
Rendel St BIRK CH41 11 H3
Rendlesham Cl
GOL/RIS/CU WA3 107 K7
Renfrew Av PS/BROM CH62 144 A8
RNFD/HAY WA11 90 A6
Renfrew Cl WGNS/IIMK WN3 79 J2
Renfrew Rd WGNE/HIN WN2 57 M8
Renfrew St EHL/KEN L7 113 J3
Renfrey Cl ORM L39 51 G5
Rennell Rd DV/KA/FCH L14 114 E2
Rennie Av ECCL WA10 101 L1
Renown Cl GOL/RIS/CU WA3 122 F1
Renown Wy SPK/HALE L24 131 J7
Renshaw St CLVPS L1 13 J8
Renton Av RUNC WA7 149 M3
Renville Rd DV/KA/FCH L14 114 E4
Renwick Av RAIN/WH L35 117 J1
Renwick Sq AIMK WN4 91 H2
Repton Av WGNS/IIMK WN3 80 B1
Repton Gv WLT/FAZ L9 84 E3
Repton Rd CHLDW L16 114 F5
EP CH65 20 F7
Reservoir Rd RF/TRAN CH42 127 K4
WLTN L25 131 H2
Reservoir Rd North
RF/TRAN CH42 127 K3
Reservoir St NPK/KEN L6 113 J1
STHEL WA9 101 L6
WGNE/HIN WN2 69 J5
Rest Hill Rd BEB CH63 127 K8
Restormel Av WGNE/HIN WN2 57 M8
Retford Rd NWD/KWIPK L33 86 B3
Reva Rd DV/KA/FCH L14 115 H3
Revesby Cl WDN WA8 133 M3
Rexmore Rd CALD/MH L18 130 C3
Rexmore Wy WAV L15 114 A6
Reynolds Av GOL/RIS/CU WA3 107 G8
STHEL WA9 103 K3
Reynolds Cl NPK/KEN L6 113 J1
Reynolds St WARRS WA4 138 B2
Reynolds Wy WLTN L25 131 J3
Rhiwlas St TOX L8 113 J8
Rhodesia Rd WLT/FAZ L9 84 D7
Rhodes St WARRN/WOL WA2 15 G1
Rhodesway HES CH60 141 K6
Rhona Cl BEB CH63 154 E1
Rhona Dr WARRW/BUR WA5 120 A7
Rhosesmor Cl KKBY L32 86 B7
Rhosesmor Rd KKBY L32 86 B7
Rhuddlan Ct EP CH65 163 M3
Rhum Cl EP CH65 163 L4
Rhyl St TOX L8 113 H8
WDN WA8 * 16 B6
Rialto Cl TOX L8 113 H6
Ribbesford Rd WGNS/IIMK WN3 78 E1
Ribble Av CHTN/BK PR9 25 L1
MGHL L31 73 G3
RAIN/WH L35 117 L2
Ribble Cl GOL/RIS/CU WA3 107 H3
WDN WA8 135 H2
Ribble Crs WGNW/BIL/O WN5 89 L2
Ribbledale Rd CALD/MH L18 130 C1
Ribble Dr WGNW/BIL/O WN5 67 L6
Ribble Gv LEIGH WN7 81 L8
Ribble Rd WGNE/HIN WN2 80 C3
WGNNW/ST WN6 55 K3
WLTN L25 131 L2
Ribbler's La KKBY L32 85 M6
PR/KW L34 86 B7
Ribblesdale EP CH65 20 A9
Ribblesdale Av WLT/FAZ L9 84 D6
Ribblesdale Cl PS/BROM CH62 144 B8
Ribblesdale Pl CHLY/EC PR7 32 D6
Ribble St BIRK CH41 111 H4
Ribchester Gdns
GOL/RIS/CU WA3 107 J2
Ribchester Wy RAIN/WH L35 116 C6
Rice Hey Rd WAL/EG CH44 95 L8
Rice La WAL/EG CH44 95 L8
WLT/FAZ L9 97 J1
Rice St CLVPS L1 113 G5
Richard Allen Wy EV L5 13 K2
Richard Gv WD/CROXPK L12 99 G8
Richard Hesketh Dr KKBY L32 85 L3
Richard Kelly Cl ANF/KKDL L4 * 97 M5
Richard Kelly Dr ANF/KKDL L4 97 M3
Richard Kelly Pl ANF/KKDL L4 * 97 M5
Richard Martin Rd LITH L21 * 83 L4
Richard Rd CSBY/BLUN L23 70 C7
Richards Gv STHEL WA9 103 G1
Richardson Rd RF/TRAN CH42 128 A4
Richardson St EHL/KEN L7 113 L6
WARRN/WOL WA2 121 L5
Richards Rd WGNNW/ST WN6 55 K2
Richard St WGNS/IIMK WN3 5 H7
Richland Rd CLB/OSW/ST L13 98 B8
Richmond Av BRSC L40 52 A2
LITH L21 83 J5
RNFD/HAY WA11 90 D6
RUNC WA7 150 A3
WARRS WA4 138 B1
WARRS WA4 138 E2
Richmond Cl BEB CH63 128 B7
ECCL WA10 101 H1
GOL/RIS/CU WA3 106 F1
HTWN L38 70 B3
WGN WN1 56 D6
Richmond Ct CHLY/EC PR7 32 E7
EP CH65 20 F9
LITH L21 * 83 K6
Richmond Crs NTHTN L30 84 B2
Richmond Gdns NEWLW WA12 104 E3
Richmond Gv MGHL L31 73 G2
Richmond Hl WGNW/BIL/O WN5 67 L7
Richmond Ms BRSC L40 52 A2
Richmond Pk NPK/KEN L6 97 K7
Richmond Rd AIMK WN4 79 H8
BEB CH63 128 B7
CHLY/EC PR7 30 E6
CHLYE PR6 33 G7
CSBY/BLUN L23 71 G8
STHP PR8 35 H3
WGNE/HIN WN2 81 J2
Richmond Rw VAUX/LVPD L3 13 J3
Richmond St CLVPS L1 * 13 G7
WAL/NB CH45 95 K4
WARRS WA4 138 C2
WDN WA8 17 G1
WGN WN1 4 D3
WGNS/IIMK WN3 68 C8
Richmond Ter NPK/KEN L6 97 J8
Richmond Wy HUY L36 116 C6
PEN/TH CH61 * 126 C7
PEN/TH CH61 141 H3
Rickaby Cl BEB CH63 143 L5
Rickman St ANF/KKDL L4 96 F5
Rickman Wy HUY L36 116 B5
Ridding La RUNC WA7 150 D8
The Riddings EP CH65 20 A7
Riddock Rd LITH L21 83 K8
Ridge Av WGN WN1 56 D6
Ridgeborne Cl
WARRW/BUR WA5 120 F3
Ridge Cl CHTN/BK PR9 22 E8
Ridgefield Rd PEN/TH CH61 126 B8
Ridgemere Rd PEN/TH CH61 126 B8
Ridge Rd CHLYE PR6 33 G6
The Ridge HES CH60 140 F3
Ridgetor Rd WLTN L25 131 J2
Ridgeview Rd CL/PREN CH43 110 F8
Ridgeway GOL/RIS/CU WA3 93 G6
Ridgeway Cl GTS/LS CH66 162 E3
Ridgeway Dr MGHL L31 72 F2
Ridgeway Gdns LYMM WA13 139 M2
The Ridgeway BEB CH63 127 M5
FROD/HEL WA6 167 J3
HES CH60 141 K6
HOY CH47 109 G6
RUNC WA7 150 F7
WDN WA8 117 L7
WLTN L25 131 J2
Ridgewell Av GOL/RIS/CU WA3 92 F5
Ridgewood Dr PEN/TH CH61 141 H1
STHEL WA9 102 F7
Ridgewood Wy WLT/FAZ L9 84 C6
Ridgmont Av NG/CROX L11 98 B3
Ridgway HOR/BR BL6 57 L3
Ridgway St WARRN/WOL WA2 15 J1
Riding Cl STHEL WA9 * 118 E1
Riding Fold HLWD L26 131 M3
Riding Hill Rd PR/KW L34 99 M3
Riding La AIMK WN4 80 A8
ORM L39 61 G1
Ridings Hey CL/PREN CH43 126 F1
The Ridings CHTN/BK PR9 25 J2
CL/PREN CH43 110 F8
Riding St STHP PR8 3 G6
VAUX/LVPD L3 13 L6
Ridley Dr WARRW/BUR WA5 136 E1
Ridley Gv WKBY CH48 124 C2
Ridley La BRSC L40 41 H3
CROS/BRETH PR26 29 M2
MGHL L31 72 F4
Ridley Rd NPK/KEN L6 113 L2
Ridley St CL/PREN CH43 10 E7
Ridsdale WDN WA8 133 L5
Ridyard St WGNE/HIN WN2 80 D2
WGNW/BIL/O WN5 68 A6
Riesling Dr NWD/KWIPK L33 74 A8
Rigby Av HOR/BR BL6 * 57 L3
Rigby Dr GR/UP/WCH CH49 125 M3
Rigby Rd MGHL L31 72 D2
Rigbys Houses CHLY/EC PR7 * 44 A7
Rigbys La AIMK WN4 91 M2
Rigby St AIMK WN4 91 J2
ECCL WA10 8 F4
GOL/RIS/CU WA3 92 C5
VAUX/LVPD L3 12 D5
Rigby Wk CHLY/EC PR7 * 32 E5
Riley Av BTL L20 7 K1
Riley Dr RUNC WA7 19 H7
Riley La WGNE/HIN WN2 57 K6
Riley Sq WGN WN1 5 H3
Rilston Av GOL/RIS/CU WA3 106 F2
Rimington Av GOL/RIS/CU WA3 92 E4
Rimington Cl GOL/RIS/CU WA3 107 G2
Rimmer Av CHLDW L16 115 J4
Rimmer Cl LITH L21 83 K6
Rimmer Gn STHP PR8 36 F4

Rimmer Gv STHEL WA9 .....103 G2
Rimmer's Av FMBY L37 .....47 G7
 STHP PR8 .....3 G6
Rimmers Ct BIRK CH41 * 111 H6
Rimmer St VAUX/LVPD L3 .....13 K5
Rimmington Av AIG/SPK L17 .....130 A3
Rimrose Rd BTL L20 .....6 D2
Rimrose Valley Rd
 CSBY/BLUN L23 .....83 K1
Ringcroft Rd CLB/OSW/ST L13 .....114 D2
Ringley Av GOL/RIS/CU WA3 .....92 B4
Ring O'bells La BRSC L40 .....52 D5
Ringo Starr Dr NPK/KEN L6 * 113 K2
Ringsfield Rd SPK/HALE L24 .....147 J2
Ringtail Ct BRSC L40 .....51 K4
Ringtail Pl BRSC L40 .....51 K2
Ringtail Rd BRSC L40 .....51 K4
Ringway CHLY/EC PR7 .....32 C6
 GTS/LS CH66 .....163 G4
 NSTN CH64 .....153 H6
Ringway Rd RUNC WA7 .....149 M3
 WLTN L25 .....131 L1
Ringways PS WGNN CH62 .....143 M2
Ringwood CL/PREN CH43 .....127 J2
Ringwood Av DV/KA/FCH L14 .....115 H3
Ringwood Cl GOL/RIS/CU WA3 .....107 K8
Ringwood Ct CL/PREN CH43 * 127 J2
Rio Ct PR/KW L34 .....100 F6
Ripley Av LITH L21 .....83 K4
Ripley Cl MGHL L31 .....73 H4
Ripley Dr WGNS/IIMK WN3 .....78 E1
Ripley St WARRW/BUR WA5 .....121 G6
Ripon Av GOL/RIS/CU WA3 .....92 F5
Ripon Cl HUY L36 .....116 C2
 NEWLW WA12 .....104 E1
 NTHTN L30 .....84 B4
 STHP PR8 .....36 B2
Ripon Dr AIMK WN4 .....91 M3
Ripon Rd WAL/EG CH45 .....95 G3
Ripon St ANF/KKDL L4 .....97 H4
 BIRK CH41 .....11 J3
Rippon Av GTS/LS CH66 .....155 L8
Risbury Cl NG/CROX L11 .....98 B3
The Rise WGNNW/ST WN6 .....67 L2
Rishton Cl EV L5 .....97 J8
Risley Rd GOL/RIS/CU WA3 .....107 H7
Ritchie Av WLT/FAZ L9 .....84 E6
Ritherup La RAIN/WH L35 .....117 L1
Ritson St TOX L8 .....113 K7
Rivacre Brow GTS/LS CH66 .....156 A6
Rivacre Rd GTS/LS CH66 .....156 A6
 PS/BROM CH62 .....155 J1
River Avon St TOX L8 * 113 L6
Riverbank Cl HES CH60 .....141 H7
Riverbank Rd ALL/GAR L19 .....130 C6
 HES CH60 .....141 G7
River Cl FMBY L37 .....59 K4
Riverdale Cl WGNNW/ST WN6 .....67 M2
River Gv PS/BROM CH62 .....128 D5
Rivermeade STHP PR8 .....36 F5
River Rd WARRS WA4 .....14 F7
Riversdale FROD/HEL WA6 .....160 E4
 WARR WA1 .....123 H6
Riversdale Ct CSBY/WL L22 * 86 A1
Riversdale Ct AIG/SPK L17 .....130 B5
Riversdale Ms ALL/GAR L19 .....130 B5
Riversdale Rd ALL/GAR L19 .....130 B5
 LITH L21 .....83 H6
 RUNC WA7 .....150 A4
 WAL/EG CH44 .....111 J8
 WKBY CH48 .....124 C3
Riverside HTWN L38 .....70 B1
 PS/BROM CH62 .....128 D8
 WD/CROXPK L12 .....99 G4
 WKBY CH48 .....124 D5
Riverside Av WGN WN1 .....5 H1
Riverside Cl BTL L20 .....83 J8
 CROS/BRETH PR26 .....29 J3
 WARR WA1 .....14 H7
Riverside Crs CROS/BRETH PR26 .....29 J3
Riverside Dr AIG/SPK L17 .....129 J3
Riverside Dr STHEL WA9 .....90 F7
Riverside Wk NSTN CH64 .....152 F8
Riverslea Rd CSBY/WL L23 .....82 D3
Rivers St WCGNW/BIL/O WN5 .....67 G7
River St BIRK CH41 .....11 G6
River Vw CSBY/WL L22 .....82 D3
Riverview Rd NSTN CH64 .....153 H8
 WAL/EG CH44 .....112 A2
Riverview Wk TOX L8 .....129 H1
River Wy RUNC WA7 * 150 B6
Riverwood Rd PS/BROM CH62 .....144 B4
Riviera Dr RF/TRAN CH42 .....127 M4
 WD/CROXPK L12 .....99 G2
Rivington Av CHLY/EC PR6 .....44 C6
 CL/PREN CH43 .....127 C1
 ECCL WA10 .....89 C7
 GOL/RIS/CU WA3 .....92 E4
 WGN WN1 .....68 D3
 WGNE/HIN WN2 .....80 D2
Rivington Cl STHP PR8 .....35 J2
Rivington Ct WARR WA1 * 123 G5
Rivington Dr BRSC L40 .....52 E1
 SKEL WN8 .....66 E6
 WGNE/HIN WN2 .....81 H4
Rivington La CHLYE PR6 .....44 F6
 HOR/BR BL6 .....45 H4
Rivington Pl CHLY/EC PR7 .....42 F7
Rivington Rd CHLYE PR6 .....33 G4
 ECCL WA10 .....8 A4
 EP CH65 .....20 B5
 WAL/EG CH44 .....111 J4
Rivington St ECCL WA10 .....8 A7
 HOR/BR BL6 .....57 M3
Rivington Wy WGNNW/ST WN6 .....56 D5
Rixton Av WARRW/BUR WA5 .....121 H5
Roach Gn WGN WN1 .....5 K2
Roadside Ct GOL/RIS/CU WA3 .....92 E5
Roadwater Cl WLTN L25 .....115 K6
Robarts Rd ANF/KKDL L4 .....97 J7
Robeck Rd CLB/OSW/ST L13 .....114 D4
Robert Dr GR/UP/WCH CH49 .....126 A2
Robert Gv WD/CROXPK L12 .....99 G8
Roberts Av RNFD/HAY WA11 .....90 C8
Roberts Ct RUNC WA7 .....150 A7
Roberts Dr BTL L20 .....83 J8
Robertson St TOX L8 .....113 G8
Roberts St CHLY/EC PR7 .....32 E6
 VAUX/LVPD L3 .....12 C4
Robert St BIRK CH41 .....11 H4
 RUNC WA7 .....19 L3
 WARRW/BUR WA5 .....14 A4
 WDN WA8 .....16 F2
 WGNE/HIN WN2 .....80 C2
Robina Rd STHEL WA9 .....102 F5
Robin Cl CHLY/EC PR7 .....42 F2
 RUNC WA7 .....150 F6
Robin Hill Dr WGNNW/ST WN6 .....55 L3
Robin Hill La WGNNW/ST WN6 .....55 K2
Robin Hood La FROD/HEL WA6 * 160 D5
 WGNNW/ST WN6 .....54 D7
Robin La SKEL WN8 .....40 E8
Robin Park Rd
 WGNW/BIL/O WN5 .....4 A1
Robins Cft GTS/LS CH66 .....163 H3
Robins La GOL/RIS/CU WA3 .....106 F3
 RNFD/HAY WA11 .....77 H3
 STHEL WA9 .....102 E5

Robinson Ms BIRK CH41 * 11 L5
Robinson Pl STHEL WA9 .....9 M5
Robinson Rd LITH L21 .....83 L4
Robin Wy GR/UP/WCH CH49 .....126 D3
Rob La NEWLW WA12 .....105 L1
Robsart St CLB/OSW/ST L13 .....97 G8
 EV L5 .....97 H7
 WARR WA1 .....15 J3
Robson Wy GOL/RIS/CU WA3 .....93 H5
Roby Cl RAIN/WH L35 .....117 L1
Roby Gv WARRW/BUR WA5 .....120 C2
Roby Ml SKEL WN8 .....66 D2
Roby Mount Av HUY L36 .....115 M3
Roby Rd HUY L36 .....115 J3
Roby St BTL L20 .....7 A2
 ECCL WA10 .....8 A9
 WAV L15 .....114 A6
Roby Well Wy
 WGNW/BIL/O WN5 .....77 M8
Rocastle Cl NPK/KEN L6 .....113 J2
Rochester Av NTHTN L30 .....84 B4
Rochester Dr GOL/RIS/CU WA3 .....92 C5
 WARRW/BUR WA5 .....120 E8
Rochester Dr EP CH65 .....20 F9
Rochester Gdns ECCL WA10 .....8 A9
Rochester Rd RF/TRAN CH42 .....128 C3
Roch Pl WGNE/HIN WN2 .....80 B3
Rock Av HES CH60 .....141 H4
Rockbank Rd CLB/OSW/ST L13 .....98 B8
Rockbourne Av WLTN L25 .....115 H8
Rockbourne Cl WGNE/HIN WN2 .....80 F1
Rockbourne Gn WLTN L25 .....115 H8
Rockbourne Wy WLTN L25 .....115 H8
Rock Ct RF/TRAN CH42 .....128 B3
Rock Ct CLB/OSW/ST L13 .....114 C2
Rock Dr FROD/HEL WA6 .....160 E4
Rock Farm Cl NSTN CH64 .....153 J7
Rock Farm Dr NSTN CH64 .....153 J7
Rock Farm Gv NSTN CH64 * 153 J7
Rock Ferry By-Pass
 RF/TRAN CH42 .....128 C3
Rockfield Cl WDN WA8 .....133 M3
Rockfield Dr FROD/HEL WA6 .....166 E3
Rockford Av KKBY L32 .....86 A6
Rockford Cl KKBY L32 .....86 A6
Rockford Wk KKBY L32 .....86 A6
Rock Gv CLB/OSW/ST L13 .....114 C2
Rockhill Rd WLTN L25 .....131 K4
Rockhouse St NPK/KEN L6 .....97 L8
Rockingham Ct
 GOL/RIS/CU WA3 .....107 K7
Rockingham Ct
 NWD/KWIPK L33 * 86 B3
Rockingham Dr
 WGNE/HIN WN2 .....80 E1
Rockland Rd CSBY/WL L22 .....82 F3
Rocklands Av BEB CH63 .....128 C6
Rocklands La BEB CH63 .....142 H6
Rock La MGHL L31 .....73 H8
 WDN WA8 .....134 B1
Rock La East RF/TRAN CH42 .....128 C4
Rock La West RF/TRAN CH42 .....128 B4
Rocklee Gdns NSTN CH64 .....153 J7
Rockley St ANF/KKDL L4 .....97 G5
Rock Mount Cl WLTN L25 .....131 H2
Rockmount Rd AIG/SPK L17 .....130 B4
Rock Park Rd RF/TRAN CH42 .....128 D4
Rocksavage Expy RUNC WA7 .....149 L8
Rockside Rd CALD/MH L18 .....130 C3
Rock St CLB/OSW/ST L13 .....114 C2
 GOL/RIS/CU WA3 .....92 C3
 WALL WA9 .....101 L5
The Rock FROD/HEL WA6 .....166 D3
Rock Vw EV L5 .....97 G7
 MGHL L31 .....85 J1
Rockville Rd DV/KA/FCH L14 .....114 E4
Rockville St RF/TRAN CH42 .....128 B3
Rockybank Rd WGNE/HIN WN2 .....98 F5
Rockybank Rd RF/TRAN CH42 .....127 M2
Rocky Bank Ter
 WGNS/IIMK WN3 * 5 J9
Rocky La CHLDW L16 .....114 F4
 HES CH60 .....141 H5
 NPK/KEN L6 .....97 L8
Rocky La South HES CH60 .....141 J5
Roderick Rd ANF/KKDL L4 .....97 J3
Roderick St VAUX/LVPD L3 * 13 K4
Rodgers Cl FROD/HEL WA6 .....160 D4
Rodick St WLTN L25 .....131 H3
Rodmell Rd WLT/FAZ L9 .....84 D7
Rodney St BIRK CH41 .....11 H8
 CLVPS L1 .....13 K9
 ECCL WA10 .....14 L3
 WARRN/WOL WA2 .....14 E3
 WGN WN1 .....4 F5
Roe Aly CLVPS L1 * 13 H8
Roebuck St WGNE/HIN WN2 .....81 L2
Roeburn Wy WARRW/BUR WA5 .....135 M2
Roecliffe Cl WGNS/IIMK WN3 .....4 C8
Roedean Cl MGHL L31 .....72 F3
 WLTN L25 .....131 J1
Roehampton Dr CSBY/BLUN L23 .....70 E7
 RUNC WA7 .....150 A6
Roe Hey Dr CHLY/EC PR7 .....43 H5
Roe La CHTN/BK PR9 .....25 G5
Roemarsh Ct RUNC WA7 .....150 A7
Roe Park Ms CHTN/BK PR9 .....3 M2
Roe St CLVPS L1 .....13 H7
Rogers Av BTL L20 .....7 M1
Rogerson's Gn HLWD L26 .....132 A3
Rokeby Av GOL/RIS/CU WA3 .....92 F4
Rokeby Cl VAUX/LVPD L3 .....13 K3
Rokeby St VAUX/LVPD L3 .....13 K3
Rokeden NEWLW WA12 .....104 F1
Roker Av WAL/EG CH44 .....111 J2
Rokesmith Av EHL/KEN L7 .....113 L5
Roland Av BEB CH63 .....127 M7
 RNFD/HAY WA11 .....89 L4
 RUNC WA7 .....18 F4
Roleton Cl NTHTN L30 .....84 D1
Rolleston Dr BEB CH63 .....143 J1
 WAL/NB CH45 .....95 H6
Rolleston St WARRN/WOL WA2 .....14 C4
Rolling Mill La STHEL WA9 .....103 H5
Rollo St ANF/KKDL L4 .....97 H5
Rollos CLVPS L1 .....13 H6
Roman Cl NEWLW WA12 .....104 E3
 RUNC WA7 .....150 A4
Roman Rd NSTN CH64 .....153 H6
Roman Rd AIMK WN4 .....79 J8
 BEB CH63 .....127 J6
 HOY CH47 .....108 F5
 WLTN L25 .....131 L4
Rome Cl HUY L36 .....115 M4
Romer Rd NPK/KEN L6 .....113 L2
Romford St WGNE/HIN WN2 .....69 M8
Romford Wy HLWD L26 .....132 B7
Romiley Dr SKEL WN8 .....66 B5
Romiley Rd GTS/LS CH66 .....156 A3
Romilly St NPK/KEN L6 .....113 J2
Romley St ANF/KKDL L4 .....97 H4
Romney Cl WDN WA8 .....134 B3
Romney Wy NSTN CH64 .....153 H6
 WGN WN1 .....68 D2
Romsey Av FMBY L37 .....59 K5

Romsey Gv WGNS/IIMK WN3 .....78 F3
Romulus St EHL/KEN L7 .....113 M5
Rona Av EP CH65 .....163 L4
Ronald Cl CSBY/WL L22 .....83 H4
Ronald Dr WARRN/WOL WA2 .....122 D3
Ronald Ross Av NTHTN L30 .....84 B2
Ronald St CLB/OSW/ST L13 .....114 B2
Ronaldsway WDN WA8 .....135 G3
Ronald St CLB/OSW/ST L13 .....114 B2
Ronaldsway AIN/FAZ L10 .....85 J6
 CSBY/BLUN L23 .....71 J7
 GR/UP/WCH CH49 .....110 B7
 HES CH60 .....141 H7
 HLWD L26 .....132 C5
Ronan Cl BTL L20 .....6 D2
Ronan Rd WDN WA8 .....134 A8
Rone Cl MOR/LEA CH46 .....109 M5
Roocroft Sq HOR/BR BL6 .....57 L3
Rookery Av AIMK WN4 .....91 K3
 WGNW/BIL/O WN5 .....54 C6
Rookery Cl CHLY/EC PR7 .....32 C7
Rookery Dr ALL/GAR L19 .....130 B5
 RNFD/HAY WA11 .....76 C8
Rookery Rd CHTN/BK PR9 .....25 G4
 RNFD/HAY WA11 .....76 C8
Rook Rd WARRS WA4 .....15 M8
Rooks Wy HES CH60 .....141 G5
Rookwood CHLY/EC PR7 .....30 D7
Rookwood Cl CHLY/EC PR7 .....32 E5
The Rooley HUY L36 .....115 M4
Roome St WARRN/WOL WA2 .....15 G1
Roosevelt Dr WLT/FAZ L9 .....84 D5
Ropers Bridge Cl RAIN/WH L35 .....116 F3
Roper St STHEL WA9 .....113 H8
 TOX L8 .....113 H8
The Ropewalk NSTN CH64 .....152 E5
Rosalind Av BEB CH63 .....128 A6
Rosalind Wy BTL L20 .....7 K8
Rosam Ct RUNC WA7 .....150 A7
Rosclare Dr WAL/NB CH45 .....95 H7
Roscoe Av NEWLW WA12 .....105 G2
 WARRN/WOL WA2 .....121 M5
Roscoe Cl RAIN/WH L35 .....116 C5
Roscoe La CLVPS L1 .....13 J9
Roscoe Lowe Brow CHLYE PR6 .....44 F6
Roscoe Pl CLVPS L1 .....13 J9
Roscoe St CLVPS L1 .....113 G5
 ECCL WA10 .....8 B6
 WGN WN1 .....5 J1
Roscommon St EV L5 .....13 J1
Roscote Cl HES CH60 .....141 H6
Roscote Cl ORM L39 .....51 G7
Roscrest Ct HOY CH47 * 108 C7
Rosedale Av CSBY/BLUN L23 .....83 G1
 GOL/RIS/CU WA3 .....92 E6
 WARR WA1 .....14 E1
Rosedale Cl WLT/FAZ L9 .....97 K1
Rosedale Rd CALD/MH L18 .....130 C1
 RF/TRAN CH42 .....128 A2
Rose Dr RNFD/HAY WA11 .....76 C8
Rosefield Av BEB CH63 .....128 A6
Rosefield Rd WLTN L25 .....131 L4
Roseheath Dr HLWD L26 .....132 B7
Rose Hl STHP PR8 .....3 G6
 VAUX/LVPD L3 .....13 H3
Rosehill Av STHEL WA9 .....103 K8
Rose Hill Av WGNW/BIL/O WN5 .....67 L7
Rosehill Ct WLTN L25 .....131 J1
Rosehill Dr ORM L39 .....89 M6
Rose Hill Vw AIMK WN4 .....79 H6
Roseland Cl MGHL L31 .....72 F1
Roselands Ct RF/TRAN CH42 .....128 A4
Rose La CALD/MH L18 .....130 B2
Rose Lea Cl WDN WA8 .....134 C1
Roselea Dr CHTN/BK PR9 .....25 L1
Rosemary Av RUNC WA7 .....150 B8
 WARRS WA4 .....138 A3
Rosemary Cl CL/PREN CH43 .....111 G5
 EHL/KEN L7 .....113 J5
 WARRW/BUR WA5 * 120 E7
Rosemary Crs WGN WN1 .....68 F3
Rosemary Dr NEWLW WA12 .....105 G2
Rosemary La FMBY L37 .....59 G2
Rosemead Av PEN/TH CH61 .....141 H1
Rosemere Dr GTS/LS CH66 .....163 H6
Rosemont Rd AIG/SPK L17 .....130 B3
Rosemoor Dr CSBY/BLUN L23 .....71 J8
Rosemoor Gdns WARRS WA4 .....138 B8
Rose Mt CL/PREN CH43 .....127 K2
 CSBY/WL L22 * 82 E4
 RUNC WA7 * 151 H7
Rose Mount Cl CL/PREN CH43 .....127 J2
Rose Mount Dr WAL/NB CH45 .....95 J7
Rose Pl ORM L39 .....51 L8
 RF/TRAN CH42 .....127 M3
 RNFD/HAY WA11 .....76 C8
 VAUX/LVPD L3 .....13 J3
Rose St CLVPS L1 * 13 H6
 WDN WA8 .....16 B5
 WGN WN1 .....5 L5
 WGNE/HIN WN2 .....69 M8
 WLTN L25 .....131 L5
Rose View Av WDN WA8 .....134 C3
Rose Vis WAV L15 .....114 A4
Rosewarne Cl AIG/SPK L17 .....129 K5
Rosewell St CSBY/WL L22 .....19 K7
Rosewood Av FROD/HEL WA6 .....160 F6
 WARR WA1 .....15 L1
Rosewood Cl NTHLY L27 .....116 A8
 STBRV L28 .....99 K6
 WGNE/HIN WN2 .....80 D5
Rosewood Dr MOR/LEA CH46 .....109 M5
Rosewood Gdns NG/CROX L11 .....98 D4
Roseworth Av WLT/FAZ L9 .....84 C6
Rosina Cl AIMK WN4 .....79 H7

Roskell Rd WLTN L25 .....131 L6
Rosklyn Rd CHLYE PR6 .....33 G6
Rosley Rd WGNS/IIMK WN3 .....79 K2
Roslin Rd CL/PREN CH43 .....127 K1
 PEN/TH CH61 .....125 M7
Roslyn St BIRK CH41 .....128 B2
Rossall Av AIN/FAZ L10 .....84 F2
Rossall Gv GTS/LS CH66 .....155 M7
Rossall Rd CHLYE PR6 .....33 G4
 CLB/OSW/ST L13 .....114 D3
 MOR/LEA CH46 .....110 B4
 WARRN/BUR WA5 .....136 C5
Ross Av WAR/LEA CH46 .....110 A5
Rossbank Rd EP CH65 .....156 C6
Rosscliffe Rd EP CH65 .....156 C7
Ross Cl PR/KW L34 .....99 M2
 WARRW/BUR WA5 .....120 F5
 WGNE-HIN WN2 .....69 H3
 WGNW/BIL/O WN5 .....78 A8
Rossdale Gv WGNNW/ST WN6 .....56 C6
Ross Dr GTS/LS CH66 .....155 L8
Rossendale Cl CL/PREN CH43 .....126 F1
Rossendale Dr GOL/RIS/CU WA3 .....107 J7
Rossett Av AIG/SPK L17 .....113 K4
Rossett Cl WARRN/BUR WA5 .....121 G3
 WGNS/IIMK WN3 .....78 F2
Rossett Rd CSBY/BLUN L23 .....82 E2
Rossett St NPK/KEN L6 .....97 L8
Rossfield Rd EP CH65 .....156 C4
Rossini St LITH L21 .....83 J7
Rosslyn Av MGHL L31 .....72 D5
Rosslyn Crs MOR/LEA CH46 .....110 A5
Rosslyn Dr MOR/LEA CH46 .....110 A5
Rosslyn Pk MOR/LEA CH46 .....110 A5
Rosslyn St AIG/SPK L17 .....129 K2
Rossmore Gdns ANF/KKDL L4 * 97 K6
 GTS/LS CH66 .....155 M7
Rossmore Rd East EP CH65 .....156 B6
Rossmore Rd West
 GTS/LS CH66 .....155 M6
Rossmount Rd EP CH65 .....156 C7
Ross Rd EP CH65 .....156 C7
Ross St STHEL WA9 .....9 M4
 WDN WA8 .....16 F2
Ross Tower Ct WAL/NB CH45 .....95 L5
Rosswood Rd EP CH65 .....156 C7
Rostherne Av GOL/RIS/CU WA3 .....92 E3
 WAL/EG CH44 .....111 J2
Rostherne Crs WDN WA8 .....133 M3
Rosthwaite Cl WGNS/IIMK WN3 .....79 J1
Rosthwaite Gv RNFD/HAY WA11 .....89 K4
Rosthwaite Rd WD/CROXPK L12 .....98 E7
Rostron Crs FMBY L37 .....59 G4
Rothay Dr WARRW/BUR WA5 .....135 M2
Rothbury Cl MOR/LEA CH46 .....109 L5
 RUNC WA7 .....149 J7
Rothbury Ct WLTN L25 .....118 D3
Rothbury Rd DV/KA/FCH L14 .....99 H7
Rother Dr EP CH65 .....156 C6
Rotherham Cl HUY L36 .....116 A1
Rotherwick Av CHLY/EC PR7 .....32 D6
Rotherwood Cl BEB CH63 .....127 M7
Rothesay Dr CSBY/BLUN L23 .....83 G2
 PS/BROM CH62 .....154 F1
Rothesay Gdns CL/PREN CH43 * 127 H4
Rothley Av STHP PR8 .....47 J1
Rothwell Cl RNFD/HAY WA11 .....90 A6
Rothwell Dr ORM L39 .....50 F8
Rothwell Dr ORM L39 .....50 F8
 STHP PR8 .....54 C8
Rothwell Rd CHLYE PR6 .....44 D6
 GOL/RIS/CU WA3 .....92 E4
Rothwells La CSBY/BLUN L23 .....71 J2
Rothwell St NPK/KEN L6 .....113 J1
Rotten Rw STHP PR8 .....2 B7
Rotunda St EV L5 .....96 F8
Roughdale Av KKBY L32 .....86 B6
 STHEL WA9 .....118 D1
Roughdale Cl KKBY L32 .....86 B6
Roughlea Av GOL/RIS/CU WA3 .....106 F1
Roughley Av WARRW/BUR WA5 .....136 F1
Roughwood Dr
 NWD/KWIPK L33 .....86 B2
The Roundabout WDN WA8 .....117 M7
Round Hey STBRV L28 .....99 J5
The Round Meade MGHL L31 .....72 D3
Roundmoor Rd
 WGNNW/ST WN6 .....56 C6
Round Thorn GOL/RIS/CU WA3 .....106 C6
The Roundway HTWN L38 .....70 B2
Roundwood Dr RF/TRAN CH42 .....3 K9
Routledge St WDN WA8 .....16 F1
Rowan Av GOL/RIS/CU WA3 .....93 H6
 WD/CROXPK L12 .....99 H4
 WGNNW/ST WN6 .....68 B2
Rowan Cl BRSC L40 .....39 H7
 RNFD/HAY WA11 .....89 M6
 RUNC WA7 .....19 L3
 WARRW/BUR WA5 .....120 B7
Rowan Ct AIG/SPK L17 .....130 A3
 CL/PREN CH43 .....125 K3
Rowan Dr KKBY L32 .....85 L5
Rowan Gv BEB CH63 .....143 G1
 CHLYE PR6 .....32 E2
 HUY L36 .....115 M5
Rowanhill Wk WARRS WA4 * 5 H1
Rowan La SKEL WN8 .....65 K6
The Rowans ORM L39 .....62 G6
Rowan Tree Cl
 GR/UP/WCH CH49 .....125 K2
Rowbottom Sq WGN WN1 .....4 E4
Rowena Cl CSBY/BLUN L23 .....83 H1
Rowland Cl WARRN/WOL WA2 .....122 C4
Rowsley Gv WLT/FAZ L9 .....84 D6
Rowson St PR/KW L34 .....100 F6
 WAL/NB CH45 .....95 G5
Rowthorn Cl WDN WA8 .....134 A5
Rowton Cl CL/PREN CH43 .....127 H2
Rowton Ri WGN WN1 .....56 D5
Roxborough Cl
 WARRW/BUR WA5 .....104 C3
Roxborough Wk WLTN L25 .....131 L2
Roxburgh Av AIG/SPK L17 .....129 L2
 RF/TRAN CH42 .....127 M3
Roxburgh Rd GTS/LS CH66 .....155 H7
Roxburgh St ANF/KKDL L4 .....7 L7
Royal Ar WGN WN1 .....4 F3
Royal Av WDN WA8 .....133 M5
Royal Cl FMBY L37 .....59 J4
Royal Crs FMBY L37 .....59 J4
Royal Cft WD/CROXPK L12 .....114 F1
Royal Gv ECCL WA10 .....101 M4
Royal Mail St VAUX/LVPD L3 .....13 J4
Royal Standard Wy RF/TRAN CH42 .....128 E2
Royal Ter STHP PR8 .....2 B7
The Royal HOY CH47 .....108 B7
Royden Av RUNC WA7 .....18 F7
 WAL/EG CH44 .....95 M8
 WGNS/IIMK WN3 .....79 H3
Royden Rd GR/UP/WCH CH49 .....110 A7
 WGNW/BIL/O WN5 .....78 A8
Royden Wy VAUX/LVPD L3 .....129 G2
Royhsay Cl EV L5 .....13 K1

Royleen Dr FROD/HEL WA6 .....160 F7
Royle Rd CHLY/EC PR7 .....33 G5
Royal Ar WGN WN1 .....45 K7
Roynton Rd HOR/BR BL6 .....45 K7
Roysten Gdns STHEL WA9 .....102 F3
Royston Av WAL/EG CH44 .....111 M1
 WARR WA1 .....122 B6
Royston St GOL/RIS/CU WA3 .....93 G5
 GTS/LS CH66 .....163 H3
Royton St STHEL/KEN L7 .....113 K4
Royton Rd CSBY/WL L22 .....83 H3
Rozel Crs WARRW/BUR WA5 .....136 A3
Ruabon Crs WGNE/HIN WN2 .....81 H1
Rubbing Stone WKBY CH48 * 124 F7
Ruby Cl LITH L21 .....83 L2
Ruby St TOX L8 .....129 H2
Ruby St STHEL WA9 .....103 J3
Ruddington Rd STHP PR8 .....36 A3
Rudd St HOY CH47 .....108 D6
Rudgate RAIN/WH L35 .....117 G3
Rudgrave Ms WAL/EG CH44 .....95 M8
Rudgrave Pl WAL/EG CH44 .....95 M8
Rudgrave Sq WAL/EG CH44 .....95 M8
Rudloe Ct WARRN/WOL WA2 .....122 B4
Rudstone Cl GTS/LS CH66 .....155 K8
Rudston Rd CHLDW L16 .....114 F8
Rudyard Av WGNNW/ST WN6 .....56 A3
Rudyard Cl DV/KA/FCH L14 .....114 E2
Rudyard Rd DV/KA/FCH L14 .....114 E2
Ruecroft Cl WGNNW/ST WN6 .....54 F8
Ruff La ORM L39 .....63 J1
Rufford Av AIN/FAZ L10 .....85 H4
 RAIN/WH L35 .....101 H8
 WDN WA8 .....133 L3
Rufford Dr CHTN/BK PR9 .....23 H8
Rufford Park La BRSC L40 .....28 C8
Rufford Rd BRSC L40 .....40 B4
 BTL L20 .....83 L8
 CHTN/BK PR9 .....25 L2
 NPK/KEN L6 .....113 L2
 RNFD/HAY WA11 .....76 B5
 WAL/EG CH44 .....111 L2
Rugby Dr AIN/FAZ L10 .....85 G4
Rugby Rd EP CH65 .....20 E9
 WAL/EG CH44 .....84 D5
 WLT/FAZ L9 .....84 D5
Rugby Wk EP CH65 .....20 E8
Ruislip Cl WLTN L25 .....122 D4
Ruislip Ct WARRN/WOL WA2 .....122 B4
Rullerton Rd WAL/EG CH44 .....111 J1
Rumford Pl VAUX/LVPD L3 .....12 D6
Rumford St CLVP L2 .....12 D6
Rumney Pl ANF/KKDL L4 .....96 F5
Rumney Rd ANF/KKDL L4 .....96 F5
Rumney Rd West ANF/KKDL L4 .....96 F5
Runcorn Docks Rd RUNC WA7 .....18 D4
Runcorn Rd WARRS WA4 .....136 E8
Runcorn Spur Rd RUNC WA7 .....18 C3
Runcorn-Widnes Br WDN WA8 .....149 J1
Rundle Rd AIG/SPK L17 .....130 A3
Rundle St TOX L8 .....129 H1
Runic St CLB/OSW/ST L13 .....114 B3
Runnells La CSBY/BLUN L23 .....71 J2
The Runnell NSTN CH64 .....152 F1
The Runnel ORM L39 .....49 K3
Runnymede WLTN L25 .....131 J1
Runnymede Dr
 RNFD/HAY WA11 * 90 C7
Runnymede Wk WDN WA8 .....55 C5
Runshaw Av WGNNW/ST WN6 .....55 G5
Runshaw Hall La CHLY/EC PR7 .....31 J1
Runton Rd WLTN L25 .....115 L8
Rupert Dr NPK/KEN L6 .....113 J2
Rupert Rd HUY L36 .....115 M5
Rupert St WGN WN1 .....5 H5
Ruscar Cl HLWD L26 .....132 A3
Ruscolm Cl WARRW/BUR WA5 .....119 M6
Ruscombe Rd DV/KA/FCH L14 .....99 H7
Rushdene WGNS/IIMK WN3 .....79 J1
Rushden Rd KKBY L32 .....86 C4
Rushey Hey Rd KKBY L32 .....86 A4
Rushfield Crs RUNC WA7 .....150 D8
Rushford Cl CL/PREN CH43 .....110 E6
Rushlake Dr NTHLY L27 .....115 M8
Rushmere Rd NG/CROX L11 .....98 B3
Rushmoor Gv WARR WA1 .....122 C6
Rusholme Cl HLWD L26 .....132 C7
Rushton Av LEIGH WN7 .....81 M5
Rushton Cl WDN WA8 .....16 A2
Rushton Cl WDN WA8 .....134 B3
Rushton Pl WLTN L25 .....131 J1
Rushy Vw NEWLW WA12 .....104 C1
Ruskin Av NEWLW WA12 .....104 E1
 RF/TRAN CH42 * 128 B4
 WAL/EG CH44 .....111 J2
 WARRN/WOL WA2 .....121 L3
 WGNE/HIN WN3 .....79 H2
Ruskin Cl BTL L20 .....7 G5
Ruskin Crs WCNE/HIN WN2 .....80 D4
Ruskin Dr ECCL WA10 .....8 B3
 EP CH65 .....20 F8
Ruskin St ANF/KKDL L4 .....97 G5
Ruskin Wy CL/PREN CH43 .....126 F2
 HUY L36 .....115 M4
Rusland Av PEN/TH CH61 .....141 H1
Rusland Rd KKBY L32 .....86 C3
Russeldene Rd WGNS/IIMK WN3 .....79 G2
Russell Av CHTN/BK PR9 .....25 J6
Russell Rd ALL/GAR L19 .....130 D2
 CALD/MH L18 .....130 B6
 CHTN/BK PR9 .....25 J6
 HUY L36 .....116 D3
 RF/TRAN CH42 .....128 B2
 RUNC WA7 .....18 C7
 WAL/EG CH44 .....95 G8
Russell Sq CHLYE PR6 .....32 F4
Russell Sq West CHLYE PR6 .....32 F4
Russell St BIRK CH41 .....11 J4
 VAUX/LVPD L3 .....13 K5
 WGNE/HIN WN2 .....69 J5
 WGN WN1 .....81 L8
Russet Cl ECCL WA10 .....8 F2
 NTHLY L27 .....116 A8
Russian Dr CLB/OSW/ST L13 .....98 B8
Rutherford Cl CLB/OSW/ST L13 .....114 A4
Rutherford Rd CALD/MH L18 .....114 C7
 ECCL WA10 .....88 B7
 MGHL L31 .....73 G4
Rutherglen Av CSBY/BLUN L23 .....83 H3
Ruth Evans Ct RAIN/WH L35 .....117 H3
Ruthin Cl WARRW/BUR WA5 * 121 G2
Ruthin Ct CLB/OSW/ST L13 .....114 D4
 LITH L21 .....83 H6
Rutland Av AIG/SPK L17 .....133 M7
 HLWD L26 .....132 B5
 WARRS WA4 .....137 K5
Rutland Cl EV L5 .....97 J8
Rutland Crs ORM L39 .....50 F6
Rutland Dr AIMK WN4 .....91 J1
Rutland Rd STHP PR8 .....36 A3
Rutland St BTL L20 .....7 G7
 ECCL WA10 .....8 E2
 RUNC WA7 .....18 F7

Rutter Av WARRW/BUR WA5 121 H3
Rutter St TOX L8 113 G8
Ryburn Rd ORM L39 62 F1
Rycot Rd SPK/HALE L24 146 E1
Rycroft Rd AIN/FAZ L10 85 G5
HOY CH47 109 G5
WAL/EG CH44 111 L3
Rydal Av CL/PREN CH43 110 E8
CSBY/BLUN L23 83 H3
FMBY L37 58 F3
PR/KW L34 101 H7
WARRS WA4 137 J3
WGNW/BIL/O WN5 67 H6
Rydal Bank BEB CH63 128 C6
WAL/EG CH44 111 L1
Rydal Cl AIMK WN4 91 L1
AIN/FAZ L10 85 H3
EP CH65 163 L3
HOR/BR BL6 57 L2
NSTN CH64 153 H7
NWD/KWIPK L33 85 M1
PEN/TH CH61 141 H1
Rydal Gv FROD/HEL WA6 166 D4
RNFD/HAY WA11 89 J6
RUNC WA7 19 K8
Rydal Pl CHLY/EC PR7 32 E7
WGNE/HIN WN2 69 K5
WGNE/HIN WN2 80 D5
Rydal Rd HUY L36 116 A4
Rydal St EV L5 97 J8
NEWLW WA12 104 E2
Rydal Wy WDN WA8 133 L5
Ryder Cl ORM L39 62 E3
RAIN/WH L35 117 J1
Ryder Crs ORM L39 62 E4
STHP PR8 35 G5
Ryder Rd WARR WA1 122 E5
WDN WA8 134 D1
Ryde St WGNW/BIL/O WN5 68 A7
The Rydinge FMBY L37 47 J7
Rye Cl STHEL WA9 118 E1
Ryecote KKBY L32 86 A6
Ryecroft CHNE CH2 165 K2
Rye Cft LITH L21 83 K2
Ryecroft Av GOL/RIS/CU WA3 93 G4
Ryecroft Rd HES CH60 141 L6
Ryedale Cl TOX L8 113 K6
Ryefield La LITH L21 83 K2
Ryeford Cl WGNS/IIMK WN3 5 L8
Ryegate Rd ALL/GAR L19 130 D6
Rye Gv WD/CROXPK L12 99 G7
Rye Hey Rd KKBY L32 86 A3
Rye Moss La FMBY L37 60 C5
Ryland Pk PEN/TH CH61 126 C8
Rylands Hey GR/UP/WCH CH49 125 M1
Rylands Rd CHLY/EC PR7 32 D6
Rylands St WARR WA1 14 E6
WDN WA8 16 E3
WGNNW/ST WN6 68 C3
Ryleys Gdns CLVP L2 12 F6
Rymer Gv ANF/KKDL L4 97 J4
Rymers Gn FMBY L37 59 G1
Ryton Cl WGNS/IIMK WN3 4 C8

S

Sabden Brook Dr
WGNE/HIN WN2 * 80 B3
Sabre Cl RUNC WA7 * 150 F6
Sackville Rd ECCL WA10 88 E7
Sackville St CHLYE PR6 33 G6
Saddleback Crs
WGNW/BIL/O WN5 67 K6
Saddleback Rd
WGNW/BIL/O WN5 67 K6
Saddle Cl WLT/FAZ L9 84 F5
Saddlers Ri RUNC WA7 150 E5
Sadler's La RNFD/HAY WA11 88 A6
Sadler St WDN WA8 17 G1
Saffron Cl GOL/RIS/CU WA3 93 G5
WARRN/WOL WA2 122 D4
Saffron Gdns STHEL WA9 102 F3
Saffron Ms CSBY/BLUN L23 71 K7
Sagar Fold ORM L39 62 F5
Sagar St CHLY/EC PR7 30 E7
Sage Cl WARRN/WOL WA2 122 E3
St Agnes Rd ANF/KKDL L4 96 F5
HUY L36 116 B3
St Aidan's Cl WGNW/BIL/O WN5 78 A7
St Aidans Ct CL/PREN CH43 111 H7
St Aidan's Ter CL/PREN CH43 111 H7
EV L5 96 F7
St Aidan's Wy NTHTN L30 83 M2
St Aiden's Gv PR/KW L34 99 L6
St Alban Rd WARRW/BUR WA5 120 A8
St Albans NPK/KEN L6 97 K8
St Albans Cl RNFD/HAY WA11 91 H6
St Albans Ct EV L5 96 E8
St Alban's Pl CHLY/EC PR7 32 F8
St Alban's Rd BTL L20 7 H5
CL/PREN CH43 10 A4
WAL/EG CH44 111 K1
St Alban's Sq BTL L20 7 H6
St Alexander Cl BTL L20 7 J9
St Ambrose Cft NTHTN L30 84 A1
St Ambrose Gv ANF/KKDL L4 97 K7
St Ambrose Rd WDN WA8 17 H1
St Ambrose Wy EV L5 13 K2
St Andrew Rd ANF/KKDL L4 97 K7
St Andrews Av WD/CROXPK L12 99 G7
St Andrews Cl CHLYE PR6 31 M1
WARRN/WOL WA2 122 C1
St Andrew's Crs WGNE/HIN WN2 69 M8
St Andrew's Dr CSBY/BLUN L23 70 D7
PR/KW L34 99 L6
WGNNW/ST WN6 68 B3
St Andrew's Gv NTHTN L30 * 83 L2
RNFD/HAY WA11 89 K7
St Andrew's Pl STHP PR8 3 G5
St Andrews Rd BEB CH63 143 J2
BTL L20 83 L8
CL/PREN CH43 10 C6
CSBY/BLUN L23 70 D6
EP CH65 20 F8
St Andrew St VAUX/LVPD L3 13 K7
St Andrew's Vw
NWD/KWIPK L33 74 A8
St Annes Av WARRS WA4 138 D3
St Annes Av East WARRS WA4 138 D3
St Anne's Cl BIRK CH41 11 H4
FMBY L37 47 H7
St Annes Ct VAUX/LVPD L3 * 13 J3
WGNNW/ST WN6 55 H8
St Anne's Dr WGNNW/ST WN6 55 J8
St Annes Gdns AIG/SPK L17 130 B4
St Anne's Gv AIG/SPK L17 130 A4
BIRK CH41 10 E2
St Anne's Pth FMBY L37 47 H7
St Anne's Pl BIRK CH41 10 E2
St Anne's Rd AIG/SPK L17 130 A4
Saint Annes Rd CHLYE PR6 33 G6
St Annes Rd CHTN/BK PR9 25 H1
FMBY L37 47 H7
HUY L36 116 A4
ORM L39 62 F1
WDN WA8 134 D3
St Annes Ter BIRK CH41 10 E3
St Anne St BIRK CH41 10 F3
VAUX/LVPD L3 13 J3
St Anne Wy BIRK CH41 11 H4
St Ann Pl RAIN/WH L35 117 L1
St Anns Rd ECCL WA10 101 L2
St Anthony Pl
WARRN/WOL WA2 105 K7
St Anthony's Cl PR/KW L34 99 L6
St Anthony's Gv NTHTN L30 83 M2
St Anthony's Rd
CSBY/BLUN L23 82 D1
St Asaph Dr WARRW/BUR WA5 120 F3
St Asaph Gv NTHTN L30 84 B4
St Asaph Rd GTS/LS CH66 163 G5
St Aubyn's Rd WGN WN1 * 68 E2
St Augustine's Av WARRS WA4 138 B1
St Augustine St EV L5 * 96 F8
St Augustine's Wy NTHTN L30 83 M1
St Austel Cl WARRW/BUR WA5 136 A2
St Austell Cl MOR/LEA CH46 109 K4
RUNC WA7 150 D7
St Austells Rd ANF/KKDL L4 7 M7
St Austins La WARR WA1 14 D7
St Barnabas Pl
WARRW/BUR WA5 121 G7
St Bedes Cl ORM L39 62 F2
St Benard's Cl TOX L8 113 K6
St Benedicts Cl
WARRN/WOL WA2 14 F2
St Benedict's Gv PR/KW L34 99 L6
St Benet's Wy NTHTN L30 84 A2
St Bernard's Cl NTHTN L30 83 M2
St Bernard's Dr NTHTN L30 83 M2
St Brendan's Cl HUY L36 99 L6
St Brides Cl WARRW/BUR WA5 136 A2
St Bride's Rd WAL/EG CH44 95 M8
St Bride St EHL/KEN L7 113 H5
St Bridget's Cl
WARRN/WOL WA2 122 B2
St Bridget's Gv NTHTN L30 * 83 M2
St Bridget's La WKBY CH48 * 124 D4
St Brigids Crs EV L5 96 E8
St Catherine's RF/TRAN CH42 127 M1
St Catherines Cl HUY L36 116 A4
St Catherines Gdns
RF/TRAN CH42 127 M1
St Catherine's Rd BTL L20 7 G5
St Chad's Dr KKBY L32 86 A3
St Christopher Ct
WGNNW/ST WN6 * 67 L1
St Christopher's Av NTHTN L30 83 M1
St Christopher's Dr PR/KW L34 99 L6
St Clair Dr CHTN/BK PR9 25 J4
St Clement's Rd WGN WN1 68 E2
St Clement's St WGNS/IIMK WN3 80 B1
St Columba's Cl WAL/EG CH44 * 95 M8
St Cuthbert's Cl
WD/CROXPK L12 * 99 G2
St Cuthbert's Rd CHTN/BK PR9 25 K3
St Cyrils Cl NTHLY L27 115 L6
St Damian's Cft NTHTN L30 84 A2
St David Rd CL/PREN CH43 10 A5
PS/BROM CH62 144 C7
St Davids Cl RAIN/WH L35 117 L1
St David's Crs WGNE/HIN WN2 57 K8
St Davids Dr GTS/LS CH66 163 H5
WARRW/BUR WA5 121 G3
St Davids Gv NTHTN L30 83 M3
St Davids La CL/PREN CH43 110 F8
St David's Rd ANF/KKDL L4 97 K7
DV/KA/FCH L14 99 K8
St Domingo Gv EV L5 97 J7
St Domingo Rd EV L5 97 G7
St Domingo V EV L5 97 J7
St Dunstan's Gv NTHTN L30 83 M3
St Edmond's Rd BTL L20 7 G6
St Edmunds Rd BEB CH63 128 B8
St Edwards Cl BIRK CH41 10 D2
St Edwards Ms BIRK CH41 * 10 D2
St Elizabeth's Rd
WGNE/HIN WN2 57 K8
St Elmo Rd WAL/EG CH44 95 M8
St Elphins Cl WARR WA1 15 H5
St Gabriel's Av HUY L36 116 C3
St George's Av ECCL WA10 88 E8
GTS/LS CH66 163 H5
RF/TRAN CH42 127 M3
St Georges Ct WDN WA8 133 M5
St Georges Gv NTHTN L30 83 M3
St George's Hl EV L5 97 H8
St George's Mt WAL/NB CH45 95 K5
St George's Pk WAL/NB CH45 95 K5
St George's Pl CHTN/BK PR9 3 G3
CLVPS L1 13 H6
St Georges Rd ECCL WA10 8 A7
FMBY L37 59 G1
HTWN L38 59 H8
HUY L36 100 A8
WAL/NB CH45 95 G7
St George's St CHLY/EC PR7 32 E6
St George's Wy BEB CH63 142 C6
St Gregory's Cft NTHTN L30 84 A1
St Gregory's Pl CHLY/EC PR7 32 E8
St Helen's Cl BIRK CH41 10 D6
St Helens Linkway STHEL WA9 9 H8
St Helens Rd LEIGH WN7 93 L4
ORM L39 51 H8
Saint Helens Rd ORM L39 63 H1
St Helens Rd ORM L39 63 K3
PR/KW L34 100 F7
Saint Helens Rd PR/KW L34 101 H6
St Helens Rd RNFD/HAY WA11 88 D3
St Hilary Brow WAL/EG CH44 111 H1
St Hilary Dr WAL/EG CH44 95 H8
St Hilda's Cl CHLY/EC PR7 43 L1
St Hilda's Dr FROD/HEL WA6 160 E4
St Hilda St ANF/KKDL L4 * 97 G5
St Hugh's Cl CL/PREN CH43 10 D6
St Ives Gv CLB/OSW/ST L13 114 B2
St Ives Rd CL/PREN CH43 10 A5
St Ives Wy HLWD L26 132 B5
St James Cl BRSC L40 63 L2
GR/UP/WCH CH49 125 M1
WD/CROXPK L12 98 C7
St James Crs WGNE/HIN WN2 81 H5
St James Dr BTL L20 6 E3
St James Gv WGNS/IIMK WN3 4 D8
St James Mt RAIN/WH L35 117 L3
St James Pl TOX L8 113 G6
St James Rd CL/PREN CH43 111 H5
CLVPS L1 113 G6
HUY L36 116 A4
PR/KW L34 101 G7
RAIN/WH L35 117 L3
WAL/NB CH45 95 K5
WGNW/BIL/O WN5 77 M1
St James's Pl CHLYE PR6 33 G6
St James St CLVPS L1 112 F6
STHP PR8 3 H7
St Jerome's Wy NTHTN L30 84 A1
St John Av WARRS WA4 137 K3
St John's Av WLT/FAZ L9 84 C8
St John's Brow RUNC WA7 * 19 J2
St John's Cl HOY CH47 108 F5
St Johns Ct STHP PR8 * 47 M1
St John's La CLVPS L1 13 H6
St John's Pl CSBY/WL L22 82 F4
St John's Rd BTL L20 6 F8
CSBY/WL L22 82 F4
HUY L36 116 B4
PS/BROM CH62 144 C8
STHP PR8 35 H4
WAL/NB CH45 95 G8
WGNE/HIN WN2 57 K8
St John's St RUNC WA7 19 J2
WGNE/HIN WN2 80 D5
St John's Ter BTL L20 6 F8
St John St BIRK CH41 11 H6
ECCL WA10 101 M5
NEWLW WA12 104 C2
WGNW/BIL/O WN5 67 K7
St Josephs Cl PR/KW L34 99 L6
STHEL WA9 9 L9
WARRW/BUR WA5 120 A8
St Josephs Crs VAUX/LVPD L3 13 J4
St Josephs Pl CHLYE PR6 32 F4
St Jude's Cl HUY L36 * 99 L6
St Katherines Dr HOR/BR BL6 57 L2
St Katherines Wy WARR WA1 15 J5
St Kilda Cl EP CH65 163 L4
St Kilda's Rd MOR/LEA CH46 109 M6
St Laurence Cl BIRK CH41 11 H4
St Laurence Dr BIRK CH41 11 H5
St Laurence Gv KKBY L32 * 86 B5
St Lawrence Cl TOX L8 129 J1
St Lawrence Rd FROD/HEL WA6 160 D6
St Leonard's Cl NTHTN L30 83 M1
St Lucia Rd WAL/EG CH44 95 M8
St Luke's Av GOL/RIS/CU WA3 92 F5
St Luke's Church Rd FMBY L37 58 E3
St Lukes Cl DV/KA/FCH L14 99 H7
St Lukes Ct ANF/KKDL L4 97 J3
St Luke's Crs WDN WA8 134 D1
St Luke's Dr FMBY L37 58 E3
WGNW/BIL/O WN5 77 M1
St Luke's Gv CHTN/BK PR9 3 M4
NTHTN L30 83 M1
St Luke's Rd CHTN/BK PR9 3 M5
CSBY/BLUN L23 82 F1
ECCL WA10 8 A5
St Luke's Wy FROD/HEL WA6 160 D4
HUY L36 99 L6
St Malo Rd WGN WN1 68 E1
St Margaret's Av
WARRN/WOL WA2 121 M4
St Margaret's Gv NTHTN L30 83 L3
St Margaret's Rd HOY CH47 108 C6
St Mark's Av WGNW/BIL/O WN5 68 B6
St Marks Crs GTS/LS CH66 163 H6
St Mark's Gv NTHTN L30 83 L1
St Mark's Rd HUY L36 116 B4
St Mark's St RNFD/HAY WA11 90 C7
St Martins Dr GTS/LS CH66 162 F3
St Martins Gv KKBY L32 86 B5
St Martins La RUNC WA7 150 F6
St Martin's Ms EV L5 13 J1
St Marys Ar ECCL WA10 * 9 H6
St Mary's Av ANF/KKDL L4 * 97 J3
WGNW/BIL/O WN5 89 L1
St Mary's Cl BTL L20 6 F4
WARRS WA4 137 L7
WGNE/HIN WN2 * 57 K8
St Marys Ct WLTN L25 131 J3
St Mary's Dr NTHTN L30 83 L3
St Mary's Gdns STHP PR8 35 H6
St Mary's Ga BIRK CH41 11 L6
CHLY/EC PR7 31 L2
St Mary's Gv ANF/KKDL L4 * 97 J3
St Mary's La ANF/KKDL L4 97 J3
St Marys Market ECCL WA10 * 9 H6
St Mary's Pl ANF/KKDL L4 * 97 J3
WLTN L25 131 J3
St Mary's Rd ALL/GAR L19 130 E7
CSBY/WL L22 83 H5
HUY L36 116 A3
RUNC WA7 150 B4
WARRW/BUR WA5 120 B8
WDN WA8 149 J1
WGNE/HIN WN2 57 K7
St Mary's St WAL/EG CH44 111 K1
WARRS WA4 15 H9
St Mathews Cl ANF/KKDL L4 97 M3
St Matthews Av LITH L21 83 M5
St Matthew's Cl HUY L36 * 116 B2
WARRS WA4 137 M6
WGNS/IIMK WN3 78 E1
St Matthews Gv ECCL WA10 101 L5
St Mawes Cl WDN WA8 134 A3
St Mawes Wy ECCL WA10 88 D7
St Mawgan Ct WARRN/WOL WA2 122 B4
St Michael Rd ORM L39 62 B6
St Michael's Church Rd
AIG/SPK L17 129 K3
St Michael's Cl AIG/SPK L17 129 L3
CHLY/EC PR7 32 D4
CHTN/BK PR9 25 H2
WDN WA8 133 L6
St Michaels Ct HUY L36 116 A2
WGN WN1 4 F1
St Michael's Gv NPK/KEN L6 113 K1
NTHTN L30 83 L2
St Michaels Pk ORM L39 62 C6
St Michael's Rd AIG/SPK L17 129 K2
CSBY/BLUN L23 70 E7
STHEL WA9 118 C2
WDN WA8 133 L6
St Monicas Cl WARRS WA4 137 M6
St Monica's Dr NTHTN L30 83 M1
St Nicholas' Dr NTHTN L30 83 M2
St Nicholas Gv STHEL WA9 * 102 F6
St Nicholas Pl VAUX/LVPD L3 12 D7
St Nicholas Rd GOL/RIS/CU WA3 93 J4
RAIN/WH L35 116 E4
WAL/NB CH45 94 F8
St Oswald's Av CL/PREN CH43 110 E5
St Oswalds Cl
WARRN/WOL WA2 * 105 K7
St Oswalds Ct NTHTN L30 * 84 B2
St Oswald's La NTHTN L30 84 B1
St Oswald's Ms CL/PREN CH43 110 E4
St Oswalds Rd AIMK WN4 91 J3
St Oswald's St CLB/OSW/ST L13 114 C3
St Paschal Baylon Bvd
CHLDW L16 115 H5
St Patrick's Cl NWD/KWIPK L33 * 74 A8
St Patrick's Dr NTHTN L30 * 83 M1
St Patrick St WGN WN1 5 H4
St Patricks Wy WGN WN1 5 H4
St Pauls Av WAL/EG CH44 112 A3
WGNS/IIMK WN3 79 H1
St Paul's Cl CHLYE PR6 44 C5
NWD/KWIPK L33 73 M8
RF/TRAN CH42 128 A3
St Pauls Gdns GTS/LS CH66 155 K6
St Pauls Ms RUNC WA7 * 19 H3
St Paul's Pas STHP PR8 2 F6
St Paul's Rd RF/TRAN CH42 128 B3
WAL/EG CH44 111 M3
WDN WA8 16 D5
St Paul's Sq STHP PR8 2 E6
VAUX/LVPD L3 12 E5
St Paul's St STHP PR8 2 E6
St Paul St ECCL WA10 8 D5
St Paul's Vls RF/TRAN CH42 128 A3
St Peter's Av FMBY L37 58 F1
St Peter's Cl FMBY L37 58 F1
HES CH60 141 H6
NWD/KWIPK L33 73 M8
St Peters Ct AIG/SPK L17 * 129 K1
St Peter's Ms RF/TRAN CH42 128 D4
St Peter's Rd RF/TRAN CH42 128 C4
STHP PR8 35 J2
WLT/FAZ L9 84 E6
St Peter's St CHLYE PR6 33 G4
St Peter's Wy CL/PREN CH43 126 E1
WARRN/WOL WA2 14 F4
St Philip's Av LITH L21 83 L5
St Richards Cl BTL L20 7 J9
St Seiriol Gv CL/PREN CH43 10 A6
St Stephen Rd WARRW/BUR WA5 120 B8
St Stephen's Av WARRN/WOL WA2 121 K2
WGN WN1 69 G3
St Stephens Cl HES CH60 141 L7
WLTN L25 115 L8
St Stephen's Gv NTHTN L30 83 M2
St Stephen's Rd HTWN L38 70 B1
RF/TRAN CH42 127 K3
WGNNW/ST WN6 55 L4
St Teresa's Rd ECCL WA10 8 A4
St Thomas Ct WDN WA8 * 134 A4
St Thomas's Ct SKEL WN8 * 66 E6
St Thomas's Dr NTHTN L30 83 M2
St Thomas's Rd CHLY/EC PR7 32 E5
St Thomas St WGNS/IIMK WN3 4 E6
St Thomas' Vw EP CH65 20 A7
St Vincent Rd CL/PREN CH43 10 A6
WAL/EG CH44 95 M8
WARRW/BUR WA5 120 B8
St Vincent's Cl WD/CROXPK L12 99 G7
St Vincent St VAUX/LVPD L3 13 K6
St Vincent's Wy STHP PR8 2 E9
St Vincent Wy VAUX/LVPD L3 13 K6
St Werburgh's Sq BIRK CH41 11 J6
St Wilfrid's Dr WARRS WA4 138 E4
St Wilfrid's Rd WGNNW/ST WN6 56 B5
St William Rd CSBY/BLUN L23 71 K8
St Winifred Rd RAIN/WH L35 101 K8
WAL/NB CH45 95 K6
Saker St ANF/KKDL L4 97 H6
Salacre Cl GR/UP/WCH CH49 126 C1
Salacre Crs GR/UP/WCH CH49 126 C1
Salacre La GR/UP/WCH CH49 110 C8
Salacre Ter GR/UP/WCH CH49 * 110 C8
Salcombe Cl WGN WN1 69 G3
Salcombe Dr CHTN/BK PR9 22 C8
WLTN L25 131 K6
Salem Vw CL/PREN CH43 127 K2
Salerno Dr HUY L36 115 M2
Salesbury Wy WGNS/IIMK WN3 79 J2
Saleswood Av ECCL WA10 101 J2
Salford Rd STHP PR8 34 E8
Saline Cl DV/KA/FCH L14 99 J7
Salisbury Av NTHTN L30 84 C4
WKBY CH48 124 C3
Salisbury Cl GTS/LS CH66 163 H5
Salisbury Dr PS/BROM CH62 128 D6
Salisbury Pk CHLDW L16 115 G8
Salisbury Rd AIMK WN4 * 79 J8
ALL/GAR L19 130 C7
BTL L20 6 E2
EV L5 97 J7
RNFD/HAY WA11 91 G4
WAL/NB CH45 95 J5
WAV L15 113 M6
Salisbury St BIRK CH41 11 G7
CHLY/EC PR7 * 32 F6
CHTN/BK PR9 25 J7
GOL/RIS/CU WA3 92 C5
PR/KW L34 100 F6
RUNC WA7 19 G5
VAUX/LVPD L3 13 L3
WARR WA1 15 J4
WDN WA8 16 E3
Salisbury Ter WAV L15 114 B5
Salkeld Av AIMK WN4 91 H2
Sallowfields WGNW/BIL/O WN5 66 F8
Sally's La CHTN/BK PR9 25 J3
Salmon St WGN WN1 * 5 J1
Salop St ANF/KKDL L4 97 H5
Saltash Cl HLWD L26 132 A5
RUNC WA7 150 D7
Saltburn Rd WAL/NB CH45 94 F8
Saltersgate GTS/LS CH66 163 H3
Salthouse Quay VAUX/LVPD L3 12 E9
Saltney St VAUX/LVPD L3 12 C1
Salton Gdns WARRW/BUR WA5 121 G6
Salt Pit La CHLY/EC PR7 41 H1
Saltpit La MGHL L31 73 G4
Saltram Rd WGNS/IIMK WN3 78 E1
Saltwood Dr RUNC WA7 150 E8
Saltworks Cl FROD/HEL WA6 160 F3
Salvin Cl AIMK WN4 91 M2
Salvia Wy NWD/KWIPK L33 73 M8
Salwick Cl CHTN/BK PR9 22 B8
WGNS/IIMK WN3 79 G1
Samaria Av PS/BROM CH62 128 E6
Sambourn Fold STHP PR8 34 C8
Samphire Gdns STHEL WA9 103 K6
Samuel St STHEL WA9 101 M6
WARRW/BUR WA5 137 G1
Sanbec Gdns WDN WA8 117 M8
Sandalwood RUNC WA7 150 D4
Sandalwood Cl NPK/KEN L6 97 K8
WARRN/WOL WA2 121 M3
Sandalwood Dr CL/PREN CH43 126 F1
WGNNW/ST WN6 68 B2
Sandalwood Gdns STHEL WA9 102 E6
Sandbeck St TOX L8 129 H2
Sandbrook Gdns
WGNW/BIL/O WN5 66 F8
Sandbrook La MOR/LEA CH46 110 A5
Sandbrook Rd STHP PR8 34 F8
STHP PR8 47 L2
WGNW/BIL/O WN5 66 E8
WLTN L25 115 J5
Sandcliffe Rd WAL/NB CH45 95 G5
Sandeman Rd ANF/KKDL L4 97 M4
Sanderling Rd NWD/KWIPK L33 86 C2
Sanders Hey Cl RUNC WA7 150 C8
Sanderson Cl
WARRW/BUR WA5 * 119 M7
Sanderson La CHLY/EC PR7 41 J5
Sanderson St LEIGH WN7 81 M8
Sandfield HUY L36 115 M3
Sandfield Av HOY CH47 108 F4
Sandfield Cl BEB CH63 * 127 M7
GOL/RIS/CU WA3 93 G5
WD/CROXPK L12 98 E8
Sandfield Ct FROD/HEL WA6 160 D5
Sandfield Crs ECCL WA10 8 E6
Sandfield Pk HES CH60 140 F5
ORM L39 62 F3
Sandfield Pk East
WD/CROXPK L12 98 E7
Sandfield Pl BTL L20 6 E2
Sandfield Rd BEB CH63 127 M7
BTL L20 7 K6
ECCL WA10 88 C8
GR/UP/WCH CH49 126 D4
WAL/NB CH45 95 K6
WLTN L25 131 K1
Sandfields FROD/HEL WA6 160 D5
Sandfield Wk CLB/OSW/ST L13 114 D1
Sandford Dr MGHL L31 72 F3
Sandford St BIRK CH41 11 K4
Sandforth Cl WD/CROXPK L12 98 C8
Sandforth Ct WD/CROXPK L12 * 98 C8
Sandforth Rd WD/CROXPK L12 98 C8
Sandgate CHLY/EC PR7 32 F8
Sandgate Cl SPK/HALE L24 146 D1
Sandham Gv HES CH60 141 L6
Sandham Rd SPK/HALE L24 147 J2
Sandham St CHLYE PR6 32 F5
Sandhead St EHL/KEN L7 113 M5
Sandhey Rd HOY CH47 108 E5
Sandheys NSTN CH64 152 E4
Sandheys Av CSBY/WL L22 82 E4
Sandheys Cl ANF/KKDL L4 97 G6
Sandheys Dr CHTN/BK PR9 25 H4
Sandheys Gv CSBY/WL L22 82 E3
Sandheys Rd WAL/NB CH45 95 K6
Sandheys Ter CSBY/WL L22 82 E4
Sandhills HTWN L38 70 B2
Sandhills La EV L5 96 E6
The Sandhills MOR/LEA CH46 110 A2
Sandhills Vw WAL/NB CH45 94 F8
Sandhurst Cl FMBY L37 58 E4
LITH L21 83 H6
Sandhurst Dr AIN/FAZ L10 85 G3
Sandhurst Rd HLWD L26 132 C7
RAIN/WH L35 101 J8
Sandhurst St AIG/SPK L17 129 K2
WARRS WA4 138 B2
Sandhurst Wy MGHL L31 61 K8
Sandiacre WGNNW/ST WN6 56 A5
Sandicroft Cl GOL/RIS/CU WA3 106 E8
Sandicroft Rd WD/CROXPK L12 99 H3
Sandilands Gv HTWN L38 70 B2
Sandino St TOX L8 113 G7
Sandirngham Dr AIG/SPK L17 129 K1
Sandiway BEB CH63 143 L7
HOY CH47 108 F4
HUY L36 116 B4
RAIN/WH L35 116 F3
Sandiway Av WDN WA8 133 J4
Sandiways Av NTHTN L30 84 B3
Sandiways Rd WAL/NB CH45 95 G7
Sandlea Pk WKBY CH48 124 C3
Sandlewood Gv
NWD/KWIPK L33 86 B1
Sandling Dr GOL/RIS/CU WA3 92 C3
Sandon Cl RAIN/WH L35 117 K1
Sandon Crs NSTN CH64 153 G8
Sandon Gv RNFD/HAY WA11 76 C7
Sandon Pl WDN WA8 17 K1
Sandon Rd STHP PR8 35 H4
WAL/EG CH44 111 M1
Sandon St CSBY/WL L22 82 F4
EHL/KEN L7 113 H5
Sandon Wy EV L5 96 D7
Sandown Cl GOL/RIS/CU WA3 * 107 H1
RUNC WA7 149 L7
Sandown La WAV L15 114 B5
Sandown Park Rd AIN/FAZ L10 85 G2
Sandown Rd WAV L15 114 B5
WGNNW/ST WN6 68 A2
Sandpiper Cl GR/UP/WCH CH49 109 M7
NEWLW WA12 104 E1
Sandpiper Gv HLWD L26 * 132 A4
Sandpiper Rd WGNS/IIMK WN3 78 D1
Sandra Dr NEWLW WA12 104 F2
Sandridge Av CHLY/EC PR7 32 D6
Sandridge Rd PEN/TH CH61 126 B8
WAL/NB CH45 * 95 K6
Sandringham Av CSBY/WL L22 83 G5
FROD/HEL WA6 166 D2
HOY CH47 108 E5
Sandringham Cl CHLY/EC PR7 44 A7
HOY CH47 * 108 E6
NWD/KWIPK L33 74 A8
PS/BROM CH62 128 C6
WGNW/BIL/O WN5 68 A8
Sandringham Ct CHTN/BK PR9 3 H2
Sandringham Dr STHEL WA9 102 E7
WAL/NB CH45 95 J5
WARRW/BUR WA5 136 E1
Sandringham Gdns EP CH65 163 M3
Sandringham Ms HOY CH47 * 108 E5
Sandringham Rd CHLY/EC PR7 30 E6
CHLY/EC PR7 32 D5
CLB/OSW/ST L13 98 A7
CSBY/WL L22 83 G5
FMBY L37 59 G4
MGHL L31 * 72 E5
STHP PR8 34 E8
STHP PR8 35 G2
WDN WA8 134 B1
WGNE/HIN WN2 81 G1
Sandrock Cl WAL/NB CH45 95 K6
Sandrock Rd WAL/NB CH45 95 K6
Sands Rd CALD/MH L18 130 B1
Sandstone Cl RAIN/WH L35 117 L4
Sandstone Dr RAIN/WH L35 101 H8
WKBY CH48 125 G3
Sandstone Rd WGNS/IIMK WN3 78 F3
Sandstone Rd East
CLB/OSW/ST L13 114 C1
Sandstone Rd West
CLB/OSW/ST L13 114 B1
Sandstone Trail
FROD/HEL WA6 167 H3
Sandstone Wk HES CH60 141 J6
Sandwash Cl RNFD/HAY WA11 88 D1
Sandway WGNNW/ST WN6 68 B3
Sandway Crs NG/CROX L11 98 C3
Sandwith Cl WGNS/IIMK WN3 79 K3
Sandy Brow La
GOL/RIS/CU WA3 106 A3
NWD/KWIPK L33 87 G6
Sandycroft Av WGN WN1 4 E1
Sandy Gn WLT/FAZ L9 84 E7
Sandy Gv CLB/OSW/ST L13 98 B7
Sandy Knowe WAV L15 * 114 C5
Sandy La BRSC L40 28 A8
BRSC L40 40 C3
BRSC L40 51 M6
CHLY/EC PR7 44 B6
CLB/OSW/ST L13 98 B7
FROD/HEL WA6 166 D3
GOL/RIS/CU WA3 93 J3
GOL/RIS/CU WA3 106 C4
HES CH60 141 J4
HTWN L38 70 C2
KIRK/FR/WA PR4 27 L7
LITH L21 83 H6
MGHL L31 61 L8
MGHL L31 73 J8
NEWLW WA12 92 B5
NSTN CH64 153 J7
ORM L39 62 D7
PEN/TH CH61 125 L6
RNFD/HAY WA11 88 F5
RUNC WA7 18 B9
RUNC WA7 151 G7
SKEL WN8 53 H4
SKEL WN8 64 F4
WAL/NB CH45 95 G7
WARRN/WOL WA2 121 K2
WARRS WA4 137 M5
WARRW/BUR WA5 136 C1
WDN WA8 119 K7
WDN WA8 134 A1
WGNW/BIL/O WN5 77 M1

WKBY CH48.................124 D5
WLT/FAZ L9.................84 D7
Sandy La North *PEN/TH* CH61 ..125 L5
Sandy La West
 WARRN/WOL WA2.................121 J2
Sandy Moor La *RUNC* WA7.......150 F2
Sandymoor La *RUNC* WA7.......150 F2
Sandymount Dr *BEB* CH63 *......143 H1
 WAL/NB CH45.................95 J6
Sandy Rd *LITH* L21.................83 J6
Sandy Wy *WARRW/BUR* WA5 ..120 D7
Santon Av *CLB/OSW/ST* L13 ...98 A8
Santon Dr *GOL/RIS/CU* WA3 .....93 C5
Sanvino Av *STHP* PR8.................34 E8
Sapphire Dr *NWD/KWIPK* L33 ...74 A8
Sapphire St *CLB/OSW/ST* L13 ..114 B4
Sarah's Cft *NTHTN* L30.................84 A2
Sarah St *WGNE/HIN* WN2.................81 K3
Sark Av *EP* CH65.................163 H4
Sark Rd *CLB/OSW/ST* L13.......114 A1
Sarscow La *CROS/BRETH* PR26...30 B4
Sarsfield Av *GOL/RIS/CU* WA3 ....92 F5
Sartfield Cl *CHLDW* L16.................115 C5
Sarum Rd *WLTN* L25.................115 J6
Satinwood Av *AIMK* WN4.................91 H2
Satinwood Cs *MGHL* L31.................85 J3
Saughall Massie La
 CR/UP/WCH CH49.................110 A8
Saughall Massie Rd
 GR/UP/WCH CH49.................109 L7
 WKBY CH48.................125 J1
Saughall Rd *MOR/LEA* CH46......109 J8
Saunby St *ALL/GAR* L19.................145 L1
Saunders Av *RAIN/WH* L35.......116 F1
Saundersfoot Cl
 WARRW/BUR WA5.................121 J4
Saunders Ms *CHLY/EC* PR7 *......43 L2
Saunders St *CHTN/BK* PR9.........24 D4
Saunderton Cl *RNFD/HAY* WA11 ..90 E6
Saville Av *WARRW/BUR* WA5 ....14 B1
Saville Rd *CLB/OSW/ST* L13.....114 D3
 MGHL L31.................72 E2
Saville St *CHLY/EC* PR7.................32 E8
Savon Hook *FMBY* L37.................59 K4
Savoylands Cl *AIG/SPK* L17......129 L3
Sawdon Av *STHP* PR8.................36 A1
Sawley Av *GOL/RIS/CU* WA3 ....92 F4
 WGNNW/ST WN6.................68 D2
Sawley Ct *GOL/RIS/CU* WA3 .....107 J3
 RUNC WA7.................151 G6
Sawpit La WA1.................116 B3
Sawyer Dr *AIMK* WN4.................91 M2
Saxby Rd *DV/KA/FCH* L14.................99 J7
Saxon Cl *NPK/KEN* L6.................97 K8
 WARRS WA4.................137 K8
Saxonia Rd *ANF/KKDL* L4.................97 K3
Saxon Rd *CSBY/BLUN* L23.........82 F2
 HOY CH47.................108 C3
 MOR/LEA CH46.................110 B4
 RUNC WA7.................19 L4
 STHP PR8.................2 F5
Saxon Ter *WDN* WA8 *.................16 F2
Saxon Wy *GTS/LS* CH66.................163 H5
 NWD/KWIPK L33.................74 A7
Saxony Rd *EHL/KEN* L7.................113 J3
Saxthorpe Cl *WGNS/IIMK* WN3 ..78 F2
Sayce St *WDN* WA8.................16 F5
Scafell Av *WARRN/WOL* WA2 ....121 L2
Scafell Cl *BEB* CH63.................154 C1
Scafell Dr *WDN/BIL/O* WN5 *......67 K7
Scafell La *WGNE/HIN* WN2.................80 D3
Scafell Lawn *WLTN* L27.................132 C2
Scafell Rd *ECCL* WA10.................9 J5
Scaffold La *HTWN* L38.................59 L8
Scape La *CSBY/BLUN* L23.........71 G8
Scargreen Av *LITH* L21.................83 K6
 SKEL WN8.................53 L3
 STHP PR8.................2 F5
Scarisbrick Cl *MGHL* L31.................73 G2
Scarisbrick Crs *NG/CROX* L11 ...97 M2
Scarisbrick Dr *NG/CROX* L11 ....97 M2
Scarisbrick New Rd *STHP* PR8 ....3 J1
Scarisbrick Pl *NG/CROX* L11......97 M3
 RNFD/HAY WA11.................76 B6
Scarisbrick Cl *CHTN/BK* PR9 ......3 H4
 ORM L39.................51 G7
 WGN WN1.................4 F1
Scarlet St *CHLYE* PR6.................33 G6
Scarsdale Rd *NG/CROX* L11.......98 A4
Scarth Hill La *ORM* L39.................63 G3
Scarth Pk *SKEL* WN8.................65 L6
Scawfell Rd *CHLY/EC* PR7.................43 L2
Sceptre Cl *NEWLW* WA12.................104 C2
Sceptre Rd *NG/CROX* L11.................98 E2
Sceptre Wk *NG/CROX* L11 *.................98 E2
Scholar St *EHL/KEN* L7.................113 L6
Scholefield La *WGN* WN1.................5 H3
Scholes *WGN* WN1.................5 H3
Scholes Bank *HOR/BR* BL6.........45 J8
Scholes La *ECCL* WA10.................101 K6
Scholes Pk *ECCL* WA10.................101 K6
Schomberg St *NPK/KEN* L6.......113 J2
School Av *FMBY* L37.................59 H2
 NSTN CH64.................153 H7
 WDN WA8.................18 A4
School Brow *WARR* WA1.................5 G5
 WGNW/BIL/O WN5.................78 A8
School Cl *MOR/LEA* CH46.........110 B3
 NTHLY L27.................115 J2
 ORM L39 *.................62 E4
 STHP PR8.................35 J7
School Dr *WGNW/BIL/O* WN5 ....78 A8
Schoolfield Cl
 GR/UP/WCH CH49.................126 D3
Schoolfield Rd
 GR/UP/WCH CH49.................126 D3
School Hl *HES* CH60.................141 H6
School House Gn *ORM* L39.........51 H8
School Houses *SKEL* WN8.........65 K5
School La *AIMK* WN4.................90 E2
 AIN/FAZ L10.................84 F4
 BEB CH63.................127 M8
 BRSC L40.................39 H8
 BRSC L40.................40 D4
 BRSC L40.................64 A2
 CHLY/EC PR7.................31 M2
 CHNE CH2.................142 E8
 CL/PREN CH43.................110 E4
 CLVPS L1.................13 G8
 FMBY L37.................59 H2

FROD/HEL WA6.................160 E6
FROD/HEL WA6.................167 J8
GOL/RIS/CU WA3.................107 L8
GTS/LS CH66.................155 J5
HOY CH47.................108 D6
HOY CH47.................108 F4
HUY L36.................116 C3
LITH L21.................83 J4
MGHL L31.................73 J8
MGHL L31.................73 J8
NSTN CH64.................152 D4
NSTN CH64.................153 H7
NSTN CH64.................153 K3
ORM L39.................61 H2
PEN/TH CH61.................125 K7
PR/KW L34.................86 C8
PS/BROM CH62.................128 D6
RAIN/WH L35.................118 B4
RUNC WA7.................150 B5
SKEL WN8.................64 F4
SKEL WN8.................66 D2
SKEL WN8.................66 G8
WAL/EG CH44.................111 G1
WDN WA8.................119 G6
WCN WN1.................5 G3
WGNE/HIN WN2.................57 G5
WGNNW/ST WN6.................55 M4
WLTN L25.................131 J4
School Ter *GOL/RIS/CU* WA3 *.....92 C5
School Wy *SPK/HALE* L24.........146 D2
 WDN WA8.................134 F2
 WGNW/BIL/O WN5.................67 L7
Schooner Cl *RUNC* WA7.................150 F7
Schwartzman Dr *CHTN/BK* PR9 ..2 J7
Science Rd *SPK/HALE* L24.........146 E1
Scilly Cl *EP* CH65.................163 L4
Scone Cl *NG/CROX* L11.................98 E2
Scorecross *STHEL* WA9.................102 D5
Score La *CHLDW* L16.................114 F5
Scoresby Rd *MOR/LEA* CH46 ....110 D2
The Score *STHEL* WA9.................102 C7
Scorpio Cl *DV/KA/FCH* L14.........99 J4
Scorton St *NPK/KEN* L6.................97 L8
Scotchbarn La *PR/KW* L34.........101 G7
Scoter Rd *NWD/KWIPK* L33.........86 B3
Scotia Av *PS/BROM* CH62.........128 E6
Scotia Rd *CLB/OSW/ST* L13.....114 C1
Scotland Pl *VAUX/LVPD* L3.........13 H4
Scotland Rd *EV* L5.................96 F8
 VAUX/LVPD L3.................13 H3
 WARR WA1.................14 E5
Scot La *WGNE/HIN* WN2.................57 M7
 WGNW/BIL/O WN5.................68 A4
Scott Av *HUY* L36.................116 C5
 RAIN/WH L35.................117 H2
 WDN WA8.................18 A8
Scott Cl *ANF/KKDL* L4.................97 H6
 WARRS WA4.................72 F4
Scott Dr *ORM* L39.................51 H6
Scotton Av *GTS/LS* CH66.........155 K8
Scott Rd *GOL/RIS/CU* WA3.........92 F4
Scotts Av *STHEL* WA9.................118 C2
Scotts Pl *BIRK* CH41.................111 H6
Scotts Quays *BIRK* CH41.........112 A4
Scott St *BTL* L20.................6 E1
 CHTN/BK PR9.................25 J6
 LEIGH WN7.................64 F8
 WAL/NB CH45.................95 K8
 WARRN/WOL WA2.................14 A2
 WGNNW/ST WN6.................4 C2
Scow Croft La *CHLYE* PR6.........33 K1
The Scythes *GR/UP/WCH* CH49..125 L1
 NTHTN L30.................84 D1
Scythia Cl *PS/BROM* CH62.........128 D5
Seabank Rd *CHTN/BK* PR9.........3 H1
 HES CH60.................141 G7
 WAL/NB CH45.................95 L6
Seabury St *WARRS* WA4.................138 C2
Seacombe Dr *GTS/LS* CH66.......163 G2
Seacombe Prom *WAL/EG* CH44 ..112 A2
Seacombe Vw *WAL/EG* CH44 ....112 A3
Seacroft Cl *DV/KA/FCH* L14.........99 J7
Seacroft Crs *DV/KA/FCH* L14 .....99 J7
Seacroft Rd *DV/KA/FCH* L14.........99 J7
Seafield *ANF/KKDL* L4.................97 G6
Seafield Av *CSBY/BLUN* L23.......83 H1
 HES CH60.................141 G7
Seafield Cottages
 ALL/GAR L19 *.................130 E7
Seafield Rd *BTL* L20 *.................6 E2
 PS/BROM CH62.................128 D5
 STHP PR8.................34 E7
Seaford Cl *RUNC* WA7.................150 F4
Seaford Pl *WARRN/WOL* WA2 ....121 J1
Seafore Cl *MGHL* L31.................72 D1
Seaforth Dr *MOR/LEA* CH46 ......110 A6
Seaforth Rd *LITH* L21.................83 J1
Seaforth V North *LITH* L21.........83 J6
Seaforth V West *LITH* L21.........83 J7
Seagram Cl *WLT/FAZ* L9.................84 E5
Sealand Av *FMBY* L37.................59 F3
Sealand Cl *FMBY* L37.................58 F3
 WARRN/WOL WA2.................122 A5
Sea La *RUNC* WA7.................149 M3
Sealy Cl *BEB* CH63.................143 J4
Seaman St *WAV* L15.................114 A6
Seaman Wy *WGNE/HIN* WN2 ......9 K6
Seaport St *TOX* L8.................113 J7
Sea Rd *WAL/NB* CH45.................95 H5
Seascale Av *ECCL* WA10.................101 K5
Seascale Crs *WGN* WN1.................68 A2
Seath Av *STHEL* WA9.................103 G1
Seathwaite Cl *CSBY/BLUN* L23 ..82 D2
Seathwaite Crs *NWD/KWIPK* L33 ..85 M1
Seathwaite Grove *RUNC* WA7 ...150 A4
Seatoller Pl *WGNW/BIL/O* WN5 ..67 K6
Seaton Cl *WD/CROXPK* L12.........99 J3
Seaton Gv *STHEL* WA9.................101 M7
Seaton Pk *RUNC* WA7.................151 G6
Seaton Rd *RF/TRAN* CH42.........10 C7
 WAL/EG CH44.................111 G1
Seaton St *PSKEL* WN8.................65 G2
Servite Cl *CSBY/WL* L22.................82 E3
 EP CH65.................156 B7
Sessions Rd *ANF/KKDL* L4.................97 G5
Seth Powell Wy *HUY* L36.................99 J7
Settringtion Rd *CSBY/BLUN* L23 ..71 K8
Seven Acre Rd *CSBY/BLUN* L23 ..71 K8
Seven Acres La *PEN/TH* CH61 ...126 C7
Sevenoaks Av *STHP* PR8.................34 D8
Sevenoaks Cl *EV* L5.................97 G8
Seven Stars Rd *WGNS/IIMK* WN3 ..4 B5
Severn Av *WLT/FAZ* L9 *.................84 E5

WGNNW/ST WN6.................68 C3
WLT/FAZ L9.................84 E6
Sedbergh Av *AIN/FAZ* L10.........84 E2
Sedbergh Gv *RUNC* WA7.................150 A4
Sedburgh Rd *WAL/EG* CH44.......95 H8
Sedburn Rd *KKBY* L32.................86 C6
Seddon Cl *ECCL* WA10.................101 H2
Seddon House Dr
 WGNNW/ST WN8.................68 A2
Seddon Pl *SKEL* WN8.................65 G2
Seddon Rd *ALL/GAR* L19.................130 E7
 ECCL WA10.................101 K4
Seddon St *CLVPS* L1.................13 G9
Sedgefield Dr *WGNNW/ST* WN6 ..68 A2
Sedgefield Rd *MOR/LEA* CH46 ..110 C5
Sedgely *WGNNW/ST* WN6.................56 C5
Sedgemoor Rd *NG/CROX* L11 .....98 A2
Sedgewick Crs
 WARRW/BUR WA5.................104 A3
Sedley St *NPK/KEN* L6.................97 K7
Sedum Gv *NWD/KWIPK* L33.........73 M8
Sedwyn St *WAV* L15.................5 J1
Seeds La *WLT/FAZ* L9.................84 E6
Seeley Av *BIRK* CH41.................10 A3
Seel Rd *HUY* L36.................116 B3
Seel St *CLVPS* L1.................13 H9
Sefton Av *LITH* L21.................83 K6
 WDN WA8.................134 C2
 WGNW/BIL/O WN5.................66 F8
Sefton Cl *KKBY* L32.................85 L2
 WGNW/BIL/O WN5.................66 F8
Sefton Coastal Footpath
 CSBY/WL L22.................82 D3
 HTWN L38.................70 B7
Sefton Dr *AIN/FAZ* L10.................85 C3
 CSBY/BLUN L23.................71 J4
 KKBY L32.................85 L2
 MGHL L31.................72 D5
 TOX L8.................113 L8
Sefton Fold Dr
 WGNW/BIL/O WN5.................77 M8
Sefton Fold Gdns
 WGNW/BIL/O WN5.................77 M8
Sefton Gdns *ORM* L39.................62 F6
Sefton Gv *AIG/SPK* L17.................129 L1
Sefton La *MGHL* L31.................72 D5
Sefton Mill Ct *SFTN* L29 *.................72 B6
Sefton Mill La *SFTN* L29.................72 B6
Sefton Moss La *NTHTN* L30.........83 M2
Sefton Moss Vls *LITH* L21.................83 K4
Sefton Park Rd *TOX* L8.................113 K7
Sefton Rd *AIMK* WN4.................79 H7
 BTL L20.................83 M8
 FMBY L37.................59 J3
 LITH L21.................83 K5
 RF/TRAN CH42.................128 C5
 WAL/NB CH45.................95 K6
 WGNS/IIMK WN3.................79 H1
 WGNW/BIL/O WN5.................66 F8
 WLT/FAZ L9.................97 J1
Sefton St *LITH* L21.................83 K6
 NEWLW WA12.................104 B2
 STHP PR8.................3 H8
 TOX L8.................112 F7
Sefton Vw *CSBY/BLUN* L23.........83 H1
 WGNW/BIL/O WN5.................66 F8
Sefton Vls *BTL* L20 *.................7 L2
Segar's La *STHP* PR8.................34 E8
Selborne *RAIN/WH* L35.................117 J6
Selborne Cl *TOX* L8.................113 J6
Selbourne Cl *GR/UP/WCH* CH49 .126 D2
Selby Cl *ECCL* WA10.................8 B7
 RUNC WA7.................151 L1
Selby Dr *FMBY* L37.................59 K3
 WGNS/IIMK WN3.................78 E1
Selby Gn *GTS/LS* CH66.................155 K8
Selby Gv *HUY* L36.................116 D1
Selby Pl *SKEL* WN8.................64 F2
Selby Rd *WLT/FAZ* L9.................97 J1
Selby St *WAL/NB* CH45.................95 K8
 WARRW/BUR WA5.................121 G8
Seldon St *EHL/KEN* L7 *.................113 K3
Selkia Rd *ANF/KKDL* L4.................97 M6
Selkirk Av *AIMK* WN4.................90 F1
 EP CH65.................144 A8
 WARRS WA4.................138 C2
Selkirk Cl *GTS/LS* CH66 *.................155 H8
Selkirk Dr *WGNW/BIL/O* WN5 .....67 K5
Selkirk Rd *CLB/OSW/ST* L13.......114 B3
Sellar St *ANF/KKDL* L4.................97 G6
Selsey Cl *EHL/KEN* L7.................113 K5
Selside *WGNS/IIMK* WN3.................79 K3
Selside Wk *NTHLY* L27.................132 C2
Selston Cl *BEB* CH63.................143 J3
Selworthy Dr *WARRS* WA4.........138 F2
Selworthy Gn *CHLDW* L16.........114 F7
Selworthy Rd *STHP* PR8.................34 F2
 WAL/NB CH45.................95 H5
Selwyn Cl *NEWLW* WA12.................91 K8
 WDN WA8.................134 F2
Selwyn St *ANF/KKDL* L4.................7 L8
Senator Point
 NWD/KWIPK L33 *.................86 D5
Senecar Cl *WGNE/HIN* WN2 ....69 K3
Seneschal Ct *RUNC* WA7.................150 B6
Sennen Cl *RUNC* WA7.................150 D8
Sennen Rd *KKBY* L32.................86 B5
Sennicar La *WGN* WN1.................5 E8
Sentinel Wy *NTHTN* L30.................84 D5
Sephton Av *GOL/RIS/CU* WA3 ....107 C2
Sephton Dr *ORM* L39.................51 H6
Sephton St *WGNS/IIMK* WN3.......5 L7
September Rd *NPK/KEN* L6.........97 K8
Serenade Rd *NWD/KWIPK* L33 ...74 B7
Sergeant York Loop
 WARRW/BUR WA5.................120 D8
Sergrim Rd *HUY* L36.................116 M2
Serin Cl *NEWLW* WA12.................104 E2
Serpentine Rd *WAL/EG* CH44 .....95 L8
The Serpentine South
 CSBY/BLUN L23.................82 C1
The Serpentine *ALL/GAR* L19......130 C5
 CSBY/BLUN L23.................82 C1
 ORM L39.................62 F5
Servia Rd *LITH* L21.................83 K6
Severn Rd *AIMK* WN4.................80 A8
 GOL/RIS/CU WA3.................107 H3
 NWD/KWIPK L33.................74 B7
 RAIN/WH L35.................117 K2
Severn St *BIRK* CH41.................111 J4
 EV L5.................97 H7
Severnvale *EP* CH65.................20 A8
Severs St *NPK/KEN* L6.................113 J1
Sewell St *PR/KW* L34.................100 F7
 RUNC WA7.................19 K4
Sextant Cl *RUNC* WA7.................150 F7
Sexton Av *STHEL* WA9.................103 K3
Sexton Wy *DV/KA/FCH* L14.........115 J1
Seymour Dr *GTS/LS* CH66.........156 A7
Seymour Pl *MGHL* L31.................73 G2
Seymour Pl West *WAL/NB* CH45 ..95 K5
Seymour Rd *DV/KA/FCH* L14.......114 F4
 LITH L21.................83 K6
Seymour St *BTL* L20.................7 G2
 CHLYE PR6.................32 F6
 RF/TRAN CH42.................127 M1
 STHP PR8.................3 G3
 WAL/NB CH45.................13 K6
 WAL/NB CH45.................95 K5

WGNW/BIL/O WN5.................67 J7
Shelley Gv *ALL/GAR* L19.................130 E8
 STHP PR8.................35 H6
 WARRS WA4.................138 D1
Shelley Pl *RAIN/WH* L35.................117 H2
Shelley Rd *WDN* WA8.................16 C1
Shelley St *BTL* L20.................81 C6
 LEIGH WN7.................81 L6
 STHEL WA9.................103 D3
Shelley Wy *WKBY* CH48.................124 D5
Shellfield Rd *CHTN/BK* PR9.........25 J2
Shellingford Rd *WGNNW/ST* WN6 ..54 F6
Shelly Rd *DV/KA/FCH* L14.........115 J1
Shellway Rd *EP* CH65.................21 J3
Shelmore Dr *TOX* L8.................129 G1
Shelton Cl *CLB/OSW/ST* L13.....114 C3
 WDN WA8.................135 H2
Shelton Dr *STHP* PR8.................47 J1
Shelton Rd *WAL/NB* CH45.................95 J7
Shenley Cl *BEB* CH63.................128 B2
Shenley Rd *WAV* L15 *.................114 E5
Shenley Wy *CHTN/BK* PR9 *.........32 F6
Shenton Av *RNFD/HAY* WA11......113 K4
Shenton Cl *CR/UP/WCH* CH49.....115 L1
Shepherds Cl *HOR/BR* BL6.........57 L2
Shepherds Fold Cl *TOX* L8.................113 J7
Shepherd's La *ORM* L39.................49 M8
Shepherds Wy *CHLY/EC* PR7.......32 F5
Sheppard Av *CHLDW* L16.................115 C5
Shepperton Cl *WARRS* WA4.......137 M7
Shepsides Cl *GTS/LS* CH66.........162 E2
Shepston Av *ANF/KKDL* L4.................97 J4
Shepton Av *GTS/LS* CH66.........163 G3
 HUY L36.................99 M7
Sheraton Cl *WGNW/BIL/O* WN5 ....67 K4
Sherborne Av *WLTN* L25.................131 M5
Sherborne Cl *RUNC* WA7.................151 H2
Sherborne Rd
 WGNW/BIL/O WN5.................67 J5
Sherbourne Pl *WGNS/IIMK* WN3 ...3 J9
Sherbourne Rd *EP* CH65.................67 J5
Sherbourne St *CHLYE* PR6.........32 F6
Sherbourne Wy
 WARRW/BUR WA5.................104 B7
Sherbrooke Cl *WD/CROXPK* L12 ..99 H1
Sherburn Cl *WLT/FAZ* L9.................84 F5
Sherdley Park Dr *STHEL* WA9ST ..102 D7
Sherdley Rd *STHEL* WA9.................102 C5
Sheridan Av *GOL/RIS/CU* WA3 ....92 F6
Sheridan Pl *WARRN/WOL* WA2 ...104 F3
Sheri Dr *NEWLW* WA12.................104 F3
Sheriff Cl *EV* L5.................13 K4
Sheringham Cl
 CR/UP/WCH CH49.................110 C6
 STHEL WA9.................102 F2
Sheringham Rd
 WARRW/BUR WA5.................104 B7
Sherlock Av *RNFD/HAY* WA11......91 G6
Sherlock La *WAL/EG* CH44.................111 K2
Sherman Dr *RAIN/WH* L35.................117 M4
Sherrat St *SKEL* WN8.................64 F4
Sherringham Rd *STHP* PR8.................35 G3
Sherry Ct *AIG/SPK* L17 *.................114 A8
Sherry La *GR/UP/WCH* CH49.......126 C3
Sherwell Cl *WAV* L15.................114 A4
Sherwood Av *AIMK* WN4 *.................91 L1
 CSBY/BLUN L23.................71 G2
 ORM L39.................62 E3
 PEN/TH CH61.................125 L6
Sherwood Cl *RAIN/WH* L35.........101 K8
 WDN WA8.................133 L4
 WD/CROXPK L12.................99 H3
Sherwood Crs
 WARRW/BUR WA5.................104 A7
 WGNE/HIN WN2.................80 C3
 WGNW/BIL/O WN5.................67 M6
Sherwood Dr *BEB* CH63.................128 A6
 RAIN/WH L35.................117 H3
 SKEL WN8.................53 H5
Sherwood Gv *FROD/HEL* WA6.....166 C2
 HOY CH47.................109 H6
 HOY CH47.................109 M6
Sherwood Pl *CHLYE* PR6.................42 E5
Sherwood Rd *CSBY/BLUN* L23 ....70 E8
 HOY CH47.................109 H5
 WAL/EG CH44.................111 L2
Sherwood's La *AIN/FAZ* L10.........85 H5
Sherwood St *VAUX/LVPD* L3.......12 F2
Sherwyn Rd *ANF/KKDL* L4.................97 L6
Shetland Cl *WARRN/WOL* WA2 ...122 A1
 WDN WA8.................135 G2
Shetland Dr *EP* CH65.................163 L4
 PS/BROM CH62.................144 A5
Shevington Cswy
 CROS/BRETH PR26.................29 J3
Shevington Cl *STHEL* WA9.........102 E6
 WDN WA8.................135 G2
Shevington Moor
 WGNNW/ST WN6.................55 J3
Shevington's La
 NWD/KWIPK L33.................74 A8
Shewell Cl *RF/TRAN* CH42.................11 H9
Shiel Rd *WAL/NB* CH45.................95 J4
Shiggins Cl *WARRW/BUR* WA5 ...120 F7
Shildon Cl *WGNE/HIN* WN2.........69 H3
Shillingford Ct *WARRS* WA4.......138 A8
Shimmin St *EHL/KEN* L7.................113 J4
Shipham Cl *LEIGH* WN7.................81 M5
Ship St *FROD/HEL* WA6.................160 F6
Shipton Cl *ALL/GAR* L19.................130 D5
 CL/PREN CH43.................127 C4
 WARRW/BUR WA5.................133 M2
Ship Yd *WGN* WN1.................4 F4
Shirdley Av *KKBY* L32.................86 D5
Shirdley Crs *STHP* PR8.................47 L2
Shirdley Wk *KKBY* L32.................86 D5
Shirebourne Av
 RNFD/HAY WA11.................89 K6
Shireburn Rd *FMBY* L37.................46 E8
Shires, The *ECCL* WA10.................9 D7
Shirewell Rd *WGNW/BIL/O* WN5 ..55 C3
Shirley Dr *WARRS* WA4.................138 C3
Shirley Rd *ALL/GAR* L19.................130 E6
Shirley St *WAL/EG* CH44.................112 A4
Shirwell Gv *STHEL* WA9.................118 C5
Shobdon Cl *WD/CROXPK* L12.......99 H1
Shones Cft *NSTN* CH64.................153 J8
Shop La *MGHL* L31.................72 E4
Shore Bank *PS/BROM* CH62.......128 E5
Shore Dr *PS/BROM* CH62.................128 E5
Shorefields *PS/BROM* CH62.......128 E4
Shorefields Village *TOX* L8.........129 H2
Shoreham Dr
 WARRW/BUR WA5.................136 C2
Shore Rd *BIRK* CH41.................11 L3
 BTL L20.................6 B1
 STHP PR8.................34 B7
 WKBY CH48.................124 E6
Short Cl *NEWLW* WA12.................104 A2

Shortfield Rd
GR/UP/WCH CH49 ....126 C1
Shortfield Wy
GR/UP/WCH CH49 * 126 C1
Shortland Pl WGNE/HIN WN2 ....81 J7
Short St GOL/RIS/CU WA3 * 92 D4
  NEWLW WA12 ....104 A2
  RNFD/HAY WA11 ....91 F7
  WDN WA8 ....134 C8
  WGNW/BIL/O WN5 ....67 K7
Shortwood Rd DV/KA/FCH L14 ....115 H2
Shorwell Cl WARRW/BUR WA5 ....119 L6
Shotwick La CH/BCN CH1 ....162 A7
Shrewsbury Av AIN/FAZ L10 ....82 F2
  CSBY/WL L22 ....82 F2
Shrewsbury Dr
GR/UP/WCH CH49 ....110 C7
Shrewsbury Rd ALL/GAR L19 ....130 C7
  CL/PREN CH43 ....10 D9
  HES CH60 ....141 J4
  WAL/NB CH45 ....95 H8
  WKBY CH48 ....124 C4
Shrewsbury St WARRS WA4 ....15 J9
Shrewton Rd WLTN L25 ....115 J6
Shropshire Cl NTHTN L30 ....84 C1
  WARR WA1 ....123 G7
Shropshire Gdns ECCL WA10 ....8 E7
Shropshire Rd EP CH65 ....21 J9
Shuttle Hillock Rd
WGNE/HIN WN2 ....81 H6
Sibbering Brow Preston Rd
CHLY/EC PR7 ....31 L6
Sibford Rd WD/CROXPK L12 ....98 F8
Sibley Av RUNC WA4 ....91 M1
Sidbrook St WGNE/HIN WN2 ....69 L8
Siddall St ECCL WA10 ....8 H6
Siddeley Dr NEWLW WA12 ....104 B2
Siddeley St AIG/SPK L17 ....129 G2
  LEIGH 81 M8
Sidgreave St ECCL WA10 ....8 D6
Siding La RNFD/HAY WA11 ....75 M4
The Sidings RF/TRAN CH42 ....128 C2
Sidlaw Av STHEL WA9 ....103 H2
Sidlaw Cl GTS/LS CH66 ....155 H1
Sidmouth Cl ECCL WA10 ....88 C8
  WARRW/BUR WA5 ....136 A1
Sidmouth Gv WGNS/IIMK WN3 ....95 G2
Sidney Av WAL/NB CH45 ....95 J1
Sidney Gdns RF/TRAN CH42 ....128 A1
Sidney Pl EHL/KEN L7 ....113 J4
Sidney Powell Av KKBY L32 ....85 L3
Sidney Rd BIRK CH41 ....128 A1
  BTL L20 ....7 K6
  CHTN/BK PR9 ....25 H5
  NSTN CH64 ....155 H4
Sidney St BIRK CH41 ....11 K4
  ECCL WA10 ....8 B4
Sidney Ter RF/TRAN CH42 ....128 A2
Sidwell St ALL/GAR L19 ....130 E8
Signal Works Rd WLT/FAZ L9 ....85 G5
Silcock St GOL/RIS/CU WA3 ....92 C5
Silcroft Rd KKBY L32 ....86 A5
Silkstone Cl ECCL WA10 ....8 B6
  EHL/KEN L7 ....113 K5
Silkstone Crs RUNC WA7 ....150 D6
Silkstone St ECCL WA10 ....8 C6
Sillitoe Dr WGNNW/ST WN6 ....56 C5
Silsbury Gv WGNNW/ST WN6 ....56 C5
Silsden Av GOL/RIS/CU WA3 ....93 K5
Silver Av RNFD/HAY WA11 ....90 C6
Silverbeech Av CALD/MH L18 ....130 D1
Silverbeech Rd WAL/EG CH44 ....111 L2
Silver Birch Gv AIMK WN4 ....79 J8
Silverbirch Rd GTS/LS CH66 ....163 H5
Silver Birch Wy MGHL L31 ....61 K8
Silverbrook Rd NTHLY L27 ....115 L6
Silverburn Av MOR/LEA CH46 ....110 A4
Silverdale Av CLB/OSW/ST L13 ....98 A3
  WGNE/HIN WN2 ....69 J5
Silverdale Cl FROD/HEL WA6 ....160 E6
  MGHL L31 ....116 A5
Silverdale Ct WGNW/BIL/O WN1 ....5 H4
Silverdale Dr LITH L21 ....83 M5
Silverdale Gv RNFD/HAY WA11 ....89 G3
Silverdale Rd BEB CH63 ....128 B6
  CHLYE PR6 ....33 G5
  CL/PREN CH43 ....10 A9
  NEWLW WA12 ....104 D1
  WARRS WA4 ....15 M7
  WGNW/BIL/O WN5 ....67 K5
Silver La GOL/RIS/CU WA3 ....107 J6
Silverlea Av WAL/NB CH45 ....111 J1
Silver Leigh AIG/SPK L17 ....129 M4
Silverlime Gdns STHEL WA9 ....101 L6
Silverne Dr EP CH65 ....163 J3
Silverstone Dr HUY L36 ....115 M5
Silverstone Gv MGHL L31 ....61 K8
Silver St WARRS WA2 ....14 E3
  WGNW/BIL/O WN1 ....80 D3
Silver Ter WGN WN1 ....80 B7
Silverthorne Dr CHTN/BK PR9 ....25 H4
Silverton Rd AIG/SPK L17 ....130 A5
Silverwell Rd NG/CROX L11 ....85 M8
Silvester Rd CHLY/EC PR7 ....32 E7
Silvester St EV L5 ....96 F8
  HOR/BR BL6 ....57 M3
Silvington Wy WGNE/HIN WN2 ....69 J4
Simfield Cl WGNNW/ST WN6 ....55 M4
Simkin Av WARRS WA4 ....138 A5
Simms Av STHEL WA9 ....103 G2
Simm's Rd NPK/KEN L6 ....97 M7
Simnel Cl WLTN L25 ....135 J2
Simonsbridge WKBY CH48 * 124 F7
Simons Cl NTHTN L30 ....116 E5
Simon's Cft NTHTN L30 ....83 L2
Simonside WDN WA8 ....133 H7
Simons La FROD/HEL WA6 ....160 D7
Simonstone Gv STHEL WA9 ....102 F6
Simonswood La
NWD/KWIPK L33 ....86 C3
  ORM L39 ....74 B2
Simpkin St WGNE/HIN WN2 ....80 D4
Simpson St BIRK CH41 ....11 H5
  CLVPS L1 ....9 G8
Sim St VAUX/LVPD L3 ....13 K4
Sinclair Av RAIN/WH L35 ....101 H8
  WARRN/WOL WA2 ....121 K3
  WDN WA8 ....16 B3
Sinclair Cl RAIN/WH L35 ....101 H8
Sinclair Dr CALD/MH L18 ....114 D7
Sinclair Pl WGNW/BIL/O WN5 ....68 A1
Sinclair St ALL/GAR L19 ....130 E8
Sineacre La ORM L39 ....75 G4
Singleton Av RF/TRAN CH42 ....128 A1
  RNFD/HAY WA11 ....89 M8
Singleton Ct RNFD/HAY WA11 ....160 E5
Singleton Dr PR/KW L34 ....99 M2
Singleton Rd EP CH65 ....163 H1
Sirdar Cl EHL/KEN L7 ....113 H5
Sir Howard Wy EHL/KEN L7 ....113 H5
Sir Thomas St CLVPS L1 ....12 F6
Siskin Cl NEWLW WA12 ....104 A2
Siskin Gn WLTN L25 ....131 J1
Sisters Wy BIRK CH41 ....11 G5
Sittingbourne Rd WGN WN1 ....68 E1
Six Acre Gdns WARRS WA4 ....136 C8

Six Acre La RUNC WA7 ....136 C8
Sixpenny La STHP PR8 ....47 M4
Sixth Av WLT/FAZ L9 ....84 F6
Skeffington RAIN/WH L35 ....117 G3
Skelmersdale Rd ORM L39 ....64 C6
Skelton Cl RNFD/HAY WA11 ....89 H3
Skelton St AIMK WN4 ....79 H7
Skerries Rd ANF/KKDL L4 ....97 J7
Skiddaw Cl RUNC WA7 ....150 C7
Skiddaw Pl WGNW/BIL/O WN5 ....67 L7
Skiddaw Rd PS/BROM CH62 ....144 A3
Skipton Av CHTN/BK PR9 ....22 E7
Skipton Rd ANF/KKDL L4 ....81 J1
  ANF/KKDL L4 ....97 K6
  HUY L36 ....116 D2
Skirving Pl EV L5 ....96 F7
Skirving St EV L5 ....96 F7
Skull House La WGNNW/ST WN6 ....54 E5
Skull House Ms WGNNW/ST WN6 ....54 E5
Skye Cl EP CH65 ....163 L4
Slackey Fold WGNE/HIN WN2 ....81 K4
Slack La CHTN/BK PR9 ....25 L1
Slack's La CHLYE PR6 ....44 E3
Slag La GOL/RIS/CU WA3 ....93 H3
  RNFD/HAY WA11 ....90 D6
Slaidburn Cl WGNS/IIMK WN3 ....78 J2
Slaidburn Crs CHTN/BK PR9 ....22 B7
  GOL/RIS/CU WA3 ....92 B3
Slate La SKEL WN8 ....64 E5
Slater Pl CLVPS L1 ....13 H9
Slater St CLVPS L1 ....9 H8
  WARRS WA4 ....15 H8
Slatey Rd CL/PREN CH43 ....10 C6
Sleaford Rd DV/KA/FCH L14 ....99 K8
Sledbrook St
WGNW/BIL/O WN5 * 67 L8
Sleepers HI ANF/KKDL L4 ....97 H6
Slessor Av WKBY CH48 ....124 F2
Slim Rd HUY L36 ....116 C1
Slingsby Dr GR/UP/WCH CH49 ....110 E5
Sluice La BRSC L40 ....39 K2
Slutchers La WARR WA1 ....14 D8
Small Av WARRN/WOL WA2 ....121 J5
Small Crs WARRN/WOL WA2 ....121 M5
Smalley St WGNNW/ST WN6 ....56 A4
The Smallholdings MGHL L31 * 73 J2
Small La BRSC L40 ....38 A5
  ORM L39 ....62 B2
  ORM L39 ....63 H1
Small La North ORM L39 ....49 M3
Small La South ORM L39 ....49 L8
Smallridge Cl PEN/TH CH61 * 141 G1
Smallshaw Cl AIMK WN4 ....91 J3
Smallwoods Ms HES CH60 ....141 G4
Smeaton St ANF/KKDL L4 * 7 L9
Smethurst La WGNW/BIL/O WN5 ....67 L3
Smethurst Park Hall
WGNW/BIL/O WN5 ....77 L3
Smethurst Rd WGNE/HIN WN2 ....57 L3
  WGNW/BIL/O WN5 ....67 L3
Smilie Av MOR/LEA CH46 ....109 L4
Smith Av BIRK CH41 ....11 J5
  WARRN/WOL WA2 ....121 M5
Smith Brow HOR/BR BL6 ....57 L3
Smith Crs WARRN/WOL WA2 ....121 M5
Smithdown Gv EHL/KEN L7 ....113 J5
Smithdown La EHL/KEN L7 ....113 J5
Smithdown Pl WAV L15 ....113 L6
Smithdown Rd EHL/KEN L7 ....113 L6
Smithfield St CLVP L2 ....12 F5
  STHEL WA9 ....102 F5
Smithford Wk RAIN/WH L35 ....135 G4
Smithills Cl CHLYE PR6 ....33 G4
  GOL/RIS/CU WA3 ....106 F3
Smith Pl EV L5 ....96 F7
Smith Rd WDN WA8 ....16 B5
Smith's La KIRK/FR/WA PR4 ....24 B4
  WGNE/HIN WN2 ....81 J5
Smith St CHLY/EC PR7 ....32 F7
  EV L5 ....97 G6
  PR/KW L34 * 101 G7
  SKEL WN8 ....64 F4
  STHEL WA9 ....105 G6
  WARR WA1 ....14 F6
  WGNE/HIN WN2 ....57 L3
Smithy Brow GOL/RIS/CU WA3 ....106 B3
  SKEL WN8 ....53 J4
  WGNNW/ST WN6 ....41 L5
Smithy Cl FMBY L37 ....59 K1
  WDN WA8 ....117 L7
Smithy Gn FMBY L37 ....59 K1
Smithy Hey WKBY CH48 ....124 F3
Smithy Hts BEB CH63 ....142 C7
Smithy La BRSC L40 ....40 D3
  BRSC L40 ....50 E1
  FROD/HEL WA6 ....159 L8
  GOL/RIS/CU WA3 ....106 C3
  GTS/LS CH66 ....155 L7
  KIRK/FR/WA PR4 ....27 L7
  NSTN CH64 ....154 C5
  ORM L39 ....49 J7
  ORM L39 ....62 B7
  WDN WA8 ....117 L8
Smock La AIMK WN4 ....90 F1
Smollett St BTL L20 ....83 J7
Smugglers Wy WAL/NB CH45 ....95 G5
Smyth Rd WDN WA8 ....134 F3
Snabwood Cl NSTN CH64 ....153 G8
Snaefell Av CLB/OSW/ST L13 ....98 A8
Snaefell Cl KKBY L32 ....85 K3
Snaefell Ri WARRS WA4 ....137 L5
Snaefell Rd ALL/GAR L19 ....131 G6
Snape Gn STHP PR8 ....47 L3
Snave Cl LITH L21 ....83 K8
Snipewood CHLY/EC PR7 ....30 D7
Snottlesbrook Gn NG/CROX L11 ....98 B2
Snowberry Cl WDN WA8 ....135 G1
Snowberry Rd DV/KA/FCH L14 ....99 H7
Snowden Av WGNS/IIMK WN3 ....79 J1
Snowden Cl MOR/LEA CH46 ....109 L4
Snowdon Cl GTS/LS CH66 ....155 J1
  WARRW/BUR WA5 ....120 A7
Snowdon Dr HOR/BR BL6 ....45 L8
Snowdon Gv STHEL WA9 ....102 E8
Snowdon La EV L5 ....96 E8
Snowdon Rd RF/TRAN CH42 ....127 M3
Snowdrop Av BIRK CH41 ....111 H3
Snowdrop Cl RUNC WA7 ....161 H1
Snowdrop Ms LITH L21 ....83 K7
Snowdrop St EV L5 ....96 F6
Snowhill Dr WGNS/IIMK WN3 ....78 L1
Soane Cl WGNE/HIN WN2 ....81 M2
Soho Pl VAUX/LVPD L3 ....13 K3
Soho Sq VAUX/LVPD L3 ....13 K3
  WGNW/BIL/O WN5 ....68 B6
Solar Rd WLT/FAZ L9 ....5 L3
Sole St WGN WN1 ....5 L3
Sollom La BRSC L40 ....38 D3
Solly Av RF/TRAN CH42 ....128 A3
Solomon St EHL/KEN L7 ....113 K3

Solway Cl AIMK WN4 ....91 J1
  WARRN/WOL WA2 ....122 B1
Solway Gv RUNC WA7 ....149 M8
Solway St West TOX L8 ....113 K6
Sova Av LITH L21 ....83 L5
Somerford Rd DV/KA/FCH L14 ....115 J1
Somerset Av CHLY/EC PR7 ....32 C4
Somerset Dr STHP PR8 ....27 L2
Somerset Pl NPK/KEN L6 ....97 M8
Somerset Rd BTL L20 ....7 K2
  CSBY/WL L22 ....82 E3
  PEN/TH CH61 ....141 G1
  WAL/NB CH45 ....95 G8
  WGNW/BIL/O WN5 ....67 J8
  WKBY CH48 ....124 C4
Somerset St STHEL WA9 ....102 F3
Somerset Wy WARR WA1 ....122 C5
Somerton Av WAV L15 ....114 A5
Somerville Cl BEB CH63 ....143 K7
  NSTN CH64 ....153 G8
Somerville Crs EP CH65 ....20 D7
Somerville Ct CSBY/WL L22 ....82 F3
  WDN WA8 ....133 M5
  WGN WN1 ....68 E1
Sommer Av WD/CROXPK L12 * 98 C6
Sonning Av ANF/KKDL L4 ....83 J4
Sonning Rd ANF/KKDL L4 ....97 M3
Sorany Cl CSBY/BLUN L23 ....71 J2
Sorbus Cl CHNE CH2 ....9 L6
Sorogold St STHEL WA9 ....9 L6
Sorrel Cl CL/PREN CH43 ....110 F8
  WARRN/WOL WA2 ....122 E3
Sougher's La AIMK WN4 ....79 M1
South Albert Rd AIG/SPK L17 ....129 K1
Southampton Wy RUNC WA7 ....151 G7
South Av CHLY/EC PR7 ....30 E8
  PR/KW L34 ....100 F4
  WARRN/WOL WA2 ....14 F1
  WARRS WA4 ....15 L4
South Bank CL/PREN CH43 ....127 K2
South Bank Rd ALL/GAR L19 ....130 D6
  EHL/KEN L7 ....113 M5
Southbank Rd STHP PR8 ....3 K1
South Bank Ter RUNC WA7 ....18 F2
South Barcombe Rd
CHLDW L16 ....115 G6
South Boundary Rd
NWD/KWIPK L33 ....86 D5
Southbourne Rd WAL/NB CH45 ....94 F8
Southbrook Rd NTHLY L27 ....115 J7
South Cantril Av
WD/CROXPK L12 ....99 H6
South Chester St TOX L8 ....113 G7
South Cloughton Rd BIRK CH41 * 10 F6
Southcroft Rd WAL/NB CH45 ....94 F8
South Dl WARRW/BUR WA5 ....120 B8
Southdale Rd RF/TRAN CH42 ....128 A3
  WARR WA1 ....122 C6
  WAV L15 ....114 A3
Southdean Rd DV/KA/FCH L14 ....99 K7
Southdene SKEL WN8 ....53 K4
Southdowns Rd CHLY/EC PR7 ....32 F8
South Dr GR/UP/WCH CH49 ....110 C8
  HES CH60 ....141 H6
  PEN/TH CH61 ....125 L8
  WAV L15 ....114 A3
  WD/CROXPK L12 ....98 C8
  WGNNW/ST WN6 ....54 E7
Southern Crs TOX L8 ....113 G8
Southern Rd SPK/HALE L24 ....147 G5
  STHP PR8 ....2 B1
Southern's Fold
WGNE/HIN WN2 ....69 J2
Southern's La RNFD/HAY WA11 ....76 D1
Southern St WARRS WA4 ....137 L4
  WGNW/BIL/O WN5 ....67 K7
Southey Av WGNS/IIMK WN3 ....78 A3
Southey Cl WDN WA8 ....16 A3
Southey Gv MGHL L31 ....72 F7
Southey Rd ECCL WA10 ....101 L5
Southey St BTL L20 ....6 F7
  WAV L15 ....114 A4
South Ferry Quay VAUX/LVPD L3 ....112 F7
Southfield WGNE/HIN WN2 ....80 D3
Southfield Rd GTS/LS CH66 ....155 L7
  WLT/FAZ L9 ....84 B7
Southfields Av
WARRW/BUR WA5 ....120 B7
South Front RAIN/WH L35 ....117 G5
Southgate Cl WD/CROXPK L12 ....99 G3
Southgate Rd CLB/OSW/ST L13 ....114 D2
Southgates CHLY/EC PR7 ....42 F7
South Gv CALD/MH L18 ....130 E4
  TOX L8 ....129 J1
South Hey LEIGH WN7 ....81 L8
South Hey Rd PEN/TH CH61 ....140 F4
South Highville Rd CHLDW L16 ....114 F7
South Hill Gv CL/PREN CH43 ....10 D9
  TOX L8 ....129 J1
South Hill Rd CL/PREN CH43 ....10 D9
  TOX L8 ....129 J1
South Hunter St CLVPS L1 ....13 L9
South John St CLVPS L1 ....12 F7
  STHEL WA9 ....9 L5
Southlands Av
WARRW/BUR WA5 ....136 B2
  WGNNW/ST WN6 ....56 B4
Southlands Ms RUNC WA7 ....18 F7
South La WDN WA8 ....16 F6
South Manor Wy WLTN L25 ....131 L4
South Meade MGHL L31 ....72 D4
South Mossley Hill Rd
ALL/GAR L19 ....130 C4
Southney Cl KKBY L32 ....85 K3
South Pde KKBY L32 ....86 A3
  RUNC WA7 ....18 A4
  SPK/HALE L24 ....147 G3
  WKBY CH48 ....124 C5
South Park Ct RAIN/WH L35 ....112 A2
South Park Rd KKBY L32 ....85 L2
South Parkside Dr
WD/CROXPK L12 ....98 E6
South Park Wy BTL L20 ....7 J6
South Pier Rd EP CH65 ....156 F5
Southport New Rd
CHTN/BK PR9 ....26 D7
  KIRK/FR/WA PR4 ....27 M1
Southport Old Rd FMBY L37 ....47 K6
Southport Rd BTL L20 ....7 G2
  CHLY/EC PR7 ....43 G4
  CROS/BRETH PR26 ....30 C3
  CSBY/BLUN L23 ....71 J6
  FMBY L37 ....47 J8
  MGHL L31 ....61 J6
  ORM L39 ....49 J5
  ORM L39 ....50 F5
  STHP PR8 ....36 C3
Southport St STHEL WA9 ....103 J2
Southport Ter CHLYE PR6 ....33 G6
South Rd AIG/SPK L17 ....129 K3
  ALL/GAR L19 ....130 B7
  CHLY/EC PR7 ....43 G4
  CSBY/WL L22 ....82 E3
  DV/KA/FCH L14 ....114 F2

  EP CH65 ....20 D8
  EP CH65 ....21 J5
  SPK/HALE L24 ....147 G1
  WKBY CH48 ....124 C4
  WLT/FAZ L9 ....84 F7
Southside CHLY/EC PR7 ....31 L5
South Station Rd WLTN L25 ....115 K8
South St EHL/KEN L7 ....113 J8
  WDN WA8 ....16 D8
South Sudley Rd ALL/GAR L19 ....130 C4
South Ter ORM L39 ....63 G1
South Vw CSBY/WL L22 * 83 G5
  HUY L36 ....116 D3
  PS/BROM CH62 ....128 F8
  TOX L8 * 129 J1
South Vis WAL/NB CH45 ....95 K6
Southward Rd RNFD/HAY WA11 ....91 H6
South Wy WAV L15 ....114 A5
Southway RUNC WA7 ....150 A6
  SKEL WN8 ....65 L4
  WDN WA8 ....133 M5
Southway Av WARRS WA4 ....137 M6
Southwell Pl TOX L8 ....113 G8
Southwick Rd RF/TRAN CH42 ....128 A2
Southwood Av RUNC WA7 ....150 A6
Southwood Cl AIG/SPK L17 ....129 K3
Southworth Av
WARRW/BUR WA5 ....121 H5
Southworth La
WARRN/WOL WA2 ....105 M4
Southworth Rd NEWLW WA12 ....105 H1
Sovereign Cl GOL/RIS/CU WA3 ....93 G6
  RUNC WA7 ....150 F5
Sovereign Ct GOL/RIS/CU WA3 ....122 E1
  NG/CROX L11 ....98 E2
Sovereign Wy BIRK CH41 ....111 K4
  NG/CROX L11 ....98 E2
Spa Fold BRSC L40 ....64 C1
Spa La BRSC L40 ....64 D1
Spark La BRSC L40 ....28 D7
Sparks La PEN/TH CH61 ....126 D7
Sparling St CLVPS L1 ....112 F6
Sparrow Hall Cl WLT/FAZ L9 * 98 B1
Sparrow Hall Rd WLT/FAZ L9 ....98 B1
Sparrowhawk Cl HLWD L26 ....132 A4
  RUNC WA7 ....150 F5
Sparrow Ml SKEL WN8 ....54 C5
Spawell Cl GOL/RIS/CU WA3 ....92 F5
Speakman Av NEWLW WA12 ....91 K8
Speakman Av WGNNW/ST WN6 ....54 E7
Speakman Rd ECCL WA10 ....88 C8
Speakman St RUNC WA7 ....18 F2
Speedwell Cl GOL/RIS/CU WA3 ....93 G5
  HES CH60 ....141 L5
Speedwell Dr HES CH60 ....141 L5
Speke Bvd SPK/HALE L24 ....146 E1
Speke Church Rd SPK/HALE L24 ....146 D2
Speke Hall Av SPK/HALE L24 ....146 D2
Speke Hall Rd WLTN L25 ....131 J6
Spekeland Rd EHL/KEN L7 ....113 L5
Speke Rd ALL/GAR L19 ....130 D7
  HLWD L26 ....132 D7
  WDN WA8 ....133 H7
  WLTN L25 ....131 K4
Speke Town La SPK/HALE L24 ....146 D1
Spelding Dr WGNNW/ST WN6 ....67 M2
Spellow Av ANF/KKDL L4 ....97 H5
Spellow La ANF/KKDL L4 ....97 H5
Spence Av BTL L20 ....83 M8
Spencer Cl HUY L36 * 116 C4
  WDN WA8 ....134 B4
Spencer Gdns STHEL WA9 ....102 F5
Spencer Pl BTL L20 ....83 M6
  CHTN/BK PR9 * 3 K3
Spencer Rd WGN WN1 ....68 D2
Spencer Rd West
WGNW/BIL/O WN5 ....68 C2
Spencer's La MGHL L31 ....85 H2
  ORM L39 ....48 D2
  SKEL WN8 ....65 K5
  WGNW/BIL/O WN5 ....68 F6
Spencer St BTL L20 ....6 C2
  NPK/KEN L6 ....13 M2
Spendmore La CHLY/EC PR7 ....42 F5
Spennymoor Ct RUNC WA7 ....150 D4
Spenser Av RF/TRAN CH42 ....128 B4
Spenser Rd NSTN CH64 ....153 G5
Spey St WGNNW/ST WN6 ....56 A3
Spicer Gv KKBY L32 ....86 A3
Spice St WLT/FAZ L9 ....84 D8
Spilsby Sq WGNS/IIMK WN3 ....79 J3
Spindle Cl NPK/KEN L6 ....13 M1
Spindle Hillock AIMK WN4 ....90 F7
Spindlewood Rd
WGNS/IIMK WN3 ....5 K8
Spindus Rd SPK/HALE L24 ....146 C2
Spinnaker Cl RUNC WA7 ....150 F7
Spinney Av WDN WA8 ....133 G4
Spinney Cl NWD/KWIPK L33 ....86 E5
  ORM L39 ....62 F2
  STHEL WA9 ....118 E1
Spinney Crs CSBY/BLUN L23 ....70 D7
Spinney Dr GTS/LS CH66 ....160 A1
Spinney Gn ECCL WA10 ....101 J3
Spinney Houses CLVPS L1 * 13 G8
The Spinney BEB CH63 ....143 K2
  CHLYE PR6 ....32 F6
  FMBY L37 ....47 J8
  HES CH60 ....141 L6
  NSTN CH64 ....152 F5
  PR/KW L34 ....100 C6
  RNFD/HAY WA11 ....76 B3
  STBRV L28 ....99 J8
  WGNW/BIL/O WN5 ....68 C2
  WKBY CH48 ....124 F3
Spinney Wy NWD/KWIPK L33 ....86 F5
Spion Kop AIMK WN4 ....91 J3
Spiredale Brow
WGNNW/ST WN6 ....56 B4
Spires Cl WARRN/WOL WA2 ....105 J4
Spital Heyes BEB CH63 ....143 K5
Spital Rd BEB CH63 ....143 K5
Spitfire Rd ALL/GAR L19 ....131 H4
Spofforth Rd WAV L15 ....113 M5
Spooner Av LITH L21 ....83 M5
Sportsman St LEIGH WN7 ....81 M8
Sprainger St VAUX/LVPD L3 ....12 C2
Sprakeling Pl BTL L20 ....84 A3
Spray St ECCL WA10 ....8 D4
Spreyton Cl NG/CROX L11 ....98 E2
Sprig Cl WLT/FAZ L9 ....84 F5
Spring Av GTS/LS CH66 ....155 L7
Springbank Cl RUNC WA7 ....149 M2
Springbourne FROD/HEL WA6 ....160 F2
Springbrook Cl ECCL WA10 ....101 J1
Spring Cl NWD/KWIPK L33 * 74 D1
  STHP PR8 ....2 B1
Spring Ct RUNC WA7 ....19 H3

Springcroft NSTN CH64 ....152 E4
Springdale Cl WD/CROXPK L12 ....98 E6
Springfld RNFD/HAY WA11 ....76 A3
Springfield VAUX/LVPD L3 ....13 K4
Spring Fld RNFD/HAY WA11 ....76 A3
Spring Gdns GOL/RIS/CU WA3 ....93 B5
  LITH L21 ....83 L5
  WARR WA1 ....122 B5
  WARRS WA4 ....138 D2
  WKBY CH48 ....125 G2
Springfield Cl BRSC L40 ....51 M3
  FMBY L37 ....58 E3
  GR/UP/WCH CH49 ....126 E3
Springfield La ECCL WA10 ....88 C8
Springfield Pk RNFD/HAY WA11 ....90 E6
Springfield Rd CHLY/EC PR7 ....32 E5
  CHLYE PR6 ....43 G5
  ECCL WA10 ....44 C5
  ORM L39 ....62 B8
  WDN WA8 ....133 J5
  WGNE/HIN WN2 ....69 K7
  WGNNW/ST WN6 ....68 B3
Springfield Rd North
CHLY/EC PR7 ....43 G4
Springfield Sq ANF/KKDL L4 ....97 H5
Springfield St WARR WA1 ....16 E3
  WGN WN1 ....5 G3
Springfield Wy WD/CROXPK L12 ....99 G5
Spring Gdns GTS/LS CH66 ....155 L7
  MGHL L31 ....73 G3
Spring Gv WD/CROXPK L12 ....98 E6
Springhill Av PS/BROM CH62 ....143 M7
Spring La GOL/RIS/CU WA3 ....108 D8
Springmeadow Rd WLTN L25 ....115 J8
Springmount Dr SKEL WN8 ....53 G6
Springpool STHEL WA9 ....102 F6
  WGNS/IIMK WN3 ....78 D3
Spring Rd WGNW/BIL/O WN5 ....67 H5
Springs Cl BTL L20 * 7 J3
Springs Rd CHLYE PR6 ....32 F3
Spring St RF/TRAN CH42 ....128 A2
  WDN WA8 ....16 D7
  WGN WN1 ....80 A1
Spring V WAL/NB CH45 ....95 G6
Springvale CL/PREN CH43 ....127 K1
Springville Rd WLT/FAZ L9 * 84 L6
Springwell Rd BTL L20 ....83 L6
Springwood Av ALL/GAR L19 ....130 F5
  WLTN L25 ....130 F5
Springwood Dr BRSC L40 ....28 C8
  CHLYE PR6 ....33 G6
Springwood Gv KKBY L32 ....86 B6
Springwood Wy RF/TRAN CH42 ....128 C5
Sprodley Dr WGNNW/ST WN6 ....54 D3
Spruce Cl GOL/RIS/CU WA3 ....93 H6
  RF/TRAN CH42 ....11 G9
  WARR WA1 ....123 G2
Spruce Gv STBRV L28 ....99 K6
Spruce Rd WGNNW/ST WN6 ....68 A2
Spruce Wy FMBY L37 ....58 E2
Sprucewood Cl NPK/KEN L6 ....97 K8
Spunhill Av GTS/LS CH66 ....162 E2
Spur Cl NG/CROX L11 ....98 E2
Spurgeon Cl EV L5 ....97 G7
Spurling Rd WARRW/BUR WA5 ....104 B7
Spurrier's La MGHL L31 ....73 M5
Spurstow Cl CL/PREN CH43 ....127 K4
The Spur CSBY/BLUN L23 ....82 F2
Spymers Cft FMBY L37 ....47 J7
Square House La CHTN/BK PR9 ....23 K6
Squires Av BTL L20 ....84 C3
Squires Cl RNFD/HAY WA11 ....90 D7
Squires St EHL/KEN L7 ....113 J4
Squirrel Gn FMBY L37 ....46 F6
Stable Cl GR/UP/WCH CH49 ....125 L1
The Stables CSBY/BLUN L23 * 125 G2
The Stackfield WKBY CH48 ....125 G2
Stadium Rd PS/BROM CH62 ....144 D1
  WGNW/BIL/O WN5 ....68 A4
Stadium Wy WGNNW/ST WN6 ....68 A4
Staffin Av EP CH65 ....163 K5
Stafford Gdns EP CH65 ....20 D7
Stafford Cl HUY L36 ....116 C1
Stafford Moreton Wy
MGHL L31 * 72 E4
Stafford Rd ECCL WA10 ....8 A9
  STHP PR8 ....137 L3
  WARRS WA4 ....137 L3
Staffordshire Cl EV L5 ....97 G7
Stafford St SKEL WN8 ....64 D4
  VAUX/LVPD L3 ....13 K5
  WGNE/HIN WN2 ....69 L8
Stainburn Av NG/CROX L11 ....98 B2
Staincliffe Cl WGNE/HIN WN2 ....57 J7
Stainer Cl DV/KA/FCH L14 ....99 H7
  NEWLW WA12 ....91 K8
Staines Cl WARRS WA4 ....138 A8
Stainforth Cl GOL/RIS/CU WA3 ....107 K7
Stainton Cl HLWD L26 ....132 A5
  RNFD/HAY WA11 ....89 F4
Stairgate WGN WN1 ....4 F4
Stairhaven Rd ALL/GAR L19 ....130 C5
The Stakes MOR/LEA CH46 ....110 A2
Stalbridge Av CALD/MH L18 ....114 B8
Staley Av CSBY/BLUN L23 ....70 B3
Staley St BTL L20 ....83 L7
Stalisfield Av NG/CROX L11 ....98 C3
Stalisfield Gv NG/CROX L11 ....98 C3
Stalisfield Pl NG/CROX L11 ....98 C3
Stalmine Rd WLT/FAZ L9 ....97 H1
Stamfordham Dr ALL/GAR L19 ....130 E5
Stamfordham Gv ALL/GAR L19 ....130 F6
Stamfordham Pl ALL/GAR L19 ....130 E6
Stamford Rd STHP PR8 ....35 K2
Stamford St EHL/KEN L7 ....113 L3
  EP CH65 ....156 C3
Stanbury Av BEB CH63 ....143 L5
Stancliffe Av WGNE/HIN WN2 ....57 L7
Standale Rd WAV L15 ....114 B5
Standard Pl RF/TRAN CH42 ....128 C2
Standard Rd NG/CROX L11 ....98 E1
Standen Cl ECCL WA10 ....8 D4
Stand Farm Rd WD/CROXPK L12 ....99 G2
Standhouse La ORM L39 ....62 B3
Standish Av WGNW/BIL/O WN5 ....54 A8
Standish Dr RNFD/HAY WA11 ....76 C5
Standish Gallery WGN WN1 * 4 F3
Standishgate WGN WN1 ....4 F3
Standish St CHLY/EC PR7 ....9 L2
  ECCL WA10 ....9 L2
  VAUX/LVPD L3 ....13 G5
Standish Wood La
WGNNW/ST WN6 ....56 A6
Stand Park Av BEB CH63 ....143 L5
Stand Park Cl NTHTN L30 ....84 B3
Stand Park Rd CHLDW L16 ....114 F7
Stand Pkwy NTHTN L30 ....84 A3
Standring Gdn ECCL WA10 ....101 K5
Standedge Gv WGNS/IIMK WN3 ....79 K3
Stanfield Av EV L5 ....97 H8
Stanfield Dr BEB CH63 ....143 H2

Stanford Av WAL/NB CH45 ....95 K6
Stanford Crs WLTN L25 ....131 M5
Stangate WLTN L31 ....72 D3
Stanhope Dr HUY L36 ....115 G2
  PS/BROM CH62 ....143 M4
Stanhope St ECCL WA10 ....8 F1
  LEIGH WN7 ....81 M7
Stanier Wy EHL/KEN L7 ....113 L4
Staniforth PI CHLDW L16 ....114 H4
Stanlawe Rd EP CH65 ....20 D6
Stanley Av BEB CH63 ....127 L6
  RNFD/HAY WA11 ....76 A6
  STHP PR8 ....35 H3
  WAL/NB CH45 ....94 F7
  WARRS WA4 ....138 B3
  WARRW/BUR WA5 ....119 M6
Stanley Bank Rd
  RNFD/HAY WA11 ....90 C6
Stanley Bungalows PR/KW L34 * 99 L1
Stanley CI ANF/KKDL L4 ....96 F6
  WAL/EG CH44 ....112 A3
  WDN WA8 ....134 E3
Stanley Ct BIRK CH41 ....128 B2
  BRSC L40 ....39 G8
Stanley Crs PR/KW L34 ....100 E7
Stanley Dr LEIGH WN7 ....81 M5
Stanley Gdns WLT/FAZ L9 ....84 B8
Stanley Gv PS/BROM CH62 ....144 B8
  WGNE/HIN WN2 ....57 L6
Stanley Pk LITH L21 ....83 K4
Stanley Park Av North
  ANF/KKDL L4 ....97 K4
Stanley Park Av South
  ANF/KKDL L4 ....97 K5
Stanley PI CHLY/EC PR7 ....32 E5
  WARRS WA4 * 138 B3
  WGN WN1 ....5 J3
Stanley Prec BTL L20 ....7 H6
Stanley Rd BIRK CH41 ....111 H4
  BTL L20 ....7 G5
  CSBY/WL L22 ....83 G5
  EP CH65 ....156 E6
  FMBY L37 ....47 G7
  HOY CH47 ....108 C7
  HUY L36 ....116 A3
  LITH L21 ....83 K7
  MGHL L31 ....72 E7
  RF/TRAN CH42 ....128 C3
  SKEL WN8 ....66 C6
  WGNE/HIN WN2 ....57 L7
  WGNW/BIL/O WN5 ....80 C2
Stanley St ALL/GAR L19 ....145 L1
  CHTN/BK PR9 ....3 G5
  CLVP L2 ....7 F7
  EHL/KEN L7 ....114 A2
  NEWLW WA12 * 104 C2
  RUNC WA7 ....19 J2
  WAL/EG CH44 ....112 A3
  WARR WA1 ....14 D6
  WGNW/BIL/O WN5 ....68 B7
Stanley Vis RUNC WA7 * 18 F6
Stanley Wy SKEL WN8 ....65 G2
Stanlowe Vw ALL/GAR L19 ....130 B7
Stanmoor Dr WGNE/HIN WN2 ....57 L8
Stanmore Pk
  GR/UP/WCH CH49 ....125 K2
Stanmore Rd WAL/NB CH45 ....114 D7
Stannanought Rd SKEL WN8 ....65 M2
Stanner CI WARRW/BUR WA5 ....120 F3
Stanney CI PS/BROM CH62 ....155 G2
Stanney La EP CH65 ....20 B7
Stanney Mill La CHNE CH2 ....164 E6
Stanney Mill Rd EP CH65 ....164 B3
Stanney Woods Av EP CH65 ....163 L4
Stannyfield CI CSBY/BLUN L23 ....71 H7
Stanny Field Dr CSBY/BLUN L23 ....71 H7
Stansfield Rd MGHL L31 ....113 H4
  WARR WA1 ....122 B7
Stansfield Dr WARRS WA4 ....138 C6
Stanstead Av WGNS/IIMK WN3 ....68 C8
Stanstead CI WGNE/HIN WN2 ....69 H3
Stansted CHLY/EC PR7 ....32 C6
Stanton Av LITH L21 ....83 J4
Stanton CI NTHTN L30 ....71 M8
  RNFD/HAY WA11 ....90 E7
  WGNS/IIMK WN3 ....79 K2
Stanton Crs KKBY L32 ....85 L3
Stanton Rd BEB CH63 ....143 G2
  CALD/MH L18 * 114 B8
  WARRS WA4 ....138 F2
Stanwood CI ECCL WA10 ....101 H2
Stanwood Gdns RAIN/WH L35 ....117 G2
Stapehill CI CLB/OSW/ST L13 ....114 C8
Stapeley Gdns HLWD L26 ....132 C7
Staplands Rd DV/KA/FCH L14 ....114 F3
Stapleford Ct GTS/LS CH66 ....156 B5
Stapleford Rd WLTN L25 ....115 L7
Staplehurst CI WD/CROXPK L12 ....99 H2
  WGNE/HIN WN2 ....81 L3
Stapleton Av
  GR/UP/WCH CH49 ....125 M1
  RAIN/WH L35 ....117 L1
  SPK/HALE L24 ....146 F2
  WARRN/WOL WA2 ....121 M5
Stapleton CI WLTN L35 ....117 L1
  WLTN L25 ....115 K6
Stapleton Rd FMBY L37 ....58 F5
  RAIN/WH L35 ....101 K4
Stapleton Wy WGNE/HIN WN2 ....80 C3
Stapley CI RUNC WA7 ....19 G8
Starbeck Dr GTS/LS CH66 ....155 K7
Starkey Gv WARRS WA4 * 138 B1
Star La LYMM WA13 ....139 L1
Starling CI RUNC WA7 ....150 F6
Starling Gv WD/CROXPK L12 ....99 H4
Star St TOX L8 ....113 G7
Startham Av
  WGNW/BIL/O WN5 ....89 M2
Starworth Dr PS/BROM CH62 ....128 E6
Statham Av LYMM WA13 ....139 L2
Statham CI LYMM WA13 ....139 L2
Statham Dr LYMM WA13 ....139 M2
Statham La LYMM WA13 ....123 K8
Statham Rd CL/PREN CH43 ....110 C5
  SKEL WN8 ....64 F2
Statham Wy ORM L39 ....63 G1
Station Ap BRSC L40 ....39 G8
  HOY CH47 ....109 G5
  MOR/LEA CH46 ....110 A3
  ORM L39 ....51 H8
Station Av FROD/HEL WA6 ....166 D0
  GTS/LS CH66 ....155 H6
  WGNE/HIN WN2 ....80 F4
  WGNW/BIL/O WN5 ....66 F8
Station CI NSTN CH64 ....153 H6
Station Gn GTS/LS CH66 ....155 L6
Station Ms AIMK WN4 *
  KKBY L32 ....85 L2
Station Rd AIMK WN4 ....90 E2
  BEB CH63 ....127 J8
  BIRK CH41 ....111 H4
  BRSC L40 ....39 M1
  CHLY/EC PR7 ....43 G3
  CHLY/EC PR7 ....44 B7
  CHNE CH2 ....158 C8

CHTN/BK PR9 ....23 H8
CROS/BRETH PR26 ....29 K2
EP CH65 ....20 D3
GTS/LS CH66 ....155 L7
HES CH60 ....141 H7
HOY CH47 ....108 D7
HUY L36 ....115 L3
MGHL L31 ....61 J7
MGHL L31 ....73 G5
MGHL L31 ....85 J3
NSTN CH64 ....152 E5
ORM L39 ....49 H5
ORM L39 ....51 H7
PEN/TH CH61 ....127 G8
PR/KW L34 ....100 F7
RAIN/WH L35 ....117 L2
RNFD/HAY WA11 ....90 E7
RUNC WA7 ....18 F3
RUNC WA7 ....161 K1
SKEL WN8 ....53 L3
STHEL WA9 ....104 E8
STHP PR8 ....34 E8
WAL/EG CH44 ....111 J1
WARRS WA4 ....138 A3
WARRW/BUR WA5 ....120 E3
WARRW/BUR WA5 ....135 M2
WGN WN1 4
WLTN L25 ....115 K8
Station Rd North
  WARRN/WOL WA2 ....122 C3
Station Rd South
  WARRN/WOL WA2 ....122 C4
Station Rd RAIN/WH L35 * 117 L2
Station Yd WARRN/WOL WA2 * 122 L5
Statton Rd CLB/OSW/ST L13 ....114 D4
Staveley Av BRSC L40 ....52 A1
Staveley Rd ALL/GAR L19 ....130 D5
  SKEL WN8 ....65 G2
  STHP PR8 ....47 M1
Stavert CI LITH L21 ....98 D2
Staverton Rd KKBY L32 ....85 L4
Stavordale Rd MOR/LEA CH46 ....110 F7
Steble St TOX L8 ....113 H8
Stechford Av WAL/NB CH45 ....95 L4
Steel Ct EV L5 ....96 E8
Steeley La CHLYE PR6 ....32 F6
Steel St WARR WA1 ....15 K1
Steeplechase CI WLT/FAZ L9 ....84 E5
Steeple CI NSTN CH64 ....153 G6
The Steeple WKBY CH48 ....124 F7
Steers Cft STBRV L28 ....99 H5
Stein Av GOL/RIS/CU WA3 ....93 G5
Steinberg Ct VAUX/LVPD L3 ....12 E1
Stela Prec LITH L21 * 83 J7
Stenhills Crs RUNC WA7 ....19 L5
Stephens La CLVP L2 * 12 L4
Stephenson Ct EHL/KEN L7 * 113 L4
Stephenson Rd
  CLB/OSW/ST L13 * 114 C3
  NEWLW WA12 ....104 E3
Stephenson St WGNE/HIN WN2 ....80 D5
Stephenson Wy FMBY L37 ....59 L2
  WAV L15 ....114 A4
Stephens Ter GTS/LS CH66 ....155 K7
Stephen St WAV L15 ....15 K3
  WGNE/HIN WN2 ....80 C3
Stephen Wy RAIN/WH L35 * 101 K8
Stepney Gv ANF/KKDL L4 ....97 J4
Sterling Wy EV L5 ....96 F7
Sterndale Av WGNS/IIMK WN3 ....56 A3
Sterndale CI EHL/KEN L7 ....113 K5
Sterrix Av LITH L21 ....83 L3
Sterrix Gn LITH L21 ....83 L3
Sterrix La LITH L21 ....83 L3
Steve Biko CI TOX L8 ....113 K6
Stevenage CI STHEL WA9 ....102 B6
Steven Dr BEB CH63 ....143 H2
Stevenson Crs WGNS/IIMK WN3 ....68 C8
Stevenson Dr BEB CH63 ....143 H2
Stevenson St WAV L15 ....114 B5
Stevens Rd HES CH60 ....141 L6
Stevens St STHEL WA9 ....101 M5
Steventon RUNC WA7 ....151 G1
Steward CI RAIN/WH L35 ....101 H8
Steward's Av WDN WA8 ....16 A3
Stewart Ar BTL L20 ....7 L3
Stewart CI PEN/TH CH61 ....141 H2
Stewart Rd WGNS/IIMK WN3 ....79 J2
Stewerton CI GOL/RIS/CU WA3 ....92 B3
Stile Hey CSBY/BLUN L23 ....71 K8
Stiles Rd NWD/KWIPK L33 ....74 H7
The Stiles ORM L39 ....51 G8
Stillington Rd TOX L8 ....129 J1
Stiperstones CI GTS/LS CH66 ....155 H7
Stirling Av CSBY/BLUN L23 ....83 G2
Stirling CI CHLYE PR6 *
  WARR WA1 ....123 G6
Stirling Crs STHEL WA9 ....102 D7
Stirling Dr AIMK WN4 ....90 F1
Stirling Rd SPK/HALE L24 ....146 D2
  WGNE/HIN WN2 ....81 H1
Stirling St WAL/EG CH44 ....111 K3
  WGN WN1 ....68 D3
Stirrup CI WARRN/WOL WA2 ....122 C2
Stockbridge La HUY L36 ....99 L8
Stockbridge PI EV L5 ....97 H2
Stockbridge St EV L5 ....97 J3
Stockdale CI VAUX/LVPD L3 * 12 F4
Stockham La RUNC WA7 ....150 C5
Stockham La RUNC WA7 ....150 D6
Stockley Crs ORM L39 ....64 A7
Stockmoor Rd NG/CROX L11 ....98 B2
Stockpit Rd NWD/KWIPK L33 ....66 H6
Stockport Rd WARRS WA4 ....138 F2
Stocks Av STHEL WA9 ....103 G2
Stocks La CHLY/EC PR7 ....42 A7
Stockswell Rd RAIN/WH L35 ....133 H1
Stockton Gv STHEL WA9 ....101 M7
Stockton La WARRS WA4 ....138 A4
Stockton Wood Rd
  SPK/HALE L24 ....146 E2
Stockville Rd CALD/MH L18 ....131 G1
Stockwell CI WGNS/IIMK WN3
Stoddart Rd ANF/KKDL L4 ....97 J3
Stoke Ct PS/BROM CH62 ....155 G2
Stoke Gdns EP CH65 ....20 D7
Stoker Wy WLT/FAZ L9 ....84 C8
Stokesay CL/PREN CH43 ....110 F7
Stokesay Ct EP CH65 ....21 L8
Stokesley Av WGNE/HIN WN2
Stokes St BIRK CH41 *
Stoke Wk EP CH65 ....20 D6
Stonebarn Dr NSTN CH64 ....153 J7
Stone Barn La MGHL L31 ....72 B7
Stonebridge La AIN/FAZ L10 ....85 J7
Stonebridge Dr WAL/NB CH45 ....95 J6
Stonechat CI GOL/RIS/CU WA3 ....93 G5
  NTHLY L27 ....132 A3
  RUNC WA7 ....150 A4
Stonecroop CALD/MH L18 ....115 G8

Stonecrop WGNNW/ST WN6 ....54 F4
Stonecrop CI GOL/RIS/CU WA3 ....122 E1
  RUNC WA7 ....161 K1
Stonecross Dr RAIN/WH L35 ....117 M4
Stone Cross La North
  GOL/RIS/CU WA3 ....92 E4
Stone Cross La South
  GOL/RIS/CU WA3 ....92 E7
Stonedale Crs NG/CROX L11 ....98 D1
Stonedale Pk NG/CROX L11 * 98 C1
Stonefield Rd DV/KA/FCH L14 ....115 H1
Stonegate Dr TOX L8 ....129 H1
Stone Hvn WGNS/IIMK WN3 ....78 E3
Stonehaven CI CHLDW L16 ....115 H5
Stonehaven Dr
  WARRN/WOL WA2 ....122 C2
Stone Hay RAIN/WH L35 ....116 F4
Stonehey Dr WKBY CH48 ....124 E4
Stonehey Rd KKBY L32 ....86 A5
Stonehill Av ANF/KKDL L4 ....97 K7
Stonehills Ct RUNC WA7 ....19 M4
Stonehouse Ms CALD/MH L18 ....130 F2
Stonehouse Rd WAL/EG CH44 ....95 G8
Stonelea RUNC WA7 ....150 D3
Stoneleigh CI STHP PR8 ....47 L1
Stoneleigh Gdns WARRS WA4 ....138 F4
Stoneleigh Gv RF/TRAN CH42 ....128 B5
Stone Pit CI GOL/RIS/CU WA3 ....93 G4
Stone Pit La GOL/RIS/CU WA3 ....106 B3
Stoneridge Ct CL/PREN CH43 * 110 C5
Stone Sq BTL L20 ....84 A8
Stone St VAUX/LVPD L3 ....97 J7
Stoneville Rd CLB/OSW/ST L13 ....114 C1
Stoney Brow SKEL WN8 ....66 D3
Stoneycroft WD/CROXPK L12 ....114 D1
  HOR/BR BL6 ....45 M8
Stoneycroft Crs
  CLB/OSW/ST L13 ....98 C8
Stoneygate La WGNNW/ST WN6 ....54 D3
Stoney Hey Rd WAL/NB CH45 ....95 H6
Stoney Holt RUNC WA7 ....150 E5
Stoneyhurst Av AIN/FAZ L10 ....84 E2
Stoney La CHLY/EC PR7 ....57 G1
  RAIN/WH L35 ....117 H1
  SKEL WN8 ....53 L1
Stonham CI GR/UP/WCH CH49 ....110 A3
Stonor Rd CHLY/EC PR7 ....43 L1
Stonyfield NTHTN L30 ....72 A8
Stonyhurst Av WGNS/IIMK WN3 ....5 H8
Stonyhurst CI RNFD/HAY WA11 ....89 K6
Stonyhurst Crs GOL/RIS/CU WA3 ....93 M8
Stonyhurst Rd WLTN L25 ....131 K4
Stony La WGNNW/ST WN6 ....54 A1
Stopford St TOX L8 ....129 H1
  WGNE/HIN WN2
Stopforth St WGNNW/ST WN6 ....4 A2
Stopgate La NWD/KWIPK L33 ....74 F7
  WLT/FAZ L9 ....97 M2
Store St BTL L20 ....7 K8
Storeton CI CL/PREN CH43 ....127 J2
Storeton La PEN/TH CH61 ....141 L1
Storeton Rd RF/TRAN CH42 ....127 K3
Stormont Rd ALL/GAR L19 ....130 D2
Storrington Av NG/CROX L11 ....98 D2
Storrington Heys NG/CROX L11 * 98 D2
Storrsdale Rd CALD/MH L18 ....130 D3
Stour Av RAIN/WH L35 ....117 L2
Stourcliffe Rd WAL/EG CH44 94
Stour Ct EP CH65 ....20 B1
Stourport CI
  GR/UP/WCH CH49 * 125 L1
Stourton St RKBY L32 ....86 A5
  STHP PR8 ....47 L1
Stourvale Rd HLWD L26 * 132 B6
Stout St LEIGH WN7 ....81 L8
Stowe Av AIN/FAZ L10 ....85 G3
Stowe CI WLTN L25 ....131 K6
Stowell St EHL/KEN L7 ....13 L9
Stowford CI NG/CROX L11 ....98 E3
Strada Wy VAUX/LVPD L3 ....13 L4
Stradbroke CI GOL/RIS/CU WA3 ....93 L3
Strafford Dr BTL L20 7
Straight Length
  FROD/HEL WA6 ....160 A6
Straight Up La CHTN/BK PR9 ....25 L5
Straker Av EP CH65 ....156 B7
Strand Av AIMK WN4 ....91 K1
Strand Rd BTL L20 ....6 E4
  HOY CH47 ....108 D6
Strand St CLVPS L1 ....12 E8
The Strand AIMK WN4 91
  CLVP L2 ....12 D7
Strange Rd AIMK WN4 91
Strange St LEIGH WN7 ....93 K1
Stranraer Rd WGNW/BIL/O WN5 ....67 L4
Stratford CI STHP PR8 ....34 C7
Stratford Rd ALL/GAR L19 ....130 B5
  CHLYE PR6 ....32 F5
  NSTN CH64 ....152 F7
Stratford WGNNW/ST WN6 ....4 A1
Strathallan CI HES CH60 ....141 G3
Strathcona Rd WAL/NB CH45 ....95 K7
  WAV L15 ....114 A6
Strathearn Rd HES CH60 ....141 H7
Strathlorne CI RF/TRAN CH42 ....128 B3
Strathmore Av AIMK WN4
Strathmore CI CSBY/BLUN L23 ....83 G2
Strathmore Gv CHLY/EC PR7
  STHEL WA9 ....102 E7
Strathmore Rd NPK/KEN L6 ....113 L1
Stratton CI RUNC WA7 ....150 B8
  WAL/NB CH45 ....95 L7
  WLTN L25 ....131 G3
Stratton Dr WGNE/HIN WN2 ....80 B4
Stratton Pk WDN WA8
Stratton Rd KKBY L32 ....85 L4
  WARRW/BUR WA5 ....120 D8
Strauss CI TOX L8 ....113 K7
Strawberry CI GOL/RIS/CU WA3 ....122 E1
Strawberry Cross
  CH/BCN CH1 * 163 J5
Strawberry Dr EP CH65 ....163 J5
Strawberry La CH/BCN CH1 ....162 E8
Strawberry Rd NG/CROX L11 ....98 A3
Streatham Av CALD/MH L18 ....114 B8
Street Hey La NSTN CH64 ....154 D3
Stretford St NWD/KWIPK L33 ....74 A8
Stretton Av GOL/RIS/CU WA3 * 92 D7
  STHEL WA9 ....103 H2
  WAL/EG CH44 ....111 J1
  WGNW/BIL/O WN5
Stretton CI CL/PREN CH43 ....127 G2
  PS/BROM CH62 ....155 G2
  WD/CROXPK L12 ....99 J2
Stretton Dr CHTN/BK PR9 ....25 H5
Stretton Wy RAIN/WH L35 ....116 F4
Strickland St WARRS WA4 ....138 C6
Strines CI WGNE/HIN WN2 ....69 M7
The Strine BRSC L40
Stringer CI WARRS WA4 ....15 M7
Stringhey Rd WAL/EG CH44 ....95 L8

Stroma Av EP CH65 ....163 K5
Stroma Rd CALD/MH L18 ....130 D4
Stromness CI WARRN/WOL WA2 ....122 C2
Stroud CI GR/UP/WCH CH49 ....125 L2
  WGNE/HIN WN2 ....69 H3
Stuart Av MOR/LEA CH46 ....110 B4
  WLTN L25 ....131 L6
Stuart CI MOR/LEA CH46 ....110 C5
Stuart Crs WGNW/BIL/O WN5 ....77 M8
Stuart Dr DV/KA/FCH L14 ....115 G2
  WARR WA1 ....138 B3
Stuart Gv BTL L20 ....7 K8
Stuart Rd ANF/KKDL L4
  CSBY/WL L22
  ECCL WA10 ....88 E7
  MGHL L31 ....85 K2
  RF/TRAN CH42 ....127 M2
  RUNC WA7 ....150 D1
Stuart Rd North BTL L20 ....7 M4
Stubbs La CL/PREN CH43 ....127 G2
Stub La BRSC L40 ....51 J3
Studfold CHLY/EC PR7 ....32 D3
Studholme St EV L5 ....96 E6
Studland Rd WLT/FAZ L9 ....98 A1
Studley Rd WAL/NB CH45 ....95 G7
Stump La CHLYE PR6 ....32 F5
Sturdee Rd CLB/OSW/ST L13 ....114 D4
Sturgess CI ORM L39 ....51 H6
Sturgess St NEWLW WA12 ....104 B2
Sturton Av WGNS/IIMK WN3 ....79 G2
Suburban Rd NPK/KEN L6 ....97 L7
Sudbrook CI GOL/RIS/CU WA3 * 93 G5
Sudbury CI WGNS/IIMK WN3 ....79 K3
  MGHL L31 ....85 M3
Sudbury Rd CSBY/WL L22 ....82 E3
Sudbury Wy SPK/HALE L24 ....146 D1
Sudell Av MGHL L31 ....73 H3
Sudell La MGHL L31 ....61 M7
Sudley Gra AIG/SPK L17 ....130 A4
Sudworth Rd WAL/NB CH45 ....95 J6
Suez St NEWLW WA12 ....104 C2
  WARR WA1 ....14 D6
Suffield CI ANF/KKDL L4 ....96 F5
Suffolk Av EP CH65 ....156 B8
Suffolk CI WARR WA1 ....122 F7
  WGN WN1 ....56 D5
Suffolk Gv LEIGH WN7
Suffolk PI WDN WA8 ....133 L6
Suffolk Rd STHP PR8 ....35 J5
Suffolk St BTL L20 ....7 J2
  CLVPS L1 ....13 H9
  RUNC WA7 ....18 E2
Suffton Pk KKBY L32 ....85 L4
Sugar La FROD/HEL WA6 ....167 G8
  PR/KW L34 ....99 M2
Sugar Stubbs La CHTN/BK PR9 ....26 E1
Sugnall St EHL/KEN L7 ....13 L9
Sulby Av CLB/OSW/ST L13 ....98 B8
  WARRS WA4 ....137 K2
Sulby CI STHP PR8 ....35 H2
Sulgrave CI CHLDW L16 ....114 E4
Sullington Dr NTHLY L27 116
Sullivan Av GR/UP/WCH CH49 ....126 B1
Sullivan's Wy STHEL WA9 ....102 B5
Sullivan Wy WGN WN1 ....5 J4
Sumley CI RNFD/HAY WA11 ....9 M1
Summerdale PS/BROM CH62 ....143 M3
Summerfield Av ECCL WA10 ....101 H2
  WARRW/BUR WA5 ....121 H3
Summerfields CHLY/EC PR7 ....43 H6
Summerford CI RF/TRAN CH42 ....128 A2
Summerhill Dr MGHL L31 ....73 H6
Summer La RUNC WA7 ....150 D4
  WARRS WA4 ....151 K7
Summers Av BTL L20 ....7 L4
Summer Seat BTL L20 ....7 H5
  VAUX/LVPD L3 ....12 F2
Summers Rd VAUX/LVPD L3 ....112 F8
Summer St SKEL WN8 ....65 H1
Summertrees Av
  GR/UP/WCH CH49 ....125 M1
Summertrees CI
  GR/UP/WCH CH49 ....125 M1
Summertrees Rd GTS/LS CH66 ....163 G3
Summerville Gdns WARRS WA4 ....138 B4
Summer Wy WLTN L25 ....131 H2
Summerwood PEN/TH CH61 ....125 M6
Summerwood La ORM L39 ....49 L4
The Summit WAL/EG CH44 ....95 L8
Summit Wy WLTN L25 ....131 H2
Sumner Av ORM L39 ....61 H1
Sumner CI EV L5 ....96 E8
  RAIN/WH L35 ....117 M2
Sumner Gv NWD/KWIPK L33 ....74 B8
Sumner Rd CL/PREN CH43 ....111 H5
  FMBY L37 ....59 H2
Sumner's La CROS/BRETH PR26 ....29 J6
Sumner St RNFD/HAY WA11 ....90 C7
  WGNE/HIN WN2 ....57 M7
Sunbeam Rd CLB/OSW/ST L13 ....114 C2
Sunbeam St NEWLW WA12 ....104 B2
Sunbourne Rd AIG/SPK L17 ....129 K3
Sunbury Dr STHP PR8 ....47 K1
Sunbury Gdns WARRS WA4 ....138 A6
Sunbury Rd ANF/KKDL L4 ....97 H1
  WAL/EG CH44 ....111 J2
Suncroft CI WARR WA1 ....123 G4
Suncroft Rd HES CH60 ....141 L6
Sundale Av RAIN/WH L35 ....101 J3
Sunderland PI
  WGNW/BIL/O WN5 ....67 M4
Sundew CI BTL L20 ....84 B6
Sundridge St TOX L8 ....129 J1
Sunfield CI GTS/LS CH66 ....156 C2
Sunfield Rd MOR/LEA CH46 ....110 B3
Sunflower CI STHEL WA9 ....103 J6
Sunlight St NPK/KEN L6 ....97 L8
Sunloch CI WLT/FAZ L9 ....84 F5
Sunningdale Av WDN WA8 ....133 K4
Sunningdale CI HUY L36 ....115 L4
  WARRW/BUR WA5 ....104 B7
Sunningdale Dr BEB CH63 ....143 K7
  CSBY/BLUN L23 ....70 E7
  PEN/TH CH61 ....126 C8
Sunningdale Gdns FMBY L37 ....59 G2
Sunningdale Rd WAL/NB CH45 ....95 J6
  WAV L15 ....114 B5
Sunny Bank BEB CH63 ....127 M7
  GR/UP/WCH CH49 ....110 B7
Sunnybank Av CL/PREN CH43 ....126 F1
Sunny Bank Rd CHLDW L16 ....114 F6
Sunnybank Cl NEWLW WA12 ....104 E1
Sunny Brow CHLY/EC PR7 ....43 J3
Sunnydale RAIN/WH L35 ....117 M2
Sunny Dr WGNW/BIL/O WN5 ....67 M7
Sunnyfields ORM L39 ....78 E3
Sunnygate Rd ALL/GAR L19 * 130 C5
Sunnymede Dr MGHL L31 ....72 H2
Sunny Rd CHTN/BK PR9 ....25 J3
Sunnyside EP CH65 ....20 D2
  ORM L39 ....62 A6
  STHP PR8 ....35 H2
  TOX L8 ....113 J8
  WARRW/BUR WA5 ....120 A2
Sunnyside La RUNC WA7 ....151 L1
Sunnyside Rd AIMK WN4 ....79 H7

CSBY/WL L22 ....82 E2
Sunsdale Rd CALD/MH L18 * 114 C8
Sunset CI NWD/KWIPK L33 ....74 C8
Superior CI NTHLY L27 ....116 A8
Surby CI CHLDW L16 ....115 G5
Surrey Av GR/UP/WCH CH49 ....110 A8
Surrey Dr WKBY CH48
Surrey St BTL L20 ....7 J1
  CLVPS L1 ....112 F5
  RUNC WA7 ....19 G4
  WAL/EG CH44 ....111 J2
  WARRS WA4 ....15 J9
Susan Dr WARRW/BUR WA5 ....119 M8
Susan Gv MOR/LEA CH46 ....109 M5
Susan St WDN WA8 ....134 E3
Sussex CI BTL L20 ....7 J1
  PEN/TH CH61 ....141 G1
Sussex Gv STHEL WA9 ....9 M7
Sussex Rd CHTN/BK PR9 ....5 K4
  MGHL L31 ....72 F6
  STHP PR8 ....35 J5
  WKBY CH48 ....124 E2
Sussex St BTL L20 ....7 K3
  CSBY/WL L22 * 82 E3
  WDN WA8 ....18 A1
Sutch La BRSC L40 ....52 D1
Sutcliffe St CHLY/EC PR7 ....32 F6
  NPK/KEN L6 ....113 K2
Sutherland Ct RUNC WA7 ....19 J3
Sutherland Dr PS/BROM CH62 ....155 F1
Sutherland Rd PR/KW L34 ....101 G3
  WGNS/IIMK WN3
Sutherland St WGNE/HIN WN2 ....69 L8
  WGNW/BIL/O WN5 ....68 B7
Sutton Av GOL/RIS/CU WA3 ....107 G3
  NSTN CH64 ....152 G7
Sutton Cswy FROD/HEL WA6 ....161 G3
Sutton CI PS/BROM CH62 ....155 G2
Sutton Gv CHLYE PR6 ....33 H1
Sutton Hall Dr GTS/LS CH66 ....155 J7
Sutton Hall Gdns GTS/LS CH66 ....155 J7
Sutton Heath Rd STHEL WA9 ....102 A7
Sutton La CHLYE PR6 ....44 D5
Sutton Moss Rd STHEL WA9 ....103 H5
Sutton Oak Dr STHEL WA9 ....102 E4
Sutton Park Dr STHEL WA9 ....102 E6
Sutton Rd FMBY L37 ....59 G4
  STHEL WA9 ....9 M9
  WAL/NB CH45 ....95 K6
Sutton's La FMBY L37 ....60 A2
  WDN WA8 ....16 E6
Sutton St CLB/OSW/ST L13 ....98 A8
  RUNC WA7 ....19 K4
Sutton Wy EP CH65 ....156 C8
  GTS/LS CH66 ....155 G1
Sutton Wood Rd SPK/HALE L24 ....146 C3
Swainson Rd AIN/FAZ L10 ....85 G6
Swale Av WARRN/WOL WA1 ....117 M2
Swaledale Av RAIN/WH L35 ....117 M2
Swaledale CI PS/BROM CH62 ....144 A8
  WARRW/BUR WA5 ....120 B6
Swalegate MGHL L31 ....73 G6
Swale Rd EP CH65 ....156 C6
Swallow CI GOL/RIS/CU WA3 * 93 G5
  NTHLY L27 ....116 B8
  NWD/KWIPK L33 ....74 A6
  WD/CROXPK L12 ....99 H2
Swallow Ct ECCL WA10
Swallowfield Gdns WARRS WA4 ....138 B1
Swallow Flds WLT/FAZ L9 ....98 B1
Swallowhurst Crs NG/CROX L11 ....98 E3
Swanage CI WARRS WA4 ....138 A3
Swan Av STHEL WA9 ....103 J3
Swan CI GTS/LS CH66 ....162 E3
Swan Crs WAV L15 ....114 D5
Swan Delph ORM L39 ....62 A3
Swan Hey MGHL L31 ....73 G6
Swan La ORM L39 ....81 K1
Swan Meadow Rd
  WGNS/IIMK WN3 ....4 C6
Swann St WGNS/IIMK WN3 ....4 E3
Swanpool La ORM L39 ....62 E3
Swan Rd NEWLW WA12 ....104 A1
Swanside Av DV/KA/FCH L14 ....115 G2
Swanside Rd DV/KA/FCH L14 ....115 G2
Swanston Av ANF/KKDL L4 ....97 J4
Swan St CLB/OSW/ST L13 ....114 C1
Swan Wk MGHL L31 ....73 G6
Sweden Gv CSBY/WL L22 * 82 F4
Sweet Briar Ct STHEL WA9 ....118 F2
Sweet Briar Dr STHEL WA9 ....118 F2
Sweetfield Gdns GTS/LS CH66 ....155 M6
Sweetfield Rd GTS/LS CH66 ....155 M6
Sweeting St CLVP L2 ....12 E7
Swift CI WARRN/WOL WA2 ....122 A2
Swift Gv WD/CROXPK L12 ....99 H1
Swift's CI NTHTN L30 ....83 M1
Swift's La NTHTN L30 ....83 M1
Swift St ECCL WA10
  WGNW/BIL/O WN5 ....4 A6
Swinbrook Gn NG/CROX L11 ....98 B8
Swinburne CI CHLDW L16 ....115 H5
Swinburne Rd ECCL WA10 ....8 A2
Swinburn Gv WGNW/BIL/O WN5 ....77 M4
Swindale Av WARRN/WOL WA2 ....121 M2
Swindale CI TOX L8 ....113 K6
Swinden CI RUNC WA7 * 150 F6
Swinderby Dr KKBY L32 ....85 K2
Swindon CI EV L5 ....96 F6
  GR/UP/WCH CH49 ....125 L1
Swindon St EV L5 ....96 F6
Swinford Av WDN WA8 ....135 G3
Swinley La WGN WN1 ....68 E3
Swinley St WGN WN1 ....68 E3
Swinside WGN WN1 ....5 M2
Swireford Rd FROD/HEL WA6 ....166 D3
Swisspine Gdns STHEL WA9 ....101 L6
Swiss Rd NPK/KEN L6 ....113 L2
Swords Cross CI CHLY/EC PR7 ....32 G8
Sword Wk NG/CROX L11 ....98 E2
Swynnerton Wy WDN WA8 ....118 D8
Sybil Rd ANF/KKDL L4 ....97 J3
Sycamore Av CHLY/EC PR7 ....31 M2
  CSBY/BLUN L23 ....71 H7
  GOL/RIS/CU WA3 ....109 M7
  HLWD L26 ....132 A7
  NEWLW WA12 ....104 E2
  RNFD/HAY WA11 ....90 C8
  WDN WA8 ....134 D3
  WGNE/HIN WN2 ....81 H7
  WGNNW/ST WN6 ....78 D3
Sycamore Gdns ECCL WA10 ....89 G7
Sycamore Gv FMBY L37 ....58 E4
Sycamore La WARRW/BUR WA5 ....120 D8

Sycamore Pk CALD/MH L18........130 F3
Sycamore Ri GR/UP/WCH CH49 ..125 L3
Sycamore St CHLYE PR6 ....32 F5
 CSBY/WL L22 ....83 G3
 HUY L36 ....116 A5
 RF/TRAN CH42 ....11 H5
 RUNC WA7 ....19 M7
Syd Brook La BRSC L40 ....30 A7
Sydenham Av WLT/FAZ L9 ....113 L8
Syderstone CI WGNE/HIN WN2 ...81 C3
Sydney Av LEIGH WN7 ....93 M3
Sydney St RUNC WA7 ....148 F6
 WGNE/HIN WN2 ....80 C2
 WLT/FAZ L9 ....84 C7
Syers Ct WARR WA1 ....15 L1
Sykes Crs WGNS/IIMK WN3 ....78 E4
Sylvan Ct WLTN L25 ....131 J4
Sylvandale Gv PS/BROM CH62 ...143 M5
Sylvania Rd ANF/KKDL L4 ....97 J5
Sylvia CI NG/CROX L11 ....85 K7
Sylvia Crs WARRN/WOL WA2 .....121 M4
Synge St WARRN/WOL WA2 ....15 C1
Syren St BTL L20 ....96 E5
Sresham St WGNE/HIN WN2 ....80 D3
Syston Av RNFD/HAY WA11 ....89 L7
Sytch Cft NSTN CH64 ....153 C5

T

Tabby Nook KIRK/FR/WA PR4 .....27 H4
Tabby's Nook SKEL WN8 ....53 J5
Taberner CI WGNNW/ST WN6 .....56 B4
Taberner St WGNE/HIN WN2 ......80 D3
Tabley Av WDN WA8 ....133 M3
Tabley CI CL/PREN CH43 ....127 H2
Tabley Gdns STHEL WA9 ....101 M7
Tabley Rd WAV L15 ....113 M6
Tabley St CLVPS L1 ....112 F5
Tace CI TOX L8 ....113 H6
Tadgers La FROD/HEL WA6 ....159 M4
Tadlow CI FMBY L37 ....58 E4
Taggart Av CHLDW L16 ....114 F7
Tagus CI TOX L8 ....113 K7
Tagus St TOX L8 ....113 K7
Tailor's La MGHL L31 ....73 J7
 KIRK/FR/WA PR4 ....27 M2
Talaton CI CHTN/BK PR9 ....22 C8
Talbot Av BEB CH63 ....142 C4
 NSTN CH64 ....153 H7
Talbot CI ECCL WA10 ....8 E4
 GOL/RIS/CU WA3 ....123 C2
 NSTN CH64 ....153 H7
 HUY L36 ....10 B9
Talbot Ct CL/PREN CH43 ....115 M4
 STHP PR8 ....5 H5
Talbot Gdns NSTN CH64 ....153 H7
Talbot Rd CL/PREN CH43 ....127 J1
 FROD/HEL WA6 ....166 A6
 GTS/LS CH66 ....163 H2
Talbot Rw CHLYE PR7 * 31 M4
Talbot St AIMK WN4 * 91 M1
 CHLYE PR6 * 33 C4
 LITH L21 ....92 C5
 STHP PR8 ....2 F6
Tallbottville Rd CLB/OSW/ST L13 ..114 E4
Talgarth Wy WLTN L25 ....115 J6
Taliesin St EV L5 ....96 E3
Talisman CI RUNC WA7 ....150 F6
Talisman Wy BTL L20 ....6 D2
Talland CI HLWD L26 ....132 A4
Tallarn Rd KKBY L32 ....85 K3
Talman Gv AIMK WN4 ....91 M2
Talton CI WAV L15 ....113 M6
Tamar CI NPK/KEN L6 ....113 J1
Tamar Gv MOR/LEA CH46 ....109 M6
Tamarisk Gdns STHEL WA9 ....101 L6
Tamar Rd RNFD/HAY WA11 ....90 E7
Tamer Gv LEIGH WN7 ....81 C5
Tamerton CI WLTN L25 ....131 C3
The Tamneys SKEL WN8 ....65 H4
Tamworth Av WGNE/HIN WN2 ....69 H3
Tamworth St ECCL WA10 ....8 C4
 TOX L8 ....113 C8
Tanar CI PS/BROM CH62 ....143 K2
Tan Dr CALD/MH L18 ....130 D1
Tancred Rd ANF/KKDL L4 ....97 J6
 WAL/NB CH45 ....53 L3
Tanfield Nook SKEL WN8 ....53 J3
Tanfields SKEL WN8 ....65 H4
Tan House CI SKEL WN8 ....53 L2
Tan House Dr WGNS/IIMK WN3 ...78 E4
Tan House La SKEL WN8 ....53 L3
 WARRW/BUR WA5 ....120 C1
 WDN WA8 ....17 H4
 WGNS/IIMK WN3 ....78 E3
Tanhouse Rd CSBY/BLUN L23 .....71 K8
 SKEL WN8 ....65 M4
Tankersley Gv
 WARRW/BUR WA5 ....120 C8
Tanner's La GOL/RIS/CU WA3 .....92 D5
 WARRN/WOL WA2 ....14 D4
Tannersmith La CHLY/EC PR7 .....30 B8
Tannery La NSTN CH64 ....153 C5
 WARRW/BUR WA5 ....135 J2
Tanning Ct WARR WA1 ....14 F6
Tansley Av CHLY/EC PR7 ....42 F5
Tansley CI WKBY CH48 ....125 C3
Tansley Sq WGNW/BIL/O WN5 ....67 M8
Tanworth Gv WARRW/BUR CH46 ..109 K4
Tanyard CI CHLY/EC PR7 ....42 F5
Taplev PI CLB/OSW/ST L13 ....114 B3
Taplow CI WARRS WA4 ....138 A4
Taplow St NPK/KEN L6 ....97 K5
Tarbock Rd HUY L36 ....115 M4
 SPK/HALE L24 ....146 F1
Tarbot Hey MOR/LEA CH46 ....109 K4
Target Rd HES CH60 ....140 D5
Tariff St EV L5 ....96 F8
Tarleswood SKEL WN8 ....65 H6
Tarleton CI HLWD L26 ....132 A5
Tarleton Rd CHTN/BK PR9 ....25 J5
Tarleton St CLVPS L1 ....13 C7
Tarlscough La BRSC L40 ....38 E4
Tarlton CI RAIN/WH L35 ....101 J8
Tarnbeck RUNC WA7 ....150 A6
Tarnbeck Dr BRSC L40 ....40 E3
Tarnbrook Gv WGNE/HIN WN2 ....57 H8
Tarn Brow ORM L39 ....62 E2
Tarn CI AIMK WN4 ....79 K8
Tarn Ct WARR WA1 ....123 J4
Tarn Gv RNFD/HAY WA11 ....89 K5
Tarn Hows CI CHLY/EC PR7 * 32 D8
Tarnrigg CI WGNS/IIMK WN3 ......79 C2
Tarn Rd FMBY L37 ....58 F2
Tarnside Rd WGNW/BIL/O WN5 ...67 J1
Tarnway GOL/RIS/CU WA3 ....93 H6
Tarporley CI CL/PREN CH43 ....127 H1
Tarporley Rd GTS/LS CH66 ....163 C1
Tarran Dr MOR/LEA CH46 ....109 M3
Tarran Rd MOR/LEA CH46 ....109 M3
Tarran Wy East MOR/LEA CH46 ..109 M3
Tarran Wy North
 MOR/LEA CH46 ....109 M3

Tarran Wy South
 MOR/LEA CH46 ....109 M3
Tarran Wy West MOR/LEA CH46 ..109 M3
Tarvin CI CHTN/BK PR9 ....22 F1
 EP CH65 ....20 D7
 GOL/RIS/CU WA3 ....93 G6
 RUNC WA7 ....149 L2
 STHEL WA9 ....118 D1
Tarvin Rd FROD/HEL WA6 ....166 F3
 PS/BROM CH62 ....155 H1
Tasker Ter WARRW/BUR WA5 .....117 L1
Tasman Gv WARRW/BUR WA5 ....120 E5
Tasman Dr WARRW/BUR WA5 ....102 A6
Tate CI WDN WA8 * 133 M3
Tate St ANF/KKDL L4 ....97 H5
Tatham Gv WGNS/IIMK WN3 ......78 H4
Tatlock CI WGNW/BIL/O WN5 .....78 A8
Tatlock St EV L5 ....12 F1
Tattersall Rd LITH L21 ....83 J6
Tattersall Wy EHL/KEN L7 ....114 A3
Tatton Ct WARR WA1 * 122 F5
Tatton Dr AIMK WN4 ....91 H1
Tatton Rd RF/TRAN CH42 ....11 C8
 WLT/FAZ L9 ....84 D7
Taunton Av LEIGH WN7 ....81 M3
 STHEL WA9 ....102 F8
Taunton Dr AIN/FAZ L10 ....85 J3
 WAL/NB CH45 ....95 C2
Taunton St WAV L15 ....114 A5
Taurus Pk WARRW/BUR WA5 .....120 F1
Taurus CI DV/KA/FCH L14 ....115 J1
Tavistock Dr STHP PR8 ....34 D7
Tavistock Rd WAL/NB CH45 ....95 G7
 WARRW/BUR WA5 ....196 A1
 WGNE/HIN WN2 ....81 A1
Tavlin Av WARRW/BUR WA5 ......121 H4
Tavy CI NPK/KEN L6 ....113 J1
Tawd Rd SKEL WN8 ....64 E2
Tawd St ANF/KKDL L4 ....97 C5
Tawny Ct RUNC WA7 ....150 A6
Tayleur Ter NEWLW WA12 * 104 F3
Taylor Av ORM L39 ....51 J8
Taylor CI STHEL WA9 ....101 M7
Taylor Gv WGNE/HIN WN2 ....81 C2
Taylor Rd RNFD/HAY WA11 ....91 H7
 WGNE/HIN WN2 ....81 C2
Taylors CI WLT/FAZ L9 ....97 H2
Taylor's La BTL L20 ....97 G2
 KIRK/FR/WA PR4 ....27 M2
 WARRW/BUR WA5 ....135 J3
 WGNS/IIMK WN3 ....80 B2
Taylor St BIRK CH41 ....11 K3
 CHLY/EC PR7 ....32 D8
 LEIGH WN7 ....81 M5
 SKEL WN8 ....64 F4
 STHEL WA9 ....103 C5
 WARRS WA4 ....137 J4
 WDN WA8 ....17 C1
 WGNS/IIMK WN3 ....4 C4
Teakwood CI NPK/KEN L6 ....97 K8
Teal CI ORM L39 ....62 E3
 RNFD/HAY WA11 ....89 K7
 WARRN/WOL WA2 ....122 A2
 WGNS/IIMK WN3 ....4 C3
Teal Gv GOL/RIS/CU WA3 ....123 H2
 HLWD L26 ....132 A4
Teals Wy HES CH60 ....140 F5
Tears La SKEL WN8 ....53 H5
Teasville Rd CALD/MH L18 ....131 C1
Teasvale Rd SKEL WN8 ....65 H4
Tebay Rd PS/BROM CH62 ....144 A3
Tebay CI MGHL L31 ....73 H1
Tebworth Dr WGNE/HIN WN2 .....81 C5
Teck St EHL/KEN L7 ....113 J3
Tedburn CI WLTN L25 ....131 L1
Tedbury CI KKBY L32 ....86 A5
Tedder Av CHTN/BK PR9 ....25 J6
Tedder Sq WDN WA8 ....133 M5
Teddington CI WARRS WA4 ....138 A8
Teehey CI BEB CH63 ....127 M7
Teehey Gdns BEB CH63 ....127 M7
Teehey La BEB CH63 ....127 M7
Tees CI ANF/KKDL L4 ....7 L9
Tees Ct EP CH65 ....156 C6
Teesdale Rd BEB CH63 ....143 G1
 RNFD/HAY WA11 ....90 E6
Tees PI ANF/KKDL L4 ....7 L9
Tees St ANF/KKDL L4 ....7 L9
 BIRK CH41 ....111 H4
Teilo St TOX L8 ....113 J8
Telary CI EV L5 ....96 E8
Telegraph Rd WKBY CH48 ....125 J3
Telford CI CL/PREN CH43 ....10 C9
 WDN WA8 ....133 M1
Telford Crs LEIGH WN7 ....81 M5
Telford Rd EP CH65 ....21 D7
Temperance St CHLYE PR6 ....33 C5
Tempest Hey CLVP L2 ....12 F4
Temple Ct CLVP L2 ....12 F7
 GOL/RIS/CU WA3 ....107 G2
Temple Flds CHLYE PR6 * 33 J2
Templegate Ct WGNNW/ST WN6 .56 B3
Temple La CLVP L2 ....12 F7
Templemore Av CALD/MH L18 ....130 C2
Templemore Rd CL/PREN CH43 ..127 J3
Temple Rd RF/TRAN CH42 ....127 L3
Temple St CLVP L2 * 12 F6
Templeton Crs WD/CROXPK L12 ..99 C7
Templeton Rd WGNE/HIN WN2 ...80 C4
Tenby Av LITH L21 ....83 J4
Tenby CI WARRW/BUR WA5 ......121 H5
Tenby Dr MOR/LEA CH46 ....110 B6
 RUNC WA7 ....149 M3
Tenby St EV L5 ....97 J7
Tenement St WGNE/HIN WN2 .....80 D4
Tennis St ECCL WA10 ....8 C1
Tennis St North ECCL WA10 ....8 C1
Tennyson Av CHLY/EC PR7 ....32 E7
 LEIGH WN7 ....81 L5
 RF/TRAN CH42 * 128 B4
Tennyson Dr ORM L39 ....50 F7
 WARRN/WOL WA2 ....121 L3
Tennyson Rd EP CH65 ....163 C1
 HUY L36 ....116 C5
Tennyson St BTL L20 ....6 E1
 WDN WA8 ....16 C1
Tensing CI WARRW/BUR WA5 ....120 F1
Tensing Rd MGHL L31 ....72 F4
Tenterden St EV L5 ....13 J8
Tenter Dr WGNNW/ST WN6 ....56 D6
Tenth Av WLT/FAZ L9 ....84 F6
Terence Av WARR WA1 ....122 B6
Terence Rd CHLDW L16 ....114 F7
Terminus Rd HUY L36 ....99 H8
 PS/BROM CH62 ....143 M2
Tern CI NWD/KWIPK L33 ....74 A6
 WDN WA8 ....134 D1
Ternhall Rd WLT/FAZ L9 ....98 B1
Ternhall Wy WLT/FAZ L9 ....98 B1

Tern Wy MOR/LEA CH46 ....109 K4
 PR/KW L34 ....101 J6
Terrace Rd WDN WA8 ....134 C4
Terret CI WGNW/BIL/O WN5 ....67 M4
Tetbury Rd WGNW/BIL/O WN5 ....67 M4
Tetbury St BIRK CH41 ....10 F7
Tetchill CI GTS/LS CH66 ....162 F3
 RUNC WA7 ....150 F5
Tetlow St ANF/KKDL L4 ....97 H5
Tetlow Wy ANF/KKDL L4 ....97 H5
Teversham SKEL WN8 ....65 H3
Tewit Hall CI SPK/HALE L24 ......146 E2
Tewit Hall Rd SPK/HALE L24 .....146 E2
Tewkesbury CI GTS/LS CH66 .....163 G6
 WD/CROXPK L12 ....99 H1
 WLTN L25 ....131 L3
Tewkesbury Rd
 GOL/RIS/CU WA3 ....92 D5
Teynham Av PR/KW L34 ....109 M1
Teynham Crs NG/CROX L11 ....98 B5
Thackeray CI TOX L8 * 113 H7
Thackeray Gdns NTHTN L30 ....83 H5
Thackeray PI TOX L8 ....113 H7
 WGNS/IIMK WN3 ....68 C8
Thackeray Sq TOX L8 ....113 H7
Thackray Rd ECCL WA10 ....101 L5
Thamesdale EP CH65 ....20 A7
Thames CI WGNW/BIL/O WN5 .....67 H6
Thames Gdns EP CH65 ....163 J2
Thames Rd GOL/RIS/CU WA3 ....107 H3
 STHEL WA9 ....102 E7
Thames Side EP CH65 ....20 A8
Thames St TOX L8 ....113 H7
Thanet CI WDN WA8 ....65 G3
Thatto Heath Rd ECCL WA10 .....101 M5
Thealby CI SKEL WN8 ....65 G3
Thelwall CI LEIGH WN7 ....93 K1
Thelwall La WARRS WA4 ....138 D2
Thelwall New Rd WARRS WA4 ...138 D2
Thermal Rd PS/BROM CH62 ......143 M1
Thetford CI WGNE/HIN WN2 ....81 C5
Thetford Rd WARRW/BUR WA5 ..120 A7
The Uplands RUNC WA7 ....150 B6
Thewlis St WARRW/BUR WA5 ....121 G8
Thicknesse Av WGNNW/ST WN6 .68 B2
Thickwood Moss La
 RNFD/HAY WA11 ....76 B8
Thingwall Av AIG/SPK L17 ....114 F3
Thingwall Dr PEN/TH CH61 ....126 C7
Thingwall Hall Dr
 DV/KA/FCH L14 ....114 F3
Thingwall La DV/KA/FCH L14 .....114 F2
Thingwall Rd PEN/TH CH61 ....126 B7
Thingwall Rd East
 PEN/TH CH61 ....126 C7
Third Av CL/PREN CH43 ....110 D7
 CSBY/BLUN L23 * 82 F1
 RUNC WA7 ....150 B6
 WGNNW/ST WN6 ....68 C3
 WLT/FAZ L9 ....84 F6
Thirlmere Av AIMK WN4 ....91 L1
 CL/PREN CH43 ....110 E7
 FMBY L37 ....59 J3
 LITH L21 ....83 M5
 RNFD/HAY WA11 ....89 L3
 SKEL WN8 ....66 D6
 WARRN/WOL WA2 ....121 L2
 WGNE/HIN WN2 ....69 K6
 WGNE/HIN WN2 ....80 C6
 WGNNW/ST WN6 ....56 C6
 WGNW/BIL/O WN5 ....67 H6
Thirlmere CI CHLYE PR6 ....44 D5
 FROD/HEL WA6 ....160 F5
 MGHL L31 ....73 G3
Thirlmere Dr LITH L21 ....83 M5
 STHP PR8 ....47 K2
 WAL/NB CH45 ....95 K8
Thirlmere Gv RUNC WA7 ....149 L7
Thirlmere Ms HTWN L38 * 70 C1
Thirlmere Rd CHLY/EC PR7 ....32 C7
 EP CH65 ....163 J1
 EV L5 ....97 J8
 GOL/RIS/CU WA3 ....92 E4
 HOR/BR BL6 ....57 K2
 HTWN L38 ....70 C1
 NSTN CH64 ....153 G7
 WGNS/IIMK WN3 ....79 H8
Thirlmere Wk NWD/KWIPK L33 * .85 M1
Thirlmere Wy WDN WA8 ....133 K5
Thirlstane St AIG/SPK L17 ....129 K2
Thirsk SKEL WN8 ....65 G3
Thirsk CI RUNC WA7 ....149 L7
Thistle CI CHLYE PR6 ....33 G5
Thistledown CI AIG/SPK L17 ....129 J2
 WGNNW/ST WN6 ....68 C3
Thistleton Av BIRK CH41 ....111 H5
Thistleton Ms CHTN/BK PR9 ....3 K2
Thistleton Rd EHL/KEN L7 ....114 A3
Thistley Hey Rd KKBY L32 ....86 B3
Thomas CI ALL/GAR L19 ....130 E8
 EP CH65 ....163 K3
Thomas Dr DV/KA/FCH L14 ....114 A3
 RAIN/WH L35 ....116 E1
Thomas La DV/KA/FCH L14 ....114 F2
Thomasons Bridge La
 WARRS WA4 ....137 G7
Thomas St BIRK CH41 ....11 K7
 CSBY/BLUN L23 ....71 H6
 RUNC WA7 ....19 J2
 WDN WA8 ....16 C6
 WGNE/HIN WN2 ....81 K2
Thomaston St EV L5 ....96 F7
Thomas Winder Ct EV L5 * 96 F7
Thompson Av GOL/RIS/CU WA3 * .107 J2
 ORM L39 ....51 J8
Thompson St AIMK WN4 ....91 M1
 BIRK CH41 ....11 J9
 ECCL WA10 ....101 M4
 GOL/RIS/CU WA3 ....107 G2
 LEIGH WN7 ....81 K8
 WGN WN1 ....5 J1
Thomson Rd LITH L21 ....83 J5
Thomson St ANF/KKDL L4 ....97 G4
Thorburn Rd RF/TRAN CH42 .....128 D5
Thorburn Crs PS/BROM CH62 ....128 D5
Thorburn Rd PS/BROM CH62 .....128 D5
 WGNW/BIL/O WN5 ....77 M4
Thorburn Rd EP CH65 ....163 C1
Thorburn St EHL/KEN L7 ....113 K4
Thoresby CI WGNS/IIMK WN3 .....79 G2
Thoriby Rd GOL/RIS/CU WA3 ....107 H2
Thornaby CI WLTN L25 ....114 C4
Thornaby Gv STHEL WA9 ....101 M7
Thornbeck Av HTWN L38 ....70 D1
Thornbeck CI WD/CROXPK L12 ...99 G2
Thornbridge Av BRSC L40 ....52 A2
 LITH L21 ....83 J6
Thornbrook CI WD/CROXPK L12 ..98 F5
Thornbury SKEL WN8 ....65 G3
Thornbury Rd GOL/RIS/CU WA3 ..93 G6
Thornbush CI GOL/RIS/CU WA3 ..93 G4
Thorn CI RUNC WA7 ....19 M9
Thorncliffe Rd WAL/EG CH44 .....111 J5
Thorn CI RUNC WA7 ....19 M9
 WARRW/BUR WA5 ....136 B2

Thorncroft Dr PEN/TH CH61 ......141 K1
Thorndale Rd CSBY/WL L22 ....82 F3
Thorndyke CI RAIN/WH L35 ....118 A4
Thorne Dr GTS/LS CH66 ....162 D1
Thornes Rd NPK/KEN L6 ....113 K2
Thorneycroft St BIRK CH41 ....10 A2
Thornfield CI GOL/RIS/CU WA3 ...92 E5
Thornfield Hey BEB CH63 ....143 J3
Thornfield Rd CSBY/BLUN L23 ....71 J7
 WLT/FAZ L9 ....84 D6
Thornham Av GOL/RIS/CU WA3 ..92 E5
Thornham CI GR/UP/WCH CH49 .110 C6
Thornhead La WD/CROXPK L12 ...98 F7
Thornhill ORM L39 ....62 D4
Thornhill Rd AIMK WN4 ....90 E1
 CHLYE PR6 ....32 F5
 WAV L15 ....114 C6
Thornholme Crs NG/CROX L11 ....98 C4
Thornhurst KKBY L32 ....86 A6
Thornleigh Av PS/BROM CH62 ...155 H2
Thornleigh Gv CTS/LS CH66 ......163 C1
Thornley Rd LYMM WA13 ....139 L2
 MOR/LEA CH46 ....109 K6
Thorn Rd ECCL WA10 ....101 L2
 RUNC WA7 ....19 M9
 WARR WA1 ....122 C5
Thorns Dr GR/UP/WCH CH49 ....125 L3
The Thorns MGHL L31 ....72 D3
Thornton WDN WA8 * 134 A5
Thornton Av BEB CH63 ....127 M5
 BTL L20 ....83 M7
Thornton CI AIMK WN4 ....90 H1
 BRSC L40 ....39 L2
Thornton Common Rd
 BEB CH63 ....142 D6
Thornton Crs HES CH60 ....141 K7
Thorntondale Dr
 WARRW/BUR WA5 ....120 B6
Thornton Green La CHNE CH2 ....163 L8
Thornton Gv BEB CH63 ....127 L5
Thornton Rd BEB CH63 ....127 M5
 BTL L20 ....83 M7
 CHLDW L16 ....115 C4
 CHTN/BK PR9 ....25 H6
 EP CH65 ....21 C7
 WAL/NB CH45 ....95 J7
 WARRW/BUR WA5 ....136 D1
Thornton St BIRK CH41 ....10 A2
 LITH L21 ....83 K7
Thorntree CI AIG/SPK L17 ....129 J2
Thorntree Gn WARRS WA4 ....138 D8
Thornvale WGNE/HIN WN2 ....80 C6
Thornwood SKEL WN8 ....65 H3
Thornway BEB CH63 ....143 J5
 GR/UP/WCH CH49 ....125 L3
Thornwythe Gv CTS/LS CH66 ....163 C1
Thornycroft Rd WAV L15 ....113 M7
Thoroughgood CI BRSC L40 ....51 M3
Thorpe SKEL WN8 ....65 H3
Thorpe Bank RF/TRAN CH42 .....128 B5
Thorstone Dr PEN/TH CH61 ....125 L6
Thorsway RF/TRAN CH42 ....128 B3
 WKBY CH48 ....124 F5
Three Butt La WD/CROXPK L12 ...98 D5
Three Oaks CI BRSC L40 ....52 D3
Three Pools CHTN/BK PR9 ....25 L2
Three Sisters Rd AIMK WN4 ....91 J4
Three Tuns La FMBY L37 ....59 H2
Threlfall CHLY/EC PR7 ....32 B3
Threlfalls La CHTN/BK PR9 ....25 L2
Threlfall St TOX L8 ....129 J1
Thresher Av
 GR/UP/WCH CH49 * 125 L1
The Threshers NTHTN L30 * 84 D7
Throne Rd NG/CROX L11 ....98 E2
Throstle Nest Av
 WGNNW/ST WN6 ....4 A1
Thrurcroft Dr SKEL WN8 ....65 C3
Thurlby CI AIMK WN4 ....91 M1
Thurlow GOL/RIS/CU WA3 ....93 C6
Thurne Wy WLTN L25 ....115 J7
Thurnham St NPK/KEN L6 ....97 L8
Thursby CI KKBY L32 ....86 B5
Thursby Crs KKBY L32 ....86 B5
Thursby Rd PS/BROM CH62 ....155 A3
Thursford Gv PEN/BR BL6 ....57 M4
Thurstaston Rd HES CH60 ....141 C4
 PEN/TH CH61 ....141 K1
Thurston SKEL WN8 ....65 C3
Thurston Av WGNS/IIMK WN3 .....79 K2
Thurston La WARRW/BUR WA5 ..120 F7
Thurston Rd ANF/KKDL L4 ....97 K7
Thynne St WARR WA1 ....14 C7
Tibbs Cross La WDN WA8 ....118 F4
Tichbourne Wy NPK/KEN L6 ....13 M4
Tickle Av STHEL WA9 ....102 F2
Tidal La WARRN/WOL WA2 ....122 B5
Tideswell CI WGNW/BIL/O WN5 ...67 J4
Tidewell CI EHL/KEN L7 ....113 L5
Tide Wy WAL/NB CH45 ....95 C5
Tilbrook Dr STHEL WA9 ....102 F7
Tilbury Gv WGNNW/ST WN6 ....54 F6
Tilbury PI RUNC WA7 ....151 C7
Tilcroft SKEL WN8 ....65 H4
Tildsley Crs RUNC WA7 ....149 H7
Tilley St WARR WA1 ....14 E5
Tillotson CI TOX L8 ....113 C8
Tilman CI WARRW/BUR WA5 ......120 D5
Tilney St WLT/FAZ L9 ....84 C7
Tilstock Av PS/BROM CH62 ....128 D5
Tilstock Crs CL/PREN CH43 ....127 H4
Tilston Av WARRS WA4 ....138 C1
Tilston CI WLT/FAZ L9 ....97 M2
Tilston Rd KKBY L32 ....85 J3
 WAL/NB CH45 ....95 J7
 WLT/FAZ L9 ....97 M1
Timberscombe Gdns
 WARRS WA4 ....123 C7
Time Pk RAIN/WH L35 ....101 H8
Timmis CI WARRN/WOL WA2 .....122 C2
Timmis Crs WDN WA8 ....16 C2
Timmins Av LEIGH WN7 ....93 M3
Timms CI FMBY L37 ....47 H8
Timms La FMBY L37 ....47 H8
Timon Av BTL L20 ....7 L2
Timor Av WARRS WA4 ....102 A5
Timperley Av WARRS WA4 ....138 C1
Timperley St WDN WA8 * 16 E4
Timpron St EHL/KEN L7 ....113 L5
Timway Dr WD/CROXPK L12 ....99 H1
Tinas Wy GR/UP/WCH CH49 .....110 C8
Tincklers La CHLY/EC PR7 ....30 B7
Tinkersfield LEIGH WN7 ....81 M6
Tinling CI PR/KW L34 ....99 H1
Tinsley Av STHP PR8 ....36 A2
Tinsley's La STHP PR8 ....36 B4
Tinsley St ANF/KKDL L4 ....97 H3
 WARRS WA4 ....138 B2
Tintagel SKEL WN8 ....65 H6
Tintagel CI RUNC WA7 ....150 E7
Tintagel Rd NG/CROX L11 ....85 M8
 WGNE/HIN WN2 ....91 M2
Tintern Av WARRN/WOL WA2 .....91 M2
 CHLY/EC PR7 ....32 F8
Tintern CI WARRW/BUR WA5 * ...121 C3
Tintern Dr FMBY L37 ....59 K3
 MOR/LEA CH46 ....110 A5

Tinwald PI WGN WN1 ....5 L2
Tipping St WGNS/IIMK WN3 ....4 C8
Tiptree CI WD/CROXPK L12 ....99 H1
Titchfield St EV L5 ....12 F1
Tithebarn CI HES CH60 * 141 H6
 CHLYE PR6 ....33 J1
 SKEL WN8 ....85 M4
Tithebarn Dr NSTN CH64 ....152 D3
Tithebarn La AIMK WN4 ....79 J8
 CSBY/BLUN L23 ....71 H8
 PR/KW L34 ....99 M1
 STHP PR8 ....3 M5
Tithebarn Rd AIMK WN4 ....90 E1
 CHLYE PR6 ....32 F5
 WAV L15 ....114 C6
The Tithings RUNC WA7 ....150 A4
 SKEL WN8 ....65 C3
 WAL/EG CH44 ....111 K1
Tiverton CI HUY L36 ....116 D3
 WDN WA8 ....133 L2
Tiverton Sq WARRW/BUR WA5 ...136 A1
Tiverton St WAV L15 ....114 A5
Tobermory CI RNFD/HAY WA11 ...90 C8
Tobin CI EV L5 ....12 F1
Tobin St WAL/EG CH44 ....111 H1
Tobruk Rd HUY L36 ....115 M1
Toddington La WGNE/HIN WN2 ...57 K5
Todd Rd STHEL WA9 ....9 J8
Todd's La CHTN/BK PR9 ....28 F3
Toft CI WDN WA8 ....16 A2
Toft St EHL/KEN L7 ....113 L3
Toftwood Av RAIN/WH L35 ....117 M4
Tokenspire Pk
 NWD/KWIPK L33 * 86 D6
Toll Bar La FMBY L37 ....86 D6
Tollemache Rd BIRK CH41 ....111 C5
Tollemache St WAL/NB CH45 ......95 L5
Tollerton Rd WD/CROXPK L12 ....98 B7
Tollgate Rd BRSC L40 ....51 K3
Tollgreen CI WGNE/HIN WN2 ......69 M6
Toll St WGNE/HIN WN2 ....69 M6
Tolpuddle Rd WLTN L25 ....131 H2
Tolpuddle Wy ANF/KKDL L4 ....96 F5
Tolver St ECCL WA10 ....9 H4
Tomlinson Av WARRN/WOL WA2 .121 M5
Tonbridge CI SPK/HALE L24 ......146 D1
Tonbridge Dr AIN/FAZ L10 ....84 F2
Tongbarn SKEL WN8 ....65 C3
Tontine SKEL WN8 ....66 E7
Toogood La WGNNW/ST WN6 ......41 M6
Tootell St CHLY/EC PR7 ....32 D7
Toothill CI AIMK WN4 ....79 K8
Tootle La BRSC L40 ....39 H2
Top Acre Rd SKEL WN8 ....65 L6
Topaz CI ANF/KKDL L4 ....7 M7
Topaz Wy CHLYE PR6 ....33 G3
Topcliffe Gv WD/CROXPK L12 ......99 J2
Top Rd FROD/HEL WA6 ....160 E8
Topgate CI HES CH60 ....141 K5
Topham Dr WLT/FAZ L9 ....84 D3
Topping Ct GOL/RIS/CU WA3 .....122 D1
Topsham CI WLTN L25 ....131 L1
Torcross CI CHTN/BK PR9 ....22 C8
Torcross Wy HLWD L26 ....132 A5
 WLTN L25 ....131 L1
Tordelow CI NPK/KEN L6 ....113 J1
Tormore CI CHLYE PR6 ....33 J2
Toronto CI HUY L36 ....99 M7
Toronto St WAL/EG CH44 ....112 A2
Torquay Dr WGNW/BIL/O WN5 ....78 A3
Torridon CI WARRW/BUR WA5 .....56 C6
Torridon Gv GTS/LS CH66 ....163 H2
Torrington Dr HLWD L26 ....132 A5
 PEN/TH CH61 ....126 D7
Torrington Gdns PEN/TH CH61 ..126 D6
Torrington Rd ALL/GAR L19 ....130 D6
 WAL/EG CH44 ....111 J1
Torrisholme Rd WLT/FAZ L9 ....97 M2
Torr St EV L5 ....97 C3
Torside CI WGNE/HIN WN2 ....69 M7
Torus Rd CLB/OSW/ST L13 ....114 C1
Torver CI WGNS/IIMK WN3 ....79 J3
Tor View Rd WAV L15 ....114 C7
Torwood CL/PREN CH43 ....110 C6
Tothale Turn NTHLY L27 ....132 B1
Totland CI WARRW/BUR WA5 .....119 L6
Totnes Av HLWD L26 ....132 B4
Totnes Dr CHTN/BK PR9 ....22 F1
Totnes Rd NG/CROX L11 ....85 L8
Toulston Rd WGNNW/ST WN6 .....68 D3
Tourney Gn WARRW/BUR WA5 ...120 C3
Towcester St LITH L21 ....83 K7
Tower Buildings CHTN/BK PR9 * ...3 J1
Tower End FMBY L37 ....46 E8
Tower Gdns VAUX/LVPD L3 ....51 J8
Tower Hill ORM L39 ....51 J8
 RF/TRAN CH42 ....127 M2
Tower Hill Rd SKEL WN8 ....66 C8
Tower La RUNC WA7 ....150 E6
Tower Nook SKEL WN8 ....66 C8
Tower Prom WAL/NB CH45 ....95 C3
Tower Quays BIRK CH41 * 11 J2
Tower Rd BIRK CH41 ....11 J2
 RF/TRAN CH42 ....127 M2
Tower Rd North HES CH60 ....141 K5
Tower Rd South HES CH60 ....141 H4
Towers Av MGHL L31 ....71 H8
Towers La FROD/HEL WA6 ....166 D6
Towers Rd CHLDW L16 ....114 E7
The Towers RF/TRAN CH42 * 127 M4
Tower St VAUX/LVPD L3 ....112 F8
Tower Wy WLTN L25 ....131 G2
Tower Whf BIRK CH41 ....11 J2
Towneley Ct WDN WA8 ....16 C2
Townfield Av AIMK WN4 ....91 K3
Townfield CI CL/PREN CH43 ......127 G2
Townfield Gdns BEB CH63 ....128 B6
Townfield La BEB CH63 ....128 B6
 CL/PREN CH43 ....127 H2
 FROD/HEL WA6 ....160 E6
Townfield Rd RUNC WA7 ....150 D4
 WARRN/WOL WA2 * 105 J8
 WKBY CH48 ....124 D3
Townfields AIMK WN4 ....91 J2
Townfield Vw RUNC WA7 ....150 D4
Towngate CHLY/EC PR7 ....30 D5
Town Green La ORM L39 ....62 E5
Town HI WARR WA1 ....14 E5
Town La BEB CH63 ....128 A7
 CHLY/EC PR7 ....42 D6
 CHLY/EC PR7 ....42 D6
 NSTN CH64 ....153 H7
 SPK/HALE L24 ....147 M4
 STHP PR8 ....35 H1
Town La (Kew) STHP PR8 ....35 L2
Townley St CHLYE PR6 ....32 F4
Town Meadow La MOR/LEA CH46 .109 K3
Town Rd CROS/BRETH PR26 ....29 K3
 RF/TRAN CH42 ....127 M2
Town Rw WD/CROXPK L12 ....98 E7
Town's End La MGHL L31 ....73 J3
Townsend Av NG/CROX L11 ....98 C4
Townsend La CLB/OSW/ST L13 * ..97 M6
Townsend St BIRK CH41 ....111 G4

EV L5 ....96 D7
Townsend Vw LITH L21 ....83 K3
NG/CROX L11 ....98 A2
Townshend Av PEN/TH CH61 ....125 M8
Town Sq RUNC WA7 * 150 B6
Town Vw CL/PREN CH43 ....10 C1
Town Wk RUNC WA7 * 150 B6
Towson St EV L5 ....97 H7
Toxteth St EV L5 ....129 J1
Toxteth St TOX L8 ....113 H8
Tracks La WGNW/BIL/O WN5 ....77 M2
Tracy Dr NEWLW WA12 ....104 A2
Trafalgar Av WAL/EC CH44 ....95 M8
Trafalgar Cl BEB CH63 ....16 C8
Trafalgar Dr BEB CH63 ....143 J1
Trafalgar St RUNC WA7 ....35 C3
WAL/EC CH44 ....95 L8
WGN WN1 ....4 E1
WGNE/HIN WN2 ....69 M8
Trafalgar Wy NPK/KEN L6 ....13 M4
Trafford Av WARRW/BUR WA5 ....121 G5
Trafford Crs RUNC WA7 ....150 B6
Trafford Rd WGNE/HIN WN2 ....69 L8
Tragan Dr WARRW/BUR WA5 ....135 M2
Tram St WGNE/HIN WN2 ....80 C4
Tramway Rd AIG/SPK L17 ....129 C4
Trans Pennine Trail CHLDW L16 ....115 H6
CLVPS L1 ....12 F8
MGHL L31 ....72 D7
NTHTN L30 ....84 D2
TOX L8 ....113 K8
WARRW/BUR WA5 ....135 M4
WD/CROXPK L12 ....114 E1
WDN WA8 ....134 C8
WLT/FAZ L9 ....84 D8
Trap HI FMBY L37 ....58 E4
Trapwood Cl ECCL WA10 ....101 K2
Travandon Cl NG/CROX L11 * 85 K7
Travers' Entry WARR WA1 ....103 J7
Traverse St STHEL WA9 ....9 L5
Travis St WD/CROXPK L12 ....16 E3
Treborth St TOX L8 ....113 J8
Trecastell Cl WGN WN1 ....5 L3
Trecastle Rd NWD/KWIPK L33 ....86 C1
Tree Bank Cl RUNC WA7 ....19 G7
Treen Cl CHTN/BK PR9 ....22 D7
Treesdale Cl STHP PR8 ....35 H1
Tree Tops NSTN CH64 ....153 G8
Treetops Cl WARR WA1 ....122 B6
Treetops Dr BIRK CH41 ....110 F4
Treetops Vls CHTN/BK PR9 ....25 H1
Trefoil Cl GOL/RIS/CU WA3 ....106 E8
Treforris Rd WAL/NB CH45 ....95 H6
Trefula Pk WD/CROXPK L12 ....99 H1
Tregaron Gv WGNE/HIN WN2 ....80 C4
Trelawney Cl WLTN L25 ....115 K7
Tremore Cl NG/CROX L11 ....98 A4
Trenance Cl RUNC WA7 ....150 D8
Trencherfield MI
WGNS/IIMK WN3 ....4 D6
Trendeal Rd NG/CROX L11 ....85 M8
Trent Av DV/KA/FCH L14 ....115 H3
MGHL L31 ....73 H3
Trent Cl BRSC L40 ....39 H8
RAIN/WH L35 ....117 K2
STHEL WA9 ....102 E8
WD/CROXPK L12 ....98 F2
WDN WA8 ....134 D1
Trentdale EP CH65 ....20 B9
Trent Dr WGNE/HIN WN2 ....81 L2
Trent Gv LEIGH WN7 ....93 L1
Trentham Cl CALD/MH L18 ....114 D8
Trentham Cl WDN WA8 ....134 D1
Trentham Rd KKBY L32 ....85 L4
Trentham St RUNC WA7 ....18 E2
Trent Rd AIMK WN4 ....79 L8
RAIN/WH L35 ....117 K2
WGNW/BIL/O WN5 ....67 L6
WGNW/BIL/O WN5 ....89 C1
Trent St EV L5 ....96 E7
GOL/RIS/CU WA3 ....92 C5
Trent Wy HES CH60 ....141 K7
LITH L21 ....83 J4
Trescott Ms WGNNW/ST WN6 ....56 A5
Tresham Dr WARRS WA4 ....138 C5
Tressel Dr STHEL WA9 ....118 C2
Tressell St WLT/FAZ L9 ....97 H2
Trevelyan Dr WGNW/BIL/O WN5 ....77 M4
Trevelyan St WLT/FAZ L9 ....97 J2
Treviot Cl NWD/KWIPK L33 ....73 M7
Trevor Dr CSBY/BLUN L23 ....83 H7
Trevor Rd BRSC L40 ....51 M1
STHP PR8 ....47 L1
WLT/FAZ L9 ....84 C7
The Triad BTL L20 ....7 G3
Trident Pk RUNC WA7 * 150 A6
Trimley Cl GR/UP/WCH CH49 ....110 A8
Tring Cl GR/UP/WCH CH49 ....110 C6
Trinity Cl GOL/RIS/CU WA3 ....107 H8
Trinity Gdns AIMK WN4 ....91 H1
STHP PR8 ....2 F6
Trinity Gv CSBY/BLUN L23 ....82 D5
Trinity La BIRK CH41 ....11 J4
Trinity Ms CHTN/BK PR9 ....3 K3
Trinity Pl BTL L20 ....7 J5
WDN WA8 ....16 E5
Trinity Rd BTL L20 ....7 J5
CHLY/EC PR7 * 32 D6
HOY CH47 ....108 D6
WAL/EC CH44 ....95 K8
Trinity St BIRK CH41 ....11 J4
STHEL WA9 * 9 H1
Trinity Wk VAUX/LVPD L3 ....13 K4
Trispen Cl HLWD L26 ....132 A5
Trispen Rd NG/CROX L11 ....98 F1
Triumph Wy SPK/HALE L24 ....131 H7
Trlam Rd BTL L20 ....6 E3
Troon Cl BEB CH63 ....143 L8
CHLYE PR6 ....31 M1
RNFD/HAY WA11 ....90 C8
WD/CROXPK L12 ....99 H7
Trossachs Cl WARRN/WOL WA2 ....122 A3
Trotwood Cl WLT/FAZ L9 ....84 F5
Troutbeck Av MGHL L31 ....73 C3
NEWLW WA12 ....104 A1
WARRW/BUR WA5 ....14 A1
Troutbeck Cl GR/UP/WCH CH49 ....110 C8
RUNC WA7 ....150 C3
Troutbeck Rd RNFD/HAY WA11 ....90 K3
Troutbeck Ri WGNW/BIL/O WN5 ....67 K7
Troutbeck Rd AIMK WN4 ....79 L8
CALD/MH L18 ....114 F8
CHLY/EC PR7 ....32 D6
Trouville Rd ANF/KKDL L4 ....97 M1
Trowbridge St VAUX/LVPD L3 ....13 K7
Trueman Cl CHTN/BK PR9 ....110 E3
Trueman Ct VAUX/LVPD L3 ....13 G5
Trumans La GTS/LS CH66 ....155 L6
Trundle Pie La ORM L39 ....49 L7
Truro Av CHTN/BK PR9 ....22 D8
NTHTN L30 ....84 B1
Truro Cl GTS/LS CH66 ....163 H5
RNFD/HAY WA11 ....89 M6
WARR WA1 ....122 D5
Truro Rd WAV L15 ....114 C7

Truscott Rd BRSC L40 ....51 M1
Tucker's Hill Brow
WGNNW/HIN WN2 ....57 K4
Tudor Av BEB CH63 ....143 J2
WAL/EC CH44 ....112 A3
Tudor Cl EHL/KEN L7 ....13 M8
GTS/LS CH66 ....163 H5
RNFD/HAY WA11 ....76 A5
WAV L15 ....138 C3
Tudor Ct WARRS WA4 * 138 A4
Tudor Gra GR/UP/WCH CH49 ....125 M2
Tudor Gv WGNS/IIMK WN3 ....79 G3
Tudor Rd CSBY/BLUN L23 ....82 F2
RF/TRAN CH42 ....128 A2
RUNC WA7 ....150 D2
STHP PR8 ....34 D7
WLTN L25 ....131 L6
Tudor St NPK/KEN L6 ....113 K2
Tudor Vw NWD/KWIPK L33 ....74 A8
Tudorville Rd BEB CH63 ....128 B8
Tudorway HES CH60 ....141 K5
Tue La WDN WA8 ....117 K7
Tuffins Cnr NTHLY L27 ....115 M8
Tulip Av BIRK CH41 ....111 H5
Tulip Dr WGNNW/ST WN6 ....68 B2
Tulip Rd RNFD/HAY WA11 ....91 H7
WAV L15 ....114 C6
Tulketh St STHP PR8 ....3 H4
Tullimore Rd CALD/MH L18 ....130 C4
Tullis St ECCL WA10 ....8 D7
Tulloch St NPK/KEN L6 ....113 K2
Tully Av NEWLW WA12 ....104 A2
Tumilty Av BTL L20 ....97 J3
Tunbridge Cl WARRW/BUR WA5 ....120 C5
Tunley La WGNNW/ST WN6 ....42 A8
Tunley Moss WGNNW/ST WN6 ....55 C1
Tunnel Rd BIRK CH41 ....11 L7
EHL/KEN L7 ....113 K5
Tunstall Cl GR/UP/WCH CH49 ....110 A4
Tunstall La WGNW/BIL/O WN5 ....67 M8
Tunstall St EHL/KEN L7 ....113 L6
Tunstall's Wy STHEL WA9 ....118 F1
Tupelo Cl WD/CROXPK L12 ....99 H1
Tupman St TOX L8 ....113 H8
Turflands CROS/BRETH PR26 ....29 K4
Turmar Av PEN/TH CH61 ....142 B1
Turmarce DV/KA/FCH L14 ....115 C2
FMBY L37 ....47 K7
Turnall Rd WDN WA8 ....133 K6
Turnberry SKEL WN8 ....64 F3
Turnberry Cl HUY L36 ....115 L2
LYMM WA13 ....139 L1
MOR/LEA CH46 ....109 K4
WD/CROXPK L12 ....99 H7
Turnberry Wy WGNNW/ST WN6 ....67 G7
Turnbridge Rd MGHL L31 ....72 E2
Turnbury Cl CHLYE PR6 ....31 M1
Turnditch Cl WGNNW/ST WN6 ....68 C1
Turner Av BTL L20 ....84 A7
WGNE/HIN WN2 ....81 G4
Turner Gv NWD/KWIPK L33 ....74 A7
Turner St BIRK CH41 ....10 E3
WGN WN1 ....5 L3
WGNE/HIN WN2 ....69 M7
Turners Yd WAL/EC CH44 ....111 J1
Turney Rd WAL/EC CH44 ....111 J1
Turnill La WGNW/HIN WN4 ....91 K3
Turning La STHP PR8 ....36 C5
Turnpike Rd ORM L39 ....62 C4
Turnstone Av NEWLW WA12 ....104 E1
Turnstone Cl WD/CROXPK L12 ....99 C2
Turnstone Dr HLWD L26 ....132 A4
Turret Hall Dr GOL/RIS/CU WA3 ....92 G5
Turret Rd WAL/NB CH45 ....95 J7
Turriff Dr BEB CH63 ....154 E1
Turriff Gv WGNE/HIN WN2 ....69 J4
Turrocks Cl WDN WA8 ....115 J1
Turrocks Cft NSTN CH64 ....153 G8
Turton Cl GOL/RIS/CU WA3 ....106 E8
Turton Dr CHLYE PR6 ....33 C5
Turton St EV L5 * 96 F7
GOL/RIS/CU WA3 ....92 C5
Tuscan Cl WDN WA8 ....118 D8
Tuson Dr WDN WA8 ....134 B1
Tutor Bank NEWLW WA12 ....104 F2
Tweed Cl NPK/KEN L6 ....113 L1
Tweedsmuir Cl
WARRN/WOL WA2 ....122 C1
Tweed St BIRK CH41 ....111 J4
Twenty Acre Rd
WARRW/BUR WA5 ....120 E5
Twickenham Dr HUY L36 ....115 L4
MOR/LEA CH46 ....110 C2
Twigden Cl AIN/FAZ L10 ....85 H5
Twig La HUY L36 ....115 L1
MGHL L31 ....72 F4
Twiss Green Dr
GOL/RIS/CU WA3 ....107 G1
Twiss Green La
GOL/RIS/CU WA3 ....106 F1
Twist Av GOL/RIS/CU WA3 ....92 E5
Twistfield Cl STHP PR8 ....2 D7
Twist La LEIGH WN7 ....81 M8
Twomey Cl EV L5 * 12 F1
Twyford Av LITH L21 ....83 K4
Twyford Cl MGHL L31 * 73 G4
WDN WA8 ....134 D1
Twyford La WDN WA8 ....118 F7
Twyford Pl STHEL WA9 ....9 M5
Twyford St WLTN L25 ....131 L7
Tyberton Pl WLTN L25 ....131 L7
Tyburn Cl BEB CH63 ....143 H3
Tyburn Rd BEB CH63 ....143 H3
Tyldesley Ar WGN WN1 * 4 F3
Tyndall Av CSBY/WL L22 ....81 H5
Tyne ANF/KKDL L4 ....97 G5
STHEL WA9 ....101 M7
WARRN/WOL WA2 ....122 A3
Tynemouth Cl EV L5 ....97 J8
Tynemouth Rd RUNC WA7 ....150 E7
Tyne St BIRK CH41 ....111 H4
Tynron Gv CL/PREN CH43 ....110 F8
Tynville Rd WLT/FAZ L9 ....84 B6
Tynwald Cl CLB/OSW/ST L13 ....98 B8
Tynwald Crs WDN WA8 ....118 D8
Tynwald Dr WARRS WA4 ....137 L6
Tynwald Hill CLB/OSW/ST L13 ....114 B1
Tynwald Pl CLB/OSW/ST L13 ....114 B1
Tynwald Rd WKBY CH48 ....124 C3
Tyrer Av WGNS/IIMK WN3 ....68 B8
Tyrer La CL/PREN CH43 ....51 H6
Tyrer's Av MGHL L31 ....61 L8
Tyrers Cl FMBY L37 ....59 H3
Tyrer St BIRK CH41 ....111 H4
CLVPS L1 * 13 H7

U

Uldale Cl NG/CROX L11 ....98 A1
STHP PR8 ....47 K2
Uldale Wy NG/CROX L11 ....98 A1
Ullapool Cl GTS/LS CH66 ....155 H7
Ullet Rd AIG/SPK L17 ....113 H6
Ullswater Av CL/PREN CH43 ....110 E7
RNFD/HAY WA11 ....89 J5
WARRN/WOL WA2 ....121 L6
WGNW/BIL/O WN5 ....67 L6
Ullswater Cl NWD/KWIPK L33 ....85 M1
Ullswater Dr WGNE/HIN WN2 ....69 K4
Ullswater Rd CHLY/EC PR7 ....32 D7
EP CH65 ....163 L3
GOL/RIS/CU WA3 ....92 C4
Ullswater St EV L5 ....97 J7
Ulnes Walton La
CROS/BRETH PR26 ....30 B1
Ulster Rd CLB/OSW/ST L13 ....114 D2
Ultonia St ALL/GAR L19 ....145 L1
Ulverscroft CL/PREN CH43 ....127 H1
Ulverston Av WARRN/WOL WA2 ....121 K2
Ulverston Cl WGNNW/ST WN6 ....73 C3
RNFD/HAY WA11 ....90 C7
Ulverston Lawn NTHLY L27 ....132 B3
Ulverston Rd WGNS/IIMK WN3 ....79 H2
Umbria St ALL/GAR L19 ....145 L1
Underbridge La WARRS WA4 ....157 G7
Undercliffe Rd CLB/OSW/ST L13 ....114 C1
Underhill Rd ECCL WA10 ....8 D7
Underley St EHL/KEN L7 ....113 L6
The Underway RUNC WA7 ....150 B5
Underwood Dr EP CH65 ....163 L3
Unicorn Rd NG/CROX L11 ....98 C1
Unicorn Wy BIRK CH41 ....11 L8
Union Bank La WDN WA8 ....118 C4
Union Ct CLVP L2 ....12 F7
Union St BIRK CH41 ....11 L8
CHLY/EC PR7 ....32 E5
CHTN/BK PR9 ....3 J1
EV L5 ....96 D8
RUNC WA7 ....19 K4
VAUX/LVPD L3 ....12 D6
WAL/EC CH44 ....111 M1
WGNE/HIN WN2 ....69 J1
Unit Rd STHP PR8 ....34 F8
Unity Gv PR/KW L34 ....86 D5
University Rd BTL L20 ....7 J5
Unsworth Av GOL/RIS/CU WA3 ....92 F4
Unsworth Ct
WARRN/WOL WA2 * 122 B4
Upavon Av GR/UP/WCH CH49 * 125 K2
Upchurch Cl TOX L8 ....129 H1
Upholland Rd
WGNW/BIL/O WN5 ....77 M2
Upland Cl ECCL WA10 ....101 L5
Upland Dr AIMK WN4 ....91 M1
Upland Rd ECCL WA10 ....101 K5
GR/UP/WCH CH49 ....110 B7
Uplands Cl ECCL WA10 * 101 K5
Uplands Rd PS/BROM CH62 ....143 L4
Upper Aughton Rd STHP PR8 ....2 B7
Upper Baker St NPK/KEN L6 ....113 J2
Upper Beau St VAUX/LVPD L3 ....13 J2
Upper Beckwith St BIRK CH41 ....10 C2
Upper Brassey St BIRK CH41 ....10 A2
Upper Bute St EV L5 ....13 K2
Upper Dicconson St WGN WN1 ....4 F2
Upper Duke St CLVPS L1 ....113 C5
Upper Essex St TOX L8 ....113 H8
Upper Flaybrick Rd CL/PREN CH43 ....111 G6
Upper Frederick St CLVPS L1 ....112 F5
Upper Hampton St TOX L8 ....113 H7
Upper Harrington St TOX L8 ....113 G7
Upper Hill St TOX L8 ....113 H7
Upper Hope PI TOX L8 * 113 J7
Upper Huskisson St TOX L8 ....113 J6
Upper Mann St TOX L8 ....113 G8
Upper Mersey Rd WDN WA8 ....16 C9
Upper Mersey St EP CH65 ....20 D1
Upper Newington CLVPS L1 ....13 J8
Upper Park St TOX L8 ....113 H8
Upper Parliament St TOX L8 ....113 G6
Upper Pitt St CLVPS L1 ....112 F5
Upper Pownall St CLVPS L1 ....112 F5
Upper Raby Rd NSTN CH64 ....153 J3
Upper Rice La WAL/EC CH44 ....95 L8
Upper St Stephen St
WGNNW/ST WN6 ....4 C3
Upper Stanhope St TOX L8 ....113 H6
Upper Warwick St TOX L8 ....113 H7
Upper William St VAUX/LVPD L3 ....12 D1
Uppingham SKEL WN8 ....64 F4
Uppingham Av AIN/FAZ L10 ....85 C3
Uppingham Rd CLB/OSW/ST L13 ....98 B8
WAL/EC CH44 ....95 H8
Upton Av STHP PR8 ....34 D7
Upton Barn MGHL L31 ....72 E3
Upton Bridle Pth WDN WA8 ....134 B1
Upton By-Pass
GR/UP/WCH CH49 ....110 A8
Upton Cl GOL/RIS/CU WA3 ....92 F5
GR/UP/WCH CH49 ....110 B8
SPK/HALE L24 * 147 G2
Upton Dr WARRW/BUR WA5 ....120 B8
Upton Gra WDN WA8 ....133 M2
Upton Gn SPK/HALE L24 * 147 G2
Upton La WDN WA8 ....134 B1
Upton Park Dr
GR/UP/WCH CH49 ....110 C7
Upton Rd CL/PREN CH43 ....110 E7
GTS/LS CH66 ....162 F1
Upwood Rd GOL/RIS/CU WA3 ....92 F6
Ure Ct STHP PR8 ....47 K2
Urmson Rd WAL/NB CH45 ....95 K8
Urmston Av NEWLW WA12 ....91 K8
Urmston Dr LEIGH WN7 ....81 M8
Ursula St BTL L20 ....7 K8
Utkinton Cl CL/PREN CH43 ....127 H2
Utting Av ANF/KKDL L4 ....97 K5
Utting Av East NG/CROX L11 ....98 A4
Uxbridge St EHL/KEN L7 ....113 K5

V

Vahler Ter RUNC WA7 ....19 L3
Vale Cl WARRN/WOL WA2 ....121 L5
Vale Cl WGNNW/ST WN6 ....55 C5
WLTN L25 ....131 H5
Vale Crs STHP PR8 ....47 L3
Vale Dr WAL/NB CH45 ....95 L6
Vale Gdns EP CH65 ....20 C7
FROD/HEL WA6 ....166 D1
Vale Gv KKBY L32 ....72 C8
Vale La BRSC L40 ....53 G8
Vale Ldg WLT/FAZ L9 * 97 J2
Valencia Gv PR/KW L34 ....101 J4
Valencia Rd WAV L15 ....114 C5

Valentia Rd HOY CH47 ....108 C7
Valentine Gv AIN/FAZ L10 ....85 G4
Valentine Rd NEWLW WA12 ....104 B2
Valentines Wy WLT L9 ....84 C1
Vale Owen Rd
WARRN/WOL WA2 ....121 M4
Valerian Rd BIRK CH41 ....111 H6
Valerie Cl AIN/FAZ L10 ....85 K7
Vale Rd CSBY/BLUN L23 ....82 F1
EP CH65 ....20 C7
WLTN L25 ....131 L2
Valescourt Rd WD/CROXPK L12 ....98 E5
The Vale WGNNW/ST WN6 ....54 F5
WARRN/WOL WA2 ....121 L5
WD/CROXPK L12 ....99 J3
Valiant Rd WGNW/BIL/O WN5 ....67 M5
Valiant Wy BIRK CH41 ....11 L9
Valkyrie Rd WAL/NB CH45 ....95 J8
Vallance Rd ANF/KKDL L4 ....97 L6
Valleybrook Gv BEB CH63 ....143 K3
Valley Av AIN/FAZ L10 ....85 J6
CSBY/BLUN L23 ....83 K1
Valley Ct WARRN/WOL WA2 ....122 B4
Valley Dr GTS/LS CH66 ....155 M8
Valley Rd AIN/FAZ L10 ....85 J6
ANF/KKDL L4 ....110 F5
BIRK CH41 ....110 F5
PS/BROM CH62 ....143 M5
WGNW/BIL/O WN5 ....67 M8
Valley Vw CHLYE PR6 ....33 C6
GTS/LS CH66 ....155 M8
NEWLW WA12 ....104 A2
Vanbrugh Crs WARRN/WOL WA2 ....122 B4
Vanbrugh Gv WGNNW/ST WN6 ....67 K4
Vanbrugh Rd ANF/KKDL L4 ....97 L5
Vancouver Rd NTHLY L27 ....132 B4
Vanderbilt Av WLT/FAZ L9 ....84 D5
Vanderbyl Av PS/BROM CH62 ....143 K3
Vandries St VAUX/LVPD L3 ....12 C2
Vandyke St TOX L8 ....113 L6
Vanguard Cl WARRW/BUR WA5 ....122 F1
Vanguard St EV L5 ....97 H7
Vanguard Wy BIRK CH41 ....128 B2
Vardon St BIRK CH41 ....11 G2
Varley Rd ALL/GAR L19 ....130 C4
STHEL WA9 ....102 C8
Varthen St EV L5 ....97 J7
Varthen St EV L5 ....97 J7
Vaudrey Dr WARR WA1 ....122 F6
Vaughan Rd STHP PR8 ....35 K1
WAL/NB CH45 ....95 K1
Vaughan St BIRK CH41 ....111 H5
Vaux Crs BTL L20 ....83 M8
Vauxhall Cl WARRW/BUR WA5 ....136 B1
Vauxhall Rd VAUX/LVPD L3 ....12 F4
Vaux PI BTL L20 ....7 K1
Vauze Av HOR/BR BL6 ....57 M4
Vauze House CH HOR/BR BL6 ....57 M3
Venables Cl BEB CH63 ....143 K4
Venables Dr BEB CH63 ....143 J3
Venice St EV L5 ....97 H7
Venmore St EV L5 ....97 H7
Venns Rd WARRN/WOL WA2 ....15 J3
Ventnor Cl WARRW/BUR WA5 ....119 M6
Ventnor Rd CHLY/EC PR7 ....32 D7
WAV L15 ....114 D5
Verdala Pk CALD/MH L18 * 130 F3
Verda St WGNE/HIN WN2 ....80 C5
Verdi Av LITH L21 ....83 H8
Verdi St LITH L21 ....83 H8
Verdi Ter LITH L21 ....83 H8
Vere St TOX L8 ....113 G8
Vermont Av CSBY/BLUN L23 ....82 F1
Vermont Cl NWD/KWIPK L33 ....73 M7
WARRW/BUR WA5 ....120 E6
Vermont Rd CSBY/BLUN L23 ....82 F1
Vermont Wy BTL L20 ....7 G3
Verney Crs ALL/GAR L19 ....144 E4
Verney Crs South ALL/GAR L19 ....156 D1
Vernon Av GTS/LS CH66 ....155 J3
WAL/EC CH44 ....111 M3
Vernon Ct CHTN/BK PR9 ....25 J5
Vernon St CLVP L2 ....12 F5
STHEL WA9 ....9 L4
WARR WA1 ....14 F7
Verona St EV L5 ....97 H7
Veronica Wy GTS/LS CH66 ....155 M6
Verulam Cl TOX L8 ....113 J6
Verulam Rd CHTN/BK PR9 ....25 J5
Verwood Cl PEN/TH CH61 ....125 M6
Verwood Dr WD/CROXPK L12 ....99 J2
Veryan Cl HLWD L26 ....132 B4
Vescock St EV L5 ....13 G1
Vesta Rd ALL/GAR L19 ....145 M1
Vesuvius PI EV L5 ....96 F7
Vetch Hey NTHLY L27 ....116 A8
Viaduct St NEWLW WA12 ....104 C2
Vicarage Cl CALD/MH L18 ....130 D3
CHLY/EC PR7 ....31 M2
CHLYE PR6 ....33 C6
FMBY L37 ....58 E1
ORM L39 ....53 J8
RF/TRAN CH42 ....127 K4
SPK/HALE L24 ....148 A4
WGNE/HIN WN2 ....80 C3
Vicarage Dr RNFD/HAY WA11 ....90 C7
Vicarage Gdns BRSC L40 ....51 M1
Vicarage Gv WAL/EC CH44 ....95 L8
Vicarage HI FROD/HEL WA6 ....166 E1
Vicarage La BRSC L40 ....63 H7
CHTN/BK PR9 ....23 H6
FROD/HEL WA6 ....166 E1
WGNNW/ST WN6 ....55 J1
Vicarage Lawn WLTN L25 ....115 J8
Vicarage PI PR/KW L34 ....100 E7
Vicarage Rd AIMK WN4 ....91 K3
FMBY L37 ....58 F1
HOR/BR BL6 ....57 M3
RNFD/HAY WA11 ....90 D6
WDN WA8 ....16 D5
WGNE/HIN WN2 ....80 D4
WGNW/BIL/O WN5 ....77 M1
Vicarage Rd West HOR/BR BL6 ....57 M4
Vicarage St ORM L39 ....53 J8
Vicarage Wk ORM L39 ....51 G8
Vicar Rd NPK/KEN L6 ....97 L6
Viceroy St EV L5 ....97 H7
Vickers Rd WDN WA8 ....149 G1
Victor Cl WGNNW/ST WN6 ....67 M5
Victoria Av CSBY/BLUN L23 ....82 E1
DV/KA/FCH L14 ....114 C1
HES CH60 ....141 H7
RNFD/HAY WA11 ....89 J5
WARRS WA4 ....138 C3
WARRW/BUR WA5 ....95 K4
WAV L15 ....114 B5
WGNE/HIN WN2 ....81 M4
WGNNW/ST WN6 ....56 A5
Victoria Bridge Rd STHP PR8 ....3 J5
Victoria Cl AIG/SPK L17 ....130 A2
WGNE/HIN WN2 ....57 K7
Victoria Ct BIRK CH41 ....11 G4
WAV L15 ....114 C1

Victoria Dr RF/TRAN CH42 ....128 C4
WKBY CH48 ....124 C3
WLT/FAZ L9 ....84 B7
Victoria Flds RF/TRAN CH42 ....127 L1
Victoria Gdns CL/PREN CH43 ....10 C9
Victoria Gv WDN WA8 ....134 C9
Victoria La CL/PREN CH43 ....127 K1
Victoria Mt CL/PREN CH43 ....127 K1
Victoria Pde WAL/NB CH45 ....95 L4
Victoria Pk SKEL WN8 ....64 E4
Victoria Park Rd RF/TRAN CH42 ....127 M3
Victoria Pl CLB/OSW/ST L13 ....114 C2
RAIN/WH L35 ....117 L3
WARRS WA4 ....137 L4
Victoria Rd AIG/SPK L17 ....130 A3
AIMK WN4 ....91 M1
BEB CH63 ....127 M7
CLB/OSW/ST L13 ....98 A7
CSBY/BLUN L23 ....82 A7
CSBY/WL L22 ....81 H4
EP CH65 ....20 B4
FMBY L37 ....46 D8
HTWN L38 ....71 G2
HUY L36 ....116 B5
NEWLW WA12 ....104 B1
NSTN CH64 ....153 J7
ORM L39 ....62 G2
RF/TRAN CH42 ....11 G9
RUNC WA7 ....95 K5
WAL/NB CH45 ....95 K5
WARRS WA4 ....135 M1
WDN WA8 ....80 C4
WGNE/HIN WN2 ....80 C3
WKBY CH48 ....124 C4
Victoria Sq ECCL WA10 ....9 G4
WDN WA8 ....16 D5
Victoria St BRSC L40 ....39 C8
CHLY/EC PR7 ....32 F6
CLVP L2 ....12 F7
ECCL WA10 ....9 G2
HOR/BR BL6 ....57 M2
PS/BROM CH62 ....128 D8
RAIN/WH L35 ....117 L2
RNFD/HAY WA11 ....76 B6
STHP PR8 ....3 J6
WARR WA1 ....15 G5
WDN WA8 ....16 E5
WGNE/HIN WN2 ....80 C3
WGNW/BIL/O WN5 ....68 A7
Victoria Ter CHLYE PR6 ....32 F4
RAIN/WH L35 ....117 L2
WAV L15 ....114 B5
WGNE/HIN WN2 ....81 H5
Victoria Wy FMBY L37 ....46 F8
STHP PR8 ....3 D4
Victor St WAV L15 ....113 M5
Victory Av CHTN/BK PR9 ....25 J4
Victory Cl NTHTN L30 ....84 A5
Vienna St EV L5 ....97 H7
Viennese Rd WLTN L25 * 115 K6
Viewpark Cl CHLDW L16 ....115 J3
View Rd RAIN/WH L35 ....117 L3
Vigo St WGNE/HIN WN2 ....83 J6
Viking Cl LITH L21 ....83 J8
Villa Av WGNNW/ST WN6 ....68 C1
Villagate La WARRS WA4 ....138 E8
Village Cl RUNC WA7 ....150 C5
SKEL WN8 ....64 F5
WAL/NB CH45 ....95 G7
WARRS WA4 ....139 G1
Village Ct AIG/SPK L17 ....130 A2
Village Cft CHLY/EC PR7 ....31 L2
Village Green Ct
CL/PREN CH43 ....110 E5
Village Nook AIN/FAZ L10 * 85 J6
Village Rd BEB CH63 ....127 M7
CL/PREN CH43 ....141 H6
HES CH60 ....141 H6
WKBY CH48 ....124 E4
Village St NPK/KEN L6 ....113 K2
Village Vw WGNW/BIL/O WN5 ....78 A8
Village Wy HTWN L38 ....70 F1
SKEL WN8 ....64 F5
WAL/NB CH45 ....95 G8
Villa Gloria Cl ALL/GAR L19 ....130 C5
Villars St WARR WA1 ....15 H5
Villas Rd MGHL L31 ....73 K3
Villiers Crs ECCL WA10 ....8 D8
Villiers Rd PR/KW L34 ....86 D7
Vincent Cl WARRW/BUR WA5 ....135 M4
Vincent Ct CLVPS L1 * 112 F5
Vincent Rd LITH L21 ....83 L4
RAIN/WH L35 ....117 L3
Vincent St CLB/OSW/ST L13 ....114 B4
ECCL WA10 ....9 H2
Vincent Wy WGNW/BIL/O WN5 ....67 M5
Vine Crs WARRW/BUR WA5 ....135 M1
The Vineries WLTN L25 ....131 G2
Vine Rd GTS/LS CH66 ....155 L4
Vineside Rd WD/CROXPK L12 ....98 F3
Vine St CHLY/EC PR7 ....32 E4
EHL/KEN L7 ....113 J5
RUNC WA7 ....16 D1
WDN WA8 ....16 D5
WGN WN1 ....4 D5
WGNE/HIN WN2 ....69 M7
Vine Tree Rain/WH L35 * 133 J3
Vineyard St ALL/GAR L19 ....131 G8
Vining Rd RAIN/WH L35 ....101 H7
Vining St TOX L8 ....113 H7
Viola Cl WGNNW/ST WN6 ....55 M3
Viola St BTL L20 ....7 H8
Violet Cl GOL/RIS/CU WA3 ....122 E1
Violet Rd BIRK CH41 ....111 H6
LITH L21 ....83 K7
Violet St AIMK WN4 ....16 C6
WDN WA8 ....16 D5
Virgil St ECCL WA10 ....8 C4
Virginia Av MGHL L31 ....72 E2
Virginia Gdns
WARRW/BUR WA5 ....120 D5
Virginia Gv MGHL L31 ....72 F2
Virginia Rd WAL/NB CH45 ....95 K4
Virginia St STHP PR8 ....3 J5
VAUX/LVPD L3 * 12 E1
Virginia Wy WGNW/BIL/O WN5 ....67 L5
Virgin's La CSBY/BLUN L23 ....82 C1
Viscount Rd WARRN/WOL WA2 ....122 A3
Vista Av NEWLW WA12 ....104 C1
Vista Rd NEWLW WA12 ....104 C1
RUNC WA7 ....19 H7
Vista Wy NEWLW WA12 ....104 C1
Vitesse Rd ALL/GAR L19 ....131 H7
Vittoria Cl BIRK CH41 ....11 G4
Vittoria Ct BIRK CH41 ....10 F4
Vittoria St BIRK CH41 ....11 G4
Vivian Av WAL/EC CH44 ....95 L8
Vivian Dr STHP PR8 ....35 J3
Voelas St TOX L8 ....113 J8
Vogan Av CSBY/BLUN L23 ....83 J2
Volunteer St ECCL WA10 ....8 F3

FROD/HEL WA6 160 E4
Vose Cl WARRW/BUR WA5 120 F7
Vronhill Cl TOX L8 113 J7
Vulcan Cl CL/PREN CH43 111 H5
NEWLW WA12 104 E4
WARRN/WOL WA2 122 B3
Vulcan Dr WGN WN1 5 H5
Vulcan Rd WGNW/BIL/O WN5 67 M5
Vulcan St ALL/GAR L19 145 L1
BTL L20 6 D3
CHTN/BK PR9 3 J4
VAUX/LVPD L3 12 C2
Vyner Cl CL/PREN CH43 111 G7
Vyner Rd WAL/NB CH45 95 H8
Vyner Rd North CL/PREN CH43 110 F6
WLTN L25 115 J8
Vyner Rd South CL/PREN CH43 110 F7
WLTN L25 115 J8
Vyrnwy St EV L5 97 H6

W

Waddicar La MGHL L31 85 J2
Waddington Cl
GOL/RIS/CU WA3 * 93 H5
WARRN/WOL WA2 122 B4
Wadebridge Rd NG/CROX L11 85 J7
Wadeson Rd ANF/KKDL L4 97 M3
Wadeson Wy GOL/RIS/CU WA3 106 D6
Wadham Pk BTL L20 7 H8
Wadham Rd BTL L20 7 G8
Wadsworth Dr WGNNW/ST WN6 68 B3
Wagon La RNFD/HAY WA11 90 D7
Waine Gv RAIN/WH L35 101 J8
Waine St RNFD/HAY WA11 90 B7
STHEL WA9 102 F1
Wainfleet Cl WGNS/IIMK WN3 79 G2
Wainwright Cl EHL/KEN L7 * 113 K5
Wainwright Gv ALL/GAR L19 130 E7
Wakefield Crs WGNNW/ST WN6 56 C6
Wakefield Dr MOR/LEA CH46 110 B1
Wakefield Rd GTS/LS CH66 163 G4
NTHTN L30 84 D2
Wakefield St GOL/RIS/CU WA3 92 C6
VAUX/LVPD L3 13 J4
Walby Cl GR/UP/WCH CH49 126 E3
Walcot Pl WGNS/IIMK WN3 79 J3
Walden Cl WARRS WA4 138 F2
Walden Rd DV/KA/FCH L14 114 E2
Waldgrave Pl WAV L15 114 D4
Waldgrave Rd WAV L15 114 C4
Waldon Cl WGNE/HIN WN2 81 H1
Waldorf Cl WGNS/IIMK WN3 78 F3
Walford Cl BEB CH63 143 H3
Walford Rd AIMK WN4 91 L2
Walgarth Dr CHLY/EC PR7 32 C6
Walkden Av WGN WN1 68 D3
Walkden Av East WGN WN1 68 E3
Walker Av STHEL WA9 118 D2
Walker Cl FMBY L37 59 H3
Walker Dr BTL L20 83 L6
Walker Ms RF/TRAN CH42 127 M2
Walker Pl RF/TRAN CH42 127 M2
Walker Rd LITH L21 83 J6
Walker's Cft WAL/NB CH45 95 H8
Walkers La GTS/LS CH66 155 L7
STHEL WA9 118 C2
WARRW/BUR WA5 136 A2
Walker St HOY CH47 108 D6
NPK/KEN L6 113 J2
PS/BROM CH62 * 128 D7
RF/TRAN CH42 127 M2
WARRN/WOL WA2 14 C4
Walker Wy WLT/FAZ L9 84 B7
The Walk SPK/HALE L24 146 C3
STBRV L28 * 99 L6
STHP PR8 2 E8
Wallace Av HUY L36 116 B1
Wallace Dr HUY L36 116 B1
Wallace La WGN WN1 5 J1
Wallace St WDN WA8 16 D3
WLT/FAZ L9 84 C7
Wallacre Rd WAL/EG CH44 111 G1
Wallasey Bridge Rd BIRK CH41 111 H4
Wallasey Rd WAL/EG CH44 111 J1
Wallasey Village WAL/EG CH44 95 G8
Wallbrook Av
WGNW/BIL/O WN5 77 M4
Wallcroft NSTN CH64 154 C6
Wallcroft St SKEL WN8 65 G5
Waller Cl ANF/KKDL L4 97 G6
Waller St BTL L20 83 J7
Walletts Rd CHLY/EC PR7 32 D7
Wallgarth Cl WGNS/IIMK WN3 78 F3
Wallgate WGN WN1 4 E5
Wallgate Rd WLTN L25 115 H7
Wallgate Wy WLTN L25 115 H7
Wallingford Rd
GR/UP/WCH CH49 110 B8
Wallis St WARRS WA4 137 K2
Wallrake HES CH60 141 H6
Wallsend Ct WDN WA8 134 A2
Walls St WGNE/HIN WN2 81 L3
Wall St WGNNW/ST WN6 68 B4
Walmer Ct STHP PR8 35 H2
Walmer Rd CSBY/WL L22 83 G5
STHP PR8 35 J2
Walmesley Av WGNS/IIMK WN3 4 E7
Walmesley Dr RNFD/HAY WA11 76 C8
WGNE/HIN WN2 69 K6
Walmesley Rd ECCL WA10 88 C8
Walmesley St WGN WN1 5 G5
Walmsley St EV L5 96 E8
NEWLW WA12 104 F1
WAL/EG CH44 95 L8
WDN WA8 17 H3
Walney Rd WD/CROXPK L12 98 C5
WGNS/IIMK WN3 78 F3
Walnut Av WGN WN1 68 F3
WLT/FAZ L9 97 L2
Walnut Cl WARR WA1 123 G6
Walnut Gv GTS/LS CH66 163 H4
MGHL L31 85 J2
Walnut St STHP PR8 3 K9
Walpole Av RAIN/WH L35 117 H2
WGNS/IIMK WN3 79 H2
Walpole Gv WARRN/WOL WA2 121 L3
Walpole Rd RUNC WA7 149 K7
Walro Ms CHTN/BK PR9 25 J2
Walsh Cl EV L5 12 F1
NEWLW WA12 91 L8
Walsh Rd DV/KA/FCH L14 114 E3
Walsingham Ct WAL/EG CH44 111 M2
Walsingham Dr RUNC WA7 150 F3
Walsingham Rd CHLDW L16 115 G5
WAL/EG CH44 111 M2
WARRW/BUR WA5 120 B8
Walter Beilin Ct AIG/SPK L17 * 114 A8
Walter Gv STHEL WA9 103 H6
Walter Scott Av WGN WN1 68 D1
Walters Green Crs
GOL/RIS/CU WA3 92 C3
Walter St AIMK WN4 * 91 M1
LEIGH WN7 81 K8
VAUX/LVPD L3 96 D8
WARR WA1 15 L1
WDN WA8 17 J1
WGNW/BIL/O WN5 67 M7
Waltham Av WGNNW/ST WN6 68 B2
Waltham Ct RUNC WA7 151 G1
Waltham Rd NPK/KEN L6 97 L7
Walthew House La
WGNW/BIL/O WN5 67 K4
Walthew La WGNE/HIN WN2 80 C3
WGNW/BIL/O WN5 67 M3
Waltho Av MGHL L31 73 G4
Walton Av WARRW/BUR WA5 120 A8
Walton Breck Rd ANF/KKDL L4 97 J7
Walton Hall Av ANF/KKDL L4 97 K3
Walton Heath Rd WARRS WA4 137 K4
Walton La ANF/KKDL L4 97 J4
Walton Lea Rd WARRS WA4 137 J6
Walton New Rd WARRS WA4 137 K5
Walton Pk WLT/FAZ L9 97 J1
Walton Park Gdns ANF/KKDL L4 97 J3
Walton Rd ANF/KKDL L4 97 G5
ECCL WA10 88 F7
GOL/RIS/CU WA3 107 G8
GOL/RIS/CU WA3 107 H2
WARRS WA4 137 L5
Walton St BIRK CH41 * 11 J6
CHLY/EC PR7 44 C7
CHTN/BK PR9 3 J2
RUNC WA7 19 H4
Walton V WLT/FAZ L9 84 C7
Walton Village ANF/KKDL L4 97 H3
Wambo La WLTN L25 115 L8
Wandsworth Rd NG/CROX L11 98 B4
Wandsworth Wy WDN WA8 16 B8
Wanes Blades Rd BRSC L40 53 G1
Wango La AIN/FAZ L10 85 H4
Wanishar La ORM L39 49 J8
Wansfell Pl WARRN/WOL WA2 121 J2
Wantage Vw HUY L36 115 L5
Wapping VAUX/LVPD L3 112 F6
Wapping Quay VAUX/LVPD L3 112 E6
Wapshare Rd NG/CROX L11 98 A4
Warbeck Cl WGNE/HIN WN2 81 G2
Warbler Cl HLWD L26 131 M3
Warbreck Av WLT/FAZ L9 84 C6
Warbreck Moor WLT/FAZ L9 84 D6
Warbreck Rd WLT/FAZ L9 84 C7
Warburton Hey RAIN/WH L35 117 K1
Warburton St WARRS WA4 137 M4
Ward Av FMBY L37 58 F3
Ward Cl WARRW/BUR WA5 120 D4
Warden St ANF/KKDL L4 97 G5
Wardgate Av WD/CROXPK L12 99 G2
Ward Gv RF/TRAN CH42 128 B5
Wardley St WGNW/BIL/O WN5 67 K8
Wardlow Av WGNW/BIL/O WN5 67 J5
Wardour St WARRW/BUR WA5 121 G7
Ward Rd CSBY/BLUN L23 70 C7
Ward St CHLYE PR6 33 G6
ECCL WA10 9 G3
PR/KW L34 100 F6
VAUX/LVPD L3 13 J6
WGNE/HIN WN2 69 M6
Wareham Cl WARR WA1 122 E5
Wareing Rd WLT/FAZ L9 84 E7
Waresley Crs WLT/FAZ L9 98 A1
Wargrave Ms NEWLW WA12 104 E4
Wargrave Rd NEWLW WA12 104 E2
Warham Rd ANF/KKDL L4 97 L6
Waring Av RF/TRAN CH42 127 M3
STHEL WA9 103 K3
WARRS WA4 122 B8
The Warings CHLY/EC PR7 41 M1
Warkworth Cl WDN WA8 133 L2
Warlow Dr LEIGH WN7 81 M4
Warmington Rd
DV/KA/FCH L14 114 E2
Warminster Gv WGNS/IIMK WN3 78 F3
Warncliffe St WGNW/BIL/O WN5 67 M8
Warner Dr ANF/KKDL L4 97 L5
Warnerville Rd CLB/OSW/ST L13 114 E4
Warnford St WGN WN1 68 E3
Warnley Cl WDN WA8 133 M2
Warpers Moss Cl BRSC L40 39 H8
Warper's Moss La BRSC L40 39 J8
Warren Ct FROD/HEL WA6 160 F7
GTS/LS CH66 162 F2
STHP PR8 2 B7
Warren Cft RUNC WA7 150 E6
Warrender Dr BIRK CH41 111 H5
Warren Dr CL/PREN CH43 110 E7
GTS/LS CH66 156 A6
NEWLW WA12 105 H1
WAL/NB CH45 95 H5
WARRS WA4 137 L5
Warren Gn FMBY L37 58 F1
Warren Hey BEB CH63 143 J4
Warren House Rd CSBY/WL L22 82 D3
Warrenhouse Rd
NWD/KWIPK L33 86 C1
Warren La WARR WA1 122 F5
Warren Rd CHTN/BK PR9 25 J5
CSBY/BLUN L23 70 C8
HOY CH47 108 C6
WARRN/WOL WA2 121 M4
WARRS WA4 137 L6
The Warren GR/UP/WCH CH49 110 D8
Warren Wy HES CH60 140 F4
Warrington Av EP CH65 163 K3
Warrington La WGN WN1 5 G4
Warrington New Rd STHEL WA9 9 K6
Warrington Old Rd STHEL WA9 9 J7
Warrington Rd AIMK WN4 91 K3
GOL/RIS/CU WA3 105 K2
GOL/RIS/CU WA3 122 E2
LYMM WA13 139 K1
NEWLW WA12 92 C7
RAIN/WH L35 101 H8
RUNC WA7 150 C1
WARRS WA4 137 H7
WARRW/BUR WA5 135 M1
WDN WA8 17 G4
WGNE/HIN WN2 80 C3
WGNS/IIMK WN3 5 H8
WGNS/IIMK WN3 79 H1
Warrington St BIRK CH41 11 J9
Warton Cl WARRW/BUR WA5 136 C2
Warton Pl CHLY/EC PR7 32 C5
Warton St BTL L20 83 J7
Warton Ter BTL L20 83 J7
Warwick Av AIMK WN4 91 M3
CSBY/BLUN L23 82 F2
NEWLW WA12 104 F3
WARRW/BUR WA5 14 A1
WARRW/BUR WA5 119 M6
Warwick Cl CL/PREN CH43 10 F7
HUY L36 116 C2
NSTN CH64 153 G8
STHP PR8 35 K2
Warwick Ct EP CH65 164 A3
Warwick Dr WAL/NB CH45 95 L7
WKBY CH48 124 E5
Warwick Rd BTL L20 7 K3
CHLY/EC PR7 30 E6
GR/UP/WCH CH49 110 B7
HUY L36 116 C2
WGNE/HIN WN2 * 57 L8
Warwick St CHLY/EC PR7 44 B7
ECCL WA10 8 A6
STHP PR8 35 K1
TOX L8 113 G8
Wasdale Av MGHL L31 73 H3
RNFD/HAY WA11 89 K5
Wasdale Rd AIMK WN4 79 J5
WLT/FAZ L9 84 C8
Washbrook Av CL/PREN CH43 * 110 E5
Washbrook Cl ECCL WA10 101 K1
Washbrook Wy ORM L39 63 G1
Washington Dr NWD/KWIPK L33 73 M7
WARRW/BUR WA5 120 E6
Washington La CHLY/EC PR7 32 B3
Washington Pde BTL L20 7 G4
Wash La WARRS WA4 138 A3
Washway La ECCL WA10 89 J6
Wasley Cl WARRN/WOL WA2 122 B2
Wastdale Ct MOR/LEA CH46 109 L4
Wastdale Dr MOR/LEA CH46 109 L4
Wastdale Ms MOR/LEA CH46 109 L4
Wastle Bridge Rd HUY L36 100 A8
Watchyard La FMBY L37 59 J2
Waterbeck Cl WGN WN1 5 L2
Waterbridge Ct WARRS WA4 137 M5
Waterdale Crs STHEL WA9 102 F6
Waterdale Pl STHEL WA9 102 F6
Water Dr WGNNW/ST WN6 56 D6
Waterfield Cl BEB CH63 127 M8
Waterfoot Av STHP PR8 47 K2
Waterford Cl CHLYE PR6 44 C4
Waterford Dr NSTN CH64 153 J6
Waterford Rd CL/PREN CH43 111 G8
NTHLY L27 115 L7
Waterford Wy RUNC WA7 150 E7
Waterfront WARRS WA4 151 H7
Watergate La WLTN L25 131 K3
Watergate Wy WLTN L25 131 K3
Waterhouse Cl NPK/KEN L6 97 K8
Waterhouse St EV L5 13 L1
Waterland La STHEL WA9 103 H3
Water La CHTN/BK PR9 22 F8
RAIN/WH L35 132 F1
Waterloo Cl CSBY/WL L22 82 F5
EP CH65 20 D5
Waterloo La FROD/HEL WA6 167 L4
Waterloo Pl BIRK CH41 11 K7
Waterloo Rd CSBY/WL L22 83 G5
RUNC WA7 18 F3
STHP PR8 35 G4
VAUX/LVPD L3 12 C2
WAL/NB CH45 95 K4
WDN WA8 16 C9
Waterloo St CHLY/EC PR7 32 F4
ECCL WA10 8 F5
WAV L15 114 C6
WGNNW/ST WN6 4 A1
Watermead Dr RUNC WA7 151 H8
Watermede WGNW/BIL/O WN5 78 A2
Waterpark Cl CL/PREN CH43 127 H4
Waterpark Dr STBRV L28 99 J5
Waterpark Rd CL/PREN CH43 127 J4
Watersedge FROD/HEL WA6 160 F3
Watersedge Apartments
WAL/NB CH45 * 95 L4
Waterside NTHTN L30 72 A8
STHEL WA9 9 K3
WARRS WA4 137 M5
Waterside Ct STHEL WA9 9 K3
Waterside Dr FROD/HEL WA6 160 F3
WGNS/IIMK WN3 4 D7
Waterside Pk HUY L36 115 M4
Waters Reach WGN WN1 5 L4
Water St BIRK CH41 11 L5
CHLY/EC PR7 32 F4
CHLY/EC PR7 44 C7
CSBY/BLUN L23 71 K7
CSBY/WL L22 * 82 F5
ECCL WA10 8 F5
NEWLW WA12 104 E1
PS/BROM CH62 128 D7
RUNC WA7 19 H2
VAUX/LVPD L3 12 D7
WAL/EG CH44 111 M1
WDN WA8 16 C8
WGN WN1 4 F3
Water Tower Rd NSTN CH64 153 G3
Waterway Av NTHTN L30 84 D2
Waterways WARRW/BUR WA5 120 F7
Waterworks Dr NEWLW WA12 105 H1
Waterworks La GTS/LS CH66 155 G5
WARRN/WOL WA2 105 K6
Waterworks Rd ORM L39 51 J7
Waterworks St BTL L20 7 J4
Watery La FROD/HEL WA6 161 G8
STHEL WA9 103 G5
WARRN/WOL WA2 105 G7
Watford Rd ANF/KKDL L4 97 K6
Watkin Cl NTHTN L30 84 D4
Watkins Av NEWLW WA12 104 B2
Watkinson St CLVPS L1 112 F6
Watkinson Wy WDN WA8 17 G3
WDN WA8 118 B6
Watkin St WARRN/WOL WA2 14 E2
WGN WN1 4 F3
Watling Av LITH L21 83 J4
Watling Wy RAIN/WH L35 101 J8
Watmough St EV L5 13 K2
Watson Av AIMK WN4 91 L2
GOL/RIS/CU WA3 92 B4
Watson St BIRK CH41 11 H4
Watton Beck Cl MGHL L31 73 H3
Watton Cl WARRS WA4 138 E2
WD/CROXPK L12 99 J3
Watts Cl NWD/KWIPK L33 86 C1
Watts La BTL L20 84 A7
Wauchope St WAV L15 114 A5
Wavell Av CHTN/BK PR9 25 K6
WDN WA8 133 L5
Wavell Cl CHTN/BK PR9 25 K6
Wavell Rd HUY L36 116 A1
Waverley SKEL WN8 64 F4
Waverley Av WARRS WA4 137 M5
Waverley Ct WGNS/IIMK WN3 78 F2
Waverley Dr HUY L36 100 B8
Waverley Gv RF/TRAN CH42 127 L3
Waverley Rd AIG/SPK L17 129 L1
CSBY/BLUN L23 82 E2
GOL/RIS/CU WA3 92 F4
HOY CH47 108 E6
WGNE/HIN WN2 69 L8
Waverley St BTL L20 6 F4
STHP PR8 2 F3
Waverton Av CL/PREN CH43 127 G3
Waverton Rd GTS/LS CH66 156 A8
Wavertree Av CLB/OSW/ST L13 114 A4
WDN WA8 16 C3
Wavertree Bvd EHL/KEN L7 113 M4
Wavertree Bvd South
EHL/KEN L7 114 A4
Wavertree Ct GTS/LS CH66 156 B6
Wavertree Gn WAV L15 114 C6
Wavertree Nook Rd WAV L15 114 E5
Wavertree Rd EHL/KEN L7 113 K4
Wavertree V WAV L15 113 M6
Wayfarers Ar STHP PR8 * 3 G3
Wayfarers Dr NEWLW WA12 105 G3
Wayford Cl FROD/HEL WA6 160 D4
Waylands Dr WLTN L25 131 K6
Wayside Cl LYMM WA13 139 M3
Wayville Cl CALD/MH L18 130 D3
Waywell Cl WARRN/WOL WA2 122 B2
Weald Dr GTS/LS CH66 155 J7
Weardale Rd WAV L15 114 A7
Wearhead Cl GOL/RIS/CU WA3 92 C6
Weasdale Cl STHEL WA9 102 F6
Weaste La WARRS WA4 138 F3
Weates Cl WDN WA8 135 G2
Weaver Av BRSC L40 39 H8
NWD/KWIPK L33 74 B7
RAIN/WH L35 117 K2
Weaver Crs FROD/HEL WA6 160 F4
Weaver Gv LEIGH WN7 93 L1
STHEL WA9 103 J2
Weaver La FROD/HEL WA6 160 D3
Weaver Rd EP CH65 20 D9
FROD/HEL WA6 160 F4
GOL/RIS/CU WA3 107 J3
RUNC WA7 149 J7
Weaver's Brow CHLYE PR6 33 J8
Weaverside Av RUNC WA7 161 H1
Weavers La MGHL L31 73 H7
Weaver St WLT/FAZ L9 97 H2
Webb Cl EHL/KEN L7 113 L4
Webb Dr WARRW/BUR WA5 104 B7
Webber Rd NWD/KWIPK L33 86 D4
Webb St EHL/KEN L7 113 L6
STHEL WA9 102 F4
Webster Av BTL L20 7 L2
WAL/EG CH44 95 M8
Webster Dr KKBY L32 86 A3
Webster Rd WAV L15 113 M6
Websters La GTS/LS CH66 163 H3
Webster's St WGNE/HIN WN2 80 C3
Webster St LITH L21 83 K7
VAUX/LVPD L3 13 G5
Weddell Cl WARRW/BUR WA5 120 F6
Wedge Av RNFD/HAY WA11 90 C8
Wedgewood Dr
WGNNW/ST WN6 67 M2
Wedgewood Gdns STHEL WA9 101 K7
Wedgewood St EHL/KEN L7 113 L3
Wedgwood Dr WDN WA8 134 D1
Wednesbury Dr
WARRW/BUR WA5 120 B7
Weedon Av NEWLW WA12 91 K8
Weightman Gv WLT/FAZ L9 84 C7
Weir La WARR WA1 123 G7
Weir St WARRS WA4 137 J4
Welbeck Av CALD/MH L18 114 B8
NEWLW WA12 104 F3
Welbeck Ct CSBY/WL L22 * 82 F4
Welbeck Rd AIMK WN4 79 K8
STHP PR8 35 H1
WGNS/IIMK WN3 79 G2
Welbeck Ter STHP PR8 35 H1
Welbourne Rd CHLDW L16 114 E4
Weld Av CHLY/EC PR7 32 E8
Weldbank La CHLY/EC PR7 32 E8
Weldbank St CHLY/EC PR7 32 E8
Weld Blundell Av MGHL L31 72 D1
Weld Dr FMBY L37 58 F1
Weldon Dr ORM L39 63 H1
Weldon Gv WGN WN1 69 G3
Weldon St ANF/KKDL L4 97 H3
Weld Pde STHP PR8 2 D9
Weld Rd CSBY/BLUN L23 82 E2
STHP PR8 2 C8
Welfield Pl TOX L8 129 J1
Welford Av CL/PREN CH43 127 H3
GOL/RIS/CU WA3 92 E6
Welland Cl HLWD L26 132 A8
Welland Rd AIMK WN4 80 A8
BEB CH63 * 127 M8
Wellbank Dr HLWD L26 132 C4
Wellbrae Cl GR/UP/WCH CH49 109 M8
Wellbrook Cl RUNC WA7 150 E8
SPK/HALE L24 * 146 F1
Wellbrooke Cl AIMK WN4 91 L2
Wellbrook Gn SPK/HALE L24 * 146 F2
Well Brow Rd ANF/KKDL L4 97 K3
Wellcroft Rd HUY L36 116 A1
Wellcross Rd SKEL WN8 66 D7
Weller St TOX L8 113 H8
Weller Wy TOX L8 129 J1
Wellesbourne Pl NG/CROX L11 98 C3
Wellesbourne Rd NG/CROX L11 98 C2
Wellesley Av EP CH65 20 D5
Wellesley Cl NEWLW WA12 91 K8
WGNW/BIL/O WN5 68 A5
Wellesley Gv BEB CH63 128 C7
Wellesley Rd TOX L8 129 J1
WAL/EG CH44 111 K1
Wellesley Wk EP CH65 20 D5
Well Farm Cl WARR WA1 122 F5
Wellfield RNFD/HAY WA11 88 C1
RUNC WA7 151 G8
WDN WA8 134 C1
Wellfield Av KKBY L32 86 A4
Wellfield La BRSC L40 63 L3
Wellfield Rd GOL/RIS/CU WA3 107 G1
WGNE/HIN WN2 81 J1
WGNNW/ST WN6 68 B1
WLT/FAZ L9 97 J1
Wellfield St WARRW/BUR WA5 121 G8
Wellgreen Rd WLTN L25 115 H6
Wellham Rd WGNS/IIMK WN3 79 K2
Wellington Av WAV L15 113 M6
Wellington Cl AIN/FAZ L10 84 E2
EP CH65 20 D4
WARRN/WOL WA2 122 B3
Wellington Flds WAV L15 113 M7
Wellington Ga SPK/HALE L24 147 M3
Wellington Gv WAV L15 * 114 A5
WGNS/IIMK WN3 5 H9
Wellington Rd BEB CH63 128 C7
CL/PREN CH43 10 A8
EP CH65 20 B6
LITH L21 83 J6
TOX L8 129 H1
WAL/NB CH45 95 K4
WAV L15 114 A6
Wellington Rd North EP CH65 20 D5
Wellington St ALL/GAR L19 130 E8
CHLY/EC PR7 32 E4
CSBY/WL L22 82 F4
NEWLW WA12 104 C2
RUNC WA7 19 G2
STHP PR8 2 E5
VAUX/LVPD L3 13 G3
WARR WA1 15 G6
WDN WA8 16 C8
WGN WN1 5 H4
Wellington Ter BIRK CH41 11 H8
ECCL WA10 9 G2
TOX L8 113 J8
Well La BEB CH63 127 M7
BTL L20 7 J4
GR/UP/WCH CH49 125 L2
HES CH60 141 J7
NSTN CH64 153 H8
ORM L39 49 G7
RF/TRAN CH42 128 A3
WARRW/BUR WA5 136 A2
WLTN L25 115 H6
Well Lane Gdns BTL L20 7 J4
Wells Av WGNW/BIL/O WN5 77 M8
Wells Cl GTS/LS CH66 163 G5
WARR WA1 122 D5
Wells Dr WGNE/HIN WN2 69 H3
Wells Pl WGN WN1 5 K3
Wells St WAV L15 114 B6
Wellstead Cl WAV L15 114 C5
Wellstead Rd WAV L15 114 C5
Wellswood Rd GTS/LS CH66 156 A6
Welsby Cl WARRN/WOL WA2 122 B2
Welshampton Cl GTS/LS CH66 162 F3
Welshpool Cl WARRW/BUR WA5 120 F2
Welsh Rd GTS/LS CH66 155 J4
Welton Av GR/UP/WCH CH49 110 B8
Welton Cl SPK/HALE L24 146 F2
Welton Gn SPK/HALE L24 146 F2
Welton Rd PS/BROM CH62 143 M3
Welwyn Av STHP PR8 34 F7
Welwyn Cl STHEL WA9 102 A7
WARRS WA4 138 E2
Wembley Gdns WLT/FAZ L9 84 B7
Wembley Rd CALD/MH L18 114 D8
CSBY/BLUN L23 * 83 H2
Wendell St TOX L8 113 L6
Wendover Av AIG/SPK L17 129 L2
Wendover Cl CL/PREN CH43 126 F1
Wendron Rd NG/CROX L11 * 85 M8
Wenger Rd WDN WA8 118 D8
Wenlock Cl HOR/BR BL6 45 L7
WARR WA1 122 C5
Wenlock Dr HLWD L26 132 A6
Wenlock Gdns GTS/LS CH66 163 H3
Wenlock Gv WGNE/HIN WN2 80 F1
Wenlock La GTS/LS CH66 163 H3
Wenlock Rd ANF/KKDL L4 97 K6
RUNC WA7 161 J1
WGNE/HIN WN2 69 M8
Wenlock St WGNE/HIN WN2 * 80 F1
Wenning Av MGHL L31 73 G3
Wennington Rd CHTN/BK PR9 25 H5
Wensley Av HLWD L26 132 A6
Wensleydale WLT/FAZ L9 84 C6
Wensleydale Av
PS/BROM CH62 144 A8
RAIN/WH L35 117 M2
Wensleydale Cl MGHL L31 72 D3
WARRW/BUR WA5 120 B5
Wensley Rd GOL/RIS/CU WA3 93 G6
WLT/FAZ L9 84 C6
Wentworth Av WAL/NB CH45 95 K6
WARR WA1 122 D6
Wentworth Cl CL/PREN CH43 126 F1
STHP PR8 47 L1
WDN WA8 118 C8
Wentworth Dr BEB CH63 143 K8
CHLYE PR6 31 M1
EV L5 13 M1
Wentworth Gv HUY L36 115 K3
Wentworth Rd AIMK WN4 79 H8
Wernbrook Cl CL/PREN CH43 126 F1
Wernbrook Rd ANF/KKDL L4 97 L6
Wervin Cl CL/PREN CH43 127 G3
Wervin Rd CL/PREN CH43 127 G3
KKBY L32 85 M4
Wescoe Cl WGNW/BIL/O WN5 67 G8
Wesley Av RNFD/HAY WA11 91 G6
WAL/EG CH44 95 L8
Wesley Cl NSTN CH64 152 F6
Wesley Gv WAL/EG CH44 112 A2
Wesley St CSBY/WL L22 82 F5
STHP PR8 3 G5
WGNW/BIL/O WN5 78 F1
Wessex Cl WARR WA1 122 F6
WGN WN1 56 D4
Wessex Rd WGNW/BIL/O WN5 67 M4
West Albert Rd AIG/SPK L17 129 K1
West Av GOL/RIS/CU WA3 92 D4
WARRN/WOL WA2 121 K5
WARRS WA4 137 L4
West Bank CHLY/EC PR7 32 E5
Westbank Av WAL/NB CH45 95 L6
West Bank Dock WDN WA8 16 B9
West Bank Dock Est WDN WA8 133 M8
West Bank Rd EHL/KEN L7 114 A3
Westbank Rd RF/TRAN CH42 127 L2
West Bank St WDN WA8 16 C9
Westbourne Av CSBY/BLUN L23 71 K7
Westbourne Gdns STHP PR8 2 A9
Westbourne Gv WKBY CH48 124 C3
Westbourne Rd CHLY/EC PR7 32 D7
CL/PREN CH43 10 E7
STHP PR8 34 F1
WAL/EG CH44 111 H1
WARRS WA4 137 K6
WKBY CH48 124 C3
Westbridge Ms WGN WN1 4 F5
Westbrook Av PR/KW L34 100 D7
WARRS WA4 137 M3
Westbrook Centre
WARRW/BUR WA5 120 E4
Westbrook Crs
WARRW/BUR WA5 120 E4
Westbrook Rd MOR/LEA CH46 109 L6
WLTN L25 115 L8
Westbrook Wy
WARRW/BUR WA5 120 D4
Westbury Av WGNS/IIMK WN3 78 F3
Westbury Cl AIG/SPK L17 129 L4
WARR WA1 122 C5
Westbury St BIRK CH41 * 11 J9
Westcliffe Rd STHP PR8 2 B8
WD/CROXPK L12 98 C6
West Cl CL/PREN CH43 110 F8
PR/KW L34 101 J6
Westcombe Rd ANF/KKDL L4 97 L6
Westcott Dr WGNS/IIMK WN3 78 E1
Westcott Rd ANF/KKDL L4 97 K7
Westcott Wy CL/PREN CH43 126 F1
Westcroft WGNE/HIN WN2 80 D3
Westdale Rd RF/TRAN CH42 128 A3
WARR WA1 122 C6
WAV L15 114 B5
Westdale Vw WAV L15 114 B5
West Dene SKEL WN8 53 K3
West Derby Rd CLB/OSW/ST L13 98 A8
NPK/KEN L6 113 K1
West Derby St VAUX/LVPD L3 13 M6
West Derby Village
WD/CROXPK L12 98 D6
West Dr GR/UP/WCH CH49 110 C8
HES CH60 141 J6
NSTN CH64 152 F7
WARRW/BUR WA5 136 D1
Westend Av CHLY/EC PR7 42 F4
West End Gv RNFD/HAY WA11 90 B7
West End Rd RNFD/HAY WA11 90 B7
Westenra Av EP CH65 156 B7
Westerdale Dr CHTN/BK PR9 23 K8
Western Av HUY L36 115 K2
PS/BROM CH62 143 M1
SPK/HALE L24 146 E2
Western Dr ALL/GAR L19 130 C6
Westerton Rd WD/CROXPK L12 99 G7
Westfield Av AIMK WN4 91 J1
DV/KA/FCH L14 115 G3
Westfield Crs RUNC WA7 18 E6
Westfield Dr WD/CROXPK L12 99 G2
Westfield Gv WGN WN1 68 D2
Westfield Ms RUNC WA7 18 E5
Westfield Rd RUNC WA7 18 D6
WAL/EG CH44 111 M4
WLT/FAZ L9 84 A7
Westfields CROS/BRETH PR26 29 J3
Westfield St ECCL WA10 8 E6

Westfield Wk KKBY L32 ....85 K4
West Float BIRK CH41 * 111 K4
Westford Rd WARRS WA4 ....137 J2
Westgate SKEL WN8 ....64 F5
Westgate Dr WGNW/BIL/O WN5 ....66 F8
Westgate Rd PS/BROM CH62 ....143 K1
WAV L15 * 114 C8
West Gv HES CH60 ....141 H5
Westhaven Crs ORM L39 ....62 E5
Westhay Crs GOL/RIS/CU WA3 ...107 J8
Westhead Av GOL/RIS/CU WA3 .....93 G5
NWD/KWIPK L33 ....86 C4
Westhead Rd NWD/KWIPK L33 ....86 C4
Westhead Rd CROS/BRETH PR26 ..29 K3
Westhead Wk NWD/KWIPK L33 ....86 B3
West Heath Gv LYMM WA13 ....139 L1
Westhill STHP PR8 * 2 E6
Westhoughton Rd CHLY/EC PR7 ...44 B4
Westhouse CI BEB CH63 ....143 L8
West Hyde LYMM WA13 ....139 L2
Westinghouse CI
  WGNNW/ST WN6 ....4 B4
West Kirby Rd WKBY CH48 ....109 L8
West Knowe CL/PREN CH43 * 127 H1
Westlake Gv WGNE/HIN WN2 ......81 K1
Westlands CI NSTN CH64 ....153 H4
West La FMBY L37 ....47 H7
RUNC WA7 ....150 A6
Westleigh La LEIGH WN7 ....81 M3
Westleigh PI STHEL WA9 ....102 E8
Westlock WGNS/IIMK WN3 ....4 B8
West Mains SKP/HALE L24 ....147 J2
Westmead WGNNW/ST WN6 ....56 A5
West Meade MGHL L31 ....72 D3
Westminster CI NTHTN L30 ....84 A1
Westminster CI WARRS WA4 ......138 E3
WDN WA8 ....133 K5
Westminster Dr
  PS/BROM 143 M7
  RNFD/HAY WA11 ....91 H6
  STHP PR8 ....34 C8
Westminster Gv EP CH65 ....20 C5
PR/KW L34 ....100 C3
Westminster Rd ANF/KKDL L4 .....97 C6
BTL L20 ....7 K8
CHLY/EC PR7 ....32 E6
EP CH65 ....20 C2
WAL/EG CH44 ....111 K1
Westminster St
  WGNW/BIL/O WN5 * 68 B7
Westmoreland St WGNW/WN1 ......5 J4
Westmoreland PI EV L5 ....96 F8
Westmoreland Rd STHP PR8 ....3 K8
WAL/NB CH45 ....5 L6
Westmorland Av NTHTN L30 ....83 L2
WDN WA8 ....133 K5
Westmorland Dr VAUX/LVPD L3 ...12 F4
Westmorland PI EV L5 ....96 F8
Westmorland Rd HUY L36 ....116 A3
West Mt WGN WN1 ....68 F3
WGNW/BIL/O WN5 ....67 H7
West Oakhill Pk
  CLB/OSW/ST L13 ....114 C3
Westonby Ct AIMK WN4 ....91 M2
Weston Crs RUNC WA7 ....149 H7
Weston Gv HLWD L26 ....132 C7
MGHL L31 ....72 F7
Weston Pk WGNNW/ST WN6 ......67 M2
Weston Point Dock RUNC WA7 ..148 C6
Weston Point Expy RUNC WA7 .....18 C5
West Orchard La WLT/FAZ L9 ......84 F1
WARR WA1 ....122 B6
Westover Rd MGHL L31 ....72 E4
West Park Dr GTS/LS CH66 ....163 H5
West Park Rd ECCL WA10 ....14 D7
West Quay Rd
  WARR/WOL WA2 ....121 H2
West Rd CL/PREN CH43 ....110 F8
DV/KA/FCH L14 ....114 A3
EP CH65 ....20 D8
RUNC WA7 ....18 A9
WLT/FAZ L9 ....97 H2
Westry CI MOR/LEA CH46 ....109 K5
West Side STHEL WA9 ....9 L7
West Side Av RNFD/HAY WA11 ....90 C7
West St CHLY/EC PR7 ....32 E6
ECCL WA10 ....14 A5
PR/KW L34 ....100 E7
STHP PR8 ....3 K8
WAL/NB CH45 * 95 K8
WARRN/WOL WA2 ....14 F1
WGNE/HIN WN2 ....69 J5
WGNE/HIN WN2 ....8 C2
WGNNW/ST WN6 ....4 C2
West V NSTN CH64 ....153 G7
West Vw HOR/BR BL6 * 45 M8
HUY L36 ....116 D3
RNFD/HAY WA11 * 76 B7
SKEL WN8 ....53 K3
WARRN/WOL WA2 ....122 C4
West View Av HUY L36 ....116 D3
Westview CI CL/PREN CH43 ....116 F1
West View CI HUY L36 ....116 D3
Westward Ho WKBY CH48 ....124 F7
Westward Av AIG/SPK L17 ....129 J2
CSBY/WL L22 ....82 D3
West Wy CHLY/EC PR7 ....32 D5
MOR/LEA CH46 ....110 A4
RUNC WA7 ....150 A5
Westway CL/PREN CH43 ....126 F1
GR/UP/WCH CH49 ....93 G6
HES CH60 ....141 H7
HTWN L38 ....70 B1
MGHL L31 ....72 D3
WAV L15 ....114 D5
Westwell Rd CHLYE PR6 ....32 F4
Westwick PI WLT/FAZ L9 ....115 K2
Westwood CI STHP PR8 ....36 A2
Westwood Ct NSTN CH64 ....153 G4
Westwood Gv WAL/EG CH44 ......111 J1
Westwood La WGNS/IIMK WN3 .....5 H9
Westwood Rd CALD/MH L18 ......130 D3
CL/PREN CH43 ....110 E7
WGNS/IIMK WN3 ....4 E7
Westwood Ter WGNS/IIMK WN3 * ..5 J9
Westy La WARRS WA4 ....15 M8
Wetheral CI WGNE/HIN WN2 ....81 J7
Wetherby Av WAL/NB CH45 ....95 G8
Wetherby Ct NEWLW WA12 ....91 L8
Wetherby Ct HUY L36 ....99 L8
Wetherby Wy GTS/LS CH66 ....155 K8
Wethersfield Rd
  CL/PREN CH43 ....127 G1
Wetstone La STHEL WA9 ....9 L7
Wexford Av SPK/HALE L24 ....147 M3
Wexford CI CL/PREN CH43 ....127 H1
Wexford Rd CL/PREN CH43 ....127 H1
Wexham Gdns WGNE/HIN WN2 ...80 C2
Wexwood Gv RAIN/WH L35 ....117 G3
Weybourne CI
  GR/UP/WCH CH49 ....110 C6
Weybourne Dr WGNS/IIMK WN3 ...3
Weybridge CI WARRS WA4 ....138 A6
Weyman Av RAIN/WH L35 ....117 G2
Weymoor CI BEB CH63 ....143 H3
Weymouth Av STHEL WA9 ....103 H4

Weymouth CI CHLDW L16 ....115 H5
RUNC WA7 ....151 G7
Weymouth Dr WGNE/HIN WN2 ...81 J1
Weymouth Rd
  WARRW/BUR WA5 ....104 B7
Whaley La PEN/TH CH61 ....126 B7
Whalley Av ECCL WA10 ....89 G6
RNFD/HAY WA11 ....76 B7
Whalley CI WGNS/IIMK WN3 ....79 J2
Whalley Ct NTHTN L30 ....84 B1
Whalley Dr FMBY L37 ....59 J3
ORM L39 ....62 E6
Whalley Gv LEIGH WN7 ....81 M4
WDN WA8 ....134 F2
Whalley Rd CHLY/EC PR7 ....41 M1
RF/TRAN CH42 ....11 C8
Whalleys Rd SKEL WN8 ....53 J8
Whalley St CHLY/EC PR7 * 32 E6
TOX L8 * 129 H1
Wharf La BRSC L40 * 50 B1
Wharfdale CI WARRW/BUR WA5 ..120 C6
Wharfedale RUNC WA7 ....150 D7
Wharfedale Dr RF/TRAN CH42 ....127 K3
Wharfedale Dr PS/BROM CH62 ...144 B8
RAIN/WH L35 ....117 M2
Wharfe La EP CH65 ....156 C6
Wharford La RUNC WA7 ....151 G2
Wharf Rd NEWLW WA12 ....104 A3
Wharfside Ct WARRS WA4 ....138 A5
Wharf St PS/BROM CH62 ....128 D8
Wharmby Rd RNFD/HAY WA11 ....91 C7
Wharncliffe Rd
  CLB/OSW/ST L13 ....114 C2
Wharncliffe St
  WGNE/HIN WN2 * 69 M8
Wharton CI GR/UP/WCH CH49 ...109 M7
Wharton St STHEL WA9 ....102 D4
Whatcroft CI RUNC WA7 ....149 M7
Wheatacre SKEL WN8 ....65 G5
Wheat Cft WARRW/BUR WA5 * ...120 E2
Wheatcroft Rd CALD/MH L18 .....130 E3
Wheatear CI NTHLY L27 ....132 A1
Wheatfield CI GTS/LS CH66 ....162 E2
MOR/LEA CH46 ....110 B6
NTHTN L30 ....84 D2
Wheatfield Vw LITH L21 ....83 K3
Wheat Hill Rd NTHLY L27 ....116 A6
Wheatland CI STHEL WA9 ....118 E1
Wheatland La WAL/EG CH44 ......111 M2
Wheatland Rd HES CH60 ....141 L6
Wheatlands CI NTHLY L27 ....115 M7
Wheat La BRSC L40 ....52 C2
Wheatlea Rd WGNS/IIMK WN3 ....79 H4
Wheatley Av BTL L20 ....84 A8
NEWLW WA12 ....91 L8
Wheatsheaf Av STHEL WA9 ....102 F7
Wheatsheaf Wk
  WGNNW/ST WN6 ....55 M4
Wheeler Dr MGHL L31 ....85 K2
Whelan Gdns STHEL WA9 ....102 A7
Whelley GTS/LS CH66 ....155 K8
Whelley WGN WN1 ....5 J8
Whernside WDN WA8 ....133 L3
Whetstone Hey GTS/LS CH66 ....155 M8
Whetstone La BIRK CH41 ....11 G6
RF/TRAN CH42 ....127 M3
Whickham CI WDN WA8 ....134 B2
Whimberry CI CHLYE PR6 ....33 G5
Whimbrel Av NEWLW WA12 ....104 E2
Whimbrel CI RUNC WA7 ....150 B8
Whimbrel Pk HLWD L26 ....132 A4
Whinbury Ct STHEL WA9 ....118 E1
Whinchat Av NEWLW WA12 ....104 E1
Whinchat CI GOL/RIS/CU WA3 .....93 C6
Whinchat Dr GOL/RIS/CU WA3 ...123 H2
Whinfell Gv RUNC WA7 ....150 A3
Whinfell Rd WD/CROXPK L12 ....98 E8
Whinfield Av STHEL WA9 ....32 F4
Whinfield CI WGNNW/ST WN6 ......4 B8
Whinfield Rd CSBY/BLUN L23 .....71 J7
WLT/FAZ L9 ....84 B7
Whinhowe Rd NG/CROX L11 ....98 D3
Whinmoor CI CL/PREN CH43 ......110 F7
Whinmoor Rd AIN/FAZ L10 ....85 J8
WD/CROXPK L12 ....98 E8
Whinney Gv East MGHL L31 ....72 E7
Whinney Gv West MGHL L31 ....72 E7
Whinny La CHLY/EC PR7 ....32 A2
Whistlecroft Ct WGNS/IIMK WN3 ...5 L8
Whistley St WGNE/HIN WN2 ....80 D2
Whiston La HUY L36 ....116 C1
Whitbarrow Rd LYMM WA13 ....139 L1
Whitbeam Gv WGNE/HIN WN2 ....81 G3
Whitburn CI AIMK WN4 ....90 F1
Whitburn Rd NWD/KWIPK L33 .....86 C1
Whitby Av CHTN/BK PR9 ....27 K2
WAL/NB CH45 ....95 G8
WARRN/WOL WA2 ....121 M5
Whitby La HI/BCN CH1 ....163 A6
Whitby Rd EP CH65 ....20 B6
RUNC WA7 ....19 H6
Whitby St NPK/KEN L6 ....97 M7
Whitchurch CI WARR WA1 ....122 C5
Whitchurch Wy RUNC WA7 ....149 M7
Whitcroft Rd NPK/KEN L6 ....113 M2
Whiteacre WGNNW/ST WN6 ....55 J3
Whitebeam CI GTS/LS CH66 ......163 G5
Whitebeam CI NWD/KWIPK L33 ...74 B7
RUNC WA7 ....150 E4
Whitebeam Dr WD/CROXPK L12 ...98 F2
Whitebeam Gdns STHEL WA9 .....101 K7
Whitebeam Wk
  GR/UP/WCH CH49 ....125 K3
White Br BRSC L40 ....39 M1
Whitechapel CLVPS L1 ....13 G7
Whitecroft Av GOL/RIS/CU WA3 ...93 G4
Whitecroft Rd GTS/LS CH66 ....163 G3
WGN WN1 ....79 J3
Whitefield Dr WD/CROXPK L12 ...98 F2
Whitefield CI GR/UP/WCH CH49 .126 D2
HTWN L38 ....70 B3
Whitefield Dr KKBY L32 ....85 K3
Whitefield La BRSC L40 ....116 C7
RAIN/WH L35 ....116 C7
Whitefield Rd ECCL WA10 ....13 A1
NPK/KEN L6 ....113 K1
WARRS WA4 ....137 K5
WLT/FAZ L9 ....84 C8
Whitefields CHNE CH2 ....165 K2
Whitefield Wy NPK/KEN L6 ....113 J1
Whitegate CI GR/UP/WCH CH49 .107 J3
Whitegate Gv PR/KW L34 ....99 M1
White Gate Fold CHLY/EC PR7 ....43 D7
Whitegates CI NSTN CH64 ....154 A5
Whitehall Av WGNW/ST WN6 ......55 G5
Whitehall CI ANF/KKDL L4 ....7 J1
Whitehall La HOR/BR BL6 ....57 M2
Whitehall PI FROD/HEL WA6 ....160 D5
Whitehall St WGNS/IIMK WN3 ....5 J8

Whitehart CI ANF/KKDL L4 ....97 K4
Whitehaven CI STHEL PR8 ....47 K2
Whitehedge Rd ALL/GAR L19 .....130 E6
Whitehey Rd SKEL WN8 ....65 L5
Whitehorn Dr STBRV L28 ....99 K6
White Horse La HOR/BR BL6 ....45 L4
White House CI RNFD/HAY WA11 ..90 D7
White House Dr WARR WA1 ....123 C6
Whitehouse Expy RUNC WA7 .....150 D8
White House La BRSC L40 ....37 L4
HES CH60 ....141 M4
Whitehouse Rd
  CLB/OSW/ST L13 ....114 D3
Whitehouse V RUNC WA7 * 151 H8
Whitelands Meadow
  GR/UP/WCH CH49 ....110 A8
Whiteledge Rd SKEL WN8 ....65 K5
Whiteley's La BRSC L40 ....63 L3
White Lodge Av HUY L36 ....115 M2
White Lodge CI PS/BROM CH62 ..144 A8
White Lodge Dr AIMK WN4 ....91 J1
Whitely Gv NWD/KWIPK L33 ....74 C7
White Meadow Dr
  CSBY/BLUN L23 ....71 J7
Whitemere Ct EP CH65 * 20 C1
White Moss Rd SKEL WN8 ....64 E6
White Moss Rd South SKEL WN8 ..65 G6
Whiterails Dr ORM L39 ....50 A7
Whiterails Ms ORM L39 ....50 E7
White Rock St NPK/KEN L6 ....113 K1
Whitesands Rd LEIGH WN7 ....81 L1
Whiteside Av RNFD/HAY WA11 ....90 A8
WGNE/HIN WN2 ....69 M6
WGNNW/ST WN6 ....4 A1
Whiteside CI EV L5 ....96 F8
Whiteside Rd RNFD/HAY WA11 ....90 D7
Whitestock SKEL WN8 ....65 G5
Whitestone CI PR/KW L34 ....99 L3
White St CLVPS L1 ....112 F5
WARR WA1 ....14 C6
WARRS WA4 ....137 L4
NSTN CH64 ....154 C8
WGNW/BIL/O WN5 ....67 K7
Whitethorn Av
  WARRW/BUR WA5 ....120 B8
Whitewell Dr
  GR/UP/WCH CH49 ....110 B7
Whitewood CI AIMK WN4 ....79 J7
Whitewood Pk WLT/FAZ L9 ....84 F7
Whitfield Av WARR WA1 ....122 B6
Whitfield Ct RF/TRAN CH42 ....11 H9
Whitfield Gv RNFD/HAY WA11 .....90 C7
Whitfield La HES CH60 ....141 J4
Whitfield St RF/TRAN CH42 ....127 M1
Whitford Rd RF/TRAN CH42 ....127 L1
Whithorn Av CSBY/BLUN L23 ......83 H1
Whithorn St EHL/KEN L7 ....113 M5
Whitland Rd RNFD/HAY WA11 .....90 D7
Whitledge Gn AIMK WN4 ....79 J8
Whitledge Rd AIMK WN4 ....79 J8
Whitley Av WARRS WA4 ....138 C1
Whitley CI RUNC WA7 ....18 F7
Whitley Crs WGN WN1 ....68 D1
WGNE/HIN WN2 ....80 D6
Whitley Rd SKEL WN8 ....65 L5
Whitley St VAUX/LVPD L3 ....12 D2
Whitlow Av GOL/RIS/CU WA3 ....92 B4
Whitman St WAV L15 ....114 A6
Whitmoor CI RAIN/WH L35 ....118 A4
Whitney PI WLTN L25 ....131 L3
Whitney Rd WLTN L25 ....131 L2
Whitsbury Av WGNE/HIN WN2 .....80 F1
Whitstable Pk WDN WA8 ....134 A1
Whitstone CI WLTN L25 ....131 G3
Whitstone Dr SKEL WN8 ....65 M6
Whittaker Av
  WARRN/WOL WA2 ....121 M3
Whittaker CI
  CLB/OSW/ST L13 * 114 B4
Whittam Rd CHLY/EC PR7 ....32 D8
Whittier St TOX L8 ....113 L6
Whittle Av RNFD/HAY WA11 ....90 C8
WARRW/BUR WA5 ....120 C4
Whittle CI EV L5 ....97 G7
Whittle La WGNS/IIMK WN3 ....79 J5
Whittle Rd ORM L39 ....51 G6
Whittle Hall La
  WARRW/BUR WA5 ....120 B7
Whittle La WGNNW/ST WN6 ....41 G8
Whittle St ECCL WA10 ....101 M4
EV L5 ....97 G7
Whittlewood CI
  GOL/RIS/CU WA3 ....107 J3
Whittlewood Ct
  NWD/KWIPK L33 ....86 B1
Whitwell CI WARRW/BUR WA5 ...119 M6
Whitworth Av WGNW/ST WN6 .....55 M3
Whitworth Dr CHLY/EC PR7 ....32 C7
Wholesome La CHTN/BK PR9 ......37 L3
Wicket CI AG/CROX L11 ....85 M8
Wickham CI WAL/EG CH44 ....111 M3
Wicklow La GTS/LS CH66 ....155 G2
Wicks Crs FMBY L37 ....58 E1
Wicks Gdns FMBY L37 ....59 G2
Wicks Gn FMBY L37 ....58 E2
Wicks Green FMBY L37 ....58 E1
Wicks La FMBY L37 ....58 F2
Wicksten Dr RUNC WA7 ....19 L4
Widdale Av RAIN/WH L35 * 117 M2
Widdale CI WARRW/BUR WA5 ....120 B6
Widdrington Rd WGN WN1 ....5 H8
Widgeons Covert BEB CH63 ....142 B8
Widmore Rd WLTN L25 ....131 L1
Widnes Rd WDN WA8 ....16 E4
Wiend WGN WN1 ....4 F1
The Wiend BEB CH63 ....128 C8
RF/TRAN CH42 ....127 M4
Wigan La CHLY/EC PR7 ....43 M6
WGN WN1 ....4 F1
Wigan Lower Rd
  WGNNW/ST WN6 ....67 L1
Wigan Pier WGNS/IIMK WN3 * 5 H9
Wigan Rd AIMK WN4 ....79 H6
CHLY/EC PR7 ....31 L2
GOL/RIS/CU WA3 ....92 D2
LEIGH WN7 ....81 L6
ORM L39 ....51 H8
SKEL WN8 ....65 H5
WGNE/HIN WN2 ....69 J2
WGNNW/ST WN6 ....55 K8
WGNW/ST WN6 ....56 C7
WGNW/BIL/O WN5 ....78 B6
Wigan Sq WGN WN1 * 4 F1
Wigan St WGNE/HIN WN2 ....4 D3
Wiggins La BRSC L40 ....27 J3
Wight CI EP CH65 ....163 L4
Wightman Av NEWLW WA12 ....91 L7
Wightman Rd NPK/KEN L6 ....113 K2
Wight Moss Wy STHP PR8 ....35 M2
Wigmore CI GOL/RIS/CU WA3 ....107 J7
Wignall CI KKBY L32 * 86 A6
Wignalls Meadow HTWN L38 ......70 B2
Wigshaw La GOL/RIS/CU WA3 ...106 F3
Wigton CI STHP PR8 ....48 E1
Wilberforce Rd ANF/KKDL L4 ....97 K4
Wilbraham PI EV L5 ....96 F8

Wilbraham St EV L5 ....96 F8
LEIGH WN7 ....81 L8
STHEL WA9 ....119 G2
Wilburn St ANF/KKDL L4 ....97 H4
Wilbur St STHEL WA9 ....103 G6
Wilcock CI EV L5 ....96 F8
Wilcock Rd RNFD/HAY WA11 ....68 B6
Wilcock St WGNS/IIMK WN3 ....4 B5
Wilcote CI WDN WA8 ....134 C1
Wilcove SKEL WN8 ....65 H4
Wild Arum CI GOL/RIS/CU WA3 ....93 C5
Wildbrook Dr BIRK CH41 ....110 F3
Wildcherry Gdns STHEL WA9 .....101 K6
Wilderspool Cswy WARRS WA4 ....14 C8
Wilderspool Rd WARRS WA4 .....137 K4
Wilde St VAUX/LVPD L3 * 12 F2
Wilding Av RUNC WA7 ....19 K3
Wilding St WGNS/IIMK WN3 ....5 J8
Wilding Wy WGNS/IIMK WN3 ....9 J8
Wild PI BTL L20 ....84 A9
Wildwood Gv WARR WA1 ....122 C6
Wilfer CI EHL/KEN L7 ....113 L5
Wilfred Owen Dr CL/PREN CH43 .111 G3
Wilfred Rd RNFD/HAY WA11 ....90 B8
Wilfrid's PI WGNNW/ST WN6 ....56 A4
Wilkes Av MOR/LEA CH46 ....134 E1
Wilkesley Av WGNNW/ST WN6 ....55 M5
Wilkie St WAV L15 ....114 A6
Wilkin St ANF/KKDL L4 ....97 G6
Wilkinson Av WARR WA1 ....122 B7
Wilkinson CI WDN WA8 ....134 C8
Wilkinson St BIRK CH41 ....10 F7
Wilkinson St North EP CH65 ....20 C2
Wilkin St ANF/KKDL L4 * 97 G6
Willan St CL/PREN CH43 ....127 K1
Willard Av WAL/NB CH45 ....95 J7
Willard St BTL L20 ....84 A8
Willaston Dr HLWD L26 ....132 C7
Willaston Rd ANF/KKDL L4 ....97 K4
BEB CH63 ....142 F7
MOR/LEA CH46 ....109 M4
NSTN CH64 ....154 C8
Wildedsan Av CSBY/BLUN L23 ....83 G2
William Brown St CLVPS L1 ....13 H6
William Harvey CI NTHTN L30 ......84 B2
William Henry St BTL L20 ....84 B2
VAUX/LVPD L3 ....13 K3
William Jessop Wy
  VAUX/LVPD L3 ....12 C5
William Morris Av BTL L20 ....84 A8
William Moult St EV L5 ....96 F8
William Penn CI
  WARRW/BUR WA5 * 136 A1
William Rd RNFD/HAY WA11 ....90 B8
William Roberts Av KKBY L32 ....85 L3
Williams Av BTL L20 ....7 M1
NEWLW WA12 ....91 M1
Williamson CI WLTN L25 ....131 L4
Williamson Sq CLVPS L1 ....13 G7
Williamson St CLVPS L1 ....13 G7
STHEL WA9 ....9 M4
William St PR/KW L34 ....100 F7
BIRK CH41 ....11 K5
ECCL WA10 ....9 G4
WAL/EG CH44 ....111 K1
WDN WA8 ....134 E3
WGNS/IIMK WN3 ....5 K8
William Wall Rd LITH L21 ....83 K3
Willingdon Av WGNE/HIN WN2 ....80 A6
Willington Av PS/BROM CH62 ....155 C2
Willink Rd RNFD/HAY WA11 ....89 L6
Willis CI RAIN/WH L35 ....116 F3
Willis La WGNW/BIL/O WN5 ....77 J5
Willis St WARR WA1 ....15 J3
Willmer Rd ANF/KKDL L4 ....97 K6
RF/TRAN CH42 ....10 F8
Willoughby CI
  WARRW/BUR WA5 ....120 E4
Willoughby Dr ECCL WA10 ....101 K5
Willoughby Rd CSBY/WL L22 ....82 E5
DV/KA/FCH L14 ....115 G3
WAL/EG CH44 ....111 J1
Willow Av HUY L36 ....116 A5
KKBY L32 ....85 L2
NEWLW WA12 ....104 F1
RAIN/WH L35 ....116 F2
WDN WA8 ....134 D3
Willow Bank FROD/HEL WA6 ......160 D5
Willowbank CI HUY L36 ....99 L8
Willow Bank Est WARRW/BUR WA5 ..120 C6
Willowbank Rd PS/BROM CH62 ..128 D7
RF/TRAN CH42 ....127 M2
Willow Brook ORM L39 ....36 C7
Willowbrook Dr
  WGNNW/ST WN6 ....55 K6
Willowbrow Rd BEB CH63 ....153 M3
Willow CI CHLYE PR6 ....44 D5
RUNC WA7 ....19 K9
Willow Ct TOX L8 * 129 J1
Willow Dene RAIN/WH L35 * 117 L3
Willowdale NEWLW WA12 ....105 G2
Willowdale Rd CALD/MH L18 .....114 B8
WLT/FAZ L9 ....97 J1
Willowdale Wy GTS/LS CH66 .....163 H5
Willow Dr CHLY/EC PR7 ....42 F2
SKEL WN8 ....65 H4
WGNE/HIN WN2 ....81 H2
Willow End BRSC L40 ....51 H8
Willowfield Gv AIMK WN4 ....91 J3
Willow Gn BRSC L40 ....39 J2
ORM L39 ....51 H8
WLTN L25 ....131 G3
Willow Gv AIMK WN4 ....80 A8
CHNE CH2 ....165 J2
CHTN/BK PR9 ....25 C6
FMBY L37 ....59 H1
GOL/RIS/CU WA3 ....107 J8
GTS/LS CH66 ....163 J4
MOR/LEA CH46 ....109 M6
RAIN/WH L35 ....101 G8
WAV L15 ....114 C5
Willowhey CHTN/BK PR9 ....25 G7
Willow Hey MGHL L31 ....71 H5
SKEL WN8 ....65 H4
Willow Lea CL/PREN CH43 ....127 H1
Willow Ldg WGNE/HIN WN2 ....80 C3
Willow Moss CI MOR/LEA CH46 ..110 C5
Willow Rd CHLYE PR6 ....33 G3
ECCL WA10 ....101 L2
NEWLW WA12 ....104 F1
RNFD/HAY WA11 ....91 G6
WAV L15 ....114 C5
WGNNW/ST WN6 ....68 B1
The Willows BRSC L40 ....43 K1
FROD/HEL WA6 ....160 E5
STHEL WA9 ....118 C1
Willow Tree Av STHEL WA9 ....118 F1
Willow Tree CI WGN WN1 ....68 D1
Willow Wk SKEL WN8 ....65 K1
NG/CROX L11 ....85 M8
Wills Av MGHL L31 ....72 E3
Willsford Av KKBY L32 ....85 K2
Wilmere La WDN WA8 ....118 C7
Wilmot Av WARRW/BUR WA5 ....120 B7
Wilmot Dr RNFD/HAY WA11 ....92 B6
Wilmslow Av GTS/LS CH66 ....156 A6
Wilmslow Crs WARRS WA4 ....138 F2
Wilmslow Dr GTS/LS CH66 ....156 A6
Wilne Rd WAL/NB CH45 ....95 J7
Wilsden Rd WDN WA8 ....133 K4
Wilsford CI GOL/RIS/CU WA3 ....92 D4
Wilsham Rd WGNW/BIL/O WN5 ...67 G8
Wilson Av WAL/EG CH44 ....112 A1
WGNNW/ST WN6 ....68 D3

Willow Tree Av STHEL WA9 ....118 F1
Willow Tree CI WGN WN1 ....68 D1
Willow Wk SKEL WN8 ....65 K1
NG/CROX L11 ....85 M8
Wills Av MGHL L31 ....72 E3
Willsford Av KKBY L32 ....85 K2
Wilmere La WDN WA8 ....118 C7
Wilmot Av WARRW/BUR WA5 ....120 B7
Wilmot Dr RNFD/HAY WA11 ....92 B6
Wilmslow Av GTS/LS CH66 ....156 A6
Wilmslow Crs WARRS WA4 ....138 F2
Wilmslow Dr GTS/LS CH66 ....156 A6
Wilne Rd WAL/NB CH45 ....95 J7
Wilsden Rd WDN WA8 ....133 K4
Wilsford CI GOL/RIS/CU WA3 ....92 D4
Wilsham Rd WGNW/BIL/O WN5 ...67 G8
Wilson Av WAL/EG CH44 ....112 A1
WGNNW/ST WN6 ....68 D3
Wilson CI WARR WA1 ....138 F2
STHEL WA9 ....17 K1
WDN WA8 ....16 F6
Wilson Dr ALL/GAR L19 ....130 E7
Wilson La GOL/RIS/CU WA3 ....107 G8
Wilson Rd PR/KW L34 ....100 C7
RAIN/WH L35 ....116 B3
WAL/EG CH44 ....112 A1
Wilsons La LITH L21 ....83 K5
Wilson St TOX L8 ....129 J1
WARR/BUR WA5 ....14 C1
Wilson Av AV BEB CH63 ....127 M8
Wilstan Av WGNE/HIN WN2 ....69 H3
Wilton Gv CLB/OSW/ST L13 ....114 C3
Wilton La GOL/RIS/CU WA3 ....93 J8
Wilton Rd HUY L36 ....115 M3
RF/TRAN CH42 ....128 C4
WGNNW/ST WN6 ....55 J7
Wiltons Dr PR/KW L34 ....99 L2
Wilton St AIMK WN4 ....79 H7
WAL/EG CH44 ....111 K1
WGN WN1 ....5 G6
Wiltshire CI WARR WA1 ....122 F7
Wiltshire Gdns ECCL WA10 ....13 L5
Wiltshire PI WGNW/BIL/O WN5 ....67 L7
Wimbledon St WAL/NB CH45 ....95 K8
WAV L15 ....114 A6
Wimborne CI DV/KA/FCH L14 ......99 K7
Wimborne PI DV/KA/FCH L14 ......99 K7
Wimborne Rd DV/KA/FCH L14 .....99 K8
WGNW/BIL/O WN5 ....67 J5
Wimborne Av PEN/TH CH61 ....126 C3
Wimborne Wy WGNE/HIN WN2 .125 M6
Wimbourne Av PEN/TH CH61 .....126 C8
Wimbrick CI MOR/LEA CH46 ......110 B5
ORM L39 ....62 F1
Wimbrick Ct MOR/LEA CH46 * ...110 B5
Wimbrick Crs ORM L39 ....62 F2
Wimbrick Hey MOR/LEA CH46 ...110 B5
Wimpole St EHL/KEN L7 ....113 K3
Winchester Av AIMK WN4 ....91 J2
AIN/FAZ L10 ....84 F2
CHLY/EC PR7 ....44 A7
CSBY/WL L22 ....82 E3
EP CH65 ....20 F7
WARRW/BUR WA5 ....120 E8
Winchester CI
  WGNW/BIL/O WN5 ....67 H6
WLTN L25 ....131 K6
Winchester Dr WAL/EG CH44 ......95 J8
Winchester Gv WGNS/IIMK WN3 ...5 H8
Winchester PI WDN WA8 ....133 L5
Winchester Rd NPK/KEN L6 ....97 L7
RNFD/HAY WA11 ....91 G4
WGNW/BIL/O WN5 ....77 M4
Winchfield Rd WAV L15 ....114 B7
Windbourne Av
  RNFD/HAY WA11 ....89 J5
WARRN/WOL WA2 ....121 J2
WDN WA8 ....134 D2
Windermere Av
  RNFD/HAY WA11 ....89 J5
WARRN/WOL WA2 ....121 J2
WDN WA8 ....134 D2
Windermere Crs STHP PR8 ....47 L2
Windermere Dr CHLYE PR6 ....44 D3
MGHL L31 ....73 G3
NWD/KWIPK L33 ....85 M1
RNFD/HAY WA11 ....76 B3
WD/CROXPK L12 ....98 E4
Windermere Rd CHLYE PR6 * 33 G4
CL/PREN CH43 ....110 E8
EP CH65 ....163 L5
HTWN L38 ....70 C1
RNFD/HAY WA11 ....90 D7
WGNE/HIN WN2 ....69 J2
WGNE/HIN WN2 ....80 D5
WGNW/BIL/O WN5 ....67 J5
Windermere St EV L5 ....97 J7
WDN WA8 ....134 D1
WGN WN1 ....5 H1
Windermere Ter TOX L8 * 113 K8
Windfield CI NWD/KWIPK L33 ......74 C7
Windfield Gdns GTS/LS CH66 ....155 M6
Windfield Gn ALL/GAR L19 ....145 M1
Windfield Rd ALL/GAR L19 ....145 M1
Windle Ash MGHL L31 ....72 E4
Windle Av CSBY/BLUN L23 ....83 J1
Windlebrook Crs ECCL WA10 ......88 D7
Windle City ECCL WA10 ....89 H7
Windle Ct GOL/RIS/CU WA3 * 122 E1
NSTN CH64 ....153 G3
Windle Gv ECCL WA10 ....88 E7
Windle Hall Dr ECCL WA10 ....89 G6
Windlehurst Av ECCL WA10 ....89 G7
Windleshaw Rd ECCL WA10 ....8 B1
Windleshaw St WGNS/IIMK WN3 ...8 B1
Windle St ECCL WA10 ....8 E2
Windle V ECCL WA10 ....8 C2
Windmill Av CSBY/BLUN L23 ....71 H8
ORM L39 ....51 H8
Windmill Gdns STHEL WA9 ....102 F1
Windmill Hts SKEL WN8 ....66 C5
Windmill Hill Av RUNC WA7 ....150 F5
Windmill Hill Av East
  RUNC WA7 ....150 F5
Windmill Hill Av North
  RUNC WA7 ....150 F4
Windmill Hill Av South
  RUNC WA7 ....150 F4
Windmill Hill Av West
  RUNC WA7 ....150 E3
Windmill La WARRS WA4 ....137 L7
WARRS WA4 ....151 J4
WGN WN1 ....5 H1
Windmill St RUNC WA7 ....19 K3
Window La ALL/GAR L19 ....145 L1
Windrows SKEL WN8 ....65 H4
Windscale Rd
  WARRN/WOL WA2 ....122 C3
Windsor Av CHLY/EC PR7 ....44 A7
LITH L21 ....83 J5
NEWLW WA12 ....104 C3
Windsor CI BRSC L40 ....52 A2
CHLY/EC PR7 ....32 C6
GR/UP/WCH CH49 ....125 M2
NTHTN L30 ....72 B8
PS/BROM CH62 ....128 C6

Windsor Ct BTL L20 ...84 A8
  STHP PR8 ...2 B9
  WARRS WA4 * ...138 A4
Windsor Cresent
  WGNE/HIN WN2 ...57 M8
Windsor Dr EP CH65 ...163 J2
  RNFD/HAY WA11 ...91 J6
  WARRS WA4 ...138 D2
Windsor Gv RUNC WA7 ...19 K7
  WGNE/HIN WN2 ...81 K2
Windsor Ms PS/BROM CH62 ...128 D6
Windsor Park Rd AIN/FAZ L10 ...85 J2
Windsor Rd AIMK WN4 ...91 K3
  BTL L20 ...84 A8
  CHLY/EC PR7 ...30 E6
  CHLY/EC PR7 ...32 D6
  CHTN/BK PR9 ...3 L4
  CLB/OSW/ST L13 ...97 M7
  ECCL WA10 ...8 A5
  FMBY L37 ...59 G4
  GOL/RIS/CU WA3 ...92 E5
  HUY L36 ...115 K3
  MGHL L31 ...72 E5
  RAIN/WH L35 ...117 G1
  SKEL WN8 ...66 C5
  WDN WA8 ...134 C1
  WGNW/BIL/O WN5 ...78 B8
Windsor St CL/PREN CH43 ...10 F7
  TOX L8 ...113 H6
  WAL/NB CH45 ...95 K4
  WARRW/BUR WA5 ...121 C7
  WGN WN1 ...5 L4
Windsor Vw TOX L8 ...113 K6
Windus St ECCL WA10 ...8 D5
Windways GTS/LS CH66 ...155 M6
Windy Arbor Cl LEIGH WN7 ...81 M4
  NEWLW WA12 ...104 F3
Windy Arbor Rd RAIN/WH L35 ...116 F4
Windy Bank PS/BROM CH62 ...128 D7
Windy Bank Av
  GOL/RIS/CU WA3 ...93 G5
Windy Harbour Rd STHP PR8 ...35 G6
Wineva Gdns CSBY/BLUN L23 ...83 H2
Winfield Cl WGNNW/ST WN6 ...4 F4
Winfield Wy WDN WA8 ...16 B1
Winford St WAL/EC CH44 ...111 H2
Winfrith Cl BEB CH63 ...143 H3
Winfrith Dr BEB CH63 ...143 H3
Winfrith Rd WARRN/WOL WA2 ...122 C4
  WLTN L25 ...131 L1
Wingate Av STHEL WA9 ...101 M7
Wingate Cl CL/PREN CH43 * ...127 G1
Wingate Rd AIG/SPK L17 ...130 A3
  NWD/KWIPK L33 ...86 B1
  PS/BROM CH62 ...128 D2
Wingates Rd WGN WN1 ...56 E8
Wingfield Cl SFTN L29 ...71 M5
  WGNNW/ST WN6 ...68 C1
Wingrave Wy NG/CROX L11 ...99 D4
Winhill WLTN L25 ...131 J1
Winifred La ORM L39 ...62 D4
Winifred Rd AIN/FAZ L10 ...85 K6
Winifred St EHL/KEN L7 ...113 K4
  WARRN/WOL WA2 ...15 G2
  WGNS/IIMK WN3 ...5 K8
Winkle St TOX L8 ...113 H8
Winmarleigh St WARR WA1 ...14 C6
Winmoss Dr NWD/KWIPK L33 ...74 B8
Winnington Cl HOY CH47 ...124 C1
Winnipeg Dr NTHLY L27 ...116 A8
The Winnows RUNC WA7 ...149 M4
Winscar Rd WGNE/HIN WN2 ...69 M7
Winsford Cl RNFD/HAY WA11 ...91 H6
Winsford Dr WARRW/BUR WA5 ...104 A6
Winsford Gv GTS/LS CH66 ...162 E2
Winsford Rd CLB/OSW/ST L13 ...98 B7
Winsham Cl KKBY L32 ...86 A5
Winsham Rd KKBY L32 ...86 A5
Winskill Rd NG/CROX L11 ...98 C4
Winslade Cl ANF/KKDL L4 ...97 K3
Winslade Rd ANF/KKDL L4 ...97 K4
Winslow Cl RUNC WA7 ...150 H1
Winslow St ANF/KKDL L4 ...97 J2
Winsmoor Dr WGNE/HIN WN2 ...81 G1
Winstanley Cl
  WARRW/BUR WA5 ...120 E8
Winstanley Pl WGNS/IIMK WN3 ...5 L1
Winstanley Rd CSBY/WL L22 ...83 G3
  NSTN CH64 ...153 G8
  PS/BROM CH62 ...128 D6
  SKEL WN8 ...65 H5
  WGNE/HIN WN2 ...80 B5
  WGNW/BIL/O WN5 ...78 B2
  WGNW/BIL/O WN5 ...78 C5
Winstanley St
  WGNW/BIL/O WN5 ...68 B7
Winster Dr NTHLY L27 ...132 C2
  WGNE/HIN WN2 ...80 B7
The Winsters SKEL WN8 ...65 H4
Winston Av NEWLW WA12 ...104 D2
  STHEL WA9 ...103 K3
Winston Crs STHP PR8 ...36 A3
Winston Dr CL/PREN CH43 ...110 E8
Winstone Rd DV/KA/FCH L14 ...115 J1
Winston Gv MOR/LEA CH46 ...110 A5
Winterburn Crs
  WD/CROXPK L12 ...98 F6
Winter Gv STHEL WA9 ...103 K3
Winterhey Av WAL/EC CH44 ...111 K4
Winterlea Dr HLWD L26 ...132 C7
Winter St NPK/KEN L6 ...113 J2
Winthrop Pk CL/PREN CH43 ...111 G8
Winton Av WGNW/BIL/O WN5 ...67 M8
Winton Cl WAL/NB CH45 ...95 J5
Winton Gv RUNC WA7 * ...150 H4
Winton Rd GOL/RIS/CU WA3 ...93 G8
Winward St LEIGH WN7 ...81 K8
Winwick Cl GOL/RIS/CU WA3 ...105 M3
Winwick Link Rd
  WARRN/WOL WA2 ...105 K2
Winwick Park Av
  WARRN/WOL WA2 ...105 J8
Winwick Rd NEWLW WA12 ...14 E3
  WARRN/WOL WA2 ...14 E1
Winwick St WARR WA1 ...14 E3
Winwick Vw WARRW/BUR WA5 ...103 M4
Wirral Cl BEB CH63 ...143 H2
  GOL/RIS/CU WA3 ...107 G2
Wirral Crs NSTN CH64 ...153 H8
Wirral Dr WGNS/IIMK WN3 ...78 E3
Wirral Gdns BEB CH63 ...143 H2
Wirral Mt WAL/NB CH45 ...95 H8
  WKBY CH48 ...124 F3
Wirral Vw ALL/GAR L19 ...138 B7
Wirral Vis WAL/NB CH45 ...95 C7
Wirral Wy CL/PREN CH43 ...110 E8
  NSTN CH64 ...152 E2
  NSTN CH64 ...153 J6
  WKBY CH48 ...124 D3
Wisenholme Cl RUNC WA7 ...161 G1
Witham Cl NTHTN L30 ...84 C1
  WGNNW/ST WN6 ...55 M4
Witham Rd SKEL WN8 ...64 F4
Withburn Cl WGNW/BIL/O WN5 ...110 K8
Withensfield WAL/NB CH45 ...95 K7
Withen's La WAL/NB CH45 ...95 K8
Withens Rd MGHL L31 ...72 F2
The Withens STBRV L28 ...99 K6
Withers Av WARRN/WOL WA2 ...121 M5
Wither's La KNUT WA16 ...139 L8

Withert Av BEB CH63 ...127 M5
Witherwin Av WARRS WA4 ...138 C6
Withington Av
  GOL/RIS/CU WA3 ...107 J1
Withington Gra
  WGNE/HIN WN2 ...69 K3
Withington La CHLY/EC PR7 ...42 A3
  WGNE/HIN WN2 ...69 K3
Withington Rd SPK/HALE L24 ...147 H2
  WAL/EC CH44 ...111 L2
Withins Fld HTWN L38 ...70 B2
Withins La HTWN L38 ...60 B6
Withins Rd GOL/RIS/CU WA3 ...107 H1
  RNFD/HAY WA11 ...91 G5
Within Wy SPK/HALE L24 ...148 A4
Withnell Cl CLB/OSW/ST L13 ...114 D3
  WGNNW/ST WN6 ...68 B4
Withnell Gv CHLYE PR6 ...33 C4
Withnell Rd CLB/OSW/ST L13 ...114 D5
Withy Cl FROD/HEL WA6 ...160 E5
Withycombe Rd
  WARRW/BUR WA5 ...136 A1
Witley Av MOR/LEA CH46 ...110 A4
Witley Cl MOR/LEA CH46 ...110 A4
Witney Cl GR/UP/WCH CH49 ...125 L2
Witney Gdns WARRS WA4 ...138 B7
Wittenham Cl
  GR/UP/WCH CH49 * ...126 B1
Wittering La CHLY/EC PR7 ...140 F6
Witton Rd CLB/OSW/ST L13 ...97 M7
Witton Wy RNFD/HAY WA11 ...91 H6
Witt Rd WDN WA8 ...16 C6
Wivern Pl RUNC WA7 ...19 K2
Woburn Av LEIGH WN7 ...81 M4
  NEWLW WA12 ...104 F3
Woburn Cl CLB/OSW/ST L13 ...114 B1
  RNFD/HAY WA11 ...91 H6
Woburn Dr WDN WA8 ...117 M8
Woburn Hl CLB/OSW/ST L13 ...114 B1
Woburn Pl RF/TRAN CH42 * ...128 B3
Woburn Rd WAL/NB CH45 ...95 K7
  WARRN/WOL WA2 ...123 G1
Wokefield Wy ECCL WA10 ...101 K1
Wokingham Gv HUY L36 ...116 A5
The Wold CHLYE PR6 ...33 J2
Wolfe Cl WARRS WA4 ...138 D5
Wolfe St TOX L8 ...113 G8
Wolfrick Dr BEB CH63 ...143 K4
Wolfson Sq AIMK WN4 ...91 H1
Wollaton Dr STHP PR8 ...36 B2
Wolmer St AIMK WN4 ...91 J2
Wolseley Rd ECCL WA10 ...8 E2
Wolsey Cl AIMK WN4 ...79 J8
Wolsey St BTL L20 ...7 H9
Wolstenholme Sq CLVPS L1 ...13 H9
Wolverham Rd EP CH65 ...20 D8
Wolverton SKEL WN8 ...65 H5
Wolverton St NPK/KEN L6 ...97 L7
Woodacre Gv GTS/LS CH66 ...156 B5
Woodacre Rd GTS/LS CH66 ...156 B5
Woodale Cl WARRW/BUR WA5 ...120 A6
Woodall Dr RUNC WA7 ...19 J6
Wood Av BTL L20 ...7 M1
Woodbank Cl CHLDW L16 ...115 H5
Woodbank Pk CL/PREN CH43 ...127 C1
Woodbank Rd EP CH65 ...163 K5
  WARRW/BUR WA5 ...136 C1
Woodberry Cl CL/PREN CH43 ...126 F1
  NWD/KWIPK L33 ...74 B7
Woodbine St EV L5 ...96 F5
Woodbourne Rd
  DV/KA/FCH L14 ...114 F1
Woodbridge Av HLWD L26 ...131 M3
Woodbrook Av WGNS/IIMK WN3 ...78 F1
Woodburn Bvd BEB CH63 ...128 A5
Woodburn Dr HES CH60 ...141 H7
Woodchurch WGN WN1 ...5 L1
Woodchurch La CL/PREN CH43 ...127 L2
Woodchurch La GTS/LS CH66 ...156 A8
  RF/TRAN CH42 ...127 K3
Woodchurch Rd
  CLB/OSW/ST L13 ...114 C1
  CL/PREN CH43 ...126 D4
  RF/TRAN CH42 ...127 L2
Wood Cl BIRK CH41 ...11 H3
Woodclose GTS/LS CH66 ...155 J4
Wood Cl KKBY L32 ...85 M3
Woodcock Dr WGNE/HIN WN2 ...80 D3
Woodcock Sq AIMK WN1 * ...4 E3
Woodcock Fold CHLY/EC PR7 ...30 D8
Woodcote Bank
  RF/TRAN CH42 ...128 B6
Woodcote Cl NWD/KWIPK L33 ...86 C1
  WARRN/WOL WA2 ...121 M4
The Woodcotes
  PS/BROM CH62 ...143 M7
Woodcot La HES CH60 ...141 G4
Woodcourt WGNS/IIMK WN3 ...4 D8
Woodcroft SKEL WN8 ...65 H5
  WGNNW/ST WN6 ...55 C7
Woodcroft Dr PEN/TH CH61 ...141 H1
Woodcroft La BEB CH63 ...128 A5
Woodcroft Rd WAV L15 ...113 M6
Woodcroft Wy STHEL WA9 ...118 F1
Woodedge AIMK WN4 ...91 J2
Woodend PEN/TH CH61 ...141 H1
Woodend Av CSBY/BLUN L23 ...71 G7
  MGHL L31 ...72 E6
  SPK/HALE L24 ...131 L8
Woodend La GOL/RIS/CU WA3 ...123 M3
  SPK/HALE L24 ...146 B1
Woodend Rd EP CH65 ...20 B7
Woodene Cl KKBY L32 ...86 C6
Woodfall CHLY/EC PR7 ...32 D3
Woodfall Cl NSTN CH64 ...153 J7
Woodfall Gv NSTN CH64 ...153 H7
Woodfall La NSTN CH64 ...153 H7
Woodfarm Hey STBRV L28 ...99 J5
Woodfield Av BEB CH63 ...128 A5
Woodfield Crs AIMK WN4 ...91 J3
Woodfield Rd BEB CH63 ...143 G6
  CHLY/EC PR7 ...32 E4
  ORM L39 ...62 G2
  PEN/TH CH61 ...141 G1
  WLT/FAZ L9 ...84 B7
Woodfield Rd North EP CH65 ...20 C4
Woodford Cl WGNE/HIN WN2 ...69 J2
Woodford Gv GOL/RIS/CU WA3 ...93 F6
Woodford Rd FROD/HEL WA6 ...166 D3
  RUNC WA7 ...149 K7
  WARRS WA4 ...138 C2
Woodford Copse CHLY/EC PR7 ...32 B6
Woodford Rd DV/KA/FCH L14 ...115 G1
  ECCL WA10 ...88 E7
  PS/BROM CH62 ...128 D8
Woodford St WGNW/BIL/O WN5 ...67 K7
Woodgate LEIGH WN7 ...81 L8
Woodgarth LEIGH WN7 * ...81 L8
Woodger St ALL/GAR L19 ...138 A2
Wood Gn CL/PREN CH43 * ...110 E5
  PR/KW L34 ...100 E7
Woodgreen Cl WGNE/HIN WN2 ...80 F1

Woodgreen Rd
  CLB/OSW/ST L13 ...114 C1
Wood Gv CLB/OSW/ST L13 ...114 B3
Woodhall Av WAL/EC CH44 ...111 M4
Woodhall Rd CLB/OSW/ST L13 ...114 C2
Woodhall Rd WARRW/BUR WA5 ...120 C5
Woodhart La CHLY/EC PR7 ...30 E8
Woodhatch Rd RUNC WA7 ...150 D8
Woodhead Gv PS/BROM CH62 ...128 K3
Woodhead La PS/BROM CH62 ...128 D6
Woodhey Gv BEB CH63 ...128 B6
Woodhey Rd ALL/GAR L19 ...130 C5
  BEB CH63 ...128 B6
Woodhouse Cl ANF/KKDL L4 ...97 G6
  GOL/RIS/CU WA3 ...123 H1
Woodhouse Gv WGNNW/ST WN6 ...68 A2
Woodhouse La WGNNW/ST WN6 ...4 A1
Woodhurst Dr WGNNW/ST WN6 ...55 M4
Woodin Rd RF/TRAN CH42 ...128 C5
Woodkind Hey BEB CH63 ...143 J4
Woodland Av BRSC L40 ...37 H6
  HOY CH47 ...108 F4
  NEWLW WA12 * ...105 H2
  WDN WA8 ...16 B1
Woodland Dr AIMK WN4 ...79 K8
  GR/UP/WCH CH49 ...126 C2
  WAL/NB CH45 ...95 L6
  WGNNW/ST WN6 ...56 A3
Woodland Gv RF/TRAN CH42 ...128 B5
  WGN WN1 ...68 D3
Woodland Rd ANF/KKDL L4 ...97 M5
  EP CH65 ...163 K3
  GR/UP/WCH CH49 ...126 C2
  HLWD L26 ...132 A6
  LITH L21 ...83 G6
  MGHL L31 ...85 J1
  RF/TRAN CH42 ...128 B5
  WKBY CH48 ...125 M1
Woodlands Av WGNS/IIMK WN3 ...5 L8
  WD/CROXPK L12 ...98 C8
Woodlands Meadow
  CHLY/EC PR7 ...43 L2
Woodlands Pk NEWLW WA12 * ...91 L8
  WD/CROXPK L12 ...98 C8
Woodlands Rd AIG/SPK L17 ...130 A3
  FMBY L37 ...58 F3
  HUY L36 ...115 K3
  NSTN CH64 ...152 F5
  PEN/TH CH61 ...125 M8
  RNFD/HAY WA11 ...89 L6
  WLT/FAZ L9 ...84 F7
Woodland Vw CSBY/BLUN L23 ...71 J6
Wood La BRSC L40 ...29 M8
  BRSC L40 ...40 A8
  CHLY/EC PR7 ...42 A1
  FMBY L37 ...60 F4
  GR/UP/WCH CH49 ...109 M8
  HUY L36 ...116 D3
  NSTN CH64 ...152 E3
  NTHLY L27 ...116 B8
  PR/KW L34 ...100 D2
  RUNC WA7 ...161 H2
  SKEL WN8 ...53 M3
  WAL/NB CH45 ...95 G7
  WARRS WA4 ...138 A5
Wood Lea NG/CROX L11 ...99 G2
Woodlea Cl CHTN/BK PR9 ...22 F8
  PS/BROM CH62 ...143 M8
Woodlee Rd WLTN L25 ...131 L1
Woodleigh Cl MGHL L31 ...61 K8
Woodley Fold
  WARRW/BUR WA5 ...136 B1
Woodley Gv LEIGH WN7 ...81 L8
Woodley Park Rd SKEL WN8 ...65 K1
Woodleys Rd MGHL L31 ...72 E7
Woodmancote CHLY/EC PR7 ...32 D3
Woodmoss La STHP PR8 ...37 G3
Woodnook Rd WGNNW/ST WN6 ...55 C5
Woodpecker Cl
  GOL/RIS/CU WA3 ...123 H1
  GR/UP/WCH CH49 ...109 M8
  WD/CROXPK L12 ...99 H4
Woodpecker Dr HLWD L26 ...132 A3
Woodridge RUNC WA7 ...150 E4
Woodrock Rd WLTN L25 ...131 K3
Woodrow SKEL WN8 ...53 H4
Woodruff St TOX L8 ...129 H1
Woodrush Rd WGNNW/ST WN6 ...67 M2
Woods Cl ORM L39 ...61 H4
Woodside CHLY/EC PR7 ...31 L2
  CHLY/EC PR7 ...44 A1
Woodside Av WGNW/BIL/O WN5 ...79 J5
  FROD/HEL WA6 ...160 F6
  MOR/LEA CH46 ...109 M5
  RNFD/HAY WA11 ...89 H5
  STHP PR8 ...47 K2
Woodside La GOL/RIS/CU WA3 ...123 M3
  WD/CROXPK L12 ...98 D5
Woodside of SKEL WN8 ...66 E5
Woodside Ferry Ap BIRK CH41 ...11 M4
Woodside Rd PEN/TH CH61 ...126 A1
  RNFD/HAY WA11 ...91 G6
  WARRW/BUR WA5 ...120 B7
Woodside St EHL/KEN L7 ...113 K4
Woodside Wy NWD/KWIPK L33 ...74 B8
Woodsome Cl AIMK WN4 ...91 L1
Woodsome Cl EP CH65 ...163 K4
Woodsorrel Rd BIRK CH41 ...111 H6
  WAV L15 ...114 D6
Wood Sorrel Wy
  GOL/RIS/CU WA3 ...93 G5
Wood's St WGNS/IIMK WN3 ...4 L1
Woodstock Av NEWLW WA12 ...104 F3
Woodstock Gdns WARRS WA4 ...138 B7
Woodstock Gv WDN WA8 ...133 M3
Woodstock Rd WAL/EC CH44 ...95 F8
Woodstock St EV L5 ...96 E8
Wood St ALL/GAR L19 ...130 E7
  BIRK CH41 ...11 J3
  CLVPS L1 ...13 H8
  GOL/RIS/CU WA3 ...92 D5
  HOY CH47 * ...108 D6
  LITH L21 ...83 H6
  PR/KW L34 ...100 F7
  PS/BROM CH62 ...128 D8
  STHEL WA9 ...88 F2
  WARR WA1 ...15 K4
  WDN WA8 ...18 B4
  WGNE/HIN WN2 ...81 K2
  WGNS/IIMK WN3 ...5 J4
  WGNW/BIL/O WN5 ...68 B6

Woodthorn Cl RUNC WA7 ...151 H1
Wood V STHEL WA9 ...102 A7
Woodvale Cl WGNNW/ST WN6 ...68 B4
  WARRN/WOL WA2 ...122 A5
Woodvale Dr GTS/LS CH66 ...93 G4
  STHP PR8 ...47 M3
  WD/CROXPK L12 ...99 H2
  WLTN L25 ...131 K3
Woodview WGNNW/ST WN6 ...55 J8
Woodview Av WAL/EC CH44 ...111 K4
Woodview Crs WDN WA8 ...133 J5
Woodview Rd WDN WA8 ...133 J5
Wood View Rd WLTN L25 ...115 H8
Woodville Av CSBY/BLUN L23 ...82 F2
Woodville Pl WDN WA8 ...133 M4
Woodville Rd CHLY/EC PR7 ...44 B4
  RF/TRAN CH42 ...127 L1
  WGNS/IIMK WN3 ...80 B1
Woodville St ECCL WA10 ...9 J1
Woodville Ter NPK/KEN L6 ...97 K8
Woodward Rd NWD/KWIPK L33 ...86 D1
  RF/TRAN CH42 ...127 L1
Woodway GR/UP/WCH CH49 ...125 M1
Woodyates St
  WGNW/BIL/O WN5 ...68 B7
Woodyear Rd PS/BROM CH62 ...144 A6
Woolacombe Av STHEL WA9 ...102 E8
Woolacombe Cl GOL/RIS/CU WA3 ...93 G4
Woolacombe Rd CHLDW L16 ...115 H7
Woolden Rd WGNW/BIL/O WN5 ...55 B7
Wooler Cl MOR/LEA CH46 ...109 L5
Woolfall Cl HUY L36 ...115 K1
Woolfall Crs HUY L36 ...115 K1
Woolfall Heath Av HUY L36 ...99 M8
Woolfall Ter LITH L21 ...83 J7
Woolhope Rd WLT/FAZ L9 ...97 K3
Woolley Cl FROD/HEL WA6 ...166 ...
Woolmer Cl GOL/RIS/CU WA3 ...107 K7
Woolston Grange Av
  WARR WA1 ...123 G5
  WARRN/WOL WA2 ...122 E3
Woolton Bvd WLTN L25 ...131 K4
Woolton Cl AIMK WN4 ...79 H8
Woolton Ct GTS/LS CH66 ...156 A5
Woolton Hill Rd WLTN L25 ...131 J1
Woolton Mt WLTN L25 ...131 J2
Woolton Pk WLTN L25 ...131 J2
Woolton Park Cl WLTN L25 ...131 J2
Woolton Rd ALL/GAR L19 ...130 E7
  WAV L15 ...114 C6
  WLTN L25 ...115 H8
Woolton St WLTN L25 ...131 J1
Worcester Av CLB/OSW/ST L13 * ...97 M6
  CSBY/WL L22 ...82 E3
  GOL/RIS/CU WA3 ...92 D5
Worcester Cl ECCL WA10 ...8 E7
  WARRW/BUR WA5 ...120 D3
Worcester Dr CLB/OSW/ST L13 ...97 M6
Worcester Dr North
  CLB/OSW/ST L13 ...97 M6
Worcester Pl CHLY/EC PR7 ...44 A2
Worcester Rd BTL L20 ...7 K2
  CL/PREN CH43 ...110 F5
Worcester St EP CH65 ...20 D2
Worcester Wk EP CH65 ...20 D2
Wordsworth Av LEIGH WN7 ...81 M6
  RF/TRAN CH42 ...128 B4
  STHEL WA9 ...118 C2
  WARRS WA4 ...137 K2
  WDN WA8 ...16 A3
Wordsworth Cl ORM L39 ...50 F7
Wordsworth St BTL L20 ...6 D1
  TOX L8 ...113 L6
Wordsworth Ter CHLYE PR6 ...32 F3
Wordsworth Wk WKBY CH48 ...126 E8
Wordsworth Wy GTS/LS CH66 ...163 G4
  HUY L36 ...116 B4
Worrow Cl NG/CROX L11 ...98 D2
Worrow Rd NG/CROX L11 ...98 D2
Worsborough Av
  WARRW/BUR WA5 ...120 D8
Worsley Av WARRS WA4 ...138 B1
Worsley Brow STHEL WA9 ...103 C5
Worsley Cl WGNW/BIL/O WN5 * ...67 K8
Worsley Gn WGNW/BIL/O WN5 ...67 K8
Worsley Mesnes Dr
  WGNS/IIMK WN3 ...68 C8
Worsley Rd WARRS WA4 ...137 K4
Worsley St GOL/RIS/CU WA3 ...92 C5
  RNFD/HAY WA11 ...90 B7
  WGNW/BIL/O WN5 ...67 K8
Worsley Ter WGN WN1 ...4 F2
Worthing St STHP PR8 ...35 H2
Worthing St CSBY/WL L22 ...82 E1
Worthington Cl RUNC WA7 ...150 C6
Worthington St TOX L8 ...112 F7
  WGNE/HIN WN2 ...69 M7
Worthington Wy
  WGNS/IIMK WN3 ...79 G3
Worthy St CHLYE PR6 ...33 G6
Wortley Rd AIN/FAZ L10 ...85 G6
Wotton Dr AIMK WN4 ...91 M2
Wraxhall Crs LEIGH WN7 ...81 M6
Wray Av STHEL WA9 ...118 F1
Wrayburn Cl EHL/KEN L7 ...113 L5
Wray St WGN WN1 ...5 K4
Wrekin Cl WLTN L25 ...131 K5
Wrekin Dr AIN/FAZ L10 ...85 G6
Wrenbury Cl CL/PREN CH43 * ...127 H3
  WGNW/BIL/O WN5 ...67 K8
Wrenbury St EHL/KEN L7 ...113 L3
Wren Cl GOL/RIS/CU WA3 ...123 H1
  RUNC WA7 ...150 C7
  WGNW/BIL/O WN5 ...67 K8
Wrenfield Gv AIG/SPK L17 ...129 L3
Wren Gv HLWD L26 ...132 A4
Wrennalls La CHLY/EC PR7 ...30 D8
Wrexham Cl WARRW/BUR WA5 ...149 J1
Wright Crs WDN WA8 ...148 ...
Wrightington St WGN WN1 ...4 E1
Wrights Gn WARRS WA4 * ...138 C1
Wright's La WARRW/BUR WA5 ...135 H3
  WDN WA8 ...135 ...
Wrights Ter STHP PR8 ...35 K2
Wright St AIMK WN4 ...114 C6
  CHLYE PR6 ...33 G5
  CHTN/BK PR9 ...3 H3
  EV L5 ...96 F6
  WAL/EC CH44 ...111 M1
  WARRW/BUR WA5 ...124 D5
Wrigley Rd RNFD/HAY WA11 ...91 G7
Wrigleys Cl FMBY L37 ...47 H8
Wrington Cl LEIGH WN7 ...81 M5
Wroxham Cl FROD/HEL WA6 ...166 D1
  GR/UP/WCH CH49 ...110 C8
Wroxham Dr
  GR/UP/WCH CH49 ...126 C1

Wroxham Rd
  WARRW/BUR WA5 ...120 A7
Wroxham Wy
  GR/UP/WCH CH49 * ...110 C8
Wryneck Cl ECCL WA10 ...101 K6
Wrynose Rd PS/BROM CH62 ...144 A5
Wulstan St ANF/KKDL L4 ...96 F6
Wyatt Cl AIMK WN4 ...96 ...
Wycherley Rd RF/TRAN CH42 ...127 M2
Wycherley St PR/KW L34 * ...100 F7
Wychwood GR/UP/WCH CH49 ...110 B8
Wychwood Av WLDM WA13 ...139 L2
Wycliffe Rd ANF/KKDL L4 ...97 L6
  GTS/LS CH66 ...163 H2
  RNFD/HAY WA11 ...91 G6
Wycliffe St RF/TRAN CH42 * ...128 B3
Wye Cl RF/TRAN CH42 ...128 B2
Wyedale EP CH65 ...20 H6
Wyedale Rd RNFD/HAY WA11 ...91 G7
Wye St EV L5 ...97 H7
Wyke Cop Rd STHP PR8 ...36 F2
Wykeham Cl WGNS/IIMK WN3 ...5 L8
Wykeham St ANF/KKDL L4 ...96 F6
Wykeham Wy ANF/KKDL L4 ...96 F6
Wyke La CHTN/BK PR9 ...25 L6
Wyke Gv RNFD/HAY WA11 ...9 M1
Wyke Rd RAIN/WH L35 ...101 G8
Wyke Wood La CHTN/BK PR9 ...26 B5
Wylin Rd NWD/KWIPK L33 ...86 C3
Wylva Av CSBY/BLUN L23 ...82 ...
Wylva Rd ANF/KKDL L4 ...97 J7
Wymundsley CHLY/EC PR7 ...32 B4
Wynard Av WGN WN1 ...5 H7
Wyncroft Cl EP CH65 ...163 J2
  WDN WA8 ...133 L6
Wyncroft Rd WDN WA8 ...133 L6
Wyncroft St TOX L8 ...129 J1
Wyndale Cl CALD/MH L18 ...130 D2
Wyndcote Rd CALD/MH L18 ...114 D8
Wyndham Av DV/KA/FCH L14 ...115 J3
Wyndham Cl GTS/LS CH66 ...155 ...
Wyndham Rd WAL/NB CH45 ...94 F8
Wyndham St ANF/KKDL L4 ...97 H3
Wynne Rd ECCL WA10 ...8 D2
Wynnstay Av MGHL L31 ...72 F2
Wynnstay St TOX L8 ...113 J7
Wynstay Rd HOY CH47 ...108 E5
Wynwood Pk HUY L36 ...115 L4
Wyre Av WGNE/HIN WN2 ...80 C3
Wyre Rd EV L5 ...97 H6
Wyrescourt Rd WD/CROXPK L12 ...98 F3
Wyresdale Av ECCL WA10 ...89 G6
  STHP PR8 ...36 ...
Wyresdale Rd WLT/FAZ L9 ...84 D6
Wyrevale Gv AIMK WN4 ...91 L2
Wysall Cl RNFD/HAY WA11 ...89 M8
Wyswall Cl HLWD L26 ...132 A4
Wythburn Crs RNFD/HAY WA11 ...89 K5
Wythburn Gv RUNC WA7 ...150 A3
Wyvern Rd MOR/LEA CH46 ...110 A5

Y

Yanwath St TOX L8 ...113 K6
Yarcombe Cl HLWD L26 ...132 B4
Yardley Av WARRW/BUR WA5 ...121 H5
Yardley Dr BEB CH63 ...143 J4
Yardley Rd NWD/KWIPK L33 ...86 E4
Yarmouth Rd
  WARRW/BUR WA5 ...120 A7
Yarrow Av MGHL L31 ...73 H3
Yarrow Cl CROS/BRETH PR26 ...29 K3
Yarrow Ga CHLY/EC PR7 ...33 G7
Yarrow Gn CHLYE PR6 ...33 G7
Yarrow St WGNE/HIN WN2 ...80 E1
Yates Cl WARRW/BUR WA5 ...120 D3
Yates' Ct PR/KW L34 ...100 F8
Yates Gv WGNNW/ST WN6 ...68 B1
Yates Rd CHNE CH2 ...165 G4
Yates St CHLY/EC PR7 ...32 D8
  TOX L8 ...113 G8
  WGNS/IIMK WN3 ...5 K4
Yeadon SKEL WN8 ...65 K4
Yeadon Gv CHLY/EC PR7 ...32 C6
Yeald Brow LYMM WA13 ...139 K2
Yellow Brook Cl WGNE/HIN WN2 ...57 L7
Yellow House La STHP PR8 ...3 G6
Yelverton Cl HLWD L26 ...132 B4
Yelverton Rd ANF/KKDL L4 ...97 L6
  RF/TRAN CH42 ...127 M2
Yeoman Cottages HOY CH47 ...108 F2
Yeoman Wy GTS/LS CH66 ...163 G4
Yeovil Cl WARR WA1 ...122 E5
Yew Bank Rd CHLDW L16 ...114 F4
Yewdale SKEL WN8 ...65 J4
  WGNNW/ST WN6 ...55 K7
Yewdale Av RNFD/HAY WA11 ...89 K4
Yewdale Crs WGN WN1 ...68 D3
Yewdale Dr GTS/LS CH66 ...163 H4
Yewdale Pk CL/PREN CH43 ...127 K1
Yewdale Rd AIMK WN4 ...79 J6
  WLT/FAZ L9 ...97 K1
Yew Gv WGNNW/ST WN6 ...68 B2
Yewlands CHLY/EC PR7 ...42 B2
Yew Tree Av CHLY/EC PR7 ...44 C1
  NEWLW WA12 ...104 C1
  STHEL WA9 ...102 E7
Yew Tree Cl CHNE CH2 ...165 G4
  WD/CROXPK L12 ...99 G7
Yewtree Cl CHLY/EC PR7 ...43 L2
  GR/UP/WCH CH49 ...126 C3
  NSTN CH64 ...153 H6
Yew Tree Ct GOL/RIS/CU WA3 * ...107 J3
Yew Tree Gn MGHL L31 ...85 K1
Yew Tree La WARRS WA4 ...138 C1
  WD/CROXPK L12 ...99 G7
Yewtree La WKBY CH48 ...124 D2
Yewtree Rd CALD/MH L18 ...130 F2
Yew Tree Rd BEB CH63 ...143 G1
  HUY L36 ...115 M5
  MOR/LEA CH46 ...110 B3
  ORM L39 ...51 H7
  WLT/FAZ L9 ...97 K1
  WLTN L25 ...131 ...
Yew Tree Vls CHLY/EC PR7 * ...42 D2
Yew Tree Wy GOL/RIS/CU WA3 ...92 G5
Yorkaster Rd CALD/MH L18 ...130 E4
York Av AIG/SPK L17 ...113 M7
  CSBY/BLUN L23 ...82 F1
  GOL/RIS/CU WA3 ...107 J3
  STHP PR8 ...2 E9
  WAL/EC CH44 ...111 M2
  WARRW/BUR WA5 ...120 B4
  WKBY CH48 ...124 D5
York Cl ECCL WA10 ...8 E3
  FMBY L37 ...57 J8
  NTHTN L30 ...72 B8
York Ct WARRS WA4 * ...138 E4
York Dr WARRS WA4 ...138 C3
York Gdns STHP PR8 ...2 E9
York Mnr FMBY L37 * ...59 H2
York Pl CHLYE PR6 ...44 C5

RUNC WA7 ....19 H4
York Rd AIMK WN4 ....91 L3
CSBY/BLUN L23 ....83 G1
EP CH65 ....20 C5
FMBY L37 ....59 H2
HUY L36 ....116 C2
MGHL L31 ....72 F7
STHP PR8 ....2 D9
WAL/EG CH44 ....111 M3
WARRS WA4 ....138 C3
WDN WA8 ....133 L5
York Rd South AIMK WN4 ....91 L3
Yorkshire Gdns ECCL WA10 ....8 E8
York St ALL/GAR L19 ....145 L1
CHLY/EC PR7 ....32 F6
CLVPS L1 ....13 G9
CSBY/WL L22 ....82 F5
GOL/RIS/CU WA3 ....92 C4
PS/BROM CH62 ....128 F8
RUNC WA7 ....19 G4
WARRS WA4 ....15 G8
WGNS/IIMK WN3 ....4 C5
WLT/FAZ L9 ....97 H2
York Ter CHTN/BK PR9 ....3 K2
EV L5 ....97 G7
York Vls EV L5 * 97 H6
York Wy ALL/GAR L19 ....145 M2
Youatt Av RAIN/WH L35 ....117 G1
Youens Wy DV/KA/FCH L14 ....115 G1
Yoxall Dr NWD/KWIPK L33 ....74 A7
Yvonne Cl AIMK WN4 ....79 M8

Z

Zander Gv WD/CROXPK L12 ....99 J2
Zante Cl EV L5 ....97 G7
Zara Ct RNFD/HAY WA11 ....90 E6
Zenith Wk WLTN L25 ....115 J6
Zetland Rd CALD/MH L18 * 114 B8
WAL/NB CH45 ....95 H6
Zetland St CHTN/BK PR9 ....3 L4
Zig Zag Rd WAL/NB CH45 ....95 K7
WD/CROXPK L12 ....98 F8
Zircon Cl LITH L21 ....83 L5

Index - featured places

59 Rodney Street (NT)
CLVPS L1 ....113 G5
Abbey Farm Caravan Park
BRSC L40 ....51 L5
Abbey Lakes Sports Centre
WGNW/BIL/O WN5 ....66 F6
Abbey Lane Industrial Estate
BRSC L40 ....51 L4
Abbey Sefton Hospitals
CSBY/WL L22 ....83 G4
Abbeystead Medical Centre
WAV L15 ....114 D6
Abbotsfield Road Industrial Park STHEL WA9 ....103 G8
Abbots Lea Special School
WLTN L25 ....131 G1
ABC Cinema
CALD/MH L18 ....130 D1
STHP PR8 ....3 G4
Abercromby Health Centre
TOX L8 ....113 J5
Abingdon Medical Centre
ANF/KKDL L4 ....97 L4
Abraham Guest High School
WGNW/BIL/O WN5 ....67 J7
Abram Bryn Gates Primary School WGNE/HIN WN2 ....80 B6
Abram CE Primary School
WGNE/HIN WN2 ....80 D4
Ackhurst Business Park
CHLY/EC PR7 ....32 B5
Ackhurst Park Industrial Estate CHLY/EC PR7 ....32 A5
Acorn Business Centre
NWD/KWIPK L33 ....86 D4
Acorn Special School
CLB/OSW/ST L13 ....98 A5
Adlington Cricket Club
CHLY/EC PR7 ....44 C7
Adlington Medical Centre
CHLYE PR6 ....44 D5
Adlington Primary School
CHLY/EC PR7 ....44 B6
Ainscough Business Park
WGNNW/ST WN6 ....42 A7
Ainsdale CE Primary School
STHP PR8 ....47 M1
Ainsdale Clinic
STHP PR8 ....47 M2
Ainsdale High School
STHP PR8 ....34 E7
Ainsdale Sand Dunes
FMBY L37 ....47 G3
Aintree Hospitals
WLT/FAZ L9 ....84 F6
Aintree Industrial Estate
WLT/FAZ L9 ....84 D8
Aintree Osteopathic Clinic
WLT/FAZ L9 ....84 E6
Aintree Racecourse
WLT/FAZ L9 ....84 E4
Aintree Racecourse Retail & Business Park WLT/FAZ L9 ....84 E4
AK Business Park
CHTN/BK PR9 ....25 J7
Alban Retail Park
WARRN/WOL WA2 ....121 J3
Albany High School
CHLYE PR6 ....33 G8
Albert Dock Village
VAUX/LVPD L3 ....112 D5
Albert Road Medical Centre
WDN WA8 ....16 F1
Albert Street Business Park
HOR/BR BL6 ....45 K8
Alderman Bolton Community School WARRS WA4 ....15 M9
Alder Root Golf Club
WARRW/BUR WA5 ....104 F6
Alexander House Health Centre WGNE/HIN WN2 ....80 D2
Alexandra Industrial Estate
WDN WA8 ....16 B6
Alicia Hotel
AIG/SPK L17 ....129 L1
Allanson Street CP School
STHEL WA9 ....102 F3
Allerton Cemetery
WLTN L25 ....131 H6
Allerton Health Centre
WAV L15 ....114 C8
Allerton Park Golf Club
CALD/MH L18 ....130 F3
Allerton Remedial Clinic
AIG/SPK L17 ....114 A8
All Saints Catholic School
KKBY L32 ....86 A4
All Saints CE Primary School
CHLY/EC PR7 ....32 D8
RUNC WA7 ....19 G2
All Saints Junior School
NPK/KEN L6 ....97 L7
All Saints RC Infant School
ANF/KKDL L4 ....97 K7
All Saints RC Primary School
GOL/RIS/CU WA3 ....92 D5
All Saints Upton Primary School
WDN WA8 ....133 K2
All Seasons Leisure Centre
CHLY/EC PR7 ....32 F4
Alsop High School
ANF/KKDL L4 ....97 J3
Alt Bridge Secondary Support Centre HUY L36 ....116 B1
Alternative Medical Centre
ECCL WA10 ....8 F4
Alvanley Primary School
FROD/HEL WA6 ....166 F4
Andersons Industrial Estate
WDN WA8 ....16 D7
Anderton Primary School
CHLYE PR6 ....44 C5
Anfield Cemetery
ANF/KKDL L4 ....97 J5
Anfield Comprehensive School
ANF/KKDL L4 ....97 K6
Anfield Crematorium
ANF/KKDL L4 ....97 J5
Anfield J & I School
ANF/KKDL L4 ....97 K7
Anfield Medical Centre
ANF/KKDL L4 ....97 K6
Appleton Thorn Trading Estate WARRS WA4 ....138 F8
Appley Bridge All Saints CE Primary School
WGNNW/ST WN6 ....54 D4
Archbishop Beck Catholic Secondary School
WLT/FAZ L9 ....84 C7
Archbishop Blanch CE High School EHL/KEN L7 ....113 J4
Argyle Health Centre
BIRK CH41 ....11 J6
Argyle Lawn Tennis Club
CHTN/BK PR9 ....25 G3
Arncot County Primary School
ANF/KKDL L4 ....97 H4
Arrowe Country Park
GR/UP/WCH CH49 ....126 B4
Arrowe Hill Primary School
GR/UP/WCH CH49 ....126 C2
Arrowe Park Hospital
GR/UP/WCH CH49 ....126 C4
Ashley Business Centre
PR/KW L34 ....100 F7
Ashley Retail Park
WDN WA8 ....16 F5
Ashley School
WDN WA8 ....133 M4
Ashton Grange Industrial Estate AIMK WN4 ....79 K7
Ashton-in-Makerfield Golf Club AIMK WN4 ....91 G3
Ashton Leisure Centre
AIMK WN4 ....91 J1
Ashton Medical Centre
AIMK WN4 ....79 J8
Ashton Town AFC
AIMK WN4 ....91 M1
Ashurst Health Centre
SKEL WN8 ....65 K1
Ashurst Primary School
RNFD/HAY WA11 ....89 M7
Ashville FC
WAL/NB CH45 ....110 F1
Ashworth Hospital
MGHL L31 ....73 J3
Asmall Primary School
ORM L39 ....50 F6
Aspull Clinic
WGNE/HIN WN2 ....57 L8
Aspull Holy Family RCP School
WGNE/HIN WN2 ....69 J3
Astley Hall Museum & Art Gallery CHLY/EC PR7 ....32 C4
Astley Park School
CHLY/EC PR7 ....32 D5
Astmoor Industrial Estate
RUNC WA7 ....149 M2
Astmoor Primary School
RUNC WA7 ....150 B3
Aston Primary School
RUNC WA7 ....161 L4
Atherton House School
CSBY/BLUN L23 ....82 F1
Atherton Infant School
EP CH65 ....156 B8
Atkinson Art Gallery
STHP PR8 ....3 G4
Auckland College
AIG/SPK L17 ....129 K2
Aughton Christ Church CE Primary School ORM L39 ....62 E2
Austin Rawlinson Sports Centre SPK/HALE L24 ....147 G2
Avalon School
WKBY CH48 ....124 E5
Balmoral Lodge Hotel
CHTN/BK PR9 ....3 K1
Balshaw Lane Primary School
CHLY/EC PR7 ....32 A4
Bankfield School
WDN WA8 ....133 M4
Bank Quay Trading Estate
WARRW/BUR WA5 ....14 B8
Banks Health Centre
CHTN/BK PR9 ....23 H7
Banks Methodist Primary School CHTN/BK PR9 ....23 K7
Banks Road Primary School
ALL/GAR L19 ....145 M1
Barlows Primary School
WLT/FAZ L9 ....84 F6
Barnston Primary School
HES CH60 ....141 L6
Barrow Hall County Primary School WARRW/BUR WA5 ....120 A6
Baycliff Road Health Centre
WD/CROXPK L12 ....99 H6
BBC North & BBC Radio Merseyside CLVPS L1 ....12 F8
Beach Road Primary School
LITH L21 ....83 J6
The Beacon CE Primary School
EV L5 ....97 G8
Beacon Country Park
SKEL WN8 ....66 A2
Beacon Park Public Golf Centre
SKEL WN8 ....66 A2
Beacon School
SKEL WN8 ....66 A5
Beamont Infant School
WARRN/WOL WA2 ....15 H1
The Beatles Story
VAUX/LVPD L3 ....112 D5
Beaufort Hotel
BRSC L40 ....51 K4
Beaufort Park County Primary School TOX L8 ....113 H8
Beaufort Park School
TOX L8 ....129 H1
Bebington High School Sports College BEB CH63 ....128 A7
Bechers Business Centre
NTHTN L30 ....84 C3
Bedford Primary School
BTL L20 ....7 K6
Beechenhurst School
CALD/MH L18 ....114 F8
Beech Hill Primary School
WGNNW/ST WN6 ....68 C2
Beechwood County Primary School HUY L36 ....99 L7
Beechwood Primary School
RUNC WA7 ....149 M8
Bel-Air Hotel
WGN WN1 ....68 E1
Belair Industrial Estate
CSBY/BLUN L23 ....83 H2
Belle Green Industrial Estate
WGNE/HIN WN2 ....69 J5
Bellerive High School
TOX L8 ....113 K8
Belle Vale Health Centre
WLTN L25 ....115 K7
Belle Vale JMI School
WLTN L25 ....115 L8
Belle Vale Shopping Centre
WLTN L25 ....115 K7
Belle Vale Swimming Pool
WLTN L25 ....115 L7
The Belvedere School
TOX L8 ....129 K1
The Bennett House School
CHLYE PR6 ....33 G4
Bewsey Business Centre
WARRW/BUR WA5 ....14 B3
Bewsey Industrial Estate
WARRW/BUR WA5 ....14 B2
Bewsey Lodge Primary School
WARRW/BUR WA5 ....14 A2
BICC Athletic Club
RAIN/WH L35 ....101 H8
Bickershaw CE Primary School WGNE/HIN WN2 ....81 H5
Bickerstaffe CE Primary School ORM L39 ....64 A8
Bidston Avenue Primary School CL/PREN CH43 ....111 G6
Bidston Golf Club
MOR/LEA CH46 ....110 E2
Bidston Industrial Estate
WAL/EG CH44 ....110 F2
Bigdale Medical Centre
NWD/KWIPK L33 ....86 C2
Bigham Road Medical Centre
NPK/KEN L6 ....113 L2
Billinge Chapel End Primary School WGNW/BIL/O WN5 ....90 A1
Billinge Clinic
WGNW/BIL/O WN5 ....89 M1
Billinge Hospital
WGNW/BIL/O WN5 ....77 M3
Binns Road Industrial Estate
CLB/OSW/ST L13 ....114 A3
Birchwood CE Primary School
GOL/RIS/CU WA3 ....123 H1
Birchwood Community High School GOL/RIS/CU WA3 ....122 F2
Birchwood Golf Club
GOL/RIS/CU WA3 ....106 F7
Birchwood Medical Centre
GOL/RIS/CU WA3 ....123 G2
Birchwood One Business Park
GOL/RIS/CU WA3 ....123 G2
Birkdale Cemetery
STHP PR8 ....35 G6
Birkdale High School
STHP PR8 ....35 G6
Birkdale Primary School
STHP PR8 ....35 K2
Birkdale RC Cemetery
STHP PR8 ....35 G7
Birkdale Trading Estate
STHP PR8 ....35 H3
Birkenhead County Court
BIRK CH41 ....11 K6
Birkenhead High School for Girls CL/PREN CH43 ....10 B7
Birkenhead Park Cricket Club
BIRK CH41 ....10 C5
Birkenhead Park RUFC
BIRK CH41 ....10 B3
Birkenhead Priory
BIRK CH41 ....11 M6
Birkenhead Priory and Museum
BIRK CH41 ....11 M6
Birkenhead School
CL/PREN CH43 ....111 H8
Birkenhead Sixth Form College
CL/PREN CH43 ....111 H6
Birleywood Health Centre
SKEL WN8 ....65 M7
Bishop David Sheppard CE Primary School
CHTN/BK PR9 ....25 K6
Bishop Martin CE Primary School SKEL WN8 ....65 M6
WLTN L25 ....131 J3
Bispham Hall Business Park
WGNW/BIL/O WN5 ....77 L3
Blackbrook St Marys Catholic Primary School
RNFD/HAY WA11 ....90 A7
Black Cat Industrial Estate
WDN WA8 ....16 B7
Black Horse Hill Infant School
WKBY CH48 ....124 F2
Black Horse Hill Junior School
WKBY CH48 ....124 F2
Blacklow Brow Primary School
HUY L36 ....115 M4
Blackmoor Park Infant School
WD/CROXPK L12 ....98 F7
Blackmoor Park Junior School
WD/CROXPK L12 ....98 F8
Black Moss School
SKEL WN8 ....64 F3
Blackrod Church School
HOR/BR BL6 ....57 L3
Bleak Hill Primary School
ECCL WA10 ....88 D7
Blessed Sacrament RC Infant School WLT/FAZ L9 ....84 D7
Blessed Sacrament RC Junior School WLT/FAZ L9 ....84 D7
Blowick Business Centre
CHTN/BK PR9 ....25 J7
Blueberry Park CP School
DV/KA/FCH L14 ....99 J7
The Blue Coat School
WAV L15 ....114 C7
Blue Planet Aquarium
EP CH65 ....163 M4
Blundells Hill Golf Club
RAIN/WH L35 ....117 K4
Boaler Street Industrial Estate
NPK/KEN L6 ....113 J2
Boat Museum
EP CH65 ....20 E1
Bold Business Centre
STHEL WA9 ....103 K6
Bold Hotel
CHTN/BK PR9 ....3 H2
Bold Industrial Estate
WDN WA8 ....118 E8
Bold Industrial Park
STHEL WA9 ....103 K7
Bold Street Medical Centre
WARR WA1 ....14 D7
Booker Avenue J & I School
CALD/MH L18 ....130 D4
Bootle Cricket Club
BTL L20 ....7 J7
Bootle Golf Club
NTHTN L30 ....84 A4
Bootle High School
NTHTN L30 ....84 C1
Bootle Leisure Centre
BTL L20 ....7 G1
Bootle Stadium Sports Centre
BTL L20 ....7 M3
Borough Cemetery
ECCL WA10 ....88 F6
WDN WA8 ....134 C2
Borron Road Industrial Estate
NEWLW WA12 ....104 E1
Botanic Estate
EHL/KEN L7 ....113 M4
Botanic Gardens Museum
CHTN/BK PR9 ....25 K3
Bousfield Health Centre
ANF/KKDL L4 ....97 G6
Bowers Business Park
WDN WA8 ....17 G5
The Bowler Hat Hotel
CL/PREN CH43 ....127 J1
Bowling Alley
CLB/OSW/ST L13 ....114 B4
NTHTN L30 ....84 C2
PS/BROM CH62 ....143 M2
WAL/NB CH45 ....95 K4
WGNS/IIMK WN3 ....4 D5
Bowring Comprehensive School HUY L36 ....115 K2
Bowring Park Golf Club
HUY L36 ....115 K4
The Bowry Health Centre
STHEL WA9 ....101 M5
Brackenwood Golf Club
BEB CH63 ....142 F1
Brackenwood Infant School
BEB CH63 ....128 B8
Brackenwood Junior School
BEB CH63 ....128 A8
Bradley Hall Trading Estate
WGNNW/ST WN6 ....56 C3
Bradshaw Primary School
WARRS WA4 ....138 D3
Breckfield Community Comprehensive School EV L5 ....97 H8
Breckfield County Primary School EV L5 ....97 J7
Bridgehouse Clinic
BEB CH63 ....127 M7
Bridge Industrial Estate
SPK/HALE L24 ....131 K8
Bridgewater Community High School (Lower) WARRS WA4 ....137 M7
Bridgewater Upper School
WARRS WA4 ....137 M6
Brindley Arts Centre
RUNC WA7 ....19 H3
Britannia Bridge Primary School WGNS/IIMK WN3 ....5 J7
The British Lawnmower Museum STHP PR8 ....3 G7
Britonwood Trading Estate
NWD/KWIPK L33 ....86 D6
Broadgreen Community Comprehensive School
CLB/OSW/ST L13 ....114 D3
Broad Green JMI School
CLB/OSW/ST L13 ....114 D3
Broad Oak Community Primary School
STHEL WA9 ....103 J2
Broad Square Primary School
NG/CROX L11 ....98 B5
Broadway Community High School ECCL WA10 ....101 L5
Bromborough Golf Club
BEB CH63 ....143 K7
Bromborough Pool Primary School PS/BROM CH62 ....128 F8
Brook Acre Primary School
WARRN/WOL WA2 ....122 A4
Brookdale Primary School
GR/UP/WCH CH49 ....126 A2
Brookfield Comprehensive School KKBY L32 ....85 M5
Brookfield High School
WGNE/HIN WN2 ....81 G1
Brookfield School
WDN WA8 ....134 F3
Brookfields Primary School
SKEL WN8 ....64 F3
Brook House Business Centre
WKBY CH48 ....124 D3
Brookhurst Primary School
BEB CH63 ....143 L7
Brook Lodge Primary School
RNFD/HAY WA11 ....76 B5
Brooklyn Park and Country Club CHTN/BK PR9 ....26 C1
Brookside Primary School
DV/KA/FCH L14 ....99 K6
GTS/LS CH66 ....163 G1
Brookvale Primary School
RUNC WA7 ....150 D8
Brookvale Recreation Centre
RUNC WA7 ....150 E7
Broomfield County Junior School WARRS WA4 ....138 A6
Broughton Hall High School Technology College
WD/CROXPK L12 ....99 G8
The Brow Primary School
RUNC WA7 ....150 B4
Bruche Community Primary School WARR WA1 ....122 C6
Brunswick Business Park
VAUX/LVPD L3 ....128 F1
Buckshaw Primary School
CHLY/EC PR7 ....32 C3
Burscough Bridge Methodist Primary School BRSC L40 ....38 F8
Burscough Cricket Club
BRSC L40 ....52 B1
Burscough Health Centre
BRSC L40 ....39 G8
Burscough Industrial Estate
BRSC L40 ....38 D8
Burscough Primary School
BRSC L40 ....39 H8
Burscough Priory High School
BRSC L40 ....38 F8
Burscough RC Primary School
BRSC L40 ....52 A3
Burscough Sports Centre
BRSC L40 ....39 G8
Burtonwood Industrial Centre
WARRW/BUR WA5 ....104 B6
Burtonwood Primary School
WARRW/BUR WA5 ....104 A6
Business Development Centre
STHEL WA9 ....9 K3
Business Resource Centre
NWD/KWIPK L33 ....86 E5
Byrchall High School
AIMK WN4 ....91 K4
Byrne Avenue Recreation Centre RF/TRAN CH42 ....128 B4
Cabinet War Rooms
CLVP L2 ....12 E6
Cables Retail Park
PR/KW L34 ....100 F7
Calday Grange Grammar School WKBY CH48 ....124 F4
Calderstones Comprehensive School CALD/MH L18 ....130 E1
Caldy Golf Club
WKBY CH48 ....125 G7
Camberley Medical Centre
WLTN L25 ....131 L5
Cambridge Road Primary School EP CH65 ....20 D5
Camelot Theme Park
CHLY/EC PR7 ....42 C1
Cammell Laird's Sports Club
RF/TRAN CH42 ....128 C4
Campanile Hotel
RUNC WA7 ....19 G3
VAUX/LVPD L3 ....112 E6
Campion Catholic High School
EV L5 ....13 K1
Canalside Industrial Estate
EP CH65 ....20 F2
Canning Road Industrial Estate CHTN/BK PR9 ....25 J7
Cansfield High School
AIMK WN4 ....91 J1
Capenhurst CE Primary School
CH/BCN CH1 ....162 D5
Capenhurst Grange Special School GTS/LS CH66 ....162 F3
Capenhurst Learning Centre
CH/BCN CH1 ....162 D4
Capitol Trading Estate
NWD/KWIPK L33 ....86 F3
Cardinal Heenan Catholic High
WD/CROXPK L12 ....98 F8
Cardinal Newman RC High School WARRS WA4 ....122 B8
Carleton House Preparatory School CALD/MH L18 ....130 B2
Carlton Lawn Tennis Club
STHP PR8 ....35 H3
Carmel College
ECCL WA10 ....101 K4
Carr Lane Industrial Estate
HOY CH47 ....108 E6
Carr Mill Infant School
RNFD/HAY WA11 ....89 K5
Carr Mill Junior School
RNFD/HAY WA11 ....89 L4
Castlefields Health Centre
RUNC WA7 ....150 C3
The Castle
HOR/BR BL6 ....45 H7
Castleview Primary School
RUNC WA7 ....149 M5
Castleway Primary School
MOR/LEA CH46 ....110 C1
Catalyst Science Discovery Centre WDN WA8 ....134 C8
Cathcart Street Primary School
BIRK CH41 ....11 G3
Causeway Medical Centre
WARRS WA4 ....137 K2
Cavendish Medical Centre
BIRK CH41 ....10 C2
Cavendish Special School
RUNC WA7 ....149 K8
Cavern Club
CLVP L2 ....12 F7

Cedar Cross Medical Centre *RAIN/WH* L35 ....116 F2
Centec Business Centre *NG/CROX* L11 ....85 K8
Central Clinic *ECCL* WA10 ....9 G3
Central Library *VAUX/LVPD* L3 ....13 H5
Chadwick Court Industrial Centre *VAUX/LVPD* L3 ....12 D3
Chaigley School *WARRS* WA4 ....139 G1
Chalon Way Industrial Estate *STHEL* WA9 ....9 H7
Chapelfield Clinic *WDN* WA8 ....133 K4
Chapel Lane Business Park *CHLY/EC* PR7 ....43 G3
Chapel Street Clinic *WDN* WA8 ....16 D6
Charnock Richard Golf Club *CHLY/EC* PR7 ....42 D1
Cherryfield Primary School *KKBY* L32 ....86 A6
Cherry Tree Community School *LYMM* WA13 ....139 L3
Cheshire Oaks Retail Outlet *EP* CH65 ....164 A3
Chesnut Lodge School *WDN* WA8 ....134 A4
Chesterfield High School *CSBY/BLUN* L23 ....83 J1
Childer Thornton Primary School *GTS/LS* CH66 ....155 K5
Childwall CE Primary School *CHLDW* L14 ....114 F8
Childwall College: A specialist sports colleage *WAV* L15 ....114 A6
The Childwall Golf Club *NTHLY* L27 ....116 A6
Chinese Arch *CLVPS* L1 ....113 G5
Chorley AFC *CHLY/EC* PR7 ....32 E7
Chorley Business & Technology Centre *CHLYE* PR6 ....32 A1
Chorley Cricket Club *CHLY/EC* PR7 ....32 D5
Chorley East Business Centre *CHLYE* PR6 ....33 H6
Chorley Golf Club *CHLYE* PR6 ....44 C2
Chorley North Business Park *CHLYE* PR6 ....32 F2
Chorley North Industrial Park *CHLYE* PR6 ....32 F3
Chorley Retail Park *CHLY/EC* PR7 ....32 E6
Chorley & South Ribble District General Hospital *CHLY/EC* PR7 ....32 E2
Chorley West Business Park *CHLY/EC* PR7 ....32 B5
Christchurch CE Primary School *BIRK* CH41 ....10 F9
Christ Church CE Primary School *BTL* L20 ....7 J3; *EP* CH65 ....163 K3; *MOR/LEA* CH46 ....110 A5
Christchurch Charnock Richard CE Primary School *CHLY/EC* PR7 ....42 F1
Christian Fellowship School *EHL/KEN* L7 ....113 K5
Christina Hartley Maternity Hospital *STHP* PR8 ....3 M7
Christ the King Catholic Primary School *WAV* L15 ....114 E5
Christ the King RC High School *STHP* PR8 ....35 K2
Christ the King RC Primary School *PS/BROM* CH62 ....144 A6
Chromolyte Industrial Estate *STHP* PR8 ....3 C8
Church Drive Primary School *PS/BROM* CH62 ....128 D7
Churchill Industrial Estate *WLT/FAZ* L9 ....84 E5
Church Road Medical Centre *BEB* CH63 ....143 J1
Church Square Shopping Centre *ECCL* WA10 ....9 G5
Church Street Industrial Estate *WARR* WA1 ....15 G6
Churchtown Medical Centre *CHTN/BK* PR9 ....25 J3
Churchtown Primary School *CHTN/BK* PR9 ....25 K3
Cineworld *ECCL* WA10 ....9 G5; *RUNC* WA7 ....150 B6
Cinnamon Brow CE Primary School *WARRN/WOL* WA2 ....122 B2
The Citadel *ECCL* WA10 ....9 G5
City of Liverpool Community College *VAUX/LVPD* L3 ....13 K8
Civic Building *WGN* WN1 ....4 E2
Civic Centre *WGN* WN1 ....4 F4
Civic Hall *EP* CH65 ....20 B6; *ORM* L39 ....51 C8
Claremont Medical Centre *MGHL* L31 ....72 D5
Claremont Special School *WAL/NB* CH45 ....95 H7
Claremount School *MOR/LEA* CH46 ....110 C4
Clarence House School *FMBY* L37 ....47 G7
Clatterbridge Hospital *BEB* CH63 ....142 F4
Claughton Medical Centre *BIRK* CH41 ....10 A3
Clayton Square Shopping Centre *CLVPS* L1 ....13 H7
Cleveland Business Park *BIRK* CH41 ....10 F2
Clifford Holroyde Centre of Expertise *DV/KA/FCH* L14 ....114 F2
Clinic for the Handicapped *WARRN/WOL* WA2 ....14 D4
Clock Face Country Park *STHEL* WA9 ....119 H2
Clough Fold Primary School *SKEL* WN8 ....65 L3
Cobbs Brow Primary School *SKEL* WN8 ....65 J2
The Cobbs Infant School *WARRS* WA4 ....138 A5
Cockhedge Centre *WARR* WA1 ....14 F5
Cole Street Primary School *BIRK* CH41 ....10 E6
Collins Industrial Estate *STHEL* WA9 ....9 M1

Commercial Business Centre *RAIN/WH* L35 ....117 L2
Common Bank Employment Area *CHLY/EC* PR7 ....32 B6
Common Bank Industrial Estate *CHLY/EC* PR7 ....32 B6
Common Ground Sign Dance Theatre *CLVPS* L1 ....13 C8
Community Care for Health *WDN* WA8 ....16 D5
Concourse Shopping Centre *SKEL* WN8 ....65 K4
Conservation Centre *CLVPS* L1 ....13 G6
Constance Industrial Estate *WDN* WA8 ....16 D8
Coppenhouse Medical Centre *AIN/FAZ* L10 ....85 J6
Coppull Community Leisure Centre *CHLY/EC* PR7 ....43 G5
Coppull Parish CE Primary School *CHLY/EC* PR7 ....43 H4
Coppull Primary School *CHLY/EC* PR7 ....42 F4
Corinthian Industrial Estate *CLB/OSW/ST* L13 ....114 D1
Corner House Clinic *WKBY* CH48 ....124 D3
Cornerways Medical Centre *HUY* L36 ....99 L8
Corpus Christi Catholic Primary School *RNFD/HAY* WA11 ....76 D4
County Sessions House *VAUX/LVPD* L3 ....13 J5
Cowley Language College *ECCL* WA10 ....88 F7
Cowling Brow Industrial Estate *CHLYE* PR6 ....33 G7
Craighurst JMI School *WLTN* L25 ....115 J4
Craven Business Centre *BIRK* CH41 ....11 G5
Crawford Village Primary School *SKEL* WN8 ....77 G2
The Cricketer Sports Club *WGNS/IIMK* WN3 ....39 G3
Cricket Street Business Centre *WGNS/IIMK* WN6 ....4 B4
Croft Business Park *PS/BROM* CH62 ....144 A2
Croft County Primary School *GOL/RIS/CU* WA3 ....106 D5
Cromdale Way Community Hall & Health Centre *WARRW/BUR* WA5 ....120 F1
Cronton CE Primary School *WDN* WA8 ....117 J1
Crosby Baths *CSBY/BLUN* L23 ....82 D3
Crosby High School *CSBY/BLUN* L23 ....71 G7
Crossens CE Primary School *CHTN/BK* PR9 ....22 E8
Crossens Cricket Club *CHTN/BK* PR9 ....25 M1
Cross Farm Primary School *NTHLY* L27 ....132 D1
Croston Medical Centre *CROS/BRETH* PR26 ....29 L2
Croston Sports Club *CROS/BRETH* PR26 ....29 K3
Crowland Street Industrial Estate *CHTN/BK* PR9 ....25 M1
Crow Orchard Primary School *SKEL* WN8 ....65 H3
Croxteth Comprehensive School *NG/CROX* L11 ....85 L8
Croxteth Country Park *WD/CROXPK* L12 ....98 F3
Croxteth Family Health Centre *NG/CROX* L11 ....98 E1
Croxteth Hall *WD/CROXPK* L12 ....98 F4
Croxteth Primary School *NG/CROX* L11 ....98 F1
Croxteth Sports Centre *NG/CROX* L11 ....98 E1
Culcheth Clinic *GOL/RIS/CU* WA3 ....107 G2
Culcheth Primary & High School *GOL/RIS/CU* WA3 ....107 J2
Culcheth Sports Club *GOL/RIS/CU* WA3 ....107 H2
Cunard Building *VAUX/LVPD* L3 ....12 D7
Daleacre Primary School *NTHTN* L30 ....83 L2
Dallam Community Primary School *WARRW/BUR* WA5 ....121 H4
Dalton CE Primary School *SKEL* WN8 ....53 M8
Dalweb Industrial Park *CHTN/BK* PR9 ....26 E2
Daresbury Park Business Park *WARRS* WA4 ....151 H5
Daresbury Park Hotel *WARRS* WA4 ....151 J5
Daresbury Primary School *WARRS* WA4 ....151 K3
Davenhill Primary School *AIN/FAZ* L10 ....84 F3
Dawpool CE Primary School *PEN/TH* CH61 ....125 K7
Deacon Trading Estate *NEWLW* WA12 ....104 C3
Deanery CE High School *WGN* WN1 ....4 D3
Dean Wood Golf Club *SKEL* WN8 ....66 E5
De La Salle RC High School *NG/CROX* L11 ....98 D3
De La Salle School *ECCL* WA10 ....101 L1
The Dell Primary School *RF/TRAN* CH42 ....128 D4
Delph Side Primary School *SKEL* WN8 ....65 M4
Dental Hospital *VAUX/LVPD* L3 ....13 M6
Derby Lane Medical Centre *CLB/OSW/ST* L13 ....114 C2
Devaney Medical Centre *CL/PREN* CH43 ....10 D8
Devonshire Park Primary School *RF/TRAN* CH42 ....127 L4
Deyes High School *MGHL* L31 ....72 F4
Deysbrook Medical Centre *WD/CROXPK* L12 ....98 C4
Diamond Business Park *RNFD/HAY* WA11 ....88 D1
Dinas Lane Medical Centre *HUY* L36 ....115 L1
The District CE Primary School *NEWLW* WA12 ....104 C2
Ditton CE Primary School *WDN* WA8 ....133 J4

Ditton Medical Centre *WDN* WA8 ....133 L4
Dobson Park Industrial Estate *WGNE/HIN* WN2 ....69 J7
Douglas Valley Business Park *WGN* WN1 ....56 E8
Dovecot Health Clinic *DV/KA/FCH* L14 ....115 H1
Dovecot JMI School *DV/KA/FCH* L14 ....115 J2
Dovedale County Infant School *CALD/MH* L18 ....114 C8
Dovedale Junior School *CALD/MH* L18 ....114 C8
Downall Green RC Primary School *AIMK* WN4 ....79 G7
Downholland Haskayne CE Primary School *ORM* L39 ....61 G2
Drug Dependency Clinic *CLVPS* L1 ....13 K8; *WDN* WA8 ....16 D6
Duke Street Primary School *CHLY/EC* PR7 ....32 E7
Dunham Hill Primary School *FROD/HEL* WA6 ....166 A7
Dunkirk Trading Estate *CH/BCN* CH1 ....162 F7
Dunmys Sports Club *WLT/FAZ* L9 ....97 J1
Durnings Endowed Primary School *BRSC* L40 ....40 F6
Duxbury Jubilee Park Golf Club *CHLY/EC* PR7 ....43 M2
Duxbury Park Golf Club *CHLY/EC* PR7 ....43 M1
Eagle Sports Club *WARRW/BUR* WA5 ....136 C1
Earle Road Medical Centre *EHL/KEN* L7 ....113 L5
East Chorley Business Centre *CHLYE* PR6 ....32 F5
Eastcroft Park CP School *NWD/KWIPK* L33 ....74 B8
East Gillbrands Industrial Estate *SKEL* WN8 ....65 J6
Eastham Country Park *PS/BROM* CH62 ....144 C6
Eastham Lodge Golf Club *PS/BROM* CH62 ....144 C7
Eastside Industrial Estate *STHEL* WA9 ....9 M7
Eastway Primary School *MOR/LEA* CH46 ....110 A4
Eaton Road Medical Centre *WD/CROXPK* L12 ....98 E8
Eaves Primary School *STHEL* WA9 ....102 E7
Eccleston Lane Ends Primary School *PR/KW* L34 ....101 H6
Eccleston Medical Centre *ECCL* WA10 ....88 D8
Eccleston Mere Primary School *ECCL* WA10 ....101 J2
Eccleston Park Golf Club *STHEL* WA9 ....101 K7
Eccleston Primary School *CHLY/EC* PR7 ....30 D7
The Edgebright Clinic *CLVPS* L1 ....113 G5
Edge Hill Enterprise Training Centre *WLT/FAZ* L9 ....85 G7
Edge Hill Health Centre *EHL/KEN* L7 ....113 L4
Edge Hill University Sector College *ORM* L39 ....63 H2
Edge Lane Medical Centre *EHL/KEN* L7 ....113 K4
Edge Lane Retail Park *CLB/OSW/ST* L13 ....114 B3
Edwards Lane Industrial Estate *SPK/HALE* L24 ....131 L7
Egremont Medical Centre *WAL/EC* CH44 ....111 M1
Egremont Primary School *WAL/EC* CH44 ....111 M1
Elaine Norris Sports Centre *VAUX/LVPD* L3 ....12 F1
Elimu Academy *TOX* L8 ....113 K6
Elleray Park School *WAL/NB* CH45 ....95 J6
Ellergreen Medical Centre *NG/CROX* L11 ....98 B3
Ellesmere Port Business Centre *EP* CH65 ....20 B5
Ellesmere Port Catholic High School *EP* CH65 ....163 H2
Ellesmere Port Clinic *EP* CH65 ....20 B7
Ellesmere Port Golf Centre *GTS/LS* CH66 ....155 K5
Ellesmere Port Hospital *EP* CH65 ....20 C7
Ellesmere Port Stadium *EP* CH65 ....21 H8
Elmers Green Community Primary School *SKEL* WN8 ....65 M4
The Elms Special School *STBRV* L28 ....99 K5
Eltham Green Clinic *GR/UP/WCH* CH49 ....126 D3
Elton Primary School *CHNE* CH2 ....165 J1
Emmaus Primary School *WD/CROXPK* L12 ....99 H2
Empress Industrial Estate *WGNE/HIN* WN2 ....5 L5
English Martyrs RC Primary School *LITH* L21 ....83 K5; *RNFD/HAY* WA11 ....90 F6
Epic Leisure Centre *EP* CH65 ....20 C7
Eric Moore Health Centre *WARRN/WOL* WA2 ....14 D4
Ernest Cookson Special School *WD/CROXPK* L12 ....98 D7
Erskine Street Industrial Estate *NPK/KEN* L6 ....13 M5
Estuary Business Park *SPK/HALE* L24 ....146 B1
Europa Pool *BIRK* CH41 ....11 H5
Euxton CE Primary School *CHLY/EC* PR7 ....31 L2
Euxton Hall Hospital *CHLY/EC* PR7 ....31 L4
Euxton St Marys RC Primary School *CHLY/EC* PR7 ....31 L2
Evelyn Primary School *WAV* L34 ....101 G6
Evelyn Street Primary School *WARRW/BUR* WA5 ....137 G1
Everite Road Industrial Estate *WDN* WA8 ....133 K6
Everton FC (Goodison Park) *ANF/KKDL* L4 ....97 H5
Everton Park Sports Centre *EV* L5 ....97 G8

Everton Road Health Clinic *NPK/KEN* L6 ....13 M2
Everyman Theatre *VAUX/LVPD* L3 ....13 L8
Express by Holiday Inn *VAUX/LVPD* L3 ....112 D5
Express Industrial Estate *WDN* WA8 ....133 J6
Expressway Business Park *RF/TRAN* CH42 ....128 B2
Fairfield High School *WDN* WA8 ....134 D2
Fairfield Hospital *RNFD/HAY* WA11 ....89 G3
Fairfield J & I School *WDN* WA8 ....134 D3
Fairfield Medical Centre *NPK/KEN* L6 ....113 L2
Fairfield Primary School *WARR* WA1 ....15 H3
Fairfield RFC *RF/TRAN* CH42 ....128 B3
Fairlie CP School *SKEL* WN8 ....65 K2
Fairway Trading Estate *WDN* WA8 ....134 A6
Faith House Yoga & Natural Health Centre *WAL/NB* CH45 ....95 K5
Falcongate Industrial Estate *BIRK* CH41 ....111 K4
Family Health Centre *KKBY* L32 ....85 L3
Farnborough Road J & I School *STHP* PR8 ....35 H5
Farnworth CE Primary School *WDN* WA8 ....134 C1
Fazakerley High School *AIN/FAZ* L10 ....85 H6
Fazakerley Primary School *AIN/FAZ* L10 ....85 H6
Fazakerley Sports Centre *AIN/FAZ* L10 ....85 H6
Fearnhead Cross Medical Centre *WARRN/WOL* WA2 ....122 B3
Fender Primary School *GR/UP/WCH* CH49 ....126 E2
Fernhill Sports Centre *BTL* L20 ....28 M7
Ferries Industrial Estate *RF/TRAN* CH42 ....128 B2
Fingerprints of Elvis *VAUX/LVPD* L3 ....12 D9
Fir Grove Hotel *WARRS* WA4 ....138 C2
Firsdale Industrial Estate *LEIGH* WN7 ....81 L7
Fir Tree Drive South Medical Centre *WD/CROXPK* L12 ....99 H2
Fishwicks Industrial Estate *RNFD/HAY* WA11 ....91 H5; *STHEL* WA9 ....102 F5
Fleet Lane Industrial Estate *STHEL* WA9 ....103 G3
Fleming Building *WARR* WA1 ....15 G5
Floral Pavilion Theatre *WAL/NB* CH45 ....95 L4
Florence Melly Comm Primary School *ANF/KKDL* L4 ....97 L4
Fordton Leisure Centre *WARRN/WOL* WA2 ....121 J2
Forefield Junior School *CSBY/BLUN* L23 ....83 J1
Forefield Infant School *CSBY/BLUN* L23 ....83 H1
Forest Hills Hotel & Leisure Complex *FROD/HEL* WA6 ....160 D7
The Forge Shopping Centre *WARRS* WA4 ....137 L4
Formby AFC *FMBY* L37 ....59 H2
Formby Business Park *FMBY* L37 ....59 J2
Formby Cricket Club *FMBY* L37 ....47 H8
Formby Golf Club *FMBY* L37 ....46 F8
Formby Hall Golf Club *FMBY* L37 ....47 L5
Formby High School *FMBY* L37 ....59 G1
Formby Junior Sports Club *FMBY* L37 ....47 J8
Formby Ladies Golf Club *FMBY* L37 ....46 F8
Formby Lawn Tennis Club *FMBY* L37 ....47 H8
The Fountains Abbey *ANF/KKDL* L4 ....97 G6
Four Acre Lane Shopping Centre *STHEL* WA9 ....118 D1
Foxfield School *MOR/LEA* CH46 ....109 M5
Foyer & Coops Business Centre *WGN* WN1 ....4 D4
Freshfield Primary School *FMBY* L37 ....59 J1
Freshlea Private Clinic *FMBY* L37 ....58 F4
Friary Primary School *EV* L5 ....13 K2
Frodsham CE Primary School *FROD/HEL* WA6 ....160 E6
Frodsham Golf Club *FROD/HEL* WA6 ....160 D8
Frodsham Science & Technology College *FROD/HEL* WA6 ....160 D5
Funland *STHP* PR8 ....2 F2
Fylde Road Industrial Estate *CHTN/BK* PR9 ....25 K1
Gallagher Industrial Estate *WAL/EG* CH44 ....111 K3
The Galleries Shopping Centre *WGN* WN1 ....4 E3
Garston CE Primary School *ALL/GAR* L19 ....130 F7
Garston Industrial Estate *ALL/GAR* L19 ....145 L1
Garston Leisure Centre *ALL/GAR* L19 ....130 E7
Garston Sports Centre *ALL/GAR* L19 ....130 E6
Garswood FC *AIMK* WN4 ....78 D8
Garswood Primary School *AIMK* WN4 ....90 E1
Garven Place Clinic *WARR* WA1 ....14 C6
Gateacre Comprehensive School *WLTN* L25 ....115 J8
Gateworth Industrial Estate *WARRW/BUR* WA5 ....136 F2
Gathurst Golf Club *WGNNW/ST* WN6 ....55 H8
Gayton Primary School *HES* CH60 ....141 J7

Gemini Business Park *WARRW/BUR* WA5 ....121 G2
Gidlow Cemetery *WGNNW/ST* WN6 ....56 C8
Gilbrook School *BIRK* CH41 ....11 L5
Gilded Hollins Primary School *LEIGH* WN7 ....93 L4
Gillibrand Primary School *CHLY/EC* PR7 ....32 D7
Gillmoss Industrial Estate *NG/CROX* L11 ....85 K7
Gillmoss Medical Centre *NG/CROX* L11 ....85 L8
Gilmour Infant School *ALL/GAR* L19 ....130 D6
Gilmour Junior School *ALL/GAR* L19 ....130 D6
Glenburn High School *SKEL* WN8 ....65 J5
Glenda Jackson Theatre *RF/TRAN* CH42 ....127 L2
Golborne Clinic *GOL/RIS/CU* WA3 ....92 D4
Golborne CP School *GOL/RIS/CU* WA3 ....92 C5
Golborne High School *GOL/RIS/CU* WA3 ....92 C4
Golden Square Shopping Centre *WARR* WA1 ....14 D6
Golden Triangle Industrial Estate *WDN* WA8 ....133 L7
Good Shepherd School *LITH* L21 ....83 L3
Gorse Covert Primary School *GOL/RIS/CU* WA3 ....107 K7
Gorsewood Primary School *RUNC* WA7 ....151 G6
Gorsthills Primary School *GTS/LS* CH66 ....162 E2
Grain Industrial Estate *TOX* L8 ....129 G1
Granada TV *VAUX/LVPD* L3 ....12 E9
The Grand National Experience *WLT/FAZ* L9 ....84 D2
The Grange Comprehensive School *RUNC* WA7 ....19 M6
The Grange Country Club *NSTN* CH64 ....153 H1
The Grange Infant School *RUNC* WA7 ....19 M5
The Grange Junior School *RUNC* WA7 ....19 M5
Grange Park Golf Club *ECCL* WA10 ....101 L4
Grange Primary School *NTHTN* L30 ....72 A8
The Grange Shopping Precinct *BIRK* CH41 ....11 H6
Grange Valley Primary School *RNFD/HAY* WA11 ....90 F2
Grappenhall Clinic *WARRS* WA4 ....138 D3
Grappenhall Cricket Club *WARRS* WA4 ....138 C4
Grappenhall Hall School *WARRS* WA4 ....138 D4
Grappenhall Heys Primary School *WARRS* WA4 ....138 C6
Grappenhall Sports Club *WARRS* WA4 ....138 B4
Greasby Health Centre *GR/UP/WCH* CH49 ....125 M2
Greasby Infant School *GR/UP/WCH* CH49 ....125 L3
Greasby Junior School *GR/UP/WCH* CH49 ....125 M4
Great Crosby RC Primary School *CSBY/BLUN* L23 ....83 H1
Great Homer Street Medical Centre *EV* L5 ....97 G6
Great Meols Primary School *HOY* CH47 ....109 G4
Great Sankey County High School *WARRW/BUR* WA5 ....120 A6
Great Sankey Primary School *WARRW/BUR* WA5 ....120 C8
Great Sutton Health Centre *GTS/LS* CH66 ....162 F1
Greenbank High School *STHP* PR8 ....35 G4
Greenbank Industrial Estate *WGNE/HIN* WN2 ....81 J2
Greenbank Primary School *CALD/MH* L18 ....114 B8
Green Lane Medical Centre *CLB/OSW/ST* L13 ....98 A4
Green Lane Special School *WARR* WA1 ....122 D5
Greenleas School *WAL/NB* CH45 ....94 E7
Greenoaks Farm Industrial Estate *WDN* WA8 ....17 H3
Green Oaks Shopping Centre *WDN* WA8 ....16 F3
Green Park Primary School *MGHL* L31 ....72 D3
Greenways Special School *ALL/GAR* L19 ....130 B6
Gresford Medical Centre *DV/KA/FCH* L14 ....115 H2
Grimeford Industrial Estate *CHLYE* PR6 ....44 F7
Grove House Hotel *WAL/NB* CH45 ....95 G6
Grove Park Industrial Estate *CHLY/EC* PR7 ....30 D8
Grove Street Primary School *PS/BROM* CH62 ....128 C6
Guardian Medical Centre *WARRW/BUR* WA5 ....14 A4
Guardian Street Industrial Estate *WARRW/BUR* WA5 ....14 B4
Guinea Gap Baths & Recreation Centre *WAL/EG* CH44 ....112 A2
Gulliver's World Theme Park *WARRW/BUR* WA5 ....121 G4
Guys Industrial Estate *BRSC* L40 ....51 K3
Gwladys Street County Pri School *ANF/KKDL* L4 ....97 J4
Haigh Hall Country Park *WGNE/HIN* WN2 ....57 H7
Hale CE Primary School *SPK/HALE* L24 ....148 A4
Hale Road Industrial Estate *WDN* WA8 ....133 L8
Halewood CE Primary School *HLWD* L26 ....132 C4
Halewood Comprehensive School *HLWD* L26 ....132 A6
Halewood Health Centre *HLWD* L26 ....132 B6
Halewood St Marks Catholic Primary School *HLWD* L26 ....132 C5

Halewood Sports Centre *HLWD* L26 ... **132** C6
Hallgate Bus Station *WGN* WN1 ... **4** E3
Hall Green Clinic *SKEL* WN8 ... **66** D6
Hall Street Medical Centre *ECCL* WA10 ... **9** H5
Halewood Park Primary School *RUNC* WA7 ... **150** A7
Halsall St Cuthberts CE Primary School *ORM* L39 ... **49** K4
Halsnead Community Primary School *RAIN/WH* L35 ... **116** F3
Halton College *WDN* WA8 ... **16** D5
Halton College of Further Education *WDN* WA8 ... **16** C4
Halton General Hospital *RUNC* WA7 ... **150** B7
Halton High School *RUNC* WA7 ... **150** E8
Halton House School *RUNC* WA7 ... **150** A4
Halton Lodge Primary School *RUNC* WA7 ... **149** M5
Halton Magistrates Court *RUNC* WA7 ... **150** B5
Hamblett School *ECCL* WA10 ... **88** F7
Hanson Road Business Park *WLT/FAZ* L9 ... **84** E8
The Hardshaw Shopping Centre *ECCL* WA10 ... **9** H5
Harold Magnay Special School *WLTN* L25 ... **131** H1
Hartley Trading Estate *WLT/FAZ* L9 ... **84** D8
Haslemere Industrial Estate *AIMK* WN4 ... **79** J5
Hatton Garden Industrial Estate *CLVP* L2 ... **12** F5
Hatton Hill Primary School *LITH* L21 ... **83** K3
Hawkley Brook Trading Estate *WGNS/IIMK* WN3 ... **79** G3
Hawkley Hall High School *WGNS/IIMK* WN3 ... **79** K2
Hawthorne Business Park *WARRW/BUR* WA5 ... **121** H5
Haydock Cricket Club *RNFD/HAY* WA11 ... **90** E7
Haydock High School *RNFD/HAY* WA11 ... **90** E7
Haydock Lane Industrial Estate *RNFD/HAY* WA11 ... **91** C5
Haydock Medical Centre *RNFD/HAY* WA11 ... **90** F7
Haydock Park Golf Club *NEWLW* WA12 ... **92** B8
Haydock Park Racecourse *NEWLW* WA12 ... **91** L4
Hayfield School *GR/UP/WCH* CH49 ... **110** C7
Hazel Business Park *RNFD/HAY* WA11 ... **88** E1
The Heath Comprehensive School *RUNC* WA7 ... **149** K6
Heath Road Medical Centre *RUNC* WA7 ... **19** J7
Helsby Golf Club *FROD/HEL* WA6 ... **166** D6
Helsby Health Centre *FROD/HEL* WA6 ... **166** D2
Helsby High School *FROD/HEL* WA6 ... **159** M8
Hesketh Centre (Hospital) *CHTN/BK* PR9 ... **24** E4
Hesketh Golf Club *CHTN/BK* PR9 ... **25** G3
Heskin FC *CHLY/EC* PR7 ... **41** M2
Heskin Pembertons CE Primary School *CHLY/EC* PR7 ... **42** A3
Heswall FC *HES* CH60 ... **141** L6
Heswall Golf Club *HES* CH60 ... **141** J8
Heswall Health Centre *HES* CH60 ... **141** H4
Heswall Preparatory School *HES* CH60 ... **141** G3
Heswall Primary School *PEN/TH* CH61 ... **141** J4
Hewitt Business Park *WGNW/BIL/O* WN5 ... **78** A1
Heygarth Primary School *PS/BROM* CH62 ... **144** A8
Heygreen Comm Primary School *WAV* L15 ... **114** A5
Higher Bebington Junior School *BEB* CH63 ... **127** L7
Higher Side Community Comprehensive School *RAIN/WH* L35 ... **117** H2
Highfield CE Primary School *WGNS/IIMK* WN3 ... **78** E1
Highfield Cricket Club *WGNS/IIMK* WN3 ... **78** E1
Highfield Industrial Estate *CHLYE* PR6 ... **32** E3
Highfield Primary School *CHLYE* PR6 ... **32** F5
Highfield School *CL/PREN* CH43 ... **111** G7
Highfield Special School *HLWD* L26 ... **132** C6
Hilbre High School *WKBY* CH48 ... **124** F2
Hillcrest Hotel *WDN* WA8 ... **118** B8
Hillside Golf Club *STHP* PR8 ... **35** G4
Hillside Health Centre *SKEL* WN8 ... **65** L4
Hillside High School *BTL* L20 ... **7** M5
Hillside Primary School *CL/PREN* CH43 ... **110** F8
 FROD/HEL WA6 ... **159** M8
Hill Street Business Centre *TOX* L8 ... **112** F7
Hillview Primary School *RUNC* WA7 ... **161** G1
Hinderton School *EP* CH65 ... **163** J2
Hindley Business Centre *WGNE/HIN* WN2 ... **69** M8
Hindley Green Primary School *WGNE/HIN* WN2 ... **80** B1
Hindley Hall Golf Club *WGNE/HIN* WN2 ... **69** M5
Historic Warships *BIRK* CH41 ... **111** M4
HM Coroners Court *CLVP* L2 ... **12** F7
HM Customs & Excise National Museum *VAUX/LVPD* L3 ... **12** C9

HM Prison Altcourse *WLT/FAZ* L9 ... **84** F7
HM Prison Hindley *WGNE/HIN* WN2 ... **80** F3
HM Prison Liverpool *WLT/FAZ* L9 ... **84** B8
HM Remand Centre (Risley) *GOL/RIS/CU* WA3 ... **107** G5
Holcroft Clinic *GOL/RIS/CU* WA3 ... **107** G2
Holiday Inn *RNFD/HAY* WA11 ... **91** K5
 RUNC WA7 ... **161** H1
 WARR WA1 ... **123** H6
Holland Business Park *BRSC* L40 ... **64** L1
Holland Moor Primary School *SKEL* WN8 ... **66** A6
Holly Lodge Girls College *WD/CROXPK* L12 ... **98** C7
Holmeswood Methodist Primary School *KIRK/FR/WA* PR4 ... **27** L7
Holy Angels RC Primary School *KKBY* L32 ... **85** L3
Holy Cross Primary School *VAUX/LVPD* L3 ... **13** G4
Holy Cross RC High School *CHLY/EC* PR7 ... **43** L1
Holy Cross RC Primary School *BIRK* CH41 ... **111** C4
 ECCL WA10 ... **9** J4
Holy Family Catholic Primary School *CHTN/BK* PR9 ... **25** G6
Holy Family RC High School *CSBY/BLUN* L23 ... **71** J7
Holy Family RC Primary School *WDN* WA8 ... **117** M7
 WGNE/HIN WN2 ... **80** C1
 WLTN L25 ... **131** M4
Holy Name RC Primary School *WLT/FAZ* L9 ... **85** G6
Holy Rosary RC Junior School *AIN/FAZ* L10 ... **84** F2
Holy Rosary RC Primary School *AIN/FAZ* L10 ... **84** E2
Holy Spirit Catholic Primary School *STHEL* WA9 ... **103** J2
The Holy Spirit RC Aided Primary School *RUNC* WA7 ... **149** M5
Holy Spirit RC Primary School *NTHTN* L30 ... **83** M2
Holy Trinity CE Primary School *CHTN/BK* PR9 ... **3** J2
 FMBY L37 ... **59** C2
 HOY CH47 ... **108** E6
Holy Trinity RC Primary School *ALL/GAR* L19 ... **130** F8
Homoeopathic Medical Centre *CLB/OSW/ST* L13 ... **114** C2
Hood Manor Medical Centre *WARRW/BUR* WA5 ... **120** E8
Hope School *HUY* L36 ... **115** M6
Hope Special School *WGNS/IIMK* WN3 ... **79** H3
Hope Street Natural Health Centre *CLVPS* L1 ... **113** C5
Hope Valley County Primary School *EV* L5 ... **97** H6
Horns Mill Primary School *FROD/HEL* WA6 ... **166** C4
Hornspit Medical Centre *NG/CROX* L11 ... **98** C5
Hotel Ibis *HUY* L36 ... **112** E5
Houghwood Golf Club *WGNW/BIL/O* WN5 ... **77** K6
Howard Johnson Hotel *PR/KW* L34 ... **86** B7
Howley Quay Industrial Estate *WARR* WA1 ... **15** J5
Hoylake Business Centre *HOY* CH47 ... **108** E5
Hoylake Cottage Hospital *HOY* CH47 ... **108** E5
Hoylake Golf Club *HOY* CH47 ... **108** D7
Hoylake RFC *HOY* CH47 ... **108** D6
Hudson Primary School *MGHL* L31 ... **72** F6
Hugh Baird College of Technology *BTL* L20 ... **7** H7
Hulmes Bridge Business Centre *ORM* L39 ... **49** L3
Hunts Cross JMI School *WLTN* L25 ... **131** L7
Hunts Cross Shopping Park *SPK/HALE* L24 ... **131** J7
Hurlston Hall Country Caravan Park *BRSC* L40 ... **50** E3
Hurlston Hall Golf Club *BRSC* L40 ... **50** E3
Hurst School *ECCL* WA10 ... **89** C7
Huyton & Prescot Golf Club *HUY* L36 ... **100** C8
Huyton with Roby CE Primary School *HUY* L36 ... **115** M2
Ince Clinic & Community Centre *WGNE/HIN* WN2 ... **69** J6
Ince in Makerfield Primary School *WGNE/HIN* WN2 ... **69** J6
Innkeeper's Lodge Hotel *ALL/GAR* L19 ... **130** C5
 CLB/OSW/ST L13 ... **114** D1
 GOL/RIS/CU WA3 ... **93** G7
Interactive College *CLVP* L2 ... **12** F6
Interchange Motorway Industrial Estate *HUY* L36 ... **116** C4
International Business Centre *WARRW/BUR* WA5 ... **120** E3
International Swimming Pool *WGN* WN1 ... **4** F5
Irby Cricket Club *PEN/TH* CH61 ... **125** M5
Irby Primary School *PEN/TH* CH61 ... **126** A6
Irwin Road Health Centre *STHEL* WA9 ... **102** F6
Isle of Man Ferry Terminal *VAUX/LVPD* L3 ... **12** C6
Islington House Medical Centre *NPK/KEN* L6 ... **13** M4
Job's Ferry *PS/BROM* CH62 ... **144** C4
John Street Medical Centre *GOL/RIS/CU* WA3 ... **92** C5
John Street Primary School *EP* CH65 ... **20** C2
Jubilee Medical Centre *NG/CROX* L11 ... **98** E3
Junction 1 Retail Park *WAL/EG* CH44 ... **110** F2
Kensington CP J & I Schools *EHL/KEN* L7 ... **113** K3

Kensington Industrial Estate *CHTN/BK* PR9 ... **3** K5
Kensington Medical Centre *NPK/KEN* L6 ... **113** J2
Kerfoot Business Park *WARRN/WOL* WA2 ... **121** J5
Kew Medical Centre *STHP* PR8 ... **36** A2
Kew Retail Park *STHP* PR8 ... **36** C1
Kew Woods Primary School *STHP* PR8 ... **36** A2
Kilgarth School *BIRK* CH41 ... **10** D1
Kilhey Court Hotel *WGN* WN1 ... **56** E3
The King David High School *WAV* L15 ... **114** E6
King David Primary School *WAV* L15 ... **114** E6
King Edward Industrial Estate *VAUX/LVPD* L3 ... **12** C4
Kingfisher Business Park *BTL* L20 ... **83** J3
 LITH L21 ... **83** K6
King George V College *STHP* PR8 ... **25** C8
Kingsbury School *ORM* L39 ... **50** F8
Kings Business Park *PR/KW* L34 ... **100** C8
Kingsdown High School *WGNW/BIL/O* WN5 ... **67** L6
Kings Gap Court Hotel *HOY* CH47 ... **108** C7
Kingsley Community School *TOX* L8 ... **113** J6
Kings Meadow Primary School *STHP* PR8 ... **47** L2
Kingsmead School *HOY* CH47 ... **108** E5
Kingsway Industrial Park *VAUX/LVPD* L3 ... **13** H2
Kingsway Primary School *WAL/EG* CH44 ... **111** L3
Kingsway Surgery *CSBY/WL* L22 ... **83** G3
Kingswood College *BRSC* L40 ... **37** J7
Kirby-Liverpool Municipal Golf Club *AIN/FAZ* L10 ... **85** K5
Kirkby CE Primary School *KKBY* L32 ... **85** M2
Kirkby Sports Centre *KKBY* L32 ... **85** L5
Kirkdale St Lawrence CE School *ANF/KKDL* L4 ... **96** F5
Kirkfield Hotel *NEWLW* WA12 ... **105** G1
Kirkless Industrial Estate *WGNE/HIN* WN2 ... **69** J3
Knotty Ash Primary School *DV/KA/FCH* L14 ... **114** F1
Knowsley Business Park *KNOW* L34 ... **86** D8
Knowsley Central Primary Support Centre *HUY* L36 ... **116** B1
Knowsley Community College *HUY* L36 ... **115** L3
 KKBY L32 ... **85** M3
Knowsley Hey School *HUY* L36 ... **116** B3
Knowsley Industrial Park *NWD/KWIPK* L33 ... **86** C7
Knowsley Magistrates Court *HUY* L36 ... **116** A3
Knowsley Medical Centre *PR/KW* L34 ... **99** M2
Knowsley Northern Primary Support Centre *NWD/KWIPK* L33 ... **86** B1
Knowsley Safari Park *PR/KW* L34 ... **100** D4
Knowsley Village Primary School *KNOW* L34 ... **99** L3
Lady Lever Art Gallery *PS/BROM* CH62 ... **128** D7
Ladymount RC Primary School *PEN/TH* CH61 ... **141** M2
Lairdside Technology Park *BIRK* CH41 ... **128** B1
Lakeside School *HUY* L36 ... **115** M6
Lamberhead Green Primary School *WGNW/BIL/O* WN5 ... **67** J8
Lamberhead Industrial Estate *WGNW/BIL/O* WN5 ... **67** K8
Lancashire College *CHLY/EC* PR7 ... **32** C5
Lancaster House Medical Centre *ECCL* WA10 ... **9** G3
Lance Lane Medical Centre *WAV* L15 ... **114** C6
Lander Road Primary School *LITH* L21 ... **83** L7
Landgate Industrial Estate *AIMK* WN4 ... **79** J5
Landican Cemetery *GR/UP/WCH* CH49 ... **126** D4
Landican Crematorium *CR/UP/WCH* CH49 ... **126** D5
Langbank Medical Centre *NG/CROX* L11 ... **98** B4
Langham Street Industrial Estate *ANF/KKDL* L4 ... **97** H5
Larkfield Primary School *CHTN/BK* PR9 ... **25** J2
Latchford CE Primary School *WARRS* WA4 ... **14** F8
Latchford Medical Centre *WARRS* WA4 ... **138** A2
Lathom County High School *SKEL* WN8 ... **65** H2
Lathom Park CE Primary School *BRSC* L40 ... **52** C5
Lathom Road Health Centre *HUY* L36 ... **116** A2
Laurel Business Centre *EHL/KEN* L7 ... **113** M3
Lea Green Business Park *STHEL* WA9 ... **118** B1
Leamington Community School *NG/CROX* L11 ... **97** M3
Leasowe Castle Hotel *MOR/LEA* CH46 ... **110** A1
Leasowe Golf Club *MOR/LEA* CH46 ... **110** B1
Leasowe Millennium Centre *MOR/LEA* CH46 ... **110** C2
Leasowe Primary School *MOR/LEA* CH46 ... **110** D1
Leasowe Recreation Centre *MOR/LEA* CH46 ... **110** C2
Leeds Street Industrial Estate *WGNS/IIMK* WN3 ... **4** C5
Lee Park Golf Club *NTHLY* L27 ... **131** M1

Legh Vale Primary School *RNFD/HAY* WA11 ... **90** D7
Leigh Golf Club *GOL/RIS/CU* WA3 ... **106** F1
Leisure Lakes *CHTN/BK* PR9 ... **26** F5
Library & Rainford Gallery *RNFD/HAY* ... **9** G4
Lifeboat House *HOY* CH47 ... **108** C6
Linacre Primary School *BTL* L20 ... **83** L8
Linaker Primary School *STHP* PR8 ... **35** H8
Lincoln Road Health Centre *STHP* PR8 ... **35** J4
Lindley Hotel *WAV* L15 ... **53** L2
Lingham Primary School *MOR/LEA* CH46 ... **109** M4
Lingholme Health Centre *ECCL* WA10 ... **8** F4
Lingley Mere Business Park *WARRW/BUR* WA5 ... **120** C3
Lister Drive Infant School *CLB/OSW/ST* L13 ... **114** A1
Lister Drive Junior School *CLB/OSW/ST* L13 ... **114** A1
Litherland High School *STHEL* WA9 ... **83** M3
Litherland Moss Primary School *LITH* L21 ... **83** M4
Little Digmoor Primary School *SKEL* WN8 ... **65** K7
Little Sutton Ce Primary School *GTS/LS* CH66 ... **155** J7
Little Theatre *CHLY/EC* PR7 ... **32** E5
 CHTN/BK PR9 ... **3** H3
 CL/PREN CH43 ... **10** F6
Liver Industrial Estate *WLT/FAZ* L9 ... **97** L1
Liverpool Anglican Cathedral *CLVPS* L1 ... **113** G6
Liverpool College *CALD/MH* L18 ... **130** B1
Liverpool Community College *VAUX/LVPD* L3 ... **12** E3
Liverpool Cricket Club *ALL/GAR* L19 ... **130** B5
Liverpool Empire Theatre *CLVPS* L1 ... **13** H6
Liverpool FC (Anfield) *ANF/KKDL* L4 ... **97** J6
Liverpool FC Museum *ANF/KKDL* L4 ... **97** J6
Liverpool Hope University College *CHLDW* L16 ... **114** F7
 VAUX/LVPD L3 ... **13** L4
Liverpool John Lennon International Airport *SPK/HALE* L24 ... **146** E3
Liverpool John Moores University *AIG/SPK* L17 ... **130** B4
 CLVPS L1 ... **13** L8
 VAUX/LVPD L3 ... **13** G5
 VAUX/LVPD L3 ... **13** H4
 VAUX/LVPD L3 ... **13** K6
 VAUX/LVPD L3 ... **13** K7
Liverpool Magistrates Court *CLVP* L2 ... **12** F6
Liverpool Marriott Hotel *CLVPS* L1 ... **13** H6
 SPK/HALE L24 ... **146** B1
Liverpool Museum *VAUX/LVPD* L3 ... **13** H5
Liverpool Playhouse Theatre *CLVPS* L1 ... **13** H7
Liverpool St Helens RUFC *RNFD/HAY* WA11 ... **88** C4
Liverpool Womens Hospital *TOX* L8 ... **113** J5
Locking Stumps Primary School *GOL/RIS/CU* WA3 ... **106** E8
Longbarn County Primary School *WARRN/WOL* WA2 ... **122** D4
Long Lane County Primary School *WARRN/WOL* WA2 ... **121** K4
Long Lane Medical Centre *WLT/FAZ* L9 ... **98** B1
Longmoor Community Primary School *WLT/FAZ* L9 ... **84** D7
Longshoot Health Centre *WGN* WN1 ... **5** L1
Longton Lane Community Primary School *RAIN/WH* L35 ... **101** K8
Longton Medical Centre *RAIN/WH* L35 ... **117** K2
Longview J & I School *HUY* L36 ... **100** A7
Lordsgate Township Primary School *BRSC* L40 ... **52** A2
Lourdes Hospital *CALD/MH* L18 ... **130** B1
Loushers Lane Special School *GOL/RIS/CU* WA3 ... **123** C2
 WARRS WA4 ... **137** M3
Lower Lee Special School *WLTN* L25 ... **131** C1
Lowfield Industrial Estate *STHEL* WA9 ... **102** B8
Low Hall Primary School *WGNE/HIN* WN2 ... **80** C1
Lowton Business Park *GOL/RIS/CU* WA3 ... **93** J5
Lowton High School *GOL/RIS/CU* WA3 ... **93** K5
Lowton J & I School *GOL/RIS/CU* WA3 ... **93** J6
Lowton St Marys CE Primary School *GOL/RIS/CU* WA3 ... **93** J5
Lowton West Primary School *GOL/RIS/CU* WA3 ... **92** E5
Lunts Heath Primary School *WDN* WA8 ... **118** D8
Lydiate Primary School *MGHL* L31 ... **72** E1
Lyme Community Primary School *NEWLW* WA12 ... **104** D1
Lymm Golf Club *LYMM* WA13 ... **123** M8
Lymm Hotel *LYMM* WA13 ... **139** M2
The Lyndale School *PS/BROM* CH62 ... **144** B8
Lyon Industrial Estate *STHEL* WA9 ... **118** C5
Mab Lane Primary School *STBRV* L28 ... **99** H6
Mabs Cross Primary School *WGN* WN1 ... **5** C1
Mackets Primary School *WLTN* L25 ... **131** M4
Maghull Health Centre *MGHL* L31 ... **72** F4
Maghull High School *MGHL* L31 ... **72** E6

Manley County Primary School *FROD/HEL* WA6 ... **167** J7
Manor Farm Medical Centre *HUY* L36 ... **116** B4
Manor High School *CSBY/BLUN* L23 ... **70** F7
The Manor House Primary School *FROD/HEL* WA6 ... **160** E4
Manor Industrial Estate *WARRS* WA4 ... **15** M8
Manor Primary School *CL/PREN* CH43 ... **110** E6
Mansfield Primary School *EP* CH65 ... **163** H2
Marble Place Shopping Centre *STHP* PR8 ... **3** G4
Margaret Beavan Special School *WD/CROXPK* L12 ... **98** C6
The Margaret Thompson Medical Centre *SPK/HALE* L24 ... **147** J1
Maricourt Catholic High School *MGHL* L31 ... **73** G5
Marine FC *CSBY/BLUN* L23 ... **82** F2
Marketgate Shopping Centre *WGN* WN1 ... **4** F3
Market Street Medical Centre *CHLY/EC* PR7 ... **69** M7
Market Walk Shopping Centre *CHLY/EC* PR7 ... **32** E5
Marsh Green County Primary School *WGNW/BIL/O* WN5 ... **67** M5
Marsh Green Health Centre *WGNW/BIL/O* WN5 ... **67** M4
Marston Bentley Industrial Estate *WGNE/HIN* WN2 ... **69** K3
Martland Mill Business Park *WGNW/ST* WN6 ... **67** M3
Martland Mill Industrial Estate *WGNW/ST* WN6 ... **67** L3
Martlew Day Hospital *STHEL* WA9 ... **101** L8
Marus Bridge Health Centre *WGNS/IIMK* WN3 ... **79** H3
Marus Bridge School *WGNS/IIMK* WN3 ... **79** G3
Maryland Health Centre *CLVPS* L1 ... **13** L4
Mason Street Industrial Estate *WGNS/IIMK* WN3 ... **4** C5
Massey Hall School *WARRS* WA4 ... **139** H1
Maternity & Child Welfare Clinic *STHEL* WA9 ... **103** H2
 WGNE/HIN WN2 ... **69** L8
Matthew Arnold Primary School *TOX* L8 ... **129** J2
Mawdesley CE Primary School *BRSC* L40 ... **40** F2
Mayfield School *CHLY/EC* PR7 ... **32** E8
Mayflower Industrial Estate *FMBY* L37 ... **59** J4
Maypole Industrial Estate *WGNE/HIN* WN2 ... **80** E6
McKee School of Education *CALD/MH* L18 ... **130** E3
Meadow Bank Special School *AIN/FAZ* L10 ... **85** H5
Meadow Lane Industrial Park *EP* CH65 ... **20** E3
Meadow Primary School *GTS/LS* CH66 ... **163** G3
Meadowside School *CR/UP/WCH* CH49 ... **126** C3
Media Arts College *WAL/EG* CH44 ... **111** H2
Melling Primary School *MGHL* L31 ... **85** K1
Melrose Abbey *ANF/KKDL* L4 ... **7** K9
Mendell Primary School *PS/BROM* CH62 ... **144** A5
Meols Cop High School *STHP* PR8 ... **25** H8
Meols Cop Retail Park *STHP* PR8 ... **36** B1
Merchant Taylors Junior School for Girls *CSBY/BLUN* L23 ... **82** F2
Merchant Taylors School for Boys *CSBY/BLUN* L23 ... **83** G3
Merchant Taylors School for Girls *CSBY/BLUN* L23 ... **82** F1
Mere Brow CE Primary School *KIRK/FR/WA* PR4 ... **27** H3
Merefield Special School *STHP* PR8 ... **47** K1
Mere Oaks School *WGN* WN1 ... **56** D8
Mersey Ferries *VAUX/LVPD* L3 ... **12** D8
Mersey Park Primary School *RF/TRAN* CH42 ... **127** M2
Merseyside Maritime Museum *VAUX/LVPD* L3 ... **12** C9
Mersey View *FROD/HEL* WA6 ... **160** D6
Mersey View Special School *AIG/SPK* L17 ... **130** A4
Merton Bank Primary School *STHEL* WA9 ... **9** M3
Met Quarter *CLVP* L2 ... **13** G7
Metropole Hotel *STHP* PR8 ... **2** F5
Metropolitan Cathedral of Christ the King *SPK/HALE* L24 ... **13** L7
Middlefield Primary School *SPK/HALE* L24 ... **147** G2
Millbrook Business Centre *RNFD/HAY* WA11 ... **88** E2
Millbrook Primary School *KKBY* L32 ... **85** M2
Millennium Centre *WGNW/ST* WN6 ... **55** K7
Millfields Primary School *PS/BROM* CH62 ... **155** G1
Mill Green Special School *NEWLW* WA12 ... **105** G2
Mill Hotel *CROS/BRETH* PR26 ... **30** A2
Millingford Industrial Estate *GOL/RIS/CU* WA3 ... **92** D5
Mill Lane Industrial Estate *EP* CH65 ... **21** J9
Millstead Special School *WAV* L15 ... **114** C5
Mill Street Medical Centre *ECCL* WA10 ... **8** F7
Miriam Centre *BIRK* CH41 ... **111** H5
Model Village *STHP* PR8 ... **2** E3
Monksdown Primary School *NG/CROX* L11 ... **98** C4
Montrose School *WGNW/BIL/O* WN5 ... **67** M6

Moore Primary School
  WARRS WA4 ....136 C8
Moore RUFC
  WARRS WA4 ....136 D7
Moorfield Primary School
  WDN WA8 ....134 F2
Moorfoot Road Industrial Estate
  STHEL WA9 ....103 H1
Moor Lane Business Centre
  WDN WA8 ....16 C6
Moorside Primary School
  SKEL WN8 ....66 A6
Moreton Medical Centre
  MOR/LEA CH46 ....110 A5
Mosscroft Primary School
  HUY L36 ....116 C2
Moss Industrial Estate
  LEIGH WN7 ....93 K4
Mosslands School
  WAL/EG CH44 ....111 L1
Moss Lane Sports Centre
  LITH L21 ....83 M4
Mossley Hill Hospital
  CALD/MH L18 ....130 A1
Mossock Hall Golf Club
  ORM L39 ....74 A1
Mosspits J & I School
  WAV L15 ....114 D7
Mossy Lea Primary School
  WGNNW/ST WN6 ....42 B7
Mother Teresa RC JMI School
  EV L5 ....13 G1
Mount Carmel Preparatory
  School *ORM* L39 ....62 F3
Mount Primary School
  WAL/NB CH45 ....95 J5
The Mount-St Marys
  Preparatory School
  CSBY/BLUN L23 ....82 D2
Much Woolton Catholic School
  WLTN L25 ....131 K3
Murdishaw Health Centre
  RUNC WA7 ....150 F6
Murrayfield Hospital
  PEN/TH CH61 ....126 F8
Museum of Liverpool Life
  VAUX/LVPD L3 ....12 D9
National Discovery Park
  CLVPS L1 ....12 F8
National Museums & Galleries
  Merseyside
  CLVPS L1 ....13 H6
National Wildflower Centre
  CHLDW L16 ....115 H4
Natural Health Clinic
  PR L34 ....100 F7
Nature Reserve
  BEB CH63 ....143 K6
  FMBY L37 ....46 F4
  FMBY L37 ....58 C5
Neptune Theatre
  CLVPS L1 ....13 G8
Neston Cricket Club
  NSTN CH64 ....152 E5
Neston High School
  NSTN CH64 ....153 H4
Neston Medical Centre
  NSTN CH64 ....153 G5
Neston Primary School
  NSTN CH64 ....153 G6
Neston Recreation Centre
  NSTN CH64 ....153 H4
Netherfield Family Health
  Clinic *EV* L5 ....97 G8
Netherley Health Centre
  NTHLY L27 ....116 A8
Netherley Sports Centre
  NTHLY L27 ....115 M8
Netherton Industrial Estate
  NTHTN L30 ....84 B5
Netherton Moss Primary
  School *NTHTN* L30 ....84 A2
Netherton Park Primary
  School *NTHTN* L30 ....84 B3
Newborough School
  WLTN L25 ....131 H2
New Brighton Primary School
  WAL/NB CH45 ....95 L5
New Brighton RUFC
  MOR/LEA CH46 ....110 B1
Newburgh CE Primary School
  SKEL WN8 ....53 J4
Newburgh Cricket Club
  SKEL WN8 ....53 J4
Newfield Special School
  CSBY/BLUN L23 ....71 K8
New Heys Community
  School *CALD/MH* L18 ....130 F4
New Hutte County Primary
  School *HLWD* L26 ....132 A7
New Lodge Industrial Estate
  NWD/KWIPK L33 ....86 D5
New Market Hall
  RUNC WA7 ....19 H2
New Mersey Retail Park
  SPK/HALE L24 ....131 H8
New Park Primary School
  NPK/KEN L6 ....93 K4
Newstead Abbey
  TOX L8 ....113 L6
Newton Bank Preparatory
  School *NEWLW* WA12 ....105 G1
Newton Community Hospital
  NEWLW WA12 ....104 D2
Newton Health Clinic
  NEWLW WA12 ....104 D1
Newton-Le-Willows Cemetery
  NEWLW WA12 ....104 F3
Newton-Le-Willows
  Community High School
  NEWLW WA12 ....91 M8
Newton-Le-Willows Primary
  School
  NEWLW WA12 ....104 E2
Newton-Le-Willows Sports
  Club *NEWLW* WA12 ....104 E1
Newton Westpark Primary
  School *LEIGH* WN7 ....81 L5
New Way Business Centre
  WAL/EG CH44 ....111 M3
Nicol Mere School
  AIMK WN4 ....79 J4
Nine Tree Primary School
  STBRV L28 ....99 J4
Norley Hall Cricket Club
  WGNW/BIL/O WN5 ....67 K6
Norman Pannell JMI School
  NTHLY L27 ....116 A8
Norris Green Family Health
  Clinic *NG/CROX* L11 ....98 A4
North Cheshire Trading Estate
  CL/PREN CH43 ....127 G5
North Clinic
  CL/PREN CH43 ....111 J6
Northcote Primary School
  WLT/FAZ L9 ....97 J2
Northern Cricket Club
  CSBY/BLUN L23 ....71 H7

North Meols Community
  Leisure Centre
  CHTN/BK PR9 ....23 J8
North Meols Lawn Tennis Club
  CHTN/BK PR9 ....25 K1
North Mersey Business Centre
  NWD/KWIPK L33 ....86 G1
North Mersey Community
  Hospital *WLT/FAZ* L9 ....84 F7
North Park Health Centre
  BTL L20 ....6 F1
North Quarry Business Park
  WGNNW/ST WN6 ....54 F4
Northway Primary School
  MGHL L31 ....73 G2
  WAV L15 ....114 D4
North Western Hall
  CLVPS L1 ....13 J6
North Wirral Coastal Park
  MOR/LEA CH46 ....109 M1
Norton Priory Museum and
  Gardens *RUNC* WA7 ....150 D2
Norton Priory Recreation
  Centre *RUNC* WA7 ....150 D3
Norwood Primary School
  CHTN/BK PR9 ....25 G6
Notre Dame Catholic High
  School *ANF/KKDL* L4 ....97 G6
Nugent House School
  WGNW/BIL/O WN5 ....89 M1
Nutgrove Methodist Primary
  School *STHEL* WA9 ....101 M6
Nye Bevan Swimming Pool
  SKEL WN8 ....65 K4
Oak Cottage Medical Centre
  HUY L36 ....116 A4
Oakdene Primary School
  RAIN/WH L35 ....117 L3
Oakfield Junior School
  WDN WA8 ....133 K5
Oak Remedial Clinic
  WD/CROXPK L12 ....99 G1
The Oaks Community Primary
  School *EP* CH65 ....20 F9
Oakwood Avenue Primary
  School *WARR* WA1 ....15 K1
Odeon Cinema
  CLVPS L1 ....13 H6
  NTHTN L30 ....84 C2
  PS/BROM CH62 ....143 M3
Old Boston Trading Estate
  RNFD/HAY WA11 ....91 J5
Oldershaw School
  WAL/NB CH45 ....95 J8
Old Foundry Estate
  WDN WA8 ....16 F6
Old Hall Farm Business Park
  CHTN/BK PR9 ....25 J8
Old Hall Primary School
  WARRW/BUR WA5 ....120 F5
Old Mill Leisure Club
  CHLYE PR6 ....33 H7
Old Parkonians RFC
  CLVPS L1 ....127 J2
Old Rockerrians RFC
  CL/PREN CH43 ....127 H5
Old Swan Health Centre
  CLB/OSW/ST L13 ....114 C3
Ormskirk Business Park
  ORM L39 ....51 H7
Ormskirk CE Primary School
  ORM L39 ....51 H7
Ormskirk Cricket Club
  ORM L39 ....63 H1
Ormskirk & District General
  Hospital *ORM* L39 ....63 H1
Ormskirk Golf Club
  BRSC L40 ....52 A6
Ormskirk RUFC
  ORM L39 ....51 G7
Ormskirk School
  BRSC L40 ....51 K8
Orrell Clinic
  WGNW/BIL/O WN5 ....67 G6
Orrell Newfold C P School
  WGNW/BIL/O WN5 ....77 M1
Orrell Primary School
  BTL L20 ....83 M8
Orrell RUFC
  WGNW/BIL/O WN5 ....67 G8
Orrell Water Park
  WGNW/BIL/O WN5 ....78 A1
Orrets Meadow School
  MOR/LEA CH46 ....110 B5
Our Lady & All Saints RC
  Primary *SKEL* WN8 ....53 L3
Our Lady Catholic High School
  NPK/KEN L6 ....113 J1
Our Lady Immaculate RC
  Primary School *EV* L5 ....97 G7
Our Lady Mother of the
  Saviour Catholic Primary
  RUNC WA7 ....150 C4
Our Lady of Compassion RC
  Primary School *FMBY* L37 ....59 J2
Our Lady of Good Help RC
  Primary School *WAV* L15 ....114 C5
Our Lady of Lourdes RC
  Primary School
  MOR/LEA CH46 ....110 D1
  STHP PR8 ....35 J4
Our Lady of Mount Carmel
  RC Primary School
  TOX L8 ....113 H8
Our Lady of Perpetual Succour
  RC Primary School
  WDN WA8 ....133 H5
Our Lady of Pity Primary
  School *GR/UP/WCH* CH49 ....125 M3
Our Lady of Reconciliation
  Primary School
  VAUX/LVPD L3 ....12 F2
Our Lady of the Assumption
  Primary School
  WLTN L25 ....115 K7
Our Lady of the Rosary RC
  Primary School
  LEIGH WN7 ....81 K8
Our Lady of Walsingham RC
  Infant School *NTHTN* L30 ....84 A3
Our Lady of Walsingham RC
  Junior School *NTHTN* L30 ....84 A3
Our Lady Queen of Peace RC
  High School *SKEL* WN8 ....65 H1
Our Lady Queen of Peace RC
  Primary School *LITH* L21 ....83 J3
Our Lady RC Primary School
  WARRS WA4 ....138 G3
  WGNE/HIN WN2 ....57 L8
Our Lady & St Edwards RC
  Primary School *BIRK* CH41 ....10 C2
Our Lady & St Philomenas
  Primary School *WLT/FAZ* L9 ......98 B1
Our Lady & St Swithins
  Catholic Primary School
  NG/CROX L11 ....85 L8
Our Ladys Bishop Eton RC
  Primary School
  CALD/MH L18 ....114 E8

Our Ladys Catholic Infant
  School *EP* CH65 ....163 J2
Our Ladys RC Junior School
  EP CH65 ....163 J2
Our Ladys RC Primary School
  PR/KW L34 ....100 F6
Our Lady Star of the Sea RC
  Primary School *LITH* L21 ....83 J7
The Oval Sports Centre
  BEB CH63 ....128 C6
Overchurch J & I School
  GR/UP/WCH CH49 ....110 B7
Overdale Primary School
  NWD/KWIPK L33 ....86 B1
Oxton Cricket Club
  CL/PREN CH43 ....127 H1
Paddington House Hotel
  WARR WA1 ....122 C6
Padgate Business Centre
  WARR WA1 ....122 C5
Padgate CE Primary School
  WARRN/WOL WA2 ....122 C4
Padgate Community High
  School *WARRN/WOL* WA2 ....122 B3
Padgate Medical Centre
  WARRN/WOL WA2 ....122 C4
Paerr Hall
  WARR WA1 ....14 D7
Pagefield Industrial Estate
  WGNW/BIL/O WN5 ....68 B4
Palacefields Primary School
  RUNC WA7 ....150 C7
Palace Theatre
  WARR WA1 ....14 E6
Palatine Industrial Estate
  WARRS WA4 ....15 G9
Palmerston Special School
  WLTN L25 ....131 G2
Paradise Street Bus Station
  CLVPS L1 ....12 F8
Parbold Douglas CE Primary
  School *SKEL* WN8 ....53 M2
Parish CE Primary School
  ECCL WA10 ....9 J3
Park Brow Primary School
  KKBY L32 ....86 C5
Park Business Centre
  WGNE/HIN WN2 ....80 F1
Parkdale Industrial Estate
  WARR WA1 ....15 H7
Parkfield Medical Centre
  RF/TRAN CH42 ....128 C5
Parkfield Special School
  KKBY L32 ....86 A5
Parkgate Primary School
  NSTN CH64 ....152 E4
Park Hall Hotel
  CHLY/EC PR7 ....42 C1
Park Hall Leisure Centre
  CHLY/EC PR7 ....42 C1
Park High School Sports
  College *CL/PREN* CH43 ....10 C6
Park House Medical Centre
  PR/KW L34 ....100 F7
Park Industrial Estate
  AIMK WN4 ....91 G2
Parklands High School
  CHLY/EC PR7 ....32 C5
  SPK/HALE L24 ....147 G2
Parklands Primary School
  GTS/LS CH66 ....155 M8
The Park Lane Hotel
  AIG/SPK L17 ....129 L2
Park Medical Centre
  WKBY CH48 ....124 C3
Park Pool
  ORM L39 ....51 G8
Park Primary School
  WAL/EG CH44 ....111 K2
The Park Primary School
  RUNC WA7 ....150 C4
Park Road Primary School
  WARRW/BUR WA5 ....120 A7
Park Road Sports Centre
  TOX L8 ....113 H8
Park View Primary School
  HUY L36 ....115 L1
Parliament Street North
  Waterfront Business Area
  VAUX/LVPD L3 ....112 E6
Parliament Street South
  Waterfront Business Area
  CLVPS L1 ....113 G6
Parr Industrial Estate
  STHEL WA9 ....103 G3
Parrs Corner Trading Estate
  BTL L20 ....7 H2
Parr Swimming Baths
  STHEL WA9 ....9 M5
Pasture Road Health Centre
  MOR/LEA CH46 ....110 A4
Patterdale Lodge Medical
  Centre *NEWLW* WA12 ....104 C2
Peatwood Medical Centre
  KKBY L32 ....86 B6
Pemberton Business Centre
  WGNW/BIL/O WN5 ....67 L7
Pemberton Clinic
  WGNW/BIL/O WN5 ....67 M7
Pemberton Primary School
  WGNW/BIL/O WN5 ....67 L7
Peninsula Business Park
  MOR/LEA CH46 ....110 C3
Penketh Business Park
  WARRW/BUR WA5 ....136 D1
Penketh County High School
  WARRW/BUR WA5 ....120 B8
Penketh Health Clinic
  WARRW/BUR WA5 ....136 A1
Penketh Primary School
  WARRW/BUR WA5 ....135 M1
Penketh South Community
  Primary School
  WARRW/BUR WA5 ....136 B2
Penketh Swimming Baths
  WARRW/BUR WA5 ....120 A8
Penkford School
  NEWLW WA12 ....104 A3
Penlake Industrial Estate
  STHEL WA9 ....103 G7
Pennington Flash Country
  Park *LEIGH* WN7 ....93 L3
Penpoll Industrial Estate
  BTL L20 ....83 L7
Penpoll Trading Estate
  BTL L20 ....83 L7
Pensby Clinic
  PEN/TH CH61 ....141 J2
Pensby High School for Boys
  PEN/TH CH61 ....140 F2
Pensby High School for Girls
  PEN/TH CH61 ....140 F1
Pensby Infant School
  PEN/TH CH61 ....141 H2
Pensby Junior School
  PEN/TH CH61 ....141 H2
Pensby Park Primary School
  PEN/TH CH61 ....141 G1

Pensby Recreation Centre
  PEN/TH CH61 ....126 C8
Pepper Mill Business Park
  WGN WN1 ....5 G5
Peterhouse School
  CHTN/BK PR9 ....25 K2
Peter Lloyd Leisure Centre
  CLB/OSW/ST L13 ....98 B8
Pewithall Primary School
  RUNC WA7 ....19 J9
Philharmonic Hall
  CLVPS L1 ....13 J9
  TOX L8 ....113 H5
Phoenix Medical Centre
  ECCL WA10 ....8 F4
Phoenix Primary School
  EHL/KEN L7 ....114 A3
Picture House Cinema
  WLTN L25 ....131 J3
Pinehurst Primary School
  ANF/KKDL L4 ....97 L6
Pinfold Primary School
  BRSC L40 ....50 B2
Pinners Brow Retail Park
  WARRN/WOL WA2 ....14 F4
Pioneer Industrial Estate
  WGNW/BIL/O WN5 ....68 A7
Pius XII RC Primary School
  GTS/LS CH66 ....155 M7
Plantation Business Park
  PS/BROM CH62 ....144 B3
Plantation Primary School
  HLWD L26 ....132 B5
Platt Bridge Clinic
  WGNE/HIN WN2 ....80 C3
Platts Lane Industrial Estate
  BRSC L40 ....52 A3
Plaza Cinema
  CSBY/WL L22 ....82 F4
Pleasant Primary School
  VAUX/LVPD L3 ....13 K8
Pleasureland
  STHP PR8 ....2 C3
Plessington Catholic High
  School *BEB* CH63 ....128 C6
Pontville School
  ORM L39 ....62 F2
Poole Hall Industrial Estate
  EP CH65 ....156 B4
Pooltown Junior School
  EP CH65 ....156 B8
Port Arcades
  EP CH65 ....20 C5
Portland Primary School
  BIRK CH41 ....10 A1
Port of Liverpool
  LITH L21 ....83 G7
Port of Liverpool Building
  VAUX/LVPD L3 ....12 E8
Poulter Road Medical Centre
  WLT/FAZ L9 ....84 D6
Poulton Lancelyn Primary
  School *BEB* CH63 ....143 J3
Poulton Park Golf Club
  WARRN/WOL WA2 ....122 C1
Poulton Primary School
  WAL/EG CH44 ....111 J2
Premier Lodge
  AIMK WN4 ....91 K3
  CHLYE PR6 ....33 G8
  CLVPS L1 ....12 F6
  GR/UP/WCH CH49 ....126 A1
  HUY L36 ....115 K3
  RAIN/WH L35 ....84 B3
  VAUX/LVPD L3 ....112 E5
  WARR WA1 ....123 H7
  WARRN/WOL WA2 ....105 J7
  WCNNW/ST WN6 ....55 K4
Prenton Golf Club
  CL/PREN CH43 ....127 K5
Prenton High School for Girls
  RF/TRAN CH42 ....127 M4
Prenton Infant & Junior Schools
  CL/PREN CH43 ....127 J4
Prenton Preparatory School
  CL/PREN CH43 ....127 K2
Prescot AFC
  PR/KW L34 ....100 F6
Prescot Leisure Centre
  RAIN/WH L35 ....101 G8
Prescot Medical Centre
  PR/KW L34 ....100 F7
Prescot Museum
  PR/KW L34 ....100 E7
Prescot Primary School
  PR/KW L34 ....101 H7
Prescot School
  PR/KW L34 ....100 E6
Presfield Special School
  CHTN/BK PR9 ....25 J2
Price Street Business Centre
  BIRK CH41 ....10 E2
Priestley Business Centre
  WARRW/BUR WA5 ....14 A5
Priestley Sixth Form College
  WARRS WA4 ....137 L2
Primrose Hill Primary School
  CHLY/EC PR7 ....31 K1
Prince Edwin Alseth Centre
  EV L5 ....13 J1
Princes Park Health Centre
  TOX L8 ....113 K7
Princess Drive Medical Centre
  DV/KA/FCH L14 ....99 J7
Princes Special School
  TOX L8 ....113 J6
The Priory CE Primary School
  BIRK CH41 ....10 F3
The Priory Medical Centre
  NPK/KEN L6 ....97 L8
Prospect House Medical Centre
  WGNW/BIL/O WN5 ....67 J7
Prospect Industrial Estate
  WGNE/HIN WN2 ....69 M8
Pump House Museum
  BIRK CH41 ....11 L4
Pyramid
  WARR WA1 ....14 D7
Pyramids Shopping Centre
  BIRK CH41 ....11 H6
The Quadrangle Business
  Centre *WGNE/HIN* WN2 ....81 K1
Quality Hotel
  GTS/LS CH66 ....155 H7
  SKEL WN8 ....77 H1
  WGN WN1 ....5 G3
Quay Business Centre
  WARRN/WOL WA2 ....121 J2
Queen Elizabeth II Law Courts
  CLVPS L1 ....12 E8
Queenscourt Hospice
  STHP PR8 ....36 A1
Queens Dock Business Centre
  VAUX/LVPD L3 ....112 F6
Queens Drive Family Health
  Clinic *WLT/FAZ* L9 ....97 J2
Queens Park CE & RC Primary
  School *ECCL* WA10 ....8 B3

Queens Park Community
  Leisure Centre
  ECCL WA10 ....8 D4
Queensway Business Centre
  WDN WA8 ....16 C9
Racecourse Retail Park
  WLT/FAZ L9 ....84 E3
Radio City
  CLVP L2 ....12 F6
Radnor Medical Centre
  NPK/KEN L6 ....97 M8
Raeburn Primary School
  PS/BROM CH62 ....143 M7
RAF Burtonwood
  WARRW/BUR WA5 ....120 C6
Railway Centre
  STHP PR8 ....3 J5
Rainbow Medical Centre
  STHEL WA9 ....103 G6
Rainford CE Primary School
  RNFD/HAY WA11 ....76 B7
Rainford Health Centre
  RNFD/HAY WA11 ....76 C7
Rainford High School
  RNFD/HAY WA11 ....76 C5
Rainford Industrial Estate
  RNFD/HAY WA11 ....88 D1
Rainhill Clinic
  RAIN/WH L35 ....117 L2
Rainhill High School
  RAIN/WH L35 ....117 M3
Range High School
  FMBY L37 ....58 F5
Ravenhead Retail Park
  STHEL WA9 ....9 H9
Ravenscroft Primary School
  NWD/KWIPK L33 ....74 A8
Rawson Road Primary School
  LITH L21 ....83 H7
Record Business Park
  WARRN/WOL WA2 ....121 J5
Rectory CE Primary School
  AIMK WN4 ....78 F8
Redbridge High School
  AIN/FAZ L10 ....85 L6
Redgate Primary School
  FMBY L37 ....59 J3
Red Lion Shopping Centre
  MGHL L31 ....72 F4
Reginald Road Industrial Park
  STHEL WA9 ....103 H7
Renacres Hall Hospital
  ORM L39 ....36 D8
Rice Lane J & I Schools
  WLT/FAZ L9 ....84 C8
Richard Evans Community
  Primary School
  RNFD/HAY WA11 ....90 B7
Richard Evans Infant School
  RNFD/HAY WA11 ....90 C7
Ridgeway High School
  CL/PREN CH43 ....126 F1
Rimrose Business Park
  BTL L20 ....6 C1
Rimrose Valley Country Park
  CSBY/BLUN L23 ....83 J3
Ringtail Industrial Estate
  BRSC L40 ....51 K3
Risley Moss Nature Park
  GOL/RIS/CU WA3 ....123 K1
Rivacre Business Centre
  GTS/LS CH66 ....156 A8
Rivacre Valley Country Park
  GTS/LS CH66 ....156 A5
Rivacre Valley CP School
  GTS/LS CH66 ....156 A6
Riverhill Hotel
  CL/PREN CH43 ....127 J2
Riverside Primary School
  WAL/EG CH44 ....112 A2
Riverside Retail Park
  WARR WA1 ....15 G7
Riverside Trading Estate
  WARRW/BUR WA5 ....135 M4
Rivington & Blackrod High
  School *HOR/BR* BL6 ....45 K7
Rivington Country Park
  HOR/BR BL6 ....45 J5
Rivington Park Independent
  School *HOR/BR* BL6 ....45 H4
Rivington Primary School
  ECCL WA10 ....8 C1
  HOR/BR BL6 ....45 H4
R L Hughes Primary School
  AIMK WN4 ....91 J2
Roberts Primary School
  BTL L20 ....83 K6
Robin Park Arena
  WGNW/BIL/O WN5 ....68 A5
Robin Park Sports Centre
  WGNW/BIL/O WN5 ....68 B5
Robins Lane Primary School
  STHEL WA9 ....102 E5
Robson Street Clinic
  WARR WA1 ....15 J4
Roby Medical Centre
  HUY L36 ....115 J3
Roby Mill CE Primary School
  SKEL WN8 ....66 D2
Roby Park Primary School
  HUY L36 ....115 K2
Rocket Trading Centre
  DV/KA/FCH L14 ....114 E4
Rock Ferry High School
  RF/TRAN CH42 ....128 B5
Rock Ferry Medical Centre
  RF/TRAN CH42 ....128 B2
Rock Ferry Primary School
  RF/TRAN CH42 ....128 B3
Rock Retail Park
  BIRK CH41 ....11 L8
Rodney Fertility Clinic
  CLVPS L1 ....13 K9
Roscoe Primary School
  CLB/OSW/ST L13 ....98 B6
Rose Bridge High School
  WGN WN1 ....5 J3
Roseheath Primary School
  HLWD L26 ....132 B6
Rosehill Business Centre
  CHTN/BK PR9 ....3 M5
Ross Business Centre
  WGNW/BIL/O WN5 ....67 M8
Rossmore Primary School
  GTS/LS CH66 ....155 L6
Rossmore Trading Estate
  EP CH65 ....156 C6
Rother Drive Business Park
  EP CH65 ....156 C6
Rowan Park Special School
  LITH L21 ....83 M3
Royal Albert Edward Infirmary
  WGN WN1 ....68 E3
The Royal Birkdale Golf Club
  STHP PR8 ....34 F4
Royal Clifton Hotel
  STHP PR8 ....2 F3
Royal College of Nursing
  CLVP L2 ....12 E7

Royal Court Theatre
  CLVPS L1 ....13 H6
The Royal Hotel
  CSBY/WL L22 ....82 F5
Royal Liver Building
  VAUX/LVPD L3 ....12 D7
Royal Liverpool Childrens
  Hospital (Alder Hey)
  WD/CROXPK L12 ....114 C4
Royal Liverpool Golf Club
  HOY CH47 ....108 D2
Royal Liverpool University
  Hospital EHL/KEN L7 ...13 M6
  EHL/KEN L7 ....113 J3
Royal Mail Sorting Office
  VAUX/LVPD L3 ....13 K7
Royal School for the Blind
  WAV L15 ....114 B6
Royal Umpire Caravan Park
  CROS/BRETH PR26 ....30 A3
Roy Castle International
  Centre for Lung Research
  EHL/KEN L7 ....13 M5
Rudston J & I School
  CHLDW L16 ....114 F5
Rufford CE Primary School
  BRSC L40 ....39 K1
Ruffwood Community School
  NWD/KWIPK L33 ....86 B2
Runcorn AFC
  RUNC WA7 ....19 K2
Runcorn County Court
  RUNC WA7 ....150 B2
Runcorn Golf Club
  RUNC WA7 ....19 H9
Runcorn Rowing Club
  RUNC WA7 ....160 F1
Runcorn Ski Slope
  RUNC WA7 ....150 D6
Runcorn Swimming Pool
  RUNC WA7 ....19 J2
Rutherford Medical Centre
  CALD/MH L18 ....114 D7
Sacred Heart Catholic Primary
  School WGNE/HIN WN2 ...81 K2
Sacred Heart RC High School
  CSBY/WL L22 ....83 G1
Sacred Heart RC Primary
  School CHLYE PR6 ......33 G4
  EHL/KEN L7 ....113 J3
  MOR/LEA CH46 ....110 B4
  WARRW/BUR WA5 ....121 G8
  WGNW/BIL/O WN5 ....68 B3
St Aelreds RC Technology
  College NEWLW WA12 ...104 F1
St Agnes RC Primary School
  HUY L36 ....116 B4
St Aidans CE Primary School
  WGNW/BIL/O WN5 ....78 A8
St Aidans RC Primary School
  HUY L36 ....116 B2
  WGNS/IIMK WN3 ....78 F3
St Albans RC Primary School
  WAL/EG CH44 ....111 J1
  WARRW/BUR WA5 ....14 B3
St Alberts RC Primary School
  STBRV L28 ....99 J4
St Aloysius RC Primary School
  HUY L36 ....115 L1
St Ambrose Barlow RC High
  School NTHTN L30 ......72 C8
St Ambrose RC Primary School
  SPK/HALE L24 ....147 J3
St Andrews CE Primary School
  BEB CH63 ....128 B7
  WARRN/WOL WA2 ......121 L2
  WGNNW/ST WN6 ....68 B3
St Andrews Maghull CE Primary
  School
  MGHL L31 ....72 F4
St Andrews RC Primary School
  WLTN L25 ....131 M6
St Annes CE Primary School
  CLB/OSW/ST L13 ......114 B2
  WGNNW/ST WN6 ....67 M2
St Annes RC Primary School
  EHL/KEN L7 ....113 K5
  HUY L36 ....115 M4
  ORM L39 ....62 F1
  RF/TRAN CH42 ....128 B5
  STHEL WA9 ....102 F6
St Anns CE Primary School
  RAIN/WH L35 ....117 L2
  WARRN/WOL WA2 ......121 L5
St Anselms College
  CL/PREN CH43 ....10 B6
St Anselms Redcourt
  CL/PREN CH43 ....10 B7
St Anthony of Padua RC
  Primary School
  CALD/MH L18 ....130 B1
St Anthony's Shopping
  Centre EV L5 ....97 G8
St Augustine of Canterbury
  RC High School
  RNFD/HAY WA11 ....90 A8
St Augustines Catholic Primary
  School WARRS WA4 ....138 B1
St Augustines RC Primary
  School RUNC WA7 .....150 C3
St Austins RC Primary School
  ALL/GAR L19 ....130 D6
  STHEL WA9 ....101 L6
St Barnabas CE Primary School
  WARRW/BUR WA5 ....14 A5
St Bartholomews RC Primary
  School RAIN/WH L35 ..118 A4
St Basil RC Primary School
  RAIN/WH L35 ....133 J2
St Bedes Catholic High School
  ORM L39 ....62 F1
St Bedes RC J & I School
  WDN WA8 ....16 D1
St Benedicts RC Primary School
  WARRN/WOL WA2 ....15 J1
  WGNE/HIN WN2 ....69 L7
St Benets RC Primary School
  NTHTN L30 ....72 B8
St Bernadettes Catholic
  Primary School
  WGNNW/ST WN6 ....55 J7
St Bernards RC Primary School
  EP CH65 ....20 E8
  EP CH65 ....163 M3
St Berteline CE Primary School
  RUNC WA7 ....150 E5
St Bridgets CE Primary
  School WARRN/WOL WA2 .122 B2
St Bridgets CE Primary School
  WKBY CH48 ....124 D4
St Brigids RC Primary School
  STBRV L28 ....99 J6
St Catharines CE Primary
  School WGN WN1 ....5 J4
St Catherines Centre for Girls
  RNFD/HAY WA11 ....90 A7
St Catherine's Hospital
  RF/TRAN CH42 ....127 M2

St Catherines RC Primary
  School GOL/RIS/CU WA3 .93 G5
St Cecilias RC Infant School
  CLB/OSW/ST L13 ....98 A8
St Chads Catholic High School
  RUNC WA7 ....149 M6
St Charles RC Primary School
  AIG/SPK L17 ....129 L3
St Christophers RC Primary
  School SPK/HALE L24 ..146 F1
St Clares RC Primary School
  WAV L15 ....113 M6
St Clements RC Primary School
  RUNC WA7 ....19 G6
St Cleopas CE Primary School
  TOX L8 ....129 H1
St Columbas RC Primary
  School HUY L36 ......100 A8
St Cuthberts Catholic High
  School STHEL WA9 ....103 H4
St Cuthberts RC Primary
  School CLB/OSW/ST L13 .114 B2
  WGNW/BIL/O WN5 ....67 M7
St Davids CE Primary School
  WGNE/HIN WN2 ....57 K6
St Dominics RC J & I School
  DV/KA/FCH L14 ....99 K7
St Edmund Arrowsmith
  Catholic High School
  AIMK WN4 ....91 J3
St Edmund Arrowsmith RC
  Comprehensive School
  RAIN/WH L35 ....101 H8
St Edmund of Canterbury
  High School
  DV/KA/FCH L14 ....99 K7
St Edmunds & St Thomas
  Catholic Primary School
  CSBY/WL L22 ....82 F4
St Edwards Catholic Primary
  School RUNC WA7 ......19 K2
  WGNW/BIL/O WN5 ....68 B6
St Edwards College (Secondary)
  WD/CROXPK L12 ....98 D8
St Edwards Runnymede
  Junior School
  WD/CROXPK L12 ....98 D8
St Elizabeths Catholic Primary
  School LITH L21 ......83 L7
St Finbars Catholic Primary
  School TOX L8 ....129 J2
St Francis de Sales RC Infant
  School ANF/KKDL L4 ....7 M7
St Francis de Sales RC Junior
  School ANF/KKDL L4 ....7 M8
St Francis of Assisi RC Primary
  School ALL/GAR L19 ..130 E7
St Francis Xavier RC College
  WLTN L25 ....131 G1
St Gabriels CE Primary School
  HUY L36 ....116 C3
St George of England High
  School BTL L20 ....83 M7
St Georges CE Primary School
  CHLY/EC PR7 ....33 G8
St George's Hall
  CLVPS L1 ....13 H6
St Georges Medical Centre
  WAL/NB CH45 ....95 K6
St Georges Primary School
  WAL/NB CH45 ....95 G8
St Georges RC Primary School
  MGHL L31 ....72 F6
St Gerards RC School
  EV L5 ....96 F7
St Gregorys Catholic Primary
  School CHLY/EC PR7 ...32 E8
  MGHL L31 ....72 E1
St Gregorys RC High School
  WARRW/BUR WA5 ....120 F8
St Gregorys RC JMI School
  NTHLY L27 ....116 A8
St Helens AFC
  STHEL WA9 ....103 H6
St Helens Bus Station
  ECCL WA10 ....9 H5
St Helens College
  ECCL WA10 ....8 F5
St Helens Crematorium
  ECCL WA10 ....88 E6
St Helens Cricket Club
  ECCL WA10 ....8 C2
St Helens Hospital
  STHEL WA9 ....102 E4
St Helens Museum & Art
  Gallery ECCL WA10 .....9 H4
St Helens Retail Park
  STHEL WA9 ....9 K6
St Helens RLFC
  (Knowsley Road Stadium)
  ECCL WA10 ....101 L2
St Helens Theatre Royal
  ECCL WA10 ....9 H5
St Hildas CE High School
  AIG/SPK L17 ....113 M8
St Hughs JMI School
  WAV L15 ....113 M6
St James Catholic Primary
  School WGNW/BIL/O WN5 .77 M1
St James CE Primary School
  BRSC L40 ....64 A1
  CHLYE PR6 ....33 G6
  WGNS/IIMK WN3 ....68 B8
St James Primary School
  RNFD/HAY WA11 ....91 G7
St James RC Primary School
  BTL L20 ....6 E2
  SKEL WN8 ....65 K1
St Joan of Arc RC Primary
  School BTL L20 ....6 C1
St John Almond RC Secondary
  School ALL/GAR L19 ..130 F7
St John Bosco RC Primary
  School MGHL L31 ......72 D3
St John Bosco RC Secondary
  School NG/CROX L11 ...98 D2
St John Fisher Catholic High
  School WGNNW/ST WN6 ..68 B2
St John Fisher Junior & Infant
  School WDN WA8 ....17 K1
St John Fisher RC Primary
  School PR/KW L34 .....99 L1
St John Rigby RC 6th Form
  College WGNW/BIL/O WN5 .67 H3
St John's Beacon
  CLVPS L1 ....13 H7
St Johns Catholic Junior and
  Infant School BEB CH63 .128 B6
St Johns CE J & I School
  WGNE/HIN WN2 ....69 H2
St Johns CE Primary School
  BRSC L40 ....39 H8
  CHLY/EC PR7 ....42 F6
  CSBY/WL L22 ....82 F4
  WGNW/BIL/O WN5 ....67 K7
St Johns Primary School
  ANF/KKDL L4 ....97 G5
St Johns RC Primary School
  SKEL WN8 ....65 L4

St John's Shopping Centre &
  Market CLVPS L1 ......13 H7
St John Stone Catholic Primary
  School STHP PR8 ......47 M3
St John Vianney RC Primary
  School STHEL WA9 ....102 A7
St Josephs Catholic Primary
  School WARRW/BUR WA5 .120 A8
St Josephs Catholic Primary
  School CHLYE PR6 .....32 F3
  CHLYE PR6 ....44 D6
  WGNNW/ST WN6 ....55 H2
St Josephs RC Infant School
  KKBY L32 ....86 A4
St Josephs RC Primary School
  GR/UP/WCH CH49 .....110 C8
St Josephs RC Primary School
  HUY L36 ....116 B2
  WAL/EG CH44 ....111 M3
St Judes Catholic Primary
  School WGNS/IIMK WN3 .68 B8
St Julie RC Primary School
  ECCL WA10 ....101 J1
St Julies RC High School
  WLTN L25 ....131 J3
St Laurence Medical Centre
  KKBY L32 ....86 B4
St Laurence RC Primary School
  KKBY L32 ....86 B4
St Laurences RC Primary
  School BIRK CH41 .....11 H4
St Leos RC Primary School
  RAIN/WH L35 ....117 G3
St Lewis's Catholic Primary
  School GOL/RIS/CU WA3 .106 D4
St Lukes CE Primary School
  FMBY L37 ....58 F4
  GOL/RIS/CU WA3 ....93 G6
St Lukes Halsall CE Primary
  School CSBY/BLUN L23 .70 F8
St Lukes RC Primary School
  FROD/HEL WA6 ....160 E5
  RAIN/WH L35 ....117 H1
  SKEL WN8 ....65 A7
St Malachys RC Primary
  School TOX L8 ....113 G8
St Margaret Marys RC J & I
  School DV/KA/FCH L14 .115 H2
St Margarets Anfield CE
  Primary School
  NPK/KEN L6 ....97 L8
St Margarets CE Controlled
  Infant School
  WARRN/WOL WA2 ......121 L3
St Margarets CE High School
  AIG/SPK L17 ....129 M4
St Margarets CE Primary
  School TOX L8 ....113 H6
  WARRN/WOL WA2 ......121 L4
St Marie RC Primary School
  NWD/KWIPK L33 ....86 C2
St Maries RC Primary School
  WGNNW/ST WN6 ....56 A3
St Marks Catholic Primary
  School SKEL WN8 ......66 A5
St Marks CE Primary School
  BRSC L40 ....36 F5
  WGNW/BIL/O WN5 ....68 B6
St Martins Catholic Primary
  School RUNC WA7 ....151 G2
St Mary & St Paul Primary
  School RAIN/WH L35 ..116 F1
St Marys Catholic College
  WAL/NB CH45 ....95 G7
St Marys Catholic Junior
  School NEWLW WA12 ...104 D1
St Marys CE Primary School
  NEWLW WA12 ....104 E1
St Marys CE Primary School
  BTL L20 ....6 F5
  CHLY/EC PR7 ....30 E7
  PS/BROM CH62 ....144 B8
  RUNC WA7 ....150 C5
St Marys' Market
  ECCL WA10 ....9 H6
St Marys RC Primary School
  BRSC L40 ....37 J4
  CHLY/EC PR7 ....32 C6
  CSBY/BLUN L23 ....71 G5
  WGNW/BIL/O WN5 ....89 M1
St Marys & St Johns RC Primary
  School WGN WN1 ....5 G2
St Marys West Derby Primary
  School WD/CROXPK L12 .98 D6
St Mary & Thomas CE Primary
  School ECCL WA10 .....8 E4
St Matthews Catholic Primary
  School ANF/KKDL L4 ...97 M5
St Matthews CE Primary
  School STHEL WA9 ...101 L6
St Matthews RC Primary
  School SKEL WN8 ......65 M6
St Michael in the Hamlet
  Primary School AIG/SPK L17 .129 K2
St Michael Jubilee Golf Club
  WDN WA8 ....134 A6
St Michaels Catholic Primary
  School NPK/KEN L6 ...113 K1
  WDN WA8 ....133 L6
St Michaels CE High School
  CHLY/EC PR7 ....32 E3
St Michaels CE Primary School
  ORM L39 ....62 D4
St Monicas RC Primary School
  BTL L20 ....7 L1
St Monicas RC Primary School
  WARRS WA4 ....137 M6
St Nathaniels CE Primary
  School WGNE/HIN WN2 .80 D2
St Nicholas Catholic Primary
  School VAUX/LVPD L3 ..13 L8
St Nicholas CE Primary School
  CSBY/BLUN L23 ....82 D2
St Oswalds Catholic Infant
  School CLB/OSW/ST L13 .114 C2
St Oswalds Catholic Junior
  School CLB/OSW/ST L13 .114 C3
St Oswalds CE Primary School
  CL/PREN CH43 ....110 E4
  NTHTN L30 ....84 B2
St Oswalds RC J & I School
  AIMK WN4 ....91 K2
St Oswalds RC Primary School
  CHLY/EC PR7 ....42 E5
  WARR WA1 ....122 A5
St Paschal Baylon RC Primary
  School WLTN L25 ....115 H5
St Patricks Catholic Primary
  School TOX L8 ....113 H7
St Patricks RC Primary School
  CHTN/BK PR9 ....25 J3
  WGN WN1 ....5 H4
St Paul of the Cross Catholic
  Primary School
  WARRW/BUR WA5 ....104 A7
St Pauls CE Primary School
  CHLYE PR6 ....44 C5
  WGNS/IIMK WN3 ....79 H2

St Pauls RC Primary School
  CL/PREN CH43 ....110 D6
St Pauls & St Timothys RC J
  & I School WD/CROXPK L12 .98 E6
St Peter & Paul RC Primary
  School RNFD/HAY WA11 .89 K6
  WAL/NB CH45 ....95 J5
St Peter & St Paul RC High
  School WDN WA8 .....134 B3
St Peter & St Pauls RC Primary
  School BRSC L40 ......41 H3
St Peters Catholic High School
  WGNW/BIL/O WN5 ....67 H6
St Peters CE Primary School
  WARR WA1 ....122 E6
St Peters CE Infant School
  LEIGH WN7 ....81 L8
St Peters CE Junior School
  LEIGH WN7 ....81 L8
St Peters CE Primary School
  AIMK WN4 ....79 H7
  CHLYE PR6 ....33 G3
  FMBY L37 ....47 J8
  HES CH60 ....141 H6
  NEWLW WA12 ....104 F1
  WGNE/HIN WN2 ....69 G8
St Peters RC Primary School
  GR/UP/WCH CH49 .....126 E1
St Philips CE Primary School
  CHTN/BK PR9 ....85 L5
  STHP PR8 ....3 K6
St Philips Church Community
  School WARRW/BUR WA5 .120 D4
St Raymonds RC Primary
  School NTHTN L30 ....83 M1
St Richards Catholic Primary
  School SKEL WN8 .....64 E4
St Robert Bellarmine RC
  Primary School
  BTL L20 ....83 M6
St Saviours CE Aided Primary
  School CL/PREN CH43 .127 J2
St Saviours RC J & I School
  GTS/LS CH66 ....163 G2
St Sebastians Primary School
  EHL/KEN L7 ....113 M3
St Silas CE Primary School
  TOX L8 ....113 J8
Saints Peter & Paul Catholic
  School NWD/KWIPK L33 .74 B8
St Stephens Catholic Primary
  School WARRN/WOL WA2 .121 K2
St Stephens CE Primary School
  WGN WN1 ....69 G3
St Stephens Primary School
  CHTN/BK PR9 ....23 J8
St Stephens School
  CHTN/BK PR9 ....23 H7
St Teresas Catholic Primary
  School ECCL WA10 .....8 A4
St Teresas County Primary
  School SKEL WN8 .....66 D4
St Teresas Junior School
  NG/CROX L11 ....98 B3
St Teresa of Lisieux Infant
  School NG/CROX L11 ...98 B3
St Teresas RC Infant School
  STHP PR8 ....2 F9
  STHP PR8 ....35 J1
St Theresas Primary School
  STHEL WA9 ....118 E2
St Thomas Becket School
  HUY L36 ....116 C2
St Thomas CE Primary School
  AIMK WN4 ....91 L2
  GOL/RIS/CU WA3 ....92 D4
  MGHL L31 ....72 F1
  WARRS WA4 ....137 M4
St Thomas More Catholic High
  School WGNW/BIL/O WN5 .68 B6
St Thomas of Canterbury
  Catholic Primary School
  ECCL WA10 ....88 F7
St Thomas of Canterbury RC
  School CSBY/WL L22 ..83 G5
St Thomas the Martyr CE
  Primary School
  SKEL WN8 ....66 D6
St Vincents Catholic Primary
  School WARRW/BUR WA5 .136 A2
St Vincents School
  WD/CROXPK L12 ....99 C7
St Weburgh CE Primary School
  WARRS WA4 ....137 K3
St Werburghs RC Primary
  School BIRK CH41 .....11 G8
St Wilfrids CE Aided Primary
  School WARRS WA4 ...138 D4
St Wilfrids CE Primary School
  WGNW/ST WN6 ....56 B4
St Wilfrids RC High School
  LITH L21 ....83 L6
St William of York RC Primary
  School CSBY/BLUN L23 .71 K8
St Williams CE Primary School
  WGNE/HIN WN2 ....57 H6
St Winefrides Catholic Primary
  School BTL L20 ....6 F5
St Winefrides RC Primary
  School NSTN CH64 ...153 H6
Sandfield Medical Centre
  ECCL WA10 ....8 E6
Sandfield Park Special School
  WD/CROXPK L12 ....98 D8
Sandhills Business Park
  EV L5 ....96 E7
Sandon Industrial Estate
  VAUX/LVPD L3 ....96 D7
Sandringham Medical Centre
  TOX L8 ....129 K1
Sandy Lane Health Centre
  SKEL WN8 ....64 E4
Sankey Bridge Industrial Estate
  WARRW/BUR WA5 ....136 C1
Sankey Medical Centre
  WARRW/BUR WA5 ....120 A6
Sankey Valley Country Park
  WARRW/BUR WA5 ....120 F4
Sankey Valley Industrial Estate
  NEWLW WA12 ....104 D3
Sankey Valley St James CE
  Primary School
  WARRW/BUR WA5 ....120 E7
Savio Catholic High School
  WARR WA1 ....84 A4
Scarisbrick Hotel
  STHP PR8 ....2 F7
Scholes Shopping Precinct
  WGN WN1 ....5 H1
School of Good Shepherd
  ANF/KKDL L4 ....97 H4
Scot Lane Primary School
  WGNW/BIL/O WN5 ....68 B0
Seabank Medical Centre
  WAL/NB CH45 ....95 K6
Seaforth Health Clinic
  LITH L21 ....83 J6
Sefton Business Park
  NTHTN L30 ....84 C5

Sefton Cricket Club
  AIG/SPK L17 ....129 L1
Sefton Lane Industrial Estate
  MGHL L31 ....72 C5
Sefton Park Medical Centre
  WAV L15 ....113 M7
Sefton Road Health Clinic
  LITH L21 ....83 K5
Senate Business Park
  NTHTN L30 ....84 B5
Shaw Hall Caravan Park
  BRSC L40 ....50 D1
Sherdley Business Park
  STHEL WA9 ....102 D5
Sherdley Park Golf Club
  STHEL WA9 ....102 C6
Sherdley Primary School
  STHEL WA9 ....102 E7
Shevington County Primary
  School WGNNW/ST WN6 ..55 H7
Shevington Vale Primary
  School WGNNW/ST WN6 ..55 G5
Shorefields Community
  Comprehensive School
  AIG/SPK L17 ....129 K1
  TOX L8 ....129 J2
Shoreside Primary School
  STHP PR8 ....47 K1
Shorrocks Hill Country Club
  FMBY L37 ....58 D4
Showcase Cinemas
  NG/CROX L11 ....98 C1
Silverdale Medical Centre
  HES CH60 ....141 H5
Simms Cross County Primary
  School WDN WA8 ......16 C4
Simonswood Industrial Park
  NWD/KWIPK L33 ....74 D7
Sir Alfred Jones Memorial
  Hospital ALL/GAR L19 .130 E7
Sir Thomas Boteler High
  School WARRS WA4 ...138 A2
Skelmersdale & Ormskirk
  Colleges SKEL WN8 ...65 J4
Skelmersdale Park Primary
  School SKEL WN8 .....65 G4
Skelmersdale Sports Centre
  SKEL WN8 ....65 L6
Skelmersdale United FC
  SKEL WN8 ....64 E5
Skylark Industrial Estate
  SPK/HALE L24 ....146 D2
Slaidburn Industrial Estate
  CHTN/BK PR9 ....25 J1
Small Business Centre
  VAUX/LVPD L3 ....112 F8
Smithdown County Primary
  School EHL/KEN L7 ..113 K5
SMM Business Park
  WAL/EG CH44 ....111 L4
Somerville Primary School
  WAL/EG CH44 ....111 L2
Southbank Tennis Club
  STHP PR8 ....36 A1
Southdene Medical Centre
  KKBY L32 ....86 C5
Southern Primary Support
  Centre WLTN L25 ....131 M5
South Lancashire Industrial
  Estate AIMK WN4 .....79 K7
Southlands High School
  CHLY/EC PR7 ....32 C8
Southmead Primary School
  RAIN/WH L35 ....117 G3
Southport & Ainsdale Golf
  Club STHP PR8 ....34 E7
Southport & Birkdale Cricket
  Club STHP PR8 ....35 G2
Southport Business Centre
  CHTN/BK PR9 ....3 H3
Southport Business Park
  STHP PR8 ....35 J2
Southport College
  CHTN/BK PR9 ....3 J3
Southport Crematorium
  STHP PR8 ....36 B3
Southport FC
  STHP PR8 ....25 G8
Southport Flower Show Site
  STHP PR8 ....2 D4
Southport & Formby District
  General Hospital
  STHP PR8 ....36 A1
Southport & Formby Hospital
  CHTN/BK PR9 ....3 H3
Southport General Infirmary
  STHP PR8 ....3 M7
Southport Girls FC
  STHP PR8 ....25 H7
Southport Municipal Golf Club
  CHTN/BK PR9 ....24 E3
Southport New Synagogue
  STHP PR8 ....3 G5
Southport Old Links Golf Club
  CHTN/BK PR9 ....25 K4
Southport Pier
  STHP PR8 ....24 B4
Southport RFC
  STHP PR8 ....35 G4
Southport Sailing Club
  STHP PR8 ....24 C4
Southport Swimming Baths
  STHP PR8 ....2 D4
Southport Town Hall
  STHP PR8 ....3 G4
Southport Zoo & Conservation
  Trust STHP PR8 ....2 D3
South Sefton Business Centre
  BTL L20 ....6 F6
South Wirral High School
  PS/BROM CH62 ....154 F1
Sovereign Business Park
  WGN WN1 ....5 H6
Speke Family Health Clinic
  SPK/HALE L24 ....147 G2
Speke Hall Industrial Estate
  SPK/HALE L24 ....146 D2
Sphynx Tennis Club
  STHP PR8 ....36 A1
The Sporting Edge Track
  ORM L39 ....63 J2
Springbank Industrial Estate
  WGNE/HIN WN2 ....80 D2
Springfield Special School
  KKBY L32 ....86 A6
Spring View Cricket Club
  WGNE/HIN WN2 ....5 H6
Springwood Crematorium
  WLTN L25 ....131 H5
Springwood Primary School
  ALL/GAR L19 ....131 G5
Ss Michael & All Angels RC
  Primary School
  GR/UP/WCH CH49 .....126 E3
The Stables Business Centre
  CLB/OSW/ST L13 ....98 A6
Standish Clinic
  WGNNW/ST WN6 ....56 A5

Standish Community High
School *WGNW/ST* WN6 ....55 L3
Standish Court Golf Club
WGNW/ST WN6 ....56 B4
Standish Cricket Club
WGNW/ST WN6 ....56 A5
Stanley High School
CHTN/BK PR9 ....25 H1
Stanley Medical Centre
EV L5 ....96 F7
Stanley School
PEN/TH CH61 ....126 C7
Stanney High School
EP CH65 ....163 L3
Stanney Mill Industrial Estate
CHNE CH2 ....164 B4
Stanney Mill Industrial Park
EP CH65 ....21 H3
Stanney Ten Industrial Estate
EP CH65 ....164 B3
Stanney Woods Country Park
EP CH65 ....163 K4
Stanton Road Primary School
BEB CH63 ....143 H2
Statham Primary School
LYMM WA13 ....139 L4
Station Road Industrial Estate
WARRS WA4 ....138 B3
Stockbridge Village Health
Centre *STBRV* L28 ....99 J3
Stockton Heath Community
Primary School
WARRS WA4 ....137 L4
Stockton Heath Medical
Centre *WARRS* WA4 ....137 L4
Stockton Wood Community
Primary School
SPK/HALE L24 ....146 E2
Stonebridge Business Park
NG/CROX L11 ....85 J8
Stone Cross Business Park
GOL/RIS/CU WA3 ....92 D6
Stopgate Medical Centre
WLT/FAZ L9 ....97 M2
Storrsdale Medical Centre
CALD/MH L18 ....130 D2
The Strand Medical Centre
BTL L20 ....7 G2
Strand Shopping Centre
BTL L20 ....7 G3
Streatham House School
CSBY/BLUN L23 ....82 E1
Stutelea Hotel & Leisure Club
CHTN/BK PR9 ....24 E1
Sudley House
AIG/SPK L17 ....130 B3
Sudley Infant School
AIG/SPK L17 ....130 A3
Sudley Junior School
AIG/SPK L17 ....130 A4
Summerhill Primary School
MGHL L31 ....73 G5
Summersales Industrial Estate
WGNS/IIMK WN3 ....78 D1
Sunnymede School
STHP PR8 ....2 D6
Sutton Community Leisure
Centre Track
STHEL WA9 ....102 C7
Sutton Cricket Club
STHEL WA9 ....102 E7
Sutton Green Primary School
GTS/LS WA9 ....155 K8
Sutton Hall Golf Club
RUNC WA7 ....161 J2
Sutton High School
GTS/LS WA9 ....156 A4
Sutton High Sports College
STHEL WA9 ....102 D7
Sutton Manor Community
Primary School
STHEL WA9 ....118 C3
Sutton Oak CE Primary School
STHEL WA9 ....103 G5
Swan Meadow Industrial
Estate *WGNS/IIMK* WN3 ....4 C7
Sycamore Lane Community
Primary
WARRW/BUR WA5 ....120 D8
Sylvester Primary School
HUY L36 ....116 B4
Tanhouse Industrial Estate
WDN WA8 ....17 L5
Tanning Court Industrial Estate
WARR WA1 ....14 F7
Tate Gallery
VAUX/LVPD L3 ....112 D5
Taylor Street Industrial Estate
EV L5 ....96 F8
Thatto Heath Community
Primary School
STHEL WA9 ....102 A5
Theatre & Floral Hall
STHP PR8 ....3 G1
Thelwall Infant School
WARRS WA4 ....138 E2
Thelwall Junior School
WARRS WA4 ....138 F2
Thelwall New Road Industrial
Estate *WARRS* WA4 ....138 L1
Thingwall Primary School
PEN/TH CH61 ....126 C1
Thingwall Recreation Centre
PEN/TH CH61 ....126 D7
Thomas Gray Infant School
BTL L20 ....6 E2
Thomas Gray Junior School
BTL L20 ....6 F1
Thornton Crematorium
CSBY/BLUN L23 ....71 G6
Thornton Hall Hotel
NSTN CH64 ....142 B8
Thornton Hough Primary
School *BEB* CH63 ....142 D6
Thornton Primary School
CSBY/BLUN L23 ....71 K7
Three Sisters Racing Circuit
AIMK WN4 ....79 L6
Titanic Memorial
VAUX/LVPD L3 ....12 C7
Tower College
RAIN/WH L35 ....117 M4

Tower Dene Preparatory
School *CHTN/BK* PR9 ....25 H3
Tower Hill Health Centre
NWD/KWIPK L33 ....74 B8
Townfield Primary School
CL/PREN CH43 ....127 G2
Town Green Primary School
ORM L39 ....62 E5
Town Lane Infant School
BEB CH63 ....128 A7
Toxteth Park Cemetery
TOX L8 ....113 M7
Toxteth Sports Centre
TOX L8 ....113 H7
Tranmere Rovers FC
(Prenton Park)
RF/TRAN CH42 ....127 L3
Tranmere Sports Centre
RF/TRAN CH42 ....127 L3
Travel Inn
CHNE CH2 ....165 L3
CLB/OSW/ST L13 ....98 C7
CLVP L2 ....12 F6
GOL/RIS/CU WA3 ....92 D6
NTHTN L30 ....84 D1
PS/BROM CH62 ....144 A4
RAIN/WH L35 ....116 D5
RUNC WA7 ....161 M1
STHEL WA9 ....118 B2
WGNS/IIMK WN3 ....79 H4
WGNW/BIL/O WN5 ....67 H6
WLT/FAZ L9 ....84 D5
Travelodge
CLVP L2 ....13 G6
KNUT WA16 ....139 K7
PS/BROM CH62 ....155 H2
RNFD/HAY WA11 ....91 G5
VAUX/LVPD L3 ....128 F1
WARR WA1 ....14 D5
WDN WA8 ....17 G4
Tree Tops Country House Hotel
FMBY L37 ....47 L4
Trentham Road Medical Centre
STHEL WA9 ....85 L3
Trident Industrial Estate
GOL/RIS/CU WA3 ....107 G7
Trident Retail Park
RUNC WA7 ....150 A6
Trinity Primary School
SKEL WN8 ....65 G4
Trinity & St Michaels CE &
Methodist Primary School
CROS/BRETH PR26 ....29 L3
Triumph Trading Park
SPK/HALE L24 ....131 J7
Twelve Apostles RC Primary
School *LEIGH* WN7 ....81 M5
Twelve Quays Ferry Terminal
BIRK CH41 ....112 B4
Twig Lane Clinic
HUY L36 ....115 L1
Twin Lakes Industrial Park
CROS/BRETH PR26 ....29 J2
Twiss Green Primary School
GOL/RIS/CU WA3 ....107 G1
UGC Cinema
CLB/OSW/ST L13 ....114 B3
WGNW/BIL/O WN5 ....68 B5
Unity Theatre
CLVPS L1 ....13 K9
University Hospital Aintree
WLT/FAZ L9 ....85 C7
University of Liverpool
EHL/KEN L7 ....13 M8
EHL/KEN L7 ....113 J4
VAUX/LVPD L3 ....13 L6
Up Holland High School
WGNW/BIL/O WN5 ....77 L1
Upper Parliament Medical
Centre *EHL/KEN* L7 ....113 K5
Upton Cricket Club
GR/UP/WCH CH49 ....110 B8
Upton Hall FCJ School
GR/UP/WCH CH49 ....110 B8
Upton Medical Centre
WDN WA8 ....133 K2
Ursuline RC Primary School
CSBY/BLUN L23 ....82 D2
Uveco Business Centre
BIRK CH41 ....111 K4
Valewood Primary School
CSBY/BLUN L23 ....70 F8
Valley Medical Centre
ANF/KKDL L4 ....97 G6
CHLDW L16 ....115 G6
Valley Road Business Park
WAV L15 ....114 D5
VAT House & HM Customs &
Excise *VAUX/LVPD* L3 ....112 E7
Vauxhall Business Centre
VAUX/LVPD L3 ....12 E3
Vauxhall Health Centre
EV L5 ....13 G1
Vernon Sangster Sports
Centre *ANF/KKDL* L4 ....97 J6
Victoria Central Hospital
WAL/EG CH44 ....111 K2
Victoria Park Arena
WARRS WA4 ....15 K4
Victoria Road Primary School
RUNC WA7 ....19 G5
Victoria Trading Estate
RAIN/WH L35 ....117 L2
Village Medical Centre
WLTN L25 ....131 J3
Villa Medical Centre
CL/PREN CH43 ....127 J5
Virgin Cinemas
CLB/OSW/ST L13 ....114 B4
Vittoria Medical Centre
BIRK CH41 ....11 G3
VUE Cinema
BIRK CH41 ....11 J5
EP CH65 ....164 A4
Vulcan Industrial Estate
NEWLW WA12 ....104 F4
Vyner Primary School
CL/PREN CH43 ....110 F4
Wade Deacon County High
School *WDN* WA8 ....134 C3
Wakefield Industrial Estate
NTHTN L30 ....84 C2

Walker Art Gallery
VAUX/LVPD L3 ....13 H5
Wallasey Golf Club
WAL/NB CH45 ....94 F6
Wallasey RFC
WAL/NB CH45 ....94 F8
Wallasey School
MOR/LEA CH46 ....110 C2
Wallasey Town Hall
WAL/EG CH44 ....112 A1
Walton Hall
WARRS WA4 ....137 J7
Walton Hall Golf Club
WARRS WA4 ....137 H6
Walton Hall Medical Centre
ANF/KKDL L4 ....97 J4
Walton Hospital
WLT/FAZ L9 ....97 H2
Walton Lea Crematorium
WARRS WA4 ....137 J4
Walton Medical Centre
ANF/KKDL L4 ....97 H1
Walton St Mary CE Primary
School *ANF/KKDL* L4 ....97 H3
Walton Sports Centre
WLT/FAZ L9 ....97 K3
Walton Village Medical Centre
ANF/KKDL L4 ....97 J4
Wargrave House School
NEWLW WA12 ....104 E4
Wargrave Primary School
NEWLW WA12 ....104 E4
Warren Golf Club
WAL/NB CH45 ....95 H6
Warrington Business Centre
WARR WA1 ....14 E5
Warrington Business Park
WARRN/WOL WA2 ....121 L4
Warrington Central Trading
Estate *WARRN/WOL* WA2 ....14 C3
Warrington Collegiate Institute
WARRN/WOL WA2 ....121 K4
Warrington Community
Health Care
WARRN/WOL WA2 ....105 H7
Warrington Golf Club
WARRS WA4 ....137 L8
Warrington Hospital
WARRW/BUR WA5 ....121 G7
Warrington Museum & Library
WARR WA1 ....14 D7
Warrington New Town
Cricket Club
WARRW/BUR WA5 ....120 E8
Warrington Road Industrial
Estate *WCNS/IIMK* WN3 ....68 A8
Warrington Sports Club
WARRS WA4 ....137 J6
Warrington Town AFC
WARRS WA4 ....138 A3
Warrington Wolves RLFC
(Halliwell Jones Stadium)
WARRN/WOL WA2 ....14 D3
Waterfront Business Area
VAUX/LVPD L3 ....112 E6
Watergate North Primary
School *AIN/FAZ* L10 ....85 H5
Watergate Special School
WLTN L25 ....131 K3
Waterloo FC
CSBY/BLUN L23 ....70 D8
Waterloo Primary School
CSBY/WL L22 ....83 G4
Wavertree Athletics Centre
WAV L15 ....114 B6
Wavertree CE Primary School
WAV L15 ....114 B6
Wavertree Cricket Club
WAV L15 ....114 B5
Wavertree Health Clinic
WAV L15 ....114 C7
Wavertree Retail Park
EHL/KEN L7 ....113 L4
Wavertree Technology Park
EHL/KEN L7 ....114 A4
Wavertree Town Hall
WAV L15 ....114 C6
Wavertree Trading Estate
WAV L15 ....114 A6
Weatherhead High School
WAL/EG CH44 ....111 H2
Weatherstone Business Centre
NSTN CH64 ....153 L5
Weaver Industrial Estate
ALL/GAR L19 ....145 L2
Weaver Park Industrial Estate
FROD/HEL WA6 ....160 F3
Weaver Vale Primary School
FROD/HEL WA6 ....160 E3
Welcome Lodge
CHLY/EC PR7 ....42 D2
WARRW/BUR WA5 ....120 D2
Wellesbourne Primary School
NG/CROX L11 ....98 B3
Wellington Employment Park
EV L5 ....96 E7
Wellington Street Industrial
Estate *WDN* WA8 ....16 C7
Well Lane Primary School
RF/TRAN CH42 ....128 A2
Wesley House
ECCL WA10 ....9 H4
West Bank Medical Centre
WDN WA8 ....16 C9
West Bank Primary School
WDN WA8 ....149 H1
Westbourne School
WAL/NB CH45 ....95 L7
Westbrook Medical Centre
WARRW/BUR WA5 ....120 E4
West Derby Cemetery
NG/CROX L11 ....98 C1
West Derby Comprehensive
School *CLB/OSW/ST* L13 ....98 C8
West Derby Golf Club
WD/CROXPK L12 ....99 G7
West End Primary School
ORM L39 ....51 G6
Westfield Primary School
RUNC WA7 ....18 E5
West Gillbrands Industrial
Estate *SKEL* WN8 ....65 G6

West Kirby Foot Health Clinic
WKBY CH48 ....124 D3
West Kirby Girls Grammar
School *WKBY* CH48 ....124 C1
West Kirby Health Centre &
Swimming Pool
WKBY CH48 ....124 C3
West Kirby Primary School
WKBY CH48 ....124 C3
West Kirby Residential School
WKBY CH48 ....124 B2
West Kirby Sailing Club
WKBY CH48 ....124 D5
West Lancashire Golf Club
CSBY/BLUN L23 ....70 C7
West Lancs Yacht Club
STHP PR8 ....24 C4
Westleigh Cricket Club
LEIGH WN7 ....81 M8
Westleigh High School
LEIGH WN7 ....81 M4
Westleigh Methodist Primary
School *LEIGH* WN7 ....81 M5
Westminster Industrial Park
EP CH65 ....156 B7
Westminster Medical Centre
ANF/KKDL L4 ....7 G1
Westminster Retail Park
EP CH65 ....20 E2
Westminster Road Swimming
Pool *ANF/KKDL* L4 ....97 G6
Weston Point Primary School
RUNC WA7 ....18 D9
Weston Primary School
RUNC WA7 ....149 J7
West Park RFC
ECCL WA10 ....101 K4
Westside Industrial Estate
STHEL WA9 ....9 J4
Westvale Health Centre
KKBY L32 ....85 L3
Westvale Primary School
KKBY L32 ....85 K3
Westwood Cemetery
WGNS/IIMK WN3 ....5 G9
Wheathill Industrial Estate
NTHLY L27 ....115 M7
Wheatland Business Park
WAL/EG CH44 ....111 M3
Wheatlea Industrial Estate
WGNS/IIMK WN3 ....79 H3
Whelley Hospital
WGN WN1 ....69 G3
Whetstone Lane Health Centre
BIRK CH41 ....11 G7
Whiston Health Centre
RAIN/WH L35 ....116 F2
Whiston Hospital
RAIN/WH L35 ....117 H1
Whitbyheath Primary School
EP CH65 ....20 A9
The Whitby High School
GTS/LS CH66 ....163 J4
Whitefield Cricket Club
WDN WA8 ....115 H4
Whitefield JMI School
NPK/KEN L6 ....113 J1
Whiteledge Centre
SKEL WN8 ....65 K5
White Thorn Special School
WLT/FAZ L9 ....84 E5
Widnes Community Midwifery
& Ante-natal Centre
WDN WA8 ....134 B3
Widnes Crematorium
WDN WA8 ....134 B2
Widnes Cricket Club
WDN WA8 ....134 D1
Widnes Golf Club
WDN WA8 ....16 B1
Widnes Public Baths
WDN WA8 ....16 D4
Widnes & Runcorn 6th Form
College *WDN* WA8 ....118 A8
Widnes Vikings RLFC
(Halton Stadium)
WDN WA8 ....16 B4
The Wiend Centre
WGN WN1 ....4 F4
Wigan Athletic FC & Wigan
Warriors RLFC
(The JJB Stadium)
WGNW/BIL/O WN5 ....68 A5
Wigan Borough Cemetery
WGNS/IIMK WN3 ....68 F8
Wigan Crematorium
WGNS/IIMK WN3 ....79 M1
Wigan Golf Club
CHLY/EC PR7 ....56 F3
Wigan & Leigh College
WGN WN1 ....4 D2
Wigan Little Theatre
WGN WN1 ....5 G3
Wigan Magistrates Court
WGN WN1 ....5 G5
Wigan Pier
WGNS/IIMK WN3 ....4 C6
Wigan RUFC
WGN WN1 ....56 F8
Wildfowl and Wetlands Trust
Martin Mere
CHTN/BK PR9 ....38 D4
Willaston Primary School
NSTN CH64 ....154 B5
William Beamont Community
School
WARRN/WOL WA2 ....121 K4
William Gladstone CE Primary
School *LITH* L21 ....83 J6
Williamson Art Gallery &
Museum *CL/PREN* CH43 ....10 C8
William Stockton Primary
School *EP* CH65 ....20 A4
Willowbank Holiday Home
& Touring Park
STHP PR8 ....47 K3
Willow Grove School
AIMK WN4 ....80 A8
Willow Tree Primary School
STHEL WA9 ....118 F1
Wilson Business Centre
HUY L36 ....116 C4

Windlehurst Primary School
ECCL WA10 ....89 G7
Windmill Farm
BRSC L40 ....38 D1
Windmill Hill Primary School
RUNC WA7 ....150 E3
Windmill Shopping Centre
WDN WA8 ....16 F3
Windsor Primary School
TOX L8 ....113 H7
Wingate Medical Centre
NWD/KWIPK L33 ....86 C2
Winstanley College
WGNW/BIL/O WN5 ....78 A2
Winstanley Industrial Estate
WARRN/WOL WA2 ....121 K4
Winstanley Medical Centre
WGNS/IIMK WN3 ....78 F2
Winstanley Primary School
WCNS/IIMK WN3 ....78 E3
Winwick CE Primary School
WARRN/WOL WA2 ....105 K7
Winwick Parish Leisure Centre
WARRN/WOL WA2 ....105 K7
Wirral Borough Magistrates
Court *BIRK* CH41 ....11 M5
Wirral Business Centre
WAL/EG CH44 ....111 L4
Wirral Business Park
GR/UP/WCH CH49 ....126 B2
Wirral Country Park
NSTN CH64 ....154 A6
PEN/TH CH61 ....140 B2
Wirral Grammar School for
Boys *BEB* CH63 ....143 G1
Wirral Grammar School for
Girls *BEB* CH63 ....143 G1
Wirral Hospital
BEB CH63 ....142 F4
Wirral Hospital School
WAL/NB CH45 ....110 E1
Wirral International Business
Park *PS/BROM* CH62 ....144 B3
Wirral Ladies Golf Club
CL/PREN CH43 ....111 G7
Wirral Metropolitan College
BIRK CH41 ....11 J5
BIRK CH41 ....11 K2
PS/BROM CH62 ....144 C6
Wirral Museum
BIRK CH41 ....11 L5
Wirral Stroke & Head Injury
Clinic *CL/PREN* CH43 ....127 K4
Wirral Tennis & Sports Centre
BIRK CH41 ....110 F3
Wirral Transport Museum
BIRK CH41 ....11 L3
Wolverham Primary School
EP CH65 ....20 E6
Woodchurch CE Primary
School *GR/UP/WCH* CH49 ....126 D3
Woodchurch High School
GR/UP/WCH CH49 ....126 E3
Woodchurch Leisure Centre
GR/UP/WCH CH49 ....126 E2
Woodchurch Road Primary
School *RF/TRAN* CH42 ....127 L1
Woodcote Hotel
GTS/LS CH66 ....155 H4
Woodend Industrial Estate
SPK/HALE L24 ....131 L8
Woodfall Infant School
NSTN CH64 ....153 J7
Woodfall Junior School
NSTN CH64 ....153 J7
Woodfield Primary School
WGN WN1 ....68 E1
Wood Fold Primary School
WGNNW/ST WN6 ....55 M5
Woodlands Industrial Estate
NEWLW WA12 ....91 L7
Woodlands Infant School
GTS/LS CH66 ....163 H3
Woodlands Junior School
GTS/LS CH66 ....163 H4
Woodlands Primary School
BIRK CH41 ....11 H8
FMBY L37 ....58 F2
Woodlands Works
NWD/KWIPK L33 ....86 E2
Woodside Business Park
BIRK CH41 ....11 M3
Woodside County Primary
School *RUNC* WA7 ....150 A6
Woodside Ferry Landing Stage
VAUX/LVPD L3 ....112 C9
Woodslee Primary School
PS/BROM CH62 ....143 M3
Woodvale Airfield
FMBY L37 ....47 H5
Woolston CE Primary School
WARR WA1 ....122 E5
Woolston Community High
School *WARR* WA1 ....122 D6
Woolston Community Primary
School *WARR* WA1 ....122 E6
Woolton Golf Club
WLTN L25 ....131 K5
Woolton House Medical Centre
WLTN L25 ....131 J3
Woolton J & I School
WLTN L25 ....131 K2
Woolton Swimming Pool
WLTN L25 ....131 J3
World of Glass
ECCL WA10 ....9 H6
Worsley Mesnes Primary
School *WCNS/IIMK* WN3 ....79 J1
Worthington Lakes Business
Park *WGN* WN1 ....56 E5
Wrightington Hospital
WGNNW/ST WN6 ....55 G4
Wrightington Hotel & Country
Club *WGNNW/ST* WN6 ....55 H2
Yew Tree Trading Estate
RNFD/HAY WA11 ....90 F5

Acknowledgements

The Post Office is a registered trademark of Post Office Ltd. in the UK and other countries.

Schools address data provided by Education Direct.

Petrol station information supplied by Johnsons

One-way street data provided by © Tele Atlas N.V. Tele Atlas

The statement on the front cover of this atlas is sourced, selected and quoted
from a reader comment and feedback form received in 2004.

Garden centre information provided by

Garden Centre Association  Britains best garden centres

Wyevale Garden Centres

Notes

Notes

 **AA** **Street by Street** QUESTIONNAIRE

Dear Atlas User
Your comments, opinions and recommendations are very important to us. So please help us to improve our street atlases by taking a few minutes to complete this simple questionnaire.

You do not need a stamp (unless posted outside the UK). If you do not want to remove this page from your street atlas, then photocopy it or write your answers on a plain sheet of paper.

Send to: The Editor, AA Street by Street, FREEPOST SCE 4598, Basingstoke RG21 4GY

ABOUT THE ATLAS...

Which city/town/county did you buy?

_____

Are there any features of the atlas or mapping that you find particularly useful?

_____
_____
_____

Is there anything we could have done better?

_____
_____
_____

Why did you choose an AA Street by Street atlas?

_____
_____
_____

Did it meet your expectations?

Exceeded ☐   **Met all** ☐   **Met most** ☐   **Fell below** ☐

Please give your reasons

_____
_____
_____
_____
_____
_____

MX048z

continued overleaf

Where did you buy it?

_____

For what purpose? (please tick all applicable)

To use in your own local area ☐   To use on business or at work ☐

Visiting a strange place ☐   In the car ☐   On foot ☐

Other (please state)

_____

LOCAL KNOWLEDGE...

Local knowledge is invaluable. Whilst every attempt has been made to make the information contained in this atlas as accurate as possible, should you notice any inaccuracies, please detail them below (if necessary, use a blank piece of paper) or e-mail us at *streetbystreet@theAA.com*

_____
_____
_____
_____
_____
_____

ABOUT YOU...

Name (Mr/Mrs/Ms)
Address
                                          Postcode
Daytime tel no
E-mail address

Which age group are you in?

Under 25 ☐   25-34 ☐   35-44 ☐   45-54 ☐   55-64 ☐   65+ ☐

Are you an AA member?   YES ☐   NO ☐

Do you have Internet access?   YES ☐   NO ☐

Thank you for taking the time to complete this questionnaire. Please send it to us as soon as possible, and remember, you do not need a stamp (unless posted outside the UK).

We may want to contact you about other products and services provided by us, or our partners (by mail, telephone) but please tick the box if you DO NOT wish to hear about such products and services from us by mail or telephone. ☐   MX048z